Biological Psychology

ABOUT THE **AUTHOR**

James W. Kalat (rhymes with ballot) is Professor of Psychology at North Carolina State University. Born in 1946, he received an A.B. degree *summa cum laude* from Duke University in 1968 and a Ph.D. in psychology in 1971 from the University of Pennsylvania. He is also the author of *Introduction to Psychology* (the fourth edition was published by Brooks/Cole in 1996).

SIXTH**EDITION**

BIOLOGICAL PSYCHOLOGY

James W. Kalat
North Carolina State University

Brooks/Cole Publishing Company
I**T**P® An International Thomson Publishing Company

Pacific Grove • Albany, NY • Belmont, CA • Bonn • Boston • Cincinnati • Detroit • Johannesburg • London
Madrid • Melbourne • Mexico City • New York • Paris • Singapore • Tokyo • Toronto • Washington

Sponsoring Editor: *Jim Brace-Thompson*
Project Development Editor: *Penelope Sky*
Marketing Team: *Lauren Harp, Romy Taormina*
Editorial Assistant: *Terry Thomas*
Production Editor: *Kirk Bomont*
Copyeditor: *William Heckman*
Permissions Editor: *May Clark*
Interior and Cover Design: *Roy R. Neuhaus*

Interior Illustration: *Precision Graphics*
Cover Photo: *A. Pasieka, Science Source/Photo Researchers*
Art Editor: *Lisa Torri*
Photo Editor: *Kathleen Olson*
Photo Researcher: *Sue C. Howard*
Indexer: *Do Mi Stauber*
Typesetting: *GTS Graphics, Inc.*
Printing and Binding: *World Color*

For more information, contact:

BROOKS/COLE PUBLISHING COMPANY
511 Forest Lodge Road
Pacific Grove, CA 93950
USA

International Thomson Publishing Europe
Berkshire House 168-173
High Holborn
London WC1V 7AA
England

Thomas Nelson Australia
102 Dodds Street
South Melbourne, 3205
Victoria, Australia

Nelson Canada
1120 Birchmount Road
Scarborough, Ontario
Canada M1K 5G4

International Thomson Editores
Seneca 53
Col. Polanco
11560 México, D. F., México

International Thomson Publishing GmbH
Königswinterer Strasse 418
53227 Bonn
Germany

International Thomson Publishing Asia
221 Henderson Road
#05-10 Henderson Building
Singapore 0315

International Thomson Publishing Japan
Hirakawacho Kyowa Building, 3F
2-2-1 Hirakawacho
Chiyoda-ku, Tokyo 102
Japan

Printed in the United States of America

10   9   8   7   6   5

Library of Congress Cataloging-in-Publication Data

Kalat, James W.
    Biological psychology / James W. Kalat. — 6th ed.
        p.   cm.
    Includes bibliographical references and indexes.
    ISBN 0-534-34893-9
    1. Neuropsychology.   2. Psychobiology.   I. Title.
QP360.K33   1998
612.8—dc21
                                            97-25089
                                            CIP

To Ann

Brief Contents

Contents

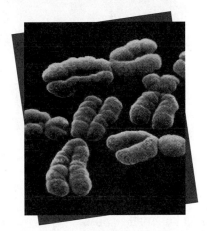

CHAPTER **TWO**

NERVE CELLS AND NERVE IMPULSES   22

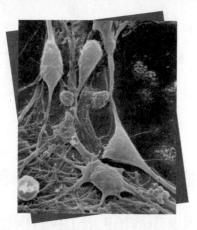

CHAPTER **THREE**

SYNAPSES AND DRUGS   46

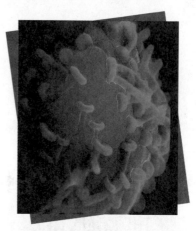

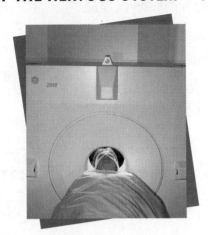
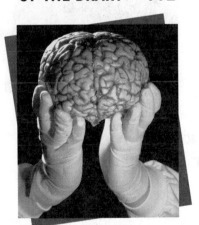

CHAPTER **SIX**

VISION   140

CHAPTER **SEVEN**

THE NONVISUAL SENSORY SYSTEMS   178

CHAPTER **EIGHT**

MOVEMENT   210

CHAPTER **NINE**

RHYTHMS OF WAKEFULNESS AND SLEEP   240

CHAPTER **TEN**

THE REGULATION OF INTERNAL BODY STATES   268

CHAPTER **ELEVEN**

HORMONES AND SEXUAL BEHAVIOR   296

CHAPTER **THIRTEEN**

THE BIOLOGY OF LEARNING AND MEMORY   344

CHAPTER **TWELVE**

EMOTIONAL BEHAVIORS AND STRESS   322

CHAPTER **FOURTEEN**

LATERALIZATION AND LANGUAGE 372

CHAPTER **FIFTEEN**

RECOVERY FROM BRAIN DAMAGE 398

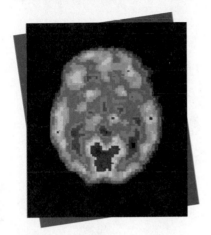

Preface

The most challenging aspect of writing a text is selecting what to include and what to omit. My primary goal in writing this text has been to engage readers' interest. I have focused on the biological mechanisms that are most relevant to key issues in psychology—including language, learning, sexual behavior, anxiety, aggression, recovery from brain damage, depression, schizophrenia, and the mind–body problem. I hope that by the end of the book readers will clearly see what the study of the brain has to do with "real psychology" and that they will be interested in learning more.

Each chapter is divided into modules; each module begins with its own introduction and finishes with its own summary and questions. This organization makes it easy for instructors to assign part of a chapter per day instead of a whole chapter per week. Parts of chapters can also be covered in a different order. (Indeed, of course, whole chapters can be taken in different orders as well. I know some instructors who like to start with Chapter 14 on lateralization and language as an attention grabber.)

I assume that the reader has a basic background in psychology and biology and understands such terms as *classical conditioning, reinforcement, vertebrate, mammal, gene, chromosome, cell, mitochondrion, liver, intestine,* and *digestion.* Naturally, the stronger the background, the better. Those whose memories of chemistry have faded a bit may consult Appendix A for a review.

Changes in This Edition

The changes in this text are my attempt to keep pace with the rapid progress in biological psychology. There are more than 500 new references from 1994 through 1997, and additions, corrections, and deletions in almost every paragraph. There are many new or improved illustrations and the overall layout has been redesigned. Note the newly added icon "Try It Yourself," which calls attention to simple demonstrations described in the text. Because this book is used in a number of European colleges, I have tried to remove terms and examples that are unfamiliar or ambiguous outside the United States; for example, the term "CB radio." I also changed certain descriptions; for example, "football shaped" becomes "avocado shaped," and "corn" is now "maize."

The major changes in the text are listed in the *Instructor's Manual*, chapter by chapter. Here are a few highlights:

• **Introduction: The Goals of Biological Psychology** Covers the types of biological explanation that were previously in Chapter 1.

• **Chapter 1: Human Behavior in the Context of the Animal Kingdom** The first module is on genetics and evolution. Some of the material was imported from Appendix A (on genetics) in the fifth editon; the rest is new. The second module, on ethics of experimentation, is revised from material in Chapter 1 of the previous edition.

• **Chapter 2: Nerve Cells and Nerve Impulses** New digression on the investigator Santiago Ramón y Cajal.

• **Chapter 3: Synapses and Drugs** New major section on reinforcement and addiction. New information on several drugs of abuse.

• **Chapter 4: The Anatomy and Investigation of the Nervous System** Added discussion of microdialysis and fMRI.

• **Chapter 5: The Development and Evolution of the Brain** Much revision and reorganization. Expanded section on the effects of experience on brain development. New digression on Rett syndrome. Important new study showing that the size of various subareas of the mammalian brain is predictable from the size of the overall brain. Emphasis on two partly competing and partly complementary explanations for human brain evolution: Growth in size and change in organization. Deleted controversy on ethnic differences.

• **Chapter 6: Vision** New digression on suppressed vision during saccadic eye movements. Changed the term "parallel processing" to "concurrent processing." Added spatial-frequency sensitivity as an alternative description of the role of V1 neurons.

• **Chapter 7: The Nonvisual Sensory Systems** New section on the auditory cortex. New or expanded discussions of phantom pain, headache, and sensitization of pain. Explanation of why opiates block postsurgical pain but not the pain from a cut.

• **Chapter 8: Movement** Revised descriptions of the behavioral functions of the cerebellum, basal ganglia, and motor cortex. Deleted discussion of the pyramidal and extrapyramidal systems, with concentration instead on the dorsolateral tract and ventromedial tract. Updated discussions of Parkinson's disease and Huntington's disease.

• **Chapter 9: Rhythms of Wakefulness and Sleep** New section on melatonin. Completely new discussion of brain mechanisms and pharmacology of arousal and sleep. Revised digression on the evolution of REM sleep.

• **Chapter 10: The Regulation of Internal Body States** Much revision of the hunger module. Note especially the virtually all-new sections on genetics of body weight, effects of leptin, and the effects of NPY and other neurotransmitters and hormones.

• **Chapter 11: Hormones and Sexual Behavior** Greatly revised section on the activating effects of hormones on sexual behaviors, emphasizing the effects of dopamine and the medial preoptic nucleus of the hypothalamus. A new section on activating effects of hormones on nonsexual behaviors replaces the old section on activating effects of hormones on aggressive behavior. Updated discussion of parental behaviors. Brief updates on antiandrogens for sex offenders, premenstrual syndrome, and harms from steroid abuse.

• **Chapter 12: Emotional Behaviors and Stress** Deleted section on ulcers (because new data indicate that bacteria, not stress, cause most ulcers). Removed reinforcement, placing it in Chapter 3. Changed order of presentation within modules. New discussion of hormones and aggression; new discussion of amygdala damage in humans.

• **Chapter 13: The Biology of Learning and Memory** Reordered presentation of material within modules. Downplayed the distinction between implicit and explicit memory; new discussion of working memory and its mechanisms. New material on hippocampus and spatial memory, including comparative material on food-storing and nonstoring birds. Updated and revised the section on age and memory. New information on Alzheimer's disease.

• **Chapter 14: Lateralization and Language** New section, "Beyond Broca and Wernicke." Revised discussion of dyslexia to emphasize multiple types and multiple explanations. Note that Williams syndrome is now known to be genetic in origin.

• **Chapter 15: Recovery from Brain Damage** Much new information on mechanisms of cell death after a stroke, and new strategies for minimizing such brain damage. Completely rewritten description of assessment after brain damage. Updates on collateral sprouting, denervation supersensitivity, and neural transplants.

• **Chapter 16: Depression and Schizophrenia** Reorganized the module on mood disorder, separating the discussions of major depression, bipolar disorder, and seasonal affective disorder. Also reorganized order of presentation in schizophrenia module. New section on the neurodevelopmental hypothesis. Revised description of the role of neurotransmitters, with discussion of the glutamate hypothesis as a plausible rival to the dopamine hypothesis. New digression on differential diagnosis of schizophrenia. Deleted the section on autism.

• **Epilogue: Mind and Brain** A revised presentation of some material previously in Chapter 1.

Supplements

An exciting new **CD-ROM** called *The Integrator* has been prepared by Art and Wendy Kohn and their associates. This program provides video clips, computer simulations, interviews, and many other audiovisual aids for instructors to use in the classroom and for students to use on their own. A new **Biopsych Web Site** has been designed to accompany the textbook to help students learn the concepts of biological psychology and have fun at the same time. Students and instructors will find annotated links, online tutorial modules, practice tests, an online biopsych dictionary, discussion forums, Kalat's "Biological Psychology Updates" newsletter, and more at http://psychstudy.brookscole.com. Instructors who adopt the book may also obtain from the publisher a copy of the *Instructor's Manual,* written by Ron Ruiz of Riverside Community College and Teri Rust of Lewis-Clark State College. The manual contains approximately two thousand multiple-choice test items (also available on diskette for IBM and Macintosh computers), chapter outlines, class demonstrations and projects, a list of video resources, and the author's answers to the Thought Questions at the end of text modules. A set of **overhead transparencies** is also available to U.S. adopters, as is a **videotape** containing teaching modules edited from "The Brain" video series. The *Study Guide,* written by Elaine Hull of SUNY–Buffalo, may be purchased by students. I am grateful for the excellent work of the Kohns, Ruiz, Rust, and Hull.

Acknowledgments

Let me tell you something about researchers in this field: As a rule, they are amazingly cooperative with textbook authors. A number of my colleagues have sent me comments, ideas, and published materials; others supplied me with photos. I thank especially the following: Ralph Adolphs, University of Iowa Hospitals and Clinics; Dawna Armstrong, Baylor College of Medicine; Kim Barke, Union College; Francine M. Benes, McLean Hospital, Belmont, MA; Stephen Black, Bishop's University; Jennifer Brown and colleagues, Harvard Medical School; Suzanne Corkin, Massachusetts Institute of Technology; James Croxton, Santa Monica, CA; Thomas Elbert, University of Konstanz; Barbara Finlay, Cornell University; Riita Hari, Helsinki University of Technology; David Hubel, Harvard Medical School; Elaine Hull, SUNY–Buffalo; Masao Ito, Frontier Research Program (Saitama, Japan); Bob Jacobs, Colorado College; Eric Kandel, Columbia University; Jerre Levy, University of Chicago; Jacqueline Ludel, Guilford College; James McGaugh, University of California, Irvine; Linda Mealey, University of Queensland; Adrian Morrison, University of Pennsylvania; Eviatar Nevo; Duane Rumbaugh, Georgia State University; J. N. Sanes, Brown University; Tony Santucci, Manhattanville College; Sue Savage-Rumbaugh, Georgia State University; Robert E. Schmidt, Washington University School of Medicine; Jan A. W. M. Weijnen, Tilburg University (Netherlands); Torsten Wiesel, Rockefeller University; and David Yells.

I have received an enormous number of letters and e-mail messages from students. Many included helpful suggestions; some managed to catch errors or inconsistencies that everyone else had overlooked. I thank especially the following: Andrea Hunter; Corey Lafferty, North Carolina State University; Chiga Miyake, North Carolina State University; Esther Nobbe, Catholic University of Tilburg, Netherlands; Alan Oursland, North Carolina State University; Iris Schino, Catholic University of Tilburg, Netherlands; Hanneke Schuurmans, University of Nijmegen; Karen Todd-Turla, University of New Hampshire; Debby Wimer, Indiana University–Purdue University at Indianapolis; and Karen Woodward.

I appreciate the helpful comments provided by the following reviewers: Michael Anch, St. Louis University; Debora Baldwin, University of Tennessee–Knoxville; David Berger, SUNY–Cortland; Peter Brunjes, University of Virginia; Verne Cox, University of Texas–Arlington; Kenneth Guttman, Citrus College; Leonard Hamilton, Rutgers University; Merrill Hiscock, University of Houston; Elaine Hull, SUNY–Buffalo; Bart Hoebel, Princeton University; Jon Kaas, Vanderbilt University; Jonathan Kahane, Springfield College; Scott Kraly, Colgate University; Robert McCaffrey, SUNY–Albany; Ilyse O'Desky, Kean College of New Jersey; Maria-Teresa Romero, SUNY–Binghamton; Susan Schenk, Texas A & M University; Thomas Scott, University of Delaware; Robert L. Spencer, University of Colorado; Timothy Teyler, Didactic Systems; Carl Thompson, Wabash College; AnnJane Tierney, Colgate University; Robin Timmons, Drew University; and James Torcivia, California State University–Northridge.

In preparing this text I have been most fortunate to work with Jim Brace-Thompson, an amazingly supportive and patient acquisitions editor, and with Terry Thomas, his editorial assistant. Penelope Sky, my developmental editor, has repeatedly examined every word and illustration to improve the clarity of presentation. I greatly appreciate her excellent detailed comments. Kirk Bomont, the production editor, has overseen a complex project with impossible deadlines; without his expertise, publishing this text would have been impossible. The artists assigned to this edition have had to deal with an author who cannot draw well enough to show them what he wants, but who nevertheless is hard to please. I thank Precision Graphics and art editor Lisa Torri for both their skills and their patience. I thank Roy Neuhaus for the text and cover design, Bill Heckman for the copyediting, Kathleen Olson and Sue Howard for the photos, and Do Mi Stauber for the indexes. Faith Stoddard has done an excellent job of coordinating all the supplements for this text. All these people have been splendid colleagues.

Thanks to my wife, Ann, and my daughter, Robin, who listened whenever I wanted to talk about the latest thing I had read. And thanks to my department head, David Martin, for his support and encouragement.

I welcome correspondence from both students and faculty. Write: James W. Kalat, Department of Psychology, Box 7801, North Carolina State University, Raleigh, NC 27695-7801, U.S.A. E-mail: kalat@poe.coe.ncsu.edu.

James W. Kalat

THE GOALS OF BIOLOGICAL PSYCHOLOGY

A biological psychologist tries to explain any behavior not in terms of subjective experiences like "love" but in terms of its physiology, development, evolution, and function.
Source: Courtesy of the Cincinnati Zoo.

INTRODUCTION

MAIN**IDEAS**

1. Biological psychologists attempt to relate behavior and experience to the activities of the brain and the rest of the body.
2. Biological explanations of behavior fall into several categories, including physiology, development, evolution, and function.

Biological psychology is the study of behavior and experience in terms of genetics, evolution, and physiology, especially the physiology of the nervous system. Some of the many specializations most directly related to this field are listed in Table 1.

Biological psychology is the most interesting topic in the world. I am sure every professor and every textbook author feels that way about his or her field. But the others are wrong; this topic really *is* the most interesting. I do not mean that memorizing the names and functions of brain parts and chemicals is any more interesting than is memorizing geographical terms or dates in history. I mean that biological psychology deals with some deep theoretical questions that almost anyone should find exciting. Actually, I shall back off a bit and assert that biological psychology is perhaps tied with cosmology as the most interesting topic. Cosmologists ask why the universe exists at all. Why is there *something* instead of *nothing?* And given that there is a universe, why this particular kind of universe instead of some other? Biological psychologists ask, given the existence of a universe composed of matter and energy, why is there such a thing as consciousness? How does the physical brain give rise to vision, hearing, hunger, sexual desire, anger, fear, and other experiences?

I hasten to add that we have only partial answers to what philosophers call the "easy" questions: which aspects of brain functioning correspond to vision, which aspects correspond to hunger, and which aspects correspond to other specific states. We have even less satisfactory answers to the "hard" questions: why consciousness exists at all, and what enables the brain to produce it.

The great challenge of biological psychology is to improve our answers to all these questions. It is that challenge that makes biological psychology a topic of compelling interest.

TABLE **1**

Some of the Major Specializations in Biological Psychology

Physiological psychologist (also known as psychobiologist, biopsychologist, or behavioral neuroscientist)	Ph.D., probably in psychology or related field. May hold position in a research institution, but more likely in a college or university. Conducts research on how behavior relates to the physiology of the brain and other organs of the body.
Comparative psychologist	Ph.D. in psychology. Conducts research on animal behavior, comparing different species. Similar to an ethologist, a zoologist who studies animal behavior.
Neuroscientist	Ph.D. or M.D. Conducts research on the nervous system, from brain anatomy to behavior.
Neurologist	M.D. specializing in treatment of brain damage. Likely to hold position in hospital or clinic.
Neuropsychologist	Ph.D. in psychology, probably with some medical courses. Tests the abilities and disabilities of brain-damaged or otherwise impaired people.

Biological Explanations of Behavior

Biological explanations of behavior fall into four major categories: physiological, ontogenetic, evolutionary, and functional (Tinbergen, 1951). A **physiological explanation** relates a behavior to the activity of the brain and other organs. It deals with the machinery of the body—for example, how the body converts the chemical energy of foods into the kinetic energy of body movements, and how the machinery of the brain organizes those movements.

The term *ontogenetic* comes from Greek roots meaning "to be" and "origin" (or genesis). Thus, an **ontogenetic explanation** describes the development of a structure or a behavior. So far as possible, it traces the influences of genes, nutrition, early experiences, and the interactions among these influences in producing behavioral tendencies.

An **evolutionary explanation** examines a structure or a behavior in terms of evolutionary history. For example, when people become frightened, they sometimes get "goosebumps"—erections of the hairs, especially on the arms and shoulders. Goosebumps are useless in humans, because our shoulder and arm hairs are so short. In hairier animals, however, erection of the hairs makes a frightened animal look larger and more intimidating (Figure 1). Thus, an evolutionary explanation of human goosebumps is that the behavior evolved in our remote (hairier) ancestors and that we still have the mechanism for producing goosebumps even though they are no longer useful for us.

A **functional explanation** describes *why* a structure or behavior evolved as it did. In a large population, a gene will spread only if it is linked to some advantage. A functional explanation identifies the advantage that some structure or behavior has provided. For example,

FIGURE **1**
A frightened cat with erect hairs
When a frightened mammal erects its hairs, it looks larger and more intimidating than it would otherwise. (Consider, for example, the "Halloween cat.") Frightened humans sometimes also erect their body hairs, forming "goosebumps." An evolutionary explanation for goosebumps is that we inherited the tendency from ancestors who had enough hair for the behavior to be useful.

certain species can change color to match their background (Figure 2). A functional explanation is that such a change makes the animal inconspicuous to predators and therefore likely to survive longer than it would otherwise.

To illustrate the four types of biological explanation, consider how they all apply to one example, birdsong (Catchpole & Slater, 1995):

Physiological explanation: A particular area of the songbird brain grows under the influence of testosterone; hence it is larger in breeding males than in females or immatures. That brain area enables a mature male to sing.

Ontogenetic explanation: In certain species, a young male bird learns its song by listening to adult males. He must hear the appropriate song during a sensitive period early in life, even though he cannot begin his own singing until he is at least a year old.

Evolutionary explanation: In certain cases, one species of bird has a song that closely resembles that of a different species. For example, dunlins and Baird's sandpipers, two kinds of shorebird, give their calls in distinct pulses, unlike other shorebirds. This similarity suggests that the two species evolved from a single ancestor.

Unlike all other birds, doves and pigeons can drink with their heads down. A physiological explanation would describe these birds' unusual pattern of nerves and throat muscles. An evolutionary explanation states that all doves and pigeons share this behavioral capacity because they inherited their genes from a common ancestor.

FIGURE **2**
A chameleon changes its appearance to match its background
A functional explanation addresses why a behavior has evolved, or what function it serves. In this case, the function is that an animal that matches its background becomes inconspicuous, so that potential predators overlook it.

Functional explanation: In most bird species, only the male sings, and he sings only during the reproductive season and only in his territory. The functions of the song are to attract a female and to warn other males that he is defending his territory. As a rule, a bird sings only loud enough to be heard in the territory he is capable of defending, not beyond it. In short, each bird has evolved a tendency to sing in a way that improves its chances for successful mating.

Note that biological explanations do not require an individual to understand the reasons for his or her behavior. A male bird does not need to understand what his singing will accomplish, any more than a frightened person needs to understand the relationship between goosebumps and the fur displays of hairier mammals. Indeed, we have a number of behaviors that no one fully understands (Provine, 1986, 1996). For example, exactly why do we yawn? Why did we evolve a tendency to laugh? Why do we cry? According to the biological view, our behavior does not require any conscious understanding of its functions; we act as we do because some ancient animals that acted this way survived and reproduced more successfully than other animals did; the first group of animals therefore became our ancestors and the second group became extinct.

IN**CLOSING**

The Biology of Experience

Among the biological explanations, you may notice the absence of any reference to *mind* or to any mental processes. We shall come back to the topic of mind and brain in the epilogue, after we have examined biological explanations of behavior in more detail. At this point, however, let us jump to the summary: Yes, of course "mind" or "conscious experience" exists, but we have no evidence that they are anything other than synonyms for "brain activity." In short, biological psychology is a very ambitious field. We are setting out to explain as much as we can of psychology in strictly biological, physical terms.

Summary

1. Biological psychology encompasses the work of many kinds of specialists, including psychologists, biologists, and medical doctors. (p. 1)
2. Biological psychologists try to answer four types of questions about any given behavior: How does it relate to the physiology of the brain and other organs? How does it develop within the individual? How did the capacity for the behavior evolve? And why did the capacity for this behavior evolve? (That is, what function does it serve?) (p. 2)
3. Biological explanations of behavior do not necessarily assume that the individual understands the purpose or function of the behavior. (p. 3)

Review Question

1. What is the difference between an evolutionary explanation and a functional explanation? (p. 2)

Terms

biological psychology   study of the physiological and evolutionary principles underlying behavior (p. 1)

physiological explanation   understanding in terms of the machinery of the body (p. 2)

ontogenetic explanation   understanding in terms of how a structure or a behavior develops (p. 2)

evolutionary explanation   understanding in terms of the evolutionary history of a species (p. 2)

functional explanation   understanding why a structure or behavior evolved as it did (p. 2)

HUMAN BEHAVIOR IN THE CONTEXT OF THE ANIMAL KINGDOM

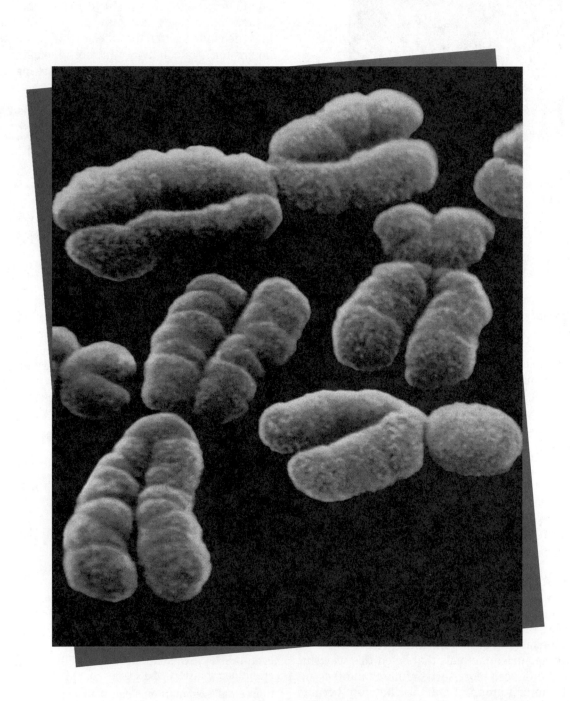

CHAPTER **ONE**

It is often said that Man is unique among animals. It is worth looking at this term "unique" before we discuss our subject proper. The word may in this context have two slightly different meanings. It may mean: Man is strikingly different—he is not identical with any animal. This is of course true. It is true also of all other animals: Each species, even each individual is unique in this sense. But the term is also often used in a more absolute sense: Man is so different, so "essentially"
different (whatever that means) that the gap between him and animals cannot possibly be bridged—he is something altogether new. Used in this absolute sense the term is scientifically meaningless. Its use also reveals and may reinforce conceit, and it leads to complacency and defeatism because it assumes that it will be futile even to search for animal roots. It is prejudging the issue.

—Niko Tinbergen (1973)

The "animal roots" of which Tinbergen wrote have become more and more evident with further research. We have long recognized similarities between ourselves and other species in our body structure and in the ways we eat, drink, grow, reproduce, and eventually die. Research at the molecular level has uncovered even more detailed similarities. More than 98 percent of human genes are the same as those of chimpanzees, and most of the chemicals in our brains are similar or identical to those of other animals, even microorganisms.

In the first module of this chapter we shall examine the ways in which genes affect behavior and some basic principles of evolution as it applies to behavior. The similarities between humans and other animal species make it possible for us to learn a great deal about ourselves by studying other species. Those similarities also raise questions about the ethics of animal research, which we shall consider in the brief second module.

The Genetics and Evolution of Behavior

Ultimately, the ability of any biological organism to do anything at all—metabolize food, grow, reproduce, or read textbooks—depends on the genes. Without your genes, there would not be any *you*. So far, so good; no controversy. The controversies start to arise when we discuss individual differences, especially in humans. People differ in their learning and memory, their eating and weight, their sexual orientation, their use of alcohol and other drugs, their mood, and so forth. To what extent, if any, can we trace those differences to genetic differences, as opposed to differences in experience? Many arguments on such issues are intense, even angry, but often uninformative.

In later chapters we shall consider the evidence for genetic influences on certain specific behaviors. Here we deal with the general principles of genetics and evolution. This chapter will certainly not resolve all the controversies, but it should at least enable you to distinguish between reasonable questions and meaningless questions, between plausible statements and blatant nonsense.

The Genetics of Behavior

We begin with a review of elementary genetics. Readers already familiar with the concepts may skim quickly over the next two pages.

Mendelian Genetics

Prior to the work of Gregor Mendel, a late-nineteenth-century monk, scientists thought that inheritance was a blending process, in which the properties of the sperm and the egg simply mixed, much as one might mix red paint and yellow paint.

Mendel demonstrated that inheritance occurs through **genes,** units of heredity that maintain their structural identity from one generation to another and do not blend with one another. As a rule, genes come in pairs because they are aligned along **chromosomes** (strands of genes), which also come in pairs. (The sex chromosomes are an exception to this rule; so are all the chromosomes of certain insects.) An individual that has an identical pair of genes on the two chromosomes is said to be **homozygous** for that gene. An individual with an unmatched pair of genes—for example, a gene for blue eyes on one chromosome and a gene for brown eyes on the other—is said to be **heterozygous** for that gene.

Certain genes can be identified as dominant or recessive. A **dominant** gene shows a strong effect in either the homozygous or heterozygous condition; a **recessive** gene shows its effects only in the homozygous condition. For example, someone with a gene for brown eyes (dominant) and one for blue eyes (recessive) will have brown eyes, although he or she is a "carrier" for the blue-eye gene and can transmit it to a child. For a behavioral example, the gene for ability to taste moderate concentrations of phenylthiocarbamide (PTC) is dominant; the gene for ability to taste it only in high concentrations is recessive. Only someone with two recessive genes will have trouble tasting the substance. Figure 1.1 illustrates the possible results of a mating between two parents who are both heterozygous for the PTC-tasting gene. Because each of them has one taster (T) gene, each can taste PTC. However, each parent can transmit either a taster gene (T) or a nontaster gene (t) to a given child, with equal probability. Therefore, a child in this family has a 25 percent chance of being a homozygous (TT) taster, a 50 percent chance of being a heterozygous (Tt) taster, and a 25 percent chance of being a homozygous (tt) nontaster.

Many instances show effects far more complicated than the simple case of one dominant and one recessive gene. The medical condition diabetes, for example, is affected by more than a dozen genes, some with major effects and some with minor effects. Some genes are said to have **partial penetrance**—they "penetrate" into

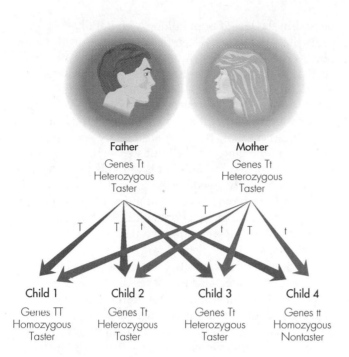

Father
Genes Tt
Heterozygous
Taster

Mother
Genes Tt
Heterozygous
Taster

Child 1
Genes TT
Homozygous
Taster

Child 2
Genes Tt
Heterozygous
Taster

Child 3
Genes Tt
Heterozygous
Taster

Child 4
Genes tt
Homozygous
Nontaster

FIGURE **1.1**
Four equally likely outcomes of a mating between two parents who both are heterozygous for a given gene (Tt)
A child in this family has a 25 percent chance of being homozygous for the dominant gene (TT), a 25 percent chance of being homozygous for the recessive gene (tt), and a 50 percent chance of being heterozygous (Tt).

someone's life under certain conditions and not others. For example, genes that increase the risk of alcohol abuse will obviously have little effect if the person lives in a culture that provides no access to alcohol. Even in the presence of alcohol, the effect of such genes will also depend on the person's family life, perhaps on diet, even on what other genes the person has.

Chromosomes and crossing over In certain cases, the inheritance of one gene is linked to inheritance of another gene. Genes are located on strands of DNA called chromosomes. Each chromosome participates in reproduction independently of the others, and each species has a certain number of chromosomes (23 pairs in humans, 4 pairs in fruit flies). For example, if an individual has a *BbCc* genotype, and if the *B* and *C* genes are on different chromosomes, its contribution of a *B* or *b* gene has nothing to do with whether it contributes a *C* or a *c*. But suppose they are on the same chromosome. If one chromosome has the *BC* combination and the other has *bc*, then an individual who contributes a *B* gene will probably also contribute a *C*.

The exception to this statement comes about as a result of **crossing over.** During reproduction, a pair of chromosomes may break apart and reconnect such that part of one chromosome attaches to the other part of the second chromosome. If one chromosome has the *BC* combination and the other chromosome has the *bc* combination, crossing over between the *B* locus and the *C* locus leaves new chromosomes with the combinations *Bc* and *bC*. The closer the *B* locus is to the *C* locus, the less often crossing over will occur between them.

Sex-linked and sex-limited genes All but one pair of mammalian chromosomes are known as autosomal chromosomes; genes located on these chromosomes are referred to as **autosomal genes.** The other two chromosomes are the sex chromosomes; genes located on them are known as **sex-linked genes.**

In mammals, the two sex chromosomes are designated X and Y. (Unlike the symbols *B* and *C* that I introduced to illustrate gene pairs, X and Y are standard symbols for sex chromosomes used by all geneticists.) A female mammal has two X chromosomes; a male has an X and a Y. During reproduction, the female necessarily contributes an X chromosome, and the male contributes either an X or a Y. If he contributes an X, the offspring will be female; if he contributes a Y, the offspring will be male. (Birds are different. Male birds have two sex chromosomes alike, designated ZZ; the female has two different sex chromosomes, designated ZW.)

The **Y chromosome** is small and carries few if any genes other than the genes that cause the individual to develop as a male. The **X chromosome,** however, carries many genes. Thus, when biologists speak of sex-linked genes, they ordinarily mean X-linked genes.

A characteristic that is controlled by a sex-linked recessive gene—for example, red-green color blindness—produces its effects only in the absence of the dominant gene. Any man who has the recessive gene for red-green color blindness will necessarily be color-blind, because he has no other X chromosome that might overrule the recessive gene. A woman, however, will be color-blind only if she has that recessive gene on both of her X chromosomes. So, for example, if 8 percent of human X chromosomes contain the gene for color blindness, then 8 percent of all men will be color-blind, but less than 1 percent of women will be color-blind (.08 × .08).

Distinct from sex-linked genes are the **sex-limited genes.** A sex-limited gene has an effect in one sex only, or at least it has a much stronger effect in one sex than the other. For instance, genes control the amount of chest hair in men, breast size in women, the amount of crowing in roosters, and the rate of egg production in hens. Such genes need not be on the sex chromosomes; both sexes have the genes, but the genes exert their effects only after activation by the sex hormones testosterone or estrogen.

Sources of variation   If reproduction always produced offspring that were exact copies of the parents, evolution would not be possible. One source of variation is **recombination.** The effects of a gene depend on what other genes are present. An offspring, in receiving some genes from one parent and some from the other, may have a new combination of genes that together yield characteristics not found in either parent.

Another source of variation is a **mutation,** or change, in a single gene. For instance, a gene for brown eyes might mutate into a gene for blue eyes. Mutation of a given gene is a rare event, but because each of us has millions of genes, mutations provide a constant source of variation.

A mutation is a random event; that is, the needs of the organism do not guide it. A mutation is analogous to having an untrained person add, remove, or distort something on the blueprints for your new house. Only rarely would the random change improve the house.

Most mutations produce recessive genes, however. Thus, if you or one of your recent ancestors had a harmful mutation on one of the genes, your children would not show the harmful effects unless you happened to mate with someone who had the same harmful mutant gene. Your mate is unlikely to have the same mutant genes that you have, unless the two of you got that gene from the same ancestor. For this reason, it is unhealthy for people to marry their close relatives.

Heritability

Unlike PTC sensitivity and color blindness, most variations in human behavior depend on the combined influence of many genes and many environmental influences. You may occasionally hear someone ask about a behavior, "Which is more important, heredity or environment?" That question, as stated, is meaningless, because heredity and environment are equally important. (No behavior can develop in the absence of either heredity or environment.)

Consider, however, a more meaningful question: "Do the observed *differences* among individuals in this population depend more on differences in heredity or differences in environment?" For example, you could not sing at all without both heredity and environment, but if you sing better than I do, the reason could be that you inherited genes that produced better vocal cords, or that you have practiced singing more extensively, or, of course, a combination of both factors.

In measuring the relative contribution of heredity to variations in outcome, researchers use the concept of **heritability,** an estimate of variance due to heredity that ranges from 0 to 1. If the heritability of a given characteristic is 0, then hereditary differences account for none of the observed variations in that characteristic within the tested population. A heritability of 1 indicates that hereditary differences account for all of the observed differences. Naturally, an intermediate value, such as .5, indicates an intermediate role for heredity.

How do researchers determine the heritability of some human trait? First, they compare the resemblances between monozygotic (identical) twins and dizygotic (fraternal) twins. A stronger resemblance between monozygotic twins indicates high heritability; equal resemblance in both kinds of twins indicates low or zero heritability. Second, they examine adopted children and their biological and adoptive parents. Resemblance to the biological parents indicates high heritability; resemblance to the adoptive parents indicates low heritability.

Heritability is difficult to measure precisely, especially with humans. Our estimates of human heritabilities depend on uncertain assumptions about the extent to which people choose mates who are genetically similar to themselves and the extent to which they choose mates from similar environments (Reynolds, Baker, & Pedersen, 1996). Furthermore, heritability can vary from one population to another. For example, in a community in which everyone is closely related to everyone else, the heritability of most behaviors will be low. (Differences in heredity cannot account for much if people have almost no differences in heredity!) Conversely, if the people in some other community differ in their heredity but all have virtually the same environment, the heritability of most behaviors will be high for that community. (Environmental differences cannot account for much, so the remaining variability must be largely hereditary.) In short, any estimate of heritability is necessarily imprecise and may or may not apply to people at a different time and place.

Even if we find that a trait has high heritability, it is still possible for environmental interventions to influence that trait. (A measure of heritability applies to a specific population in a specific environment; it cannot tell us about the possible effects of a different environment.) For example, **phenylketonuria** (FEE-nil-KEET-uhn-YOOR-ee-uh), or **PKU,** is a common genetically caused form of mental retardation. One to two percent of Europeans and Asians carry a recessive gene for PKU; few if any Africans have the gene (Wang et al., 1989). The gene prevents the body from metabolizing the amino acid *phenylalanine.* The consequent buildup of phenylalanine leads to structural malformations of the brain, leaving children mentally retarded, restless, irritable, and sometimes prone to temper tantrums. Under ordinary conditions, the heritability of PKU would be virtually 1.0.

However, it is possible to create conditions that minimize the effects of the PKU gene. In many countries, physicians routinely measure the level of phenylalanine or its metabolites in the blood or urine of every baby. If the results are abnormal, they advise the parents to put the baby on a strict diet to minimize the buildup of phenylalanine and thereby reduce the resulting abnormalities (Waisbren, Brown, de Sonneville, & Levy, 1994). Our ability to prevent PKU provides particularly strong evidence that *heritable* or *genetic* does not mean *unmodifiable.*

A couple of notes about PKU: First, a person with the condition can relax the diet after reaching maturity (about age 12–15), although a woman with PKU should return to the diet during pregnancy and nursing. Even a genetically normal baby cannot handle the enormous amounts of phenylalanine that an affected mother might pass through the placenta. Second, you may have noticed that beverages containing the artificial sweetener aspartame (NutraSweet) carry this advisory: "Phenylketonurics: Contains Phenylalanine." Aspartame is a compound of phenylalanine and one other amino acid. Anyone with PKU must be certain to avoid aspartame, and even genetically normal women should probably avoid large amounts during pregnancy.

How Genes Affect Behavior

We customarily speak of a "gene for brown eyes" or a "gene for" some other trait. In fact, a gene does not literally produce brown eyes. When we say "a gene for brown eyes," what we really mean is "a gene that produces a protein which, under ordinary circumstances, combines with other body products and environmental conditions to make the eyes brown instead of another color." Similarly, if we speak of a "gene for depression," or for any other psychological condition, we should not imagine that the gene itself produces depression. Rather, certain genes produce proteins that, under certain circumstances, increase the probability of depression. (Under other circumstances, the effects might be different.)

Exactly how a gene increases the probability of a given behavior is another matter, and in some cases the route can be indirect. In later chapters, we shall encounter a few examples of genes that control chemicals with known functions in the brain. In other cases, however, the heritability of a behavior can be traced to genes that affect processes outside the nervous system. For example, most people's livers metabolize ethanol (the kind of alcohol that people drink) to acetaldehyde, and then metabolize acetaldehyde to acetic acid, a harmless substance. However, some people lack the gene that enables them to convert acetaldehyde to acetic acid. When they drink alcohol, they accumulate acetaldehyde, a poison, and become ill. (See Figure 1.2.) The presence of the alternative gene in Southeast Asians may help explain their relatively low prevalence of alcohol abuse (Tu & Israel, 1995). In other words, the

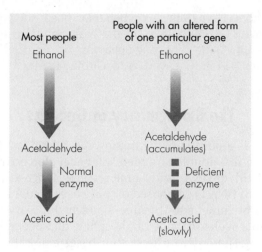

FIGURE **1.2**
How a gene controlling a digestive enzyme can influence alcohol consumption
Most people metabolize ethanol (ethyl alcohol) to acetaldehyde (a poison), then quickly convert acetaldehyde to acetic acid (a harmless substance). However, a gene common in Southeast Asian people impairs the conversion of acetaldehyde to acetic acid. People with this altered gene become ill after drinking alcohol; they are therefore less likely than others to abuse alcohol. This example illustrates how a gene can affect behavior even if it does not directly affect brain development.

heritability of alcohol abuse depends partly on a gene that affects functions in the liver, not the brain.

In other cases, genes affect behavior through even more indirect routes. For example, a gene that increases a person's height also increases the probability that the person will spend time playing basketball (if he or she lives in a community where people play basketball). Because time spent on a basketball court is necessarily time not spent doing something else, the increased-height gene probably decreases the time that the person spends playing the violin, talking on the telephone, and so forth.

Consequently, we should not be amazed by reports that almost every human behavior has some heritability. Research on monozygotic twins and adopted children indicates significant heritability of even such culturally specific behaviors as television watching (Plomin, Corley, DeFries, & Fulker, 1990), religious devoutness (Waller, Kojetin, Bouchard, Lykken, & Tellegen, 1990), social attitudes (Posner, Baker, Heath, & Martin, 1996), and interests and hobbies (Lykken, McGue, Tellegen, & Bouchard, 1992). I do not know what gene or combination of genes might increase the probability of watching television, but we can imagine many possibilities. (Genes for low physical activity, perhaps?) The point is, genes that affect the body in any way will also affect behavior, and a gene that affects one behavior will indirectly affect many other behaviors. Heritability of a behavior need not imply a gene with a direct effect on the brain, and we should not assume "one gene, one behavior" or "one gene, one disorder" (Plomin, Owen, & McGuffin, 1994).

The Biochemistry of Genetics

A gene is a portion of a chromosome, which is a molecule of the double-stranded chemical **deoxyribonucleic acid,** or **DNA** (with some proteins attached). Each strand of DNA is composed of four bases—guanine, cytosine, adenine, and thymine—attached in varying orders to a skeleton made of phosphate and deoxyribose, a sugar. The order of these four bases along the chromosome constitutes the genetic information for development of the body.

A strand of DNA serves as a **template,** or model, for the synthesis of **ribonucleic acid** (**RNA**) molecules. RNA is a single strand composed of a sequence of bases—guanine, cytosine, adenine, and uracil—attached to a skeleton made of phosphate and the sugar ribose. The RNA bases are arranged in a manner complementary to those of DNA: Where a DNA chain has guanine, the RNA chain has cytosine; similarly, DNA's cytosine, adenine, and thymine pair up with RNA's guanine, uracil, and adenine, as Figure 1.3 illustrates.

After they are synthesized from the DNA template, RNA molecules disperse to various places in the cell, where different kinds of RNA serve different functions. One kind, messenger RNA (mRNA), serves as a template for the formation of proteins. An mRNA chain uses a code to determine the amino-acid structure of a protein: Each sequence of three RNA bases codes for one amino acid. For instance, the RNA sequence guanine-cytosine-guanine codes for the amino acid arginine. The order of RNA bases determines the order of the protein's amino acids. Figure 1.4 summarizes the main steps in translating information from DNA through RNA into proteins, which then determine the development and properties of the organism. Some proteins form part of the structure of the body; others serve as **enzymes,** biological catalysts that regulate chemical reactions in the body.

Through the marvels of modern biochemistry, researchers can identify the exact location of genes on chromosomes. In fact, biologists hope to map the location of all human genes by the early 2000s. During the 1990s, researchers located the genes responsible for Huntington's disease (Chapter 8), most cases of Alzheimer's disease (Chapter 13), and a number of other conditions. We can expect research to continue identifying genes with profound psychological effects.

Locating a gene has at least two important benefits. First, it enables physicians to detect a harmful condition before symptoms begin. For example, Huntington's

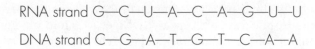

RNA strand G—C—U—A—C—A—G—U—U

DNA strand C—G—A—T—G—T—C—A—A

FIGURE 1.3

A strand of RNA is formed by pairing the complementary base to each base in the DNA.

disease, controlled by a single dominant gene, is a fatal condition with an average age of onset of about 40 years. If one of your parents had Huntington's disease, would you want to know whether you also have the gene? (The answer might affect your decision about having children, for example.) A chromosomal examination can give you the answer. There are evidently several genes (most of them not yet localized) that increase the probability of alcohol abuse. Psychologists know that once someone has become a severe alcoholic, relieving the problem is extremely difficult. If we could identify young people who are likely to become alcoholics, perhaps we could find more effective ways to prevent or minimize their alcohol abuse. (Perhaps not, I admit, but it seems worth a try.)

The second benefit of locating a gene is that researchers can determine what protein the normal gene produces and what distorted protein the abnormal gene produces. With that knowledge, researchers try to design more effective drugs or other treatments, with fewer years of trial-and-error testing. Identifying a gene and understanding its protein product will not guarantee a solution, but it certainly is an important step.

Gene localization offers potential dangers as well as benefits: What if employers insisted that job applicants take chromosome tests so that the employer could hire only people who had little risk of serious medical or psychological problems? What if insurance companies refused to insure people with high-risk genes? We do not face such threats at present, partly because chromosome tests are too expensive for routine use. If the tests become more widespread in the future, should we legally require insurance companies to offer coverage to all applicants at the same rate, regardless of their genetic predispositions? On the one hand, it seems unfair to discriminate against people on the basis of their genes. On the other hand, the insurance companies reply, "We won't require you to get a chromosome test, but if you get one on your own, and find out that you are likely to get some dreaded disease at an early age, and then we have to offer you insurance at the same rate as everyone else, what are you going to do? You may decide to buy ten million dollars' worth of health insurance and ten million dollars' worth of life insurance—far more than you would have wanted otherwise—and we would have to charge the same rate

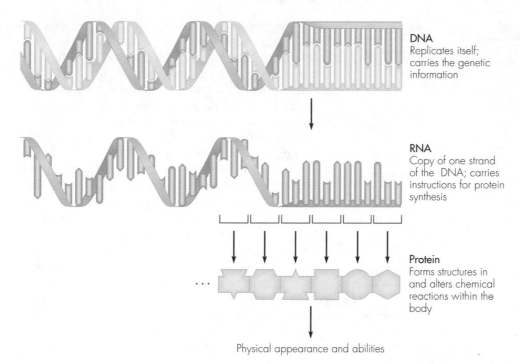

DNA
Replicates itself; carries the genetic information

RNA
Copy of one strand of the DNA; carries instructions for protein synthesis

Protein
Forms structures in and alters chemical reactions within the body

Physical appearance and abilities

FIGURE **1.4**
How DNA controls the development of the organism
The sequence of bases along a strand of DNA determines the order of bases along a strand of RNA; RNA in turn controls the sequence of amino acids in a protein molecule.

that we charge to someone who has no known risk. The insurance will be a great bargain for you, but our rates will have to go up for everyone else."

In short, genetic testing poses some problems and will undoubtedly create difficulties in the way we handle health and life insurance. How we shall resolve those difficulties is far from certain.

The Evolution of Behavior

Every gene that influences behavior, whether through direct effects on the brain or through roundabout effects on other organs, is subject to evolution by natural selection. **Evolution** is a change over generations in the frequencies of various genes in a population. Note that by this definition, evolution includes *any* change in gene frequencies. If a given gene increases in frequency for a few generations and then decreases, both the increase and the decrease are examples of evolution.

We must distinguish two questions about evolution: How *did* species evolve, and how *do* species evolve? To ask how species did evolve is to ask what evolved from what, and any answer is an inference based on fossils and detailed comparisons of living species. For example, biologists find that humans are more similar to chimpanzees than to other species in a wide variety of details, including the specific chemical structure of our proteins and our chromosomes. These similarities point to the probability of a common ancestor from which both humans and chimpanzees inher-

Sometimes a sexual display, like the spread tail feathers of a peacock, leads to great reproductive success and therefore to the spread of the associated genes. In a slightly changed environment, this "successful" gene could prove to be extremely harmful. For example, if an aggressive predator with good color vision enters the range of the peacock, the bird's slow movement and colorful feathers could spell its doom.

ited most of their genes. Similarly, humans and chimpanzees together have some striking resemblances to monkeys, and presumably shared a common ancestor with monkeys in the even more remote past. Using similar reasoning, evolutionary biologists have constructed an "evolutionary tree" that shows the relationships

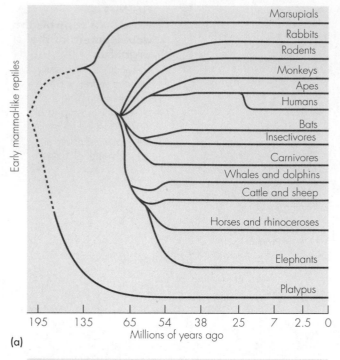

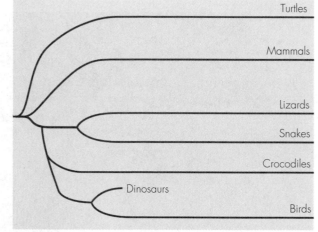

FIGURE 1.5
Evolutionary trees

(**a**) Evolutionary relationships among various species of mammals. (**b**) Evolutionary relationships among mammals, birds, and several kinds of reptiles.

among various species (see Figure 1.5). However, as new evidence becomes available, biologists occasionally change their opinions of what evolved from what, so any evolutionary tree is tentative.

Nevertheless, the question of how species *do* evolve is a question of how the process works, and that process is, in its basic outlines, a logical necessity. That is, any species that reproduces more or less the way we do *must* evolve. The study of genetics has demonstrated that offspring generally resemble their parents, but that mutations and recombinations of genes occa-

sionally introduce new inheritable variations. Some individuals survive longer and reproduce more abundantly than others; the individuals who reproduce the most will pass on the greatest number of genes to the next generation, which will in turn resemble the older individuals who reproduced most successfully. Any new gene or gene combination that is consistently associated with reproductive success will become more and more prevalent in later generations.

For hundreds of years, this principle has been well known by plant and animal breeders, who choose individuals with a desired trait and make them the parents of the next generation. This process of **artificial selection** over many generations has produced chickens that lay enormous numbers of eggs, cows that produce great volumes of milk, breeds of dogs ranging from Great Danes to Chihuahuas, and so forth. Darwin's (1859) insight was that nature also selects. If certain individuals are more successful than others in finding food, escaping enemies, attracting mates, or protecting their offspring, then their genes will become more prevalent in later generations.

Common Misunderstandings About Evolution

Let us clarify the principles of evolution by addressing a few misconceptions.

• *Does "evolution" mean "improvement"?* In the long run, the answer is *not necessarily.* For example, in some cases an individual may reproduce successfully because of its elaborate sexual displays. (Consider, for example, the colorful tail feathers of the peacock.) If the environment changes by the introduction of a new predator that responds to bright colors, the previously advantageous display may become a serious handicap. Evolutionary changes indicate what genes have been successful in the past, not necessarily what genes will be successful in the future.

• *Have humans stopped evolving?* Because modern medicine can keep almost anyone alive, and because welfare programs in prosperous countries provide the necessities of life for almost everyone, some people assert that humans are no longer subject to the principle of "survival of the fittest." Therefore, the argument goes, human evolution has stopped or at least slowed down a great deal.

The flaw in this argument is that evolution really relies not on survival of the fittest but on different rates of reproduction. A person who lives to age 100 without having children is an evolutionary failure, whereas someone who has many children but dies young is an evolutionary success—presuming that those children can survive long enough to reproduce. That is, the genes of the people who have the most children will spread in the population, and human evolution will continue. (Recall, however, the previous point: The evolution occurring today is not necessarily making the human species healthier, more intelligent, or "better." It is just making the species more like the types of people who are currently having the most children.)

• *Does the use or disuse of some structure or behavior cause an evolutionary increase or decrease in that feature?* You have probably heard someone say something like "because we hardly ever use our little toes for anything, they will get smaller and smaller in each succeeding generation." This is nonsense. Before Darwin, the biologist Jean Lamarck proposed the idea of evolution through the inheritance of acquired characteristics, an idea known as **Lamarckian evolution.** According to this idea, if giraffes stretch their necks as far out as possible, their offspring will be born with longer necks. Similarly, if you exercise your arm muscles, your children will be born with bigger arm muscles, and if you fail to use your little toes, your children's little toes will be smaller than yours. However, biologists have found no mechanism for Lamarckian evolution to occur and no evidence that it does occur. Using or failing to use some part of the body does not change the genes that control that part of the body. (People's little toes would shrink from generation to generation only if those people who have genes for smaller-than-usual little toes had some sort of advantage—for example, if extra-tiny little toes were considered sexy.)

• *Does evolution act to benefit the individual or the species?* Neither: It acts for the benefit of the genes! In a very real sense, you do not carry your genes around as a way of reproducing yourself; your genes carry *you* around as a way of reproducing *themselves* (Dawkins, 1989). A gene will spread through a population if—and only if—the individuals bearing that gene reproduce more than do the individuals bearing other genes. So, for example, imagine a gene that causes you to risk your own life in order to protect your children. That gene will spread through the population (if it really does benefit your children), even though it endangers you personally. Imagine a gene that causes you to attack other members of the species in order to provide more food for your children. If the others do not retaliate against you or your children, your aggressiveness will benefit your children's reproductive potential and your "uncooperative" genes will spread—even though they are probably harmful to the species.

Given that a gene spreads only if the individuals who bear it reproduce more than others, how can we explain the (admittedly rare) phenomenon of altruistic behavior in animals? **Altruistic behavior** benefits someone other than the individual doing the behavior. Altruism is common in humans: We contribute to charities, we try to help people in distress, a student may

It is possible to slow the rate of evolution, but not just by keeping everyone alive. China has enacted a policy that attempts to limit each family to one child. If the government managed to enforce the policy, human evolution would indeed reach a near standstill in China.

even explain something to a classmate who is competing for a good grade in a course. In humans it is especially hard to know whether such behaviors reflect "altruism genes" or the influence of deliberate teaching. However, we can observe a few apparently altruistic behaviors that are so widespread within certain animal species that it is hard to believe that each individual learned them. For example, when a crow finds food, it emits a call that attracts other crows to the food—where they may in fact compete with the first crow for as much food as possible. The "here's food" call benefits the other crows, but does not directly benefit the one who calls.

We do not know whether any genes are responsible for such behavior, but for the sake of illustration, suppose they are. How could such genes spread through the population? One common reply is that the altruistic behavior costs a crow very little. True, but being almost harmless is not good enough; a gene will spread only if the individuals that have it reproduce more than those that do not. Another common reply is that the altruistic behavior benefits the species. True again, but the rebuttal is the same. A gene that benefits the species but not the individual will die out with that individual.

A suggestion that sounds good at first is *group selection.* According to this idea, some groups within a species are altruistic toward one another and some groups are not; the altruistic groups survive and the uncooperative groups do not (Wilson & Sober, 1994). However, if a gene provides even a slight disadvantage to the individual, group selection will be unstable at best. Consider: Even if cooperative groups survive better than uncooperative groups, what will happen when an uncooperative mutation occurs within a cooperative group? If the uncooperative individual has even a slight reproductive advantage within its group, its genes will spread until the group as a whole is uncooperative.

One acceptable explanation for the spread of altruistic genes is **reciprocal altruism,** the idea that animals help those who will help them in return. Clearly, two individuals who cooperate with each other will prosper; however, reciprocal altruism can operate only in individuals capable of recognizing each other, and of distinguishing cooperators from cheaters. In other words, reciprocal altruism can arise only in a species with good sensory organs and a fairly well-developed brain. The other acceptable explanation is **kin selection,** selection in favor of a gene because it benefits the individual's relatives. I noted earlier that a gene could spread if it caused you to risk your life to protect your children. In a sense, such an act is altruistic; you are endangering yourself in order to help others, but because those others are your children, they share half of your genes, including perhaps the altruistic gene. Therefore, altruistic behavior toward your children helps spread your altruistic genes. Natural selection can favor altruism toward less close relatives—such as cousins, nephews, or nieces—if the benefits to them are enough greater than the cost to you (Dawkins, 1989; Hamilton, 1964; Trivers, 1985). Because groups of animals ordinarily include a number of close relatives, the kin-selection theory explains how genes for certain kinds of altruistic behavior may spread.

Sociobiology

Sociobiology deals with issues that concern the evolution of social behaviors, such as altruism. The emphasis is on *functional* explanations, as defined earlier (how a behavior might be useful and why natural selection would favor it). For example, why do males of so many species show more sexual jealousy than females do (Wilson & Daly, 1996)? Why do wolves live in packs and bears live singly? Why do males of some species help with infant care and males of other species do not?

Although sociobiologists make important contributions to our understanding, the field is subject to two major criticisms. First, functional explanations are often speculative. If we ask why male wrens share nesting and parental activities with the female and male grouse do not, it is relatively easy to devise a speculative explanation. One might then conduct either field studies or mathematical modeling to test that explanation. In the presence of such research, we may find that our explanation is sound; without research, however, it is just a guess. Second, sociobiological explanations sometimes imply that human behavior is what it is be-

cause it evolved that way, and because it evolved that way it should stay that way. For example, sociobiologists offer a plausible explanation for why mothers in all cultures contribute at least as much to child care as fathers do, and generally much more: A mother can be sure that a baby is her own, whereas a father may not be equally certain. Sociobiologists also explain why men tend to be more interested than women are in having casual sex with multiple partners: Males sometimes spread their genes this way, whereas a female with many sex partners cannot have babies more frequently than a female with one partner (Buss, 1994). The objection many people raise, however, is that the way things *are* is not necessarily the same as the way they *should be.* Agreeing that men tend to be more promiscuous than women does not mean that we should encourage men to be sexually irresponsible or that we should insist that every woman remain faithful to a single partner. Indeed, various human societies have differing rules and expectations about sexual behavior. Even if our genes predispose men and women to behave differently, we still have great flexibility in acting on our predispositions.

IN CLOSING

Genes and Behavior

In the control of behavior, genes are neither all-important nor irrelevant. Certain behaviors have a very high heritability; the ability to taste PTC is a clear, if not very important, example. Many other behaviors are influenced by many genes, but also subject to strong influence by experience. Our genes and our evolution make it possible for us to be what we are today, but they also make it possible for us to change our behavior as circumstances warrant.

Summary

1. Genes are chemical particles. A dominant gene affects development regardless of whether a person has pairs of that gene or only a single copy per cell. A recessive gene affects development only in the absence of the dominant gene. (p. 6)
2. Some behavioral differences demonstrate simple effects of dominant and recessive genes. More often, however, behavioral variations reflect the combined influences of

many genes and many environmental factors. Heritability is an estimate of the amount of variation that is due to variation in genes, as opposed to environmental variation. (p. 6)

3. The fact that some behavior shows high heritability for a given population does not necessarily indicate that it will show an equal heritability for a different population. It also does not deny the possibility that a change in the environment might significantly alter the behavioral outcome. (p. 8)

4. Genes influence behavior directly, by altering chemicals in the brain, and also indirectly, by affecting height, digestive enzymes, or virtually any other aspect of the body. (p. 9)

5. Genes are composed of DNA, which forms RNA copies, which in turn direct the formation of proteins. Locating a gene with known effects enables an early warning for a condition and may also facilitate research to control the condition; however, such knowledge can also be used in harmful ways. (p. 10)

6. The process of evolution through natural selection is a logical necessity, because mutations sometimes occur in genes and individuals with certain sets of genes reproduce more successfully than others do. (p. 12)

7. Evolution does not necessarily lead to the improvement of the species. It merely spreads the genes associated with the individuals who have reproduced the most. (p. 12)

Review Questions

1. Suppose you can taste PTC. If your mother can also taste PTC, what (if anything) can you predict about your father's ability to taste it? If your mother cannot taste it, what (if anything) can you predict about your father's ability to taste it? (p. 6)

2. How does a sex-linked gene differ from a sex-limited gene? (p. 7)

3. Suppose researchers measure the heritability of a trait in two populations, one in which everyone shares a good, supportive environment, and one in which certain individuals have a much better environment than others do. Which population will show the higher heritability, and why? (p. 8)

4. What example illustrates the point that changes in the environment can alter a behavioral outcome, even if that behavioral outcome shows high heritability under ordinary circumstances? (p. 8)

5. Many people believe that the human appendix is useless. Should we therefore expect that it will get smaller from generation to generation? Why, or why not? (p. 13)

6. What is a plausible way for possible altruistic genes to spread in a population? (p. 14)

Thought Questions

1. Huntington's disease has a heritability of virtually 1. What human behaviors, if any, would have a heritability of 0?

2. Certain conditions, including Alzheimer's disease, have a high heritability and ordinarily have their onset in old age. Genetic differences probably account for the fact that some people seem to age more slowly and more gracefully than others. Given that the genes affecting old age do not begin to show their effects *until* old age—long after people have stopped having children—how could evolution have any effect on such genes? Or should we assume that genes affecting only old people will just drift at random and that evolution will select neither for nor against them?

Suggestions for Further Reading

Plomin, R., DeFries, J. C., & McClearn, G. E. (1990). *Behavioral genetics: A primer* (2nd ed.). New York: W. H. Freeman. A textbook covering topics from the chemistry of chromosomes to the political implications of behavior genetics.

Plomin, R., Owen, M. J., & McGuffin, P. (1994). The genetic basis of complex human behaviors. *Science, 264,* 1733–1739. Fine review in a special issue of *Science* containing many articles on behavior genetics.

Weiner, J. (1994). *The beak of the finch.* New York: Alfred Knopf. Excellent description of observations of evolution in action, at a surprisingly rapid pace, in the birds of the Galapagos Islands.

Terms

gene   a physical particle that determines some aspect of inheritance (p. 6)

chromosome   strand of DNA bearing the genes (p. 6)

homozygous   having two identical genes for a given characteristic (p. 6)

heterozygous   having two unlike genes for a given trait (p. 6)

dominant gene   gene that exerts noticeable effects even in an individual who has only one copy of the gene per cell (p. 6)

recessive gene   a gene that exerts noticeable effects only in an individual who has two copies of the gene per cell (p. 6)

partial penetrance   tendency of a gene to be expressed only under certain conditions (p. 6)

crossing over   exchange of parts between two chromosomes during replication (p. 7)

autosomal gene   gene on any of the chromosomes other than the sex chromosomes (X and Y) (p. 7)

sex-linked gene   gene on either the X or the Y chromosome (p. 7)

Y chromosome   a chromosome of which female mammals have none and males one (p. 7)

X chromosome   a chromosome of which female mammals have two and males have one (p. 7)

sex-limited gene gene whose effects are seen only in one sex, although members of both sexes may have the gene (p. 7)

recombination a reassortment of genes during reproduction, sometimes leading to a characteristic that is not apparent in either parent (p. 8)

mutation change in a gene during reproduction (p. 8)

heritability an estimate of variance due to heredity, ranging from 0 to 1.0, indicating the degree to which variations in a characteristic depend on variations in heredity for a given population (p. 8)

phenylketonuria (PKU) inherited inability to metabolize phenylalanine, leading to mental retardation unless the afflicted person stays on a strict low-phenylalanine diet throughout childhood (p. 8)

deoxyribonucleic acid (DNA) the chemical that composes the chromosomes (p. 10)

template model from which copies are made (p. 10)

ribonucleic acid (RNA) a chemical whose structure is determined by DNA and that in turn determines the structure of proteins (p. 10)

enzyme any protein that catalyzes biological reactions (p. 10)

evolution change in the frequencies of various genes in a population over generations (p. 11)

artificial selection change in the frequencies of various genes in a population because of a breeder's selection of desired individuals for mating purposes (p. 12)

Lamarckian evolution discredited theory that evolution proceeds through the inheritance of acquired characteristics (p. 13)

altruistic behavior behavior that benefits someone other than the individual engaging in the behavior (p. 13)

reciprocal altruism helping individuals who may later be helpful in return (p. 14)

kin selection selection in favor of a gene because it benefits the individual's relatives (p. 14)

sociobiology field concerned with how and why various social behaviors evolved (p. 14)

The Use of Animals in Research

Certain ethical disputes seem to linger on forever, resistant to either solution or compromise. One is abortion; another is the death penalty; still another is the use of animals for research. For the purposes of biological psychology, the most relevant of these is animal research. As you will see throughout this book, most of what we know about the functioning of the nervous system stems from research done on laboratory animals. Some of that research is painful, stressful, or at least unpleasant for the animals. How shall we deal with the fact that on the one hand we want more knowledge and on the other hand we wish to minimize animal distress?

Reasons for Animal Research

Given that most biological psychologists want to understand the human brain and human behavior, why do they study nonhuman animals? Here are five reasons.

1. *The underlying mechanisms of behavior are similar across species and sometimes are easier to study in a nonhuman species.* If you wanted to understand how a complex machine works, you might begin by examining a smaller, simpler machine that operates on the same principle. We also learn about brain-behavior relationships by starting with simpler cases. The brains and behavior of nonhuman vertebrates resemble those of humans in many aspects of their chemistry and anatomy (see Figure 1.6 on the next page). Even invertebrate nerves follow the same basic principles as our own. Much research on nerve cells has been conducted on squid nerves, which are similar to human nerves but thicker and therefore easier to study.

2. *Sometimes a certain process is more exaggerated in certain animals than it is in humans.* For example, research has demonstrated that birds that have to learn their song can do so more easily during an early sensi-

tive period than they can later in life. When we find a clear phenomenon such as this in nonhumans, we can look for evidence of similar phenomena in ourselves.

3. *We are interested in animals for their own sake.* Humans are by nature curious. We would like to understand why the Druids built Stonehenge, where the moon came from, how the rings of Saturn formed, and why certain animals do the strange things they do, regardless of whether or not such information turns out to have any practical applications.

4. *What we learn about animals sheds light on human evolution.* What is our place in nature? How did we come to be the way we are? One way of approaching such questions is by examining other species. Can we find any trace of language capacity in chimpanzees and other nonhuman species? How intelligent are monkeys, rats, and other species? Humans did not evolve from chimpanzees, monkeys, or rats, but we do share common ancestors with these modern animals, so comparing the structure and function of various animal nervous systems with our own provides important clues to our evolution.

5. *Certain experiments cannot use human subjects because of legal or ethical restrictions.* For example, investigators insert electrodes into the brain cells of rats and other animals to determine the relationship between brain activity and behavior. Such experiments answer questions that investigators cannot address in any other way. They also raise an ethical issue: If it is unacceptable to do such research on humans, should we not also object to using nonhumans?

The Ethical Debate

In some experiments on animals, researchers observe their behavior as a function of different times of day, different seasons of the year, changes in diet, and so

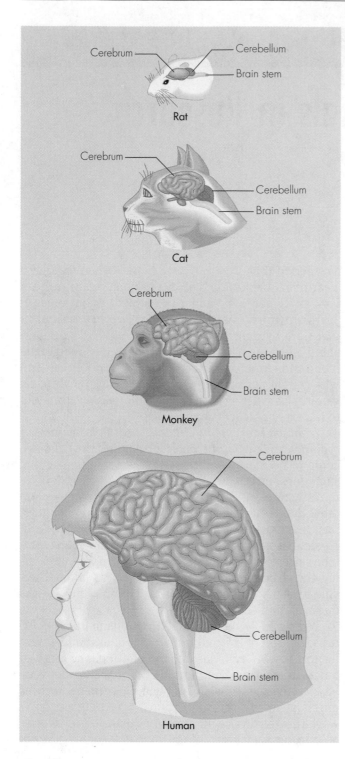

Cerebrum — — Cerebellum

— Brain stem

Rat

Cerebrum — — Cerebellum

— Brain stem

Cat

Cerebrum

— Cerebellum

— Brain stem

Monkey

— Cerebrum

— Cerebellum

— Brain stem

Human

FIGURE **1.6**
Brains of several species
The general plan and organization of the brain are similar for all mammals, even though the size varies from species to species.

however, including many discussed in this book, animals have been subjected to brain damage, electrode implantation, injections of drugs or hormones, and other treatments that would not be given to human beings. Many people regard such experimentation as cruelty to animals and have reacted either with peaceful (though vociferous) demonstrations, or with more extreme tactics, such as breaking into research labs, stealing lab animals, vandalizing lab property, and threatening researchers. Surveys have found that although most Americans support continuing animal research, a significant minority sees no value in animal research or thinks that such research is immoral regardless of the benefits (Compton, Dietrich, Smith, & Johnson, 1995). (See Figure 1.7.)

The issues are indeed difficult. On the one hand, many laboratory animals undergo painful or debilitating procedures that are *not* intended for their own benefit. Anyone with a conscience (including scientists) is bothered by this fact. On the other hand, experimentation with animals is essential for answering many research questions (American Medical Association, 1988; Miller, 1985). It has been critical to the medical research that led to methods for prevention or treatment of polio, diabetes, measles, smallpox, massive burns, heart disease, and other serious conditions. Most Nobel prizes in physiology or medicine have been awarded for research conducted on nonhuman animals. The hope of finding methods to treat or prevent AIDS and various brain diseases (such as Alzheimer's disease) depends largely on animal research. In biological psychology, when we deal with certain questions about brain functioning, our choice is to conduct research on animals or not to answer the questions at all.

Opposition to animal research ranges considerably in degree. At one end are the moderates, the "minimalists" who agree that some animal research is acceptable, but who wish it reduced to a minimum. That is, they would accept some kinds of research but prohibit others, depending on the probable value of the research, the amount or type of distress to the animal, and perhaps the type of animal. (Most people have fewer qualms about hurting an insect or a worm, say, than about hurting a dog or a dolphin.)

At the other end are the "abolitionists," who see no room for compromise. Abolitionists maintain that all animals have the same rights as humans. Keeping an animal (presumably even a pet) in a cage is, in their view, slavery. They regard killing an animal as murder, regardless of whether the intention is to eat it, to use its fur, or to gain scientific knowledge. Because they believe animals have the same right as humans to choose how to spend their lives, and because animals cannot give informed consent to an experiment, abolitionists insist it is wrong to use them in any experiment, re-

forth—procedures that we could ethically perform on humans, except that it is difficult to get people to stay in a laboratory long enough. In other experiments,

FIGURE 1.7
For many years, animal-rights activists have protested against experimentation with animals. This ad was placed by supporters of such research.

gardless of the circumstances. According to one opponent of animal research, "We have no moral option but to bring this research to a halt. Completely. . . . We will not be satisfied until every cage is empty" (Regan, 1986, pp. 39–40). Advocates of this position sometimes claim that much animal research is extremely painful or that no animal research ever leads to important results. Note, however, that for a true abolitionist, none of those facts really matter. The moral imperative would remain that people have no right to use animals in research, regardless of how useful or painless the research may be.

Some abolitionists have come into conflict with environmental protection groups as well. For example, red foxes, which humans introduced into California, so effectively rob bird nests that they have severely endangered several populations, including least terns and clapper rails. To protect the endangered birds, the U.S. Fish and Wildlife Service began trapping and killing red foxes in the areas where endangered birds breed. Their efforts were temporarily thwarted by the Animal Lovers Volunteer Organization, which argued that killing any animal was immoral even when the motive was to pro-

tect another species (Alper, 1991). Similar objections were raised when conservationists proposed to kill the pigs (again a human-introduced species) that were destroying the habitat of native Hawaiian wildlife.

At times in the animal-rights dispute, people on both sides have taken shrill "us versus them" positions. Some defenders of animal research have claimed that such research is almost always useful and seldom painful, and some opponents have argued that the research is usually painful and never useful. In fact, the truth is messier (Blum, 1994): Much of the research is both useful and painful. Those of us who value both knowledge and animal life look for compromises instead of either-or solutions.

Nearly all animal researchers sympathize with the desire to minimize painful research. That is, just about everyone draws a line somewhere and says, "I will not do this experiment. The knowledge I might gain is not worth the distress I would cause to these animals." To be sure, most experimenters would draw that line at a different point from where animal-rights activists would draw it. Deciding where to draw the line is not easy; researchers often cannot predict how useful a

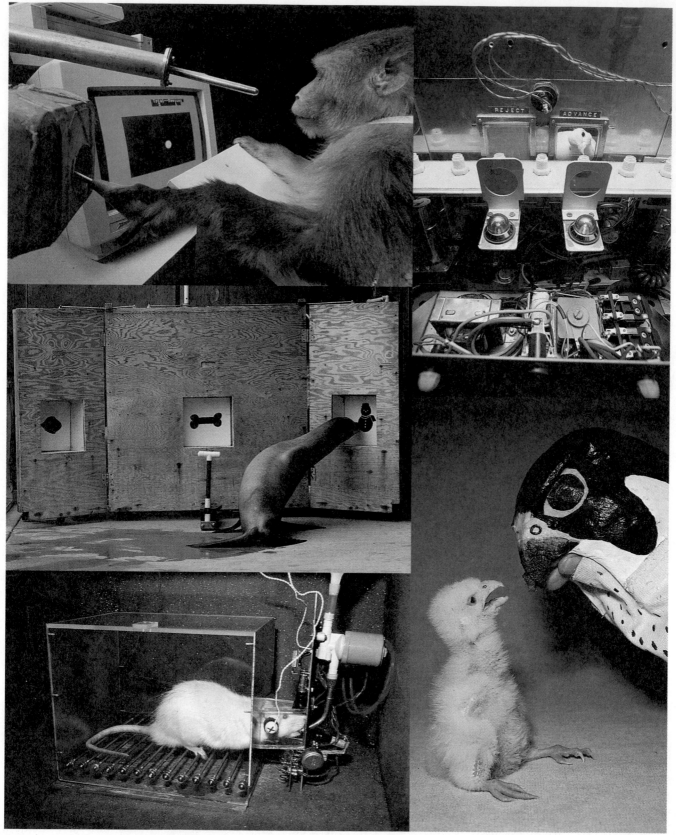

Animals are used in many kinds of research studies, some dealing with behavior and others with the functions of the nervous system.

given experiment will be, and no one has found a way to measure "distress to the animals" and "value of the results" in comparable units, in order to determine whether the value outweighs the distress.

Although it is very difficult to decide whether the probable value of proposed research justifies the probable distress to the animals, at least it is possible to compromise by letting a group of people decide, not the experimenter alone. In the United States, every college or other research institution that receives federal funds is required to have an Institutional Animal Care and Use Committee, composed of veterinarians and community representatives as well as scientists, that will evaluate proposed experiments, decide whether they are acceptable, and specify procedures designed to minimize pain and discomfort. (Similar regulations and committees govern research on human subjects.) In addition, all research laboratories must abide by national laws requiring certain standards of cleanliness and animal care. Professional organizations such as the Society for Neuroscience publish guidelines for the use of animals in research (see Appendix B).

Is this sort of compromise satisfactory? The disagreement between animal researchers and the abolitionists who object even to carefully regulated research is not a dispute between ethical standards and the absence of ethics. The dispute is between one ethical position ("Do no intentional harm to any other being, regardless of circumstances") and another one ("Sometimes a little harm leads to a greater good"). On the one hand, permitting research has the undeniable consequence of inflicting pain or distress. On the other hand, banning the use of animals for human purposes (including but not limited to research) means a great setback in medical research, as well as the end of animal-to-human transplants (such as using pig heart valves to help people with heart diseases). Many victims of serious diseases have organized to oppose animal-rights groups and to support animal research (Feeney, 1987).

IN **CLOSING**

Humans and Animals

We began this chapter with a quote from the Nobel Prize–winning biologist, Niko Tinbergen. Tinbergen argued that no fundamental gulf separates humans from other animal species. Because we are similar in many ways to other species, we can learn much about ourselves from animal studies. Also because of that similarity, we identify with animals and we wish not to inflict pain or distress upon them. Neuroscience researchers who have decided to conduct animal research have not, as a rule, taken this decision lightly. They want to minimize harm to animals, but they also want to increase knowledge. They believe it is better to inflict limited distress under controlled conditions than permit ignorance and disease to inflict uncontrolled and unregulated distress. We hope that at least most of the time we are making the right decision.

Summary

1. Researchers study animals because the mechanisms are sometimes easier to study in nonhumans, because they are interested in animal behavior for its own sake, because they want to understand the evolution of behavior, and because certain kinds of experiments would be difficult or impossible with humans. (p. 17)
2. The ethics of using animals in research is controversial. Some research does inflict stress or pain on animals; however, many research questions can be investigated only through animal research. (p. 18)
3. Animal research today is conducted under legal and ethical controls that attempt to minimize animal distress. (p. 20)

Review Questions

1. Describe at least one reason why biological psychologists sometimes conduct their research on nonhuman animals. (p. 17)
2. How does the "minimalist" position differ from the "abolitionist" view on animal research? (p. 18)

Suggestion for Further Reading

Blum, D. (1994). *The monkey wars.* New York: Oxford University Press. Informative and evenhanded account of the disputes between animal researchers and animal-rights activists.

NERVE CELLS AND NERVE IMPULSES

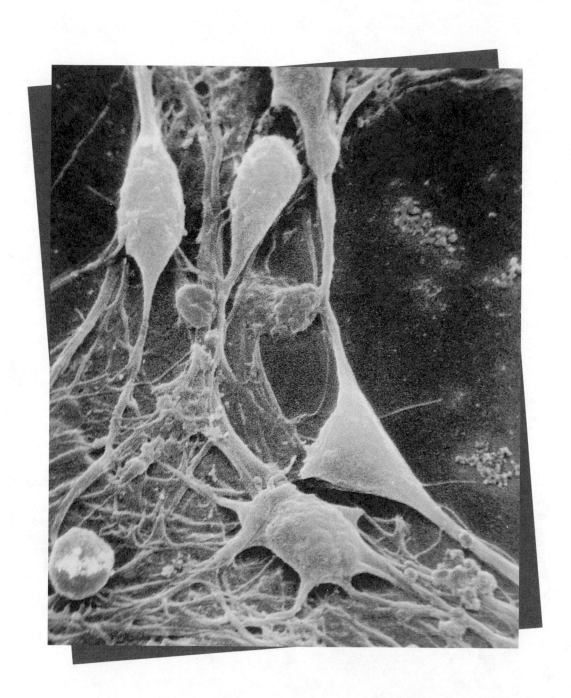

CHAPTER TWO

MAIN IDEAS

1. Two kinds of cells compose the nervous system: neurons and glia. Only the neurons transmit impulses from one location to another.
2. The structure of a neuron remains plastic throughout life. Its fibers can increase or decrease their branching pattern as a function of experience, age, and chemical influences.
3. Many molecules in the bloodstream that can enter other body organs are unable to enter the brain.
4. The action potential, an electrical change across the membrane of a neuron, is caused by the sudden flow of sodium ions into the neuron and is followed by a flow of potassium ions out of the neuron.
5. Many small neurons convey information through graded electrical potentials that vary in intensity, instead of through action potentials.

A nervous system, composed of many individual cells, is in some regards like a society of people who work together and communicate with one another, or even like elements that form a chemical compound: In each case, the combination has properties and functions that are unlike those of its individual components. We begin our study of the nervous system by examining single cells; later we shall try to understand the compounds of many cells acting together.

Advice: Parts of this chapter and the next require a knowledge of some basic chemical concepts such as *positively charged ions.* If you need to refresh your memory, read Appendix A.

The Cells of the Nervous System

Until the late 1800s, the best microscopic views of the nervous system revealed little detail about the organization of the brain. Without special staining techniques, the tiny cells, or *neurons*, of the brain are hard to distinguish from one another or from their background. Observers noted long, thin fibers between one neuron and another, but they could not determine whether each fiber stopped before the next cell or whether they actually merged. Then, in the late 1800s, Santiago Ramón y Cajal (see Digression 2.1 on page 26) demonstrated that a single neuron does not merge with its neighbors. A small gap separates the tip of one neuron's fibers from the surface of the next neuron.

Philosophically, we can see the appeal of the once-popular concept that neurons merge. We each experience our consciousness as a single thing, not as the sum of separate parts. It would seem right that all the cells in the brain should join together physically as one unit. Yet we now know that they do not. The adult human brain contains a great many neurons (Figure 2.1)—approximately 100 billion, according to one estimate (Williams & Herrup, 1988). (Because certain areas of the brain contain large numbers of very small cells, an accurate count is difficult.) Those billions of cells combine to produce both unified experience and coordinated, organized behavior. Before we can begin to contemplate how they act together, we need to know a little about the properties of the individual cell.

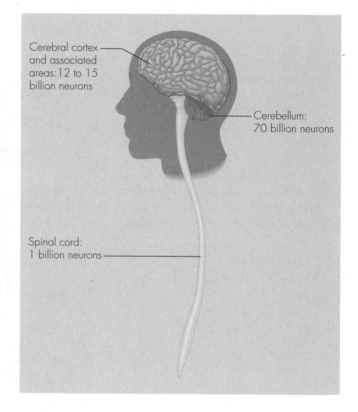

FIGURE **2.1**
Estimated numbers of neurons in humans, according to Williams & Herrup, 1988
Because of the small size of many neurons and the variation in cell density from one spot to another, obtaining an accurate count is difficult.

Neurons and Glia

It may not be obvious why a student of psychology needs to know details about the cells of the nervous system. However, many explanations of behavior do reflect specific details about neurons. For example, a kind of memory loss called Korsakoff's syndrome (Chapter 13) is caused by a deficiency in the nutrition of nerve cells; alcohol induces structural changes in nerve cells; anesthetic drugs prevent the transmission of nerve impulses. To follow these and other examples, one needs a basic understanding of nerve cells and their activities.

The nervous system consists of two kinds of cells, neurons and glia. **Neurons** receive information and transmit it to other cells by conducting electrochemical impulses; they are what people usually mean when

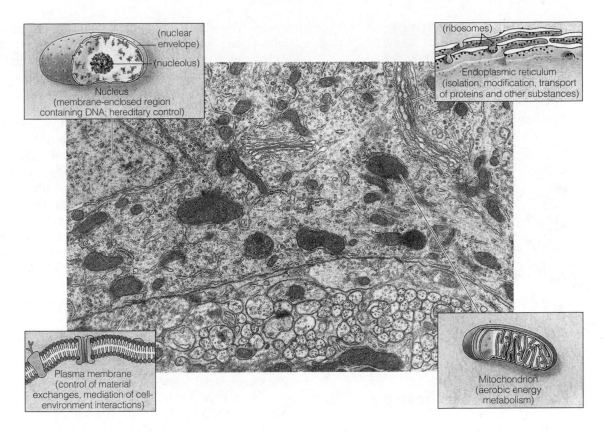

FIGURE **2.2**
An electron micrograph of a neuron from the cerebellum of a mouse
The nucleus, membrane, and other structures are characteristic of most animal cells. Magnification × 23,000.   Source: Micrograph courtesy of Dennis M. D. Landis.

they refer to "nerve cells." Later we shall examine the various types of glia and their functions. Because neurons resemble other body cells in many ways, we shall begin with the properties that all animal cells have in common.

The Structures of an Animal Cell

Figure 2.2 illustrates a neuron from the cerebellum of a mouse, magnified × 23,000. It contains the same basic structures as most other animal cells, even though its size and shape are quite distinctive.

Every cell is surrounded by a **membrane** (often called a *plasma membrane*), a structure composed of two layers of fat molecules that are free to flow around one another. (Figure 2.12 shows this arrangement in more detail.) The membrane controls the flow of materials between the inside of the cell and the outside environment. A few chemicals, such as water, oxygen, carbon dioxide, and many fat-soluble molecules, move fairly freely across the membrane. A few larger mole-

cules can cross through specialized protein channels. Other large or electrically charged molecules, for which no specialized protein channels exist, do not cross the membrane at all. The fluid inside the cell membrane is the **cytoplasm.**

All animal cells (except red blood cells) have a **nucleus,** the structure that contains the chromosomes. A **mitochondrion** (plural: mitochondria) is the site where the cell performs metabolic activities, providing the energy that the cell requires for all its other activities. Mitochondria require fuel and oxygen to function. **Ribosomes** are the sites at which the cell synthesizes new protein molecules. Proteins provide building materials for the cell and facilitate various chemical reactions. Some ribosomes float freely within the cell; others are attached to the **endoplasmic reticulum,** a network of thin tubes that transport newly synthesized proteins to other locations. **Lysosomes** contain enzymes that break down many chemicals into their component parts so they can be recycled for other uses. The **Golgi complex** is a network of vesicles that prepare hormones and other products for secretion.

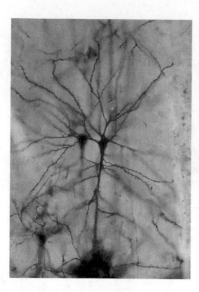

FIGURE **2.3**
Neurons, stained to appear dark
Note the small, fuzzy-looking spines on the dendrites.

The Structure of a Neuron

A neuron (Figure 2.3) contains a nucleus, a membrane, mitochondria, ribosomes, and the other structures typical of animal cells. What sets neurons apart from other cells is their shape. From the central bodies of neurons emanate variable numbers of small, thin fibers, which may extend their branches over short or very wide dis-

tances. The shape of a given neuron determines its connections with other neurons and thereby determines how it will contribute to the overall functioning of the nervous system. The wider the branching, the greater the number of possible connections with other neurons.

Figure 2.4 shows a motor neuron. It would be misleading to call this a typical neuron; no one neuron is typical of all others any more than an artichoke is typical of all vegetables. Nevertheless, the motor neuron contains all the parts found in other neurons.

Most neurons have three major components: the cell body, dendrites, and an axon. The **cell body,** or **soma** (Greek for *body*), contains the nucleus, some ribosomes and mitochondria, and other structures found in most cells. Much of the metabolic work of the neuron occurs here. Cell bodies of neurons range in diameter from 0.005 mm to 0.1 mm in mammals and up to a full millimeter in certain invertebrates.

The **dendrites** are thin, widely branching fibers that get narrower as they extend from the cell body toward the periphery. (The term *dendrite* comes from a Greek root word meaning *tree;* a dendrite's shape resembles that of a tree.) The dendrites form the information-receiving pole of the neuron (Bodian, 1962); that is, either direct sensory information or input from other neurons stimulates the dendrites, and the dendrites convey that information to the rest of the neuron.

The dendrite's surface is lined with specialized junctions, called *synapses,* at which the dendrite receives information from other neurons. (Chapter 3 fo-

---

DIGRESSION **2.1**

Santiago Ramón y Cajal

One of the major pioneers in the study of the nervous system—many rank him as the greatest of all—was the Spanish investigator Santiago Ramón y Cajal (1852–1934). Cajal's career did not progress altogether smoothly. At one point he was imprisoned in a solitary cell, limited to one meal a day, and taken out daily for public floggings . . . at the age of ten . . . for the crime of not paying attention during his Latin class (Cajal, 1937). (And you thought *your* teachers were strict!)

Cajal wanted to become an artist, but his father, who believed he could never earn a living at art, insisted that he study medicine. Cajal managed to combine the two fields, becoming an outstanding anatomical researcher and illustrator. His detailed drawings of the nervous system are still consulted today as a definitive source.

Before the late 1800s, microscopy could reveal few details about the nervous system. Then the Italian investigator Camillo Golgi discovered a method of using silver salts to stain nerve cells. For reasons unknown, this method completely stained some cells without affecting others at all. Consequently, it became possible to examine the structure of a single cell. Cajal used Golgi's methods, but applied them to infant brains, in which the cells are smaller, more compact, and therefore easier to examine on a single slide. Cajal's research demonstrated the structure of nerve cells and the fact that they remain separate instead of merging into one another.

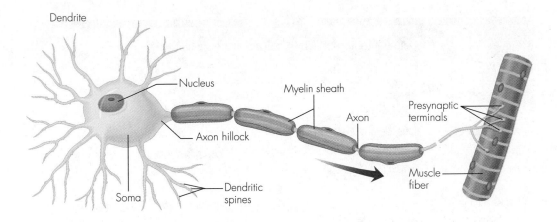

FIGURE **2.4**
The components of a vertebrate motor neuron
The cell body of a motor neuron is located in the spinal cord. The various parts are not drawn to scale; in particular, a real axon is much longer in proportion to the size of the soma.

cuses on the synapses.) The greater the surface area of a dendrite, the more information it can receive. Some dendrites branch widely, and therefore have a large surface area. Some also contain **dendritic spines,** the short outgrowths shown in Figure 2.5. The specialized synapses that form on dendritic spines apparently play an important role in the formation of learning and memory (Koch & Zador, 1993).

The **axon** is also a thin fiber, in most cases much longer than the dendrites. (The term *axon* comes from a Greek word meaning *axis.*) The axon is the information-sending pole of the neuron, conveying an impulse either toward other neurons or toward a gland or muscle (Bodian, 1962).

A mature neuron has either one axon or none, whereas it may have any number of dendrites. An axon may have many branches, however, which generally depart from the main trunk of the axon at a point far from the cell body. The axon maintains a constant diameter along its entire length. Some axons are a meter or more in length—for example, the axons going from your spinal cord to your feet. A neuron without an axon can convey information only to other neurons immediately adjacent to it.

The axon of a motor neuron is covered with an insulating material called a **myelin sheath.** Myelin covers some but not all vertebrate axons. Invertebrate axons do not have myelin sheaths.

Each branch of an axon swells at its tip, forming a **presynaptic terminal,** or *end bulb.* This is the point from which the axon releases chemicals that cross through the synapse (the junction between one neuron

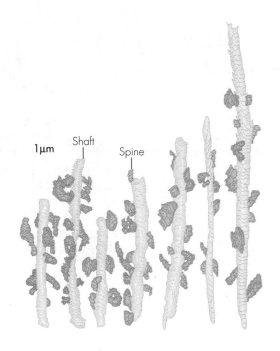

FIGURE **2.5**
Dendritic spines
The dendrites of certain neurons are lined with spines, short outgrowths that receive specialized incoming information. That information apparently plays a key role in long-term changes in the neuron that mediate learning and memory.   Source: From Harris & Stevens, 1989.

and the next) and influence the next cell. Because synthesizing and using these chemicals requires considerable energy, the presynaptic terminals have many mitochondria. Table 2.1 lists the anatomical distinctions between dendrites and axons.

TABLE **2.1**

Anatomical Distinctions Between Dendrites and Axons

	Dendrites	**Axons**
Number per cell	Can be many	One or none
Branches	Variable number; can have many	Variable number; can have many
Angle of branches	Usually branch at acute angles	Usually branch at right angles to the trunk of the axon
Length	Usually shorter than axon	Can be any length, in some cases 1 meter or longer
Tapering?	Diameter tapers toward periphery of the dendrite	Diameter constant over length of axon until presynaptic terminal
Hillock?	No hillock	Some axons begin at a hillock attached to the soma
Myelin?	Not covered with myelin	Among vertebrates, some axons are covered with a myelin sheath
Contain ribosomes?	Many ribosomes in larger dendrites	Few or no ribosomes
Receive synapses?	Yes; most are virtually covered with synapses	Only at or near the presynaptic terminal

Variations Among Neurons

Neurons vary enormously in size, shape, and function. We can distinguish between large neurons that relay information over great distances and small neurons with only local connections. We can also distinguish among sensory neurons, motor neurons, and interneurons. A **receptor** or **sensory neuron** is specialized to be highly sensitive to a particular type of stimulation, such as a certain wavelength of light, a certain kind of touch, or a particular chemical. A vertebrate sensory receptor receives touch information from the skin (Figure 2.6). Note that the dendrites of such a neuron merge directly into the axon; the soma is located on a little stalk off the main trunk. The nerve impulse, or action potential, begins at the start of the axon.

A **motor neuron** (Figure 2.4) receives excitation from other neurons and conducts impulses from its soma in the spinal cord to muscle or gland cells. The dendrites enter the soma and the axon exits from the soma. In such neurons, the action potential begins at the **axon hillock,** where the axon exits the soma.

Interneurons receive information from receptor neurons or other interneurons and send it to either motor neurons or other interneurons. Many interneurons connect only to other interneurons, not to receptor or motor neurons. Most of the neurons in the human nervous system are interneurons.

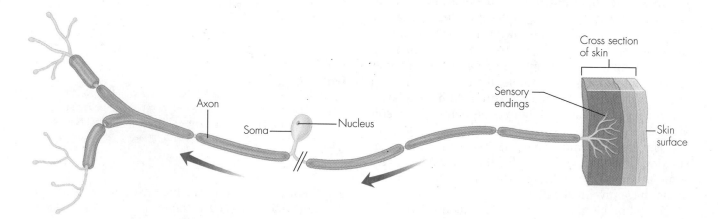

FIGURE **2.6**
A vertebrate sensory neuron
Note that the soma is located in a stalk off the main trunk of the axon. As in Figure 2.4, the various structures are not drawn to scale.

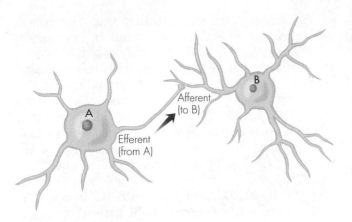

FIGURE **2.7**
Cell structures and axons
It all depends on the point of view. An axon from A to B is an *efferent* axon from A; it is an *afferent* axon to B—just as a train from Washington to New York is *exiting* Washington and *approaching* New York.

Other terms associated with neurons are *afferent, efferent,* and *intrinsic.* An **afferent axon** brings information into a structure; an **efferent axon** carries information away from a structure. Every sensory neuron is an afferent to the rest of the nervous system; every motor neuron is an efferent from the nervous system. Within the nervous system, a given neuron can be efferent from the standpoint of one structure and afferent from the standpoint of another; for example, an axon that is efferent from the thalamus may be afferent to the cerebral cortex (Figure 2.7). If a cell's dendrites and axon are entirely contained within a single structure, the cell is an interneuron or **intrinsic neuron** of that structure. For example, an intrinsic neuron of the cerebral cortex has all its dendrites or axons within the cortex; it communicates only with other cells of the cortex.

The function of a neuron is closely related to its shape (Figure 2.8). For example, the dendrites of the Purkinje cell of the cerebellum (Figure 2.8a) branch extremely widely within a single plane; this cell is capable of integrating an enormous amount of incoming information. The neurons in Figures 2.8c and 2.8e also have widely branching dendrites that receive and integrate information from many sources. By contrast, certain cells in the retina (Figure 2.8d) have only short branches of their dendrites and therefore pool input from only a few sources.

Glia

Glia (or *neuroglia*) are the other major components of the nervous system. The term *glia* is derived from a Greek word meaning *glue;* early investigators believed that glia were like glue or putty that held the neurons

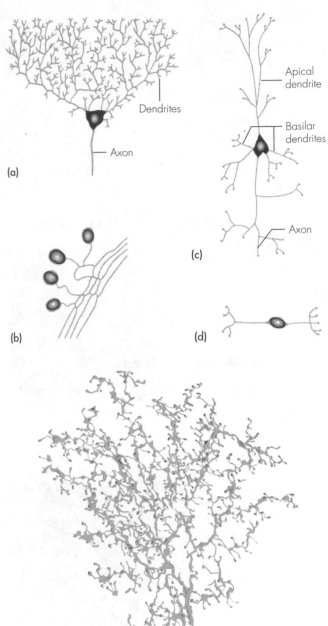

FIGURE **2.8**
The diverse shapes of neurons
(**a**) Purkinje cell, a cell type found only in the cerebellum; (**b**) sensory neurons from skin to spinal cord; (**c**) pyramidal cell of the motor area of the cerebral cortex; (**d**) bipolar cell of retina of the eye; (**e**) Kenyon cell, from a honeybee.

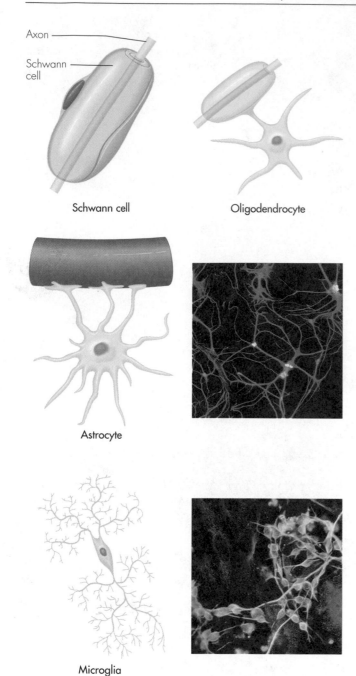

FIGURE **2.9**
Shapes of some glia cells
Glia perform a number of important roles in the nervous system. Among other functions, they guide the growth and migration of neurons, produce the myelin sheaths that insulate certain vertebrate axons, and remove waste products from the brain.

together (Somjen, 1988). Although that concept is obsolete, the term remains.

The average glial cell is about one-tenth the size of a neuron. However, because glia are about ten times more numerous than neurons in the human brain, they occupy about the same total space as the neurons (see Figure 2.9).

Because neurons are larger than glia, investigators can measure the electrical and chemical properties of neurons much more easily than they can those of glia. Consequently, our knowledge of glia is less extensive. In contrast to neurons, glia do not transmit information over long distances, although the possibility remains that glia may exchange information with immediately adjacent neurons. Among other functions, glia, particularly the star-shaped glia called **astrocytes,** absorb chemicals released by neurons, store those chemicals, and then either return them to the neurons or transfer them to the blood (Sontheimer, 1995a, 1995b). Glia also remove waste material, particularly that created when neurons die. **Oligodendrocytes** (OL-i-go-DEN-druh-sites) in the brain and spinal cord and **Schwann cells** in the periphery of the body are specialized types of glia that build the myelin sheaths that surround and insulate certain vertebrate axons. **Radial glia,** a type of astrocyte, guide the migration of neurons and the growth of their axons and dendrites during embryonic development. Schwann cells perform a related function after damage to axons in the periphery, guiding a regenerating axon to the appropriate target.

Glia probably perform other functions, contributing to the structural changes that occur in neurons as a result of experience (Raisman, 1991). Even such functions as learning and memory may depend not just on the neurons but on the glia-neuron combinations. Future research may identify additional functions.

Structural Changes in Neurons and Glia

Skin cells and cells in many other parts of the body can divide at any time to replace cells that have died. However, in most areas of the adult vertebrate brain, lost neurons cannot be replaced. As neurons develop their complex shape and function, they lose their ability to divide and reproduce. In the adult vertebrate brain, a few immature neurons are capable of dividing and maturing into new neurons—at least it is possible to get them to do so in tissue culture—but they ordinarily do not form new neurons. Evidently, the chemical environment of the brain prevents these cells from dividing (Goldman, 1995). In other words, virtually all of the neurons present in an adult vertebrate brain have been there since infancy.

Neuroscientists have identified a very few exceptions to this rule. Olfactory receptors, which are exposed to the outside world and its toxic chemicals, have a short life expectancy; if we could not replace them, we would lose our sense of smell at an early age. Fortunately, a small population of neurons in the nose remain immature until one of the mature olfactory recep-

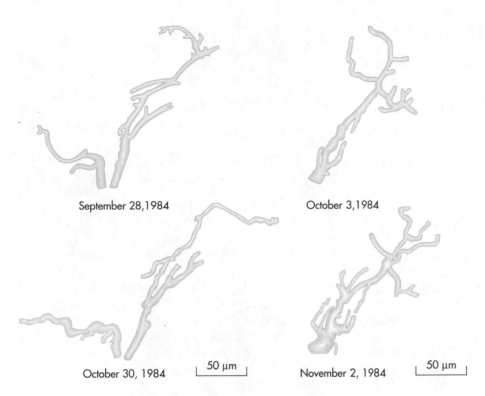

September 28, 1984   October 3, 1984

October 30, 1984   └ 50 µm ┘   November 2, 1984   └ 50 µm ┘

FIGURE **2.10**
Changes over time in dendritic trees of two neurons
During a month, some branches elongated and others retracted. The shape of the neuron is in flux even during adulthood.   Source: From Purves & Hadley, 1985.

tors dies. Then an immature neuron divides, forming one neuron that will become mature and one that will remain immature (Graziadei & deHan, 1973; Graziadei & Monti Graziadei, 1985).

Another exception to the "no new neurons in adulthood" rule is in the song-producing areas of canaries, where researchers have found a fairly steady process of old neurons dying and being replaced by new neurons (Nottebohm, 1985). A similar process occurs in certain areas of the rat brain (Bayer, 1985; Kaplan, 1985). In both the canary and the rat, the new neurons are always small ones with strictly local connections. Researchers have not found evidence of any new neurons in adult monkeys (Rakic, 1985).

Cancer is an abnormal proliferation of cells. Because most neurons cannot reproduce, brain cancers are generally—maybe always—limited to glial cells, which can and do divide throughout life.

Although new neurons do not develop in most of the adult vertebrate brain, existing neurons can change their shapes and connections. Indeed, such phenomena as learning and memory require some sort of alteration in the nervous system, and many such changes are demonstrable, as we shall see in Chapter 13. Dale Purves and R. D. Hadley (1985) developed a method of injecting a dye that enabled them to examine the structure of a living neuron at different times, days to weeks apart. They demonstrated that some dendritic branches grow and extend, while others retract or disappear altogether (see Figure 2.10). Evidently, the anatomy of the brain is in constant plasticity at the microscopic level as neurons change their connections.

People gradually lose neurons throughout life; as they age beyond about age 60, they also begin to have some shrinkage of dendrites of the remaining neurons, at least in certain brain areas (Jacobs & Scheibel, 1993). However, other processes partly compensate for these losses. For example, although dendrites tend to get shorter as people age, some of the shrinking dendrites increase their branching; thus the brain may have shorter but more numerous dendritic segments. Also, although dendrites tend to shrink in many brain areas, they may actually grow wider branching patterns in other areas. S. J. Buell and P. D. Coleman (1981) found that alert elderly people had widely branching dendrites, whereas senile elderly people had dendrites that were both short and poorly branched.

The Blood-Brain Barrier

Medical doctors sometimes find that a drug that they would like to administer cannot enter the brain. For example, certain chemotherapy drugs that fight cancer elsewhere in the body cannot get into the brain to attack brain cancers. Dopamine would be helpful in alleviating Parkinson's disease except that it too is unable to enter the brain. The mechanism that keeps most chemicals out of the vertebrate brain is known as the **blood-brain barrier.** Before we examine how it works, let us consider why we need it.

Why We Need a Blood-Brain Barrier

From time to time, harmful substances enter the body—viruses, for example. When a virus enters a cell, mechanisms within the cell extrude a virus particle through the cell membrane, so that *natural killer cells* (part of the immune system) can find the virus. When the natural killer cells attack the virus, they also kill the cell that contains it. In effect, the cell that exposes the virus through its membrane is committing suicide; it says, "Look, immune system, I'm infected with this virus. Kill me and save the others."

That plan works fine if the virus-infected cell is, say, a skin cell or a blood cell: The body can simply make a replacement. But the mature vertebrate brain does not make replacement neurons; a neuron that it loses is gone forever. To minimize any neuron loss, the body literally builds a wall along the sides of the brain's blood vessels, a wall that keeps most viruses, bacteria, and other dangerous intruders out.

"If that works so well for the brain," you might ask, "why don't we have similar walls around the rest of our organs?" The answer is that we pay a price for having a blood-brain barrier: The barrier that keeps out the viruses also keeps out most forms of nutrition.

"What happens if a virus does enter the brain?" you might also ask. After all, certain viruses do break through the blood-brain barrier. Neurons, unlike other body cells, do not commit suicide by exposing a virus through the membrane (Joly, Mucke, & Oldstone, 1991). The brain has some defenses against viral reproduction (Levine et al., 1991), but no way to kill a virus. Consequently, a virus that enters your nervous system will probably remain with you for life. The herpes virus, for example, enters spinal-cord cells. Even though it may remain dormant for years, and even though the immune system may have eliminated the herpes virus outside the nervous system, virus particles can emerge from the spinal cord at any time and reinfect the rest of the body.

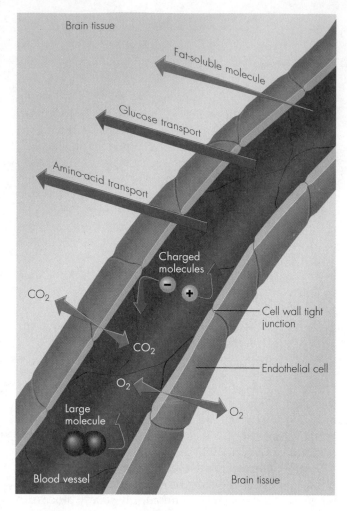

FIGURE **2.11**
The blood-brain barrier
Most large molecules and electrically charged molecules cannot cross from the blood to the brain. A few small, uncharged molecules such as O_2 and CO_2 can cross; so can certain fat-soluble molecules. Active transport systems pump glucose and certain amino acids across the membrane.

How the Blood-Brain Barrier Works

The blood-brain barrier (Figure 2.11) depends on the arrangement of endothelial cells that form the walls of the capillaries (Bundgaard, 1986; Rapoport & Robinson, 1986). In most parts of the body, such cells are separated by gaps large enough to allow the passage of large molecules. In the brain, the endothelial cells are tightly joined to one another. Many molecules simply cannot pass through those joints.

Molecules that freely cross the blood-brain barrier include oxygen, carbon dioxide, and a few other small, uncharged molecules. Because heroin, nicotine, and cannabinol (the active substance in marijuana) are soluble in fats, they can dissolve in the fats of the capillary walls and cross. Heroin crosses more freely than morphine does and therefore produces stronger effects on the brain.

A mechanism called an **active transport system** (an energy-using protein) pumps into the brain certain important chemicals that would not be able to pass through the barrier otherwise. One transport system pumps in glucose; another pumps in certain large amino acids.

The Nourishment of Vertebrate Neurons

Most cells use a wide variety of fuels, but vertebrate neurons derive almost all of their nutrition from **glucose,** a simple sugar. (Cancer cells and the testis cells that make sperm also rely overwhelmingly on glucose.) The metabolic pathway that uses glucose requires oxygen; consequently, the neurons—especially their dendrites—consume an enormous amount of oxygen compared with other body organs (Wong-Riley, 1989).

Why do neurons depend so heavily on glucose? Actually, they have the enzymes necessary to metabolize fats and several sugars. However, in most parts of the adult vertebrate nervous system, nutrients other than glucose cannot cross the blood-brain barrier (Gjedde, 1984). When the blood-brain barrier is weak, as it is in infants, neurons can and do use other fuels.

Even for neurons that depend exclusively on glucose, a glucose shortage is rarely a problem. The liver can convert many carbohydrates, proteins, and fats into glucose; thus, the glucose level in the blood is almost always sufficient to meet the brain's needs. An inability to *use* glucose can be a problem, however. Many chronic alcoholics have a diet deficient in vitamin B_1, **thiamine,** which is necessary for the use of glucose. Prolonged thiamine deficiency can lead to death of neurons and a condition called Korsakoff's syndrome, marked by severe memory impairments (Chapter 13).

IN**CLOSING**

Neurons

What does the study of individual neurons tell us about behavior? Perhaps the main lesson is that our experience and behavior *do not* follow from the properties of any one neuron. Just as a chemist must know about atoms to make sense of compounds, a biological psychologist must know about cells to understand the nervous system. Still, the nervous system is no more the sum of the individual cells than water is the sum of oxygen and hydrogen. Our behavior emerges from the communication among neurons.

Summary

1. In the late 1800s, Santiago Ramón y Cajal used newly discovered staining techniques to establish that the nervous system is composed of separate cells, now known as neurons. (pp. 24, 26)
2. Neurons receive information and convey it to other cells. The nervous system also contains *glia,* cells that serve many functions but do not transmit information over long distances. (pp. 24, 29)
3. Neurons have four major parts: a cell body, dendrites, an axon, and presynaptic terminals. Their shapes vary greatly, depending on the function of the neuron and the connections that it makes with other cells. (p. 26)
4. As a rule, the mature vertebrate nervous system cannot form new neurons to replace damaged ones. The olfactory receptors are among the few exceptions to this rule. (p. 30)
5. Neurons can alter their shape as a result of experience or aging. (p. 31)
6. Because of a set of mechanisms known as the blood-brain barrier, many molecules, especially large ones, cannot enter the brain. Adult neurons rely heavily on glucose, the only nutrient that can cross the blood-brain barrier. (pp. 31, 33)

Review Questions

1. Identify nucleus, mitochondrion, and ribosomes. (p. 25)
2. Suppose you are looking at a small fiber in the brain; how can you tell whether it is a dendrite or an axon? (p. 28)
3. Distinguish among receptor neurons, motor neurons, and interneurons. Distinguish between afferent and efferent. (p. 28)
4. Give an example of how a neuron's shape relates to its function. (p. 29)
5. What are some functions of the glia? (p. 30)
6. What is the current belief about whether new neurons can form in an adult vertebrate brain? (p. 30)
7. What mechanisms cause the blood-brain barrier? (p. 32)
8. What is the primary fuel of neurons in the adult vertebrate brain? Why do most brain neurons use very little of other fuels? (p. 33)
9. Which vitamin is necessary for neurons to use their primary fuel? (p. 33)

Suggestion for Further Reading

Kimelberg, H. K., & Norenberg, M. D. (1989, April). Astrocytes. *Scientific American, 260* (4), 66–76. An overview of the functions of glia.

Terms

neuron   cell that receives information and transmits it to other cells by conducting electrochemical impulses (p. 24)

membrane   structure that surrounds a cell (p. 25)

cytoplasm   fluid inside the cell membrane (p. 25)

nucleus   structure within a cell that contains the chromosomes (p. 25)

mitochondrion (plural: **mitochondria**)   the structure where the cell performs the metabolic activities that provide energy (p. 25)

ribosome   the site at which the cell synthesizes new protein molecules (p. 25)

endoplasmic reticulum   a network of thin tubes within a cell that transports newly synthesized proteins to other locations (p. 25)

lysosome   structure within a cell that contains enzymes that break down many chemicals into their component parts (p. 25)

Golgi complex   a network of vesicles within a cell that prepare hormones and other products for secretion (p. 25)

cell body or **soma**   structure of a cell that contains the nucleus (p. 26)

dendrite   thin, widely branching fiber that emanates from a neuron (p. 26)

dendritic spine   short outgrowth along the dendrites (p. 27)

axon   a single fiber that extends from a neuron (p. 27)

myelin sheath   an insulating material that covers many vertebrate axons (p. 27)

presynaptic terminal   the tip of an axon, the point from which the axon releases chemicals (p. 27)

receptor or **sensory neuron**   a neuron specialized to be highly sensitive to a specific type of stimulation (p. 28)

motor neuron   a neuron that receives excitation from other neurons and conducts impulses from its soma in the spinal cord to muscle or gland cells (p. 28)

axon hillock   a swelling of the soma, the point where the axon begins (p. 28)

interneuron   a neuron that receives information from other neurons and sends it to either motor neurons or interneurons (p. 28)

afferent axon   a neuron that brings information into a structure (p. 29)

efferent axon   a neuron that carries information away from a structure (p. 29)

intrinsic neuron   a neuron whose axons and dendrites are all confined within a given structure (p. 29)

glia   a type of cell in the nervous system that, in contrast to neurons, does not conduct impulses to other cells (p. 29)

astrocyte (astroglia)   a relatively large, star-shaped glia cell (p. 30)

oligodendrocyte   glia cell that surrounds and insulates certain axons in the vertebrate brain and spinal cord (p. 30)

Schwann cell   glia cell that surrounds and insulates certain axons in the periphery of the vertebrate body (p. 30)

radial glia   a type of glia cell that guides the migration of neurons and the growth of their axons and dendrites during embryological development (p. 30)

blood-brain barrier   the mechanism that keeps many chemicals out of the brain (p. 31)

active transport   transfer of chemicals across a membrane by expenditure of energy, as opposed to passive diffusion (p. 32)

glucose   a simple sugar, the main fuel of vertebrate neurons (p. 33)

thiamine (vitamin B_1)   a chemical necessary for the metabolism of glucose (p. 33)

The Nerve Impulse

Think about the axons that convey information from your feet's touch receptors toward your spinal cord and brain. If the axons could convey information by electrical conduction, they could transfer that information extremely rapidly. However, given that your body is made of carbon compounds and not copper wire, the strength of the impulse would decay greatly on the way from your toes to your spinal cord and brain. If you could feel the impulses at all, you would experience a pinch on your shoulder much more strongly than a pinch on your abdomen, which in turn would feel much stronger than a pinch on your toes. Short people would be able to feel their toes better than tall people could.

The way your axons actually function avoids that problem. Instead of simply conducting an electrical impulse, the axon regenerates an impulse at each point along the way, analogous to the way a burning string conveys a stimulus without loss of strength from its start to its finish. (Unlike a string, of course, an axon can transmit repeated impulses.)

Although the axon's method of transmitting an impulse prevents a pinch on your shoulder from feeling stronger than a pinch on your toes, it introduces a different problem: Because the axon transmits information at only a moderate speed (10–100 m/s), a pinch on your shoulder will reach your brain *faster* than does a pinch on your toes. Now, if you get some friend to pinch you simultaneously on your shoulder and your toe, you probably will not notice that your brain received one stimulus before the other. Your brain is not set up to register small differences in time of arrival of touch messages. After all, why should it be? You almost never need to know whether a touch on one part of your body occurred slightly before or after a touch somewhere else.

In vision, however, your brain *does* need to know whether one stimulus began slightly before or after another one. If two adjacent spots on your retina—let's call them spots A and B—send impulses at almost the same time, an extremely small difference in timing of the impulses indicates whether a flash of light moved from A to B or from B to A. In order to detect movement as accurately as possible, your visual system compensates for the fact that some parts of the retina are slightly closer to your brain than other parts are. Without some sort of compensation, simultaneous flashes arriving at two spots on your retina would reach your brain at different times and you might perceive a flash of light moving from one spot to the other. What prevents that illusion is the fact that axons from more distant parts of your retina transmit impulses slightly faster than axons that are closer to the brain (Stanford, 1987)!

In short, the properties of impulse conduction in an axon are well adapted to the exact needs for information transfer in the nervous system. Let us now examine the mechanics of impulse transmission in more detail.

The Resting Potential of the Neuron

The membrane of a neuron is specialized to control the exchange of chemicals between the inside and outside of the cell; it also maintains an electrical gradient necessary for neural signaling. All parts of a neuron are covered by a membrane about 8 nanometers (nm) thick (just less than 0.00001 mm), composed of two layers (an inner layer and an outer layer) of phospholipid molecules (molecules containing chains of fatty acids and a phosphate group). Embedded among the phospholipids are some cylindrical protein molecules (see Figure 2.12). The structure of the membrane provides it with a good combination of flexibility and firmness and retards the flow of chemicals between the inside and the outside of the cell.

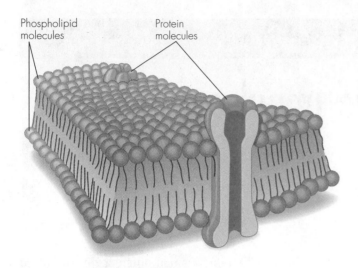

Phospholipid
molecules

Protein
molecules

FIGURE **2.12**
The membrane of a neuron
Embedded in it are protein channels that permit certain ions to
cross through the membrane at a controlled rate. Each membrane molecule has a water-attracting "head" and two fatty
water-repelling "tails."

In the absence of any outside disturbance, the
membrane maintains an electrical **polarization;** that is,
the neuron inside the membrane has a slightly negative
electrical potential with respect to the outside. In a resting neuron, this electrical potential, or difference in
voltage, is called the **resting potential.** It is produced
by the unequal distribution of ions between the inside
and outside of the neuron.

When the neuron is at its resting potential, a number of common ions are distributed unequally across
the membrane. The difference in distribution is called a
concentration gradient. Sodium is more than ten times
more concentrated outside the membrane than it is inside; potassium is more than twenty times more concentrated inside than outside (Guyton, 1974). However,
because the body has far more total sodium ions than
potassium ions, the concentration of sodium ions outside the membrane is far greater than the concentration
of potassium ions inside the membrane. Thus, the outside of the cell is more positively charged, the inside
more negatively. (The actual negative charges are
borne mostly by chloride ions and by some large proteins inside the cell.)

Researchers can measure the resting potential by
inserting a very thin **microelectrode** into the cell body,
as Figure 2.13 shows. The diameter of the electrode
must be as small as possible so that it can enter the cell
without causing damage. By far the most common electrode is a fine glass tube filled with a concentrated salt
solution, such as 2 to 3 molar (M) potassium chloride,
and tapering to a tip diameter of 0.0005 mm or less.
This electrode, inserted into the neuron, is connected to

recording equipment. A reference electrode placed
somewhere outside the cell completes the circuit.
When we connect the electrodes to a voltmeter, we find
that the neuron's interior has a potential somewhere in
the range of approximately −30 to −90 millivolts (mV)
relative to its exterior.

The Forces Behind the Resting Potential

One mechanism that maintains the resting potential is
the **selective permeability** of the neuron membrane,
the fact that some molecules pass much more freely
through the membrane than others do. Oxygen, carbon
dioxide, urea, and water cross in both directions at all
times. Most larger or electrically charged ions and molecules cannot cross the membrane at all. However, a
few biologically important ions, such as potassium,
chloride, and sodium, cross through channels (or gates)
in specialized proteins embedded in the membrane.
Each of these ions travels through a different kind of
channel, and the channels control the rate at which
their ions pass. When the membrane is at rest, the
potassium and chloride channels permit potassium and
chloride ions to pass at a moderate rate, but the sodium
channels are closed, restricting sodium flow to a very
low rate. These channels are shown in Figure 2.14. As
we shall see later, certain kinds of stimulation can open
the sodium channels.

What causes sodium ions to become so much more
concentrated outside the neuron than inside it? The driving force is a protein complex called the **sodium-
potassium pump,** which transports sodium ions out of
the cell while simultaneously drawing potassium ions
into the cell. To be precise, the pump ejects three
sodium ions for every two potassium ions that it brings
in. Because both sodium and potassium ions carry a +1
electrical charge, the result is a net movement of positive ions out of the cell. The sodium-potassium pump is
an **active transport,** requiring energy.

The sodium-potassium pump is effective only because of the selective permeability of the membrane.
Without the selective permeability, the sodium ions
pumped out of the neuron would leak right back in
again. As it is, the sodium ions pumped out stay out.
However, some of the potassium ions pumped into the
neuron do leak out, carrying a positive charge with
them. That leakage actually increases the electrical gradient across the membrane, as shown in Figure 2.15 on
page 38.

The number of potassium ions inside the membrane reflects an equilibrium of competing forces. The
concentration gradient for potassium tends to push
potassium out; that is, the numerous potassium ions
inside the neuron are more likely to move out than the

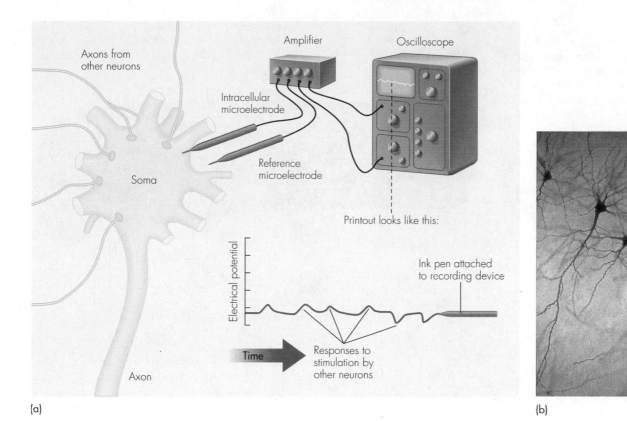

(a)

(b)

FIGURE **2.13**
Methods for recording activity of a neuron
(**a**) Diagram of the apparatus and a sample recording. (**b**) A microelectrode and stained neurons, magnified hundreds of times by a light microscope. Brain tissue has been sliced and stained to make the neurons easy to see. In a living organism, microelectrodes like this one can record the electrical activity of a neuron.

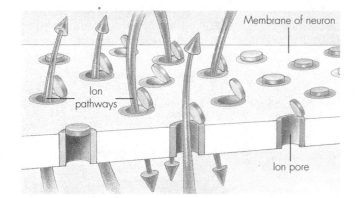

FIGURE **2.14**
Ion channels in the membrane of a neuron
When a channel opens, it permits one kind of ion to cross the membrane. When it closes, it prevents passage of that ion.

few potassium ions outside the neuron are likely to move in. However, the **electrical gradient** pushes potassium in the opposite direction: Because the inside of the cell is negatively charged in relation to the outside, potassium ions are attracted into the neuron.

When the membrane is at rest, the concentration gradient and the electrical gradient are almost in balance for potassium.

On the contrary, sodium tends to be driven into the neuron by both the concentration (more sodium outside, less inside) and the electrical gradient (positively charged sodium ions outside, negative charge inside). Sodium remains mostly outside the cell because the sodium-potassium pump drives them out and because the sodium gates are so tightly closed that sodium ions can leak only very slowly into the cell.

Why a Resting Potential?

Presumably, evolution could have equipped us with neurons that were electrically neutral at rest. The sodium-potassium pump uses energy; presumably, it must provide some benefit to justify this expense. The advantage is that the resting potential prepares the neuron to respond rapidly to a stimulus. As we shall see in the next section, an excitation of the neuron opens the sodium channels, enabling sodium to enter the cell

FIGURE **2.15**

Factors controlling sodium and potassium gradients for a membrane at rest

The sodium-potassium pump brings two potassium (K$^+$) ions into the cell for every three sodium (Na$^+$) ions it pumps out. As a result of the pump and of the low ability of Na$^+$ ions to diffuse back through the membrane, sodium ions are much more concentrated outside the cell; the potassium ions are more concentrated inside the cell. Because ions tend to move from an area of greater concentration to an area of lesser concentration, the concentration gradient tends to push Na$^+$ ions into the cell and K$^+$ ions out. Because the total positive charge is greater outside the cell than inside, the electrical gradient tends to push both Na$^+$ and K$^+$ ions into the cell. For K$^+$ ions the two gradients almost cancel each other out. For Na$^+$ ions, both gradients push in the same direction; sodium stays outside the cell only because the sodium channels are closed.

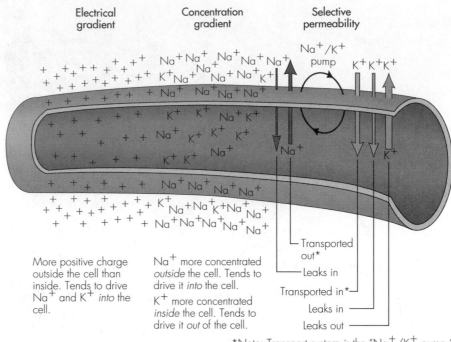

Electrical gradient

More positive charge outside the cell than inside. Tends to drive Na$^+$ and K$^+$ *into* the cell.

Concentration gradient

Na$^+$ more concentrated *outside* the cell. Tends to drive it *into* the cell.

K$^+$ more concentrated *inside* the cell. Tends to drive it *out* of the cell.

Selective permeability

Na$^+$/K$^+$ pump

Transported out*
Leaks in
Transported in*
Leaks in
Leaks out

*Note: Transport system *is* the "Na$^+$/K$^+$ pump."

explosively. Because the membrane did its work in advance by maintaining the concentration gradient for sodium, the cell is prepared to respond strongly and rapidly to a stimulus.

The resting potential of a neuron can be compared to a poised bow and arrow: An archer who pulls the bow in advance and then waits is ready to fire as soon as the appropriate moment comes. Evolution has applied the same strategy to the neuron.

The Action Potential

The resting potential remains stable as long as the animal remains healthy and the neuron is not stimulated. Ordinarily, stimulation of the neuron takes place at the synapse, which we shall consider in Chapter 3. In the laboratory, it is also possible to stimulate a neuron by inserting an electrode into it.

We can measure a neuron's potential with a microelectrode, as shown in Figure 2.13b. To stimulate the axon, an extra electrode is placed on the membrane surface close to the intracellular electrode. When the membrane is at rest, the recordings show a steady negative potential within the axon. The potential varies from one axon to another, but let's take −70 mV as a

representative value. If we now use an additional electrode to apply a negative charge, we can further increase the negative charge inside the neuron. The change is called **hyperpolarization,** which means increased polarization. As soon as the artificial stimulation ceases, the charge returns to its original resting level. The recording looks like this:

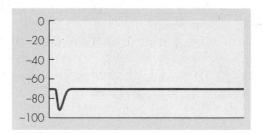

Now let us apply currents for **depolarization** of the neuron—that is, reduction of its polarization toward zero. If we apply a small depolarizing current, we get a result like this:

With a slightly stronger depolarizing current, the potential rises slightly higher, but again it returns to the resting level as soon as the stimulation ceases:

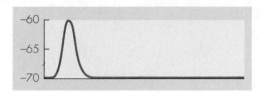

Now let us see what happens when we apply a still stronger current: If the depolarization passes a certain level, called the **threshold,** the membrane produces a disproportionately large response. When the potential reaches the threshold, the membrane suddenly opens its sodium channels and permits a rapid, massive flow of ions across the membrane. The potential then shoots up far beyond the strength of the stimulus that brought the membrane to threshold:

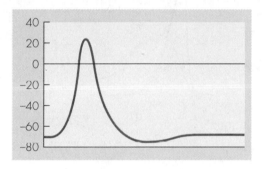

Any *subthreshold* stimulation produces a small response proportional to the amount of current. Any stimulation *beyond the threshold,* regardless of how far beyond, produces the same response, like the one shown above. That response is referred to as an **action potential.** Action potentials occur in axons. As a rule, dendrites produce potentials that are proportional to the magnitude of the stimulation.

Within a given cell, all action potentials are approximately equal in size and shape (amplitude) under normal circumstances. This is the **all-or-none law:** *The size and shape of the action potential are independent of the intensity of the stimulus that initiated it.* For an analogy, think about flushing a toilet: You have to make a press of at least a certain strength (the threshold), but pressing even harder will not make the toilet flush any faster or more vigorously.

As a consequence of this law, a neuron's messages are analogous to those of a telegraph. An axon cannot send larger action potentials any more than a telegraph operator could send louder dots and dashes. In both cases, the message is conveyed by the time sequence of impulses and pauses. For instance, an axon might signal "dim light" by a low frequency of action potentials

per second and "brighter" or "more than" by a higher frequency.

The Molecular Basis

The action potential can be related to the distribution of ions across the membrane of an axon. Remember that the sodium concentration is much higher outside the neuron than inside. In addition to this concentration gradient, sodium ions are attracted to the inside of the neuron by an electrical gradient, because of the negative charge inside the neuron. If sodium ions were free to flow across the membrane, they would diffuse rapidly into the cell. Ordinarily, the membrane is almost impermeable to sodium, but during the action potential its permeability increases sharply.

The membrane proteins that control sodium entry are **voltage-activated channels;** that is, their permeability to sodium depends on the voltage difference across the membrane. As the membrane of the neuron becomes even slightly depolarized, the sodium channels begin to open and sodium flows more freely. If the depolarization is less than the threshold, the increased entry of sodium ions is balanced by an increased exit of potassium ions. (Potassium ions ordinarily cross the membrane at a restricted rate through potassium channels that are independent of voltage. Some additional, voltage-activated potassium channels open when the membrane is depolarized and the electrical gradient no longer holds the potassium ions inside the cell.)

When the potential across the membrane reaches threshold, the sodium channels open wide enough to let sodium enter the cell faster than potassium can exit. The entering sodium ions depolarize the cell still further, opening the sodium channels even wider. Sodium ions rush into the neuron until the electrical potential across the membrane passes beyond zero to a reversed polarity, as shown in the diagram below:

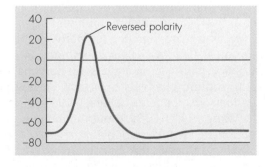

Compared to the total number of sodium and potassium ions in and around the axon, only a small percentage cross the membrane during an action potential. Even at the peak of the action potential, sodium ions continue to be far more concentrated outside the neuron than inside. An action potential increases the sodium concentration inside a neuron by less than 1 percent in most cases. Because of the persisting concentration gradient, sodium ions should still tend to diffuse into the cell. However, they are no longer attracted into the cell by an electrical gradient; in fact, the interior of the neuron has become temporarily positive with respect to the outside. This reversed electrical gradient impedes the further entry of sodium.

After the peak of the action potential, what brings the membrane back to its original state of polarization? The answer is *not* the sodium-potassium pump, which is simply too slow for this purpose. The sodium channels close at about the time that the action potential reaches its peak; however, positively charged potassium ions flow out of the axon through several kinds of channels, beginning at the start of the action potential and continuing until the membrane is repolarized (C. Smith, 1996). Potassium ions leave the axon simply because they are much more concentrated inside than outside, and because they are no longer held inside by a negative charge. The exit of potassium ions returns the membrane to its original state of polarization. In fact, because certain potassium channels open wider than usual, enough potassium ions leave to drive the potential a bit beyond the normal resting level to a temporary hyperpolarization. Figure 2.16 summarizes the movements of ions during an action potential.

At the end of this process, the membrane has returned to its resting potential and everything is back to normal, except that the inside of the neuron has slightly more sodium ions and slightly fewer potassium ions than before. Eventually, the sodium-potassium pump restores the original distribution of ions, but that process takes time. In fact, if a series of action potentials occurs at a sufficiently rapid rate, the pump cannot keep up with the action, and sodium may begin to accumulate within the axon. If it accumulated long enough, the axon would "fatigue" and stop firing action potentials. (Ordinarily, the synapses—to be discussed in Chapter 3—fatigue faster than the axon, so we seldom face a threat of too much sodium within the axon.)

For the neuron to function properly, sodium and potassium must flow across the membrane at just the right pace. Scorpion venom attacks the nervous system by keeping sodium channels open and closing potassium channels (Pappone & Cahalan, 1987; Strichartz, Rando, & Wang, 1987). As a result, the membrane goes into a prolonged depolarization that makes it useless for conveying information. **Local anesthetic** drugs, such as Novocain and Xylocaine, attach to the sodium channels of the membrane, preventing sodium ions from entering (Ragsdale, McPhee, Scheuer, & Catterall, 1994). In doing so, such drugs block action potentials in the affected area. If anesthetics are applied to sensory nerves carrying pain messages, they prevent the

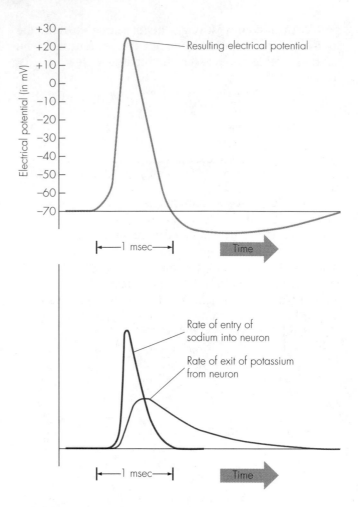

FIGURE **2.16**
The movement of sodium and potassium ions during an action potential
Note that sodium ions cross during the peak of the action potential and that potassium ions cross later in the opposite direction, returning the membrane to its original polarization.

messages from reaching the brain. **General anesthetics,** such as ether and chloroform, decrease brain activity in a different way. They open certain potassium channels wider than usual (Nicoll & Madison, 1982). With the potassium channels wide open, as soon as any stimulus starts to excite a neuron by opening sodium channels, potassium ions exit about as fast as the sodium ions enter. The balance of flows prevents most action potentials.

The Refractory Period

While the electrical potential across the membrane is returning from its peak toward the resting point, it is still above the threshold. Why does the cell not produce another action potential during this period? Immediately after an action potential, the cell is in a **refractory**

period, during which it resists further action potentials. In the first part of this period, the **absolute refractory period,** the sodium gates are incapable of opening and the membrane cannot produce an action potential, regardless of the stimulation. During the second part, the **relative refractory period,** the sodium gates are reverting to their usual state, but the potassium gates remain open. Because of the free flow of potassium, a stronger-than-usual stimulus is necessary to initiate an action potential. Most of the axons that have been tested have an absolute refractory period of about 1 millisecond (ms) and a relative refractory period of another 2–4 ms.

The refractory period sets a maximum on the firing frequency of a neuron. For example, with an axon that has a combined absolute and relative refractory period lasting 5 ms, only very strong stimuli could produce more than 200 action potentials per second.

Propagation of the Action Potential

Up to this point, we have dealt with the action potential at one location on the axon. Now let us consider how it moves down the axon toward some other cell. Remember that it is important for axons to convey impulses without any loss of strength over distance.

An action potential begins on the axon hillock. It cannot travel any great distance down the axon in the manner that a wire conducts electricity, because the axon is a poor conductor of electricity. Rather, each point along the membrane regenerates the action potential in much the same way that it was generated initially.

At the time of the action potential, sodium ions enter a point on the axon, bearing positive charges. Temporarily, that location is positively charged in comparison with neighboring areas along the axon. The positive ions flow down the axon and across the membrane, as shown in Figure 2.17. If the resistance to electrical flow is great across the membrane and lower inside the axon, the ions will flow relatively far along the axon. If, on the other hand, the resistance is slight across the membrane and greater inside the axon—as it is in the thinnest axons—the ions will flow only a short distance along the axon before crossing the membrane.

As sodium ions move down the axon, they slightly depolarize the adjacent areas of the membrane. The areas closest to the action potential are depolarized enough to reach their threshold and to generate an action potential of their own. In this manner, the action potential is regenerated. The action potential passes like a wave along the axon. If we could record the electrical potentials from all points along the axon simultaneously, the result would resemble Figure 2.18.

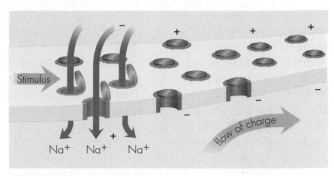

(a)

(b)

FIGURE 2.17
Current that enters an axon at the point of the action potential flows down the axon, thereby depolarizing adjacent areas of the membrane. The current flows more easily through relatively thick axons. Behind the area of sodium entry, potassium ions exit.

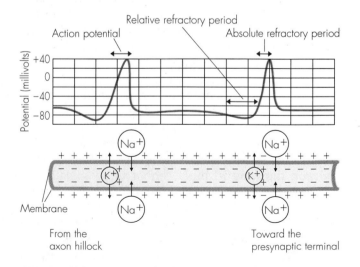

FIGURE 2.18
Two action potentials as waves traveling along the axon
Note that they are depicted here as a function of location on the axon rather than as a function of time.

The term **propagation of the action potential** describes the transmission of an action potential down an axon. The propagation of an animal species is the production of babies; in a sense, the action potential gives birth to a new action potential at each point along the axon. In this manner, the action potential can be just as strong at the end of the axon as it was at the beginning. The action potential is much slower than electrical conduction because it requires the diffusion of sodium ions at successive points along the axon. The thinnest axons are the slowest; their action potentials travel at a velocity of less than 1 meter per second (m/s). In the thickest unmyelinated axons, action potentials reach a velocity of about 10 m/s. In axons surrounded by myelin, which we shall discuss in the next section, the velocity may reach or exceed 100 m/s. In comparison, electricity travels at 300 million m/s.

Let us reexamine Figure 2.17 for a moment. What is to prevent the electrical charge from flowing in the direction opposite the direction that the action potential is traveling? Nothing. In fact, the electrical charge does flow in both directions. In that case, what prevents an action potential near the center of an axon from reinvading the areas that it has just passed? The answer is that those areas are still in their refractory period.

The Myelin Sheath and Saltatory Conduction

As just noted, the maximum velocity of action potentials in the thickest unmyelinated axons of vertebrates is about 10 m/s. At that speed, an impulse from a giraffe's foot would take about a second to reach the brain. Even in smaller animals, a speed of 10 m/s is too slow for the coordination of rapid responses. Myelin sheaths increase speed to make such coordination possible.

Consider the following analogy. Suppose it were my job to carry written messages over a distance of 3 kilometers (km), without using any mechanical device. Taking each message and running with it would be analogous to the propagation of the action potential along an unmyelinated axon: It would get the job done, but not very rapidly. I could try tying each message to a ball and throwing it, but I cannot throw a ball even close to 3 km. The ideal compromise would be to station people at moderate distances along the 3 km and to throw the message-bearing ball from person to person.

The principle behind **myelinated axons** is the same. Many vertebrate axons are covered with a myelin sheath, a coating made up largely of fats. The myelin sheath is interrupted at intervals of approximately 1 mm by short unmyelinated sections of axon called **nodes of Ranvier** (RAHN-vee-ay), as shown in Figure 2.19. Each node is only about one micrometer wide.

Suppose that an action potential is initiated at the

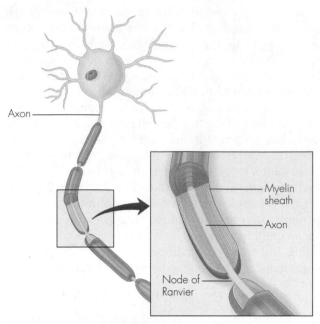

Cutaway view of axon wrapped in myelin

FIGURE **2.19**
An axon surrounded by a myelin sheath and interrupted by nodes of Ranvier
The lower part shows a cross section through both the axon and the myelin sheath. Magnification approximately × 30,000.

axon hillock and propagated along the axon until it reaches the first myelin segment. The action potential cannot regenerate along the membrane between one node and the next for two reasons. First, the myelin sheath increases the resistance to electrical transmission at every point between the nodes. Second, sodium channels are located in abundance at the nodes but are virtually absent in the myelinated areas between them (Catterall, 1984). Thus, sodium ions cannot cross the membrane between one node and the next. After an action potential occurs at a node, sodium ions that enter the axon diffuse in both directions within the axon, repelling positive ions that were already present, and thus pushing a chain of positive ions along the axon to the next node, where they regenerate the action potential (see Figure 2.20). This flow of ions is considerably faster than the regeneration of an action potential at each point along the axon; consequently, the transmission of impulses is faster in myelinated axons than in axons without myelin—in some cases as fast as 120 m/s. The jumping of action potentials from node to node is referred to as **saltatory conduction,** from the Latin word *saltare*, meaning *to jump*. (The same root shows up in the word *somersault*.) In addition to providing very rapid conduction of impulses, saltatory conduction has the added benefit of conserving energy: Instead of admitting sodium ions at every point along the axon, and then having to pump them out via the

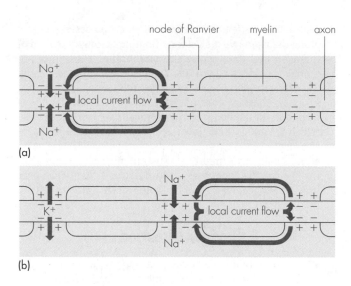

node of Ranvier   myelin   axon

(a)

(b)

FIGURE **2.20**
Saltatory conduction in a myelinated axon
An action potential at the node triggers flow of current to the next
node, where the membrane regenerates the action potential.

sodium-potassium pump, a myelinated axon admits sodium only at its nodes.

Some diseases, including multiple sclerosis, destroy myelin sheaths, thereby slowing down action potentials or stopping them altogether. An axon that has lost its myelin is not the same as one that has never had any myelin. A myelinated axon develops sodium channels almost exclusively at the nodes (Waxman & Ritchie, 1985). After the axon loses its myelin, it still lacks sodium channels in the areas previously covered. Therefore, depolarization of the unmyelinated areas of an axon does not produce an action potential.

Signaling Without Action Potentials

Unlike axons, dendrites and somas do not produce action potentials; they produce small depolarizations and hyperpolarizations, depending on the stimulation affecting them. The action potential, with its all-or-none law, starts at the beginning of the axon. The depolarizations and hyperpolarizations of the dendrites and soma do not follow the all-or-none law, but decay as they travel.

Very small neurons, known as **local neurons,** also do not produce action potentials, because they have either a very short axon or no axon at all and cannot transmit information to more distant cells. A local neuron receives information from other neurons in its immediate vicinity and produces **graded potentials,** membrane potentials that vary in magnitude and do not follow the all-or-none law. When a local neuron is stimulated, it depolarizes or hyperpolarizes in proportion to the intensity of the stimulus. The change in membrane potential is conducted to adjacent areas of the cell, gradually decaying as it travels. At various points along the cell, it may transmit information to other cells, also in its immediate vicinity.

Local neurons are somewhat difficult to study, just because they are small; it is difficult to insert an electrode into a small cell without damaging it. A disproportionate amount of our knowledge, therefore, has come from large neurons. (See Digression 2.2.) A large neuron with a long axon is specialized to transmit messages over long distances, such as from the spinal cord to the muscles, or from one part of the brain to another.

DIGRESSION **2.2**

On the Growth of Neurons and the Growth of Misconceptions

The nervous system contains enormous numbers of very small "local" neurons that play special roles in processing information. Many years ago, long before neuroscientists could investigate these local neurons, all they knew about them was that they were small. Given that nearly all knowledge about the nervous system was based on the activities of large neurons, the small neurons seemed an anomaly, a mistake. Many scientists assumed that they were "baby" neurons. As one textbook author put it, "Many of these [neurons] are small and apparently undeveloped, as if they constituted a reserve stock not yet utilized in the individual's cerebral activity" (Woodworth, 1934, p. 194). In other words, the small cells would contribute to behavior only if they grew.

Perhaps the misunderstanding of local neurons led to the origin of that widespread, nonsensical belief that "they say we use only 10 percent of our brain." It is difficult to imagine any reasonable justification for that belief. Surely no one maintained that a person could lose 90 percent of the brain and still behave as before, or that only 10 percent of neurons are active at any given moment. Whatever its origin, that belief became popular, presumably because people wanted to believe it. Eventually, they were simply quoting one another long after everyone forgot what evidence they had (or didn't have) for it in the first place.

Its dendrites receive information at one end of the cell, and its axon transmits information to a target at the other end. Local neurons do not have such a polarity between one end and the other; they can receive information at various points along their membrane and transmit it in either direction. In Chapter 6, we shall discuss in some detail a particular local neuron, the *horizontal cell.*

IN**CLOSING**

Neural Messages

In this chapter we have examined what happens within a single neuron, as if each neuron acted independently. It does not, of course; all its functions depend on communication with other neurons, as we shall consider in the next chapter. We may as well admit from the start, however, that neural communication is pretty amazing. Unlike human communication, in which a speaker sometimes presents a complicated message to an enormous audience, a neuron delivers only an action potential—merely an on/off message—to only that modest number of other neurons that receive branches of its axon. At various receiving neurons, an "on" message can be converted into either excitation or inhibition (yes/no). From this limited system, all of our behavior and experience emerges.

Summary

1. The inside of a resting neuron has a negative charge with respect to the outside. Sodium ions are actively pumped out of the neuron, and potassium ions are pumped in. Potassium ions are moderately free to flow across the membrane of the neuron, but the flow of sodium ions is greatly restricted. (p. 36)
2. When the charge across the membrane is reduced, sodium ions can flow more freely across the membrane. When the change in membrane potential is sufficient to reach the threshold of the neuron, sodium ions enter explosively and the charge across the membrane is suddenly reduced and reversed. This event is known as the action potential. (p. 38)
3. The magnitude of the action potential is independent of the size of the stimulus that initiated it; this statement is the all-or-none law. (p. 39)
4. Immediately after an action potential, the membrane enters a refractory period, during which it is resistant to starting another action potential. (p. 40)

5. The action potential is regenerated at successive points along the axon by sodium ions flowing through the core of the axon and then across the membrane. The action potential maintains a constant magnitude as it passes along the axon. (p. 41)
6. In axons that are covered with myelin, action potentials form only in the nodes between myelinated segments. Between the nodes, ions flow faster than through axons without myelin. (p. 42)
7. Many small local neurons transmit messages over relatively short distances by graded potentials that decay over time and space, instead of by action potentials. (p. 43)

Review Questions

1. What is the difference between a hyperpolarization and a depolarization? What is an action potential? (p. 38)
2. State the all-or-none law of the action potential. (p. 39)
3. Explain the ion movements responsible for the action potential and the return to the resting potential. (p. 39)
4. Distinguish between the absolute refractory period and the relative refractory period. (p. 41)
5. How does the refractory period limit the maximum frequency of action potentials in an axon? (p. 41)
6. How does an action potential propagate along an axon? (p. 41)
7. How does myelin increase the velocity of the action potential? Why does myelin loss severely impair the ability of an axon to conduct action potentials? (p. 42)
8. What is a graded potential? How does a local neuron differ from a neuron with a long axon? (p. 43)

Thought Questions

1. Suppose that the threshold of a neuron were the same as the neuron's resting potential. What would happen? At what frequency would the cell produce action potentials?
2. In the laboratory, researchers can apply an electrical stimulus at any point along the axon, making action potentials travel in both directions from the point of stimulation. An action potential moving in the usual direction, away from the axon hillock, is said to be traveling in the *orthodromic* direction. An action potential traveling toward the axon hillock is traveling in the *antidromic* direction. If we started an orthodromic action potential at the axon hillock and an antidromic action potential at the opposite end of the axon, what would happen when they met at the center? Why? What research might make use of antidromic impulses?
3. If a drug partly blocked a membrane's potassium channels, how would it affect the action potential?

Suggestion for Further Reading

Smith, C. U. M. (1996). *Elements of molecular neurobiology* (2nd ed.). New York: Wiley. A detailed treatment of the molecular biology of neurons, including both action potentials and synaptic activity.

Terms

polarization   an electrical gradient across a membrane (p. 36)

resting potential   electrical potential across a membrane when a neuron is not being stimulated (p. 36)

concentration gradient   difference in concentration of a solute across some distance (p. 36)

microelectrode   a very thin electrode, generally made of glass and filled with an electrolyte solution (p. 36)

selective permeability   tendency to permit certain chemicals but not others to cross a membrane (p. 36)

sodium-potassium pump   mechanism that actively transports sodium ions out of the cell while simultaneously drawing potassium ions in (p. 36)

active transport   mechanism that uses energy to move chemicals across a membrane (p. 36)

electrical gradient   difference in electrical potential across some distance (p. 37)

hyperpolarization   increased polarization across a membrane (p. 38)

depolarization   reduction in the level of polarization across a membrane (p. 38)

threshold   level of depolarization at which a brief stimulation triggers a rapid, massive electrical change by the membrane (p. 39)

action potential   depolarization of an axon produced by a stimulation beyond the threshold (p. 39)

all-or-none law   principle stating that the size and shape of the action potential are independent of the intensity of the stimulus that initiated it (p. 39)

voltage-activated channel   channel in the neuronal membrane that opens as the membrane becomes depolarized (p. 39)

local anesthetic   drug that blocks action potentials in the nerves in a particular area where the drug is applied (p. 40)

general anesthetic   chemical that depresses brain activity as a whole (p. 40)

refractory period   brief period following an action potential, when the cell resists reexcitation (p. 40)

absolute refractory period   time immediately after an action potential, when the membrane cannot produce an action potential in response to stimulation of any intensity (p. 41)

relative refractory period   time after an action potential, when a stimulus must exceed the usual threshold to produce an action potential (p. 41)

propagation of the action potential   transmission of an action potential down an axon (p. 42)

myelinated axon   axon covered with myelin (p. 42)

node of Ranvier   short unmyelinated section of axon between segments of myelin (p. 42)

saltatory conduction   alternation between action potentials at nodes and a more rapid conduction by the flow of ions between nodes (p. 42)

local neuron   a small neuron with no more than a short axon (p. 43)

graded potential   membrane potential that varies in magnitude (p. 43)

SYNAPSES AND DRUGS

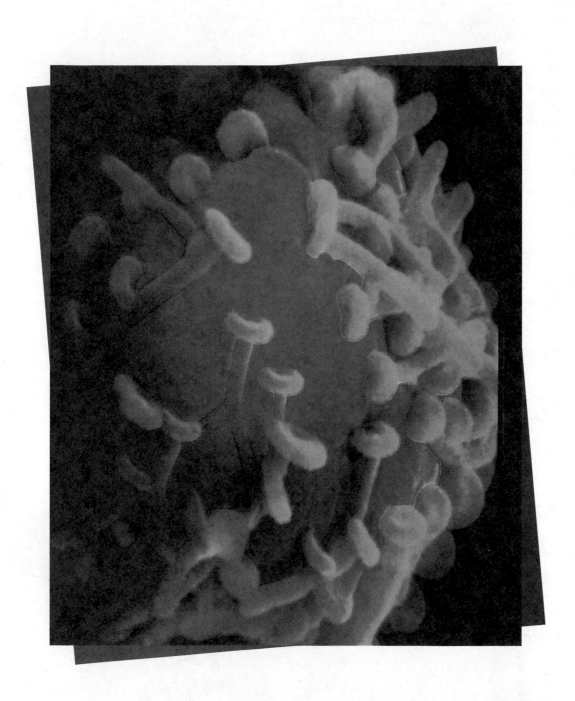

CHAPTER THREE

MAIN IDEAS

1. At a synapse, a neuron releases a chemical known as a neurotransmitter that excites or inhibits another cell.
2. A single release of neurotransmitter produces only a subthreshold response in the receiving cell. This response summates with other subthreshold responses to determine whether or not the cell will produce an action potential.
3. Because different neurotransmitters contribute to behavior in different ways, many behavioral abnormalities can be traced to excessive or deficient transmission at a particular type of synapse.
4. Many of the drugs that affect behavior and experience do so by altering activity at synapses.

If you had to communicate with someone and you were not allowed to use speech or any other auditory information, what would you do? Chances are, your first choice would be a visual code, such as sign language or written words. If that failed, you might try some sort of touch code or a system of electrical impulses. You might not even think of communicating by passing chemicals back and forth. Chemical communication is, however, the primary method of communication for the neurons in your nervous system. Considering how well the human nervous system works, chemical communication is evidently a more versatile system than we might have guessed. Neurons communicate by transmitting chemicals at specialized junctions called *synapses*. The synapses are central to all comparison and integration of information in the brain.

The Concept of the Synapse

In the late 1800s, Ramón y Cajal demonstrated that neurons do not physically merge into one another, that a narrow gap separates one from the next. As far as anyone knew, information might be transmitted across the gap in the same way that it was transmitted along an axon.

Then, in 1906, Charles Scott Sherrington inferred that a specialized type of communication occurs at the gap, which he labeled the **synapse.** Sherrington also deduced most of the major properties of the synapse. What makes his accomplishment particularly impressive is that he based his conclusions almost entirely on behavioral data. Decades later, when investigators developed techniques for measuring and recording neural processes, most of Sherrington's predictions turned out to be correct.

The Properties of Synapses

Sherrington conducted most of his experiments on **reflexes,** automatic responses to stimuli. In a simple reflex, receptors excite interneurons, which excite motor neurons, which excite muscles, as Figure 3.1 shows. This circuit is called a **reflex arc.** Because a reflex depends on communication from one neuron to another—not just on the transmission of action potentials along an axon—Sherrington reasoned that the properties of a reflex might reveal some of the special properties of synapses.

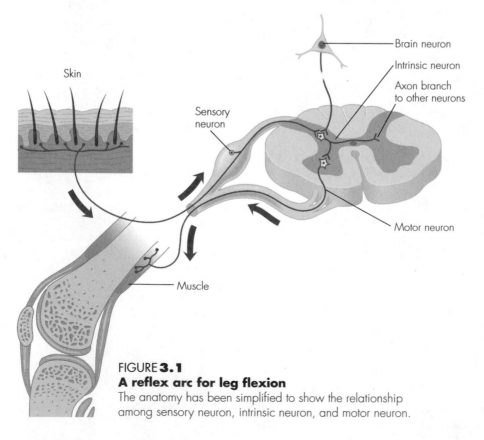

FIGURE **3.1**
A reflex arc for leg flexion
The anatomy has been simplified to show the relationship among sensory neuron, intrinsic neuron, and motor neuron.

In a typical experiment, a dog was strapped into a harness suspended above the ground. Sherrington pinched one of the dog's feet; after a short delay, the dog *flexed* (raised) the pinched leg and *extended* the others. Both the flexion and the extension were reflexive movements—automatic reactions to the stimulus. Furthermore, Sherrington found the same movements after he made a cut that disconnected the spinal cord from the brain; evidently, the flexion and extension were controlled by the spinal cord itself. In an intact animal, the brain could modify the reflexive movements, but it was not necessary for their occurrence.

Sherrington observed several properties of reflexes suggesting that some special process must occur at the junctions between neurons: (1) Reflexes are slower than conduction along an axon; consequently, there must be some delay at the synapses. (2) Several weak stimuli presented at slightly different times or slightly different locations produce a stronger reflex than a single stimulus does. Therefore, the synapse must be able to *summate* different stimuli. (3) When one set of muscles becomes excited, a different set becomes relaxed. Evidently, synapses are connected so that the excitation of one leads to a decreased excitation, or even an inhibition, of others. We shall consider each of these points in some detail.

Speed of a Reflex and Delayed Transmission

When Sherrington pinched a dog's foot, the dog flexed that leg after a short delay. During the delay, an impulse had to travel up an axon from a skin receptor to the spinal cord, then an impulse had to travel from the spinal cord back down the leg to a muscle. Sherrington measured the total distance that the impulse traveled from skin receptor to spinal cord to muscle and calculated the speed at which the impulse must have traveled to produce a muscle response after the measured delay. He found that the overall speed of conduction through the reflex arc was significantly slower than the known speed of conduction along an axon. Therefore, he deduced, transmission between one neuron and another at the synapse must be slower than transmission along an axon (see Figure 3.2).

Temporal Summation

Sherrington's work with reflex arcs suggested that repeated stimuli occurring within a brief time can have a cumulative effect. He referred to this phenomenon as **temporal summation.** When Sherrington pinched a dog's foot very lightly, the leg did not move. However, when he repeated the same light pinch several times in rapid succession, the leg flexed slightly. The more rapid the series of pinches, the greater the response. Sher-

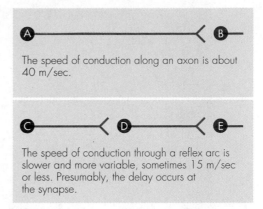

The speed of conduction along an axon is about 40 m/sec.

The speed of conduction through a reflex arc is slower and more variable, sometimes 15 m/sec or less. Presumably, the delay occurs at the synapse.

FIGURE **3.2**
Sherrington's evidence for synaptic delay
An impulse traveling through a synapse in the spinal cord is slower than one traveling a similar distance along an uninterrupted axon.

rington surmised that a single pinch produced a synaptic transmission that was too weak to produce an action potential in the next cell. That is, the excitation would be less than the threshold of the second cell, the **postsynaptic neuron.** (The neuron that delivers the synaptic transmission is the **presynaptic neuron.**) Sherrington proposed that this subthreshold excitation begins to decay within a fraction of a second but is capable of combining with a second small excitation that quickly follows it. A rapid succession of pinches produces a series of weak activations at the synapse, each adding its effect to what was left of the previous excitations. If the excitations occur rapidly enough, they combine to exceed the threshold and therefore produce an action potential in the postsynaptic neuron.

Decades after Sherrington's studies, it became possible to measure some of the single-cell properties he had inferred. To record the activity evoked in a neuron by synaptic input, researchers insert a microelectrode into the neuron to measure changes in the electrical potential across the membrane. Using this method, John Eccles (1964) demonstrated temporal summation in single cells. He attached stimulating electrodes to some of the axons that formed synapses onto a neuron. He then recorded from the neuron while stimulating one or more of those axons. For example, after he had briefly stimulated an axon, Eccles recorded a slight depolarization of the membrane of the postsynaptic cell (point 1 in Figure 3.3 on the next page).

Note that this partial depolarization is a graded potential. Unlike action potentials, which are always depolarizations, graded potentials may be either depolarizations (excitatory) or hyperpolarizations (inhibitory). A graded depolarization is known as an **excitatory postsynaptic potential (EPSP).** Like an action potential, an EPSP results from sodium ions entering the cell (see Chapter 2). The synaptic activation opens sodium

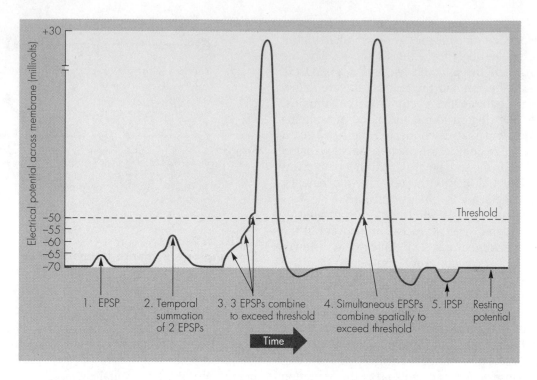

FIGURE **3.3**
Recordings from a postsynaptic neuron during synaptic activation

gates and increases the flow of sodium ions across the membrane. However, transmission at a single synapse does not open enough sodium gates to provoke an action potential. Unlike an action potential, an EPSP is a subthreshold event that decays over time and space; that is, its magnitude decreases as it travels along the membrane.

When Eccles stimulated the axon twice in close succession, two consecutive EPSPs were recorded in the postsynaptic cell. If the delay between EPSPs was short enough, temporal summation occurred; that is, the second EPSP added to what was left of the first one (point 2 in Figure 3.3). The summation of two EPSPs might or might not be enough to exceed the threshold of the postsynaptic cell, depending on the size of the EPSP, the time between the two, and the threshold of the postsynaptic cell. In point 3 in Figure 3.3, three consecutive EPSPs combine to exceed the threshold and produce an action potential.

Spatial Summation

Sherrington's work with reflex arcs also suggested that synapses have the property of **spatial summation:** Several synaptic inputs originating from separate locations can exert a cumulative effect on a neuron. Sherrington again began with a pinch that was too weak to elicit a

response. But this time, instead of pinching the dog twice, he gave simultaneous pinches at two points on the foot. Although neither pinch alone would elicit a response, the two together did. Sherrington concluded that pinching two points on the foot activated two sensory neurons, each of which sent an axon to the same interneuron. Excitation from either axon would excite a synapse on the interneuron, but one excitation would be insufficient for an action potential. When both excitations were present at the same time, however, their combined effect exceeded the threshold for producing an action potential (see point 4 in Figure 3.3).

Again, Eccles confirmed Sherrington's inference, demonstrating the spatial summation of EPSPs by recording from single cells. Note that temporal and spatial summation produce the same result (Figure 3.4): Either one generates an action potential in the postsynaptic cell.

Inhibitory Synapses

When Sherrington vigorously pinched a dog's foot, the flexor muscles of that leg contracted, and so did the extensor muscles of the other three legs (see Figure 3.5). At the same time, the dog relaxed the extensor muscles of the stimulated leg and the flexor muscles of the other legs. Sherrington's explanation for this series of coordi-

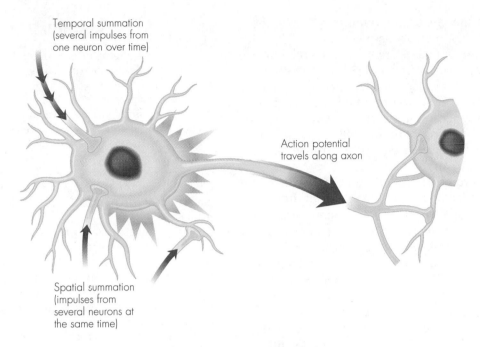

Temporal summation
(several impulses from
one neuron over time)

Action potential
travels along axon

Spatial summation
(impulses from
several neurons at
the same time)

FIGURE **3.4**
Temporal and spatial summation

nated and adaptive movements depended, again, on the synapses and in particular on the connections among neurons in the spinal cord: A pinch on the foot sends a message along a sensory neuron to an interneuron in the spinal cord, which in turn excites the motor neurons connected to the flexor muscles of that leg. Sherrington surmised that the interneuron also sends a message that decreases excitation of motor neurons connected to the extensor muscles in the same leg. He did not know whether the interneuron actually formed an inhibitory synapse onto the motor neuron to the extensor muscles or whether it simply decreased the amount of excitation. In either case, the flexor and extensor muscles of the leg were prevented from contracting at the same time.

Eccles and other later researchers demonstrated that the interneuron actually has inhibitory synapses onto the motor neuron of the extensor muscle. At these synapses, input from the axon hyperpolarizes the postsynaptic cell, increasing the cell's negative charge and decreasing the probability of an action potential by moving the potential further from the threshold (point 5 in Figure 3.3). This temporary hyperpolarization—called an **inhibitory postsynaptic potential,** or **IPSP**—resembles an EPSP in many ways. An IPSP occurs when synaptic input selectively opens the gates for potassium ions to leave the cell (carrying a positive charge with them) or for chloride ions to enter the cell (carrying a negative charge). Inhibition is more than just the absence of excitation; it is an active "brake" that can suppress excitatory responses.

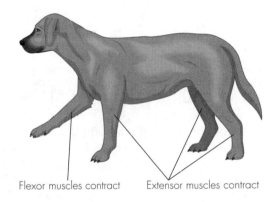

Flexor muscles contract   Extensor muscles contract

FIGURE **3.5**
Antagonistic muscles
Flexor muscles draw an extremity toward the trunk of the body, whereas extensor muscles move an extremity away from the body.

Relationship Among EPSP, IPSP, and Action Potential

A neuron is rarely exposed to a single EPSP or IPSP at a time. A neuron may have thousands of synapses along its surface, some that excite the neuron and others that inhibit it. Any number and combination of synapses may be active at any time, yielding a continuing combination of temporal and spatial summation. The greater the number of EPSPs, the greater the probability of an action potential; the greater the number of IPSPs, the lower the probability of an action potential.

Moreover, some synapses are more influential than others because of their locations. EPSPs and IPSPs are graded potentials; they decrease in strength as they flow from their point of origin toward other parts of the neuron. A synapse located near the far end of a dendrite has only a weak effect on the cell; a synapse on the closer end of a dendrite has a much stronger effect (Soltesz, Smetters, & Mody, 1995).

In many neurons, the EPSPs and IPSPs merely modify the frequency of action potentials that the neuron would fire spontaneously. That is, many neurons have a **spontaneous firing rate,** producing many action potentials per second even without synaptic input. EPSPs increase the frequency of action potentials in these neurons, while IPSPs decrease it. For example, if the neuron's spontaneous firing rate were 10 per second, a steady stream of EPSPs might increase the rate to 15 or 20 or more, whereas a steady stream of IPSPs might decrease the rate to 5 or fewer action potentials per second.

IN **CLOSING**

The Neuron as Decision Maker

The neuron can be compared to a thermostat, a smoke detector, or any other device that detects something and triggers a response: When input reaches a certain level, the neuron triggers an action potential. That is, the synapses enable the postsynaptic neuron to integrate information. The EPSPs and IPSPs reaching a neuron at a given moment compete against one another, and the net result is a complicated, not exactly algebraic summation of the two effects. We could regard the summation of EPSPs and IPSPs as a "decision," because they determine whether or not the postsynaptic cell will fire an action potential, but we should not imagine that any neuron decides between cereal and pancakes for breakfast. A great many neurons are involved in any behavior, and behavior depends on the whole neural network, not on a single neuron. Moreover, we cannot even assume, for instance, that an inhibitory synapse inhibits bodily activity. Activity at an inhibitory synapse may stop one neuron from inhibiting another neuron, and thus yield a net excitation. Such disinhibition (inhibition of inhibition) is commonplace in the nervous system.

Summary

1. The synapse is the point of communication between two neurons. Charles S. Sherrington's observations of reflexes enabled him to infer the properties of synapses. (p. 48)
2. Because transmission through a reflex arc is slower than transmission through an equivalent length of axon, Sherrington concluded that there is a delay of transmission at the synapse. (p. 49)
3. Graded potentials (EPSPs and IPSPs) summate their effects. The summation of graded potentials from stimuli at different times is temporal summation. The summation of graded potentials from different locations is spatial summation. (p. 49)
4. A single stimulation at a synapse produces a brief graded potential in the postsynaptic cell. An excitatory graded potential (depolarizing) is an EPSP. An inhibitory graded potential (hyperpolarizing) is an IPSP. (pp. 49, 51)
5. An EPSP occurs when sodium gates open in the membrane; an IPSP occurs when potassium or chloride gates open. (pp. 49, 51)
6. At any time, the EPSPs on a neuron compete with the IPSPs; the balance between the two determines the rate of firing of the neuron. (p. 51)

Review Questions

1. What evidence did Sherrington use to support his conclusion that transmission at a synapse is different from transmission along an axon? (p. 49)
2. What is the difference between temporal summation and spatial summation? What evidence did Sherrington have that they exist? (pp. 49, 50)
3. What evidence did Sherrington have for inhibition in the nervous system? (p. 50)
4. What ion gates in the membrane open during EPSPs? What gates open during IPSPs? (pp. 49, 51)
5. What is meant by the *spontaneous firing rate* of a neuron? (p. 52)

Thought Questions

1. When Sherrington measured the reaction time of a reflex (that is, the delay between stimulus and response), he found that the response occurred faster after a strong stimulus than after a weak one. How could you explain this finding? Remember that all action potentials—whether produced by strong or weak stimuli—travel at the same speed along a given axon.
2. A pinch on an animal's right hind foot leads to excitation of an interneuron that excites the motor neurons connected to the flexor muscles of that leg; the interneuron also inhibits the motor neurons connected to the extensor muscles of the leg. In addition, this interneuron sends impulses that reach the motor neuron connected to the extensor muscles of the left hind leg. Would you expect the interneuron to excite or inhibit that motor neuron? (Hint:

The connections are adaptive. When an animal lifts one leg, it must put additional weight on the other legs to maintain balance.)

3. Neuron X has a synapse onto neuron Y, and Y has a synapse onto Z. Presume here that no other neurons or synapses are present. An experimenter finds that excitation of neuron X causes an action potential in neuron Z after a short delay. However, she determines that the synapse of X onto Y is inhibitory. Explain how the stimulation of X might produce excitation of Z.

Terms

synapse   point of communication between two neurons or between a neuron and a muscle (p. 48)

reflex   automatic response to a stimulus (p. 48)

reflex arc   circuit of neurons and their connections that is responsible for producing a reflex (p. 48)

temporal summation   combination of effects of more than one synaptic input at different times (p. 49)

postsynaptic neuron   neuron on the receiving end of a synapse (p. 49)

presynaptic neuron   neuron on the releasing end of a synapse (p. 49)

excitatory postsynaptic potential (EPSP)   graded depolarization of a neuron (p. 49)

spatial summation   combination of effects of activity from two or more synapses onto a single neuron (p. 50)

inhibitory postsynaptic potential (IPSP)   temporary hyperpolarization of a membrane (p. 51)

spontaneous firing rate   speed of action potentials that a neuron produces in the absence of synaptic input (p. 52)

Chemical Events at the Synapse

Although Charles Sherrington accurately inferred many properties of the synapse, he drew one conclusion that was wrong, or at least greatly overstated: Although he knew that synaptic transmission was slower than transmission along an axon, he thought it was still too fast to depend on a chemical process and therefore concluded that it must be electrical. We now know that although *some* synaptic transmission is indeed electrical, in most cases it relies on chemical processes that are much faster than Sherrington thought possible and far more versatile than anyone would have guessed.

The Discovery That Most Synaptic Transmission Is Chemical

T. R. Elliott, a young British scientist, demonstrated in 1905 that the hormone *adrenaline* closely mimics the effects of the sympathetic nervous system, a set of nerves that control the internal organs (see Chapter 4). For example, stimulation of the sympathetic nerves accelerates the heartbeat, relaxes the stomach muscles, and dilates the pupils of the eyes. Applying adrenaline directly to the surface of the heart, the stomach, and the pupils produces those same effects. Elliott therefore suggested that the sympathetic nerves stimulate muscles by releasing adrenaline or a similar chemical, and that synapses in general operate by releasing chemicals. Elliott's evidence was not decisive, however; perhaps adrenaline merely mimicked certain effects that are ordinarily produced by electrical stimulation. At the time, Sherrington's prestige was so great that most scientists ignored Elliott's results and continued to assume that synapses transmitted information by electrical impulses.

Otto Loewi, a German physiologist, was also attracted to the idea that synapses operate by releasing chemicals, but as he did not see how he could test the theory decisively, he set it aside for almost twenty years. Then one night in 1920, he aroused from sleep

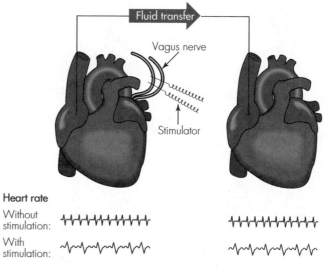

Heart rate

Without stimulation:

With stimulation:

FIGURE **3.6**

Loewi's experiment demonstrating that nerves send messages by releasing chemicals

He stimulated the vagus nerve to one heart, decreasing the heartbeat. Then he transferred fluid from that heart to another heart, and observed a decrease in its heartbeat.

with a sudden idea. He wrote himself a note and went back to sleep. Unfortunately, the next morning he could not read his own writing. The following night at 3 A.M., when he awoke with the same idea, he rushed to the laboratory and performed the experiment at once.

He repeatedly stimulated the vagus nerve to a frog's heart, causing the heart rate to decrease. He then collected fluid from that heart, transferred it to a second frog's heart, and found that the second heart also decreased its rate of beating. (This experiment is illustrated in Figure 3.6.) In a later experiment, Loewi stimulated the accelerator nerve to the first frog's heart, causing the heart rate to increase. When he collected fluid from that heart and transferred it to the second heart, the heart rate increased. That is, stimulating one nerve released something that inhibited heart rate, and

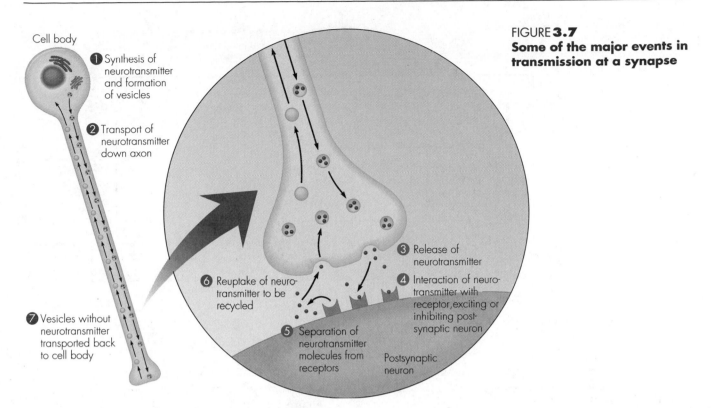

FIGURE **3.7**
Some of the major events in transmission at a synapse

Cell body

① Synthesis of neurotransmitter and formation of vesicles

② Transport of neurotransmitter down axon

③ Release of neurotransmitter

④ Interaction of neurotransmitter with receptor, exciting or inhibiting postsynaptic neuron

⑤ Separation of neurotransmitter molecules from receptors

⑥ Reuptake of neurotransmitter to be recycled

⑦ Vesicles without neurotransmitter transported back to cell body

Postsynaptic neuron

stimulating a different nerve released something else that increased heart rate. Those somethings had to be chemicals, not loose electricity. Therefore, Loewi concluded, nerves send messages by releasing chemicals.

Loewi later remarked that if he had thought of this experiment in the light of day he probably never would have tried it (Loewi, 1960). Even if synapses did release chemicals, his daytime reasoning went, there was little chance that they would release enough of the chemicals to make collecting them easy. Fortunately, by the time he realized that the experiment was unlikely to work, he had already completed the research, for which he later won the Nobel prize.

Although we now know that most synapses operate by transmitting chemicals, a few electrical synapses do exist. They occur mostly where it is important for two neurons to synchronize their activities exactly, such as synapses controlling rapid escape movements in certain fish and invertebrates.

The Sequence of Chemical Events at a Synapse

A great many medical conditions and drugs that affect behavior do so by altering neurotransmission. Consequently, understanding the chemical events occurring at a synapse is fundamental to much current research in biological psychology. The major events at a synapse are as follows:

1. The neuron synthesizes chemicals that serve as neurotransmitters.
2. The neuron transports these chemicals to the axon terminals.
3. An action potential causes the release of the neurotransmitters from the terminals.
4. The released molecules attach to receptors and alter the activity of the postsynaptic neuron.
5. The molecules separate from their receptors and (in some cases) are converted into inactive chemicals.
6. In some cells, as many as possible of the neurotransmitter molecules are taken back into the presynaptic cell for recycling.
7. In some cells, empty *vesicles* return to the cell body.

Figure 3.7 summarizes these steps. We shall discuss each step in more detail.

Types of Neurotransmitters

The chemicals released at the synapse are **neurotransmitters.** Each neuron synthesizes its neurotransmitters from materials in the blood. Neuroscientists believe that dozens of chemicals function as neurotransmitters in the brain, and research has been gradually adding to the list of known or suspected neurotransmitters (C. Smith, 1996). We shall consider many of these transmitters repeatedly; for now, you can familiarize yourself with some of their names (see Figure 3.8 on the next page). Some major categories are:

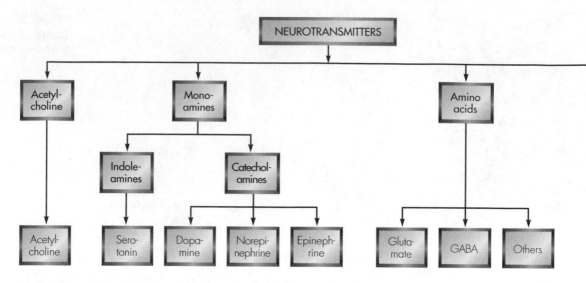

FIGURE **3.8**
Some neurotransmitters

amino acids   acids containing an amine group (NH_2)

peptides   chains of amino acids (A protein is also a chain of amino acids; the term *peptide* is generally used for shorter chains, *protein* for longer chains.)

acetylcholine (a one-member "family")   a chemical similar to an amino acid, except that the NH_2 group has been replaced by an $N(CH_3)_3$ group

monoamines   nonacidic neurotransmitters containing an amine group (NH_2), formed by a metabolic change of certain amino acids

purines   specifically, adenosine and several of its derivatives

gases   specifically, nitric oxide and possibly others

The chemicals used as neurotransmitters are a diverse lot. The most surprising is *nitric oxide* (chemical formula NO), a gas (!) released by many small local neurons. Nitric oxide is poisonous in large quantities, and very difficult to make in a laboratory. Yet many neurons contain an enzyme that enables them to make this gas with relatively little energy. Nitric oxide serves many functions in the brain (Dawson & Dawson, 1995), including dilation of blood vessels to get more blood to areas that have been active. It also has specialized functions that are apparently necessary for learning, and may well have other functions not yet discovered. (Do not confuse nitric oxide, NO, with nitrous oxide, N_2O, sometimes known as "laughing gas.")

Synthesis of Transmitters

Every cell in the body uses chemical reactions to build some of the materials that it needs, converting substances provided by the diet into other chemicals necessary for normal functioning. The neuron is no exception, synthesizing its neurotransmitters from precursor molecules derived originally from foods.

Figure 3.9 illustrates the chemical steps in the synthesis of acetylcholine, serotonin, dopamine, epinephrine, and norepinephrine. Note the relationship among epinephrine, norepinephrine, and dopamine—three closely related compounds known as **catecholamines.** Some neurons synthesize dopamine; others have an additional enzyme that converts dopamine to norepinephrine; still others can convert norepinephrine to epinephrine.

Each pathway in Figure 3.9 begins with substances found in the diet. Acetylcholine, for example, is synthesized from choline, which is abundant in cauliflower and milk. The body can also make choline from lecithin, a component of egg yolks, liver, soybeans, butter, peanuts, and several other foods. The amino acids phenylalanine and tyrosine, constituents of most proteins, are precursors of dopamine, norepinephrine, and epinephrine.

The amino acid *tryptophan* is the precursor to serotonin, and a special "transport system" enables it to cross the blood-brain barrier. However, tryptophan shares its transport system with several other amino acids (including phenylalanine) that are almost always more prevalent in the diet. Thus, after a meal rich in protein, the level of tryptophan reaching the brain may be low because of competition from the other amino acids. One way to increase the amount of tryptophan entering the brain is to eat carbohydrates with the protein. Carbohydrates increase release of the hormone **insulin,** which takes a number of competing amino acids out of the bloodstream and into cells throughout the body, thus decreasing the competition against tryptophan for entry into the brain (J. J. Wurtman, 1985).

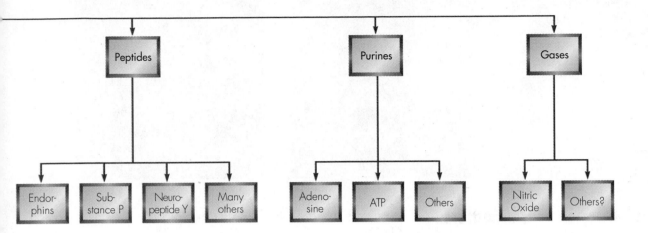

Transport of Transmitters

Peptide neurotransmitter molecules are synthesized in the cell body. From there, the peptide is transported down the axon to the terminal, where it can be released. The speed of transport varies from only 1 millimeter per day in thin axons to more than 100 mm per day in thicker ones.

Even at the highest speeds, transport from cell body to terminal may take hours or days in the longest axons. Consequently, after releasing peptides, neurons take a long time to replenish their supply. Furthermore, neurons reabsorb and recycle many of the nonpeptide transmitters, but not the peptides. For these reasons, a neuron can exhaust its supply of a peptide relatively quickly.

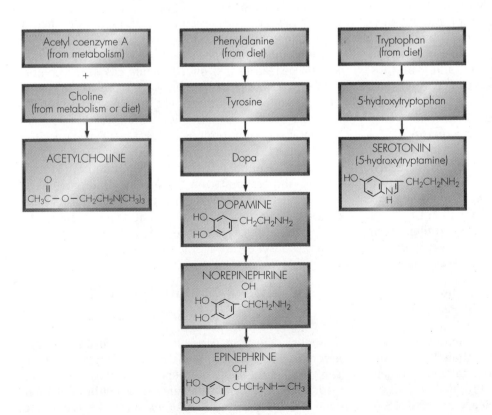

FIGURE **3.9**
Steps in the synthesis of acetylcholine, dopamine, norepinephrine, epinephrine, and serotonin
Arrows represent chemical reactions.

FIGURE **3.10**

Left: An electron micrograph, showing a synapse from the cerebellum of a mouse, magnified × 93,000. The small round structures are vesicles.   Source: From Landis, 1987.   *Right:* Electron micrograph showing axon terminals onto the soma of a neuron. Magnified × 11,000.   Source: From Lewis et al., 1969.

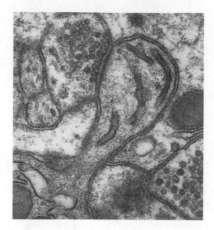
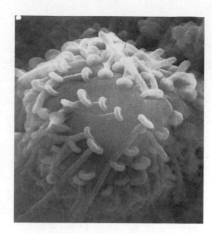

Release and Diffusion of Transmitters

The presynaptic terminal stores high concentrations of neurotransmitter molecules in **vesicles,** tiny near-spherical packets (Figure 3.10). (Nitric oxide, the gaseous neurotransmitter mentioned earlier, is an exception to this rule. Neurons do not store nitric oxide for future use; they synthesize it immediately before they release it.) In addition to the neurotransmitter stored in vesicles, the presynaptic terminal also maintains substantial amounts outside the vesicles.

When an action potential reaches the end of an axon, the depolarization changes the voltage across the membrane and opens voltage-dependent calcium gates in the presynaptic terminal. As calcium flows through specialized channels into the presynaptic terminal, it causes the neuron to release a certain amount of its neurotransmitter during the next 1 or 2 milliseconds. The result is not the same every time; many action potentials fail to release any transmitter, and even those that succeed do not all release the same amount (Südhof, 1995).

The presynaptic terminal releases neurotransmitter in outbursts of a fixed quantity, called a **quantum.** The quantum is the minimum amount of transmitter that a neuron terminal can release at one time. Larger amounts that it might release are in most cases integral multiples of the quantum. For example, an EPSP might be 10 or 11 times the quantum, but not 10.5. Does each vesicle represent one quantum of release? It might seem obvious that the answer must be yes; however, the evidence for that conclusion remains weak (Vautrin, 1994).

After the presynaptic cell releases the neurotransmitter, the chemical diffuses across the synaptic cleft to the postsynaptic membrane, where it attaches to a receptor. The cleft is only 0.02 to 0.05 microns wide, and the neurotransmitter takes no more than 10 microseconds to diffuse across the cleft. The total delay in transmission across the synapse, including the time that it takes for the presynaptic cell to release the neurotrans-

mitter, is 0.5 to 2 milliseconds (Martin, 1977; Takeuchi, 1977).

The brain as a whole uses dozens of neurotransmitters, but no single neuron releases them all. For many years, investigators believed that each neuron released just one neurotransmitter. This generalization is known as *Dale's law* or *Dale's principle,* after the first investigator to propose it. According to later studies, it appears that many, perhaps most, neurons release two, three, or even more transmitters (Hökfelt, Johansson, & Goldstein, 1984). However, consistent with the general idea behind Dale's law, each neuron probably releases the *same combination* of transmitters from all branches of its axon. For example, if one branch of the axon releases norepinephrine and enkephalin, then all its branches release norepinephrine and enkephalin—though perhaps in different ratios at different branches or at different times (Eccles, 1986).

Why does a neuron release a combination of transmitters instead of just one? In some cases, the combination makes the neuron's message more complex. For example, one transmitter might quickly initiate salivation; a second transmitter with a slower but longer-lasting effect might prolong salivation (Crawley, 1990).

Although a neuron releases only a limited number of neurotransmitters (generally at its terminal), it may receive and respond to a number of different neurotransmitters at various synapses (generally on its dendrites and soma). For example, it might respond to acetylcholine released at one synapse, serotonin at another synapse, GABA at still another, and so on.

Activation of Receptors of the Postsynaptic Cell

In English, the term *fern* refers to a plant. In German, *fern* means far away. In French, it means nothing at all. The meaning of any word depends on who hears it or reads it. Similarly, the meaning of a neurotransmitter depends on its receptor. For example, acetylcholine

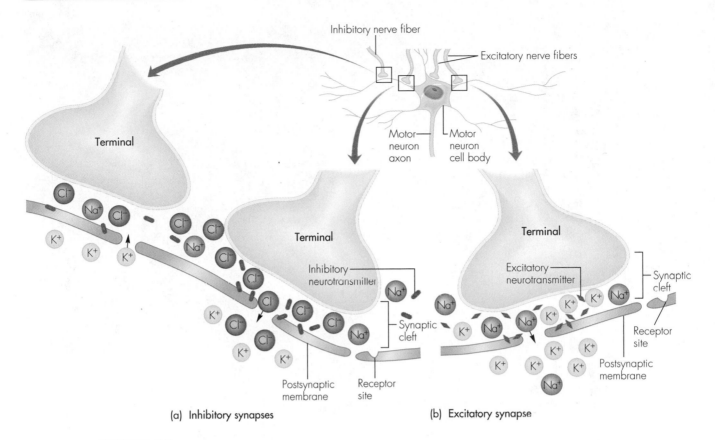

FIGURE **3.11**
Ionotropic synapses
At an ionotropic synapse, a neurotransmitter may open (**a**) chloride or potassium gates, hyperpolarizing the membrane, or (**b**) sodium gates, depolarizing the membrane.

may excite one neuron, inhibit another, and have no effect at all on still another, depending on those neurons' receptors.

A neurotransmitter receptor is a protein embedded in the membrane. When the neurotransmitter attaches to the active site of the receptor, the receptor can directly open a channel or it can exert slower but longer-lasting effects. For convenience, we distinguish three major types of effects: ionotropic, metabotropic, and modulatory.

Ionotropic effects Some neurotransmitters exert **ionotropic effects** on the postsynaptic neuron. This means that the neurotransmitter attaches to a receptor on the membrane, almost immediately opening the gates for some type of ion (see Figure 3.11). For example, when the neurotransmitter *glutamate* attaches to certain receptors, it opens sodium gates, thereby enabling sodium ions to enter the postsynaptic cell. The sodium ions, bearing a positive charge, partially depolarize the membrane. Consequently, glutamate is generally an *excitatory* neurotransmitter.

GABA is another neurotransmitter that exerts ionotropic effects, but its effects are generally *inhibitory*. When GABA attaches to its receptors on the membrane, it opens chloride gates, enabling chloride ions, with their negative charge, to cross the membrane into the cell more rapidly than usual.

Acetylcholine exerts ionotropic effects at some synapses, which are known as *nicotinic* synapses because they can be stimulated by the drug *nicotine*. When acetylcholine attaches to one of these receptors, as shown in Figure 3.12 on the next page, it slightly rotates the walls of the cylindrical channel into a position that lets sodium ions cross through the membrane (Unwin, 1995). Ionic effects at synapses are rapid but short-lived. Typically, a neurotransmitter opens the ion channels within 10 ms after its release and keeps them open for less than 20 ms (North, 1989; Westbrook & Jahr, 1989). Ionotropic synapses are therefore useful for conveying information about visual and auditory stimulation, muscle movements, and other rapidly changing events.

Metabotropic effects and second messenger systems
At certain other synapses, neurotransmitters exert

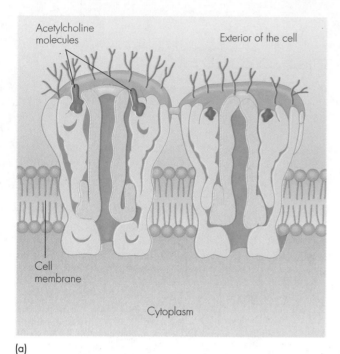

Acetylcholine molecules

Exterior of the cell

Cell membrane

Cytoplasm

(a)

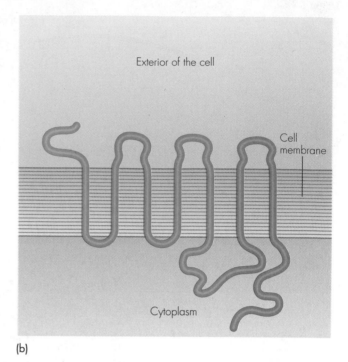

Exterior of the cell

Cell membrane

Cytoplasm

(b)

FIGURE **3.12**
(a) Acetylcholine receptors embedded in a membrane
The receptors on the left have acetylcholine molecules attached to them; consequently, their ion pores are open. **(b) A neurotransmitter receptor, as it would look if folded out**
Source: Part (a) adapted from Lindstrom, 1979.

Native South Americans cover arrow tips with curare, a poison that kills by blocking acetylcholine synapses at nerve-muscle junctions.

metabotropic effects. These effects take place through a sequence of metabolic reactions; they are slower, longer lasting, and more complicated than the ionic effects. The effects emerge about 30 ms after the release of the transmitter (North, 1989); they may last seconds or longer—in some cases, much longer.

When the neurotransmitter attaches to a metabotropic receptor, it alters the configuration of the rest of the protein, enabling a portion of the protein inside the neuron to react with other molecules, as described in Figure 3.13 (Levitzki, 1988; O'Dowd, Lefkowitz, & Caron, 1989). The receptor molecule, which loops back and forth across the membrane, has a portion outside the membrane that binds to a neurotransmitter. It also has a portion inside the membrane that binds to a **G-protein,** which is a protein coupled to guanosine triphosphate (GTP), an energy-storing molecule. When the neurotransmitter binds to its site outside the membrane, the receptor molecule activates the G-protein, which in turn increases the concentration of a **second messenger,** such as cyclic adenosine monophosphate (cyclic AMP), inside the cell. Just as the "first messenger" (the neurotransmitter) carries a message to the postsynaptic cell, the second messenger carries a message to areas within the cell. The message may vary from cell to cell; the second messenger may open or close an ion channel in the membrane or alter the production of proteins or activate a portion of a chromosome. Metabotropic changes are relatively slow and long lasting compared with the effects of ionotropic synapses.

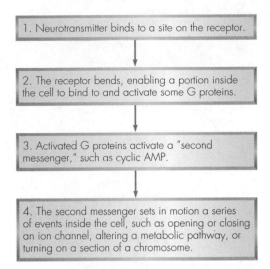

1. Neurotransmitter binds to a site on the receptor.

2. The receptor bends, enabling a portion inside the cell to bind to and activate some G proteins.

3. Activated G proteins activate a "second messenger," such as cyclic AMP.

4. The second messenger sets in motion a series of events inside the cell, such as opening or closing an ion channel, altering a metabolic pathway, or turning on a section of a chromosome.

FIGURE **3.13**
Sequence of events at a metabotropic synapse, using a second messenger within the postsynaptic neuron

Neuromodulators A neurotransmitter is like a telephone line: It conveys a message directly and exclusively from the sender to the receiver. Hormones (discussed mainly in Chapter 11) are more like a radio station: They convey a message to any receiver that happens to be tuned in to the right station. A **neuromodulator** is intermediate between a neurotransmitter and a hormone. Like a hormone, it conveys a message to any receiver that happens to be tuned in, but the signal weakens before it travels very far.

Neurons release neuromodulators generally but not necessarily at their terminals. The neuromodulators diffuse to other neurons in the region, perhaps even to the neuron that released them. They affect all those nearby cells that have receptors for them—that is, all the cells "tuned to the right station" (Vizi, 1984).

The distinction between a neurotransmitter and a neuromodulator is not sharp. After all, any chemical can diffuse away from its point of release and affect nearby cells. In most cases the neuromodulators exert their effects by second messengers, like the metabotropic neurotransmitters.

As a rule, neuromodulators by themselves produce little effect on a neuron. This is why they are called "modulators"; they modulate (alter) the effect of neurotransmitters (Millhorn et al., 1989). For example, certain neuromodulators prolong or limit the effect of a neurotransmitter. Such neuromodulators are said to have a conditional effect: They produce an effect only when the neurotransmitter is present. Other neuromodulators have other effects, such as limiting the release of neurotransmitter from the presynaptic neuron.

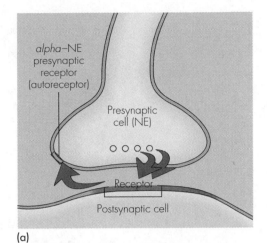

(a)

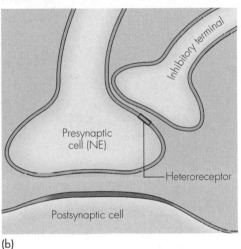

(b)

FIGURE **3.14**
Two types of presynaptic receptors
(**a**) An axon releases a neurotransmitter—in this case, norepinephrine—which may return to a spot on the axon containing a special kind of receptor known as an autoreceptor. Stimulation of the autoreceptor probably decreases further release of the neurotransmitter. (**b**) At heteroreceptors on the presynaptic terminal, a neurotransmitter, neuromodulator, or hormone may either excite or inhibit the presynaptic cell, thus facilitating or decreasing the release of neurotransmitter from the cell.

Presynaptic Receptors

In one special interaction, the receptor is located on the terminal at the tip of an axon. Such a receptor is known as a **presynaptic receptor.** One kind of presynaptic receptor, an **autoreceptor,** is sensitive to the neurotransmitter released by the axon itself. After the axon releases the neurotransmitter, some of the released molecules return to the autoreceptors on the axon, probably providing negative feedback. That is, activation of the autoreceptors probably decreases further release of the neurotransmitter (see Figure 3.14a). However, note that word "probably"; research has not yet

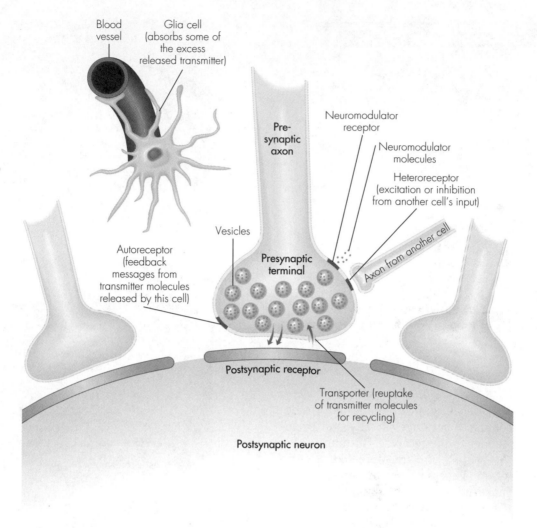

FIGURE **3.15**
Factors influencing the release and disposal of a neurotransmitter
Neuromodulators and heteroreceptors can either increase or decrease the release of transmitter.
Stimulation of autoreceptors decreases release. The transporter molecule facilitates the recycling of
transmitter for future use.

fully determined the function of the autoreceptors (Kalsner, 1990).

Another kind of presynaptic receptor, a **heteroreceptor,** responds to a chemical other than the neurotransmitter released by the axon itself. That other chemical might be a neurotransmitter released at an axon-to-axon synapse, as shown in Figure 3.14b, or a hormone or neuromodulator that diffuses from another location. Some heteroreceptors produce an excitatory effect; others produce an inhibitory effect (Starke, 1981).

Inactivation and Reuptake of Neurotransmitters

A neurotransmitter does not normally linger at the postsynaptic membrane. If it did, it might continue exciting or inhibiting the postsynaptic neuron indefinitely. Various neurotransmitters are inactivated in different ways.

After acetylcholine activates a receptor, it is broken down by the enzyme **acetylcholinesterase** (a-SEE-til-ko-lih-NES-teh-raze) into two fragments, acetate and choline. The choline diffuses back to the presynaptic neuron, which takes it up and reconnects it with acetate already in the cell to form acetylcholine again. This recycling process is highly efficient but not perfect and not instantaneous. At any synapse, not just one using acetylcholine, a sufficiently rapid series of action potentials can release the neurotransmitter faster than the presynaptic cell resynthesizes it, thus bringing transmission to a halt (Liu & Tsien, 1995).

If the enzyme acetylcholinesterase is not present in adequate amounts, acetylcholine may remain at the synapse for an abnormally long time and continue to excite it. Drugs that block acetylcholinesterase can be useful for certain purposes. For example, myasthenia gravis is a condition associated with a deficit of transmission at acetylcholine synapses. One way to alleviate the symptoms is to give drugs that inhibit acetylcholinesterase, thereby prolonging the activity of acetylcholine.

Serotonin and the catecholamines (DA, NE, and epinephrine) are not broken down into inactive fragments at the postsynaptic membrane, but simply detach from the receptor. The presynaptic neuron takes up most of these neurotransmitter molecules intact and reuses them. This process, called **reuptake**, occurs through special membrane proteins called **transporters.**

Some of the serotonin and catecholamine molecules, either before or after reuptake, are converted into inactive chemicals that cannot stimulate the receptor. The enzymes that convert catecholamine transmitters into inactive chemicals are **COMT** (catechol-o-methyl-transferase) and **MAO** (monoamine oxidase, which affects serotonin as well as catecholamines). We shall return to MAO in the discussion of antidepressant drugs. Figure 3.15 summarizes the influences on release and disposal of a neurotransmitter.

IN**CLOSING**

Neurotransmitters and Behavior

The brain uses a great many chemicals as neurotransmitters and neuromodulators, and each of the widely investigated neurotransmitters has more than one type of receptor. For example, acetylcholine has at least four types of nicotinic receptors and five types of muscarinic receptors (McCormick, 1989). Dopamine has at least five types of receptors (Schwartz, Giros, Martres, & Sokoloff, 1992), serotonin at least ten (Humphrey, Hartig, & Hoyer, 1993), and glutamate at least sixteen (Westbrook, 1994). In each case the transmitter itself activates all types of its receptor, although different receptors may respond to different drugs.

Why are there so many neurotransmitters and so many types of receptors? It is probably for the same reason that our alphabet has more than just three or four letters. The nervous system needs a large number of elements that can be combined in different ways to produce complex behavior. Different transmitters and different receptors play different roles in brain functioning and behavior. Indeed, one major reason why people differ from one another in what we call "personality" may be that their neurotransmitter receptors differ.

Summary

1. Most synapses operate by transmitting a neurotransmitter from the presynaptic cell to the postsynaptic cell. (p. 54)
2. Many chemicals are used as neurotransmitters. As far as we know, each neuron releases the same combination of neurotransmitters from all branches of its axon. (pp. 56, 58)
3. At certain synapses, a neurotransmitter exerts its effects by attaching to a receptor that opens the gates to allow a particular ion, such as sodium, to cross the membrane more readily. At other synapses, a neurotransmitter may lead to slower but longer-lasting changes inside the postsynaptic cell. (p. 59)
4. Presynaptic receptors are on the terminal of an axon. Activation of such receptors may inhibit or facilitate the release of a neurotransmitter from that axon. (p. 61)
5. After a neurotransmitter has activated its receptor, some of the transmitter molecules reenter the presynaptic cell through transporter molecules in the membrane. This process, known as reuptake, enables the presynaptic cell to recycle its neurotransmitter. (p. 62)

Review Questions

1. What evidence did Loewi offer to show that transmission at a synapse depends on the release of chemicals? (p. 54)
2. What is a "quantum" of neurotransmitter? (p. 58)
3. Distinguish between ionotropic and metabotropic effects at synapses. (p. 59)
4. What does a "second messenger" do? (p. 60)
5. What is an autoreceptor and how does it contribute to negative feedback? How does an autoreceptor differ from a heteroreceptor? (p. 61)
6. After acetylcholine excites its receptor and then detaches from it, what prevents it from attaching and exciting the receptor again? (p. 62)

Thought Question

1. Suppose that axon A enters a ganglion (a cluster of neurons) and axon B leaves on the other side. An experimenter who stimulates A can shortly thereafter record an impulse traveling down B. We would like to know whether axon B is just an extension of axon A, or whether A formed an excitatory synapse on some neuron in the ganglion, whose axon is axon B. How could an experimenter determine the answer? You should be able to think of more than one good method. Presume that the anatomy within the ganglion is so complex that you cannot simply trace the course of an axon through it.

Suggestions for Further Reading

Allman, W. F. (1989). *Apprentices of wonder.* New York: Bantam Books. Certain neuroscientists have developed mathematical models of how enormous populations of neurons and synapses mediate complex behavior. This book describes those attempts in nontechnical language.

Levitan, I. B., & Kaczmarek, L. K. (1991). *The neuron*. New York: Oxford University Press. A thorough treatment of the mechanisms of synaptic communication.

Terms

neurotransmitter chemical released at a synapse (p. 55)

amino acids acids containing an amine group (NH_2) (p. 56)

peptides chains of amino acids (p. 56)

monoamines nonacidic neurotransmitters containing an amine group (NH_2), formed by a metabolic change of certain amino acids (p. 56)

purines category of chemicals including adenosine (p. 56)

acetylcholine, glutamate, GABA, endorphins, substance P, neuropeptide Y, ATP, nitric oxide, adenosine, serotonin, dopamine, norepinephrine, and **epinephrine** chemicals believed to act as neurotransmitters at various places in the nervous system (pp. 56–57)

catecholamine compound such as dopamine, norepinephrine, and epinephrine that contains both catechol and an amine (NH_2) (p. 56)

insulin hormone that increases the conversion of glucose into stored fat and facilitates the transfer of glucose across the cell membrane (p. 56)

vesicle tiny, nearly spherical packet near the axon terminals filled with the neurotransmitter (p. 58)

quantum the minimum size of an EPSP or IPSP in a postsynaptic neuron (p. 58)

ionotropic effect synaptic effect that depends on the rapid opening of some kind of gate in the membrane (p. 59)

metabotropic effect effect at a synapse that produces a relatively slow but long-lasting effect through metabolic reactions (p. 60)

G-protein a protein coupled to GTP (guanosine triphosphate, an energy-storing molecule); an important part of the receptor molecule found in many synapses (p. 60)

second messenger chemical activated by a neurotransmitter, which in turn initiates processes that carry messages to several areas within the neuron (p. 60)

neuromodulator chemical that has properties intermediate between those of a neurotransmitter and those of a hormone (p. 61)

presynaptic receptor receptor located on the terminal at the tip of an axon (p. 61)

autoreceptor presynaptic receptor that responds to its own neurotransmitter (p. 61)

heteroreceptor presynaptic receptor that responds to some chemical other than the neurotransmitter released by the axon itself (p. 62)

acetylcholinesterase enzyme that breaks acetylcholine into acetate and choline (p. 62)

reuptake reabsorption of a neurotransmitter by the presynaptic terminal (p. 63)

transporter membrane protein responsible for the reuptake of a neurotransmitter after its release (p. 63)

COMT catechol-o-methyltransferase, an enzyme that converts catecholamines into synaptically inactive forms (p. 63)

MAO monoamine oxidase, enzyme that converts catecholamines and serotonin into synaptically inactive forms (p. 63)

Synapses, Drugs, and Behavior

Drugs that affect the brain can be either helpful or harmful. Physicians prescribe antidepressants, tranquilizers, and so forth, to help people deal with psychological troubles; meanwhile, society tries to combat the use of recreational drugs. Many drugs, including morphine, amphetamine, and cocaine, have legitimate medical uses as well as dangerous or addictive uses. The difference between a "good" drug and a "bad" drug is partly a matter of the drug itself and partly a matter of how much of the drug a person is taking, and when, and why.

Most drugs that strongly affect the brain influence behavior mainly by influencing the synapses. We shall consider here a few of the basic mechanisms by which drugs operate, especially some frequently abused drugs. In later chapters, we shall discuss drugs that are prescribed for their psychiatric value. Although we are focusing on drugs, the underlying point is more general: Each transmitter and each receptor plays a specialized role in behavior and experience.

How Drugs Can Affect Synapses

A drug can mimic or increase the effects of a given neurotransmitter, or it can block those effects. A drug that blocks the effects is called an **antagonist;** a drug that mimics or increases the effects is called an **agonist.** (*Antagonist,* meaning *enemy,* is used in everyday speech, whereas *agonist* is seldom used except to describe drug effects. The term *agonist* is derived from a Greek word meaning *contestant;* an antagonist is an "anti-agonist," or member of the opposing team.)

Drugs work in a wide variety of ways, facilitating or inhibiting the synthesis of a neurotransmitter, increasing or decreasing the release of a neurotransmitter, or altering what happens to the transmitter after it attaches to its receptors. Figure 3.16 illustrates the sequence of events at a norepinephrine synapse and some of the ways that drugs can alter the events. Ordinarily, tyrosine from the diet is converted into dopa, which in turn gives rise to dopamine and then to norepinephrine. Action potentials in this axon release norepinephrine, which diffuses to the postsynaptic cell and binds with receptors there. After detaching from the receptors, some of the norepinephrine is reuptaken by the presynaptic cell, and the rest is broken down into inactive chemicals by the enzymes MAO and COMT.

Drugs can facilitate or interfere at any step along the way (see Figure 3.16). For example, *alpha-methyl-para-tyrosine (AMPT)* blocks the enzyme that converts tyrosine into dopa; the result is a decreased production of dopa and ultimately a decreased production of norepinephrine. *Reserpine* causes the vesicles that store norepinephrine to leak. *Tricyclic antidepressant* drugs inhibit the reuptake of norepinephrine as well as several other transmitters; *amphetamine* increases the release of those transmitters as well as blocking their reuptake. *MAO inhibitors* prevent the enzyme MAO from breaking down norepinephrine and other catecholamines into inactive chemicals.

Some drugs also attach directly to the receptors. Investigators say that a particular drug has an **affinity** for a particular type of receptor if it attaches to that receptor, fitting somewhat like a lock and key. Drugs vary in their affinities, from strong to weak. The **efficacy** of a drug is its tendency to activate the receptor. So, for example, a drug that binds tightly to a receptor but fails to stimulate it has a high affinity but a low efficacy. Such a drug is, in fact, an antagonist, because by occupying the receptor it prevents the effects of the transmitter.

If you or anyone you know has ever taken any drug that affects the brain—tranquilizers, antidepressants, even high-blood-pressure drugs—you are probably aware that both the effectiveness and the side effects vary from one person to another. For example, antipsychotic drugs sometimes produce serious movement disorders, sexual impotence, dizziness, drowsiness, exces-

FIGURE **3.16**
Events at a norepinephrine synapse and the drugs that can inhibit each step
AMPT blocks the conversion of tyrosine to dopa. Reserpine causes leakage from the vesicles that store norepinephrine. Amphetamine increases the release. Clonidine stimulates the presynaptic receptors that inhibit release of norepinephrine. Tricyclic antidepressants block reuptake. MAO inhibitors block MAO (monoamine oxidase), an enzyme that breaks down norepinephrine and similar transmitters.

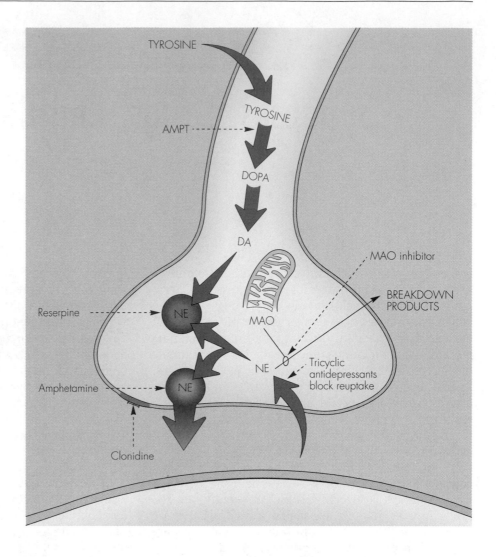

sive salivation, and other undesirable effects. Some people experience these effects to a great degree; others, to a mild degree or not at all. Why such differences in effects? Part of the explanation is that each drug affects more than one kind of synapse. Antipsychotic drugs are beneficial because they can block certain dopamine pathways in the brain. However, the brain has several kinds of dopamine receptors with varying behavioral effects, and an individual may have more than the usual amount of one receptor or less than the usual amount of another. Consequently, drugs have different effects on different people. A major research goal is to find drugs that affect just one kind of receptor and not others.

Synapses, Reinforcement, and Addiction

Researchers have gradually built a strong case that links reinforcement, drug addiction, and related behaviors to the *inhibition* of certain cells in several parts of the brain, especially a small subcortical area known as the **nucleus accumbens** (see Figure 3.17). The surest way to inhibit this area is to increase activity of dopamine, which is an inhibitory transmitter in the nucleus accumbens and other locations. Another way is to *decrease* activity of glutamate, which is an excitatory transmitter in the nucleus accumbens and elsewhere. However, because glutamate has such a diverse set of roles throughout the brain, drugs that inhibit it have a mixture of reinforcing and punishing effects. Most abused drugs (and indeed most real-life reinforcing activities) act by increasing the activity at dopamine synapses.

Electrical Self-Stimulation of the Brain

The discovery of the brain's reinforcement systems began decades ago with an accidental discovery: Two young scientists, James Olds and Peter Milner (1954), put rats in a situation in which they had to choose between turning left and turning right. Olds and Milner wanted to test whether stimulation of a particular brain

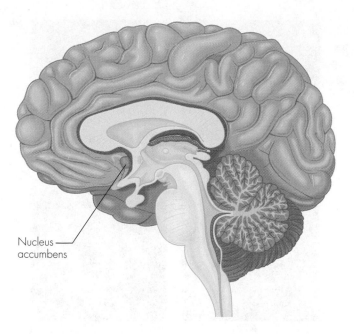

FIGURE **3.17**
Location of the nucleus accumbens in the human brain
This area, considered essential for reinforcement or reward, is in the interior of each hemisphere—that is, slightly behind the plane shown in this midline diagram.

area would cause a rat that was looking in one direction to turn in that direction. However, they accidentally implanted the electrode in an unintended area of the brain, the septum. To their surprise, when the rat received the brain stimulation, it sometimes sat up, looked around, and sniffed, as if reacting to a favorable stimulus.

Olds and Milner later placed rats in Skinner boxes, where they could repeatedly press a lever for electrical brain stimulation as a reinforcement (see Figure 3.18). Rats worked, sometimes extremely vigorously, for such **self-stimulation of the brain.** Olds found that a number of other areas in the limbic system also produce reinforcement; in some cases rats pressed a lever to stimulate certain brain areas as often as 2,000 times per hour, continuing for hours until collapsing from exhaustion (Olds, 1958). In similar experiments, monkeys pressed a lever as often as 8,000 times per hour (Olds, 1962). The results of later experiments have indicated that brain stimulation is reinforcing almost exclusively in tracts of axons that release dopamine; it is only weakly reinforcing, if at all, in other areas (Wise, 1996).

Do such results indicate that dopamine activity equates to pleasure? Not necessarily. As Kent Berridge (1996) has pointed out, "wanting" something or working for it is not always the same as "liking" it. You might want very much to take your medicine or to eat your vegetables, even though you dislike their taste, and at the end of a big meal you might not want to eat

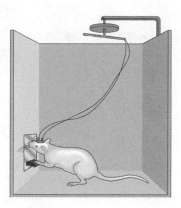

FIGURE **3.18**
A rat pressing a lever for self-stimulation of its brain

dessert, even though you know it would taste wonderful. Long-term drug addicts will work furiously to get their drug, even though it provides them with little if any pleasure (Berridge & Robinson, 1995). Similarly, drugs that stimulate or inhibit dopamine synapses alter how hard a rat will work for, say, a food reinforcement, but they have little effect on the rat's facial expressions when it gets the reinforcement. (Yes, rats do have facial expressions. For example, they gape and shake their heads after tasting something bitter; they have characteristic mouth and tongue movements after tasting something sweet.)

Most of the research on dopamine does not distinguish whether it enhances reinforcement by increasing pleasure or attention. In either case, however, most experiences that prove reinforcing to either humans or laboratory animals increase the activity at dopamine synapses, especially dopamine receptor types D_2, D_3, and D_4. For example, sexual excitement depends on the release of dopamine at D_2 receptors. When monkeys learn to respond to a visual or auditory signal by pressing a lever to receive fruit juice, either the signal or the presentation of the juice itself can activate the release of dopamine (Mirenowicz & Schultz, 1996).

Effects of Stimulant Drugs on Dopamine Synapses

Further evidence for the importance of dopamine for reinforcement comes from research on drugs that many people self-administer for nonmedical reasons. Many highly addictive drugs are **stimulant drugs,** producing excitement, alertness, elevated mood, decreased fatigue, and sometimes increased motor activity. The drugs exert these effects mainly by activating dopamine receptors types D_2–D_4, either directly or indirectly (Harris, Brodie, & Dunwiddie, 1992; Wise & Bozarth, 1987).

Amphetamine stimulates dopamine synapses by increasing the release of dopamine from the presynaptic terminal. The presynaptic terminal has a mechanism for reabsorbing dopamine after its release. Amphetamine apparently reverses that mechanism, causing the cell to release dopamine instead of reabsorbing it (Giros, Jaber, Jones, Wightman, & Caron, 1996). Amphetamine also increases the release of several other neurotransmitters. **Cocaine** blocks the reuptake of dopamine, norepinephrine, and serotonin, thus prolonging their effects. Because both amphetamine and cocaine increase and prolong dopamine activity, their behavioral effects are similar.

The effects of cocaine and amphetamine on dopamine synapses are necessarily temporary. By increasing the release of dopamine or decreasing its reuptake, the drugs increase the accumulation of dopamine in the synaptic cleft. However, the excess dopamine eventually washes away from the synapse faster than the presynaptic cell can resynthesize dopamine. Furthermore, the excess dopamine in the synaptic cleft activates autoreceptors on the presynaptic terminal, exerting a negative feedback effect that reduces further release of dopamine (North, 1992). The net result is that within hours after taking amphetamine or cocaine, a user "crashes" into a depressed state, nearly the opposite of the pleasant, aroused state that the drug initially produced.

Methylphenidate (Ritalin), another stimulant drug, is often prescribed for people with **attention-deficit disorder (ADD),** a condition marked by impulsiveness and poor control of attention. Methylphenidate, like cocaine, acts by blocking the reuptake of dopamine by presynaptic terminals; in fact, methylphenidate and cocaine attach to the same receptor sites in the brain. However, people with attention-deficit disorder ordinarily take methylphenidate in a carefully measured dosage, so the effects build up much more slowly than the effects of cocaine, producing an increase in attention and arousal without the sudden rush of excitement. The effects of methylphenidate's effects last four to five times as long as those of cocaine (Volkow et al., 1995). Although some people do abuse methylphenidate, few people with ADD develop an addiction. In fact, many think of the drug as "that medicine they made me take when I was a child," not as an exciting or desirable substance.

Because dopamine is mostly an inhibitory transmitter, drugs that increase activity at dopamine synapses decrease the activity of many other neurons and decrease total activity in many brain areas (London et al., 1990). (See Figure 3.19.) How, you might wonder, could drugs that decrease overall brain activity lead to increased arousal, activity, and (with appropriate doses) improved concentration? One explanation is that

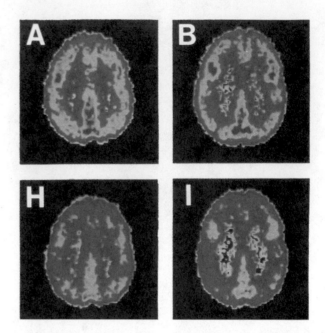

FIGURE 3.19

Sometimes "your brain on drugs" is not like something in a frying pan, a popular analogy; it is more like something in the refrigerator. As these positron emission tomography (PET) scans show, the brain has lower metabolism and lower overall activity under the influence of cocaine than it has ordinarily. Red indicates highest activity, followed by yellow, green, and blue. A and B represent brain activity under normal conditions; H and I show activity after a cocaine injection.   Source: From London et al., 1990.

high dopamine activity mostly decreases "background noise" in the brain and therefore increases the signal-to-noise ratio (Mattay et al., 1996).

Synaptic Effects of Other Abused Drugs

A number of other abused drugs also activate dopamine receptors. For example, **nicotine,** a compound present in tobacco, has long been known to stimulate one type of acetylcholine receptor, conveniently known as the *nicotinic receptor*, found both in the central nervous system and at the nerve-muscle junction of skeletal muscles. However, acetylcholine stimulation is not ordinarily reinforcing; in fact, most addicting drugs decrease the release of acetylcholine (Pothos, Rada, Mark, & Hoebel, 1991; Rada, Pothos, Mark, & Hoebel, 1991). Nicotine is reinforcing because it attaches to receptors that increase the release of dopamine in the nucleus accumbens (Levin & Rose, 1995; Pontieri, Tanda, Orzi, & DiChiara, 1996).

Morphine and other opiate drugs also increase dopamine activity, although they do so indirectly. Opiates stimulate endorphin synapses, which inhibit cells releasing GABA, which would otherwise inhibit dopamine release. Thus, through inhibition of an inhibitor, the net effect of opiates is to increase the release of dopamine. Both opiate addiction and opiate withdrawal symptoms depend largely on how opiates affect dopamine synapses. Ordinarily, anyone who quits opiates after long-term use will suffer withdrawal symptoms, such as rapid breathing, perspiration, crying, tremors, and muscle twitches. It is possible to decrease the withdrawal symptoms by procedures that stimulate D_2 receptors (including electrical stimulation of a brain area rich in dopamine); conversely, any drug that blocks D_2 receptors will increase opiate withdrawal symptoms (Harris & Aston-Jones, 1994). Still, opiate drugs retain some of their reinforcing effects even after dopamine synapses are blocked (Nader, Vechara, Roberts, & van der Kooy, 1994). That is, opiates exert part of their reinforcing effects through pathways independent of dopamine.

Phencyclidine (**PCP,** or "angel dust") is a commonly abused drug that does *not* affect dopamine synapses. Instead, it inhibits certain kinds of glutamate receptors, including those located in the nucleus accumbens. Because rats will work to deliver phencyclidine to their brains even after dopamine synapses have been blocked, we can conclude that the reinforcing effects of the drug do not require some indirect effect on dopamine (Carlezon & Wise, 1996). Inhibition of glutamate synapses is not always reinforcing; in fact, administration of phencyclidine to specific parts of the brain can be either reinforcing or punishing, depending on the location. In the nucleus accumbens, however, it is reinforcing. Because glutamate axons converge on the same postsynaptic cells as dopamine axons, the simplest explanation is that reinforcement depends on the inhibition of those postsynaptic cells—either by increasing dopamine (an inhibitory transmitter) or by decreasing glutamate (an excitatory transmitter). The nucleus accumbens is not the brain's only reinforcement system, but it appears to be a very prominent one.

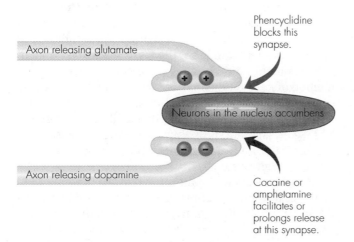

Axon releasing glutamate

Phencyclidine blocks this synapse.

Neurons in the nucleus accumbens

Axon releasing dopamine

Cocaine or amphetamine facilitates or prolongs release at this synapse.

Variations in Synapses and Variations in Personality

Each of the various neurotransmitters has a number of receptor types, each with a different function in behavior. For example, serotonin type 3 receptors ($5\text{-}HT_3$) are evidently responsible for nausea. That fact makes it possible to design and market drugs such as ondansetron, which block nausea without impairing other kinds of serotonin function (Perez, 1995).

The specialization of receptors has theoretical implications. Presumably, people differ from one another in their amounts of different receptors and possibly also in the sensitivity of different receptors. Any variation in receptors should lead to a particular behavioral predisposition. Or, to put it the other way, some part of the variation we see in people's personalities may be attributable to differences in their neurotransmitter receptors (Zuckerman, 1995).

The first apparent example of such a relationship came from studies of dopamine receptors. In 1990, researchers identified the gene that controls the development of the D_2 (dopamine type 2) receptor in humans. They also reported that people with the less common form of this gene, and therefore an alternative form of the receptor, were somewhat more likely than other people to develop severe alcoholism. Later research suggested that this gene is not a "gene for alcoholism," but instead apparently increases the probability of a variety of unrestrained pleasure-seeking behaviors, including alcoholism, other kinds of drug abuse, obesity, and habitual gambling (Blum, Cull, Braverman, & Comings, 1996). Researchers described this combination of effects as "reward deficiency syndrome." The theory is that people who have the alternative form of the D_2 receptor fail to get the normal amount of reinforcement or pleasure from everyday experiences and therefore try more adventurous ways of stimulating their D_2 receptors. However, the correlation between pleasure seeking and alternative forms of the D_2 receptor is at best a weak one, and several other laboratories have been unable to replicate the finding. Furthermore, the results, if replicated, could be interpreted in other ways, such as altered attention as opposed to altered pleasure.

Similarly, researchers have identified the gene that controls the development of the human D_4 receptor. Like other neurotransmitter receptors, it consists of a long string of amino acids that loops back and forth across the membrane. In individuals with an alternative form of the receptor gene, one of the loops is longer than usual; these people tend to have a stronger than average "novelty seeking" aspect of personality, as measured by a standardized personality test (Benjamin et al., 1996; Ebstein et al., 1996). (See Figure 3.20.)

FIGURE **3.20**

Relationship between D₄ receptor type and personality test scores

The top three comparisons represent the results of Benjamin et al. (1996); the bottom comparison represents the results of Ebstein et al. (1996). In each comparison, the yellow bar represents the mean score for people with a shorter loop of the D₄ receptor (that is, the standard form of the gene, as found in most people). The blue bar represents the mean score for people with a longer loop of the receptor. Note that people with the alternative, less common form of the gene tend to score higher in novelty seeking and extraversion, lower in conscientiousness. The difference between the Benjamin et al. results and the Ebstein et al. results reflects the fact that the two studies used different questionnaires to measure personality.

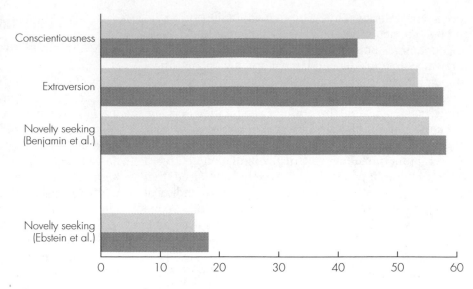

Novelty seeking consists of being impulsive, exploratory, and quick-tempered. Again, of course, it is prudent to await further research to test the strength of the D₄–novelty seeking relationship. Note that reward deficiency syndrome and novelty seeking are not necessarily bad; they predispose people to risky behaviors, but sometimes risk-taking is a successful strategy.

Recall from Chapter 1 that personality differences among people are partly heritable. Here we see one of the few examples documented so far in which we can identify genes that (perhaps) contribute to a personality trait and understand to some extent how those genes work. Obviously, a given individual's actual behavior depends not just on the D₂ or D₄ receptor, but also on his or her experiences, current environment, health, nutrition, and other genes. The shape of a receptor does not force a given behavior; it merely changes the probabilities.

Some Other Self-Administered Drugs

So far we have examined drugs whose effects on the reinforcement systems of the brain are fairly simple and well established. The drugs we shall consider next are often self-administered, but they have less direct effects on dopamine and some prominent effects on other transmitters.

Opiates

Opiate drugs are derived from (or are similar to those derived from) the opium poppy. Familiar opiates include morphine, heroin, and methadone. Opiates give rise to a generally pleasant state, an overall withdrawal from reality, and decreased sensitivity to pain. Opiate drugs, when taken as painkillers under medical supervision, are very seldom habit-forming; when taken recreationally, they are strongly addictive.

People smoked or injected morphine and other opiates for centuries before anyone knew how they affected the brain. Then Candace Pert and Solomon Snyder found that opiates attach to specific receptors in the brain (Pert & Snyder, 1973). It was a safe guess that vertebrates had not evolved such receptors just to enable us to become addicted to derivatives of the opium poppy; the brain must produce some chemical of its own that attaches to these receptors. And, indeed, investigators soon found that the brain has a class of neurotransmitters now known as the *endorphins*—a contraction of *endo*genous mor*phines*. We shall discuss the endorphins in more detail in the section on pain (Chapter 7); at this point, let us simply note that they serve as a brake on pain and probably contribute to pleasant experience. Opiate drugs are an artificial way of tapping into that brain system.

Opiates activate dopamine synapses, but only indirectly. Endorphin synapses inhibit neurons that release GABA, a transmitter that inhibits dopamine release

(North, 1992). Because of this inhibition of inhibition, the net effect of opiates is increased dopamine release.

Marijuana

The leaves of the marijuana plant contain the chemical Δ^9-*tetrahydrocannabinol (Δ^9-THC)* and other **cannabinoids** (chemicals related to Δ^9-THC), which people absorb when they smoke or eat the leaves. The results may include an intensification of sensory experience and an illusion that time is passing very slowly. Marijuana users sometimes also experience impairments of attention, learning, and memory, especially the first few times that they use the substance. Marijuana is sometimes used medically to relieve pain or nausea or to combat glaucoma (an eye disorder).

Marijuana can be habit-forming, although few users experience the same intense cravings that cocaine or opiate users do. Cannabinoids dissolve in the body's fats and leave the body very slowly. One consequence is that users seldom experience strong withdrawal effects after quitting the drug, as cocaine and opiate users do. Another consequence is that a marijuana user can test positive for cannabinoids in the urine days or weeks after the last use.

Marijuana users face certain health risks. Driving while under the influence of marijuana is analogous to driving under the influence of alcohol. Also, long-term marijuana smoking increases the risk of lung cancer. However, marijuana users do not typically overdose the way that cocaine and opiate users do; even an unusually large dose of marijuana is unlikely to interfere with breathing or heartbeat.

For years, investigators could not explain the effects of marijuana on the brain. The drug was known to have some general effects on neuronal membranes, but nothing spectacular. Then, investigators localized specific receptors for cannabinoids (Devane, Dysarz, Johnson, Melvin, & Howlett, 1988). Those receptors are abundant in the hippocampus, the basal ganglia, and the cerebellum (Herkenham, 1992; Herkenham, Lynn, de Costa, & Richfield, 1991). However, they are virtually absent from the medulla and the rest of the brain stem. That absence is significant, because the medulla and brain stem include the centers that control breathing and heartbeat; we begin to understand why even large doses of marijuana do not threaten breathing or heartbeat.

Just as the discovery of opiate receptors in the brain led to a successful search for the brain's endogenous opiates, the discovery of cannabinoid receptors prompted investigators to search for a brain chemical that binds to those receptors. One such chemical has

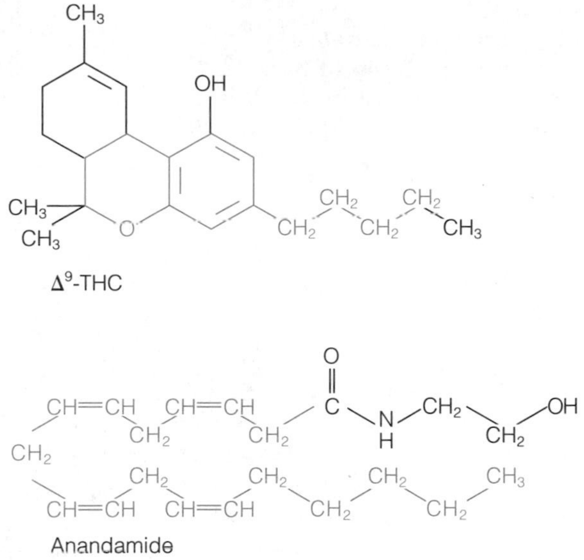

FIGURE **3.21**
Anandamide and Δ^9-tetrahydrocannabinol
Note the similarity between one part of the naturally occurring brain chemical and one part of the marijuana derivative.

been found, **anandamide,** from the Sanskrit word *ananda,* meaning *bliss* (see Figure 3.21). Anandamide is synthesized within neurons and probably released as a neurotransmitter (DiMarzo et al., 1995). However, researchers are only beginning to identify its behavioral functions. One is that it inhibits activity at serotonin type 3 (5-HT$_3$) synapses (Fan, 1995). Recall that those synapses mediate nausea; Δ^9-THC, which is known to decrease nausea, apparently does so by activating anandamide synapses that block 5-HT$_3$ synapses.

Hallucinogenic Drugs

Drugs that distort perception are called **hallucinogenic drugs.** Phencyclidine has already been mentioned; other examples are lysergic acid diethylamide (LSD) and mescaline. Their effects vary from person to person and from one use to another; most often, the effect is described as a dreamlike state.

Hallucinogens chemically resemble the neurotransmitter serotonin (see Figure 3.22) and produce some of their effects at serotonin synapses. LSD attaches to and stimulates serotonin receptors. (That is, it is a serotonin agonist.) Contrast this mode of action to that of amphetamine, which acts by releasing norepinephrine and dopamine from the presynaptic neurons. If the neurons have a low supply of these neurotransmitters, amphetamine is ineffective. In contrast, even after the com-

FIGURE **3.22**
Resemblance of the neurotransmitter serotonin to two chemicals with hallucinogenic effects

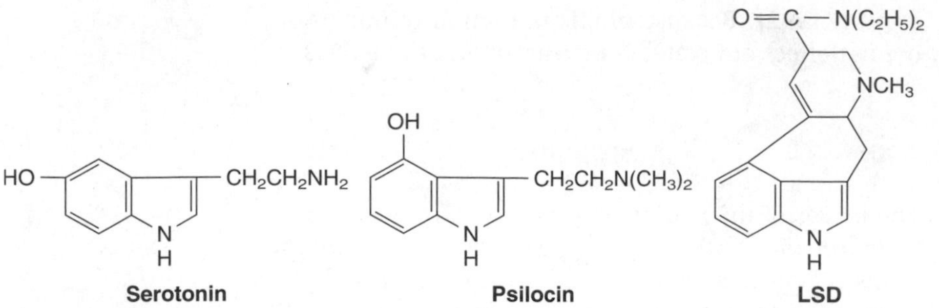

plete removal of the presynaptic neurons that release serotonin, LSD still exerts its full effect. It may even produce a greater-than-normal effect: After the removal of the serotonin-containing neurons, the postsynaptic neuron may develop an increased number of serotonin receptors as a kind of compensation. More receptors make LSD more effective (Jacobs, 1987).

Serotonin (5-HT) has several types of receptors, each with slightly different properties and, no doubt, different roles in behavior. LSD, it turns out, has a strong affinity for only one of these types, the 5-HT_2 receptor (Jacobs, 1987). Receptors of that type are abundant in much of the brain. By binding to this receptor, LSD stimulates it at abnormal times and blocks serotonin from stimulating it in the normal way.

Note that we now know *where* in the brain LSD exerts its effects, but not *why* those effects include hallucinations and other changes in perception. Presumably, the 5-HT_2 receptors contribute in some way to perception, and an abnormal pattern of stimulation of those receptors leads to abnormal perceptions. But certainly we can explain the chemistry better than we can explain the psychological effects.

MDMA ("Ecstasy")

The drug methylenedioxymethamphetamine, mercifully abbreviated **MDMA** (also known as "ecstasy"), is a chemical derivative of methamphetamine, and like other drugs in the amphetamine family, it stimulates the release of dopamine, especially at low doses. At higher doses, MDMA produces greater and greater effects on serotonin synapses, producing hallucinogenic effects similar to those of LSD. Unfortunately, MDMA not only stimulates serotonin synapses, it also destroys them. (At least it does so in rats and monkeys; we can only assume it does the same in humans.) After repeated doses of MDMA, some users remark that its effects seem weaker and weaker; the probable explanation is that it can no longer stimulate serotonin synapses because previous doses have destroyed them. If a user stops taking MDMA, would the damaged serotonin axons grow back? We do not know about humans, but in monkeys that were exposed to MDMA and

then deprived of it, serotonin synapses regenerated in some parts of the brain and not others. Even where they did grow back, the restoration was gradual and took more than a year (Fischer, Hatzidimitriou, Wlos, Katz, & Ricaurte, 1995).

Caffeine

Caffeine, a drug found in coffee, tea, and many soft drinks, affects brain functioning in at least two ways. First, it alters blood flow, slightly increasing heart rate but also constricting the blood vessels to the brain, thereby decreasing the blood flow to the brain. (Because of that effect, abstention from caffeine after repeated use increases blood flow to the brain and can cause a headache.) Second, caffeine interferes with the effects of the neurotransmitter *adenosine.* Recall that many neurons have presynaptic receptors—receptors on the presynaptic terminal that facilitate or inhibit the release of transmitter. Adenosine acts at certain presynaptic receptors to inhibit the release of a number of neurotransmitters, including glutamate and dopamine. Because caffeine blocks the effects of adenosine, which inhibits the release of glutamate and dopamine, the net effect of caffeine is to increase the release of those transmitters (Silinsky, 1989).

Alcohol

Societies vary enormously in their attitudes toward alcohol, ranging from those that strictly forbid its use to those where a glass of beer or wine is a routine part of almost any dinner. Drunk in moderation, alcohol can help people overcome social inhibitions and reduce their tension and anxiety. Unfortunately, many people cross the vague line between social drinker and problem drinker, and someone who has crossed that line can seldom cross back. I expect that almost every reader of this book knows people whose lives have been harmed by alcohol.

Many problem drinkers suffer serious health hazards, including diseases of the liver and other internal organs, and the risk of accidents and injuries while drunk. Alcohol can impair the dendritic branching of neurons, especially in infancy but in adulthood as well (Riley & Walker, 1978). Long-term alcoholics have been reported to have somewhat smaller-than-average brains, although we do not know which is the cause and which is the effect (Harper & Kril, 1993).

People who drink heavily also suffer a variety of cognitive deficits, including impairments of reasoning and memory. Problem drinkers who abstain from alcohol will gradually improve in their performance of cognitive tasks, although the recovery process may require as many as 15 years and even then may not be complete (Parsons, 1993). Generally, people who give up alcohol early in life will recover faster and more completely than will people who quit later.

Alcohol exerts its effects on behavior through many routes. It inhibits the flow of sodium across the membrane, expands the surface of membranes, and generally interferes with nervous system activity. In addition to these nonspecific effects on neurons throughout the brain, alcohol decreases serotonin activity (Fils-Aime et al., 1996) and facilitates the $GABA_A$ receptor, making it more responsive.

Risk factors for alcohol abuse A number of researchers have attempted to identify the risk factors that make some people more likely than others to become problem drinkers. Identifying those factors might make it possible to prevent some cases of alcohol abuse, or to recognize alcohol abuse in its earliest stages, when treatment is more likely to be effective. One important risk factor is a genetic predisposition. A person who is closely related to one or more alcoholics has an increased probability of becoming an alcoholic too, even if raised in an adoptive family without alcohol abusers (Cloninger, Bohman, & Sigvardsson, 1981; Gabrielli & Plomin, 1985; Vaillant & Milofsky, 1982).

The genes that increase the risk of alcoholism—and I do mean genes, not just one gene—alter people's reactions to alcohol in a number of ways. We have already encountered the idea that people may be predisposed to alcohol abuse and other risky behaviors because of a gene that affects the D_2 or D_4 receptor. Research has also found that the sons of alcoholics (many of whom will go on to become alcoholics themselves) tend to experience more than the usual amount of relief from anxiety after drinking alcohol (Levenson, Oyama, & Meek, 1987) and tend to experience greater-than-average increases in endorphins after drinking alcohol (Gianoulakis, Krishnan, & Thavundayil, 1996). In another study, investigators tested hundreds of young men for their ability to estimate their own intoxication after drinking. Eight years later, they followed up on those men to determine which ones had developed alcohol problems. The findings were (1) that 18- to 29-year-old men who had an alcoholic father were likely to underestimate their own intoxication after they had

been drinking, and (2) 18- to 29-year-old men who underestimated their own intoxication after drinking were much more likely than other men to develop a habit of alcohol abuse within the next eight years. Young men who *did not* have any alcoholic relatives but who *did* underestimate their own intoxication were also at high risk for an alcohol problem (Schuckit & Smith, 1996). In other words,

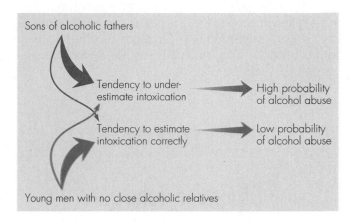

How would underestimating one's intoxication increase the risk of alcohol abuse? Imagine two people who have drunk the same amount of alcohol. One correctly ascertains the beginning of intoxication and therefore decides to quit drinking. The other fails to notice the intoxication and therefore continues drinking.

Alcohol consumption and alcohol metabolism Another gene affects alcohol consumption by controlling proteins that alter the rate of alcohol's metabolism. After a person drinks **ethyl alcohol,** enzymes in the liver metabolize it to **acetaldehyde,** a poisonous substance. The enzyme *acetaldehyde dehydrogenase* then converts acetaldehyde to **acetic acid,** which the body can use as a source of energy:

$$\text{Ethyl alcohol} \rightarrow \text{Acetaldehyde} \xrightarrow{\text{Acetaldehyde dehydrogenase}} \text{Acetic acid}$$

Repeated exposure to acetaldehyde can cause cirrhosis of the liver and damage to other organs. Even in the short term, acetaldehyde can cause illness if it reaches a high concentration. People who for genetic reasons produce little acetaldehyde dehydrogenase feel ill after drinking alcohol and are unlikely to abuse alcohol (see Chapter 1).

The drug *disulfiram*, which goes by the trade name **Antabuse,** decreases a person's levels of acetaldehyde dehydrogenase. Antabuse inactivates all copper-containing enzymes, including acetaldehyde dehydrogenase. For at least a couple of days after taking an

Antabuse pill, preferably longer, people must avoid all contact with alcohol, at the risk of grave illness. Antabuse is sometimes used to help people stop abusing alcohol (Peachey & Naranjo, 1983). The idea is that a person will learn an aversion to the taste of alcohol because of the illness that follows. In fact, however, the drug may be effective mostly because of its threat value. Many people who take Antabuse abstain from drinking completely, never experiencing the illness that alcohol would cause them (Fuller & Roth, 1979). Those who drink in spite of taking the pill do get ill, but they are as likely to stop taking the pill as to stop drinking alcohol. Evidently, Antabuse functions mostly as a way for an alcoholic to make a daily reaffirmation of the decision to abstain from alcohol.

IN CLOSING

Drugs and Behavior

We study drugs because they are an important part of human society; we need to understand how they work so that we can prevent or relieve some of the problems that they cause. We also study drugs because they shed light on the normal processes of behavior. Investigations of drugs have been responsible for much of our understanding of the brain processes behind reinforcement. As we shall see in later chapters, studies of drugs also contribute much to our understanding of anxiety, depression, and schizophrenia.

Summary

1. Drugs can act as agonists (facilitators) or antagonists (inhibitors) of a neurotransmitter by altering any step in the total sequence of transmission, from synthesis of the transmitter to its reuptake or breakdown following transmission. (p. 65)
2. Reinforcement depends to a great extent on the inhibition of cells in a few brain areas, including the nucleus accumbens. Reinforcing brain stimulation, reinforcing experiences, and most self-administered drugs act largely by increasing the activity of axons that release dopamine (an inhibitory transmitter) at dopamine receptor types D_2, D_3, and D_4 in the nucleus accumbens. A few other self-administered drugs act by decreasing the activity of glutamate (an excitatory transmitter) in that same region. (p. 66)
3. Amphetamine acts mostly by increasing the release of

dopamine. Cocaine and methylphenidate act by decreasing the reuptake of dopamine after its release. Opiate drugs stimulate endorphin synapses, which block GABA synapses, which would otherwise inhibit the release of dopamine. Phencyclidine inhibits glutamate synapses, which excite some of the same neurons that dopamine inhibits. (p. 68)
4. The genes responsible for dopamine receptor types D_2 and D_4 have been identified. People with the less common form of these genes produce a less sensitive form of the receptors. A few studies have linked the alternative receptor form to an increased probability of substance abuse, overeating, gambling, and a novelty-seeking personality. (p. 69)
5. Opiates, marijuana, hallucinogens, MDMA, and caffeine also act by increasing or decreasing the activity at various kinds of synapses. (p. 70)
6. Alcohol affects behavior by many routes, including effects on GABA and serotonin synapses. Risk factors for alcohol abuse include having biological relatives with a history of alcohol abuse, a tendency to get more than the usual pleasure from alcohol, and a tendency to underestimate one's own intoxication. (p. 73)
7. The liver metabolizes alcohol into acetaldehyde (a toxic substance) and then metabolizes acetaldehyde into acetic acid (a harmless substance). People who are slow to metabolize acetaldehyde into acetic acid (either for genetic reasons or because they have taken Antabuse) will feel ill after drinking alcohol and are less likely than other people are to continue drinking. (p. 73)

Review Questions

1. Why do drugs have stronger effects for some people than for others, and different side effects from one person to another? (p. 66)
2. Why is methylphenidate generally less disruptive to behavior than cocaine is, despite the drugs' similarity of effects? (p. 68)
3. Does cocaine increase or decrease overall brain activity? Explain. (p. 68)
4. What naturally occurring transmitters attach to the same receptors as opiates? As Δ^9-THC? (pp. 70, 71)
5. Why does repeated use of MDMA cause the drug to become less and less effective? (p. 72)
6. How might a tendency to underestimate one's intoxication increase the risk of alcohol abuse? (p. 73)

Thought Question

1. Young people who take methylphenidate (Ritalin) for control of attention-deficit disorder often report that although the drug increases their arousal for a while, they feel a decrease in alertness and arousal a few hours later. Explain.

Suggestions for Further Reading

Julien, R. M. (1995). *A primer of drug action* (7th ed.). New York: W. H. Freeman. Extremely informative description of the effects of both legal and illegal drugs.

Zuckerman, M. (1995). Good and bad humors: Biochemical bases of personality and its disorders. *Psychological Science, 6,* 325–332. Discussion of how alterations in brain structures, transmitters, and receptors might contribute to variations in personality.

Terms

antagonist   drug that blocks the effects of a neurotransmitter (p. 65)

agonist   drug that mimics or increases the effects of a neurotransmitter (p. 65)

affinity   tendency of a drug to bind to a particular type of receptor (p. 65)

efficacy   tendency of a drug to activate a particular kind of receptor (p. 65)

nucleus accumbens   small subcortical brain area that is rich in dopamine receptors and evidently a major part of the brain's reinforcement system (p. 66)

self-stimulation of the brain   response reinforced by direct electrical stimulation of a brain area (p. 67)

stimulant drugs   drugs that tend to increase activity and arousal, at least in most people under most circumstances (p. 67)

amphetamine, cocaine, and **methylphenidate**   stimulant drugs that increase the stimulation of dopamine synapses. Cocaine and methylphenidate block the reuptake of dopamine by the presynaptic neuron; amphetamine increases the release of dopamine (p. 68)

attention-deficit disorder (ADD)   a condition marked by impulsiveness and poor control of attention (p. 68)

nicotine   a drug that, among other effects, stimulates certain acetylcholine receptors (p. 68)

phencyclidine (PCP)   drug that blocks certain glutamate synapses (p. 69)

opiate   class of drugs that stimulate endorphin receptors in the nervous system (p. 70)

cannabinoids   chemicals related to Δ^9-THC, the component of marijuana that alters experience (p. 71)

anandamide   a naturally occurring brain chemical that stimulates the same receptors as cannabinoids (p. 71)

hallucinogenic drugs   drugs that grossly distort perception, such as LSD (p. 71)

MDMA (methylenedioxymethamphetamine)   a drug that excites dopamine and serotonin synapses, evidently damaging the serotonin axons in the process (p. 72)

caffeine   a drug that dilates blood vessels and prevents adenosine from inhibiting glutamate release (p. 72)

ethyl alcohol (or ethanol)   the type of alcohol that people drink (in contrast to methyl alcohol, isopropyl alcohol, and others) (p. 73)

acetaldehyde   toxic substance produced in the metabolism of alcohol (p. 73)

acetic acid   chemical that the body uses as a source of energy (p. 73)

Antabuse   trade name for disulfiram, a drug that helps people break an alcohol habit by impairing their ability to convert acetaldehyde to acetic acid (p. 73)

THE ANATOMY AND INVESTIGATION OF THE NERVOUS SYSTEM

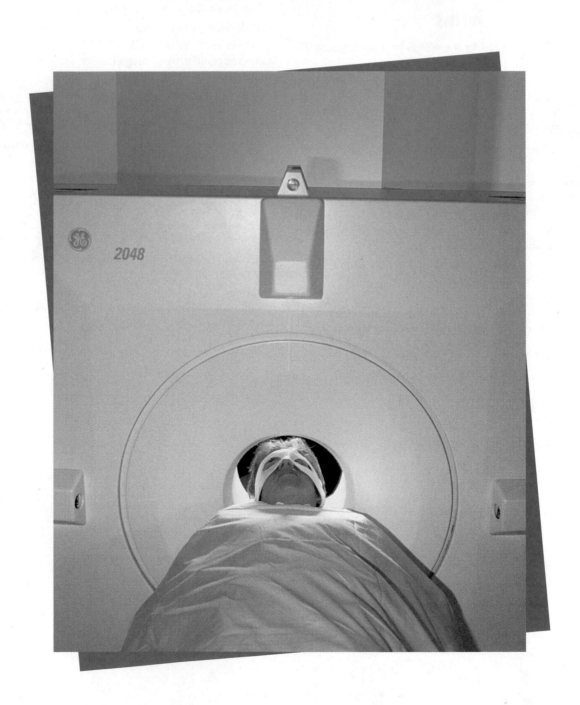

CHAPTER **FOUR**

MAIN **IDEAS**

1. Each part of the nervous system has specialized functions, although the parts work together to produce behavior. Damage to different areas results in different types of behavioral deficits.
2. The cerebral cortex, the largest structure in the mammalian brain, elaborately processes sensory information and provides fine control of movement.
3. Various investigative techniques explore the roles of brain areas in behavior.

Trying to learn **neuroanatomy** (the anatomy of the nervous system) from a book is like trying to learn geography from a road map. A map can tell you that Mystic, Georgia, is about 40 km north of Enigma, Georgia, and that the two cities are connected by a combination of roads including U.S. Route 129. Similarly, a book can tell you that the habenula is about 4.6 mm from the interpeduncular nucleus in a rat's brain (slightly farther in a human brain) and that the two structures are connected by a set of axons known as the habenulopeduncular tract (also sometimes known as the fasciculus retroflexus). But these two little gems of information will seem both mysterious and enigmatic unless you are concerned with that part of Georgia or that area of the brain.

This chapter does not provide a detailed road map of the nervous system. It is more like a world globe, describing the large, basic structures (analogous to the continents) and a few distinctive features of each. The focus is entirely on the nervous systems of vertebrates, especially mammals. Most of the illustrations are of the human brain, but its structure is similar to that of other mammals. The chapter also surveys some common methods of studying how brain structures control behavior. Later chapters contain additional detail on specific parts of the brain.

The Divisions of the Vertebrate Nervous System

Your nervous system is composed of many structures, each with substructures made up of many neurons, each of which receives and makes many synapses. How do all those little parts work together to make one behaving unit, namely, you? Does each neuron have an independent function—so that, for example, one cell recognizes your grandmother, another controls your desire for pizzas, and another makes you smile at babies? Do individual neurons send partial messages to some "monarch" center that adds up all the information into a single experience? Or does the brain operate as an undifferentiated whole, with each part doing the same thing as every other part?

The answers are no, no, and no. Each area, and each cell within an area, does have a specialized function, but in general the activity of a single cell by itself has no more meaning than the letter *h* does out of context. Different brain areas do communicate with one another, but they do not funnel all their activity into any central processor or "little person in the head." Meaningful activity emerges from an enormous number of partly independent, partly interdependent processes occurring simultaneously throughout your nervous system. Throughout this text we shall go back and forth between the special contributions of particular brain areas and the ways in which different areas communicate with one another and combine into functioning systems.

The vertebrate nervous system consists of the central nervous system and the peripheral nervous system (see Figure 4.1). The **central nervous system (CNS)** is the spinal cord and the brain, which in turn include a great many substructures. The **peripheral nervous system (PNS)** has two divisions: the **somatic nervous system,** which consists of the nerves that convey messages from the sense organs to the CNS and from the CNS to the muscles and glands, and the **autonomic nervous system,** a set of neurons that control the heart, the intestines, and other organs. In this text, and in this chapter particularly, our focus is mainly on the central nervous system and secondarily on the autonomic nervous system.

In this first module we examine the terminology of neuroanatomy and survey some large and important nervous system structures. In the second module we focus on the structures and functions of the cerebral cortex, the largest part of the mammalian central nervous system. In the final module, we consider the most common methods of brain-behavior research.

Some Terminology

To follow a road map, you first must understand the terms *north, south, east,* and *west.* Because the nervous system is a complex three-dimensional structure, we need more terms to describe it. In Figure 4.2 and Table 4.1, note that the terms **dorsal** and **ventral** mean toward the back and toward the stomach. In a four-legged animal, the top of the brain (with respect to gravity) is dorsal (on the same side as the animal's back), and the bottom of the brain is ventral (on the stomach side). When humans evolved an upright posture, the position of our head changed relative to the spinal cord. For convenience, we still apply the terms *dorsal* and *ventral* to the same parts of the human brain as of other vertebrate brains. Consequently, the dorsal-ventral axis of the human brain is at right angles to the dorsal-ventral axis of the spinal cord.

Table 4.2 introduces some additional terminology that relates to clusters of neurons and anatomical structures of the brain. Such technical terms may be confusing at first, but they help investigators communicate clearly with one another.

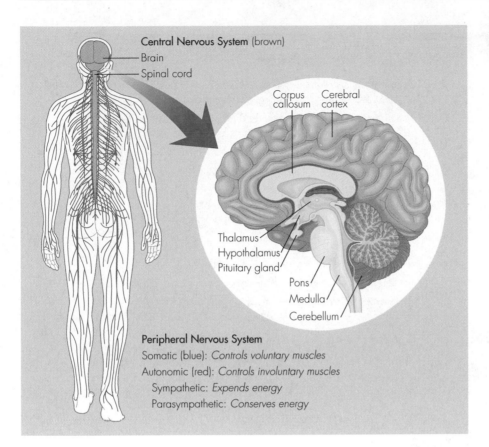

Central Nervous System (brown)
— Brain
— Spinal cord

Corpus callosum   Cerebral cortex

Thalamus
Hypothalamus
Pituitary gland
Pons
Medulla
Cerebellum

Peripheral Nervous System
Somatic (blue): *Controls voluntary muscles*
Autonomic (red): *Controls involuntary muscles*
  Sympathetic: *Expends energy*
  Parasympathetic: *Conserves energy*

FIGURE **4.1**
The human nervous system consists of the central nervous system and the peripheral nervous system, each with major subdivisions. The close-up of the brain shows the right hemisphere as seen from the midline.

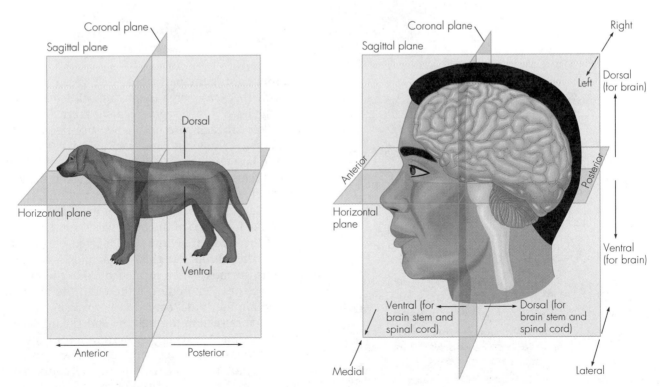

FIGURE **4.2**
Terms for anatomical directions in the nervous system
In four-legged animals, dorsal and ventral point in the same direction for the head as they do for the rest of the body. However, humans' upright posture has tilted the head relative to the spinal cord, so the dorsal and ventral directions of the head are not parallel to the dorsal and ventral directions of the spinal cord.

TABLE 4.1
Anatomical Terms Referring to Directions

Dorsal	Toward the back, away from the ventral (stomach) side. The top of the brain is considered dorsal because it has that position in four-legged animals.
Ventral	Toward the stomach, away from the dorsal (back) side. (*Venter* is the Latin word for belly. It also shows up in the word *ventriloquist,* literally meaning *stomach-talker.*)
Anterior	Toward the front end.
Posterior	Toward the rear end.
Superior	Above another part.
Inferior	Below another part.
Lateral	Toward the side, away from the midline.
Medial	Toward the midline, away from the side.
Proximal	Located close (approximate) to the point of origin or attachment.
Distal	Located more distant from the point of origin or attachment.
Ipsilateral	On the same side of the body (left or right).
Contralateral	On the opposite side of the body (left or right).
Coronal plane (or **frontal plane**)	A plane that shows brain structures as they would be seen from the front.
Sagittal plane	A plane that shows brain structures as they would be seen from the side.
Horizontal plane (or **transverse plane**)	A plane that shows brain structures as they would be seen from above.

The Spinal Cord

TABLE 4.2
Terms Referring to Parts of the Nervous System

Lamina	A row or layer of cell bodies separated from other cell bodies by a layer of axons and dendrites.
Column	A set of cells perpendicular to the surface of the cortex, with similar properties.
Tract	A set of axons within the CNS, also known as a *projection*. If axons extend from cell bodies in structure A to synapses onto B, we say that the fibers "project" from A onto B.
Nerve	A set of axons in the periphery, either from the CNS to a muscle or gland, or from a sensory organ to the CNS.
Nucleus	A cluster of neuron cell bodies within the CNS.
Ganglion	A cluster of neuron cell bodies, usually outside the CNS (as in the sympathetic nervous system), or any cluster of neurons in an invertebrate species.
Gyrus (plural: **gyri**)	A protuberance on the surface of the brain.
Sulcus (plural: **sulci**)	A fold or groove that separates one gyrus from another.
Fissure	A long, deep sulcus.

The **spinal cord** is the part of the CNS that communicates with the sense organs and muscles below the level of the head. It is a segmented structure, and each segment has on each side both a sensory nerve and a motor nerve, as shown in Figures 4.3 and 4.4. The **Bell-Magendie law** refers to the observation that the entering dorsal roots carry sensory information and the exiting ventral roots carry motor information to the muscles and glands. (This was one of the first discoveries about the functions of the nervous system.) The cell bodies of the sensory neurons are located outside the cord in the **dorsal root ganglia.** (A ganglion is a cluster of neurons, in most cases located outside the central nervous system.) Cell bodies of the motor neurons are located within the spinal cord.

In the cross section through the spinal cord shown in Figure 4.5, the H-shaped **gray matter** in the center of the cord is densely packed with cell bodies and dendrites. Many of the interneurons of the spinal cord (those that are neither sensory nor motor) send axons that leave the gray matter and travel toward the brain or to other parts of the spinal cord through the **white matter,** which is composed mostly of myelinated axons.

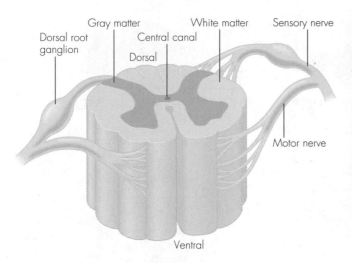

Dorsal root ganglion · Gray matter · Central canal · Dorsal · White matter · Sensory nerve · Motor nerve · Ventral

FIGURE **4.3**
Diagram of a cross section through the spinal cord
The dorsal root on each side conveys sensory information to the spinal cord; the ventral root conveys motor commands to the muscles.

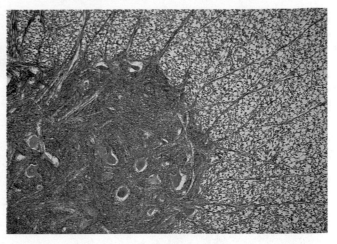

FIGURE **4.5**
A section of gray matter of the spinal cord (lower left) and white matter surrounding it
Cell bodies and dendrites reside entirely in the gray matter. Axons travel from one area of gray matter to another in the white matter.

Each segment of the spinal cord sends sensory information to the brain and receives motor commands from the brain. All that information passes through tracts of axons in the spinal cord. If the spinal cord is cut at a given segment, the brain loses sensation from that segment and all segments below it; the brain also loses motor control over all parts of the body served by that segment and the lower ones.

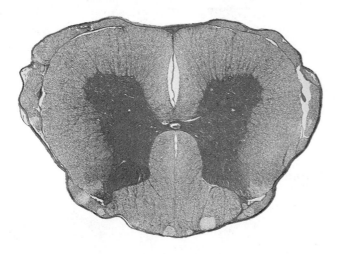

FIGURE **4.4**
Photo of a cross section through the spinal cord
The H-shaped structure in the center is gray matter, composed largely of cell bodies. The surrounding white matter is composed of axons. The axons are organized in tracts; some carry information from the brain and higher levels of the spinal cord downward, while others carry information from lower levels upward.

The Autonomic Nervous System

The autonomic nervous system is a set of neurons that receives information from and sends commands to the heart, intestines, and other organs. It is composed of two parts: the sympathetic and parasympathetic nervous systems (see Figure 4.6). The **sympathetic nervous system** consists of two paired chains of **ganglia** (collections of neuron cell bodies) lying just to the left and right of the spinal cord in its central regions (the thoracic and lumbar areas) and connected by axons to those spinal cord regions. *Postganglionic* axons extend from the sympathetic ganglia to the body's organs. The sympathetic nervous system prepares the body for "fight or flight" activities: It accelerates breathing and heart rate and decreases digestive activity. Because all the sympathetic ganglia are closely linked, they often act as a single system, "in sympathy" with one another. It is possible, however, to activate one part of the sympathetic nervous system more than others. The sweat glands, the adrenal glands, the muscles that constrict blood vessels, and the muscles that erect the hairs of the skin have sympathetic input only. (See Digression 4.1.)

The term *para* means *beside* or *related to;* the **parasympathetic nervous system** has functions that

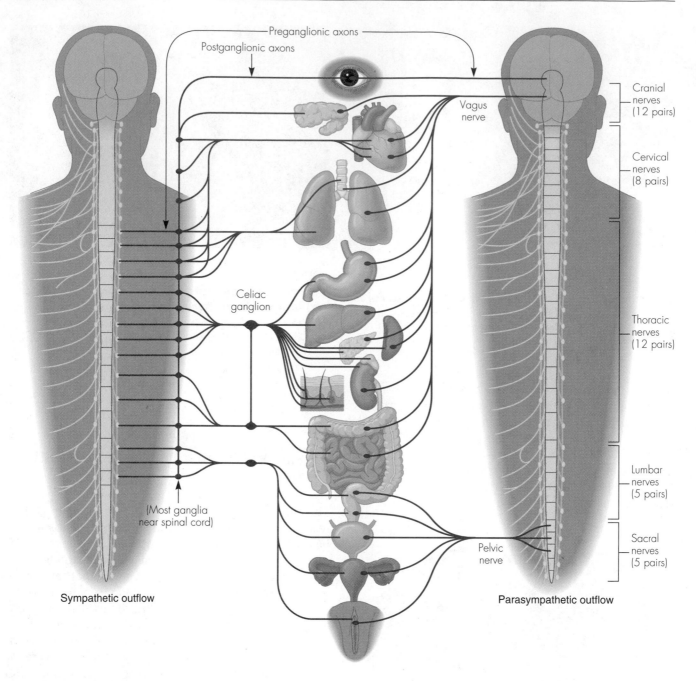

Preganglionic axons
Postganglionic axons

Vagus
nerve

Cranial
nerves
(12 pairs)

Cervical
nerves
(8 pairs)

Celiac
ganglion

Thoracic
nerves
(12 pairs)

(Most ganglia
near spinal cord)

Lumbar
nerves
(5 pairs)

Pelvic
nerve

Sacral
nerves
(5 pairs)

Sympathetic outflow

Parasympathetic outflow

FIGURE **4.6**
The sympathetic nervous system (red lines) and parasympathetic nervous system (blue lines)
Source: From Starr & Taggart, 1989.

are related to, and generally opposite to, those of the sympathetic nervous system. For example, the sympathetic nervous system increases heart rate; the parasympathetic nervous system decreases it. The parasympathetic nervous system increases digestive activity; the sympathetic nervous system decreases it. Although the sympathetic and parasympathetic systems act in opposition to one another, they are both constantly active to varying degrees, and some stimuli arouse parts of one system and parts of the other.

The parasympathetic nervous system is sometimes also known as the craniosacral system because it consists of the cranial nerves and nerves from the sacral spinal cord (Figure 4.6). Unlike the ganglia in the sympathetic system, the parasympathetic ganglia are not arranged in a chain near the spinal cord. Rather, long *preganglionic* axons extend from the spinal cord to parasympathetic ganglia close to each internal organ; shorter *postganglionic* fibers then extend from the parasympathetic ganglia into the organs themselves.

Because the parasympathetic ganglia are not linked to one another, they sometimes act more independently than the sympathetic ganglia do. Parasympathetic activity decreases heart rate, increases digestive rate, and in general promotes energy-conserving, nonemergency functions.

The parasympathetic nervous system's postganglionic axons release the neurotransmitter acetylcholine. Most of the postganglionic synapses of the sympathetic nervous system use norepinephrine, although a few, such as the ones that control the sweat glands, use acetylcholine. Because the two systems use different transmitters, certain drugs may excite or inhibit one system or the other. For example, over-the-counter cold remedies exert most of their effects either by blocking parasympathetic activity or by increasing sympathetic activity. This action is useful because the flow of sinus fluids is a parasympathetic response; thus, drugs that block the parasympathetic system inhibit sinus flow. The common side effects of cold remedies also stem from their pro-sympathetic, anti-parasympathetic activities: They inhibit salivation and digestion and increase heart rate.

The Hindbrain

The brain itself (as distinct from the spinal cord) consists of three major divisions: the hindbrain, the midbrain, and the forebrain. (See Figure 4.7 and Table 4.3.) Brain investigators unfortunately use a variety of terms synonymously. For example, instead of the English terms *hindbrain*, *midbrain*, and *forebrain*, some people prefer words with Greek roots: *rhombencephalon*,

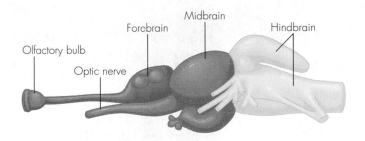

FIGURE **4.7**
Three major divisions of the vertebrate brain
In a fish brain, as shown here, the forebrain, midbrain, and hindbrain are clearly visible as separate bulges. In adult mammals, the forebrain grows so large that it surrounds the entire midbrain and part of the hindbrain.

TABLE **4.3**

Major Divisions of the Vertebrate Brain

Area	Also Known as	Major Structures
Hindbrain	**Rhombencephalon** (literally, parallelogram-brain)	Medulla, pons, cerebellum
Midbrain	**Mesencephalon** (literally, middle-brain)	Tectum, tegmentum, superior colliculus, inferior colliculus, substantia nigra
Forebrain	**Prosencephalon** (literally, forward-brain)	
	Diencephalon (literally, between-brain)	Thalamus, hypothalamus
	Telencephalon (literally, end-brain)	Cerebral cortex, hippocampus, basal ganglia)

DIGRESSION **4.1**

Gooseflesh

Erection of the hairs, known as "gooseflesh" or "goose bumps," is controlled by the sympathetic nervous system. What does this response have to do with the "fight or flight" functions that are usually associated with the sympathetic nervous system?

Human body hairs are so short that erecting them accomplishes nothing of importance; the response is an evolutionary relic from ancient ancestors with furrier bodies. Erecting the hairs helps nonhuman mammals to conserve their body warmth in a cold environment by increasing their insulation. It also serves several species as a defense against enemies in fight-or-flight situations. Consider, for example, the

Halloween cat, or any other frightened, cornered animal; by erecting its hairs, it looks larger and thereby may deter its opponent.

The porcupine's quills, which are an effective defense against potential predators, are actually modified body hairs. In a fight-or-flight situation, sympathetic nervous system activity leads to erection of the quills, just as it leads to erection of the hairs in other mammals (Richter & Langworthy, 1933). The behavior that makes the quills so useful, their erection in response to fear, evidently evolved before the quills themselves did.

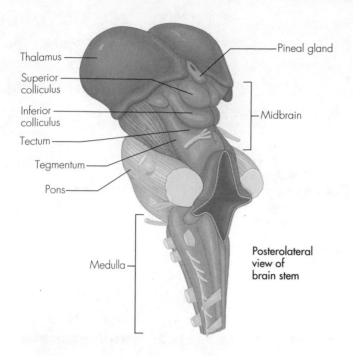

Thalamus

Superior colliculus

Inferior colliculus

Tectum

Tegmentum

Pons

Medulla

Pineal gland

Midbrain

Posterolateral view of brain stem

FIGURE 4.8
The human brain stem
This composite structure extends from the top of the spinal column into the center of the forebrain. The pons, pineal gland, and colliculi are ordinarily surrounded by the cerebral cortex.

mesencephalon, and *prosencephalon.* You may encounter those terms in other reading.

The **hindbrain,** the posterior part of the brain, consists of the medulla, the pons, and the cerebellum. The medulla and pons, the midbrain, and certain central structures of the forebrain constitute the **brain stem** (see Figure 4.8).

The **medulla,** or medulla oblongata, is located just above the spinal cord and could be regarded as an enlarged, elaborated extension of the spinal cord, although it is located in the skull rather than in the spine. The medulla controls a number of vital reflexes—including breathing, heart rate, vomiting, salivation, coughing, and sneezing—through the **cranial nerves;** thus, damage to the medulla is frequently fatal, as are large doses of drugs that affect it, such as opiates or cocaine. Drugs that have little effect on the medulla—such as marijuana—are seldom life-threatening, even though they produce major effects on other parts of the brain (Herkenham et al., 1990).

Just as the lower parts of the body are connected to the spinal cord via sensory and motor nerves, the skin and muscles of the head and the internal organs are connected to the brain by twelve pairs of cranial nerves (one of each pair on the right of the brain and one on the left). Most cranial nerves have both sensory and motor components, although some include just one or the other (see Table 4.4). Each cranial nerve originates in a **nucleus** (a cluster of neurons within the CNS) that integrates the sensory information and regulates the motor output. The cranial nerve nuclei for nerves V

TABLE 4.4
The Cranial Nerves

Number and Name	Function of Sensory Component	Function of Motor Component
I. Olfactory	Smell	(No motor nerve)
II. Optic	Vision	(No motor nerve)
III. Oculomotor	Sensations from eye muscles	Eye movements, pupil constriction
IV. Trochlear	Sensations from eye muscles	Eye movements
V. Trigeminal	Sensations from skin of face, nose, and mouth	Chewing, swallowing
VI. Abducens	Sensations from eye muscles	Eye movements
VII. Facial	Taste from the anterior two-thirds of the tongue, visceral sensations from head	Facial expressions, crying, salivation, and dilation of blood vessels in the head
VIII. Statoacoustic	Hearing, equilibrium	(No motor nerve)
IX. Glossopharyngeal	Taste and other sensations from throat and posterior third of tongue	Swallowing, salivation, dilation of blood vessels
X. Vagus	Taste and sensations from neck, thorax, and abdomen	Swallowing, control of larynx, parasympathetic nerves to heart and viscera
XI. Accessory	(no sensory nerve)	Movements of shoulders and head; parasympathetic to viscera
XII. Hypoglossal	Sensation from tongue muscles	Movement of tongue

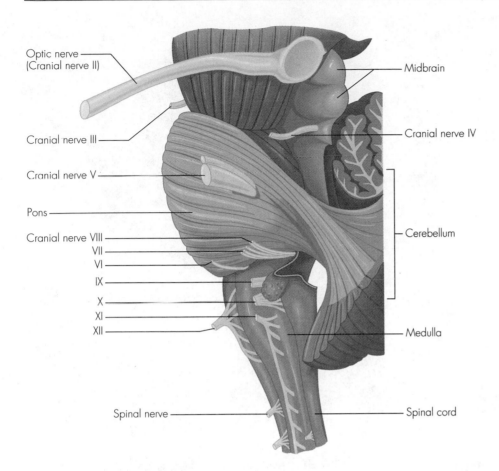

Optic nerve
(Cranial nerve II)

Cranial nerve III

Cranial nerve V

Pons

Cranial nerve VIII
VII
VI
IX
X
XI
XII

Spinal nerve

Midbrain

Cranial nerve IV

Cerebellum

Medulla

Spinal cord

FIGURE **4.9**
Cranial nerves II through XII
Source: Based on Braus, 1960.

through XII are in the medulla and pons of the hindbrain. Those for cranial nerves I through IV are in the midbrain and forebrain (see Figure 4.9).

The **pons** lies anterior to the medulla; like the medulla, it contains nuclei for several cranial nerves. The term *pons* is Latin for *bridge;* the name reflects the fact that many axons in the pons cross from one side of the brain to the other.

The medulla and pons also contain the **reticular formation,** which has axons both up into the brain and down into the spinal cord, and the **raphe system,** which sends axons diffusely throughout the forebrain. These two systems and several others regulate brain arousal; they do not provide sensory information themselves, but they increase or decrease the brain's readiness to respond to other sources of information (Mesulam, 1995).

The **cerebellum** is a large hindbrain structure with a great many deep folds. It has long been known for its contributions to the control of movement (see Chapter 8). Many researchers now believe that the cerebellum may be more active in organizing the sensory information that guides movement than it is in controlling the movement itself. People with damage to the cerebellum have trouble responding to abstract stimuli or shifting their attention back and forth between auditory and visual stimuli (Canavan, Sprengelmeyer, Diener, & Hömberg, 1994). Malformation of the cerebellum is com-

mon among autistic children and may be responsible for their attentional deficits (Courchesne et al., 1994).

The Midbrain

The **midbrain** starts in the middle of the brain, although in adult mammals it is dwarfed and surrounded by the forebrain. In birds, reptiles, amphibians, and fish, the midbrain is proportionately much larger than it is in mammals. The roof of the midbrain is called the **tectum.** (*Tectum* is the Latin word for *roof;* the same root shows up in the geological term *plate tectonics.*) The two swellings on each side of the tectum are the **superior colliculus** and the **inferior colliculus** (see Figures 4.8 and 4.12), both part of important routes for sensory information.

Under the tectum is the **tegmentum,** the middle part of the midbrain. (In Latin, *tegmentum* means a covering, such as a rug on the floor.) The tegmentum includes the nuclei for the third and fourth cranial nerves, parts of the reticular formation, and extensions of the pathways between the forebrain and the spinal cord or hindbrain. Another midbrain structure is the **substantia nigra,** which deteriorates in Parkinson's disease (see Chapter 8).

FIGURE **4.10**
The limbic system, a set of subcortical structures that form a border (or limbus) around the brain stem

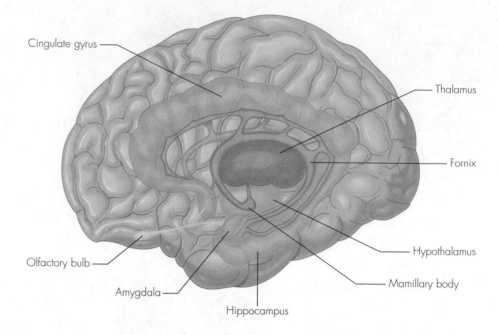

The Forebrain

The **forebrain** is the most anterior and most prominent part of the mammalian brain. The outer portion is the cerebral cortex. (*Cerebrum* is a Latin word meaning *brain; cortex* is a Latin word meaning *bark* or *covering*.) Under the cerebral cortex are other structures, including the thalamus, which provides the main source of input to the cerebral cortex. A set of structures known as the basal ganglia plays a major role in certain aspects of movement. A number of other structures, known as the **limbic system,** form a border (or *limbus,* the Latin word for border) around the brain stem. These interlinked structures are particularly important for motivated and emotional behaviors, such as eating, drinking, sexual activity, anxiety, and aggression. The larger structures of the limbic system are the olfactory bulb, hypothalamus, hippocampus, amygdala, and cingulate gyrus of the cerebral cortex. Figure 4.10 shows the positions of these structures in a three-dimensional perspective. Figures 4.11 and 4.12 show coronal and sagittal sections through the human brain (that is, sections showing structures as seen from the front and from the side). Figure 4.11 also includes a view of the ventral surface of the brain.

In describing the forebrain, we shall begin with the subcortical areas; the next module focuses on the cerebral cortex. In later chapters we shall return to each of these areas.

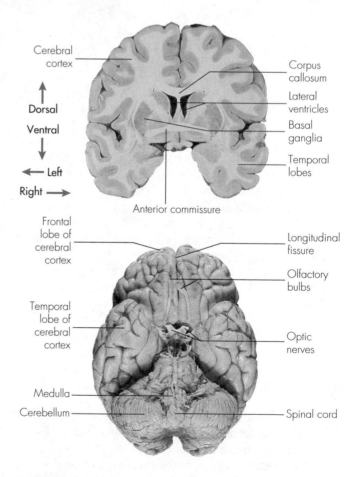

FIGURE **4.11**
Views of the human brain
Top: Coronal section. Bottom: Ventral surface.   Source: Photos courtesy of Dana Copeland.

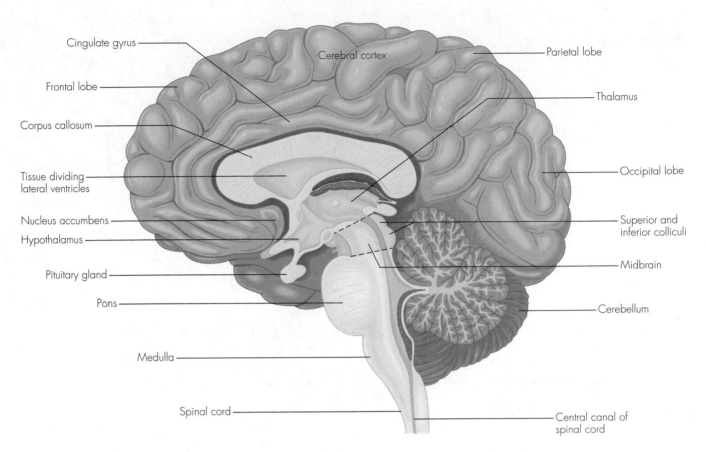

FIGURE **4.12**
A sagittal section through the human brain
Source: After Nieuwenhuys, Voogd, & vanHuijzen, 1988.

Hypothalamus

The **hypothalamus** is a small area near the base of the brain just ventral to the thalamus (see Figures 4.10 and 4.12). It has widespread connections with the rest of the forebrain and the midbrain. The hypothalamus contains a number of distinct nuclei, which we shall examine in Chapters 10 and 11. Activity in various nuclei of the hypothalamus controls daily rhythms of activity and sleep, as well as many aspects of motivated and emotional behavior. Damage to a hypothalamic nucleus leads to abnormalities in one or more motivated behaviors, such as feeding, drinking, temperature regulation, sexual behavior, fighting, or activity level. Because of these spectacular effects, the rather small hypothalamus attracts more than its share of attention from biological psychologists.

Through its effects on the pituitary gland, the hypothalamus also regulates the secretion of hormones. Partly through nerves and partly through hypothalamic hormones, it conveys messages to the pituitary gland, altering its release of hormones.

Pituitary Gland

The **pituitary gland** is an **endocrine** (hormone-producing) **gland** attached to the base of the hypothalamus by a stalk that contains neurons, blood vessels, and connective tissue (see Figure 4.12). In response to messages from the hypothalamus, the pituitary synthesizes and releases hormones into the bloodstream, which carries them to other organs. The pituitary is sometimes called the "master gland" because its secretions control the timing and amount of hormone secretion by the other endocrine organs, such as the thyroid, the adrenal glands, and the ovaries or testes.

Basal Ganglia

The **basal ganglia,** a group of subcortical structures left and right of the thalamus, include three major structures: the caudate nucleus, the putamen, and the globus pallidus (see Figure 4.13). Some authorities include several other structures as well.

FIGURE**4.13**
The basal ganglia
Source: After Nieuwenhuys, Voogd, & vanHuijzen, 1988.

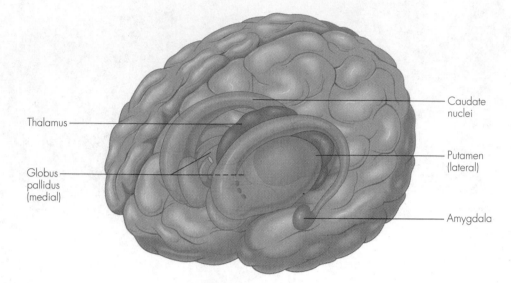

Thalamus

Globus pallidus (medial)

Caudate nuclei

Putamen (lateral)

Amygdala

The basal ganglia have multiple subdivisions, each of which exchanges information with a different part of the cerebral cortex. The connections are most abundant with the frontal areas of the cortex, which are responsible for planning sequences of behavior and for certain aspects of memory and emotional expression (Graybiel, Aosaki, Flaherty, & Kimura, 1994). In conditions such as Parkinson's disease and Huntington's disease, in which the basal ganglia deteriorate, the most prominent symptoms are impairments of movement, but people also show depression, deficits of memory and reasoning, and attentional disorders.

Hippocampus

The **hippocampus** (from a Latin word meaning *sea horse*) is a large structure between the thalamus and the cerebral cortex, mostly toward the posterior of the forebrain, as shown in Figure 4.10. A major axon tract, the **fornix,** links the hippocampus with the hypothalamus and several other structures. (The fornix was named after an ancient Roman arch that was a famous gathering place for prostitutes. That arch also gave us the word *fornication.*) We shall consider the role of the hippocampus in memory in Chapter 13.

Thalamus

The **thalamus** (derived from a Greek word meaning *anteroom, inner chamber,* or *bridal bed*) resembles two avocados joined side by side, one in the left hemisphere and one in the right. Most sensory information goes first to the thalamus, which then processes it and sends the output to the cerebral cortex. The one clear exception to this rule is olfactory information, which progresses from the olfactory receptors to the olfactory

bulbs and from the bulbs directly to the cerebral cortex. The cortex also receives certain other axons that do not pass through the thalamus; these, however, appear to be more important for activation or arousal than for sensation (Foote & Morrison, 1987).

Many nuclei of the thalamus receive their primary input from one of the sensory systems, such as vision, and then transmit the information to a single area of the cerebral cortex, as in Figure 4.14, while also receiving feedback information from the same cortical area. Certain other thalamic nuclei receive their input from several sources, including neighboring thalamic nuclei, various subcortical structures, and several areas of the cortex; they then transmit information either to other parts of the thalamus or to multiple parts of the cortex. In other words, some thalamic nuclei have simple, discrete functions such as vision; other thalamic nuclei convey more complex or general messages, such as arousal (Barth & MacDonald, 1996).

The cerebral cortex is the largest structure of the mammalian brain. Because we consider it in detail in the next module, we shall not examine it here.

The Ventricles

The nervous system begins its development as a tube surrounding a fluid canal. The canal persists into adulthood as the **central canal** of the spinal cord and, with much expansion, as the **ventricles,** fluid-filled cavities within the brain. Each hemisphere contains one of the two large lateral ventricles (see Figure 4.15). Toward the posterior, they connect to the third ventricle, which connects to the fourth ventricle in the medulla.

The ventricles and the central canal of the spinal cord contain **cerebrospinal fluid (CSF),** a clear fluid

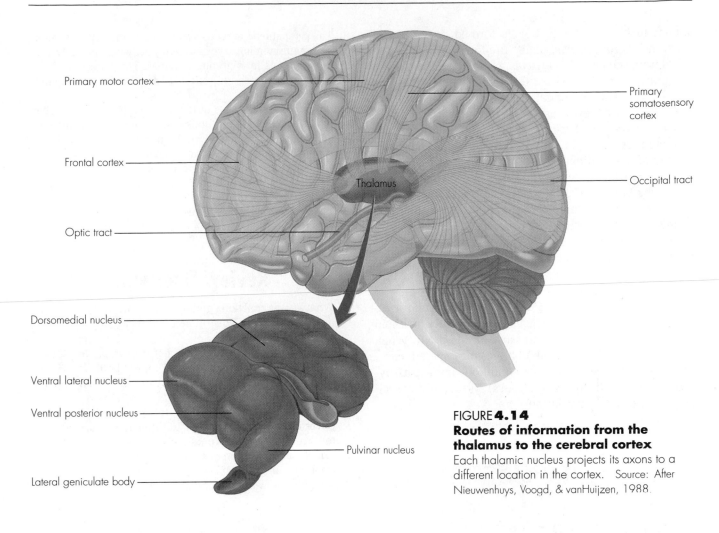

Primary motor cortex

Frontal cortex

Optic tract

Thalamus

Primary somatosensory cortex

Occipital tract

Dorsomedial nucleus

Ventral lateral nucleus

Ventral posterior nucleus

Lateral geniculate body

Pulvinar nucleus

FIGURE **4.14**
Routes of information from the thalamus to the cerebral cortex
Each thalamic nucleus projects its axons to a different location in the cortex.   Source: After Nieuwenhuys, Voogd, & vanHuijzen, 1988.

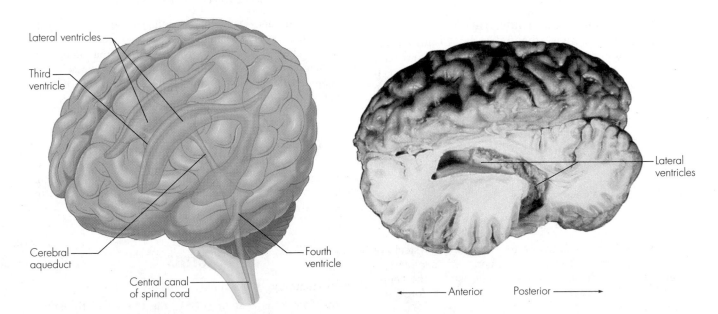

Lateral ventricles

Third ventricle

Cerebral aqueduct

Central canal of spinal cord

Fourth ventricle

Lateral ventricles

← Anterior   Posterior →

FIGURE **4.15**
The cerebral ventricles
Left: Diagram showing positions of the four ventricles. Right: Photo of a human brain, viewed from above, with a horizontal cut through one hemisphere to show the position of the lateral ventricle. Note that the two parts of this figure are seen from different angles.   Source: Photo courtesy of Dana Copeland.

similar to blood plasma. CSF is formed by groups of cells, the *choroid plexus,* inside the four ventricles. CSF flows from the lateral ventricles to the third and then to the fourth ventricle. From the fourth ventricle, some flows into the central canal of the spinal cord, but more goes through an opening into the thin **subarachnoid space,** between the brain and one of the thin **meninges** (membranes) that surround it. (Meningitis is an inflammation of the meninges surrounding the brain or spinal cord.) From the subarachnoid space, CSF is gradually reabsorbed into the blood vessels of the brain.

Cerebrospinal fluid cushions the brain against mechanical shock when the head moves. It also provides buoyancy; just as a person weighs less in water than on land, the cerebrospinal fluid helps support the weight of the brain. The CSF also provides a reservoir of hormones and nutrition for the brain and spinal cord.

Sometimes the flow of CSF is obstructed and it accumulates within the ventricles or in the subarachnoid space, thus increasing the pressure on the brain. When this occurs in infants, the skull bones may spread, causing an overgrown head. This condition, known as **hydrocephalus** (HI-dro-SEFF-ah-luss), is usually associated with mental retardation.

IN**CLOSING**

Structures of the Nervous System

The brain is a complex structure. This module has introduced a great many terms and facts; do not be discouraged if you have trouble remembering them. You didn't learn world geography all at one time, either. It will help to refer back to this section to review the anatomy of certain structures as you encounter them again in later chapters. Gradually, the material will become more familiar.

Summary

1. The main divisions of the vertebrate nervous system are the central nervous system and the peripheral nervous system. The central nervous system consists of the spinal cord, the hindbrain, the midbrain, and the forebrain. (p. 78)
2. Each segment of the spinal cord has a sensory nerve on each side and a motor nerve on each side. Several spinal pathways convey information to the brain. (p. 80)

3. The sympathetic nervous system (one of the two divisions of the autonomic nervous system) activates the body's internal organs for vigorous activities. The parasympathetic system promotes digestion and other nonemergency processes. (p. 81)
4. The hindbrain consists of the medulla, pons, and cerebellum. The medulla and pons control breathing, heart rate, and other vital functions through the cranial nerves. The cerebellum contributes to movement. (p. 84)
5. The subcortical areas of the forebrain include the hypothalamus, pituitary gland, basal ganglia, hippocampus, and thalamus. (p. 86)
6. The cerebral cortex receives its sensory information, except for olfaction, from the thalamus. (p. 88)

Review Questions

1. What are the functions of the sympathetic and parasympathetic nervous systems? Where are their ganglia located? (p. 81)
2. Why do certain drugs excite either the sympathetic or the parasympathetic nervous system but not both? (p. 83)
3. Name the principal structures of the hindbrain and the midbrain. (p. 84)
4. What do the cranial nerves do? (p. 84)
5. Cover the labels in Figures 4.10 through 4.14 and identify the structures shown. (pp. 86–89)
6. Which subcortical area is the main source of input to the cerebral cortex? (p. 88)
7. What do the ventricles contain? (p. 88)

Thought Question

1. The drug phenylephrine is sometimes prescribed for people suffering from a sudden loss of blood pressure or other medical disorders. It acts by stimulating norepinephrine synapses, including those that constrict blood vessels. One common side effect of this drug is gooseflesh. Explain why. What other side effects might be likely?

Suggestion for Further Reading

Heimer, L. (1995). *The human brain and spinal cord* (2nd ed.). New York: Springer-Verlag. Well-illustrated overview of the structure of the entire nervous system.

Terms

neuroanatomy   the anatomy of the nervous system (p. 77)

central nervous system (CNS)   the brain and the spinal cord (p. 78)

peripheral nervous system (PNS)   nerves outside the brain and spinal cord (p. 78)

somatic nervous system nerves that convey messages from the sense organs to the CNS and from the CNS to muscles and glands (p. 78)

autonomic nervous system set of neurons that regulates functioning of the internal organs (p. 78)

dorsal toward the back, away from the ventral (stomach) side (p. 78)

ventral toward the stomach, away from the dorsal (back) side (p. 78)

anterior toward the front end (p. 80)

posterior toward the rear end (p. 80)

superior above another part (p. 80)

inferior below another part (p. 80)

lateral toward the side, away from the midline (p. 80)

medial toward the midline, away from the side (p. 80)

proximal located close (approximate) to the point of origin or attachment (p. 80)

distal located more distant from the point of origin or attachment (p. 80)

ipsilateral on the same side of the body (left or right) (p. 80)

contralateral on the opposite side of the body (left or right) (p. 80)

coronal plane a plane that shows brain structures as they would be seen from the front (p. 80)

sagittal plane a plane that shows brain structures as they would be seen from the side (p. 80)

horizontal plane a plane that shows brain structures as they would be seen from above (p. 80)

lamina a row or layer of cell bodies separated from other cell bodies by a layer of axons and dendrites (p. 80)

column a set of cells perpendicular to the surface of the cortex (p. 80)

tract a set of axons within the CNS (p. 80)

nerve a set of axons in the periphery, either from the CNS to a muscle or gland, or from a sensory organ to the CNS (p. 80)

nucleus a cluster of neuron cell bodies within the CNS (p. 80)

ganglion a cluster of neuron cell bodies, usually outside the CNS (as in the sympathetic nervous system), or any cluster of neurons in an invertebrate species (p. 80)

gyrus (plural: **gyri**) a protuberance or elevation of the brain, separated from another gyrus by a sulcus (p. 80)

sulcus (plural: **sulci**) a fold or groove that separates one gyrus from another (p. 80)

fissure a long, deep sulcus (p. 80)

spinal cord portion of the central nervous system found within the spinal column (p. 80)

Bell-Magendie law observation that the dorsal roots of the spinal cord carry sensory information and that the ventral roots carry motor information toward the muscles and glands (p. 80)

dorsal root ganglion set of sensory neuron somas on the dorsal side of the spinal cord (p. 80)

gray matter areas of the nervous system with a high density of cell bodies and dendrites, with few myelinated axons (p. 80)

white matter area of the nervous system consisting mostly of myelinated axons (p. 80)

sympathetic nervous system network of nerves innervating the internal organs that prepare the body for vigorous activity (p. 81)

ganglion (plural: **ganglia**) a cluster of neuron cell bodies (p. 81)

parasympathetic nervous system system of nerves innervating the internal organs, tending to conserve energy (p. 81)

hindbrain most posterior part of the brain, including the medulla, pons, and cerebellum (p. 84)

brain stem the hindbrain, midbrain, and posterior central structures of the forebrain (p. 84)

medulla hindbrain structure located just above the spinal cord (p. 84)

cranial nerve part of a set of nerves controlling sensory and motor information of the head, connecting to nuclei in the medulla, pons, midbrain, or forebrain (p. 84)

nucleus a cluster of neurons within the central nervous system (p. 84)

pons hindbrain structure, anterior or ventral to the medulla (p. 85)

reticular formation network of neurons in the medulla and higher brain areas, important for behavioral arousal (p. 85)

raphe system group of neurons in the pons and medulla whose axons extend throughout much of the forebrain (p. 85)

cerebellum a large, highly convoluted structure in the hindbrain (p. 85)

midbrain middle part of the brain, including superior colliculus, inferior colliculus, tectum, and tegmentum (p. 85)

tectum roof of the midbrain (p. 85)

superior colliculus midbrain structure active in vision, visuomotor coordination, and other processes (p. 85)

inferior colliculus part of the auditory system located in the midbrain (p. 85)

tegmentum dorsal part of the midbrain (p. 85)

substantia nigra area in the midbrain that gives rise to a dopamine-containing pathway (p. 85)

forebrain the most anterior part of the brain, including the cerebral cortex and other structures (p. 86)

limbic system interconnected set of subcortical structures in the forebrain, including the hypothalamus, hippocampus, amygdala, olfactory bulb, septum, other small structures, and parts of the thalamus and cerebral cortex (p. 86)

hypothalamus forebrain structure located just ventral to the thalamus (p. 87)

pituitary gland endocrine gland whose secretions regulate the activity of many other hormonal glands (p. 87)

endocrine gland   gland that releases hormones (p. 87)

basal ganglia   set of subcortical forebrain structures including the caudate nucleus, putamen, and globus pallidus (p. 87)

hippocampus   large forebrain structure between the thalamus and cortex (p. 88)

fornix   tract of axons connecting the hippocampus with the hypothalamus and other areas (p. 88)

thalamus   structure in the center of the forebrain (p. 88)

central canal   fluid-filled channel in the center of the spinal cord (p. 88)

ventricle   any of the four fluid-filled cavities in the brain (p. 88)

cerebrospinal fluid (CSF)   liquid similar to blood serum, found in the ventricles of the brain and in the central canal of the spinal cord (p. 88)

subarachnoid space   area filled with CSF, located beneath the arachnoid membrane that surrounds the nervous system (p. 90)

meninges   membranes surrounding the brain and spinal cord (p. 90)

hydrocephalus   accumulation of excessive fluid in the head (p. 90)

The Cerebral Cortex

The surface of the forebrain consists of two cerebral hemispheres, one on the left side and one on the right, that surround all the other forebrain structures (Figure 4.16). Each hemisphere is organized to receive sensory information, mostly from the contralateral (opposite) side of the body, and to control muscles, mostly on the contralateral side, through axons to the spinal cord and the cranial nerve nuclei.

The cellular layers on the outer surface of the cerebral hemispheres form gray matter known as the **cerebral cortex** (from the Latin word *cortex,* meaning *bark*). Large numbers of axons extend inward from the cortex, forming the white matter of the cerebral hemispheres (Figure 4.11). Neurons in each hemisphere communicate with neurons in the corresponding part of the other hemisphere through two bundles of axons, the **corpus callosum** (Figures 4.11, 4.12, and 4.16) and the smaller **anterior commissure** (Figure 4.11). (Several other commissures link subcortical structures.)

Organization of the Cerebral Cortex

The microscopic structure of the cells of the cerebral cortex varies substantially from one cortical area to another. The differences in appearance relate to differences in function. Much research has been directed toward understanding the relationship between structure and function.

Laminae and Columns

In humans and most other mammals, the cerebral cortex contains up to six distinct **laminae,** layers of cell bodies that are parallel to the surface of the cortex and separated from each other by layers of fibers (see Figure 4.17). The laminae vary in thickness and prominence from one part of the cortex to another, and a given

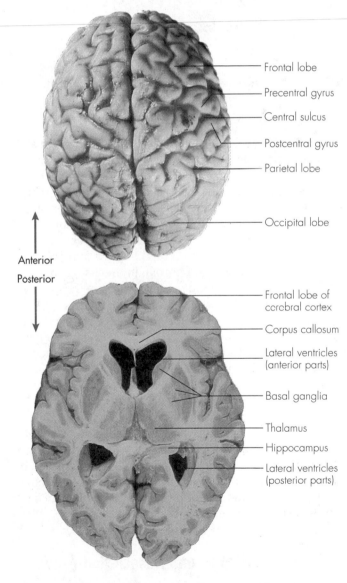

Anterior

Posterior

- Frontal lobe
- Precentral gyrus
- Central sulcus
- Postcentral gyrus
- Parietal lobe
- Occipital lobe

- Frontal lobe of cerebral cortex
- Corpus callosum
- Lateral ventricles (anterior parts)
- Basal ganglia
- Thalamus
- Hippocampus
- Lateral ventricles (posterior parts)

FIGURE **4.16**
Dorsal view of the brain surface and a horizontal section through the brain
Source: Photos courtesy of Dana Copeland.

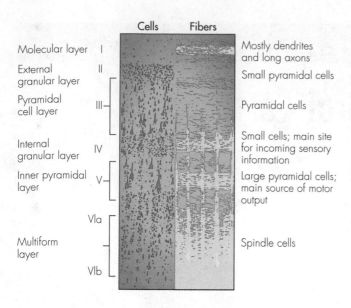

Cells   Fibers

Molecular layer   I   Mostly dendrites and long axons

External granular layer   II   Small pyramidal cells

Pyramidal cell layer   III   Pyramidal cells

Internal granular layer   IV   Small cells; main site for incoming sensory information

Inner pyramidal layer   V   Large pyramidal cells; main source of motor output

Multiform layer   VIa   Spindle cells

VIb

FIGURE 4.17
The six laminae of the human cerebral cortex
Source: From Ranson & Clark, 1959.

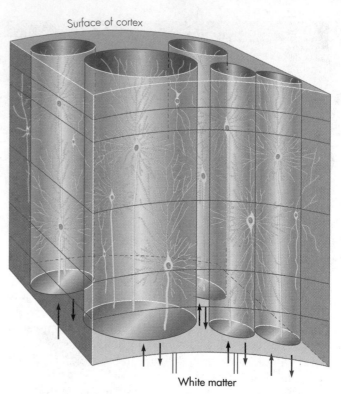

Surface of cortex

White matter

FIGURE 4.18
Columns in the cerebral cortex
Each column extends through several laminae. Neurons within a given column have similar properties. For example, in the somatosensory cortex, all the neurons within a given column respond to stimulation of the same area of skin.

lamina may be absent from certain areas. Lamina V, which sends long axons to the spinal cord and other distant areas, is thickest in the motor cortex, which has the greatest control of the muscles. Lamina IV, which receives axons from the various sensory nuclei of the thalamus, is prominent in all the primary sensory areas (visual, auditory, and somatosensory) but absent from the motor cortex. Anecdotal reports have found lamina IV to be even thicker than normal in the visual cortex of a person with photographic memory and in the auditory cortex of a musician with perfect pitch (Scheibel, 1984).

The cells of the cortex are also organized into **columns** of cells perpendicular to the laminae. Figure 4.18 illustrates the idea of columns, although in fact they do not all have such a straight, columnar shape. The cells within a given column have similar or related properties and many connections to one another. For example, if one cell in a given column responds to touch on the palm of the left hand, then the other cells in that column also respond to touch on the palm of the left hand. If one cell responds to a particular pattern of light at a particular location in the retina, then the other cells in the column respond to the same pattern of light in the same location.

Sensory, Motor, and Association Areas

Many authorities describe the cerebral cortex as having three types of areas: sensory, motor, and association (see Figure 4.19). This division reflects assumptions about the brain that were popular long ago. Although the idea is not exactly right, it is not exactly wrong, either. It is, however, misleading.

The original reasoning behind the sensory-motor-association distinction was as follows. The brain has distinct sensory and motor areas. For example, visual information from the thalamus goes directly to the primary visual cortex. Damage to the primary visual cortex results in blindness. The primary auditory cortex and primary somatosensory cortex play analogous roles for hearing and the skin senses. We can also distinguish certain motor areas in the cortex; damage to those areas impairs movement in various ways. After accounting for the primary sensory and motor areas, we have certain other areas left over. Damage to those areas does not lead to complete loss of any sense, nor does it produce paralysis. So what do those areas do? Perhaps, the reasoning went, those areas "associate." They link vision with hearing, or hearing with touch, or touch with taste; or they link current sensory impressions with memories. This description fits a commonsense view of the mind: First it gets sensory information, then it thinks about it, then it acts. The idea of an association cortex quickly became popular because it matched the popular view of the mind (Zeki, 1993).

But does the association cortex really associate? Well, not exactly. The association areas process infor-

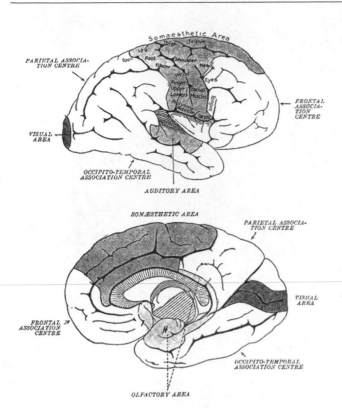

FIGURE 4.19

An old, somewhat misleading view of the cortex

Note the designation "association areas" in this illustration of the cortex in an old introductory psychology textbook (Hunter, 1923). Today's researchers are more likely to regard those areas as "additional sensory areas." They do not associate one kind of sensory information with another.

mation more elaborately than the primary sensory areas do (Van Hoesen, 1993), but they do not link one kind of sensory information with another. For example, the association cortex next to the primary visual cortex consists of cells that are responsive to visual information; few if any of its cells respond selectively to anything else. Similarly, the association cortex next to the primary auditory cortex consists of cells that respond to auditory information. Furthermore, input to the "association" areas does not come exclusively from other areas of the cerebral cortex, as early neuroanatomists supposed, but from sensory areas of the thalamus as well (I. T. Diamond, 1979, 1983). It is better, therefore, to describe these areas as "additional sensory areas" to avoid the implication that they link different senses or that they are the exclusive locations for thinking.

"But, then," you might ask, "what about the idea that the sensory areas get the sensation, the association areas think about it, and the motor cortex acts? If the association cortex doesn't think about the information, what area does?" So far as we can determine, the brain has no single site at which all information funnels into a hidden observer—a "little person in the brain." Thinking, or information processing, depends on sepa-

rate, simultanous processes throughout the brain. And how all those processes produce what appears to be a unified consciousness remains a puzzle, one we shall return to later, especially in discussing the visual system. But frankly, we shall not solve it.

We now turn to specific parts of the cortex. We can distinguish fifty or more areas of the cerebral cortex, based on differences in the thickness of the six laminae and on the appearance of cells and fibers within each lamina. For convenience, however, we group these areas into four *lobes* named for the skull bones that lie over them: occipital, parietal, temporal, and frontal.

The Occipital Lobe

The **occipital lobe,** located at the posterior (caudal) end of the cortex (see Figure 4.20), is the main target for axons from the thalamic nuclei that receive input from the visual pathways. The very posterior pole of the occipital lobe is known as the *primary visual cortex* or as the *striate cortex* because of its striped appearance in cross section. Destruction of any part of the striate cortex causes *cortical blindness* in the related part of the visual field. For example, extensive damage to the striate cortex of the right hemisphere causes blindness in the left visual field (the left side of the world from the viewer's perspective). A person with cortical blindness has normal eyes, normal pupillary reflexes, and some eye movements, but no pattern perception.

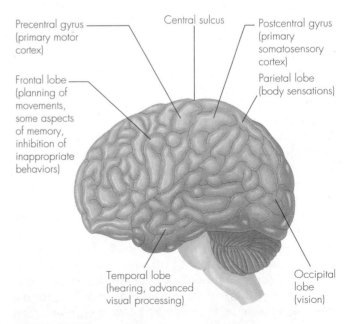

FIGURE 4.20

Some major subdivisions of the human cerebral cortex, with a few of their primary functions

FIGURE **4.21**
Approximate representation of sensory and motor information in the cortex
(**a**) Each location in the somatosensory cortex represents sensation from a different body part. (**b**) Each location in the motor cortex regulates movement of a different body part.
Source: Adapted from Penfield & Rasmussen, 1950.

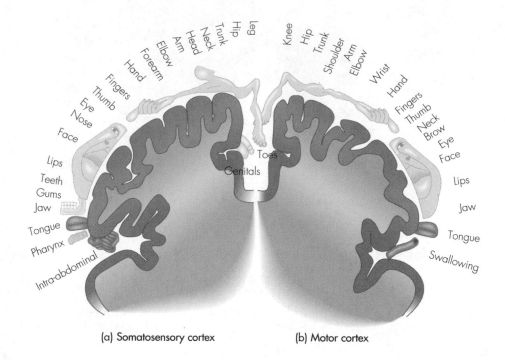

(a) Somatosensory cortex   (b) Motor cortex

The Parietal Lobe

The **parietal lobe** lies between the occipital lobe and the **central sulcus,** one of the deepest grooves in the surface of the cortex (see Figure 4.20). The parietal lobe is specialized for processing body information, including touch, muscle-stretch receptors, and joint receptors.

The area just posterior to the central sulcus, called the **postcentral gyrus** or the *primary somatosensory cortex,* is the primary target for touch sensations and other skin and muscle information. Direct electrical stimulation of the postcentral gyrus in one hemisphere evokes sensations on the opposite side of the body that people often describe as tingling or unnatural. The postcentral gyrus includes four bands of cells that run parallel to the central sulcus. Separate areas along each band receive information from different parts of the body, as shown in Figure 4.21a. Two of the bands receive mostly light-touch information, one receives deep-pressure information, and one receives a combination of both (Kaas, Nelson, Sur, Lin, & Merzenich, 1979). In effect, the postcentral gyrus contains four separate representations of the body.

Information about touch and body location is important not only for its own sake but also for interpreting visual and auditory information. For example, if you see something in the upper left portion of the visual field, your brain needs to know which direction your eyes are turned, the position of your head, and the tilt of your body before it can determine the location of the object that you see, and therefore the direction you

should go if you want to approach or avoid it. The parietal lobe monitors all the information about eye, head, and body positions and passes it on to other brain areas that control movement (Gross & Graziano, 1995).

People with damage to the parietal lobe do not completely lose the sense of touch, or the muscle and joint senses. Rather, they suffer a variety of symptoms that suggest difficulty in interpreting and using such information (Lynch, 1980). Common symptoms include:

1. Impaired ability to identify objects by touch. For example, a blind person who suffers damage to the parietal lobe loses the ability to read Braille (Gloning, Gloning, Weingarten, & Berner, 1954).
2. Clumsiness on the side of the body opposite the damage.
3. Inability to draw and follow maps, describe how to get somewhere, or say what something might look like when viewed from a different angle.
4. Neglect of the opposite side of the body, especially of the left side after right-hemisphere parietal lobe damage. People may fail to dress the left side of the body, read mostly the right side of a page, draw mostly the right side of an object, and describe from memory mostly the right side of a familiar scene. How do you suppose such a person would respond if asked to look at drawings of animals or letters and "name the colors in the background" as in Figure 4.22? Regardless of how the cow drawing is tilted, parietal-damaged people name more colors on their own right than on their own left; they do not, however, neglect the cow's left side in a rotated drawing. However, if they are viewing a drawing of a letter, they often neglect not only the left side of the paper but also the

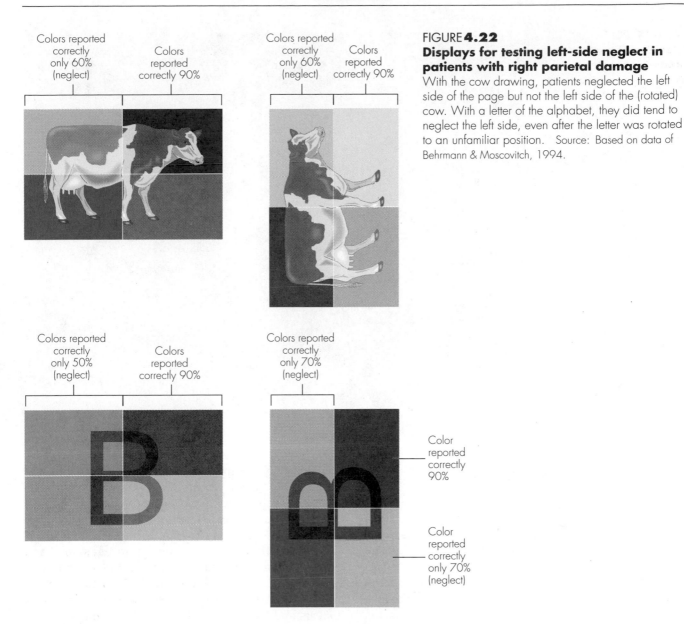

Colors reported correctly only 60% (neglect)

Colors reported correctly 90%

Colors reported correctly only 60% (neglect)

Colors reported correctly 90%

Colors reported correctly only 50% (neglect)

Colors reported correctly 90%

Colors reported correctly only 70% (neglect)

Color reported correctly 90%

Color reported correctly only 70% (neglect)

FIGURE **4.22**

Displays for testing left-side neglect in patients with right parietal damage

With the cow drawing, patients neglected the left side of the page but not the left side of the (rotated) cow. With a letter of the alphabet, they did tend to neglect the left side, even after the letter was rotated to an unfamiliar position. Source: Based on data of Behrmann & Moscovitch, 1994.

left side of the rotated page (Behrmann & Moscovitch, 1994). Evidently, under some circumstances they mentally rotate the drawing and then neglect what would appear on the left after the rotation.

The Temporal Lobe

The **temporal lobe** is located laterally in each hemisphere, near the temples (see Figure 4.20). It is the primary cortical target for auditory information. In humans, the temporal lobe—especially the left temporal lobe in most cases—is essential for understanding spoken language. It also contributes to some of the more complex aspects of vision, including recognition of faces. A tumor in the temporal lobe may give rise to

elaborate visual hallucinations, whereas a tumor in the occipital lobe ordinarily evokes only simple sensations, such as flashes of light.

The temporal lobes also play a part in emotional and motivational behaviors. Temporal lobe damage can lead to a set of behaviors known as the **Klüver–Bucy syndrome** (named for the investigators who first described it). Previously wild and aggressive monkeys fail to display normal fears and anxieties after temporal lobe damage (Klüver & Bucy, 1939). They put almost anything they find into their mouths, and attempt to pick up snakes and lighted matches (which intact monkeys consistently avoid). It is hard to determine how much of this behavior results from emotional change and how much from a visual or cognitive deficit. For example, a monkey might handle a snake either because it is no longer afraid of snakes or because it no longer recognizes what a snake is.

FIGURE **4.23**
Species differences in prefrontal cortex
Note that the prefrontal cortex (shaded area) constitutes a larger proportion of the human brain than of the brains of these other species. Source: After Fuster, 1989.

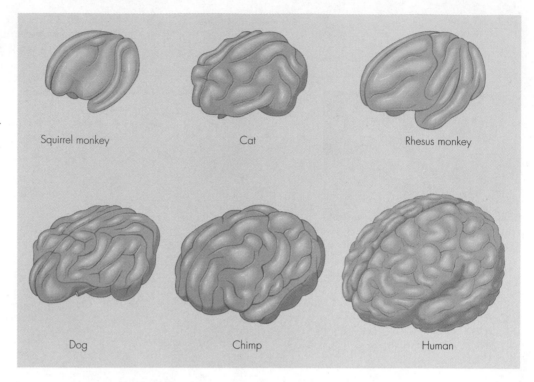

Squirrel monkey

Cat

Rhesus monkey

Dog

Chimp

Human

The Frontal Lobe

The **frontal lobe,** which contains the motor cortex and the prefrontal cortex, extends from the central sulcus to the anterior limit of the brain (see Figure 4.20). The posterior portion of the frontal lobe, the **precentral gyrus,** is specialized for the control of fine movements, such as moving one finger at a time. Separate areas are responsible for different parts of the body (Figure 4.21), mostly on the contralateral (opposite) side but with slight control of the ipsilateral (same) side, too.

The most anterior portion of the frontal lobe, the **prefrontal cortex,** is a fairly large structure, especially in species with a large cortex overall, such as humans (see Figure 4.23). It is not the primary target for any single sensory system, but it receives information from all the sensory systems, including the interior of the body. The prefrontal cortex is the only cortical area known to receive input from all sensory modalities (Stuss & Benson, 1984).

The prefrontal cortex was the target of **prefrontal lobotomies,** an infamous type of brain surgery that used to be conducted in attempts to control psychological disorders (see Digression 4.2). People with lobotomies generally lost their initiative and failed to inhibit socially unacceptable impulses. They also showed impairments in certain aspects of memory and in their fa-

cial expressions of emotion. However, lobotomy cases provided only a superficial understanding of the prefrontal lobes. Later researchers, working with brain-damaged people and monkeys, have tried to establish the functions of the prefrontal cortex. Among other functions, the prefrontal cortex is important for *working memory,* the ability to remember recent stimuli and events, such as where I parked the car today (Goldman-Rakic, 1988). The prefrontal cortex is especially important for a **delayed response task,** in which a stimulus appears and then disappears, and after some delay the individual must respond to the remembered stimulus. The prefrontal cortex is much less important for *reference memory,* the ability to remember unchanging information, such as the fact that a green traffic light means "go" or that the Summer Olympics occur once every four years.

The prefrontal cortex also contributes to the shifting of attention (Dias, Robbins, & Roberts, 1996). It monitors recent events, calculates possible actions in response to those events, ascertains from memory the probable outcomes of the actions, and determines the emotional value of each of those outcomes (Tucker, Luu, & Pribram, 1995). If all operates properly, the result is a good choice of movements and an emotionally satisfying outcome. If the prefrontal cortex is damaged, however, the person may fail either to remember the likely outcomes or to imagine the emotional consequences. The result may be an incomplete or badly planned movement: The person showers with clothes

The Rise and Fall of Prefrontal Lobotomies

In the late 1940s and early 1950s, about 40,000 prefrontal lobotomies were performed in the United States (Shutts, 1982). The surgery consists of damaging the prefrontal cortex or cutting the connections between the prefrontal cortex and the rest of the cortex. The impetus for the operation was a report that damaging the prefrontal cortex of laboratory primates had made them tamer without impairing their sensory or motor capacities in any striking way. It was reasoned that the same operation might help people who suffered from severe and otherwise untreatable psychiatric disorders.

The largest number of lobotomies in the United States were performed by Walter Freeman, a medical doctor who had never been trained in surgery. His techniques were amazingly crude, even by the standards of the 1940s. He performed many operations in his office or in other sites outside the hospital. (Freeman carried his equipment, such as it was, around with him in his car, which he called his "lobotomobile.")

Freeman and others became increasingly casual about deciding who should get a lobotomy. At first, the technique was used only in cases of severe, untreatable schizophrenia. Lobotomy did calm some schizophrenic people, but the effects were often disappointing, even to Freeman and others who performed the operations. (We now know that the frontal lobes of many severe schizophrenics are partly shrunken and less active than normal; lobotomy was therefore damaging a structure that had already been impaired.) As time went on, Freeman lobotomized people with an assortment of other major and minor disorders, some of whom would, in fact, be considered normal by today's standards.

After effective drug therapies became available in the mid-1950s, the use of lobotomy declined sharply. Freeman, who had been praised by some of his colleagues and barely tolerated by others, lost his privilege to practice at most hospitals and faded into the same obscurity as lobotomy itself.

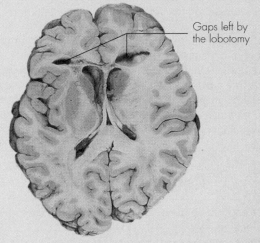

Gaps left by the lobotomy

A horizontal section of the brain of a person who had a prefrontal lobotomy many years earlier. The two holes in the frontal cortex are the visible results of the operation. Source: Photo courtesy of Dana Copeland.

Lobotomy has been an exceedingly rare operation since the mid-1950s (Lesse, 1984; Tippin & Henn, 1982).

Among the common consequences of prefrontal lobotomy were apathy, a loss of the ability to plan and take initiative, memory disorders (Chapter 13), distractibility, generally blunted emotions, and a loss of facial expression (Stuss & Benson, 1984). People with prefrontal damage lose their social inhibitions; they behave in a tactless, callous manner and ignore the rules of polite, civilized conduct. They may also seem impulsive, simply because they fail to calculate adequately the probable outcomes of their behaviors.

on, or shakes the salt into the tea instead of onto the food, or pours water on the tube of toothpaste instead of on the toothbrush (Schwartz, 1995).

IN **CLOSING**

Functions of the Cerebral Cortex

The cerebral cortex is prominent in the mammalian brain but only rudimentary in reptiles and fish. Obviously, it is not a *necessary* part of a nervous system; reptiles and fish can find food, escape predators, repro-

duce, learn, and remember, just like mammals. Our cortex does not enable us to do something we could not do otherwise; it merely helps us perform certain functions better. The cortex provides greater detail in our sensory discriminations, control of movement, and retention of information.

Summary

1. The cerebral cortex is composed of six laminae (layers) of neurons. A given lamina may be absent from certain parts of the cortex. The cortex is organized into columns of cells arranged perpendicular to the laminae. (p. 93)

2. Almost every cortical area has sensory, associational, and motor functions, although the degree of each varies. (p. 94)
3. The occipital lobe of the cortex is primarily responsible for vision. Damage to part of the occipital lobe leads to blindness in part of the visual field. (p. 95)
4. The parietal lobe processes body sensations. The postcentral gyrus contains four separate representations of the body. (p. 96)
5. The temporal lobe contributes to hearing and to complex aspects of vision. (p. 97)
6. The frontal lobe includes the precentral gyrus, which controls fine movements. It also includes the prefrontal cortex, which contributes to memories of current and recent stimuli, planning of movements, and regulation of emotional expressions. (p. 98)

Review Questions

1. In what way do the neurons within a given column resemble one another? (p. 94)
2. Why is the term *association cortex* misleading? (p. 95)
3. How does cortical blindness differ from blindness caused by damage to the eyes? (p. 95)
4. What kind of brain damage leads to sensory neglect of the left half of the body? (p. 96)
5. What is a delayed-response task? (p. 98)

Thought Question

1. When monkeys with Klüver–Bucy syndrome pick up lighted matches and snakes, we do not know whether they are displaying an emotional deficit or a difficulty identifying the object. What kind of research might help answer this question?

Suggestions for Further Reading

Klawans, H. L. (1988). *Toscanini's fumble and other tales of clinical neurology.* Chicago: Contemporary Books. Fascinating description of cases of human brain damage and other neurological conditions.

Calvin, W. H., & Ojemann, G. A. (1994). *Conversations with Neil's brain.* Reading, MA: Addison-Wesley. A discussion of brain anatomy and brain damage, written for a popular audience.

Valenstein, E. S. (1986). *Great and desperate cures.* New York: Basic Books. Account of the rise and fall of prefrontal lobotomies.

Terms

cerebral cortex layer of cells on the outer surface of the cerebral hemispheres of the forebrain (p. 93)

corpus callosum large set of axons that connects the two hemispheres of the cerebral cortex (p. 93)

anterior commissure set of axons connecting the two cerebral hemispheres; smaller than the corpus callosum (p. 93)

lamina (plural: **laminae**) a layer of cells (p. 93)

column collection of cells having similar properties, arranged perpendicular to the laminae (p. 94)

occipital lobe one of the four lobes of the cerebral cortex (p. 95)

parietal lobe one of the lobes of the cerebral cortex (p. 96)

central sulcus a large groove in the surface of the primate cerebral cortex, separating frontal from parietal cortex (p. 96)

postcentral gyrus gyrus of the cerebral cortex just posterior to the central gyrus; a primary projection site for touch and other body sensations (p. 96)

temporal lobe one of the lobes of the cerebral cortex (p. 97)

Klüver–Bucy syndrome condition in which monkeys with damaged temporal lobes fail to display normal fears and anxieties (p. 97)

frontal lobe one of the lobes of the cerebral cortex (p. 98)

precentral gyrus gyrus of the cerebral cortex just anterior to the central sulcus; site of the primary motor cortex (p. 98)

prefrontal cortex the most anterior portion of the frontal lobe of the cerebral cortex (p. 98)

prefrontal lobotomy surgical disconnection of the prefrontal cortex from the rest of the brain (p. 98)

delayed-response task assignment in which an animal must respond on the basis of a signal that it remembers but that is no longer present (p. 98)

Investigating How the Brain Controls Behavior

In the nineteenth century, Franz Joseph Gall observed (or so he thought) that people with an excellent verbal memory had bulging, protruding eyes. He concluded that verbal memory depended on a part of the brain immediately behind the eyes and that overdevelopment in this area pushed the eyes forward. If this were so, Gall reasoned, bulges and depressions elsewhere on the skull might also reflect development in the underlying brain areas. Thus, by comparing people's skulls and comparing their features to behavior, it should be possible first to identify the activities conducted by each part of the brain and then to interpret people's personalities by feeling their head bumps. These were the basic premises of **phrenology.** Figure 4.24 is a typical phrenological map of the human skull.

Phrenology is a classic example of pseudoscience. In many cases, phrenologists identified an area on their map of the brain by observing only one or two people. Moreover, they ignored discrepancies when someone's behavior did not fit the theory. Nevertheless, researchers today maintain one of phrenology's basic assumptions: Different parts of the brain control different aspects of

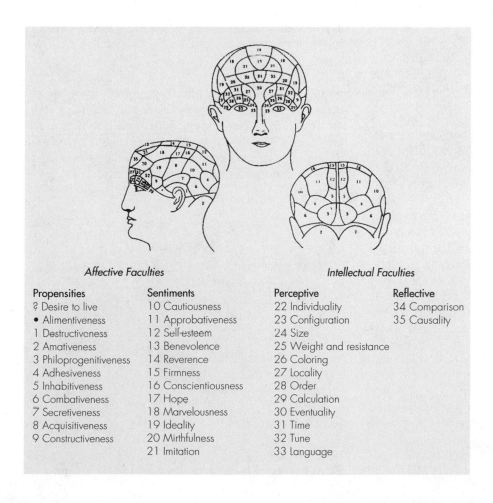

Affective Faculties

Propensities
? Desire to live
• Alimentiveness
1 Destructiveness
2 Amativeness
3 Philoprogenitiveness
4 Adhesiveness
5 Inhabitiveness
6 Combativeness
7 Secretiveness
8 Acquisitiveness
9 Constructiveness

Sentiments
10 Cautiousness
11 Approbativeness
12 Self-esteem
13 Benevolence
14 Reverence
15 Firmness
16 Conscientiousness
17 Hope
18 Marvelousness
19 Ideality
20 Mirthfulness
21 Imitation

Intellectual Faculties

Perceptive
22 Individuality
23 Configuration
24 Size
25 Weight and resistance
26 Coloring
27 Locality
28 Order
29 Calculation
30 Eventuality
31 Time
32 Tune
33 Language

Reflective
34 Comparison
35 Causality

FIGURE **4.24**
A phrenologist's map of the brain
Source: From Spurzheim, 1908.

behavior. If brain area A controls behavior X, then individuals with a deficiency of behavior X probably have some deficiency in brain area A. Individuals with a greater-than-normal amount of behavior X should have some advantage in area A.

Current research differs from phrenology in several major respects, however. Psychologists no longer attempt to localize such personality traits as self-esteem, reverence, or "marvelousness." Rather, we attempt to understand how the brain produces such biological functions as vision, control of finger movements, and temperature regulation. We consider not only localized brain areas but also systems of neurons that are not confined to one region. And we examine the electrical and chemical activity of brain areas and systems, not just their size, because behavior depends on differences in brain activity, not just differences in structure.

In this module we consider a few of the most common research techniques. The fundamental strategies are to examine behavior after brain damage, to examine behavior after extra stimulation of a brain area, and to examine correlations between spontaneous brain activity and spontaneous behavior.

The Stereotaxic Instrument

A **stereotaxic instrument** is a useful device for implanting an electrode, with which investigators can damage, stimulate, or record from a brain area. Figure 4.25 shows a stereotaxic instrument for a rat, by far the most commonly used animal in research of this type. An anesthetized rat is positioned in the device with ear bars and a clamp around the nose and mouth to hold the head in place. Any part of the brain can be located fairly accurately from the position of two landmarks on the head: the ear bars and **bregma,** the point where the frontal and parietal skull bones join (see Figure 4.26).

To calculate the position, the researcher refers to a **stereotaxic atlas** (or map) of the animal's brain areas in relation to the external landmarks. Such atlases have been published for the brains of many species. Figure 4.27, from Pellegrino and co-workers' (1979) atlas, illustrates one slice through the brain of an adult rat. The scale at the bottom indicates distances in millimeters left or right from the center of the skull. The scales at the left and right indicate distances dorsal and ventral from the top surface of the brain and from the ear bars, respectively. The notations in the upper corners indicate that this slice is 6.0 mm anterior to the ear bars and 0.2 mm anterior to bregma. Other pages of the atlas illustrate slices at 0.2-mm intervals.

An experimenter who wants to insert an electrode into, say, the ventromedial hypothalamus (VMH in Fig-

FIGURE **4.25**
A stereotaxic instrument for locating brain areas in small animals

ure 4.27) places an anesthetized animal in the stereotaxic instrument, drills holes at the appropriate spots on the skull, inserts the electrode, and lowers it to the target area. The investigator can then use the electrode to record from cells in that area, stimulate the cells, or overstimulate and thereby destroy them.

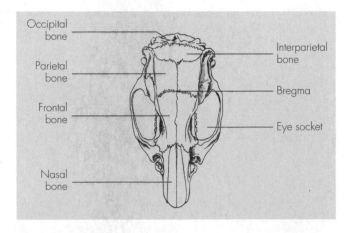

FIGURE **4.26**
Skull bones of a rat and the position of bregma

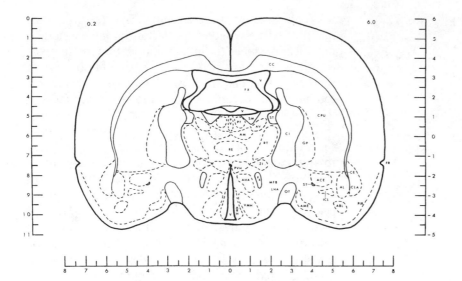

FIGURE **4.27**
A typical page from a stereo-taxic atlas of the rat brain, showing a coronal section 6.0 mm anterior to the ear bars
The surrounding unlabeled area is the cerebral cortex. Abbreviations refer to various areas of the brain; for example, CC = corpus callosum.   Source: From Pellegrino et al., 1979.

Lesions and Ablations

A **lesion** is the destruction or functional disruption of an area of the brain. An **ablation** is the removal of part of the brain. Lesions and ablations can be produced intentionally by experimenters with laboratory animals, and they can occur naturally, as the result of a stroke or a head wound. When a lesion or ablation leads to a deficit in some behavior, we assume that the damaged area had some role in the control of that behavior, although its exact role may be difficult to determine. The lesion technique has been widely used throughout the history of biological psychology.

Methods of Producing Lesions and Ablations

Brain damage occurs in humans as a result of strokes, surgery to remove brain tumors, and so forth. To gain better control of the location and size of the damage, the age of damage, or the experience before or after the damage, researchers turn to laboratory animals.

Lesions and ablations can be produced in experimental animals in several ways. To remove a large area on the external surface of the brain, an experimenter cuts back a flap of skull and removes tissue with a knife or with vacuum suction. To make small lesions, especially beneath the surface of the brain, the investigator uses a stereotaxic instrument to insert an electrode and then applies a current. The electrode inevitably kills a few cells on the way to the target. To find out the effects of such accidental damage and to separate them from the effects of the lesion itself, an experimenter produces a **sham lesion** in a control group, performing all the same procedures but without the electrical current. Any behavioral difference between the lesioned group and the sham-lesion group must result from the lesion itself and not from damage caused by inserting the electrode.

Another method of creating a lesion is to inject chemicals that are toxic to neurons. Certain chemicals are selectively toxic to particular kinds of neurons. For example, 6-hydroxydopamine damages cells that release dopamine or norepinephrine as their neurotransmitter. By injecting such a chemical, researchers can damage one set of neurons in an area while sparing the others.

Still another lesion method is the *gene-knockout* approach, in which researchers use biochemical methods to direct a mutation at a particular gene, one that produces a particular transmitter, for example, or one that produces a protein that is important for certain cells (Joyner & Guillemot, 1994). The gene-knockout approach can destroy or alter widespread systems of cells or subsystems within cells, and therefore provides information that other methods cannot. However, we must remember that if an animal develops without a particular chemical or a particular kind of cell, the abnormal internal environment will affect other chemicals and other cells as well.

Histological Techniques

Suppose that an investigator has made a lesion in a rat's brain and then tested the behavioral effects of the lesion. When the experiment is over, the investigator

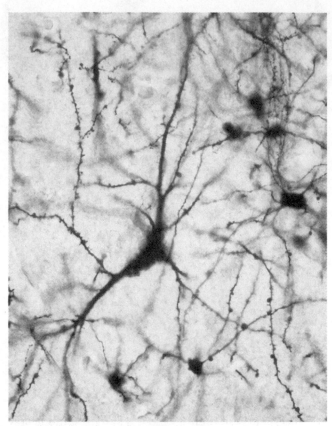

Human brain section treated with Golgi stain, which enters only some neurons but stains those neurons completely. (Magnification × 400.)

usually examines the rat's brain to determine the size and the exact location of the lesion.

The rat is deeply anesthetized, then perfused with chemicals that preserve the tissues. Then the brain is removed and stained. Without special treatment, brain tissue looks fairly uniform; it is difficult to identify even the major nuclei and tracts. Therefore, investigators use various histological procedures to highlight the brain tissues that they wish to examine. (*Histology* is the study of the minute structure of tissues.) First, investigators harden the brain, either by freezing it or by forcing a chemical into it that hardens it ("embedding" the tissue). Then the brain is divided into slices just a few microns thick by means of a device called a microtome. Finally, the tissue is stained with chemicals that selectively attach to certain structures. For example, Nissl stain attaches selectively to cell bodies; Weigert stain attaches to axons.

Difficulties of Interpretation

The results of a lesion experiment are seldom easy to interpret. Suppose, for example, that some lesion in a rat's brain disrupts maze learning. That result by itself does not tell us whether the lesion impairs vision, or body location sense, or hunger motivation, or some aspect of memory, or any of a number of other behavioral processes. To determine the effect of a lesion, researchers must determine what the lesion impairs and what it *does not* impair.

For analogy, suppose that investigators studying the functioning of an automobile discover that by removing one structure from the engine they prevent the radio from working. If everything else in the car still works fine, then the investigators know they have damaged either the radio itself or the wires leading to it. If, however, the removal of a structure has stopped not only the radio but also the horn, the lights, and the windshield wipers, then what they damaged is not specifically part of the radio. (Maybe they removed the battery.)

Similarly, in studying the brain, investigators try to demonstrate a **double dissociation of function:** a demonstration that lesion 1 impairs behavior A more than behavior B, while lesion 2 impairs behavior B more than behavior A. For example, damage to one set of axons in the hindbrain impairs use of the trunk muscles (those needed for standing, sitting, turning, and other bilateral movements), whereas damage to a different set spares the trunk muscles but impairs use of the peripheral muscles (those needed for movements of the hands, fingers, and toes). The contrast between the two lesions gives us better information than either lesion would alone; the contrast tells us that the lesions are not just impairing arousal or motivation or some other process that might apply to all movements. In some cases, even the results of a double dissociation of function remain difficult to interpret (Plaut, 1995), but at least they provide an important step in clarifying the effects of each lesion.

The analogy between damage to an automobile and damage to the human brain fails if we take it too seriously, and the reason for that failure is important: An automobile, unlike the human brain, contains some structures whose functions are entirely independent of one another. That is, it is possible to damage the radio, the horn, or the lights without having any effect on anything else. In human brain damage, we seldom if ever see such a complete dissociation of function. A particular kind of brain damage may impair one behavior much more than others, but it does not destroy one behavior while leaving all others fully intact. Furthermore, we do not find sharp boundaries between the brain areas controlling one function and those controlling another function (as we do in an automobile). Rather, we find a gradual progression from cells having predominantly one function to cells having another (Goldberg, 1995). In other words, the division of labor among brain areas is relative, not complete.

Stimulating and Recording Brain Activity

Lesion methods determine what behaviors occur when certain areas of the brain are damaged. An alternative way of studying brain functioning is to stimulate a brain area to extra activity, either by applying a brief, mild electrical current to the area or by injecting neurotransmitters or other chemicals that will increase brain activity. Another strategy is to record the activity of the brain and determine what patterns of increased or decreased activity accompany various kinds of behavior. Here are three methods of recording activity in animal brains; later we shall examine some methods appropriate for use with humans.

Microdialysis

Researchers who wish to determine which neurotransmitters are released during a behavioral activity, and in what amounts, often use **microdialysis,** a method for measuring the concentrations of chemicals in a small area. Using stereotaxic procedures, an investigator implants into the brain a thin stainless-steel tube filled with fluid (generally a dilute salt solution with the same molarity as the blood). Brain fluids, which contain neurotransmitters, diffuse across the thin dialysis membrane at the tip of the tube and thus enter the tube, from which they are carried up and out of the brain for chemical analysis (Westerink, 1995). In this manner, the researchers can measure the amounts of neurotransmitter released during various behaviors.

Autoradiography

An autograph is a signature. An autoradiograph is a "signature" produced radioactively by a chemical. **Autoradiography** is a method of determining where a chemical is located in the brain.

An investigator begins by injecting a radioactively labeled chemical into a laboratory rat. After the injection, the investigator waits a few minutes for the chemicals to reach the brain and then kills the rat, removes the brain, and slices it into thin sections. The investigator then places each section against a piece of x-ray film, which records all the radioactivity that the labeled chemicals emit, creating a map of the relative amounts of radioactivity in different parts of the rat's brain.

For example, an investigator might inject radioactively labeled glucose or 2-deoxy-D-glucose, which neurons take up when they absorb glucose. (The advantage of 2-deoxy-D-glucose is that it is metabolized much more slowly than glucose and so remains in the cell longer.) The most active neurons take up more glucose than less active neurons do; consequently, autoradiography provides a map of relative activity levels in the brain (Hibbard, McGlone, Davis, & Hawkins, 1987).

Immunohistochemistry

The term *immunohistochemistry* is a combination of *immuno,* which refers to the immune system, *histo,* which means tissues, and *chemistry.* **Immunohistochemistry,** therefore, is a method of using the immune system to label particular types of tissues.

First, investigators purify a protein or peptide in which they are interested—say, the acetylcholine receptor of rhesus monkeys. Then they inject that protein into a different species, such as rabbits, whose immune system will form antibodies to it. (The acetylcholine receptors are very similar across species but not identical; thus, the rabbit's immune system attacks the monkey's acetylcholine receptors as intruders.) Investigators collect the antibodies from the rabbit's blood, chemically attach them to dyes, and expose the dyed antibodies to a slice of a monkey's brain. The rabbit's antibodies, carrying the dye with them, attach to acetylcholine receptors. The investigators then observe where the dye attaches and use this distribution to map the location of acetylcholine receptors. Immunohistochemistry cannot detect moment-by-moment changes in the brain, but it can detect long-term changes, such as the fact that animals subjected to some treatment have a decreased number of acetylcholine receptors.

Studying the Structure of Living Human Brains

Many of the methods commonly used in animal research damage the brain, or at least endanger it. For many years, researchers had few techniques suitable for research on humans, other than examining the behavior of people who had suffered strokes or other brain damage. Current technology, however, enables researchers to examine the structure and activity of living, working human brains, healthy or not.

Computerized Axial Tomography

Is Alzheimer's disease associated with loss of brain tissue? Is schizophrenia? One way to find out is to use **computerized axial tomography,** better known as a **CT** or **CAT scan** (Andreasen, 1988). A CT scan uses x-rays, but x-rays ordinarily reveal very little contrast

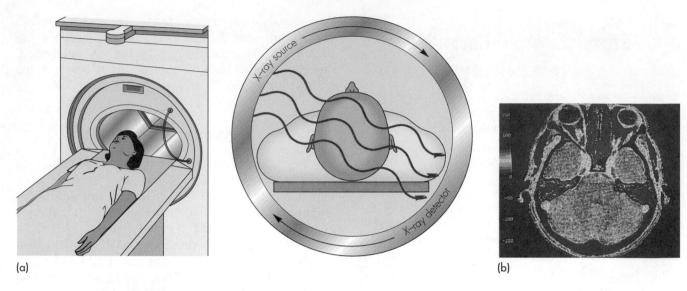

(a)   (b)

FIGURE **4.28**
CT scanner
(**a**) A person's head is placed into the device and then a rapidly rotating source sends x-rays through the head while detectors on the opposite side make photographs. A computer then constructs an image of the brain. (**b**) A view of a normal human brain generated by computerized axial tomography (CT scanning).

between one part of the brain and another. To increase the contrast, a physician injects a dye into the blood and then places the person's head into a CT scanner like the one shown in Figure 4.28a. X-rays are passed through the head and recorded by detectors on the opposite side. The CT scanner is rotated 1 degree at a time and the procedure is repeated until a measurement has been taken at each angle over 180 degrees. From the 180 measurements, a computer can reconstruct images of the brain. Figure 4.28b is a CT scan of a normal brain. CT scans show that the cortex is atrophied (shrunken) in patients with Alzheimer's disease and that the cerebral ventricles are enlarged in certain people with schizophrenia.

Magnetic Resonance Imaging

A second method of examining brain anatomy in a living person is **magnetic resonance imaging (MRI),** also known as nuclear magnetic resonance (NMR). Magnetic resonance imaging produces images with a high degree of resolution without exposing the brain to any radiation at all (Warach, 1995). This method is based on the fact that any atom with an odd atomic weight—such as hydrogen—has an inherent axis of rotation. An MRI device applies a magnetic field of 1.5 tesla (about 25,000 times the magnetic field of the earth), thereby aligning all the axes of rotation. A brief radio-frequency

field can then perturb (tilt) these axes. When the radio-frequency field is turned off, the atomic nuclei release electromagnetic energy as they relax and return to their original axis. By measuring that energy, MRI devices form an image of the brain, like the one in Figure 4.29. Different kinds of molecules release energy at different electromagnetic frequencies; most MRI scans are set to detect the energy released by the hydrogen atoms in water molecules, which are the most abundant molecules in the body. The MRI procedure is not terribly expensive, and it poses no known health risks. Like CT scans, an MRI image can reveal structural defects such as an enlarged ventricle or an atrophied cortex. A modified version of MRI, called *functional MRI*, is discussed in the next section, as it is used to measure activity and not just structure.

Measuring Human Brain Activity

At any moment, certain areas of the brain are more active than others. For example, the visual cortex becomes more active during visual stimulation, and the olfactory bulb becomes more active during olfactory stimulation. Investigators have developed several noninvasive ways to measure changes in brain activity.

lay) over a limited area of the cerebral cortex. A meaningful or attention-getting stimulus evokes another electrical response with a latency of about 0.3 second. Among many other uses, evoked potentials can identify which stimuli attract the attention of different people.

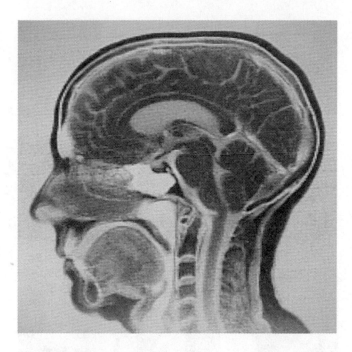

FIGURE **4.29**
A view of a living brain generated by magnetic resonance imaging
Any atom with an odd atomic weight (such as hydrogen) has an inherent rotation. An outside magnetic field can align the axes of rotation. A radio-frequency field can then make all these atoms move like tiny gyros. When the radio-frequency field is turned off, the atomic nuclei release electromagnetic energy as they relax. By measuring that energy, we can obtain an image of a structure such as the brain without damaging it.

Electroencephalography

A device called the **electroencephalograph (EEG)** records electrical activity of the brain through electrodes attached to the scalp. It enables investigators to make gross determinations of brain activity in humans and other animals without actually cutting into the skull. Electrodes, generally eight or fewer, are attached with glue or other adhesive to various locations on the surface of the scalp. The electrodes do not record the activity of any one neuron, but an average of the whole population of cells in the area under the electrode. The output of the electrodes is then amplified and recorded. An investigator can determine from EEG records whether the person is asleep, dreaming, awake, or excited. Abnormalities in the EEG record may also suggest the presence of epilepsy, a tumor, or other medical problems in the region under a particular electrode.

With the **evoked potential** method, experimenters use the EEG apparatus to record the brain's activity in response to sensory stimuli. Any sensory stimulus evokes electrical activity with a very short latency (de-

Magnetoencephalography

The electrical currents in the brain generate very weak magnetic fields (less than 10^{-8} as strong as the Earth's magnetic field), and by using suitable amplification, investigators can monitor the magnetic fields just as they can the electrical currents. **Magnetoencephalography (MEG)** is the measurement of the brain's magnetic fields by devices that record simultaneously from many portions of the brain. It produces results similar in many ways to those of electroencephalography (Hari, 1994).

Figure 4.30, one example of MEG results, shows the magnetic fields in many brain areas as evoked by a brief tone heard in the right ear. The diagram represents a human head as viewed from above, with the nose at the top. Note that the areas of greatest response are in the temporal lobes, with a slightly greater response in the left hemisphere than in the right hemisphere (Hari, 1994). Using MEG with more complicated tasks, such as naming a picture, researchers can identify the brain location that responds most quickly, the areas that respond slightly later, those that respond still later, and so on. In such a manner, researchers can trace a wave of brain activity from its origin in one of the sensory systems to its output in the motor cortex (Salmelin, Hari, Lounasmaa, & Sams, 1994).

PET Scans

Positron-emission tomography (PET) provides a high-resolution image of brain activity. PET scans rely on the fact that the radioactive decay of certain elements emits a positron, an antimatter particle with the same mass as an electron but an opposite charge.

First, the person receives an injection of glucose or some other chemical with a radioactive label of ^{11}C, ^{18}F, or ^{15}O. (These chemicals have half-lives ranging from 110 minutes for ^{18}F to 2 minutes for ^{15}O. Because their half-lives are so short, the investigators must make them in a cyclotron near the PET scanner. Cyclotrons are very large and expensive. Consequently, PET scans are available only at the largest research hospitals.) The chemical chosen for injection depends on the nature of the research question. For example, glucose goes to the most active areas of the brain, so it is suitable for finding which areas are most active at a given moment.

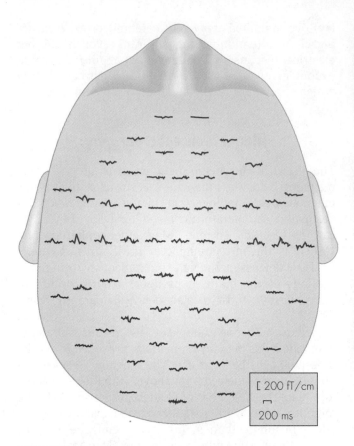

FIGURE **4.30**
A result of magnetoencephalography, showing responses to a tone in the right ear
The nose is at the top. For each spot on the diagram, the display shows the changing response over a few hundred ms following the tone (calibration is at lower right). The tone evoked responses in many areas, with the largest responses in the temporal cortex, especially on the left side.   Source: From Hari, 1994.

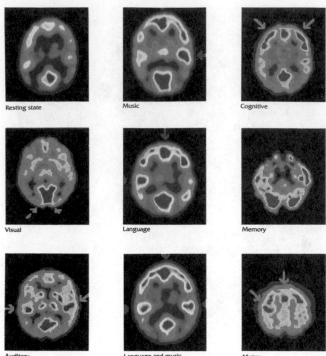

FIGURE **4.31**
PET scans of normal brains, showing differences during various tasks
Red indicates the greatest level of brain activity; blue indicates the least. Left column: Brain activity with no special stimulation and during passive exposure to visual and auditory stimuli. Center column: Activity while listening to music, language, or both. Right column: Activity during performance of a cognitive task, an auditory memory task, and a task of moving fingers of the right hand in a fixed sequence. Arrows indicate regions of greatest activity.   Source: From Phelps & Mazziotta, 1985.

When a radioactive label decays, releasing a positron, the positron immediately collides with a nearby electron. When a positron and an electron collide, they emit two gamma rays in exactly opposite directions. The person's head is surrounded by a set of gamma-ray detectors. When the detectors record two gamma rays at the same time, they identify a spot halfway between the detectors as the point of origin of the gamma rays. Using this information, a computer can determine how many gamma rays are coming from each spot in the brain—and, therefore, how much of the radioactively labeled chemical is located in each area (Phelps & Mazziotta, 1985). PET scans are useful for locating tumors and epileptic foci, as well as for research on how different brains react to different stimuli. Figure 4.31 includes several examples of PET scans of the human brain.

Regional Cerebral Blood Flow

When an area of the brain becomes more active, its blood supply, its use of glucose, and its synthesis of proteins increase. Researchers can capitalize on this fact by administering small amounts of certain radioactive chemicals and then monitoring them to measure the relative activity of various areas of the brain. We already encountered this strategy in autoradiography. With a few changes in procedure, it can be applied to a living human brain.

In the **regional cerebral blood flow (rCBF)** method, an investigator uses a chemical that dissolves in the blood. One such substance is xenon (^{133}Xe), a radioactive gas. After a person inhales xenon, it enters the bloodstream. Because it does not react chemically with anything in the body, the xenon goes wherever the blood goes. Thus, the radioactivity recorded from a particular part of the brain will be proportional to the amount of blood flow to it. The investigator places the person's head in a PET scanner or similar device (see

FIGURE **4.33**
An rCBF image of a normal human brain
Red indicates the greatest amount of blood flow and therefore of brain activity. Yellow shows the next greatest amount, followed by green and blue.   Source: Karen Berman and Daniel Weinberger, National Institute of Mental Health.

FIGURE **4.32**
No, it's not a state-of-the-art hairdo; it's a type of PET scanner. A person engages in a cognitive task while attached to this apparatus that records regional cerebral blood flow in the brain to determine which areas become more active, and by how much.

Figure 4.32), and a computer constructs a colored image of the brain, like those in Figure 4.33. Areas with a great deal of radioactivity appear red; those with less activity appear orange, yellow, green, blue, and violet.

I have told you that blood flow is greatest in the brain areas with the greatest activity. You might ask, how does the blood "know" which brain areas are most active? The answer is that certain neurons, when active, release chemicals that dilate the nearby blood vessels. As a natural result of a series of action potentials, potassium ions leave the neuron and accumulate in the glia cells, which pump them to the walls of nearby arteries. Potassium dilates (expands) the artery walls and thereby increases the flow of blood to that part of the brain (Paulson & Newman, 1987). A second, evidently more important mechanism is that certain neurons, when active, release nitric oxide (NO), which strongly but briefly dilates nearby blood vessels (Iadecola, 1993). The result of the released potassium and NO is to increase blood flow to the most active areas of the brain, as the rCBF method reveals.

A typical way of using the rCBF method is to ask a person to engage in a series of tasks, such as listening to music, solving a problem, and moving the fingers in a certain way. The investigator then uses the rCBF results to compare the type of brain activity that occurs during the various tasks, and to compare the results for different kinds of people (Andreasen, 1988).

Functional MRI

For a number of years, researchers had to choose between methods that show brain structure and methods that show brain activity. For example, EEGs and MEGs

have excellent temporal resolution (that is, they can report changes in activity from one millisecond to the next) but they have poor spatial resolution (they tell us only approximately where the signal originates). CT scans and standard MRI scans have excellent spatial resolution but no useful temporal resolution. A standard MRI, recording the energy released by water molecules, can accurately show a structure smaller than a millimeter in diameter, but it shows no changes from one time to another (because the brain has very little net flow of water). A PET scan is a reasonable compromise, with spatial resolution sometimes as good as a few millimeters and temporal resolution as good as a second or two. However, PET requires radioactive chemicals; researchers cannot test the same person repeatedly because they would exceed the maximum safe exposure to radioactivity. Another way to study both structure and function is to combine one method with another. However, researchers could not perform EEG or MEG measurements at the same time as an MRI; the enormous magnetic field of the MRI would interfere with the very delicate measures of the brain's electrical activity.

A newer method that enables researchers to get both good spatial resolution and good temporal resolution is **functional magnetic resonance imaging (fMRI),** a modified version of MRI (Cohen, Noll, & Schneider, 1993). The fMRI procedure takes advantage of the fact that hemoglobin (the blood protein that binds oxygen) slightly changes its paramagnetic properties after it has released its oxygen. Because blood flow and oxygen consumption increase in the brain areas with the greatest activity, researchers can set the fMRI scanner to detect energies released by hemoglobin, distinguish between hemoglobin with oxygen and hemoglobin without oxygen, and thereby measure the relative activity of various brain areas. Such images have spatial resolution of 1 or 2 mm (almost as good as standard MRI) and temporal resolution of less than a second. Researchers have just begun to tap the potential of fMRI; the technique does not have enough resolution to enable neuroscientists to "watch people think," but it may bring us closer to that goal than we have ever been before.

IN **CLOSING**

Identifying the Functions of Brain Areas

When I was in graduate school, I heard an address by the great Hungarian neuroscientist Georg von Békésy. Békésy advised young investigators to test any new hypothesis by at least three methods. A conclusion demonstrated by any one method, he argued, was suspect. The method might have some hidden flaw, or the results might depend on some very particular set of conditions. However, if several studies using different methods converge on the same conclusion, the conclusion stands much firmer. Neuroscientists use a variety of methods because each method shows us something that others do not, and because using a combination guards against the ways in which any single method might mislead us.

Summary

1. A stereotaxic device enables an investigator to implant electrodes deep in the brain to make lesions or to stimulate neurons or record from them. (p. 102)
2. One of the most common methods of studying brain functioning is by examining the effects of lesions (brain damage). (p. 103)
3. Lesion studies help locate the brain areas most critical to a particular behavioral function, but they do not indicate how that area controls behavior. (p. 104)
4. Autoradiography is a way of measuring the activity of various brain areas at a given time. Histochemistry is a method of identifying the distribution of a particular chemical in various parts of the brain. Microdialysis determines the amount of a neurotransmitter or other chemical that is present in a brain area at a given time. (p. 105)
5. CT scans and MRI images reveal the structure of the brain in a living person. (p. 105)
6. Electroencephalographs, magnetoencephalographs, PET scans, and rCBF images indicate the activity taking place in various parts of a human brain at a given time. Of current technologies, functional MRI scans provide the best combination of spatial and temporal resolution. (p. 107)

Review Questions

1. Describe the method for inserting an electrode into an area of an animal's brain that cannot be seen from the surface. (p. 102)
2. What are some of the difficulties in interpreting the results of a lesion experiment? (p. 104)
3. Describe methods used to study the structure of a living human brain. (p. 105)
4. Describe methods used to study the functioning of a living human brain. (p. 107)

Thought Question

1. Multiple sclerosis destroys the myelin sheaths of axons. Why should we expect that evoked potentials would have longer-than-normal latencies in people with this disease?

Suggestion for Further Reading

Damasio, H. (1995). *Human brain anatomy in computerized images.* Oxford, England: Oxford University Press. A collection of MRI scans of human brains.

Terms

phrenology   nineteenth-century theory that personality types are related to bumps on the skull (p. 101)

stereotaxic instrument   device for the precise placement of electrodes in the head (p. 102)

bregma   a point on the skull where the frontal and parietal bones join (p. 102)

stereotaxic atlas   an atlas of the location of brain areas relative to external landmarks (p. 102)

lesion   damage to a structure (p. 103)

ablation   removal of a structure (p. 103)

sham lesion   control procedure for an experiment, in which an investigator inserts an electrode into a brain but does not pass a current (p. 103)

double dissociation of function   demonstration that one lesion impairs behavior A more than it impairs behavior B, while a second lesion impairs behavior B more than it impairs behavior A (p. 104)

microdialysis   method for measuring the concentrations of chemicals in a small brain area by enabling them to cross a membrane into an implanted tube (p. 105)

autoradiography   method of injecting a radioactively labeled chemical and then mapping the distribution of radiation in the brain (p. 105)

immunohistochemistry   method of using the immune system to label particular types of tissues (p. 105)

computerized axial tomography (CT scan, CAT scan) method of visualizing a living brain by injecting a dye into the blood and then passing x-rays through the head and recording them by detectors on the other side (p. 105)

magnetic resonance imaging (MRI) method of imaging a living brain by using a magnetic field and a radio-frequency field to make atoms with odd atomic weights all rotate in the same direction and then removing those fields and measuring the energy that the atoms release (p. 106)

electroencephalography (EEG) measurement of the brain's electrical activity through electrodes on the scalp (p. 107)

evoked potential electrical activity recorded from the brain, usually via electrodes on the scalp, in response to sensory stimuli (p. 107)

magnetoencephalography (MEG) the measurement of the brain's magnetic fields (p. 107)

positron-emission tomography (PET) a method of mapping activity in a living brain by recording the emission of radioactivity from injected chemicals (p. 107)

regional cerebral blood flow (rCBF) method of estimating activity of different areas of the brain by dissolving radioactive xenon in the blood and measuring radioactivity from different brain areas (p. 108)

functional magnetic resonance imaging (fMRI) a modified version of MRI that measures energies released by hemoglobin molecules in an MRI scan, and then determines the brain areas receiving the greatest supply of blood and oxygen (p. 109)

THE DEVELOPMENT AND
EVOLUTION OF THE BRAIN

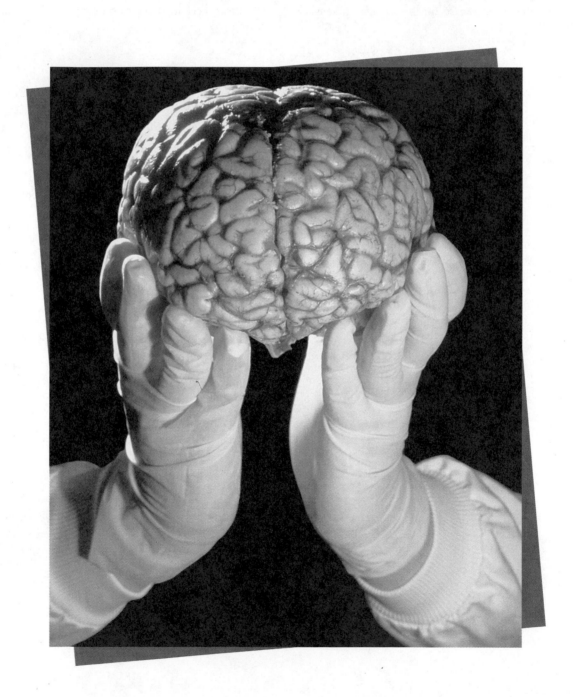

CHAPTER **FIVE**

MAIN**IDEAS**

1. The nervous system at first forms far more neurons than it needs and then eliminates those that do not establish suitable connections. It also forms more synapses than will survive, and discards the less active or less useful ones. Initial connections form largely by chemical attraction; later adjustment of synapses depends on experiences.
2. The human brain is the product of an evolutionary modification of the general mammalian neural organization. Brain differences among species are partly the result of changes in overall size and partly the result of detailed changes of connections.

"Some assembly required." Have you ever bought a device with those ominous words on the package? Sometimes all you have to do is attach two or three parts and tighten a few bolts. But in other cases you face page after page of incomprehensible instructions. I remember putting together my daughter's bicycle and wondering how something that appeared to be so simple could in fact be so complicated.

The human nervous system requires an enormous amount of assembly. Its structure and potential have changed enormously over the course of evolution; they also change enormously as we progress from the embryonic stage to adulthood. The instructions for assembling the nervous system are different from those for, say, a bicycle. Instead of "Put this piece here and that piece there," the instructions for the brain are "Put these axons here and those dendrites there, and then wait to see what happens. Keep the connections that seem to be working well, move some of the others around, throw away the rest, and then make some new ones similar to the ones that you kept." Moreover, the brain continues moving connections around; it literally takes a lifetime to put your brain together.

The Development of the Brain

As a college student you can probably perform a number of feats that you could not have done a few years ago: solve calculus problems, perhaps, or read a foreign language, or convincingly pretend that you understand James Joyce's novels. Have you developed these new skills because your brain has grown? No. Your brain has no doubt moved a number of synapses around, but its overall size and structure are about the same as they were before.

Now think of all the things that 1- or 2-year-old children can do that they could not do at birth. Have *they* developed these new skills because of brain growth? To a large extent, yes. Consider, for example, Jean Piaget's object permanence task, in which an observer shows a toy to an infant and then places it behind a barrier. Generally, a child younger than 9 months old does not reach around the barrier to retrieve the toy (Figure 5.1). Why not? The biological explanation is that the prefrontal cortex is necessary for responding to a signal that appears and then disappears, and the synapses of the prefrontal cortex develop massively between the ages of $7\frac{1}{2}$ and 12 months (Goldman-Rakic, 1987). Developing the ability to solve the object permanence task is a matter of developing the necessary neurons and synapses.

Behavioral development does not depend entirely on brain growth, of course; it also requires experience and synaptic readjustments in much the same way as an adult brain does. Furthermore, as we shall see, many processes of brain development depend on experience in complex ways that blur the distinction between learning and maturation. In this module we consider three major issues: the production of neurons, the growth of axons, and fine-tuning by experience.

The Growth and Differentiation of the Vertebrate Brain

The human central nervous system begins to form when the embryo is about two weeks old. First, the dorsal surface of the embryo thickens and then long thin

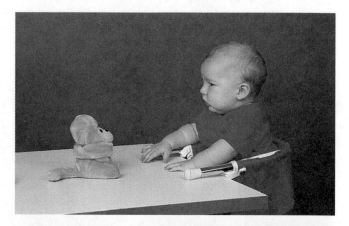
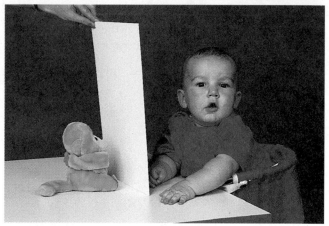

FIGURE **5.1**
Piaget's object permanence task
An infant sees a toy, then an investigator places a barrier in front of the toy. Infants younger than about 9 months old fail to reach for the hidden toy. Tasks that require a response to a stimulus that is no longer present depend on the prefrontal cortex, a structure that is slow to mature.

lips rise, curl, and merge, forming a neural tube surrounding a fluid-filled cavity (see Figure 5.2). The tube sinks under the surface of the skin and continues to develop. The forward end enlarges and differentiates into the hindbrain, midbrain, and forebrain (see Figure 5.3); the rest becomes the spinal cord. The fluid-filled cavity within the neural tube becomes the central canal of the

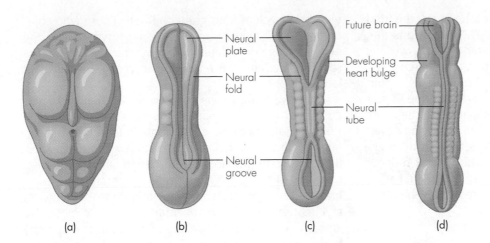

FIGURE **5.2**
Early development of the human central nervous system
The brain and spinal cord begin as folding lips surrounding a fluid-filled canal. Stages shown occur at approximately ages 2 to 3 weeks.

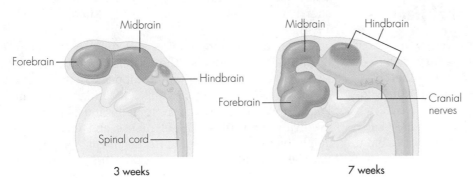

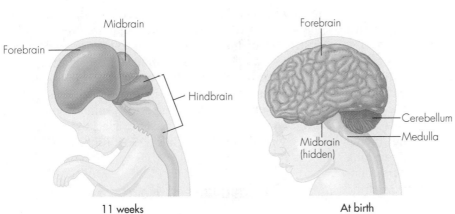

FIGURE **5.3**
Human brain at five stages of development
The brain already shows an adult structure at birth, although it continues to grow during the first year or so.
Source: Photo courtesy of Dana Copeland.

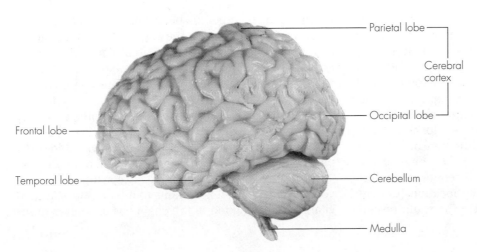

spinal cord and the four ventricles of the brain; the fluid is the cerebrospinal fluid (CSF). The developmental process is about the same in all vertebrates, varying mainly in speed, duration, and, ultimately, size.

At birth, the average human brain weighs about 350 grams (g). Certain areas of the forebrain are immature for the first few weeks, as indicated by their low levels of glucose use. Development is rapid, however, and areas of the brain that are almost silent at birth approach adult patterns of arousal within 7 to 8 months (Chugani & Phelps, 1986). At the end of the first year, the brain weighs 1,000 g, not much less than the adult weight of 1,200 to 1,400 g.

The Growth and Development of Neurons

The development of the nervous system naturally includes the production and alteration of neurons. Neuroscientists distinguish four major stages in the development of neurons: proliferation, migration, differentiation, and myelination.

Proliferation is the production of new cells. Early in development, cells lining the ventricles of the brain divide. Some of the new cells remain where they are, continuing to divide and redivide. Others become primitive neurons and glia that **migrate** (move) toward their eventual destinations in the brain. The cerebral cortex develops from the inside out; that is, each arriving wave of new cells migrates beyond the previous cells.

At first, a primitive neuron looks like any other cell. Gradually, the neuron **differentiates,** forming the axon and dendrites that provide its distinctive shape. Generally, the axon grows before the dendrites; in fact, the axon may grow while the neuron is migrating. (Some neurons leave an axon growing behind them like a long tail.) After the neuron reaches its final location, dendrites begin to form, very slowly at first. Most dendritic growth occurs later, when incoming axons are due to arrive.

Not only does a neuron look different from other kinds of body cells, but neurons in different parts of the brain differ from one another in their shapes and chemical components. When and how does a neuron "decide" which kind of neuron it is going to be? Evidently it is not a sudden all-or-none decision. In some cases, immature neurons experimentally transplanted from one part of the developing cortex to another develop all the properties characteristic of their new location (McConnell, 1992). However, immature neurons transplanted at a slightly later stage develop some of the properties of their new location while retaining some of the properties of neurons in their old location (Cohen-Tannoudji, Babinet, & Wassef, 1994). The result resembles the speech of immigrant children: Those who enter a country when they are very young may master the new language completely, whereas those entering at a slightly older age will retain the accent of their original language.

Finally, some axons **myelinate,** as glial cells produce the insulating sheaths that make rapid transmission possible. Neurons can operate before they develop myelin, although the myelin certainly improves their functioning. In humans, myelin forms first in the spinal cord and then in the hindbrain, midbrain, and forebrain. Unlike proliferation and migration of neurons, myelination continues for many years. A moderate amount of myelin is still forming at age 20, and in some brain areas it continues for additional decades, as shown in Figure 5.4 (Benes, Turtle, Khan, & Farol, 1994).

Brain maturation requires not only the development of neurons but also the organization of brain areas. As the brain grows, what happens at the microscopic level? Anthony-Samuel LaMantia and Dale Purves (1989) created a way to stain and photograph the living brain of an infant mouse and then photograph the same area later in development. They found that the brain adds new subdivisions during at least the first three weeks of life. As Figure 5.5b shows, the olfactory bulb has *glomeruli,* analogous to the columns of the visual cortex. The glomeruli that are present in the first week of life are somewhat expanded two weeks later, but additional glomeruli have also appeared. Evidently, the brain develops partly by the expansion of old units and partly by the addition of new units. A similar principle holds across species: Animals with large brains have many columns and specialized subdivisions within the cortex (Kaas, 1989; Killackey, 1990).

Determinants of Neuron Survival

Getting just the right number of neurons for each area of the nervous system is more complicated than it might seem. In order to be of any use, each neuron must receive axons from the right source and send its own axons to a cell in the right area. The various areas do not all develop at the same time, so in some cases the neurons in one area develop before any incoming axons have arrived or before any receptive sites are available for their own axons. If we examine a healthy adult nervous system, we find no leftover neurons that failed to make appropriate connections. How does the nervous system get the numbers to come out right?

Consider a specific example. The sympathetic nervous system chain sends axons to internal muscles and glands; each ganglion in the chain has enough neurons

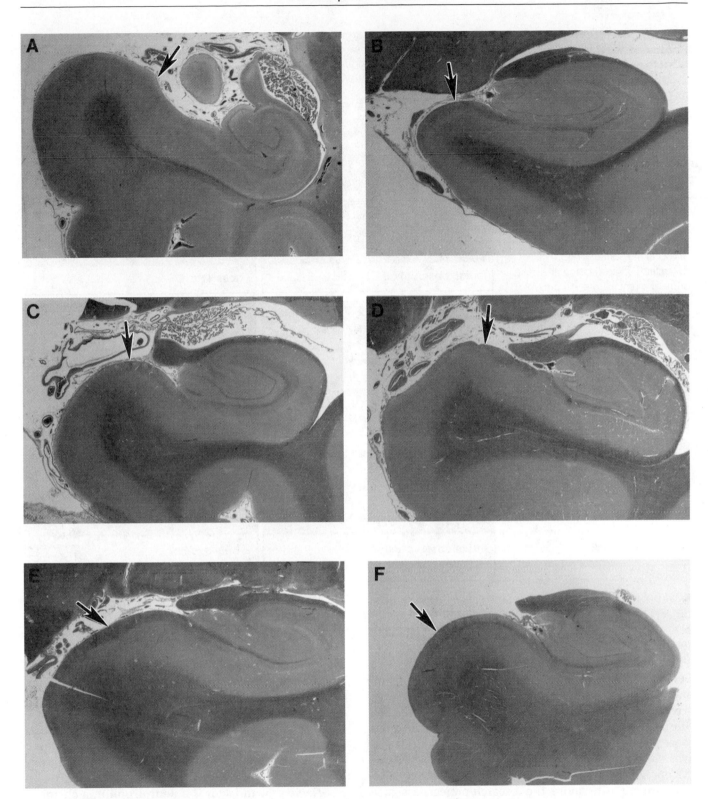

FIGURE **5.4**
Prolonged development of myelin in the human brain
In each part, the arrow points to the blue-stained myelinated axons in one layer of the hippocampus. This layer grows rapidly until age 20 and then more slowly until about age 60. The timetable for myelination varies from one brain area to another. A = birth, B = 8 years, C = 13 years, D = 24 years, E = 36 years, F = 57 years.   Source: Benes, Turtle, Khan, & Farol, 1994.

FIGURE **5.5**
Photos of sections of the olfactory bulbs of mice
Each of the numbers indicates a glomerulus, a cluster of neurons analogous to a column in the cerebral cortex. The initial observations (left) were taken in mice 4 to 6 days old. The later observations (right) were taken an hour later or two weeks later, using a different staining procedure. In (**a**), note the consistency of appearance over one hour; each glomerulus is easily recognized and is in the same position. In (**b**), after a 2-week delay, the 30 original glomeruli are still present and noticeably larger, and five new glomeruli have appeared, each indicated by a (+). The brain develops partly by growth of old units and partly by addition of new units.   Source: LaMantia & Purves, 1989.

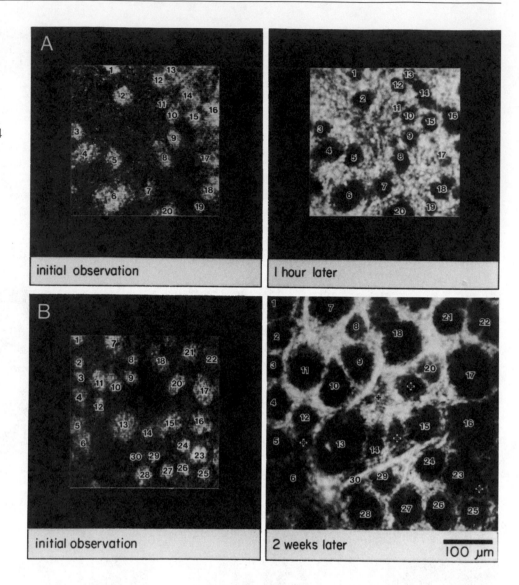

to supply all the muscles or glands in its area, but no more. Long ago, one explanation was that the muscles sent chemical messages to the sympathetic ganglion to tell it how many neurons to form. One of the researchers who disconfirmed that hypothesis was Rita Levi-Montalcini. If you were going to plan life circumstances to encourage scientific success, you certainly would not have planned Levi-Montalcini's early life. She was a young Italian Jewish woman. The Nazis were persecuting and exterminating Jews, World War II was destroying the Italian economy, and almost no one encouraged any woman to pursue a scientific or medical career. Furthermore, the research projects assigned to her as a young medical student were virtually impossible, as she described in her autobiography (Levi-Montalcini, 1988). Nevertheless, she developed a love for research and eventually discovered that each sympathetic ganglion generates a certain number of axons regardless of the size of the muscles or glands that they will eventually innervate. The muscles do not determine how many axons *form;* they determine how many *survive.*

When a neuron of the sympathetic nervous system forms a synapse onto an organ muscle, the muscle delivers a protein called **nerve growth factor (NGF)** that promotes the survival and growth of the axon (Levi-Montalcini, 1987). An axon that does not receive enough NGF degenerates, and its cell body dies. Each neuron starts life with a "suicide program": If its axon does not make contact with an appropriate postsynaptic cell by a certain age, the neuron kills itself, through a process called **apoptosis.** NGF is the postsynaptic cell's way of telling the incoming axon, "I'll be your partner. Don't kill yourself."

Nerve growth factor is a **neurotrophin,** a chemical that promotes the survival and activity of neurons. (The word *trophin* is derived from an ancient Greek word for *nourishment.*) In addition to NGF, the nervous system responds to *brain-derived neurotrophic factor* (BDNF), *neurotrophins 3, 4/5,* and 6 (NT-3, NT-4/5, and NT-6), and others (Götz et al., 1993; Mendell, 1995). The neurotrophins act in several ways. First, early in development they cause selected axons to survive instead of submitting to apoptosis; different neurotrophins are active for different kinds of axons. Second, at later ages, activation of a neuron by synapses or hormones causes it to secrete neurotrophins that increase the branching of incoming axons and enhance the behaviors they control (Calandrei & Alleva, 1995; Cohen-Cory & Fraser, 1995). Third, in response to nervous system injury, neurotrophins decrease pain and increase regrowth of damaged axons (Beck et al., 1995; Ren, Thomas, & Dubner, 1995; Tomac et al., 1995). Researchers hope eventually to harness the power of neurotrophins to relieve certain diseases that attack the nervous system.

Not only the sympathetic ganglia but all areas of the developing nervous system initially overproduce neurons, in some cases developing two or three times as many as will actually survive into adulthood. Each part of the brain has a period of massive cell death, becoming littered with dead and dying cells (Figure 5.6). This loss of cells does not indicate that something is wrong; it is a natural part of development (Finlay & Pallas, 1989).

Why does the CNS produce more neurons than it needs? Here are two possible explanations:

• The extra neurons allow for error correction. Even if some axons fail to reach appropriate targets, enough others will. In a sense, overproduction followed by death of superfluous cells is an opportunity for survival of the fittest.
• The extra neurons enable the CNS to compensate for unpredictable variations in body size. For example, when the motor neuron axons begin growing from the spinal cord toward the leg muscles, there is no way to predict exactly how large that leg will be or how many muscle fibers it will have. The spinal cord starts by producing an abundance of neurons; by discarding the excess, it ends with just the necessary number.

Pathfinding by Axons

For the nervous system to operate properly, axons must reach their proper targets and form synapses with the correct neurons. How do they find their way?

Basic Strategies for Directing an Axon to Its Target

Suppose you operate a government office in Washington, D.C. You decide to install private telegraph cables to convey secret messages. You tell one of your employees, "Here, Carlos, take this cable and run it across the street to the Office of Bureaucratic Mismanagement." Because it is so near, you hardly give a thought

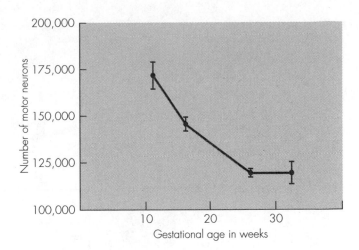

FIGURE **5.6**
Cell loss during development of the nervous system
The graph shows the number of motor neurons in the ventral spinal cord of human fetuses. Note that the number of motor neurons is highest at 11 weeks and drops steadily until about 25 weeks. This is when motor neuron axons make synapses with muscles. Those that fail to make synapses die.   Source: From Forger & Breedlove, 1987.

as to how he is going to find the way. Then you tell another employee, "Here, Carla, take this very long cable and stretch it to the mayor's office in Truth or Consequences, New Mexico." (Carla got the tough job.) Now you definitely have to worry: Will Carla find a reasonably direct route from here to there? Will she find her way at all? You have to make sure that she has a map and a compass. Or, if some other employee made the same trip last week and carefully left a trail, you can just tell Carla to follow the purple arrows along the side of the road.

The developing nervous system faces a similar problem. It sends some of its axons over enormous distances. For example, the cerebral cortex sends certain axons all the way to the spinal cord, and the spinal cord sends motor axons to muscles in the arms, legs, and elsewhere. How do these axons find their way to the correct locations?

Chemical Pathfinding by Axons

A famous biologist, Paul Weiss (1924), conducted an experiment in which he grafted an extra leg to a salamander and then waited for axons to grow into it. (Such an experiment could never work with a mammal. Salamanders and other amphibians can regenerate many parts of their bodies that mammals cannot. They also generate new axon branches to an extra, grafted-on limb.) After the axons reached the muscles, the extra leg, positioned next to one of the hind legs, moved in perfect synchrony with the normal adjacent leg.

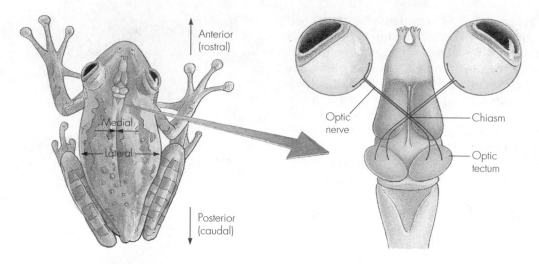

FIGURE 5.7

The optic tectum is a large structure in fish, amphibians, reptiles, and birds. Its location corresponds to the midbrain of mammals, but its function is more elaborate, analogous to what the cerebral cortex does in mammals.
Source: After Romer, 1962.

One interpretation of these results is that each axon to the normal limb had developed a branch that found its way to exactly the same muscle in the extra limb. Weiss dismissed that possibility as unbelievable. He suggested instead that the nerves attached to muscles at random and then sent a variety of messages, each one tuned to a different muscle. In other words, it did not matter which axon was attached to which muscle. The muscles were like a series of radios, each tuned to a different station. They all received the same signals through the air, but each one responded only to the station to which it was tuned.

Specificity of axon connections   Weiss's theory has not stood the test of time. Later evidence supported the interpretation he dismissed as unbelievable: The salamander's extra leg moved in synchrony with its neighbor because each axon had sent a branch to each leg and each branch had attached to exactly the same muscle. That is, a growing axon finds its way to the correct target.

Since the time of Weiss's work, most of the research on axon growth has dealt with how sensory axons find their way to the correct targets in the brain. (The issues and difficulties are the same as those for axons finding their way to muscles in the periphery.) Roger Sperry, who had been a student of Weiss, conducted much of the decisive research in this area. In one study, he cut the optic nerves of some newts. In amphibians, unlike mammals, a damaged optic nerve grows back and contacts the *tectum*, the main visual area of fish, amphibians, reptiles, and birds (see Figure 5.7). Sperry found that when the new synapses formed, the newt regained normal vision.

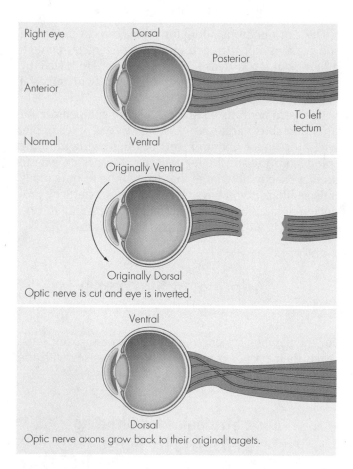

FIGURE 5.8

Summary of Sperry's experiment on nerve connections in newts

After he cut the optic nerve and inverted the eye, the optic nerve axons grew back to their original targets, not to the targets corresponding to the eye's current position.

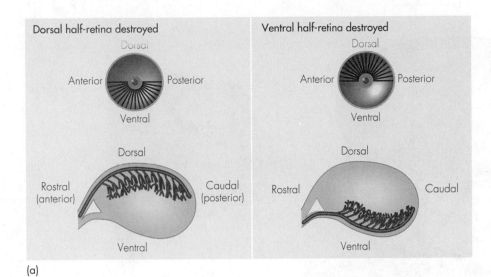

Dorsal half-retina destroyed

Ventral half-retina destroyed

(a)

FIGURE **5.9**
After half of the goldfish retina is destroyed and the optic nerve from the other half is cut, the optic nerve grows back to just half of the optic tectum, the part that it ordinarily innervates. (**a**) After the destruction of the dorsal or ventral half-retina, axons from the remaining half-retina regenerate to the medial-dorsal or lateral-ventral half of the tectum, respectively. (**b**) After the destruction of the anterior or posterior half-retina, axons from the remaining half of the retina regenerate to the appropriate half of the tectum.
Source: Based on Attardi & Sperry, 1963.

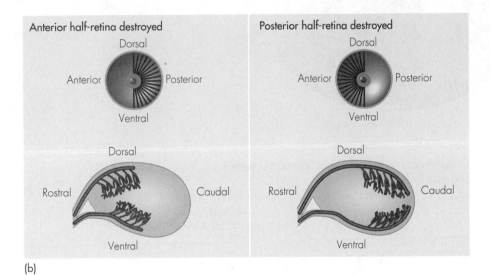

Anterior half-retina destroyed

Posterior half-retina destroyed

(b)

To discover how axons find their targets, Sperry (1943) repeated the experiment, but this time, after he cut each optic nerve, he rotated the eye by 180 degrees. When the axons grew back to the tectum, would the axons rotated to the dorsal side of the eye go where axons from the dorsal side ordinarily go, and would the axons now on the ventral side go where axons on the ventral side ordinarily go? Or would each axon ignore the fact that it was in a new position and find its way back to its *original* target, indicating that it "knew" where to go? Sperry found that the axons from what had originally been the dorsal side of the retina (which was now on the ventral side) grew back to their original target area of the tectum—the area responsible for vision in the dorsal side of the retina. Likewise, axons from what had once been the ventral side of the retina (now on the dorsal side) grew back to the tectal area responsible for vision on the ventral side of the retina. The newt now saw the world upside down and backward. It responded to stimuli in the sky as if they were on the ground, to stimuli on the left as if they were on the right (see Figure 5.8). Evidently, each axon regenerated to

the area of the tectum where it had originally been.

In another experiment, Domenica Attardi and Roger Sperry (1963) damaged parts of goldfish retinas and cut their optic nerves. The optic nerve from the intact part of each retina grew back to the tectal area that it ordinarily innervated, as Figure 5.9 shows. Again, each axon found its appropriate target. The tectal areas originally innervated by the damaged parts of the retina now had vacant synapses, with no incoming axons. As with the previous experiment, these results suggested that each axon might be following a chemical trail to its destination, like a bloodhound sniffing its way through the forest. We now know that some cells emit chemicals that attract a given axon, while other cells emit chemicals that repel the axon (Tessier-Lavigne & Goodman, 1996).

Chemical gradients   The next question was, how specific a target might the axon have? Did an axon from a newt's or goldfish's retina have to find the tectal cell with exactly the right chemical marker on its surface, like a key finding the right lock? Such a mechanism

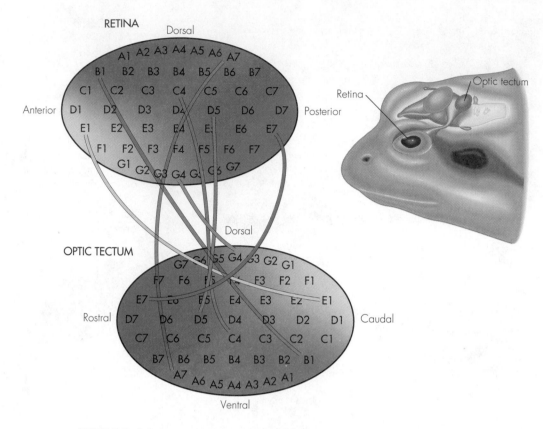

FIGURE **5.10**
**Retinal axons match up with neurons in the tectum by
following two gradients**

The protein TOP_{DV} is concentrated mostly in the dorsal retina and the ventral tectum. Axons rich in TOP_{DV} attach to tectal neurons that are also rich in that chemical. Similarly, a second protein directs axons from the posterior retina to the rostral portion of the tectum.

hardly seems plausible. Just think of the billions of axons in the nervous system. Does the body have to synthesize a separate chemical marker for each one of them?

No. Neurons in the retina are marked with a gradient of chemicals, and so are the neurons in the tectum. One such chemical is a protein known as TOP_{DV}. (TOP for *top*ography; DV for *d*orso-*v*entral.) This protein is 30 times more concentrated in the neurons of the dorsal retina than it is in the neurons of the ventral retina, and it is 10 times more concentrated in the ventral tectum than in the dorsal tectum. As axons from the retina grow toward the tectum, the retinal axons with the greatest concentration of TOP_{DV} connect to the tectal cells with the highest concentration of that chemical; the axons with the lowest concentration connect to the tectal cells with the lowest concentration. A similar gradient of another protein aligns the axons along the anterior–posterior axis (Sanes, 1993). (See Figure

5.10.) Other chemical gradients have been found for other brain areas and other species (Yuasa, Hirano, Yamagata, & Noda, 1996). Evidently, chemical gradients are a widespread mechanism.

Once an axon reaches the correct brain location, it does not have to search for its one and only target. For example, axons from the anterior ventral part of an amphibian retina might reach the tectum, only to find that something has destroyed the tectal neurons to which these axons ordinarily should connect. The axons then make contact with the nearest approximations that they can find to their normal targets. In two similar experiments, investigators removed the caudal half of the tectum of a goldfish and cut the optic nerve. Ordinarily, axons from the anterior side of the retina make contact with the caudal tectum. When those axons reached the tectum, they formed synapses with the most caudal portion of what was left of the tectum (Figure 5.11). That is, the whole optic nerve made a compressed pro-

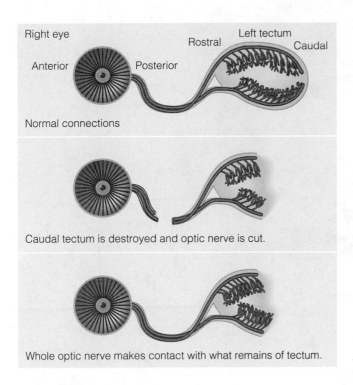

Right eye   Left tectum
                                Rostral   Caudal
Anterior   Posterior

Normal connections

Caudal tectum is destroyed and optic nerve is cut.

Whole optic nerve makes contact with what remains of tectum.

FIGURE **5.11**
Regeneration of the goldfish optic nerve after damage to the optic tectum
Experimenters cut the optic nerve and destroyed the caudal part of the tectum. Then the axons that ordinarily innervate the caudal tectum grew back to the most caudal part of the remaining tectum. Other axons arranged themselves in the correct order as before, though not on the same target cells as before.   Source: Based on results of Gaze & Sharma, 1970; Yoon, 1971.

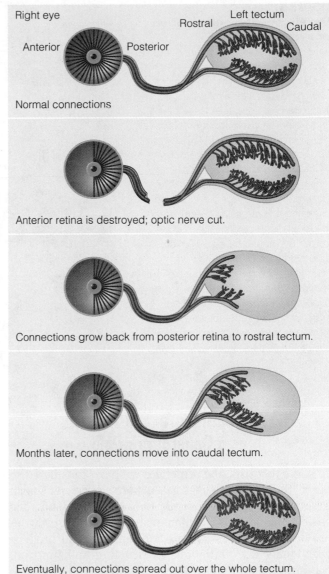

Right eye   Left tectum
                                Rostral   Caudal
Anterior   Posterior

Normal connections

Anterior retina is destroyed; optic nerve cut.

Connections grow back from posterior retina to rostral tectum.

Months later, connections move into caudal tectum.

Eventually, connections spread out over the whole tectum.

FIGURE **5.12**
Regrowth of a goldfish's optic nerve after damage to half of the retina
Experimenters destroyed the anterior retina and cut the optic nerve. At first, axons from the posterior retina grew back to their original target cells in the rostral tectum (as they did in the earlier experiment by Attardi and Sperry). However, as months passed, connections moved into the vacant caudal portion of the tectum and eventually spread out over the whole tectum.   Source: Based on results of Schmidt, Cicerone, & Easter, 1977.

jection onto the now-small tectum (Gaze & Sharma, 1970; Yoon, 1971).

In a related experiment, investigators destroyed the anterior half of the retina of a goldfish and then cut the optic nerve, letting the axon from the posterior half-retina regenerate. Initially, it connected only to its normal area, the rostral part of the tectum. Months later, however, some of the axons began creeping from the edge of the rostral tectum into the adjacent areas of the caudal tectum (Figure 5.12). This process continued until the axons had spread themselves evenly over the entire tectum (Schmidt, Cicerone, & Easter, 1977).

As these experiments suggest, when axons initially reach their targets, each one forms synapses onto several target cells in approximately the correct location, and each target cell receives synapses from a large number of axons. Gradually, the postsynaptic cell strengthens its synapses with some of those axons and weakens or discards its connections with others. Figure 5.13 summarizes the results: At first, axons and post-

synaptic cells have many tentative connections with one another; later they develop fewer but stronger attachments. (It's a little like dating.) They do not have to find an exact match chemically; they accept the available partner that is closest to their chemical preference.

FIGURE **5.13**
Development by elimination of synapses

(**a**) Early in development, each muscle fiber receives synapses from branches of several motor axons. The muscle fiber gradually strengthens its synapse with one axon and rejects the others. (However, an axon can form synapses with many muscle fibers.) (**b**) Early in development, neurons in the ganglia of the sympathetic nervous system receive synapses from many axons. Later, each cell rejects the incoming axons from some neurons and accepts the axons from others. Although the cell as a whole may accept axons from numerous different neurons, typically, each dendrite forms lasting synapses with only one axon. That axon may, however, form a great many branches and therefore a great many synapses onto that dendrite. Source: After Purves & Lichtman, 1980.

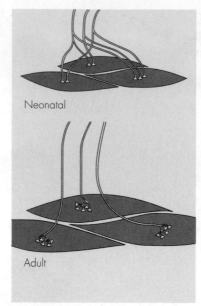

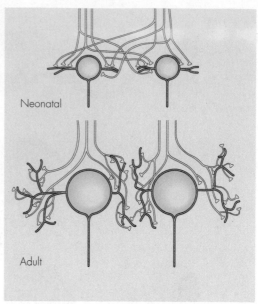

(**a**) Muscle fibers

(**b**) Sympathetic ganglion cells

Competition Among Axons as a General Principle

To some theorists, the principles we have considered so far in this chapter suggest a general principle, which Gerald Edelman (1987) calls **neural Darwinism.** The basic principle of Darwinian evolution is that during reproduction, gene mutations and reassortment produce individuals with variations in structure and function. Natural selection favors some variations while weeding out the rest.

Similarly, in the development of the nervous system we start with more neurons and synapses than we shall keep. Synapses form somewhat randomly at first, and then a selection process keeps some and rejects others. A muscle fiber selects only one incoming axon, based mostly on chemical factors. A neuron selects the most active incoming axon, or combinations of two or more incoming axons, especially if they often send synchronized signals. In this manner, the most successful axons or axon combinations survive; the less active or less informative ones fail to sustain active synapses.

The principle of competition among axons is an important one, although we should use the analogy with Darwinian evolution cautiously. So far as we know, mutations in the genes occur completely at random. The growth of axonal branches and new synapses is partly random but partly controlled by chemical guidance and trophic factors. Still, in both cases, the most successful types proliferate at the expense of the less

successful, and for both, a change in the environment can cause a different type of individual to thrive.

Fine-Tuning by Experience

The genetic instructions for assembling your nervous system are only approximate. Because of the unpredictability of life, we have evolved the ability to redesign our brains (within limits) in response to our experience (Shatz, 1992). Our genes set up an enormous number of neurons, connections, and potential connections, and our experience determines which ones will survive.

Let's start with a relatively simple example of this principle. If you live in a complex and challenging environment, you need an elaborate nervous system. Ordinarily, a laboratory rat lives in a simple and most unchallenging environment: alone in a small, bare, gray cage with food and water. Imagine a rat that spends its life in a more stimulating environment: in a larger cage, among ten or so other rats, with a few little pieces of junk to explore or play with. Researchers sometimes call this an enriched environment, but it is enriched only in contrast to the impoverished environment of the usual rat cage.

Compared to a rat kept in an individual cage, a rat in the more stimulating environment develops a thicker

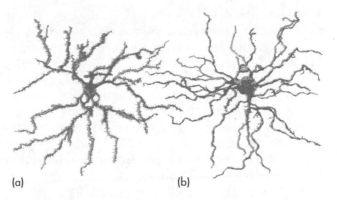

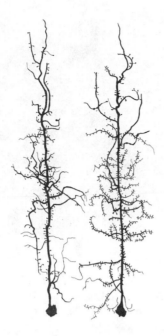

FIGURE **5.14**
Effect of a stimulating environment on neuronal branching
A jewel fish reared in isolation develops neurons with fewer branches (left). A fish reared with others has more neuronal branches (right).   Source: Photo courtesy of Richard Coss.

FIGURE **5.15**
Dendritic spines in the song-control area of a mynah bird's brain
(**a**) Early in the bird's first year of life, the dendrites have an enormous number of tiny spines, each of them evidently corresponding to one of the enormous variety of potential song elements that the bird might learn. (**b**) About a year later, the dendrites have far fewer spines, but the surviving spines have grown much larger. These presumably correspond to song elements that the bird has actually learned to produce.   Source: Rausch & Scheich, 1982.

cortex, more dendritic branching, and improved performance on many tests of learning (Rosenzweig & Bennett, 1996). Similar results have been reported for species as remote as jewel fish (Coss & Globus, 1979) and honeybees (Coss, Brandon, & Globus, 1980). (See Figure 5.14.) Humans with extensive education tend to have longer and more widely branched dendrites than less-educated people do, although we cannot be sure whether learning promotes the dendritic branching or whether people with wide dendritic branching succeed in school and therefore stay longer (Jacobs, Schall, & Scheibel, 1993).

Although the effects of environmental enrichment can occur at any time, some effects are more prominent if they occur early. For example, young birds of certain species learn their song by selecting some elements out of a set of possible song components and discarding other possible elements (Marler & Nelson, 1992). In doing so, they apparently magnify some dendritic branches and shrink others. One portion of a mynah bird's brain is essential to its ability to sing. (Mynah birds, like parrots and mockingbirds, excel at imitating other birds' songs.) In that brain area, one kind of neuron has a great many *dendritic spines* (little outgrowths) early in the first year of life. At this time, the mynah bird is rapidly learning a variety of new songs. By the end of the first year, each of those neurons has fewer dendritic

spines than it had at the start of the year, but the surviving spines are larger than they used to be (Figure 5.15). Evidently, the multitude of tiny dendritic spines at the start of the year made it possible for the bird to learn an unpredictable variety of new songs. By the end of the year, the mynah bird has learned many songs and strengthened the spines needed for those songs, but by losing other spines it has decreased its ability to learn additional songs.

Profound effects also occur if an animal is deprived of normal experience in early life. In one experiment, kittens were raised without visual experience. One part of cats' parietal lobe, known as the *anterior ectosylvian region,* ordinarily responds only to visual stimuli. In the visually deprived kittens, however, many of the neurons in this area became responsive to auditory or touch stimuli, enabling the kittens to localize sounds with a greater degree of accuracy than normal cats do (Rauschecker, 1995). Similarly, in people who become blind early in life, certain parts of the visual cortex become responsive to auditory and touch stimuli, including Braille symbols (Kujala et al., 1995; Sadato et al., 1996).

Particularly powerful evidence of the effects of early experience on brain development comes from studies of children with extensive early music training. Some people develop absolute pitch—the ability to hear a note and identify it, such as B♭ or C♯. Perhaps it is more accurate to say they "retain" the ability rather than "develop" it; many children have absolute pitch, and nearly all lose it by adulthood. In any case, almost every adult who shows this ability began extensive music training early, generally by age 6 or 7, and continued practicing into adulthood (Takeuchi & Hulse, 1993). Adults who have absolute pitch also have larger than usual development in one area of the temporal cortex in the left hemisphere (Schlaug, Jäncke, Huang, & Steinmetz, 1995). If we assume that absolute pitch is the result of the early music training (rather than the cause of it), the extra development of the temporal cortex is also the result of the music training.

A related study used magnetoencephalography (MEG; see Figure 4.30) to compare the postcentral gyrus of nonmusicians to people who had extensive experience in playing stringed instruments, especially the violin. As you may recall from Chapter 4, the postcentral gyrus is the primary somatosensory cortex, with each area along the gyrus responding to a particular area of the body. In string players, who use the left hand to finger the strings, the postcentral gyrus of the right hemisphere has a larger than usual area responding to sensations from the fingers of the left hand (Elbert, Pantev, Wienbruch, Rockstroh, & Taub, 1995). The left hemispheres had a normal-sized area devoted to sensations from the right hand. As shown in Figure 5.16b, the area devoted to the left fingers was larger in those who began learning a stringed instrument early. However, those who started early had also continued for more years than those who started later; therefore we do not know whether the difference in brain structure depends on total years of study or on the age of starting. Nevertheless, it is clear that, within limits, practicing a skill can reorganize or restructure the brain.

Combinations of Chemical and Experiential Effects

The results discussed so far suggest a two-stage process. First, axons find their approximate targets by following a chemical gradient, and then they strengthen some connections and discard others, in response to experience. Like many generalizations about the nervous system, this one is not entirely correct. Even during early prenatal development, when axons are first reaching their destinations, they produce spontaneous action potentials, and if those are blocked, the axons fail to produce normal branches and connections (Herrmann & Shatz, 1995).

What use could action potentials have during prenatal development, when the embryo has only very limited and not very meaningful experience? Consider an example: One part of the thalamus, the *lateral geniculate* (Figure 4.14), receives its input from the retinas of the eyes. During prenatal development, each lateral

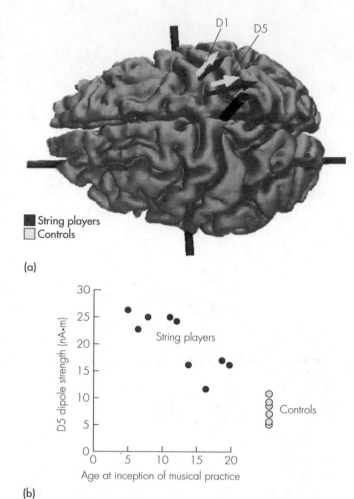

(a)

(b)

FIGURE **5.16**
Expanded cortical representation of fingers on string players' left hand
(**a**) The yellow and black arrows show the dipole moments (an MEG measure of neuronal activity) in response to stimulation of the thumb (D1) and little finger (D5), superimposed on an MRI scan of a brain. The red bars merely show the left-right, dorsoventral, and anterior–posterior axes. Note that the representation of the left thumb is equal for string players and controls, but that the representation of the fifth finger is significantly greater for the string players. Representations of the right hand, not shown in the figure, were equal for musicians and nonmusicians. (**b**) The brain representation of the little finger (D5) was greater in those who had started learning a stringed instrument early than in those who had started late.   Source: From Elbert, Pantev, Wienbruch, Rockstroh, & Taub, 1995.

geniculate cell initially receives input from a number of retinal axons, which produce spontaneous action potentials. Repeated waves of activity sweep over the retina from one side to the other. Consequently, axons from adjacent areas of the retina are almost simultaneously activated. Each lateral geniculate cell selects a group of axons that are simultaneously active at this time; as a result, it becomes responsive to a group of receptors adjacent to one another on the retina (Meister, Wong, Baylor, & Shatz, 1991).

The Vulnerable Developing Brain

Brain development requires a complicated interplay of cells, chemicals, and timing that can easily go wrong. For example, a genetic mutation might cause the brain to produce chemically abnormal neurotrophins or receptors, or to produce the neurotrophins or receptors in abnormal amounts or at the wrong time. The possibilities are so numerous that it is sometimes difficult to determine the cause of a brain abnormality. (See Digression 5.1.) As of 1994, researchers had identified more than 200 genetic mutations capable of producing mental retardation (Thapar, Gottesman, Owen, O'Donovan, & McGuffin, 1994).

The developing brain is also more vulnerable than the mature brain is to the effects of malnutrition (Levitsky & Strupp, 1995), toxic chemicals, and infections. For example, impaired thyroid function in adulthood produces lethargy and decreased alertness (among other symptoms), from which the person can recover by thyroid replacement. A similar thyroid impairment in infancy produces permanent mental retardation and slowed body growth; animal studies have noted a loss of the normal fear that is usually evoked by an unfamiliar setting (Darba et al., 1995). Thyroid deficiency was more widespread in the past because of inadequate iodine in the diet; today's table salt is almost always fortified with iodine.

Exposure to alcohol also impairs the developing brain much more than it does the mature brain. The children of mothers who drink heavily during pregnancy may be born with **fetal alcohol syndrome,** a condition marked by decreased alertness, hyperactivity, varying degrees of mental retardation, motor problems, heart defects, and facial abnormalities (Figure 5.17). Dendrites tend to be short, with few branches. Researchers are not sure what amount of alcohol, if any, it is safe to drink during pregnancy, and the risk probably depends on the stage of pregnancy as well as on the amount of alcohol. Even in children who do not show any facial or other visible abnormalities, the more the mother drank during pregnancy, the more impulsive the child and the worse the school performance (Hunt, Streissguth, Kerr, & Carmichael-Olson, 1995). To play it safe, pregnant women should avoid alcohol and other drugs (even tobacco) as much as possible during pregnancy (Rush & Callahan, 1989).

FIGURE **5.17**
Child with fetal alcohol syndrome
Note the folds around the eyes. Many children exposed to smaller amounts of alcohol before birth will have behavioral deficits without facial signs.

IN CLOSING

Brain Development

Considering the number of ways in which abnormal chemicals can disrupt brain development, let alone the possible varieties of abnormal experience, it is a wonder that any of us develop normally. Evidently, the system has enough redundancies or margin for error that we can function even if all our connections do not develop quite perfectly. There are many ways for development to go wrong, but somehow the system usually manages to work.

Summary

1. In vertebrate embryos, the central nervous system begins as a tube surrounding a fluid-filled cavity. Developing neurons proliferate, migrate, differentiate, and myelinate. (p. 114)
2. Initially, the nervous system develops far more neurons than will actually survive. As they send out their axons, some make synaptic contacts with cells that release to them nerve growth factor or other neurotrophins. The neurons that receive neurotrophins survive; the others die. (p. 118)
3. Growing axons manage to find their way close to the right locations by following a chemical gradient. (p. 121)

Rett Syndrome: An Anomaly of Brain Development

Rett syndrome is regarded as the most common cause of severe mental retardation in girls; if it occurs at all in boys, it is very rare. (The neurological literature has reported two apparent cases in boys.) Girls with Rett syndrome seem almost normal for the first year or two after birth, but during the next few years they gradually lose their ability to speak and to use their hands usefully; they also develop a number of repetitive movements (Percy, 1995).

Because Rett syndrome develops almost exclusively in girls, researchers originally assumed that it reflected an abnormality of the X chromosome—perhaps an X-linked dominant gene or a fragile X chromosome. According to this assumption, Rett syndrome occurs only in girls because a boy with the mutant gene or fragile chromosome would not survive, having no second X chromosome. However, research has failed to find any evidence for abnormal X chromosomes either in the girls with Rett syndrome or in their parents (Migeon, Dunn, Thomas, Schmeckpeper, & Naidu, 1995). Some girls with Rett syndrome have a fragile X chromosome, but most do not. Broken chromosomes are indeed more common than average in children with Rett syndrome—found in 16 percent of their cells as opposed to 8 percent of the cells of normal girls—but the number of chromosome breaks does not correlate consistently with the presence or absence of Rett syndrome (Telvi, Leboyer, Chiron, Feingold, & Ponsot, 1994).

How, then, can we explain why Rett syndrome is limited almost exclusively to girls? A sex-limited gene is a possibility, but most sex-limited genes exert their effects at or after puberty—such as the genes that control breast growth or chest and facial hair. At present, the sex ratio for Rett syndrome remains unexplained.

A further puzzle is that the progressive loss of speech and hand function suggests that Rett syndrome is associated with gradual brain degeneration. However, autopsies of the brains of Rett syndrome girls who died at various ages have shown neuronal abnormalities that do not increase with age. The autopsies fail to show any evidence of the glial proliferation that usually occurs around dead neurons (Percy, 1995). The underlying problem in Rett syndrome appears to be not a loss of neurons but an abnormality in their development. In particular, neurons in many brain areas have relatively short dendrites with few branches and spines. Many dendrites have long bare regions that are apparently devoid of synapses (Armstrong, Dunn, Antalffy, & Trivedi, 1995; Belichenko & Dahlström, 1995).

The currently popular hypothesis is that Rett syndrome is caused by a deficit or aberration in neurotrophins, such that

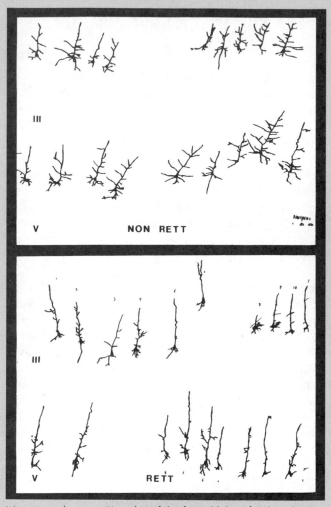

Neurons in laminae III and V of the frontal lobe of girls without Rett syndrome (above) and with Rett syndrome (below). Note the bare areas on the dendrites of the Rett girls.   Source: Armstrong, Dunn, Antalffy, & Trivedi, 1995.

neurons fail to develop their normal synaptic connections. Perhaps, as the children grow older, they may even lose synaptic connections. If so, Rett syndrome may turn out to be a new type of neurodegenerative condition, in which the person loses synapses but not neurons.

4. Axons identify their targets relatively, not absolutely. For example, an axon that ordinarily connects to the extreme caudal part of the tectum will, if deprived of its normal target, connect to the most caudal area available. (p. 122)
5. Variations in experience can increase or decrease the amount of brain devoted to a particular sensory system. (p. 124)
6. The action potentials of an axon are important in synapse formation even at the earliest stages of development. (p. 126)
7. The brain is vulnerable during early development; abnormalities of genes, nutrition, or the chemical environment can produce disorders of various magnitudes. (p. 127)

Review Questions

1. What biological explanation applies to the inability of an 8-month-old child to reach around a barrier to find a hidden toy? (p. 114)
2. What process enables the nervous system to have only as many neurons as target cells for the axons to innervate? (p. 118)
3. Who has more neurons, an infant or an adult? Why? (p. 119)
4. How did Roger Sperry establish that each axon finds its way to a relatively specific target, instead of connecting at random? (p. 121)
5. What does the term *neural Darwinism* mean? (p. 124)
6. How does the brain of a stringed instrument player differ from that of other people? (p. 126)
7. What evidence indicates that Rett syndrome is not due to a progressive loss of neurons, even though the behavior deteriorates over time? (p. 128)

Thought Question

1. Biologists can develop antibodies against nerve growth factor (that is, molecules that inactivate nerve growth factor). What would happen if someone injected such antibodies into a developing nervous system?

Suggestions for Further Reading

Levi-Montalcini, R. (1988). *In praise of imperfection.* New York: Basic Books. Autobiography by the discoverer of nerve growth factor.

Science. (15 November 1996). A special issue with a series of articles devoted to the development of the brain.

Shatz, C. J. (1992, September). The developing brain. *Scientific American, 267* (3), 60–67. Excellent review of brain development, by one of the leading researchers.

Terms

proliferation the production of new cells (p. 116)

migration movement of neurons toward their eventual destinations in the brain (p. 116)

differentiation formation of the axon and dendrites that gives a neuron its distinctive shape (p. 116)

myelination the development of a myelin sheath around an axon (p. 116)

nerve growth factor (NGF) protein that promotes the survival and growth of axons in the sympathetic nervous system and certain axons in the brain (p. 118)

apoptosis the developmental program by which a neuron kills itself if its axon has not made contact with an appropriate postsynaptic cell by a certain age (p. 118)

neurotrophin chemical that promotes survival and activity of neurons (p. 118)

neural Darwinism principle that, in the development of the nervous system, synapses form somewhat randomly at first, and then a selection process keeps some and rejects others (p. 124)

fetal alcohol syndrome condition resulting from prenatal exposure to alcohol and marked by decreased alertness, hyperactivity, varying degrees of mental retardation, motor problems, heart defects, and facial abnormalities (p. 127)

Rett syndrome condition found exclusively or almost exclusively in girls, marked by a gradual deterioration of hand use and language abilities beginning at age 1 or 2 years (p. 128)

The Evolution of the Brain and Its Capacities

We humans pride ourselves on being the dominant animal species on earth. By "dominant," we do not mean that we are the most numerous, but that we control the environment. We tear down and replant forests, extract gas and oil from the ground, and bury our garbage. We capture and domesticate animals we consider useful and kill animals we consider dangerous, until their numbers dwindle to near-extinction, when we start to protect them. In one way or another, we make decisions that affect nearly all other species.

Human genes differ from those of chimpanzees and gorillas by only a few percent. Somehow, a relatively slight amount of genetic change enormously altered what our brains can do. What made the human brain capable of language, culture, and all its other accomplishments? If we could explain the evolution of the human brain, we would probably understand a great deal more than we now do about intelligence.

Inferring the Evolution of the Brain and Behavior

Shortly we shall examine some differences among animal brains, as shown in Figure 5.18. No doubt you have seen similar illustrations in other texts, and you will probably see them again in the future. If I do not explain carefully, you may assume that you are looking at an evolutionary sequence—for example, the codfish brain evolved into the frog brain, which evolved into the alligator brain, and so forth, until it reached the human brain. In reality, nothing of the sort is true (Campbell & Hodos, 1991). The remote ancestors that gave rise to today's species were not the same as any of today's fish, amphibians, reptiles, and so forth.

What *did* the brains of our ancient ancestors look like, and how did ancient animals behave? We cannot

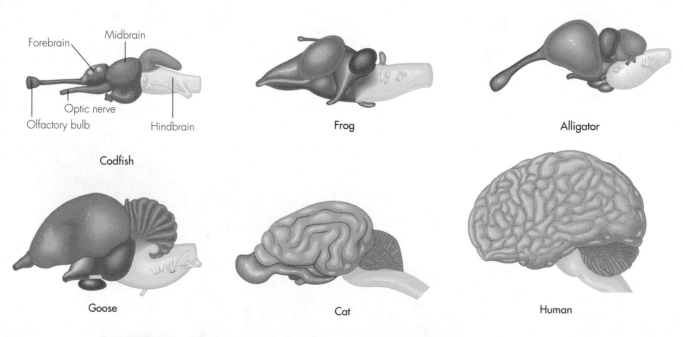

FIGURE **5.18**
The brains of five vertebrates (not drawn to the same scale)
The human forebrain surrounds the midbrain and part of the hindbrain. Source: After Romer, 1962.

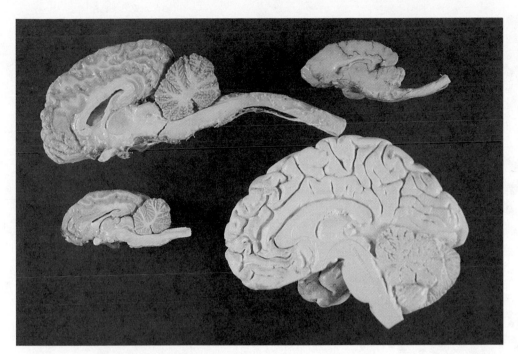

FIGURE **5.19**
Similarities and differences in mammalian brains
The general structure and organization of the brain is the same across species, but each species has adaptations to its own way of life. For example, primates have large visual areas and small olfactory bulbs. Species that rely heavily on hearing have elaborations in the auditory area. Raccoons have large areas of the cortex devoted to touch. Source: Photo by David Hinds.

answer with certainty. Behavior, with very few exceptions, does not fossilize. ("Exceptions?" you might ask. "How could any behavior ever leave fossils?" Occasionally investigators find fossil footprints, from which they can reconstruct the animal's gait, or fossilized animals with what appears to be their fossilized food. Fossils can tell us a little about behavior, but not much.) Investigators find no fossil brains, although they do find fossil skulls. From the size and shape of a skull, researchers can infer the approximate structure of the brain and note how brains have changed over the past two million years (Tobias, 1996).

With due caution, we can also use current species to make limited inferences about the brains of their ancestors. For example, researchers have identified about 20 areas of the cortex that have nearly the same position, function, and structure in all mammals; presumably, all species derived those areas by inheritance from an original common ancestor (Kaas, 1995). Cortical areas that appear in some species and not others, however, are presumably later evolutionary additions. Still, we must be ever cautious when discussing the primitive mammalian brain; the line separating reasonable inferences from mere guesswork can become blurry (Deacon, 1990b).

What Makes the Human Brain Special?

Throughout this text are references to studies of rat and other nonhuman brains, conducted by investigators who are ultimately concerned with the human brain.

The justification is that the fundamental principles of neurons, axons, and synapses are largely the same throughout the animal kingdom; species throughout the animal kingdom even use the same chemicals as neurotransmitters (Erbas, Meinertzhagen, & Shaw, 1991). Among vertebrate species, the details of neuroanatomy vary, but the overall structure is recognizably the same. (See Figure 5.18.)

Given all these similarities, what enables the human brain to do so much that other species' brains cannot? The theories fall into two main categories: the size of the human brain, and its special organization.

Size

If we compare the brains of different mammals, the first difference that we notice is size (Figure 5.19). Across mammalian species, the bigger the body, the bigger the brain. However, the correlation between brain mass and body mass is imperfect, and researchers have tried to make sense of the exceptions. For example, fruit-eating monkeys have larger brains than leaf-eating monkeys, and for a time researchers speculated that it takes a bigger brain to find fruits than to find leaves. An alternative view was that fruit-eating monkeys tend to live in larger social groups, and perhaps they need larger brains to deal with social complexities. Both interpretations are unconvincing, however, in light of the fact that fruit-eating bats have larger brains than insect-eating bats. Finding insects should be at least as difficult as finding fruits, and both kinds of bats have about the same kind of social structure. The more likely hypothesis is that fruits are a richer source of energy, and

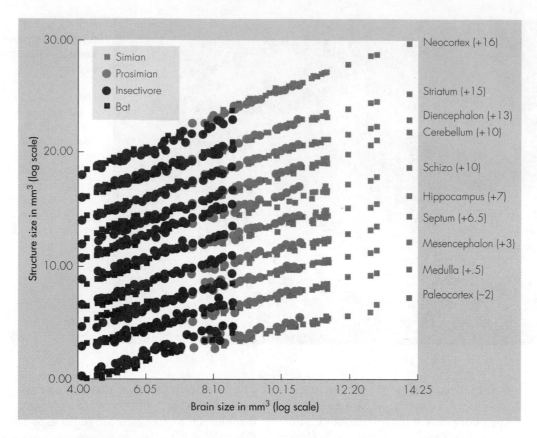

FIGURE **5.20**

Relationship between total brain mass and mass of individual structures within the brain

Each point represents the data for one species of placental (nonmarsupial) mammal; the points at the far right represent humans, which have the largest brains of the species studied. Each line represents a different part of the brain. The lines have been separated by adding or subtracting a constant from each; if the authors had not done so, the lines would be almost perfectly superimposed on one another, except for the neocortex.

Neocortex = cerebral cortex, including white matter and corpus callosum; *striatum* = caudate nucleus, putamen, and nucleus accumbens; *diencephalon* = thalamus, hypothalamus, and globus pallidus; *schizocortex* = parts of the medial temporal cortex; *septum* = an area ventral to the center of the corpus callosum; *mesencephalon* = the midbrain; *paleocortex* = anterior portion of the temporal lobe.   Source: From Finlay & Darlington, 1995.

therefore make it possible to form a large brain. Across species, the brain mass at birth correlates highly with the mother's **basal metabolic rate,** her rate of using energy when at rest (R. Martin, 1996). In other words, the genetic program for mammals says, "Build as big a brain as possible, within the limits of the mother's energy resources." Note that, because brain growth is nearly complete before or soon after birth, its development depends more on the mother's health and energy supplies than on the individual's own health and energy later in life.

Although metabolic rate is a powerful determinant of brain size, it is not the only one. For example, **primates** (monkeys, apes, and humans) devote more of their energy than other species do to brain develop-ment, and therefore develop larger brains than one would predict based on just their body mass or their mothers' basal metabolic rate. Many of the larger primates' brains also have a greater degree of folding (sulci and gyri) than one would predict from the overall volume of their brains (Zilles, Armstrong, Moser, Schleicher, & Stephan, 1989).

Growth of the whole brain and its structures   To what extent does overall brain size determine the size of substructures within the brain? The answer is, to a greater extent than most of us probably would have guessed. As shown in Figure 5.20, if all you know about a mammal is the overall mass of its brain, you can predict fairly accurately the mass of its medulla, cerebel-

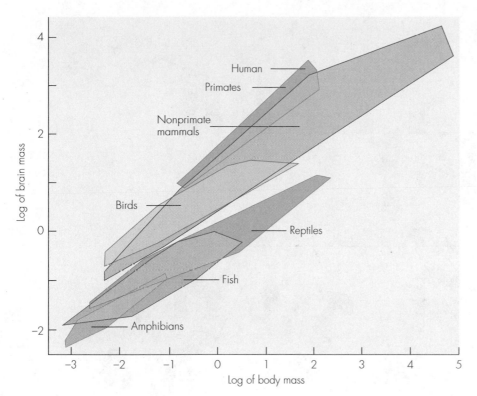

FIGURE **5.21**
Relationship between brain mass and body mass across species
Each species is one point within one of the polygonal areas. Note that primates in general and humans in particular have a high ratio of brain mass to body mass.   Source: Adapted from Jerison, 1985.

lum, hippocampus, cerebral cortex, and so forth (Finlay & Darlington, 1995). The only major exception to this rule is the olfactory bulb, which comprises a large percentage of some mammals' brains (such as rats') and only a tiny percentage of others' brains (such as humans'). In addition to this major exception, there are an enormous number of minor exceptions. For example, species that need a particularly accurate spatial memory have an expanded hippocampus; bats and dolphins have an especially large auditory cortex; and so forth (Aboitiz, 1996). Differences in brain organization that appear minor in Figure 5.20 might have important consequences for the animal's functioning. Nevertheless, the point is that different brain areas grow in parallel with one another; an increase in one area is generally linked to increases in others. Evidently, it is difficult to expand one part of the brain without expanding the rest of it as well (Finlay & Darlington, 1995).

Do not misread Figure 5.20 as indicating that all brain components increase in direct proportion with one another; the graph is a logarithm–logarithm function. Because the cerebral cortex has a higher exponent than the other brain areas do, as overall brain mass increases, the percentage of the brain occupied by the cerebral cortex increases. However, it increases in an orderly, predictable way; the greater the total brain mass, the greater the percentage of it devoted to the cerebral cortex. Note that the results for humans fall almost exactly on the lines determined by the other species; the sizes of our cerebral cortex, hippocampus, and other structures are close to the predictions for a mammalian brain the size of ours.

Is bigger better? (And if so, why?)   The larger the lungs, the more air they can absorb. The larger the stomach, the more food it can digest. Brain functioning is not that simple, however. Although it seems almost self-evident that larger brains must have some advantage over smaller brains, increased size could have some disadvantages as well. Various brain areas have to communicate with one another, and in a very large brain the increased distances among areas will slow the communication. The extra delay in traveling the greater distance, probably no more than a few milliseconds, may not be important for most purposes, but it might be for some. Therefore, an increase in brain size probably requires some reorganization or at least an increase in myelination.

Does an increase in brain size lead to greater behavioral complexity, to greater intelligence? Most neuroscientists doubt that brain size itself is critical; if it were, a cow would be more intelligent than a monkey. A more popular view is that brain-to-body ratio is important to intelligence. Figure 5.21 illustrates the relationship between logarithm of body mass and logarithm of brain mass for various kinds of vertebrates (Jerison, 1985). Note that the species we regard as most intelligent—ourselves, for example—have the highest brain-to-body ratio, and that the species we consider less impressive—frogs, for example—have a lower brain-to-body ratio.

The differences among animals in what we regard as intelligent behavior are largely if not entirely quantitative, and those quantitative differences relate to differences in brain size and complexity. Figure 5.22

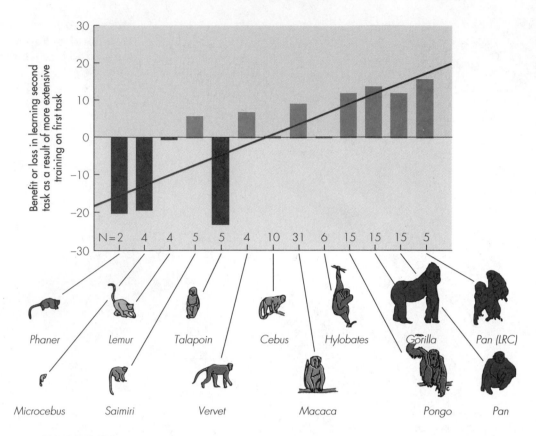

FIGURE **5.22**
Relationship between brain complexity and problem solving among twelve primate species
Along the x-axis are twelve primate species, arranged in order of estimated brain complexity, based on a combination of brain mass and ratio of brain mass to body mass. Chimpanzees (Pan) that received extensive language training are represented separately from other chimpanzees. Each animal was trained on a first task either moderately or more extensively and then shifted to a second task. For the smaller-brained primates (left), the more extensive training interfered with learning the second task, as shown by the downward bars. For the larger-brained primates (right), the more extensive training facilitated learning the second task.   Source: From Rumbaugh, 1995.

summarizes experiments with twelve nonhuman primate species. In each case, an animal was trained first on one task (such as picking up a square object instead of a triangle to get food). Some received a moderate amount of training; others much more. Then they were shifted to learning a second task (such as picking up a circle instead of a hexagon). For some species, extensive training on the first task actually interfered with learning the second task, as if the monkeys were still trying to find the previously correct object (the square). For other species, extensive training on the first task facilitated learning the second task, indicating that practice at learning had made them better at new learning. As you can see in Figure 5.22, the general trend was for primates rated higher in "brain complexity" to show

greater facilitation of the second task (Rumbaugh, Savage-Rumbaugh, and Washburn, 1996). Loosely speaking, larger and more complex brains are associated with more intelligent behaviors.

Problems arise, however, when we try to move beyond informal estimates of animal intelligence, especially if we try comparing species that are not closely related and do not share the same way of life. The study of animal learning is littered with examples in which investigators underestimated the potentials of animals by testing them under circumstances that may seem reasonable to us but were not to them (Davis, 1996; Thomas, 1996). For example, suppose that we offer an animal three objects. Two look the same, one looks different; the animal can find food by looking under the different one. Monkeys master this principle quickly; rats do not. For years, psychologists maintained that rats "could not grasp the idea of oddity." And then other investigators demonstrated that rats readily learned to pick the object that *smelled* different from the others (Langworthy & Jennings, 1972). Evidently, rats do not lack the concept of oddity; they simply do not apply it to visual discriminations. (How quickly would humans learn to pick the object that smells different from the others? Might a rat experimenter conclude that humans lack the concept of oddity?)

Animals certainly differ in their learning abilities, but the only differences we can clearly demonstrate are differences in degree—such as speed of learning or ability to learn under more varied circumstances—and not differences in kind (Macphail, 1985). It is difficult to determine how much of any difference in speed of learning is due to "intellect" as opposed to differences in sensation, motor control, or motivation. So we are left with the following. Animal intelligence (or behavioral complexity, if you prefer) is related to brain size and complexity, but we have trouble specifying exactly what we mean by either behavioral complexity or brain complexity. Brain complexity probably corresponds approximately to brain-to-body ratio, but brain-to-body ratio may not be the best predictor of intelligence either. (If it were, then an animal or person who lost weight would get smarter.) There might be some better correlate of intelligence; perhaps brain-to-basal-metabolic-rate ratio, or brain-to-muscle ratio, or brain-to-blood-volume ratio. The problem is that, without a good measurement of animal intelligence, we can hardly expect to determine which of various physical measurements correlates best with it.

Brain size and IQ performance among humans

You are no doubt familiar with the difficulties and controversies associated with measurements of intelligence in humans. However, compared with the concept of animal intelligence, human intelligence is actually a simpler problem. At least we have measurements (IQ tests) that are reasonably useful if we limit their use to people who grew up within a given culture. The tests are hardly perfect, and we can even debate whether or not they are measuring intelligence, but at least they are measuring something reasonably consistent and nontrivial. (IQ scores correlate moderately well with school performance, which in turn is important preparation for many jobs.)

Do differences in IQ scores correspond to any differences in brain size or structure? For many years the answer appeared to be, for all practical purposes, *no*. One typical study found a correlation of only 0.1 be-

tween IQ score and estimated brain size—too low to have any practical value or even much theoretical interest (Passingham, 1979).

However, those results were based on inaccurate estimates of brain size. Investigators either weighed the brains of recently deceased people—whose brains tend to dry out and gradually shrink—or they estimated brain size from the size of the skull. Either method produces sloppy estimates of brain size. If we take an inaccurate estimate of brain size and an IQ score, which is admittedly also an imperfect measure, the correlation between them can hardly be strong.

Investigators today use the modern MRI technique (Chapter 4) to visualize and measure accurately the brains of living people. In one such study, investigators measured the brains of 20 male and 20 female college students who were selected on the basis of their IQ scores. Half of the students (10 male and 10 female) had IQ scores of 130 or above; half had IQ scores of 103 or below. The investigators found that the higher-IQ students had significantly larger brains than did the lower-IQ students (Willerman, Schultz, Rutledge, & Bigler, 1991). They further found that IQ scores correlated 0.51 with brain-to-body ratio and slightly less with absolute brain volume. That correlation is somewhat inflated because the sample consisted of two groups differing by at least 27 IQ points; the authors estimated that the correlation for a representative population would be about 0.35. (See Digression 5.2.)

Do these results mean that human IQ is strongly related to brain size? Maybe; we need to see more data, drawn from larger and more representative samples. However, these results do suggest that we should no longer disregard the possibility of a relationship between IQ and brain size.

If IQ does correlate with brain size, does that correlation tell us anything about the role of genetics in IQ development? No. Genetic factors certainly do contribute to variations in total brain size, which is partly determined by the genes that control early body growth up to about 1 year of age. (Adult body size also depends on genes that control the adolescent growth spurt, which does not affect the brain.) However, variations in health and nutrition (especially the mother's health and nutrition during pregnancy) also contribute strongly to brain development. People today are taller and have larger heads and larger brains than did people in the 1700s and 1800s. Evolution is too slow to account for such a striking change; the change presumably relates to the enormous improvements in public health and nutrition. Similarly, differences in brain size among individuals within a given generation could easily reflect differences in health and nutrition, not just genetic differences.

Organization

Even if we concede that an important part of human brain evolution was an increase in size, size does not explain everything. For example, Albert Einstein (Figure 5.23), who was widely acknowledged as an extraordinarily intelligent person, had a brain of normal size. After he died, neuroscientists examined selected areas of his brain in great detail to see whether they could discover possible reasons for his brilliance. They found only minor differences that might or might not be relevant to his intellectual achievements: In part of Einstein's prefrontal cortex, neurons were more densely packed than usual (Anderson & Harvey, 1996), and part of his parietal cortex had an unusually high ratio of glia to neurons (Diamond, Scheibel, Murphy, & Harvey, 1985). Regardless of whether such differences were the key to Einstein's success, the point is that brain functioning depends on the microscopic details of its structure, not just its size.

Similarly, the differences between human brains and other brains may include changes in organization as well as variation in overall growth. The reorganization of the human brain included expansion of some areas necessary for language, increased specialization of function between the left and right hemispheres, and relative expansion of the secondary sensory areas of the cortex at the expense of the primary sensory areas (Holloway, 1996; Wilkins & Wakefield, 1995). To compare human brains with other primate brains, Terence Deacon (1990a) calculated how much of each brain is devoted to the primary visual cortex, primary motor cortex, prefrontal cortex, and so forth. Then he determined how much larger or smaller each area is in the human brain than the average for other primates. As Figure 5.24 shows, the primary visual cortex, primary motor cortex, and olfactory bulb occupy a smaller portion in the human brain than in other primate brains. In contrast, the prefrontal cortex, important for recent memory and certain aspects of language production, occupies about twice as much of the human cortex as it does in other primates. The auditory cortex, also important for language, is also slightly expanded.

Figure 5.25 illustrates several other distinctive features of the human brain (Deacon, 1992, 1994). Compared with other primates, humans have a larger number of axons from one cortical area to another and from the basal ganglia to the cortex, enabling different kinds of communication than occurs in other primates. The control of vocalizations in apes depends mostly on the limbic system, which produces emotional grunts and squeals. Humans have that system too, but we also have a more extensive set of connections from the cortex, which are responsible for our more precise control

DIGRESSION 5.2

Brain, IQ, and Sex

The relationship between human brain size and IQ is complicated by sex differences. In a study conducted by Willerman et al. (1991), if we look at the data just for men or just for women, the results fit a simple pattern: Brain size correlates moderately well with IQ scores. However, on the average, men have significantly larger brains than women do. How, then, might we explain the fact that men and women do equally well on IQ tests?

Appealing to brain-to-body ratio helps somewhat, but does not resolve the issue. On the average, women are smaller than men, and therefore their brain-to-body ratio is nearly the same as men's. However, even brain-to-body ratio would not predict IQ equality between men and women. Furthermore, if IQ correlated strongly with brain-to-body ratio, we should expect short, light people to get higher IQ scores than tall, heavy people; in fact, body size shows no consistent relationship with IQ.

Is there, then, some difference in organization that enables the smaller female brain to perform as well as the larger male brain? Researchers have found a number of differences, most of them small, inconsistent, or hard to interpret. Here are several examples of possibly relevant findings:

• In a part of the temporal cortex important for language functioning, women have a greater density of neurons per volume (Witelson, Glezer, & Kigar, 1995).
• Women tend to have a proportionately larger corpus callosum relative to total brain size, presumably facilitating greater communication between the hemispheres (Johnson, Pinkston, Bigler, & Blatter, 1996).
• Some brain areas develop more strongly in men, others in women. In both humans and monkeys, males on the average perform better than females on tasks that depend on the orbital prefrontal area of the frontal cortex; females perform better on tasks that depend on the inferior temporal cortex (Overman, Bachevalier, Schuhmann, & Ryan, 1996).

Overall, the safest conclusion is that we do not know how sex differences in the brain may relate to intellectual performance. Indeed, we do not even know what causes the differences between male and female brains. Because of the uncertainty about sex differences, we must remain cautious in interpreting the role of brain size in intelligence.

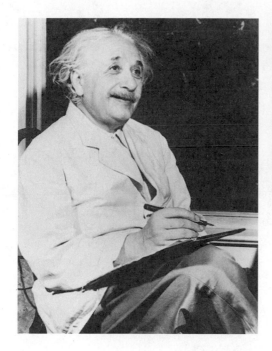

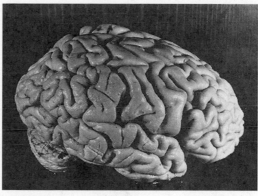

FIGURE **5.23**
After the death of the great scientist Albert Einstein, biological researchers dissected his brain to look for clues to his genius. Einstein's brain was normal in its size and structure; the differences were at a microscopic level and may or may not be relevant to his intellectual accomplishments.   Source: Left photo: Historical Pictures Services, Chicago/FPG; right photo: Courtesy of Dr. Thomas Harvey.

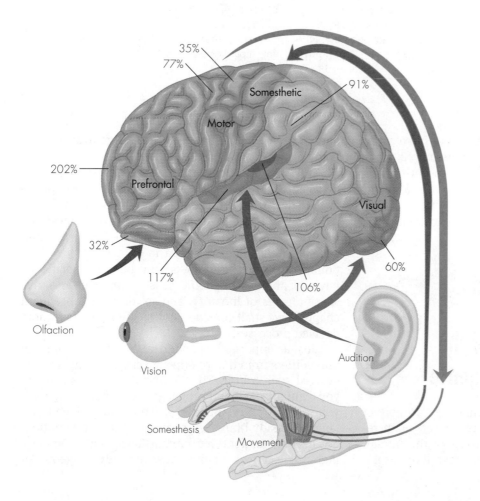

FIGURE **5.24**
Sizes of human cortex areas compared to those in other primates
T. W. Deacon calculated how large each cortical area would be in an "average" nonhuman primate if its overall brain size were as large as that of humans. He then determined how large each human area is in comparison with that of the nonhuman primates. Note that the motor and visual areas are proportionately smaller in humans than they are in other primates, whereas the prefrontal area is substantially larger.   Source: From Deacon, 1990a.

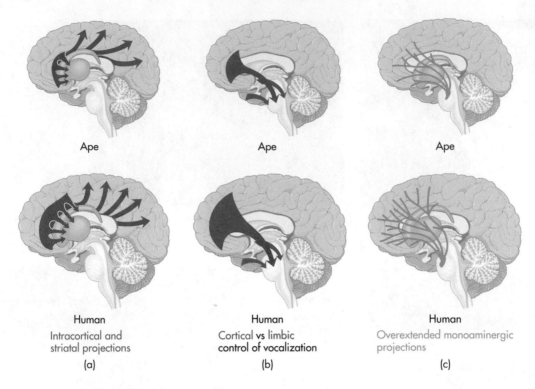

FIGURE **5.25**

Ape and human brains, drawn as if they were the same size
The size and branching of the colored arrows indicate the relative amounts of
certain connections. (**a**) The human brain has more axons between cortical
areas and between the cortex and the basal ganglia. (**b**) Although ape and
human have similar areas in the limbic system that control vocalizations, the
human cortex also has a great deal of control. (**c**) Axons releasing monoamines,
such as dopamine and norepinephrine, are proportionately more widespread in
humans than in apes.   Source: From Deacon, 1992.

of vocalizations. Note also that humans have more
widespread monoamine axons (dopamine, norepinephrine, and related transmitters) than other primates
have. In short, our brains have evolved to differ from
other primate brains in several respects that probably
facilitate language and other human characteristics.

IN**CLOSING**

The Evolution of the Brain and Intelligence

Neuroscientists will readily admit that they do not yet
understand how the structure of the human brain relates to intelligence. Overall expansion of the human
brain is one reason for its success; the rest of the expla-

nation pertains to changes in its organization, but
many details remain uncertain.

If we are ever going to understand the relationship
between brain structures and intelligence, our understanding will have to come from studies at a microscopic level. That is, we can never get very far by studying the relationship between whole-brain size and
general intelligence. We need to know how the functioning of specific brain areas contributes to specific behavioral abilities—specific sensory and motor skills,
specific types of memory, and so forth. In subsequent
chapters, we shall consider investigations of these more
detailed processes.

Just as important as understanding *how* the human
brain differs from that of other species is asking *why* we
evolved such a brain. If the answer seems obvious to
you ("Intelligence and language are useful"), then ask
yourself why other animals have not also evolved large,
language-ready brains. At some point in our evolutionary history, unidentified circumstances either made a
high-intellect way of life especially advantageous or

made the key set of genetic and structural variations possible. Many scientists have speculated on those circumstances, ranging from tool use to a change in diet or habitat. Eventually, one hopes, these speculations will yield to research data.

Summary

1. The fossil record leaves us only limited information about how the brain evolved and how ancient animals behaved. We can make certain inferences based on current animals. For example, we infer that brain structures common to all current mammals must have derived from a common remote ancestor. (p. 130)
2. Differences in the size of different mammals' brains relate largely to the basal metabolic rate of the mother, that is, the amount of energy she had available during pregnancy. (p. 131)
3. Among mammals, the size of the brain as a whole correlates almost perfectly with the size of its major components. That is, the factors of health, nutrition, and genetics that control development of any one brain area also govern development of the other areas. (p. 132)
4. The animals that we informally regard as intelligent, including ourselves and other primates, have a high ratio of brain mass to body mass. However, researchers cannot measure animal intelligence and therefore cannot accurately determine whether it correlates best with brain-to-body ratio, brain-to-metabolic-rate ratio, or some other ratio. (p. 133)
5. Among humans, one study indicates a moderately large correlation between brain size and IQ. The meaning of this correlation is unclear for several reasons, including the confusing issue of why males and females differ in brain size but not in IQ. (p. 135)
6. The human brain differs from other brains not only in size but also in certain details of organization that are presumably adapted to language and other specifically human characteristics. (p. 136)

Review Questions

1. What evidence suggests that certain cortical areas derive from the common mammalian ancestor, whereas other

cortical areas evolved more recently in separate mammalian lines? (p. 131)
2. Which brain area is an exception to the rule that the size of an area is determined by the size of the total brain? (p. 133)
3. In what way might increased brain size be a disadvantage for certain functions? (p. 133)
4. Why is it difficult to speak meaningfully about species differences in intelligence? In what way would it be useful to research if we had a decent measure of animal intelligence? (p. 134)
5. Why did old studies find such a low correlation between human IQ and brain size? What advance in research methods led to a higher estimate? (p. 135)
6. Why should we not assume that differences among people in brain size are necessarily due to genetic differences? (p. 135)
7. In what ways did Albert Einstein's brain differ from that of other people? (p. 136)

Thought Question

1. How can we study the evolution of behavior? Behavior leaves no fossils, with the exception of occasional footprints. (*Hint:* How might you study the evolution of the heart, kidney, or other internal organs, which also leave few fossils?)

Suggestions for Further Reading

Changeux, J.-P., & Chavaillon, J. (Eds.). (1996). *Origins of the human brain.* Oxford, England: Oxford University Press. Collection of articles ranging from fossil human skulls to the history of writing.

Kaas, J. H. (1995). The evolution of isocortex. *Brain, Behavior, and Evolution, 46,* 187–196. Excellent review of the differences among mammals in the structure and organization of the cerebral cortex.

Terms

basal metabolic rate a body's rate of using energy when at rest (p. 132)

primate member of the mammalian order that includes humans, monkeys, apes, and their relatives (p. 132)

VISION

CHAPTER SIX

MAIN IDEAS

1. Vertebrate vision depends on two kinds of receptors: cones, which contribute to color vision, and rods, which do not.
2. Activity of one set of neurons produces visual sensation; activity of another set produces auditory sensation. The difference between one visual experience and another depends largely on which visual neurons are most active at a given time.
3. Within the retina, a process called lateral inhibition enhances the contrast between a brightly lit area and a neighboring dimmer area.
4. After visual information reaches the brain, different pathways analyze different aspects, such as shape, color, and movement.
5. Neurons of the visual system establish approximately correct connections and properties through chemical gradients that are present before birth. Especially during infancy, visual experience can fine-tune those properties or alter them drastically.

Some years ago, a graduate student taking his final oral exam for a Ph.D. degree in psychology had answered without difficulty many questions, most of them about animal behavior, his specialty. Then one member of his committee asked, "How far can an ant see?" The student suddenly turned pale. He did not know the answer, and evidently he was supposed to. (Do you know the answer? Think about it for a minute before you read on.)

Quickly, the poor graduate student mentally reviewed everything he had read about the compound eye of insects. He remembered much about insects' light perception, color vision, and ability to detect movement . . . but nothing about how far they can see. Finally, he gave up and admitted he did not know.

With an impish grin, the professor told him, "Presumably, an ant can see 93 million miles—the distance to the sun." Yes, this was a trick question—a beaut, as trick questions go. But it illustrates an important point: How far an ant can see, or how far you or I can see, depends on how far the light travels. Good eyes cannot see farther than bad eyes. We fall into a trap because we perceive the objects we see as being "out there," when in fact the stimulation is on the retinas of our eyes. The light activates the retinas, which in turn stimulate the brain, which somehow makes sense of an enormous amount of information. How does all this happen?

Visual Coding and the Retinal Receptors

Imagine that you are a piece of iron. I admit that's not easy to do. A piece of iron doesn't have a brain, and even if it did it would not have much experience. But try to imagine it anyway.

So there you are, sitting around doing nothing, as usual, when along comes a drop of water. What will be your perception, your experience, of the water?

You will have the experience of rust. From your point of view, water is above all else *rustish*. Now return to your perspective as a human. You know that rustishness is not really a property of water itself but of the way water interacts with iron.

The same is true of human perception. In vision, for example, when you look at the leaves of a tree, you perceive them as *green*. But green is no more a property of the leaves themselves than rustish is a property of water. The greenness is what happens when the light bouncing off the leaves interacts with the neurons in the back of your eye, and eventually with the neurons in your brain. That is, the greenness is really in us—just as the rust is really in the piece of iron.

Reception, Transduction, and Coding

When any stimulus reaches any receptor, it starts a series of three steps that take us from stimulus to perception: reception, transduction, and coding (see Figure 6.1). **Reception** is simply the absorption of physical energy by the receptors. **Transduction** is the conversion of that physical energy to an electrochemical pattern in the neurons. **Coding** is the one-to-one correspondence between some aspect of the physical stimulus and some aspect of the nervous system activity. For example, molecules from a squeezed lemon strike receptors in the nose (reception); they lead to a chemical reaction that changes the polarization across the membrane of the receptor cell (transduction); and the resulting activity in that neuron and other neurons sends a distinctive message to the brain (coding).

Each receptor is specialized to absorb one kind of energy and transduce it into an electrochemical pattern

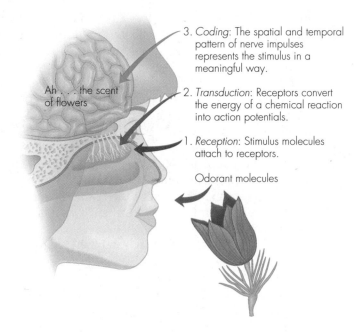

3. *Coding:* The spatial and temporal pattern of nerve impulses represents the stimulus in a meaningful way.

2. *Transduction:* Receptors convert the energy of a chemical reaction into action potentials.

1. *Reception:* Stimulus molecules attach to receptors.

Ah . . . the scent of flowers

Odorant molecules

FIGURE **6.1**
Three steps in the sensation and perception of a stimulus

that the brain can read. For example, visual receptors can absorb and respond to as little as a single photon of light and transduce it into a **generator potential,** a local depolarization or hyperpolarization of a neuron membrane. The generator potential determines what message the neuron passes along to the next neuron on the way to the brain.

From Neuronal Activity to Perception

After the information gets to the brain, how does the brain make sense of it? Let us consider what is *not* an answer. The seventeenth-century philosopher René Descartes believed that the brain's representation of a physical stimulus would have to resemble the stimulus itself. That is, when you look at something, the nerves from the eye would project a picture-like pattern of impulses onto your visual cortex. The problem with this theory is that it assumes a little person in the head who can look at the picture. There is no little person in the head, and even if there were, we would have to explain how he or she perceives the picture. (Maybe there is an even littler person inside *that* person's head?) One wonders whether the early scientists and philosophers might have avoided this error if they had started by studying olfaction instead of vision; we are less tempted to imagine that we create a little flower for a little person in the head to smell.

The main point is that the coding of visual information in your brain *does not duplicate* the shape of the object that you see. For example, when you see a table, the representation of the top of the table does not have to be on the top of your retina or on the top of your head.

General Principles of Sensory Coding

An important aspect of all sensory coding is *which* neurons are active. A given frequency of impulses may mean one thing when it occurs in one neuron and something quite different in another. In 1838, Johannes Müller described this basic insight as the **law of specific nerve energies**. Müller held that whatever excited a particular nerve established a special kind of energy unique to that nerve. In modern terms, any activity by a particular nerve always conveys the same kind of information to the brain. The brain "sees" the activity of the optic nerve and "hears" the activity of the auditory nerve.

We can state the law of specific nerve energies another way: No nerve has the option of sending the message "high C note" at one time, "bright yellow" at another time, and "lemony smell" at yet another. It sends only one kind of message—action potentials. The brain somehow interprets the action potentials from the auditory nerve as sounds, the action potentials from the olfactory nerve as odors, and those from the optic nerve as light. (Admittedly, that word *somehow* glosses over a deep mystery.)

If you poke your eye or rub it hard, you may see spots or flashes of light even if the room is totally dark.

The reason is that the mechanical pressure excites receptors in the retina of the eye; anything that excites those receptors is perceived as light. (If you wish to try this experiment, first remove your contact lenses, if your wear them.) Then shut your eye and press gently on your eyeball.)

If it were possible to take the nerves from your eyes and ears and cross transplant them so that the visual receptors were connected to the auditory nerve and vice versa, you would literally see sounds and hear lights. Perceptions depend on which neurons are active and how active each one is at a given time.

Although the law of specific nerve energies is fundamentally correct, we must add some important qualifications. First, cells with a spontaneous rate of firing may signal one kind of stimulus by an increase in firing and a different kind by a decrease in firing. For instance, a particular cell might signal "green" by increasing its firing rate and "red" by decreasing its firing rate.

Second, in some cases information depends on the timing of action potentials, not just their total number (Hopfield, 1995). Imagine a neuron that receives two incoming synapses, designated A and B. Whether A fires a millisecond before or after B might tell a cell in the visual system in which direction a light is moving. A similar difference might tell a cell in the auditory system whether a sound is coming from the left or from the right. Conceivably, a cell might even recognize complex patterns based on the timing of inputs from a large number of synapses.

Third, the exact meaning of an impulse in a single neuron may depend on what other neurons are active. Just as the letter *h* has no meaning by itself but can be part of many meaningful words, the activity of a given neuron might contribute to the sensation of green, yellow, or white, depending on the simultaneous level of activity of other neurons.

To understand how we perceive light and color, we begin with the reception and transduction by the receptors in the eyes.

The Eye and Its Connections to the Brain

We can explain a few phenomena of perception in terms of the structure of the eye (Figure 6.2). Light enters through an opening in the eyeball called the **pupil.** It is focused by the cornea and lens and projected onto the **retina,** the rear surface of the eye, which is lined with visual receptors. Light from the left side of the world strikes the right half of the retina and vice versa. Light from above strikes the bottom half of the retina; light from below strikes the top half of the retina. (As in a camera, the image is reversed. However, the inversion of the image poses no problems for the nervous system. Remember, the visual system does not simply duplicate the image. There is no more need to present the image right side up than there is for a computer to use the top of its memory bank to store commands for the top of the screen.)

The Fovea

An area called the **fovea** (meaning *pit*) in the center of the human retina is specialized for acute, detailed vision. Because blood vessels and ganglion cell axons are almost absent near the fovea, it has the least impeded

FIGURE **6.2**
Cross section of the vertebrate eye
Note how an object in the visual field produces an inverted image on the retina.

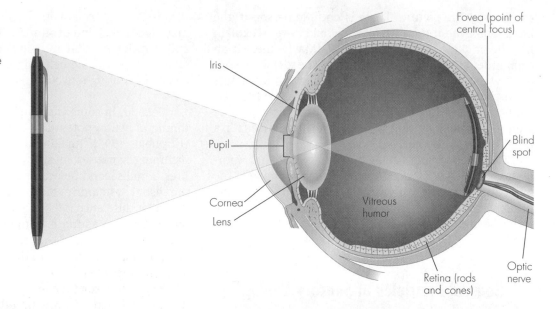

Iris

Fovea (point of central focus)

Pupil

Blind spot

Cornea

Lens

Vitreous humor

Retina (rods and cones)

Optic nerve

vision available. The tight packing of receptors further aids perception of detail.

Different species have their greatest visual sensitivity in different parts of the retina, not always in the center (Land & Fernald, 1992). For example, in both rabbits and cheetahs a highly sensitive *visual streak* stretches horizontally through the center of the retina, suited to scanning the horizon.

You have heard the expression "eyes like a hawk." In many bird species, the eyes occupy more than half the volume of the head, compared to only 5 percent of the head in humans. Furthermore, many bird species have two foveas per eye, one pointing ahead and one pointing to the side (Wallman & Pettigrew, 1985). The two foveas enable such birds to perceive detail in their peripheral vision.

Hawks and other birds of prey have a greater density of visual receptors on the top half of their retinas (looking down) than they have on the bottom half of their retinas (looking up). That arrangement is highly adaptive, because predatory birds spend most of their day soaring high in the air, looking down. However, when the bird lands and needs to see above it, it must turn its head, as Figure 6.3 shows (Waldvogel, 1990).

Conversely, in certain animals that hawks prey on, such as rats, the greater density of receptors is on the bottom half of the retina (Lund, Lund, & Wise, 1974). As a result, they can see objects above them in more detail than the objects below them.

The Route Within the Retina

In a sense, the retina is built inside-out. If you or I were designing an eye, we would probably let the light strike the receptors and then have the receptors send their messages directly back to the brain. In the vertebrate

FIGURE **6.3**
One owlet has turned its head almost upside down to see above itself. Birds of prey have a great density of receptors on the upper half of the retina, enabling them to see below them in great detail during flight. But they see objects above themselves very poorly, unless they turn their heads. Take another look at the prairie falcon at the start of this chapter. It is not a one-eyed bird; it is a bird that has tilted its head. Do you now understand why?

retina, however, the receptors, located on the back of the eye, send their messages not toward the brain but to **bipolar cells,** neurons located closer to the center of the eye. The bipolar cells send their messages to **ganglion cells,** located still closer to the center of the eye. Only at that point do the axons from the ganglion cells join one another, loop around, and travel from the eye to the brain. (See Figure 6.4.)

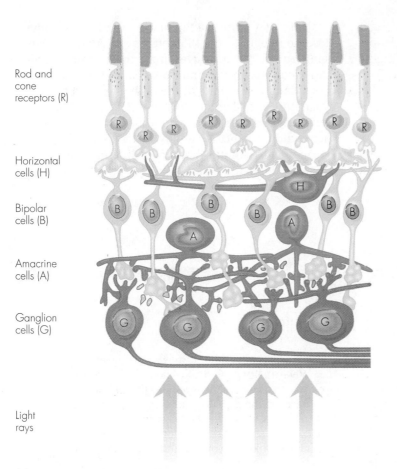

Rod and
cone
receptors (R)

Horizontal
cells (H)

Bipolar
cells (B)

Amacrine
cells (A)

Ganglion
cells (G)

Light
rays

Outer
segment

Inner
segment

Optic
nerve
fibers

(a)

FIGURE 6.4

(a) Diagram of the neurons of the retina. The top of the figure is the back of the retina. All the optic nerve fibers group together and then turn around to exit through the back of the retina, in the "blind spot" of the eye.   Source: Based on Dowling & Boycott, 1966.
(b) Photo of a cross section through the retina. This section from the periphery of the retina has relatively few ganglion cells; a slice closer to the fovea would have a greater density.

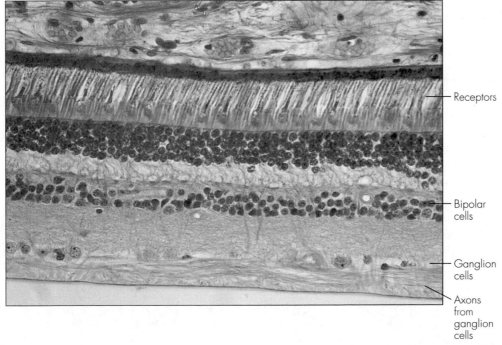

Receptors

Bipolar
cells

Ganglion
cells

Axons
from
ganglion
cells

(b)

One consequence of this anatomy is that light passes through the ganglion cells and bipolar cells before it reaches the receptors. These cells are highly transparent, so they distort vision only minimally.

A more important consequence of the eye's anatomy is the *blind spot*. The ganglion cell axons band together to form the **optic nerve** (or optic tract), which exits through the back of the eye. The point at which it leaves is called the **blind spot** because it has no receptors. (See Figure 6.2 and Digression 6.1). Blood vessels also enter the eye through the blind spot.

Note that some ganglion cells are located much closer to the blind spot than others are. All other things being equal, the messages from the nearer ganglion cells would reach the brain sooner, and we would see events in different parts of the retina just slightly out of synchrony. But all other things are not equal: The axons from ganglion cells farther from the blind spot conduct their action potentials slightly faster (Stanford, 1987). Consequently, stimuli that strike different parts of the retina at the same time reach the brain at the same time.

DIGRESSION **6.1**

Blind Spots and Blindsight

Every person is blind in the part of each eye where the optic nerve exits the eye. You can demonstrate your own blind spot using Figure 6.5. Close your left eye and focus your right eye on the **o** at the top. Then move the page toward you and away, noticing what happens to the **x**. When the page is about 25 cm away, the **x** disappears because its image has struck the blind spot of your retina.

Now repeat the procedure with the lower part of the figure. When the page is again about 25 cm away from your eyes, what do you see? The *gap* disappears! But although you no longer see the gap, do you see something *inside* the gap? You might say that you see an **x** in the middle of the gap. Whether you actually *see* an **x** or just infer it is controversial, and it is possible that you literally fill in a gap under some cir-

FIGURE **6.5**
Two demonstrations of the blind spot of the retina
Close your left eye and focus your right eye on the **o** in the top part. Move the page toward you and away, noticing what happens to the **x**. At a distance of about 25 cm (10 inches), the **x** disappears. Now repeat this procedure with the bottom part. At that same distance, what do you see?

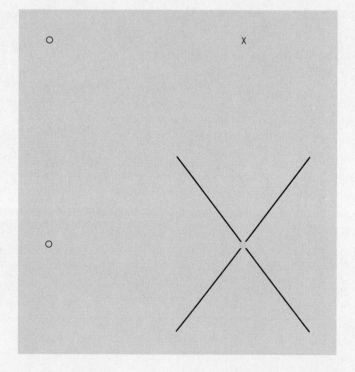

Visual Receptors: Rods and Cones

The vertebrate retina contains two types of receptors: **rods** and **cones** (see Figure 6.7). The rods, which are most abundant in the periphery of the human retina, are responsive to faint light, but reach their peak firing levels quickly and are not very useful in bright daylight. Cones, which are most abundant in and around the fovea, are less active in dim light but more useful in bright light. Color vision, for species that have it, depends on the cones.

In and near the fovea, only a few receptors (mostly cones) convey their input to any given cell at the next level of processing. Toward the periphery, larger and larger numbers of receptors (mostly rods) send their input to a given postsynaptic cell. We can see dim lights better in the periphery of the retina partly because rods are so sensitive to dim light and partly because so many of them pool their responses to influence the next layer of cells. The cost is that, by funneling responses from a wide area, they sacrifice information about detail.

cumstances and not others (Dennett, 1991; DeWeerd, Gattass, Desimone, & Ungerleider, 1995; Ramachandran, 1992).

Some people have much larger blind spots in their retinas, because glaucoma or another disease has destroyed receptors or parts of the optic nerve. Generally, they do not notice their blind spots; some are quite surprised, in fact, when an optician's test reveals that they have lost virtually half of their visual field. Why don't they notice their loss of vision? Mainly, what they "see" in their blind areas is not blackness, but simply *nothing*—no sensation at all, the same as other people experience in their smaller blind spots.

Here is another way that people can "see" something in a blind part of the retina. Suppose that your retina and optic nerve were intact, but your visual cortex were damaged. Now, depending on the location and extent of the damage, you would be blind in some part of your visual field. If someone showed you something on the corresponding part of your retina and asked what it was, you would insist that you saw nothing.

However, if instead of asking you to *say* what the object was, the investigator asked you to point to it or to turn your eyes toward it, your accuracy would be surprisingly good—surprising even to yourself, since you would continue to insist that you saw nothing (Bridgeman & Staggs, 1982; Weiskrantz, Warrington, Sanders, & Marshall, 1974). This ability to localize visual objects within an apparently blind field of vision is called **blindsight.**

The explanation for blindsight remains controversial. One possibility is that an apparently blind person may have tiny islands of healthy tissue within an otherwise damaged visual cortex, not large enough to provide any conscious perception, but nevertheless enough for blindsight (Fendrich, Wessinger, & Gazzaniga, 1992). Surviving tissue may contribute to blindsight in some cases, but it appears not to be necessary. Monkeys with complete removal of the visual cortex in one hemisphere have behaved much like humans with

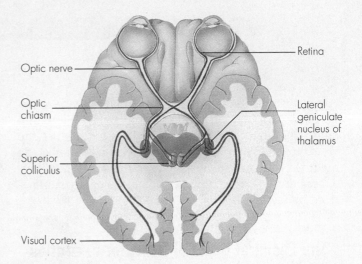

FIGURE **6.6**
Major connections in the visual system of the brain
Part of the visual input goes to the thalamus and from there to the visual cortex. Another part of the visual input goes to the superior colliculus.

blindsight (Cowey & Stoerig, 1995; Moore, Rodman, Repp, & Gross, 1995).

The other explanation is that although the visual cortex is damaged, intact branches of the optic tract send information to the superior colliculus (Figure 6.6) and other noncortical structures. The superior colliculus is important for the control of eye movements and other visually guided movements, and may provide nonconscious responses to visual stimuli (Rafal et al., 1990).

FIGURE **6.7**
(**a**) Diagram of a rod and a cone.
(**b**) Photo of rods and a cone, produced with a scanning electron microscope and magnified × 7,000.
Source: Micrograph courtesy of E. R. Lewis, F. S. Werblin, and Y. Y. Zeevi.

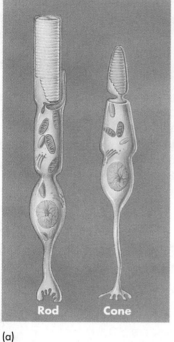

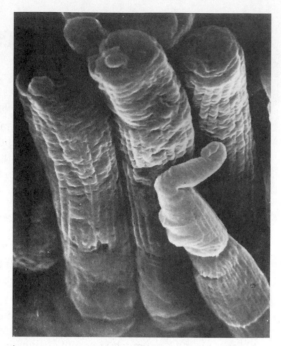

(a)   (b)

Foveal vision thus has better *acuity* (sensitivity to detail) and peripheral vision has better sensitivity to dim light. Therefore, for reading we look straight at the words to get foveal vision; to perceive a faint star in the night sky, we may focus slightly to the side. The differences between foveal and peripheral vision are summarized in Table 6.1.

The Chemical Basis of Receptor Excitation

Both rods and cones contain **photopigments,** chemicals that release energy when struck by light. Photopigments consist of 11-*cis*-retinal (a derivative of vitamin

A) bound to proteins called *opsins*. The 11-*cis*-retinal is stable in the dark; light energy converts it extremely quickly and efficiently to another form, all-*trans*-retinal (Wang, Schoenlein, Peteanu, Mathies, & Shank, 1994). (The light is absorbed in this process; it does not continue to bounce around in the eye.)

The conversion of 11-*cis*-retinal to all-*trans*-retinal changes hundreds of second-messenger molecules to their active state, ultimately closing the sodium channels in the cell membrane (Lamb & Pugh, 1990). The closing of sodium channels hyperpolarizes the receptor; the greater the light, the greater the hyperpolarization. Do not be confused by the fact that light inhibits the receptor cell. Receptors have inhibitory synapses

TABLE **6.1**
Human Foveal Vision and Peripheral Vision

Characteristic	Foveal Vision	Peripheral Vision
Receptors	Cones in the fovea itself; cones and rods mix in the surrounding area.	Proportion of rods increases toward the periphery; the extreme periphery has only rods.
Funneling of receptors	Just a few receptors send their input to each postsynaptic cell.	Increasing numbers of cells send input to each postsynaptic cell.
Brightness sensitivity	Useful for distinguishing among bright lights; responds poorly to faint lights.	Responds well to faint lights; less useful for making distinctions in bright light.
Sensitivity to detail	Detail vision is good because few receptors funnel their input to a postsynaptic cell.	Detail vision is poor because so many receptors send their input to the same postsynaptic cell.
Color vision	Good (many cones)	Poor (few cones)

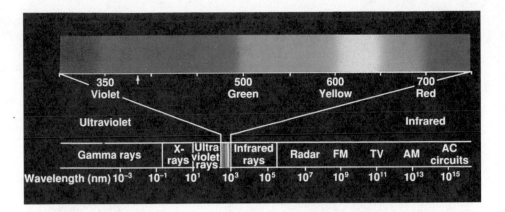

FIGURE **6.8**
A beam of light separated into its wavelengths
Although the wavelengths vary over a continuum, we perceive them as several distinct colors.

onto the next cells, known as bipolar cells, and therefore the hyperpolarization and inhibition of receptor cells decreases the inhibition of the bipolar cells, producing an excitation.

Color Vision

Almost all vertebrates have at least some cones in the retina, and apparently all mammals do (Jacobs, 1993). However, to have color vision, an individual must be able to compare the responses of different kinds of cones. For example, rats, which have just one kind of cone (Neitz & Jacobs, 1986), can probably see better during the day than they would with only rods, but they cannot discriminate among colors. Mice have only one kind of cone in the ventral half of their retina, but two kinds in the dorsal half (Szél et al., 1992). Presumably, they see some color in the upper part of their visual field only.

In the human visual system, the shortest visible wavelengths, about 400 nm (1 nm = nanometer, or 10^{-9} m), are perceived as violet; progressively longer wavelengths are perceived as blue, green, yellow, orange, and red, near 700 nm (Figure 6.8). Again, species differ; unlike humans, the kestrel, a small hawk, can see ultraviolet light. Curiously, voles, small rodents that kestrels prey on, have urine and feces that reflect ultraviolet light (Viitala, Korpimäki, Palokangas, & Koivula, 1995).

Discrimination among colors poses some special coding problems for the nervous system. A cell in the visual system, like any other neuron, can vary only its frequency of action potentials or, in a cell with graded potentials, its membrane polarization. If the cell's response indicates brightness, then it cannot simultaneously signal color. Conversely, if each response indicates a different color, the cell cannot signal brightness. The inevitable conclusion is that no single neuron can simultaneously indicate brightness and color; our perceptions must depend on patterns of responses by a number of different neurons. Two major interpretations of color vision were described in the 1800s: the trichromatic theory and the opponent-process theory.

The Trichromatic (Young-Helmholtz) Theory

The **trichromatic theory** of color vision, also known as the **Young-Helmholtz theory,** was first proposed by Thomas Young and later modified by Hermann von Helmholtz. According to this theory, we perceive color through the relative rates of response by three kinds of cones, with each kind maximally sensitive to a different set of wavelengths. (*Trichromatic* means *three colors*.) Figure 6.9 shows wavelength-sensitivity functions for the three cone types, *short-wavelength, medium-wavelength*, and *long-wavelength*. Note that each cone is more responsive to some wavelengths than to others but is at least moderately responsive to a broad band of wavelengths.

According to the trichromatic theory, we discriminate among wavelengths by the ratio of activity across the three types of cones. For example, light at 500 nm excites the medium-wavelength cone to about 65 percent of its maximum, the long-wavelength receptor to 40 percent of its maximum, and the short-wavelength receptor to 10 or 15 percent of its maximum. This ratio of responses among the three cones determines what color is perceived, in this case blue-green. More intense light would increase the activity of all three cones but would not greatly alter the ratio of responses. When all three types of cones are equally active, we see white (or gray).

Note that, in the trichromatic theory, a given response rate by a given cone is ambiguous. For example,

FIGURE **6.9**
Response of rods and three kinds of cones to various wavelengths of light
Note that each kind responds somewhat to a wide range of wavelengths but best to wavelengths in a particular range.   Source: Adapted from Bowmaker & Dartnall, 1980.

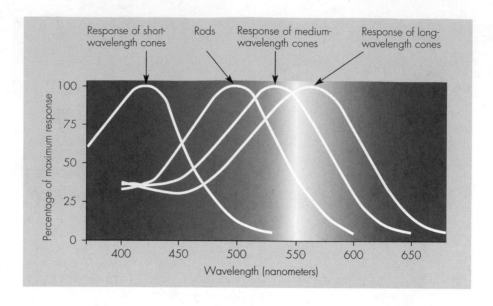

a low response rate by a middle-wavelength cone might indicate low-intensity 540-nm light, or brighter 500-nm light, or still brighter 460-nm light. Even a high response rate is ambiguous; it could indicate either bright light specifically at 540 nm or bright white light, which includes 540 nm. The nervous system can determine the color and brightness of the light only by comparing the responses of the three types of cones.

The Young-Helmholtz theory was based strictly on **psychophysical observations,** reports by human observers concerning their perceptions of various stimuli. For example, they found they could match any color by mixing appropriate amounts of just three wavelengths, so three types of cones are sufficient to account for human color vision. Modern methods have clearly established that different opsins bound to 11-*cis*-retinal in the three kinds of cones modify the sensitivity of the photopigment to produce the three different peaks of wavelength absorption (Wald, 1968).

The Opponent-Process Theory

When the information from the cones passes to later stages of the visual system, messages from the three kinds of cones converge onto the same cells (DeValois & Jacobs, 1968). For example, certain neurons receive excitatory input from both long- and medium-wavelength cones and inhibitory input from all three kinds of cones. Therefore, the trichromatic theory does not apply at levels beyond the receptors themselves.

Consider the response of the type of cell I just mentioned—excited by both long- and medium-wavelength cones and inhibited by all three types (see Figure 6.10). Your first assumption might be that this convergence of information might confuse perception. In fact, it helps reduce ambiguity. This cell responds most vigorously to

yellow light, which stimulates the long and medium cones *without* stimulating the short-wavelength cones. The cell responds much less to white light, which provides some excitation but also strong inhibition. Blue light, which inhibits the cell without exciting it, lowers the response to less than the spontaneous level of activity. By subtracting one kind of input from another, the cell determines the dominant wavelength of light more accurately than any cone does.

The **opponent-process theory** of Ewald Hering, a nineteenth-century rival of Helmholtz, describes this manner of coding color information. According to the opponent-process theory, we perceive color in terms of paired opposites: white versus black, red versus green, and yellow versus blue (Hurvich & Jameson, 1957). In modern terms, some neurons are excited by green and inhibited by red, or excited by red and inhibited by green, and so forth. Hering supported his view with psychophysical observations, such as the phenomenon of color afterimages: If you stare at something yellow for about a minute and then look at a white background, you see blue. Similarly, if you stare at blue, red, or green, you see a yellow, green, or red afterimage, respectively (Figure 6.11). **Negative afterimages** result from fatiguing one or another kind of response by opponent-process visual cells. For example, in the prolonged presence of green light, a particular cell may undergo prolonged excitation. When the green light is removed, the cell becomes hyperpolarized, and its output is perceived as red.

Color Blindness

A colleague once sent a survey to me and a number of other psychologists asking what discoveries psychologists had made. The encyclopedias are full of examples

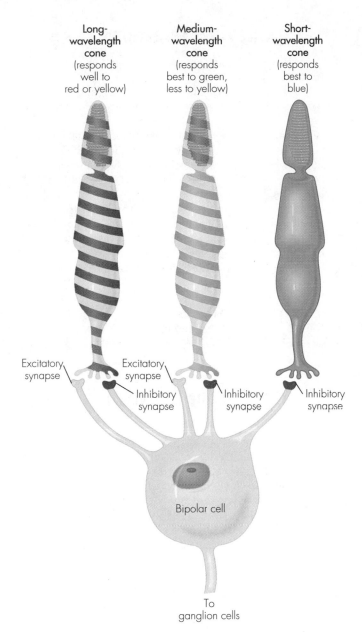

Long-
wavelength
cone
(responds
well to
red or yellow)

Medium-
wavelength
cone
(responds
best to green,
less to yellow)

Short-
wavelength
cone
(responds
best to
blue)

Excitatory
synapse

Excitatory
synapse

Inhibitory
synapse

Inhibitory
synapse

Inhibitory
synapse

Bipolar cell

To
ganglion cells

FIGURE **6.10**
Possible wiring for one bipolar cell
This cell responds best to yellow light, which excites both the long- and medium-wavelength cones. Blue light inhibits the bipolar cell to less than its usual level of firing. (In fact, receptors excite by decreasing their usual inhibitory messages. Here we translate that double negative into "excitation" for simplicity.)

FIGURE **6.11**
Stimulus for demonstrating negative color afterimages
Stare at the dot in the center under bright light for about a minute and then look at a white field. You should see a red rose with green leaves.

in astronomy, biology, chemistry, and physics, but they seldom designate anything as a "discovery in psychology." What are psychologists' discoveries?

You might give that question some thought. A psychological discovery should be clearly part of psychology, formerly unknown, but now well established. I shall leave it to you to devise your own list, but let me tell you what I believe was the first real discovery in psychology: the phenomenon of color blindness. Before color blindness was discovered in the 1600s (Fletcher &

Voke, 1985), people took it for granted that vision copies the objects we see. That is, if an object is round, we see the roundness; if it is yellow, we see the yellowness; if it is moving, we see the movement. Investigators *discovered* that it is possible to have otherwise satisfactory vision without seeing color.

We now recognize several types of color blindness. For genetic reasons, some people lack the long-wavelength, medium-wavelength, or short-wavelength cones. Some lack two kinds of cones (Nathans et al., 1989). Other people have all three types of cones but have low numbers or unusual forms of one of them.

In the most common form of color blindness, people have trouble distinguishing red from green, due to an alteration of the genes that code for the opsins in the long- and medium-wavelength cones (Nathans, Piantanida, Eddy, Shows, & Hogness, 1986). Those are recessive genes on the X chromosome. About 8 percent of males are red-green color blind, compared with about 1 percent of females.

IN**CLOSING**

Visual Receptors

I remember trying to explain to my then-teenaged son a newly discovered detail about the visual system of the brain, only to have him reply, "I didn't realize it would be so complicated. I thought the light strikes your eyes and then you see it." As you should now be starting to realize—and if not, the next module should convince you—vision requires extremely complicated processing. If you tried to build a robot with vision, you would quickly discover that shining light into its eyes accomplishes nothing unless its visual detectors are connected to devices that will identify the useful information and use it to select the proper action. We have such devices in our brains, although we are still far from fully understanding them.

Summary

1. Each type of receptor transduces a particular kind of energy into a generator potential. (p. 142)
2. Sensory information is coded so that the brain can process it. The coded information bears no physical similarity to the stimuli it describes. (p. 142)
3. According to the law of specific nerve energies, the brain interprets any activity of a given sensory neuron as representing the sensory information that neuron is tuned to. (p. 143)
4. Light passes through the pupil of a vertebrate eye and stimulates the receptors lining the retina at the back of the eye. (p. 143)
5. Visual receptors are most densely packed in the fovea, the central area of the retina. (p. 143)
6. The axons from the retina loop around to form the optic tract, which exits from the eye at a point called the blind spot. (p. 144)
7. The retina has two kinds of receptors, rods and cones. Rods are more sensitive to faint light, cones more useful in bright light. Rods are more numerous in the periphery of the eye, cones in the fovea. (p. 147)
8. Because so many receptors in the periphery funnel their messages into each cell at the next level of processing, our peripheral vision is highly sensitive to faint light but poorly sensitive to detail. (p. 147)
9. Light stimulates the receptors by triggering a molecular change in 11-*cis*-retinal, releasing energy and thereby activating second messengers within the cell. (p. 148)
10. According to the trichromatic (or Young-Helmholtz) theory of color vision, color perception begins with a given wavelength of light stimulating a distinctive ratio of responses by the three types of cones. (p. 149)
11. According to the opponent-process theory of color vision, visual system neurons beyond the receptors themselves respond with an increase in activity to indicate one color of light and a decrease to indicate the opposite color. The three pairs of opposites are red-green, yellow-blue, and white-black. (p. 150)
12. For genetic reasons, certain people are unable to distinguish one color from another. Red-green color blindness is the most common type. (p. 151)

Review Questions

1. What is the difference between transduction and coding? (p. 142)
2. What is the law of specific nerve energies, and how must it be modified in light of modern knowledge of the nervous system? (p. 143)
3. When light from the environment strikes the retina, it is reversed left-right and up-down. Does the nervous system turn the image right side up? If so, where and how? If not, does the reversal of the image cause any difficulties? (p. 143)
4. What makes the blind spot of the retina blind? (p. 146)
5. Why is perception of detail better in the fovea than it is toward the periphery of the retina? Why is perception of dim light better in the periphery? (p. 147)
6. How does 11-*cis*-retinal contribute to the detection of light? (p. 148)
7. Describe the Young-Helmholtz theory and the opponent-process theory. (p. 149)
8. Why is color blindness more common in men than in women? (p. 151)

Thought Question

1. How could you test for the presence of color vision in a bee? Examining the retina will not help; invertebrate receptors resemble neither rods nor cones. It is possible to train bees to approach one visual stimulus and not another. The difficulty is that if you trained some bees to approach, say, a yellow card and not a green card, you would not know whether they solved the problem by color or by brightness. Because brightness is different from physical intensity, you cannot equalize brightness by any physical measurement, nor can you assume that two colors that are equally bright to humans are also equally bright to bees. How might you get around the problem of brightness to study the possibility of color vision in bees?

Suggestion for Further Reading

Dowling, J. E. (1987). *The retina*. Cambridge, MA: Harvard University Press. Detailed, well-illustrated review of research on retinal receptors and their connections to other neurons within the eye.

Terms

reception   the absorption of physical energy by the receptors (p. 142)

transduction   the conversion of that physical energy to an electrochemical pattern in the neurons (p. 142)

coding   the one-to-one correspondence between some aspect of the physical stimulus and some aspect of the nervous system activity (p. 142)

generator potential a local depolarization or hyperpolarization of a neuron membrane (p. 142)

law of specific nerve energies statement that each nerve always conveys the same kind of information to the brain (p. 143)

pupil opening in the eyeball through which light enters (p. 143)

retina the rear surface of the eye, lined with rods and cones (p. 143)

fovea area in the center of the human retina specialized for acute, detailed vision (p. 143)

bipolar cell type of neuron in the retina that receives input directly from the receptors (p. 144)

ganglion cell type of neuron in the retina that receives input from the bipolar cells (p. 144)

optic nerve (or optic tract) bundle of axons that travel from the ganglion cells of the retina to the brain (p. 146)

blind spot point in the retina that lacks receptors because the optic nerve exits at this point (p. 146)

blindsight ability to point toward or turn the eyes toward objects in a damaged area of the visual field (p. 147)

rod a type of retinal receptor that does not contribute to color perception (p. 147)

cone a type of retinal receptor that contributes to color perception (p. 147)

photopigment chemical that releases energy when struck by light (p. 148)

trichromatic theory or **Young-Helmholtz theory** theory that we perceive color through the relative rates of response by three kinds of cones, with each kind maximally sensitive to a different set of wavelengths (p. 149)

psychophysical observations reports by human observers concerning their perceptions of various stimuli (p. 150)

opponent-process theory theory that we perceive color in terms of paired opposites: white versus black, red versus green, and blue versus yellow (p. 150)

negative afterimages perceptions resulting from the fatigue of one kind of neuron, such as seeing green after staring at something red (p. 150)

The Neural Basis of Visual Perception

Before the discovery of color blindness, people assumed that anyone who saw an object at all would see everything about the object—its shape, its color, its movement. Because you have heard about color blindness since childhood, you may wonder why its discovery was so surprising. And yet you yourself may be surprised—as were late twentieth-century psychologists—by the analogous phenomenon of *motion blindness:* Some people with otherwise satisfactory vision fail to detect that an object is moving, or at least have great trouble determining its direction and speed. "How could anyone see something and not see that it is moving?" you might ask. Your question is not very different from the question raised in the 1600s, "How could anyone see something without seeing what color it is?"

The fundamental fact about the visual cortex takes a little getting used to: You have no little person in the head, no central processor that sees every aspect of a visual stimulus at once. Different parts of your cortex process different aspects of the visual stimulus somewhat independently of one another.

An Overview of the Mammalian Visual System

Let us begin with a general outline of the anatomy of the mammalian visual system and then examine certain stages in more detail. The rods and cones make synaptic contact with **horizontal cells** and bipolar cells (Figure 6.12). The bipolars make synapses onto *amacrine cells* and ganglion cells. All these cells are within the eyeball.

The axons of the ganglion cells form the optic nerve, which leaves the retina and travels along the lower surface of the brain. The optic nerve from the left eye and the optic nerve from the right eye meet at the optic chiasm (Figure 6.6), where, in humans, half of the

FIGURE **6.12**

A bipolar cell from the retina of a carp, stained with Procion yellow

Bipolar cells get their name from the fact that a fibrous process is attached to each end (or pole) of the neuron.   Source: Dowling, 1987.

axons from each eye cross to the opposite side of the brain. The percentage of crossover varies from one species to another, depending on the location of the eyes. In species with eyes on the sides of the head, like rabbits and guinea pigs, nearly all the axons cross to the opposite side.

Most of the axons go to the **lateral geniculate nucleus** of the thalamus. (The term *geniculate* comes from the Latin root *genu,* meaning *knee.* To *genuflect* is to bend the knee. In some species, the lateral geniculate looks a little like a knee . . . if you use some imagination.) Some axons go to the superior colliculus, and a smaller number go to several other areas. A very few axons go to a section of the hypothalamus that keeps waking-sleeping schedules synchronized with day-night cycles. (See Chapter 9.) At any rate, most of the axons, and thus most of the visual information, goes to the lateral geniculate, which in turn sends its axons to the visual areas of the cerebral cortex.

The cerebral cortex has a number of visual areas with distinct functions and ways of analyzing visual information. However, the division of labor begins much earlier. Way back at the level of the ganglion cells are several types of cells, with different sizes of cell bodies and different conduction speeds, playing different roles in perception. Those cells form different pathways that remain largely separate in the lateral geniculate and in the cerebral cortex. To understand the story of these different pathways, we need to begin with some general principles.

Mechanisms of Processing in the Visual System

The human retina contains roughly 120 million rods and 6 million cones. We cannot intelligently process 126 million independent messages; we need to extract the meaningful patterns—what are the objects in space, where are they, and are they moving? To provide this information, the cells of our visual system have to compare what is happening in different parts of the retina.

Receptive Fields

In tracing what happens to visual information as it passes from the retina to various points in the brain, we rely on the concept of **receptive field,** the portion of the retina in which light affects the activity of a given neuron. For example, the receptive field of a cell in the visual cortex is a part of the retina where the receptors stimulate bipolar cells, which in turn stimulate ganglion cells, and so forth until eventually the message reaches the corresponding cortical cell. If light in a retinal area leads to excitation of the cortical cell, that area is part of the cell's excitatory receptive field. If light in another retinal area inhibits the cortical cell, that area is part of the cell's inhibitory receptive field. And, of course, if light neither excites nor inhibits, then it is not part of the cell's receptive field at all. (It is presumably part of the receptive fields of other cortical cells.)

We can describe the receptive field of a visual cell in two ways. The first is as an area of the retina, as in

Figure 6.13. The second is as an area of the visual field. Because every spot on the retina receives input from its own point in the visual field, the two descriptions are equivalent.

To map the receptive fields of neurons in the visual system, an investigator can shine light on specific receptors in the retina while recording from a cell in the brain. If light on a particular receptor increases or decreases the firing rate of a brain cell, then that receptor is part of the cell's receptive field. Otherwise, it is outside the receptive field.

Neuroscientists often informally say that a particular neuron in the visual system responds to a particular pattern of light: For example, "This cell in the cerebral cortex responds best to a green horizontal line." The investigator does not mean that light shining on the neuron excites it. Rather, the neuron is excited when that pattern of light shines on the neuron's receptive field in the retina.

Lateral Inhibition

Neurons in the cerebral cortex have complicated receptive fields. Instead of simply being excited or inhibited by light, a cortical cell may respond only to some complicated pattern, such as a horizontal green line moving

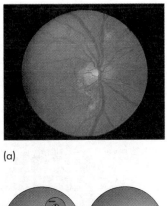

(a)

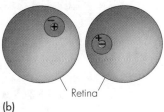

Retina

(b)

FIGURE **6.13**

(**a**) View of the retina through an ophthalmoscope. (**b**) Diagrams of two typical receptive fields of bipolar cells (greatly magnified).

FIGURE **6.14**
An illustration of lateral inhibition
Do you see dark diamonds at the "crossroads"?

upward through the receptive field. Complicated receptive fields arise through interactions among various cells in the visual system. One of the most basic examples is lateral inhibition.

Lateral inhibition is the reduction of activity in one neuron by activity in a neighboring neuron (Hartline, 1949). Lateral inhibition ordinarily serves to heighten the contrast at borders; it also produces other curious effects. For example, examine Figure 6.14. Do you see dark diamonds at the crossroads among the black squares? By the end of this section, you should be

able to explain how lateral inhibition produces the illusion of diamonds.

Suppose that Figure 6.15a represents the receptive fields in some portion of the retina. (Don't think of these as individual receptors but as receptive fields of bipolar or ganglion cells.) Figure 6.15b shows light falling on a rectangular area of the retina. Now, suppose that each receptive field is excited in proportion to the amount of light falling on it. In addition, in proportion to this excitation, each receptive field *inhibits* each of its immediate neighbors. What will be the result?

Each of the fields near the center of the rectangle will get a certain amount of excitation from the light, plus a certain amount of inhibition from each of the fields surrounding it. The net result is a limited degree of excitation. Now consider the fields around the rim of the rectangle. They too are excited by the light, but they are inhibited from one side and not the other. (They are inhibited only by neighbors that are excited.) As a result, the receptive fields along the rim of the rectangle will be more excited than any of the receptive fields on the interior. In this manner, lateral inhibition increases the apparent contrast at the edges of an illuminated area of the retina, and thereby helps define the borders of an object.

To further clarify the principle, consider an analogy: If I place a wooden block on a surface of gelatin, the block depresses the gelatin beneath it while raising the surrounding surface (Figure 6.16a). The depression is analogous to the excitation of a neuron; the rise in the surrounding gelatin is analogous to lateral inhibition of surrounding neurons. Then I place a second block next to the first. As the second block sinks into the gelatin, it slightly raises the first (Figure 6.16b). Fi-

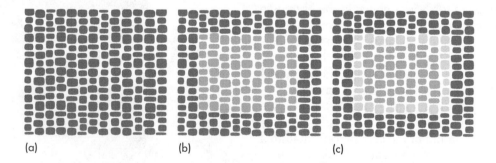

(a)   (b)   (c)

FIGURE **6.15**
(**a**) Diagram representing receptive fields in part of the retina.
(**b**) Diagram showing the same fields while light is falling on one part of the retina (highlighted). Because each excited receptive field inhibits those next to it (via lateral inhibition), the cells on the outer rim of the stimulated region will receive the greatest net excitation, as shown in
(**c**). The fields along the rim get the same amount of stimulation as those on the interior, but they get less inhibition.

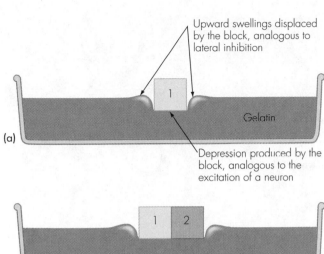

Upward swellings displaced by the block, analogous to lateral inhibition

Gelatin

(a)

Depression produced by the block, analogous to the excitation of a neuron

(b)

(c)

FIGURE **6.16**
Blocks on a surface of gelatin, analogous to lateral inhibition

nally, I try placing a row of blocks on the gelatin. The blocks at the beginning and end of the row sink deeper than the others (Figure 6.16c). Why? Because each block in the interior of the row is subject to an upward pressure from both sides, whereas the blocks at the beginning and end of the row are subject to pressure from one side only.

To understand how the connections in the retina accomplish lateral inhibition, let us start with a simpli-

fied case. Imagine light shining on just one receptor. That receptor excites the nearest bipolar cell and a large, widely branching horizontal cell. The horizontal cell inhibits the excited bipolar cell and several other nearby bipolar cells. So, one bipolar cell is being excited and inhibited; the net result here is a limited degree of excitation. The surrounding bipolars get inhibition alone, and therefore become less active than they are spontaneously. That is, lateral inhibition reduces their response.

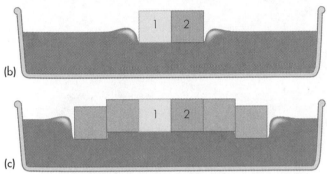

Now imagine a string of receptors equally excited by light. Each directly stimulates its nearest bipolar cell. Each also stimulates the horizontal cell, which sends a graded response, strongly inhibiting the bipolars near the center of its excitation and producing less inhibition at the edge of its excitation. The bipolars at the edge thus have greater net excitation than those near the center.

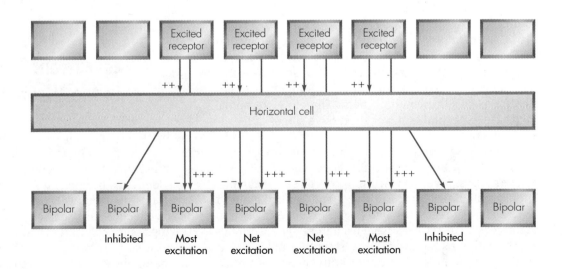

FIGURE **6.17**
Diagram of connections in the vertebrate retina
Receptors excite horizontal and bipolar cells; horizontal cells inhibit bipolars.
Source: Based on Dowling & Boycott, 1966.

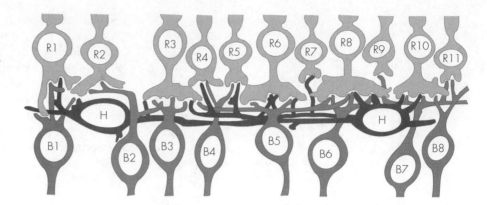

The situation in the retina is more complicated because most receptors connect to several bipolar cells, and several horizontal cells may contact a given bipolar, as shown in Figure 6.17. The basic principle, however, is the same.

How Receptive Fields Are Built

Lateral inhibition is one element of the receptive field of a neuron in the visual system. Examine cell B3 in Figure 6.17. Cell B3 is excited when light strikes receptor R3. It is also connected to a horizontal cell that receives input from receptors R1 through R8, and thus receives lateral inhibition from those cells. Receptors R1 through R8 constitute the receptive field of cell B3; that is, stimulation anywhere in that area affects the cell by either exciting or inhibiting it. Figure 6.17 shows cells along only one dimension. If we view the entire retina in two dimensions, the receptive field of a cell such as B3 looks like the drawing in Figure 6.13b. Some bipolar cells have the reverse receptive field, with an inhibitory region in the center and an excitatory field in the surround.

A group of bipolar cells sends its output to ganglion cells; in turn, a group of ganglion cells sends its output to cells in the lateral geniculate, and so on. The receptive fields of neurons at each level combine the receptive fields of all incoming fibers. Therefore, receptive fields are larger and larger at successive stages of the visual system.

When a set of neurons sends its axons to a cell at the next level, the sum of their receptive fields constitutes the receptive field of the next cell. For example, suppose that six neurons in the lateral geniculate each have a circular receptive field on the retina, as shown in Figure 6.18. All six cells have excitatory synapses onto a cell in the visual cortex. The receptive field of that cortical cell is the sum of the receptive fields of the six lateral geniculate cells—a bar shape, as shown in the

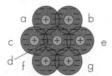

Receptive fields of 7 bipolar cells

Receptive field of one ganglion cell, which is excited by the bipolar cell with receptive field d and inhibited by the other 6 bipolar cells

Receptive fields of 6 lateral geniculate cells

Receptive field of one cell in the visual cortex that is excited by the 6 lateral geniculate cells

FIGURE **6.18**
The construction of a receptive field by the summation of axons
One neuron in the visual cortex receives its input from six lateral geniculate cells, whose receptive fields line up in a row on the retina, as shown on the left. Consequently, this visual cortex cell has a bar-shaped receptive field.

lower right of Figure 6.18 (Ferster, Chung, & Wheat, 1996).

Concurrent Pathways in the Visual System

Look out your window. Perhaps you see someone walking by. Although your perception of that person seems to be a single, integrated whole, different parts of your brain are analyzing different aspects. One set of neurons identifies the person's shape, another set concentrates on the colors of skin and clothing, and another sees which direction the person is walking and how fast (Livingstone, 1988; Livingstone & Hubel, 1988; Zeki & Shipp, 1988). Although the various pathways necessarily communicate with one another, they function more independently than we might have imagined.

TABLE **6.2**		
Distinctions Between Parvocellular and Magnocellular Neurons		
	Parvocellular Neurons	**Magnocellular Neurons**
Cell bodies	Smaller	Larger
Receptive fields	Smaller	Larger
Color sensitive?	Yes	No
Response	Sustained response; adapted for detailed analysis of stationary objects	Fast, transient responses; adapted to detect movement and broad outlines of shape

Source: Based on Livingstone, 1988; Livingstone & Hubel, 1988; Marrocco, 1986.

In the Retina and Lateral Geniculate

Your visual pathway begins its division of labor before it reaches the cerebral cortex. Even at the level of the ganglion cells in the retina, different cells are already reacting in different ways to the same input.

Remember that the bipolar cells connect to ganglion cells, whose axons form the optic nerve. Most primate ganglion cells fall into two major categories (see Table 6.2), parvocellular and magnocellular (Shapley, 1995). The **parvocellular cells,** with smaller cell bodies, are located mostly in or near the fovea. (Parvocellular means *small celled,* from the Latin root *parv,* meaning *small.*) The **magnocellular cells,** with larger cell bodies, are distributed fairly evenly throughout the retina. (Magnocellular means *large celled,* from the Latin root *magn,* meaning *large.* The same root appears in *magnify* and *magnificent.*) (A third category, the *koniocellular cells,* are the least numerous, the least responsive, and the least understood.)

The parvocellular cells have small receptive fields, so they are well suited to respond to visual details. They are also highly sensitive to color, each responding more to some colors than to others. The high sensitivity to detail and color reflects the fact that parvocellular cells are located mostly in and around the fovea, where we have many cones.

The magnocellular cells, in contrast, have larger receptive fields and do not respond selectively to colors. They respond best to moving stimuli, responding only briefly to a stationary stimulus. Magnocellular cells are found throughout the retina, including the periphery, where we are highly sensitive to movement but not to color or details.

(Try this demonstration: Take a stack of small colored objects, pick one without looking at it, and slowly move it into the extreme periphery of your vision. When you can just barely see it, you cannot clearly see its shape or color, but if you shake it, you will have no trouble detecting the movement.)

TRY IT YOURSELF

Most magnocellular cells and apparently all parvocellular cells send their axons to the lateral geniculate nucleus of the thalamus. The parvocellular ganglion cells contact mostly smaller (parvocellular) cells of the lateral geniculate, whereas magnocellular ganglion cells contact mostly the larger (magnocellular) lateral geniculate cells. Thus, the two kinds of pathways remain fairly distinct.

The distinction between parvocellular and magnocellular pathways has certain implications for human vision (Livingstone, 1988; Livingstone & Hubel, 1988). For example, consider Figure 6.19. The artist used distinct colors to indicate shadows. The result does not look entirely realistic, and yet the shadows enable us to

FIGURE **6.19**
The artist André Derain (1880–1954) showed depth with colored shadows in this portrait of painter Henri Matisse (1905). Although the painting does not look realistic, we perceive the depth easily because the magnocellular pathway (responsible for depth perception) is color blind. Note that we perceive depth about equally well in the color reproduction and in the black-and-white version.

perceive the illusion of depth about as well in the color version as in the black-and-white version. The reason is that the magnocellular pathway, which is important for depth perception, is highly sensitive to brightness and not to color.

In the Cerebral Cortex

Most visual information from the lateral geniculate area of the thalamus goes first to the **primary visual cortex,** also known as area **V1** or as the *striate cortex* because of its striped appearance. Much of the information is sent from the primary visual cortex to the **secondary visual cortex** (area **V2**), which processes it and sends it on to additional areas, as shown in Figure 6.20. The connections in the visual cortex are reciprocal; for example, V1 sends information to V2 and V2 returns information to V1. Each area of the visual cortex has subdivisions that send information to additional brain areas. Neuroscientists have distinguished about thirty to forty visual areas in the brain of a macaque monkey (Van Essen & DeYoe, 1995) and suspect that the human brain has even more.

Within the cerebral cortex, the parvocellular and magnocellular pathways split from two pathways into three. Part of the parvocellular pathway continues as a system that is sensitive primarily to details of shape. The main part of the magnocellular pathway continues as a system that is highly sensitive to movement. A third system that receives input from both the parvocellular and the magnocellular pathways is sensitive to brightness and color. Although the parvocellular cells and magnocellular cells lie side by side within this system, their responses do not mingle much. The parvocellular components are sensitive to color (Ts'o & Gilbert, 1988); the magnocellular components are sensitive to black-and-white brightness.

You will note a number of unfamiliar terms in Figure 6.20, including blobs and interblobs, thin stripes and thick stripes, that refer to anatomical structures that stand out when stained in particular ways; they also receive different kinds of input and apparently process the input in different ways (Roe & Ts'o, 1995). Do not be too concerned about those details unless you plan to become a visual cortex researcher. The key point of Figure 6.20 is that the three paths are largely independent. Neurons within a given path connect heavily to other neurons in the same path but only sparsely to neurons in other paths. The anatomy therefore suggests a division of labor, with each path specializing in a different aspect of perception, such as shape, color, or movement. The exact division remains controversial, as some researchers report that most

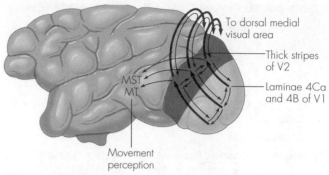

(a) Mostly magnocellular path

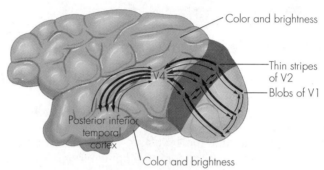

(b) Mixed magnocellular/parvocellular path

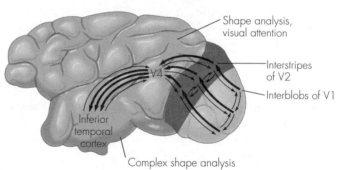

(c) Mostly parvocellular path

FIGURE **6.20**
Three visual pathways in the cerebral cortex
(**a**) A pathway originating mainly from magnocellular neurons. (**b**) A mixed magnocellular/parvocellular pathway. (**c**) A mainly parvocellular pathway. Neurons are heavily connected with other neurons in their own pathway but only sparsely connected with neurons of other pathways. Area V1 gets its primary input from the lateral geniculate nucleus of the thalamus; the other areas get some input from the thalamus but most from cortical areas.   Source: Based on DeYoe, Felleman, Van Essen, & McClendon, 1994; Ts'o & Roe, 1995; Van Essen & DeYoe, 1995.

cells are at least partly sensitive to all aspects of a stimulus—shape, color, and movement (Leventhal, Thompson, Liu, Zhou, & Ault, 1995). Further research will be necessary to resolve the amount of specialization and cooperation among pathways.

The Cerebral Cortex: The Shape Pathway

In the 1950s, David Hubel and Torsten Wiesel began a research project in which they shone various light patterns on the retina while using microelectrodes to record from cells in the animal's brain. They found that each cell was highly responsive to a particular "preferred" stimulus, and less responsive or unresponsive to other stimuli in the same part of the retina. This project, for which Hubel and Wiesel received a Nobel prize, has often been called "the research that launched a thousand microelectrodes" because it inspired so much further research. By now, their research has probably launched a million microelectrodes.

Hubel and Wiesel (1959) found that most neurons in the primary visual cortex of cats and monkeys respond to portions of both eyes and have receptive fields shaped like a bar or an edge. They and others have distinguished three categories of neurons in the visual cortex: simple, complex, and end-stopped or hypercomplex cells (von der Heydt, 1995).

Hubel and Wiesel's Cell Types in the Primary Visual Cortex

The receptive fields shown in Figure 6.21 are typical of **simple cells,** which are found exclusively in the primary visual cortex. The receptive field of a simple cell has fixed excitatory and inhibitory zones. A mere point of light in the excitatory zone will produce only a slight response, if any, but as the light extends to a larger portion of the excitatory zone, the response increases. However, the more light that falls in the inhibitory field, the less the cell responds. For example, a cell with a receptive field like that depicted in Figure 6.21c is maximally responsive to a vertical bar of light in its receptive field. The response decreases sharply if the bar of light is moved to the left or right or tilted from the vertical, because light then strikes the inhibitory regions as well (see Figure 6.22). Most simple cells have bar-shaped or edge-shaped receptive fields, which may be at vertical, horizontal, or intermediate orientations.

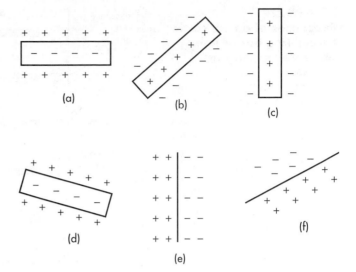

FIGURE **6.21**
Typical receptive fields for simple visual cortex cells of cats and monkeys
Areas marked with a plus (+) are the excitatory receptive fields; areas marked with a minus (−) are the inhibitory receptive fields.   Source: Based on Hubel & Wiesel, 1959.

Unlike simple cells, **complex cells,** located in either area V1 or V2, have receptive fields that cannot be mapped into fixed excitatory and inhibitory zones. A complex cell responds to a pattern of light in a particular orientation (for instance, a vertical bar) anywhere within its large receptive field, regardless of the exact location of the stimulus (see Figure 6.23). It responds most strongly to a stimulus moving perpendicular to its axis—for example, a vertical bar moving horizontally or a horizontal bar moving vertically. If a cell in the visual cortex responds to a bar-shaped pattern of light, the best way to classify the cell is to move the bar slightly in different directions. If the cell responds to the light in only one location, it is a simple cell; if it responds strongly to the light throughout a large area, it is a complex cell.

End-stopped or **hypercomplex** cells resemble complex cells with one additional feature: An end-stopped cell has a strong inhibitory area at one end of its bar-shaped receptive field. The cell responds to a bar-shaped pattern of light anywhere in its broad receptive field, provided that the bar does not extend beyond a certain point (see Figure 6.24).

Table 6.3 summarizes the properties of simple, complex, and end-stopped cells.

FIGURE **6.22**
Responses of a cat's cortical cell to a bar of light presented at varying angles
The short horizontal lines indicate when light is on.   Source (top): From Hubel & Wiesel, 1959.

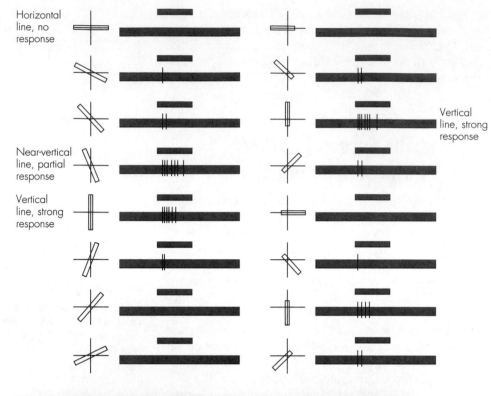

Horizontal line, no response

Near-vertical line, partial response

Vertical line, strong response

Vertical line, strong response

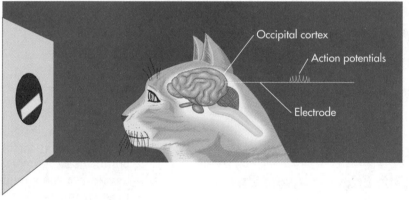

Occipital cortex

Action potentials

Electrode

TABLE **6.3**

Summary of Cells in the Primary Visual Cortex

Characteristic	Simple Cells	Complex Cells	End-Stopped Cells
Location	V1	V1 and V2	V1 and V2
Binocular input?	Yes	Yes	Yes
Size of receptive field	Smallest	Medium	Largest
Receptive field	Bar- or edge-shaped, with fixed excitatory and inhibitory zones	Bar- or edge-shaped, without fixed excitatory or inhibitory zones; responds to stimulus anywhere in receptive field, especially if moving perpendicular to its axis	Same as complex cell, but with strong inhibitory zone at one end

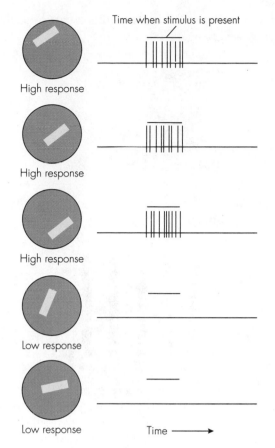

Time when stimulus is present

High response

High response

High response

Low response

Low response

Time ⟶

FIGURE 6.23
The receptive field of a complex cell in the visual cortex
It is like a simple cell in that its response depends on a bar of light's angle of orientation. It is unlike a simple cell in that its response is the same for a bar in any position within the receptive field.

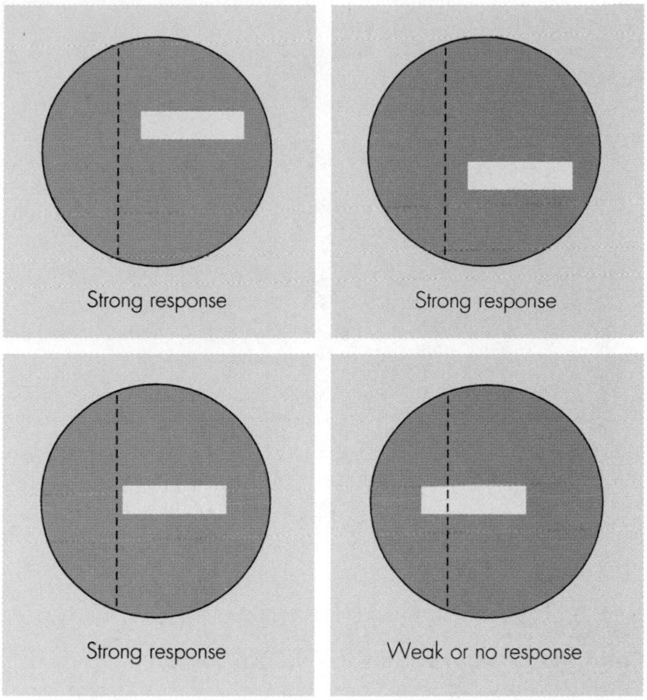

Strong response

Strong response

Strong response

Weak or no response

FIGURE 6.24
The receptive field of an end-stopped cell responds to a bar in a particular orientation (in this case, horizontal) anywhere in its receptive field, provided that the bar does not extend into a strongly inhibitory area.

The Columnar Organization of the Visual Cortex

Cells with various properties are grouped together in the visual cortex in columns perpendicular to the surface (Hubel & Wiesel, 1977). (See Figure 4.18.) For example, cells within a given column respond either mostly to the left eye, mostly to the right eye, or to both eyes about equally. Also, cells within a given column respond best to lines of a single orientation.

Figure 6.25 shows what happens when an investigator lowers an electrode into the visual cortex and records from each cell that it encounters. Each red line represents a neuron and shows the angle of orientation of its receptive field. In electrode path A, the first 12 cells show orientation preferences parallel to one another. Because electrode path B is not perpendicular to the surface of the cortex, it crosses through columns and encounters cells with different properties. In short, the cells within one column process similar information; cells in different columns process different information.

Are Visual Cortex Cells Feature Detectors?

Given that neurons in areas V1 and V2 respond strongly to bar- or edge-shaped patterns, it seems natural to

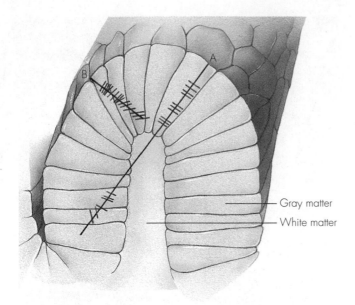

- Gray matter
- White matter

FIGURE **6.25**
Columns of neurons in the visual cortex
When an electrode passes perpendicular to the surface of the cortex (A), it encounters a sequence of neurons with parallel receptive fields. (The colored lines show the angle of orientation of the receptive field for each cell.) When an electrode passes at some other angle (B), it encounters neurons with a variety of receptive fields.   Source: From Hubel, 1963.

suppose that the activity of such a cell *is* (or at least is necessary for) the perception of a bar, line, or edge. That is, such cells might be **feature detectors**—neurons whose responses indicate the presence of a particular feature.

Supporting the concept of feature detectors is the fact that prolonged exposure to a given visual feature makes one less sensitive to that feature, as if one had fatigued the relevant detectors. For example, if you stare at a waterfall for a minute or more and then look away, the rocks and trees next to the waterfall appear to be flowing upward. This effect, the *waterfall illusion*, suggests that you have fatigued the neurons that detect downward motion, leaving unopposed the detectors that detect the opposite motion.

However, the fact that a cell responds best to a particular stimulus does not make it a detector of that stimulus only. Just as a medium-wavelength cone responds somewhat to the whole range of wavelengths, a cortical cell that responds best to one stimulus will also respond to many others. The response of any cell, from rod or cone through any part of the cortex, is ambiguous unless it is compared to the responses of other cells.

Furthermore, Hubel and Wiesel tested only a limited range of stimuli. Later researchers have tried some

other kinds of stimuli and found that a cortical cell that responds well to a single bar or line

will also respond, generally even more strongly, to a sine-wave grating of bars or lines:

Different cortical neurons respond best to gratings of different spatial frequencies (i.e., wide bars or narrow bars). Most visual researchers now believe that neurons in area V1 respond to spatial frequencies rather than to bars or edges. How do we translate a series of spatial frequencies into our perception of an environment? Many researchers are struggling with this issue (Hughes, Nozawa, & Kitterle, 1996). Although we might with effort convince ourselves that we see the world as a great many lines and edges, we obviously do not perceive it as an assembly of sine-wave gratings. Mathematicians have demonstrated by Fourier analysis that any scene can be decomposed into a series of sine waves, but how the brain uses them to identify objects is not yet clear. Several kinds of evidence suggest that the activity of area V1 is at least a step or two removed from our identification of visual objects (He, Cavanagh, & Intiligator, 1996).

Shape Analysis Beyond Areas V1 and V2

As visual information goes from the simple cells in the primary visual cortex to the complex cells in both the primary and the secondary visual cortex, receptive fields become larger and more complex. As visual information proceeds to areas specialized for further shape analysis, the receptive fields are still larger and still more complex.

One important area for shape analysis is the **inferior temporal cortex** (see Figure 6.20c). Because cells in this area have huge receptive fields, always including the fovea, their responses provide almost no information about stimulus location. However, many of these cells do provide detailed information about stimulus shape, responding preferentially to such complex visual stimuli as a hand or a face (Desimone, 1991; Desimone, Albright, Gross, & Bruce, 1984). Their responses to their preferred shapes have little relationship to many distinctions that are critical for other cells. For example, some square-responsive cells in the inferior temporal cortex respond about equally to a black square on a white background, a white square on a black background, and a square-shaped pattern of dots moving across a stationary pattern of dots (Sáry, Vogels, & Orban, 1993). Face-sensitive cells in macaque monkeys respond equally to a given face in left and right profiles. The ability of such cells to ignore changes in size and direction probably contributes to our capacity for **shape constancy**— the ability to recognize an object's shape even as it approaches or retreats or rotates.

Disorders of Object Recognition

Damage to the pattern pathway of the cortex should lead to specialized deficits in the ability to recognize objects. Neurologists have reported such cases for decades, although they frequently met with skepticism. Now that we understand *how* such specialized defects might arise, we find them easier to accept.

An inability to recognize objects is called **visual agnosia** (literally meaning *lack of knowledge*). A brain-damaged person might be able to point to visual objects and slowly describe them, but fail to recognize what they are. For example, one patient, when shown a key, said, "I don't know what that is; perhaps a file or a tool of some sort." When shown a stethoscope, he said that it was "a long cord with a round thing at the end." When he could not identify a pipe, the examiner told him what it was. He then replied, "Yes, I can see it now," and pointed out the stem and bowl of the pipe. Then the examiner asked, "Suppose I told you that the last object was not really a pipe?" The patient replied, "I would take your word for it. Perhaps it's not really a pipe" (Rubens & Benson, 1971).

Some brain-damaged people experience **prosopagnosia,** an inability to recognize faces. They may be able to read and write and to recognize many other objects, and they can recognize their friends and relatives from their voices, so the problem is not an overall loss of memory. When they look at a face, they can describe whether the person is old or young, male or female, and so forth. However, they cannot identify the person, and they may even be unsure whether the face is familiar or unfamiliar (Etcoff, Freeman, & Cave, 1991).

Many people with prosopagnosia also have trouble recognizing different kinds of animals, plants, and cars (Farah, 1990). So the deficit is, at least in some cases, a general difficulty with complex visual discriminations, and not exclusively a problem with faces. Typically, however, the people who cannot recognize faces can still read. Conversely, brain-damaged patients who lose the ability to read seldom complain of trouble in recognizing faces. Evidently, the human brain has different mechanisms for different kinds of pattern perception (Farah, 1992).

Functional MRI scans indicate that when people with intact brains recognize faces, activity increases in their inferior temporal cortex and in several other cortical areas (Puce, Allison, Gore, & McCarthy, 1995). The inferior temporal cortex contains some cells that respond vigorously to certain faces, less vigorously to other faces, and hardly at all to stimuli other than faces (Gross & Sergent, 1992; Ojemann, Ojemann, & Lettich, 1992). What do such cells record? We might imagine that each cell identifies a particular face—one cell for your grandmother, another for your psychology professor, another for your roommate. Such a mechanism would be extremely vulnerable. For example, if you happened to suffer damage to your "grandmother neuron," you would suddenly become unable to recognize your grandmother, even though you could still recognize everyone else. That kind of loss simply does not occur. People who have trouble recognizing faces have trouble with many or all faces, not just certain ones.

Research on monkeys has found that, although each cell responds more to some faces than it does to others, each responds fairly strongly to a large number of faces (Gross & Sergent, 1992; Young & Yamane, 1992). Therefore, no one cell acts as a detector for your grandmother or for any other individual. In order to perceive a face, you rely on a distinctive pattern across a population of face-selective neurons.

The Cerebral Cortex: The Color Pathway

Color perception depends mostly on the parvocellular path, as one might expect because both color perception and parvocellular cells predominate in and near the fovea. A path of cells highly sensitive to color emerges in parts of area V1 known as the *blobs*. (These blob-shaped clusters of neurons can be identified because a chemical called cytochrome oxidase stains them without staining other cells.) The blobs also have cells of the magnocellular path, which probably contribute to brightness perception or other noncolor functions. The cells in the blobs then send their output through particular parts of areas V2, V4, and the posterior inferior temporal cortex, as shown in Figure 6.20b.

Several investigators have argued that either area V4 or a nearby area is particularly important for **color constancy**—the ability to recognize the color of an object despite changes in lighting (Kennard, Lawden, Morland, & Ruddock, 1995; Zeki, 1980, 1983). If you put on green-tinted glasses or replace your white light bulb with a green-tinted one, you will still be able to identify all the objects in the room. You will of course notice the greenish tint, but you will still identify bananas as yellow, paper as white, walls as brown (or whatever), and so forth. You do so by comparing the color of one object with the color of another, in effect subtracting a fixed amount of green from each. Color constancy requires a comparison; if you focused the green light on just one object, it would look green, not its original color.

It has been reported that monkeys with damage to area V4 can learn to pick up a yellow object to get food, but if the overhead lighting is changed from white to blue, the monkeys can no longer find the yellow object (Wild, Butler, Carden, & Kulikowski, 1985). That is, the brain-damaged monkeys retain some color vision but lose color constancy. Other researchers, however, are uncertain whether the key area is V4 or some other area.

In addition to a role in color vision, area V4 has cells that contribute to visual attention (Leopold & Logothetis, 1996). Animals with damage to V4 have trouble shifting their attention from a larger or brighter stimulus to a less prominent stimulus.

The Cerebral Cortex: The Motion and Depth Pathways

Many of the cells of the magnocellular pathway are specialized for **stereoscopic depth perception,** the ability to detect depth by differences in what the two eyes see. To illustrate, hold a finger in front of your eyes and look at it, first with just the left eye and then with just the right eye. Try again, holding your finger at different distances. Note that the two eyes see your finger differently and that the closer your finger is to your face, the greater the difference is between the two views. Certain cells in the magnocellular pathway are highly sensitive to the discrepancy between the two views, presumably mediating stereoscopic depth perception. (When you look at something with just one eye, the same cells are almost unresponsive.)

TRY IT YOURSELF

Structures Important for Motion Perception

A branch of the magnocellular pathway that is specialized for motion perception goes to an area in the middle of the temporal lobe, known as area **MT** (for middle-temporal cortex, also known as area **V5**), and to an adjacent region, area **MST** (medial superior temporal cortex). (See Figure 6.20a.) The cells in those areas respond selectively to the speed and direction of movement. For example, a particular cell might respond most vigorously in the presence of an object moving to the left at 15 degrees of visual arc per second; another cell might respond best to something moving upward at 10 degrees per second. Such cells are almost indifferent to *what* is moving; that is, they respond about equally to a large or small, bright or dark object, provided that it is moving in the correct direction at the correct speed (Albright, 1992; Lague, Raiguel, & Orban, 1993).

Monkeys with damage to areas MT or MST respond inaccurately to moving visual stimuli. If those brain areas are stimulated electrically in an intact monkey, the monkey responds as if it saw movement in a particular direction (Celebrini & Newsome, 1995). Humans show similar results. Functional MRI scans indicate that neurons in approximately the MT or MST area become active when people look at moving or flickering stimuli (Tootell et al., 1995). People who have damage in this area show no impairment in describing or responding to stationary visual stimuli but cannot identify the speed and direction of moving objects (Greenlee, Lang, Mergner, & Seeger, 1995).

Especially in area MT, many cells respond best to moving borders within their receptive fields. Cells in the dorsal part of area MST respond best to the expansion, contraction, or rotation of a large visual scene, as illustrated in Figure 6.26. That kind of experience occurs when you move forward or backward or tilt your head. These two kinds of cells—the ones that record movement of single objects and the ones that record movement of the entire background—funnel their messages into neurons in the ventral part of area MST, where cells respond whenever an object moves in a certain direction *relative to its background*. Such a cell responds both when a small object moves against a stationary background and when the observer's head and the object itself move in the same direction at the same time (Tanaka, Sugita, Moriya, & Saito, 1993). (See Figure 6.27.) In such a case, the object stays at a single point on the retina, but moves in relation to its background.

A cell with such properties is enormously useful in determining the motion of objects. When you move your head from left to right, all the objects in your visual field move across your retina as if the world itself

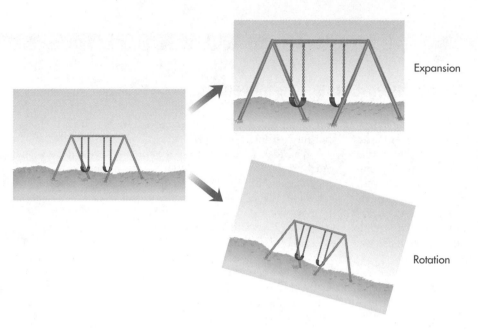

FIGURE **6.26**
Stimuli that excite certain cells in the dorsal part of area MST Cells in this area have large receptive fields; they respond not to the movement of a single object or border but rather to the expansion, contraction, or rotation of a large scene, as when an observer moves forward or backward or tilts his or her head.

Expansion

Rotation

had moved right to left. (Go ahead; try it.) Yet you do not perceive anything as moving; the world looks stationary. Indeed, all the objects are stationary—with respect to one another. But if, while you are moving your head from left to right, some object in your visual field really is moving, you see the movement. Cells in the ventral part of area MST in your brain evidently detect the motion of objects in relation to their background. Such cells enable you to perceive moving objects whether or not your head itself is moving. Digression 6.2 describes another mechanism that prevents us from confusing movements of the eyes with movements of objects.

TRY IT YOURSELF

Motion Blindness

After damage in and around area MT, a person becomes **motion blind.** That is, he or she can see objects but has trouble determining whether they are moving or stationary. One patient with extensive damage reported that she felt uncomfortable with people walking around, because "people were suddenly here or there but I have not seen them moving." She could not cross a street without someone to help her: "When I'm looking at the car first, it seems far away. But then, when I want to cross the road, suddenly the car is very near." Even such a routine task as pouring coffee became very

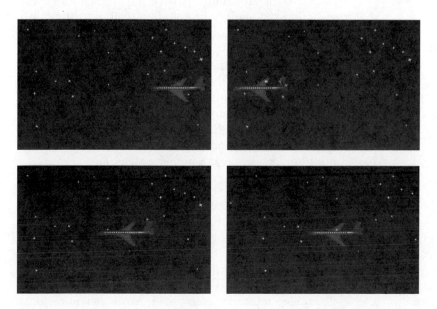

FIGURE **6.27**
Stimuli that excite certain cells in the ventral part of area MST
Cells in this area respond best when a small object moves relative to its background—either when the object's image moves on the retina or when the object remains in one place as the background moves.

Suppressed Vision During Eye Movements

In the temporal cortex are cells that distinguish between moving objects and visual changes due to head movements. An additional mechanism prevents confusion or blurring during eye movements. Before the explanation, try this demonstration: Look at yourself in a mirror and focus on your left eye. Then shift your focus to your right eye. *(Please do this now.)* Did you see your eyes move? No, you did not. *(I said to try this. I bet you didn't. None of this is going to make any sense unless you try the demonstration!)*

TRY IT YOURSELF

Why didn't you see your eyes move? Your first impulse is to say that the movement was too small or too fast. Wrong. Try looking at someone else's eyes while he or she focuses first on your left eye, then on your right. You *do* see the other person's eyes move. So an eye movement is neither too small nor too fast for you to see.

The reason you do not see your own eyes move is that your brain actually shuts down its visual cortex during eye movements! In effect, certain brain areas that monitor eye movements send the visual cortex the message, "We're about to move the eye muscles, so shut off for the next split second, or you will see nothing but a blur anyway." Regardless of what is in the visual field—in fact, even if the person is in total darkness—neural activity and blood flow in the visual cortex decrease during eye movements. The shutdown is especially prominent in the magnocellular pathway (Burr, Morrone, & Ross, 1994; Paus, Marrett, Worsley, & Evans, 1995).

difficult; the flowing liquid appeared to be frozen and unmoving, so she would not stop pouring until she had overfilled the cup (Zihl, von Cramon, & Mai, 1983).

IN **CLOSING**

Coordinating Separate Visual Pathways

The main points of this module have been as follows:

• Each cell in the visual system has a receptive field, a portion of the retina to which it responds.
• Each cell in the visual system responds to specific features of a stimulus in its receptive field, such as shape, color, or movement.
• Separate pathways in the visual system attend to different aspects of the visual system.
• Certain kinds of brain damage can impair specific aspects of visual perception.

How do we put together the information from different pathways? For example, when you look at a rabbit, you do not see a rabbit-shaped thing, a brown thing, and a hopping thing; you see one thing, a rabbit. What part of the brain puts the rabbit together?

So far as researchers can determine, no *part* of the brain puts it together. Each visual pathway gets input from the others, and area V1 gets feedback from all of the specialized areas, but researchers find no point where all the various pathways converge. At no one spot does damage cause us to lose the unity of perception.

"But, then," you might ask, "if different parts of my brain see color, shape, location, motion, and so forth, how do I perceive all of those as aspects of a single object?" You are reformulating the mind-brain question: "What is the relationship between conscious experience and the activity of countless cells in the brain?" The answer is not obvious. Perhaps information does converge in some place or in some way that researchers have not yet identified; perhaps we do not need it to converge. Perhaps the link among different aspects of visual perception is that they happen at the same time (Sillito, Jones, Gerstein, & West, 1994). What is most remarkable is that this question of how we perceive a unified stimulus has begun to look like a scientific question, and not just a philosophical one.

Summary

1. The optic tracts of the two eyes join at the optic chiasm, where half of the axons from each eye cross to the opposite side of the brain. Most of the axons then travel to the

lateral geniculate nucleus of the thalamus, which communicates with the visual cortex. (p. 154)

2. Each neuron in the visual system has a receptive field, an area of the retina to which it is connected. Light on the receptive field excites or inhibits the neuron, depending on the light's location, color, movement, and so forth. (p. 155)

3. Lateral inhibition is a mechanism by which stimulation in any area of the retina suppresses the responses in neighboring areas, thereby enhancing the contrast at light-dark borders. (p. 155)

4. Receptive fields of higher-level neurons are built up by excitatory and inhibitory connections from lower-level neurons. In the simplest case the receptive field of a higher-level neuron is the sum of the receptive fields of all the lower-level neurons connected to it. (p. 158)

5. The mammalian vertebrate visual system has a partial division of labor. In general, the parvocellular system is specialized for perception of color and fine details; the magnocellular system is specialized for perception of depth, movement, and overall patterns. (p. 159)

6. One system in the cerebral cortex is responsible for shape perception. Within the primary visual cortex, neuroscientists distinguish simple cells, which have a fixed excitatory and inhibitory field, from complex cells, which respond to a light pattern of a particular shape regardless of its exact location. End-stopped cells are similar to complex cells, except that they have a strong inhibitory field at one end. (p. 161)

7. Within the cortex, cells with similar properties cluster together in columns perpendicular to the surface of the cortex. (p. 163)

8. Neurons sensitive to shapes or other visual aspects may or may not act as feature detectors. In particular, cells of area V1 are highly responsive to spatial frequencies, even though we are not subjectively aware of spatial frequencies in our visual perception. (p. 164)

9. Damage to specific areas beyond the primary visual cortex can impair specific aspects of vision, such as facial recognition, color constancy, and motion perception. (pp. 165–168)

Review Questions

1. Where in the brain do axons from the retina go? (p. 154)

2. What is and where is the receptive field of a cell in the visual cortex? (p. 155)

3. Suppose light shines equally on all the receptors in a square-shaped area of the retina. In which part of the retina will the bipolar cells show the greatest activity? Why? (p. 156)

4. How does a horizontal cell produce lateral inhibition in the vertebrate eye? (p. 157)

5. How are the receptive fields of simple cells in the cortex built up from the input from lateral geniculate cells that have circular receptive fields? (p. 158)

6. What are the differences between parvocellular neurons and magnocellular neurons? (p. 159)

7. How could an investigator determine whether a given cell in the visual cortex is simple or complex? (p. 161)

8. What is shape constancy, and what part of the brain is especially important for this function? (p. 165)

9. What does the study of agnosias tell us about the possible existence of separate shape representation systems in the visual cortex? (p. 165)

10. What is color constancy? (p. 166)

11. How does the visual system distinguish between a moving object and an image moving across the retina because of the observer's own movement? Why do we not see a blur during our eye movements? (pp. 166–168)

Thought Questions

1. Explain the dark diamonds you see in Figure 6.14 in terms of lateral inhibition.

2. After a receptor cell is stimulated, the bipolar cell receiving input from it shows an immediate burst of response. A fraction of a second later, the bipolar's response rate decreases, even though the stimulation from the receptor cell remains constant. How can you account for that decrease? (*Hint*: What does the horizontal cell do?)

Suggestions for Further Reading

Livingstone, M. S. (1988, January). Art, illusion and the visual system. *Scientific American, 258* (1), 78–85. Interesting discussion of the three pathways in the visual system of the cerebral cortex.

Gazzaniga, M. S. (Ed.) (1995). *The cognitive neurosciences.* Cambridge, MA: MIT Press. A collection of 92 chapters by various researchers, including 14 chapters on various aspects of vision.

Terms

horizontal cell a cell type in the vertebrate eye, responsible for lateral inhibition (p. 154)

lateral geniculate a thalamic nucleus that receives incoming visual information (p. 154)

receptive field region of the receptive surface (such as retina or skin) that can excite or inhibit a given neuron (p. 155)

lateral inhibition restraint of activity in one neuron by activity in a neighboring neuron (p. 156)

parvocellular neuron small-celled neuron of the visual system that is sensitive to color differences and visual details (p. 159)

magnocellular neuron large-celled neuron of the visual system that is sensitive to changing or moving stimuli (p. 159)

primary visual cortex or area **V1** area of the cortex responsible for the first stage of visual processing (p. 160)

secondary visual cortex or area **V2**   area of the visual cortex responsible for the second stage of visual processing (p. 160)

simple cell   type of visual cortex cell that can be excited by a point of light anywhere in the excitatory part of its receptive field and inhibited by light anywhere in the inhibitory part (p. 161)

complex cell   cell type of the visual cortex that responds best to a light stimulus of a particular shape anywhere in its receptive field; its receptive field cannot be mapped into fixed excitatory and inhibitory zones (p. 161)

end-stopped or **hypercomplex cell**   cell of the visual cortex that responds best to stimuli of a precisely limited type, anywhere in a large receptive field, with a strong inhibitory field at one end of its field (p. 161)

feature detector   neuron whose responses indicate the presence of a particular feature (p. 164)

inferior temporal cortex   portion of the cortex where neurons are highly sensitive to complex aspects of the shape of visual stimuli within very large receptive fields (p. 164)

shape constancy   ability to perceive the shape of an object despite the movement or rotation of the object (p. 165)

visual agnosia   impaired ability to identify visual objects, despite otherwise satisfactory vision (p. 165)

prosopagnosia   impaired ability to recognize or identify faces (p. 165)

color constancy   ability to recognize the color of an object despite changes in lighting (p. 166)

stereoscopic depth perception   ability to detect depth by differences in what the two eyes see (p. 166)

MT or area **V5**   a portion of the middle temporal cortex, where neurons are highly sensitive to the speed and direction of movement of visual stimuli (p. 166)

MST   medial superior temporal cortex, an area in which neurons are sensitive to expansion, contraction, or rotation of the visual field or to the movement of an object relative to its background (p. 166)

motion blindness   impaired ability to perceive the direction or speed of movement, despite otherwise satisfactory vision (p. 167)

The Development of the Visual System

Suppose that you had lived all your life in the dark. And then today, for the first time, you came out into the light and looked around. Would you be able to make any sense of what you saw?

Chances are, you did have this experience once—on the day you were born. We cannot know how much sense babies make of what they see; presumably, the world looks fairly mysterious to them. Yet, within a few months to a year or so, they can recognize familiar faces, they can crawl toward a toy they see at the other side of a room, and they may even show signs of recognizing themselves in a mirror. How do they develop these impressive skills?

As we shall see, much of visual development depends on the formation and selection of synapses: Once axons get to approximately their correct targets, they form a large number of synapses, only some of which will survive. The selection of synapses depends partly on experience.

Infant Vision

When cartoonists want to show us a character as an infant, they draw the eyes large in proportion to the head. Infant eyes look large because they approach full size sooner than the rest of the head does. There is a good reason for this tendency: Infant eyes form an enormous number of complex attachments to the brain. If the eyes grew substantially after making those attachments and then sent new axons to the brain, the brain would have to reorganize its connections continually to use the additional information.

Human newborns have better-developed sensory capacities than psychologists once imagined. Newborns less than two days old spend more time looking at faces, circles, or stripes than at a patternless display (see Figure 6.28). However, because the receptors in and around the fovea are immature at birth (Abramov

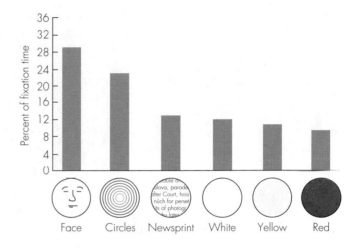

FIGURE **6.28**

Amount of time infants spend looking at various patterns

Even in the first two days after birth, infants look more at faces and other complex patterns than at a plain color or incomprehensible newsprint.   Source: Based on Fantz, 1963.

et al., 1982), infants see better in the periphery than they do in the center of vision.

Another special feature of infant vision is that infants have trouble shifting their attention. For example, infants less than 4 months old may stare at a highly attractive display, such as twirling dots on a computer screen, and be unable to shift their gaze onto another object (Johnson, Posner, & Rothbart, 1991). Occasionally, infants stare at one object until they begin crying in distress! Slightly older infants can look away from the most attractive display in the room, but they quickly shift their gaze back to it (Clohessy, Posner, Rothbart, & Veccra, 1991). Not until about age 6 months can an infant explore one object and then shift attention to something else.

To examine visual development in more detail, investigators turn to studies of animals. The research in this area has greatly expanded our understanding of

FIGURE **6.29**
The anatomical basis for binocular vision in cats and primates
Light from a point in the visual field strikes one point in the left retina and another point in the right retina. Then those two retinal areas send their axons to separate layers of the lateral geniculate. In turn, neurons in the lateral geniculate send axons to the visual cortex, where the inputs from the two eyes finally converge onto a single cell. That cell is connected (via the lateral geniculate) with corresponding areas of the two retinas.

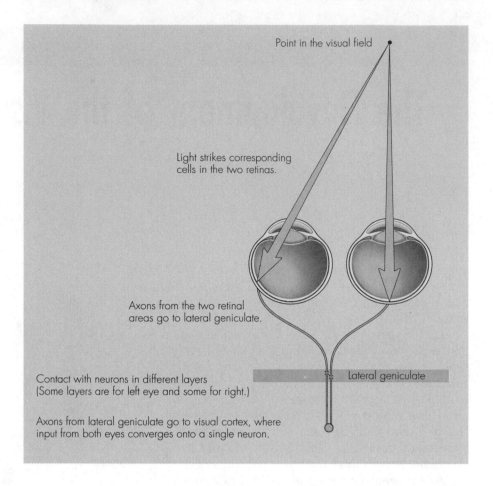

Point in the visual field

Light strikes corresponding cells in the two retinas.

Axons from the two retinal areas go to lateral geniculate.

Contact with neurons in different layers (Some layers are for left eye and some for right.)

Lateral geniculate

Axons from lateral geniculate go to visual cortex, where input from both eyes converges onto a single neuron.

brain development and has helped alleviate certain human abnormalities.

Effects of Experience on Visual Development

Developing axons of the visual system approach their targets by following chemical gradients, as discussed in Chapter 5. In newborn kittens and monkeys, the lateral geniculate and visual cortex already resemble those of adults (Gödecke & Bonhoeffer, 1996; Horton & Hocking, 1996), and they can develop many, though not all, of their normal properties even if the eyes are damaged (Rakic & Lidow, 1995; Shatz, 1996). Normal development, however, requires normal experience.

Effects of Early Lack of Stimulation of One Eye

To illustrate the effects of abnormal experience, consider the effects of nonstimulation of one eye early in life. For mammals with both eyes pointed in the same

direction—cats and primates—most neurons in the visual cortex receive **binocular** input (stimulation from both eyes). As soon as a kitten opens its eyes (at about age 9 days), each neuron responds to approximately corresponding areas in the two retinas—that is, areas that ordinarily focus on the same point in space (Figure 6.29).

If an experimenter sutures shut one eyelid so that a kitten sees with the other eye only for the first 4 to 6 weeks of life (see Figure 6.30a), thalamic axons representing the deprived eye gradually lose most of their synapses onto cortical cells (Hockfield & Kalb, 1993). The kitten becomes almost blind in the deprived eye (Wiesel, 1982; Wiesel & Hubel, 1963). Similar results occur in other species, including mice (Gordon & Stryker, 1996) and monkeys.

Effects of Early Lack of Stimulation of Both Eyes

What do you suppose happens if *both* eyes are kept shut for the first few weeks of a kitten's life? Surprisingly, cortical cells remain responsive to both eyes, although they respond sluggishly (Figure 6.30b). Evi-

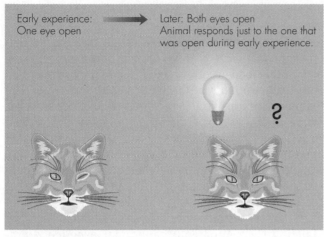

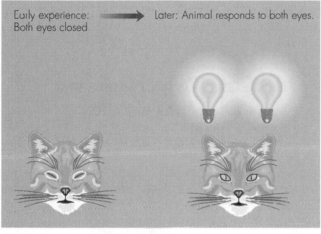

FIGURE 6.30

Reduced activity in either or both eyes affects the responsiveness of neurons in the visual cortex. Visual cortex neurons lose responsiveness to an inactive input only if there is competition from a more active input.

dently, when one eye remains shut during early development, the active synapses from the open eye displace the inactive synapses from the closed eye. If neither eye is active, no axon displaces any other.

Occasionally, human infants are born blind because of a problem that can be corrected surgically at a later age; although they have no visual experience in early infancy, they begin to see later. Such people respond to visual stimuli after the operation; for example, they can identify the brightness of light and the direction from which it is coming. However, they find it difficult to identify objects just by looking at them, or even to describe the shapes of the objects they see. They also have trouble using vision to find their way around

(Valvo, 1971). In some cases, they may even choose to close their eyes and rely on familiar touch and sound cues to maneuver through a hallway or down the stairs.

Because abnormal experience early in life produces such powerful effects on the cortex, we refer to this time as the **sensitive period** or **critical period.** The length of the sensitive period varies from one species to another and from one part of the cortex to another (Crair & Malenka, 1995); it lasts a bit longer if an animal has almost no relevant experience—for example, if a kitten is kept in total darkness for the first couple of months (Kirkwood, Lee, & Bear, 1995). Abnormal experience after the sensitive period can also alter cortical neurons, but the effects are relatively small and slow to develop (Darian-Smith & Gilbert, 1995; Sugita, 1996).

Restoration of Response After Early Deprivation of Vision

After the cortical neurons have become insensitive to the inactive eye, can experience restore their sensitivity? Yes and no. If the cat simply lives a normal life with both eyes open, it does not become responsive to the deprived eye. However, if the previously active eye is covered for a few months, the cortical cells become somewhat responsive to the previously deprived eye (Kim & Bonhoeffer, 1994).

This animal research has clear relevance to the human condition called **lazy eye,** also known by the fancier term **amblyopia ex anopsia,** in which a child ignores the vision in one eye, sometimes not even focusing it in the correct direction. The animal results imply that the best way to facilitate normal vision in the ignored eye is to prevent the child from using the active eye. A physician puts a patch over the active eye, and the child gradually increases his or her attention to vision in the previously ignored eye. Eventually, the child is permitted to use both eyes together. Although an eyepatch is likely to be most effective if it is used in early childhood, we do not know exactly how long the sensitive period lasts in humans.

Uncorrelated Stimulation in Both Eyes

Almost every neuron in the human visual cortex responds to approximately corresponding areas of both eyes. (A few neurons that respond to the extreme left or extreme right of the visual field respond to only one eye.) By comparing the slightly different inputs from the two eyes, you achieve **stereoscopic depth perception,** a versatile method of perceiving distance.

Stereoscopic depth perception requires the brain to detect **retinal disparity,** the discrepancy between what the left eye sees and what the right eye sees. But how do cortical neurons adjust their connections to detect retinal disparity? Genetic instructions could not by themselves be sufficient; different individuals have slightly different head sizes, and the genes cannot predict exactly how far apart someone's two eyes will be. The fine-tuning of binocular vision must depend on experience.

And indeed it does. Suppose an experimenter sets up a procedure in which a kitten can see with the left eye one day, the right eye the next day, and so forth. The kitten therefore receives the same amount of stimulation in both eyes, but it never sees with both eyes at the same time. After several weeks, almost every neuron in the visual cortex responds to one eye or the other, but not to both. The kitten, therefore, cannot detect retinal disparities and has no stereoscopic depth perception.

Similarly, suppose a kitten has defective or damaged eye muscles, so that its two eyes cannot focus in the same direction at the same time. In this case, both eyes are active simultaneously, but no neuron in the visual cortex gets the same message from both eyes at the same time. Again, the result is that each neuron in the visual cortex chooses one eye or the other and becomes fully responsive to it, ignoring the other eye (Blake & Hirsch, 1975; Hubel & Wiesel, 1965).

A similar phenomenon occurs in humans. Certain children are born with **strabismus,** a condition in which the eyes do not point in the same direction. Such children do not develop stereoscopic depth perception; they perceive depth no better with two eyes than they do with one. Muscle surgery in adulthood to correct the strabismus does not improve their depth perception (Banks, Aslin, & Letson, 1975; Mitchell, 1980), presumably because the sensitive period for cortical development is over long before then.

The mechanism behind all these results is apparently that each cortical cell identifies groups of axons with synchronized activity and increases its responsiveness to them (Singer, 1986). For example, if a portion of the left retina frequently focuses on the same object as some portion of the right eye, then axons from those two retinal areas frequently carry synchronous messages, and a cortical cell strengthens its synapses with both of them. However, if the eye muscles are damaged, or if one eye at a time is always covered, the cortical cell does not receive simultaneous inputs from the two eyes, and it strengthens its synapses with axons from only one eye.

Recall from Chapter 5 that postsynaptic cells promote the survival of certain axons by delivering nerve growth factor (NGF) or other neurotrophins. The same process apparently happens in the visual cortex. In one experiment, investigators closed one eye of infant ferrets. Ordinarily, that procedure causes cells in the lateral geniculate and visual cortex to become responsive only to the open eye; however, if the brain was supplied with extra amounts of the neurotrophin NT-4, all cells remained responsive to both eyes (Riddle, Lo, & Katz, 1995). In another experiment, experimenters produced strabismus in infant rats, but also injected large amounts of NGF into their brains. Instead of becoming responsive to just one eye—the usual result of infant strabismus—the cortical cells maintained a strong response to both eyes, just as if the rats had grown up with normal visual experiences (Domenici, Parisi, & Maffei, 1992). Apparently, abnormal experience produces its effects by causing neurons to release neurotrophins to the active incoming axons and not to inactive ones; if the brain is bathed in extra neurotrophins, all the axons survive and experience becomes irrelevant.

Effects of Early Exposure to a Limited Array of Patterns

If a kitten spends its entire early sensitive period wearing goggles with horizontal lines painted on them (Figure 6.31), nearly all its visual cortex cells become responsive primarily to horizontal lines (Stryker & Sherk, 1975; Stryker, Sherk, Leventhal, & Hirsch, 1978). Even after months of later normal experience, the cat ignores vertical lines and objects (Mitchell, 1980).

What would happen if human infants were exposed mainly to vertical or horizontal lines, and not to both equally? You might wonder how such a bizarre thing could happen. No parents would let an experimenter subject their child to such a procedure, and it would never happen accidentally in nature. Right?

Wrong. In fact, it probably happened to you! About 70 percent of all infants have **astigmatism,** a blurring of vision for lines in one direction (such as horizontal, vertical, or one of the diagonals). Astigmatism is caused by an asymmetric curvature of the eyes (Howland & Sayles, 1984). The prevalence of astigmatism declines to about 10 percent in 4-year-old children as a result of normal growth.

You can informally test yourself for astigmatism with Figure 6.32. Do the lines in one direction look darker or sharper than those in another direction? If so, rotate the page. You will notice that the faintness or blurriness of certain lines depends on their position. If you wear corrective lenses, try this demonstration with and without

TRY IT YOURSELF

them. If you see a difference in the lines only without your lenses, then the lenses have corrected your astigmatism.

If your eyes had strong astigmatism during your early childhood, during the sensitive period for the development of your visual cortex, you saw lines more clearly in one direction than in another direction. If your astigmatism was not corrected early, then the cells of your visual cortex probably became more responsive to the kind of lines you saw more clearly, and you will continue throughout life to see lines in other directions as slightly faint or blurry (Freedman & Thibos, 1975). However, if you began wearing corrective lenses before age 3 to 4 years, you thereby improved your capacity for adult vision (Friedburg & Klöppel, 1996). The moral of the story: Children should be tested for astigmatism early and given corrective lenses as soon as possible.

Effects of Not Seeing Objects in Motion

What would happen if kittens grew up without seeing anything move? You can imagine the difficulty of arranging such a world; even if nothing else in the world moved, the kitten's head would be sure to move. Max Cynader and Garry Chernenko (1976) used an ingenious procedure: They raised kittens in an environment illuminated only by a strobe light, which flashed eight times a second for 10 microseconds each. In effect, the

FIGURE **6.32**
An informal test for astigmatism
Do the lines in one direction look darker or sharper than the other lines do? If so, notice what happens when you rotate either the page or your head. The lines really are identical; certain lines appear darker or sharper because of the shape of your eye. If you wear corrective lenses, try this demonstration both with and without your lenses.

kittens' visual world was a series of still photographs. After 4 to 6 months in this odd environment, each kitten's visual cortex had neurons that responded normally to shapes but few neurons that responded strongly to moving stimuli. In short, the kittens had become motion blind.

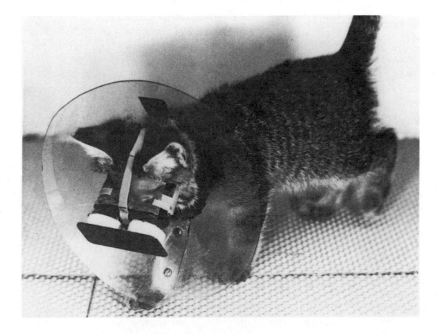

FIGURE **6.31**
Procedure for restricting a kitten's visual experience during early development
For a few hours a day, the kitten wears goggles that show just one stimulus, such as horizontal stripes or diagonal stripes. For the rest of the day, the kitten stays with its mother in a dark room without the mask.

IN**CLOSING**

Visual Research

Neuroscientists understand the visual system more thoroughly than any of the other sensory systems, and certainly more than motivation, emotion, and other topics that we shall consider in later chapters. One reason for our progress in understanding vision is that the research is relatively easy to conduct. Vision researchers may be stunned to have me call their work "easy," so let me explain: Good research leads to more good research. Because of advances long ago in physics and engineering, today's researchers can readily control light stimuli, varying intensity, wavelength, timing, and so forth. Controlling olfactory stimuli is more difficult; controlling motivational or emotional stimuli is still more difficult. Furthermore, we have better ways of measuring visual responses than of measuring many other kinds of behavior.

Neuroscientists have also concentrated so much effort on vision because for most of us our eyes are our "windows on the world." Understanding our vision helps us to understand much about the brain and about the mind–brain relationship; when research does not answer all the questions, it at least clarifies what the questions mean.

Summary

1. Human infants have nearly normal peripheral vision at birth, but foveal vision matures later. In mammals, the eyes approach their full size earlier than the rest of the head does. (p. 171)
2. The cells in the visual cortex of infant kittens have nearly normal properties. However, visual experience is necessary to maintain and fine-tune those properties. For example, if a kitten has visual experience in one eye and not in the other during the early sensitive period, its cortical neurons become responsive only to the open eye. (p. 172)
3. Cortical neurons become unresponsive to axons from the inactive eye mainly because of competition from axons from the active eye. If both eyes are closed, cortical cells remain responsive to axons from both eyes. (p. 172)
4. If cortical cells have become unresponsive to an eye because it was inactive during the early sensitive period, normal visual experience later does not restore normal responsiveness. However, prolonged closure of the previously active eye can increase the response to the previously inactive eye. (p. 173)

5. Ordinarily, most cortical neurons of cats and primates respond to portions of both retinas. However, if the two eyes are seldom open at the same time during the sensitive period, or if they consistently focus in different directions, then each cortical neuron becomes responsive to the axons from just one eye and not the other. (p. 174)
6. If a kitten sees only horizontal or vertical lines during its sensitive period, most of the neurons in its visual cortex become responsive only to lines in that direction. For the same reason, children who have a strong astigmatism early in life may have a permanently decreased responsiveness to one or another kind of lines. (p. 174)
7. Deprivation of early motion perception also impairs visual development. (p. 175)

Review Questions

1. In what way is the visual attention of human infants different from that of adults? (p. 171)
2. What happens to neurons in a kitten's visual cortex if one of its eyes is closed throughout its early development? What if both eyes are closed? (p. 172)
3. How could an investigator determine the duration of the sensitive period for development of the visual cortex? (p. 173)
4. What is "lazy eye"? How can it be treated? (p. 173)
5. What experience is necessary in early life to maintain binocular input to the neurons of the visual cortex? (p. 174)
6. What is strabismus, and how does it affect the development of the visual cortex? (p. 174)
7. Does an injection of NGF increase or decrease the effects of abnormal visual experience? Why? (p. 174)
8. What is astigmatism, and how can early childhood astigmatism affect the development of the nervous system? (p. 174)
9. What evidence indicates that perception of movement depends on early experience in watching movement? (p. 175)

Thought Questions

1. A rabbit has eyes on the sides of its head instead of in front. Would you expect rabbits to have many cells with binocular receptive fields—that is, cells that respond to both eyes? Why or why not?
2. Would you expect the cortical cells of a rabbit to be just as sensitive to the effects of experience as are the cells of cats and primates? Why or why not?

Suggestion for Further Reading

Hubel, D. H. (1988). *Eye, brain, and vision.* New York: Scientific American Library. Excellent source by co-winner of the Nobel prize. See especially Chapter 9.

Terms

binocular   based on simultaneous stimulation of two eyes (p. 172)

sensitive period or **critical period**   time of development when experiences produce major, lasting effects (p. 173)

lazy eye or **amblyopia ex anopsia**   reduced vision resulting from disuse of one eye, usually associated with failure of the two eyes to point in the same direction (p. 173)

stereoscopic depth perception   sensation of depth by comparing the slightly different inputs from the two eyes (p. 173)

retinal disparity   discrepancy between what the left eye sees and what the right eye sees (p. 173)

strabismus   condition in which the two eyes point in different directions (p. 174)

astigmatism   blurring of vision for lines in one direction because of the nonspherical shape of the eye (p. 174)

THE NONVISUAL SENSORY SYSTEMS

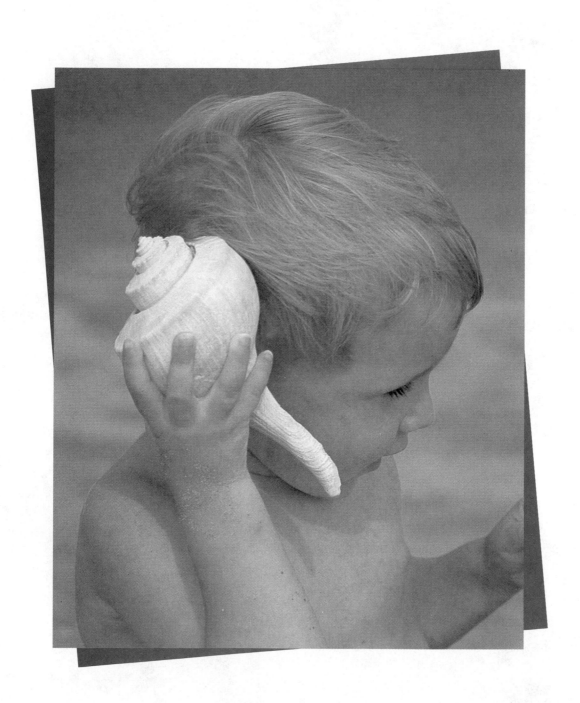

CHAPTER **SEVEN**

MAIN**IDEAS**

1. Our senses have evolved not to give us complete information about all the stimuli in the world but to give us the information most useful to us.
2. Different sensory systems code information in different ways. As a rule, the activity in a single sensory axon is ambiguous by itself; its meaning depends on its relationship to a pattern across a population of axons.

According to an American Indian saying, "A pine needle fell. The eagle saw it. The deer heard it. The bear smelled it" (Herrero, 1985). Different species are sensitive to different kinds of information. Bees and many other insects can see short-wavelength (ultraviolet) light that is invisible to humans; conversely, humans see long-wavelength (red) light that these insects cannot see. Bats produce sonar waves at 20,000 to 100,000 hertz (cycles per second) and use the echoes to locate insect prey. Most adult humans cannot hear in this range, although children may hear in the lower part of the range (Griffin, Webster, & Michael, 1960).

Many animal species are sensitive to only the small range of stimuli that are most useful in their way of life.

For example, certain cells in a frog's eyes respond selectively to small, dark, moving objects such as insects (Lettvin, Maturana, McCulloch, & Pitts, 1959). The ears of the green tree frog, *Hyla cinerea,* are highly sensitive to sounds at two frequencies—900 and 3,000 Hz—the frequencies found in the adult male's mating call (Moss & Simmons, 1986). The auditory systems of other species of frogs are tuned to hear best at frequencies that match their calls.

We generally assume that human sensory systems simply reflect the physical world. Granted, our visual and auditory abilities are broader and less specialized than those of frogs, perhaps because a wider range of stimuli is biologically relevant to us than to them. However, humans too have important sensory specializations. For example, our sense of taste can alert us to the bitter taste of certain poisons even at very low concentrations (Richter, 1950; Schiffman & Erickson, 1971), whereas it has virtually no response to substances such as cellulose that are neither helpful nor harmful to us. Our olfactory systems are unresponsive to gases that it would be useless for us to detect (nitrogen, for example) and highly responsive to such biologically useful stimuli as the smell of rotting meat. Thus, this chapter concerns not how our sensory systems enable us to perceive reality, but how they process biologically useful information.

Audition

If a tree falls in a forest where no one is present to hear it, does it make a sound? The answer depends on what we mean by "sound." If we were to define it simply as a vibration, then of course a falling tree would make a sound. However, we usually define sound as a psychological phenomenon, a vibration that some organism hears. By the standard definition, a vibration is not a sound unless someone is present to hear it.

The human auditory system enables us to hear not only falling trees but also the birds singing in the branches and the wind blowing through the leaves. Some blind people learn to click their heels as they walk and use the echoes to locate walls and other obstructions. Our auditory systems are amazingly well adapted for detecting and interpreting an enormous variety of information.

Sound

Sound waves are periodic compressions of air, water, or other media. When a tree falls, both the tree and the ground vibrate, setting up sound waves in the air that strike the ears. If something hit the ground on the moon, where there is no air, people would not hear it—unless, perhaps, they put an ear to the ground.

Sound waves vary in two ways, amplitude and frequency. The **amplitude** of a sound wave is its intensity. A very intense compression of air, like that produced by a bolt of lightning, produces sound waves of great amplitude, which a listener hears as great loudness. **Loudness**, the *perception* of intensity, is not the same thing as amplitude. If the amplitude of a sound doubles, its perceived loudness increases, but it does not double.

The **frequency** of a sound is the number of compressions per second, measured in hertz (Hz, cycles per second). **Pitch** is a perception closely related to fre-

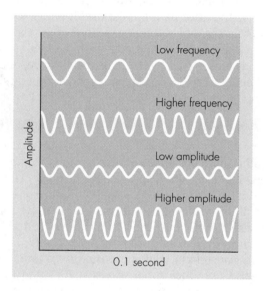

FIGURE **7.1**
Four sound waves
The time between the peaks determines the frequency of the sound, which we experience as pitch. Here, the top line represents 5 sound waves in 0.1 second, or 50 Hz—a very low-frequency sound that we would experience as a very low pitch. The other three lines represent 100 Hz. The vertical extent of each line represents its amplitude or intensity, which we experience as loudness.

quency. As a rule, the higher the frequency of a sound, the higher its pitch. Figure 7.1 illustrates the amplitude and frequency of sounds. The height of each wave corresponds to amplitude, and the number of waves per second corresponds to frequency.

Most adult humans can hear air vibrations ranging from about 15 or 20 Hz to somewhat less than 20,000 Hz. Children can hear high-frequency sounds much better than adults, whose ability to perceive high frequencies decreases with age and with exposure to loud noises (B. A. Schneider, Trehub, Morrongiello, & Thorpe, 1986).

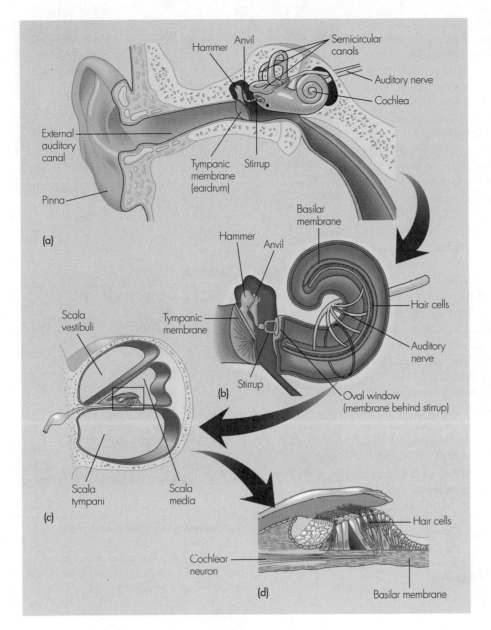

(a)

(b)

(c)

(d)

Hammer
Anvil
Semicircular canals
Auditory nerve
Cochlea
External auditory canal
Pinna
Tympanic membrane (eardrum)
Stirrup

Basilar membrane
Hammer
Anvil
Tympanic membrane
Stirrup
Hair cells
Auditory nerve
Oval window (membrane behind stirrup)

Scala vestibuli
Scala tympani
Scala media

Hair cells
Cochlear neuron
Basilar membrane

FIGURE **7.2**
Structures of the ear
When sound waves strike the tympanic membrane in (**a**), they cause it to vibrate three tiny bones—the hammer, anvil, and stirrup—that convert the sound waves into stronger vibrations in the fluid-filled cochlea (**b**). Those vibrations displace the hair cells along the basilar membrane in the cochlea. (**c**) A cross section through the cochlea. The array of hair cells in the cochlea is known as the organ of Corti. (**d**) A close-up of the hair cells.

Structures of the Ear

Rube Goldberg (1883–1970) drew cartoons that featured enormously complicated, far-fetched inventions. For example, a person's tread on the front doorstep would pull a string that raised a cat's tail, awakening the cat, which would then chase a bird that had been resting on a balance, which would swing up to strike a doorbell. The functioning of the ear may remind you a little of a Rube Goldberg device, because sound waves are transduced into action potentials through a many-step, roundabout process. Unlike Rube Goldberg's inventions, however, the ear actually works.

Anatomists distinguish among the outer ear, the middle ear, and the inner ear (see Figure 7.2). The outer ear includes the **pinna,** the familiar structure of flesh and cartilage attached to the side of the head. By altering the reflections of sound waves, the pinna helps us locate the source of a sound. It is unnecessary for hearing, however.

After sound waves pass through the auditory canal (Figure 7.2), they strike the **tympanic membrane,** or eardrum, in the middle ear. The tympanic membrane vibrates at the same frequency as the sound waves that strike it. The tympanic membrane is attached to three tiny bones that transmit the vibrations to the **oval window,** a membrane of the inner ear. These bones are sometimes known by their English names (hammer, anvil, and stirrup) and sometimes by their Latin names (malleus, incus, and stapes). The tympanic membrane is about 20 times larger than the footplate of the stirrup, connected to the oval window. As in a hydraulic pump, the vibrations of the tympanic membrane are transformed into more forceful vibrations when they reach the smaller stirrup. The net effect of the system is to convert the sound waves into waves of greater pressure on the small oval window. This transformation is important because more force is required to move the viscous fluid inside the oval window than to move the eardrum, which has air on both sides of it.

In the inner ear is a snail-shaped structure called the **cochlea** (KOCK-lee-uh, Latin for *snail*). A cross section through the cochlea, as in Figure 7.2c, shows three long, fluid-filled tunnels: the scala vestibuli, scala media, and scala tympani. The stirrup makes the oval window vibrate at the entrance to the scala vestibuli, thereby setting in motion all the fluid in the cochlea. The auditory receptors, known as **hair cells,** lie between the **basilar membrane** of the cochlea on one side and the **tectorial membrane** on the other (Figure 7.2d). Because the tectorial membrane is more rigid and the basilar membrane more flexible, the fluid in the cochlea vibrates with a shearing action that stimulates hair cells. A hair cell responds within microseconds to a displacement as small as 10^{-10} meter (0.1 nanometer, about the diameter of one atom), thereby opening ion channels in the membrane of the neuron (Fettiplace, 1990; Hudspeth, 1985). Figure 7.3 shows electron micrographs of the hair cells of three species. The hair cells stimulate the cells of the auditory nerve, which is part of the eighth cranial nerve.

Pitch Perception

Our ability to understand speech or enjoy music depends on our ability to differentiate among sounds of different frequencies, even when the sounds are presented briefly in rapid succession. How do we do so?

Frequency Theory and Place Theory

According to the early **frequency theory,** the basilar membrane vibrates in synchrony with a sound, causing auditory nerve axons to produce action potentials at the same frequency. For example, a sound at 500 Hz would cause 500 action potentials per second in the auditory nerve. The downfall of this theory in its simplest form is that some people can distinguish frequencies up to 20,000 Hz and many small animals can hear even higher frequencies. The refractory period of neurons prevents them from maintaining such high rates of action potentials.

FIGURE **7.3**
Hair cells from the auditory systems of three species
(**a, b**) Hair cells from a frog sacculus, an organ that detects ground-borne vibrations. (**c**) Hair cells from the cochlea of a cat. (**d**) Hair cells from the cochlea of a fence lizard. Kc = kinocilium, one of the components of a hair bundle.   Source: Hudspeth, 1985.

According to the **place theory,** the basilar membrane resembles the strings of a piano in that each area along the membrane is tuned to a specific frequency and vibrates whenever that frequency is present. Each frequency thus activates the hair cells at only one place along the basilar membrane, and the nervous system distinguishes among frequencies on the basis of which neurons are activated. The downfall of this theory in its original form is that the various parts of the basilar membrane are bound together and no one part can resonate like a piano string.

The currently prevalent theory combines modified versions of both frequency and place theories. For low-frequency sounds (up to about 100 Hz), the basilar membrane vibrates in synchrony with the sound waves (in accordance with the frequency theory), and auditory nerve axons generate one action potential per wave. Weak sounds activate only a small number of neurons, whereas stronger sounds activate greater numbers. Thus, at low frequencies, the frequency of impulses identifies the pitch, and the number of firing cells identifies the loudness.

Beyond about 100 Hz, a neuron cannot keep up with the frequency of the sound waves, but it may nevertheless produce action potentials phase-locked to the peaks of the sound waves (that is, always occurring at the same phase in the sound wave), as illustrated here:

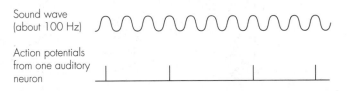

Additional auditory neurons also produce action potentials that are phase-locked with peaks of the sound wave but not necessarily in phase with one another's action potentials:

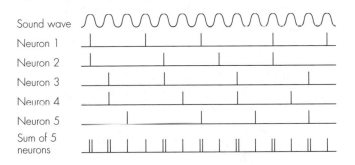

If we consider the auditory nerve as a whole, we find that each sound wave of moderately high frequency produces a volley of impulses by various fibers; that is, at least a few neurons fire synchronously with each wave in, say, a 600 Hz tone. According to the **volley principle** of pitch discrimination, the auditory nerve as a whole can have volleys of impulses up to about 5,000 per second, even though no individual axon can approach that frequency by itself (Rose, Brugge, Anderson, & Hind, 1967). (Beyond about 5,000 Hz, even staggered volleys of impulses cannot keep pace with the sound waves.) Do such volleys really contribute to pitch perception? Although biological psychologists generally assume that the brain can use any information that the neurons produce, we do not know whether or how the brain uses the volleys.

Most of human hearing takes place below 5,000 Hz, the apparent limit of the volley principle. Higher frequencies sound squeaky; they play little role in either music or speech. We do, nevertheless, hear such frequencies, and our ability to do so requires an explanation similar to the original place theory.

At its **base**, where the stirrup meets the cochlea,

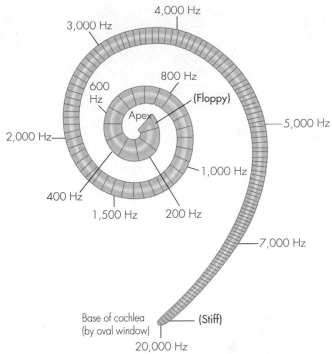

FIGURE 7.4
The basilar membrane of the human cochlea
High-frequency sounds produce their maximum displacement near the base. Low-frequency sounds produce their maximum displacement near the apex.

the basilar membrane is narrow (about 0.15 mm) and stiff. It is wider (0.5 mm) and only one-hundredth as stiff at the other end of the cochlea, the **apex** (von Békésy, 1956; Yost & Nielsen, 1977). (See Figure 7.4.) You may be surprised that the basilar membrane is narrowest at the base, where the cochlea itself is widest. At the base the cochlea has a wide bony shelf attached to the basilar membrane. When a vibration strikes the basilar membrane, it sets up a **traveling wave.** As the wave travels along the membrane, it produces some displacement at all points, but the amount of displacement varies because of differences in the thickness and stiffness of the membrane.

Vibrations at different frequencies set up traveling waves that peak at different points along the basilar membrane, as in Figures 7.4 and 7.5. The traveling wave for a low-frequency vibration peaks at or near the apex, where the membrane is large and floppy. For progressively higher frequencies, the point of maximum displacement is closer to the base. In fact, the highest frequencies produce practically no displacement of the membrane near the apex. The waveforms in Figure 7.5 are drawn broadly to be easily visible. In healthy tissues, however, the waves are sharply defined, falling rapidly on both sides of the maximum displacement (Zwislocki, 1981). Only the neurons near the point of maximum displacement respond significantly to a tone.

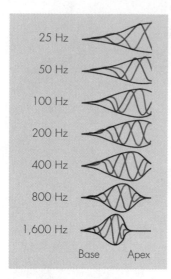

FIGURE **7.5**
Traveling waves in the basilar membrane set up by different frequencies of sound
Note that the peak displacement is closer to the base of the cochlea for high frequencies and is toward the apex for lower frequencies. In reality, the peak of each wave is much narrower than shown here.

To summarize, we identify the lowest-frequency sounds by the frequency of impulses. We discriminate among high frequencies according to the place along the basilar membrane at which the receptors show their greatest activity; the higher the frequency, the closer the maximum displacement to the base of the cochlea. We discriminate intermediate frequencies (about 60 to 5,000 Hz) through a combination of frequency and place.

Pitch Perception in the Cerebral Cortex

Information from the auditory system passes through several subcortical structures, with an important cross-over between the superior olive and inferior colliculus that enables each hemisphere of the forebrain to get its major auditory input from the opposite ear (Glenden-ning, Baker, Hutson, & Masterton, 1992). The information ultimately reaches the **primary auditory cortex** in the temporal lobes, as shown in Figure 7.6. Within the primary auditory cortex, each cell responds best to one tone, and the cells preferring a given tone cluster together, as shown in Figure 7.7 (Scheich & Zuschratter, 1995). Thus, the location of strong responses within the auditory cortex indicates the frequency of a sound.

Someone with massive damage to the primary visual cortex becomes completely blind, except for the very limited functions described as "blindsight" (p. 147). In contrast, people with similar damage to the primary auditory cortex do not become deaf. They can hear and respond to simple sounds with only slight impairments, unless the damage extends into subcortical brain areas (Tanaka, Kamo, Yoshida, & Yamadori, 1991). Damage limited to the primary auditory cortex produces clear impairments only when a brain-dam-

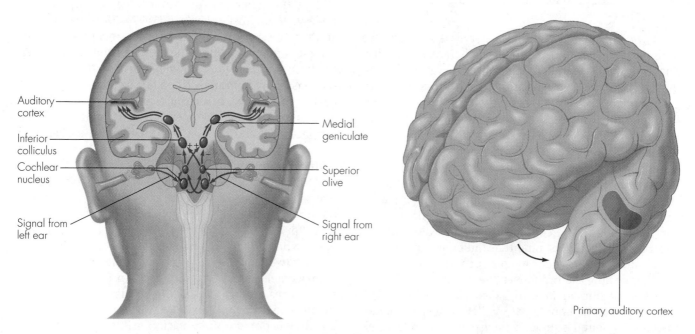

FIGURE **7.6**
Route of auditory impulses from the receptors in the ear to the auditory cortex
The cochlear nucleus receives input from the ipsilateral ear only (the one on the same side of the head). All later stages have input originating from both ears.

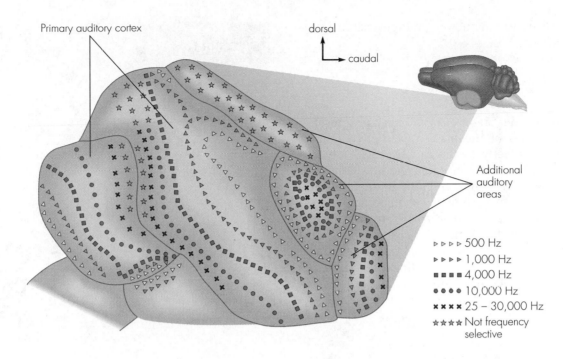

Primary auditory cortex

dorsal

caudal

Additional
auditory
areas

▷ ▷ ▷ ▷ 500 Hz
▶ ▶ ▶ ▶ 1,000 Hz
■ ■ ■ ■ 4,000 Hz
● ● ● ● 10,000 Hz
✕ ✕ ✕ ✕ 25 – 30,000 Hz
★ ★ ★ ★ Not frequency
              selective

FIGURE **7.7**
Responses of cells in a gerbil's primary auditory cortex
Each dot represents the location of a single cell in the primary auditory cortex of a gerbil.
The color of each dot indicates the approximate frequency of tone that produces the
greatest response. For example, the yellow dots represent neurons that respond best to
tones of about 500 Hz. Gray dots respond about equally to all tones. Note that the neurons are arranged in a gradient, with cells responding to low-frequency tones at one end
and cells responding to high-frequency tones at the other end. Note also that the gerbil
cortex has several separate representations of the auditory world, each presumably serv
ing a different function.   Source: Adapted from Scheich & Zuschratter, 1995.

aged individual must respond to combinations or sequences of sounds, such as in a melody or human
speech.

Just as the primary visual cortex (V1) adjoins additional visual areas such as V2 and V3, the primary auditory cortex adjoins several additional auditory areas.
Cells in the **secondary auditory cortex** respond weakly
if at all to any single tone. Instead, each cell responds
best to a complex combination of sounds. In rhesus
monkeys, most neurons in the secondary auditory cortex respond vigorously to one or another of the various
calls that male rhesus monkeys make (Rauschecker,
Tian, & Hauser, 1995). The corresponding area of the
human temporal cortex responds best to speech
sounds.

Deafness

Complete deafness is rare. About 99 percent of deaf
people can hear at least certain frequencies if the tones
are loud enough. We distinguish two categories of hear-

ing impairment: nerve deafness and conductive deafness.

Nerve deafness, or **inner-ear deafness,** results
from damage to the cochlea, the hair cells, or the auditory nerve. The damage can occur in any degree. It may
be confined to one part of the cochlea or to neurons in
one part of the cochlea. The result is a permanent impairment of hearing in one range of frequencies, most
often the high frequencies. Hearing aids cannot compensate for extensive nerve damage but can be designed to help people who have lost receptors in a portion of the cochlea. Nerve deafness can be inherited, or
it can develop from a variety of prenatal problems or
disorders of early childhood (Cremers & van Rijn, 1991;
Robillard & Gersdorff, 1986), including:

- Exposure of one's mother to rubella (German
  measles), syphilis, or other contagious diseases during pregnancy
- Exposure of one's mother to various toxins during
  pregnancy
- Inadequate oxygen to the brain during the birth
  process
- Inadequate activity of the thyroid gland

- Certain diseases, including multiple sclerosis and meningitis
- Childhood reactions to certain drugs, including aspirin
- Prolonged exposure to loud noises

Conductive deafness, or **middle-ear deafness,** occurs if the bones of the middle ear fail to transmit sound waves properly to the cochlea. Such deafness can be caused by certain diseases and infections or by a tumorous bone growth in and around the middle ear. Conductive deafness is sometimes temporary. If it persists, it can be corrected either by surgery or by hearing aids that amplify the stimulus. Because people with conductive deafness have a normal cochlea and auditory nerve, they can hear sounds that bypass the middle ear. For example, they can hear their own voices, which can be conducted through the bones of the skull directly to the cochlea.

Localization of Sounds

You are walking alone when suddenly you hear a loud noise. You want to know *what* produced the noise (friend or foe), but equally you want to know *where* the sound originated (so you can approach or escape it). Determining the direction and distance of a sound requires a comparison between the responses of the two ears—which are in effect just two points in space. And yet this system is accurate enough for you to turn almost immediately toward a sound, and for owls to locate mice in the middle of the night (Konishi, 1995).

We localize sounds through many cues, including differences between the ears in intensity and timing. First, intensity: If a sound has a high frequency and therefore a wavelength shorter than the width of the head, the head creates a *sound shadow* (Figure 7.8). Consequently, the sound is more intense for the closer ear. In adult humans, this mechanism produces accurate sound localization for frequencies above 2,000 to 3,000 Hz. Another method of localization is the difference in *time of arrival* at the two ears. A sound coming from a source directly in front of a person reaches both ears at the same time. A sound coming directly from the left will reach the left ear about 600 microseconds (6 × 10^{-4} seconds) before it reaches the right ear. Sounds coming from intermediate locations will reach the two ears at times 0 to 600 microseconds apart. Time of arrival is useful for localizing sounds with a distinct, sudden onset, such as the sound of an object hitting the floor. It is less useful for localizing sounds with a gradual onset. When threatened, many birds give alarm calls that increase gradually in loudness; such calls are

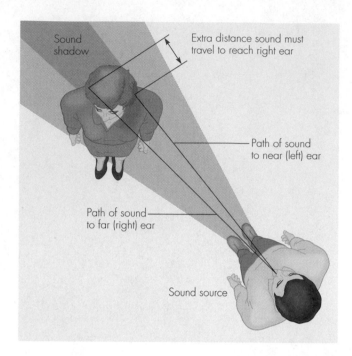

FIGURE **7.8**
Differential loudness as a cue for sound localization
The sound shadow shown here does not include the effects of diffraction, or "bending" of sound waves around the head.
Source: After Lindsay & Norman, 1972.

difficult for the predator to localize. Their mating calls are much easier to localize.

However, for low-frequency sound waves, even gradual-onset sounds can be localized. Every sound wave has phases, with two consecutive peaks 360 degrees apart. Figure 7.9 shows sound waves that are in phase and sound waves that are 45, 90, and 180 degrees out of phase. If a sound originates to the side of the head, the sound wave that strikes one ear will be slightly out of phase with the same sound wave as it strikes the other ear. In Figure 7.10a, note that the sound waves in the left ear are out of phase with those in the right ear. For each wave, the receptors in the ear closer to the sound source will fire slightly sooner than those in the farther ear will. A large difference in phase between the two ears indicates that the sound source is almost directly to the side; a small difference indicates that the sound source is approximately straight ahead or straight behind. However, phase differences are useless for localizing high-frequency sounds. As Figure 7.10b shows, it would be easy to confuse the phase of one high-frequency wave with the phase of another wave. Phase differences provide information that is useful for localizing sounds with frequencies up to about 1,500 Hz.

In short, humans localize low frequencies (up to 1,500 Hz) mostly by differences in phase and time of onset. We localize high frequencies (above 2,000 to

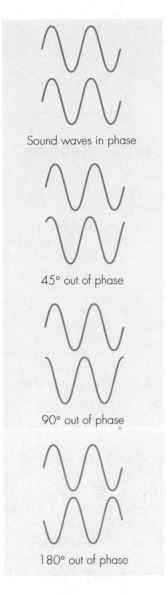

FIGURE **7.9**
Sound waves can be in phase or out of phase

Sound waves in phase

45° out of phase

90° out of phase

180° out of phase

3,000 Hz) by loudness differences. We are less accurate at localizing intermediate frequencies.

The usefulness of both methods of localization depends on the size of the head (Masterton, Heffner, & Ravizza, 1969). A mouse's ears are so close together that it cannot detect phase differences even with a low-frequency sound. Mice and other small animals can localize sounds only by differences in loudness, but loudness is a good localization cue only for high frequencies. (At lower frequencies, the head does not produce much of a sound shadow.) The smaller the animal, the higher a frequency must be before the animal can use loudness as a cue to direction.

Mammals with small heads have tended to evolve the greatest sensitivity to high-frequency sounds. For example, many species of rodents are sensitive to frequencies up to 40,000, 60,000, or even 100,000 Hz. Mammals with large heads are more sensitive to low frequencies, which they can localize readily. For example, the upper limit for elephants is just 10,000 Hz (Heffner & Heffner, 1982). These findings underscore a point made at the beginning of this chapter: Each species is most sensitive to the information that is most useful to it.

IN **CLOSING**

Distinctive Features of Hearing

Evolution has adapted the human auditory system to the highly complex process of language, and we sometimes

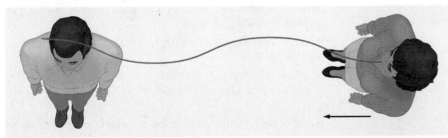

(a)

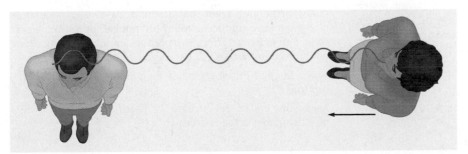

(b)

FIGURE **7.10**
Phase differences between the ears as a cue for sound localization
Note that a low-frequency tone (**a**) arrives at the ears slightly out of phase. The ear for which the receptors fire first (here, the person's left ear) is interpreted as being closer to the sound. If the difference in phase between the ears is small, then the sound source is close to the center of the body. However, with a high-frequency sound (**b**), the phase differences become ambiguous. The person cannot tell which sound wave in the left ear corresponds to which sound wave in the right ear.

forget that the original, primary function of hearing has to do with simpler but extremely important issues: What do I hear? Where is it? Is it coming closer? Is it a potential mate, a potential enemy, a potential food, or something irrelevant? The organization of the auditory system is well suited to resolving these questions.

Summary

1. We detect the pitch of low-frequency sounds by the frequency of action potentials in the auditory system. We detect the pitch of high-frequency sounds by the area of greatest response along the basilar membrane. (p. 182)
2. Each cell in the primary auditory cortex responds best to a particular frequency of tones. Cells in the adjoining secondary auditory cortex respond poorly to any one tone but more vigorously to combinations of sounds, such as human speech or monkey vocalizations. (p. 184)
3. Deafness may result from damage to the nerve cells or to the bones that conduct sounds to the nerve cells. (p. 185)
4. We localize high-frequency sounds according to differences in loudness between the ears. We localize low-frequency sounds on the basis of differences in phase. (p. 186)

Review Questions

1. Contrast the frequency theory, the volley principle, and the place theory of pitch perception. (p. 182)
2. How do our mechanisms of pitch perception vary among low-, medium-, and high-pitched tones? (p. 182)
3. In what way do the effects of damage to the primary auditory cortex differ from the effects of damage to the primary visual cortex? (p. 184)
4. What are the two major categories of deafness, and what causes each? (p. 185)
5. What mechanisms enable an animal to localize sounds? How does the effectiveness of each method depend on the size of the animal's head? (p. 186)

Thought Questions

1. Why do you suppose that the human auditory system evolved sensitivity to sounds in the range of 20 to 20,000 Hz instead of some other range of frequencies?
2. The text explains how we might distinguish loudness for low-pitched sounds. How might we distinguish loudness for high-pitched sounds?
3. Which would stimulate a larger portion of the basilar membrane—a high-frequency tone or a low-frequency tone? Why?

4. The medial part of the superior olive (a structure in the medulla) is critical for sound localization based on phase differences. The lateral part of the superior olive is critical for localization based on loudness. Which part of the superior olive would you expect to be better developed in mice? In elephants?

Suggestions for Further Reading

Goldstein, E. B. (1996). *Sensation and perception* (4th ed.). Belmont, CA: Wadsworth. A general textbook on the sensory systems, emphasizing vision and hearing.

Webster, D. B., Fay, R. R., & Popper, A. N. (Eds.). (1992). *The evolutionary biology of hearing.* New York: Springer Verlag. Collection of articles about hearing in humans and other species.

Terms

amplitude   the intensity of a sound or other stimulus (p. 180)

loudness   perception of the intensity of a sound (p. 180)

frequency   the number of sound waves per second (p. 180)

pitch   the experience that corresponds to the frequency of a sound (p. 180)

pinna   the outer-ear structure of flesh and cartilage that sticks out from the side of the head (p. 181)

tympanic membrane   the eardrum (p. 181)

oval window   a membrane of the inner ear, adjacent to the stirrup (p. 181)

cochlea   structure in the inner ear, containing auditory receptors (p. 182)

hair cell   a type of sensory receptor shaped like a hair; auditory receptors are hair cells (p. 182)

basilar membrane   floor of the scala media, within the cochlea (p. 182)

tectorial membrane   roof of the scala media, within the cochlea (p. 182)

frequency theory   concept that pitch perception depends on differences in frequency of action potentials by auditory neurons (p. 182)

place theory   concept that pitch perception depends on which part of the inner ear has cells with the greatest activity level (p. 182)

volley principle   tenet that a sound wave of a moderately high pitch may produce a volley of impulses by various fibers even if no individual fiber can produce impulses in synchrony with the sound waves (p. 183)

base   the part of the tympanic membrane closest to the stirrup (p. 183)

apex   one end of the cochlea, farthest from the point where the stirrup meets the cochlea (p. 183)

traveling wave   wave that travels along a surface, producing some displacement at all points, though possibly more at some than at others (p. 183)

primary auditory cortex   area in the temporal lobes in which cells respond best to tones of a particular frequency (p. 184)

secondary auditory cortex   area adjoining the primary auditory cortex; cells here respond best to complex combinations of sounds, such as human speech or monkey vocalizations (p. 185)

nerve deafness or **inner-ear deafness**   hearing loss that results from damage to the cochlea, the hair cells, or the auditory nerve (p. 185)

conductive deafness or **middle-ear deafness**   hearing loss that occurs if the bones of the middle ear fail to transmit sound waves properly to the cochlea (p. 186)

The Mechanical Senses

The next time you turn on your radio or stereo set, place your hand on its surface. The vibrations you feel in your hand are the same vibrations you hear.

If you practiced enough, could you learn to "hear" the vibrations with your fingers? No. They would remain just vibrations. If an earless species had enough time, might its vibration detectors evolve into sound detectors? Yes! In fact, that is probably how our remote ancestors did evolve the ability to hear. Fish have no ears as such; they have on each side of the body a *lateral line system* consisting of touch receptors that respond to vibrations in the water. Primitive vertebrates probably had similar touch receptors, from which we ultimately evolved our organs of hearing. But we also retained receptors that are responsive to mechanical stimulation. Psychologists generally pay little attention to them, but their importance becomes clear as soon as we contemplate what it would be like to live without them.

The *mechanical senses*—called that because they respond to pressure, bending, or other distortions of a receptor—include touch, pain, temperature, and other body sensations, as well as vestibular sensation, a system specialized to detect the position and movement of the head and to adjust posture and eye movements. Audition could be regarded as a mechanical sense as well, because the hair cells are modified touch receptors. However, it is convenient to consider audition separately because it provides information about much higher vibrational frequencies.

Vestibular Sensation

Try this demonstration: Attempt to read this text while you jiggle your head up and down, back and forth. It is a little inconvenient, you will find, but not too bad. Now hold your head steady and jiggle the book up and down, back and forth. Suddenly, reading becomes much more difficult. Why?

TRY IT YOURSELF

When you move your head, the **vestibular organ** adjacent to the cochlea monitors each movement and directs compensatory movements of your eyes. When your head moves left, your eyes move right; when your head moves right, your eyes move left. Almost effortlessly, you keep your eyes focused on what you want to see. When you move the page, however, the vestibular organ cannot help you keep your eyes on target. Sensations from the vestibular organ detect the direction of tilt and the amount of acceleration of the head. We are seldom aware of our vestibular sensations except under unusual conditions such as riding a roller coaster; they are nevertheless critical for guiding eye movements and maintaining balance.

The anatomy of the vestibular organ, shown in Figure 7.11, consists of two **otolith organs** (the *saccule* and *utricle*) and three semicircular canals. Like the hearing receptors, the vestibular receptors are modified touch receptors. One otolith organ has a horizontal patch of hairs; the other has a vertical patch. Calcium carbonate particles called *otoliths* lie next to the hair cells in the otolith organs. When the head tilts in different directions, the otoliths push against different sets of hair cells and excite them (Gresty, Bronstein, Brandt, & Dieterich, 1992).

The three **semicircular canals,** oriented in three different planes, are filled with a jellylike substance and lined with hair cells. An acceleration of the head in any plane causes the jellylike substance in one of these canals to push against the hair cells. Action potentials initiated by cells of the vestibular system travel through part of the eighth cranial nerve to the brain stem and cerebellum. (The eighth cranial nerve contains both an auditory component and a vestibular component.)

Somatosensation

The **somatosensory system,** the sensation of the body and its movements, is not one sense but many. We can distinguish the shape of an object (discriminative

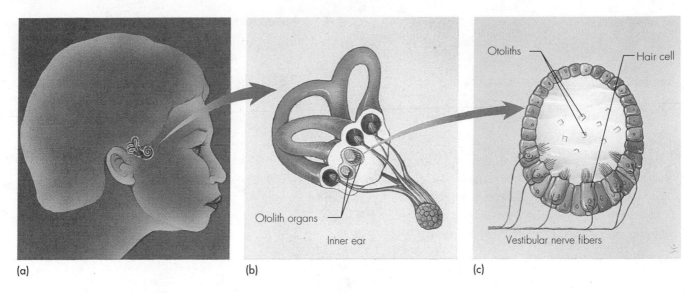

(a) (b) (c)

FIGURE **7.11**

(**a**) Location of the vestibular organs. (**b**) Structures of the vestibular organs. (**c**) Cross section through an otolith organ. Calcium carbonate particles, called otoliths, press against different hair cells, depending on the direction of tilt and rate of acceleration of the head.

touch), deep pressure, cold, warmth, pain, and the position and movement of joints.

Somatosensory Receptors

The skin is packed with a variety of somatosensory receptors. Some of the major receptor types found in mammalian skin are shown in Figure 7.12; their probable functions are listed in Table 7.1 (Iggo & Andres, 1982). However, each receptor contributes in some degree to several kinds of somatosensory experience. Many respond to more than one kind of stimulus, such as touch and temperature. Others (not shown on the list) respond to deep stimulation, joint movement, or muscle movement.

A touch receptor may be a simple bare neuron ending (such as many pain receptors), an elaborated neuron ending (Ruffini endings and Meissner's corpuscles), or a bare ending surrounded by nonneural cells that modify its function (Pacinian corpuscles). Some of the more sensitive areas of skin, such as the fingertips, have as many as 350 touch cells per square millimeter of surface.

One example of a receptor is the **Pacinian corpuscle** (see Figure 7.13), which detects sudden displacements or high-frequency vibrations on the skin. Inside the onionlike surround is a neuron membrane. When mechanical pressure bends the membrane, its resistance to sodium flow decreases, and sodium ions enter, depolarizing the membrane (Loewenstein, 1960). Only a sudden or vibrating stimulus can bend the membrane; the onionlike outer structure provides mechani-

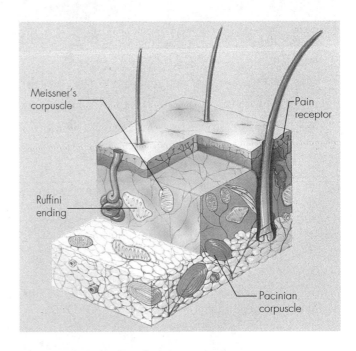

FIGURE **7.12**

Some sensory receptors found in the skin, the human body's largest organ

cal support that resists gradual or constant pressure on the skin.

We need practice to use touch information effectively, just as we do for vision or hearing. In one study, the whiskers of infant rats were trimmed daily until the rats were 45 days old. After their whiskers grew back, the rats learned to use them to feel surfaces and discriminate rough from smooth, but they never learned to

TABLE **7.1**
Somatosensory Receptors and Their Probable Functions

Receptor	Location	Responds to	Rate of Adaptation to a Prolonged Stimulus
Free nerve ending (unmyelinated or thinly myelinated fibers)	Around base of hairs and elsewhere in skin	Pain, warmth, cold	Uncertain
Hair-follicle receptors	Hair-covered skin	Movement of hairs	Rapid
Meissner's corpuscles	Hairless areas	Sudden displacement of skin; low-frequency vibration (flutter)	Rapid (?)
Pacinian corpuscles	Both hairy and hairless skin	Sudden displacement of skin; high-frequency vibration	Very rapid
Merkel's disks	Both hairy and hairless skin	Indentation of skin	Slow
Ruffini endings	Both hairy and hairless skin	Stretch of skin	Slow
Krause end bulbs	Hairless areas, perhaps including genitals; maybe some hairy areas	Uncertain	Uncertain

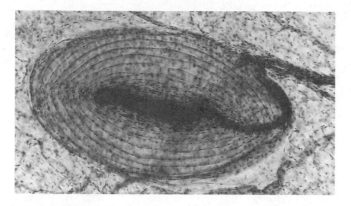

FIGURE **7.13**
A Pacinian corpuscle
Pacinian corpuscles respond best to sudden displacement of the skin or to high-frequency vibrations. They respond only briefly to steady pressure on the skin. The onionlike outer structure provides a mechanical support to the neuron inside it so that a sudden stimulus can bend it but a sustained stimulus cannot.

distinguish one rough surface from another, as normally experienced rats do (Carvell & Simons, 1996).

Input to the Spinal Cord and the Brain

Information from touch receptors in the head enters the CNS through the cranial nerves. Information from receptors below the head enters the spinal cord and passes toward the brain. The spinal cord has 31 segments and therefore 31 sets of sensory and motor nerves. Beginning at the top, the **spinal nerves** (see Figure 7.14) include eight cervical nerves, twelve thoracic nerves, five lumbar nerves, five sacral nerves, and one coccygeal nerve.

Each spinal nerve *innervates* (connects to) a limited area of the body. The skin area connected to a single sensory spinal nerve is called a **dermatome** (see Figure 7.15). For example, the third thoracic nerve (T3) innervates a strip of skin just above the nipples as well as the underarm area. But the borders between dermatomes are not so distinct as Figure 7.15 implies; there is actually an overlap of one-third to one-half between adjacent pairs.

The sensory information that enters the spinal cord travels in well-defined pathways toward the brain, with different kinds of information, such as touch and temperature, taking different routes and projecting to different parts of the thalamus and cerebral cortex (Dykes, Sur, Merzenich, Kaas, & Nelson, 1981). The various areas of the somatosensory thalamus send their impulses to different areas of the somatosensory cortex, located in the parietal lobe. Two parallel strips in the somatosensory cortex respond mostly to touch on the skin; two other parallel strips respond mostly to deep pressure and movement of the joints and muscles (Kaas, 1983). In short, various aspects of somatosensation remain at least partly separate from one another at all levels, from the receptors to the cortex.

The somatosensory cortex receives input primarily from the contralateral side of the body, although many cells also receive input across the corpus callosum from the somatosensory cortex of the opposite hemisphere. Such crossed input enables somatosensory cortex cells to compare, for example, left-hand sensation and right-hand sensation (Iwamura, Iriki, & Tanaka, 1994). After damage to the somatosensory cortex, people generally experience an impairment of body perceptions. One patient with Alzheimer's disease, who had damage in the somatosensory cortex as well as elsewhere, had much trouble getting her clothes on correctly, and she could

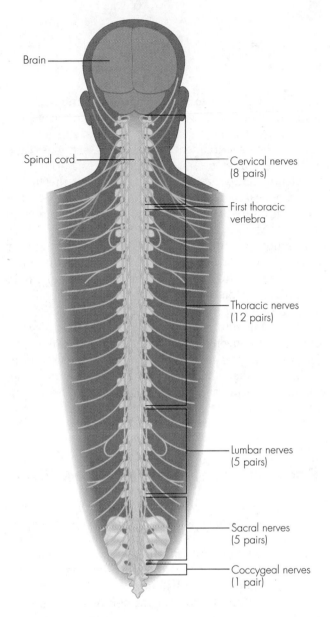

FIGURE **7.14**
The human central nervous system (CNS)
Spinal nerves from each segment of the spinal cord exit through
the correspondingly numbered opening between vertebrae.
Source: From Starr & Taggart, 1989.

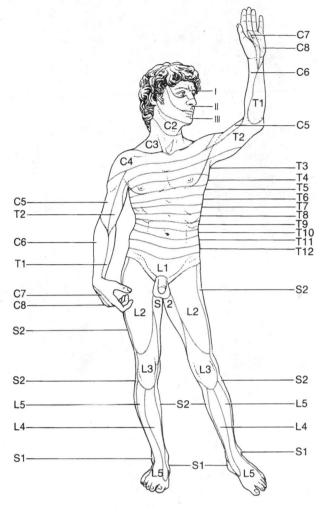

FIGURE **7.15**
**Dermatomes innervated by the 31 sensory spinal
nerves**
Areas I, II, and III of the face are not innervated by the spinal
nerves, but instead by three branches of the fifth cranial nerve.
Although this figure shows distinct borders, the dermatomes
actually overlap one another by about one-third to one-half of
their width.

not point correctly in response to such directions as
"show me your elbow" or "point to my knee," although
she pointed correctly to various nonbody objects in the
room. When told to touch her elbow, her most frequent
response was to feel her wrist and arm and suggest that
the elbow was probably around there, somewhere. She
acted as if she had only a blurry map of her own body
parts (Sirigu, Grafman, Bressler, & Sunderland, 1991).

Because touch perception itself depends on activity
in the cerebral cortex, people with an intact cortex but
damage in the periphery may experience a **phantom**
limb, the continuing sensation of an amputated body
part. That experience can range from an occasional tingling sensation to intense pain. The area of the somatosensory cortex that formerly responded to the amputated part is likely to reorganize its connections,
becoming responsive to other body parts. The stimulation of other parts, however, is sometimes experienced
as if it had come from the amputated part. Magnetoencephalography (see Chapter 4) indicates that the people
who have the greatest amount of reorganization of the
somatosensory cortex after an amputation are the most
likely to experience a painful phantom limb (Flor et al.,
1995).

FIGURE **7.16**

People with a phantom limb report sensation in the amputated limb—for example, pain as if fingernails were digging into the skin. By looking in a mirror placed as shown here, such a person can "see" the amputated limb (actually a reflection of the normal limb). If the normal limb moves, the phantom limb now also feels as if it is moving. If the normal fist relaxes, some people with a phantom limb feel their phantom fist relaxing—with consequent reduction of pain.

Is there anything one can do to relieve the phantom pain? In some cases, yes. In one study, five people with painful phantom limbs who felt "as if fingernails were digging into the skin," sat with a tall mirror perpendicular to the chest, as shown in Figure 7.16, so that they saw a mirror image of their normal arm superimposed on the phantom that they felt. Four of them found that if they made a fist with the normal hand, and then looked into the mirror while opening that hand, they felt the phantom hand opening also, and the pain subsiding (Ramachandran, Rogers-Ramachandran, & Cobb, 1995). Evidently, the combination of the visual experience and the tactile experience of the opposite hand, transferred via the corpus callosum, had somehow altered the activity in the somatosensory cortex that had been producing the phantom pain.

Pain

Pain, the sensation evoked by a harmful stimulus, alerts us to a danger. People who are born with an insensitivity to pain sustain a seemingly endless series of injuries. They have frequent severe burns, scratches, and cuts, because they do not receive an early warning signal of impending harm. They may bite off the tips of their tongues, scorch their mouths by drinking very hot coffee, or injure their feet by exposing them too long to the cold. Many such people also damage their bones and tendons by sitting or standing in one position for too long. Most of us shift position every few minutes without even thinking about it because we feel a mild discomfort. People lacking a sense of pain generally do not feel even that discomfort.

A woman with pain insensitivity once took a casserole out of the oven and carried it with her bare hands. Her husband screamed because the casserole was burning hot, but she calmly set it on their cardboard table. Not until the table burst into flames did she realize what a mistake she had made (Comings & Amromin, 1974).

Pain Neurons and Their Neurotransmitters

The term *pain* refers to a wide variety of sensations, ranging from sharp cuts to dull headaches (see Digression 7.1). Many kinds of pain depend on certain unmyelinated and thinly myelinated axons carrying information to the spinal cord and releasing a neurotransmitter known as **substance P** (Levine, Fields, & Basbaum, 1993). The spinal cord neurons in turn send the information to certain thalamic nuclei that relay it to parts of the cerebral cortex, especially the insula, the cingulate cortex, and the somatosensory cortex (Craig, Bushnell, Zhang, & Blomqvist, 1994; Talbot et al., 1991). (See Figure 7.17.) The projection to the cingulate cortex is interesting, because that part of the brain has been linked to emotional responses.

What effect would you expect if an investigator injected substance P, an important pain transmitter, into an animal's spinal cord? The animal would whimper, scratch, bite, and show other indications of pain—not pain in the spinal cord itself, but in the part of the body that ordinarily sends information to that section of the spinal cord. An animal also shows signs of pain and distress after a spinal injection of **capsaicin,** a chemical that causes neurons containing substance P to release it suddenly. An injection of capsaicin causes an animal to

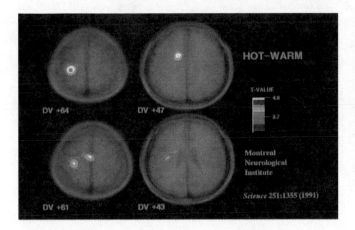

HOT-WARM

T-VALUE

DV +64   DV +47

DV +61   DV +43

Montreal
Neurological
Institute

Science 251:1355 (1991)

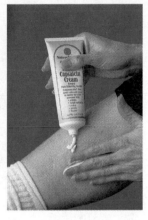

When people rub a medication containing capsaicin into a sore spot, they experience a burning sensation followed by relief from pain.

FIGURE **7.17**
Representation of pain in the human brain
Investigators used PET scans and MRI data to record the activity of various brain areas during exposure to painful heat and to nonpainful warmth, both on the right arm. Then the investigators subtracted the activity during warm stimulation from the activity during painful heat to find the activity attributable to pain itself. The areas marked in white showed the greatest response to pain, followed by the red, yellow, blue, and violet areas. Response was greatest in a portion of the somatosensory cortex contralateral to the stimulated arm.   Source: Talbot et al., 1991.

react about the same way as it would after an injection of substance P itself. After a few minutes, however, because the neurons released substance P far faster than they could resynthesize it, their ability to release it de-

clines. Consequently, the animal becomes relatively insensitive to pain for a long time, even months (Gamse, Leeman, Holzer, & Lembeck, 1981; Jancsó, Kiraly, & Jancsó-Gábor, 1977; Yarsh, Farb, Leeman, & Jessell, 1979).

Capsaicin occurs in nature in jalapeños and other hot peppers. When you eat a hot pepper, the capsaicin causes certain neurons in your tongue to release substance P, giving you a sensation of pain or heat. After the heat sensation wears off, you may experience a pleasant state of relief, probably accompanied by a decreased sensitivity to pain on your tongue. Capsaicin is therefore sometimes used for pain relief. Capsaicin rubbed onto a sore shoulder, an arthritic joint, or other

DIGRESSION **7.1**

Headaches

Most headaches are the result of tension in the neck muscles, sinus infections, anxiety or depression, sleeplessness, or withdrawal from caffeine. Such headaches can be treated with rest, aspirin, or, in some cases, antidepressant drugs or tranquilizers; they are not a cause for great concern. Less commonly, a headache may be a sign of a serious medical problem, such as a brain tumor, encephalitis or other brain infection, a burst blood vessel, head injury, or migraine.

Here are a few questions to ask to determine whether a headache is probably a serious medical problem or probably a "don't worry about it" headache (Diamond, 1994; Pincus & Tucker, 1985):

• Have you had headaches like this before? (If yes, especially if you have had them occasionally for a year or more, your headache is almost certainly *not* a serious problem.)

• Is this headache the worst you have ever had? (If it is, it may be a serious problem.)
• Are you able to go to work or school in spite of the headache? (If yes, the headache is probably not serious.)
• Does the headache awaken you when you are sleeping? (If it does, it might be serious.)
• Is the headache worse on some days than on others? (If it is worse during the week and not so bad on weekends, it is probably a tension headache.)
• Does your headache make you vomit? Lose consciousness? (If it does, it is a serious problem, perhaps migraine.)
• Have any of your relatives had similar headaches? (Most people with migraine headaches will say yes.)

FIGURE **7.18**
Synapses responsible for pain and its inhibition
The pain afferent neuron releases substance P as its neurotransmitter. Another neuron releases enkephalin at presynaptic synapses; the enkephalin inhibits the release of substance P and therefore alleviates pain.

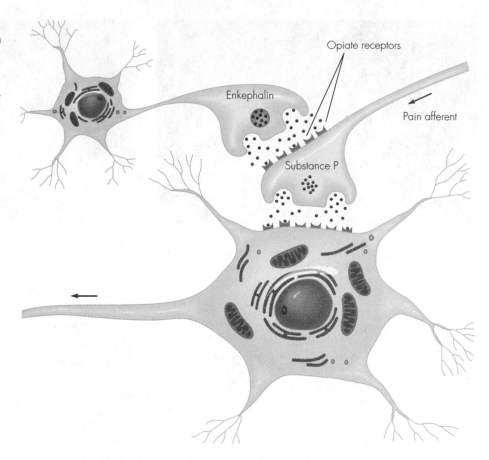

painful area produces a temporary, mild sting followed by a longer period of decreased pain. Do not, however, try eating hot peppers to help reduce pain in, say, your legs. Because little if any of the ingested capsaicin enters the blood, the capsaicin you eat will not relieve your pain—unless it is your tongue that hurts (Karrer & Bartoshuk, 1991).

Events That Limit Pain

How much pain someone feels is often poorly related to the amount of tissue damage. On the one hand, some people complain of severe and lasting pain after a minor injury. On the other hand, athletes and soldiers sometimes ignore serious injuries until their competition or battle is over. An infant rat reacts vigorously to a burning stimulus when it is by itself, but reacts only slightly if it is next to its mother (Blass, Shide, Zaw-Mon, & Sorrentino, 1995).

To account for certain of these phenomena, Ronald Melzack and P. D. Wall (1965) proposed a highly influential theory of pain known as the **gate theory.** According to this theory, certain areas of the spinal cord receive messages not only from pain receptors but also from other receptors in the skin and from axons descending from the brain. If these other inputs to the spinal cord are sufficiently active, they close the "gates"

for the pain messages. In other words, the brain can increase or decrease its own exposure to pain information.

Although Melzack and Wall's gate theory included certain details that turned out to be wrong, the general principle is valid: Nonpain stimuli can increase or decrease the intensity of pain. Much of that regulation takes place through **opioid mechanisms**—systems that are responsive to opiate drugs and similar chemicals. For centuries, although people have been using opiates to relieve pain, induce sleep, and stimulate pleasure, no one knew how they worked. Then, in 1973, Candace Pert and Solomon Snyder identified brain receptors that bind specifically to morphine and related drugs. They also demonstrated that the opiate receptors are concentrated in the same brain areas where substance P is concentrated (McLean, Skirboll, & Pert, 1985). Apparently, opiate receptors inhibit or limit the pain-producing effects of substance P (see Figure 7.18).

The discovery of opiate receptors implied that the brain must have its own chemicals with opiatelike effects. Before long, those substances were discovered. Two of them are peptide neurotransmitters: **met-enkephalin** and **leu-enkephalin.** (The term *enkephalin* refers to the fact that these chemicals were first found in the brain, or encephalon. The two enkephalins are the same except at one end, where met-enkephalin has methionine and leu-enkephalin has leucine.) Although the enkephalins have chemical structures very unlike mor-

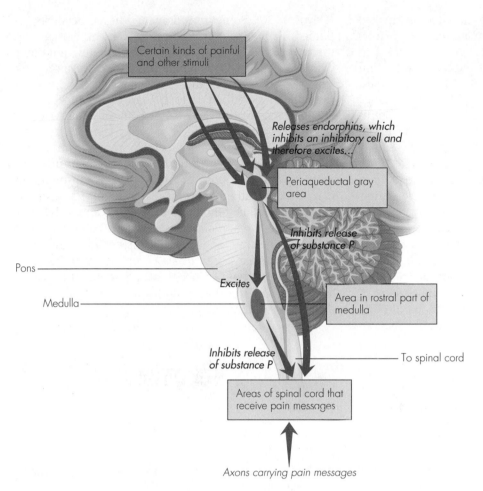

FIGURE **7.19**
The periaqueductal gray area, where electrical stimulation relieves pain
Periaqueductal means "around the aqueduct," a passageway of cerebrospinal fluid between the third and fourth ventricles.

Certain kinds of painful and other stimuli

Releases endorphins, which inhibits an inhibitory cell and therefore excites...

Periaqueductal gray area

Inhibits release of substance P

Pons

Excites

Medulla

Area in rostral part of medulla

Inhibits release of substance P

To spinal cord

Areas of spinal cord that receive pain messages

Axons carrying pain messages

phine, they interact with the same receptors as morphine, as do a number of other brain chemicals, including *dynorphin*, β-*endorphin*, α-*neoendorphin*, and *nociceptin*. Collectively, these chemicals are known as **endorphins** (a contraction of *endogenous morphines*) because they are the brain's own morphines. (Nociceptin, unlike the others, increases pain.)

Among the many roles of endorphins in behavior, the best documented one is **analgesia** (relief from pain). According to a theoretical review by Basbaum and Fields (1984), certain stimuli, particularly certain painful stimuli, activate neurons that release endorphins in the **periaqueductal gray area** and surrounding areas in the midbrain. Under the influence of the endorphins, the periaqueductal gray area excites cells in the medulla, and then the axons from both the medulla and the periaqueductal gray area itself send messages to appropriate areas of the spinal cord and brain stem, blocking the release of substance P and therefore decreasing pain (Reichling, Kwiat, & Basbaum, 1988; Terman, Shavitt, Lewis, Cannon, & Liebeskind, 1984). Figure 7.19 summarizes these effects.

Have you ever wondered why morphine and other opiates relieve slow, dull pain but not sharp pain? For example, morphine relieves postsurgical pain, but it would not be effective during the surgery itself. Also,

patients under the influence of morphine to relieve postsurgical pain feel the sharp pain of a needle injection. The explanation is that sharp pain is carried in large-diameter pain fibers (with cell bodies larger than 40 μm), which are unaffected by endorphins, whereas dull pain is carried by smaller pain fibers (with cell bodies smaller than 30 μm), which do respond to endorphins (Taddese, Nah, & McCleskey, 1995).

Stimuli That Produce Analgesia

Pain inhibits pain; that is, certain kinds of painful stimuli evoke the release of endorphins, which put the brakes on further pain. Presumably, the evolutionary function of this mechanism is that pain alerts the animal to danger, then shuts off the pain message before it throws the animal into an unproductive panic.

A number of situations loosely characterized as stressful can also reduce pain. For example, the mere presence of a cat temporarily decreases rats' response to pain (Lester & Fanselow, 1985). Pain-induced and stress-induced analgesia sometimes depend on the release of endorphins and sometimes do not. For example, exposure to intermittent or low-intensity continuous shock induces the release of endorphins. We know that endorphins are necessary because the effect is blocked by **naloxone,** a drug that blocks opiate receptors. However, exposure to continuous, high-intensity shock also decreases pain sensitivity without inducing endorphin release (Terman & Liebeskind, 1986). In many cases, the nonendorphin analgesia can be blocked by drugs that interfere with glutamate synapses (Mogil, Sternberg, & Liebeskind, 1993). Evidently, animals have several mechanisms for inhibiting pain, not just the endorphin system.

Physicians and physical therapists sometimes try to control patients' pain with stimuli that release endorphins. Two examples are acupuncture, an ancient Chinese technique of gently twisting thin needles placed in the skin, and **transcutaneous electrical nerve stimulation (TENS),** a prolonged, mild electrical shock applied to the arms, legs, or back. TENS provides relief for more than half of people in pain, with almost none of the side effects or risks associated with painkilling drugs (Pomeranz, 1989). Note that, because TENS decreases pain through nonpain stimulation, it supports the gate theory of pain.

The Pros and Cons of Morphine Analgesia

Suppose that a patient is suffering serious pain after surgery or from cancer. Should a physician prescribe enough morphine to suppress the pain? Or should the patient just suffer through it?

Some physicians hesitate to prescribe morphine, partly because of the fear of addiction. Actually, morphine taken under hospital conditions almost never becomes addictive. Very large doses of morphine can suppress breathing, but moderate doses do not pose that risk.

A more serious worry is that opiates temporarily weaken the immune system and leave the body vulnerable to disease and even to the spread of certain kinds of cancer. That danger, however, lasts only a couple of days before the immune system returns to full force. Prolonged pain or stress, in contrast, weakens the immune system for much longer (Mogil, Sternberg, & Liebeskind, 1993). Morphine, by alleviating pain, in the long run actually strengthens the immune system and enhances the defenses against the spread of certain cancers (Page, Ben-Eliyahu, Yirmiya, & Liebeskind, 1993). Consequently, vigorous efforts to relieve pain are beneficial not just because they comfort the patient, but also because they promote long-term recovery.

The Sensitization of Pain

In addition to opioid and other mechanisms of decreasing pain, the body has mechanisms that increase pain

(Devor, 1996). Sometimes damaged tissue becomes inflamed, activating the immune system and triggering the release of histamine, nerve growth factor, and other chemicals that help to repair the damage. Among the less pleasant effects of those chemicals is an increase in the number of sodium gates in nearby receptors and axons. Because of the increase in sodium gates, a weak stimulus that would ordinarily evoke few if any action potentials will suddenly evoke a rapid train of responses. Even a gentle touch becomes painful, and what would have been a mildly painful tap or bump can be excruciatingly painful. Even without any stimulus at all, action potentials arise spontaneously, producing a burning or stinging sensation. The spinal cord may also become sensitized, causing an increase in painful sensations even in areas remote from the damage. In short, pain is a complex phenomenon, with some mechanisms that inhibit it and others that exaggerate and prolong it.

IN CLOSING

The Mechanical Senses

We humans generally pay so much attention to vision and hearing that we take our mechanical senses for granted. However, a mere moment's reflection should reveal how critical they are for survival. At every moment your vestibular sense tells you whether you are standing or falling; your sense of pain can tell you that you have in fact fallen. If you moved to a television-like universe with only vision and hearing, you might get by if you had already learned what all the sights and sounds mean. But it is hard to imagine how you could have learned their meaning if you had not had extensive experience of touch and pain.

Summary

1. The vestibular system is a sensory system that detects the position and acceleration of the head and adjusts body posture and eye movements accordingly. (p. 190)
2. The somatosensory system depends on a variety of receptors that are sensitive to different kinds of stimulation of the skin and internal tissues. The brain maintains several parallel somatosensory representations of the body. (p. 190)
3. Because body sensation lies in the brain, not in the body itself, people sometimes experience sensations from amputated parts. Such "phantom limbs" reflect a reorganization of the somatosensory cortex. (p. 193)

4. Pain messages are transmitted by axons that predominantly release substance P as a neurotransmitter. (p. 194)

5. A certain harmful stimulus may give rise to a greater or lesser degree of pain, depending on other current and recent stimuli. According to the gate theory of pain, other stimuli can close certain gates and block the transmission of pain. (p. 196)

6. Opiate drugs attach to a particular type of receptor in the brain. The brain produces its own opiate-like chemicals, known collectively as endorphins, which decrease pain sensations, probably by blocking the release of substance P. (p. 196)

7. Pain and stress can release endorphins and thereby decrease sensitivity to pain. (p. 197)

8. Although morphine by itself temporarily impairs the immune system, pain impairs it more. Morphine, by relieving pain, actually produces a net enhancement of the immune system. (p. 198)

Review Questions

1. If a person suffers damage to the vestibular system, he or she has trouble reading street signs while walking. Why? (p. 190)

2. In what way is touch several senses instead of just one? (p. 190)

3. By what method is it sometimes possible to relieve phantom pain? (p. 194)

4. Why is lifelong insensitivity to pain dangerous? (p. 194)

5. Which neurotransmitter do pain-receptor neurons release? (p. 194)

6. How do jalapeño peppers produce a hot sensation? (p. 195)

7. Why does morphine relieve dull pain but not sharp pain? (p. 197)

8. What evidence indicates that we have more than one mechanism for inhibiting pain? (p. 197)

Thought Questions

1. Why is the vestibular sense generally useless under conditions of weightlessness?

2. Sometimes you can temporarily relieve a pain by scratching the skin around the painful area. Explain how this procedure may work.

Suggestions for Further Reading

Hamill, O. P., & McBride, D. W., Jr. (1995). Mechanoreceptive membrane channels. *American Scientist, 83,* 30–37. Describes the mechanisms of various somatosensory receptors.

Snyder, S. (1989). *Brainstorming: The science and politics of opiate research.* Cambridge, MA: Harvard University Press. Fascinating insider's history of the discovery of endorphins.

Terms

vestibular organ component in the inner ear that detects tilt of the head (p. 190)

otolith organ an organ responsible for vestibular sensation (p. 190)

semicircular canal canal lined with hair cells and oriented in three planes, sensitive to the direction of tilt of the head (p. 190)

somatosensory system sensory network that monitors the surface of the body and its movements (p. 190)

Pacinian corpuscle a receptor that responds to a sudden displacement of the skin or high-frequency vibration on the skin (p. 191)

spinal nerve nerve that conveys information between the spinal cord and either sensory receptors or muscles in the periphery (p. 192)

dermatome area of skin connected to a particular spinal nerve (p. 192)

phantom limb a sensation that feels like a body part even after that part has been amputated (p. 193)

substance P a neurotransmitter released by nerves that are sensitive to pain (p. 194)

capsaicin a chemical that causes neurons containing substance P to release it suddenly (p. 194)

gate theory assumption that stimulation of certain nonpain axons in the skin or in the brain can inhibit transmission of pain messages in the spinal cord (p. 196)

opioid mechanisms systems responsive to opiate drugs and similar chemicals (p. 196)

leu-enkephalin and **met-enkephalin** each, a chain of five amino acids believed to function as a neurotransmitter that inhibits pain (p. 196)

endorphin category of chemicals the body produces that stimulate the same receptors as do opiates (p. 197)

analgesia relief from pain (p. 197)

periaqueductal gray area of the brain stem that is rich in enkephalin synapses (p. 197)

naloxone drug that blocks opiate receptors (p. 197)

transcutaneous electrical nerve stimulation (TENS) method of relieving pain by applying prolonged, mild electrical shock to the arms, legs, or back (p. 198)

The Chemical Senses

Suppose you had the godlike power to create a new species of animal, but you could equip it with only one sensory system. Which sense would you give it?

Your first impulse might be to choose either vision or hearing. After all, those senses are extremely versatile and valuable to humans. But an animal with only one sensory system is not going to be much like humans, is it? To have any chance of survival, it will probably have to be small and slow, probably even one-celled. What sense will be most useful to such an animal?

Most theorists believe that the first sensory system of the earliest animals was probably a chemical sensitivity (Parker, 1922). A chemical sense enables a small animal to cope with the basics of survival: finding food, distinguishing food from nonfood, identifying certain kinds of danger, and even locating mates.

Now, imagine that you have to choose one of your senses to *lose*. Which one will it be? Most of us would not choose to lose vision, hearing, or touch. Losing sensitivity to pain can be dangerous. You might choose to sacrifice your olfaction or taste.

Curious, isn't it? If an animal is going to survive with only one sense, it almost has to be a chemical sense, and yet to humans, who have many other well-developed senses, the chemical senses seem dispensable. Perhaps we underestimate the importance of these senses.

General Issues About Chemical Coding

Suppose you run a bakery and you need to send frequent messages to your supplier two blocks away. Suppose further that you can communicate only by ringing three large bells on the roof of your bakery. You would have to work out a code.

One possibility would be to label the three bells: The high-pitched bell means "I need flour." The medium-pitched bell means "I need sugar." And the low-pitched bell means "I need eggs." Then you simply ring the right bell at the right moment. The more you need something, the faster you ring the bell. We shall call this the "labeled-line code" because each bell has a single, unchanging label. The problem with this simple code is that it can signal only flour, sugar, or eggs.

Another possibility would be to set up a code that depends on a relationship among the three bells. Ringing the high and medium bells equally means that you need flour. The medium and low bells together call for sugar; the high and low bells together call for eggs. Ringing all three together means you need vanilla extract. Ringing mostly the high bell while ringing the other two bells slightly means you need hazelnuts. And so forth. We call this the "across-fiber pattern code" because the meaning depends on the pattern across bells. This code is versatile and can be highly useful, provided that we do not make it too complicated.

A sensory system could theoretically use either type of coding. In a system relying on the **labeled-line principle,** each receptor responds to a limited range of stimuli and would send a direct line to the brain. In a system relying on the **across-fiber pattern principle,** each receptor responds to a wider range of stimuli and contributes to the perception of each of them. In other words, a given level of response by a given sensory axon means little unless the brain knows what a number of other axons are doing at the same time.

In vertebrate sensory systems, it is hard to find a pure labeled-line code. In color perception, we encountered a clear case of an across-fiber pattern code; each color-sensitive cell responds best to certain stimuli, but, because it also responds to other stimuli, its message out of context is ambiguous. For example, a medium-wavelength cone might produce the same level of response to a moderately bright green light, a brighter blue light, or a white light. In auditory pitch perception, the responses of the hair cell receptors are rather narrowly tuned, but even in this case the meaning of a particular receptor's response depends on the context: A given receptor may respond best to a certain high-frequency tone, but it will also respond in phase with a number of low-frequency tones (as will all the other receptors). Each receptor will also respond to white noise

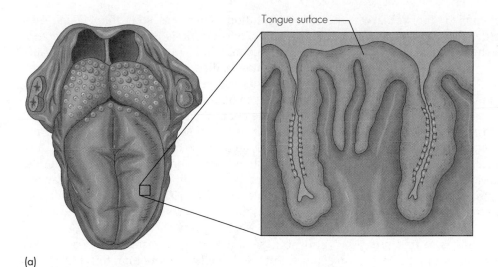

Tongue surface

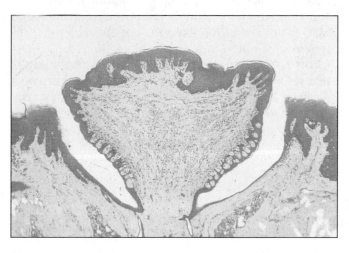

(a)

(b)

FIGURE **7.20**
FIGURE **7.20**
The organs of taste

(**a**) The tip, back, and sides of the tongue are covered with taste buds. Taste buds are located in papillae. (**b**) Photo showing cross section of a taste bud. Each taste bud contains about 50 receptor cells.

(static) and to various mixtures of tones. To decode any cell's response, the nervous system must compare it with the simultaneous responses of other cells.

Also, in the case of taste and smell, many stimuli can excite several kinds of receptors, and the meaning of a particular response by a particular receptor depends on the context of responses by other receptors. However, our understanding of the chemical senses is noticeably incomplete. Even on fairly basic questions of how we code stimuli or how many kinds of receptors we have, we cannot draw conclusions for taste and smell with nearly the same confidence that we can for vision and hearing.

Taste

When we talk about the taste of food, we generally mean a combination of taste and smell. The term *flavor* would be better for that purpose; *taste* should refer to

the stimulation of the taste buds. Most people who complain of losing their sense of taste actually have an impaired sense of smell. Only rarely does a person lose the sense of taste, except temporarily after burning the tongue.

Taste Receptors

The receptors for taste are not true neurons but modified skin cells. Like neurons, taste receptors have excitable membranes and release neurotransmitters to excite neighboring neurons, which in turn transmit information to the brain. Like skin cells, however, taste receptors are gradually sloughed off and replaced, each one lasting about 10 to 14 days (Kinnamon, 1987).

Mammalian taste receptors are located in **taste buds,** located in **papillae,** structures on the surface of the tongue (see Figure 7.20). A given papilla may contain any number of taste buds from none to ten or more (Arvidson & Friberg, 1980), and each taste bud contains about 50 receptor cells. Each of the neurons carrying impulses from the taste bud receives synaptic contacts from a number of receptors (Altner, 1978).

In adult humans, taste buds are located almost exclusively along the outside edge of the tongue, with few or none in the center. You can demonstrate this to yourself as follows: Soak one end of a cotton swab in sugar water, salt water, or vinegar. You might try one of each. Then touch it lightly on various portions of your tongue. You should experience a clear taste when you touch the edges of your tongue, but very little in the center.

TRY IT YOURSELF

Now change the procedure a bit. Wash your mouth out with water and prepare a cotton swab as before. Touch the soaked portion to one edge of your tongue and then slowly stroke it to the center of your tongue. Now it will seem as if you are moving the taste to the center of your tongue. In fact, you are getting only a touch sensation from the center of your tongue; you attribute the taste you had on the side of your tongue to every other spot you stroke (Bartoshuk, 1991).

How Many Kinds of Taste Receptors?

We can describe most if not all tastes with combinations of the four terms *sweet, sour, salty,* and *bitter,* though a few tastes defy such categorization (Schiffman & Erickson, 1980; Schiffman, McElroy, & Erickson, 1980). Do we have separate receptors for sweet, sour, salty, and bitter tastes? And do we have any additional taste receptors?

One way to answer these questions is to find procedures that affect one kind of receptor without affecting others. For example, certain chemicals can alter the response of sweetness receptors without affecting other taste receptors (see Digression 7.2). Therefore, we conclude that there must be a sweetness receptor, independent of receptors for other tastes.

Further evidence for at least four taste receptors comes from studies of the following type: Soak your tongue for 15 seconds in a sour solution, such as unsweetened lemon juice. Then try tasting some other sour solution, such as dilute vinegar. You will find that

the second solution tastes less sour than usual. Depending on the concentrations of the lemon juice and vinegar, the second solution may not taste sour at all. This phenomenon, called **adaptation,** presumably reflects the fatigue of receptors sensitive to sour tastes. Now try tasting something salty, sweet, or bitter. Those substances taste about the same as usual. In short, you experience little or no **cross-adaptation,** a reduced response to one taste because of exposure to another. Additional tests show that exposure to sodium chloride produces adaptation to all other salty substances (Smith & van der Klaauw, 1995) but no cross-adaptation to sweet, sour, or bitter substances (McBurney & Bartoshuk, 1973).

In short, we must have at least four kinds of taste receptors. But might we have more than four receptors? Research suggests a possible separate receptor for "umami," the taste of MSG (monosodium glutamate). MSG tastes somewhat like salt, but chemicals that interfere with salty tastes do not block the taste of MSG (Scott & Plata-Salaman, 1991). Another possibility is that we may have more than one kind of bitter or sweet receptor. The enormous variety of substances that taste bitter have little in common with one another chemically, except that nearly all of them are in some way harmful to the body. The strongest evidence for multi-

DIGRESSION 7.2

Miracle Berries and the Modification of Taste Receptors

Although the miracle berry of West Africa is practically tasteless, it temporarily changes the taste of other substances. Miracle berries contain a protein, *miraculin,* that modifies sweet receptors in such a way that they can be stimulated by acids (Bartoshuk, Gentile, Moskowitz, & Meiselman, 1974). If you ever get a chance to chew a miracle berry (and I do recommend it), for about the next half hour all acids (which are normally sour) will taste sweet, while continuing to taste sour as well.

Miraculin was, for a time, commercially available in the United States as a diet aid. The idea was that dieters could coat their tongue with a miraculin pill and then eat and drink unsweetened, slightly acidic substances. Such substances would taste sweet without providing many calories.

A colleague and I once spent an evening experimenting with miracle berries. We drank straight lemon juice, sauerkraut juice, even vinegar. All tasted extremely sweet. Somehow we forgot how acidic these substances are. We awoke the next day to find our mouths full of ulcers.

Other taste-modifying substances include an extract from the plant *Gymnema sylvestre,* which makes people temporarily insensitive to a great variety of sweet tastes (Frank, Mize, Kennedy, de los Santos, & Green, 1992), and the chemical *theophylline,* which reduces the bitterness of many substances (Kodama, Fukushima, & Sakata, 1978). After eating artichokes, some people report a sweet taste from water (Bartoshuk, Lee, & Scarpellino, 1972).

Have you ever tasted orange juice just after brushing your teeth? And did you wonder why something that usually tastes so good suddenly tasted so bad? Most toothpastes contain sodium lauryl sulfate, a chemical that intensifies bitter tastes while weakening sweet tastes (DeSimone, Heck, & Bartoshuk, 1980; Schiffman, 1983). Evidently, it disrupts the membrane surfaces, preventing molecules from binding to sweetness receptors. Fortunately, the effect wears off in a few minutes.

ple bitter receptors comes from studies of the taste of PTC (phenylthiocarbamide) and related chemicals that most people describe as strongly bitter. For genetic reasons, certain people have a greatly reduced sensitivity to PTC, as well as to caffeine and saccharin, although they have a normal ability to detect the bitter taste of quinine (Gent & Bartoshuk, 1983; Hall, Bartoshuk, Cain, & Stevens, 1975). Such results suggest that we may have several kinds of bitter receptors.

Mechanisms of Taste Receptors

Neuroscientists do not yet know the properties of all taste receptors, and even their total number is still in doubt. The best-understood taste receptor is the salty detector (or, at least, one type of salty detector). Recall that a neuron produces an action potential when sodium ions cross its membrane. A saltiness receptor, which detects the presence of sodium, does not need a specialized membrane site sensitive to sodium. It simply permits sodium ions on the tongue to cross its membrane. The higher the concentration of sodium on the tongue, the greater the response of this receptor. Chemicals such as amiloride, which prevents sodium from crossing the membrane, reduce the intensity of salty tastes (DeSimone, Heck, Mierson, & DeSimone, 1984; Schiffman, Lockhead, & Maes, 1983).

Sourness receptors operate on a different principle. When an acid binds to the receptor, it closes potassium channels, preventing potassium from leaving the cell. The result is an increased accumulation of positive charges within the neuron and therefore a depolarization of the membrane (Shirley & Persaud, 1990).

Sweetness and bitterness receptors apparently operate like a metabotropic synapse (Chapter 3). After a molecule binds to one of these receptors, it activates a G protein that releases a second messenger within the cell. Sweetness and bitterness rely on the same G protein; animals that have lost that protein become insensitive to both sweet and bitter substances but remain normally sensitive to salty and sour substances (Wong, Gannon, & Margolskee, 1996).

The Coding of Taste Information

How do we perceive tastes? Although you may consider it self-evident that the four kinds of receptors imply four labeled lines to the brain, the research suggests a more complicated system (Hettinger & Frank, 1992). Each cell in the taste system responds best to a particular taste, but it responds somewhat to other stimuli also.

The neurons that respond best to sweet substances are necessary for the perception of sweet tastes; in their absence, the remaining cells would not be able to distinguish sweetness from other tastes (Smith, VanBuskirk, Travers, & Bieber, 1983). However, the "sweet-best" neurons may not be sufficient for perception of sweets. If we examine *only* the responses of the sweet-best cells, we find ambiguous information (Scott, 1987). For example, a moderate level of response could indicate either a dilute sugar solution or a fairly concentrated salt solution. (Remember, the "sweet-best" cells respond somewhat to other stimuli also.) Only by comparing these cells' responses with those of other neurons, such as the "salt-best" neurons, can the brain determine what the tongue is tasting. In other words, although a given cell or axon may contribute significantly more to one taste than it does to others, its response contributes to the response of the other tastes also (Erickson, DiLorenzo, & Woodbury, 1994).

Taste Coding in the Brain

Information from the receptors in the anterior two-thirds of the tongue is carried to the brain along the chorda tympani, a branch of the seventh cranial nerve (the facial nerve). Taste information from the posterior tongue and the throat is carried along branches of the ninth and tenth cranial nerves. Those three nerves project to different parts of the **nucleus of the tractus solitarius (NTS)** in the medulla (Travers, Pfaffmann, & Norgren, 1986). From the NTS, information branches out, reaching the pons, the lateral hypothalamus, the amygdala, the ventral-posterior thalamus, and two areas of the cerebral cortex, one responsible for taste and one responsible for the sense of touch on the tongue (Pritchard, Hamilton, Morse, & Norgren, 1986; Yamamoto, 1984). A few of these major connections are illustrated in Figure 7.21.

With any sensory system, the brain must determine not only what the stimulus is, but also what it means. Meaning is particularly critical in taste, which tells the brain whether to swallow something or to spit it out. In rats, even cells in the NTS (the first stop in the brain) code the meaning of the taste and not just its physical identity. For example, rats deficient in sodium show an increased preference for salty tastes. Recordings from the NTS show that after rats become sodium-deficient, salty substances excite cells that ordinarily respond mostly to sweets! Researchers cannot yet say whether the salty substance actually tastes sweet to the rat or whether it just tastes good. In either case, it is impressive that neurons at the level of the medulla have already classified the acceptability of a taste.

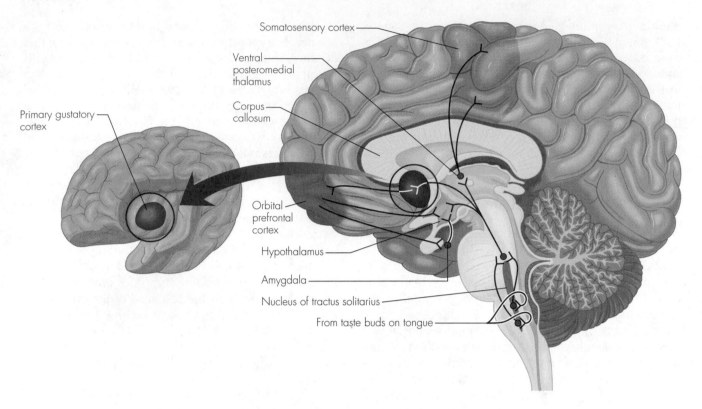

FIGURE **7.21**
Major routes of impulses related to the sense of taste in the human brain
The thalamus and cerebral cortex receive impulses from both the left and the right sides of the tongue.   Source: Based on Rolls, 1995.

Conversely, a rat that has become nauseated after drinking sugar water decreases its preference for sugar, and its NTS now responds to sugar in almost the same way that it responds to quinine, a bitter substance. In short, if experience has shown a substance to be good for the rat, the substance actually starts to taste good; if experience has shown a substance to be dangerous, it starts to taste bad (Scott, 1992). Monkeys show similar results in their cerebral cortex, although not in their NTS.

mention it (Schiffman, 1983). Nevertheless, olfaction is more important than we may realize. We rely on it for appreciating food, for discriminating good wine from poor wine, and for recognizing that old meat is rotting. Natural gas companies add a strong odor to their gas so that people can smell a leak in the gas line. Most mammals, including humans to some extent, alter their social responses to one another because of odors (see Digression 7.3).

Olfaction

Olfaction, the sense of smell, is the detection and recognition of chemicals in contact with the membranes inside the nose. In an ordinary day most of us pay little attention to what we smell, and an entire industry—the deodorant industry—is dedicated to removing one type of smell from our experience. Although many people lose their sense of smell temporarily as a result of medication, physicians seldom ask about this side effect, and patients seldom

Olfactory Receptors

The neurons responsible for smell are the **olfactory cells,** which line the olfactory epithelium in the rear of the nasal air passages (see Figure 7.22). In mammals, each olfactory cell has cilia (threadlike dendrites) that extend from the cell body into the mucous surface of the nasal passage. The fundamental structure of an olfactory receptor is about the same in all species, with variations reflecting each species' nose shape and way of life (Menco, 1992). Olfactory receptors, almost alone among mature mammalian neurons, are replaceable. Each receptor survives for about a month or two and then a new one develops to take its place.

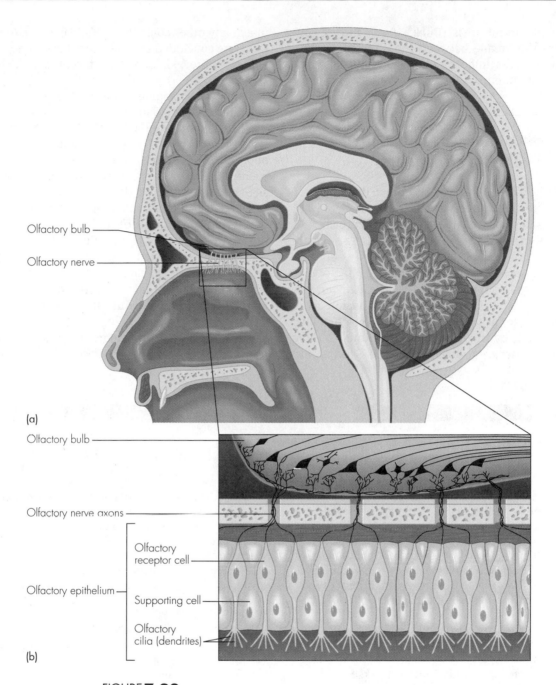

Olfactory bulb

Olfactory nerve

(a)

Olfactory bulb

Olfactory nerve axons

Olfactory
receptor cell

Olfactory epithelium

Supporting cell

Olfactory
cilia (dendrites)

(b)

FIGURE **7.22**
Olfactory receptors
(**a**) Location of receptors in nasal cavity. (**b**) Close-up of olfactory cells.

The olfactory receptor sites are located on the cilia. Because odorant molecules must pass through a mucous fluid before they reach the receptors, we experience a delay—perhaps as long as 300 ms—between inhaling a substance and smelling it (Getchell & Getchell, 1987). After a molecule excites the receptors, continuing stimulation actually suppresses their activity (Kurahashi, Lowe, & Gold, 1994). So, unlike vision, olfaction does not respond rapidly enough to record sudden changes or movements, nor does it provide a steady response, such as what you see when you watch an unmoving object.

When an olfactory receptor is stimulated, its axon carries an impulse directly to the olfactory bulb (Figure 4.11). Each receptor excites only a limited part of the olfactory bulb, and different receptors excite different parts. The olfactory bulb sends its axons to at least five areas of the cerebral cortex, which in turn send their output to still further areas (Buck, 1996). Strong connections are thus made between the olfactory system and the brain areas important for feeding and reproduction. (Many mammals find mates largely by smell.)

Behavioral Methods of Identifying Olfactory Receptors

How many kinds of olfactory receptors do we have? Certainly more than one; a single receptor could not signal differences in both type of smell and intensity. At the other extreme, we could hardly imagine a separate receptor for every possible smell.

But do we have two or three kinds of olfactory receptors, or seven, or twenty, or what? Researchers answered the analogous question for color vision more than a century ago, using only behavioral observations. They found that, by mixing various amounts of three colors of light—say, red, green, and blue—they could

match any other color that people can see. Researchers therefore concluded that we must have three, and probably only three, kinds of color receptors (which we now call cones).

We could imagine doing the same experiment for olfaction. Take a small number of odors—say, almond, lilac, and skunk—and test whether people can mix various proportions of those odors to match all other odors. If three odors are not enough, add more until eventually we can mix them to match every other possible odor. Because we do not know what are the "primary odors" (if indeed there is such a thing), we might have to do a great deal of trial-and-error testing to find the best set of odors to use. So far as we know, however, no one ever tried such an experiment, or anyone who did try it must have given up in discouragement. (It may turn out, in fact, that in order to match all the identifiable odors we would need to use a thousand or so "primaries.")

A second way to estimate the number of olfactory receptor types is to study people who have trouble

DIGRESSION 7.3

Pheromones

A **pheromone** is an odorous chemical released by an animal that affects the behavior of other members of the same species. Most mammals use pheromones in sexual attraction; they can determine from an individual's smell whether it is an infant, an adult male, a female in estrus, or a female not in estrus. Pheromones can also produce certain long-lasting effects (Bronson, 1974): The odor of a group of female mice can stop another female mouse's estrous cycle, and the odor of a male can restore it.

Most of the effects of pheromones depend on activity of the vomeronasal organ, not on the olfactory system itself. The vomeronasal organ is a set of receptors located near, but separate from, the olfactory receptors. Although it is a reasonably prominent structure in most mammals and easy to find in a human fetus, it is so small in adult humans that for years biologists were not sure that it was present at all. Research has now established that most adults do have a small vomeronasal organ (Monti-Bloch, Jennings-White, Dolberg, & Berliner, 1994). It responds best to some chemicals found in human skin, and only weakly or not at all to most of the chemicals that stimulate the olfactory receptors. Extremely small amounts of those human skin chemicals (human pheromones?) can stimulate the vomeronasal receptors, leading to autonomic responses such as increases or decreases in sweating and skin temperature (Monti-Bloch et al., 1994). The effects of most such chemicals differ between women and men (Monti-Bloch & Grosser, 1991). As a rule, people are not consciously aware of any vomeronasal sensations; the effects take place automatically.

So, do pheromones influence human behaviors, particularly sexual behaviors, as they do in other mammals? A number of researchers have sought evidence for such effects, mostly finding only unimpressive results. One of the stronger effects relates to the timing of women's menstrual cycles. In many cases, female college roommates who become close friends and spend much time together find that their menstrual cycles become synchronized (McClintock, 1971; Weller, Weller, & Avinir, 1995). (They do not become synchronized if either of them is taking birth-control pills, or if they spend little time together.) To test whether pheromones are responsible for the synchronization, researchers in two studies exposed young volunteer women to the underarm secretions of a donor woman. In both studies, most of the women exposed to these secretions became synchronized to the donor woman's menstrual cycle (Preti, Cutler, Garcia, Huggins, & Lawley, 1986; Russell, Switz, & Thompson, 1980).

Another study dealt with the phenomenon that a woman who has an intimate relationship with a man tends to have more regular menstrual periods than other women do. One hypothesis is that the man's pheromones somehow promote this regularity. In one study, young women who were not sexually active were exposed daily to a man's underarm secretions. (Getting volunteers for a study like this isn't easy.) Gradually, over 14 weeks, most of these women's menstrual periods became more regular than before, with a mean of 29–30 days each (Cutler et al., 1986). In short, human body secretions apparently do act as pheromones, although the effects are more subtle than they are in nonhuman mammals.

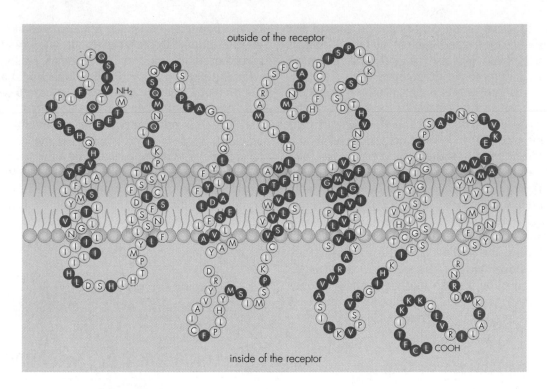

FIGURE **7.23**
One of the olfactory receptor proteins

If you compare this protein with the synaptic receptor protein shown in Figure 3.12b, you will notice great similarity. Each protein traverses the membrane seven times; each responds to a chemical outside the cell and triggers activity of a G protein inside the cell. The protein shown is one of a family; different olfactory receptors contain different proteins, each with a slightly different structure. Each of the little circles in this diagram represents one amino acid of the protein. The white circles represent amino acids that are the same in most of the olfactory receptor proteins; the darker circles represent amino acids that vary from one protein to another.   Source: Based on Buck & Axel, 1991.

smelling one type of chemical. A general lack of olfaction is known as **anosmia;** the inability to smell a single chemical is a **specific anosmia.** For example, about 2 to 3 percent of all people are insensitive to the smell of isobutyric acid, the smelly component of sweat (Amoore, 1967). (They seldom complain about this disability.) Because people can lose the ability to smell just this one chemical, we may assume that there is a receptor specific to isobutyric acid. We might then search for additional specific anosmias on the theory that each specific anosmia represents the loss of a different type of receptor.

One investigator identified at least five other specific anosmias—musky, fishy, urinous, spermous, and malty—and less convincing evidence suggested 26 other possible specific anosmias (Amoore, 1977). Additional research indicates that specific anosmias are partly inherited but also partly dependent on experience: After prolonged exposure to some chemical, an individual with a specific anosmia to that chemical starts to smell it, presumably by developing new olfactory receptors (Wang, Wysocki, & Gold, 1993).

Research on specific anosmias suggests that humans probably have a fairly large number of olfactory receptors. However, the more receptors, the more discouraging the prospects for identifying them all through specific anosmias. That is, if researchers found, for example, just five specific anosmias, with a large number of cases of each, we would begin to believe that people have just five kinds of receptors. But if researchers report 31 kinds of specific anosmias, some of them very rare, we must begin to wonder how many other rare specific anosmias might exist.

Biochemical Identification of Receptor Types

Ultimately, the best way to determine the number of olfactory receptor types is to isolate the receptor molecules themselves. In 1991, Linda Buck and Richard Axel (1991) identified in olfactory receptors a family of proteins, as shown in Figure 7.23. Like many neurotransmitter receptors, each of these proteins traverses the cell membrane seven times and responds to a chemical outside the cell (here, an odorant molecule instead of a neurotransmitter) by triggering changes in a G protein inside the cell; the G protein then provokes chemical activities that lead to an action potential.

Olfactory receptor proteins occur only in the olfactory receptors, not in other parts of the brain or other organs of the body. Moreover, different receptor cells have different receptor proteins. Buck and Axel identified 18 different receptor proteins, varying in their amino acid composition at certain sites (Figure 7.23). Other researchers since then have identified additional receptor proteins (Raming et al., 1993). Investigators now estimate that humans have hundreds, perhaps even a thousand or more, different types of olfactory receptor proteins. We know that the receptors are arranged in a nonrandom order, because the arrangement is the same for the left and right nasal cavities (Ressler, Sullivan, & Buck, 1994). The exact basis for the order is not yet clear, however.

Implications for Coding

We have only three kinds of cones and either four or slightly more than four kinds of taste receptors, so most researchers assumed that we might have only a few kinds of olfactory receptors. Having so many makes possible a great specialization of olfactory receptors. To illustrate: Because we have only three kinds of cones with which to see a great variety of colors, each cone must contribute to almost every color perception. In olfaction, we can afford to have specialist receptors that contribute strongly to the perception of just a few odors. The response of one olfactory receptor might mean "I smell a fatty acid with a straight chain of about 3–5 carbon atoms." The response of another receptor might mean "I smell either a fatty acid or an aldehyde, with a straight chain of about 4–6 carbon atoms." The responses of other cells could identify alcohols, alkanes, and other types of odorous molecules (Imamura, Mataga, & Mori, 1992; Mori, Mataga, & Imamura, 1992). In short, the response of a single receptor can identify the approximate nature of the molecule, with some ambiguity; the response of a larger population of receptors enables more precise recognition of the molecule; and, of course, the total population can identify a complex mixture of many odorous chemicals.

The question may have occurred to you, "Why did evolution go to the bother of designing hundreds of different olfactory receptor types? After all, color vision gets by with just three types of cones." The main reason is that vision deals with light energy, which can be arranged along a single dimension, the wavelength. Olfaction, however, deals with an enormous variety of airborne chemicals, which are not arranged along any single continuum. To detect them all, we probably need a great variety of receptors. A secondary reason has to do with localization. Granted that olfaction has to have hundreds of receptor types, why couldn't color vision also have hundreds of receptor types? The answer is that several hundred receptors take up a lot of space. In olfaction, space is no problem; we arrange our olfactory receptors over the entire surface of the nasal passages. In vision, however, the brain needs to determine precisely where on the retina some stimulus originates. Hundreds of different kinds of receptors to identify different colors could not be compacted into each spot on the retina.

IN CLOSING

The Unity of Perception

Chapters 6 and 7 have considered each sensory system in isolation—how we see, how we hear, how we detect odors, and so forth. In life, however, we need to combine information from various senses. For example, if you play a violin, you have to see the score that you are trying to play, feel your hands on the strings and bow, and hear the music you play to determine whether it matches what the score said you should play. How do you combine the senses? Relatively few researchers have addressed this question. The brain is dominated by areas that are responsive mainly to a single sense, such as vision. Even in the frontal cortex, which receives input from all the senses, most subareas are responsive to just one sense. The brain does have a few areas that apparently combine visual, auditory, and other inputs—such as the superior colliculus (Stein & Meredith, 1993). Still, a great deal remains to be learned about how we combine different senses to perceive a unified object.

Summary

1. Sensory information can be coded either in terms of a labeled-line system or in terms of an across-fiber pattern system. (p. 200)
2. Taste receptors are modified skin cells located in taste buds in papillae on the tongue. (p. 201)
3. The tongue has at least four kinds of receptors, one each for sweet, sour, salty, and bitter, and perhaps additional re-

ceptors, such as more than one kind of bitter receptor. (p. 202)

4. Salty receptors respond simply to sodium ions crossing the membrane. At sweet receptors, sucrose or other substances activate a second messenger within the neuron. (p. 203)

5. Each taste axon responds best to one kind of substance but also responds somewhat to other kinds. (p. 203)

6. Brain neurons change their response to a taste to reflect its meaning. Sodium deficiency makes salt taste more pleasant; associating a taste with nausea makes it taste less pleasant. These changes in response occur even in the nucleus of the tractus solitarius (NTS) of rats, but not until the cortex in primates. (p. 203)

7. Olfactory receptors are proteins, each showing its strongest response to one chemical, weaker responses to similar chemicals, and little or no response to unrelated chemicals. Vertebrates have many olfactory receptor types, probably in the hundreds. (p. 207)

Review Questions

1. What is the difference between the labeled-line theory and the across-fiber pattern theory? (p. 200)
2. How long does a taste receptor last before it is replaced? (p. 201)
3. What are the effects of miraculin and *Gymnema sylvestre* extract on sweetness receptors? (p. 202)
4. What evidence indicates that we have more than one kind of bitter receptor? (p. 202)
5. How does amiloride block salty tastes? (p. 203)
6. Why is the response of any single taste neuron in the brain somewhat ambiguous? How does comparing it with other neurons remove the ambiguity? (p. 203)
7. What is a pheromone? (p. 206)
8. What is a specific anosmia? (p. 207)
9. How do olfactory receptors resemble neurotransmitter receptors? (p. 207)

Thought Questions

1. In the English language, the letter "t" has no meaning out of context; its meaning depends on its relationship to other letters. Indeed, even a word, such as *to*, has little meaning except in its connection to other words. So is language a labeled-line system or an across-fiber pattern system?

2. Suppose a chemist synthesizes a new chemical, which turns out to have an odor. Presumably we do not have a specialized receptor for that chemical. Explain how our receptors would detect it.

Suggestions for Further Reading

Farbman, A. I. (1992). *The cell biology of olfaction*. Cambridge, England: Cambridge University Press.

McLaughlin, S., & Margolskee, R. F. (1994). The sense of taste. *American Scientist, 82*, 538–545. Excellent discussion of how taste receptors work.

Terms

labeled-line principle   concept that each receptor responds to a limited range of stimuli and has a direct line to the brain (p. 200)

across-fiber pattern principle   notion that each receptor responds to a wide range of stimuli and contributes to the perception of every stimulus in its system (p. 200)

taste bud   structure on the tongue that contains taste receptors (p. 201)

papilla (plural: **papillae**)   structure on the surface of the tongue, containing taste buds (p. 201)

adaptation   decreased response to a stimulus as a result of recent exposure to it (p. 202)

cross-adaptation   reduced response to one stimulus because of recent exposure to some other stimulus (p. 202)

nucleus of the tractus solitarius (NTS)   area in the medulla that receives input from taste receptors (p. 203)

olfaction   sense of smell (p. 204)

olfactory cell   neuron responsible for smell, located on the olfactory epithelium in the rear of the nasal air passages (p. 204)

pheromone   odorous chemical released by one animal that affects the behavior of other members of the same species (p. 206)

anosmia   general lack of olfaction (p. 207)

specific anosmia   inability to smell one type of chemical (p. 207)

MOVEMENT

CHAPTER **EIGHT**

MAIN**IDEAS**

1. At different times different combinations of muscles are used to achieve similar outcomes. Movement depends on overall plans, not just connections between a stimulus and a muscle contraction.
2. Movements vary in sensitivity to feedback, skill, and variability in the face of obstacles.
3. Different parts of the brain control different aspects of movement, and damage to different brain locations produces different kinds of impairment.
4. Many kinds of brain damage impair both movement and cognitive processes.

Imagine that you are a limpet, a small shellfish that lives on a rock at the edge of the ocean. When the tide is out, you cling tightly to the rock. When the tide is in, you loosen your grip enough to capture and eat algae and other tiny plants that float in on the waves. Your main enemies are shorebirds. Whenever you loosen your grip on the rock, a bird might rip you right out of your shell and swallow you whole. You are almost defenseless against this attack; the birds can see exactly where you are, but you can barely distinguish light from dark. Even if you could see them, you would be unable to defend yourself; the shorebirds are bigger, stronger, faster, and smarter than you are. Under the circumstances, what hope do you have?

Your one chance is that you might happen to be in a crevice or beneath an overhang where the shorebirds cannot reach you. You have no way of knowing whether you are in a safe location, but the longer you have been in one place without getting eaten, the better your chances. If you move around, sooner or later you are going to wander into a dangerous spot, and then the birds will probably get you. So your best bet is to stay right where you are. Most limpets do exactly that (Frank, 1981). The moral of the story: If your enemies are big and strong and fast, and you have almost no brains, you might as well stay in one place and hope they don't find you. The reverse is also true: If you are not going to move much, you do not need an elaborate nervous system.

Although the final outcome of neural activity is to control behavior, most psychologists pay little attention to movement. The study of muscle contractions seems somehow less "psychological" than the study of visual perception, learning, social interactions, motivation, or emotion. And yet the rapid movements of a skilled typist, musician, or athlete require very complex brain activities. Understanding movement is a significant challenge for psychologists as well as biologists.

The Control of Movement

Athletic skills require amazingly precise timing of neural activity, not just muscle strength.

Think for a moment about how impressive human movement can be. Take what seems a pretty simple movement—throwing a ball. Throwing with decent speed, not to mention accuracy, requires stepping forward with one leg, pushing backward with the other leg, moving all the joints in the throwing arm in the proper sequence, and moving the opposite arm to maintain balance, making each movement at just the right time. Experienced pitchers learn to move all their joints almost exactly the same way every time; most bad throws come from opening their fingers a few milliseconds too soon or too late at the end of the sequence (Hore, 1996). It is a tribute to the motor control systems of our brains that we ordinarily put together complex sequences of movement without even thinking about them.

Muscles and Their Movements

All animal movement depends on the contraction of muscles. Vertebrate muscles fall into three categories (see Figure 8.1): **smooth muscles,** which control movements of internal organs; **skeletal,** or **striated, muscles,** which control movement of the body in relation to the environment; and **cardiac muscles** (the heart muscles), which have properties intermediate between those of smooth and skeletal muscles.

Each muscle is composed of many individual muscle fibers, as Figure 8.2 illustrates. A given axon may innervate more than one muscle fiber. For example, the

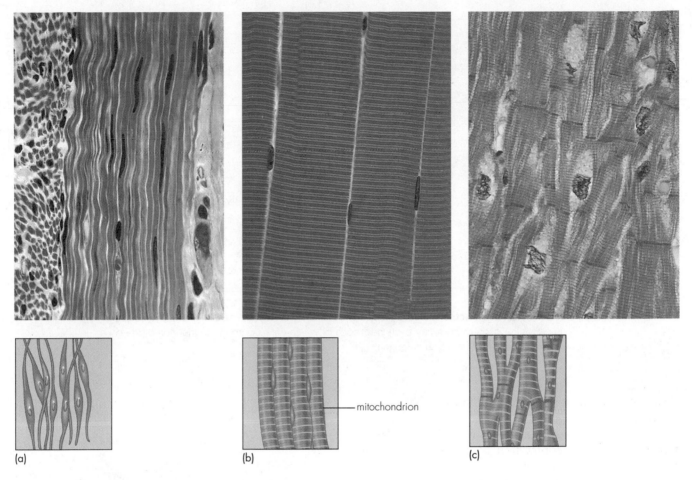

(a)   (b)   —— mitochondrion   (c)

FIGURE **8.1**
The three main types of vertebrate muscles
(**a**) Smooth muscle, found in the intestines and other organs, consists of long, thin cells. (**b**) Skeletal, or striated, muscle consists of long, cylindrical fibers with stripes. (**c**) Cardiac muscle, found in the heart, consists of fibers that fuse together at various points. Because of those fusions, cardiac muscles contract together, not independently.   Source: Illustrations after Starr & Taggart, 1989.

eye muscles have a ratio of about one axon per three muscle fibers, and the biceps muscles of the arm have a ratio of one axon to more than a hundred fibers (Evarts, 1979). This difference enables eye movements to be more precise than biceps movements.

A **neuromuscular junction** is a synapse where a motor neuron axon meets a muscle fiber (Figure 8.3). In skeletal muscles, every axon releases acetylcholine at the neuromuscular junction, and the acetylcholine always excites the muscle to contract.

Each muscle can make just one movement—contraction—in just one direction. In the absence of excitation it relaxes, but it never moves actively in the opposite direction. Moving a leg or arm in two directions requires opposing sets of muscles, called **antagonistic muscles.** An arm, for example, has a **flexor** muscle that

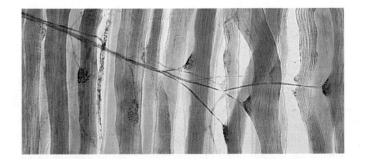

FIGURE **8.2**
An axon branching to innervate separate muscle fibers
Movements can be much more precise where each axon innervates only a few fibers, as with the eye muscle, than where it innervates many fibers, as with the biceps muscle.

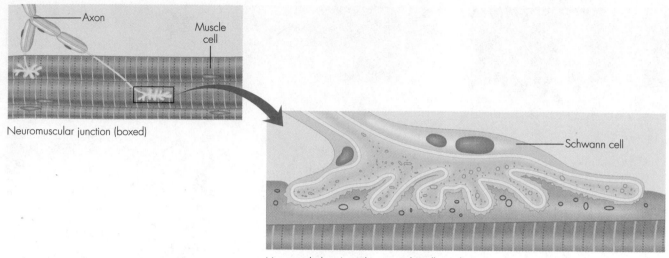

Neuromuscular junction (boxed)

Motor end plate (troughs in muscle cell membrane)

FIGURE **8.3**
A neuromuscular junction, the synapse between a motor neuron and a muscle
The terminal of the axon forms many branches, each of which enters a trough in the membrane of
the muscle cell.   Source: From Starr & Taggart, 1989.

flexes or raises it and an **extensor** muscle that extends
or straightens it (Figure 8.4). Walking, clapping hands,
and other coordinated sequences require a regular alternation between contraction of one set of muscles
and contraction of another.

The motor nerves of mammals originate from neurons in the spinal cord or the medulla. Their axons all
exit the ventral side of the spinal cord, in contrast to
sensory axons, which all enter the dorsal side (see Figure 4.3). The axon of a motor neuron extends all the
way from the spinal cord or medulla to the muscle that
it innervates.

Fast and Slow Muscles

At the start of this chapter I asked you to imagine that
you were a limpet. Now imagine that you are a small
fish. You are in constant danger of attack by larger fish,
turtles, and birds; your only defense is your ability to
get away (Figure 8.5). The temperature of a fish is the
same as the temperature of the water. Are you in particular danger when the water is cold? If the temperature drops from 20°C to 5°C, your body temperature
drops from 20° to 5°.

All muscle fibers contract more vigorously at high
temperatures than at low temperatures. Therefore, you
should be able to swim faster at high temperatures; at
low temperatures, your sluggish movements should
leave you extremely vulnerable to attack, especially by

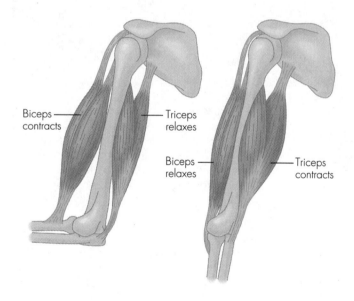

FIGURE **8.4**
A pair of antagonistic muscles
The biceps of the arm is a flexor; the triceps is an extensor.
Source: From Starr & Taggart, 1989.

warm-blooded animals such as birds. Right? Strangely,
a fish swims just as fast at low temperatures as it does
at high temperatures. It maintains its swimming speed
by recruiting more muscles at low temperatures (Rome,
Loughna, & Goldspink, 1984).

FIGURE **8.5**
Fish are "cold blooded," but many of their predators (such as this pelican) are not. At cold temperatures, a fish must maintain its normal swimming speed, even though every muscle in its body contracts more slowly than usual. To do so, a fish calls upon white muscles that it would otherwise use only for brief bursts of speed.

A fish has three kinds of muscles: red, pink, and white. Red muscles produce rather slow movements, but they can respond almost indefinitely without fatigue, like the muscles you use for sitting or standing. White muscles produce the fastest movements, but they fatigue rapidly. Pink muscles are intermediate in both speed and fatigue. At high temperatures, a fish relies on its red muscles and a few pink muscles, using its white muscles only when it needs a brief burst of speed. At colder temperatures, the red and pink muscles produce only slow and weak contractions, and the fish relies more and more on its white muscles. By recruiting enough white muscles, the fish can maintain its usual swimming speed in all water temperatures, although it fatigues faster at low temperatures because of its dependence on white muscles.

All right, you can stop imagining that you are a fish. Now consider birds. A chicken's breast muscle is white and its leg muscles are dark. The difference corresponds to function: A chicken uses its breast muscles only for quick acceleration to fly a short distance. Those muscles fatigue rapidly, so a chicken cannot fly

very far. The dark muscles of its legs, however, enable it to walk slowly for hours at a time. Because a duck has dark muscle in its breast, it may not be able to accelerate as powerfully as a chicken, but it can fly much longer without fatigue.

In humans and other mammals, various kinds of muscle fibers are mixed together, not in separate bundles as in fish and birds. Our muscle types are graded, from **fast-twitch fibers** that produce fast contractions but fatigue rapidly, to **slow-twitch fibers** that produce less vigorous contractions without fatiguing (Hennig & Lømo, 1985). For standing, walking, and nonstrenuous activities, we rely on our slow-twitch and intermediate fibers. For running up a flight of stairs at full speed, we use more fast-twitch fibers.

People have varying percentages of fast-twitch and slow-twitch fibers, and exercise apparently increases the percentage of one kind or the other. For example, competitive sprinters have about 70 percent intermediate- and fast-twitch fibers in certain leg muscles, which allow for brief bursts of great speed. Marathon runners, however, have about 60 percent slow-twitch fibers, with increased capillary blood flow to those muscles (Crenshaw, Fridén, Thornell, & Hargens, 1991; Sjöström, Johansson, & Lorentzon, 1988). The Swedish ultramarathon runner Bertil Järlaker built up so many slow-twitch fibers in his legs that he once ran 3,520 km (2,188 miles) in 50 days (an average of 1.7 marathons per day), with only minimal signs of pain or fatigue (Sjöström, Fridén, & Ekblom, 1987). However, because he developed these slow-twitch fibers at the expense of his fast-twitch fibers, his speed for short-distance races was a mediocre 6 minutes per kilometer (more than 9 minutes per mile).

Muscle Control by Proprioceptors

You are walking along on a slightly bumpy road. What happens if the messages from your spinal cord to your leg muscles are not exactly correct? You might set your foot down a little too hard or not quite hard enough. Nevertheless, you adjust your posture almost immediately and maintain your balance without even thinking about it. How do you do that? A baby is lying on its back. You playfully tug its foot and then let go. At once the leg bounces back to its original position. How did that happen?

In both cases, the mechanism is under the control of proprioceptors (see Figure 8.6). A **proprioceptor** is a receptor that is sensitive to the position and movement of a part of the body—in these cases, a muscle. Muscle proprioceptors detect the stretch and tension of a muscle and send messages that enable the spinal cord to

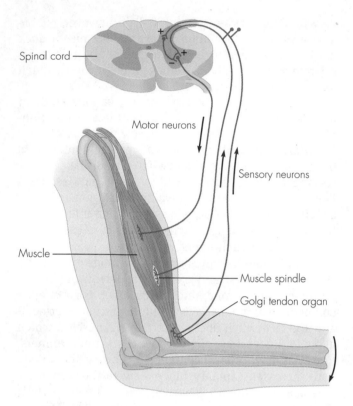

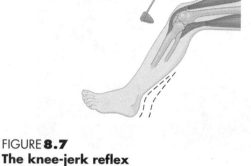

FIGURE **8.7**
The knee-jerk reflex

FIGURE **8.6**
Two kinds of proprioceptors regulate the contraction of a muscle

When a muscle is stretched, the nerves from the muscle spindles transmit an increased frequency of impulses, resulting in a contraction of the surrounding muscle. Contraction of the muscle stimulates the Golgi tendon organ, which acts as a brake or shock absorber to prevent a contraction that is too quick or extreme.

adjust its signals. When a muscle is stretched, the spinal cord sends a reflexive signal to contract that muscle. This **stretch reflex** is *caused* by a stretch; it does not *result* in a stretch.

One kind of proprioceptor is the **muscle spindle,** a stretch receptor parallel to the muscle (Merton, 1972; Miles & Evarts, 1979). Whenever the muscle spindle is stretched, its sensory nerve sends a message to a motor neuron in the spinal cord, which in turn sends a message back to the muscles surrounding the spindle, causing a contraction. Note that this reflex provides for negative feedback: When a muscle and its spindle are stretched, the spindle sends a message that results in a muscle contraction that opposes the stretch.

When you set your foot down on a slight bump on the road, your knee bends a bit, stretching the extensor muscles of that leg. The sensory nerves of the spindles send action potentials to the motor neuron in the spinal cord, and the motor neuron sends action potentials to the extensor muscle. Contraction of the extensor mus-

cle straightens the leg, adjusting for the bump on the road.

A physician who asks you to cross your legs and then taps you just below the knee (Figure 8.7) is testing your stretch reflexes. The tap below the knee stretches the extensor muscles and their spindles, resulting in a message that jerks the lower leg upward.

Another proprioceptor, the **Golgi tendon organ,** responds to increases in muscle tension. Located in the tendons at opposite ends of a muscle, it acts as a brake against an excessively vigorous contraction. Some muscles are so strong that they could damage themselves if too many fibers contracted at once. Golgi tendon organs detect muscle contraction. The more vigorous the contraction, the greater the response of the Golgi tendon organs. Their impulses travel to the spinal cord, where they inhibit the motor neurons through messages from interneurons. In short, a vigorous muscle contraction inhibits further contraction by activating the Golgi tendon organs.

The proprioceptors not only control important reflexes but also provide the brain with information about the location of body parts. If you have ever tried walking after your legs have "fallen asleep," you know how difficult it is to control movement without proprioception. One 19-year-old man suffered a complete loss of touch and proprioception from the neck down, the result of a virus that attacked his sensory neurons. For about a year afterward, he hardly moved a muscle. He still *could* move his muscles, but because of the lack of proprioception, he had no control of the distance, direction, or velocity of his movements, so he found it safer to make no movements at all. (Again, you may note parallels to the experience of having your legs fall asleep. The difference is that his loss of sensation included all his body except the head, and that it was permanent.) Over several years, he gradually regained the ability to walk, write, and so forth, but only by watching every movement carefully. In a dim or dark room, he is still unable to control his movements (Cole, 1995). In short, do not underestimate the importance of your proprioceptors.

Units of Movement

The stretch reflex is a simple example of movement. More complex kinds include speaking, walking, threading a needle, and throwing a basketball through a hoop while off balance and trying to evade two defenders. In many ways, these movements are different from one another, and they depend on different kinds of control by the nervous system.

Voluntary and Involuntary Movements

Reflexes are consistent automatic responses to stimuli. The stretch reflex is one example; another is the constriction of the pupil in response to bright light. We generally think of reflexes as being *involuntary* because although they are sensitive to external stimuli, they are not sensitive to reinforcements, punishments, and motivations.

Many behaviors are a complex mixture of voluntary and involuntary influences. Take swallowing, for example. You can voluntarily swallow or inhibit swallowing, but only within certain limits. Try to swallow ten times in a row, voluntarily. The first swallow is easy; the second almost as easy; but before long, you will find additional swallows difficult, unpleasant, eventually almost impossible. Now try to inhibit swallowing for, say, 15 minutes. Chances are, you will give in long before you reach that goal. (No fair spitting.)

Can you think of a purely voluntary movement—that is, one that is independent of external stimuli, with no unintentional components? That question probably sounds easy, and you suggest walking, talking, scratching your head. . . . However, most examples turn out to include involuntary components. Consider walking: When you walk, you automatically compensate for the

bumps and irregularities in the surface of the road. You probably also swing your arms a bit. You could voluntarily increase or decrease the extent of the swing, but ordinarily it occurs as an automatic, involuntary consequence of walking.

Certain visual stimuli greatly facilitate walking, at least in certain people. A patient with Parkinson's disease has great trouble walking under ordinary circumstances but can walk surprisingly well when following a parade. Also, if someone marks lines across the floor at approximately one-step intervals, a Parkinson's patient can step across each line much more easily than he or she can walk down an unmarked hall (Teitelbaum, Pellis, & Pellis, 1991). So, is the walking voluntary or involuntary? Evidently, it is a mixture of both: The person chooses to walk, but the stimuli of following a parade or crossing lines greatly facilitate the behavior. In short, the distinction between voluntary and involuntary is often blurry.

Movements with Different Sensitivity to Feedback

The military distinguishes between ballistic missiles and guided missiles. A ballistic missile is simply launched toward the target, like a thrown ball. Once the missile is launched there is no way to correct its aim. A guided missile, however, detects the target location and adjusts its trajectory one way or the other to correct for error in the original aim.

Similarly, some movements are ballistic and others are corrected by feedback. A **ballistic movement** is executed as a whole; once initiated, it cannot be altered or its aim corrected. A reflex, a simple automatic response to a stimulus, such as the stretch reflex or the contraction of the pupils in response to light, is a ballistic movement. Infants have certain reflexes that are absent in adults (see Digression 8.1).

Truly ballistic movements are rare; most behaviors are subject to feedback correction. For example, when you thread a needle, you make a slight movement, check your aim, and then readjust the next movement. Similarly, a singer who holds a single note for a prolonged time hears any unintentional wavering of the pitch and corrects it. The importance of the feedback becomes apparent if we distort it. Suppose we equip you with a device that records what you sing and then plays it back over earphones so that you hear what you sang 5 seconds ago. Now when you try to sing one note, you hear the error you made 5 seconds ago and try to correct it. But you will not start to hear your correction for another 5 seconds, and by that time you have overcorrected. The result is wild swings back and forth around the intended note.

Sequences of Behaviors

Many of our behaviors consist of rapid sequences, as in speaking, writing, dancing, or playing a musical instrument. In certain cases we can attribute these sequences to **central pattern generators,** neural mechanisms in the spinal cord or elsewhere that generate rhythmic patterns of motor output. Examples include wing flapping in birds and insects, fin movements in fish, and the repetitive shaking movements that a wet animal makes to dry itself off. Although a stimulus may activate a central pattern generator, it does not control the frequency of repetition of the alternating movements. For example, dogs scratch themselves at a rate of four or five scratches per second; increased irritation can increase the vigor of each scratch, but not the frequency.

We refer to a fixed sequence of movements as a **motor program.** A central pattern generator produces a motor program, but so do other mechanisms that are not necessarily rhythmic. A motor program can be either learned or built into the nervous system. For example, a mouse periodically grooms itself by sitting up,

---

DIGRESSION 8.1

Infant Reflexes

Certain reflexes are present in infants but not in older children or adults. For example, if you place an object firmly in an infant's hand, the infant will reflexively grasp it tightly (the **grasp reflex**). If you stroke the sole of the foot, the infant will reflexively extend the big toe and fan the others (the **Babinski reflex**). If you touch the cheek of an awake infant, the head will turn toward the stimulated cheek and the infant will begin to suck (the **rooting reflex**). The rooting reflex is not a pure example of a reflex; its intensity depends on the infant's alertness, hunger, and so forth. Still, this reflex, like the others, is characteristic of infants and seldom present in healthy adults.

Although such reflexes fade away with time, their reflexive connections remain intact, not lost but suppressed by axons from the maturing brain. If the cerebral cortex is damaged, the infant reflexes are released from inhibition. In fact, neurologists and other physicians frequently test adults for infant reflexes. A physician who strokes the sole of your foot during a physical exam is probably looking for evidence of brain damage. This is hardly the most dependable test, but it is among the easiest. If a stroke of the sole of your foot makes you fan your toes like a baby, there may be an impairment of your cerebral cortex.

Infant reflexes sometimes return temporarily if activity in the cerebral cortex is depressed by alcohol, carbon dioxide, or other chemicals. (You might try testing for infant reflexes in a friend who has consumed too much alcohol.)

Infants and children also have a stronger tendency than adults do to certain *allied reflexes*. If dust blows in your face, you will reflexively close your eyes and mouth, and probably sneeze. These reflexes are *allied* in the sense that each of them tends to elicit the others. If you suddenly see a bright light—as when you emerge from a dark theater on a sunny afternoon—you will reflexively close your eyes and you may also close your mouth and perhaps sneeze. Some adults react this way; a higher percentage of young children do (Whitman & Packer, 1993).

Rooting reflex

Grasp reflex

Babinski reflex

The vigorous body shaking of a wet mammal is one example of a central pattern generator. The frequency of shakes is nearly constant for a given species.

The repetitive grooming behavior of a mouse is one example of a motor program.

licking its paws, wiping its paws over its face, closing its eyes as the paws pass over them, licking the paws again, and so forth (Fentress, 1973). Once begun, the sequence is predictable from beginning to end. In contrast to this apparently built-in mechanism, many people develop learned yet very predictable motor sequences. An expert gymnast will produce a familiar pattern of movements as a smooth, coordinated whole; the same can be said for skilled typists, piano players, and so forth.

By comparing species, we begin to understand how a motor program can be gained or lost through evolution. For example, if you hold a chicken several feet above the ground and then drop it, it will stretch its wings and flap them. Even chickens with featherless wings make the same movements, even though they fail to break their fall (Provine, 1979, 1981). On the other hand, penguins, emus, and rheas, which have not used their wings for flight in countless generations, do not extend or flap their wings when they are dropped (Provine, 1984). Although their ancient ancestors presumably had this motor program, it has been lost over the course of evolution.

Do humans have any built-in motor programs? Yawning is one example (Provine, 1986). A yawn consists of a prolonged open-mouth inhalation, often accompanied by stretching, and a shorter exhalation. Yawns are very consistent in duration, with a mean of just under 6 seconds.

IN **CLOSING**

Categories of Movement

Charles Sherrington described a motor neuron in the spinal cord as "the final common path." He meant that regardless of what sensory and motivational processes occupy the brain, the final result is always either a muscle contraction or the delay of a muscle contraction. However, a motor neuron and its associated muscle will participate in a great many different kinds of movements, and we need many brain areas to control the different kinds.

Summary

1. Vertebrates have skeletal, cardiac, and smooth muscles. (p. 212)
2. The neuromuscular junction is a specialized type of synapse. (p. 213)
3. Skeletal muscles range from slow muscles that do not fatigue to fast muscles that fatigue quickly. We rely on the slow muscles most of the time, but we recruit the fast muscles for brief periods of strenuous activity. (p. 214)

4. Proprioceptors are receptors sensitive to the position and movement of a part of the body. Two kinds of proprioceptors, muscle spindles and Golgi tendon organs, help regulate muscle movements. (p. 215)
5. Some movements, especially reflexes, proceed as a unit, with little if any guidance from sensory feedback. Other movements, such as threading a needle, are constantly guided and redirected by sensory feedback. (p. 217)
6. Someone who becomes skillful at a movement executes large sequences of the movement as a whole, with little dependence on moment-by-moment feedback. (p. 219)

Review Questions

1. Why can the eye muscles move with greater precision than the biceps muscles? (p. 213)
2. What transmitter is released at the neuromuscular junction of skeletal muscles? (p. 213)
3. How do fish swim at the same speed in water of different temperatures, even though temperature affects the vigor of contraction of each muscle fiber? (p. 214)
4. Someone who runs extraordinary distances builds up muscles that enable long-distance running without fatigue. What disadvantage is likely? Why? (p. 215)
5. If you are holding your arm straight out and someone pulls it down slightly, it immediately bounces back to its original position. What proprioceptor is responsible? (p. 215)
6. What is the function of Golgi tendon organs? (p. 216)
7. In what ways is walking not a purely voluntary movement? (p. 217)
8. Give an example of a movement that is highly sensitive to feedback and one that is relatively insensitive. (p. 217)
9. Give an example of a motor program. (p. 218)

Thought Question

1. Would you expect jaguars, cheetahs, and other great cats to have mostly slow-twitch, nonfatiguing muscles in their legs or mostly fast-twitch, quickly fatiguing muscles? What kinds of animals might have mostly the opposite kind of muscles?

Suggestions for Further Reading

Cole, J. (1995). *Pride and a daily marathon.* Cambridge, MA: MIT Press. Biography of a man who lost all his touch and proprioception from the neck down and eventually learned to control his movements strictly by vision.

Lashley, K. S. (1951). The problem of serial order in behavior. In L. A. Jeffress (Ed.), *Cerebral mechanisms in behavior* (pp. 112–136). New York: John Wiley & Sons. One of the true classic articles in psychology; thought-provoking appraisal of what a theory of movement needs to explain.

Terms

smooth muscle   muscle that controls movements of internal organs (p. 212)

skeletal muscle or **striated muscle**   muscle that controls movement of the body in relation to the environment (such as arm and leg muscles) (p. 212)

cardiac muscle   muscle of the heart (p. 212)

neuromuscular junction   synapse where a motor neuron's axon meets a muscle fiber (p. 213)

antagonistic muscle   muscle that moves a limb in opposite directions (for example, extensor and flexor) (p. 213)

flexor   muscle that flexes a limb (p. 213)

extensor   muscle that extends a limb (p. 214)

fast-twitch muscle   muscle that produces fast contractions but fatigues rapidly (p. 215)

slow-twitch muscle   muscle that produces less vigorous contractions without fatiguing (p. 215)

proprioceptor   receptor that is sensitive to the position and movement of a part of the body (p. 215)

stretch reflex   reflexive contraction of a muscle in response to a stretch of that muscle (p. 216)

muscle spindle   receptor that responds to the stretch of a muscle (p. 216)

Golgi tendon organ   receptor that responds to the contraction of a muscle (p. 216)

reflex   a consistent, automatic response to a stimulus (p. 217)

ballistic movement   motion that proceeds as a single organized unit that cannot be redirected once it begins (p. 217)

grasp reflex   reflexive grasp of an object placed firmly in the hand (p. 218)

Babinski reflex   reflexive flexion of the big toe when the sole of the foot is stimulated (p. 218)

rooting reflex   reflexive head turning and sucking after a touch on the cheek (p. 218)

central pattern generator   neural mechanism in the spinal cord or elsewhere that generates rhythmic patterns of motor output (p. 218)

motor program   fixed sequence of movements that occur as a single unit (p. 218)

Brain Mechanisms of Movement

Suppose you stand up, walk across the room, sit at the piano, place your hands in position, and start to play. So far as you are consciously aware, you merely decide to perform this sequence of actions and then do it. However, much of your nervous system is devoted to making it happen. Furthermore, different parts of your brain are responsible for different aspects of movement. Figure 8.8 outlines the major motor areas of the mammalian central nervous system. Don't get too bogged down in details at this point; we shall attend to each area in due course.

The Role of the Spinal Cord

Have you ever heard the expression "running around like a chicken with its head cut off"? A rather gruesome image, but a chicken with its head cut off *can* run around . . . for a little while. Of course, it does not run toward anything or away from anything; it just runs. Nevertheless, it keeps its balance and maintains a

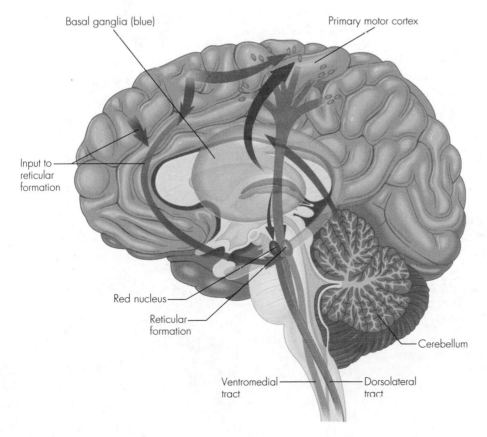

FIGURE **8.8**
The major motor areas of the mammalian central nervous system
The cerebral cortex, especially the primary motor cortex, sends axons directly to the medulla and spinal cord. So do the red nucleus, reticular formation, and other brain-stem areas. The medulla and spinal cord control all muscle movements. The basal ganglia and cerebellum influence movement indirectly through their communication back and forth with the cerebral cortex and brain stem.

normal pace, because walking and running are controlled largely by the spinal cord, even when the brain is intact, even in humans. The motor programs for chewing, swallowing, breathing, scratching, and a number of other common behaviors are also in the spinal cord and medulla (Shik & Orlovsky, 1976). The cerebral cortex does not direct the individual muscle contractions necessary for such movements; it merely turns on the appropriate motor programs. Diseases of the spinal cord can impair the control of movement in various ways. (See Table 8.1.)

The motor program for the scratch reflex has received considerable research attention. In cats, the reflex is three or four scratches per second, generated by cells in the third through fifth lumbar segments of the spinal cord (Deliagina, Orlovsky, & Pavlova, 1983). Stroking the skin stimulates certain neurons to produce impulses at a rate of three or four per second. The rate of scratching remains the same even if those neurons are isolated from all cerebral input, so it appears that the rhythm originates in the spinal cord. Furthermore, the cells generate the rhythm even if the muscles are paralyzed, so the rhythm does not require feedback from muscle movements.

The Role of the Cerebellum

The cerebellum is important for motor control, including learned motor responses. The term *cerebellum* is Latin for *little brain*. The cerebellum contains so many neurons and so many connections that its potential for information processing is comparable to that of the cerebral cortex.

The most obvious effect of cerebellar damage is trouble with rapid, ballistic movement sequences that require accurate aiming and timing. For example, people with cerebellar damage have trouble tapping a rhythm, pointing at a moving object, and adapting to prisms that distort vision (Daum et al., 1993). They also have trouble with speaking, writing, typing, playing a musical instrument, and athletics. With simple alternating movements such as hand clapping, the person has to pause after each movement to plan the next one.

The cerebellum is generally large in species that make many rapid, well-aimed movements, such as birds. The sloth, at the other extreme, is a mammal

TABLE 8.1
Some Disorders of the Spinal Cord

Disorder	Description	Cause
Paralysis	Lack of voluntary movement in part of the body.	Damage to motor neurons in the spinal cord or their axons in the periphery.
Flaccid paralysis	Inability to move one part of the body voluntarily, accompanied by low muscle tone and weak reflexive movements.	Damage to motor neurons in the spinal cord. Can be temporary result of damage to axons from brain to spinal cord.
Spastic paralysis	Inability to move one part of the body voluntarily, although reflexive movements and tremors remain. Muscles are stiff and muscle tone is higher than normal. Reflexes are strong and jerky.	Damage to axons from the brain to the spinal cord. (Such damage initially causes flaccid paralysis, which eventually gives way to spastic paralysis.)
Paraplegia	Loss of sensation and voluntary muscle control in both legs. Reflexes remain in legs. Although no messages pass between the brain and the genitals, the genitals still respond reflexively to touch. Paraplegics feel nothing in their own genitals, but they can function sexually, satisfy their partners, and still experience orgasm (Money, 1967).	Cut through the spinal cord above the segments attached to the legs.
Quadriplegia	Loss of sensation and muscle control in all four extremities.	Cut through the spinal cord above the level controlling the arms.
Hemiplegia	Loss of sensation and muscle control in the arm and leg on one side.	Cut halfway through the spinal cord or (more commonly) damage to one of the hemispheres of the cerebral cortex.
Tabes dorsalis	Impaired sensation in the legs and pelvic region, impaired leg reflexes and walking, loss of bladder and bowel control.	Late stage of syphilis. Dorsal roots of the spinal cord deteriorate gradually.
Poliomyelitis	Paralysis.	Virus that damages cell bodies of motor neurons.
Amyotrophic lateral sclerosis (Lou Gehrig's disease)	Gradual weakness and paralysis, starting with the arms and later spreading to the legs. Both motor neurons and axons from the brain to the motor neurons are destroyed.	Unknown.

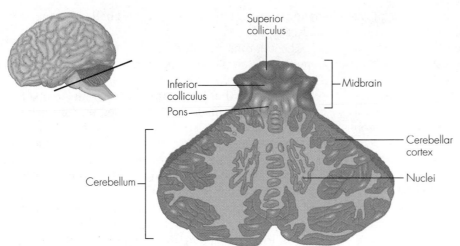

FIGURE **8.9**
Location of the cerebellar nuclei relative to the cerebellar cortex

that is proverbial for its slowness. When M. G. Murphy and J. L. O'Leary (1973) made cerebellar lesions in sloths, they detected no change in the animals' movement patterns.

Here is one quick way to test how well someone's cerebellum is functioning: Ask the person to focus on one spot, then to move the eyes quickly to another spot. **Saccades** (sa-KAHDS), ballistic eye movements from one fixation point to another, depend on impulses from the cerebellum and the frontal cortex to the cranial nerves. A normal, healthy person's eyes move from one fixation point to another by a single movement or by one large movement with a small correction at the end. Someone with cerebellar damage, however, has difficulty programming the angle and distance of eye movements (Dichgans, 1984). The eyes make many short movements until, by trial and error, they eventually focus on the intended spot.

Another test of cerebellar damage is the *finger-to-nose test*. The person is instructed to hold one arm straight out and then, at command, to touch his or her nose as quickly as possible. A normal person does so in three steps. First, the finger moves ballistically to a point just in front of the nose. This *move* function depends on the cerebellar cortex (the surface of the cerebellum), which sends messages to the nuclei (clusters of cell bodies in the interior of the cerebellum; see Figure 8.9). Second, the finger remains steady at that spot for a fraction of a second. This *hold* function depends on the nuclei alone (Kornhuber, 1974). Finally, the finger moves to the nose by a slower movement that does not depend on the cerebellum.

After damage to the cerebellar cortex, a person has trouble with the initial rapid movement. Either the finger stops too soon or it goes too far, striking the person in the face. If certain cerebellar nuclei have been damaged, the person may have difficulty with the hold seg-

ment: When the finger reaches a point just in front of the nose it wavers wildly.

The symptoms of cerebellar damage markedly resemble those of intoxication. Drunken individuals as a rule are clumsy, their speech is slurred, and their eye movements are inaccurate. A police officer testing someone for drunkenness may use the finger-to-nose test or other tests that reveal damage to the cerebellum because it is one of the first areas of the brain to show the effects of intoxication.

Evidence of a Broad Role

The cerebellum is not only a motor structure. It is unimportant for many kinds of movement and critical for some nonmotor functions. According to one experiment, neurons in the cerebellum are seldom active while a cat is walking, even if it is walking on a horizontal ladder that requires careful coordination. However, if one of the ladder rungs is moved just as the cat is about to step on it, cerebellar neurons become very active. Evidently they respond to a signal that directs movement, not just to the movement itself (Armstrong & Marple-Horvat, 1996).

In another study, functional MRI measured cerebellar activity while people performed several tasks with a single set of objects (Gao et al., 1996). When they simply lifted things, a purely motor task, the cerebellum showed little activity. When they felt objects with both hands to decide whether the objects were the same or different, the cerebellum was most active. The cerebellum even showed some activity when people held their hands steady and the experimenter rubbed an object across them. As in the cat study, the cerebellum responded to sensory stimuli that might guide movement, and responded to the use of movement to explore sensory information, but it did not respond to movement by itself.

What, then, is the role of the cerebellum? Masao Ito (1984) proposed that it is critical for establishing new motor programs that enable one to execute a sequence of actions as a whole instead of waiting for feedback. By extension, the cerebellum may also develop cognitive programs that allow us to go through several problem-solving steps in a single smooth sequence.

Richard Ivry and his colleagues have emphasized the importance of the cerebellum for behaviors that depend on precise timing of fairly short intervals (up to about 1.5 seconds). Any sequence of rapid movements, including alternating movements, obviously requires timing. Many perceptual and cognitive tasks also require timing—for example, judging which of two visual stimuli is moving faster, or listening to two pairs of beeps and judging whether the delay was longer between the first pair or the second pair.

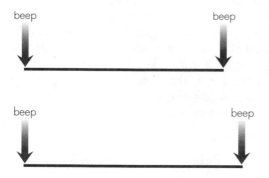

People who are accurate at one kind of timed movement, such as tapping a rhythm with a finger, also tend to be good at other timed movements, such as tapping a rhythm with a foot, and at judging which visual stimulus moved faster and which intertone delay was longer. People with cerebellar damage are impaired at all of these tasks, but unimpaired at controlling the force of a movement or at judging which tone is louder (Ivry & Diener, 1991; Keele & Ivry, 1990). Furthermore, the cerebellum has been shown to be important for learned responses that require timing (such as blinking the eyes after a signal that predicts a puff of air to the eyes 0.5 seconds later) but unimportant for learned responses that do not require timing (such as a learned change in heart rate following a fear signal). The apparent unifying pattern is that the cerebellum is important for any behavior that requires careful timing of brief intervals.

Cellular Organization

The cerebellum receives input from the spinal cord, from each of the sensory systems by way of the cranial nerve nuclei, and from the cerebral cortex. That infor-

mation eventually reaches the **cerebellar cortex,** the surface of the cerebellum (see Figure 8.9).

The neurons of the cerebellar cortex have an extremely regular pattern, as illustrated in Figure 8.10. The **Purkinje cells** are very flat cells in sequential planes. The **parallel fibers** are axons parallel to one another but perpendicular to the planes of the Purkinje cells. Action potentials in varying numbers of parallel fibers excite one Purkinje cell after another. Each of those Purkinje cells then transmits an inhibitory message to cells in the interior **nuclei of the cerebellum** and the vestibular nuclei in the brain stem, which in turn send information to the midbrain and the thalamus. Depending on which parallel fibers and how many of them are active, they might stimulate only the first few Purkinje cells or a long series of them. Because the parallel fibers' messages reach different Purkinje cells one after another, not all at the same time, the greater the number of Purkinje cells excited, the greater their collective *duration* of response. That is, if the parallel fibers stimulate only a few Purkinje cells, the result is a brief message to the target cells; if they stimulate more Purkinje cells, the message lasts longer. The controlled timing of the response may affect either movements or cognitive processes (Raymond, Lisberger, & Mauk, 1996).

The Role of the Basal Ganglia

The term *basal ganglia* applies collectively to a group of large subcortical structures in the forebrain (see Figure 8.11): the **caudate nucleus,** the **putamen,** the **globus pallidus,** the **substantia nigra,** and the **subthalamic nucleus.** Each of these areas exchanges information with the others and with the thalamus and cerebral cortex. The main receptive areas are the caudate nucleus and the putamen, which receive sensory input from much of the thalamus and the cerebral cortex. The main output area is the globus pallidus, which sends information to the thalamus, which in turn sends it to the motor cortex and the prefrontal cortex (Hoover & Strick, 1993).

Because of the multiple connections between the basal ganglia and the cerebral cortex, damage to the basal ganglia prevents much of the cortex from functioning normally. People with damage or malfunction in the basal ganglia, such as patients with Parkinson's disease or Huntington's disease, have trouble with memory and problem solving as well as with movements. In studying such patients, it is difficult to separate the effects of cell loss in the basal ganglia from the effects of impaired functioning by the still-intact cerebral cortex.

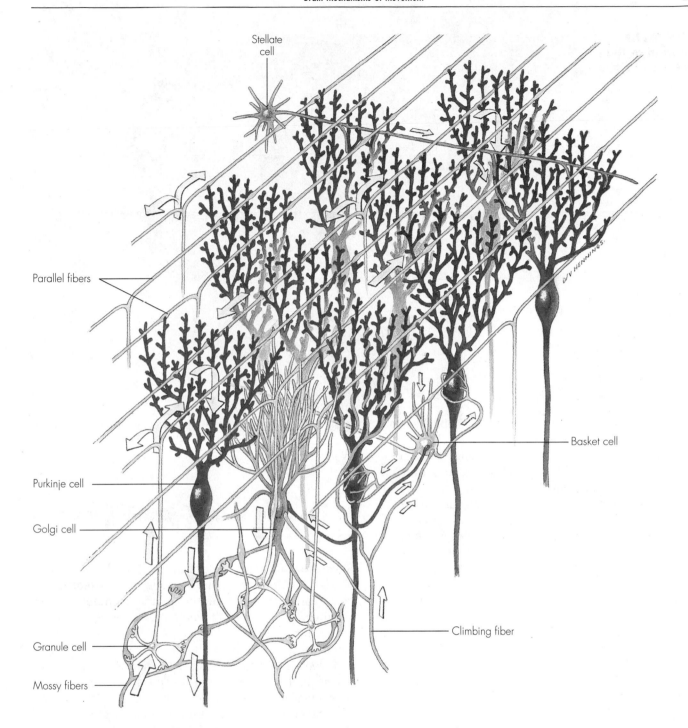

Stellate
cell

Parallel fibers

Basket cell

Purkinje cell

Golgi cell

Climbing fiber

Granule cell

Mossy fibers

FIGURE **8.10**
Cellular organization of the cerebellum
Parallel fibers activate one Purkinje cell after another. Purkinje cells inhibit a target cell in one of the nuclei of the cerebellum. The more Purkinje cells that respond, the longer the target cell is inhibited. In this way, the cerebellum controls the duration of a movement.

FIGURE **8.11**
Location of the basal ganglia

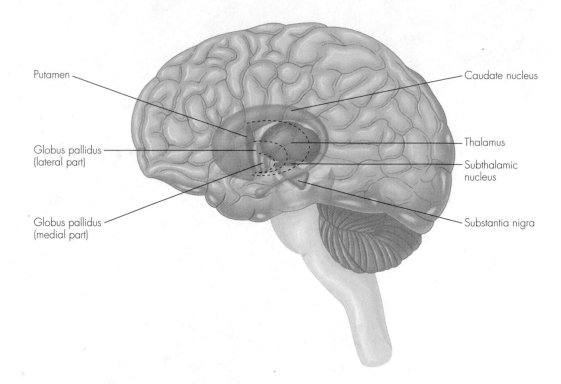

Putamen

Caudate nucleus

Globus pallidus
(lateral part)

Thalamus

Subthalamic
nucleus

Globus pallidus
(medial part)

Substantia nigra

PET scans of healthy brains have established that cells in the basal ganglia become active before movements but after activity has begun in motor areas of the cerebral cortex. Thus, basal ganglia cells do not initiate the plan for movement (the cerebral cortex does). Rather, they help organize it. Basal ganglia activity increases before both new and habitual movements, before both self-initiated movements and movements in response to a signal, before both actual movements and imagined movements (Brooks, 1995). Although the exact role of the basal ganglia remains uncertain, one attractive hypothesis is that they are important for selecting the correct movement because they inhibit the unwanted movements (Brooks, 1995). To touch your forehead, you have to prevent all kinds of muscle contractions that might move your hand somewhere else. In particular, the basal ganglia may synchronize the outputs from several parts of the cerebral cortex, first activating one group and inhibiting others, then inhibiting the first group and activating another (Graybiel, Aosaki, Flaherty, & Kimura, 1994). To make a complex sequence of movements, like signing your name, the key point is to delay each movement until its turn. If all movements start at once, the result is either slow, uncoordinated movement or no movement at all.

Some people are consistently clumsy, in many cases because of dysfunction in either the cerebellum or the basal ganglia. One study of very clumsy children found that those with cerebellar impairment were inaccurate in the timing of their movements, whereas those with basal ganglia impairments were inaccurate in their control of muscle force (Lundy-Ekman, Ivry, Keele, & Woollacott, 1991).

The Role of the Cerebral Cortex

Since the pioneering work of Gustav Fritsch and Eduard Hitzig (1870), neuroscientists have known that direct electrical stimulation of the **primary motor cortex** (Figure 8.12) can elicit movements. However, the motor cortex has no direct connections to the muscles; it sends axons to the medulla and spinal cord, which in turn send axons to the muscles. Electrical stimulation of the motor cortex generally produces coordinated movement in several muscles, not isolated movement in a single muscle (Asanuma, 1981). In other words, the cortex (unlike the spinal cord) is in charge of general movement plans, not individual muscle contractions. The cerebral cortex is particularly important in controlling complex actions. It contributes little to the control of coughing, sneezing, gagging, laughing, or crying (Rinn, 1984). (Perhaps this lack of cerebral control explains why it is hard to perform those actions voluntarily.)

Figure 4.21 shows one body area for each point along the motor cortex in a simple summary of a more complex relationship. For example, when you move a

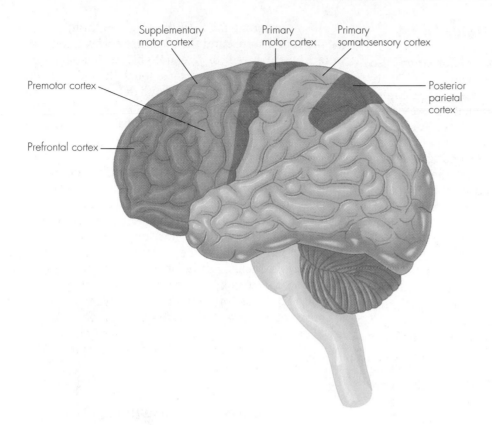

Supplementary
motor cortex

Primary
motor cortex

Primary
somatosensory cortex

Premotor cortex

Posterior
parietal
cortex

Prefrontal cortex

FIGURE **8.12**
Principal areas of the motor cortex in the human brain
Cells in the premotor cortex and supplementary motor cortex are active during the planning of movements, even if the movements are never actually executed.

finger or wrist, activity increases mainly in the cortical region associated with the hand, as Figure 4.21 indicates. However, we do not have separate regions for the thumb and each finger. Rather, movement of any one finger or the wrist activates a scattered population of cells, and the regions activated by one finger greatly overlap the regions activated by any other finger, as shown in Figure 8.13 (Sanes, Donoghue, Thangaraj, Edelman, & Warach, 1995). The reason for multiple and scattered representation of each finger is uncertain, but these results suggest that different parts of the motor cortex might control different aspects of motion, just as different parts of the primary visual cortex control different aspects of visual perception.

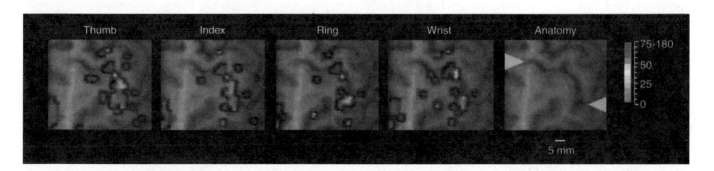

Thumb   Index   Ring   Wrist   Anatomy

75-180
50
25
0

5 mm

FIGURE **8.13**
Motor cortex during movement of a finger or the wrist
In this functional MRI scan, red indicates the greatest activity, followed by yellow, green, and blue. Note that each movement activated a scattered population of cells, and that the areas activated by any one part of the hand overlapped the areas activated by any other. The illustration at the right (anatomy) shows a section of the central sulcus (between the two yellow arrows). The primary motor cortex is just anterior to the central sulcus.   Source: Sanes, Donoghue, Thangaraj, Edelman, & Warach, 1995.

Areas Near the Primary Motor Cortex

A number of areas near the primary motor cortex also contribute to movement in diverse ways (see Figure 8.12). The **posterior parietal cortex** has some neurons that respond primarily to visual or somatosensory stimuli, some that respond mostly to current or future movements, and some that respond to a complicated mixture of the stimulus and the upcoming response (Shadlen & Newsome, 1996). Contrast the effects of posterior parietal damage with those of occipital or temporal damage. People with posterior parietal damage can accurately describe what they see, but they have trouble converting their perception into action. Although they can walk toward something they hear, they cannot walk toward something they see, nor can they reach out with a hand to grasp an object—even after fluently describing its size, shape, and angle. On the opposite extreme, people with damage to certain parts of the occipital cortex cannot describe the size, shape, or location of the objects they see, but they accurately reach out to pick up the objects, and when walking they step over or go around the objects in their way (Goodale, 1996; Goodale, Milner, Jakobson, & Carey, 1991). In short, the ability to describe what we see is separate from the influence of vision on movement, and we can lose either one without the other.

The primary somatosensory cortex is the main receiving area for touch and other body information, as mentioned in Chapter 7. It sends a substantial number of axons directly to the spinal cord and also provides the primary motor cortex with sensory information.

Cells in the prefrontal cortex, premotor cortex, and supplementary motor cortex are active during the planning of a movement, even if the movement itself is never carried out. The **prefrontal cortex** responds mostly to the sensory signals that lead to a movement (Goldman-Rakic, Bates, & Chafee, 1992). The **premotor cortex** is most active during preparations for a movement and less active during the movement itself. The **supplementary motor cortex** is most active during preparations for a rapid series of movements, such as pushing, pulling, and then turning a stick. Many cells in this area are active only in preparation for one particular order of movements (Tanji & Shima, 1994). As Karl Lashley (1951) pointed out long ago, behaviors such as typing, dancing, speaking, and playing a musical instrument require such rapid alternations of actions that we must start each movement well before we have finished the last one, sometimes as much as two or three steps ahead. Damage to the supplementary motor cortex impairs the ability to organize smooth sequences of activities.

In an experiment to contrast the contributions of the prefrontal cortex and the premotor cortex, monkeys were shown a red or green light, which signaled whether they would later have to touch the red or green pad to get food. After a 1.25-second delay, the monkeys saw a second light, which meant that it was almost time to respond. They then had to wait between 1.25 seconds and 3.5 seconds before touching the correct pad in order to receive some juice as a reinforcement. (That is, the monkeys had to time their response correctly.) The initial stimulus (the red or green light) provoked activity mostly in the prefrontal cortex. The second stimulus (indicating that the monkey must wait at least another 1.25 seconds before responding) also provoked activity mostly in the prefrontal cortex. Toward the end of that delay, just before the movement, cells in the premotor cortex became active (DiPelligrino & Wise, 1991). Thus, preparation for a movement seems to consist of waves of activity, first in the prefrontal cortex, then in the premotor cortex, then mostly in the primary motor cortex, and ultimately in the spinal cord and the muscles.

Movement Coding in the Primary Motor Cortex

Consider the area of the primary motor cortex that is responsible for arm movements. Most neurons in this area are tuned to an approximate direction of movement. For example, one neuron might be most responsive in preparation for arm movements directly toward the front, and slightly less active for movements a bit to the left or right.

An investigator can determine a *movement vector* to represent the activity of neurons in the motor cortex. For example, if the neurons tuned to a left-to-right movement are slightly more active than other neurons, we can represent this trend with a short line to the right, as in Figure 8.14(a). A longer line to the right, as in Figure 8.14(b), indicates that neurons tuned to a left-to-right movement are a great deal more active than other neurons. A line at a different angle, as in Figure 8.14(c), shows a predominant activity by neurons that prefer another angle of movement.

Now let us apply this system to the results of one experiment. Monkeys were trained to hold a lever in the center of a circle and then, under certain conditions, to pull it toward a light that flashed at some point along the radius of the circle. Under these conditions, the signal quickly elicited a movement vector pointed toward the light, the same as the direction of the movement. So far, no surprise.

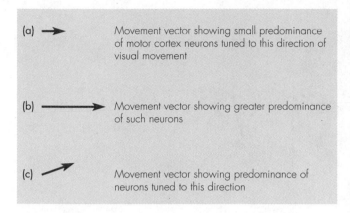

FIGURE **8.14**
Movement vectors in the primary motor cortex
The direction of the line indicates that neurons tuned to that direction of movement are more active than other neurons are. The longer the line, the greater the dominance by the neurons tuned to that direction.

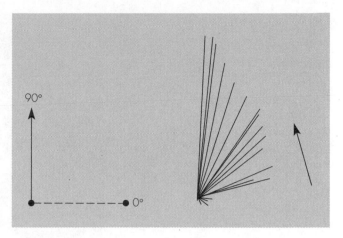

FIGURE **8.15**
Apparent mental rotation of movement vectors in a monkey experiment
The monkey saw a light appear at the 0° direction; it had to move the lever to a position 90° counterclockwise from that direction. Just after the presentation of the light, the movement vector pointed weakly in the direction of the light. Over the next 0.3 seconds, the movement vector moved toward the correct direction. In effect, these results enable us to watch the monkey's brain activity as it mentally rotates the stimulus.   Source: From Lurito, Georgakopoulos, & Georgopoulos, 1991.

Then, under other conditions, the monkey had to move the lever to a spot 90° counterclockwise from the direction of the light. Here, the results looked like those in Figure 8.15. At first, the movement vector was short and pointed almost in the direction of the light. Over the next 0.3 seconds, the movement vector gradually changed, growing longer and moving in the direction of the eventual movement (Lurito, Georgakopoulos, & Georgopoulos, 1991). The gradual change in neural activity suggests that the monkey is doing a "mental rotation" from the direction of the original stimulus to the direction of the actual movement.

Connections from the Brain to the Spinal Cord

All the messages from the brain must eventually reach the medulla and spinal cord, which control the muscles. The various outputs from the brain organize into two paths, the dorsolateral tract and the ventromedial tract.

The **dorsolateral tract** of the spinal cord is a set of axons from the primary motor cortex and surrounding areas and from the **red nucleus** of the midbrain (Figure 8.16). These axons extend without synaptic interruption to their target neurons in the spinal cord; those from the cortex to the lower spinal cord are the longest axons in the CNS. In bulges of the medulla called *pyramids,* the dorsolateral tract crosses from one side of the

brain to the opposite side of the spinal cord. This tract controls movements in peripheral areas, such as the hands, fingers, and toes. People with damage to the primary motor cortex or its axons suffer at least a temporary loss of fine movements on the opposite side of the body.

The **ventromedial tract** includes many axons from the primary motor cortex and supplementary motor cortex and also some from many other parts of the cortex. The ventromedial tract also includes axons that originate from the midbrain tectum, the reticular formation, and the **vestibular nucleus** (see Figure 8.17). Axons of the ventromedial tract do not cross from one side of the nervous system to the other, although some axons have branches to both sides of the spinal cord. The ventromedial tract controls mainly the muscles of the neck, shoulders, and trunk (Kuypers, 1989). Note that these movements are necessarily bilateral; you can move your fingers on one side and not the other, but you cannot move your neck on one side and not the other. Damage to the ventromedial tract impairs walking, turning, bending, standing up, and sitting down. Most movements rely on both dorsolateral and ventromedial tracts. The motor systems work in cooperation with each other, not independently.

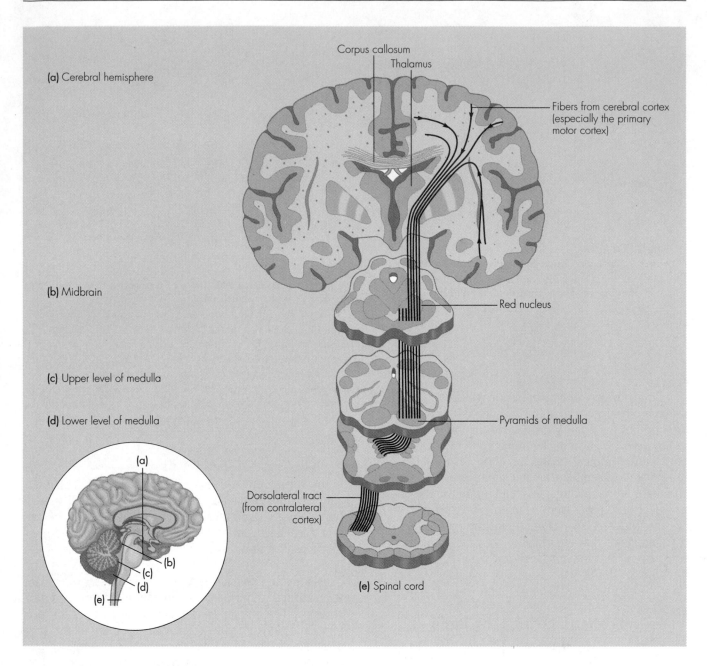

(a) Cerebral hemisphere

Corpus callosum

Thalamus

Fibers from cerebral cortex (especially the primary motor cortex)

(b) Midbrain

Red nucleus

(c) Upper level of medulla

(d) Lower level of medulla

Pyramids of medulla

(a)

(b)

(c)

(d)

(e)

Dorsolateral tract (from contralateral cortex)

(e) Spinal cord

FIGURE **8.16**
The dorsolateral tract
This tract originates from the primary motor cortex, neighboring areas, and the red nucleus. It crosses from one side of the brain to the opposite side of the spinal cord and controls precise and discrete movements of the extremities, such as hands, fingers, and feet.

IN **CLOSING**

Multiple Motor Areas

Most progress in any scientific field comes from improved measurements. In observing people's movements, it is easy to lump together a wide variety of troubles as mere clumsiness or poor coordination. The study of brain mechanisms alerts us to the importance of measuring different kinds of movements and distinguishing among timing errors, poor control of force, lost control of the extremities, lost control of the trunk muscles, and so forth. The control of movement can go wrong in many ways, and different kinds of brain damage produce different movement disorders.

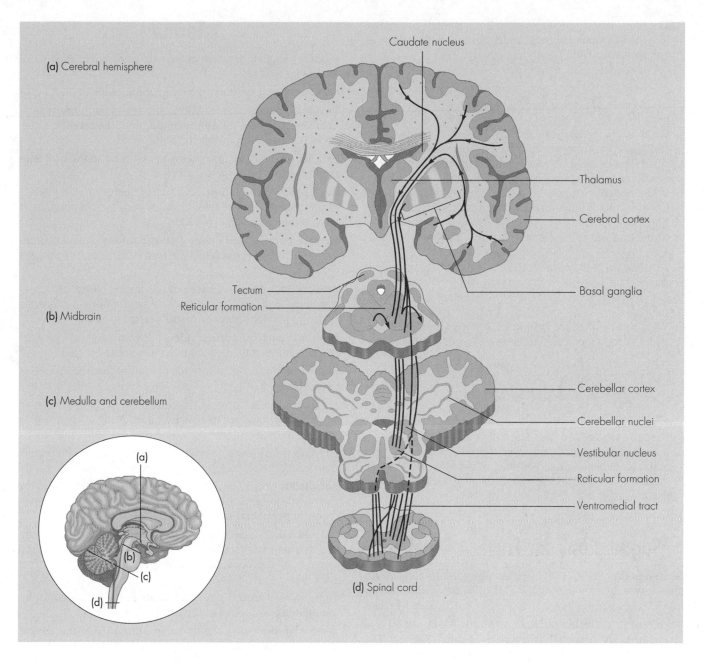

(a) Cerebral hemisphere

Caudate nucleus

Thalamus

Cerebral cortex

Basal ganglia

Tectum

Reticular formation

(b) Midbrain

(c) Medulla and cerebellum

Cerebellar cortex

Cerebellar nuclei

Vestibular nucleus

Reticular formation

Ventromedial tract

(a)

(b)

(c)

(d)

(d) Spinal cord

FIGURE **8.17**
The ventromedial tract
This tract originates from many parts of the cerebral cortex and several areas of the midbrain and medulla. It produces bilateral control of trunk muscles for postural adjustments and bilateral movements such as standing, bending, turning, and walking.

Summary

1. The spinal cord contains the mechanisms for many motor programs, including walking, running, and scratching. It can generate rhythmic movements on its own. (p. 221)

2. The cerebellum helps to develop new motor programs and is essential for any behavior that requires precise timing of short intervals. (p. 222)

3. The cells of the cerebellum are arranged in a very regular pattern that enables them to produce outputs of well-controlled duration. (p. 224)

4. The basal ganglia are a group of large subcortical structures that contribute to a wide array of movements, perhaps by inhibiting incorrect movements. (p. 224)

5. The primary motor cortex is the main source of axons to the spinal cord. Areas surrounding it contribute to particular aspects of motion, such as coordinating vision with movements, planning movements, and organizing sequences of movements. (p. 226)

6. Fibers that cross from one side of the brain to the opposite side of the spinal cord form the dorsolateral tract, which controls movements in the periphery of the body. (p. 229)

7. The fibers that do not cross sides in the spinal cord constitute the ventromedial tract, which controls bilateral movements near the midline of the body. (p. 229)

Review Questions

1. What evidence supports the conclusion that the spinal cord directly controls certain motor programs? (p. 222)
2. What kind of brain damage produces motor effects that resemble those of alcoholic intoxication, and why? (p. 223)
3. What evidence suggests that the cerebellum is important for perceptual functions and not just motor functions? (p. 223)
4. Name the structures that compose the basal ganglia. (p. 224)
5. Describe the behavioral functions of the posterior parietal cortex, the somatosensory cortex, the prefrontal cortex, the premotor cortex, and the supplementary motor cortex. (p. 228)
6. What is the difference in function between the dorsolateral and ventromedial tracts of the spinal cord? (p. 229)

Thought Question

1. Human infants are at first limited to gross movements of the trunk, arms, and legs. The ability to move one finger at a time matures gradually over more than the first year. What hypothesis would you suggest about which brain areas controlling movement mature early and which ones mature later?

Suggestions for Further Reading

Georgopoulos, A. P. (1991). Higher order motor control. *Annual Review of Neuroscience, 14,* 361–377. Review of the contributions of various brain areas to the control of movement.

Raymond, J. L., Lisberger, S. G., & Mauk, M. D. (1996). The cerebellum: A neuronal learning machine? *Science, 272,* 1126–1131. Describes the cellular mechanisms of the cerebellum.

Terms

saccade   rapid movement of the eyes from one fixation point to another (p. 223)

cerebellar cortex   outer covering of the cerebellum (p. 224)

Purkinje cell   a neuron type in the cerebellum; the type of neuron responsible for all the output from the cerebellar cortex to the cerebellar nuclei (p. 224)

parallel fiber   axon that runs perpendicular to the planes of the Purkinje cells in the cerebellum (p. 224)

nuclei of the cerebellum   clusters of neurons in the interior of the cerebellum that send axons to motor-controlling areas outside the cerebellum (p. 224)

caudate nucleus, putamen, globus pallidus, substantia nigra, subthalamic nucleus   structures of the basal ganglia (p. 224)

primary motor cortex   area of the frontal cortex just anterior to the central sulcus; a primary point of origin for axons of the pyramidal system of motor control (p. 226)

posterior parietal cortex   area important for using visual and somatosensory cues to guide movement (p. 228)

prefrontal cortex   the anterior portion of the frontal lobe of the cortex (p. 228)

premotor cortex   area of the frontal cortex, just anterior to the primary motor cortex, active during the planning of a movement (p. 228)

supplementary motor cortex   area of the frontal cortex active during the planning of a movement (p. 228)

dorsolateral tract   a path of axons in the spinal cord from the contralateral hemisphere of the brain, controlling movements of peripheral muscles (p. 229)

red nucleus   nucleus midbrain structure whose axons join the dorsolateral tract of the spinal cord, controlling distal muscles of the body such as those in the hands and feet (p. 229)

ventromedial tract   a path of axons in the spinal cord providing bilateral control of the trunk muscles (p. 229)

vestibular nucleus   cluster of neurons in the brain stem, primarily responsible for motor responses to vestibular sensation (p. 229)

Disorders of Movement

Even if your nervous system and muscles are completely healthy, you may sometimes find it difficult to move in the way you would like. For example, if you have just finished a bout of unusually strenuous exercise, your muscles may be so fatigued that you can hardly move them voluntarily, even though they constantly twitch. Or if your legs "fall asleep" while you are sitting in an awkward position, you may stumble and even fall when you try to walk.

Certain neurological disorders produce exaggerated and lasting movement impairments. Some people suffer permanent fatigue and constant twitching. Others lose the ability to perform even simple everyday movements, although their muscles are intact. We shall consider three examples of such disorders—myasthenia gravis, Parkinson's disease, and Huntington's disease.

Myasthenia Gravis

Myasthenia gravis (MY-us-THEE-nee-uh GRAHV-iss) is an *autoimmune disease,* one in which the immune system forms antibodies that attack the individual's own body. In myasthenia gravis, the immune system attacks the acetylcholine receptors at neuromuscular junctions (Shah & Lisak, 1993). Myasthenia gravis causes the deaths of two or three people per 100,000 over the age of 75 each year; it seldom affects young people (Chandra, Bharucha, & Schoenberg, 1984).

The symptoms of myasthenia gravis are progressive weakness and rapid fatigue of the striated muscles. Any repeated movement rapidly gets weaker unless the person pauses to rest. Here is what happens: Because the muscles have fewer than the normal number of acetylcholine receptors, the remaining receptors need the maximum amount of transmitter to move the muscles normally. After any motor neuron has fired a few times in quick succession, later action potentials release fewer quanta of acetylcholine. A slight decline in acetylcholine is no problem for healthy people, because they have an abundance of acetylcholine receptors. In people with myasthenia gravis, transmission at the neuromuscular junction is precarious at best, and even a slight decline in acetylcholine availability has powerful effects (Drachman, 1978).

Myasthenia gravis can be treated with drugs that suppress the immune system (Shah & Lisak, 1993), but this approach leaves the patient vulnerable to other illnesses. So, many physicians prescribe drugs that inhibit acetylcholinesterase, an enzyme that breaks down acetylcholine. Inhibiting the breakdown of acetylcholine prolongs the action of acetylcholine at the neuromuscular junction. A physician must monitor the dose carefully, however, as too much acetylcholine is just as troublesome as too little.

Parkinson's Disease

The symptoms of **Parkinson's disease** are rigidity, muscle tremors, slow movements, inaccurate aim, difficulty initiating physical and mental activity, and spatial disorientation (M. Johnson et al., 1996; Manfredi, Stocchi, & Vacca, 1995; Pillon et al., 1996). Most patients become depressed at an early stage; the depression may be part of the disease and not just a reaction to it. Because symptoms vary and overlap with those of other disorders, physicians often have trouble making an accurate diagnosis (Koller, 1992). Parkinson's disease strikes about one person per hundred above age 50, with a higher U.S. rate among whites than blacks (Chandra, Bharucha, & Schoenberg, 1984). (See Figure 8.18.)

The immediate cause of Parkinson's disease is the gradual progressive death of neurons, especially in the substantia nigra and amygdala (Braak et al., 1995). Most research attention has focused on the substantia nigra neurons, which send dopamine-releasing axons

FIGURE **8.18**
Annual deaths from causes related to Parkinson's disease
Note that the number increases rapidly after age 65 and that the disorder affects more white than black people.   Source: From Chandra et al., 1984.

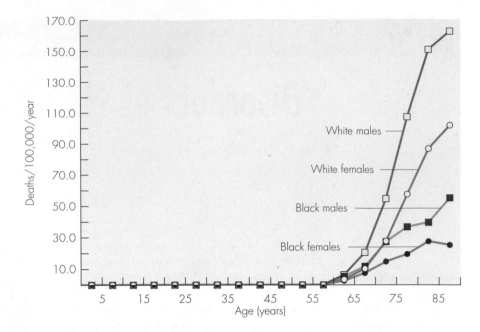

to the caudate nucleus and putamen. Those axons excite D_1 receptors and inhibit D_2 receptors; in Parkinson's disease, the loss of dopamine at both kinds of receptors produces a net increase in the inhibitory output from the globus pallidus to the thalamus, and therefore decreased excitation from the thalamus to the cerebral cortex, as shown in Figure 8.19 (Wichmann, Vitek, & DeLong, 1995).

Researchers estimate that the average person loses a little more than one percent of his or her substantia nigra neurons per year, beginning at around age 45. Most of us have neurons enough to spare, but some people either start with a smaller number or lose them at a faster rate. When the number of surviving substantia nigra neurons declines to 20–30 percent of normal, Parkinsonian symptoms begin (Knoll, 1993). The greater the cell loss, the more severe the symptoms.

Possible Causes

Unlike most other serious neurological or psychological disorders, Parkinson's disease has a relatively low heritability. Most patients have no afflicted relatives (De Michele et al., 1995). Even if one identical twin has the disease, the chance of the other twin also getting it is less than 10 percent—certainly greater than the 0.1 percent chance that other people have, but not enormous. However, when one identical twin has Parkinson's and the other does not, the non-Parkinson's twin generally has below-normal levels of dopamine synapses (Burn et al., 1992). A likely interpretation is that certain genes may increase or decrease a person's vulnerability to Parkinson's, although something in the environment determines whether the predisposition progresses to the disease itself.

Possible environmental factors include an interruption of blood flow to certain parts of the brain, prolonged exposure to certain drugs and toxins, and a history of encephalitis or other viral infections (Jenner, 1990). The possibility of a toxic cause for Parkinson's disease was discovered by accident (Ballard, Tetrud, & Langston, 1985). In northern California in 1982, several people aged 22 to 42 developed symptoms of Parkinson's disease after using a drug similar to heroin. (See Digression 8.2.) At first, physicians resisted diagnosing Parkinson's disease because the patients were so young, but eventually that diagnosis became clear. Before the investigators could alert the community to the danger of the heroin substitute, many other users had developed symptoms ranging from mild to fatal (Tetrud, Langston, Garbe, & Ruttenber, 1989).

The substance that these people used included **MPTP,** a chemical that the body converts to **MPP⁺,** which accumulates in, and then destroys, neurons that release dopamine (Nicklas, Saporito, Basma, Geller, & Heikkila, 1992). Postsynaptic neurons compensate for the dopamine loss by increasing their number of dopamine receptors (Chiueh, 1988; see Figure 8.20). The symptoms of Parkinson's disease result partly from the decreased dopamine input and partly from the jumpy overresponsiveness of the extra receptors (Miller & DeLong, 1988).

No one supposes that many cases of Parkinson's disease result from use of illegal drugs. A more likely hypothesis is that people are sometimes exposed to MPTP or similar chemicals in polluted air or water. A number of herbicides and pesticides, including *paraquat,* are likely candidates (see Figure 8.21). One study of Parkinson's patients with onset of symptoms before age 50 found that a higher-than-normal proportion of them had been exposed to large amounts of in-

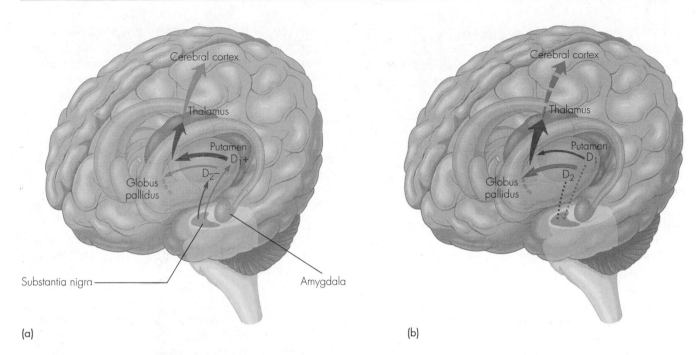

(a)   (b)

FIGURE **8.19**
Connections from the substantia nigra: normal (a), and in Parkinson's disease (b)
The substantia nigra's axons are excitatory at D_1 receptors and inhibitory at D_2 receptors. Axon loss decreases inhibitory communication and increases excitatory communication to the globus pallidus. The result is increased inhibition from the globus pallidus to the thalamus and decreased excitation from the thalamus to the cerebral cortex. People with Parkinson's disease show decreased initiation of movement. (Green arrows = excitation; red arrows = inhibition.)   Source: Based on Wichmann, Vitek, & DeLong, 1995.

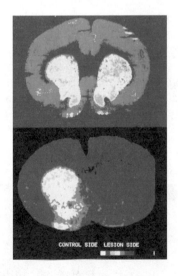

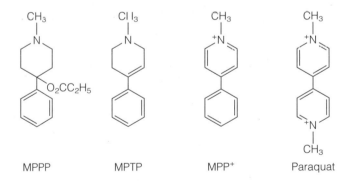

FIGURE **8.21**
The chemical structures of MPPP, MPTP, MPP⁺, and paraquat

FIGURE **8.20**
Results of injecting MPP⁺ into one hemisphere of the rat brain
The autoradiography at top shows D_2 dopamine receptors; the one at bottom shows axon terminals that contain dopamine. Red indicates the highest level of activity, followed by yellow, green, and blue. Note that the MPP⁺ greatly depleted the number of dopamine axons and that the number of D_2 receptors increased in response to this lack of input. However, the net result is a great decrease in dopamine activity.   Source: From Chiueh, 1988.

secticides and herbicides (Butterfield, Valanis, Spencer, Lindeman, & Nutt, 1993).

Most researchers doubt that exposure to a toxin is a major cause of Parkinson's disease. If it were, we should expect to find near epidemics in some geographical regions and almost no cases elsewhere. The actual patchy distribution of the disease suggests that toxins are just one factor among several in causing the disease (C. Smith et al., 1992).

L-Dopa Treatment

The traditional goal of Parkinson's therapy has been to replace the missing dopamine. However, a dopamine pill would be ineffective, because dopamine does not cross the blood-brain barrier. **L-dopa,** a precursor to dopamine, does cross the barrier. Taken as a daily pill, L-dopa reaches the brain, where neurons convert it to dopamine. Although it alleviates symptoms, L-dopa does not halt the death of neurons, and eventually the loss becomes too great to relieve.

The other limitation of L-dopa is that it enters not only the cells that need extra dopamine, but also others, producing harmful side effects that include nausea, restlessness, sleep problems, low blood pressure, stereotyped movements, hallucinations, and delusions. These effects can be relieved somewhat by additional drugs that prevent L-dopa from being converted to dopamine before it enters the brain, or by various slow-release devices.

The side effects of L-dopa generally grow worse with time, so some physicians delay giving the medication as long as possible. The research does not support the effectiveness of this approach, however (Markham & Diamond, 1981); the side effects probably grow worse simply because the disease becomes worse, not because of the cumulative effects of taking L-dopa.

Other Therapies

Given the limitations of L-dopa, researchers have alternatives and supplements. One effective drug is **deprenyl,** which slows the loss of neurons in the substantia nigra, decreases the need for L-dopa, and prolongs life in Parkinson's patients. It has also been found to increase activity and prolong life in aged but otherwise normal rats. Initially, researchers attributed the benefits of deprenyl to its ability to block the enzyme *monoamine oxidase B,* which among other effects breaks down dopamine into inactive chemicals. By blocking monoamine oxidase B, the reasoning went, deprenyl could prolong the effects of dopamine. It could also prevent monoamine oxidase B from converting harmless chemicals like MPTP into dangerous chemicals like MPP^+. However, later research found that deprenyl enhances the survival of substantia nigra neurons that do not even contain monoamine oxidase B (Knoll, 1993). Deprenyl must therefore be working partly through other routes, as yet unidentified.

Another treatment uses drugs that directly stimulate dopamine receptors (Rabey, 1995). Theoretically, drugs that inhibit glutamate synapses might also be helpful, because dopamine inhibits glutamate release (Schmidt, 1995). However, drugs that stimulate dopamine receptors produce a variety of unpleasant side effects, including nausea, and drugs that block glutamate receptors interfere with sensation, learning, and memory. Ideally, researchers would like to find a way to stimulate dopamine or inhibit glutamate in limited brain areas only. In the meantime, a common strategy is to combine a small amount of L-dopa and a small amount of a dopamine receptor stimulant, achieving a better benefit-to-side-effect ratio than that produced by a large dose of either drug.

Nicotine is also a possible treatment, although researchers have been cautious about trying it. Parkinson's disease is more common among people who do not smoke cigarettes than among those who do. The nicotine in the cigarettes increases dopamine release, facilitates binding of dopamine to D_1 receptors, blocks monoamine oxidase B, and may improve survival of certain neurons, much as neurotrophic factors do (Fowler et al., 1996; Sershen, Toth, Lajtha, & Vizi,

DIGRESSION 8.2

Designer Drugs

The United States enforces laws against the manufacture, sale, or use of many drugs that are believed to be harmful, including heroin. One way to evade the law is to sell a drug that is chemically modified, even if the difference is as minor as, say, substituting a methyl group for a single hydrogen ion. Any new drug is technically legal until the government passes a new law.

Because of this enormous loophole in the legal system, certain drug manufacturers "design" drugs to simulate the effects of prohibited substances. Although the risk to the manufacturer and dealer is low, the risk to the user is unknown and may in certain cases be more severe than the risk from the original illegal drugs.

1995). These apparent benefits do not imply that you should start smoking; the increased risk of cancer and emphysema from smoking far outweighs the decreased risk of Parkinson's disease. Still, the possibility remains that nicotine (without the tars found in tobacco) might supplement other treatments for Parkinson's disease.

Still another strategy is to graft neurons from a fetus into the damaged portion of the brain (Kupsch, Oertel, Earl, & Sautter, 1995). We shall consider that possibility more fully in Chapter 15. At this point, note that the results have been inconsistent; brain grafts are still in the experimental stage.

Huntington's Disease

Huntington's disease, also known as *Huntington's chorea,* is a severe neurological disorder that strikes about 1 person in 10,000 in the United States (Young, 1995). Motor symptoms usually begin with a facial twitch; later, tremors spread to other parts of the body and develop into purposeless writhing movements. (*Chorea* comes from the same root as *choreography;* sometimes the writhing movements of chorea look a little like dancing.) Gradually, the twitches, tremors, and writhing movements interfere more and more with the person's walking, speech, and other voluntary movements. The ability to form new movement habits is especially limited (Willingham, Koroshetz, & Peterson, 1996). The disorder is associated with widespread brain damage, especially in the caudate nucleus, putamen, and globus pallidus, and to some extent in the cerebral cortex (see Figure 8.22). Overall brain weight may decline by 15 to 20 percent before death (Sanberg & Coyle, 1984). The greatest damage is to neurons that release GABA as their transmitter; however, drugs that stimulate GABA receptors provide little or no relief from the symptoms of Huntington's disease (Young, 1995).

People with Huntington's disease also suffer psychological disorders, including depression, memory impairment, anxiety, hallucinations and delusions, poor judgment, alcoholism, drug abuse, and sexual disorders ranging from complete unresponsiveness to indiscriminate promiscuity (Shoulson, 1990). In some cases the psychological disorders develop before the motor disorders.

Huntington's disease most often appears between the ages of 30 and 50, although onset can occur at any point from childhood to old age. Once the symptoms emerge, both the psychological and the motor symptoms grow progressively worse over a period of about 15 years and culminate in death (Chase, Wexler, & Barbeau, 1979).

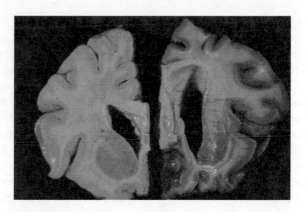

FIGURE **8.22**
Brain of a normal person (left) and a person with Huntington's disease (right)
The angle of cut through the normal brain makes the lateral ventricle look larger in this photo than it actually is. Even so, note how much larger it is in the Huntington's patient. The ventricles expand because of the loss of neurons.   Source: Courtesy of Robert E. Schmidt, Washington University.

Heredity and Presymptomatic Testing

Huntington's disease is controlled by an autosomal dominant gene. A person who has the gene will eventually develop the disease and will also transmit the gene to about half of his or her children. As a rule, a mutant gene that causes the loss of a function is recessive. The fact that the Huntington's gene is dominant implies that it produces the gain of some undesirable function.

Imagine that at the age of 20 you learn that one of your parents has Huntington's disease. You know that you have a 50 percent chance of developing it yourself, probably in about 20 years. In addition to your grief about your parent, your life will change in two ways. First, whenever you do something clumsy or experience a slight tremor anywhere in your body, you will fear that it signals the start of Huntington's disease. Second, you may have trouble deciding whether or not to have children.

Investigators worked for many years to discover an accurate **presymptomatic test** to identify which young people are at risk to develop the disease later. In the 1980s, researchers established that the gene for Huntington's disease is on chromosome number 4, although they did not yet know its exact location. To determine someone's risk for Huntington's disease, they examined a marker on that person's chromosome 4 and compared it with chromosomal markers for various relatives. If the person's marker matched those of relatives with Huntington's disease, then that person was at high risk (Folstein et al., 1985; Gusella et al., 1984). This test required the cooperation of a number of relatives; even under the best circumstances the test was only about

95 percent accurate, and it was sometimes completely indecisive. (For example, if the parent with Huntington's disease had the same markers as the other parent, then the results for the children would be ambiguous.)

In 1993 researchers identified the Huntington's gene itself (Huntington's Disease Collaborative Research Group, 1993). Now it is possible to predict with almost 100 percent accuracy whether or not someone will get Huntington's disease. No tests of relatives are necessary. Now ask yourself: If you had a parent with Huntington's disease, would you want to have your chromosomes examined? Many do; others decide they would rather live with uncertainty than run the risk of bad news. When people get good news, they are of course relieved. Those who get bad news generally accept it with less depression than we might have expected, although they find it helpful to get counseling at that point (Wiggins et al., 1992).

Identification of the Huntington's disease gene facilitates research on the disease itself. In its normal form, part of the gene includes a sequence of bases C-A-G (cytosine, adenine, guanine), repeated 11 to 24 times, less often as many as 34 times. In people with Huntington's disease, the sequence is repeated at least 37 times, sometimes far more (Huntington's Disease Collaborative Research Group, 1993; Persichetti et al., 1994). (What about someone with 35 or 36 repetitions? So few people have been found with those numbers that we do not know what to expect.) The greater the number of CAG repetitions on the gene, the earlier the probable onset of Huntington's disease. Those with about 40 repetitions sometimes escape the symptoms until old age; those with 50 or more repetitions generally begin having symptoms in their 20s or 30s, and those with still more repetitions may be affected even earlier (Claes et al., 1995; Persichetti et al., 1994). Thus, a chromosomal examination can predict not only whether a person will get Huntington's disease, but also approximately when.

Identification of the gene for Huntington's disease led to discovery of the protein for which it codes. That protein has been designated **huntingtin.** Huntingtin occurs throughout the human body and in species as remote as pufferfish (Baxendale et al., 1995). Within the brain, it is found inside neurons and not on their membranes, and more abundantly in axons and terminals rather than cell bodies (Trottier et al., 1995). Exactly what the protein does is still uncertain; research indicates that it binds to another protein, also of unknown function (Li et al., 1995), and that it interferes with the ability of brain enzymes to metabolize glucose (Burke et al., 1996). After investigators establish more clearly what the normal and mutant proteins do, the next step will be to use that information to devise methods of preventing or treating Huntington's disease.

IN CLOSING

The Psychology of Movement

The control of movement is an important topic for psychology as well as for biology. The inability to make certain movements may mean that the muscles are paralyzed, but it can also mean that the brain has difficulty planning the movements or conveying the plan from one area to another. Disorders such as Parkinson's disease and Huntington's disease are known mostly for their effect on movement, but they are also linked to abnormalities of thought and mood. In short, the brain mechanisms that control movement are not tacked on at the end of all the psychological processes; they are an integral part of everything that the brain does.

Summary

1. In myasthenia gravis, the immune system attacks the neuromuscular junctions. The disease is treated by suppressing the immune system and by prolonging the actions of acetylcholine at the neuromuscular junction. (p. 233)
2. Parkinson's disease is characterized by impaired initiation of activity, slow and inaccurate movements, tremor, rigidity, and, in most cases, depression. It is associated with the degeneration of dopamine-containing axons from the substantia nigra to the caudate nucleus and putamen. Generally, it is treated with L-dopa, often supplemented with deprenyl or other drugs. (pp. 233–237)
3. The chemical MPTP selectively damages neurons in the substantia nigra and leads to the symptoms of Parkinson's disease. Similar toxins may contribute to some cases of Parkinson's disease. (p. 234)
4. Huntington's disease is a hereditary condition marked by deterioration of motor control, plus depression, memory impairment, and other cognitive disorders. Age of onset is usually between 30 and 50. (p. 237)
5. By examining chromosome 4, physicians can determine whether someone is likely to develop Huntington's disease later in life. (p. 237)
6. The gene responsible for Huntington's disease alters the structure of a protein, known as huntingtin, which probably plays some role in the use of glucose. (p. 238)

Review Questions

1. What causes myasthenia gravis? How can the condition be treated? (p. 233)
2. What drugs are used to treat Parkinson's disease, and what additional treatments are still in the experimental stage? (p. 236)

3. What are the symptoms of Huntington's disease? What is the usual age of onset? (p. 237)
4. What procedure enables physicians to determine who is most likely to get Huntington's disease? How can they predict not only whether someone will get the disease but also at what age? (p. 237)

Thought Questions

1. Haloperidol is a drug that blocks dopamine synapses. What effect would haloperidol probably have on someone suffering from Parkinson's disease?
2. Neurologists assert that if people lived long enough, sooner or later everyone would get Parkinson's disease. Why?

Suggestions for Further Reading

Klawans, H. L. (1996). *Why Michael couldn't hit.* New York: W. H. Freeman. If you are at all interested in sports, and if you can overlook the fact that Klawans presents some reasonable guesses as if they were certainties, you should find this book fascinating.

For more information about Parkinson's disease, contact the American Parkinson Disease Association, 1250 Hylan Blvd., Suite 4B, Staten Island, NY 10305.

For more information about Huntington's disease, contact the Huntington's Disease Society of America, 140 West 22nd Street, Sixth Floor, New York, NY 10011-2420.

Terms

myasthenia gravis autoimmune disease in which the body forms antibodies against the acetylcholine receptors at neuromuscular junctions (p. 233)

Parkinson's disease malady caused by damage to a dopamine pathway, resulting in slow movements, difficulty initiating movements, rigidity of the muscles, and tremors (p. 233)

MPTP, MPP$^+$ chemicals known to be toxic to the dopamine-containing cells in the substantia nigra, capable of producing the symptoms of Parkinson's disease (p. 234)

L-dopa chemical precursor of dopamine and other catecholamines (p. 236)

deprenyl drug found to slow the progress of Parkinson's disease (p. 236)

Huntington's disease an inherited disorder characterized by tremor, movement disorder, and psychological symptoms, including depression, memory impairment, hallucinations, and delusions (p. 237)

presymptomatic test exam to predict the onset of a disease, conducted before any symptoms appear (p. 237)

huntingtin the protein produced by the gene whose mutation leads to Huntington's disease (p. 238)

RHYTHMS OF WAKEFULNESS AND SLEEP

CHAPTER NINE

MAIN IDEAS

1. Wakefulness and sleep alternate on a cycle of approximately 24 hours. The body itself generates this cycle.
2. Insomnia can result if someone's biological rhythm is out of phase with the prescribed time for sleeping.
3. Sleep progresses through four stages, which differ in brain activity, heart rate, and other signs of arousal.
4. A special type of stage 1 sleep, known as paradoxical or REM sleep, is light in some ways and deep in others. It is associated with dreaming, especially with vivid dreaming.
5. Areas in the brain stem and forebrain contribute to various aspects of arousal, attention, and sleep. Localized brain damage can result in prolonged periods of sleep or wakefulness.
6. For a variety of reasons, many people do not sleep well enough to feel rested the following day.

Suppose you are an astronaut who has just made the flight to Daynite, a planet in another solar system. Daynite rotates on its axis only once a year; that is, the same side always faces its sun, and no part of the planet alternates between day and night. Nearly all animals and plants live in the "twilight zone" between light and dark. One of the numerous peculiarities of these animals, from our point of view, is that none of them ever sleeps.

Your possible surprise at this fact hardly compares with the reaction of the Daynitian astronauts who simultaneously make their first visit to Earth. They marvel that about once every 365th of a year each animal lies down and stops moving. After these strange Earthlings appear to have been dead for a few hours, they spontaneously come back to life again! The Daynitians wonder, "What on Earth is going on?"

For the purposes of this chapter, let us adopt the perspective of the Daynitians and ask why animals as active as we are spend one-third of our lives doing so little.

The Alternation of Waking and Sleeping

When you learn that your body spontaneously generates its own rhythm of wakefulness and sleep, you are, I suspect, not particularly surprised. Psychologists of an earlier era, however, considered that idea revolutionary. The research of Curt Richter (1922) and others implied that the body generates its own cycles of activity and inactivity, but psychologists were ill-prepared to accept this news. Psychological theories prevalent from the 1920s through the 1950s assumed that nearly all behavior was in reaction to stimuli. Therefore, alternation between wakefulness and sleep must depend on something in the outside world—the cycle of sunrise and sunset, temperature fluctuations, or something else.

Gradually, the evidence became stronger, and eventually undeniable, that animals generate approximately 24-hour cycles of wakefulness and sleep even in an environment with unchanging light, temperature, noise, and other variables. Thus, at least part of the impetus for behavior comes from within the body. This conception of wakefulness and sleep was an important discovery for psychology and an important step toward viewing the organism as an active producer of behaviors, not just a responder to stimuli.

Endogenous Cycles as a Preparation for External Changes

An animal that produced its behavior entirely in response to current stimuli would be at a serious disadvantage; in many cases, an animal has to prepare for changes in sunlight and temperature before they occur. For example, most migratory birds start on their way toward their winter homes while the weather in their summer homes is still fairly warm. A bird that waited for the first frost would be in serious trouble. Similarly, squirrels begin storing nuts and putting on extra layers of fat in preparation for winter long before food becomes scarce. Animals that mate during only one season of the year change extensively in both their anatomy and their behavior as the reproductive season approaches.

How do animals know what time of day or year it is? What tells birds when to start migrating? To some extent, they respond to changes in sunlight. When the ratio of daylight hours to dark hours declines to a certain point, it is time for the bird to head south. (Temperature is a much less reliable cue.) But after a bird has wintered in the tropics, how does it know when to return north? The tropics have no distinct seasons, so neither temperature nor light is a useful cue. In one experiment, willow warblers (a European species) were captured from the wild and kept in cages with 12 hours of light alternating with 12 hours of darkness each day (Gwinner, 1986). For the next three years, the birds showed a characteristic *migratory restlessness* every fall and every spring.

Evidently, a mechanism somewhere in the bird's body generates a rhythm, an internal calendar, that prepares the bird for seasonal changes. We refer to that rhythm as an **endogenous circannual rhythm.** (*Endogenous* means *generated from within. Circannual* comes from the Latin words *circum,* for *about,* and *annum,* for *year.*) Similar mechanisms provoke mammals' seasonal changes in reproduction, body fat, and hibernation. In nature, the daily onset of light and darkness fine-tunes such mechanisms to prevent them from running too fast or too slow.

Similarly, animals produce **endogenous circadian rhythms,** rhythms that last about a day. (*Circadian* comes from *circum,* for *about,* and *dies,* for *day.*) Our most familiar endogenous circadian rhythm controls wakefulness and sleepiness. If you go without sleep all night—as most college students do, sooner or later—you feel sleepier and sleepier as the night goes on, until early morning. But as morning arrives, you actually begin to feel less sleepy. Evidently, your urge to sleep

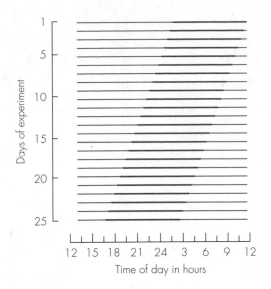

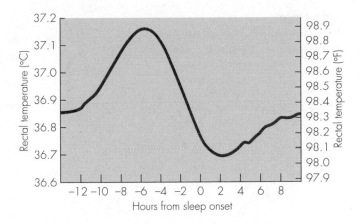

FIGURE **9.1**

Activity record of a flying squirrel kept in constant darkness

The thickened segments indicate periods of activity as measured by a running wheel. Note that the free-running activity cycle lasts slightly less than 24 hours.   Source: From DeCoursey, 1960.

FIGURE **9.2**

Mean rectal temperatures for nine adults

Body temperature reaches its low for the day about 2 hours after sleep onset; it reaches its peak about 6 hours before sleep onset.   Source: Based on data of Morris, Lack, & Dawson, 1990.

depends largely on the time of day, not just how recently you have slept.

Figure 9.1 represents the activity of a flying squirrel kept in total darkness for 25 days. Each horizontal line represents one 24-hour day. A thickening in the line represents a period of activity by the animal. Even in this unchanging environment, the animal generates a regular rhythm of activity and sleep. The self-generated cycle may be slightly shorter than 24 hours, as in Figure 9.1, or slightly longer, depending on whether the environment is constantly light or constantly dark and on whether the species is normally active in the light or in the dark (Carpenter & Grossberg, 1984). The cycle may also vary from one individual to another, even in the same environment. Nevertheless, the rhythm is highly consistent for a given individual in a given environment, month after month.

Mammals, including humans, have circadian rhythms in their waking and sleeping, frequency of eating and drinking, body temperature, secretion of certain hormones, volume of urination, sensitivity to certain drugs, and many other variables. For example, although we ordinarily think of human body temperature as 37°C, normal temperature fluctuates over the course of a day from a low of about 36.5°C at 4 A.M. to about 37.4°C in late afternoon or early evening. (See Figure 9.2.) Ordinarily, all these cycles stay in synchrony with one another, suggesting that they depend on a single master clock.

Setting and Resetting the Cycle

Although an animal's circadian rhythm persists in the absence of light, light is critical for periodically resetting the **biological clock** that underlies the rhythm. A biological clock is the internal mechanism for controlling a behavior that recurs on a regular schedule, such as sleep or migration. As an analogy, consider a wristwatch. I used to have a windup wristwatch that lost about 2 minutes per day. If I continued to wind the watch but never reset it, it would be an hour slow after a month. We could say that it had a **free-running rhythm** of 24 hours and 2 minutes. The biological clock is similar to that wristwatch. Because its free-running rhythm is not exactly 24 hours, it has to be reset daily. The stimulus that resets it is often referred to by the German term **zeitgeber** (TSITE-gay-ber), meaning *timegiver*. Light is the dominant zeitgeber for land animals (Rusak & Zucker, 1979). (The tides are a more important zeitgeber for many marine animals.)

If a consistent light cycle is not available—for people living in a cave, for example, or for blind people or astronauts in space—noises, meals, social interactions, and temperature fluctuations can also act as zeitgebers. However, the effectiveness of these nonvisual zeitgebers varies from one person to another. Most blind people maintain a nearly normal circadian rhythm, but some do not. One blind man had a circadian rhythm of about 24¹/₄ hours despite a very regular schedule of activities.

FIGURE **9.3**
Body temperatures of two men under a 28-hour cycle
Shaded areas represent time in bed. Subject K's weekly record has seven 24-hour curves, but subject R adapted fairly well to the 28-hour schedule.   Source: From Kleitman, 1963.

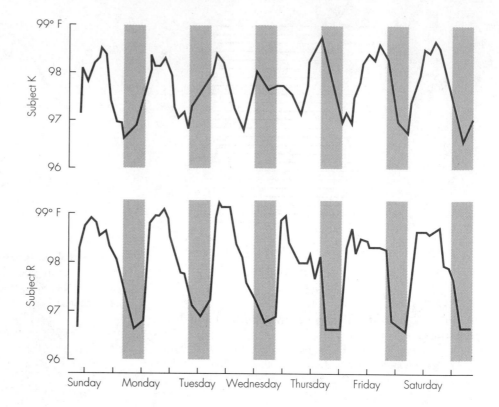

Whenever his circadian rhythm happened to be in phase with his schedule, he slept well. When it drifted out of phase, he slept poorly (Klein et al., 1993).

Attempting to Alter the Biological Clock

Is it possible to change a person's biological clock so that it will produce a different endogenous rhythm? If humans moved to a planet with 20- or 30-hour days, would they adjust easily, or would they have to undergo countless generations of evolutionary change before they felt really at home? In an effort to answer such questions, two volunteers spent a month deep in an isolated part of Mammoth Cave in Kentucky (Kleitman, 1963). The temperature (12°C) and relative humidity (100 percent) were constant at all times, and the only light they saw was artificial light controlled by a schedule set for a 28-hour day, with 19 hours of activity alternating with 9 hours of sleep.

One subject (R in Figure 9.3) adjusted reasonably well to the schedule, with lowered body temperature accompanying each sleep period. However, he was always sleepy well before the scheduled bedtime, and he had trouble awakening at the scheduled times. The other subject (K in Figure 9.3) was much less successful. He continued to feel sleepy only at his usual bedtime, once every 24 hours, and his body temperature continued to fluctuate on a 24-hour cycle. He had great trouble getting to sleep when the artificial cycle was out of phase with his original cycle.

In another experiment, a group of 12 young people lived for 3 weeks in a cavelike environment, isolated from natural light and other time cues. They agreed to go to bed when the clock indicated 11:45 P.M. and to awaken when it indicated 7:45 A.M. Although they did not know it, the clock initially ran normally and then gradually ran faster, until it was completing a day in only 22 hours. During a 23-hour day, people were alert during their wakeful periods and reported no trouble awakening or falling asleep on schedule. On a 22-hour day, however, only one subject kept pace with the clock. For the others, alertness rose and fell on a free-running 24-hour cycle that quickly drifted out of phase with the waking–sleeping schedule (Folkard, Hume, Minors, Waterhouse, & Watson, 1985). Evidently, it is difficult to adjust to a waking–sleeping cycle very different from 24 hours per day.

Resetting the Biological Clock

Instead of giving us a 24-hour clock, evolution gave us a clock of about 24½ or 24¾ hours. We have to readjust our internal workings every day to stay in phase with the outside world. On weekends, when most of us are freer to follow the dictates of our nature, we tend to stay awake later and awaken later than usual. By Monday morning, when the electric clock indicates 7 A.M., the biological clock is at about 5 A.M. (Moore-Ede,

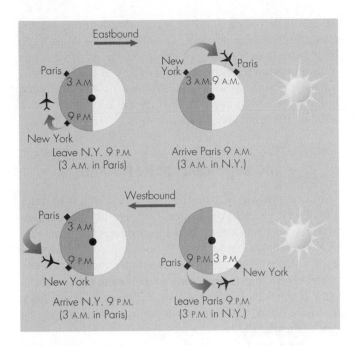

FIGURE **9.4**
Jet lag
Eastern time is later than western time. People who travel six time zones east must wake up when their biological clocks say it is the middle of the night; they must go to bed when their biological clocks say it is just late afternoon. Most people adjust more easily when they travel west; they stay up later at night and sleep later in the morning.

Czeisler, & Richardson, 1983). People who travel across time zones or who work odd schedules have special problems in resetting their biological clocks.

Jet Lag

Because the human biological clock tends to run longer than 24 hours, most of us find it easier to adjust to crossing time zones going west than going east. Going west, we stay awake later at night and awaken later in the morning than we would have at home. Going east, we go to sleep earlier and awaken earlier. A disruption of biological rhythms due to crossing time zones is known as **jet lag** (Figure 9.4). (Before air travel, transatlantic travelers knew this phenomenon as "boat lag.")

Consider Figure 9.5. According to a study of major-league baseball results in North America for three years, visiting teams that did not have to travel between one game and the next won 46 percent of their games. Teams that traveled east to west did almost as well, winning 44 percent of the games. But teams that traveled west to east won only 37 percent of the games (Recht, Lew, & Schwartz, 1995). Clearly, traveling east puts people at a definite temporary disadvantage.

Shift Work

People who have to sleep irregularly—such as pilots and truck drivers, medical interns, and shift workers in certain factories—find that their duration of sleep depends on what time they go to sleep. When they have to go to sleep in the morning or early afternoon, they sleep only briefly, even though they have been awake for 16 hours or more (Frese & Harwich, 1984; Winfree, 1983).

People who work on a night shift, such as midnight to 8 A.M., sleep during the day. Even after months or

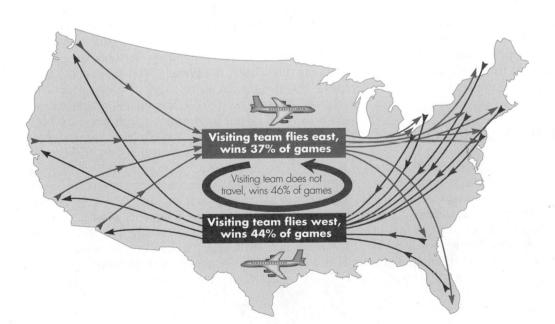

FIGURE **9.5**
Effects of jet lag on visiting teams in North American major-league baseball
Teams that had to travel from the West Coast to the East Coast before a game were less likely to win than were teams that traveled east to west or teams that did not travel at all. Source: Based on Recht, Lew, & Schwartz, 1995.

years on such a schedule, many workers fail to adjust fully. They continue to feel a little groggy while on the job, they do not sleep soundly during the day, and their body temperature continues to peak during the day, when they are trying to sleep, instead of at night while they are working. In general, night-shift workers perform less well and have more accidents than day workers do.

Working at night does not reliably shift the circadian rhythm because the rhythm is reset by bright light much more effectively than by mere activity. Ordinary indoor lighting, around 150–180 lux, as found in most nighttime work settings, is only moderately effective in resetting the rhythm (Boivin, Duffy, Kronauer, & Czeisler, 1996). In Scandinavia and other far northern areas with little or no sunlight in winter, ordinary lighting is adequate to keep circadian rhythms synchronized for most people. However, the dim artificial light needs only to resynchronize the circadian rhythm by a bit each day, just to keep it from drifting. (Even so, the rhythm does drift for some people, especially older people.) For someone working at night, the light has to shift the rhythm by many hours, and it has to compete against the brighter light that is present during the day when the person tries to sleep. People who work at night under dim light may not fully adjust their rhythms even after years. People exposed to very bright lights at night, comparable to the noonday sun, readjust their rhythms almost completely within a week (Czeisler et al., 1990). The moral of the story: People working on night shifts should work under very bright lights.

The Mechanisms of the Biological Clock

Given that our biological cycles are generated within the body, we must have a physical mechanism that produces 24-hour rhythms. Ideally, it should be like your wristwatch in its ability to keep time accurately no matter where you are or what you are doing.

Interfering with the Biological Clock

Curt Richter found that the biological clock is insensitive to most forms of interference. An animal's circadian rhythm of activity and sleep remains intact after blinding or deafening, although it may drift out of phase with the external world because of the loss of zeitgebers. The circadian rhythm is hardly disturbed at all by procedures that greatly modify an animal's activity level, including food or water deprivation, x-rays, tranquilizers, LSD, alcohol, anesthesia, lack of oxygen, long periods of forced activity or inactivity, most kinds of brain damage, or the removal of any of the hormonal organs (Richter, 1967). Even an hour or so of induced hibernation often fails to disturb the biological clock (Gibbs, 1983; Richter, 1975).

The Suprachiasmatic Nucleus

The surest way to disrupt the biological clock is to damage one key area of the hypothalamus: the **suprachiasmatic** (soo-pruh-kie-as-MAT-ik) **nucleus,** abbreviated **SCN.** It gets its name from its location just above the optic chiasm (see Figure 9.6). The optic nerve includes some axons that extend directly from the retina to the SCN. If the SCN is damaged, or if it loses its input from the optic nerve, light can no longer reset the biological clock (Rusak, 1977).

We do not know much about the visual receptors that project to the SCN, but they may not be normal rods and cones. Mice with a genetic defect that destroys nearly all their rods and cones nevertheless reset their biological clocks in synchrony with the light (Foster, 1993). Also, consider blind mole rats (Figure 9.7). Their eyes are covered with folds of skin and fur; they have neither eye muscles nor a lens with which to focus an image. They have fewer than 1,000 optic nerve axons, as compared with 100,000 in hamsters. Even a bright flash of light evokes no apparent behavior and no measurable change in brain activity. Nevertheless, light resets their circadian rhythms (de Jong, Hendriks, Sanyal, & Nevo, 1990)! Evidently the mole rat's few visual receptors send the SCN enough information to provide a zeitgeber, even though none of the visual information reaches the cerebral cortex.

The SCN generates rhythms itself. If SCN neurons are removed from an animal's brain or left in place but disconnected from the rest of the brain, they nevertheless produce a pattern of impulses that follows a circadian rhythm (Green & Gillette, 1982; Inouye & Kawamura, 1979). One group of experimenters discovered that some hamsters bear a mutant gene that causes them to produce not a 24-hour rhythm but a 20-hour rhythm (Ralph & Menaker, 1988). They surgically removed the SCN from adult hamsters and then transplanted SCN tissue from hamster fetuses into the adults. When the fetuses had a 20-hour rhythm, the recipients produced a 20-hour rhythm. When the fetuses had a 24-hour rhythm, the recipients produced a 24-hour rhythm. The recipients' rhythm no longer matched their own genes, but rather the genes of the SCN donor (Ralph, Foster, Davis, & Menaker, 1990).

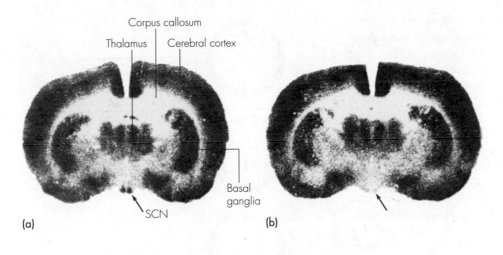

Corpus callosum

Thalamus   Cerebral cortex

Basal
ganglia

SCN

(a)   (b)

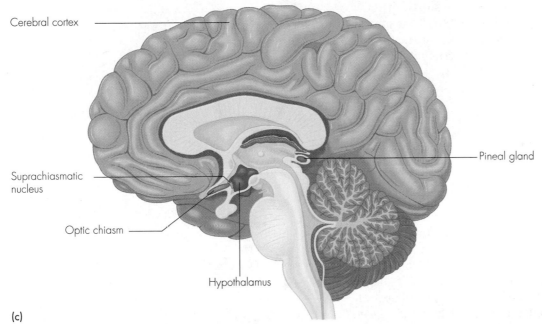

Cerebral cortex

Pineal gland

Suprachiasmatic
nucleus

Optic chiasm

Hypothalamus

(c)

FIGURE **9.6**
The suprachiasmatic nucleus (SCN) of rats
The SCN is located at the base of the brain, just above
the optic chiasm, which has torn off in these coronal
sections through the plane of the anterior hypothalamus.
Each rat was injected with radioactive 2-deoxyglucose,
which is absorbed by the most active neurons. A high
level of absorption of this chemical produces a dark
appearance on the slide. Note that the level of activity
in SCN neurons is much higher in section (**a**), in which
the rat was injected during the day, than it is in section
(**b**), in which the rat received the injection at night.
(**c**) A sagittal section through a human brain, showing
location of the SCN and the pineal gland.   Source:
Autoradiographs from Schwartz & Gainer, 1977.

FIGURE **9.7**
Although blind mole rats are indeed blind in all other regards,
they reset their circadian rhythms in response to light.   Source:
Courtesy of Eviatar Nevo.

In an intact animal, the SCN is apparently the dominant force for the circadian rhythms controlling sleep and temperature (Refinetti & Menaker, 1992). After damage to the SCN, the activity pattern becomes less consistent and no longer responds to environmental patterns of light and dark. However, cells in the retina also generate their own circadian rhythm, which apparently controls some self-repair processes in the retina (Tosini & Menaker, 1996).

Biochemically, how does the SCN produce circadian rhythms? Researchers do not yet fully understand the mechanism, but presumably it depends on a negative feedback cycle, in which SCN cells produce a protein or other chemical for a period of hours until the level inhibits further production, again for hours; when the protein level drops below some threshold, the SCN starts producing it again (see Figure 9.8). That protein affects wakefulness or sleepiness. Mechanisms of this sort have been demonstrated in invertebrates (Aronson, Johnson, Loros, & Dunlap, 1994), and the best guess is that something similar operates in vertebrates.

Melatonin

One way by which the SCN regulates waking and sleeping is by regulating production of the hormone **melatonin** by the **pineal gland** (see Figure 9.6). Melatonin increases sleepiness, and in humans the pineal gland secretes melatonin mostly at night. For most people, the onset of increased melatonin secretion begins between 8 P.M. and 10 P.M., about 2 or 3 hours before the time when they find it easiest to fall asleep. Taking a melatonin pill in the evening has very little effect on sleepiness, mostly because the pineal gland produces melatonin at that time anyway. However, people who take melatonin at any other time will become sleepy about 2 hours later (Haimov & Lavie, 1996). People who wish to sleep at an odd time in the biological cycle can sleep sooner and more satisfactorily if they take melatonin (Deacon & Arendt, 1996). People who have pineal gland tumors or any other impairment of melatonin secretion experience great difficulty falling asleep (Haimov & Lavie, 1996).

Melatonin also feeds back to reset the biological clock through its effects on receptors in the SCN (Gillette & McArthur, 1996). A moderate dose of melatonin (0.5 mg) in the afternoon *phase-advances* the clock; that is, it makes the person get sleepy earlier in the evening and wake up earlier the next morning. Melatonin in the morning *phase-delays* the clock. Curiously, exposure to bright light has nearly the opposite effects, as shown in Table 9.1 (Attenburrow, Dowling, Sargent, Sharpley, & Cowen, 1995; Lewy, Ahmed, & Sack, 1996).

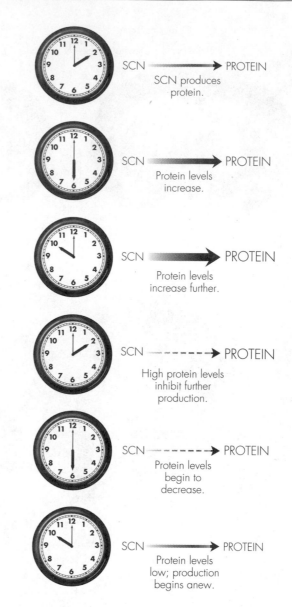

FIGURE **9.8**
Probable mechanism by which the SCN generates the circadian rhythm
The nature of the protein is as yet unknown. The times are hypothetical; the point is that the produced protein feeds back to inhibit further protein synthesis and that the cycle repeats approximately once every 24 hours.

Taking melatonin has become something of a fad. Its effect on sleep is well-established, although many people taking melatonin have no trouble sleeping without it. Many healthy people take melatonin because they think it will help keep them young or help prevent cancer, effects that are far less certain. Given that moderate, temporary use of melatonin produces no unpleasant side effects, it might seem that even the possibility of a benefit would justify taking the pills. However, we know almost nothing about the possible

TABLE **9.1**			
Resetting the Biological Clock			
	In the Morning	**In the Afternoon**	**In the Evening**
Exposure to bright lights	Phase-advances (earlier sleep)	Little effect	Phase-delays (later sleep)
Melatonin pills	Phase-delays (later sleep)	Phase-advances (earlier sleep)	Little effect

effects of taking melatonin over many years. People who do so face an unknown risk in order to gain an uncertain benefit.

The Functions of Sleep

The suprachiasmatic nucleus and other mechanisms of the biological clock control the timing of sleep, but they are not responsible for sleep itself, any more than for eating, drinking, or any other activity that follows a circadian rhythm. Presumably, mechanisms that provide alternating periods of activity and sleep would not have evolved unless sleep serves an important function. But exactly what is that function?

The Repair and Restoration Theory

According to the **repair and restoration theory of sleep,** the function of sleep is to enable the body, especially the brain, to repair itself after the exertions of the day. One way to examine these restorative functions is to observe the effects of sleep deprivation. People who have gone without sleep for a week or more, either as an experiment or as a publicity stunt, have reported dizziness, impaired concentration, irritability, hand tremors, and hallucinations (Dement, 1972; Johnson, 1969). Prolonged sleep deprivation in animals, mostly rats, has produced more severe consequences, partly because the animals were forced to stay awake, whereas the humans had volunteered for the studies and knew they could quit if necessary. (Stressors take a greater toll when they are unpredictable and uncontrollable.) During a few days of sleep deprivation, rats show increased body temperature, metabolic rate, and appetite, indicating that the body is working harder than usual. With still longer sleep deprivation, the immune system and the thyroid gland begin to fail, the animal loses its resistance to infection, and activity decreases in certain brain areas (Everson, 1995; Rechtschaffen & Bergmann, 1995). It is noteworthy that

sleep increases during illness; during sleep the body diverts energy away from other activities and toward increased function of the immune system.

However, the restorative functions of sleep are not analogous to catching your breath after running a race. If sleep were restorative in that simple sense, we should expect people to sleep significantly more after a day of great physical or mental exertion than after an uneventful day. In fact, such exertion increases sleep duration only slightly (Horne & Minard, 1985; Shapiro, Bortz, Mitchell, Bartel, & Jooste, 1981). The amount we sleep at night does not depend much on our activity level during the day.

Moreover, some people satisfy their restorative needs in far less than the customary 7 to 8 hours. Two men were reported to average only 3 hours of sleep per night and to awaken feeling refreshed (Jones & Oswald, 1968). A 70-year-old woman was reported to average only 1 hour of sleep per night; many nights, she felt no need to sleep at all (Meddis, Pearson, & Langford, 1973).

The Evolutionary Theory

Given that the duration of sleep bears little relation to the activity of the previous day, several theorists have offered an alternative explanation of why we sleep. According to the **evolutionary theory of sleep** (Kleitman, 1963; Webb, 1974), the function of sleep is similar to that of **hibernation,** a special adaptation by certain mammalian species to a season when food is scarce (see Digression 9.1). Hibernating animals have decreased heart rate, breathing, brain activity, and metabolism; they generate only enough body heat to avoid freezing. Hibernation is a true need; a ground squirrel that is prevented from hibernating can become as disturbed as a person who is prevented from sleeping. However, the function of hibernation is not to recover from a busy summer; it is simply to conserve energy when the environment is hostile.

Similarly, according to the evolutionary theory of sleep, the primary function of sleep is to force us to conserve energy when we would be relatively inefficient.

During sleep, a mammal's body temperature decreases by one or two Celsius degrees, enough to save a significant (though not an enormous) amount of energy. During food shortages, animals either increase their sleep time or decrease their body temperature during sleep (Berger & Phillips, 1995). The evolutionary theory does not deny that we need to sleep; it merely asserts that evolution built that need into us to compel us to conserve energy.

The evolutionary theory predicts that species should vary in their sleep habits in accordance with how much time each day they must devote to the search for food, how safe they are from predators when they sleep, and other aspects of their way of life. In general, the data support these predictions (Allison & Cicchetti, 1976; Campbell & Tobler, 1984). Most mammals that sleep many hours per day, such as cats and bats, eat nutrition-rich meals and face little threat of attack while they sleep. Most of the brief and fitful sleepers are herbivores (plant-eaters) that need to graze much of the day in order to get enough food, and need to be on the alert for predators even in the middle of the night. (See Figure 9.9.)

Which theory of sleep is right? Actually, adherents of each theory concede that the other is partly right. Suppose you believe that the main function of sleep is to repair and restore the brain. Surely you will grant that each species confines its sleep to those hours when it is least efficient at doing anything else and, furthermore, that species that can afford long periods of inactivity (predators) will evolve a tendency to sleep longer than species that must remain constantly vigilant (prey). Now suppose you believe that the main function of sleep is to conserve energy. Surely you will agree that if an animal is lying around doing nothing else anyway, it might profitably use that time for some repair and restoration. In short, the two theories do not directly contradict each other.

IN CLOSING

Sleep—Wake Cycles

Unlike an electric appliance that stays on until someone turns it off, the brain periodically turns itself on and off. Doing so helps save energy during times of inefficiency and provides an opportunity for repair and restoration. Regardless of the primary function of sleep, sleepiness is definitely not a voluntary or optional act. People who try to work while nature is calling for sleep are prone to errors and injuries. A person who sleeps well may not be altogether healthy or happy, but one who consistently fails to get enough sleep is almost certainly headed for troubles.

Summary

1. Animals, including humans, have internally generated rhythms of activity and other functions, approximating both a 24-hour cycle and a one-year cycle. (p. 242)
2. Although the biological clock can continue to operate in constant light or constant darkness, the onset of light at a particular time can reset the clock. (p. 243)

DIGRESSION 9.1

Some Facts About Hibernation

1. Hibernation occurs in certain small mammals such as ground squirrels and bats. Whether or not bears hibernate is a matter of definition. Bears sleep most of the winter, but they do not lower their body temperatures the way small hibernating animals do.
2. Hamsters sometimes hibernate. If you keep your pet hamster in a cold, poorly lit place during the winter, and it appears to die, make sure that it is not just hibernating before you bury it!
3. Hibernation retards the aging process. Hamsters that spend longer times hibernating have proportionately longer life expectancies than other hamsters do (Lyman, O'Brien, Greene, & Papafrangos, 1981).

4. Hibernating animals produce a chemical that suppresses metabolism and temperature regulation. H. Swan and C. Schätte (1977) injected extracts from the brains of hibernating ground squirrels into the brains of rats, a nonhibernating species. The rats decreased their metabolism and body temperature. Similar brain extracts from nonhibernating ground squirrels had no apparent effect on the rats.
5. Hibernating animals come out of hibernation for a few hours every few days, raising their body temperature to about normal. However, they do not do much during these nonhibernating hours. In fact, they spend most of the time sleeping (Barnes, 1996).

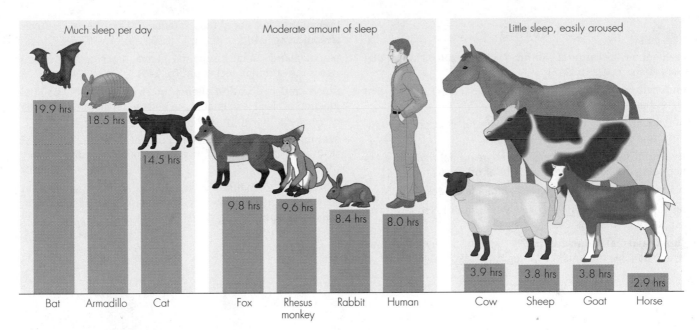

FIGURE **9.9**
Hours of sleep per day for various animal species
Generally, predators and others that are safe when they sleep tend to sleep a great deal; animals in danger of being attacked while they sleep spend less time asleep.

3. The biological clock can reset daily to match an external rhythm of light and darkness slightly different from 24 hours, but if the discrepancy exceeds about 2 hours, the biological clock generates its own rhythm instead of resetting. (p. 244)
4. It is easier for people to follow a cycle longer than 24 hours (as when traveling west) than to follow a cycle shorter than 24 hours (as when traveling east). (p. 245)
5. The suprachiasmatic nucleus (SCN), a part of the hypothalamus, generates the body's circadian rhythms for sleep and temperature. (p. 246)
6. The SCN controls the body's rhythm partly by directing the release of melatonin by the pineal gland. The hormone melatonin increases sleepiness; if it is given at certain times of day, it can also reset the circadian rhythm. (p. 248)
7. Sleep probably serves at least two functions: repair and restoration, and conservation of energy during a period of relative inefficiency. (p. 249)

Review Questions

1. How does it benefit a migratory bird to have an internal mechanism that predicts the changing seasons, instead of relying entirely on changes in the light/dark patterns in the environment? (p. 242)
2. What stimulus is the most effective zeitgeber for resetting the biological clock? (p. 243)
3. What evidence indicates that the human body has an internal biological clock, instead of timing its activities entirely on the basis of light and other external cues? (p. 244)
4. For people who consistently work at night, what proce-

dure is most effective for resetting their circadian rhythms to favor night activity? (p. 246)
5. What is the evidence that the suprachiasmatic nucleus generates circadian rhythms of activity? (p. 246)
6. At what time of day would melatonin phase-advance the circadian rhythm? At what time would it phase-delay the rhythm? (p. 248)
7. State the strengths and weaknesses of the repair and restoration theory and the evolutionary theory of the need for sleep. (p. 249)

Thought Questions

1. Is it possible for the onset of light to reset the circadian rhythms of a blind person? Does the answer depend on the cause of blindness? Explain.
2. Why would evolution have enabled blind mole rats to synchronize their SCN activity to light, even though they cannot see well enough to make any use of the light?
3. If you travel across several time zones to the east and want to use melatonin to help reset your circadian rhythm, at what time of day should you take it? What if you travel west?

Suggestion for Further Reading

Horne, J. (1988). *Why we sleep.* Oxford, England: Oxford University Press. Thorough study of the functions of sleep, including the results of sleep deprivation.

Terms

endogenous circannual rhythm   self-generated rhythm that lasts about a year (p. 242)

endogenous circadian rhythm   self-generated rhythm that lasts about a day (p. 242)

biological clock   internal mechanism for controlling rhythmic variations in a behavior (p. 243)

free-running rhythm   circadian or circannual rhythm that is not being periodically reset by light or other cues (p. 243)

zeitgeber   stimulus that resets a biological clock (p. 243)

jet lag   disruption of biological rhythms caused by travel across time zones (p. 245)

suprachiasmatic nucleus (SCN)   area of the hypothalamus where damage disrupts the biological clock (p. 246)

melatonin   hormone that, among other effects, induces sleepiness (p. 248)

pineal gland   small, unpaired gland in the brain that releases the hormone melatonin (p. 248)

repair and restoration theory of sleep   concept that the function of sleep is to enable the body to repair itself after the exertions of the day (p. 249)

evolutionary theory of sleep   concept that the function of sleep is to conserve energy at times of relative inefficiency (p. 249)

hibernation   condition in which heart rate, breathing, brain activity, and metabolism greatly decrease as an adaptation to conserve energy during winter (p. 249)

Sleeping and Dreaming

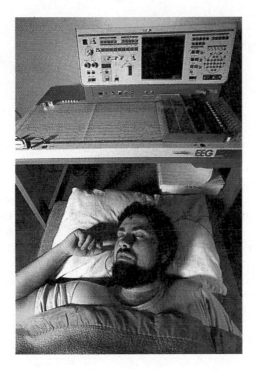

FIGURE 9.10
Sleeping person with electrodes on the scalp for recording brain activity
The printout above his head shows the readings from each electrode.

Most advances in scientific research result from improvements in our ability to measure something. Sleep research is no exception. The electroencephalograph (EEG), mentioned in Chapter 4, records a gross average of the electrical potentials of the cells and fibers in a particular part of the brain by means of an electrode attached to the scalp (see Figure 9.10). It displays a net average of all the neurons' potentials. That is, if half the

cells increase their electrical potentials while the other half decrease, the EEG recording is a flat line. The EEG record rises or falls only when a number of cells fire in synchrony—doing the same thing at the same time. You might compare it to a record of the noise in a crowded football stadium: It shows only slight fluctuations until some event makes everyone yell at once.

The EEG provides an objective way for brain researchers to determine whether people are awake or asleep without relying on self-reports, and to compare brain activity at different times of night. Such research has led to the identification of several distinct stages of sleep.

The Stages of Sleep

Figure 9.11 shows the EEG and eye movements of a male college student during the various stages of sleep. Figure 9.11a begins with a period of relaxed wakefulness for comparison. Note the steady series of **alpha waves** at a frequency of 8 to 12 per second. Alpha waves are characteristic of the relaxed state, not of all wakefulness.

In Figure 9.11b, the young man has just fallen asleep. During this period, called stage 1 sleep, the EEG is dominated by irregular, jagged, low-voltage waves. Overall brain activity is still fairly high, but it is declining. As Figure 9.11c shows, the most prominent characteristics of stage 2 are sleep spindles and K-complexes. A **sleep spindle** consists of 12- to 14-Hz waves during a burst that lasts at least half a second. A **K-complex** is a sharp, high-amplitude negative wave followed by a smaller, slower positive wave. Sudden stimuli can evoke K-complexes during other stages of sleep (Bastien & Campbell, 1992), but they are most common in stage 2.

FIGURE **9.11**
Polysomnograph records from a male college student

A polysomnograph includes records of EEG, eye movements, and sometimes other data, such as muscle tension or head movements. For each of these records, the top line is the EEG from one electrode on the scalp; the middle line is a record of eye movements; and the bottom line is a time marker, indicating 1-second units. Note the abundance of slow waves in stages 3 and 4.   Source: Records provided by T. E. LeVere.

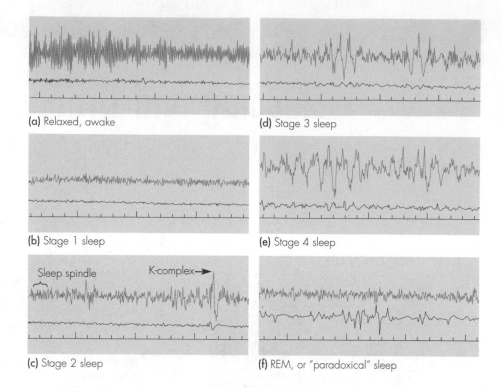

(a) Relaxed, awake

(b) Stage 1 sleep

(c) Stage 2 sleep   Sleep spindle   K-complex→

(d) Stage 3 sleep

(e) Stage 4 sleep

(f) REM, or "paradoxical" sleep

In each succeeding stage of sleep, heart rate, breathing rate, and brain activity are slower than in the previous stage, and the percentage of slow, large-amplitude waves increases (see Figure 9.11d and e). By stage 4, more than half the record includes large waves of at least a half-second duration. Stages 3 and 4 are known together as **slow-wave sleep (SWS).**

Slow waves indicate that neuronal activity is highly synchronized. In stage 1 and in wakefulness, the cortex receives much input, much of it at high frequencies. Nearly all the neurons are active, but different populations of neurons are active at different times. Thus, the EEG is full of short, rapid, choppy waves. By stage 4, however, sensory input to the cerebral cortex is greatly reduced, and the few remaining sources of input can synchronize many cells. As an analogy, imagine that the barrage of stimuli arriving at the brain of an alert person is like hundreds of rocks dropped into a pond over the course of a minute: The resulting waves largely cancel one another out. The surface of the pond is choppy, with few large waves. By contrast, the result of just one rock dropping is fewer but larger waves, like those in stage 4 sleep.

Paradoxical or REM Sleep

A person who has just fallen asleep enters stage 1 sleep. Later in the night, people may or may not return to stage 1; usually, they enter a related but very special

stage, which two sets of researchers discovered accidentally in the 1950s.

In France, Michel Jouvet was trying to test the learning abilities of cats after complete removal of the cerebral cortex. To cope with the fact that decorticate mammals hardly move at all, Jouvet recorded slight movements of the muscles and EEGs from the hindbrain. During periods of apparent sleep the cats had high levels of brain activity but their neck muscles were completely relaxed. Jouvet named this phenomenon **paradoxical sleep** because it is in some ways the deepest sleep and in other ways the lightest. (The term *paradoxical* means *apparently self-contradictory*.)

Meanwhile, in the United States, Nathaniel Kleitman and Eugene Aserinsky were observing eye movements of sleeping people as a means of measuring depth of sleep, assuming simply that eye movements would decrease during sleep. At first, they recorded only a few minutes of eye movements per hour, partly because the recording paper was expensive and partly because they did not expect to see anything interesting in the middle of the night anyway. When they occasionally found periods of eye movements in people who had been asleep for hours, the investigators assumed at first that something was wrong with their machines. Only after repeated, careful measurements did they conclude that periods of rapid eye movements do exist during sleep (Dement, 1990). They called these periods **rapid eye movement (REM) sleep** (Aserinsky & Kleitman, 1955; Dement & Kleitman, 1957a) and soon concluded that REM sleep was synonymous with what Jouvet called *paradoxical sleep*. Researchers use the

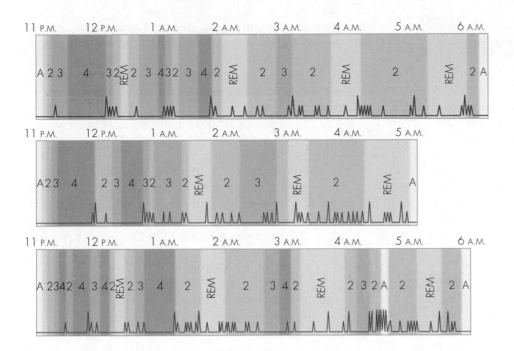

FIGURE **9.12**
Sequence of sleep stages on three representative nights
Columns indicate awake (A) and sleep stages 2, 3, 4, and REM. Deflections in the line at the bottom of each chart indicate shifts in body position. Note that stage 4 sleep occurs mostly in the early part of the night's sleep, whereas REM sleep becomes more prevalent toward the end. Source: Based on Dement & Kleitman, 1957a.

term *REM sleep* when referring to humans; most prefer the term *paradoxical sleep* when describing nonhumans, because many species lack eye movements.

During paradoxical or REM sleep, the EEG shows irregular, low-voltage fast waves, which suggest a considerable amount of brain activity. Heart and breathing rates are higher and more variable than in stages 2 through 4; in this regard, REM sleep is light. However, during REM sleep, the postural muscles of the body, such as those that support the head, are more relaxed than in any other stage; in this regard, REM sleep is deep. This stage is also associated with erections in males and vaginal moistening in females. In short, REM sleep combines deep sleep, light sleep, and features that are difficult to classify as deep or light. Consequently, it is best to avoid using the terms *deep* and *light* sleep.

In addition to its steady characteristics, REM sleep has certain intermittent characteristics, including facial twitches and the characteristic back-and-forth movements of the eyes. Figure 9.11f provides the **polysomnograph,** a combination of EEG and eye-movement records, for a period of REM sleep. The EEG record is similar to that for stage 1 sleep, but notice how different the eye-movement records are. The stages other than REM are known as **non-REM sleep (NREM).**

A person who falls asleep enters stage 1 and slowly progresses through stages 2, 3, and 4 in order. External stimuli can interrupt this progression, however. For example, noises can prolong stage 3 or cause a reversion to stage 2, stage 1, or even to wakefulness. About 60 to 90 minutes after going to sleep, the person begins gradually to cycle back from stage 4 through stages 3 and 2, and then enters a period of REM sleep. The sequence repeats, with each complete cycle lasting 90 to 100 min-

utes. Early in the night, stages 3 and 4 predominate. Toward morning, the duration of stage 4 grows shorter and the duration of REM sleep grows longer. Figure 9.12 shows typical sequences.

REM sleep is associated with dreaming, although the relationship is far from exact. William Dement and Nathaniel Kleitman (1957b) awakened adult volunteers during various stages of sleep. People awakened during REM sleep reported dreams 80 to 90 percent of the time, often including elaborate visual imagery and long, complicated plots. People awakened during slow-wave sleep reported dreams less frequently, and the dreams were shorter.

By awakening people during REM sleep, investigators have been able to answer questions that were previously a matter for speculation. For example, as far as we can determine, all normal humans dream. When people who claim they never dream are awakened during a REM period, they generally report dreams, though most of their dreams are less vivid than those of other people. Apparently, people who believe that they do not dream merely forget their dreams.

Furthermore, we now know that dreams last about as long as they seem to the dreamer to last, contrary to a once-popular belief that a dream lasts only a second or two. Dement and E. A. Wolpert (1958) awakened people who had been in REM sleep for varying periods of time. The length of the dreams they reported corresponded closely to the length of the REM period prior to awakening, up to a limit of about 15 minutes. With REM periods of more than 15 minutes, the volunteers did not report still longer dreams, perhaps because they had already forgotten the beginning of the dream by the time they got to the end of it.

The Functions of REM Sleep

From an evolutionary point of view, we look for the functions of a behavior. An average person spends about one-third of his or her life asleep and about one-fifth of that time in REM sleep, totaling about 600 hours per year. Presumably, REM sleep serves some biological function. But what? To approach this question, we can consider what kinds of people or animals get more REM sleep than others do, and examine the effects of REM sleep deprivation.

Individual and Species Differences

Nearly all mammals and birds show at least some REM sleep, indicating that the capacity for it is part of our ancient evolutionary heritage. (See Digression 9.2.) Some species, however, have a great deal more than others; as a rule, the species that get the most total sleep also have the highest percentage of REM sleep (Siegel, 1995). Cats spend up to 16 hours a day sleeping, much or most of it in REM sleep. Rabbits, guinea pigs, and sheep sleep much less and spend very little time in REM sleep.

Within a species, infants have a higher percentage of REM sleep than adults do. Figure 9.13 demonstrates this relationship for humans; a similar trend is found in other mammalian species. Again, infants get more total sleep than adults do, so the pattern remains that more total sleep is associated with a higher percentage of REM sleep. The abundance of REM sleep in infancy has led some researchers to suggest that it is important for organizing the brain, or for modifying neuronal connections in response to early experience (Marks, Shaffery, Oksenberg, Speciale, & Roffward, 1995).

Among adult humans, those who get the most sleep per night (9 or more hours) have the highest percentage of REM sleep, and those who get the least sleep (5 hours or less) have the lowest percentage of REM. In short, across age, species, or individuals, the amount of non-REM sleep varies less than REM does; an individual with extra sleep fills most of it with REM. Horne (1988) has therefore suggested that much of our REM sleep is optional; we could easily survive without it.

The Effects of REM Sleep Deprivation in Humans

Although much of our REM sleep may be optional, some of it also appears to be necessary. What would happen to someone who had almost no opportunity for REM sleep? William Dement (1960) observed the behavior of eight men who agreed to be deprived of REM sleep for 4 to 7 consecutive days. During that period, they slept only in a laboratory. Whenever the EEG and eye movements indicated that a given subject was entering REM sleep, an experimenter promptly awakened him and kept him awake for several minutes. The subject was then permitted to go back to sleep until he started REM sleep again.

Over the course of the 4 to 7 nights, the experimenters found that they had to awaken the subjects more and more frequently. On the first night, an average subject had to be awakened 12 times. By the final night, this figure had increased to 26 times. That is, the subjects had increased their attempts at REM sleep.

During the deprivation period, most subjects reported mild, temporary personality changes, including irritability, increased anxiety, and impaired concentration. Five of the eight experienced increased appetite and weight gain. Control studies found that a similar number of awakenings not linked to REM sleep did not produce similar effects. The disturbances were therefore due to REM deprivation, not just to the total number of awakenings.

After the deprivation period, seven subjects continued to sleep in the laboratory. During their first uninterrupted night, five of the seven spent more time than usual in REM sleep: 29 percent of the night, as compared with 19 percent before the deprivation. One subject showed no REM increase. (The investigators discarded the results from the seventh subject, who came to the laboratory drunk. Alcohol suppresses REM sleep, so results from this subject would be unreliable.)

The Effects of Paradoxical Sleep Deprivation in Nonhumans

Similar experiments have been done with laboratory animals, on which it is possible to impose much longer periods of paradoxical sleep deprivation. Cats have been deprived of paradoxical sleep for up to 70 consecutive days (Dement, Ferguson, Cohen, & Barchas, 1969). Do not imagine shifts of experimenters monitoring cats 24 hours a day and prodding them whenever they entered paradoxical sleep. Rather, they kept each cat on a tiny island surrounded by water. As soon as the cat entered paradoxical sleep its postural muscles relaxed, it lost its balance, and it fell into the water. It could have no more than a few seconds of paradoxical sleep at a time before awakening. Over the course of days, the cats placed in this situation made progressively more attempts to enter paradoxical sleep.

These and similar studies indicate that animals deprived of paradoxical sleep become generally disturbed in a number of ways. However, they leave unanswered

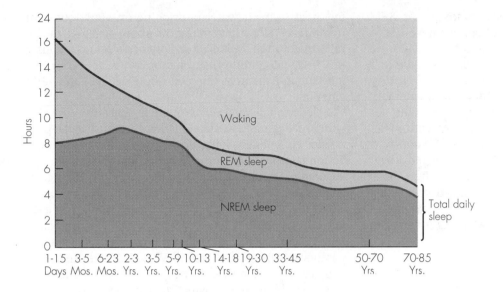

FIGURE **9.13**
Time spent by people of different ages in waking, REM sleep, and NREM sleep
REM sleep occupies about 8 hours a day in newborns but less than 2 hours in most adults. The sleep of infants is not quite like that of adults, however, and the criteria for identifying REM sleep are not the same.
Source: From Roffwarg, Muzio, & Dement, 1966.

DIGRESSION **9.2**

On the Evolutionary Origins of REM Sleep

Virtually all mammals and birds show at least some REM sleep, although birds spend much less time in it than mammals do. For many years, researchers have pondered how and why REM sleep evolved. It now appears that we have been asking the wrong question. Asking how REM sleep evolved assumes that animals first had NREM sleep and then added REM sleep as a new state. Maybe the sequence was different.

Only one species of mammal has been reported to lack REM sleep: the echidna, or spiny anteater. Echidnas, Australian egg-laying mammals, are regarded as primitive. Along with the platypus (an endangered species that is not available for research), the echidna is as close as we shall come to the original ancestors of all other mammals. The report that echidnas lack REM sleep fit the idea that NREM sleep was the primitive state and that REM sleep was a later evolutionary addition (Allison & Goff, 1968).

However, later studies found that the sleep of the echidna is not really like our NREM sleep, either. During an echnida's sleep, neurons in the brain stem show decreased overall activity (as we do during NREM sleep) but the activity has high variability from one time to another (as we have during REM sleep). In short, it is best to say that echidnas have no separation of REM from NREM sleep; they have one state that is a mixture of both (Siegel, 1995).

Relatively little is known about the sleep of fish, amphibians, and reptiles. They certainly do not have separate REM

and NREM states, but it is not clear whether we should classify their sleep as NREM or as an intermediate between REM and NREM, as we now do for echidnas. Indeed, it is not clear whether their periodic states of inactivity are really sleep in the same sense as mammalian sleep. Fish, amphibians, and reptiles do not significantly decrease their brain activity or their responsiveness to stimuli during their inactive ("sleep") periods. On the other hand, by mammalian standards their brain activity is not very high, even during wakefulness.

the question of what functions paradoxical or REM sleep actually serves. A number of studies have linked REM sleep to the process of strengthening memories. Following a new learning experience, both humans and nonhuman mammals increase their REM sleep; if they are prevented from doing so, they show memory deficits. REM sleep is particularly important for strengthening skill formation, as contrasted with memory of facts (Karni, Tanne, Rubenstein, Askenasy, & Sagi, 1994; C. Smith, 1995). NREM sleep may help strengthen certain memories also; researchers have found that patterns of brain activity that occur during new learning are often repeated during the next opportunity for NREM sleep (Skaggs & McNaughton, 1996; Wilson & McNaughton, 1994).

A Biological Perspective on Dreaming

Dreams are real while they last. Can we say more of life?

—*Havelock Ellis*

For decades, psychologists have been heavily influenced by Sigmund Freud's theory of dreams, which was based on the assumption that they reflect hidden and often unconscious wishes. Although Freud was certainly correct in asserting that dreams reflect the dreamer's personality and recent experiences, his theory of the mechanism of dreams depended on a now-obsolete view of the nervous system (McCarley & Hobson, 1977). He believed, for example, that brain cells were inactive except when nerves from the periphery brought them energy. Freud was also hampered by relying on dream reports that his patients gave him hours or days after the dreams occurred.

Contemporary investigators have offered several newer theories. According to the influential **activation-synthesis hypothesis,** during sleep various parts of the brain are activated—either by random spontaneous activity or by stimuli in the room—and the brain synthesizes a story to make sense of all the activity (Hobson & McCarley, 1977; McCarley & Hoffman, 1981). According to a slightly different version of this hypothesis, the brain is aroused and ready to process information during REM sleep, but because the environment provides few stimuli, the sleeper processes information stored in memory, treating the stream of thought and imagery as if it were the real world (Antrobus, 1986).

While we sleep, we do not completely lose contact with external stimuli. (For example, except in early childhood, we seldom roll out of bed.) We incorporate many external stimuli into our dreams, at least in a modified form: If water is dripping on your foot, you may dream about swimming or about walking in the rain. In addition, bursts of activity occur spontaneously in the visual, auditory, and motor cortexes, and in various subcortical areas that contribute to motivation and emotion.

Occasional bursts of vestibular sensation are also common during REM sleep, perhaps because a sleeping person is generally lying down. According to the activation-synthesis hypothesis, the brain incorporates vestibular sensations into dreams of falling, flying, or spinning.

Have you ever dreamt that you were trying to move, but couldn't? It is tempting to relate such dreams to the fact that the major postural muscles are virtually paralyzed during REM sleep: When you are dreaming, you really *can't* move. However, that explanation becomes less convincing when we realize how often people dream that they *are* moving. (The muscles are relaxed during both kinds of dreams.)

The activation-synthesis hypothesis and various modifications of it remain controversial. Some dream researchers consider this approach fruitful; others find it too vague. The main criticism is that it does not suggest easily tested predictions. Certainly, it does not account for all the phenomena of dreams, or explain why many people have repetitive dreams or other dreams full of personal meaning (Winson, 1993).

IN CLOSING

Stages of Sleep

In many cases, scientific progress depends on drawing useful distinctions. Chemists divide the world into different elements, biologists divide life into different species, and medical doctors distinguish one disease from another. Similarly, psychologists try to recognize the most natural or useful distinctions among types of behavior or experience. The discovery of different stages of sleep was a major landmark in psychology, because researchers found a previously unrecognized distinction that is both biologically and psychologically important. It also demonstrated that external measurements—in this case, EEG recordings—can be used to identify internal experiences. We now take it largely for granted that an electrical or magnetic recording from the brain can tell us something about a person's experience, but it is worth pausing to note what a surprising discovery that was in its time.

Summary

1. Sleep has distinct stages that EEG records can identify. Stage 1 is a transition from wakefulness to sleep; the least brain activity occurs during stage 4. (pp. 253)
2. One special stage of sleep is rapid eye movement (REM) sleep. During REM sleep the brain is more active than in other sleep stages. The postural muscles are very relaxed and the eyes move frequently. (p. 254)
3. During a night's sleep, people cycle from stage 1 or REM sleep down to stage 4 and then back to REM or stage 1 again. A complete cycle lasts 90 to 100 minutes. (p. 255)
4. People are more likely to report dreams, especially vivid ones, when they are awakened from REM sleep than when they are awakened during other stages. (p. 255)
5. REM sleep is most common in individuals and species that sleep the most total hours. (p. 256)
6. People who are deprived of REM sleep become irritable and have trouble concentrating. After a period of REM deprivation, people compensate by spending more time than usual in REM sleep. (p. 256)
7. According to the activation-synthesis hypothesis, dreams are the brain's attempts to make sense of limited, shifting, and somewhat random stimuli. (p. 258)

Review Questions

1. How can an investigator determine whether a person is in sleep stage 1, 2, 3, 4, or REM? (p. 253)
2. What is the EEG pattern when neuronal activity is synchronized? What is the pattern when activity is desynchronized? (p. 254)
3. Why do many sleep researchers avoid the terms *light sleep* and *deep sleep*? (p. 255)
4. Which sleep stages are most common early in the night? Which ones predominate later? (p. 255)
5. What kinds of dreams (if any) occur during non-REM sleep? (p. 255)
6. Do all people dream? If so, why do some people believe that they do not? (p. 255)
7. Which animal species have the largest amount of REM sleep? (p. 256)
8. What are the effects of REM sleep deprivation? (p. 256)
9. If you want to remember some new skill, why is it a good idea to learn it or practice it shortly before going to sleep? (p. 258)
10. According to the activation-synthesis hypothesis of dreams, what determines the content of our dreams? (p. 258)

Suggestions for Further Reading

Dement, W. C. (1992). *The sleepwatchers.* Stanford, CA: Stanford Alumni Association. Fascinating, entertaining account of sleep research by one of its leading pioneers.

Moorcroft, W. H. (1993). *Sleep, dreaming, & sleep disorders: An introduction* (2nd ed.). Lanham, MD: University Press of America. Excellent and thorough review of research on sleep and dreams.

Winson, J. (1990, November). The meaning of dreams. *Scientific American, 263*(5), 86–96. Discusses theories of the function of REM sleep and the meaning of dreams.

Terms

alpha wave   rhythm of 8 to 12 brain waves per second, generally associated with relaxation (p. 253)

sleep spindle   12- to 14-Hz brain waves in bursts that last at least half a second (p. 253)

K-complex   sharp, high-amplitude, negative wave followed by a smaller, slower, positive wave (p. 253)

slow-wave sleep (SWS)   stages 3 and 4 of sleep, which are occupied largely by slow, large-amplitude brain waves (p. 254)

paradoxical sleep   stage of sleep characterized by complete relaxation of the large muscles and relatively high activity in the brain (p. 254)

rapid eye movement (REM) sleep   sleep stage with rapid eye movements, high brain activity, and relaxation of the large muscles (p. 254)

polysomnograph   a combination of EEG and eye-movement records, and sometimes other data, for a sleeping person (p. 255)

non-REM sleep   sleep stages other than REM sleep (p. 255)

activation-synthesis hypothesis   hypothesis that the brain synthesizes dreams from spontaneous brain activity occurring during sleep (p. 258)

Brain Mechanisms in Sleep and Its Disorders

Suppose I buy a new radio. After I play it for 4 hours, it suddenly stops. To explain why, I try to discover whether the batteries are dead or whether the radio needs repair. Suppose I later discover that the radio always stops after playing for 4 hours, and that it will operate again a few hours later even without repairs or a battery change. I begin to suspect that the manufacturer designed it this way on purpose, perhaps to prevent me from wearing it out too fast or to prevent me from listening to the radio all day. I might then try to find the device that turns it off whenever I play it for 4 hours. Notice that I am now asking a new question. When I thought that the radio stopped because it needed repairs or new batteries, I would not have thought to ask which device turned it off. I ask that question only when I think of the stoppage as an active process.

Similarly, if we think of sleep as a passive cessation of activity, similar to catching one's breath after running a race, we do not ask which part of the brain is responsible for sleep. But if we think of sleep as a specialized state evolved to serve particular functions, we may look for the devices that regulate it.

Wakefulness and Arousal

After a cut through the midbrain separates the forebrain and part of the midbrain from all the lower structures, an animal enters a prolonged state of sleep. The brain shows no signs of wakefulness in the EEG during the next week or so, and only brief periods of wakefulness later. The explanation might seem simple: The cut isolated the brain from the sensory stimuli that come up from the medulla and spinal cord. However, when a researcher cuts each of the individual tracts that enter the medulla and spinal cord, thus depriving the brain of almost all sensory input, the animal continues to have normal periods of wakefulness and sleep. Evidently,

cutting through the midbrain is more disruptive to wakefulness than is cutting all the sensory tracts.

A cut through the midbrain decreases arousal because it damages the **reticular formation,** a structure that extends from the medulla into the forebrain. The reticular formation contains some neurons with axons ascending into the brain and some with axons descending into the spinal cord. In the discussion of movement (Chapter 8), we encountered the neurons with descending axons. In 1949, Giuseppe Moruzzi and H. W. Magoun proposed that the reticular formation neurons with ascending axons are well suited to regulate arousal. The term *reticular* (based on the Latin word *rete,* meaning *net*) describes the widespread, apparently haphazard connections among neurons in this system. These neurons receive input from many sensory systems and send their axons widely throughout the cortex. The idea was that any sensory stimulus would arouse the reticular formation, which in turn would arouse all parts of the cortex—those responsive to the original stimuli and those responsive to other kinds of stimulus. The more intense the stimulus, the greater the resulting arousal. Furthermore, in addition to responding to sensory stimuli, the reticular formation produces spontaneous activity of its own, thereby maintaining moderate arousal even during periods of little or no external stimulation.

Research since the time of Moruzzi and Magoun has confirmed a strong role for the reticular formation in arousal. When an awake but relaxed person starts performing a difficult task, activity increases in the reticular formation (Kinomura, Larsson, Gulyás, & Roland, 1996). Any stimulation of the reticular formation awakens a sleeping individual or increases alertness in one already awake, shifting the EEG from many long, slow waves to short, rapid, irregular waves. Technically, however, reticular formation activity does not desynchronize the EEG; it facilitates neuronal activity at a frequency above 30 Hz (Munk, Roelfsema, König, Engel, & Singer, 1996), thereby producing a record that looks more irregular or haphazard than it actually is.

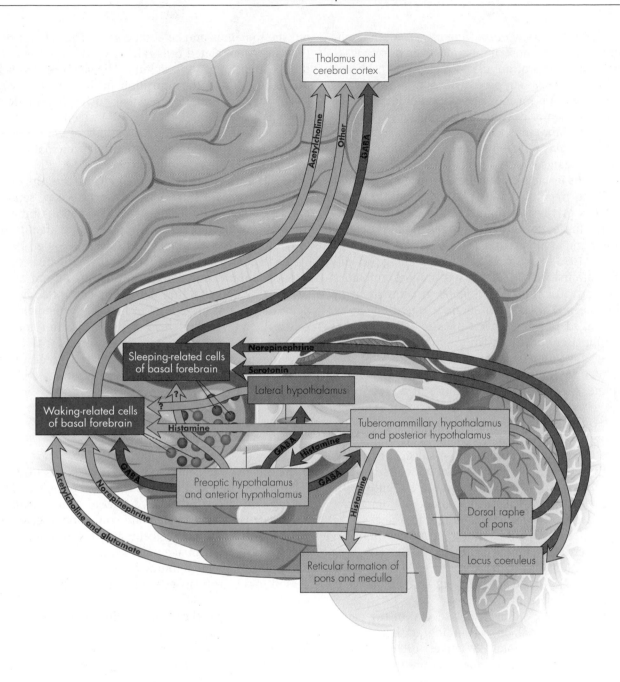

FIGURE **9.14**
Brain mechanisms of sleeping and waking
Green arrows indicate excitatory connections; red arrows indicate inhibitory connections. Neuro-
transmitters are indicated where they are known.   Source: Based on Lin, Hou, Sakai, & Jouvet, 1996;
Robbins & Everitt, 1995; and Szymusiak, 1995.

However, today neither psychologists nor neuroscientists regard arousal as a single, unitary process (Robbins & Everitt, 1995). Waking up, directing attention to
a particular stimulus, preparing to store a memory, and
increasing goal-directed effort are overlapping but different types of arousal, requiring many brain areas. The

reticular formation is now recognized as just one segment of a waking system that also includes the locus
coeruleus, the lateral hypothalamus, and scattered clusters of cells in the basal forebrain, as shown in Figure
9.14. Each of these structures plays a slightly different
role. For instance, the **locus coeruleus** (LOW-kus

ser-ROO-lee-us, literally, *dark blue place*), a hindbrain structure, is inactive most of the time, even during waking, but emits bursts of impulses in response to meaningful events such as reinforcements and punishments. It may be important for the special kind of arousal that helps us form memories (Chiara, Pompeiano, & Tononi, 1996). (The fact that the locus coeruleus is inactive during REM sleep may help explain why we quickly forget most of our dreams.)

Many cells in the **basal forebrain** (just anterior and dorsal to the hypothalamus) provide axons to widespread areas of the thalamus and cerebral cortex. In most cases these axons release acetylcholine as their transmitter and at most synapses the effect is excitatory (Mesulam, 1995; Szymusiak, 1995). Damage to the basal forebrain leads to decreased arousal, impaired learning and attention, and increased time spent in non-REM sleep. The basal forebrain is one of the areas most damaged in Alzheimer's disease (Chapter 13), leading to inattention and memory impairments.

The acetylcholine synapses responsible for arousal are inhibited by the neuromodulator *adenosine,* which accumulates in the brain during times of wakefulness. Caffeine increases arousal by inhibiting adenosine (Rainnie, Grunze, McCarley, & Greene, 1994). Drinking coffee, tea, or a cola beverage in the evening causes most people to have trouble falling asleep or staying asleep. Even a single morning cup of coffee leaves enough caffeine in the system to interfere slightly with sleep that night, increasing the likelihood of brief awakenings. Those effects are so small that most sleepers do not even notice them, but laboratory tests confirm them (Landolt, Werth, Borbély, & Dijk, 1995). The message: Just as you might use caffeine to try to keep yourself awake, you might try decreasing your caffeine intake if you have trouble sleeping.

In Figure 9.14, note also that several of the paths contributing to arousal use histamine as their neurotransmitter (Lin, Hou, Sakai, & Jouvet, 1996). Antihistamine drugs, often used for allergies, produce drowsiness if they cross the blood-brain barrier.

Sleep and REM Sleep

Not only are there kinds of brain damage that will decrease wakefulness, but there are also kinds of brain damage that decrease sleep. In Figure 9.14, note that in addition to waking-related cells, the basal forebrain also has clusters of sleep-related cells (Szymusiak, 1995). Both kinds of cells send axons widely through-

out the thalamus and cerebral cortex. The difference is that the sleep-related cells release GABA, a transmitter that is almost always inhibitory. The sleep-related cells are active during the transition from wakefulness to sleep; they continue to be active during NREM sleep, though generally not during REM sleep. Lesions to these cells result in prolonged periods of wakefulness, as do drugs that inhibit GABA, the principal neurotransmitter of the sleep-related cells.

Cells in the anterior and preoptic areas of the hypothalamus increase their activity during sleep, sending messages that excite sleep-related cells and inhibit waking-related cells in other parts of the hypothalamus and forebrain (Sherin, Shiromani, McCarley, & Saper, 1996). We shall consider the anterior and preoptic areas of the hypothalamus in more detail in Chapter 10, but at this point let us note that they detect and control body temperature. One of the effects of high body temperature, especially a fever, is increased sleepiness. You now see the mechanism: The hypothalamic areas that detect high temperature send appropriate messages to the brain areas controlling waking and sleeping.

REM-Inducing Areas

It might seem very routine to use PET scans to determine which human brain areas increase their activity during REM sleep. But PET scans require an injection of a radioactive chemical. How are you going to give people injections without awakening them? Further, a PET scan yields a clear image only if the head remains motionless for several minutes of data collection. If the person tosses or turns even slightly, the image will be worthless.

To overcome these difficulties, researchers persuaded some young men to sleep with their heads firmly attached to masks that would not permit any movement. They also inserted a cannula (plastic tube) into each man's left arm so that they could inject radioactive chemicals at various times during the night. So, imagine yourself in that setup. You have a cannula in your arm and your head is locked into position. Now try to go to sleep.

Because the researchers foresaw that it might be difficult to sleep under those conditions (!), they had the men go without sleep the entire night before. A person who is sleepy enough can sleep under trying circumstances.

Now that you appreciate the heroic nature of the procedures, here are the results. During REM sleep, activity increased in the pons, the thalamus, and the amygdala. Activity increased in certain parts of the

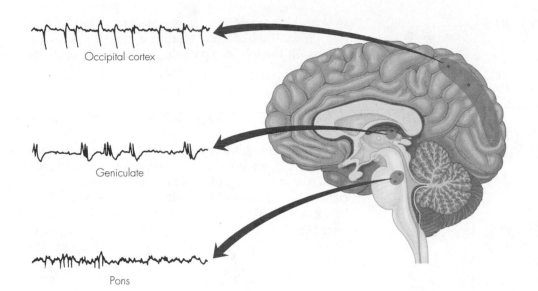

Occipital cortex

Geniculate

Pons

FIGURE **9.15**
PGO waves start in the pons (P), then show up in the lateral geniculate (G) and the occipital cortex (O). Each PGO wave is synchronized with an eye movement in REM sleep.

cerebral cortex and decreased in others, including the dorsolateral prefrontal cortex (Maquet et al., 1996). We shall consider the amygdala and the dorsolateral prefrontal cortex in much more detail in later chapters; at this point note that the amygdala is highly active during emotional experience and the dorsolateral prefrontal cortex is important for keeping track of recent memories. Perhaps the arousal of the amygdala during REM sleep has some relation to the highly emotional nature of many dreams; perhaps the suppression of the dorsolateral prefrontal cortex has some relation to the disjointed, illogical nature of many dreams. Unfortunately, it is difficult to test these appealing speculations.

Identifying the pons and thalamus as important for REM sleep came as no surprise. For many years, research on animals had found that REM sleep is associated with a distinctive pattern of high-amplitude electrical potentials known as **PGO waves,** for *p*ons-*g*eniculate-*o*ccipital (see Figure 9.15). Waves of neural activity that are detected first in the pons appear shortly afterward in the lateral geniculate nucleus of the thalamus and then in the occipital cortex (Brooks & Bizzi, 1963; Laurent, Cespuglio, & Jouvet, 1974). Because the lateral geniculate nucleus and occipital cortex are critical for vision, and because the term *REM* itself refers to eye movements, it would be natural to assume that REM is primarily a visual phenomenon. In the first minutes of a REM period, most of the activity is indeed in the visual areas of the brain. As a REM period continues, however, the waves of activity spread to more and more of the thalamus and the cerebral cortex (Amzica & Steriade, 1996). (As dreams continue, do they become less visual and more oriented to other senses? The brain data imply that they should.)

An animal compensates for lost PGO waves more precisely than for lost REM time (Dement, Ferguson, Cohen, & Barchas, 1969). During a prolonged period of REM deprivation, PGO waves begin to emerge during sleep stages 2 to 4—when they do not normally occur—and even during wakefulness, often in association with strange behaviors, as if the animal were hallucinating. At the end of the deprivation period, when an animal is permitted to sleep without interruption, the REM periods have an unusually high density of PGO waves.

Besides originating the PGO waves, cells in the pons contribute to REM sleep by sending messages to the spinal cord, inhibiting the motor neurons that control the body's large muscles. After damage to the floor of the pons, a cat still has REM sleep periods, but its muscles are not relaxed. During REM, it walks (though awkwardly), behaves as if it were chasing an imagined prey, jumps as if startled, and so forth (Morrison, Sanford, Ball, Mann, & Ross, 1995). (See Figure 9.16.) Is the cat acting out its dreams? We do not know; the cat cannot tell us, but the strong suspicion is that the answer is yes. Evidently, one function of the messages from the pons to the spinal cord is to prevent us from acting out our dreams.

REM sleep apparently depends on a combination of the neurotransmitters serotonin and acetylcholine (Benington & Heller, 1995). Drugs that block serotonin receptors in the forebrain prevent the onset of REM sleep. Drugs that block acetylcholine synapses interfere with the continuation of REM sleep. Injections of the drug *carbachol*, which stimulates ACh synapses, quickly induces a change from NREM to REM sleep (Baghdoyan, Spotts, & Snyder, 1993). Note that acetylcholine

FIGURE **9.16**
A cat with a lesion in the pons, wobbling about during REM sleep
Cells of an intact pons send inhibitory messages to the spinal cord neurons that control the large muscles.   Source: Morrison, Sanford, Ball, Mann, & Ross, 1995.

is important for both wakefulness and REM sleep, two states that are associated with activation of most of the brain.

Abnormalities of Sleep

Have you ever stayed awake extremely late at night to finish some project and then found yourself making one mistake after another the next morning? If so, you are not alone. People who work long or irregular hours are especially likely to have sleep problems; so are people with psychiatric problems such as depression, schizophrenia, and substance abuse (Benca, Obermeyer, Thisted, & Gillin, 1992). But a great many other-

wise healthy people also have at least occasional sleepless nights. Unsatisfactory sleep is a major cause of accidents on the job, comparable to the effects of drugs and alcohol.

Insomnia

How much sleep is enough? How much is too little? Some people get along fine with six hours of sleep per night. For others, eight hours may not be enough, especially if they awaken repeatedly during the night. The best gauge of **insomnia** is whether the person feels well rested the following day. Anyone who consistently feels sleepy during the day is not sleeping well enough at night.

Insomnia can have many causes, including excessive noise, worries and stress, drugs and medications, uncomfortable temperatures, sleeping in an unfamiliar place, or trying to fall asleep at the wrong time in one's circadian rhythm. It can also be the result of epilepsy, Parkinson's disease, brain tumors, or other serious illnesses (Silvestri et al., 1991). Some children suffer insomnia because they are milk-intolerant and their parents, not realizing the intolerance, give them milk to drink right before bedtime (Horne, 1992). A friend of mine suffered insomnia for months until he realized that he dreaded going to sleep because he dreaded waking up in the morning and doing his daily jogging. After he switched his jogging time to late afternoon, he no longer had any trouble sleeping. In short, before trying sleeping pills or any other method of combating insomnia, you should try to identify the reasons for your sleep troubles.

It is convenient to distinguish three categories of insomnia: onset insomnia, maintenance insomnia, and termination insomnia. People with **onset insomnia** have trouble falling asleep. Those with **maintenance insomnia** awaken frequently during the night. And those with **termination insomnia** wake up too early and cannot get back to sleep. It is possible to have more than one of the three types.

Certain cases of insomnia are related to abnormalities of biological rhythms (MacFarlane, Cleghorn, & Brown, 1985a, 1985b). Ordinarily, people fall asleep while their temperature is declining and awaken while it is rising, as in Figure 9.17a. Some people's body temperature rhythm is *phase delayed,* as in Figure 9.17b. If they try to fall asleep at the normal time, their body temperature is higher than normal for going to sleep. Such people are likely to experience onset insomnia (Morris, Lack, & Dawson, 1990). Other people's body temperature rhythm is *phase advanced,* as in Figure 9.17c. They are likely to suffer termination insomnia. Irregular fluctuations of circadian rhythms can cause maintenance insomnia.

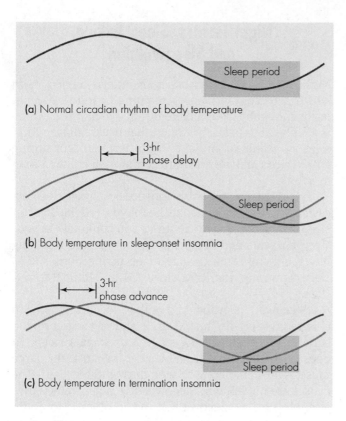

(a) Normal circadian rhythm of body temperature

3-hr phase delay

(b) Body temperature in sleep-onset insomnia

3-hr phase advance

(c) Body temperature in termination insomnia

FIGURE 9.17
Insomnia and circadian rhythms
A delay in the circadian rhythm of body temperature is associated with onset insomnia; an advance, with termination insomnia.

REM sleep occurs mostly during the rising phase of the temperature cycle. For most people, this is the second half of the night's sleep. For people with termination insomnia or anyone else who falls asleep after the temperature cycle has already hit bottom, REM sleep may start shortly after sleep begins (Czeisler, Weitzman, Moore-Ede, Zimmerman, & Knauer, 1980). Because depression is often associated with termination insomnia, most depressed people enter REM sleep earlier in the night than nondepressed people do.

Another cause of insomnia is, paradoxically, the use of tranquilizers as sleeping pills. Most sleeping pills operate at least in part by blocking the activity of norepinephrine, histamine, or other neurotransmitters that increase arousal.

Although tranquilizers may help a person fall asleep, taking such drugs a few times may cause dependence on them. Without the pills, the person goes into a withdrawal state that prevents sleep (Kales, Scharf, & Kales, 1978), and may react by taking the sleeping pills again, setting up a cycle from which it is difficult to escape.

Some tranquilizers are long-acting; others are short-acting. Either kind poses problems. A long-lasting tranquilizer may not wear off by the next morning, leaving the person sleepy during the day. A short-acting tranquilizer may wear off during the night, causing the person to awaken early. In short, frequent use of tranquilizing sleeping pills is unwise.

Sleep Apnea

One special cause of insomnia is **sleep apnea,** the inability to breathe while sleeping. Many people breathe irregularly during REM sleep, and about 10 to 15 percent of all adults have occasional periods of at least 10 seconds without breathing. Sleep apnea to that degree is considered normal and unrelated to insomnia (Kales & Kales, 1984). In serious cases, people go a minute or more without breathing and then awaken, gasping for breath. Such people may stay in bed more than 8 hours per night but sleep only about half that time. In many cases the person does not remember awakening repeatedly during the night; he or she is aware only of feeling poorly rested the next morning. When sleep apnea occurs in infancy, it is one of the possible causes of *sudden infant death syndrome* or "crib death." A family that is worried about sleep apnea in either a child or an adult can use devices that monitor the sleep and breathing and alert others when a problem occurs (White, Gibb, Wall, & Westbrook, 1995).

Obesity is one of several possible causes of sleep apnea. Some obese people, especially men, have narrower-than-normal airways and have to compensate by breathing more frequently or more vigorously than others do. During sleep this compensation fails, and the sleep posture may narrow the airways even more than usual (Mezzanotte, Tangel, & White, 1992). In other people, especially the elderly, sleep apnea results when brain mechanisms for respiration cease functioning during sleep.

Narcolepsy

Narcolepsy, a condition characterized by frequent unexpected periods of sleepiness during the day (Aldrich, 1993), strikes about one person in a thousand, generally running in families. Four symptoms are generally associated with narcolepsy, although many patients do not report all four:

1. Gradual or sudden attacks of extreme sleepiness during the day.
2. Occasional **cataplexy:** an attack of muscle weakness while the person remains awake. Cataplexy is often triggered by strong emotions, such as anger or great excitement.
3. Sleep paralysis: a complete inability to move when falling asleep or waking up. Other people may

experience sleep paralysis occasionally, but people with narcolepsy experience it more frequently.

4. *Hypnagogic hallucinations:* dreamlike experiences that the person has trouble distinguishing from reality, often occurring at the onset of sleep.

Each of these symptoms can be interpreted as an intrusion of a REM-like state into wakefulness; REM sleep is associated with muscle weakness (cataplexy), paralysis, and dreams (Mahowald & Schenck, 1992). Certain cells in the medulla become active during REM sleep, sending messages to the spinal cord to suppress muscle responsiveness. Many of those same cells in the medulla become active when a narcoleptic individual experiences cataplexy (Siegel et al., 1991). Stimulant drugs that block REM sleep, such as amphetamine, also help control narcolepsy, although many physicians are hesitant to prescribe any drug with as much potential for abuse as amphetamine has (Kryger, 1993).

Periodic Limb Movement Disorder

Another factor occasionally linked to insomnia is **periodic limb movement disorder,** a repeated involuntary movement of the legs and sometimes arms (Edinger et al., 1992). Many people, perhaps most, experience an occasional involuntary kick, especially when starting to fall asleep. Leg movements are not a problem unless they become persistent. In some people, mostly middle-aged and older, the legs kick once every 20 to 30 seconds for a period of minutes or even hours, mostly during NREM sleep. Frequent or especially vigorous leg movements may awaken the person. In some cases tranquilizers help suppress the movements (Schenck & Mahowald, 1996).

REM Behavior Disorder

For most people, the major postural muscles are relaxed and inactive during REM sleep. However, in an uncommon condition known as **REM behavior disorder,** people move around vigorously during their REM periods, apparently acting out their dreams. Many of their dreams are violent, and they may punch, kick, and leap about, often damaging property and injuring themselves or other people. Their dreams correspond to their movements; that is, they dream that they are kicking when they are actually kicking.

One study of people with REM sleep disorder found multiple areas of damage in the pons and midbrain (Culebras & Moore, 1989). Recall from the discussion of brain mechanisms of REM sleep that cells in the pons send messages to inhibit the spinal neurons that control large muscle movements; cats with damage to the pons appear to act out their dreams. The same is apparently true in humans.

Night Terrors, Sleep Talking, and Sleepwalking

Night terrors are experiences of intense anxiety from which a person awakens screaming in terror. A night terror should be distinguished from a *nightmare,* which is simply an unpleasant dream that occurs during REM sleep in people of any age. Night terrors occur during NREM sleep and are far more common in children than in adults.

Many people, probably most, talk in their sleep occasionally. Unless someone hears you talking in your sleep and later tells you about it, you could talk in your sleep for years and never know about it. Sleep talking has about the same chance of occurring during REM sleep as during non-REM sleep (Arkin, Toth, Baker, & Hastey, 1970).

Sleepwalking runs in families, occurs mostly in children, especially ages 2 to 5, and is most common early in the night, during stage 3 or stage 4 sleep. (It does not occur during REM sleep because the large muscles are completely relaxed during REM sleep.) The causes are not known. Sleepwalking is generally harmless, both to the sleepwalker and to others. No doubt you have heard people say, "You should never waken someone who is sleepwalking." In fact, it is not harmful or dangerous to awaken a sleepwalker, although the person is likely to feel very confused (Moorcroft, 1993).

In an individual case, it is often difficult to distinguish sleepwalking from REM behavior disorder. One man pleaded "not guilty" to a charge of murder because he had been sleepwalking at the time and did not know what he was doing. The jury agreed with him, partly because he had a family history of sleepwalking. However, especially for a one-time event, it is difficult to know whether he was sleepwalking, subject to REM behavior disorder, or indeed even wide awake at the time (Broughton et al., 1994).

IN CLOSING

The Physiology of Wakefulness and Sleep

Who would have guessed that the brain mechanisms for waking and sleeping would be so many and so complicated? Certainly not the psychologists or neuroscientists of an earlier era. Given the complexity of the brain controls for sleep, perhaps we should not be surprised that many people have a large variety of sleep problems. As recently as the 1960s, the medical profession had little idea how to diagnose special sleep problems and little to offer sufferers. Today, most major hospitals have a sleep-disorders clinic staffed by physicians who make a career of helping people sleep. We have come to realize that it is hard to do our waking activities right if we do not get our sleeping right.

Summary

1. Several brain areas promote wakefulness and arousal in the rest of the brain. Certain cell populations in the reticular formation, the lateral hypothalamus, and the basal forebrain arouse the rest of the brain through axons that release acetylcholine and histamine. Drugs that block those transmitters produce drowsiness. (p. 260)
2. The locus coeruleus produces bursts of arousing impulses in response to meaningful events, perhaps improving memory storage. (p. 262)
3. Another population of neurons in the basal forebrain has widespread axons that deliver GABA to the thalamus and cerebral cortex, inducing sleep. Damage to this area leads to insomnia. (pp. 262)
4. REM sleep is associated with increased activity in a number of brain areas, including the pons, thalamus, amygdala, and parts of the cortex. It is also associated with decreased activity in certain areas, including part of the frontal cortex. REM sleep depends on the neurotransmitters serotonin and acetylcholine. (p. 262)
5. REM sleep begins with PGO waves, waves of brain activity transmitted from the pons to the lateral geniculate to the occipital lobe. (p. 263)
6. Insomnia sometimes results from a shift in phase of the circadian rhythm of temperature in relation to the circadian rhythm of sleep and wakefulness. It can also result from difficulty in breathing while asleep, overuse of tranquilizers, and numerous other causes. (p. 264)
7. People with narcolepsy grow very sleepy during the day. (p. 265)
8. Among other sleep disorders are night terrors, sleep talking, sleepwalking, and REM behavior disorder. (p. 266)

Review Questions

1. How does caffeine increase arousal? (p. 262)
2. Three observations about dreams are that we forget most dreams, that many dreams are emotional, and that many dreams are disjointed and illogical. How does our knowledge of the physiology of sleep help explain these observations? (pp. 262, 263)
3. Why does someone with a fever become sleepy? Why do most antihistamines also provoke sleepiness? (p. 262)
4. What are PGO waves? Where do they originate? (p. 263)
5. Describe some of the possible causes of insomnia. (p. 264)
6. What are the disadvantages of using sleeping pills to combat insomnia? (p. 265)
7. Describe the characteristics of narcolepsy. (p. 265)
8. Are night terrors more common in REM sleep or non-REM sleep? What about sleep talking? Sleepwalking? (p. 266)

Thought Question

1. When cats are deprived of REM sleep for various periods and then permitted uninterrupted sleep, the amount of extra REM sleep increases for the first 25 to 30 days but does not increase further with a longer deprivation. What prevents the need from accumulating beyond that point? Consider PGO waves in your answer.

Suggestion for Further Reading

Moorcroft, W. H. (1993). *Sleep, dreaming, & sleep disorders* (2nd ed.). Lanham, MD: University Press of America. Chapter 4 discusses the functions of various brain areas in sleep. Chapter 8 provides a good description of sleep disorders.

Terms

reticular formation structure extending from the medulla into the forebrain, important for wakefulness and arousal (p. 260)

locus coeruleus small hindbrain structure whose widespread axons send bursts of norepinephrine in response to meaningful stimuli (p. 261)

basal forebrain forebrain area anterior and dorsal to the hypothalamus; includes cell clusters that promote wakefulness and other cell clusters that promote sleep (p. 262)

PGO wave pattern of high-amplitude electrical potentials that occurs first in the pons, then in the lateral geniculate, and finally in the occipital cortex (p. 263)

insomnia lack of sleep, leaving the person feeling poorly rested the following day (p. 264)

onset insomnia difficulty falling asleep (p. 264)

maintenance insomnia frequent awakening during the night (p. 264)

termination insomnia tendency to awaken early and to be unable to get back to sleep (p. 264)

sleep apnea inability to breathe while sleeping (p. 265)

narcolepsy condition characterized by unexpected periods of sleepiness during the day (p. 265)

cataplexy attack of muscle weakness while a person remains awake (p. 265)

periodic limb movement disorder repeated involuntary movement of the legs and sometimes arms during sleep (p. 266)

REM behavior disorder condition in which people move around vigorously during REM sleep (p. 266)

night terror experience of intense anxiety during sleep, from which a person awakens screaming in terror (p. 266)

THE REGULATION OF INTERNAL BODY STATES

CHAPTER TEN

What is life? Life can be defined in different ways depending on whether our interest is medical, legal, philosophical, or poetic. At the most basic biological level, we can say that *life is a coordinated set of chemical reactions.* Not all chemical reactions are alive, but life cannot exist without chemical reactions.

Every chemical reaction in the body takes place in a water solution at a rate that depends on the identity and concentration of molecules in the water, the temperature of the solution, and the presence of contaminants. To continue the chemical reactions that we call "life," we must follow a most precise recipe. Much of our behavior is organized to keep the ingredients present in the right proportions and at the right temperature.

Temperature Regulation

An average college student expends about 2600 kilocalories (kcal) per day. Where do you suppose all that energy goes? To physical exercise? Mental activity, perhaps? No. You use about 1700 kcal (roughly two-thirds of the total, and just less than what it takes to power a 100-watt lightbulb) just for **basal metabolism,** the energy you use to maintain a constant body temperature while at rest (Burton, 1994). Reptiles and amphibians, which do not maintain a constant body temperature, need a great deal less fuel each day than you do.

In short, temperature regulation is one of your body's top priorities, even if it is not one of your main topics of thought and conversation. I hope to convince you that it is more interesting than you had thought.

Homeostasis

Physiologist Walter B. Cannon (1929) introduced the term **homeostasis** (HO-mee-oh-STAY-sis) to refer to temperature regulation and other biological processes that keep certain body variables within a fixed range. To understand how a homeostatic process works, we can use the analogy of a thermostat in a house with both a heating and a cooling system. Someone fixes a set range of temperatures on the thermostat. When the temperature in the house drops below that range, the thermostat triggers the furnace to provide heat until the house temperature returns to the set range. When the temperature rises above the maximum of the range, the thermostat triggers the air conditioner to cool the house.

Similarly, homeostatic processes in animals trigger physiological and behavioral activities that keep certain variables within a set range. In many cases the range is so narrow that we refer to it as a **set point.** For example, if calcium is deficient in your diet and its concentration in the blood begins to fall below the set point of 0.16 g/L (grams per liter), storage deposits in your bones will release additional calcium into the blood. If the calcium level in the blood rises above 0.16 g/L, part of the excess is stored in the bones and part is excreted. Analogous mechanisms maintain constant blood levels of water, oxygen, glucose, sodium chloride, protein, fat, and acidity (Cannon, 1929).

In the mammalian body, temperature regulation, thirst, and hunger are *nearly* homeostatic processes. They are not *exactly* homeostatic, because they anticipate future needs as well as react to current needs (Appley, 1991). For example, in a frightening situation that might call for vigorous activity, you begin to experience a cold sweat even before you start to move.

Set points for body temperature, body fat, and other variables are not quite fixed; they change with time of day, time of year, and other conditions (Mrosovsky, 1990). Set points also differ among species. Most mammals have a body temperature close to that of humans, 37°C, whereas birds are significantly warmer, generally around 41°C.

Reproductive cells require a somewhat cooler environment. Birds lay eggs and sit on them because the birds' internal temperature is too hot for the embryo. Similarly, in most male mammals the scrotum hangs outside the body because sperm production requires a temperature a bit cooler than the rest of the body. (A man who wears his undershorts too tight produces fewer healthy sperm cells.) Pregnant women are advised to avoid hot baths and anything else that would overheat a developing fetus.

Mechanisms for Controlling Body Temperature

Amphibians, reptiles, and most fish are **poikilothermic** (POY-kih-lo-THER-mik): Their body temperature is the same as the temperature of their environment. They can control their body temperature to some extent by selecting their location, but they lack physiological mechanisms of temperature regulation such as shivering and sweating. A few kinds of fish maintain a nearly constant temperature in the brain, though not in the rest of the body (Block, Finnerty, Stewart, & Kidd, 1993).

Mammals and birds are **homeothermic:** They use physiological mechanisms to maintain an almost constant body temperature despite large variations in the environmental temperature. Homeothermy requires effort, and therefore fuel. An animal *generates* heat in proportion to its total mass; it *radiates* heat in proportion to its surface area. A small animal, such as a mouse or a hummingbird, has a high surface-to-volume ratio and therefore radiates heat rapidly. Such animals need a great deal of fuel each day in order to maintain their body temperature. The largest animals are best insulated against heat loss.

Why have we evolved mechanisms to control body temperature? Why is constancy of body temperature important enough to justify spending all the energy it requires? A constant body temperature enables an animal to stay active when the environment turns cold. Recall from Chapter 8 that a fish has trouble maintaining a high activity level at a low temperature. At a high temperature it can rely on its nonfatiguing slow-twitch muscle fibers; at lower temperatures it must recruit more and more of its rapidly fatiguing fast-twitch fibers. Because of their constant internal temperature, birds and mammals are ready for action at any temperature, without needing to recruit different sets of muscles.

Why did mammals evolve a body temperature of 37°C instead of 27°C or 47°C or any other possible value? Any temperature is the result of a trade-off among several competing factors. The higher the temperature, the greater the animal's potential for activity, and therefore the greater its advantage over cooler animals. However, higher temperatures require more fuel. The body needs about a 13 percent increase in metabolic rate to raise its temperature by 1°C (Long, 1996). On the other hand, maintaining a constant low temperature would be difficult also, as it would require extensive sweating, at a risk to body fluids. A further consideration is that most proteins begin to break their bonds and lose their useful properties at temperatures much above 40°C or 41°C. It would be possible to evolve proteins that are stable at higher temperatures, but only to a limited extent. Proteins have useful enzymatic properties because they have a flexible structure. A protein that had enough stabilizing bonds to hold it together at a temperature much above 41°C would be so rigid that it would lose most of its enzymatic properties (Somero, 1996). In short, the chemical properties of proteins set a theoretical upper limit to the body temperature an animal can maintain. Birds are close to that limit, and mammals are not far behind.

Brain Mechanisms

The body defends the temperature at its core—including the brain and the other internal organs—more carefully than it defends the temperature of the skin. When the body cools below the set point, the blood vessels to the skin constrict, preventing the blood from being cooled by cold air. Although the skin may be very cold, the brain, heart, and other internal organs remain warm. To generate more heat, the muscles contract rhythmically (in a shiver), or the animal runs about. The fur of a mammal becomes erect, increasing insulation from the cold environment.

If the body begins to overheat, more blood than usual flows to the skin, where it can be cooled by contact with the air (which is almost always cooler than the body). An animal may decrease heat production by decreasing activity. Depending on the species, animals sweat, pant heavily, or lick themselves. (Evaporation of sweat or saliva cools the body.)

All these physiological changes depend predominantly on certain areas within the hypothalamus, a small structure at the base of the brain (see Figure 10.1). The hypothalamus contains a number of nuclei, each of which apparently serves a different function. Most critical for temperature control is the **preoptic area,** next to the anterior hypothalamus. (It is called *preoptic* because it is near the optic chiasm, where the optic nerves cross.)

The preoptic area monitors body temperature partly by monitoring its own temperature (Nelson & Prosser, 1981). When an experimenter heats the preoptic area, an animal pants or sweats, even in a cool environment. If the same area is cooled, the animal shivers, even in a warm room. These responses are not simply reflexive. An animal will also react to a heated or cooled preoptic area by pressing a lever or doing other work for cold air or hot air reinforcements (Laudenslager, 1976; Satinoff, 1964).

Besides monitoring their own temperature, the cells of the preoptic area also receive input from temperature-sensitive receptors in the skin and spinal cord. The animal shivers most vigorously when both the preoptic area and the other receptors are cold; it sweats or pants most vigorously when both are hot.

Damage to the preoptic area impairs a mammal's ability to regulate temperature. It can no longer shiver, so its body temperature plummets in a cold environment (Satinoff, Valentino, & Teitelbaum, 1976). The preoptic area dominates temperature control, but temperature-sensitive cells also exist in other parts of the

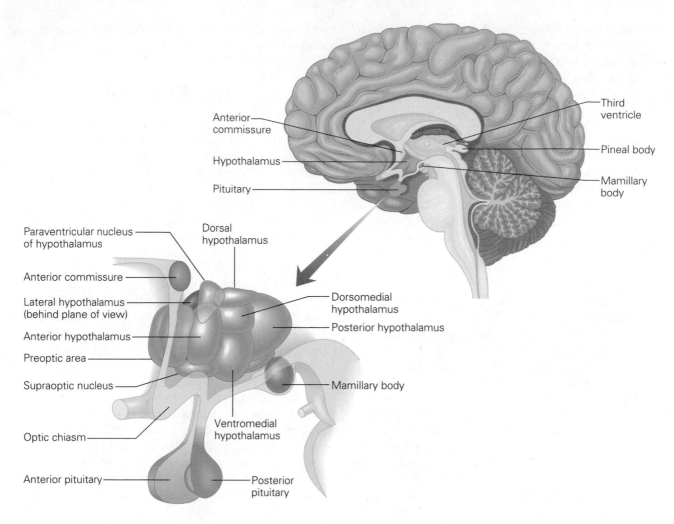

FIGURE **10.1**
Major subdivisions of the hypothalamus and pituitary
Source: After Nieuwenhuys, Voogd, & vanHuijzen, 1988.

hypothalamus, elsewhere in the brain, and in the spinal cord. Fragmentary shivering and sweating can still occur after preoptic area damage.

Behavioral Mechanisms

Although the body temperature of fish, amphibians, and reptiles matches that of their surroundings, it seldom fluctuates wildly, because they can choose their location within the environment. A desert lizard burrows into the ground in the middle of the day, when the surface is too hot, and again in the middle of the night, when the surface is too cold. On the surface, it will move from sun to shade as necessary to keep its temperature fairly constant.

Mammals, too, use behavioral means to regulate their body temperature. They do not sit shivering on an icy surface when they can build a nest, or sweat and pant in the sun when they can find a shady spot. The more they can regulate their temperature behaviorally, the less they need to rely on physiological efforts (Refinetti & Carlisle, 1986a).

During infancy, behavioral mechanisms compensate for inadequate physiological mechanisms (Alberts, 1978). For example, most young mammals and birds do not yet have their full complement of fur or feathers for insulation, and in cold air they lose a great deal of body heat to their environment. By huddling with others, they pool their body heat and decrease their heat loss (see Figure 10.2). As the ones on the outside of the group cool off, they burrow into the center of the mass while the warmer ones in the center passively drift to the outside.

Adult mammals with damaged preoptic areas can also regulate their temperature by behavioral means. In

ria, viruses, fungi, or other foreign bodies, it mobilizes, among other things, its *leukocytes* (white blood cells) to attack them. The leukocytes release a protein called *interleukin-1*, which in turn causes the production of **prostaglandin E₁** and **prostaglandin E₂,** which then cause cells in the preoptic area of the hypothalamus to raise body temperature (Scammell, Elmquist, Griffin, & Saper, 1996).

Newborn rabbits, whose hypothalamus is immature, do not shiver in response to infections. If they are given a choice of environments, however, they will select an unusually warm spot and thereby raise their body temperature (Satinoff, McEwen, & Williams, 1976). That is, they will develop a fever by behavioral rather than physiological means. Fish and reptiles do the same if they can find a warm enough environment (Kluger, 1978).

Does fever do an animal any good? Certain types of bacteria grow less vigorously at high temperatures than at normal mammalian body temperatures. Other things being equal, animals that develop moderate fevers have a better chance of surviving a bacterial infection than do animals that fail to develop a fever (Kluger, 1991). However, if the fever goes more than about 2.25° above normal body temperature, the probability of survival declines.

FIGURE **10.2**
Behavioral regulation of body temperature
A one-month-old emperor penguin chick is poorly insulated against antarctic temperatures that may easily drop to −30°C or worse. However, when a group of chicks huddle together tightly, they act in effect like one large, well-insulated organism. In fact, the cluster has to move frequently from one place to another, or it risks melting a hole in the ice and falling through!

Temperature Regulation and Behavior

When we are watching an animal's behavior and trying to interpret it, we can easily overlook the importance of temperature regulation. Let us consider two examples.

The Development of Animal Behavior

Over a number of years, psychologists observing the development of behavior in rats concluded that infant rats were incapable of certain behaviors and that the capacity for those behaviors developed at some point during the first three weeks or so of life (a much longer time in a rat's life than in a human's). The list of such behaviors included odor conditioning, female sexual behavior, certain aspects of eating and drinking, and others. After extensive attempts to study the developmental psychology of such behaviors, researchers discovered that rats could perform them all in the first week of life, sometimes even on the first day, in a warm enough room. The problem was simply that researchers generally work at "normal room temperature," perhaps 20°–23°C, which is comfortable for adult humans, but dangerously cold for an isolated baby rat. (See Figure

a cold environment, they will press a lever to keep a heat lamp on long enough to keep their body temperature near normal (Satinoff & Rutstein, 1970; Van Zoeren & Stricker, 1977). Behavioral regulation of temperature is partly under the control of the preoptic area, partly under the control of the posterior hypothalamus (Refinetti & Carlisle, 1986b), and partly under the control of other brain areas.

Fever

Bacterial and viral infections generally cause fever, an increase in body temperature. As a rule, the fever is not part of the illness; it is part of the body's defense against the illness. When the body is invaded by bacte-

FIGURE **10.3**
The special difficulties of temperature regulation for a newborn rodent
A newborn rat has no hair, thin skin, and little body fat. If left exposed in a cool room, its body temperature quickly falls. This difficulty in regulating body temperature impairs the young rat's performance in many psychological experiments.

FIGURE **10.4**
When a predator captures a young chick, the chick adopts a posture of "tonic immobility," failing to move for at least a few seconds, sometimes for hours. The cessation of this posture depends on changes in body temperature.

10.3.) In a room kept above 30°C, infant rats' behavioral capacities improve markedly (Satinoff, 1991). They also begin weaning sooner (Gerrish & Alberts, 1996).

The Tonic Immobility Response

When a baby bird is grabbed by a predator, its first response is generally to adopt a position known as **tonic immobility,** limp and almost motionless (Figure 10.4). Observers say the chick is feigning death. We should not consider this act intentional, although immobility does decrease the probability of being attacked. After all, predators attack a prey only until it stops moving. The chick gains an advantage because the predator might drop it or give it some other opportunity to escape. Granted, the chances are not good, but any chance is better than none at all.

The chick may remain limp for seconds or for hours. Within limits, the longer, the better; if it starts moving again too soon, the predator will react by attacking before the chick can escape. What determines how soon the chick stops feigning death? The answer is, simply, body temperature. A chick generates more body heat by moving than by sitting still, but moving also cools the chick by ventilation. A motionless chick gradually accumulates heat (unless the air is very cool). When its body temperature reaches 41.4°C (the normal body temperature of an adult chicken), it starts moving (Rovee-Collier, Kupersmidt, O'Brien, Collier, & Tepper, 1991). Moving incurs the risk of a possible attack by the predator, but staying still would incur the certain danger of overheating. The moral of the story: Even when we are studying dynamic behaviors such as predator-prey relations, we should not forget the importance of temperature regulation.

IN**CLOSING**

Temperature and Behavior

On one moderately warm summer day in northern Norway, I saw herds of reindeer carefully standing on patches of snow because the ground was too hot for their feet. Were they seeking snow because they need to maintain a low body temperature? No. Reindeer, like polar bears and other arctic and antarctic mammals and birds, maintain about the same body temperature as species that live in temperate or tropical environments. The difference is that polar species have so much insulation against the cold that they overheat when the environment *isn't* cold—much as you or I would if we wore our heaviest winter clothing on a normal fall afternoon.

In one way or another, every mammal and bird does what it needs to do to maintain a constant temperature. The actions include choice of location, eating, huddling with others, and a variety of other behavioral and autonomic processes. You might not think about your body temperature often, but it is essential for your survival.

Summary

1. Homeostasis is a tendency to maintain a body variable near a set point. Temperature, hunger, and thirst are almost homeostatic, but they anticipate future needs as well as reacting to current needs. (p. 270)
2. A constant body temperature enables a mammal or bird to be equally active at all environmental temperatures. (p. 271)
3. The preoptic area of the hypothalamus is critical for temperature control. It monitors both its own temperature and that of the skin and spinal cord. (p. 271)
4. Even homeothermic animals rely partly on behavioral mechanisms for temperature regulation, especially in infancy and after damage to the preoptic area. (p. 272)
5. Fever is caused by the release of prostaglandins, which stimulate cells in the preoptic area. A moderate fever helps an animal combat an infection. (p. 273)
6. Temperature regulation often influences behaviors that seem unrelated to temperature; for example, infant mammals tested in a cool environment may fail to show their full behavioral capacities. (p. 273)

Review Questions

1. In what ways are certain motivations homeostatic? (p. 270)
2. What evidence do we have that the preoptic area controls body temperature? (p. 271)
3. How can an animal regulate body temperature after damage to the preoptic area? (p. 272)
4. What processes in the brain are responsible for fevers? (p. 273)
5. After a predator has captured a chick, why does the chick feign death longer in a cool environment than in a warm environment? (p. 274)

Thought Question

1. Speculate on why birds have higher body temperatures than mammals. If you were asked to predict the body temperature of beings on some other planet, what would you first want to know about conditions on that planet?

Terms

basal metabolism   rate of energy use while the body is at rest, used largely for maintaining a constant body temperature (p. 270)

homeostasis   tendency to maintain a variable, such as temperature, within a fixed range (p. 270)

set point   level at which homeostatic processes maintain a variable (p. 270)

poikilothermic   maintaining the body at the same temperature as the environment (p. 270)

homeothermic   maintaining nearly constant body temperature over a wide range of environmental temperatures (p. 271)

preoptic area   brain area adjacent to the anterior hypothalamus, important for temperature control (p. 271)

prostaglandin E$_1$ and **prostaglandin E$_2$**   chemicals produced during an infection that stimulate an increase in body temperature (p. 273)

tonic immobility   limp and nearly motionless condition of the body's postural muscles (p. 274)

Thirst

Mammals regulate their body water either by frequent drinking, as beavers do, or by minimizing loss of water, as gerbils do.

Water constitutes about 70 percent of the mammalian body. Because the concentration of chemicals in water determines the rate of all chemical reactions in the body, the water must be regulated within narrow limits. The body also needs enough fluid in the circulatory system to maintain normal blood pressure.

Mechanisms of Water Regulation

We drink for a variety of reasons. We drink the greatest amount during meals, partly to wash down the food and partly in anticipation of the solutes about to enter the body's fluids (Kraly, 1990). We also drink just because a beverage tastes good or because we want to socialize. Thirst is activated only when drinking for these reasons does not get enough water into the system.

To maintain a constant amount of water in the body, we have to balance the water we lose with the water we take in. We take in water by drinking, of course, but also by eating. Certain foods, such as lettuce, contain a great deal of water, and even dry foods yield some water during digestion. We lose water by urinating, defecating, and sweating. We also lose a little in every breath that we exhale and a little by evaporation from the eyes, the mouth, and other moist body surfaces.

Different species have adopted different strategies for balancing water intake and loss. Beavers and other species that live in or near the water drink plenty of water and eat foods with a high water content; they excrete copious amounts of dilute urine and moist feces. However, gerbils and other desert animals may go through their entire lives without ever drinking; they gain a little water by eating, and they have many adaptations to avoid losing water. They excrete very dry feces and very concentrated urine. Unable to sweat, they avoid the heat of the day by burrowing deep under the ground. Their highly convoluted nasal passages minimize the amount of water lost when they exhale.

We humans vary our strategy, depending on circumstances. On the one hand, if you have access to ample supplies of highly palatable beverages, you will probably drink much and urinate much, as beavers do. You need not be concerned with drinking the right amount; your kidneys will discard the excess. (However, if you drink much without also eating, like many alcoholics, you will accidentally excrete enough body salts to do yourself some harm.) On the other hand, if you cannot find enough liquid that is good to drink, you will conserve your water, as gerbils do, mainly by decreasing the amount of water in your urine.

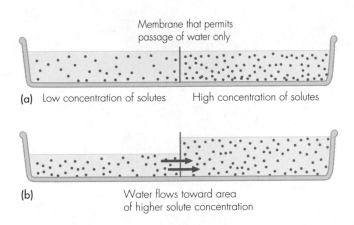

FIGURE **10.5**
Two dishes of solution separated by a semiperme-able membrane
(**a**) Two solutions of unequal solute concentration are introduced.
(**b**) Water flows by osmosis toward the area with a higher concentration of solutes.

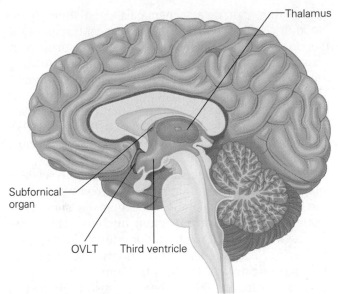

FIGURE **10.6**
The brain's receptors for osmotic pressure and blood volume
These neurons are in areas surrounding the third ventricle of the brain, where no blood-brain barrier prevents blood-borne chemicals from entering the brain. The OVLT (organum vaculosum laminae terminalis) is the primary area for detecting osmotic pressure. The subfornical organ is the primary area for detecting blood volume.   Source: Based in part on Weindl, 1973; and DeArmond, Fusco, & Dewey, 1974.

When your body needs water, it reacts not only with thirst but also with certain autonomic processes. The posterior pituitary (see Figure 10.1) releases a hormone called **vasopressin,** which raises blood pressure by constricting the blood vessels. (The term *vasopressin* comes from *vas*cular *press*ure.) The increased pressure helps compensate for the decreased volume. Vasopressin is also known as **antidiuretic hormone (ADH),** because it enables the kidneys to reabsorb water and therefore to secrete highly concentrated urine. (*Diuresis* means *urination.*) An increased need for water also provokes secretions of several other hormones that control the balance of fluid between the cells and the external spaces (Watts, Kelly, & Sanchez-Watts, 1995).

Osmotic Thirst

Although we speak about thirst as if it were a single entity, we experience one kind of thirst after an increase in the solute concentrations in the body and a different kind of thirst after a loss of overall fluid volume. Correspondingly, thirst researchers distinguish between *osmotic* thirst and *hypovolemic* thirst.

The combined concentration of all solutes in the body fluids remains at a nearly constant level of 0.15 M (molar) in mammals. (A concentration of 1.0 M has a number of grams of solute equal to the molecular weight of that solute, dissolved in 1 liter of solution.) This fixed concentration of solutes can be regarded as a set point, similar to the set point for temperature. Any deviation activates mechanisms that restore the concentration of solutes to the set point.

The solutes inside and outside a cell produce an **osmotic pressure,** the tendency of water to flow across a semipermeable membrane from the area of low solute concentration to the area of higher concentration. A semipermeable membrane is one through which water can pass, but not solutes. The membrane surrounding a cell is almost a semipermeable membrane, because water flows across it freely and various solutes flow either very slowly or not at all. The passage of water equalizes the concentrations on the two sides of the membrane (see Figure 10.5).

When someone consumes salt (NaCl), sodium ions spread through the blood and the fluid spaces between cells, but do not cross the membranes into cells. The result is a higher concentration of solutes outside the cells than inside. Similarly, loss of body water increases the concentration of solutes in the spaces outside cells. In either case, the resulting osmotic pressure draws water from the cells into the external spaces, triggering **osmotic thirst,** which helps restore the normal state. The kidneys also excrete a more concentrated urine to rid the body of excess sodium.

How does the brain know when osmotic pressure is low? It gets part of the information from receptors in areas around the third ventricle (Figure 10.6). These specialized areas are not protected by a blood-brain barrier;

hence, they can detect chemicals circulating in the blood, including the overall solute concentration of the blood (Ramsay & Thrasher, 1990). The area principally responsible for detecting osmotic pressure is known as the **OVLT** (organum vasculosum laminae terminalis). The brain also gets information from receptors in the periphery, including the stomach, that detect high levels of sodium (Kraly, Kim, Dunham, & Tribuzio, 1995), enabling the brain to anticipate an osmotic need before the rest of the body actually experiences it.

Receptors in the OVLT, the stomach, and elsewhere relay their information directly or indirectly to several parts of the hypothalamus, including the **supraoptic nucleus** and the **paraventricular nucleus,** which control the rate at which the posterior pituitary releases vasopressin. Receptors also relay information to the **lateral preoptic area** of the hypothalamus, where certain neurons control drinking. There are also a number of axons passing through the area that contribute to drinking. A lesion in the lateral preoptic area impairs osmotic thirst partly by damage to cell bodies and partly by damage to passing axons (Saad, Luiz, Camargo, Renzi, & Manani, 1996).

Hypovolemic Thirst

If blood volume, and therefore pressure, is too low, the blood cannot carry enough water and nutrients to the cells. The volume may drop sharply after a deep cut or internal hemorrhaging, triggering **hypovolemic** (HI-po-vo-LEE-mik) **thirst,** meaning *thirst based on low volume.* The body then needs to replenish not only its water but also the salts and other solutes that have been lost.

After a reduction in blood volume, an animal drinks more, but it will not drink much pure water, which would dilute its body fluids. It drinks much larger amounts of water containing salts (Stricker, 1969). If the animal is offered one container of pure water and another of excessively concentrated saltwater, it will alternate between the two to yield a mixture that matches the content of its blood.

Mechanisms

The body has two ways of detecting loss of blood volume (Epstein, 1990; Ramsay & Thrasher, 1990). First, **baroreceptors** attached to the large veins detect the pressure of blood returning to the heart. The second mechanism depends on hormones. When blood volume drops, the kidneys respond by releasing the hormone *renin.* Renin splits a portion off angiotensinogen,

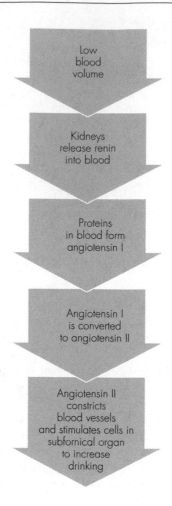

FIGURE **10.7**
Hormonal response to hypovolemia

a large protein that circulates in the blood, to form the hormone angiotensin I, which certain enzymes convert to the hormone **angiotensin II,** which constricts the blood vessels, compensating for the drop in blood pressure (see Figure 10.7).

When angiotensin reaches the brain, it stimulates neurons in the **subfornical organ,** which, like the OVLT area, adjoins the third ventricle of the brain. (See Figure 10.6.) Also like the OVLT, the subfornical organ lies outside the blood-brain barrier and is therefore well suited to monitor the blood. It relays information to the part of the preoptic area in the hypothalamus that directs drinking. Injecting angiotensin into the subfornical organ and adjacent areas can prompt drinking (Mangiapane & Simpson, 1980); injecting a drug that blocks angiotensin II receptors strongly inhibits drinking (Fregly & Rowland, 1991). These findings support the conclusion that angiotensin in the brain promotes certain types of thirst.

Angiotensin and baroreceptors have a **synergistic effect** (Epstein, 1983; Rowland, 1980). If two effects are

		TABLE **10.1**		
		Comparison of Osmotic and Hypovolemic Thirst		
Type of Thirst	Stimulus	Best Relieved by Drinking	Receptor Location	Hormone Influences
Osmotic thirst	High solute concentration outside cells causes loss of water from cells	Water	OVLT, a brain area adjoining the third ventricle	Accompanied by vasopressin secretion to conserve water
Hypovolemic thirst	Low blood volume	Saltwater or water containing other solutes	1. Baroreceptors, measuring blood flow returning to the heart 2. Subfornical organ, a brain area adjoining the third ventricle	Increased by angiotensin

synergistic, their combined effect is more than the sum of the two separate effects. That is, it may take less angiotensin to stimulate thirst if the baroreceptors also indicate low blood pressure than if they indicate normal blood pressure.

Table 10.1 summarizes the differences between osmotic thirst and hypovolemic thirst.

Sodium-Specific Cravings

Many people today limit their salt intake to control high blood pressure. However, although excessive salt can be harmful to people with high blood pressure, moderate amounts are necessary for life.

Individuals who have lost sodium and other solutes by bleeding or heavy sweating may experience a craving for salty tastes along with their hypovolemic thirst. That increased preference develops automatically, apparently without any trial-and-error learning (Richter, 1936). Sodium-specific cravings are the only known specific hunger that emerges as soon as the need exists; specific hungers for other vitamins and minerals have to be learned by trial and error (Rozin & Kalat, 1971).

Sodium hunger depends largely on hormones (Schulkin, 1991). When the body's sodium reserves are low, the adrenal glands produce the hormone **aldosterone,** which causes the kidneys, salivary glands, and sweat glands to conserve sodium and excrete more watery fluids than usual (Verrey & Beron, 1996). Aldosterone also acts on the OVLT and other areas surrounding the third ventricle to trigger an increased intake of salty foods. The body also reacts to decreased sodium reserves by increasing the blood concentrations of angiotensin II, which increases sodium hunger (Sato, Yada, & De Luca, 1996).

The effects of aldosterone and angiotensin are strongly synergistic, perhaps because they act on different parts of the brain. Either one alone produces a small increase in sodium intake; together they produce a much greater effect (Sakai & Epstein, 1990; Stricker, 1983).

IN**CLOSING**

The Psychology and Biology of Thirst

You may have thought that temperature regulation happens automatically and that water regulation depends on your behavior. You can see now that the distinction is not entirely correct. You control your body temperature partly by automatic means such as sweating or shivering, but also partly by behavioral means such as choosing a warm or a cool place. You control your body water partly by the behavior of drinking, but also by changes in kidney activity. If your kidneys cannot regulate your water and sodium adequately, your brain gets signals to change your drinking or sodium intake. In short, keeping your body's chemical reactions going depends on both skeletal and autonomic controls.

Summary

1. Different mammalian species have evolved different ways of maintaining body water, ranging from frequent drinking (beavers) to extreme conservation of fluids (gerbils). Humans alter their strategy, depending on the availability of acceptable fluids. (p. 276)

2. An increase in the osmotic pressure of the blood draws water out of cells, causing osmotic thirst. Neurons in the OVLT, an area adjoining the third ventricle, detect changes in osmotic pressure and send information to hypothalamic areas responsible for vasopressin secretion and for drinking. (p. 277)

3. Loss of blood volume causes hypovolemic thirst. Animals with hypovolemic thirst drink more water containing solutes than pure water. The subfornical organ is especially important for detecting changes in blood volume and sending information to trigger hypovolemic thirst. (p. 278)

4. Two stimuli have been identified for hypovolemic thirst: signals from the baroreceptors and the hormone angiotensin II, which increases when blood pressure falls. The two stimuli apparently act synergistically. (p. 278)
5. Loss of sodium salts from the body triggers sodium-specific cravings. The hormones aldosterone and angiotensin II synergistically stimulate such cravings. (p. 279)

Review Questions

1. What hormones help the body compensate for decreased body fluids, and what do they do? (pp. 277, 278)
2. What is osmotic pressure? (p. 277)
3. What is the difference between osmotic and hypovolemic thirst? (p. 278)
4. Which hormones synergistically promote a craving for salty tastes? (p. 279)

Thought Questions

1. An injection of concentrated sodium chloride triggers osmotic thirst, but an injection of equally concentrated glucose does not. Why not?
2. Many women crave salt during menstruation or pregnancy. Why?

Terms

vasopressin, also known as **antidiuretic hormone (ADH)** pituitary hormone that raises blood pressure and enables the kidneys to reabsorb water and therefore to secrete highly concentrated urine (p. 277)

osmotic pressure tendency of water to flow across a semipermeable membrane from the area of low solute concentration to the area of high solute concentration (p. 277)

osmotic thirst thirst that results from an increase in the concentration of solutes in the body (p. 277)

OVLT organum vasculosum laminae terminalis, a brain structure on the border of the third ventricle; it is highly sensitive to the osmotic pressure of the blood (p. 278)

supraoptic nucleus and **paraventricular nucleus** two areas of the hypothalamus that control secretion of vasopressin (p. 278)

lateral preoptic area portion of the hypothalamus that includes some cells that facilitate drinking and some that inhibit it, as well as passing axons that are important for osmotic thirst (p. 278)

hypovolemic thirst thirst provoked by low blood volume (p. 278)

baroreceptor receptor that detects the blood pressure in the largest blood veins (p. 278)

angiotensin II hormone that constricts the blood vessels, contributing to hypovolemic thirst (p. 278)

subfornical organ brain structure adjoining the third ventricle of the brain, where its cells monitor blood volume and relay information to the preoptic area of the hypothalamus (p. 278)

synergistic effect tendency for two combined influences to produce more than the sum of their separate effects (p. 278)

aldosterone adrenal hormone that causes the kidneys to conserve sodium when excreting urine (p. 279)

Hunger

FIGURE **10.8**
A python swallowing a gazelle
The gazelle weighs about 50 percent more than the snake. Although some reptiles eat enormous meals, their energy needs are much lower than those of homeothermic animals. By the time this snake eats again, your own total intake will be vastly larger than a gazelle.

Homeothermic animals, including ourselves, need to eat frequently in order to obtain adequate nutrients. Poikilothermic animals, such as reptiles, consume far less energy, although some of them eat enormous meals when they do eat. The snake shown in Figure 10.8 will not have to eat again for months. For homeothermic animals, however, the search for food is an almost constant concern.

How the Digestive System Influences Food Selection

Before discussing hunger, let's quickly examine the digestive system, diagrammed in Figure 10.9. Its function is to break the food down into smaller molecules that

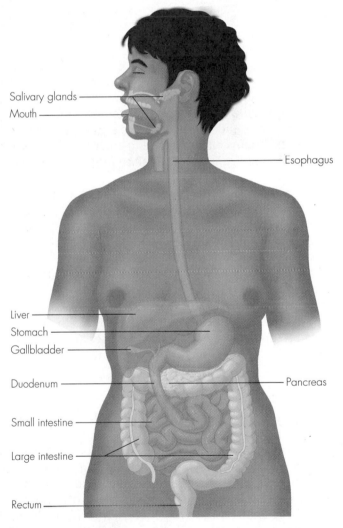

FIGURE **10.9**
The human digestive system

the cells can use. Digestion begins in the mouth, where food is mixed with saliva, which contains enzymes that help break down carbohydrates. When swallowed, the food travels down the esophagus to the stomach, where

FIGURE **10.10**
Distribution of adult lactose tolerance
People in areas with high lactose tolerance (such as Scandinavia) are likely to enjoy milk, cheese, and other dairy products throughout their lives. People in areas with low tolerance (such as much of Asia) do not ordinarily consume milk or dairy products as adults. Source: Based on Flatz, 1987; and Rozin & Pelchat, 1988.

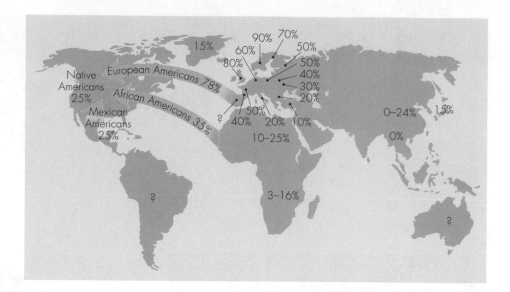

it is mixed with hydrochloric acid and several enzymes that digest proteins. Between the stomach and the intestines is a round sphincter muscle that periodically opens just briefly, allowing food to enter the intestines. Thus, the stomach is a storage place for food as well as a digestive organ.

Food then passes to the small intestine, which contains enzymes that help digest proteins, fats, and carbohydrates. It is also the main site for the absorption of digested foodstuffs into the bloodstream. Digested materials absorbed through the small intestine are carried by the blood to body cells that will use some of the nutrients and store the excess as glycogen, protein, or fat. Later, these reserves are converted into glucose, the body's primary fuel, which is mobilized into the bloodstream. The large intestine absorbs water and minerals and lubricates the remaining materials to pass them as feces.

Enzymes and Consumption of Dairy Products

Newborn mammals survive entirely on a diet of mother's milk. Why do they stop nursing when they grow older? There are several reasons: The milk dries up, the mother pushes the infants away, the infants grow large enough to try other foods. Moreover, after a certain age, most mammals lose their ability to metabolize **lactose,** the sugar in milk, because of declining levels of the intestinal enzyme **lactase.** From then on, consumption of milk can cause gas, stomach cramps, or other signs of distress (Rozin & Pelchat, 1988). Adult mammals can drink a little milk, as you may have noticed with a pet dog, but they generally limit the amount. The declining level of lactase may be an

evolved mechanism to encourage weaning at the appropriate time.

Humans are the partial exception to this rule. Many adults consume milk, cheese, ice cream, and other products derived from cow or goat milk, and their intestinal lactase levels remain at fairly high levels throughout life. Worldwide, however, most adults cannot comfortably tolerate large amounts of milk products. About two-thirds of all adult humans have low levels of lactase because of a recessive gene (Flatz, 1987). Most of these people can eat moderate amounts of dairy products but develop cramps or gas pains if they consume too much. A smaller number of people can consume almost no dairy products at all. Figure 10.10 shows the worldwide distribution of lactose tolerance. Note that most people with ancestry from northern or western Europe tolerate lactose and have no trouble digesting dairy products. Most Asians have much lower tolerance; the distribution of lactose tolerance is spotty in Africa.

Other Influences on Food Selection

For some animal species, selecting a suitable diet is easy; for others, it can be rather difficult. A **carnivore** (meat eater) has a relatively simple task; it eats any animal it can catch. However, **herbivores** (plant eaters) and **omnivores** (those that eat both meat and plants) must distinguish between edible and inedible substances.

One way to do so is to learn from the experiences of others. For example, juvenile rats tend to imitate the food selections of their elders, including some apparently unpalatable foods (Galef, 1992). Similarly, children in different cultures develop very different food preferences (Rozin, 1990). Humans will reject foods for reasons that would not concern any other species. For example, many people would refuse to eat something after watching a cockroach walk across it (Rozin, 1996).

If you parachuted onto an uninhabited island covered with unfamiliar plants, you would use a variety of behavioral strategies to select edible foods (Rozin & Vollmecke, 1986). First, you would let taste be your guide. Most naturally occurring sweet substances contain carbohydrates, an important part of our diet. If you needed more salt, you would crave salty tastes, as described earlier. You also have an innate dislike for bitter tastes, which characterize many dangerous foods (Richter, 1950).

Second, you would probably seek something that resembled a familiar food. The first time that you try anything with a strong new flavor—coffee, for example—you probably do not like it as much as you will later. After all, familiar foods are safe, and new foods may not be.

Third, you would learn the consequences of eating various foods. You are likely to associate nausea or similar distress with foods that you have eaten in the past hour or so, especially unfamiliar foods (Rozin & Kalat, 1971; Rozin & Zellner, 1985). By rejecting foods that make you ill, you select more acceptable foods. You also learn which foods satisfy your hunger. Animals prefer flavors of foods that contain sucrose or other high-calorie substances; they show much less preference for flavors paired with saccharin, a good tasting but nutritionally useless substance (Mehiel, 1991). Presumably you, too, enjoy fruit flavors because they are associated with nutrition.

How Taste and Digestion Control Hunger

Eating is far too important to be entrusted to just one mechanism. Your brain gets messages from the mouth, the stomach, the intestines, and elsewhere indicating what to eat, how much, and when.

Oral Factors

People eat partly for the sake of taste. In one experiment, college students consumed lunch five days a week without tasting it. Each swallowed one end of a rubber tube and then pushed a button to pump a liquid diet into his or her stomach (Jordan, 1969; Spiegel, 1973). After a few days of practice, each subject established a consistent pattern, pumping in a constant volume of the liquid each day and maintaining a constant body weight. Most subjects found the untasted meals unsatisfying, however, reporting a desire to taste or chew something. Moreover, when they were allowed to drink the liquid diet in the normal manner while also receiving it through the stomach tube, they drank almost as much as they would have had they received nothing through the tube (Jordan, 1969).

Eating is also sustained by other facial sensations. A rat explores a potential food with its mouth and whiskers before it starts to eat. The tactile sensations are conveyed to the brain via the fifth cranial nerve (the trigeminal nerve). After that nerve is cut, a rat decreases its exploration and biting of foods. It can still eat moist, soft foods, using its jaw as a scoop, but it loses weight. It not only fails to eat properly, but it also will not press a bar as often as normal for food reinforcement. Evidently, loss of sensation from the mouth leads to a drop in food-related motivation (Zeigler, Jacquin, & Miller, 1985).

Although taste and other oral sensations contribute to the regulation of eating, they are not sufficient by themselves to end a meal. In **sham-feeding** experiments, an animal is denied nutrition because everything it swallows leaks out a tube connected to the esophagus or stomach. Under such conditions, animals swallow several times as much as normal during each meal (Antin, Gibbs, Holt, Young, & Smith, 1975).

The Stomach and Intestines

Ordinarily, we end a meal before much of the food has reached the blood, much less the cells that need fuel. Do we stop eating simply because the stomach is full? In one experiment, researchers attached an inflatable cuff at the connection between the stomach and the small intestine (Deutsch, Young, & Kalogeris, 1978). When they inflated the cuff, food could not pass from the stomach to the duodenum. They carefully ensured that the cuff was not traumatic to the animal and did not interfere with feeding, even when inflated. With the cuff inflated, an animal would eat a normal-size meal and then stop; that is, it could become satisfied even though the food did not go beyond the stomach. These results suggested that satiety depends on stomach distension.

The stomach conveys satiety messages to the brain via the vagus nerve and the splanchnic nerves. The **vagus nerve** (cranial nerve X) conveys information about the stretching of the stomach walls, providing a major basis for satiety. The **splanchnic** (SPLANK-nik) **nerves** convey information about the nutrient contents of the stomach, carrying impulses from the thoracic and lumbar parts of the spinal cord to the digestive organs and from the digestive organs to the spinal cord (Deutsch & Ahn, 1986). After damage to the vagus nerve, messages from the splanchnic nerves can compensate well enough to control meal size under most circumstances (Davis, Smith, & Kung, 1994).

Is stomach distension the *only* part of the digestive system important for satiety? Later researchers repeated the experiment with the inflatable cuff and replicated the result that a rat ate the same amount regardless of whether the cuff was open or closed, indicating that stomach distension is *sufficient* for satiety. However, when the cuff was open, much of the food passed into the intestines before the rat stopped eating (Seeley, Kaplan, & Grill, 1995). So the rat ended its meal even though the stomach was far from full. Evidently, we monitor not just the amount of food in the stomach, but the total amount in the digestive system, and it does not matter how much is in the stomach and how much in the intestines.

The **duodenum** (DYOU-oh-DEE-num or dyuh-ODD-ehn-uhm) is the part of the small intestine adjoining the stomach; it is the first digestive site that absorbs a significant amount of nutrients. Glucose infused directly to the duodenum of human volunteers produces quick reports of satiety; the same amount of glucose infused directly to the blood has no such effect (Lavin et al., 1996). So, evidently glucose produces satiety either through receptors in the duodenum or by causing the duodenum to release hormones with a satiating effect. Curiously, although infused or eaten sugars have a quick satiating effect, fats produce only weak sensations of satiety until after they are digested several hours later (Horn, Tordoff, & Friedman, 1996). As a result, both rats and humans on high-fat diets tend to overeat.

One way by which food in the duodenum inhibits appetite is by stimulating the duodenum to release the hormone **cholecystokinin** (ko-leh-SIS-teh-KI-nehn) (**CCK**). Injections of CCK do not prevent or delay a meal, but they decrease its size (Pi-Sunyer, Kissileff, Thornton, & Smith, 1982), partly because CCK closes the sphincter muscle between the stomach and the duodenum, causing the stomach to fill more quickly than it would have (McHugh & Moran, 1985). Closing the sphincter muscle is probably not the only mechanism by which intestinal CCK decreases appetite, but the other mechanisms almost certainly relate to digestion as well. CCK is also a neurotransmitter in the brain, and in that role it does tend to decrease eating. However, the CCK from the intestines does not cross the blood-brain barrier in significant quantities. The fact that brain CCK and intestinal CCK have similar behavioral effects is an interesting coincidence suggesting that evolution uses the same chemicals in different places for similar purposes.

Blood Glucose

Much of the digested food that enters the bloodstream is in the form of glucose. An important source of energy for all parts of the body, glucose is by far the most important fuel of the brain. Jean Mayer (1953) proposed that the supply of glucose to the cells is the primary basis for hunger and satiety. According to this hypothesis, hunger is a response to too little glucose in the cells; satiety is a response to adequate glucose. Later research has demonstrated that the brain has its own receptors for glucose, concentrated in the hypothalamus (Bernardis & Bellinger, 1996).

Glucose, however, is certainly not the only factor controlling hunger and satiety. Even fructose, a sugar that does not cross the blood-brain barrier and that cannot be converted to glucose, can suppress hunger. Hunger and satiety must be based on the total availability of nutrients (Kupfermann, 1994).

The level of glucose in the blood varies little under normal conditions (LeMagnen, 1981). Even during a prolonged period of fasting, the liver converts stored nutrients into glucose to maintain blood glucose levels. However, the availability of glucose to the cells can vary significantly as a function of changes in blood levels of two pancreatic hormones, insulin and glucagon. **Insulin** facilitates the entry of glucose into the cells, which may either use the glucose for current energy needs or store it as fat or glycogen. **Glucagon** has the reverse effect, stimulating the liver to convert stored glycogen to glucose, thus raising blood glucose levels. After a meal, insulin levels rise, much glucose enters the cells, and appetite decreases. As time passes, the blood glucose level falls, the pancreas releases more glucagon and less insulin, and hunger returns (Figure 10.11).

Generally, when insulin levels are high, hunger is low, because the blood is supplying the cells with glucose. However, if the insulin level remains high well after the last meal, the body continues to move blood glucose into the cells, and liver cells and fat cells continue to store it as glycogen and fats. Consequently, the available blood glucose begins to decline. For example, in late autumn, migratory and hibernating species have high insulin levels and low glucagon levels. They rapidly deposit much of each meal as fat and glycogen, grow hungry again, and continue gaining weight in preparation for a period without food (Figure 10.12). Similarly, people with chronically high insulin levels tend to eat much and gain weight.

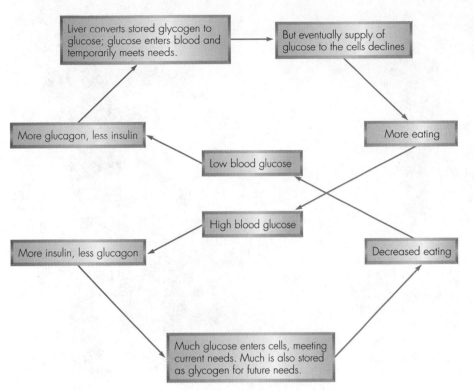

FIGURE **10.11**
Insulin and glucagon feed-back system
When glucose levels rise, the pancreas releases the hormone insulin, which causes cells to store the excess glucose as fats and glycogen. The entry of glucose into cells suppresses hunger. Lack of hunger leads to decreased eating, which lowers the glucose level; the pancreas releases glucagon, which stimulates the liver to convert stored glycogen into glucose, which enters the blood. The high ratio of glucagon to insulin also stimulates hunger, and the cycle repeats.

When the insulin level is extremely low, as in people with diabetes, blood glucose levels may exceed triple the normal level. However, little of the glucose can enter the cells (Figure 10.13). Diabetic people and animals eat more food than normal because their cells are starving (Lindberg, Coburn, & Stricker, 1984), but they lose weight because they excrete most of their glucose unused. (Note the paradox that both high and very low levels of insulin can lead to increased eating, although for different reasons. To maintain normal body

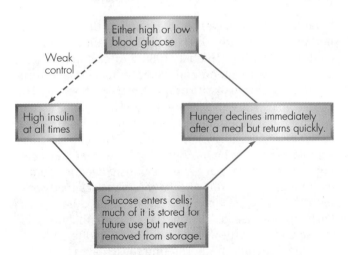

FIGURE **10.12**
Effects of steadily high insulin levels on feeding
Even when the glucose level is low, insulin remains high and much of the blood glucose is stored as fats and glycogen. Consequently, the blood's supply of glucose quickly drops and hunger returns.

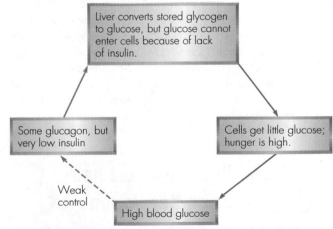

FIGURE **10.13**
Untreated diabetics eat much but lose weight
Because of their low insulin levels, the glucose in their blood cannot enter the cells, either to be stored or to be used. Consequently, they excrete glucose in their urine while their cells are starving.

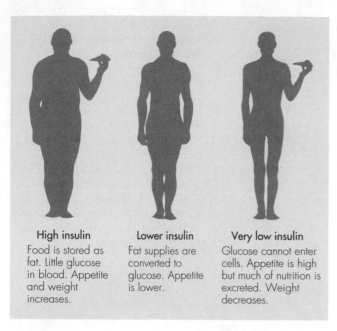

FIGURE **10.14**
Effects of insulin on glucose, appetite, and weight
People with high insulin levels eat much and gain weight; people with very low levels also eat a great deal but excrete much of what they eat.

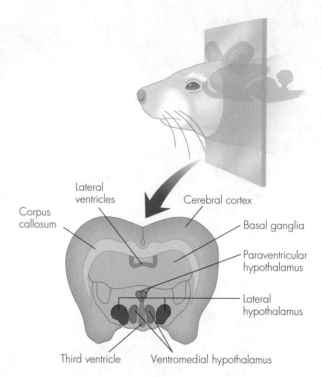

FIGURE **10.15**
The lateral hypothalamus, ventromedial hypothalamus, and paraventricular hypothalamus
The side view above indicates the plane of the coronal section of the brain below.   Source: After Hart, 1976.

weight, it is best to have an intermediate level of insulin.)

People produce more insulin not only when they eat but also when they are getting ready to eat. Increased insulin before a meal prepares the body to let more glucose enter the cells and to store the excess part of the meal as fats. However, obese people produce more insulin than do people of normal weight (Johnson & Wildman, 1983). Their high levels of insulin cause more of their food than normal to be stored as fat, and therefore their appetite returns sooner than normal after a meal (see Figure 10.14).

The Hypothalamus and Feeding Regulation

Damage to small areas of the hypothalamus can produce severe undereating or overeating. At one time, researchers described the lateral hypothalamus as a feeding center and the ventromedial hypothalamus as a satiety center. We now regard that view as an oversimplification, and we seek a better understanding of how various areas contribute to the control of feeding.

The Lateral Hypothalamus

Several kinds of evidence indicate that the **lateral hypothalamus** (Figure 10.15) is an important area for the control of feeding (Hoebel, 1988). After damage here, an animal refuses food and water, grimacing and turning its head away, as if the food were distasteful. The animal may starve to death unless it is force-fed, in which case it gradually recovers much of its ability to eat. (See Figure 10.16.) In an intact animal, electrical stimulation of the lateral hypothalamus stimulates eating and responses that have previously been reinforced with food. That is, the stimulation increases food-seeking behaviors, not just chewing or some other reflex. Furthermore, neurons in the lateral hypothalamus increase their activity when a hungry rat is offered food.

One difficulty in interpreting these data is that any electrode that damages or stimulates the lateral hypothalamus strikes not only the cell bodies in that area but also a number of dopamine-containing axons that happen to pass through. To deal with this problem, investigators developed several ways to limit the damage to either the axons or the cells. For example, they may

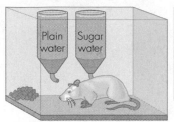

Stage 1. *Aphagia and adipsia.* Rat refuses all food and drink; must be force-fed to keep it alive.

Stage 2. *Anorexia.* Rat eats a small amount of palatable foods and drinks sweetened water. It still does not eat enough to stay alive.

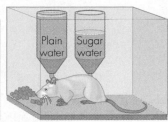

Stage 3. *Adipsia.* The rat eats enough to stay alive, though at a lower-than-normal body weight. It still refuses plain water.

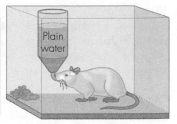

Stage 4. *Near-recovery.* The rat eats enough to stay alive, though at a lower-than-normal body weight. It drinks plain water, but only at mealtimes to wash down its food. Under slightly stressful conditions, such as in a cold room, the rat will return to an earlier stage of refusing food and water.

FIGURE **10.16**
Recovery of feeding after damage to the lateral hypothalamus
At first the rat refuses all food and drink. If kept alive for several weeks or months by force-feeding, it gradually recovers its ability to eat and drink enough to stay alive. However, even at the final stage of recovery, its behavior is not the same as that of normal rats.   Source: Based on Teitelbaum & Epstein, 1962.

inject 6-hydroxydopamine (6-OHDA), which damages passing axons that contain dopamine, but spares most of the cell bodies in the hypothalamus. Experiments of this type indicate that although damage to the dopamine-containing axons leaves an animal chronically inactive and unresponsive, it eats normally once it has food in its mouth (Berridge, Venier, & Robinson, 1989).

In other studies, experimenters found ways to damage the cell bodies without damaging the passing axons. The result was a major loss of feeding with relatively little loss of arousal or responsiveness to stimuli (Almli, Fisher, & Hill, 1979; Grossman, Dacey, Halaris, Collier, & Routtenberg, 1978; Stricker, Swerdloff, & Zigmond, 1978). Evidently, the cell bodies of the lateral hypothalamus contribute mainly to feeding, and the passing fibers contribute to overall arousal or to reinforcement of complex behaviors.

The question remains: *How* does the lateral hypothalamus contribute to feeding? It contributes in several ways (Hernandez, Murzi, Schwartz, & Hoebel, 1992). First, axons from the lateral hypothalamus extend to the NTS (nucleus of the tractus solitarius) in the medulla, part of the pathway responsive to taste (see p. 204). Information from the lateral hypothalamus modifies the activity of some of the NTS cells, either altering the taste sensation or increasing the salivation response to the tastes. Second, the lateral hypothalamus also activates a circuit that excites dopamine-containing cells, thereby initiating and reinforcing learned be-

haviors in a number of ways. Third, axons from the lateral hypothalamus extend into several forebrain structures, facilitating ingestion and swallowing, and causing cortical cells to increase their response to the taste, smell, or sight of food (Critchley & Rolls, 1996). (See Figure 10.17.) Fourth, activity in the lateral hypothalamus stimulates the release of insulin by the pancreas and digestive juices by the stomach (Morley, Bartness, Gosnell, & Levine, 1985). After damage to the lateral hypothalamus, the levels of insulin and digestive juices are low, and the animal has difficulty digesting its foods. An animal with decreased insulin levels converts much of its fat reserves into blood glucose, and thus has fairly high levels of blood sugar even without eating.

Medial Areas of the Hypothalamus

Near the lateral hypothalamus is a set of areas that contribute very differently to feeding. Neuroscientists have known since the 1940s that a large lesion centered on the **ventromedial hypothalamus** (Figure 10.15) leads to overeating and weight gain. Some people with a tumor in that area have gained more than 10 kg (22 pounds) per month (Al-Rashid, 1971; Killeffer & Stern, 1970; Reeves & Plum, 1969). Rats with similar damage sometimes double or triple their weight (Figure 10.18). Eventually, body weight levels off at a stable but high set point, and total food intake declines to nearly normal levels.

FIGURE **10.17**
Pathways from the lateral hypothalamus

Axons from the lateral hypothalamus modify activity in several other brain areas, changing the response to taste, facilitating ingestion and swallowing, and increasing food-seeking behaviors. Also (not shown), the lateral hypothalamus controls stomach secretions and insulin production.

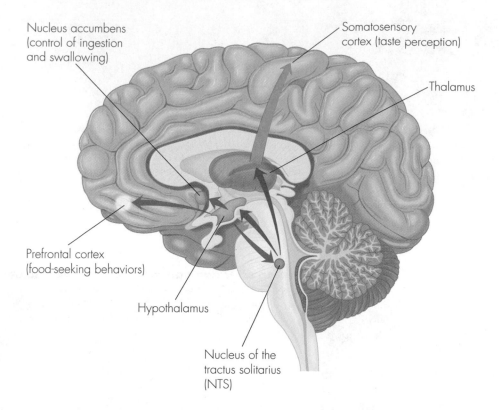

Nucleus accumbens (control of ingestion and swallowing)

Somatosensory cortex (taste perception)

Thalamus

Prefrontal cortex (food-seeking behaviors)

Hypothalamus

Nucleus of the tractus solitarius (NTS)

Although these symptoms are generally known as the *ventromedial hypothalamic syndrome,* damage limited to the ventromedial hypothalamic nucleus itself does not consistently produce large increases in eating or body weight. To produce a large effect, the lesion must extend outside the ventromedial nucleus to invade nearby medial hypothalamic cells and axons. Excess eating and increased body weight can also result from damage to the ventral noradrenergic bundle (Figure 10.19), an ascending axon pathway through the hypothalamus (Ahlskog & Hoebel, 1973; Ahlskog, Randall, & Hoebel, 1975; Gold, 1973).

Rats with damage in and around the ventromedial hypothalamus are finicky eaters. With a normal or

FIGURE **10.18**
The effects of damage to the ventromedial hypothalamus

(**a**) On the right is a normal rat. On the left is a rat after damage to the ventromedial hypothalamus. The brain-damaged rat may weigh up to three times as much as a normal rat. (**b**) Changes in weight and eating in a rat after damage to the ventromedial hypothalamus. Within a few days after the operation, the rat begins eating much more than normal. As it gains weight, its eating decreases, although it remains above normal.   Source: Adapted from Teitelbaum, 1961.

(a)

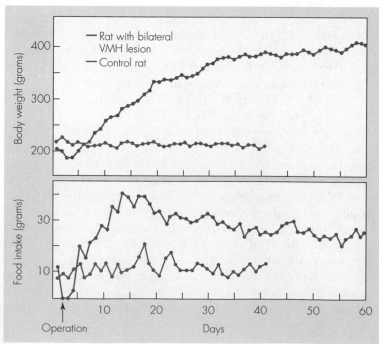

(b)

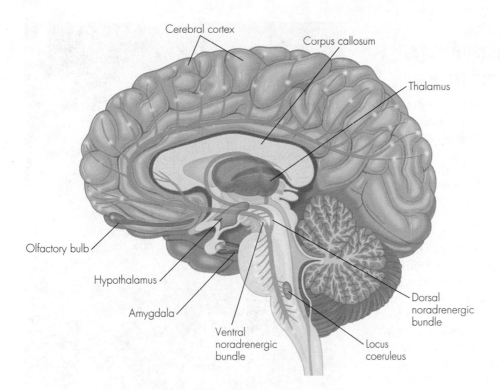

Cerebral cortex
Corpus callosum
Thalamus
Olfactory bulb
Hypothalamus
Amygdala
Ventral noradrenergic bundle
Locus coeruleus
Dorsal noradrenergic bundle

FIGURE **10.19**
Major norepinephrine pathways in the human brain
Damage to the ventral noradrenergic bundle leads to overeating and weight gain.   Source: Based on Valzelli, 1980.

sweetened diet, they overeat, sometimes eating day and night instead of sleeping. Yet they eat far less than normal on a bitter or otherwise untasty diet (Ferguson & Keesey, 1975; Teitelbaum, 1955). Consequently, we cannot say that the rats show an overall increase in hunger. We should also not say that they lack satiety. They eat normal-sized meals, demonstrating satiety at the normal time, but they eat more frequently than normal, for several reasons (Hoebel & Hernandez, 1993). First, they have increased stomach motility and secretions, and their stomachs empty faster than normal. The faster the stomach empties, the sooner an animal is ready for its next meal. Second, the damage leads to a lasting increase in insulin production (King, Smith, & Frohman, 1984), so a larger-than-normal percentage of

each meal is stored as fat. If animals with this kind of damage are prevented from overeating, they gain weight anyway! Mark Friedman and Edward Stricker (1976) have therefore proposed that the animal does not get fat because it overeats; rather, it has to overeat because it stores so much fat and has little fuel left over for its current needs.

Rats with damage in the nearby **paraventricular nucleus (PVN)** of the hypothalamus also overeat, but for a different reason. Instead of eating more frequent meals, they eat larger meals, as if they were insensitive to the usual signals for ending a meal (Leibowitz, Hammer, & Chang, 1981). Table 10.2 summarizes the effects of lesions in several areas of the hypothalamus.

TABLE **10.2**

Effects of Lesions in Certain Hypothalamic Areas

Hypothalamic Area	Effect of Lesion
Preoptic area	Deficit in physiological mechanisms of temperature regulation
Lateral preoptic area	Deficit in osmotic thirst, due partly to damage to cells and partly to interruption of passing axons
Lateral hypothalamus	Undereating, weight loss, low insulin level (because of damage to cell bodies); underarousal, underresponsiveness (because of damage to passing axons)
Ventromedial hypothalamus	Increased meal frequency, weight gain, high insulin level
Paraventricular nucleus	Increased meal size, especially increased carbohydrate intake during the first meal of the active period of the day

Genetics, Neurotransmitters, and Feeding Regulation

Contrast two possible strategies of eating: eating only what you need at the moment, and eating all you can because you might not find more food later. Which is the better strategy?

It depends on whether it is hard to find food and what the consequences are of carrying extra weight. Most small birds have almost no fat at all; their ability to survive depends on their ability to fly away from danger, so extra weight could be costly. They shift their strategies, however, when food is hard to find. Then they eat larger meals, accepting the cost of being a bit slower to decrease the risk of starving tomorrow. They also change their strategies depending on predators. The great tit, a small European bird similar to North American chickadees (Figure 10.20), is ordinarily a very slim, trim bird. During the 1960s, however, human use of the insecticide DDT almost eliminated the sparrow hawk, the tit's main predator. Tits then started eating more and getting fat. With no predators to worry about, speed was not an issue. When DDT was banned, enabling sparrow hawks to make a comeback in the 1970s, the tits "dieted" promptly, losing weight and gaining speed (Gosler, Greenwood, & Perrins, 1995).

Through evolutionary time, probably more people have died in famines than because they were too heavy to outrun a predator. As a result, we evidently evolved a strategy of eating plenty of food whenever we could find it. Today, people in prosperous countries have an abundance of tasty, high-calorie food, and an obesity problem that seldom occurred in times past. Efforts to understand the physiology of satiety have the practical prospects of helping people who have trouble restraining their appetites.

FIGURE **10.20**
A great tit, a small European bird
Ordinarily, when food is abundant, tits eat just what they need each day and maintain very low fat reserves. When food is harder to find, they eat all they can and live off fat reserves between meals. During one era when their predators were scarce, tits started putting on more fat, regardless of the food supplies.

Genetics, Metabolic Rate, and Body Weight

You have probably noticed that most thin parents have thin children and most heavy parents have heavy children. The resemblance no doubt relates in part to food choices, but genetics also plays a major role. A Danish study found that the weights of 540 adopted children correlated much more strongly with those of their biological relatives than with those of their adoptive relatives (Stunkard et al., 1986).

Genes can control body weight in many ways, including metabolic rate (Bogardus et al., 1986). People with higher metabolic rates produce more heat than others do and radiate it to their environment, thereby maintaining a low weight. People with lower metabolic rates generate less heat and conserve it better, therefore gaining weight even without overeating. Overweight people sometimes try to increase their energy expenditure through exercise. Suppose you try to lose weight by becoming more active. You walk 4.5 km (a little less than 3 miles). How much energy did you use? Enough to notice when you step on the bathroom scales tomorrow morning? Sorry. For an average person, that amount of exercise expends only about 150 kcal—the equivalent of 28 g (about an ounce) of potato chips (Burton, 1994). You could increase your energy output further by exercising longer and more strenuously, but

FIGURE **10.21**
The effects of the *obese* gene on body weight in mice
A gene that has been located on a mouse chromosome leads to increased eating, decreased metabolic rate, and increased weight gain. Source: From Zhang et al., 1994.

it is not easy to lose much weight just by exercising. Fortunately (or unfortunately, depending on your point of view), human muscles are fairly efficient and do not use enormous amounts of energy.

So the answer is to diet, right? Well, yes, but dieting often has disappointing results also. Part of the difficulty is that when someone decreases food intake, the body reacts by decreasing metabolic rate (Brownell, Greenwood, Stellar, & Shrager, 1986; McMinn, 1984). If you adhere to a low-calorie diet, your metabolic rate will decrease and you will burn fewer calories. I am not saying that weight loss is impossible; many people certainly do lose weight (sometimes a great deal) through a combination of dieting and exercise, and some even manage to keep their weight down permanently. What I am saying is that losing weight is difficult.

Leptin

Animals also have genetic differences that influence body weight, enabling researchers to study the mechanisms of certain genetic differences in greater detail. Figure 10.21 compares two normal mice to one mouse with a gene known (for obvious reasons) as *obese* (Zhang et al., 1994). After researchers located this gene, they identified a previously unknown protein that the normal gene makes, now known as **leptin** (Halaas et al., 1995). In genetically normal mammals (not just mice), fat cells throughout the body produce leptin: The more fat cells, the more leptin. Leptin circulates

through the blood, notifying the rest of the body about the current fat supplies. When leptin levels are high, hunger levels decrease (Campfield, Smith, Guisez, Devos, & Burn, 1995), the liver alters the production of enzymes that metabolize glucose (Cohen, Novick, & Rubinstein, 1996), metabolism and body activity increase, and production of several hormones changes (Ahima et al., 1996). For instance, adolescent female mammals are unlikely to reach sexual maturity before their body fat reaches a certain level. When thinner females are injected with extra leptin, the hormone glands are fooled into reacting as if the body had enough fat to start puberty (Chehab, Mounzih, Lu, & Lim, 1997).

Genetically obese mice injected daily with leptin increase energy expenditure and decrease food intake and body weight, without any apparently dangerous side effects (Pellymounter et al., 1995). For normal mice, extra leptin decreases intake but does not induce starvation. As you might imagine, news of this research suggested that leptin treatments might help people lose weight. Unfortunately, studies found that few if any overweight people lack leptin. In fact, in one study the mean leptin levels for obese people were about four times those in people of normal weight (Considine et al., 1996). That is, for obese people as well as others, the more fat cells, the more leptin. The problem is not that overweight people lack leptin but that their bodies are insensitive to it. Could we still help them lose weight by giving extremely large doses of leptin? No; at very high levels, leptin increases the risk of diabetes and other disorders (Cohen, Novick, & Rubinstein, 1996; Naggert et al., 1995). The search, therefore, turns to leptin's receptors and the activities they control.

Neuropeptide Y

Leptin activates receptors in the brain, especially the hypothalamus, to inhibit the release of **neuropeptide Y (NPY)** (Stephens et al., 1995), a neurotransmitter that (among other effects) powerfully inhibits the paraventricular nucleus (PVN) of the hypothalamus. Inhibition of the PVN, like damage, increases feeding, and prolonged inhibition can produce extreme overeating, as illustrated in Figure 10.22 (Billington & Levine, 1992; Leibowitz & Alexander, 1991; Morley, Levine, Grace, & Kneip, 1985). Injection of NPY to other parts of the hypothalamus also increases feeding (Stanley & Gillard, 1994).

Let's review. Body fat produces leptin; leptin inhibits NPY release; NPY release inhibits PVN activity; and PVN activity inhibits feeding. Most people have trouble remembering and understanding double negatives, much less triple. Study Figure 10.23, but for most

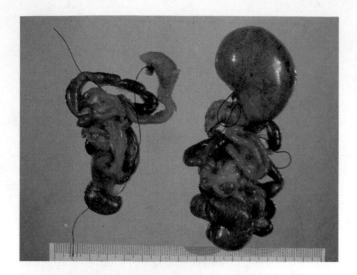

FIGURE **10.22**
The effects of inhibiting the paraventricular nucleus of the hypothalamus
On the left is the digestive system of a normal rat. On the right is the digestive system of a rat that has had its paraventricular hypothalamus inhibited by injections of peptide YY, a neurotransmitter closely related to neuropeptide Y. The rat continued eating even though its stomach and intestines distended almost to the point of bursting. . . . (All right, I'll admit this is a little bit disgusting.)   Source: From Morley, Levine, Grace, & Kneip, 1985.

purposes it will be enough to remember that leptin inhibits NPY and NPY increases feeding. Therefore, mice that fail to produce leptin (the third column in Figure 10.23) overeat. Why do overweight humans overeat? Perhaps leptin fails to inhibit NPY production; perhaps they produce excess NPY; perhaps something else is

wrong. After researchers identify the problem, we may be in a better position to seek a solution.

Other Neurotransmitters and Hormones

So far we have concentrated on NPY because of its powerful effects. A number of other neurotransmitters and hormones influence feeding. Much of the information in Table 10.3 comes from studies using microdialysis. In this procedure, an investigator implants into the brain a thin stainless steel tube filled with a dilute salt solution. At the tip is a thin membrane across which fluids can diffuse. The experimenter withdraws fluid from the tube and analyzes the brain chemicals that have diffused across the membrane. In this manner researchers discover which neurotransmitters are released during eating and which are released at the point of satiation (e.g., Stanley, Schwartz, Hernandez, Leibowitz, & Hoebel, 1989).

Let us consider several general points about the material in Table 10.3. First, the same transmitters and hormones serve the same functions with only slight variations among mammals, and many serve similar functions in nonmammalian vertebrates and even invertebrates. CCK increases satiety in species as different as humans and snails (Morley, 1995).

Second, several chemicals serve similar functions in the periphery and in the brain. For example, the peripheral hormone glucagon mobilizes stored food for current use and therefore decreases the need to eat; the very similar peptide GLP-1 acts as a transmitter in the brain to decrease eating. CCK from the intestines closes the muscle between the stomach and intestines,

Normal mice and humans		Mice homozygous for obese gene	Obese humans
Low body fat	High body fat	High body fat	High body fat
↓ Low production	↓ Much production	↓ Failure to produce	↓ Much production
Low leptin levels	High leptin levels	Low leptin levels	High leptin levels
↓ Weak inhibition of NPY release	↓ Strong inhibition of NPY release	↓ No inhibition	↓ Failure to inhibit?
Much NPY in hypothalamus	Low NPY in hypothalamus	Much NPY in hypothalamus	[NPY levels high?]
↓ Strongly inhibits PVN	↓ Lack of inhibition	↓ Strongly inhibits	↓ [?]
Low activity in PVN	High activity in PVN	Low activity in PVN	[Low activity in PVN?]
↓ Fails to inhibit eating	↓ Inhibits eating	↓ Fails to inhibit eating	↓ [?]
Much eating	Little eating	Much eating	Much eating

FIGURE **10.23**
Relation among weight, leptin, NPY, and eating

TABLE **10.3**

Neurotransmitters and Hormones That Affect Feeding

Chemical	Classification	Effects: Comments
Neuropeptide Y (NPY) and peptide YY (PYY)	Peptide neurotransmitters	Inhibit PVN activity, thereby increasing meal size; excess leads to obesity
Norepinephrine	Monoamine neurotransmitter	Different effects at different receptors. It inhibits PVN activity at alpha-2 receptors, and thereby increases meal size, especially for carbohydrates (Alexander, Cheung, Dietz, & Leibowitz, 1993; Paez, Stanley, & Leibowitz, 1993)
Galanin	Peptide neurotransmitter	Affects synapses in hypothalamus and amygdala; increases food intake, especially of fats and carbohydrates (Smith, York, & Bray, 1996; Tempel, Leibowitz, & Leibowitz, 1988)
Dynorphin	Opiate neurotransmitter	Increases feeding at certain brain sites (Morley, 1995)
Dopamine (DA)	Monoamine neurotransmitter	Increased release in the nucleus accumbens during eating, possibly related to the attention-grabbing aspects of a meal (Wilson, Nomikos, Collu, & Fibiger, 1995)
Serotonin (5HT)	Monoamine neurotransmitter	Mixed effects; mostly decreases meal size, especially for carbohydrates (Leibowitz, Alexander, Cheung, & Weiss, 1993; Leibowitz, Weiss, & Suh, 1990)
Melanocyte-stimulating hormone (MSH)	Hormone and neurotransmitter	Affects synapses in hypothalamus; inhibits feeding; inhibits NPY release (Fan, Boston, Kesterson, Hruby, & Cone, 1997)
Cholecystokinin (CCK)	Hormone and neurotransmitter	As peripheral hormone, produces satiety through effects on digestive system. As a neurotransmitter in the hypothalamus, decreases meal size (Goodison & Siegel, 1995; Cooper, Dourish, & Barber, 1990)
Glucagon-like peptide 1 (GLP-1)	Peptide very similar to the hormone glucagon	Affects synapses in PVN and amygdala; inhibits feeding (Turton et al., 1996)
Estradiol	Steroid hormone, more abundant in female than male	Inhibits feeding; responsible for decreased appetite in female during ovulation (Butera, Xiong, Davis, & Platania, 1996)

thereby increasing stomach distension; CCK in the brain also inhibits feeding. The mechanisms are different but the outcome is the same. Evidently, evolution has been conservative, using the same chemical repeatedly for related functions instead of developing new chemicals (Hoebel, 1988).

Third, note how many chemicals exert some control over feeding. One consequence is that researchers can try many kinds of drugs to help people control their appetites. The early research has focused on drugs that affect serotonin, probably because we know more about serotonin than we know about galanin, MSH, and others. Serotonin stimulates several kinds of synapses with different effects on feeding. Under most circumstances the net effect of serotonin activity is to decrease feeding, although fasting shifts the expression of different serotonin receptors so that serotonin loses its satiating effects (Nishimura, Nishihara, Torii, & Takahashi, 1996). Drugs that increase serotonin activity in the brain, such as fenfluramine, fluoxetine (Prozac), and sertraline, decrease the rate of eating and the size of meals (Simansky, 1996). A number of people now take one of these drugs to decrease appetite, with varying degrees of success. One study found the drugs most effective with a low-carbohydrate diet (Foltin, Haney, Comer, & Fischman, 1996). We can expect to see drugs designed to control appetite by altering the activity of several other neurotransmitters.

Anorexia and Bulimia

Overeating is hardly the only eating disorder. At the opposite extreme, people with **anorexia nervosa** eat much less than they need, become extremely thin, and in some cases die. Anorexia occurs mostly in women, with men constituting no more than 5 to 10 percent of cases. The condition usually begins in adolescence, much less often in the 20s, but once begun may continue for years.

People with anorexia are often interested in food; many enjoy cooking and the taste and smell of food. Their problem is not a lack of appetite but a fear of becoming fat or of losing self-control. Most people with anorexia are hardworking perfectionists who are amazingly active, unlike most other people on the verge of starvation. The perfectionism and driven activity resemble obsessive-compulsive behavior (Davis et al., 1995). Some people with anorexia also show signs of depression, and many have elevated levels of the hormone *cortisol*, as most depressed people do (Licinio, Wong, & Gold, 1996). However, antidepressant drugs are seldom effective treatments for anorexia. The biological predispositions to anorexia are as yet unknown.

Bulimia nervosa is a condition in which people (again, more women than men) alternate between dieting and overeating. Some (but not all) sometimes eat an enormous meal and then force themselves to vomit.

People with bulimia tend to have higher-than-normal levels of peptide YY (PYY), a neurotransmitter associated with increased eating (Kaye, Berrettini, Gwirtsman, & George, 1990). They have lower-than-normal levels of CCK (Brambilla et al., 1995) and signs of either decreased serotonin production or decreased receptor sensitivity for serotonin (Brewerton, 1995; Weltzin, Fernstrom, & Kaye, 1994). Both CCK and serotonin promote satiety. Drugs that increase serotonin activity are often effective in treating bulimia; drugs to increase CCK have not yet been tested (Advokat & Kutlesic, 1995).

The alterations in PYY, CCK, and serotonin are consistent with the occasional binge eating of bulimia; however, they do not explain the alternation between dieting and bingeing. Furthermore, we do not yet know whether the transmitter abnormalities precede the onset of bulimia or whether they develop as a result of abnormal eating patterns. For the answer to that question, we must await further research.

IN CLOSING

The Multiple Controls of Hunger

Eating is controlled by a number of brain areas, which monitor blood glucose, stomach distention, duodenal contents, body weight, and many other variables. Because the system is so complex, it can produce errors in many ways. However, the complexity of the system also provides a kind of security, a bit like the checks and balances in a government: If one part of the system makes a mistake, the other parts can partially counteract it. We notice how many people choose a poor diet or eat the wrong amount. Perhaps we should be even more impressed by how many people do manage to eat more or less appropriately. The regulation of eating succeeds not in spite of its complexity but because of it.

Summary

1. The ability to digest a food is one major determinant of preference for that food. For example, people who cannot digest lactose generally do not like to eat dairy products. (p. 282)
2. Other major determinants of food selection include innate preferences for certain tastes, a preference for familiar foods, and the ability to learn about the consequences of foods. (p. 282)
3. People and animals eat partly for the sake of taste. However, a sham-feeding animal, which tastes its foods but does not absorb them, eats far more than normal. (p. 283)
4. Factors controlling hunger include distension of the stomach and intestines, peripheral secretion of CCK, and the availability of glucose and other nutrients to the cells. (p. 283)
5. The hormone insulin increases the entry of glucose to the cells, including cells that store nutrients for future use. Glucagon mobilizes stored fuel and converts it to glucose in the blood. Thus, the combined influence of insulin and glucagon determines how much glucose will be available at any time. (p. 284)
6. Damage to cells in the lateral hypothalamus leads to decreased eating and loss of weight by affecting taste, salivation, swallowing, food-seeking behaviors, and insulin. (p. 286)
7. Damage to the ventromedial hypothalamus increases meal frequency; damage to the paraventricular nucleus of the hypothalamus increases meal size. Damage to either of these areas can lead to weight gain. (p. 287)
8. For people as well as mice, genetic differences influence metabolic activity and eating, and therefore weight gain. (p. 290)
9. Ordinarily, fat cells produce a protein called leptin, which inhibits hypothalamic secretion of neuropeptide Y (NPY) and thereby limits meal size. If an individual fails to produce leptin or if the leptin fails to inhibit NPY secretion, the result is overeating and obesity. (p. 291)
10. A number of other neurotransmitters also affect eating. Several current weight-control programs include drugs that increase activity at serotonin synapses. (p. 292)
11. Anorexia nervosa and bulimia nervosa are eating disorders that may be related to neurotransmitter imbalances, although the evidence is not yet convincing. (p. 293)

Review Questions

1. Why do Asian cooks seldom, if ever, use cheese and other dairy products? (p. 282)
2. What evidence points to stomach distention as a major contributor to satiety? What evidence indicates that food in the intestines is an effective signal also? (p. 283)
3. What causes release of the hormone CCK? What is one mechanism by which CCK in the periphery probably limits meal size? (p. 284)
4. Why do high and very low levels of insulin both lead to increased eating? (p. 284)
5. Describe several biological reasons why certain people may become overweight. (pp. 284–293)
6. What do cell bodies control in the lateral hypothalamus, and how does that role contrast with the contribution of dopamine-containing axons passing through the area? (p. 286)
7. Through what mechanisms does damage to the ventromedial hypothalamus lead to weight gain? (p. 287)
8. What are the advantages and disadvantages of the "eat only what you need at the moment" strategy? (p. 290)

9. In what way is the cause of obesity different for genetically obese people and mice? (p. 291)
10. What would be the probable effect on behavior of a drug that blocks serotonin receptors? A drug that stimulates galanin receptors? A drug that stimulates CCK receptors? (p. 293)

Thought Question

1. For most people, insulin levels tend to be higher during the day than at night. Use this fact to explain why people grow hungry a few hours after a daytime meal but not so quickly at night.

Suggestions for Further Reading

Capaldi, E. D. (Ed.) (1996). *Why we eat what we eat.* Washington, DC: American Psychological Association. Discusses the complex motivations that interact in food selection and eating.

Leibowitz, S. F., & Hoebel, B. G. (1997). Behavioral neuroscience and obesity. In G. A. Bray, C. Bouchard, & P. T. James (Eds.), *The handbook of obesity.* Marcel Dekker Publishers. Reviews research on neurotransmitters, hormones, brain mechanisms, and feeding.

Logue, A. W. (1991). *The psychology of eating and drinking* (2nd ed). New York: Freeman. Discussion covers both normal eating and disorders such as anorexia nervosa and bulimia.

Terms

lactose   the sugar in milk (p. 282)

lactase   enzyme necessary for lactose metabolism (p. 282)

carnivore   animal that eats meat (p. 282)

herbivore   animal that eats plants (p. 282)

omnivore   animal that eats both meat and plants (p. 282)

sham feeding   procedure in which everything that an animal swallows leaks out a tube connected to the esophagus or stomach (p. 283)

vagus nerve   tenth cranial nerve, which sends branches to the stomach and several other organs (p. 283)

splanchnic nerves   nerves carrying impulses from the thoracic and lumbar parts of the spinal cord to the digestive organs and from the digestive organs to the spinal cord (p. 283)

duodenum   part of the small intestine adjoining the stomach (p. 284)

cholecystokinin (CCK)   hormone released by the duodenum in response to food distention (p. 284)

insulin   pancreatic hormone that facilitates the entry of glucose into the cells (p. 284)

glucagon   pancreatic hormone that stimulates the liver to convert stored glycogen to glucose (p. 284)

lateral hypothalamus   area of the hypothalamus in which damage impairs eating and drinking (p. 286)

ventromedial hypothalamus (VMH)   a region of the hypothalamus, in which damage leads to faster stomach emptying and increased secretion of insulin (p. 287)

paraventricular nucleus (PVN)   area of the hypothalamus in which activity tends to limit meal size (p. 289)

leptin   peptide released by fat cells; tends to decrease eating, partly by inhibiting release of neuropeptide Y in the hypothalamus (p. 291)

neuropeptide Y   peptide found in the brain, especially the hypothalamus, that inhibits activity of the paraventricular nucleus and thereby increases eating (p. 291)

anorexia nervosa   condition characterized by unwillingness to eat as much as the body needs (p. 293)

bulimia nervosa   condition characterized by alternation between dieting and overeating (p. 293)

HORMONES AND SEXUAL BEHAVIOR

CHAPTER **ELEVEN**

MAIN**IDEAS**

1. Hormones affect behavior either by attaching to receptors on the membrane of a cell or by altering the expression of the genes.
2. The effects of sex hormones may be organizing or activating. Organizing effects, exerted during a sensitive period of early development, permanently influence genital anatomy and the brain. Activating effects are transient and may be exerted at any time.
3. In mammals, the presence or absence of testosterone determines whether the genitals and hypothalamus will develop in the male or the female manner, although for certain characteristics testosterone must first be converted to estradiol.
4. Sex hormones, including testosterone and estradiol, activate sexual, parental, and other behaviors.
5. Certain patterns of genes, hormones, and brain anatomy are related to differences in sexual identity and orientation, but exactly how is not yet clear.

Imagine that medical science has developed a new procedure—a course of drugs, let's say—that can halt the aging process. If you submit to this procedure, your body will stay as it now is, forever. If you are now 20 years old, you will always look 20 years old. Your hair will not grow gray, your skin will not wrinkle, you will continue to be as athletic and energetic as you are now, and you will not develop any of the deteriorative conditions of old age. The procedure does not guarantee immortality; you could still be killed by an accident or a deadly virus. But if you live cautiously, and if humanity manages to avoid wars and does not completely ruin the environment, you might survive for hundreds, maybe even thousands of years, looking and feeling young the whole time.

There is one catch: The government will provide this procedure free for anyone who wants it, but, in order to prevent runaway overpopulation, everyone who accepts the procedure must also submit to irreversible sterilization, because if people survive indefinitely *and* reproduce, the world will become unbearably crowded. The procedure won't destroy your sex drive, but you must give up your ability to have children.

What would you decide?

If you choose to have children, you will someday watch your childless friends continue to swim and play tennis while you hobble with a walker into a nursing home. On the other hand, all the humans of the remote future will descend from people who decided to have children instead of staying young.

The ability to reproduce is very important to most people, and it is essential for the preservation and evolution of the species. The constant reshuffling of genes enables a species to adapt evolutionarily to a changing environment. It also provides enough variability among individuals to prevent any one strain of virus or bacterium from wiping out the population.

Reproduction is not easy, however. One must find a healthy, sexually mature member of the opposite sex of the correct species, and then persuade that individual to be one's partner. The two must synchronize their behavior so that both are ready to engage in the sex act at the same time. Then, at least in mammals and birds, one or both parents must nurture the young until they reach maturity.

This chapter deals with both sexual behavior and hormonal systems. Hormones are critical for many behaviors, but especially for sexual behavior.

Hormones and Behavior

In the fall, migratory birds prepare for a long flight. They eat more and change their metabolism to store enough fat for the journey, they join into flocks with others of their species, and they start flying south. In the spring, the same birds fly back north. At that time, their feathers change to breeding colors, they start looking for appropriate mates, and males begin singing. The coordination of such widespread changes throughout the body depends on hormones.

In humans, too, hormones control a wide variety of behaviors; in Chapter 10 we considered the roles of angiotensin, aldosterone, and insulin in drinking and feeding. Hormones are so important to sexual behavior, however, that this chapter is a good context for discussing hormones in general. A **hormone** is a chemical that is secreted by a gland and conveyed by the blood to other organs, whose activity it influences. Figure 11.1 presents the major **endocrine** (hormone-producing) **glands.** Table 11.1 lists some important hormones and their principal effects.

Mechanisms of Hormone Actions

The effects of hormones on behavior overlap greatly with the effects of neurotransmitters. A number of chemicals—including epinephrine, norepinephrine, angiotensin, and CCK—serve as both neurotransmitters and hormones. The difference between a neurotransmitter and a hormone is that a neurotransmitter is released next to the target cell, and a hormone is carried by the blood to targets throughout the body. Neurotransmitters provide the better form of communication to a limited group of cells. Hormones have advantages for organizing many organs or brain areas for a single function, such as reproduction, hibernation, or migration.

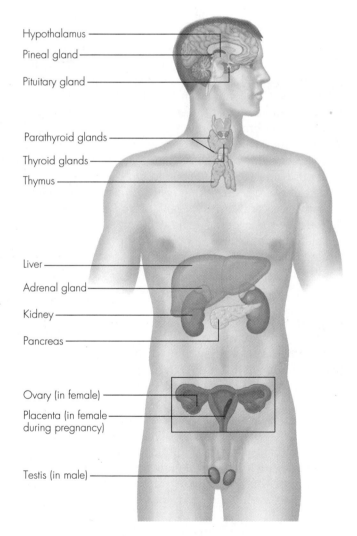

Hypothalamus
Pineal gland
Pituitary gland
Parathyroid glands
Thyroid glands
Thymus
Liver
Adrenal gland
Kidney
Pancreas
Ovary (in female)
Placenta (in female during pregnancy)
Testis (in male)

FIGURE **11.1**
Location of some of the major endocrine glands
Source: From Starr & Taggart, 1989.

Types of Hormones

Dozens of known hormones have been identified, and new ones are discovered from time to time. Most fall into a few major classes. One class is composed of **protein hormones** and **peptide hormones,** composed of chains of amino acids. (Generally, proteins are the longer chains and peptides are the shorter chains.) Insulin is one example of a protein hormone. *Glycoproteins* are a chain of amino acids attached to a carbohydrate. Protein and peptide hormones attach to receptors on the cell membrane, where they activate an enzyme that produces cyclic AMP or some other second messenger. Cyclic AMP then activates a number of enzymes that may alter the metabolism of the cell or the ability of various ions to cross the membrane (Figure 11.2).

The changes may last from minutes to hours. Note that peptide hormones affect cells by the same route as peptide neurotransmitters do (Chapter 3).

Another major class, the **steroid hormones,** contains four carbon rings, as Figure 11.3 shows. Cortisol and corticosterone, steroid hormones released by the adrenal cortex, exert their effects by entering cells and attaching to receptors in the cytoplasm, which then move to the nucleus of the cell where they determine which genes will be expressed. Cortisol and corticosterone elevate blood sugar and enhance metabolism; increased release of these steroids helps the body adapt to prolonged stress.

The "sex hormones," **estrogens, progesterone,** and the **androgens,** which are also steroids, exert their effects by attaching to a receptor that turns a gene on or

TABLE 11.1
Partial List of Hormone-Releasing Glands

Organ	Hormone	Hormone Functions
Hypothalamus	Various releasing hormones	Promote or inhibit release of various hormones by pituitary.
Anterior pituitary	Thyroid-stimulating hormone (TSH)	Stimulates thyroid gland.
	Luteinizing hormone (LH)	Increases production of progesterone (female) and testosterone (male); stimulates ovulation.
	Follicle-stimulating hormone (FSH)	Increases production of estrogen and maturation of ovum (female) and sperm production (male).
	ACTH	Increases secretion of steroid hormones by adrenal gland.
	Prolactin	Increases milk production.
	β-endorphin	Reduces pain.
Posterior pituitary	Oxytocin	Controls uterine contractions, milk release, certain aspects of parental behavior, and sexual pleasure.
	Vasopressin	Constricts blood vessels and raises blood pressure.
Pineal	Melatonin	Increases sleepiness; also has role in onset of puberty.
Thyroid	Thyroxine, Triiodothyronine	Increase metabolic rate, growth, and maturation.
Parathyroid	Parathyroid hormone	Increases blood calcium and decreases potassium.
Adrenal cortex	Aldosterone	Reduces secretion of salts by the kidneys.
	Cortisol, corticosterone	Stimulate liver to elevate blood sugar; increase metabolism of proteins and fats.
Adrenal medulla	Epinephrine, norepinephrine	Similar to effects of sympathetic nervous system.
Pancreas	Insulin	Increases entry of glucose to cells and increases storage as fats.
	Glucagon	Increases conversion of stored fats to blood glucose.
Ovary	Estrogens	Promote female sexual characteristics.
	Progesterone	Maintains pregnancy.
Testis	Androgens	Promote sperm production, growth of pubic hair, and male sexual characteristics.
Liver	Somatomedins	Stimulate growth.
Kidney	Renin	Converts a blood protein into angiotensin, which regulates blood pressure and contributes to hypovolemic thirst.
Thymus	Thymosin (and others)	Support immune responses.

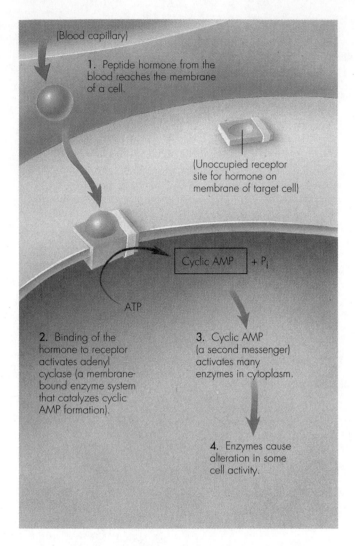

FIGURE **11.2**
Action by a peptide hormone
When it attaches to its receptor, it activates an enzyme system
that releases the second messenger, cyclic AMP, which in turn
activates other enzymes that alter the cell's activity.   Source:
From Starr & Taggart, 1989.

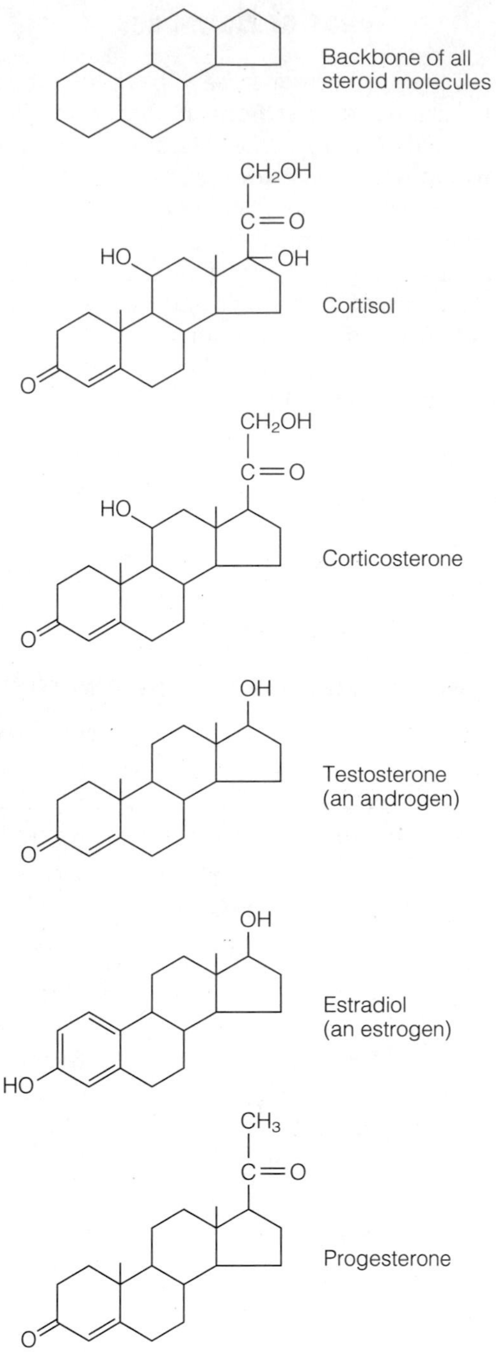

Backbone of all
steroid molecules

Cortisol

Corticosterone

Testosterone
(an androgen)

Estradiol
(an estrogen)

Progesterone

FIGURE **11.3**
Steroid hormones
Note the similarity between the sex hormones testosterone and
estradiol.

off (see Figure 11.4). In some neurons the consequence
is an increased number of dendritic spines on the cell
(Frankfurt, 1994). Estrogens and androgens may also
react with receptors on cell membranes (Ramirez,
Zheng, & Siddique, 1996). Sex hormones also affect a
number of nonneuronal cells.

Some of the genes that sex hormones activate are
called **sex-limited genes** because their effects are much
stronger in one sex than in the other. For example, estrogen activates the genes responsible for breast development in women, and androgens activate the genes
responsible for the growth of facial hair in men. Androgens stimulate the growth of pubic hair in both sexes.

Some people, especially male athletes, take steroids
to help develop their muscular strength. You might assume that a drug that increases muscle strength will
have other masculinizing effects. However, the high
levels of steroids produce negative feedback on the anterior pituitary, which secretes hormones that control

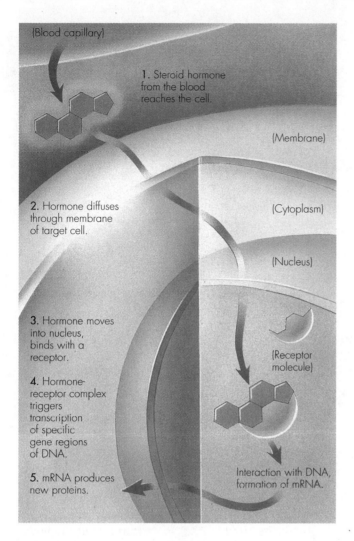

FIGURE **11.4**
Action of estrogen or androgen
The hormone enters a cell, binds with a receptor in the nucleus, and thereby activates particular genes. As a result, the cell increases its production of specific proteins.   Source: From Starr & Taggart, 1989.

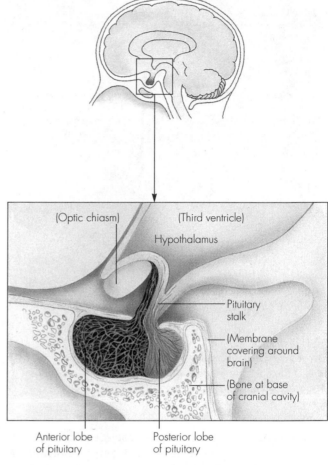

FIGURE **11.5**
Location of the hypothalamus and pituitary gland in the human brain
Source: From Starr & Taggart, 1989.

the gonads. The result is decreased testis size, sometimes breast growth, increased cholesterol levels, and a high prevalence of depression (Pope & Katz, 1994).

In addition to peptide and steroid hormones, other classes are thyroid hormones (released by the thyroid gland, all of them containing iodine) and monoamines (such as epinephrine and dopamine). Several miscellaneous hormones do not fit into any of the described categories, and researchers are still uncertain about several "possible" hormones.

Control of Hormone Release

Just as circulating hormones modify brain activity, hormones secreted by the brain control the secretion of many other hormones. The **pituitary gland,** attached to the hypothalamus, is sometimes called the "master gland" because its secretions influence so many other glands. (See Figure 11.5.) The pituitary consists of two distinct glands, the **anterior pituitary** and the **posterior pituitary,** which release different sets of hormones (Table 11.1).

The posterior pituitary, composed of neural tissue, can be considered an extension of the hypothalamus. Neurons in the hypothalamus synthesize the hormones **oxytocin** and **vasopressin** (also known as antidiuretic hormone), plus much smaller amounts of various other peptides (Morris & Pow, 1993). Hypothalamic cells then transport these hormones down their axons to their terminals in the posterior pituitary, as shown in Figure 11.6. Action potentials release these hormones into the blood.

The anterior pituitary, composed of glandular tissue, synthesizes six hormones itself, although the

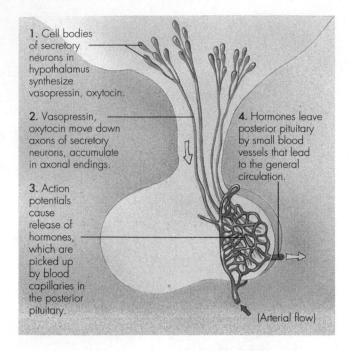

1. Cell bodies of secretory neurons in hypothalamus synthesize vasopressin, oxytocin.

2. Vasopressin, oxytocin move down axons of secretory neurons, accumulate in axonal endings.

3. Action potentials cause release of hormones, which are picked up by blood capillaries in the posterior pituitary.

4. Hormones leave posterior pituitary by small blood vessels that lead to the general circulation.

(Arterial flow)

FIGURE **11.6**
Oxytocin and vasopressin
These hormones are produced in the hypothalamus and are stored and released by the posterior pituitary.   Source: From Starr & Taggart, 1989.

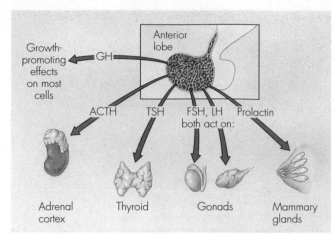

FIGURE **11.8**
Hormones secreted by the anterior pituitary and their primary targets
Source: From Starr & Taggart, 1989.

Adrenocorticotropic hormone (ACTH)	Controls secretions of the adrenal cortex
Thyroid-stimulating hormone (TSH)	Controls secretions of the thyroid gland
Follicle-stimulating hormone (FSH) Luteinizing hormone (LH)	Control secretions of the gonads
Prolactin	Controls secretions of the mammary glands
Somatotropin, also known as growth hormone (GH)	Promotes growth throughout the body

hypothalamus controls their release (see Figure 11.7). The hypothalamus secretes **releasing hormones,** which flow through the blood to the anterior pituitary. There they stimulate or inhibit the release of six known hormones, five of which control the secretions of other endocrine organs (see Figure 11.8):

FIGURE **11.7**
Hypothalamic releasing hormones and the anterior pituitary
Source: From Starr & Taggart, 1989.

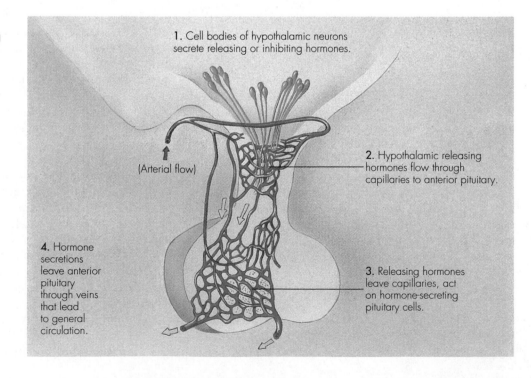

1. Cell bodies of hypothalamic neurons secrete releasing or inhibiting hormones.

2. Hypothalamic releasing hormones flow through capillaries to anterior pituitary.

3. Releasing hormones leave capillaries, act on hormone-secreting pituitary cells.

4. Hormone secretions leave anterior pituitary through veins that lead to general circulation.

(Arterial flow)

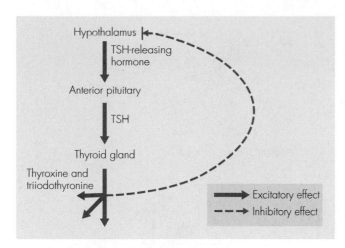

FIGURE **11.9**
Negative feedback in the control of thyroid hormones
The hypothalamus secretes a releasing hormone that stimulates the anterior pituitary to release TSH, which stimulates the thyroid gland to release its hormones. Those hormones in turn act on the hypothalamus to decrease its secretion of the releasing hormone.

The hypothalamus maintains fairly constant circulating levels of certain hormones. For example, when the level of thyroid hormone is low, the hypothalamus releases *TSH-releasing hormone,* which stimulates the anterior pituitary to release TSH, which in turn causes the thyroid gland to secrete more thyroid hormones. After the level of thyroid hormones has risen, the hypothalamus decreases its release of TSH-releasing hormone (see Figure 11.9).

Organizing Effects of Sex Hormones

We generally refer to the androgens, a group that includes testosterone and several others, as "male hormones" because their level is about ten times higher in men than in women. We refer to the estrogens, a group that includes estradiol and others, as "female hormones" because their level is ten times higher in women than in men. However, both types of hormones function in both sexes.

We distinguish between the organizing and activating effects of sex hormones. The **organizing effects,** which determine whether the brain and body will develop as a female or as a male, occur mostly at a sensitive stage of development—shortly before and after birth in rats, and well before birth in humans. **Activating effects** can occur at any time in life, when a hormone temporarily activates a particular response. Activating effects on an organ may last hours, weeks, or even months longer than the hormone remains in the

organ, but they do not last indefinitely. The distinction between the two kinds of effects is not absolute; early in life, hormones exert activating effects even while they are organizing body development, and during puberty, hormones can induce long-lasting structural changes as well as activating effects (Arnold & Breedlove, 1985; Williams, 1986).

Sex Differences in the Gonads and Hypothalamus

During an early stage of prenatal development in mammals, the **gonads** (reproductive organs) of every mammalian fetus are identical, and both male and female have a set of Müllerian ducts and a set of Wolffian ducts. Whether those primitive structures will become male or female depends on the level of testosterone during early development. A male fetus has a Y chromosome, which contains a gene that causes the primitive gonads to develop into **testes,** the sperm-producing organs. (The Y chromosome is small and has few other genes.) The developing testes produce the hormone **testosterone** (an androgen), which increases the growth of the testes, causing them to produce more testosterone, and so forth. Testosterone also causes the primitive **Wolffian ducts** to develop into *seminal vesicles* (saclike structures that store semen) and the *vas deferens* (a duct from the testis into the penis). A peptide hormone, *Müllerian inhibiting hormone (MIH)* causes the Müllerian ducts to degenerate (Graves, 1994). A genetically female fetus (XX) would also develop male structures if exposed to large enough amounts of testosterone, but under normal conditions she would not be. Her gonads develop into **ovaries,** the egg-producing organs. Her Wolffian ducts degenerate, and her primitive **Müllerian ducts** develop into female structures (including uterus and vagina). Figure 11.10 shows the hormone-dependent development of male or female genitals from the original unisex structures.

In addition to the obvious differences in the gonads and genitals, the sexes differ in the structure and function of several parts of the nervous system, especially the hypothalamus. One difference is that the female hypothalamus can generate a cyclic pattern of hormone release, as in the human menstrual cycle. The male hypothalamus cannot do so; neither can the hypothalamus of a female who was exposed to extra testosterone during early development. Another difference is that one portion of the medial preoptic nucleus of the hypothalamus is usually larger in males than in females—two to three times larger in humans, and more than that in certain other species (Hines, Davis, Coquelin, Goy, & Gorski, 1985; Swaab & Fliers, 1985).

Sexual differentiation depends on the level of testosterone during an early **sensitive period,** about the third and fourth months of pregnancy for a human

FIGURE **11.10**
Differentiation of human genitals from a single set of precursors
(**a**) At age 6 weeks, male and female look identical. (**b**) In the second trimester, male and female begin to differentiate. (**c**) Appearance at birth.   *Source: Based on Netter, 1983.*

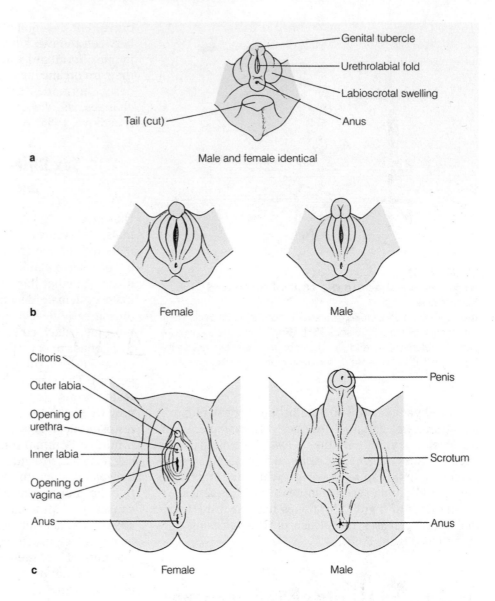

(Money & Ehrhardt, 1972). In rats, which are less well developed than humans are at birth, testosterone within the first few days controls development of the external genitals, although even weeks later it can produce profound effects on the functioning of the hypothalamus (Bloch & Mills, 1995; Bloch, Mills, & Gale, 1995). A female rat that is injected with testosterone during the last few days before being born or the first few days afterward is partly masculinized, just as if the testosterone had been produced by her own body (Ward & Ward, 1985). Her clitoris grows larger than normal; her other reproductive structures look intermediate between female and male. At maturity, her pituitary and ovaries produce steady levels of hormones instead of the cycles that are characteristic of females.

Anatomically, certain parts of her hypothalamus appear more male than female. Her behavior is also masculinized: She mounts other females and makes copulatory thrusting movements rather than arching her back and allowing males to mount her. In short, early testosterone promotes the male pattern and inhibits the female pattern (Gorski, 1985; Wilson, George, & Griffin, 1981). With enough testosterone, the individual develops as a male; without testosterone, it develops as a female. Other species show variations on this pattern, as highlighted in Digression 11.1.

Early treatment with estradiol or other estrogens does not have the reverse effect. A male that is injected with estrogens still develops male genitals; he develops a female appearance only if he is deprived of testosterone, through castration or other means.

We can summarize by saying that nature would make every mammal a female unless told to do otherwise by testosterone. A mammal with low levels of all sex hormones in early development will develop a female anatomy. Add testosterone and male characteristics develop.

According to studies on rodents, testosterone exerts a major part of its effect on the hypothalamus through a surprising route: After it enters a neuron, it is converted to estradiol! Testosterone and estradiol are chemically very similar, as you can see in Figure 11.3. In organic chemistry, a ring of six carbon atoms con-

taining three double bonds is an *aromatic* compound. An enzyme found in the brain can *aromatize* testosterone into estradiol. Other androgens that cannot be aromatized into estrogens are less effective in masculinizing the hypothalamus. Moreover, drugs that prevent testosterone from being aromatized to estradiol block the organizing effects of testosterone on sexual development. Apparently, androgens must be aromatized to estrogens to exert their organizing effects on the hypothalamus.

Why, then, is the female not masculinized by her own estradiol? During the early sensitive period, immature mammals of many species have in their blood-

---

DIGRESSION 11.1

Sexual Differentiation in the Spotted Hyena

The spotted hyena provides exceptions to many of the generalizations we usually make about males and females (Glickman et al., 1992). (See Figure 11.11.) On the average, female spotted hyenas are larger and more aggressive than males. The female's clitoris is as large as the male's penis and is capable of erections like those of a penis. The female urinates through a canal in her clitoris. During puberty, that canal enlarges enough for the male to insert his penis into it in sexual intercourse. Her babies are delivered through the canal in the clitoris. The first time a female delivers, the babies rip through the wall of the clitoris, in most cases dying in the process and causing apparently severe pain to the mother. Later-born babies have a higher chance of survival, but even then, birth is a slow process with a higher chance of infant mortality than in most mammals (Frank, Weldele, & Glickman, 1995).

Why have female hyenas evolved so many of the traits we consider typically masculine, at what appears to be a significant cost to both the mother and her babies? The explanation probably relates to the ways in which hyenas fight one another for food. The dominant females and their young get first access to any food the pack finds, followed by the next most dominant females and their young, and so on. Groups of adult females form coalitions to improve or maintain their position. Adult males always leave their home pack and join another pack, where they remain permanently subordinate to all the female coalitions. Beginning in infancy, females spend their whole lives fighting for dominance. In male–female twin pairs, the female usually dominates her brother within the first two to three weeks (Smale, Holekamp, Weldele, Frank, & Glickman, 1995).

The physiological and ontogenetic explanation for the females' behavior relates to hormones. During pregnancy, the hyena mother's ovaries produce large amounts of androstene-

FIGURE 11.11
A female spotted hyena pup
Note that her clitoris looks like a penis and that her labia are fused and swollen like a scrotum. Female spotted hyenas are exposed to large amounts of testosterone during prenatal development. Their anatomy and their aggressive behavior become highly masculinized.

dione, the precursor chemical for both testosterone and estrogen. The placenta contains relatively large amounts of the enzyme that converts androstenedione to testosterone, and small amounts of the enzyme that converts it to estrogen (Yalcinkaya et al., 1993). Therefore, at least at certain stages of development, the female fetus is exposed to much higher testosterone levels than are females of most other species.

stream a protein called **alpha-fetoprotein,** which is not present in adults (Gorski, 1980; MacLusky & Naftolin, 1981). Alpha-fetoprotein binds with estrogen and blocks it from leaving the bloodstream and entering the cells that are developing in this early period. Primates have other mechanisms for inactivating estrogen, such as breaking down estrogens into inactive substances. In any event, testosterone is neither bound to alpha-fetoprotein nor metabolized; it is free to enter the cells, where enzymes convert it into estradiol. That is, testosterone is a way of getting estradiol into the cells when estradiol itself cannot leave the blood.

This explanation of testosterone's effects makes sense of an otherwise puzzling fact: Although normal amounts of estradiol have little effect on early development, an injection of a larger amount actually masculinizes a female's development. The reason is that normal amounts are bound to alpha-fetoprotein or metabolized, whereas a larger amount may exceed the body's capacity for inactivation; the excess can thus enter the cells and masculinize them.

Testosterone also exerts organizing effects on the nerves and muscles that control the penis. In most mammalian species, a male has muscles in or near the penis that are either absent or very small in the area near the female's clitoris. Those muscles receive their neural input from two motor nuclei in the spinal cord; again, those nuclei are present in males and are either smaller or absent in females. Early in development, both male and female develop large numbers of neurons in these nuclei. The male's testosterone supports survival of those neurons; in the female the testosterone levels are lower and most of the neurons die (Goldstein & Sengelaub, 1992). A male also loses most of those neurons if he is treated with testosterone-blocking drugs during an early sensitive period (Grisham, Castro, Kashon, Ward, & Ward, 1992).

Sex Differences in Nonreproductive Characteristics

Males and females obviously differ in their organs of reproduction and in certain aspects of sexual behavior. But they also differ in many characteristics that are only indirectly related to reproduction: In most mammalian species, males tend to be larger than females and to fight with one another more than females do (Ellis, 1986). Females tend to live longer and to devote more attention to infant care. (Humans are among the few mammals in which the male helps care for the young.)

Many of these sex differences depend on prenatal hormones. For example, female monkeys exposed to testosterone during their sensitive period engage in more rough-and-tumble play than other females, are

more aggressive, and make more threatening facial gestures (Quadagno, Briscoe, & Quadagno, 1977; Young, Goy, & Phoenix, 1964). Similar effects on play and aggressive behavior have been noted in dogs (Beach, Buehler, & Dunbar, 1982; Reinisch, 1981) and ferrets (Stockman, Callaghan, Gallagher, & Baum, 1986).

In humans, too, males and females differ in their patterns of play and aggression, even at an early age, although the role of early hormones is hard to determine. Girls who were exposed to elevated androgen levels during prenatal development (because of a gene that causes inadequate cortisol production and an excess production of androgens from the adrenal gland) tend to spend more time than most other girls do playing with "boys' toys" such as cars and fire engines (Berenbaum & Hines, 1992) and are more likely than other girls are to choose boys as their favorite playmates (Hines & Kaufman, 1994). However, they are not more likely than other girls to engage in rough-and-tumble play. Although these girls' behavior suggests a possible relationship between early hormones and play preferences, it is also possible that parents and others may have treated them differently from other girls because of their somewhat masculinized appearance.

Activating Effects of Sex Hormones

At any time in life, not just during an early sensitive period, current levels of testosterone or estradiol exert activating effects, temporarily modifying sexual or other activities. Behaviors can also influence hormonal secretions; Digression 11.2 describes one example.

Sexual Behavior

After removal of the testes from a male rodent or the ovaries from a female, sexual behavior declines as the sex hormone levels in the blood decline. It may not disappear altogether, partly because the adrenal glands also produce steroid hormones. Injections of testosterone into a castrated male restore sexual behavior, as do injections of testosterone's two major metabolites, dihydrotestosterone and estradiol (Baum & Vreeburg, 1973). Estrogen followed by progesterone is the most effective combination for stimulating sexual behavior in a female (Glaser, Etgen, & Barfield, 1987).

Sex hormones activate sexual behavior partly by enhancing sensations. Estrogens enlarge the area of skin that excites the *pudendal nerve,* which transmits tactile stimulation from the pubic area to the brain (Komisaruk, Adler, & Hutchison, 1972). Sex hormones also facilitate sexual behavior by binding to receptors in the brain and thereby increasing neuronal activity, especially in the hypothalamus.

The ventromedial nucleus and the medial preoptic area (MPOA) of the hypothalamus are among the principal areas affected by sex hormones. Part of the MPOA is known as the *sexually dimorphic nucleus,* because it is distinctly larger in males than in females. Stimulation of the MPOA increases male-typical sex behavior in males and female-typical sex behavior in females (Bloch, Butler, & Kohlert, 1996). Activity increases here (and in several other brain locations) during copulation (Heeb & Yahr, 1996).

Damage to the medial preoptic area produces somewhat different effects depending on the sex and species of the animal; for example, damaging or inactivating this nucleus in male rats decreases all sexual behaviors (McGinnis, Williams, & Lumia, 1996), but in male ferrets, damage causes a loss of response to female partners and an increased response to male partners (Baum, Tobet, Cherry, & Paredes, 1996).

Two neurotransmitters in the MPOA that facilitate sexual behavior are dopamine (Hull et al., 1986) and norepinephrine (Mallick, Manchanda, & Kumar, 1996). Neurons in the MPOA increase the release of dopamine

DIGRESSION 11.2

Behavior Influences Hormonal Secretions

The mating behavior of the ring-necked dove offers a striking example of how hormones and behavior interact. A newly mated pair of doves goes through a well-synchronized series of behaviors, as outlined in the following table:

	Male	Female
Day 1	Aggressive behavior	Nonaggressive behavior
Days 2–6	Courtship (nest coos)	Courtship (nest coos)
	Copulation	Copulation
	Nest building (brings twigs)	Nest building (arranges twigs)
Day 7		Lays two eggs
Next 2 weeks	Sits on eggs during middle of the day	Sits on eggs from late afternoon to next morning
Next 3 weeks	Tends and feeds chicks	Tends and feeds chicks

The behaviors of the male and female are tightly synchronized. If the female assumes the receptive posture too early, the male may copulate but then quickly deserts her (Erickson & Zenone, 1976). But properly timed copulation establishes a pair bond that keeps the couple together through the mating season and sometimes even into later years.

Both birds normally ignore nesting materials on day 1, begin to build a nest on day 2 or 3, and, if the nest is not complete by day 6 or 7, work frantically on nest building at that time. Neither pays much attention to a nest with eggs before day 7, but they take turns sitting after that time. Both produce crop milk that they feed to chicks that hatch 14 days after the eggs are laid, but they do not provide milk if chicks hatch much earlier.

Although injections of certain hormones would induce any of the observed behaviors, it is also the case that each change in the birds' behavior induces a change in their hormone secretions. The sequence of behaviors depends on a system in which each behavior causes the production of hormones that prepare a bird for the next stage of behavior. On day 1, the male struts around and makes a cooing display. This behavior seems to excite the female; her ovaries increase production of estrogen (Erickson & Lehrman, 1964). By day 2, she is ready for courtship and soon after that for copulation. If a researcher simply injects an isolated female wih estrogen,

she is ready for courtship and copulation almost as soon as a male appears. Thus, the function of the male's behavior on the first day is to stimulate the female's hormonal secretions. Meanwhile, the male seems to be excited by observing the female on day 1; his androgen production increases. By day 2, he is ready for nest building.

A week of courtship and nest building causes the female to produce first estrogen and then a combination of estrogen and progesterone. If we give estrogen injections to an isolated female for a week, with additional progesterone on the last two days, she becomes ready to incubate eggs even if she has neither seen nor heard a male. Evidently, courting and nesting experiences produce hormonal changes that prepare her for the next behavioral stage.

Similarly, 14 days of sitting on eggs (or of watching another bird sitting on eggs) causes both males and females to produce the hormone prolactin, which stimulates the production of crop milk and disposes the birds to take care of the babies. If a dove is isolated from other birds and from nests and eggs, a researcher can still get it to care for babies by injecting it repeatedly with prolactin.

In short, one behavior causes a hormonal change, which disposes the bird toward a second behavior, which causes a further hormonal change, and so on to the end of the sequence (Lehrman, 1964; Martinez-Vargas & Erickson, 1973).

during sexual behavior, and not during other activities (Hull, Eaton, Moses, & Lorrain, 1993). If male rats are merely exposed to receptive females, but temporarily restrained from reaching them, MPOA dopamine activity increases only for those males that later attempt to copulate. In those that will later ignore the female, the MPOA does not release dopamine (Hull, Du, Lorrain, & Matuszewich, 1995). Castrated males synthesize normal amounts of dopamine in the MPOA, but they do not release much in the presence of potential sexual partners (Hull, Du, Lorrain, & Matuszewich, 1997). Such evidence shows dopamine activity in the MPOA to be critical for male sexual behavior in all species that have been studied. Sexual behavior also increases dopamine activity in the nucleus accumbens, which is important for almost all kinds of reinforcement (Pfaus, Damsma, Wenkstern, & Fibiger, 1995).

When the concentration of released dopamine is only moderately high, dopamine stimulates mostly type D_1 and the closely related D_5 receptors, which facilitate erection of the penis in the male (Hull et al., 1992) and sexually receptive postures in the female (Apostolakis et al., 1996). When the concentration of dopamine reaches a higher level, dopamine stimulates mostly type D_2 receptors, which leads to orgasm and ejaculation (Giuliani & Ferrari, 1996; Hull et al., 1992). The effects at D_1 and D_2 receptors tend to inhibit each other. As a result, the early stages of sexual excitement are characterized by arousal but not orgasm; when orgasm occurs, it is followed by a decrease in arousal.

Effects on men   Although current hormone levels are less critical for maintaining sexual behavior in humans than in other species, an influence is certainly demonstrable. Among males, sexual excitement is generally highest when testosterone levels are highest, at about ages 15 to 25. The hormone oxytocin may also contribute to sexual pleasure. The body releases enormous amounts of oxytocin during orgasm, more than tripling the usual concentration in the blood. Several studies support a relationship between oxytocin and sexual pleasure, although the results are not yet conclusive (Murphy, Checkley, Seckl, & Lightman, 1990).

Decreases in testosterone levels generally decrease sexual activity. After castration, for example, most men—though not all—report a decrease in sexual interest and activity (Carter, 1992). However, low testosterone is not the only basis for **impotence,** the inability to have an erection. Some men with normal testosterone levels are impotent, and giving them extra testosterone does not alter their condition (Carani et al., 1990).

Typically, sex offenders (exhibitionists, rapists, child molesters, committers of incest, and so forth) have about average testosterone levels (Lang, Flor-Henry, & Frenzel, 1990). Nevertheless, decreasing their

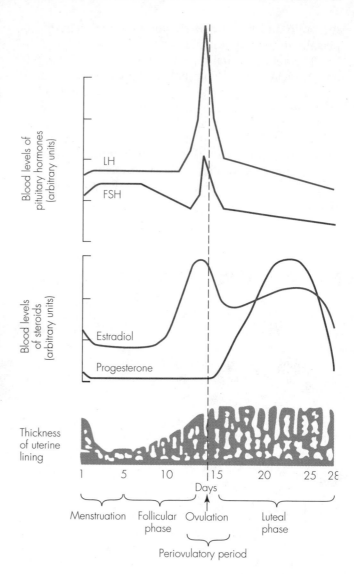

FIGURE **11.12**
Blood levels of four hormones during the human menstrual cycle

testosterone levels can reduce their troublesome sexual behaviors, as it will any other male sexual behavior. Some sex offenders have been treated with *cyproterone,* a drug that blocks the binding of testosterone to receptors within cells. Others have been treated with *medroxyprogesterone,* which decreases testosterone production and accelerates the breakdown of testosterone into inactive molecules. Within four to eight weeks of treatment with either of these drugs, most sex offenders experience a decrease in sexual fantasies and offensive sexual behaviors. However, the drugs produce a variety of unpleasant side effects, including depression, breast growth, weight gain, and blood clots. Furthermore, both drugs are ordinarily administered as daily pills, and a man with a history of sex offenses can easily quit taking the pills without telling anyone, and then revert to the offensive behaviors.

A newer drug related to one of the hypothalamic releasing hormones blocks the secretion of testosterone. Because it is given as a monthly injection, physicians or law officers can easily monitor compliance. Early results indicate that in most cases the drug greatly reduces sexual fantasies and activities without producing serious side effects. However, it is apparently necessary for the man to continue taking the drug for years, or the unwanted sexual behavior will return (Thibaut, Cordier, & Kuhn, 1996).

Effects on women A woman's hypothalamus and pituitary interact with the ovaries to produce the **menstrual cycle,** a periodic variation in hormones and fertility over the course of approximately one month (see Figure 11.12). After the end of a menstrual period, the anterior pituitary releases **follicle-stimulating hormone (FSH),** which promotes the growth of a follicle in the ovary. The follicle nurtures the *ovum* (egg cell) and produces estrogen. Toward the middle of the menstrual cycle, the follicle builds up more and more receptors to FSH; so, even though the actual concentration of FSH in the blood is decreasing, its effects on the follicle increase. As a result, the follicle produces increasing amounts of one type of estrogen, **estradiol.** Through a mechanism not well understood, the increased release of estradiol causes an increased release of FSH, as well as a sudden surge in the release of **luteinizing hormone (LH)** from the anterior pituitary. (See top graph in Figure 11.12.) FSH and LH cause the follicle to release an ovum, and the remnant of the follicle (now called the *corpus luteum*) to release the hormone progesterone, which prepares the uterus for the implantation of a fertilized ovum. Progesterone also inhibits the further release of LH. At the end of the menstrual cycle, the levels of LH, FSH, estradiol, and progesterone all decline (Feder, 1981). If the ovum is fertilized, the levels of estradiol and progesterone increase gradually throughout pregnancy. If the ovum is not fertilized, the lining of the uterus is cast off (menstruation), and the cycle begins again.

Birth-control pills prevent pregnancy by interfering with the usual feedback cycle between the ovaries and the pituitary. The most widely used birth-control pill, the *combination pill,* contains both estrogen and progesterone. It is so effective because it prevents pregnancy in a variety of ways. High levels of estrogen beginning shortly after the end of the menstrual period suppress the release of FSH, thereby preventing the development of the follicle and the release of an ovum. Progesterone blocks the secretion of luteinizing hormone, thus further guaranteeing that an ovum will not be released.

Changes in hormones over the menstrual cycle produce slight changes in women's sexual interest. The midway point, the **periovulatory period,** when ovulation occurs, is the time of maximum fertility, and gen-

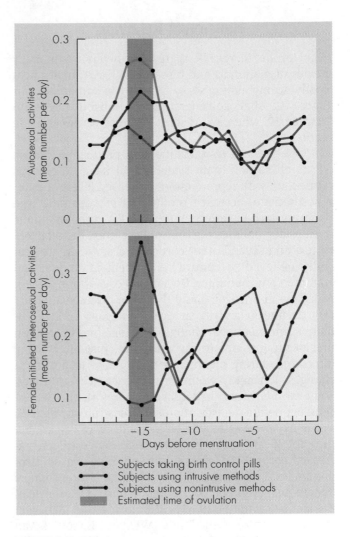

FIGURE 11.13
Female-initiated sexual activities during the monthly cycle
The top graph shows autosexual activities (masturbation and sexual fantasies); the bottom graph shows female-initiated activities with a male partner. "Intrusive" birth-control methods are diaphragm, foam, and condom; "nonintrusive" methods are IUD and vasectomy. Note that women other than pill users increase self-initiated sex activities when their estrogen levels peak.
Source: From Adams, Gold, & Burt, 1978.

erally of the highest estrogen levels. According to two studies, women not taking birth-control pills initiate more sexual activity (either with a partner or by masturbation) during the periovulatory period than at other times during the month (Adams, Gold, & Burt, 1978; Udry & Morris, 1968). (See Figure 11.13.) According to another study, women rate an erotic video as more pleasant and arousing if they watch it during the periovulatory period than if they watch it at other times (Slob, Bax, Hop, Rowland, & van der Werff ten Bosch, 1996). These effects are small, though. Women are less dependent on their current hormone levels for sexual response than are females of other species.

Nonsexual Behavior

Testosterone increases aggressive behavior in many species of mammals and birds. As a result, males fight mostly during mating season, mostly in competition for mates. We shall consider this relationship further in Chapter 12 when we discuss aggressive behavior in general.

Estrogen and testosterone also produce activating effects on several brain systems that have no obvious connection with reproduction. Increased levels of estrogen stimulate increased production of dopamine type D_2 receptors and serotonin type $5HT_{2A}$ receptors in the nucleus accumbens, the prefrontal cortex, the olfactory cortex, and several other cortical areas, which are generally believed to control reinforcement, mood, and emotion (Fink, Sumner, Rosie, Grace, & Quinn, 1996). A decline in estrogen could therefore produce a temporary decline in activity at these synapses and, potentially, some emotional changes. The declines in estrogen that occur just before menstruation, just after giving birth, and during menopause may relate to the mood changes that many women experience at those times. Some women report irritability, discomfort, and depression just before menstruation (*premenstrual syndrome*). Those experiences may have a multitude of causes, but the biological factors include decreased estrogen, increased cortisol (an adrenal hormone), decreased vasopressin, and decreased activity of the neurotransmitters dopamine, serotonin, and norepinephrine (Rosenstein, Kalogeris, Kalafut, Malley, & Rubinow, 1996; Taghavi et al., 1995; Van Goozen, Frijda, Wiegant, Endert, & Van de Poll, 1996). Many of these neural and hormonal abnormalities are found throughout the month, not just during the premenstrual period.

Increased estrogen improves verbal memory, memory of recent events, and fine motor skills, while producing either no change or a slight decline in spatial performance (such as arranging blocks to copy a pattern). The evidence comes both from studies of fluctuations of performance during the menstrual cycle and from studies of women who take estrogen supplements after **menopause** (the time when women stop menstruating) (Sherwin, 1994). Estrogen also improves memory of recent events in female rats (O'Neal, Means, Poole, & Hamm, 1996). All of these effects are small, so I do not recommend that women students try to plan their exam schedules to correspond to the right stage in the menstrual cycle. Although the effects are small, however, they are theoretically interesting, as it is not clear why we evolved a connection between sex hormones and cognitive performance.

Testosterone also has an influence on cognition. Older men who have been given extra testosterone (just enough to boost their levels back up to those typical of young men) exhibit improved performance on spatial tasks (Janowsky, Oviatt, & Orwell, 1994). Again, the effect is small, and the functional value of the testosterone–cognition connection is not obvious.

Puberty

Puberty, the onset of sexual maturity, usually begins at about age 12 to 13 for girls and a year later for boys in the United States. Because reproduction requires a great deal of energy, puberty does not begin until the body has enough energy reserves. On the average, a girl experiences **menarche** (muh-NAR-kee; her first menstruation) when she weighs about 47 kg (103 lbs). Girls who keep their weight very low because of ballet or athletic training or other reasons are slower than others to reach menarche and generally have more irregular menstrual cycles than other girls have. Girls more than 30 percent overweight also have irregular cycles (Frisch, 1983, 1984).

Weight is certainly not the only factor relevant to puberty. In several nonhuman species, exposure to the scent of males accelerates the onset of puberty, and the scent of other females retards it (Vandenbergh, 1987). The same may or may not be true of humans; it would be interesting to compare girls in coed schools with girls in all-girl elementary schools.

Puberty starts when the hypothalamus begins to release *luteinizing hormone releasing hormone* at a rate of about one burst per hour. We do not know what stimulates the hypothalamus to do so, but once it begins, it continues throughout the fertile period. This hormone stimulates the pituitary to secrete LH and FSH, which in turn stimulate the gonads to release estradiol in girls or testosterone in boys (Goldman, 1981). Estradiol causes breast development and broadening of the hips. Testosterone causes lowering of the voice, broadening of the shoulders, and hair growth on the face, chest, underarms, and pubic area. Both boys and girls undergo a growth spurt in response to the increase in hormones.

Parental Behavior

Hormones strongly influence parental behavior in most species of mammals and birds, with humans and possibly other primates standing out as apparent exceptions. Both women and men can be devoted adoptive parents without any hormonal preparation. Hormonal changes are necessary for a woman to breast-feed an infant, but we have no evidence for any other effect of hormones on human parental behavior.

FIGURE **11.14**
Brain development and maternal behavior in mice
The mouse on the left shows normal maternal behavior. The one on the right has a genetic mutation that, among other effects, impairs the development of the preoptic area of the hypothalamus. Source: Brown et al., 1996.

In rodents and most other nonprimates, however, the effects of hormones on parental behavior are clear and strong. Late in pregnancy, female rats produce a pattern of hormones that is incompatible with parental behavior; if infant rats are presented to a pregnant female 2 to 5 days before she is due to give birth, she is actually *less* responsive to them than a virgin female is (Mayer & Rosenblatt, 1984). However, by the day of delivery, her hormones have changed, with a marked increase in prolactin and oxytocin, and so has her behavior. The increase in oxytocin is necessary for the onset of maternal behavior. Ordinarily, oxytocin reaches its peak level at about the time of delivery; drugs that block oxytocin prevent the mother from gathering her young into the nest and huddling in position for them to nurse (Pedersen, Caldwell, Walker, Ayers, & Mason, 1994). Other hormones promote other aspects of maternal behavior. In one study, 30-day-old rats (just a week or so after weaning) were injected with mother rats' plasma that contained all the mothers' hormones. The young rats, especially the females, quickly showed typical rat parental behaviors (Brunelli, Shindledecker, & Hofer, 1987).

Although maternal behavior depends on hormones for the first few days, it becomes less dependent at a later stage. If a female rat that has never been pregnant is left with some 5- to 10-day-old babies, her interest in them increases over several days. (Because the babies cannot survive without parental care, the experimenter must periodically replace them with new, healthy babies.) After about six days, the adoptive mother builds a nest, assembles the babies in the nest, licks them, and does everything else that a normal mother would, except nurse them. Even males, and females whose ovaries were removed, develop most of the normal maternal behaviors if they are kept with rat pups for a few days (R. E. Brown, 1986; Mayer & Rosenblatt, 1979; Rosenblatt, 1967). The males' reactions are particularly curious, as male rats in nature do not help care for the young.

The early hormone-dependent and later experience-dependent phases of rodent parental behavior depend partly on the same and partly on different brain mechanisms. The medial preoptic area of the hypothalamus shows increased activity during both the early and the later phase, and damage to this area impairs parental behavior at either time (Brown, Ye, Bronson, Dikkes, & Greenberg, 1996; Calamandrei & Keverne, 1994; Fleming & Korsmit, 1996; Numan & Numan, 1994). (See Figure 11.14.) (This is the same preoptic area that is so important for temperature regulation, thirst, and sexual behavior. It's a crowded little place.)

A number of other brain areas are important for the later, experience-dependent phase of maternal behavior, some of which contribute by *decreasing* their activity. These areas process information from the vomeronasal organ, which, as you should remember from Chapter 7, responds to pheromones. Evidently, the pheromones from newborn or unfamiliar young inhibit maternal behavior in rodents. If the hormone-dependent activity in the MPOA is high enough, it overcomes the pheromonal inhibition. If not, maternal behavior remains low until the adult has several days of familiarization with the youngs' pheromones, enough to suppress activity in the vomeronasal system (Del Cerro et al., 1995).

Why might a mammal evolve two mechanisms for maternal behavior instead of just one? In the early phase, hormones compensate for the mother's lack of familiarity with the young. In the later phase, experience maintains the maternal behavior beyond the hormonal changes that occurred at birth (Rosenblatt, 1970). During the transitional period between the early and later phases, hormones such as oxytocin are not ordinarily necessary, but can compensate if the experience-dependent mechanisms fail (Pedersen et al., 1995).

IN**CLOSING**

Sex-Related Behaviors and Motivations

Why do humans and other animals engage in sexual and parental behaviors? "To pass on their genes and propagate the species," you may answer. Well, yes, the behaviors evolved to serve those purposes. However, in most cases the motivation for the sex act is simply that it feels good. It is hard to identify all the motivations that contribute to parental behavior, especially in non-humans, but some of the motivation is, again, simply that it feels good. For example, a mother rat licks her babies all over shortly after their birth, providing them with stimulation that is essential for their survival. But the mother presumably does not know the value of the licking for the young; she licks them because she craves the salty taste of the fluid that covers them. She licks them much less if she has access to other salty fluids (Gubernick & Alberts, 1983). In short, animals need not understand the ultimate function of their reproductive behaviors; they have evolved mechanisms that cause them to enjoy and therefore perform those acts.

Summary

1. Among the several types of hormones are peptide hormones and steroid hormones. Peptide hormones attach to membrane receptors and exert effects similar to those of neurotransmitters. Steroid hormones alter the expression of the genes. (p. 299)
2. The hypothalamus controls activity of the pituitary gland through both nerve impulses and releasing hormones. The pituitary in turn secretes hormones that alter the activity of other endocrine glands. (p. 301)
3. The organizing effects of a hormone are exerted during an early sensitive period and bring about relatively permanent alterations in anatomy or in the potential for function. (p. 303)

4. In the absence of sex hormones, an infant mammal develops the female pattern of genitals and hypothalamus. The addition of testosterone shifts development toward the male pattern. Extra estrogen, within normal limits, has little effect on early development. (p. 304)
5. During early development, testosterone is converted within certain cells to estradiol, which actually masculinizes the development of the hypothalamus. Estradiol in the blood does not masculinize development, either because it is bound to proteins in the blood or because it is metabolized. (p. 305)
6. In adulthood, sex hormones can activate sex behaviors, partly by facilitating activity in the medial preoptic area and other parts of the hypothalamus. Dopamine acts at D_1 receptors to increase sexual arousal and at D_2 receptors to stimulate orgasm. Interference with dopamine synapses suppresses sexual behavior. (p. 306)
7. A woman's menstrual cycle depends on a feedback cycle that increases and then decreases the release of several hormones. In many species, females are sexually responsive only when they are fertile. Women can respond sexually at any time in their cycle, although they may have a slight increase in sexual interest around the time of ovulation, when estrogen levels are highest. (p. 309)
8. Puberty begins when the hypothalamus begins to release bursts of luteinizing hormone releasing hormone. The onset of puberty is controlled by many factors, including weight and social stimuli. (p. 310)
9. Hormones released around the time of giving birth facilitate maternal behavior in females of many mammalian species. Nevertheless, mere prolonged exposure to young is also sufficient to induce parental behavior, even in males of certain species. Hormonal facilitation is apparently not essential to human parental behavior. (p. 311)

Review Questions

1. What are the major differences between the anterior pituitary and the posterior pituitary? (p. 301)
2. How do organizing effects differ from activating effects? (p. 303)
3. What are the effects of testosterone in the early sensitive period on the development of the genitals and the hypothalamus? What are the effects of estradiol? Why does the circulating estradiol in a female fetus have little effect on the cells? (p. 304)
4. What drugs are sometimes used in the treatment of male sex offenders? How do they work? (p. 308)
5. Describe the hormonal feedback that regulates the menstrual cycle of women. (p. 309)
6. How do combination birth-control pills prevent pregnancy? (p. 309)
7. What hormonal changes occur in women who complain of premenstrual syndrome? (p. 310)
8. What are some of the factors that control the onset of puberty? (p. 310)
9. What is responsible for maternal behavior in rats in the first few days after giving birth? What is responsible for parental behavior later? (p. 311)

10. Why should we not assume that a rat's maternal behaviors are an attempt to help her babies survive? (p. 312)

Thought Questions

1. The controversial pill RU-486 produces abortions by blocking the effects of progesterone. Explain how this process works.
2. The presence or absence of testosterone determines whether a mammal will differentiate as a male or a female; estrogens have no effect. In birds, the story is the opposite: The presence or absence of estrogen is critical (Adkins & Adler, 1972). What problems would sex determination by estrogen create if that were the mechanism for mammals? Why do those problems not arise in birds? (Hint: Think about the difference between live birth and hatching from an egg.)
3. Antipsychotic drugs, such as haloperidol and chlorpromazine, block activity at dopamine synapses. What side effects might they have on sexual behavior?

Suggestion for Further Reading

Nelson, R. J. (1995). Sunderland, MA: Sinauer Associates. *An introduction to behavioral endocrinology*. An excellent, thorough text on hormones and behavior.

Terms

hormone   chemical secreted by a gland and conveyed by the blood to other organs, whose activity it influences (p. 298)

endocrine gland   organ that produces and releases hormones (p. 298)

protein hormone   hormone composed of a long chain of amino acids (p. 299)

peptide hormone   hormone composed of a short chain of amino acids (p. 299)

steroid hormone   hormone that contains four carbon rings (p. 299)

estrogen   a class of steroid hormones that are more abundant in females than in males for most species (p. 299)

progesterone   a steroid hormone that, among other functions, prepares the uterus for the implantation of a fertilized ovum and promotes the maintenance of pregnancy (p. 299)

androgen   a class of steroid hormones that are more abundant in males than in females for most species (p. 299)

sex-limited gene   gene that exerts its effects primarily in one sex because of activation by androgens or estrogens (p. 300)

pituitary gland   an endocrine gland attached to the hypothalamus (p. 301)

anterior pituitary   portion of the pituitary gland (p. 301)

posterior pituitary   portion of the pituitary gland (p. 301)

oxytocin   hormone released by the posterior pituitary; also a neurotransmitter; important for sexual and parental behaviors (p. 301)

vasopressin (also known as antidiuretic hormone)   hormone released by the posterior hypothalamus; raises blood pressure and enables the kidneys to reabsorb water and therefore to secrete highly concentrated urine (p. 301)

releasing hormone   hormone released by the hypothalamus that flows through the blood to the anterior pituitary (p. 302)

organizing effect   long-lasting effect of a hormone that is present during a sensitive period early in development (p. 303)

activating effect   temporary effect of a hormone on behavior or anatomy, occurring only while the hormone is present (p. 303)

gonad   reproductive organ (p. 303)

testis   male gonad that produces testosterone and sperm (p. 303)

testosterone   one type of androgen (p. 303)

Wolffian ducts   early precursors to male reproductive structures (p. 303)

ovary   female gonad that produces eggs (p. 303)

Müllerian ducts   early precursors to female reproductive structures (the oviducts, uterus, and upper vagina) (p. 303)

sensitive period   time early in development during which some event (such as the presence of a hormone) has a long-lasting effect (p. 303)

alpha-fetoprotein   protein that binds with estrogen in the bloodstream of many immature mammals (p. 306)

impotence   inability to have an erection (p. 308)

menstrual cycle   in women, periodic variation in hormones and fertility over the course of approximately one month (p. 309)

follicle-stimulating hormone (FSH)   anterior pituitary hormone that promotes the growth of follicles in the ovary (p. 309)

estradiol   one type of estrogen (p. 309)

luteinizing hormone (LH)   anterior pituitary hormone that stimulates the release of an ovum and prepares the uterus for implantation of a fertilized ovum (p. 309)

periovulatory period   time just before and after the release of the ovum, when fertility is highest (p. 309)

menopause   time when middle-aged women stop menstruating (p. 310)

puberty   onset of sexual maturity (p. 310)

menarche   time of a woman's first menstruation (p. 310)

Variations in Sexual Development and Orientation

The coral goby is a species of fish in which a male and a female tend their eggs and young together. If one of them dies, the survivor looks for a new partner. But it does not go very far. This is a very stay-at-home kind of fish. If it cannot easily find an available member of the opposite sex, but does find an unmated member of its own sex, it simply changes sex and mates with the neighbor. Male-to-female and female-to-male switches are equally common (Nakashima, Kuwamura, & Yogo, 1995).

Nothing of quite this sort happens in mammals, but it shows us that male and female are not altogether distinct categories. Certain people develop anatomies that are intermediate between male and female, anatomies that do not match their genetic sex, or psychological identities that do not match their anatomies. Some people develop a heterosexual orientation; others, a homosexual orientation. Variations are interesting for their own sake and for what they reveal about sexual development in general.

Sexual development is a very sensitive issue, so let us specify from the start: "Different" does not mean "abnormal," except in the statistical sense. People naturally differ in their sexual development just as they do in their height, weight, emotions, and memory.

Determinants of Gender Identity

Gender identity is how we identify sexually and what we call ourselves. The biological differences between males and females are *sex differences;* the differences resulting from people's thinking about themselves as male or female are *gender differences.* To maintain this useful distinction, we should resist the growing trend to speak of the "gender" of dogs or even of fruit flies. Gender identity is specifically a human characteristic; sex is not.

Gender identity is closely related to, but not identical with, **gender role,** the activities and dispositions that a particular society encourages for one sex or the other. It is possible to have a female gender identity while rejecting all or part of the female gender role.

Gender roles are determined by culture and upbringing. For example, cooking is regarded as women's work in certain societies and as men's work in others. Gender identity is undoubtedly also shaped to a large degree by family experiences. From an early age a girl might be told, "You are a girl, and later if you decide to marry, you will marry a boy." She is dressed in girl's clothing and placed mostly in the company of other girls. Boys receive the reverse treatment.

And yet, a few people are clearly dissatisfied with their assigned gender, a small number of them (transsexuals) to such an extreme degree that they insist on a surgical sex change. Might a biological factor, such as prenatal hormones, influence gender identity? Several kinds of human cases shed some light on this question, though to date we have no definitive answers.

Intersexes or Pseudohermaphrodites

Recall that testosterone masculinizes the development of the genitals and the hypothalamus during a sensitive period in early development. If a genetic female is exposed to more testosterone than the average female but less than the average male, her appearance may become intermediate between male and female. The same is true of a genetic male who has low levels of testosterone or low responsiveness to it.

Rarely, human fetuses are exposed to an abnormal hormonal environment. For example, a female fetus or her mother may have an adrenal gland that produces an excess of testosterone and other androgens, or the mother may have taken an antimiscarriage drug that mimics some of the effects of testosterone. The placenta may lack the enzyme that converts testosterone to estrogen (Shozu, Akasofu, Harada, & Kubota, 1991). If for any reason a female fetus is exposed to elevated androgen levels, the result is partial masculinization of her external anatomy, as Figure 11.15 illustrates. Note in the figure the structure that appears intermediate between a clitoris and a penis, and the swellings that appear intermediate between labia and a scrotum.

Individuals whose genitals do not match the normal development for their genetic sex are referred to as **hermaphrodites** (from Hermaphroditus, son of Hermes and Aphrodite in Greek mythology). There are several types of hermaphrodites. The *true hermaphrodite,* a rarity, has some normal testicular tissue and some normal ovarian tissue—for example, a testis on one side of the body and an ovary on the other. Individuals whose development is intermediate between male and female, like the one in Figure 11.15, are variously called **intersexes, pseudohermaphrodites,** or simply hermaphrodites.

When a baby is born with an intersexual appearance, a decision must be made: Shall we call the child a boy or a girl? As a rule, intersexes are infertile, and their chromosomes are a poor predictor of their eventual genital appearance, behavior patterns, and gender identity. For decades now, the usual policy has been: When in doubt, call the child a girl. Because plastic surgeons cannot successfully enlarge the penis/clitoris to full penis size, they surgically reduce it to clitoris size and create an artificial vagina or lengthen a short natural vagina. At that point, the child looks more or less like a normal female; her parents raise her as a girl and her age-mates accept her as such.

And she lives happily ever after, right? Well, not necessarily. Listen to one intersexual adult (Chase, 1993):

> Surgical and hormonal treatment allows parents and physicians to imagine that they have eliminated the child's intersexuality. Unfortunately, the surgery is immensely destructive of sexual sensation as well as one's sense of bodily integrity. Because the cosmetic result may be good, parents and physicians complacently ignore the child's emotional pain in being forced into a socially acceptable gender. This child's body, once violated by the surgery, is again and again subjected to frequent genital examinations. Many "graduates" of medical intersex corrective programs are chronically depressed, wishing vainly for the return of body parts. Suicides are not uncommon. Some former intersexuals become transsexual, rejecting their imposed sex. (p. 3)

So, how *should* such a child be reared? On that question, psychologists do not agree. What do we learn about the causes of gender identity from a study of intersexes? Again, the answer is inconclusive. Their prenatal hormonal patterns were intermediate between male and female, their early experiences may not have

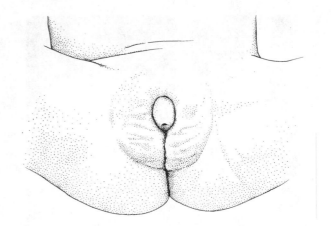

FIGURE **11.15**
External genitals of a genetic female, age 3 months
Masculinized by excess androgens from the adrenal gland before birth, the infant shows the effects of the adrenogenital syndrome.

been altogether normal, and their resulting gender identities may be male, female, or ambiguous (Ehrhardt & Money, 1967; Money, 1970; Money & Ehrhardt, 1968). Under these circumstances, we cannot clearly separate the influences of prenatal hormones and postnatal experiences.

Testicular Feminization

Certain individuals with the typical male XY chromosome pattern have the genital appearance of a female. This condition is known as **androgen insensitivity** or **testicular feminization.** Although such individuals produce normal amounts of androgens, their bodies lack the mechanism that enables androgens to bind to genes in a cell's nucleus. Consequently, the cells are insensitive to androgens, and the external genitals develop almost like those of a normal female. Two abnormalities appear at puberty. First, in spite of breast development and broadening of the hips, menstruation does not begin, because the body has two internal testes instead of ovaries and a uterus. (The vagina is short and leads to nothing.) Second, pubic hair does not develop, because it depends on androgens in females as well as males (see Figure 11.16).

A person with androgen insensitivity develops a clear female gender identity. If her condition is medically identified, typically the short vagina is surgically lengthened and the internal testes are removed, because they are likely to develop tumors and to cause additional health problems. Her female gender identity should come as no surprise: She looks like a normal

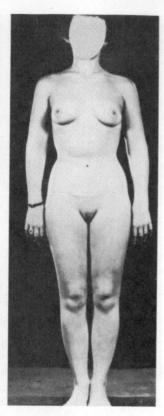

FIGURE 11.16
A woman with an XY chromosome pattern but insensitivity to androgens
Two undescended testes produce testosterone and other androgens, to which the body is insensitive. The testes and adrenal glands also produce estrogens that are responsible for the pubertal changes.   Source: Federman, 1967.

female, she has been raised unambiguously as a female, and her cells have been exposed only to estrogens since prenatal development. The only discrepancy is that her genetic sex is male (XY).

Discrepancies of Sexual Appearance

Most of the evidence from pseudohermaphrodites does not tell us anything indisputable about the roles of rearing and hormones in determining gender identity. From a scientific viewpoint, the only decisive way to settle the issue would be to raise a completely normal male baby as a female or to raise a normal female baby as a male. If the process succeeded in producing an adult who was fully satisfied in the assigned role, we would know that upbringing determines gender identity and that hormones do not. Although no one would perform such an experiment intentionally, it is possible to study accidental events. Here, we shall consider examples in which children were (presumably) exposed before birth to the hormonal pattern of one sex and then reared as members of the other sex.

Penis development delayed until puberty   Certain genetic males in the Dominican Republic were born with a gene that prevents penis growth early in life. Specifically, they have low levels of the enzyme that converts testosterone to the related hormone DHT (5-alpha-dihydrotestosterone). DHT is more effective than testosterone for masculinizing the genitals; thus, the consequence of the enzyme deficiency is a lack of penis growth before puberty. These children's testosterone levels were probably normal, however, and capable of influencing brain development. Until puberty, they were regarded as girls with slightly swollen clitorises. At puberty, their testosterone levels increased enough that, even without DHT, their penises grew. At this point, each was reassigned as a male.

If you had lived your first 12 years or so as a female and then suddenly grew a penis, and your parents said that now you were a boy, how would you react? Perhaps surprisingly, in nearly all known cases in which this has happened, the girl-turned-boy developed a clear male gender identity and directed his sexual interest toward females (Imperato-McGinley, Guerrero, Gautier, & Peterson, 1974). One interpretation of these results is that the prenatal testosterone favored a male gender identity even in children who were reared as females. Another possibility is that gender identity is established by social influences during adolescence. In either case, the results make it difficult to argue that early rearing experiences are the sole determinant of gender identity, unless we assume that these children were actually recognized as different from the start and were reared in an abnormal way. (We can only speculate about whether it would be equally easy for someone reared as a male to switch to a female identity.)

Accidental removal of the penis   Circumcision is the removal of the foreskin of the penis, a common procedure with newborn boys in the United States. One physician using an electrical procedure accidentally used too high a current and burned off the entire penis. The parents elected to rear the child as a female, with the appropriate corrective surgery. What makes this a particularly interesting case is that the child had a twin brother (whom the parents did not let the physician try to circumcise). If both twins developed satisfactory gender identities, one as a girl and the other as a boy, we would conclude that rearing was decisive in gender identity and that prenatal hormones were not. Initial reports claimed that the child reared as a girl had a normal female gender identity, despite strong tomboyish tendencies (Money & Schwartz, 1978). However, by about age 10 she had figured out that something was wrong and that "she" was really a boy. She preferred boys' activities and played only with boys' toys. She even tried urinating in a standing position, unsuccessfully. By age 14 she insisted that she wanted to live as a boy. At that time, the father tearfully explained what had happened earlier. The teenager changed names and became accepted by classmates as a boy; at age 25 he married a somewhat older woman and adopted her children. Clearly, the biological predisposition had won out over the family's attempts to rear the child as a girl (Diamond & Sigmundson, 1997).

Possible Biological Bases of Sexual Orientation

Why do some people prefer partners of the other sex and some prefer partners of their own sex? This topic is particularly difficult because it is so hard to separate scientific issues from social and political disputes. Most of our discussion will focus on male homosexuality, which is more common than female homosexuality and more heavily investigated.

Most people say that their sexual orientation "just happened," generally at an early age, and that they do not know how or why it developed as it did. Sexual orientation, like left- or right-handedness, is not something that people choose or that they can easily change.

Regardless of whether the factors controlling variations in sexual orientation are genetic, environmental, or both, we should expect to find similarities among children growing up within a family. And, indeed, investigators have consistently found that homosexual men are likely to have homosexual brothers and homosexual women are likely to have homosexual sisters. However, various studies have not agreed on whether the same families are likely to include both homosexual men and homosexual women (Bailey & Bell, 1993; Bailey & Benishay, 1993). The lack of agreement on this point is disappointing, because a consistent result would tell us whether the factors influencing sexual orientation are the same in men as in women.

Genetics

Figure 11.17 shows the frequency of homosexual and heterosexual orientations in the adult brothers of homosexual men and the adult sisters of homosexual women. Note that the probability of homosexuality is highest in monozygotic (identical) twins of the originally identified homosexual individual, lower in dizygotic twins, and still lower in adopted brothers or sisters (Bailey & Pillard, 1991; Bailey, Pillard, Neale, & Agyei, 1993). Another study with a smaller sample found similar results (Whitam, Diamond, & Martin, 1993). The results imply that genes influence sexual orientation. Note, however, two limitations:

• The results are based on limited samples, which may be unrepresentative in some way. As always, it is best to wait for replications on additional samples.
• If genetic factors completely determined sexual orientation, all pairs of identical twins would have the same sexual orientation. The frequent discrepancies indicate the importance of other, unidentified influences. Note, of course, that the explanation need not be the same for every individual.

One study that examined relatives beyond the immediate family found a higher incidence of homosexuality among the maternal relatives of homosexual men than among the paternal relatives. (See Figure 11.18.) The likely explanation is that there may be a relevant gene on the X chromosome, which a man receives only from his mother. If a gene on the X chromosome increases the probability that a male will develop a homosexual orientation, then his mother must have that gene also, even though it might have different, or even undetectable, effects on her own behavior. The gene would also occur in at least half of the mother's sisters (depending on whether they got that X chromosome from their mother or father), and any sister who had it

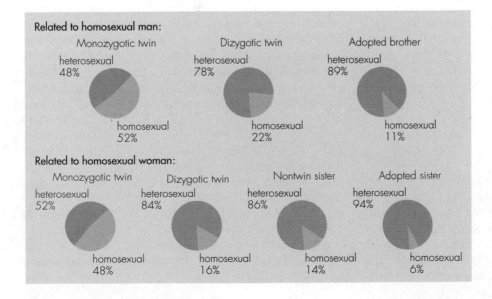

Related to homosexual man:

Monozygotic twin	Dizygotic twin	Adopted brother
heterosexual 48%	heterosexual 78%	heterosexual 89%
homosexual 52%	homosexual 22%	homosexual 11%

Related to homosexual woman:

Monozygotic twin	Dizygotic twin	Nontwin sister	Adopted sister
heterosexual 52%	heterosexual 84%	heterosexual 86%	heterosexual 94%
homosexual 48%	homosexual 16%	homosexual 14%	homosexual 6%

FIGURE 11.17
Sexual orientations in adult relatives of a homosexual man or woman
Note that the probability of a homosexual orientation is highest among monozygotic twins of a homosexual individual, lower among dizygotic twins, and still lower among adopted brothers or sisters. These data suggest a genetic contribution toward the development of sexual orientation. Source: Based on the data of Bailey & Pillard, 1991; Bailey, Pillard, Neale, & Agyei, 1993.

FIGURE **11.18**
Incidence of homosexual orientations in adult male relatives of homosexual males
Incidences are higher in relatives on the mother's side than on the father's side. Incidence is also higher in sons of the mother's sister than in sons of the mother's brother. These results are consistent with a hypothesis that a gene promoting male homosexuality is located on the X chromosome.
Source: Data of Hamer, Hu, Magnuson, Hu, & Pattatucci, 1993.

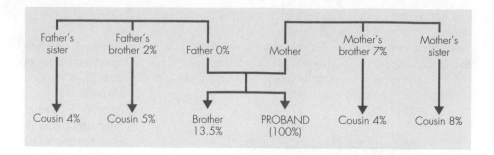

would pass it to half of her sons. Many of the mother's brothers would also have the gene, but their sons would not. (Remember, sons get their X chromosomes from their mothers.) The data in Figure 11.18 fit this set of predictions reasonably well (Hamer, Hu, Magnuson, Hu, & Pattatucci, 1993). The design of this study is interesting; however, the sample sizes are small and the effects are small. Until and unless they are replicated, we should avoid drawing premature conclusions.

You should not assume that a gene correlated with sexual orientation necessarily exerts its effects by controlling the brain structures responsible for sexual behavior. We could imagine all sorts of indirect routes by which a gene might influence the way someone reacts to various experiences, or even modify physical appearance in such a way as to elicit different treatment by other people.

If certain genes promote a homosexual orientation, no matter how directly or indirectly, then why has evolution not selected strongly against those genes, which decrease the probability of reproduction? One possible explanation is that the genes might produce different effects in different people, sometimes increasing homosexuality and sometimes increasing the likelihood of reproduction. (For example, we could hypothesize a gene that increased the probability of homosexuality in boys and increased the fertility of their sisters.) Another possibility is that homosexual men and women perhaps help their brothers or sisters to rear children, and thereby perpetuate genes that the whole family shares (LeVay, 1993). Although this hypothesis is plausible, we have no evidence to support it.

Hormones

Given the importance of hormones for sexual behavior, it seems natural to look for their possible effects on sexual orientation. We can quickly dismiss the hypothesis that sexual orientation depends on adult hormone levels: Most homosexual men have testosterone and estrogen levels well within the same range as heterosexual men; most lesbian women also have hormone levels

well within the typical female range. One study found that the more masculine or "butch" member of lesbian couples tends to have a slightly higher testosterone level than the other, more "femme" member, but these differences were small and inconsistent (Pearcey, Docherty, & Dabbs, 1996).

A more plausible hypothesis is that sexual orientation depends on testosterone levels during a sensitive period of brain development, perhaps from the middle of the second month of pregnancy until the end of the fifth month (Ellis & Ames, 1987). In studies of animals ranging from rats to pigs to zebra finches, males that were exposed to much-decreased levels of testosterone early in life have as adults shown sexual interest in other males (Adkins-Regan, 1988). Females exposed to extra testosterone during that period show an increased probability of attempting to mount sexual partners in the way that males typically do. (See Figure 11.19.)

However, in many of these animal studies the hormonal manipulation also led to abnormalities of the genitals. (Homosexual and heterosexual people are anatomically the same.) A more relevant animal study is one in which a treatment altered sexual behavior without much effect on anatomy: In several experiments, rats in the final week of pregnancy had the stressful experience of being confined in tight Plexiglas tubes for more than 2 hours each day under bright lights. Such stress increases the release of endorphins, some of which cross the placenta and evidently reach the fetus's developing hypothalamus, where endorphins produce antitestosterone effects (Ward, Monaghan, & Ward, 1986). In some cases the pregnant rats were given alcohol as well as subjected to stressful experiences (Ward, 1977; Ward, Ward, Winn, & Bielawski, 1994). Either prenatal stress or alcohol modified the males' behavior, presumably by altering development of the hypothalamus, but did not affect external anatomy. As adults, these males responded sexually to either male or female partners (Ward, Ward, Winn, & Bielawski, 1994).

Although the sexual behavior of prenatally stressed males is altered, their behavior is typically male in certain other regards, such as level of activity in an open

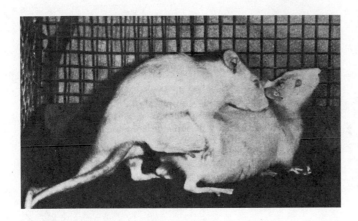

FIGURE **11.19**
A female rat mounting a male
The female was injected with androgens during an early sensitive period; the male was castrated at birth and injected with androgens at adulthood.   Source: Dörner, 1974.

field (Meisel, Dohanich, & Ward, 1979). Evidently, different aspects of sex-differentiated behavior are organized at different times in development or are sensitive to different types of androgens. Even for sexual behavior, the effects of prenatal stress varied, depending on social experiences after birth. Prenatally stressed males reared in isolation or with one another developed a sexual responsivity only to males. Those reared with nonstressed males and females became sexually responsive to both males and females (Dunlap, Zadina, & Gougis, 1978; Ward & Reed, 1985).

With regard to human sexual orientation, the rat data are suggestive, but also have limitations:

• What is true of rats may not be true of humans. Hormonal influences on sexual behavior vary even between one primate species and another.
• The female sexual behaviors shown by the male rats in these studies (such as arching their backs) do not closely mimic human behaviors. In humans, male homosexuals are characterized by their preference for male partners, not necessarily by their preference for female postures or behaviors.

Despite their limitations, the rat studies suggest that investigators should examine any possible relationship between prenatal events and later sexual orientation. One approach is to ask the mothers of homosexual men whether they experienced any unusual stress during pregnancy. One researcher contacted 283 mothers of homosexual and heterosexual men, without letting them know why or how they had been chosen. The survey made no mention of sexual orientation; it merely asked about a variety of illnesses and stressors that the woman might have experienced before, during, or after pregnancy. The mothers of homosexual men reported a significantly greater number of stressful events, especially during the second trimester of pregnancy (Ellis, Ames, Peckham, & Burke, 1988). However, a similar study failed to find increased stress during pregnancies that produced homosexual sons (Bailey, Willerman, & Parks, 1991). Both studies are limited by their reliance on mothers' memories of pregnancies more than 20 years earlier. A more decisive (though much more difficult) procedure would be to measure stress during pregnancy and follow up later to identify the sexual orientation of the offspring. At this point, the relationship between prenatal stress and human sexual orientation is uncertain.

What about the role of hormones in female homosexuality? In the 1950s and early 1960s, certain pregnant women took the synthetic estrogen **diethylstilbestrol (DES)** to prevent miscarriage or to alleviate other problems. DES can exert masculinizing effects similar to those of testosterone. One study found that of 30 adult women whose mothers had taken DES during pregnancy, 7 reported some degree of homosexual or bisexual responsiveness. By comparison, only 1 of 30 women not prenatally exposed to DES reported any homosexual or bisexual responsiveness (Ehrhardt et al., 1985). Note that although these results suggest that prenatal hormones play a role, they do not demonstrate a very strong influence.

Brain Anatomy

On the average, men's brains differ from women's in several ways, including the relative sizes of parts of the hypothalamus (Breedlove, 1992). Do the brains of homosexual men resemble those of heterosexual men or heterosexual women?

Current, rather incomplete evidence shows results that vary from one brain area to another. The anterior commissure (see p. 383) is, on the average, larger in heterosexual women than in heterosexual men; in homosexual men, it is at least as large as it is in women, perhaps even slightly larger (Gorski & Allen, 1992). The implications of this difference are unclear, as the anterior commissure has no known relationship to sexual behavior. The suprachiasmatic nucleus (SCN) is also larger in homosexual men than in heterosexual men (Swaab & Hofman, 1990). Recall from Chapter 9 that the SCN controls circadian rhythms. How might a difference in the SCN relate to sexual orientation? The answer is not clear, but male rats that are deprived of testosterone during early development also show abnormalities in the SCN, and their preference for male or female sexual partners varies with time of day. They make sexual advances toward both male and female partners early in their active period of the day, but mostly toward females as the day goes on (Swaab, Slob, Houtsmuller, Brand, & Zhou, 1995). Does human sexual behavior or orientation also vary depending on time

FIGURE **11.20**
Typical sizes of interstitial nucleus 3 of the anterior hypothalamus
On the average, the volume of this structure was more than twice as large in a sample of heterosexual men (left) than it was in a sample of homosexual men (right), for whom it was about the same size as that in women. Animal studies have implicated this structure as important for male sexual activities.   Source: From LeVay, 1991.

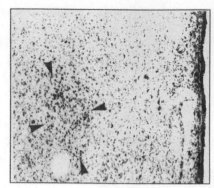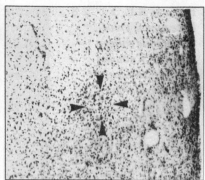

of day? Not so far as anyone has reported, but the topic certainly merits further research.

The most suggestive studies of brain differences concern a particular nucleus of the anterior hypothalamus, known as interstitial nucleus 3, which is generally more than twice as large in heterosexual men as in women. This area corresponds to part of the dimorphic nucleus of the medial preoptic area, which is important for male sexual behavior in rats. Simon LeVay (1991) examined interstitial nucleus 3 in 41 people who had died between the ages of 26 and 59. Of these, 16 were heterosexual men, 6 were heterosexual women, and 19 were homosexual men. All of the homosexual men, 6 of the 16 heterosexual men, and 1 of the 6 women had died of AIDS. LeVay found that the mean volume of interstitial nucleus 3 was 0.12 mm^3 in heterosexual men, 0.056 mm^3 in heterosexual women, and 0.051 mm^3 in homosexual men. Figure 11.20 shows typical cross-sections for a heterosexual man and a homosexual man. Figure 11.21 shows the distribution of volumes for the three groups. Note that the difference between heterosexual men and the other two groups is fairly large, and that the cause of death (AIDS versus other) has no clear relationship to the results.

These data have certain limitations. Although cause of death does not apparently relate to brain structure for heterosexual men, it would nevertheless be helpful to examine the brains of homosexual men who died of causes other than AIDS. LeVay (1993) later examined the hypothalamus of a homosexual man who died of lung cancer; he had a small interstitial nucleus 3, like the homosexual men who died of AIDS. Still, it would be helpful to examine more cases.

A second limitation is that we do not know whether the apparent brain differences were present since early childhood or whether they developed in adulthood, perhaps a result of sexual activity instead of a cause. We could debate the likelihood that sexual activity might enlarge or reduce the size of a brain structure, but there is no substitute for data on this point.

A third point is that we do not know how interstitial nucleus 3 contributes to sexual behavior. Male rats with damage to this area show a decrease in sexual be-

FIGURE **11.21**
Distribution of volumes for interstitial nucleus 3 of the anterior hypothalamus
Samples are females (F), heterosexual males (M), and homosexual males (HM). Each filled circle represents a person who died of AIDS; each triangle represents a person who died from other causes. The one open circle represents a bisexual man who died of AIDS.   Source: From LeVay, 1991.

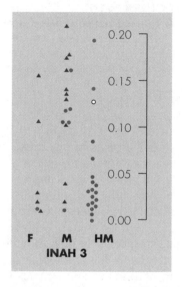

havior but no change in preference among sexual partners. Male ferrets with damage here, however, do shift to preferring male partners (Baum et al., 1996). We need to know more about the functions of this brain area.

One final point: In Figure 11.21, note that although the groups differ fairly substantially on average, they also overlap. Consequently, the data do not indicate that the structure of the hypothalamus completely determines sexual orientation. At most, it alters the probability of developing one orientation or another.

IN **CLOSING**

We Are Not All the Same

In case I have not made it sufficiently clear, let me reemphasize that research into sexual orientation is still inconclusive. The data now available suggest effects of genes, prenatal hormones, and differences in brain organization, but in no case are we certain how these factors contribute, how much of the variance they control, or how they interact with experience. Sexual preferences differ in many other ways beyond those that we have explored here, including frequency of sexual behavior and the kinds of activities that give pleasure. Regardless of whether we expect to find biological or sociological explanations for such variations, many questions remain unanswered.

Summary

1. It is difficult to determine the role, if any, of prenatal hormones in the development of gender identity. Because the sex defined by rearing usually matches the prenatal hormone pattern, the effects of rearing and hormones are hard to distinguish. (p. 314)
2. Intersexes or pseudohermaphrodites are people who were subjected to a hormonal pattern intermediate between male and female during their prenatal sensitive period for sexual development. (p. 315)
3. Although most intersexes accept their assigned sex, a number of them are somewhat or greatly dissatisfied. The contributions of prenatal hormones and rearing are hard to separate. (p. 315)
4. A limited amount of evidence suggests a genetic influence on sexual orientation, through unknown means. (p. 317)
5. Procedures that prevent testosterone from masculinizing the brains of male rats during a prenatal period lead to an adult pattern of sexual responsiveness toward other male rats. The relationship of this finding to human homosexuality is speculative. (p. 318)
6. Prenatal exposure to masculinizing hormones may contribute to some instances of female homosexuality. (p. 319)

Review Questions

1. What may cause a human to develop as an intersex? (p. 315)
2. Why are the observations on gender identity in intersexes scientifically inconclusive? (p. 315)
3. What is testicular feminization, and what are its effects on development? (p. 315)
4. What other kinds of evidence may help to evaluate the possible contribution of prenatal hormones to gender identity? (p. 316)
5. What event in early development can cause a male rat to develop sexual responsiveness to other males and not to females? Through what mechanism does this event probably operate? (p. 318)

6. What differences have been reported, on the average, between the brains of homosexual and heterosexual men? (p. 319)

Thought Questions

1. On the average, intersexes have IQ scores in the 110 to 125 range, well above the mean for the population (Dalton, 1968; Ehrhardt & Money, 1967; Lewis, Money, & Epstein, 1968). One possible interpretation is that a hormonal pattern intermediate between male and female promotes greater intellectual development. Another possibility is that intersexuality may be more common in intelligent families than in less intelligent ones or that the more intelligent families are more likely to bring their intersex children to an investigator's attention. What kind of study would be best for deciding among these hypotheses? (For one answer, see Money & Lewis, 1966.)
2. Recall LeVay's study of brain anatomy in heterosexual and homosexual men (p. 320). Certain critics have suggested that one or more of the men classified as "heterosexual" might actually have been homosexual or bisexual. If so, would that fact strengthen or weaken the overall conclusions?

Suggestions for Further Reading

LeVay, S. (1993). *The sexual brain.* Cambridge, MA: MIT Press. Discusses the biological basis of sexual behaviors, including sexual orientation.

Short, R. V., & Balaban, E. (Eds.). (1994). *The differences between the sexes.* Cambridge, England: Cambridge University Press. How do the sexes differ? Why do they differ? Why do we have two sexes at all? This outstanding book explores the research on some of the most profound questions about sex.

Terms

gender identity   the sex with which a person identifies (p. 314)

gender role   the activities and dispositions that a particular society encourages for one sex or the other (p. 314)

hermaphrodite   individual whose genitals do not match the normal development for his or her genetic sex (p. 315)

intersex or pseudohermaphrodite   individual whose sexual development is intermediate between male and female (p. 315)

androgen insensitivity or testicular feminization   condition in which a person lacks the mechanism that enables androgens to bind to genes in a cell's nucleus (p. 315)

diethylstilbestrol (DES)   a synthetic estrogen (p. 319)

EMOTIONAL BEHAVIORS AND STRESS

CHAPTER **TWELVE**

MAIN**IDEAS**

1. Frequent, intense activation of the sympathetic nervous system may increase heart rate, blood pressure, and probability of heart disease.
2. Chronic stress can suppress immune system activity and leave an individual more vulnerable to illness.
3. Aggressive behavior is associated with activity in parts of the hypothalamus and amygdala and with decreased serotonin turnover.
4. The amygdala appears to be critical for learned fears.

For most of the behaviors psychologists study, we can agree on practical operational definitions that apply equally well to all species. For example, we can run simple experiments to determine whether a housefly, a slug, or any other animal has vision, color vision, hearing, hunger, thirst, and the ability to learn and remember. We can also test robots. Most of us now feel quite comfortable talking about machines that learn or have artificial vision or intelligence. I have never heard of machine hunger, but certainly it would be possible to build a robot that periodically searches for light to recharge its solar batteries.

But we do not have equally clear definitions of emotions. Do houseflies and slugs feel anger and fear? I don't know. Is there *anything* a robot could do to convince us that it has emotions? Most of us answer either "no" or "I'm not sure." The term *emotion* generally refers to an internal experience that we can only infer. Most of us balk at the idea that a machine could feel emotion.

However, although we have trouble defining and measuring the experience of emotion, we can readily observe vigorous behaviors (such as attack and escape) that we associate with it. Research may or may not take us any closer to understanding the internal experience, but it has already discovered much about the physiological mechanisms that control the behavior.

Emotion, the Nervous System, and Health

When driving a car, you use an accelerator to increase speed and a brake to decrease speed. Although I would not push the analogy too far, some emotional states speed up your actions to deal with an emergency; others slow you down to be cautious or to conserve energy.

Where Is Emotion in the Brain?

In pioneering studies, Philip Bard (1929, 1934) found that when he removed a cat's entire cerebral cortex, the cat displayed exaggerated aggressive behaviors and postures in response to various stimuli. He concluded that subcortical structures were sufficient for vigorous emotional behaviors; the function of the cerebral cortex

was to direct those behaviors toward appropriate targets and, when appropriate, to suppress them.

In 1937, J. W. Papez (rhymes with *grapes*) proposed that emotional behaviors in general depend on a group of forebrain structures, including the hypothalamus, hippocampus, amygdala, olfactory bulb, septum, other small structures, and parts of the thalamus and cerebral cortex (see Figure 12.1). Papez noted that cells in parts of the limbic system respond to taste, smell, and pain stimuli, all of which evoke strong emotional reactions. These sensory modalities also have the properties of slow onset, slow offset, and poor localization of stimulus—properties that characterize emotions as well.

Paul MacLean revived and revised Papez's theory, giving Papez's circuit of forebrain structures the name **limbic system** (MacLean, 1949, 1958, 1970). As men-

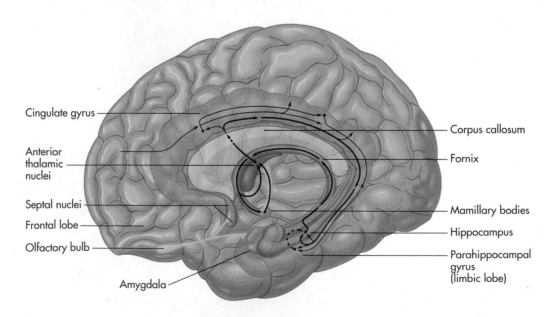

FIGURE **12.1**
The limbic system
Source: Based on MacLean, 1949.

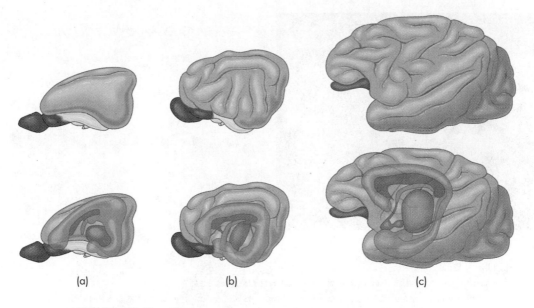

(a)   (b)   (c)

FIGURE **12.2**
Species comparisons for the limbic system
Note the similarities for the limbic systems (dark areas) of (**a**) a rabbit,
(**b**) a cat, and (**c**) a monkey, in both the lateral surface (top) and the medial
surface (bottom).   Source: From MacLean, 1954.

tioned in Chapter 4, the term *limbic* comes from *limbus,* meaning border. The limbic system forms a border around the brain stem. MacLean noted that some people with an *epileptic focus* (point of origin of epileptic attacks) in the amygdala or other limbic system structures occasionally experience aggressive impulses, fear, laughter, sexual arousal, or other emotional states immediately before, during, or after their epileptic seizures. He also noted that the size of the limbic system varies less across mammalian species than does the size of the cerebral cortex (see Figure 12.2); he inferred that the limbic system controls primitive functions that all mammals have in common, such as aggression, escape from danger, and sexual reproduction.

Later research has confirmed and clarified the role of limbic system structures for various emotional behaviors; we shall consider especially the hypothalamus and amygdala later in this chapter. Clearly, however, the full experience of emotion activates much more of the brain. Several studies indicate that the right hemisphere of the cerebral cortex may be more important than the left for certain aspects of emotion. One study tested the ability of brain-damaged people to identify other people's emotions from their facial expressions. None had any trouble recognizing happy expressions; all those who had trouble with sad or fearful expressions had damage in the right hemisphere (Adolphs, Damasio, Tranel, & Damasio, 1996). In another study, college students viewed slides of either neutral or upsetting scenes in either the right visual field (information sent first to the left hemisphere) or the left visual

field (information sent first to the right hemisphere). Emotionally upsetting information to the right hemisphere evoked greater heart rate and blood pressure changes than did the same information to the left hemisphere (Spence, Shapiro, & Zaidel, 1996).

Autonomic Nervous System Arousal

Emotional behaviors are accompanied by changes in heart and breathing rates and other internal activities that prepare the body for the increased demands it faces. The internal activities depend on the two branches of the autonomic nervous system. The sympathetic nervous system prepares the body for intense, vigorous, emergency activity. The parasympathetic nervous system increases digestion and other processes associated with conservation of energy and preparation for later events. The parasympathetic system becomes especially active after removal of a stimulus that excited the sympathetic system. Both systems are active at almost all times, although at a given moment one may be more active than the other. (To review the structure of the sympathetic and parasympathetic nervous systems, see Figure 4.6.)

Cells in the limbic system, particularly in the hypothalamus and amygdala, interpret emotionally significant events and send messages to cells in the medulla and pons, which relay the messages to the spinal cord,

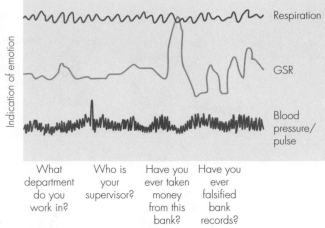

FIGURE **12.3**
The polygraph test, literally a "many measures test"
The examiner asks a series of questions and compares the autonomic responses. One major difficulty is that a heightened response may indicate either nervousness about lying or nervousness about being accused of an offense.

controlling sympathetic nervous activity (Jansen, Nguyen, Karpitskiy, Mettenleiter, & Loewy, 1995). Axons from the thoracic and lumbar portions of the spinal cord activate a chain of sympathetic ganglia outside the spinal cord; axons from those ganglia extend to the organs. Axons from the pons, medulla, and sacral portion of the spinal cord constitute the parasympathetic system.

Exactly what is the relationship between autonomic nervous system arousal and emotions? Common sense holds that we first feel an emotion, which then evokes changes in heart rate and so forth. However, according to the **James–Lange theory,** first proposed in 1884, the autonomic arousal and skeletal actions come first; what we experience as an emotion is the label we give to our responses: I am afraid *because* I run away; I am angry *because* I attack. According to an alternative view, the **Cannon–Bard theory,** an event, such as a frenzied killer running toward you with a chain saw, evokes the emotional experience and the physical arousal simultaneously but independently. The evidence suggests that neither theory is exactly correct. It is possible, by drugs or other means, to enhance or diminish autonomic responses. If the Cannon–Bard theory were correct, changes in the intensity of autonomic arousal should have no effect on emotional experience. If the James–Lange theory were correct, any change in autonomic arousal would produce a proportional change in emotion, and abolition of autonomic arousal would eliminate emotions. In fact, although changes in autonomic arousal do produce changes in reported emotional experience (Reisenzein, 1983), complete paralysis with loss of sensation from the internal organs

does not eliminate emotional experience (Lowe & Carroll, 1985).

Measurements of Autonomic Arousal

Because so many different emotional events arouse the sympathetic nervous system, researchers can measure aspects of sympathetic arousal, such as heart rate and breathing rate, to gauge emotional arousal. However, such measurements do not indicate *which* emotion someone is feeling, nor do they always distinguish between emotional arousal and responses due to exercise and so forth.

The polygraph test—the so-called lie-detector test—measures sympathetic nervous system arousal (see Figure 12.3): It typically records heart rate, blood pressure, breathing rate, and **galvanic skin response (GSR)** (measuring the electrical conductance of the skin, which varies with the slight sweating caused by sympathetic nerves). The theory behind the polygraph test is that when people lie their nervousness elevates the response of their sympathetic nervous system. Because lying is only loosely related to nervousness, the polygraph is not a highly reliable indicator of truthfulness. Some people can remain calm while lying about their criminal activities; others become nervous even when they are telling the truth. How would you react if someone strapped you into a polygraph device and then asked whether you had stolen ten thousand dollars last Thursday? About half of all innocent people "fail" the lie-detector test (Forman & McCauley, 1986; Patrick & Iacono, 1989).

Emotions, Autonomic Responses, and Health

In the early days of scientific medicine, physicians made little allowance for the relation of personality or emotions to health and disease. If someone became ill, the cause had to be a virus, a bacterium, or something else visibly identifiable. Today, **behavioral medicine** emphasizes the effects on health of diet, smoking, exercise, and other behaviors. We have also come to accept that stress and emotions influence what diseases people get, when they become ill, and how well they recover. This view does not imply any mystical concept of "mind over matter"; stress and emotions are, after all, inseparable from brain activity and, of course, the brain directs body functions.

However, it is easy to overestimate the influence of emotions on health. For example, many people assert confidently that stress increases the risk of cancer, including breast cancer. However, although some studies have found a relationship between stress and cancer, other equally large and equally well-done studies have failed to find any such relationship (Chen et al., 1995; Roberts, Newcomb, Trentham-Dietz, & Storer, 1996). Stress and emotions may indeed affect cancer onset, but their role is small compared to genes, diet, exposure to toxic substances, and other established causes of cancer. Above all, we should avoid making sick people feel guilty by implying that they must have been living wrong or thinking the wrong thoughts. We shall now consider a couple of examples of apparent relationships between emotions and health.

Voodoo Death and Related Phenomena

Almost everyone knows of someone with a strong will to live who survived well beyond others' expectations and of others who apparently "gave up" and died sooner than expected. An extreme case is *voodoo death*, in which a healthy person dies apparently just because he or she believes that a curse has destined death.

Such phenomena were generally ignored by scientists until Walter Cannon (1942) published a collection of reasonably well-documented reports of voodoo death. In a typical example, a woman who ate a fruit and then learned that it had come from a taboo place died within hours. The common pattern in such cases was that the intended victims knew about the magic spells and believed that they were sure to die. Friends and relatives, who also believed in the hex, began to treat the victim as a dying person. Overwhelmed with dread and hopelessness, the victim refused food and

water and died, usually within 24 to 48 hours. Similar examples occur in almost any society—not necessarily that people die because they believe they are hexed, but people with minor illnesses or injuries die because they expect to.

What is the cause of death in such cases? Curt Richter accidentally stumbled on a possible answer while studying the swimming abilities of rats. Ordinarily, rats can swim in turbulent warm water nonstop for 48 hours or more. However, a rat's whiskers are critical to its ability to find its way around, and Richter (1957a) found that a rat would die quickly if he cut off its whiskers just before throwing it into the tank. It would swim frantically for a minute or so and then suddenly sink to the bottom, dead. Richter found that under these conditions many, but not all, laboratory rats died quickly. Wild rats, which are more excitable, all died quickly under the same conditions. Autopsies showed that they had not drowned; their hearts had simply stopped beating.

Richter's explanation was that dewhiskering the rat and then suddenly throwing it into water greatly stimulated the rat's sympathetic nervous system and thus its heart rate. After the rat swam frantically for a minute or so and found no escape, its parasympathetic system became highly activated in rebound from the strong sympathetic activation. Massive parasympathetic response may have stopped the rat's heart altogether.

To confirm this explanation, Richter placed a rat in the water several times, rescuing it each time. Then he cut off the rat's whiskers and put it in the water again. The rescues apparently immunized the rat against extreme terror in this situation; it swam successfully for many hours. Richter's results suggest that certain cases of sudden death in a frightening situation may be due to excessive parasympathetic activity.

Does this explanation apply to many cases of heart attacks? Probably not. Most heart attacks begin when excessive sympathetic nervous system activity disrupts the normal rhythmic beating of the heart (Kamarck & Jennings, 1991). Excessive parasympathetic activity is probably a serious problem only under limited circumstances.

Sympathetic Arousal and Heart Disease

Some people consistently show stronger and quicker sympathetic responses to a wide variety of stimuli than other people do. They also tend to show more emotional expression and to be more gregarious and impulsive (Shields, 1983). Because the sympathetic nervous system increases heart rate, people with highly responsive sympathetic nervous systems may be putting extra strain on their heart muscles. Do some people eventually put themselves at risk for heart disease?

A number of studies have reported that heart disease is more common among people who are frequently hostile than among people who are relaxed and easygoing (Booth-Kewley & Friedman, 1987). Hostility could well be a marker for a specific type of over-responsive sympathetic nervous system. However, now that an enormous number of studies have been reported on hostility, heart rate, and blood pressure, we can say that there is no single, simple relationship. Some studies do find a link between a hostile or defensive personality and heart problems, but others do not, depending on many details of procedure (Jorgensen, Johnson, Kolodziej, & Schreer, 1996). A much more consistent finding is that people who have strong social support—that is, friends and family to help them through their trying experiences—tend to keep their heart rate and blood pressure low, and therefore maintain better health than people without such support (Uchino, Cacioppo, & Kiecolt-Glaser, 1996).

Chronic Stress, the Immune System, and Health

Up to this point, we have considered the effects of events that briefly or intermittently activate the sympathetic nervous system. However, people sometimes endure stressful experiences that seem to go on forever: The government builds a toxic waste dump in your neighborhood; a loved one develops a chronic illness and requires almost constant care; your business is on the verge of failure and you face a constant worry about paying the bills. The body responds to chronic stressors in a special way.

Stressors excite both the sympathetic nervous system and an axis composed of the hypothalamus, pituitary gland, and adrenal cortex. Prolonged stress increasingly activates the hypothalamus/pituitary/adrenal axis. The hypothalamus induces the anterior pituitary gland to secrete the hormone adrenocorticotropic hormone **(ACTH),** which in turn stimulates the adrenal cortex to secrete **cortisol,** which elevates blood sugar and enhances metabolism (see Figure 12.4). The increased fuel supply sustains a high, steady rate of coping with stress, as opposed to the sudden bursts of "fight-or-flight" activity associated with the sympathetic nervous system. As cortisol and other hormones direct energy toward increasing blood sugar and metabolism, they shift it away from synthesis of proteins, including the proteins necessary for the immune system. In the short term, that shift may not be a problem; however, stress that continues for weeks or months may weaken the immune system and leave the

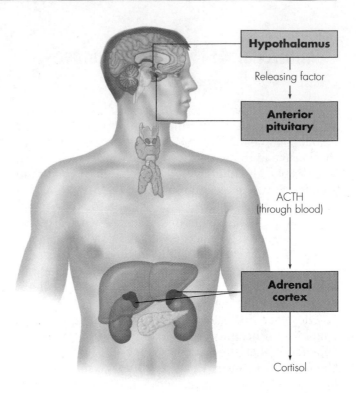

FIGURE **12.4**
The hypothalamus/anterior pituitary/adrenal cortex axis
Prolonged stress leads to the secretion of the adrenal hormone cortisol, which elevates blood sugar and increases metabolism. Those changes help the body sustain prolonged activity but at the expense of decreased immune system activity.

individual vulnerable to a variety of illnesses. In short, brief stress does not pose a threat to health, but prolonged stress does.

The Immune System

The **immune system** consists of structures that protect the body against such intruders as viruses and bacteria. (See Figure 12.5.) The immune system is like a police force: If it is too weak, the "criminals" (viruses and bacteria) run wild and create damage; if it becomes too strong or too unselective, it attacks "law-abiding citizens" (the body's own cells). When the immune system attacks normal cells, we call the result an *autoimmune disease.*

The most important elements of the immune system are the **leukocytes,** commonly known as white blood cells (Kiecolt-Glaser & Glaser, 1993; O'Leary, 1990). Leukocytes are produced in the bone marrow; they then migrate to the thymus gland, the spleen, and the peripheral lymph nodes, which store and nurture them until some foreign body causes their release. The

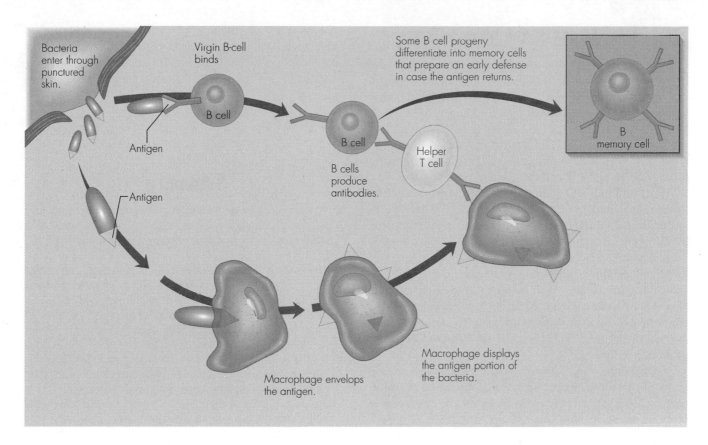

FIGURE **12.5**
Immune system responses to a bacterial infection
A macrophage cell engulfs a bacterial cell and displays one of the bacteria's antigens on its surface. Meanwhile, a B cell also binds to the bacteria and produces antibodies against the bacteria. A helper T cell attaches to both the macrophage and the B cell; it stimulates the B cell to generate copies of itself, called B memory cells, which immunize the body against future invasions by the same kind of bacteria.

leukocytes patrol the blood and other body fluids, searching for intruders. Each cell has on its surface certain proteins, called **antigens** (antibody-generator molecules). When a leukocyte finds a cell with antigens different from the rest of the body, it attacks that cell.

One type of leukocyte, a **B cell** (which matures in the bone marrow), produces specific antibodies to attack an antigen. **Antibodies** are Y-shaped proteins that circulate in the blood, each kind specifically attaching to one kind of antigen, just as a key fits only one lock. The body develops antibodies against the particular antigens that it has encountered. If you ever had measles, for example, your immune system has developed antibodies against the measles virus and will protect you against a further outbreak of the same disease. The strategy behind a vaccination is that introducing a weakened form of the virus will cause the immune system to develop antibodies against the virus without actually getting the disease.

Other leukocytes are the **T cells** (so named because

they mature in the thymus), which directly attack intruder cells or stimulate added response from other immune-system cells. A T cell may attack a cancer cell, a virus-infected cell, or any other cell that it identifies as foreign. T cells are ordinarily helpful, but after a surgical transplant they become part of the problem: They attack the foreign tissue, unless physicians can suppress their activity or trick them into accepting the transplant.

Natural killer cells are blood cells that attach to certain kinds of tumor cells and cells infected with viruses. Natural killer cells are relatively nonspecific in their targets. Unlike an antibody or a T cell, each of which attacks only one kind of intruder, a natural killer cell can attack several kinds of intruders.

The immune system also releases chemicals called **cytokines** that cross the blood-brain barrier and influence neuronal function (Cohen & Herbert, 1996). That is, the nervous system and immune system influence each other.

Effects of Stress on the Immune System

Contrary to assumptions long held in biology, we now know that the nervous system has considerable control over the immune system. The study of this relationship is called *psychoneuroimmunology* (O'Leary, 1990; Vollhardt, 1991). One of the key topics is how stress alters the immune response. The term *stress* applies to a wide variety of events, and different kinds of stress produce different effects on the body (Engel, 1985).

Certain kinds of prolonged stressful events, such as intermittent foot shocks, can stimulate the release of endorphins, which decrease pain but also suppress blood levels of natural killer cells (Mogil, Sternberg, & Liebeskind, 1993). An animal with suppressed levels of killer cells is more vulnerable to disease; if it develops a tumor, the tumor will grow faster than in other animals (Sklar & Anisman, 1981). Animals that have strong and stable social relationships tend to have stronger-than-average immune responses (Cohen, Kaplan, Cunnick, Manuck, & Rabin, 1992).

In humans, too, stressful experiences may release endorphins and suppress immune responses. For example, in 1979, at the Three Mile Island nuclear power plant, a major accident was barely contained. The people who continued to live in the vicinity during the next year had lower-than-normal levels of B cells, T cells, and natural killer cells. They also complained of emotional distress and showed impaired performance on a proofreading task (Baum, Gatchel, & Schaeffer, 1983; McKinnon, Weisse, Reynolds, Bowles, & Baum, 1989). Natural killer cells are also fewer than normal in women whose husbands are dying of cancer, women whose husbands died within the past six months, and medical students going through an exam period (Glaser, Rice, Speicher, Stout, & Kiecolt-Glaser, 1986; Irwin, Daniels, Risch, Bloom, & Weiner, 1988).

IN **CLOSING**

Emotions and Body Reactions

Research on stress and health is often difficult to interpret. For example, it is sometimes difficult to determine which chemical changes in the brain are symptoms of stress and which are mechanisms of coping with stress (Stanford, 1995). Also, most research on stress and health does not distinguish between direct and indirect effects (Cohen & Williamson, 1991). For example, when we find that people with social support recover better from an illness than people without such support, is the difference due to effects of the autonomic and immune systems? Or is it that people with social support are likely to take their prescribed medicines and exercise and eat properly? Determining the relationship between experience and illness is a major, long-term research challenge.

Summary

1. The limbic system—including the hypothalamus, hippocampus, amygdala, olfactory bulb, septum, and other structures—has important effects on emotional behaviors. (p. 324)
2. The hypothalamus includes cells that control activity of the sympathetic nervous system, which becomes aroused during many kinds of emotional experience. (p. 325)
3. The polygraph test measures emotional arousal. It is sometimes used as a lie detector, although its accuracy is not dependable for this purpose. (p. 326)
4. Frequent, intense arousal of the sympathetic nervous system appears to be associated with increased heart rate, blood pressure, and perhaps risk of heart disease. (p. 327)
5. Prolonged stressful experiences activate the adrenal cortex and increase the release of endorphins. Those changes tend to suppress the activity of the immune system. (p. 328)

Review Questions

1. Do sad and fearful experiences depend more on one brain hemisphere than the other? If so, which one? (p. 325)
2. What happens to autonomic nervous system arousal just after removal of a stimulus that excited sympathetic nervous system arousal? (p. 325)
3. What is the difference between the James–Lange theory and the Cannon–Bard theory? What evidence suggests that neither theory is fully correct? (p. 326)
4. What activity of the autonomic nervous system may be responsible for certain cases of sudden death, as in voodoo death? (p. 327)
5. What are the effects of social support on autonomic arousal and heart functioning? (p. 328)
6. What are leukocytes, and how do they contribute to the immune response? (p. 328)

Suggestions for Further Reading

Brannon, L., & Feist, J. (1997). *Health psychology* (3rd ed.). Pacific Grove, CA: Brooks/Cole. Discussion of relationships among stress, behavior, and health issues.

Goleman, D., & Gurin, J. (Eds.). (1993). *Mind/body medicine: How to use your mind for better health.* Yonkers, NY: Consumer Reports Books. A collection of articles on stress, emotions, and health.

Kagan, J. (1994). *Galen's prophecy.* New York: Basic Books. Insightful discussion of human emotion and temperament.

Leonard, B. E., & Miller, K. (Eds.). (1995). *Stress, the immune system, and psychiatry.* Chichester, England: Wiley. Presents research on how the nervous system affects the immune system.

Terms

limbic system   set of forebrain areas including the hypothalamus, hippocampus, amygdala, olfactory bulb, septum, other small structures, and parts of the thalamus and cerebral cortex (p. 324)

James–Lange theory   proposal that an event first provokes autonomic and skeletal responses, and emotion is the perception of those responses (p. 326)

Cannon–Bard theory   proposal that an event provokes emotions and autonomic arousal separately and independently (p. 326)

galvanic skin response (GSR)   measure of the electrical conductance of the skin (p. 326)

behavioral medicine   field that includes the influence of eating and drinking habits, smoking, stress, exercise, and other behavioral variables on health (p. 327)

ACTH   adrenocorticotropic hormone, which stimulates the adrenal cortex to release cortisol (p. 328)

cortisol   hormone released by the adrenal cortex that elevates blood sugar and enhances metabolism (p. 328)

immune system   set of structures that protects the body against viruses and bacteria (p. 328)

leukocyte   white blood cell, a component of the immune system (p. 328)

antigen   protein on the surface of a microorganism, in response to which the immune system generates antibodies (p. 329)

B cell   type of leukocyte that matures in the bone marrow (p. 329)

antibody   Y-shaped protein that fits onto an antigen and weakens it or marks it for destruction (p. 329)

T cell   immune system cell that matures in the thymus and directly attacks intruder cells or stimulates added response by other immune system cells (p. 329)

natural killer cell   type of leukocyte that destroys certain kinds of tumor cells and cells infected with viruses (p. 329)

cytokines   chemicals released by the immune system that cross the blood-brain barrier and influence neuronal function (p. 329)

Attack and Escape Behaviors

If you have ever watched a cat attack a rat or mouse, you may have seen it "play" with its prey before killing it. The cat kicks the rodent, bats it with its paws, tosses it in the air, and sometimes picks it up and shakes and carries it. Why? Is the cat sadistically tormenting its prey before killing it? No. Most of its play behaviors are a compromise between attack and escape: When the rodent is facing away, the cat approaches; if the rodent turns around to face the cat, and especially if it bares its teeth, the cat bats it or kicks it defensively (Pellis et al., 1988). A cat that usually plays with its prey will go for a quick kill if the rodent is small and inactive, or if the cat has been given tranquilizers to lower its anxiety. The same cat will withdraw altogether if confronted with a large and menacing rodent (Adamec, Stark-Adamec, & Livingston, 1980; Biben, 1979; Pellis et al., 1988). In sum, a cat's responses range along a continuum from attack to escape, and a mixture of the two looks to us like play.

Most of the vigorous emotional behaviors we observe in animals fall into the categories of attack and escape, and it is no coincidence that we describe the sympathetic nervous system as the "fight-or-flight" system. These behaviors and the corresponding "negative" emotions, anger and fear, are of most interest to neuroscience researchers and clinical psychologists. Other emotions, such as happiness, sadness, disgust, and surprise, elicit less distinct behaviors. (I'm not sure how we would identify a happy rat if we saw one.)

Attack Behaviors

In nonhuman animals, the behavior called **affective attack** appears highly emotional. (Do not confuse *affective* with *effective*. *Affective* comes from the noun *affect*, meaning emotion.) For example, a cat fighting or threatening another cat shrieks, erects its fur, and increases its sympathetic nervous system arousal. In contrast, a cat may attack and kill a mouse smoothly, swiftly, and with little sign of arousal.

Similarly, human attack behavior may be wildly passionate or calm and detached. For example, a soldier in battle may feel no anger toward the enemy, and people sometimes make "cold-blooded" attacks for financial gain. Therefore, we can hardly expect to find a single explanation for all aggressive behaviors. Most research focuses on affective attacks, though not all.

What actually triggers an attack is usually some sort of pain or threat, but aggression is more than simply a reaction to an event. Some individuals attack much more readily than others, and even a given individual is more ready to attack at some times than at others. Hamsters provide the clearest demonstration. If a hamster is in its home territory and another hamster intrudes, the home hamster sniffs the intruder and ultimately attacks. Suppose the intruder leaves and a little while later another hamster intrudes. The home hamster attacks faster and more vigorously than before. The exact probability of attack waxes and wanes over time but remains elevated for 30 minutes or more after the first attack (Potegal, 1994). In other words, shortly after an attack, the hamster is primed for further attacks. During that period, activity increases in the corticomedial area of the amygdala, a structure in the temporal lobe of the cortex (Potegal, Ferris, Hebert, Meyerhoff, & Skaredoff, 1996). In fact, it is possible to bypass the experience and prime an attack by stimulating the corticomedial amygdala directly (Potegal, Hebert, DeCoster, & Meyerhoff, 1996). We do not have equally good data on the role of the human amygdala in attack priming, but the behaviors are similar: After experiencing an insult or other provocation, people are more likely than usual to show aggressive behaviors for at least the next 5 to 20 minutes, and not just against the person who first provoked them (Potegal, 1994). That is, after someone has provoked you, you might yell at your roommate or kick your dog. You have probably been told that if you become angry you should count to ten before doing anything. Counting to 2000 would probably work better, but the idea is correct.

Genetics and Gene–Environment Interactions

Genetic differences control part of the variance among people in how likely they are to become angry or aggressive. Studies of thousands of twins and hundreds of adoptees have found consistent evidence of genetic contributions to many measures of aggressive, antisocial, and criminal behavior, with an estimated mean heritability of .48 (Mason & Frick, 1994). Eventually, to fully understand the genetic contributions, we shall have to distinguish different kinds of aggression and criminality. Most studies have not even distinguished between affective and nonaffective aggression, and it seems unlikely that the same genes would contribute indiscriminately to all kinds of crime (murder, embezzling money, drug trafficking, and so forth). Nevertheless, one has to start somewhere, and researchers who have lumped together many kinds of aggression and crime have at least found that genes are not irrelevant. We need additional research to tell us how many genes contribute and how, and whether different genes contribute to different kinds of undisciplined behavior. Researchers have already identified a couple of rodent genes that increase aggression, but we do not yet have similar information about humans (Dygdalo & Kalinina, 1994; Nelson et al., 1995).

Genetic and environmental influences apparently interact in ways that researchers are just beginning to explore. One study of adopted children found the highest probability of aggressive behaviors and conduct disorders among those who had biological parents with criminal records *and* adoptive parents with marital discord, depression, substance abuse, or legal problems. Either a biological predisposition or a troubled adoptive family by itself produced only moderate effects (Cadoret, Yates, Troughton, Woodworth, & Stewart, 1995). A study of thousands of twins concluded that juvenile crimes and misbehaviors depended mainly on family environment, because dizygotic twins resembled each other almost as much as monozygotic twins. However, monozygotic twins resembled each other in *adult* crimes and aggressive behaviors more than dizygotic twins did (Lyons et al., 1995). That is, the importance of genetic factors actually *increased* in adulthood, perhaps because adult twins, unlike children, choose their own environments. A twin who is predisposed to aggressive or otherwise undisciplined behaviors will choose friends and activities consistent with similar tendencies and thereby magnify the effects of the predisposition.

Hormones

Most fighting among nonhuman animals is by males competing for mates or females defending their young. Male aggressive behavior depends heavily on testosterone, which is highest for adult males in the reproductive season. Castrated males and males during nonreproductive seasons fight much less (Goldstein, 1974; Moyer, 1974).

Similarly, throughout the world, men fight more often than women, get arrested for violent crimes more often, shout insults at each other more often, and so forth. Moreover, the highest incidence of violence, as measured by crime statistics, is in men 15 to 25 years old, who have the highest levels of testosterone in the blood. The occasional studies that fail to find large sex differences generally fall into one of two categories. First, male–female differences tend to be smaller in studies of *self-reported* aggression or anger than in studies that actually observe aggressive behavior (Knight, Fabes, & Higgins, 1996). Second, women show about as much anger or aggression as men when they are seriously provoked. The difference is that some men pick fights for no apparent reason, whereas few women do (Bettencourt & Miller, 1996).

Among men of the same age, those with higher testosterone levels have, on average, slightly higher rates of violent activities and crimes than do other men (Brooks & Reddon, 1996; Dabbs, Carr, Frady, & Riad, 1995; Dabbs & Morris, 1990). Figure 12.6 shows the results of one typical study. Note that men imprisoned for rape or murder included a large percentage with high testosterone levels; those imprisoned for burglary or drug offenses had generally lower testosterone levels. Note also that this effect is of modest size; the same is true for other studies linking testosterone to violence or crime. In other words, the correlation between testosterone and attack behaviors in humans is real, but weak.

Brain Activity

As mentioned before, direct electrical stimulation of an animal's corticomedial amygdala can increase the probability of attack against an intruder. The same is true for stimulation of the ventromedial nucleus of the hypothalamus. Do not become confused: Yes, the ventromedial nucleus of the hypothalamus is an area that we considered in the last two chapters. It is important for control of eating and sexual behavior as well as aggressive behavior. Obviously, we should not think of it as an "aggression area" or a "satiety area"; like several other hypothalamic areas, it contributes to many different behaviors.

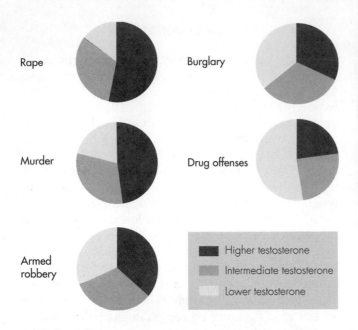

Rape

Burglary

Murder

Drug offenses

Armed
robbery

■ Higher testosterone
■ Intermediate testosterone
□ Lower testosterone

FIGURE 12.6
Testosterone levels for men convicted of various crimes
Men convicted of rape and murder have higher testosterone levels, on the average, than men convicted of burglary or drug offenses.   Source: Based on Dabbs, Carr, Frady, & Riad, 1995.

FIGURE 12.7
Effects of stimulation in the medial hypothalamus
Stimulation in some brain areas can lead to a full attack; in this case, the result was undirected growling and facial expressions, a mere fragment of a normal attack.

At any rate, increased activity in the ventromedial hypothalamus increases the likelihood of attack, and testosterone exerts part of its effect on aggression by facilitating the activity of certain synaptic receptors in this area (Delville, Mansour, & Ferris, 1996). Once these neurons are aroused, they send messages that prime the activity of many areas in the brain stem (Roberts & Nagel, 1996). Stimulation of either the ventromedial hypothalamus itself or certain areas it controls in the brainstem can increase aggressive behavior. Depending on the exact location of the brain stimulation, the animal might attack another animal or might make a series of undirected growls and facial movements (Siegel & Pott, 1988). (See Figure 12.7.)

Stimulation of the amygdala, an area in the temporal lobe (see Figure 12.8), can also lead to vigorous affective attacks. Animals with an epileptic focus (see p. 325) in the amygdala often show an increase in aggressive behavior (Pinel, Treit, & Rovner, 1977). **Rabies,** which leads to furious, violent behavior, is a disease caused by a virus that attacks much of the brain but especially the temporal lobe (including the amygdala) (Lentz, Burrage, Smith, Crick, & Tignor, 1982). (*Rabies* is the Latin term for *rage.*)

Damage to or removal of the amygdala usually leads to tameness and placidity. Monkeys with extensive damage in this area develop the *Klüver–Bucy syndrome,* as mentioned in Chapter 4. They attempt to pick up snakes, lighted matches, and other objects that they

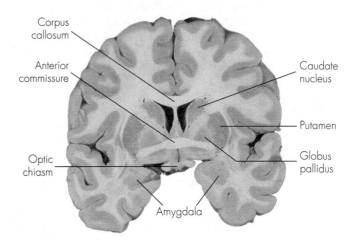

Corpus callosum

Anterior commissure

Caudate nucleus

Putamen

Optic chiasm

Globus pallidus

Amygdala

FIGURE 12.8
Coronal section through the human brain
Note the location of the amygdala.

would ordinarily avoid; male monkeys sink to the bottom of the dominance hierarchy because they do not react normally to other monkeys' threat gestures and other social signals (Rosvold, Mirsky, & Pribram, 1954). The basis for the Klüver–Bucy syndrome probably includes both impairment of emotional response and difficulty interpreting visual information.

Can irritation of the temporal lobe provoke violent behavior in humans as well? A number of investigators have looked particularly at temporal-lobe epilepsy. An epileptic attack occurs when a large group of neurons suddenly produces synchronous action potentials. When the *epileptic focus* (the point of origin) is in the temporal lobe, the symptoms include hallucinations, lip smacking or other repetitive acts, and, in certain cases, emotional behaviors.

Here is a description of a patient with temporal-lobe epilepsy who had sudden outbursts of unprovoked violent behavior (Mark & Ervin, 1970):

> Thomas was a 34-year-old engineer, who, at the age of 20, had suffered a ruptured peptic ulcer. The resulting internal bleeding deprived his brain of blood and produced brain damage. Although his intelligence and creativity were unimpaired, there were some serious changes in his behavior, including outbursts of violent rage, sometimes against strangers and sometimes against people he knew. Sometimes his episodes began when he was talking to his wife. He would then interpret something she said as an insult, throw her against the wall and attack her brutally for 5 to 6 minutes. After one of these attacks, he would go to sleep for a half hour and wake up feeling refreshed.
>
> Eventually, he was taken to a hospital, where epileptic activity was found in the temporal lobes of his cerebral cortex. For the next 7 months, he was given a combination of tranquilizers, antiepileptic drugs, and other medications. None of these treatments reduced his violent behavior. He had previously been treated by psychiatrists for 7 years without apparent effect. Eventually, he agreed to a surgical operation to destroy a small part of the amygdala on both sides of the brain. Afterwards, he had no more episodes of rage, although he continued to have periods of confusion and disordered thinking.

It is difficult to estimate how many people with temporal-lobe epilepsy have violent outbursts, because this kind of epilepsy is difficult to diagnose and violent behavior is difficult to measure (Volavka, 1990). In many instances, antiepileptic drugs have shown promise in controlling episodic violent behavior.

Many people with damage in the prefrontal cortex also fight or threaten more frequently than other people, or on less provocation (Giancola, 1995). However, people with prefrontal impairments have a general loss of inhibitions and a tendency toward many socially inappropriate behaviors, not just violent ones.

Serotonin Synapses and Aggressive Behavior

Although any behavior depends on the combined influence of many neurotransmitters, several lines of evidence indicate that low serotonin release is particularly associated with increased aggressive behavior.

Nonhuman animals Much of the earliest evidence for this conclusion came from studies on mice. Luigi Valzelli (1973) found that four weeks of social isolation induced a drop in *serotonin turnover* in the brains of the male mice. **Turnover** is the amount of release and resynthesis of a neurotransmitter by presynaptic neurons. That is, a brain with low serotonin turnover may produce a normal amount of serotonin, but the neurons fail to release it and synthesize new serotonin to take its place. Turnover can be inferred from the concentration of 5-hydroxyindoleacetic acid **(5-HIAA),** a serotonin metabolite, in the blood, cerebrospinal fluid (CSF), or urine. When 5-HIAA levels are low, serotonin turnover is low.

Valzelli further found that when social isolation lowered a male mouse's serotonin turnover it also induced increased aggressive behavior toward other males. If he placed two males with low serotonin turnover together, he could count on them to fight. Comparing different genetic strains of mice, he found that those with the lowest serotonin turnover fought the most (Valzelli & Bernasconi, 1979). Social isolation does not decrease serotonin turnover in female mice in any genetic strain, and it does not make the females aggressive. Later studies found excessive attack behaviors in mice that are deficient in one particular serotonin receptor, type 5-HT_{1B} (Saudou et al., 1994).

In a fascinating natural-environment study, investigators measured 5-HIAA levels in 2-year-old male monkeys and then observed their behavior closely. The monkeys in the lowest quartile for 5-HIAA, and therefore the lowest quartile for serotonin turnover, were the most aggressive, had the greatest probability of attacking larger monkeys, and showed the greatest number of scars and wounds. Most of them died by the age of 6, whereas all monkeys in the highest quartile for serotonin turnover were still alive at 6 (Higley et al., 1996).

Why has natural selection not eliminated the genes for low serotonin turnover? At this point, one can only speculate, but somehow the aggressive, high risk-taking behavior must be a successful enough strategy for a few monkeys to compensate for a much-enhanced probability of early death. Maybe the surviving low-serotonin monkeys become highly dominant and manage to father a great many young. We await future research for the answers.

Humans Numerous studies have found that people with a history of violent behavior tend to have lower-than-normal serotonin turnover, including people convicted of arson and other violent crimes (Virkkunen, Nuutila, Goodwin, & Linnoila, 1987) and people who commit or attempt suicide by violent means (Brown et al., 1982; Edman, Åsberg, Levander, & Schalling, 1986; Mann, Arango, & Underwood, 1990; Pandey et al., 1995). Serotonin turnover varies by 5 to 10 percent

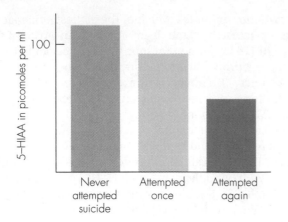

FIGURE **12.9**
Levels of 5-HIAA in the CSF of depressed people
Measurements for the two suicide-attempting groups were taken after the first attempt. Low levels of 5-HIAA indicate low serotonin turnover.   Source: Based on results of Roy, DeJong, & Linnoila, 1989.

from one time of year to another (for unknown reasons); one study in Belgium found that suicide rates were highest in spring, when serotonin turnover was lowest, and lowest in fall and winter, when serotonin turnover was highest (Maes et al., 1995).

Neuroscientists are far from understanding the mechanisms that link low serotonin turnover to aggressive behavior. According to one hypothesis, serotonin synapses inhibit actions that generally lead to unfavorable outcomes, and thus low serotonin turnover produces unrestrained, impulsive behavior (Spoont, 1992). However, even without a theoretical understanding, we may be able to use serotonin turnover measurements to make some useful predictions. For example, one study of children and adolescents with a history of aggressive behavior found that individuals with the lowest serotonin turnover were most likely to get into trouble for additional aggressive behavior during the following two years (Kruesi et al., 1992). Follow-up studies on people convicted of violent crimes or arson found that, after their release from prison, those with lower serotonin turnover had a greater probability of committing other violent crimes (Virkkunen, DeJong, Bartko, Goodwin, & Linnoila, 1989; Virkkunen, Eggert, Rawlings, & Linnoila, 1996). A follow-up study of people who had survived suicide attempts found that low serotonin turnover levels predicted additional suicide attempts within the next five years (Roy, DeJong, & Linnoila, 1989; see Figure 12.9). Thus, we can imagine mental hospitals using blood tests to identify the patients who need to be watched most carefully for suicidal tendencies, and possibly using medications to increase serotonin activity. We can also imagine courts or parole boards using blood tests to help them decide how dangerous it might be to release someone, although there are many social and political reasons why we might not *want* the legal system to base decisions on such information.

It is possible to alter serotonin synthesis by changes in diet. Neurons synthesize serotonin from tryptophan, an amino acid found in proteins, though seldom in large amounts. Tryptophan crosses the blood-brain barrier by an active transport channel that it shares with other large amino acids, such as phenylalanine. Thus a diet high in the other amino acids but low in tryptophan impairs the brain's ability to synthesize serotonin. One study found that young men on such a diet showed an increase in aggressive behavior a few hours after eating (Moeller et al., 1996). Under the circumstances, it would seem prudent for anyone with aggressive or suicidal tendencies to reduce his or her consumption of aspartame (NutraSweet), which is 50 percent phenylalanine, and maize, which is high in phenylalanine and low in tryptophan (Lytle, Messing, Fisher, & Phebus, 1975).

Escape Behaviors

We distinguish two escape emotions, fear and anxiety. Fear is a temporary experience, like what you feel in a small boat with a storm approaching. If you escape from the danger, the fear is gone. Anxiety is a longer-lasting, less escapable state. For example, a person can feel anxious about the future or about dealing with other people. General "free-floating" anxiety is not tied to any identifiable stimulus.

Anxiety, like almost anything else, can be helpful or harmful, depending on its degree. Mild anxiety promotes reasonable cautiousness; people without anxiety may take unnecessary risks. However, severe anxiety interferes with normal activity and sometimes makes people downright miserable. Many psychological disorders result in part from excess anxiety; Digression 12.1 discusses two examples. Much progress has been made toward understanding the physiological basis of fear and anxiety.

Fear, Enhanced Fears, and the Amygdala

All animals, including humans, share a fear of loud noises. We know of no exceptions to this rule, other than the deaf. The response to a loud noise, known as the **startle reflex,** is unlearned, as you can discover by watching a newborn baby. The reflex is extremely fast: Auditory information goes first to the cochlear nucleus in the medulla, and from there directly to an area in the pons that commands the tensing of the muscles, especially the neck muscles. (Tensing the neck muscles is a protective reaction, especially important because the neck is so vulnerable to injury.) Information reaches the pons within 3 to 8 milliseconds after a loud noise, and the full startle reflex is evident within two-tenths of a second (Yeomans & Frankland, 1996)—significantly faster than a response that has to wait for action by the cerebral cortex.

DIGRESSION 12.1

Panic Disorder and Obsessive-Compulsive Disorder

We may be able to learn more about the physiology of anxiety by studying clinical conditions associated with excess anxiety. **Panic disorder** afflicts about 1 percent of all adults (Robins et al., 1984). Sufferers have occasional attacks of extreme fear, breathlessness, heart palpitations, fatigue, and dizziness. The sympathetic nervous system is overresponsive, frequently stimulating the heart and other organs to high activity (Nutt, 1989).

One interpretation of panic disorder is that people misinterpret respiratory signals in the brain and react as if they were suffocating (Klein, 1993). One of the surest ways to trigger a panic attack in a susceptible person is to increase the blood levels of lactate and carbon dioxide. Those levels sometimes rise enough during exercise or stress to resemble the levels that occur in suffocation; people who are subject to panic attacks often respond as if they were in fact suffocating, especially if they believe that they have no control over the situation (Sanderson, Rapee, & Barlow, 1989).

Many people experiencing a panic attack aggravate the problem by **hyperventilating** (breathing more often or more deeply than they need to). Taking a deep breath or two can often be a good way of calming oneself, but prolonged hyperventilation lowers the levels of carbon dioxide and phosphates in the blood, which in turn decreases parasympathetic nervous system activity (George et al., 1989). Then, any stress or other event that elevates blood CO_2 will produce a very large *percentage* increase in CO_2, and in turn a sharp rise in sympathetic nervous system action.

People with panic disorder are generally treated with drugs, psychotherapy, or both. Tranquilizers and antidepressants relieve the symptoms, although many people have relapses if they stop taking the drugs (Wiborg & Dahl, 1996). Psychotherapy helps sufferers break the cycle of panic attacks leading to hyperventilation and then further attacks, and often produces long-term benefits.

People with **obsessive-compulsive disorder** have insistent, intrusive thoughts (obsessions) and feel compelled to perform repetitive acts (compulsions). Although the disorder is considered uncommon in psychiatry, mild or unreported cases affect 2 to 3 percent of all people at some point in life (Karno, Golding, Sorenson, & Burnam, 1988). Many of the relatives of obsessive-compulsive people also have obses-sions, compulsions, or anxiety disorders (Black, Noyes, Goldstein, & Blum, 1992). Thus, there may be a genetic predisposition that manifests itself in varying degrees and forms, depending on experience and other circumstances.

One clue suggesting a biological basis for obsessive-compulsive disorder is that many patients respond well to clomipramine, fluvoxamine, or other drugs that block the reuptake of serotonin into the presynaptic cell after its release (Greist, Jefferson, Kobak, Katzelnick, & Serlin, 1995). The drugs especially affect the caudate nucleus and putamen (parts of the basal ganglia) and the orbital prefrontal cortex. (See Figure 12.10.) Apparently, for most people with obsessive-compulsive disorder, these areas are structurally normal (Aylward et al., 1996) but overactive. Either drug therapy or behavior therapy lowers the metabolic rates in those areas—but only in patients who respond favorably to the therapy (Baxter et al., 1992; Schwartz, Stoessel, Baxter, Martin, & Phelps, 1996; Zald & Kim, 1996). Thus, the symptoms of obsessive-compulsive disorder appear to be closely related to increased activity in those brain areas.

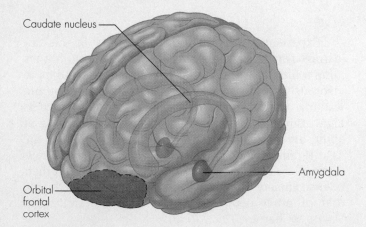

Caudate nucleus

Amygdala

Orbital frontal cortex

FIGURE 12.10
Location of the orbital prefrontal cortex
It and the amygdala send their output to some of the same structures, especially in the basal ganglia.

People's choices of activities depend in part on how easily they develop anxiety.

Experiences can modify the intensity of this un-learned fear response, however. Although you always jump a little after a loud noise, you may respond more vigorously if you are already tense, as when you are walking alone through an unfamiliar neighborhood at night. Curiously, even rats, which are active mostly at night, are startled more easily in the dark than in the light (Frankland & Ralph, 1995). People with posttrau-matic stress disorder, who are certainly known for their intense anxiety, show a startle reflex as much as double that of other people (Morgan, Grillon, Southwick, Davis, & Charney, 1995, 1996).

Psychologists can measure the enhancement of a startle reflex as a gauge of fear or anxiety in nonhu-mans as well as humans. Typically, investigators first measure an animal's muscular responses to a loud noise. Then they repeatedly pair a stimulus, such as a light, with shock. Finally, they present the light just be-fore the loud noise and determine how much more the

animal jumps after the combination of stimuli than af-ter the noise alone. (A control group is tested with a light stimulus that has not been paired with shock. We need to be sure that the effect of the light-plus-noise combination is due to what the animal has learned about the light.) Results of such studies consistently show that after animals have learned an association be-tween a stimulus and shock, that stimulus becomes a fear signal; presenting the stimulus just before a loud noise enhances the animal's response to the noise. Con-versely, a stimulus previously associated with pleasant stimuli can become a safety signal that decreases the startle reflex (Schmid, Koch, & Schnitzler, 1995).

By measuring the enhancement of the startle reflex, investigators have determined the role of various brain areas in learned fears. One key area is the amygdala. (See Figure 12.11.) Many cells in the amygdala, espe-cially in the basolateral and central nuclei, get input from more than one sensory modality, such as vision and pain, or hearing and pain, so the circuitry is well suited to establishing conditioned fears (Uwano, Nishijo, Ono, & Tamura, 1995).

Output from the amygdala to the hypothalamus controls autonomic fear responses, such as increased blood pressure. The amygdala also has axons to an area called the *central gray* in the midbrain, which in turn sends axons to the nucleus in the pons that controls the startle reflex (Fendt, Koch, & Schnitzler, 1996). By this relay, the amygdala can enhance the startle reflex, in-creasing freezing, flinching, and other skeletal re-sponses (LeDoux, Iwata, Cicchetti, & Reis, 1988). Fig-ure 12.11 shows the connections.

A rat with damage to the amygdala, particularly the central nucleus of the amygdala, still shows a normal startle reflex after a loud noise, but it shows no en-hanced startle reflex to the combination of a fear signal plus loud noise. In one typical study, rats were repeat-edly exposed to a light followed by shock, and then tested for their responses to bursts of loud noise, with or without the simultaneous presence of the light. In-tact rats showed a moderate startle reflex to the loud noise and an enhanced response to the light (fear stim-ulus) plus noise. In contrast, rats with damage at vari-ous points along the path from the central amygdala to the hindbrain showed the same startle reflex to the loud noise regardless of the presence or absence of the light (Hitchcock & Davis, 1991). A number of other studies confirm that damage to the amygdala reduces or elimi-nates learned or enhanced fears (Campeau & Davis, 1995; Lee, Walker, & Davis, 1996; Phillips & LeDoux, 1992; Young & Leaton, 1996).

Damage to the amygdala on just one side of the brain weakens learned fears but does not abolish them (LaBar & LeDoux, 1996). In other experiments, experi-menters gave rats unpleasant experiences—footshock in one experiment and smaller-than-usual reward in an-

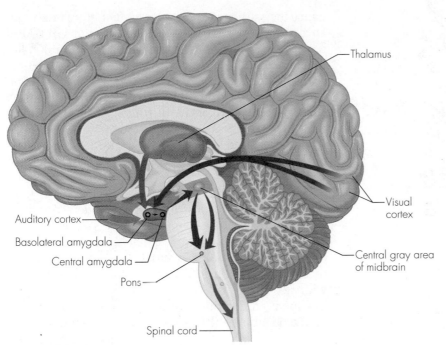

Thalamus

Auditory cortex

Basolateral amygdala

Central amygdala

Pons

Spinal cord

Visual cortex

Central gray area of midbrain

FIGURE **12.11**
Amygdala and connections relevant to learned fears
Cells in the lateral and basolateral parts of the amygdala receive visual and auditory information, and then send messages to the central amygdala, which then sends its output to the central gray area of the midbrain, which relays the information to a nucleus in the pons responsible for the startle reflex. Damage at any point along the route from amygdala to pons interferes with learned fears, although only damage to the pons would block the startle reflex itself.

other—and then infused lidocaine (an anesthetic drug) into the amygdala of just one hemisphere or the other. The suppression of amygdala activity impaired rats' memory of the unpleasant event; that is, when the rats were returned to the testing apparatus, they behaved like rats that had not been shocked or rats that had continued receiving their customary large rewards for operant activities. Curiously, in both studies, suppression of the amygdala in the right hemisphere produced a bigger effect than suppression of the left amygdala (Coleman-Mesches, Salinas, & McGaugh, 1996; Mesches & McGaugh, 1995). (Recall the studies indicating that the right hemisphere is more important than the left in humans for recognizing facial expressions, p. 325.)

The Human Amygdala

The amygdala appears to be central to the human experience of anxiety as well. One study used PET scans to measure brain activity while people looked at other people's facial expressions. Amygdala activity was greatest when people looked at a fearful expression and least when they looked at a happy expression (Morris et al., 1996). Another study examined people who had had the amygdala and surrounding tissues removed from one side of the brain for relief from severe epilepsy. These people were given conditioning trials in which a brief tone always preceded a burst of painfully loud noise. When asked to describe the events, nearly all of them stated that the tone predicted the loud noise; nevertheless, their autonomic responses showed only very weak conditioned responses to the tone (LaBar,

LeDoux, Spencer, & Phelps, 1995). That is, they remembered the tone–noise connection but showed no emotional response to the tone.

People with a rare genetic disorder known as *Urbach–Wiethe disease* suffer a gradual atrophy (dying away) of the amygdala and nearby tissues. People with this disorder experience fear and related emotions very weakly. In one study, an Urbach–Wiethe patient and some unimpaired people listened to a story featuring a traffic accident that produced severe injuries that were described and illustrated in gory detail. One week later they were asked to answer some questions about the story. The unimpaired people consistently remembered the emotionally upsetting parts of the story better than the rest of it; the Urbach–Wiethe patient had decent memory for the story overall, but failed to show any enhanced memory for the emotional parts (Cahill, Babinsky, Markowitsch, & McGaugh, 1995).

People with Urbach–Wiethe disease also have trouble recognizing fear in others. (Presumably, it is hard for someone who feels little fear to identify with someone else's fear.) One woman with this condition had no trouble identifying faces, but if she looked at photos of people with different emotional expressions, she had much trouble identifying the fearful expressions, and a little trouble with the angry and surprised expressions (Adolphs, Tranel, Damasio, & Damasio, 1994). When asked to rate the apparent intensity of the emotional expressions, she rated the intensity in the frightened, angry, or surprised faces much lower than any other observer did. Finally, when she was asked to draw faces showing certain emotions (Figure 12.12), she had no trouble drawing a happy, sad, surprised, disgusted, or

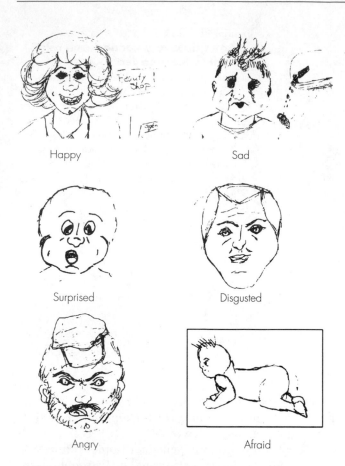

Happy

Sad

Surprised

Disgusted

Angry

Afraid

FIGURE 12.12
Drawings by a woman with a damaged amygdala

Note that her drawings of emotional expressions are fairly realistic and convincing, except for fear. She at first declined to draw a fearful expression because, she said, she could not imagine it. When urged to try, she used the fact that frightened people try to escape, and she remembered that frightened people are often depicted with their hair on end, at least in cartoons.
Source: From Adolphs, Tranel, Damasio, & Damasio, 1995. Copyright Oxford University Press.

angry face. However, when asked to draw an "afraid" face, she refused at first, saying she did not know what such a face would look like. When the researcher insisted that she try, she drew someone crawling away with hair on end (as cartoonists often indicate fear). Certainly, she seemed much less able to imagine fear than any other emotional state (Adolphs, Tranel, Damasio, & Damasio, 1995).

Anxiety-Reducing Drugs

CCK is one of the important excitatory neuromodulators in the amygdala and **GABA** (gamma amino butyric acid) is clearly the main inhibitory transmitter. Injections of CCK-stimulating drugs into the amygdala en-

hance the startle reflex (Frankland, Josselyn, Bradwejn, Vaccarino, & Yeomans, 1997), and injections of GABA-blockers can induce an outright panic (Strzelczuk & Romaniuk, 1996). In principle, tranquilizers (anxiety-reducing drugs) could act either by blocking CCK and other excitatory neurotransmitters or by increasing GABA activity. In practice, every drug that has proved useful so far acts by facilitating GABA. (CCK has so many other, unrelated behavioral effects that a CCK-blocker would probably have unacceptable side effects.)

Decades ago, **barbiturates** were the class of tranquilizers most widely used to combat anxiety. Although barbiturates are effective, they have two significant drawbacks: They are strongly habit forming, and it is fairly easy to take a fatal overdose—either intentionally or accidentally, especially by combining barbiturates with alcohol.

Today, the commonly used tranquilizers are the **benzodiazepines** (BEN-zo-die-AZ-uh-peens), such as diazepam (trade name Valium), chlordiazepoxide (Librium), and alprazolam (Xanax). Besides relieving anxiety, benzodiazepines relax the muscles, induce sleep, and decrease the likelihood of convulsions; they are used not only as tranquilizers but also as sleeping pills and as antiepileptic drugs. Benzodiazepines are ordinarily taken as pills, less often as injections; in either case, the drug reaches all parts of the body equally. However, the antianxiety effects depend mainly on how the drug affects the amygdala and, to a smaller extent, the hypothalamus. A minute amount of benzodiazepines injected directly to a rat's amygdala decreases learned shock-avoidance behaviors (Pesold & Treit, 1995) and increases social interactions with an unfamiliar partner (Sanders & Shekhar, 1995). The likely interpretation is that a rat is ordinarily slow to approach an unfamiliar partner because of anxiety about how the other will react. (The same is true for humans, of course.) Therefore, a decrease in anxiety leads to increased socialization.

Like many other drugs, benzodiazepines were found to be effective long before anyone knew how they worked. Then, in the late 1970s and early 1980s, investigators discovered specific benzodiazepine-binding sites in the CNS. The receptors are part of the **GABA$_A$ receptor,** shown in Figure 12.13. The complex includes a site that binds the neurotransmitter GABA as well as sites that bind other chemicals that modify the sensitivity of the GABA site. (The brain also has other kinds of GABA receptors, such as GABA$_B$, which have different behavioral effects.)

The heart of the GABA$_A$ receptor complex is a chloride channel. When open, it permits chloride ions (Cl$^-$) to cross the membrane into the neuron, hyperpolarizing the cell. (That is, the synapse is inhibitory.) Surrounding the chloride channel are four units, each con-

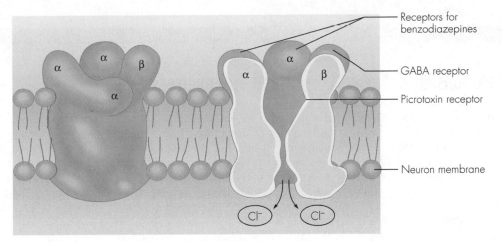

FIGURE **12.13**
The GABA_A receptor complex
Of its four receptor sites sensitive to GABA, the three α sites are also sensitive to benzodiazepines.
Source: Based on Guidotti, Ferrero, Fujimoto, Santi, & Costa, 1986.

Labels on figure: Receptors for benzodiazepines; GABA receptor; Picrotoxin receptor; Neuron membrane

taining one or more sites sensitive to GABA. Three of those four units (labeled α in Figure 12.13) also contain a benzodiazepine-binding site. When a benzodiazepine molecule attaches, by itself it neither opens nor closes the chloride channel, but it alters the shape of the receptor so that the GABA attaches more easily or binds more tightly (Macdonald, Weddle, & Gross, 1986). Benzodiazepines thus facilitate the effects of GABA. Barbiturates and alcohol also bind to the receptor complex in ways that facilitate GABA binding and thereby enhance its anxiety-reducing effects (see Digression 12.2).

Other naturally occurring chemicals bind to the same sites as benzodiazepines. One such chemical is the protein **diazepam-binding inhibitor (DBI),** which blocks the behavioral effects of diazepam and other benzodiazepines (Guidotti et al., 1983). This protein is also known as **endozepine,** a contraction of "endogenous benzodiazepine," although its effects are actually the opposite to those of benzodiazepines. So, really it is an endogenous *anti*-benzodiazepine. Many functions have been proposed for this chemical, but its actual role in behavior is not known.

IN **CLOSING**

Brain Mechanisms of Emotional Behaviors

Researchers' progress in understanding brain mechanisms of emotion has been most impressive. For example, we can now identify small areas of the amygdala, and particular types of synapses within those areas, that are necessary and perhaps even sufficient for anxiety: Damage or inactivate those areas and we diminish

anxiety; stimulate them and we evoke it. We hesitate to say that amygdala activity *is* anxiety, but only because we do not want to imply that the rest of the brain is irrelevant to the experience.

However, as is often the case, the answer to one question raises other questions or at least calls more attention to them. Identifying a small brain area as critical for anxiety raises the deep question of *why* activity in the central amygdala yields anxiety, whereas synaptic activity in other brain areas constitutes vision, thirst, or any other experience. At this point, we may as well admit our inability to answer that question.

Summary

1. Either a provoking experience, such as fighting, or the direct stimulation of the corticomedial area of the amygdala can produce a temporarily heightened readiness to attack. (p. 332)
2. There is evidence for genetic influences on aggressive and undisciplined behaviors, in humans as well as in other species, although we do not know the routes by which such genes act. (p. 333)
3. Testosterone can increase the readiness to attack by affecting cells in the hypothalamus. (p. 333)
4. Parts of the hypothalamus and amygdala are especially important for aggressive behavior. Stimulation in these areas can increase attack behaviors; damage can lead to placidity and failure to attack. (p. 333)
5. Low serotonin turnover is associated with an increased likelihood of violent behavior, including violent suicide attempts. (p. 335)
6. Researchers measure enhancement of the startle reflex as an indication of anxiety or learned fears. (p. 336)
7. The startle reflex itself depends on activity in the pons. Enhancement of the startle reflex through learning depends on the amygdala. (p. 339)

DIGRESSION **12.2**

The Relationship Between Alcohol and Tranquilizers

Ethyl alcohol, the beverage alcohol, has behavioral effects similar to those of benzodiazepine tranquilizers. It decreases anxiety and behavioral inhibitions based on the fear of punishment. Moreover, a combination of alcohol and tranquilizers depresses body activities and brain functioning more severely than either drug alone would. (A combination of alcohol and tranquilizers can be fatal.) Furthermore, alcohol, benzodiazepines, and barbiturates all exhibit the phenomenon of **cross-tolerance:** An individual who has used one of the drugs enough to develop a tolerance to it will show a partial tolerance to other depressant drugs as well.

Alcohol promotes the flow of chloride ions through the $GABA_A$ receptor complex, just as tranquilizers do (Suzdak et al., 1986), probably by facilitating the binding of GABA to its receptors. Alcohol influences the brain in other ways as well, but the effects on GABA are responsible for alcohol's antianxiety and intoxicating effects. Drugs that block the effects of alcohol on the $GABA_A$ receptor complex also block most of alcohol's behavioral effects. One experimental drug, known as Ro15-4513, is particularly effective in this regard (Suzdak et al., 1986). Besides affecting the $GABA_A$ receptor complex, Ro15-4513 blocks the effects of alcohol on motor coordination, its depressant action on the brain, and its ability to reduce anxiety (Becker, 1988; Hoffman, Tabakoff, Szabó, Suzdak, & Paul, 1987; Ticku & Kulkarni, 1988). (See Figure 12.14.)

Could Ro15-4513 be useful as a "sobering-up" pill or as a treatment to help people who want to stop drinking alcohol? Hoffman–LaRoche, the company that discovered it, eventually concluded that the drug would be too risky. People who relied on the pill might think they were sober and try to drive home when they were still somewhat impaired. Furthermore,

giving such a pill to alcoholics could easily backfire. Alcoholics generally drink to get drunk; a pill that decreased their feeling of intoxication would probably lead them to drink even more. Ro15-4513 reverses the behavioral effects of moderate alcohol doses, but a large dose can still be a health hazard or even fatal (Poling, Schlinger, & Blakely, 1988). For these reasons, Ro15-4513 is used only in experimental laboratories.

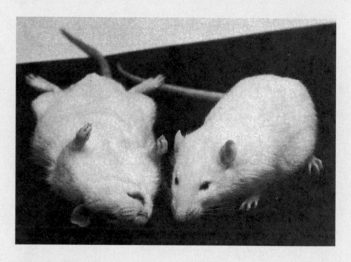

FIGURE **12.14**
Two rats that were given the same amount of alcohol
The one on the right was later given the experimental drug Ro15-4513. Within 2 minutes, its performance on motor tasks improved significantly.

8. People and nonhuman animals with damage to the amygdala lose much of their fear or anxiety. People with such damage also have trouble recognizing facial expressions of fear. (p. 339)
9. Tranquilizers decrease fear by facilitating the binding of the inhibitory neurotransmitter GABA to the $GABA_A$ receptors, especially in the amygdala. (p. 340)

Review Questions

1. What evidence supports the existence of a "readiness to attack"? (p. 332)
2. What evidence suggests that aggressive or criminal behavior depends on an interaction of genetic and environmental influences, and not on either one alone? (p. 333)
3. What are the effects of amygdala damage on aggressive behavior? (p. 334)
4. How can one measure the amount of serotonin turnover in the brain? How does serotonin turnover differ from the total amount of serotonin present? (p. 335)
5. What change in diet can alter the production of serotonin? (p. 336)
6. Why do many people with panic attacks hyperventilate? Does hyperventilation tend to alleviate or aggravate their problem? (p. 337)
7. What parts of the brain are overactive in obsessive-compulsive disorder, and what drugs sometimes alleviate the problem? (p. 337)
8 What mechanism enables the startle reflex to be so fast? (p. 337)
9. What procedure makes something a fear stimulus? (p. 338)

10. What evidence suggests that people who do not strongly feel an emotion have trouble recognizing that emotion in others? (p. 339)

11. What would be the effects of benzodiazepines on someone who had no GABA? (p. 340)

Thought Question

1. Much of the play behavior of a cat can be analyzed into attack and escape components. Is the same true for children's play?

Suggestion for Further Reading

Potegal, M., & Knutson, J. F. (Eds.). (1994). *The dynamics of aggression.* Hillsdale, NJ: Erlbaum. Collection of articles about aggressive behavior in humans and nonhumans.

Terms

affective attack attack in which an animal shows signs of emotional arousal (p. 332)

rabies disease caused by a virus that attacks much of the brain, especially the temporal lobe, causing violent behavior (p. 334)

turnover release and resynthesis of a neurotransmitter (p. 335)

5-HIAA 5-hydroxyindoleacetic acid, a serotonin metabolite (p. 335)

startle reflex the response that one makes after a sudden, unexpected loud noise or similar sudden stimulus (p. 336)

panic disorder condition characterized by occasional attacks of extreme fear, breathlessness, heart palpitations, fatigue, and dizziness (p. 337)

hyperventilation breathing more often or more deeply than necessary (p. 337)

obsessive-compulsive disorder psychological disorder characterized by intrusive thoughts and urges to perform repetitive acts (p. 337)

GABA gamma amino butyric acid, a neurotransmitter (p. 340)

barbiturates class of drugs used as anticonvulsants, sedatives, and tranquilizers (p. 340)

benzodiazepines class of widely used antianxiety drugs (p. 340)

GABA$_A$ receptor complex structure that includes a site that binds GABA, as well as sites that bind other chemicals that modify the sensitivity of the GABA site (p. 340)

diazepam-binding inhibitor (DBI) or **endozepine** brain protein that blocks the behavioral effects of diazepam and other benzodiazepines (p. 341)

cross-tolerance tolerance of a drug because of exposure to a different drug (p. 342)

THE BIOLOGY OF LEARNING AND MEMORY

CHAPTER **THIRTEEN**

MAIN**IDEAS**

1. To understand the physiology of learning we must answer two questions: What changes occur in a single cell during learning, and how do changed cells work together to produce adaptive behavior?
2. Psychologists distinguish among several types of memory, each of which can be impaired by a different kind of brain damage.
3. During learning, a variety of changes occur that are either brief or permanent and that either facilitate or decrease the activity at particular synapses.

Suppose I program my computer in BASIC as follows:

```
10 HOME
20 FOR A=1 TO 100
30 PRINT A^(0.5)
40 NEXT A
```

I can leave the computer, come back later, and type "RUN." Provided that the power has not been interrupted, the computer will print out a list of the square roots of the integers 1 to 100. How did the computer remember what to do?

That question is really two questions that call for two kinds of answers. One is: How does the computer store a representation of the keys that I type? Somehow, my hitting those keys led to a physical change in some tiny silicon chips inside the computer. To explain how that happened, we need to understand the physics of the silicon chip. The second question is: How does the computer make its response by putting together the information stored in numerous silicon chips? In other words, we have to understand the wiring diagram.

Similarly, when we try to explain how you or I remember the square root of 49, we are really answering two questions. One is: How did a pattern of sensory information create lasting changes in the input–output properties of one or more neurons in the nervous system? That question concerns the biophysics of the neuron. The second question is: After the properties of certain neurons have changed, how does the nervous system as a whole produce the appropriate behavior? That question concerns the wiring diagram. Learning requires changes in individual cells, and the properties of change for any single cell may be very different from how the organism learns as a whole (Martinez & Derrick, 1996).

We shall begin this chapter by considering how the various areas of the nervous system interact to produce learning and memory. Later, we turn to the more detailed physiology of how experience changes the properties of the individual cells and synapses.

Learning, Memory, Amnesia, and Brain Functioning

A patient known in the literature as "C" developed severe memory impairments after encephalitis damaged his temporal cortex in both hemispheres. He forgot much of what he had known before the illness, but his greatest difficulty was in remembering new events. For years after his illness, he kept a diary in which he repeatedly wrote that he had just now awakened from a long sleeplike period and was for the first time conscious. Shortly after writing each entry, he would cross it out and write it again. He could not remember writing the entry, nor any other experience since his illness. He therefore treated all previous entries as mistakes and constantly regarded the present as his first moment of consciousness (Wilson, Baddeley, & Kapur, 1995).

Life without memory is very unlike life as the rest of us know it. A study of the effects of accidental brain damage reveals much about the nature of memory and how it functions.

Localized Representations of Memory

What is the brain's physical representation of learning and memory? One early, influential idea was that it might be a strengthened connection between two brain areas. The Russian physiologist Ivan Pavlov pioneered the investigation of what we now call **classical conditioning** (Figure 13.1a), in which pairing two stimuli changes the response to one of them. Ordinarily, the experimenter starts by presenting a **conditioned stimulus (CS)**, which initially elicits no response of note, and then presents the **unconditioned stimulus (UCS)**, which automatically elicits the **unconditioned response (UCR)**. After some pairings of the CS and the UCS (perhaps just one or two pairings, perhaps many), the individual begins responding to the CS, producing a **conditioned response (CR)**, which in many cases resembles the UCR but in some cases does not. In his original experiments, Pavlov presented a dog with a sound (CS) followed by meat (UCS), which stimulated the dog to salivate (UCR). After many such pairings, the sound alone (CS) would stimulate the dog to salivate (CR).

By contrast, in **operant conditioning** (Figure 13.1b), an individual's response is followed by a reinforcement or punishment. A **reinforcement** is any event that increases the future probability of the response; a **punishment** is an event that suppresses the frequency of the response. For example, when a rat enters one arm of a maze and finds Froot Loops cereal (a potent reinforcement for a rat), the probability of its entering that arm again increases. If it receives a shock instead, the probability decreases.

Some cases of learning are difficult to label as either classical or operant. For example, a male songbird hears the song of his own species during his first spring and summer; he imitates it the following year. During the first year, the song that he heard was not paired with any other stimulus, so we cannot call this classical conditioning. He made no overt responses and received no overt reinforcements or punishments, so we cannot call it operant conditioning. That is, animals have specialized methods of learning other than classical and operant conditioning (Rozin & Kalat, 1971; Rozin & Schull, 1988).

Lashley's Search for the Engram

Pavlov believed that classical conditioning reflected a strengthened connection between a brain area that represents CS activity and a brain area that represents UCS activity. That strengthened connection lets any excitation of the CS center flow to the UCS center, evoking the unconditioned response (Figure 13.2). Karl Lashley set out to test this hypothesis. He said that he was searching for the **engram**—the physical representation of learning. (A connection between two brain areas would be one example of an engram but is hardly the only possibility.)

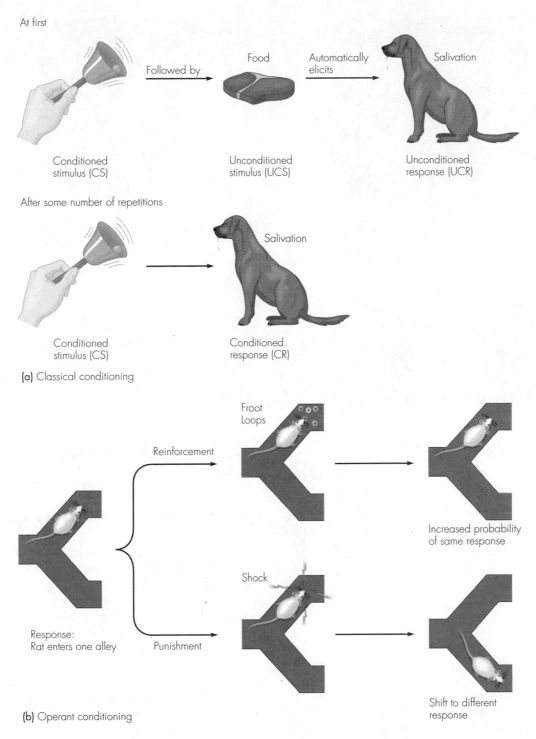

At first

Conditioned
stimulus (CS)

Followed by

Food

Unconditioned
stimulus (UCS)

Automatically
elicits

Salivation

Unconditioned
response (UCR)

After some number of repetitions

Conditioned
stimulus (CS)

Salivation

Conditioned
response (CR)

(a) Classical conditioning

Froot
Loops

Reinforcement

Increased probability
of same response

Response:
Rat enters one alley

Shock

Punishment

Shift to different
response

(b) Operant conditioning

FIGURE **13.1**
Procedures for classical conditioning and operant conditioning
In classical conditioning (**a**), two stimuli (CS and UCS) are presented at certain times, regardless of what the learner does. In operant conditioning (**b**), the learner's behavior controls the presentation of reinforcement or punishment.

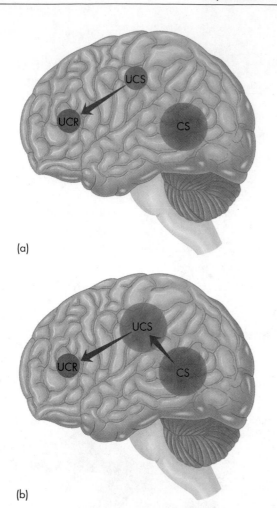

(a)

(b)

FIGURE **13.2**
Pavlov's view of the physiology of learning
Initially (**a**), the UCS excites the UCS center, which then excites the UCR center. The CS excites the CS center, which elicits no response of interest. After training (**b**), excitation in the CS center flows to the UCS center, thus eliciting the same response as the UCS.

FIGURE **13.3**
Cuts that Lashley made in the brains of various rats
He found that no cut or combination of cuts interfered with a rat's memory of a maze.   Source: Adapted from Lashley, 1950.

Lashley reasoned that if learning depends on new or strengthened connections between two brain areas, a knife cut somewhere in the brain should interrupt that connection and abolish the learned response. He trained rats on a variety of mazes and a brightness discrimination task and then made one or more deep cuts in varying locations in their cerebral cortexes (Lashley, 1929, 1950; see Figure 13.3). However, no knife cut significantly impaired the rats' performances. Evidently, the types of learning that he studied did not depend on strengthened connections across the cortex.

Lashley also tested whether any portion of the cerebral cortex is more important than others for learning. He trained rats on mazes before or after he removed large portions of the cortex. The lesions impaired performance, but the amount of retardation depended more on the amount of brain damage than on its location. Learning and memory apparently did not rely on a single cortical area.

Eventually, researchers discovered that Lashley's conclusions reflected two unnecessary assumptions: (1) that the cerebral cortex is the best place to search for an engram, and (2) that all kinds of memory are physiologically the same. As we shall see, investigators who discarded those assumptions have come to different conclusions.

The Modern Search for the Engram

Lashley studied maze learning and visual discrimination learning, which are more complex tasks than they might appear. A rat finding its way to food must attend to visual and tactile stimuli, the location of its body, the position of its head, auditory and olfactory cues if available, and so forth. No wonder the whole cortex appears to be relevant. Richard F. Thompson and his colleagues used a simpler task and managed to locate an engram of memory, not in the cerebral cortex, where Lashley sought it, but in the cerebellum.

Thompson and his colleagues have studied classical conditioning of eyelid responses in rabbits. They present first a tone (CS) and then a puff of air (UCS) to the cornea of the rabbit's eye. At first, a rabbit blinks at the air puff but not at the tone; after repeated pairings, classical conditioning takes place and the rabbit blinks at the tone also. Investigators recorded the activity in various brain cells to determine which ones change their responses during learning.

Thompson and other investigators have consistently found changes in cells in one nucleus of the cerebellum, the **lateral interpositus nucleus.** At the start of training, those cells show very little response to the tone, but as learning proceeds, the cells' responses increase (Thompson, 1986). Furthermore, damage to the lateral interpositus nucleus causes a permanent loss of the conditioned response (McCormick & Thompson, 1984; Woodruf-Pak, Lavond, & Thompson, 1985).

Now, the fact that damaging a brain area prevents a learned response does not necessarily mean that the learning took place in that area. (You could, after all, eliminate a learned response by damaging the muscles, but we would not conclude that learning occurred in the muscles.) To test the role of the cerebellum in learning, two sets of investigators temporarily suppressed activity in rabbits' lateral interpositus nucleus at the start of training, either by cooling the area or by injecting a drug into it. Then they presented the CS and UCS as usual and found no learning. Finally, they waited for the effects of the cooling or the drugs to wear off and continued training. At that point, the rabbits began to learn, but they learned at the same speed as animals that had received no previous training. (In effect, these animals *had* received no previous training, since the training took place while the relevant brain area was inactive.)

This result tells us that the interpositus nucleus has to be active, but it does not tell us that learning actually occurs here. (Maybe the nucleus just relays information to some other area.) Further evidence comes from experiments in which investigators suppressed activity in the red nucleus, a midbrain motor area that receives input from the cerebellum: When the red nucleus was suppressed during training, the rabbits showed no responses during training. However, as soon as the red nucleus had recovered from the cooling or drugs, the rabbits showed strong learned responses to the tone (Clark & Lavond, 1993; Krupa, Thompson, & Thompson, 1993). In other words, suppressing the red nucleus temporarily prevented the response but did not prevent learning. We conclude, therefore, that the learning occurred in the lateral interpositus nucleus, even though the red nucleus is necessary for the motor expression of the response. Figure 13.4 summarizes these experiments. Later experiments demonstrated that learning also occurs during suppression of other outputs from the interpositus nucleus (Krupa & Thompson, 1995; Krupa, Weng, & Thompson, 1996).

The mechanisms for this type of conditioning are probably the same in humans. In one study, PET scans revealed that classical conditioning of the eyeblink in young adults produced increased activity in the cerebellum, red nucleus, and several other areas (Logan & Grafton, 1995). People who have damage in the cerebellum are impaired at eyeblink conditioning (Woodruff-Pak, Papka, & Ivry, 1996), whereas people who have damage in other locations show normal eyeblink conditioning, even if they have other memory problems (Gabrieli et al., 1995).

Types of Memory and Amnesia

Although much of classical conditioning probably depends on the cerebellum, many other kinds of learning and memory do not. You will recall from Chapter 6 that different parts of the brain contribute to different aspects of visual perception. The same principle holds for memory, and much of our progress in understanding the physiology of memory has come from progress in distinguishing among different types of memory.

Short-Term and Long-Term Memory

Donald Hebb (1949) reasoned that no one mechanism could account for all the phenomena of learning. We can form memories almost instantaneously, and some last a lifetime. Hebb considered it unlikely that any chemical process could occur fast enough to account for immediate memory yet remain stable enough to provide permanent memory. He therefore distinguished between **short-term memory,** of events that have just occurred, and **long-term memory,** of events from previous times. Several types of evidence validate such a distinction:

- Short-term and long-term memory have somewhat different properties. For illustration, read these seven letters and then repeat them from memory: CYXGMBF. Now try eight: OBGSFKIE. Then nine: RJNWSCFPT. If you are like most adults, you can hold about seven items in short-term memory, but not more. You also forget the list quickly unless you constantly rehearse it. (Even if you correctly repeated the first set of letters, you have probably already forgotten it.) In contrast, you can store vast amounts of information in your long-term memory without removing old memories to make room for the new.
- With short-term memory, once you have forgotten something, it is probably hopelessly lost. For example, do you remember that first set of letters you read in the previous paragraph? No? What if I told you that it was either CYGXBMF or CYXGMBF. Did that help? Probably not. With long-term memory, however, you might think you have forgotten something and yet find that with enough effort or a few hints you can reconstruct it. You might, for example, try naming all your high-school teachers. You will remember some quickly and others with effort; still others you would probably recognize if someone gave you a choice of names.
- People with certain kinds of brain damage show specialized kinds of memory loss, such as impaired

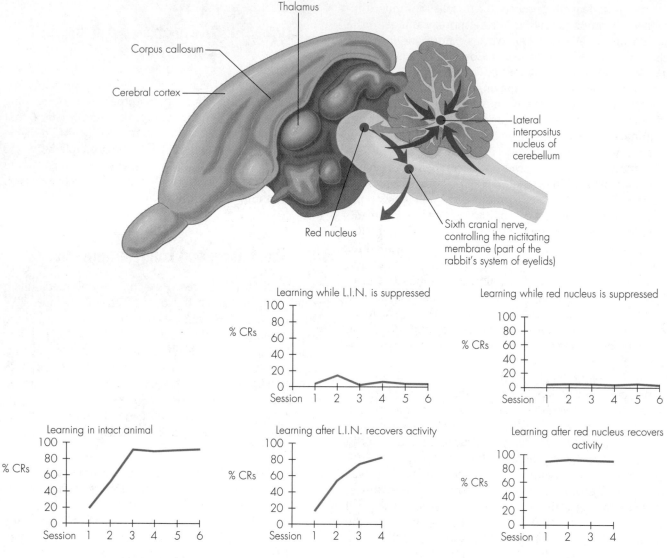

FIGURE **13.4**
Localization of an engram
Rabbits were trained on classical conditioning of an eyelid response. Temporary suppression of activity in the lateral interpositus nucleus of a rabbit blocked all indications of learning. After the suppression wore off, the rabbits learned as slowly as rabbits with no previous training. Temporary suppression of activity in the red nucleus blocked the response during the period of suppression, but the learned response appeared as soon as the red nucleus recovered from the suppression.   Source: Based on the experiments of Clark & Lavond, 1993, and Krupa, Thompson, & Thompson, 1993.

formation of new long-term memories despite normal short-term memory. We shall examine some cases later in this chapter.

Consolidation of Long-Term Memories

According to Hebb's (1949) original theory, any memory that stayed in short-term storage long enough would be gradually **consolidated** (converted and strengthened) into a long-term memory. Hebb guessed

that a short-term memory might be represented by a *reverberating circuit* of neuronal activity in the brain, with a self-exciting loop of neurons. If the reverberating circuit remained active long enough, some permanent chemical or structural change would occur.

According to later researchers, the length of time that an experience remains in short-term memory has only a minor effect on consolidation, in comparison with the meaningfulness or emotional content of the event. Suppose you try to recall as many of your high school experiences as possible. You probably spent hours trying to memorize long lists of names and terms for certain classes, and now you remember that material only vaguely, if at all. The memories that stand out are mostly the emotional ones—the first time that special person smiled at you, the time you said something foolish in class and people laughed at you, the time you won a major honor, the frightening moment when you heard that a friend had been hurt in a car accident. You may even remember irrelevant aspects of these experiences, such as where you were, what you were wearing, or what the weather was like.

One reason why we remember emotional events is that they excite the sympathetic nervous system, which increases the secretion of epinephrine and other hormones from the adrenal medulla (McGaugh, 1990). Animal research has shown that it is possible to bypass the emotional experience and simply inject moderate amounts of epinephrine; the result is still an enhanced consolidation of recent memories. (Excess epinephrine is less beneficial. Arousal aids memory; panic does not.)

How does epinephrine enhance memory storage? Little of the epinephrine released by the adrenal gland crosses the blood-brain barrier. Epinephrine in the periphery stimulates the vagus nerve, which relays activation to the brain (Williams & McGaugh, 1993). Epinephrine also increases the release of corticosterone (another adrenal medulla hormone), which stimulates norepinephrine activity in the brain, through unknown mechanisms (Roozendaal, Carmi, & McGaugh, 1996). Epinephrine also increases the conversion of glycogen to glucose and therefore raises the blood level of glucose, the brain's primary fuel. Increased glucose enhances brain activity in several ways, including increased production and release of the neurotransmitter acetylcholine (Ragozzino, Unick, & Gold, 1996). Through all these mechanisms (and probably others), emotionally arousing events increase activity in the amygdala, which itself stores some memories (as we saw in Chapter 12), but also strengthens memories stored elsewhere. After damage to the amygdala, both humans and nonhumans can still store memories, but emotional arousal does not enhance the storage (Cahill, Babinsky, Markowitsch, & McGaugh, 1995; McGaugh, et al., 1995).

A Modified Theory: Working Memory

Hebb believed that short-term memory was a temporary holding station on the way to long-term memory. Later researchers modified this view. We do have a temporary storage, but we hold material there *while we are using it,* not for the time it takes to store it in long-term memory. For example, even if you have to rehearse a telephone number a long time before you get to dial it,

it might not pass into long-term memory. Most modern researchers now call the temporary storage **working memory,** because we temporarily attend to or work with certain memories. According to A. D. Baddeley and G. J. Hitch (1994), working memory has three components:

- a **phonological loop,** which stores auditory information, including words;
- a **visuospatial sketchpad,** which stores visual information; and
- the **central executive,** which directs attention toward one stimulus or another and determines which items will be stored in working memory.

The phonological loop and visuospatial sketchpad
Working memory enables an individual to respond to a stimulus that was heard or seen a short while earlier, as tested in various forms of the **delayed response task.** For example, an animal might see a light shine above one of several doors. When the light goes off, the animal waits through a specified delay, and then has to go to the door where it saw the light. Animals are tested for how accurately they can remember the signal over various delays.

In several studies, investigators recorded from cells in various brain areas while animals performed such tasks. In one study, a monkey had to press a lever and watch a television monitor, where it would see a stimulus presented briefly, once every 0.5 to 5 seconds, one to four times before it saw a new stimulus. To get a reward, it had to keep the lever down until it saw the new stimulus. After the monkey learned to respond well on this task, a number of cells in the temporal cortex would respond when the monkey saw the first stimulus and continue responding until it saw a new stimulus. In trials when those cells stopped responding before the new stimulus appeared, the monkey released the lever too soon. Evidently those cells were temporarily storing a visual memory by their persistent response during the delay (Nakamura & Kubota, 1995).

In other experiments, a monkey was trained to stare at a fixation point on a screen. A light appeared elsewhere on the screen, then went off. To get a reward, the monkey had to continue staring straight ahead until the fixation point disappeared, and then move its eyes to where the light had appeared several seconds before. Each location of the to-be-remembered light activated a different population of cells in the monkey's prefrontal cortex. For example, a light directly above the fixation point activated one set of cells; a light directly to the right activated a different set. Those cells remained active up to 20 seconds, until the monkey's response (Goldman-Rakic, 1995a). They were storing information about the remembered stimulus, not the upcoming response; the same cells responded if the monkey had to move its eyes toward the remembered stimulus or away from it (Goldman-Rakic, 1995b). Monkeys with damage to the relevant part of the prefrontal cortex showed a severe deficit in performance on these tasks, although they performed normally on tasks that required them to move their eyes toward a light without any delay. Monkeys with damage to tiny areas of the prefrontal cortex were impaired in their working memory for certain locations only; for example, monkeys with damage in one area had trouble remembering a light to the right of fixation, and those with damage in another area had trouble remembering a light to the left (Goldman-Rakic, 1994). This result implies that different cell populations store temporary memories of different locations or different stimuli.

The prefrontal cortex is also critical for human working memory. Here is a quick way to test your working memory: Recite the digits 0 through 9 in a haphazard order (not something predictable) without omitting or repeating any digit. To do so, you need to keep a running record of which digits you have said and which you have not. Performance on this task depends strongly on the prefrontal cortex (D'Esposito & Grossman, 1996), so if you can do it easily, your prefrontal cortex is probably intact and healthy.

The central executive   It is especially difficult to identify the brain representation of the central executive because the concept itself is not clearly stated. Saying that the central executive directs attention to various stimuli and assigns memory space makes it sound like a "little person in the head." Nevertheless, researchers have made an effort to clarify the concept and determine which brain areas are most critical for it. Imagine a task that would tax your ability to control your attention: Perhaps you have to carry on an intelligent conversation while watching for a certain unusual, complex pattern on a computer screen. (This task resembles the job of an air-traffic controller.) One study using functional MRI found that simultaneously performing a verbal task and a visuospatial task activated the prefrontal cortex far more than either task did by itself (D'Esposito et al., 1995). People with damage in the prefrontal cortex have trouble on all kinds of working memory tasks, but especially if they have to shift attention between one task and another (Cummings, 1995).

Brain Damage and Long-Term Memory

People with **amnesia** (memory loss) generally have impaired long-term memory for facts and events. Much of what psychologists have learned about amnesia comes from studies of brain-damaged people, which led to experiments on animals, which in turn have led to new studies and insights about people.

Memory Loss After Hippocampal Damage

In 1953, a man known as H. M. suffered from such frequent and severe epileptic seizures that he had to quit his job. When he failed to respond to any of the antiepileptic drugs, he and his neurosurgeon became desperate to try almost anything. Because his seizures originated from disordered activity in the hippocampus (see Figure 13.5), the neurosurgeon removed that structure from both hemispheres, as well as several neighboring structures, including the amygdala. At the time, researchers had done almost no animal studies of the hippocampus and no one knew what to expect after the surgery. As events turned out, even though the operation greatly reduced H. M.'s seizures, he probably would have preferred to remain epileptic (Milner, 1959; Penfield & Milner, 1958; Scoville & Milner, 1957).

After the surgery, H. M.'s personality and intellect remained intact; his IQ score even increased slightly, presumably because of the decrease in epileptic interference. However, he suffered moderate **retrograde amnesia** (loss of memory for events that occurred shortly before brain damage). That is, he had some trouble recalling events that happened within 1 to 3 years before the operation. He also suffered a massive **anterograde amnesia** (loss of memories for events that happened after brain damage). He could form short-term memories, but very few new long-term memories.

For example, after the operation he could not learn his way to the hospital bathroom. After reading a story, he was unable to describe what had happened in it. He could read a single magazine over and over without increased familiarity or loss of interest. He lived with his parents, and when they moved to a new address, he had great difficulty finding his way home or locating anything within the house. After eight years, he had finally memorized the floor plan and could find his way from one room to another; however, he still could not find his way home from a distance of more than two blocks (Milner, Corkin, & Teuber, 1968).

In one test of H. M.'s memory, Brenda Milner (1959) asked him to memorize the number 584. After a 15-minute delay without distractions, he was able to recall the number correctly. He explained how he did so. "It's easy. You just remember 8. You see, 5, 8, and 4 add to 17. You remember 8, subtract it from 17, and it leaves 9. Divide 9 in half and you get 5 and 4, and there you are, 584. Easy." A moment later, after H. M.'s attention had shifted to another subject, he had forgotten both the number and the complicated line of thought he had associated with it.

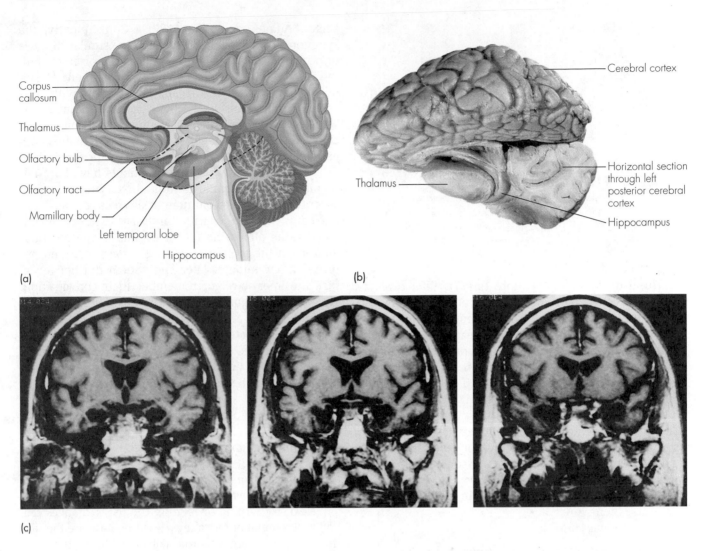

FIGURE **13.5**
The hippocampus
(**a**) Location of the hippocampus in the human brain. (**b**) Photo showing part of the hippocampus, which curves into the interior of each hemisphere. In both parts of the figure, note that the hippocampus curves around over the thalamus and under the cerebral cortex.   Source: Photo courtesy of Dana Copeland. (**c**) MRI scan of the brain of H. M., showing absence of the hippocampus.   Source: From Corkin, Amaral, González, Johnson, & Hyman, 1997.

In 1980, he moved to a nursing home. Four years later, he could not say where he lived or who cared for him. Although he watched the news on television every night, he could recall only a few fragments of events since 1953. For several years after the operation, whenever he was asked his age and the date, he answered "27" and "1953." After a few years, he started guessing wildly, generally underestimating his age by 10 years or more and missing the date by as much as 43 years (Corkin, 1984).

H. M. and similar patients are not completely unable to form new memories. They can learn to recall new material if they are given many, many repetitions under conditions designed to minimize interference. Even then, however, they do not remember when or

where they learned the material, and even when they answer correctly, they are not confident (Freed & Corkin, 1988; Hayman & Macdonald, 1993).

Although H. M. has enormous trouble learning new facts and keeping track of current events, he acquires new skills without apparent difficulty. For example, he has learned how to pass his finger through a small maze, read mirror writing, and solve the Tower of Hanoi puzzle shown in Figure 13.6 (Cohen, Eichenbaum, Deacedo, & Corkin, 1985). He does not *remember* learning these skills, however. In fact, he says he does not remember seeing the maze or the puzzle before. That is, he has impaired **declarative memory,** the ability to state a memory in words, but intact **procedural memory,** the development of motor skills.

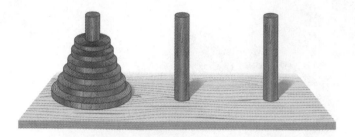

FIGURE 13.6
The Tower of Hanoi puzzle
The task is to transfer all the disks to another peg, moving just one at a time, without ever placing a larger disk on top of a smaller disk. H. M. has learned to solve this problem, although he says that he does not remember ever seeing it before.

He also shows much more *implicit* than *explicit* memory. **Explicit memory** is deliberate recall of information that one recognizes as a memory. It is tested by such questions as "What did you eat for dinner last night?" or "Who were the main characters in the last novel you read?" **Implicit memory** is the influence of recent experience on behavior, even if one does not realize that one is using memory at all. For example, if you have been reading the newspaper while ignoring a television talk show, you may not explicitly remember anything that the people on television said, and yet in your next conversation you may use some of the same words that they used. Psychologists call that phenomenon **priming,** because hearing certain words "primes" you to use them yourself.

In summary, H. M. has:

- Moderate retrograde amnesia (impaired memory of events that occurred 1 to 3 years before his operation)
- Normal short-term or working memory
- Severe anterograde amnesia for declarative memory
- Intact procedural memory
- Better implicit than explicit memory

Korsakoff's Syndrome and Other Prefrontal Damage

Korsakoff's syndrome, also known as *Wernicke–Korsakoff syndrome,* is brain damage caused by prolonged thiamine deficiency. Severe thiamine deficiency occurs almost exclusively in severe alcoholics who for days or weeks at a time eat almost nothing and drink only alcoholic beverages. The brain needs thiamine (vitamin B_1) in order to metabolize glucose, its primary fuel. Prolonged thiamine deficiency leads to a loss or shrinkage of neurons throughout the brain, especially in the mamillary bodies (part of the hypothalamus) and in the *dorsomedial thalamus,* a nucleus that projects to the prefrontal cortex (Squire, Amaral, & Press, 1990;

Victor, Adams, & Collins, 1971). Consequently, the symptoms of Korsakoff's syndrome are similar to those of people with damage to the prefrontal cortex, including apathy, confusion, and memory impairment. Hospitals in large cities report about 1 person with Korsakoff's syndrome per 1,000 hospital admissions. Treatment with thiamine can sometimes improve the condition, but the longer a person has remained thiamine deficient, the poorer the chances for recovery.

Most Korsakoff's syndrome patients have both retrograde and anterograde amnesia, in varying degrees of severity. One 59-year-old man easily recalled details of his early life and youthful military experience, but could recall almost no recent events. When an interviewer left the room after a long conversation and returned a few minutes later, the patient did not recognize the interviewer or remember their conversation. He did not recognize any doctors or nurses and could not find his way around the hospital. He read the same newspaper repeatedly, showing surprise at the news items each time. At the dinner table with an empty plate in front of him, he could not remember whether he had just finished eating or had not yet started (Barbizet, 1970).

Like H. M., people with Korsakoff's syndrome show better implicit than explicit memory. For illustration, read the following list once and then cover it: *neutral, defend, target, helium, endure, convey, ferret, modify, impale, sinker, golden, belfry, lagoon.*

Next, try writing or reciting the list. (Chances are, you will remember just a few.) Finally, here are the first three letters of some words. For each, fill in letters to make a complete word:

def____ hel____ con____ mod____ sin____ bel____

(Please try the demonstration before reading further.)

Each of these three-letter combinations is the start of many English words. Most people, however, fill in mostly words that were on the list they just read (defend, helium, convey, modify, sinker, belfry), including words they did not recall when they tried writing out the list. The contrast is even more striking with Korsakoff's patients, who in many cases cannot recall *any* of the words on the list, and may not even remember that they read a list, but nevertheless use many words from the list when completing the partial words (Schacter, 1985).

Korsakoff's patients, like other patients with frontal-lobe damage, often have great trouble recalling the temporal order of events. They cannot rank a series of world events or events from their own lives from the earliest to the most recent (Shimamura, Janowsky, & Squire, 1990). Answering questions about the timing of events calls for reasoning skills as much as for memory skills (Moscovitch, 1992). Suppose I ask, "Which happened to you most recently: graduation from high school, getting your first driver's license, or reading Chapter 2 of *Biological Psychology*?" You reason it out: "I started driving during my junior year of high school, so that came before graduation. *Biological Psychology* is one of my college texts, so I started reading it after high school." A person with frontal lobe damage has trouble with even this simple kind of reasoning; consequently, he or she will make such gross errors as saying, "I have been married for four months" and then a moment later adding, "our oldest child is 32 years old" (Moscovitch, 1989).

One of the most distinctive symptoms of Korsakoff's syndrome is **confabulation,** in which the patient takes a wild guess at the answer and then accepts that guess as if it were a memory. The tendency to confabulate produces a fascinating influence on the effects of different study techniques. Suppose you had to learn a long list of three-word sentences, such as "Medicine cured hiccups" and "Tourist desired snapshot." Would you learn it better by simply rereading the list many times? Or by alternating between reading the list and testing yourself?

Medicine cured _____.   Tourist desired _____.

Almost everyone learns better the second way. Completing the sentences forces you to be more active and calls your attention to the items you have not yet learned. Korsakoff's patients, however, learn much better the first way, by reading the list over and over, because when they test themselves, they confabulate. (*"Medicine cured headache. Tourist desired passport."*) Then they remember their confabulation instead of the correct answer (Hamann & Squire, 1995).

Alzheimer's Disease

Another cause of severe memory loss is **Alzheimer's disease,** a condition that becomes more and more prevalent with advancing age. Some people are stricken before age 50, some even before age 40. At age 65–74, it strikes less than 5 percent of the population, but in people over 85 it affects almost 50 percent (Evans et al., 1989). Many researchers believe it would eventually strike all of us if we lived long enough. The symptoms start with minor forgetfulness but progress to more serious memory loss, confusion, depression, restlessness, hallucinations, delusions, and disturbances of eating and sleeping (Cummings & Victoroff, 1990). Tasks requiring shifts of attention between one domain and another (central executive tasks) show greater deficits than single tasks do (Della Salla, Baddeley, Papagno, & Spinnler, 1995).

At the start, people with Alzheimer's disease typically have trouble keeping track of what they have just done and what has been going on around them. For example, Daniel Schacter (1983) reported playing golf with an Alzheimer's patient who remembered the rules and jargon of the game correctly but could not remember how many strokes he took on any hole. Five times he teed off, waited for the other player to tee off, and then teed off again, having forgotten his first shot. Even when he did remember not to tee off again, he could not remember where he had hit his ball.

As with H. M. and Korsakoff's patients, Alzheimer's patients have better procedural than declarative memory. They learn new hand skills, but then cannot remember learning them and may even be surprised at their good performance on what they consider an unfamiliar task (Gabrieli, Corkin, Mickel, & Growdon, 1993). Alzheimer's patients also show a bigger deficit on explicit than on implicit memory, although they also have moderate impairments on certain implicit memory tasks as well (Meiran & Jelicic, 1995), probably because of impaired attention during original exposure to the material (Randolph, Tierney, & Chase, 1995).

Researchers have identified several genes that increase the risk of Alzheimer's disease. The first clue was the fact that people with *Down syndrome* (a type of mental retardation) almost invariably get Alzheimer's disease if they survive into middle age (Lott, 1982). Down syndrome is caused by having three copies of chromosome 21 rather than the usual two copies. That fact led investigators to examine chromosome 21, where in fact they did find a gene linked to many cases of early-onset Alzheimer's disease (Goate et al., 1991; Murrell, Farlow, Ghetti, & Benson, 1991). That gene determines the structure of *amyloid precursor protein*, a large protein that is *cleaved* (broken) to form **amyloid beta protein ($A\beta$).** Ordinarily, the cleavage produces a protein of 40 amino acids, called $A\beta_{40}$, which does little harm, but it sometimes produces a slightly longer protein, $A\beta_{42}$, which forms amyloid deposits in the brain. Some people have a gene on chromosome 21 that increases the production of all $A\beta$ proteins, including $A\beta_{42}$. A more common gene, responsible for about 70 percent of early-onset Alzheimer's disease, is one on chromosome 14 (Schellenberg et al., 1992; Sherrington et al., 1995) that increases the ratio of $A\beta_{42}$ to $A\beta_{40}$ (Citron et al., 1997; Scheuner et al., 1996). A less common gene on chromosome 1 has similar effects (Levy-Lahad, 1995). Later-onset Alzheimer's disease, starting after age 60 to 65, depends on a gene on chromosome 19 (Corder et al., 1993; Pericak-Vance et al., 1991; Strittmatter & Roses, 1995). Like the others, it increases the density of amyloid deposits. Thus, although at least four different genes increase the risk of Alzheimer's disease, they produce similar effects in the brain.

FIGURE **13.7**
Brain atrophy in Alzheimer's disease
The cerebral cortex of an Alzheimer's patient (left) has gyri that are clearly shrunken in comparison with those of a normal person (right).   Source: Photos courtesy of Dr. Robert D. Terry.

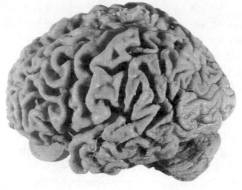
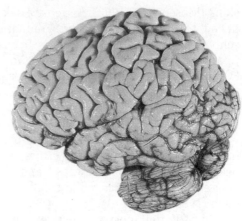

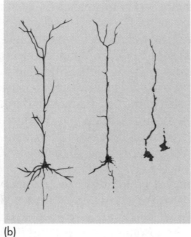

(a)   (b)

FIGURE **13.8**
Neuronal degeneration in Alzheimer's disease
(**a**) A cell in the prefrontal cortex of a normal human; (**b**) cells from the same area of cortex in Alzheimer's disease patients at three stages of deterioration. Note the shrinkage of the dendritic tree.   Source: After Scheibel, 1983.

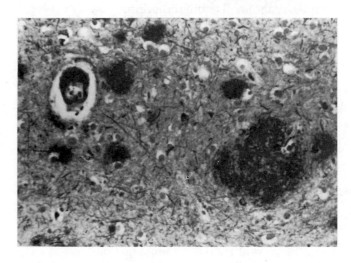

FIGURE **13.9**
Cerebral cortex of an Alzheimer's patient
The grayish areas are plaques. Magnification × 160.   Source: Rogers & Morrison, 1985.

Amyloid deposits produce widespread atrophy (wasting away) of the cerebral cortex, hippocampus, and other areas, as Figure 13.7 shows (Hyman, Van Hoesen, Damasio, & Barnes, 1984). A number of neurons degenerate (see Figure 13.8), and the dying axons and dendrites form **tangles** and **plaques,** as Figure 13.9 illustrates (Rogers & Morrison, 1985). One of the most heavily damaged areas is the entorhinal cortex, which communicates extensively with the hippocampus (Van Hoesen, Hyman, & Damasio, 1991). Another area of consistent damage is the basal forebrain, whose cells arouse the rest of the cortex by releasing acetylcholine (as discussed in Chapter 9). In rats, damage to the basal forebrain produces various deficits that are best summarized as impaired attention (Baxter, Bucci, Gorman, Wiley, & Gallagher, 1995; McGaughy, Kaiser, & Sarter, 1996).

What Amnesic Patients Teach Us

The study of amnesic patients reveals that people do not lose all aspects of memory equally. A patient with great difficulty establishing new memories may be able to remember events from long ago, and someone with greatly impaired factual memory may be able to learn new skills reasonably well. Evidently, people have several, somewhat independent kinds of memory that depend on different brain areas.

Functions of the Hippocampus in Memory

So far, we have seen that damage to the hippocampus and other areas impairs the formation of long-term explicit memories. Can we clarify their functions in more

FIGURE **13.10**
A radial maze
Food is in some arms, not in others. A rat that reenters one arm before trying other arms has made an error of working memory.

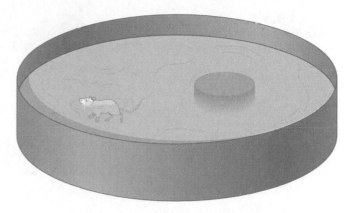

FIGURE **13.11**
The Morris search task
A rat is placed in murky water. A platform that would provide support is submerged so the rat cannot see it. Rats with hippocampal damage have trouble remembering the location of the platform.

detail? To gain greater control of the situation, neuroscientists turn to animal studies.

Damage to the Hippocampus in Rats

The discovery of how hippocampal damage impaired memory in H. M. and other patients led psychologists to experiment on rats. In early experiments, they typically made hippocampal lesions and then tested the rats' ability to learn a simple discrimination: to approach a white card instead of a black card, for example, or respond to a high-frequency tone and not a low-frequency tone. To the investigators' surprise, the rats generally did pretty well. Psychologists puzzled over why hippocampal damage seemed to impair human memory so much more than animal memory (Isaacson, 1972).

Later research highlighted distinctions among different kinds of memory. Learning to approach a particular signal requires procedural memory, the kind that is not impaired in H. M. or similar amnesic patients. Eventually, investigators discovered that rats with hippocampal lesions performed well on some memory tasks and poorly on others.

As with humans, hippocampal damage in rats impairs some kinds of memory and spares others. In a typical experiment, a rat is placed in the center of a **radial maze** (Figure 13.10) that has eight or more arms, some of which have a bit of food at the end. The rats might have to learn that the arms with a rough floor

never have food or that the arms pointing toward the window never have food. The rat stays in the maze until it has found all the food or until it has gone, say, 2 minutes without finding any more food. After enough training trials, a rat learns to go down each correct arm once and only once and not to try any of the incorrect arms. A rat can make two types of mistakes: It can go down one of the always-incorrect arms, or it can enter one correct arm repeatedly.

A normal rat makes only a few errors of either kind. Rats with damage to the hippocampus or its connections with other structures seldom enter the never-correct arms, but they frequently reenter some correct arms and fail to try others. Evidently, they forget which arms they have already tried (Jarrard, Okaichi, Steward, & Goldschmidt, 1984; Olton & Papas, 1979; Olton, Walker, & Gage, 1978).

Hippocampal damage also impairs performance on the **Morris search task** (Figure 13.11), in which a rat must swim through cloudy water to find a rest platform that is just under the surface. A rat with hippocampal damage finds the platform but, unlike normal rats, it has trouble remembering the location from one trial to the next, and therefore its escape times do not improve much (Jarrard, 1995).

Damage to the Hippocampus in Primates

Primates are generally tested on some rather complex tasks. In a **delayed matching-to-sample task,** an animal sees an object (the sample) and then, after a delay, gets a choice between two objects, from which it must choose the one that matches the sample. In the **delayed**

FIGURE **13.12**
Procedure for delayed nonmatching-to-sample task

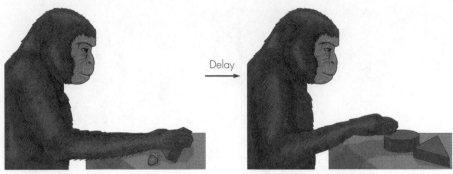

Monkey lifts sample object to get food.   Food is under the new object.

nonmatching-to-sample task (Figure 13.12), the procedure is the same except that the animal must choose the object that is *different* from the sample. In both cases, the task is to recognize which stimulus is familiar and which is new.

An animal's performance on a task like this varies enormously with apparently minor changes in procedure. For example, on either delayed matching-to-sample or delayed nonmatching-to-sample tests, the subject must remember the sample during the delay, and we might suppose that both tasks would be equally easy or equally difficult. Yet monkeys perform much better on nonmatching than on matching tests; evidently, they learn to reach for a new item more easily than they learn to reach for a familiar item. Furthermore, the results can vary depending on whether the experimenter uses the same objects repeatedly or uses new objects each time. For example, if a monkey always has to choose between a red triangle and a blue square, damage to the prefrontal cortex impairs performance, but hippocampal damage does not. If a monkey has to choose between different objects every time, damage to either the hippocampus or the prefrontal cortex greatly impairs performance (Aggleton, Blindt, & Rawlins, 1989).

Theories of the Function of the Hippocampus

Exactly how does the hippocampus contribute to memory? Clearly, we do not store memories *in* the hippocampus itself. Hippocampal damage makes it difficult to store new memories, but it does not impair old memories. Psychologists have tried to discover which memory tasks are impaired by hippocampal damage and which are not. One hypothesis is that the hippocampus is critical for declarative, explicit memory (Squire, 1992). This hypothesis is unfortunately rather imprecise because the definitions of "declarative" and "explicit" apply best to human memory. Rats and monkeys cannot describe their memories, and it is hard to

determine which of their behaviors reflect memories like human declarative memories (Nadel, 1992). Performance in a radial maze or delayed nonmatching-to-sample task requires remembering particular events (where one has been or which objects one has just seen) and does seem a reasonable match to declarative memory, but many other memory tasks are hard to classify as either declarative or procedural.

Another hypothesis is that the hippocampus is necessary for *configural conditioning*, in which the correct response depends on a combination of two or more stimuli rather than on any one stimulus—for example, stimulus A signals food and B does also, but A and B together do not. However, damage to the hippocampus sometimes impairs configural conditioning and sometimes does not (Alvarado & Rudy, 1995). According to a revised theory, the hippocampus is not necessary for configural conditioning, but it facilitates such conditioning in other brain areas (Rudy & Sutherland, 1995).

Still another hypothesis is that the hippocampus, at least in nonhumans, is especially important for spatial memories (O'Keefe, 1993). Certainly the radial maze and the Morris search task require spatial memory, as do a number of other hippocampus-dependent tasks. Electrical recordings have indicated that many neurons in a rat's hippocampus are tuned to particular spatial locations, responding best when an animal is in a particular place (O'Keefe & Burgess, 1996) or looking in a particular direction (Dudchenko & Taube, 1997; Rolls, 1996).

Particularly compelling evidence for the role of the hippocampus in spatial memory comes from comparisons of closely related species that differ in their spatial memory. Clark's nutcracker, a member of the jay family in western North America, lives year-round at high altitudes. During the summer and fall, it buries tens of thousands of seeds in thousands of locations. Unlike squirrels, which bury nuts but often cannot find them, nutcrackers return to their hiding places in the winter and find enough to survive when no other food is available. Pinyon jays, which live at slightly lower eleva-

Species	Reliance on Stored Food	Size of Hippocampus Relative to Rest of Brain	Performance on Laboratory Tests of Spatial Memory	Performance on Laboratory Tests of Color Memory
Clark's nutcracker 	Lives high in mountains; stores food in summer and relies on finding it to survive the winter.	Largest	Best	Slightly worse
pinyon jay 	Lives at fairly high altitude; depends partly on stored food to survive the winter.	Second largest	Second best	Slightly better
scrub jay 	Stores some food but less dependent on it.	Smaller	Less good	Slightly worse
Mexican jay 	Stores some food but less dependent on it.	Smaller	Less good	Slightly better

FIGURE **13.13**
Hippocampus and spatial memory in jays
Of four species of the jay family, all living in western North America, the species that rely most heavily on stored food to get through the winter have the largest hippocampus and perform best on laboratory tests of spatial memory. They have no consistent advantage on nonspatial memory.
Source: Based on results of Basil et al., 1996, and Olson et al., 1995.

tions, also in western North America, bury less food and are less dependent on it during the winter. Scrub jays and Mexican jays, living at still lower altitudes, depend even less on stored food. Researchers have found that of these four species, the Clark's nutcrackers have the largest hippocampus and perform best on radial mazes and other laboratory tests of spatial memory. Pinyon jays are second best in both respects. On nonspatial tasks, such as color memory, size of hippocampus does not correlate with success (Basil, Kamil, Balda, & Fite, 1996; Olson, Kamil, Balda, & Nims, 1995). (See Figure 13.13.)

Similarly, tits (tiny European birds) and chickadees (tiny American birds) include some species that store food and retrieve it later and some that do not. Willow tits, which store much food and retrieve it months later, have the largest hippocampus relative to the rest of the brain. Species that store a little and retrieve it days or weeks later have an intermediate hippocampus; great tits and blue tits, which never store food, have the smallest hippocampus (Healy & Krebs, 1996). In short, the species comparisons support a strong link between the hippocampus and spatial memory.

However, although hippocampal damage consistently impairs spatial memory performance, it sometimes also impairs performance on tasks with no apparent spatial component (Wan, Pang, & Olton, 1994). Whether or not performance depends on the

FIGURE **13.14**
Radial maze for children
Children could find rewards by visiting each arm once and only once. Good performance requires working memory for spatial information and is known to depend on the hippocampus.   Source: Overman, Pate, Moore, & Peuster, 1996.

hippocampus varies with a number of procedural details that might appear irrelevant. In one study, damage to a path of axons leaving the hippocampus produced memory deficits if a rat was choosing between two large goal boxes, but not if it was choosing between small goal boxes (Cassaday & Rawlins, 1995). It may prove difficult to summarize the role of the hippocampus in a few words.

Brain and Memory in Young and Old

Ideally, investigating the physiology of learning and memory should lead to insights about why some people have better memories than others do. For example, why do infants and old people sometimes have memory difficulties? Psychologists have long puzzled over **infant amnesia,** the phenomenon that adults remember very few events from their earliest years. Memories do form during this period, as 3- and 4-year-olds can clearly describe events that they experienced months ago. Nevertheless, a few years later nearly all those memories have faded beyond recall.

According to one hypothesis, early declarative memories are weak because the hippocampus is slow to mature (Moscovitch, 1985). To evaluate this hypothesis, investigators tested children of several ages on tasks that in rats are known to depend on the hippocampus. For example, they built a radial maze of human dimensions, in which children had to explore each arm to get rewards, remembering which arms they had already visited on a given day (Figure 13.14). Investigators also built a version of the Morris search task (Figure 13.15); however, instead of asking the children to

swim through murky water to find the platform, they had the children wade through little pieces of Styrofoam. The idea was the same, however; good performance required spatial memory. On both of these tasks, the performance of children less than seven years old was impaired compared to that of older children (Overman, Pate, Moore, & Peuster, 1996). This evidence suggests that poor declarative memory for early experiences may reflect slow development of the hippocampus.

The memory deficits common in aging people without Alzheimer's disease resemble those of younger people with damage to the prefrontal cortex: Both have impaired ability to reconstruct partially recalled memories and to draw plausible inferences from memory (Moscovitch & Winocur, 1995). Aged monkeys also per-

FIGURE **13.15**
Adaptation of the Morris search task for children
Unlike rats, which have to swim through murky water to find the platform, children wade through little pieces of styrofoam.
Source: Overman, Pate, Moore, & Peuster, 1996.

form poorly on the same tasks as monkeys with prefrontal damage. The memory deficits of old age may be due in part to a declining number of dopamine receptors in the prefrontal cortex (Arnsten, Cai, & Goldman-Rakic, 1995).

IN CLOSING

Different Types of Memory

Recall the discussion in Chapter 5 concerning a possible relationship between overall intelligence and overall brain size. You should now see more clearly why many investigators regard "overall intelligence" as a convenient fiction. Even "memory" is composed of separate abilities, and it is possible to impair one and not another. Intelligence is the sum of an even greater number of abilities, highly correlated with one another, but nevertheless distinct.

Summary

1. Ivan Pavlov suggested that learning depends on the growth of a connection between two brain areas. Karl Lashley showed that learning does *not* depend on new connections across the cerebral cortex. (p. 346)
2. Later researchers have demonstrated that, in certain cases, classical conditioning takes place in small areas within the cerebellum. More complex learning undoubtedly requires more widespread changes. (p. 348)
3. Psychologists distinguish between short-term memory and long-term memory. Short-term memory holds only a small amount of information and retains it only briefly unless it is constantly rehearsed. Long-term memory retains vast amounts of material indefinitely, but recalling this information sometimes requires great effort. (p. 349)
4. The consolidation of short-term memories into long-term memories depends more on arousal than on mere passage of time. Arousing events activate epinephrine and other adrenal hormones that directly or indirectly stimulate the amygdala. Even if the amygdala does not store a memory itself, it enhances storage elsewhere. (p. 350)
5. Working memory, a modern alternative to the concept of short-term memory, stores information temporarily while one is using it. The prefrontal cortex and other areas can store working memories through repetitive cellular activity. (p. 351)
6. People with damage to the hippocampus, such as the patient H. M., have great trouble forming new long-term declarative memories, although they can still recall events from before the damage and can still form new procedural memories. (p. 352)

7. Patients with Korsakoff's syndrome or other types of prefrontal damage have impairments of memory, including loss of temporal order and difficulty drawing inferences from memories. They often fill in their memory gaps with confabulations, which they then remember as if true. (p. 354)
8. Alzheimer's disease is a progressive disease, most common in old age, that is characterized by a severe impairment of memory and attention. It is caused by the deposition of amyloid in the brain. Several genes increase the deposition of amyloid. (p. 355)
9. According to research on nonhumans, the hippocampus appears to be especially important for spatial memories, although not all data fit that view. (p. 358)
10. Some memory deficits of early childhood may relate to the immaturity of the hippocampus. Deficits of memory in old people without Alzheimer's disease probably relate to decreased functioning of the prefrontal cortex. (p. 360)

Review Questions

1. What assumptions inherent in the work of Karl Lashley have later researchers discarded? (p. 348)
2. What evidence indicates that activity of the red nucleus is necessary for *performance* of a conditioned response but not for the actual *learning* of the response? (p. 349)
3. Through what mechanisms does epinephrine enhance memory storage? (p. 351)
4. Name the three components of working memory. (p. 351)
5. What is the difference between retrograde amnesia and anterograde amnesia? (p. 352)
6. What aspects of memory are least impaired in the patient H. M.? (pp. 353–354)
7. Most people learn written material best if they alternate between reading it and testing their memory. Which people learn best by reading without testing? Why? (p. 355)
8. How many genes are known to increase the risk of Alzheimer's disease? In what way do they affect the brain similarly? (p. 355)
9. Describe nonverbal tasks on which performance is impaired by hippocampal damage. (p. 357)
10. What kinds of birds have an especially large hippocampus, and why? (p. 358)
11. What evidence suggests that infant amnesia may relate to immaturity of the hippocampus? (p. 360)

Thought Questions

1. Lashley sought to find the engram, the physiological representation of learning. In general terms, how would you recognize an engram if you saw one? That is, what would someone have to demonstrate before you could conclude that a particular change in the nervous system was really an engram?
2. Benzodiazepine tranquilizers impair memory. Use what you have learned in this chapter and the previous one to propose an explanation.

Suggestions for Further Reading

Cohen, N. J., & Eichenbaum, H. (1993). *Memory, amnesia, and the hippocampal system.* Cambridge, MA: MIT Press. Discussion of memory impairments, especially as they relate to the hippocampus.

McGaugh, J. L., Bermúdez-Rattoni, F., & Prado-Alcalá, R. A. (1995). *Plasticity in the central nervous system.* Mahwah, NJ: Erlbaum. A collection of chapters on many topics related to the physiology of memory.

Terms

classical conditioning   type of conditioning produced by the pairing of two stimuli, one of which evokes an automatic response (p. 346)

conditioned stimulus (CS)   stimulus that evokes a particular response only after it has been paired with an unconditioned stimulus (p. 346)

unconditioned stimulus (UCS)   stimulus that automatically evokes an unconditioned response (p. 346)

unconditioned response (UCR)   response automatically evoked by an unconditioned stimulus (p. 346)

conditioned response (CR)   response evoked by a conditioned stimulus after it has been paired with an unconditioned stimulus (p. 346)

operant conditioning   type of conditioning in which reinforcement or punishment changes the future probabilities of a given behavior (p. 346)

reinforcement   event that increases the future probability of the preceding response (p. 346)

punishment   event that suppresses the frequency of the preceding response (p. 346)

engram   the physical representation of learning (p. 346)

lateral interpositus nucleus   a nucleus of the cerebellum that is critical for classical conditioning of the eyeblink response in rabbits (p. 348)

short-term memory   memory of an event that just happened (p. 349)

long-term memory   memory of an event that is not currently held in attention (p. 349)

consolidation   formation and strengthening of long-term memories (p. 350)

working memory   temporary storage of memories to which one is attending at the moment (p. 351)

phonological loop   aspect of working memory that stores auditory information, including (for humans) words (p. 351)

visuospatial sketchpad   aspect of working memory that stores visual information (p. 351)

central executive   mechanism that directs attention toward one stimulus or another and determines which items will be stored in working memory (p. 351)

delayed response task   task in which an individual is given a signal to which it must give a learned response after a delay (p. 351)

amnesia   memory loss (p. 352)

retrograde amnesia   loss of memory for events that occurred before brain damage (p. 352)

anterograde amnesia   loss of memory for events that happened after brain damage (p. 352)

declarative memory   memory that a person can identify verbally as a memory (p. 353)

procedural memory   memory of how to do something (p. 353)

explicit memory   deliberate recall of information that one recognizes as a memory, detectable by direct testing such as asking a person to describe a past event (p. 354)

implicit memory   influence of recent experience on memory, even if one does not recognize that influence or realize that one is using memory at all (p. 354)

priming   phenomenon that seeing or hearing a word or words increases the probability that a person will soon use those same words (p. 354)

Korsakoff's syndrome   type of brain damage caused by thiamine deficiency, characterized by apathy, confusion, and memory impairment (p. 354)

confabulation   making up an answer to a question, and then accepting the invented information as if it were a memory (p. 355)

Alzheimer's disease   condition characterized by memory loss, confusion, depression, restlessness, hallucinations, delusions, and disturbances of eating, sleeping, and other daily activities (p. 355)

amyloid beta protein (Aβ)   protein that accumulates in the brain, causing Alzheimer's disease (p. 355)

tangle   collection of disrupted axons and dendrites found in the brains of people with Alzheimer's disease (p. 356)

plaque   structure formed from degenerating axons and dendrites in the brains of people with Alzheimer's disease (p. 356)

radial maze   apparatus with many arms radiating from a central point; food is generally put at the ends of some or all of the arms (p. 357)

Morris search task   procedure in which a subject must find his or her way to a slightly submerged platform that is not visible in murky water or other opaque substance (p. 357)

delayed matching-to-sample task   task in which an animal sees a sample object and then after a delay must choose an object that matches the sample (p. 357)

delayed nonmatching-to-sample task   task in which an animal sees an object and then after a delay must choose an object that does not match the sample (p. 357)

infant amnesia   tendency for people to recall few specific events that occurred before about age 4 or 5 years (p. 360)

Storing Information in the Nervous System

When you see, hear, or do something, your experience probably leaves several traces in your nervous system. But which of these traces are important for memory?

If I walk through a field, are the footprints that I leave "memories"? How about the mud that I pick up on my shoes? If the police wanted to know who had walked across that field, a forensics expert could compare the footprints with the soles of my shoes and the mud on my shoes to the mud on the field. And yet we would not call these physical traces "memories" in the usual sense.

Similarly, when a pattern of activity passes through the brain, it leaves a path of physical changes. Any or all of those changes would be memories if something in the brain could use them appropriately. Investigators of the physiology of learning and memory try to determine how an experience lays down lasting traces in the brain and which of those traces the brain uses later. The task is a little like searching for the proverbial needle in the haystack, and researchers have explored many avenues that seemed promising for a while but now seem fruitless (see Digression 13.1).

Learning and the Hebbian Synapse

Ivan Pavlov's concept of classical conditioning lent itself readily to theorizing about the physiological basis of learning. As we have already seen, Pavlov's theories inspired Karl Lashley's unsuccessful search for new connections across the cerebral cortex. They also stimulated Donald Hebb to propose a mechanism for change at a synapse.

Hebb suggested that when the axon of neuron A "repeatedly or persistently takes part in firing [cell B], some growth process or metabolic change takes place in one or both cells" that increases the subsequent ability of axon A to excite cell B (Hebb, 1949, p. 62). In

other words, an axon that has successfully stimulated cell B in the past becomes even more successful in the future.

Consider how this relates to classical conditioning. Suppose that axon A initially excites cell B only slightly. If axon A often fires at the same time as another axon, say axon C, the combined effect on B may be great, perhaps even producing an action potential. You might think of axon A as the CS and axon C as the UCS. The pairing of activity in axons A and C causes cell B to increase its responsiveness to A. Hebb was noncommittal about where the change occurred; the terminal of axon A or the dendrites of cell B might grow, or a chemical change might occur in one or the other.

A synapse that increases in effectiveness because of simultaneous activity in the presynaptic and postsynaptic neurons is called a **Hebbian synapse.** In Chapter 5, we encountered many examples of this type of synapse; in the development of the nervous system, postsynaptic neurons increase their responsiveness to combinations of axons that are active at the same time as one another (and therefore at the same time as the postsynaptic neuron). Such synapses may also be critical for many kinds of associative learning. Neuroscientists have discovered much about the mechanisms of Hebbian (or almost Hebbian) synapses.

Single-Cell Mechanisms of Invertebrate Behavior Change

We can imagine many possible physiological mechanisms for learning and memory: changes in dendritic branching, changes in glia, increased or decreased release of a neurotransmitter, or development of new proteins within neurons. If we are going to look for the proverbial needle in a haystack, a good strategy is to look in a small haystack.

By that reasoning, many researchers have turned to

studies of invertebrates. The nervous system of an invertebrate is organized differently from that of a vertebrate; for example, many invertebrates have several widely separated ganglia instead of a single structure that we could call a "brain." But the general chemistry of the neuron, the principles of the action potential, and even many of the neurotransmitters are the same. (Many key neurotransmitters are found in one-celled animals, although we do not know what they are doing there.) If we identify the physical basis of learning and memory in an invertebrate, we cannot assume that vertebrates use the same mechanism, but at least we have a good hypothesis of what *might* work. (Biologists have long used this strategy for studying genetics, embryology, and other biological processes.)

Aplysia as an Experimental Animal

Aplysia, a marine invertebrate related to the common slug, has become a popular animal for studies of the physiology of learning (see Figure 13.17). *Aplysia* has fewer neurons than any vertebrate, and many are large (up to 1 mm in diameter) and therefore easy to study. Moreover, unlike vertebrates, *Aplysia* has neurons that are virtually identical from one individual to another, so that after an experimenter identifies the properties of the *R2* cell in one specimen, other experimenters can find the same cell in their own animals and can carry the studies further or relate that neuron to other identified neurons. Vertebrates do not show the same degree of similarity from one individual to another.

DIGRESSION 13.1

Blind Alleys and Abandoned Mines in Research

Textbook authors, myself included, write mostly about successful research, the studies that led to our current understanding of a field. You may get the impression that science progresses in a smooth fashion, that each study leads to the next and that each investigator simply contributes to an ever-accumulating body of knowledge. However, if you look at the old journals or textbooks in a field, you will find discussions of various "promising" or "exciting" findings that we disregard today. Scientific research does not progress in a straight line from ignorance to enlightenment; it explores one direction after another, a little like a rat in a complex maze, abandoning the arms that lead nowhere and pursuing those that lead further. Many promising lines of research turn out to be blind alleys.

The problem with the maze analogy is that an investigator seldom runs into a wall that clearly identifies the end of a route. Perhaps a better analogy is a prospector digging in one location after another, never entirely certain whether to abandon an unprofitable spot or to keep digging just a little longer. Many once-exciting lines of research in the physiology of learning are now of little more than historical interest. Here are three examples.

1. Wilder Penfield sometimes performed brain surgery for severe epilepsy on conscious patients who had only scalp anesthesia. When he applied a brief, weak electrical stimulus to part of the brain, the patient could describe the experience that the stimulation evoked. Stimulation of the temporal cortex sometimes evoked vivid descriptions such as:

I feel as though I were in the bathroom at school.

I see myself at the corner of Jacob and Washington in South Bend, Indiana.

I remember myself at the railroad station in Vanceburg, Kentucky; it is winter and the wind is blowing outside, and I am waiting for a train.

Penfield (1955; Penfield & Perot, 1963) suggested that each neuron in the temporal cortex stores a particular memory, almost like a videotape of one's life. However, it is doubtful that the brain stimulation actually evoked old memories. Stimulation very rarely elicited a memory of a specific event, more often evoking vague sights and sounds or repeated experiences such as "seeing a bed" or "hearing a choir sing 'White Christmas.'" Stimulation almost never elicited memories of doing anything—just of seeing and hearing. Also, some patients reported events that they had never actually experienced, such as being chased by a robber or seeing Christ descend from the sky. In short, the stimulation produced something more like a dream than an accurate memory.

2. G. A. Horridge (1962) apparently demonstrated that decapitated cockroaches can learn. First, he cut the connections between a cockroach's head and the rest of its body. Then he suspended the cockroach so that its legs dangled just above a surface of water. An electrical circuit was arranged as Figure 13.16 shows, so that the roach's leg would get a shock whenever it touched the water. Each experimental roach was paired with a control roach that got a leg shock whenever the first roach did; only the experimental roach had any control over the shock, however. (This kind of experiment is known as a "yoked-control" design.)

Over 5 to 10 minutes, roaches in the experimental group "learned" a response of tucking the leg under the body to avoid shocks. Roaches in the control group did not, on the average, change their leg position during the training period.

Much of the research on *Aplysia* concerns changes in behavior as a result of experience. Some of those changes may seem simple, and it is a matter of definition whether we call them *learning* or use the broader term *plasticity*. One commonly studied behavior is the withdrawal response: If someone touches the siphon, mantle, or gill of an *Aplysia* (Figure 13.18), the animal vigorously withdraws the irritated structure. Investigators have traced the neural path from the touch receptors through various identifiable interneurons to the motor neurons that direct the withdrawal response. Using this neural pathway, investigators have studied such phenomena as habituation and sensitization.

Habituation in *Aplysia*

Habituation is a decrease in response to a stimulus that is presented repeatedly and accompanied by no change in other stimuli. For example, if your clock chimes once an hour, you respond to it less and less after many repetitions. Habituation can be demonstrated in an *Aplysia* by repeatedly stimulating its gills with a brief jet of seawater. At first, it withdraws the gills, but after many repetitions it stops responding. In explaining this phenomenon, we can eliminate several possible mechanisms. First, we can rule out muscle fatigue because, even after habituation has occurred, direct stimulation

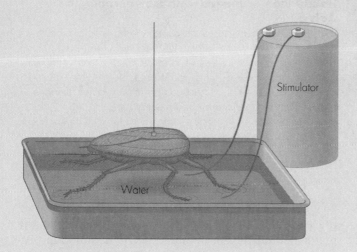

FIGURE 13.16
Learning in a headless cockroach?
This decapitated cockroach is suspended just above the water; it receives a shock whenever its hind leg touches the water. A cockroach in the control group gets a shock whenever the first roach does, regardless of its own behavior. According to some reports, the experimental roach learned to keep its leg out of the water.   Source: After Horridge, 1962.

Thus, the changed response apparently qualifies as learning and not as some accidental by-product of the shocks.

These experiments initially seemed a promising way to study learning in a very simple nervous system, a single cockroach ganglion (Eisenstein & Cohen, 1965). Unfortunately,

decapitated cockroaches learn slowly, and the results vary sharply from one individual to another, limiting the usefulness of the results. After a few studies in the 1960s and early 1970s, interest in this line of research faded.

3. In the 1960s and early 1970s, several investigators proposed that each memory is coded as a specific molecule, probably RNA or protein. The boldest test of that hypothesis was an attempt to transfer memories chemically from one individual to another. James McConnell (1962) reported that when planaria (flatworms) cannibalized other planaria that had been classically conditioned to respond to a light, they apparently "remembered" what the cannibalized planaria had learned. (At least, they learned the response faster than planaria generally do.)

Inspired by that report, other investigators trained rats to approach a clicking sound for food (Babich, Jacobson, Bubash, & Jacobson, 1965). After the rats were well trained, the experimenters ground up their brains, extracted RNA, and injected it into untrained rats. The recipient rats learned to approach the clicking sound faster than rats in the control group did.

That report led to a sudden flurry of experiments on the transfer of training by brain extracts. In *some* of these experiments, rats that received brain extracts from a trained group showed apparent memory of the task, while those that received extracts from an untrained group did not (Dyal, 1971; Fjerdingstad, 1973).

The results were inconsistent and unreplicable, however, even within a single laboratory (Smith, 1975). Many laboratories failed to find any hint of a transfer effect. By the mid-1970s, most biological psychologists saw no point in continuing such research.

FIGURE **13.17**
***Aplysia* or sea hare, a marine mollusk**
A full-grown animal is a little larger than the average human hand.

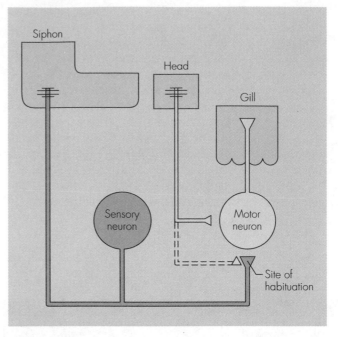

FIGURE **13.19**
Habituation of the gill-withdrawal reflex in *Aplysia*
Touching the siphon causes the gill to withdraw. After many repetitions, the response habituates (declines). The sensory neuron fires as much as before, and the motor neuron, if directly stimulated, produces as much response as before. The habituation occurs because of decreased transmission at the synapse between the sensory neuron and the motor neuron. After habituation has occurred, stimulation of another site, such as the head, sends a message that removes the habituation.   Source: After Castellucci et al., 1970.

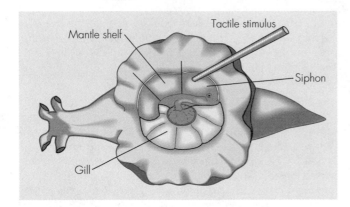

FIGURE **13.18**
Touching an *Aplysia* causes a withdrawal response
The sensory and motor neurons controlling this reaction have been identified and studied.

of the motor neuron produces a full-sized muscle contraction (Kupfermann, Castellucci, Pinsker, & Kandel, 1970). Second, habituation does not depend on a change in the firing rate of the sensory neuron. After repeated stimulation, the sensory neuron still gives a full, normal response to stimulation; it merely fails to excite the motor neuron as much as before (Kupfermann et al., 1970).

We are therefore left with the conclusion that habituation in *Aplysia* depends on a change in the synapse between the sensory neuron and the motor neuron (Figure 13.19). To determine the nature of that

change, V. Castellucci and Eric Kandel (1974) measured the excitatory postsynaptic potentials (EPSPs) in the motor neuron during habituation. As habituation proceeded, the average size of the EPSP decreased, but each EPSP was still an integral multiple of the quantum of membrane response (as described in Chapter 3), which is presumably based on a quantum of neurotransmitter release. From this evidence, Castellucci and Kandel inferred that habituation reflects a decrease in transmitter release by the presynaptic cell.

Sensitization in *Aplysia*

After a strong electrical shock or any other intense stimulus, a person undergoes **sensitization,** becoming overresponsive to mild stimuli. Similarly, a strong noxious stimulus almost anywhere on *Aplysia*'s surface can intensify later withdrawal responses to a touch on the siphon, mantle, or gill. Sensitization may last as briefly as a few seconds or as long as days, depending on the intensity and number of repetitions of the sensitizing stimulus.

As with habituation, sensitization in *Aplysia* depends on a change in the number of quanta of neurotransmitter that the presynaptic neuron releases (Dale, Schacher, & Kandel, 1988). The difference is that habituation reflects decreased release, while sensitization reflects increased release. Figure 13.20 diagrams the two relevant synapses: one between the sensory neuron and an interneuron and one between the sensory neuron and the motor neuron. Researchers have described the mechanism of that change in some detail (Cleary, Hammer, & Byrne, 1989; Kandel & Schwartz, 1982).

Strong stimulation (of the head, tail, or elsewhere) excites a particular facilitating interneuron, identifiable in any *Aplysia*, which has presynaptic synapses that release serotonin (5-HT) onto the synapses of many sensory neurons. Serotonin interacts with a receptor in each sensory neuron, ultimately blocking potassium channels in the membrane. As you will recall from Chapter 2, potassium flows out of the neuron after the peak of the action potential; the exit of potassium restores the neuron to its usual polarization. When the cyclic-AMP-dependent enzyme blocks the potassium channels, the net effect is to prolong the action potential and therefore to prolong transmitter release by the presynaptic cell.

If the sensitizing stimulus is repeated, the prolonged elevation of cyclic AMP in the sensory neuron leads to the production of new proteins responsible for long-term sensitization. Unlike the short-term variety, long-term sensitization can be blocked by drugs that interfere with protein synthesis (Schacher, Castellucci, & Kandel, 1988).

The research on *Aplysia* shows us that behavioral change can be based on increases or decreases in the activity at identifiable synapses. Learning need not rely on the same mechanisms in all situations in all species, however. Additional research may discover different mechanisms of learning.

Long-Term Potentiation in Mammals

Are the cellular mechanisms of vertebrate learning similar to those of mollusks? If not, what other mechanisms can we find? In the mammalian nervous system, the best candidate for a cellular basis of learning is a phenomenon known as **long-term potentiation (LTP).** First, a neuron is bombarded with a brief but rapid series of stimuli—typically, 100 synaptic excitations per second for 1 to 4 seconds. This burst of intense stimulation leaves the neuron "potentiated" (highly responsive to new input of the same type) for minutes, days, or weeks.

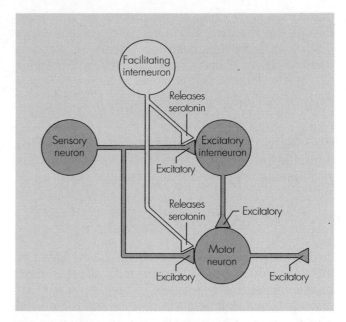

FIGURE **13.20**
Sensitization of the withdrawal response in
Aplysia
Stimulation of the sensory neuron ordinarily produces a certain amount of excitation of the motor neuron, partly by a direct path and partly by stimulation of an excitatory interneuron. Stimulation of a facilitating interneuron releases serotonin to the axon terminals of the sensory neuron, blocking potassium channels and thereby prolonging the release of neurotransmitter. This effect can be long-lasting. Source: After Kandel & Schwartz, 1982.

LTP shows the property of **cooperativity:** Nearly simultaneous stimulation by two or more axons produces LTP, whereas stimulation by just one produces it weakly, if at all. It also shows **associativity:** Pairing a weak input with a strong input enhances later response to the weak input. These observations make LTP an attractive model of learning. Furthermore, only those axons that "cooperated" become facilitated. That is, suppose that three axons—A, B, and C—all have synapses onto the same postsynaptic neuron. Now suppose that axons A and B are repeatedly active, depolarizing the postsynaptic neuron, whereas axon C is inactive. LTP strengthens the synapses of A and B, while actually weakening the synapses of C (Sejnowski, Chattarji, & Stanton, 1990). In this regard, the synapses subject to LTP are like Hebbian synapses, except that LTP requires only a depolarization of a dendrite, not necessarily an action potential by the whole cell.

LTP was first discovered in studies of hippocampal neurons (Bliss & Lømo, 1973). It can also occur in other brain areas, including the cerebral cortex (Weinberger, Javid, & Lepan, 1995). The opposite change, **long-term**

depression (LTD), also occurs in both the hippocampus (Kerr & Abraham, 1995) and the cerebellum. In the cerebellum, nearly simultaneous activity by two kinds of axons—parallel fibers and climbing fibers—attached to a single Purkinje cell produces a prolonged depression of response to the parallel fibers (Ito, 1989). Because the output of a Purkinje cell is itself inhibitory, the net effect of depression of the parallel fiber's synapses is to increase excitation at a point farther down the line. LTD is believed to be important for classical conditioning and for learning motor skills.

Cellular Mechanisms

To determine the cellular mechanisms, many investigators have studied cells in **hippocampal slices,** sections of the hippocampus removed from the animal and maintained in a culture medium with various nutrients. This procedure facilitates electrical stimulation of and recording from cells.

In the cases that have been most thoroughly studied so far, LTP depends on certain changes at glutamate synapses. The vertebrate nervous system has at least three major types of glutamate receptors, each of which comes in several subtypes (Nakanishi, 1992). You will recall that neuroscientists refer to the various dopamine receptors by number, such as D_1 and D_2. Because each dopamine receptor responds to different drugs, we could just as easily have named each receptor after a drug that stimulates it. Investigators have in fact named the glutamate receptors for the drugs that stimulate them, and we shall be interested here especially in the **NMDA glutamate receptor,** which can be stimulated by a chemical called *N*-methyl-D-aspartate (NMDA). Several other glutamate receptors can be distinguished by the various other chemicals that excite them, but for present purposes we shall lump them together as *non-NMDA receptors.*

At all the non-NMDA receptors, glutamate is an excitatory neurotransmitter, opening channels for sodium ions to enter the neuron. At the NMDA receptors, glutamate ordinarily produces neither excitatory nor inhibitory effects. In this way, NMDA receptors are different from all the other synaptic receptors that we have encountered so far. The reason for the unresponsiveness of NMDA receptors is that their ion channel is blocked by magnesium ions, which do not pass through the channel but which nevertheless block it so that no other ions can pass through. The activation of NMDA receptors requires *both* the neurotransmitter glutamate (or, in the laboratory, a substitute such as NMDA) and the *removal* of those magnesium ions. (See Figure 13.21a.)

About the only way to activate the NMDA receptors is first to activate the nearby non-NMDA glutamate receptors repeatedly, thereby depolarizing the dendrite. The depolarization repels the magnesium ions and enables glutamate to open the NMDA channels, through which both sodium and calcium ions enter. (See Figure 13.21b.) The entry of calcium induces the expression of certain otherwise inactive genes, which become active temporarily and then shut down (Meberg, Barnes, McNaughton, & Routtenberg, 1993). Those genes produce proteins that alter the structure of the dendrites and increase the future responsiveness of the active non-NMDA receptors in the area (Figure 13.21c).

In short, when glutamate massively stimulates non-NMDA receptors, the resulting depolarization enables glutamate to also stimulate nearby NMDA receptors. Stimulation of the NMDA receptors feeds back to potentiate the non-NMDA receptors. The potentiation may persist for minutes, hours, or longer.

Once LTP has been established, it no longer depends on NMDA synapses. Drugs that block NMDA synapses prevent the *establishment* of LTP, but they do not interfere with the *maintenance* of LTP that was already established (Gustafsson & Wigström, 1990). In other words, once the NMDA receptors have potentiated the non-NMDA receptors, they stay potentiated, regardless of what happens to the NMDA receptors.

Investigators do not yet agree on whether LTP depends mostly on postsynaptic changes, presynaptic changes, or a combination of both. Some investigators have found that LTP changes the properties of certain glutamate receptors on the postsynaptic cell (Liao, Hessler, & Malinow, 1995). Other investigators have found that during LTP the postsynaptic cell releases a **retrograde transmitter** (one traveling from the postsynaptic neuron to the presynaptic neuron), probably nitric oxide (NO), which signals the presynaptic neuron to release more of its neurotransmitter. Drugs that block the release or effects of NO interfere with LTP and with learning that depends on the hippocampus (Fin et al., 1995; Zhuo, Hu, Schultz, Kandel, & Hawkins, 1994). The brain probably has several forms of LTP that rely on different mechanisms (Nicoll & Malenka, 1995). It is also possible that the underlying mechanisms are more complex than anything we currently imagine. One study found that LTP facilitated responses to low-frequency stimulation but not high-frequency stimulation of the same axon (Markram & Tsodyks, 1996). That is, LTP may do more than just strengthen or weaken a synapse.

LTP and Behavior

Is LTP really a significant aspect of learning? Certainly not all neuroscientists are ready to assume that it is. Many of the experiments on LTP use hippocampal slices or other artificial conditions that may not match

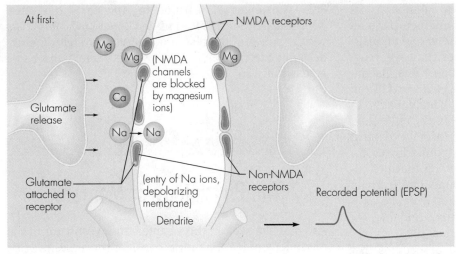

(a)

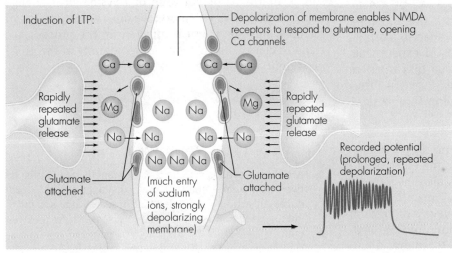

(b)

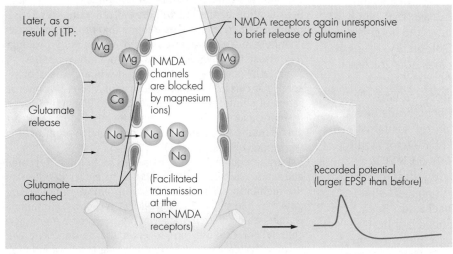

(c)

FIGURE **13.21**
One possible arrangement for LTP

(**a**) At first, glutamate stimulation moderately excites the postsynaptic neuron through the non-NMDA receptors. The nearby NMDA receptor is unresponsive. (**b**) Then LTP is induced by rapidly repeated stimulation; stimulation by two glutamate axons produces more effect than one. This stimulation strongly depolarizes the membrane. Depolarization of the membrane alters the NMDA receptor, enabling glutamate to stimulate it. Thus, the NMDA receptor is effective only when the membrane is strongly depolarized. (**c**) After induction of LTP, transmission at non-NMDA kainate and quisqualate receptors is facilitated. The exact mechanism of facilitation is not yet clear. Although the NMDA receptor was necessary for *inducing* LTP, it is not necessary for *maintaining* it.

anything that occurs in nature. Besides, a temporary facilitation of response to one axon by one neuron is remote from the complex behavior of the whole animal.

Research with intact animals does, however, suggest a link between LTP and learned behaviors. As animals undergo training, it is possible to measure LTP in recordings from single cells in the hippocampus; 90 to 180 minutes later, one can detect LTP in the *entorhinal cortex*, the area of cerebral cortex closest and most heavily linked to the hippocampus (Izquierdo, 1995). That finding fits with other data showing that the entorhinal cortex is unnecessary for immediate learning and memory but more important after a delay, as if learning occurred first in the hippocampus and then got transferred (Nagahara, Otto, & Gallagher, 1995).

Researchers have also found that procedures that impair LTP also interfere with learning. In one study, researchers produced a targeted mutation of a gene controlling NMDA receptors. Mice with this mutation had impairments of both LTP and spatial learning (Sakimura et al., 1995). Also, a series of experiments has found that a wide variety of drugs that interfere with LTP also block learning, whereas several drugs that facilitate LTP also enhance learning (Izquierdo & Medina, 1995).

An understanding of LTP may eventually lead to drugs that can help people with memory impairments. We already know that LTP depends on the entry of calcium ions into postsynaptic neurons. Calcium channels apparently become somewhat "leaky" in old age, resulting in higher-than-normal resting levels of calcium within neurons. Too much calcium flow into the neurons is just as harmful as too little; LTP requires abundant calcium flow at just the right times, with no flow at others. In aged mammals, injections of magnesium (which competes with calcium) or of drugs that block calcium channels can enhance learning and memory (Deyo, Straube, & Disterhoft, 1989). Potentially, drugs with similar effects may someday be available for human use.

LTP may also contribute to the effects of early experience. Recall from Chapter 6 that special kinds of visual experience can alter connections in the visual system only during a sensitive period of development. Apparently, the sensitive period depends on NMDA receptors. In one study, injecting a drug that blocks NMDA receptors blocked the effects of visual experience during the sensitive period (Kleinschmidt, Bear, & Singer, 1987). In another study, prolonged application of NMDA to an amphibian's brain toward the end of the sensitive period lengthened it (Udin & Scherer, 1990). These results imply that the sensitive period corresponds to a time when NMDA synapses are ordinarily easiest to stimulate.

LTP is apparently an important contributor to many kinds of vertebrate learning, though probably not all.

Some instances of learning in *Aplysia* also require NMDA-dependent LTP (Lin & Glanzman, 1994). As with so much of the rest of the nervous system, the underlying mechanisms appear to be largely the same across species.

IN CLOSING

The Physiology of Memory

As you have seen in this chapter, an investigator of the physiology of learning must consider processes ranging from molecular changes to behavior. We cannot say simply that a particular drug or physiological change improves or impairs memory; we must specify a type of memory and the way it is affected. In the process, we stand to clarify our understanding not only of the physiology but also of memory itself.

Summary

1. A Hebbian synapse is one that is strengthened if it is active at the same time that the postsynaptic neuron produces an action potential. Much research has sought to identify Hebbian synapses and to discover how they operate. (p. 363)
2. Habituation of the gill-withdrawal reflex in *Aplysia* depends on a mechanism that decreases the release of transmitter from a particular presynaptic neuron. (p. 365)
3. Sensitization of the gill-withdrawal reflex in *Aplysia* depends on the release of an enzyme that blocks potassium channels in a presynaptic neuron and thereby prolongs the release of transmitter from that neuron. (p. 366)
4. Long-term potentiation (LTP) is an enhancement of response at certain synapses because of a brief but intense series of stimuli delivered to a neuron, generally by two or more axons delivering simultaneous inputs. LTP occurs in many brain areas and is particularly prominent in the hippocampus. (p. 367)
5. LTP in hippocampal neurons occurs as follows: Repeated glutamate excitation of non-NMDA receptors depolarizes the membrane. The depolarization removes magnesium ions that had been blocking NMDA receptors. Glutamate is then able to excite the NMDA receptors, opening a channel for calcium ions to enter the neuron. The calcium activates genes that produce long-term potentiation of the nearby non-NMDA receptors. (p. 368)
6. Researchers are not yet certain whether LTP depends on increased release of neurotransmitter or changes in responsiveness of the postsynaptic neuron. (p. 368)
7. Procedures that enhance or impair LTP have similar effects on certain kinds of learning. (p. 370)

Review Questions

1. How can a Hebbian synapse account for the basic phenomena of classical conditioning? (p. 363)
2. What are the advantages of research with *Aplysia* and other mollusks as compared with vertebrates? (p. 364)
3. Why do researchers believe that habituation and sensitization in *Aplysia* depend on presynaptic rather than postsynaptic changes? (pp. 366, 367)
4. What procedures produce LTP in the mammalian brain? (p. 367)
5. What is cooperativity, and how does it relate to LTP? (p. 367)
6. What is an NMDA synapse? Are NMDA synapses responsible for maintaining LTP after it is established? (p. 368)
7. What are the possible mechanisms of LTP? (p. 368)
8. How can we explain the ability of magnesium ions to enhance certain kinds of memory in old age? (p. 370)

Thought Question

1. In one experiment (Castellucci & Kandel, 1974), habituation was attributed to a presynaptic change because the size of the quantum remained the same even though the size of the EPSP decreased. What conclusion, if any, could you draw if the size of the quantum decreased during habituation? Can you think of any other way to decide whether an alteration in EPSP size was due to presynaptic or postsynaptic changes?

Suggestion for Further Reading

Martinez, J. L., Jr., & Derrick, B. E. (1996). Long-term potentiation and learning. *Annual Review of Psychology, 47*, 173–203. Good review of research on LTP and its relationship to learning.

Terms

Hebbian synapse synapse that increases in effectiveness because the activity of the presynaptic axon was repeatedly paired with depolarization of the postsynaptic neuron (p. 363)

habituation decrease in response to a stimulus that is presented repeatedly and that is accompanied by no change in other stimuli (p. 365)

sensitization increase in response to mild stimuli as a result of previous exposure to more intense stimuli (p. 366)

long-term potentiation (LTP) increased responsiveness to axonal input as a result of a previous period of rapidly repeated stimulation (p. 367)

cooperativity tendency for nearly simultaneous stimulation by two or more axons to produce LTP much more effectively than stimulation by just one (p. 367)

associativity tendency for pairing with a stronger input to enhance the later effectiveness of a weaker input (p. 367)

long-term depression prolonged decrease in response to an axonal input that has been repeatedly paired with certain other input (in some cases requiring repetition at a low frequency) (p. 367)

hippocampal slice section of hippocampus removed from an animal and maintained in a culture medium (p. 368)

NMDA glutamate receptor glutamate receptor that also responds to *N*-methyl-D-aspartate (p. 368)

retrograde transmitter chemical released by a postsynaptic neuron that travels to the presynaptic neuron, either increasing or decreasing its later release of neurotransmitter (p. 368)

LATERALIZATION AND LANGUAGE

CHAPTER **FOURTEEN**

MAIN**IDEAS**

1. The left and right hemispheres of the brain communicate through the corpus callosum. After damage to the corpus callosum, each hemisphere has access to information solely from the opposite half of the body and from the opposite visual field.
2. In most people, the left hemisphere is specialized for language and analytical processing. The right hemisphere is specialized for certain complex visual–spatial tasks and synthetic processing.
3. The language specializations of the human brain are enormous elaborations of features that are present in other primates.
4. Abnormalities of the left hemisphere can lead to a great variety of specific language impairments.

Your brain consists of a multitude of neurons, but unlike a society of people who act together at times but still remain independent, the neurons produce a single consciousness. Although your brain parts are many, you experience yourself as a unity.

What happens if connections among brain areas are broken? After damage to the corpus callosum, people act as if they have two fields of awareness, separate "minds," if you wish. With damage to certain areas of the left hemisphere, people lose their language abilities while remaining unimpaired in other ways. Studies of such people offer fascinating clues about how the brain operates and raise equally fascinating unanswered questions.

Lateralization of Function and the Corpus Callosum

The left hemisphere of the cerebral cortex is connected to skin receptors and muscles mainly on the right side of the body. It sees only the right half of the world. The right hemisphere is connected to sensory receptors and muscles mainly on the left half of the body and sees only the left half of the world.

Each hemisphere has limited sensory input and motor control on its own side of the body, and both hemispheres can control the muscles of the face and trunk. The degree of ipsilateral control (control of the same side of the body) varies from one individual to another. *Why* humans and all other vertebrates evolved so that each hemisphere controls the contralateral (opposite) side of the body, no one knows. Perhaps there *is* no reason. For analogy, we can imagine a city in which all the doors have their hinges on the left. Why? The first housebuilder put hinges on the left and everyone else did the same. Maybe the earliest brains just happened to have contralateral control and because it worked well enough, evolution never changed it. I admit that explanation is not very convincing. You are welcome to think of a better one.

At any rate, the left and right hemispheres exchange information through a set of axons called the **corpus callosum** (Figure 14.1; see also Figures 4.11 and 4.12) and through the smaller anterior commissure and hippocampal commissure. Information that initially enters one hemisphere crosses to the opposite hemisphere with only a brief delay.

The two hemispheres are not simply mirror images of each other. In most humans, the left hemisphere is specialized for language; the functions of the right hemisphere are more difficult to summarize, as we shall see later in this chapter. Such division of labor is known as **lateralization.** If you had no corpus callosum, your left hemisphere could talk only about the information from the right side of your body, and your right hemisphere could react only to information from the left side. Because of the corpus callosum, however,

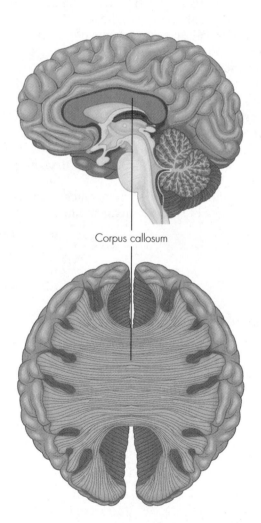

Corpus callosum

FIGURE **14.1**
Two views of the corpus callosum
The corpus callosum is a large set of axons conveying information between the two hemispheres. Top: A sagittal section through the human brain. Bottom: A dissection (viewed from above) in which gray matter has been removed to expose the corpus callosum.

each hemisphere receives information from both sides. Only after damage to the corpus callosum (or to one hemisphere or the other) do we see the effects of lateralization.

Before we can discuss lateralization in any detail, we must consider the relation of the eyes to the brain. The connections from the left and right eyes to the left and right hemispheres are more complex than you might expect.

Visual Connections to the Hemispheres

The hemispheres are connected to the eyes in such a way that each gets input from the opposite half of the visual world; that is, the left hemisphere sees the right side of the world and the right hemisphere sees the left side. In rabbits and other species that have their eyes far to the sides of the head, the connections from eye to brain are easy to describe: The left eye connects to the right hemisphere and the right eye connects to the left hemisphere. *Your* eyes are *not* connected to the brain in this way. Both your eyes face forward. You can see the left side of the world almost as well with your right eye as you can with your left eye.

Figure 14.2 illustrates the connections from the eyes to the brain in humans. Vision starts with stimulation of the receptors that line the *retina* on the back of each eye. When light from the **visual field**—what is visible at any moment—enters the eyes, light from the right visual field shines onto the left half of both retinas, and light from the left visual field shines onto the right half of both retinas. The left half of *each* retina connects to the left hemisphere, which therefore sees the right visual field. Similarly, the right half of each retina connects to the right hemisphere, which sees the left visual field. A small vertical strip down the center of each retina, covering about 5 degrees of visual arc, connects to both hemispheres (Innocenti, 1980). In Figure 14.2, note how half of the axons from each eye cross to the opposite side of the brain at the **optic chiasm** (literally, the optic "cross").

Although information about each visual field projects to just one side of the cerebral cortex, the auditory system handles information differently. Each ear receives sound waves from just one side of the head, but it sends the information to both sides of the brain, because any part of the brain that contributes to localizing sounds must receive input from both ears. However, when the two ears receive different information, each hemisphere does pay more attention to the ear on the opposite side (Hugdahl, 1996).

Cutting the Corpus Callosum

Damage to the corpus callosum prevents the exchange of information between the two hemispheres. Occasionally, surgeons sever the corpus callosum as a therapy for severe epilepsy. (See Digression 14.1.) Epilepsy can usually be controlled with drugs, but someone with frequent, severe seizures who fails to respond to medication may be willing to try almost anything. The idea behind cutting the corpus callosum is to prevent epileptic seizures from crossing from one hemisphere to the other, so they affect only half the body. In addition to this predicted benefit, a surprising bonus is that the seizures become less frequent. Evidently, the ability of epileptic activity to rebound back and forth between the hemispheres increases and prolongs the seizures.

How does severing the corpus callosum affect other aspects of behavior? Following damage to the corpus callosum, laboratory animals show normal sensation, control of movement, learning and memory, and motivated behaviors. Their responses are abnormal only when sensory stimuli are limited to one side of the body. For example, if they see something in the left visual field, they can reach out to it only with the left forepaw. If they learn to do something with the left forepaw, they have to learn the skill all over again to do it with the right forepaw (Sperry, 1961).

People who have undergone damage to the corpus callosum show similar tendencies. They can still walk, swim, and carry out other motor activities that use both sides of the body, although their coordination is sometimes slow and awkward (Zaidel & Sperry, 1977). For certain tasks, they can use their two hands independently in a way that other people cannot. For example, try drawing ⊂ with your left hand while simultaneously drawing ∪ with your right hand. Most people find this task difficult; split-brain people do it with ease because each hemisphere acts independently (Franz, Eliassen, Ivry, & Gazzaniga, 1996).

Split-brain people suffer little or no impairment of overall intellectual performance or motivation, except for difficulty in maintaining attention (Hoptman & Davidson, 1994). However, careful experiments by Roger Sperry and his students (Nebes, 1974) revealed subtle behavioral effects when stimuli were limited to one side of the body or the other. In a typical experiment, a split-brain patient stared straight ahead as pictures were flashed on the left side of a screen (see Figure 14.3). The information went to the right hemisphere and could not cross to the left, because of the damage to the corpus callosum. The picture stayed on

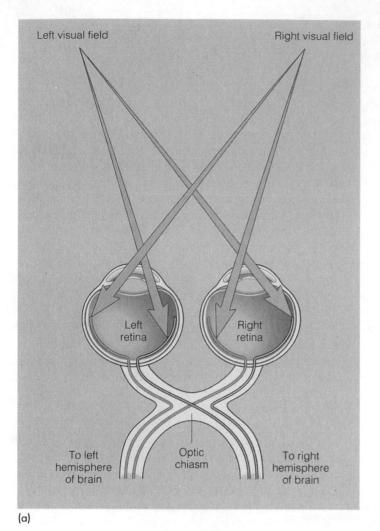

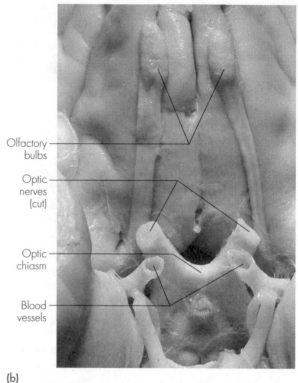

(a)   (b)

FIGURE **14.2**
Connections from the eyes to the human brain
(**a**) Route of visual input to the two hemispheres of the brain. Note that the left hemisphere is
connected to the left half of each retina and thus gets visual input from the right half of the
world, and the opposite is true of the right hemisphere. (**b**) Close-up of olfactory bulbs and the
optic chiasm. At the optic chiasm, axons from the right half of the left retina cross to the right
hemisphere, and axons from the left half of the right retina cross to the left hemisphere.   Source:
Courtesy of Dr. Dana Copeland.

the screen long enough to be visible, but not long
enough for the person to move his or her eyes.

The experimenter then told the person to put one
hand behind a cloth curtain, to feel ten or so objects,
and to hold up the one that had just been shown on the
screen. Split-brain patients consistently performed correctly if permitted to use the left hand (controlled by
the right hemisphere, which saw the display on the
screen). But if they used the right hand, accuracy fell to
the chance level. When the display flashed on the right
side of the screen, the right hand performed correctly
and the left hand failed.

For most people, the ability to speak depends on the
left hemisphere of the cerebral cortex. When a display
was flashed in the right visual field, thus going to the
left hemisphere, a split-brain person could name the object easily. But when it was flashed in the left visual
field, going to the right hemisphere, the person could
neither name nor describe it, but could point to it with
the left hand. The person would even say, "I don't know
what it is," while simultaneously pointing to the correct
choice with the left hand. (Of course, a split-brain person who watched the left hand pick up an object in the
center or right visual field could then name the object.)

Split Hemispheres: Competition and Cooperation

The two hemispheres of a split-brain person can process information and respond to questions independently of each other. Indeed, they seem at times to act like separate people sharing one body. One split-brain person sometimes found himself buttoning his shirt with one hand while unbuttoning it with the other. Another split-brain person would pick up a newspaper with the right hand, only to have the left hand (controlled by the less verbal hemisphere) put it down. Repeatedly, the right hand picked it up; an equal number

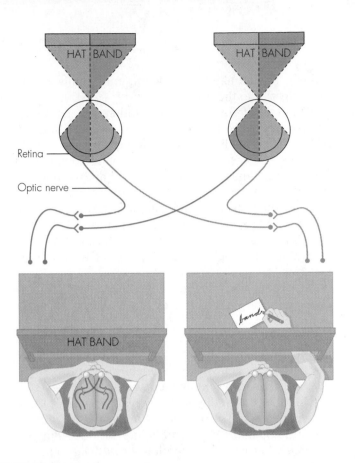

FIGURE 14.3
Effects of damage to the corpus callosum
When the word "hatband" is flashed on a screen, a woman with a split brain can report only what her left hemisphere saw, "band." However, with her left hand, she can point to a hat, which is what the right hemisphere saw.

DIGRESSION 14.1

Epilepsy

Epilepsy is a condition characterized by repeated episodes of excessive, synchronized neural activity, mainly because of decreased release of the inhibitory neurotransmitter GABA (During, Ryder, & Spencer, 1995). Epilepsy can result from a variety of causes, including genetics, birth injury or other trauma, infection in the brain, exposure to toxic substances, and brain tumors. Epilepsy of genetic origin is likely to begin during childhood or adolescence; epilepsy from other causes can begin at any age.

Epilepsy can produce a variety of symptoms, depending on which parts of the brain are affected and for how long. Two categories are *generalized seizures* and *partial seizures*. A **generalized seizure** spreads quickly across neurons over a large portion of both hemispheres of the brain. In the most spectacular form, a **grand mal seizure,** the person makes sudden, repetitive jerking movements of the head and limbs for a period of seconds or minutes and then collapses into exhaustion and sleep. In a **petit mal seizure** (or *absence seizure*), the person stares unresponsively for about 15 to 20 seconds, making few movements except for eye blinking or a drooping of the head. Observers may not even be aware of the seizure, and sometimes the affected person may not be either. The person may, however, be confused and forget what just happened.

In contrast to a generalized seizure, a **partial seizure** begins in a **focus** (point of origin) somewhere in the brain and then spreads to nearby areas. Depending on the location of the focus, someone with a partial seizure may experience a variety of sensations or involuntary movements, such as a tingling hand or a shaking leg. Sometimes the effect spreads, as when a twitch starts in a finger and moves up the arm. The person remains conscious but may become confused. A partial seizure with a focus in the temporal lobe is known as a *partial seizure with complex symptomatology* or a *temporal lobe seizure* or a *psychomotor seizure*. Such seizures produce only slight movements, such as lip smacking or chewing, but can lead to complex psychological states, including anxiety, laughter, repetitive thoughts, dreamlike hallucinations, or déjà vu experiences.

Over the years, medical researchers have developed a large array of antiepileptic drugs, which act mostly by blocking sodium flow across the membrane or by enhancing the effects of GABA. More than 90 percent of epileptic patients respond well enough to drugs to live a reasonably normal life. Some suffer only the inconvenience of taking a daily pill. A few, however, continue to have frequent seizures despite medication. In such cases, physicians consider removing the focus surgically. Surgery is, however, the method of last resort.

of times, the left hand put it down, until finally the left hand threw it to the floor (Preilowski, 1975).

One split-brain person—or, rather, his left hemisphere—described his experience as follows (Dimond, 1979): "If I'm reading, I can hold the book in my right hand; it's a lot easier to sit on my left hand, than to hold it with both hands. . . . You tell your hand—I'm going to turn so many pages in a book—turn three pages—then somehow the left hand will pick up two pages and you're at page 5, or whatever. It's better to let it go, pick it up with the right hand, and then turn to the right page. With your right hand, you correct what the left has done."

Such conflicts are more common soon after surgery than later. The severed halves of the corpus callosum do not grow back together, but the brain learns to use certain subcortical connections between the left and right hemispheres (Myers & Sperry, 1985). In some cases, the left hemisphere somehow suppresses the right hemisphere's interference and simply takes control. In other cases, the hemispheres gradually learn to cooperate. A split-brain person who was tested with the standard apparatus shown in Figure 14.3 became able to name what he saw in the left visual field, but only when the answers were restricted to two possibilities (such as yes/no or true/false), and only when he was allowed to correct himself immediately after making a guess. For example, when something was flashed in the left visual field, the experimenter might ask, "Was it a letter of the alphabet?" The left (speaking) hemisphere would take a guess: "Yes." If that guess was incorrect, the right hemisphere, which knew the correct answer, would then make the face frown. (Both hemispheres can control facial muscles on both sides of the face.) The left hemisphere, feeling the frown, would say, "Oh, I'm sorry, I meant 'no.'"

In another experiment, a split-brain patient saw two words flashed at once, one to the left hemisphere and one to the right. He was then asked to draw a picture of what he had read. Each hemisphere saw a full word, but the two words combined made a different word. For example:

Left Visual Field	Right Visual Field
hot	dog
sky	scraper
bloody	Mary
rain	bow
honey	moon

With the right hand, he almost always drew what he had seen in the right visual field (left hemisphere). However, with the left hand, he sometimes drew a literal combination of the two words. For example, after seeing *hot* and *dog,* he drew a dog that was overheated, not a wiener on a bun, and after seeing *sky* and *scraper,*

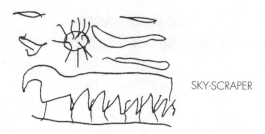

SKY-SCRAPER

FIGURE **14.4**
Left-hand drawing by a split-brain patient
He saw the word "sky" in the left visual field and "scraper" in the right visual field. His left hemisphere controlled the left hand enough to draw a scraper, and his right hemisphere controlled it enough to draw a sky. Neither hemisphere could combine the two words to make the emergent concept "skyscraper."
Source: From Kingstone & Gazzaniga, 1995.

he drew a sky and a scraper (see Figure 14.4). Evidently his left hemisphere was able to control his left hand sufficiently to draw one object (perhaps by the ventromedial spinal pathway, as described in Chapter 8) and his right hemisphere could draw another object, but neither hemisphere could combine the words into a new concept (Kingstone & Gazzaniga, 1995).

The Right Hemisphere

When investigators discovered that the left hemisphere controls speech, most psychologists thought the right hemisphere was something like a vice president, supporting the left, "major" hemisphere but always subordinate to it. Later studies indicated that the right hemisphere is capable of more than researchers first assumed.

First, although it cannot control speech or writing in most people, the right hemisphere does understand simple speech and, to a more limited extent, written words (Levy, 1983). A split-brain person who hears a verbal description can feel some objects with the left hand (right hemisphere) and pick up the one that was described. In a few split-brain patients, the left hand can write or arrange letter blocks to describe information known only by the right hemisphere (Gazzaniga, LeDoux, & Wilson, 1977; Levy, Nebes, & Sperry, 1971).

Although the right hemisphere is less important than the left for most aspects of language, it is crucial for the emotional content of speech. People who have suffered damage to the right hemisphere speak with less than normal inflection and expression (Shapiro & Danly, 1985). They have trouble interpreting the emotions that other people express through tone of voice (Tucker, 1981), and they may fail to appreciate humor and irony in speech.

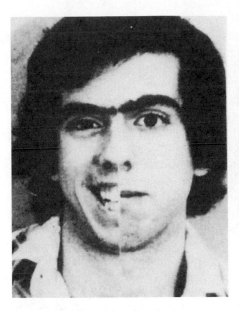 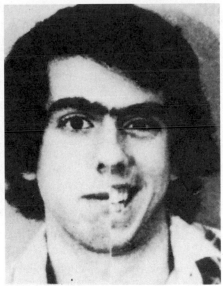

(a)   (b)

FIGURE **14.5**
Half of a smiling face combined with half of a neutral face
Which looks happier to you—the one with a smile on your left or the one with a smile on your right? Your answer may suggest which hemisphere of your brain is dominant for interpreting emotional expressions. Source: Levy et al., 1983.

The right hemisphere may be more specialized for emotional expression in general than the left hemisphere is. Although both hemispheres of a split-brain person are almost equally good at matching photographs to emotional labels, such as "sad" or "frightened," the right hemisphere does better at recognizing whether two photographs show the same or different emotions (Stone, Nisenson, Eliassen, & Gazzaniga, 1996). People with damage to the right hemisphere show less intense facial expressions and sometimes misunderstand other people's expressions (Borod, Koff, Lorch, & Nicholas, 1986; Kolb & Taylor, 1981; Rinn, 1984). Moreover, according to the studies of Jerre Levy and her colleagues on normal (brain-intact) people, when the left and right hemispheres perceive different emotions in someone's face, the response of the right hemisphere dominates. For example, examine the faces in Figure 14.5. Each of these combines half of a smiling face with half of a neutral face. Which looks happier to you: face A or face B? Most people choose face A, with the smile on the viewer's left (Heller & Levy, 1981; Hoptman & Levy, 1988). Similarly, a frown on the viewer's left looks sadder than a frown on the viewer's right (Sackeim, Putz, Vingiano, Coleman, & McElhiney, 1988).

The right hemisphere also appears to be more adept than the left at comprehending complex visual patterns. For example, one young woman, after suffering damage to her posterior right hemisphere as a result of a tumor, had great trouble finding her way through a building or around town, even in familiar areas. To reach a destination, she needed directions that listed specific visual details, such as "Walk to the corner where you see a building with a statue in front of it. Then turn left and go to the corner that has a flagpole

and turn right. . . ." Each of these directions had to include an unmistakable feature; if the instruction was "Go to the city government building—that's the one with a tower," she could easily go to a very different building that happened to have a tower (Clarke, Assal, & deTribolet, 1993).

Split-brain patients have given us additional information about the specialized functions of the right hemisphere. For example, they can arrange puzzle pieces more accurately with the left hand than with the right. Although the right hand can write words much better than the left, the left hand does better at drawing a box, a bicycle, and similar objects.

The right hemisphere is not necessary for *all* visual and spatial tasks, however. In one study, stroke patients who had suffered damage to the right hemisphere performed about as well as normal people did at estimating the positions of nine major cities on an outline map of the United States. They were also as good as normal people were at estimating the distances between points on a sheet of paper. Their impairment showed when they had to combine these tasks by imagining the positions of those same nine cities and estimating the distances between them (Morrow, Ratcliff, & Johnston, 1986). Evidently, the right hemisphere is more essential for tasks that require internal representations of visual and spatial information—visual imagination, we might say.

How can we best describe the difference in functions between the hemispheres? According to John Bradshaw and Norman Nettleton (1981), the left hemisphere is sequential, analytic, and time dependent, experiencing events as a sequence of units. The right hemisphere, in contrast, is "synthetic" and "holistic," by which Bradshaw and Nettleton mean that it perceives

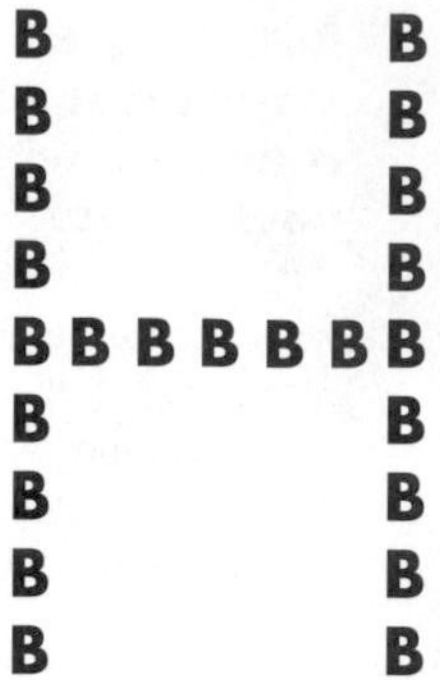

```
B                 B
B                 B
B                 B
B                 B
B B B B B B B
B                 B
B                 B
B                 B
B                 B
```

FIGURE 14.6

Stimulus to test analytical and holistic perception
When people were told to name the large composite letter, they had more activity in the right hemisphere. When told to name the small component letters, they had more activity in the left hemisphere.   Source: Based on Fink et al., 1996.

overall patterns. For example, in one study, brain-intact people examined visual stimuli, such as the one in Figure 14.6, in which many repetitions of a small letter compose a different, large letter. When they were asked to identify the small letters (in this case B), activity increased in the left hemisphere, but when they were asked to identify the large overall letter (H), activity was greatest in the right hemisphere (Fink et al., 1996). Unfortunately, the distinction between analytical and holistic perception is seldom as clear-cut as it seems in this example. Furthermore, it is important to remember that both hemispheres participate actively in all experiences, even if one may be a bit more active than the other at a given moment.

Hemispheric Specializations in Intact Brains

The differences between the two hemispheres, more apparent after damage to the corpus callosum, can also be demonstrated in people without brain damage. Most of these differences are, however, small trends apparent only as averages over large numbers of people.

In one study, people first read an incomplete or scrambled sentence; for example:

> MIGRATING BIRDS FREQUENTLY STOP TO GET
> or   GET STOP FREQUENTLY BIRDS TO MIGRATING

Then they focused on a point at the center of the screen while a set of letters flashed briefly in the left or right visual field. For example,

> WATER
> or   ERTWA

The task was to identify whether the letters formed a word. When the stimulus was flashed in the right visual field (left hemisphere), subjects answered most accurately for a real word that would logically finish the incomplete sentence, such as "Migrating birds frequently stop to get . . . water." They were less accurate for a real but irrelevant word, such as "Migrating birds frequently stop to get . . . sofas." However, when the word was flashed in the left visual field (right hemisphere), people's accuracy was not much affected by whether the flashed word was relevant or irrelevant, or even by whether the original incomplete sentence was logical or scrambled (Faust, Babkoff, & Kravetz, 1995). Evidently, an incomplete sentence primes only the left hemisphere to recognize logically related words.

Tap with a pencil in your right hand on a sheet of paper as many times as you can in 1 minute, then count the tap marks. Rest, and then do the same thing with your left hand. Then repeat the measurements while you tap and talk at the same time. For most right-handers, talking decreases the tapping rate with the right hand more than with the left hand (Kinsbourne & McMurray, 1975). Evidently, it is more difficult to do two things at once when both activities depend on the same hemisphere.

TRY IT YOURSELF

Hemispheric Differences and Cognitive Style

Occasionally, you may hear someone say something like "I don't do well in science because it is a left-brain subject and I am a right-brain person." That kind of statement is based on two reasonable scientific premises and one doubtful assumption. The scientific premises are (1) that the left hemisphere is specialized for verbal or analytic processing and the right hemisphere is specialized for nonverbal or synthetic processing, and (2) that certain tasks evoke greater activity in one hemisphere than in the other. The doubtful assumption is that any individual relies consistently on one hemisphere or the other, regardless of the task or situation.

That assumption is at best a great overstatement. For any individual, the balance of activity shifts from one hemisphere to the other, in accord with the task, and every task activates both hemispheres to some extent. Furthermore, what evidence do you suppose someone has for believing "I am a right-brain person"? Did he or she undergo an MRI or PET scan to determine which hemisphere was larger or more active? Not likely. Generally, when people say "I am right-brained," what they mean is that they perform better on creative tasks than on logical tasks. Therefore, the statement really means "I do poorly in science because I do poorly in science."

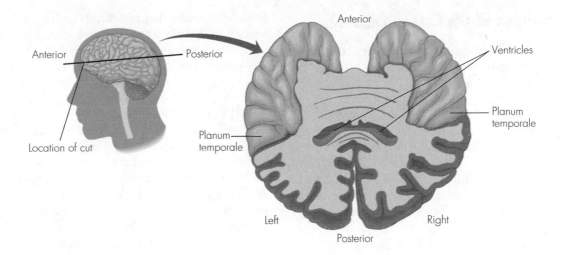

FIGURE **14.7**
Horizontal section through a human brain
This cut, taken just above the surface of the temporal lobe, shows the planum temporale, an area that is critical for speech comprehension. Note that it is substantially larger in the left hemisphere than in the right hemisphere.   Source: From Geschwind & Levitsky, 1968.

Development of Lateralization and Handedness

Because in most people language depends primarily on the left hemisphere, it is natural to ask whether the hemispheres are anatomically different. If so, is the difference present before speech develops, or does it develop later? What is the relationship between handedness and hemispheric dominance for speech?

Anatomical Differences Between the Hemispheres

The human brain is specialized to attend to language sounds. If you listen to a repeated syllable *("pack pack pack pack . . .")* and then suddenly the vowel sound changes (*". . . pack pack pack peck . . ."*), the change will catch your attention, as one could detect by recording larger evoked responses from your scalp. Changing from *pack* to *peck* also increases the evoked response from a baby, even a premature infant born only 30 weeks after conception (Cheour-Luhtanen et al., 1996). Evidently, humans attend to language sounds from the start.

But do the left and right hemispheres differ from the start? Norman Geschwind and Walter Levitsky (1968) found that one section of the temporal cortex, called the **planum temporale** (PLAY-num tem-poh-

RAH-lee), is larger in the left than in the right hemisphere for 65 percent of people (Figure 14.7). Sandra Witelson and Wazir Pallie (1973) examined the brains of 14 infants who died before age 3 months and found that the left planum temporale was larger than the right in 12 of them—on the average, about twice as large. Later studies using MRI scans on healthy children found that 5- to 12-year-olds with the biggest ratio of left to right planum temporale performed best on language tests, whereas children with nearly equal hemispheres were worse at language but better on certain nonverbal tasks (Leonard et al., 1996).

Researchers have long noted that children who suffer massive damage to the left hemisphere in the first 2 to 4 years of life recover language far better than anyone who suffers similar damage later, especially in adulthood. Such findings suggest that the right hemisphere can assume language functions if the left hemisphere is damaged before the hemispheres have completed their development. Many researchers describe early childhood as a sensitive period for language development, analogous to the sensitive period for the organizing effects of sex hormones (Chapter 11). One study of Chinese Americans who began learning English at various ages found that the earlier they started, the better their eventual pronunciation and grammar, but even starting at 13 instead of 16 made a difference for a few aspects of language mastery (Weber-Fox & Neville, 1996). In short, the window of opportunity for language acquisition closes slowly and gradually between infancy and late adolescence.

Maturation of the Corpus Callosum

The corpus callosum matures gradually over the first 5 to 10 years of human life (Trevarthen, 1974). The developmental process is not so much a matter of growing new axons, however, as of selecting certain axons and discarding others. At an early stage of development, the brain generates far more axons in the corpus callosum than it will have at maturity (Ivy & Killackey, 1981; Killackey & Chalupa, 1986). The reason is that any two neurons connected by the corpus callosum need to have corresponding functions. For example, a neuron in the left hemisphere that responds to light in the very center of the retina should be connected to a right-hemisphere neuron that responds to light in the same location. During early embryonic development, the genes cannot specify exactly where those two neurons will be. Therefore, a great many connections are made across the corpus callosum, but only those axons that happen to connect very similar cells survive (Innocenti & Caminiti, 1980).

Because the connections take years to develop their mature adult pattern, the behavior of young children in some situations resembles that of split-brain adults. An infant who has one arm restrained will not reach across the midline of the body to pick up a toy on the other side before about age 17 weeks. Evidently, in younger children, each hemisphere has too little access to information from the opposite hemisphere (Provine & Westerman, 1979).

In one study, 3- and 5-year-old children were asked to feel two fabrics, either with one hand at two times or with two hands at the same time, and say whether the materials felt the same or different. The 5-year-olds did equally well with one hand or with two. The 3-year-olds made 90 percent more errors with two hands than with one (Galin, Johnstone, Nakell, & Herron, 1979). The likely interpretation is that the corpus callosum matures sufficiently between ages 3 and 5 to facilitate the comparison of stimuli between the two hands.

Development in the Absence of a Corpus Callosum

Rarely, the corpus callosum fails to form or forms incompletely, possibly for genetic reasons, although not necessarily. People born without a corpus callosum are unlike people who have it cut later in life. First, whatever prevented formation of the corpus callosum undoubtedly affects brain development in other ways. Second, the absence or near-absence of the corpus callosum induces the remaining brain areas to develop abnormally.

People born without a corpus callosum can per-form some tasks that split-brain patients fail. They can verbally describe what they feel with either hand and what they see in either visual field; they can also feel one object with the left hand and another with the right hand and say whether they are the same or different (Bruyer et al., 1985; Sanders, 1989). How do they do so? The available evidence argues against any right-hemisphere speech in these people (Lassonde, Bryden, & Demers, 1990). A likely explanation is that each hemisphere develops pathways connecting it to both sides of the body, enabling the left (speaking) hemisphere to feel both the left hand and the right hand. Another possibility is that larger-than-normal connections develop elsewhere in the brain. In addition to the corpus callosum, people have two other major axonal connections in the forebrain: the **anterior commissure** (Figure 4.11, p. 86), which connects the anterior parts of the cerebral cortex, and the **hippocampal commissure,** which connects the left hippocampus to the right (Figure 14.8). In the absence of a corpus callosum, these other commissures probably develop beyond their usual level.

Handedness and Language Dominance

About 10 percent of all people are either left-handed or ambidextrous. (Here we shall consider ambidextrous people to be left-handed. Indeed, most left-handers are partly ambidextrous.) Of all the surviving prehistoric drawings and paintings that show people using tools, more than 90 percent show the tool in the right hand (Coren & Porac, 1977). Thus, right-handedness appears to be part of humanity's ancient heritage, not some recent development.

Although the brains of left- and right-handed people are different, they are not simply mirror images. For about 99 percent of right-handed people, the left hemisphere is strongly dominant for control of speech. Most left-handed people have a mixture of left- and right-hemisphere control of speech, although the left is dominant in most cases. Very few have strong right-hemisphere dominance (Loring et al., 1990). The corpus callosum (especially the anterior corpus callosum) is about 11 percent thicker in left-handers than in right-handers, presumably facilitating cross-hemisphere communication and bilateral representation of functions (Habib et al., 1991; Witelson, 1985).

Why are certain people left-handed and others right-handed? Genetics is hardly the only determinant. Family data on handedness do not suggest any simple Mendelian effects. Whatever the causes, left-handedness is correlated with a wide variety of seemingly disparate biological traits. Norman Geschwind and Albert Galaburda (1985) proposed that these relationships can be traced to the hormone testosterone, which in prena-

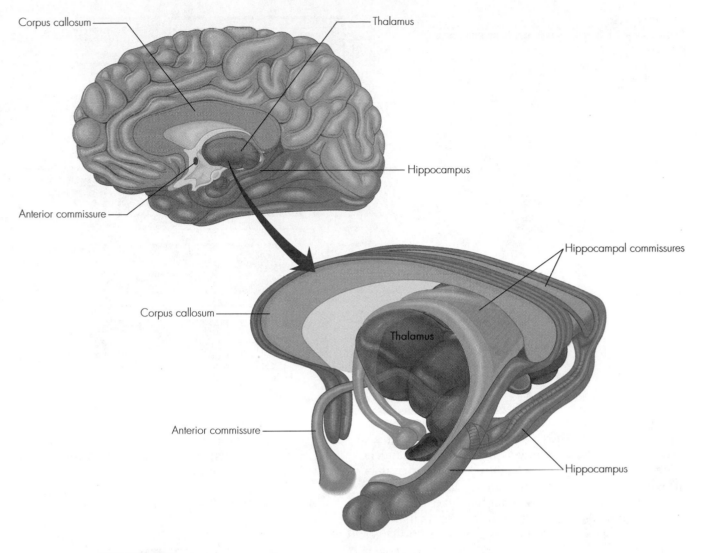

FIGURE **14.8**
The anterior commissure and hippocampal commissures
These commissures allow for the exchange of information between the two hemispheres, as does the larger corpus callosum.   Source: Based on Nieuwenhuys, Voogd, & vanHuijzen, 1988, and others.

tal and early postnatal life can impair the growth of the posterior left hemisphere, increase the probability of left-handedness and right-hemisphere language dominance, impair development of the immune system, and produce other effects, as summarized in Figure 14.9. According to this model, testosterone provides a link between left-handedness and unusual traits ranging from dyslexia to mathematical excellence, as well as medical conditions ranging from childhood allergies to immune disorders. The effects of testosterone may also account for the fact that these conditions are more common in males than in females.

These observations do *not* mean that left-handedness causes dyslexia or immune disorders, any more than they mean that immune disorders cause left-handedness. They do suggest that the factors leading to left-

handedness in some individuals overlap the factors that lead to other biological conditions.

Geschwind and Galaburda's hypothesis remains speculative. On the plus side, it brings together a number of phenomena that seemed unrelated, and proposes a mechanism for connecting them. On the negative side, the hypothesis is vague on many points and therefore difficult to test decisively (McManus & Bryden, 1991). Furthermore, the theory apparently predicts a large difference between males and females in hand preference, brain lateralization, and likelihood of developing various disorders, whereas in fact the differences are not enormous. Most studies have found that men, on average, rely on the left hemisphere for language more than women do (Hiscock, Israelian, Inch, Jacek, & Hiscock-Kalil, 1995)—apparently contradicting what

FIGURE **14.9**
Summary of hypothesis on testosterone effects
Source: Based on Geschwind & Galaburda, 1985; McManus & Bryden, 1991.

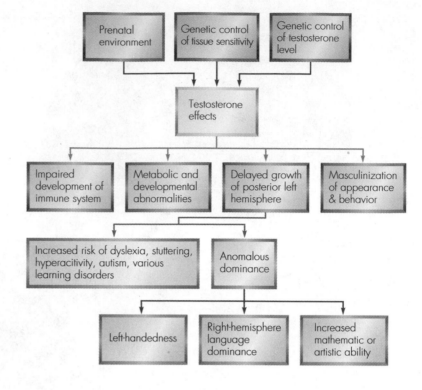

Geschwind and Galaburda predicted—although the sex difference is small. The corpus callosum is, on average, slightly larger in left-handers than in right-handers (Driesen & Raz, 1995), and slightly larger in men than in women. The left-hemisphere areas linked with language are about the same size for both sexes; however, because women's brains tend to be smaller than men's, the corpus callosum and the language areas are larger in proportion to total brain in women than in men (Driesen & Raz, 1995; Harasty, Double, Halliday, Kril, & McRitchie, 1997). Within the language areas, women have a greater density of neurons per unit volume than men do (Witelson, Glezer, & Kigar, 1995). In short, sex, handedness, brain structure, and other variables are all linked to one another, but the links are complicated and in most cases weak. We shall probably need a great deal of additional research to resolve these puzzling issues.

IN CLOSING

One Brain, Two Hemispheres

Imagine that someone asks you a question to which you honestly reply that you do not know, while your left hand points to the correct answer. It must be an unsettling experience. A split-brain person acts at times like two people sharing a single head. An intact-brain person acts and feels like a unity, even though in fact he or she has a multitude of separate brain areas. Amazingly, that unity emerges from the connections among individual cells and brain areas.

Summary

1. The corpus callosum, a set of axons connecting the two hemispheres, has been surgically cut in certain people to relieve severe, otherwise untreatable epilepsy. (p. 375)
2. The left hemisphere can answer questions verbally, and each hemisphere controls mostly the hand on the opposite side, sees the opposite side of the world, and feels the opposite side of the body. After damage to the corpus callosum, each hemisphere can respond to questions only about the information that reaches it directly, not about information reaching the other hemisphere. (p. 375)
3. Although the two hemispheres of a split-brain person are sometimes in conflict, they find many ways to cooperate and to cue each other. (p. 377)
4. The left hemisphere is apparently specialized for language or for sequential, analytic tasks. The right hemisphere is specialized to control complex visual–spatial functions, especially those that require internal representations of such information. It is also specialized for synthetic, holistic tasks. (p. 379)
5. The left and right hemispheres differ anatomically even during infancy. Young children have some trouble comparing information from the left and right hands, because the corpus callosum is not fully mature. (p. 381)

6. In a child born without a corpus callosum, the rest of the brain develops in unusual ways, and the child does not show the same deficits as an adult who sustains damage to the corpus callosum. (p. 382)
7. The brain of a left-handed person is not simply the mirror image of the brain of a right-handed person. Handedness, sex, and brain development are linked in complex ways that are not yet well understood. (p. 382)

Review Questions

1. Why is the left hemisphere of the brain connected only to the right eye in rabbits but to parts of both eyes in humans? (p. 375)
2. In the human eye, what part of each retina connects to the left hemisphere? To the right hemisphere? What part of the visual field does each hemisphere see? (p. 375)
3. Can a split-brain person name an object after feeling it with the left hand? With the right hand? Why? (p. 375)
4. Describe one way in which the two hemispheres cooperate in a split-brain person. (p. 378)
5. What kinds of tasks can the right hemisphere perform better than the left hemisphere? (p. 378)
6. A child born without a corpus callosum can name something felt by the left hand, but an adult with a damaged corpus callosum cannot. What is a likely explanation for this difference? (p. 382)
7. On the average, what differences are found between men and women in the corpus callosum and language areas? (p. 384)

Thought Question

1. When a person born without a corpus callosum moves the fingers of one hand, he or she is likely also to move the fingers of the other hand, involuntarily. What possible explanation can you suggest?

Suggestions for Further Reading

Hoptman, M. J., & Davidson, R. J. (1994). How and why do the two cerebral hemispheres interact? *Psychological Bulletin,* *116,* 195–219. Reviews research on the functions of the corpus callosum.

Springer, S. P., & Deutsch, G. (1993). *Left brain, right brain* (4th ed.). New York: W. H. Freeman. Discusses the split-brain phenomenon and the specializations of the two hemispheres evident in normal people.

Terms

corpus callosum large set of axons that connects the two hemispheres of the cerebral cortex (p. 374)

lateralization division of labor or specializations between the two hemispheres of the brain (p. 374)

visual field what is visible at a particular moment (p. 375)

optic chiasm point at which parts of the optic nerves cross from one side of the brain to the other (p. 375)

epilepsy a condition characterized by repeated episodes of excessive, synchronized neural activity, mainly because of decreased release of the inhibitory transmitter GABA (p. 377)

generalized seizure an epileptic seizure that spreads quickly across neurons over a large portion of both hemispheres of the brain (p. 377)

grand mal seizure type of generalized seizure characterized by sudden, repetitive, jerking movements of the head and limbs for a period of seconds or minutes; the person then collapses into exhaustion and sleep (p. 377)

petit mal seizure (or *absence seizure*) type of generalized seizure in which the person stares unresponsively for a period of seconds, making no sudden movements, except perhaps for eye blinking or a drooping of the head (p. 377)

partial seizure epileptic seizure that begins in a focus somewhere in the brain and then spreads to nearby areas in just one hemisphere (p. 377)

focus point in the brain from which a seizure originates (p. 377)

planum temporale area of the temporal cortex that for most people is larger in the left hemisphere than in the right hemisphere (p. 381)

anterior commissure set of axons that connects the hemispheres in the anterior part of the cerebral cortex (p. 381)

hippocampal commissure set of axons that connects the left hippocampus to the right hippocampus (p. 381)

The Biological Basis of Language

Suppose you have just learned that you have a brain tumor. It causes you few problems now, but it will become life threatening in a year or two if it is not surgically removed. After the operation—if you agree to it—you will have a normal life expectancy and will be entirely healthy, except for one thing: Because of the tumor's location, removing it will leave you incapable of understanding language. Under these conditions, will you agree to have the surgery?

Some people say yes and some say no. Even those who say yes are generally hesitant. Language is a central part of what makes us human.

The Evolution of Language Capacities

Our capacity for language enables us to profit from the experiences of people who live in other parts of the world and of people who lived long ago. Given its great usefulness, you may never have paused to wonder *why* language evolved. "Obviously," you may reply, "language enabled our ancestors to teach one another skills, to make plans. . . ."

Okay, but if language is really so useful, why have no other species evolved it?

"Maybe they just couldn't," you might reply. "Maybe a species cannot evolve language unless it first has enough intelligence, and maybe only humans are that intelligent." You have just stated one of several current theories of language evolution: that humans evolved high intelligence, and language came along as a more or less accidental by-product. Although this explanation is probably partly correct, it is not fully satisfactory. After all, can we be sure that dolphins, whales, and elephants are too unintelligent for language? An alternative view is that language evolved partly as a result of special selective pressure for social interaction among people and that our intelligence is actually a by-product of our language development (Deacon, 1992).

Still, the question of why humans and only humans evolved language remains undecided.

Another puzzle is how the process got started. Almost always, a new feature evolves as a modification of an existing feature. Bats evolved wings by modifying the forearms of their predecessors. Porcupines evolved quills by modifying hair cells. Similarly, humans' capacity for language presumably evolved from behavioral capacities present in earlier primates.

Consequently, we might expect our nearest relatives, the chimpanzees, to be able to learn at least a simple approximation of language. The early attempts to teach chimpanzees spoken language consistently failed (Premack, 1976). The next generation of experiments achieved a certain degree of success by teaching chimpanzees to use American Sign Language or various systems in which visual stimuli represented concepts (Gardner & Gardner, 1975; Premack & Premack, 1972). (See Figure 14.10.) In one version, chimps learned to punch keys bearing symbols to type messages on a computer (Rumbaugh, 1977). For example, they could make requests (such as "Please machine give apple," or "Please machine turn on movie"). They also learned to type messages to other chimps ("Please share your chocolate with me").

Although chimpanzees in these studies learned to produce correct sequences of symbols, their product was not necessarily language. For example, we humans might interpret a sequence of four symbols as "please give me apple," but the chimp might simply have learned, "If I punch these four keys in just this order, people give me an apple." In these experiments, chimps' use of symbols differed from humans' in several regards (Rumbaugh, 1990; Terrace, Pettito, Sanders, & Bever, 1979):

- The chimpanzees seldom combined symbols to make new, original "sentences" (as even very young children do).
- The chimpanzees used their symbols almost exclusively to request, almost never to describe.

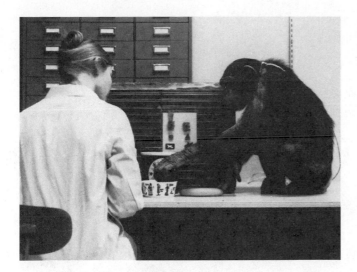

FIGURE **14.10**
One of the Premacks' chimps, Elizabeth, reacts to colored plastic chips that read "Not Elizabeth banana insert—Elizabeth apple wash." Source: Courtesy of Ann Premack.

• In spite of apparently impressive language production, the chimpanzees were limited in their comprehension of others' communications. Children, in contrast, almost invariably learn to understand speech better than they can produce it. (Consider your own ability to understand a foreign language in comparison with your ability to speak it.)

Such observations made psychologists skeptical about chimpanzees' language learning, particularly about their ability to acquire syntax, the rules for combining words to express new meanings. Then some new and surprising results emerged from studies of a rare endangered species, *Pan paniscus*, known as the pygmy chimpanzee (a misleading name because these animals are almost as large as common chimpanzees) or the bonobo (also a misleading name because it refers to a place in Africa where they do not live).

Pan paniscus has a social order resembling that of humans in several regards. Males and females form strong, sometimes long-term personal attachments. They often copulate in a face-to-face position. The female is sexually responsive at almost all times and not just during her fertile period. Unlike most other primates, these males contribute significantly to infant care. Adults often share food with one another. They stand comfortably on their hind legs. In short, they resemble humans more than any other primates do.

In the mid-1980s, Sue Savage-Rumbaugh, Duane Rumbaugh, and their associates began trying to teach a female *Pan paniscus* named Matata to press symbols that light up when touched; each symbol represents a word (see Figure 14.11). Matata made little progress. However, her infant son Kanzi seemed to learn a great deal just by watching her attempts. When given a chance to use the symbol board, he quickly surpassed the performance of his mother and of every common chimp that had been tested, even though he had never been formally trained. Furthermore, it soon became clear that Kanzi understood a fair amount of spoken language. The experimenters first noticed that whenever anyone said the word "light" he would flip the light switch. By age 5½, he understood about 150 English

FIGURE **14.11**
Language tests for Kanzi, a bonobo (Pan paniscus)
He listens to questions through the earphones and points to answers on a board. The experimenter with him does not know what the questions are or what answers are expected. Source: Georgia State University's Language Research Center, operated with the Yerkes Primate Center of Emory. Photo courtesy of Duane Rumbaugh.

FIGURE **14.12**
Language tests for Alex, a gray parrot
Alex has apparently learned to converse about objects in simple English—for example, giving the correct answer to "What color is the circle?" He receives no food rewards.

words and could respond to such complex, unfamiliar spoken commands as "Throw your ball in the river," "Go to the refrigerator and get out a tomato," and "Let's chase to the A-frame" (Savage-Rumbaugh, 1990; Savage-Rumbaugh, Sevcik, Brakke, & Rumbaugh, 1992). Kanzi has since demonstrated language comprehension comparable to that of a 2- to 2½-year-old child (Savage-Rumbaugh et al., 1993).

Kanzi and his younger sister Mulika understand far more language than they produce. Both occasionally attempt to speak, although they continue to communicate mostly by pressing symbols on their boards. Their productions exceed those of other chimpanzees in some important regards. First, they use the symbols to name and describe objects even when they are not requesting them. They also request items that they do not see, such as "bubbles" (I want to play with the bubble-blower) or "car trailer" (drive me in the car to the trailer) (Savage-Rumbaugh, 1991; Savage-Rumbaugh et al., 1993). Second, they occasionally use the symbols to describe past events. Kanzi once punched the symbols "Matata bite" to explain the cut that he had received on his hand an hour earlier. Third, Kanzi and Mulika frequently make original, creative requests. For example, after Kanzi learned to press symbols to ask someone to play "chase" with him, he asked one person to chase another person while he watched!

Why have Kanzi and Mulika developed such impressive skills where other chimpanzees have failed? One possible explanation is a species difference: Perhaps *Pan paniscus* has greater language capacities than common chimpanzees. A second explanation is that

Kanzi and Mulika began language training at an early age, unlike the chimpanzees in most other studies. A third reason may pertain to the method of training: Perhaps learning by observation and imitation promotes better understanding than the formal training methods of previous studies (Savage-Rumbaugh, Sevcik, Brakke, & Rumbaugh, 1992).

Can any nonprimate species learn any aspect of language? Maybe. Dolphins have learned to respond to a system of gestures and sounds, each representing one word. For example, after the command "Right hoop left frisbee fetch," a dolphin takes the frisbee on the left to the hoop on the right (Herman, Pack, & Morrel-Samuels, 1993). A dolphin responds correctly to new combinations of old words, but only if the result is meaningful. For example, the first time that a dolphin is given the command "Person hoop fetch," it takes the hoop to the person. But when told "Person water fetch," it does nothing (because it has no way to take water to the person). But note that this system offers the dolphins neither the opportunity nor the incentive to produce language. The dolphins cannot produce the gestures or sounds to tell a human to take the frisbee to the hoop and, even if they could, it is not clear that they would want to (Savage-Rumbaugh, 1993).

Spectacular results have been reported for Alex, an African gray parrot (Figure 14.12). Parrots are, of course, famous for imitating human sounds; Irene Pepperberg was the first to argue that parrots can learn the meaning of sounds. She kept Alex in a stimulating environment and taught him to say a variety of words in conjunction with specific objects. First, she and the other trainers would say a word many times, and then offer rewards if Alex approximated the same sound. Here is an excerpt from a conversation with Alex early in training (Pepperberg, 1981):

> **Pepperberg:** Pasta! (*Takes pasta.*) Pasta! (*Alex stretches from his perch, appears to reach for pasta.*)
> **Alex:** Pa!
> **Pepperberg:** Better . . . what is it?
> **Alex:** Pah-ah.
> **Pepperberg:** Better!
> **Alex:** Pah-ta.
> **Pepperberg:** Okay, here's the pasta. Good try.

Although pasta was used in this example, Pepperberg generally used toys. For example, if Alex said "paper," "wood," or "key," she would give him what he asked for. In no case did she reward him for saying "paper" or "wood" by giving him a piece of food.

Alex made gradual progress, learning to give spoken answers to spoken questions. He was shown a tray of 12 small objects and then asked such questions as "What color is the key?" (answer: "green") and "What object is gray?" (answer: "circle"). In one test, he gave the correct answer to 39 of 48 questions. Even many of his incorrect answers were close to being correct. In one case, he was asked the color of the "block" and he responded with the color of the "rock." In another case, the correct answer was "green," and Alex said something that sounded like "gree," but could have been "gray," so the experimenters counted his answer wrong (Pepperberg, 1993). He can also answer questions of the form "How many blue key?" in which he has to examine 10 to 14 objects, count the blue keys among objects of two shapes and two colors, and then say the answer, ranging from 1 to 6 (Pepperberg, 1994).

Is Alex actually learning language? Pepperberg simply refers to his performance as "language-like." She says that she is using the research to study the bird's concept formation, not his language capacities. Still, Alex has made far more progress than most of us would have thought possible for a nonprimate; these results prompt us to rethink some assumptions about what sort of brain development is necessary for language.

What do we learn from studies of nonhuman language abilities? At a practical level, we may gain some insights into how best to teach language to those who do not learn it easily. The methods that we develop for teaching chimpanzees may be useful for brain-damaged people or autistic children (see, for example, Glass, Gazzaniga, & Premack, 1973). At a more theoretical level, we learn something about how special humans are—and are not. Although humans undeniably develop language far more readily than any other species does, our language abilities are an elaboration of abilities that other species have to a lesser degree. Finally, these studies call attention to the difficulty of defining language: The main reason that we have such trouble deciding whether chimpanzees or parrots have language is that we have not specified exactly what language is.

Effects of Brain Damage on Human Language

Although chimpanzees and African gray parrots may learn a certain approximation of language, it does not come as easily for them as for humans. Almost every healthy child develops language, regardless of what teaching methods, if any, the parents use. Human cultures vary enormously in their use of tools, but not in the sophistication of their language. Even cultures that we might regard as technologically primitive have grammatically complex languages (Pinker, 1996). Evidently, the human brain is specialized to make language learning easy. Most of our knowledge about the brain mechanisms of language has come from studies of brain-damaged people.

Broca's Aphasia

In 1861, a patient who had been mute for 30 years was treated for gangrene by the French surgeon Paul Broca. When the man died five days later, Broca did an autopsy and found a lesion that was restricted to a small part of the frontal lobe of the left cerebral cortex near the motor cortex (Boring, 1950; Schiller, 1979). In later years Broca examined the brains of additional patients whose only problem had been **aphasia** (severe language impairment); in nearly all cases, he found damage that included this same area, which is now known as **Broca's area** (Figure 14.13). The usual cause was a stroke (an interruption of blood flow to part of the brain). We now know that damage limited to Broca's area produces only a minor or brief language impairment; serious deficits occur only with extensive damage that includes not only Broca's area but also other nearby cortical and subcortical structures.

Damage to Broca's area and surrounding areas is associated specifically with **Broca's aphasia** or *nonfluent aphasia,* characterized most prominently by impaired language production (Geschwind, 1970, 1972). For many years, neurologists asserted that people with Broca's aphasia had normal language comprehension; later studies found that both production and comprehension are normal in some ways but show deficits when the meaning of a sentence depends on prepositions, word endings, and other grammatical devices.

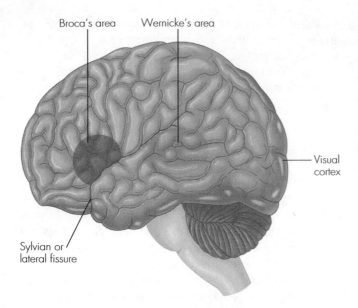

FIGURE **14.13**
Some major language areas of the cerebral cortex
In most people, only the left hemisphere is specialized for language.

Difficulty in language production   Some people with Broca's aphasia cannot utter words at all, although they may be able to produce a variety of sounds. Those with less extensive damage speak slowly and inarticulately, and also have trouble writing and expressing themselves through gestures (Cicone, Wapner, Foldi, Zurif, & Gardner, 1979). In addition, deaf people with damage in and around Broca's area have trouble producing sign language, although they can use their hands well in other ways (Hickok, Bellugi, & Klima, 1996).

Someone with Broca's aphasia speaks meaningfully but omits pronouns, prepositions, conjunctions, helper verbs, quantifiers, and tense and number endings. These omitted words and endings are sometimes known as the *closed class* of grammatical forms because a language rarely adds new prepositions, conjunctions, and the like. In contrast, new nouns and verbs (the *open-class* forms) enter a language frequently. People with Broca's aphasia use nouns and verbs more easily than they use closed-class words. They find it difficult to repeat a phrase using many prepositions and conjunctions, such as "No ifs, ands, or buts," although they can successfully repeat "The general commands the army." Furthermore, patients who cannot read aloud "To be or not to be" can read "Two bee oar knot two bee" (Gardner & Zurif, 1975). Clearly, the trouble is with the meanings of words, not just their pronunciation.

Problems in comprehending grammatical words and devices   People with Broca's aphasia understand much spoken and written language, but they have trouble understanding the same kinds of words that they have trouble speaking—prepositions, conjunctions, and other relational words—and sentences with complex grammar, such as "The girl that the boy is chasing is tall" (Zurif, 1980). Sometimes the meaning of a sentence depends on relational words and grammatical devices, and sometimes it does not. You might try deleting all the prepositions, conjunctions, articles, and word endings from a paragraph to see how the text might appear to someone with Broca's aphasia. Table 14.1 shows an example.

Still, people with Broca's aphasia have not totally lost their knowledge of grammar. For example, they generally recognize that something is wrong with the sentence "He written has songs," even if they cannot say how to improve it (Wulfeck & Bates, 1991). The speech patterns of English-speaking people with Broca's aphasia differ from those of, say, Germans or Italians, because even after brain damage, people use the word order that is normal for their language. When comprehension depends on word endings or other grammatical devices, people with Broca's aphasia are impaired, but their performance is not random. In many ways their comprehension resembles that of normal people who are greatly distracted (Blackwell & Bates, 1995).

Wernicke's Aphasia

In 1874, Carl Wernicke (generally pronounced WER-nih-kee in the United States, although the German pronunciation is VER-nih-keh), a 26-year-old junior assistant in a German hospital, discovered that damage in part of the left temporal cortex produced language impairment very different from what Broca had reported. Although patients could speak and write, they had trouble comprehending the verbal and written communications of others. Damage in and around **Wernicke's area** (Figure 14.13), located near the auditory part of the cerebral cortex, produces **Wernicke's aphasia,** also sometimes known as *fluent aphasia* because the person can still speak smoothly. Typical results are as follows:

1. *Articulate speech.* In contrast to Broca's aphasics, Wernicke's aphasics speak articulately and fluently, except when they pause to try to think of the name of something.

2. *Difficulty finding the right word.* People suffering from Wernicke's aphasia have **anomia** (ay-NOME-ee-uh), difficulty recalling the names of objects. Sometimes they make up names or substitute one name for another, and sometimes they use vague or roundabout expressions such as "the thing that we used to do with the thing that was like the other one." Such expressions no doubt mean something to the speaker, but pity the poor listener. When they do manage to find some of the right words, they arrange them improperly, saying, for example, "The Astros listened to the radio tonight" (instead of "I listened to the Astros on the radio tonight") (Martin & Blossom-Stach, 1986).

3. *Poor language comprehension.* Wernicke's aphasics have great trouble understanding both spoken and written speech. Although many sentences are clear enough without prepositions, word endings, and grammar (which confuse Broca's aphasics), almost no sentences are clear without nouns and verbs (which trouble Wernicke's patients).

The following conversation is between a woman with Wernicke's aphasia and a speech therapist trying to teach her the names of some objects. (The Duke University Department of Speech Pathology and Audiology provided this dialogue.)

Therapist: (*Holding picture of an apron*) Can you name that one?

Woman: Um . . . you see I can't, I can I can barely do; he would give me sort of umm . . .

T: A clue?

W: That's right . . . just a like, just a . . .

T: You mean, like, "You wear that when you wash dishes or when you cook a meal . . ."?

W: Yeah, something like that.

T: Okay, and what is it? You wear it around your waist, and you cook. . . .

W: Cook. Umm, umm, see I can't remember.

T: It's an apron.

W: Apron, apron, that's it, apron.

T: (*Holding another picture*) That you wear when you're getting ready for bed after a shower.

W: Oh, I think that he put under different, something different. We had something, you know, umm, you know.

T: A different way of doing it?

W: No, umm . . . umm . . . (*Pause*)

T: It's actually a bathrobe.

W: Bathrobe. Uh, we didn't call it that, we called it something else.

T: Smoking jacket?

W: No, I think we called it, uh . . .

T: Lounging . . . ?

W: No, no, something, in fact, we called it just . . . (*Pause*)

T: Robe?

W: Robe. Or something like that.

One study found that college-educated people have longer dendrites in Wernicke's area than do less educated people of the same age (Jacobs, Schall, & Scheibel, 1993). We do not know, however, whether education and associated activities caused the dendrites to grow or whether people with longer dendrites are more likely to succeed in school and therefore to continue their studies into college.

Unlike hearing people, deaf people who suffer damage to Wernicke's area continue to understand sign language. Rather, they lose that ability after damage in the parietal lobe, the area responsible for touch and other body sensations (Bellugi, Poizner, & Klima, 1983).

Table 14.2 contrasts Broca's aphasia and Wernicke's aphasia.

TABLE **14.2**

Broca's Aphasia and Wernicke's Aphasia

Type	Pronunciation	Content of Speech	Comprehension
Broca's aphasia	Very poor	Mostly nouns and verbs; omits prepositions and other grammatical connectives	Impaired if the meaning depends on prepositions, grammar, or unusual word order
Wernicke's aphasia	Unimpaired	Grammatical but sometimes nonsensical; has trouble finding the right word, especially names of objects	Seriously impaired

Beyond Broca and Wernicke

Although the definitions of Broca's aphasia and Wernicke's aphasia adequately describe the behavior of many brain-damaged people, a number of prominent neurologists believe the distinction is an oversimplification (Caramazza, 1995). First, many patients with aphasia have specialized problems that do not fall into either category. Here are a few examples:

- *Conduction aphasia:* articulate speech and reasonable language comprehension, but inability to repeat what someone else has said and general difficulty carrying on a conversation (Davis, 1993)
- *Alexia:* loss of ability to read despite adequate vision in other regards and normal comprehension of spoken language (Geschwind, 1970, 1972)
- *Optic aphasia:* ability to read only one letter at a time, never a full word (Buxbaum & Coslett, 1996; Hillis & Caramazza, 1995)
- *Word deafness:* loss of ability to understand spoken language despite adequate hearing and normal reading ability (Davis, 1993)
- *Loss of speech articulation:* poor ability to speak, as if groping for the right sound, despite normal perception of speech sounds and normal language comprehension (Dronkers, 1996)

The list could easily continue. A great many brain areas contribute to speech, no two patients have exactly the same brain damage, and there is no apparent limit to the types of possible language disorder. Dividing aphasia into distinct types is less useful than studying how each brain area contributes to language.

PET scans and functional MRI scans enable investigators to address questions that they could not answer by simply observing brain-damaged patients. Typically, investigators record brain activity while the person is engaged in a language task, such as speaking or reading, and then during some other task that does not require language. A computer then compares the activity recorded in the two tasks to find which areas are specifically activated by language. (As you can imagine, it is important but difficult to choose an appropriate non-language task for comparison.)

According to such studies, speaking increases activity in much of the frontal, temporal, and parietal cortex in the left hemisphere, and in parts of the left thalamus and basal ganglia (Wallesch, Henriksen, Kornhuber, & Paulson, 1985). (See Figure 14.14.) Reading a sentence aloud also causes widespread activity in Broca's area, Wernicke's area, other surrounding areas, and, to a lesser extent, in the corresponding areas of the right hemisphere (Just, Carpenter, Keller, Eddy, & Thulborn, 1996).

Two studies examined cortical responses while people looked at pictures and named the images. Both studies found that naming any object activated parts of the temporal lobe corresponding approximately to Wernicke's area. Additional areas also became active, depending on the kind of object. According to one study, naming people activated the anterior area of the temporal lobe, naming animals activated a posterior area, and naming tools activated a still more posterior area (Damasio, Grabowski, Tranel, Hichwa, & Damasio, 1996). The other study found that naming animals activated part of the occipital lobe, whereas naming tools activated part of the left premotor cortex in the frontal lobe (Martin, Wiggs, Ungerleider, & Haxby, 1996). These studies used different methods, so the results should not be considered contradictory. The important point is that naming activates different areas depending on the objects, and that a large part of the cortex contributes to naming in one way or another.

Figure 14.15 shows the results of a study in which people heard or read the names of objects and then either repeated the words or stated a use for the objects (such as *hammer—pound,* or *cake—eat*). Stating a use for the word activated frontal cortex areas that were not affected by simply repeating the word (Petersen, Fox, Posner, Mintun, & Raichle, 1988; Posner et al., 1988). Presumably, when people think of a function, they activate the motor or premotor areas that would enable them to perform that function. The figure indicates that the frontal cortex treats spoken and written language virtually the same way.

Genetic Abnormalities of Language and Intellect

In some cases, genetic abnormalities impair language, despite normal intellect, or impair intellect and spare language. These conditions indicate that language is not entirely a by-product of overall intelligence, but requires specific brain adaptations.

Developmental Language Impairment

In one family, 16 of 30 people in three generations show severe language deficits, despite normal intelligence in other regards. Presumably because of a dominant gene, the 16 affected people all have serious troubles with pronunciation, remaining almost unintelligible until about age 7 and decidedly inarticulate for years after that (Gopnik & Crago, 1991). They also have extreme difficulties applying simple grammatical rules, even in adulthood, as shown in the following dialogue about making plurals:

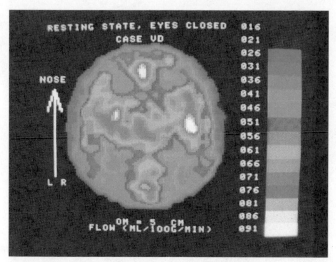

(a)

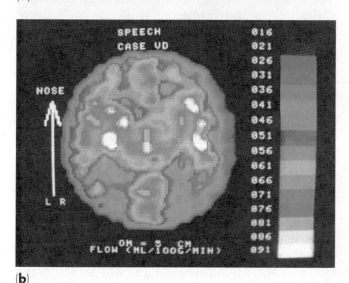

(b)

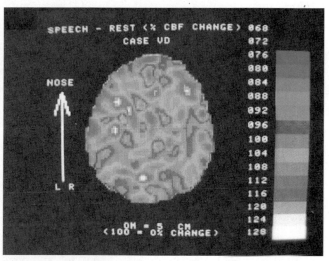

(c)

FIGURE **14.14**
Records showing rCBF for a normal adult
Red indicates the highest level of activity, followed by yellow, green, and blue. (**a**) Blood flow to the brain at rest. (**b**) Blood flow while subject describes a magazine story. (**c**) Difference between **b** and **a.** The results in **c** indicate which brain areas increased their activity during language production. Note the increased activity in many areas of the brain, especially on the left side.   Source: Wallesch, Henriksen, Kornhuber, & Paulson, 1985.

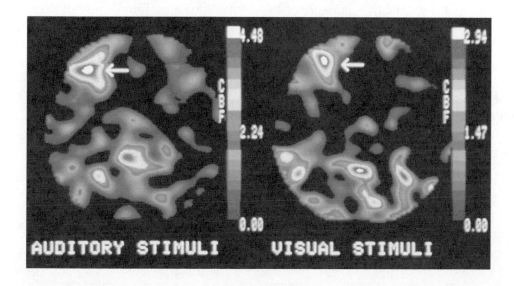

FIGURE **14.15**
Brain areas activated by thinking of a use for an object
For the scan on the left, people heard words; for the scan on the right, they read them. In both cases, the PET scan shows which brain areas were activated more by stating a use for a word (such as *cake—eat*) than by merely repeating the word (*cake—cake*). Note that for both hearing and reading, activity increased markedly in the left anterior frontal cortex (marked with arrow). Source: Petersen et al., 1988.

Experimenter	Respondent
This is a wug; these are . . .	How should I know? *[Later]* These are wug.
This is a zat; these are . . .	These are zacko.
This is a sas; these are . . .	These are sasss. *[Not sasses]*

In another test, experimenters presented sentences and asked whether each sentence was correct or, if not, how one might improve it. People with developmental language impairment frequently failed to identify errors and also misidentified many correct sentences as "ungrammatical." (Evidently, they were just guessing much of the time.) When they tried to correct a sentence, many of their results were odd. For example:

Original Item	Attempted Correction
The boy eats three cookie.	The boys eat four cookie.

The people in this family are not simply lacking in grammar; they also have trouble pronouncing, repeating, and understanding speech (Fletcher, 1990; Vargha-Khadem & Passingham, 1990). The important point is that a genetic condition that affects brain development can seriously impair language, without major effects on other aspects of intellect.

Williams Syndrome

What about the reverse pattern? Could someone have severe impairments of nonlinguistic functions and nevertheless have good language abilities? Psychologists have long assumed that all mentally retarded people have severe language deficits. They saw this rule as almost a logical necessity: Anyone who lacked the intelligence to learn simple motor skills would presumably also lack the intelligence to learn and use language.

And then, in the 1960s, psychologists discovered a rare condition called **Williams syndrome,** in which people who are retarded in most regards are skillful in their use of language. The cause is a deletion of several genes from chromosome #7 (Frangiskakis et al., 1996). Affected people are unable to learn the simple skills needed to take care of themselves; even as adults, they require constant supervision. They have impaired attention and poor visuomotor skills; they cannot hold even an unskilled job or copy even the simplest drawings. Nevertheless, they can repeat stories with great emotional expression, make up their own stories, even compose song lyrics. They can listen to a story and draw simple inferences about the knowledge and motivation of the characters (Karmiloff-Smith, Klima, Bellugi, Grant, & Baron-Cohen, 1995). They can also listen to a sentence and choose the picture that matches it (Bellugi, Wang, & Jernigan, 1994). Figure 14.16 shows the result when a young woman with Williams syndrome and an IQ of 49 was asked to draw an elephant and describe it. Contrast the high quality of the description to the almost unrecognizable drawing.

People with Williams syndrome use more than the ordinary number of unusual words. For example, if asked to "name as many animals as possible," most people list common animals such as dog, horse, and rabbit. People with Williams syndrome include a disproportionate number of exotic animals such as weasel, newt, ibex, unicorn, and triceratops (Bellugi, Wang, & Jernigan, 1994).

Given that language skills in Williams syndrome are so superior to the nonlanguage skills, we might expect to find evidence of right-hemisphere damage. In fact, however, MRI images indicate a reduction in the overall mass of the cerebral cortex and thalamus, with no trend toward any imbalance between the left and right hemispheres (Jernigan & Bellugi, 1994). We cannot explain Williams syndrome in terms of the loss or absence of a particular brain area; rather, it seems to result from an unusual organization of brain connections

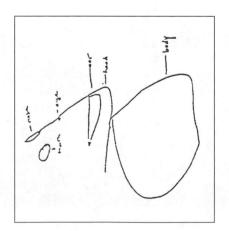

FIGURE **14.16**

A drawing and a description of an elephant by a young woman with Williams syndrome

The labels on the drawing were provided by the investigator, based on what the woman said she was drawing. Source: From Bellugi, Wang, & Jernigan, 1994. Copyright Ursula Bellugi, The Salk Institute for Biological Studies.

And what an elephant is, it is one of the animals. And what the elephant does, it lives in the jungle. It can also live in the zoo. And what it has, it has long gray ears, fan ears, ears that can blow in the wind. It has a long trunk that can pick up grass, or pick up hay . . . If they're in a bad mood it can be terrible . . . If the elephant gets mad it could stomp; it could charge, like a bull can charge. They have long big tusks. They can damage a car . . . it could be dangerous. When they're in a pinch, when they're in a bad mood it can be terrible. You don't want an elephant as a pet. You want a cat or a dog or a bird . . .

that future research will have to explore. In any case, observations of Williams syndrome support the idea that language is a specialized ability that can be kept or lost independently of other functions; it is not strictly a by-product of overall intelligence.

Dyslexia

Dyslexia is a specific difficulty with reading in a person who has adequate vision and adequate skills in other academic areas. As with backache or headache, there are many kinds of dyslexia with many different underlying causes. There is no single abnormality associated with all cases of dyslexia, but several abnormalities that occur in varying numbers of cases.

For some people with dyslexia, part of the underlying problem is perceptual. They may be able to see one letter at a time as well as anyone else but have trouble recognizing combinations of letters. Even bracketing a letter with meaningless x's (such as xex, xfx, xgx) hampers their identification of the central letter (Bouma & Legein, 1977). They may also have trouble identifying spoken syllables—for example, when they are asked to press a lever when they hear *da* but not when they hear *ga, pa,* or *ta* (Hagman et al., 1992). In short, the symptoms of dyslexia are not limited to vision.

Many but not all people with dyslexia apparently have relatively unresponsive magnocellular paths in the visual system (Livingstone, Rosen, Drislane, & Galaburda, 1991). Recall from Chapter 6 that the magnocellular path deals with overall patterns and moving objects. Many people with dyslexia have impaired perception not only of words but also of visual motion patterns (Cornelissen, Richardson, Mason, Fowler, & Stein, 1995; Eden et al., 1996; Evans, Drasdo, & Richards, 1994). However, the effects vary considerably from one individual to another, and the magnocellular path is hardly the only place to look for an explanation.

In some cases dyslexia apparently reflects an incomplete specialization of the hemispheres for language. According to one extensive review of the literature, a dyslexic person is more likely to have a bilaterally symmetrical cerebral cortex, whereas in other people the planum temporale and certain other areas are larger in the left hemisphere (Hynd & Semrud-Clikeman, 1989). In some dyslexic people, certain language-related areas are actually larger in the right hemisphere (Duara et al., 1991). These results support Geschwind and Galaburda's theory (p. 382) that links anomalous lateralization of function with a predisposition to dyslexia and other problems.

Yet another explanation of dyslexia relates it to a difference in attention or strategy. In one study, investigators asked children to examine pairs of letter combinations—such as *clid* and *cdil*—and say which one "could be" an English word. Dyslexic children were actually *better* than normal-reading children on this task, although they were worse at pronouncing pseudowords such as *batmotbem* and *monglustamer* (Siegel, Share, & Geva, 1995). Evidently, the dyslexic children attended to visual features of the words that enabled them to recognize acceptable and unacceptable letter combinations, but were not good at converting unfamiliar words into sounds.

Here is a demonstration of another process that is relevant to dyslexia. Focus your eyes on the central dot in each display below and, without moving your eyes back and forth, try to read the middle letter of each three-letter display:

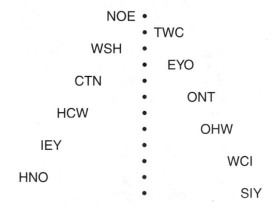

If you are like most people, you found it easier to read the letters close to the fixation point, especially those to the right. The tendency to read better to the right may be a function of our long experience in reading from left to right; several studies disagree on whether the same tendency occurs in people reading Hebrew and Farsi, which are printed right to left (Brysbaert, Vitu, & Schroyens, 1996; Faust, Kravetz, & Babkoff, 1993; Malamed & Zaidel, 1993; Pollatsek, Bolozky, Well, & Rayner, 1981).

For most people, adding a letter at the fixation point generates little interference with nearby letters but major interference with remotely placed letters. For example, the H does not mask the W in this display:

focus here

↓

HW

but it does mask the N in this display:

focus here

↓

H   N

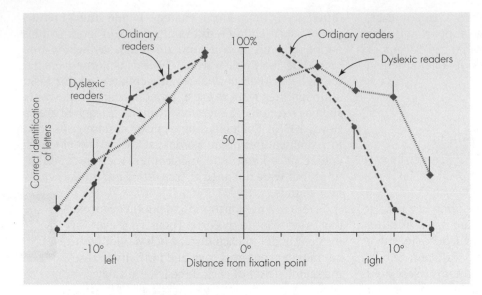

FIGURE **14.17**
Identification of a letter at various distances from the fixation point
Normal readers identify a letter most accurately when it is closest to the fixation point, and their accuracy drops steadily as letters become more remote from that point. Many people with dyslexia show a small impairment for letters just to the right of the fixation point, yet they are substantially more accurate than normal readers are in identifying letters 5–10° to the right of fixation.   Source: From Geiger, Lettvin, & Zegarra-Moran, 1992.

(Remember, we are talking about letters flashed briefly on a screen. The interference is less impressive when you can stare at letters on a page.)

Now, it turns out that the results I just described apply to most people, but not to all. For a certain minority, a letter at the fixation point produces noticeable interference for an immediately adjacent letter (like the **W** in the **HW** display) but less than the normal amount of interference for a remote letter (like the **N** in the **H   N** display). People showing this pattern suffer from dyslexia! When people with certain kinds of dyslexia focus on one letter, it blocks perception of the immediately adjacent letters but permits perception of letters farther to the right (Geiger, Lettvin, & Zegarra-Moran, 1992). So when such people focus on a word, they are worse than average at reading it but better than average at perceiving letters 5–10° to the right of fixation. That kind of attentional focus could certainly confuse attempts at reading. Figure 14.17 shows the mean results for normal readers and for people with dyslexia.

For people with this abnormality, part of an effective treatment might be to teach them to attend to just one word at a time. Some dyslexic children and adults have been told to place over the page that they are reading a sheet of paper with a window cut out of it that is large enough to expose just one word. In three months, 15 dyslexic children improved their reading skills by 1.22 grade levels (Geiger, Lettvin, & Fahle, 1994). Four dyslexic adults also made spectacular progress; one advanced from a third-grade to a tenth-grade reading level in four months (Geiger, Lettvin, & Zegarra-Moran, 1992). After about the first three weeks of practice, they no longer needed the special cut-out sheet of paper.

One final twist: Of the four dyslexic adults who went through this process, three decided that they would rather return to being dyslexic! While dyslexic, they could attend to several tasks at once, such as talking to someone, listening to news on the radio, creating a work of art, and so forth. When they learned to read one word at a time, they found themselves able to perform only one task at a time, and they missed their old way of life. In short, their reading skills were tied to their overall attentional strategies.

IN**CLOSING**

Language and the Brain

Perhaps the best summary of dyslexia is also the best summary of language impairments in general: Language and reading are sufficiently complicated that one can become impaired in these areas in many ways for many reasons. Language is not strictly a by-product of overall intelligence, but it is hardly independent of other intellectual functions either.

Summary

1. Chimpanzees can learn to communicate through gestures or nonvocal symbols, although their output lacks syntax and does not closely resemble human speech. Bonobos (pygmy chimpanzees) have made far more language progress than common chimpanzees, possibly because of

species differences and partly because of differences in training methods. (p. 386)

2. People with Broca's aphasia have difficulty speaking and writing. They find prepositions, conjunctions, and other grammatical connectives especially difficult. They also fail to understand speech when its meaning depends on grammatical connectives, sentence structure, or word order. (p. 389)

3. People with Wernicke's aphasia have trouble understanding speech and recalling the names of objects. (p. 391)

4. Because many brain areas contribute to language and because no two people have exactly the same pattern of damage, investigators find an enormous number of different kinds of language impairment. (p. 392)

5. Even naming different kinds of objects requires different brain areas. (p. 393)

6. People with certain genetic abnormalities can suffer language impairments without much loss of intellect or intellectual retardation despite good use of language. (p. 394)

7. People with reading impairments apparently have a variety of abnormalities in brain structure, perception, and attention. (p. 395)

Review Questions

1. How and why do the results of language training with *Pan paniscus* differ from those with common chimpanzees? (p. 387)

2. Describe the differences between Broca's aphasia and Wernicke's aphasia. (p. 391)

3. Why do many investigators believe it is an oversimplification to divide aphasia into a few distinct types? (p. 392)

4. How can an investigator use a PET scan to determine which areas of the brain are especially activated when a person speaks? (p. 392)

5. What problems were reported for the family with developmental language impairment? (p. 394)

6. Describe the symptoms of Williams syndrome. (p. 394)

7. What training method has helped certain people with dyslexia make rapid progress in learning to read? (p. 396)

Thought Questions

1. Most people with Broca's aphasia suffer from partial paralysis on the right side of the body. Most people with Wernicke's aphasia do not. Why?

2. In a syndrome called "word deafness," a person cannot understand spoken language, although reading, speaking, and hearing are normal in other respects. What is a possible neurological explanation?

Suggestions for Further Reading

Krasnegor, N. A., Rumbaugh, D. M., Schiefelbusch, R. L., & Studdert-Kennedy, M. (1991). *Biological and behavioral determinants of language development.* Hillsdale, NJ: Lawrence Erlbaum. Features chapters on language learning by chimpanzees, children, and language-impaired people.

Pinker, S. (1994). *The language instinct.* New York: William Morrow and Company. Discussion of both behavioral and biological aspects of language.

Terms

aphasia   severe impairment of language (p. 389)

Broca's area   portion of the human left frontal lobe associated with certain aspects of language, especially language production (p. 389)

Broca's aphasia   condition marked by loss of fluent speech and impaired use and understanding of prepositions, word endings, and other grammatical devices (p. 389)

Wernicke's area   portion of the human left temporal lobe associated with language comprehension (p. 391)

Wernicke's aphasia   condition marked by poor language comprehension and great difficulty remembering the names of objects (p. 391)

anomia   difficulty recalling the names of objects (p. 391)

Williams syndrome   type of mental retardation in which the person has good language skills in spite of extremely limited abilities in other regards (p. 394)

dyslexia   a specific difficulty with reading, despite adequate vision and at least average skills in other academic areas (p. 395)

RECOVERY FROM BRAIN DAMAGE

CHAPTER **FIFTEEN**

MAIN**IDEAS**

1. The human brain can be damaged by a sharp blow, an interruption of blood flow, and several other types of injury. Batteries of tests are available that estimate the location and extent of damage.
2. Although both humans and animals typically recover in part from brain damage, behavior is never as securely established as it would be if the injury had never occurred, and it is likely to deteriorate again under stress and in old age.
3. Many mechanisms contribute to recovery from brain damage, including restoration of undamaged neurons to full activity, regrowth of axons, readjustment of surviving synapses, and behavioral adjustments.
4. The degree of recovery from brain damage is sometimes better and sometimes worse if the damage occurs in infancy.

An American soldier who suffered a wound to the left hemisphere of his brain during the Korean War was at first unable to speak at all. Three months later he could speak in short fragments. When he was shown a letterhead, "New York University College of Medicine," and asked to read it, all he could say was, "Doctors—little doctors." Eight years later, when someone asked him again to read the letterhead, he replied, "Is there a catch? It says 'New York University College of Medicine'" (Eidelberg & Stein, 1974).

Many people show behavioral recovery after brain damage, although the recovery is seldom if ever complete. Given that the mammalian nervous system cannot replace lost neurons (with the few exceptions mentioned in Chapter 2), we face the theoretical question of how people recover from brain damage at all. From a practical standpoint, we wonder how therapists can facilitate recovery. Finally, studying recovery from brain damage may yield new insights into the functioning of the healthy brain.

Brain Damage and Mechanisms of Recovery

Your body is a partially self-repairing machine. You get a cut, it heals; you lose some blood, you make more. After brain damage, however, you do not replace the lost neurons. How, then, does recovery from brain damage take place?

Causes of Human Brain Damage

The human brain can be damaged in many ways. In young adults the most common cause is a sharp blow to the head from a fall, an automobile or motorcycle accident, an assault, or other violent trauma. Head injuries cause damage partly by subjecting the brain to rotational forces that drive brain tissue against the in-side of the skull (see Digression 15.1). Other sources of brain damage include tumors, certain infections, drugs and toxic substances, exposure to radiation, and degenerative conditions such as Parkinson's disease and Alzheimer's disease.

One of the most common causes of brain damage, especially in older people, is temporary loss of blood flow to the brain during a **stroke**, also known as a **cerebrovascular accident.** The more common type of stroke is **ischemia**, caused when a blood clot or other obstruction closes an artery; the less common type is **hemorrhage**, caused when an artery ruptures. Both types produce many of the same effects. Strokes vary in their severity from barely noticeable to immediately fatal. Figure 15.1 shows the brains of three people: one who died immediately after a stroke, one who survived for a long time after a stroke, and a victim of a bullet wound.

DIGRESSION 15.1

Why Don't Woodpeckers Get Concussions?

When a woodpecker strikes its bill against a tree, it repeatedly bangs its head against an unyielding object at a velocity of 6 to 7 meters per second (about 15 miles per hour). How does it escape brain injury?

P. R. A. May and associates (May, Fuster, Haber, & Hirschman, 1979) used slow-motion photography to observe the behavior of woodpeckers. They found that the bird often makes a pair of quick, preliminary taps against the wood before a hard strike, much like a carpenter lining up a nail with a hammer. When it makes the hard strike, it does so in an almost perfectly straight line, keeping its neck rigid. The result is a near absence of rotational forces and whiplash. The fact that woodpeckers are so careful to avoid rotating their heads during impact supports the claim that rotational forces are a major factor in traumatic brain injuries.

The researchers suggested several implications for football players, race car drivers, and others who wear protective helmets. One is that the helmet would give more protection if it extended down to the shoulders, like the metal helmets worn by medieval knights. The advice for situations in which people do not wear helmets: If you anticipate an automobile accident or similar trauma, tuck your chin to your chest and tighten your neck muscles.

A male hairy woodpecker.

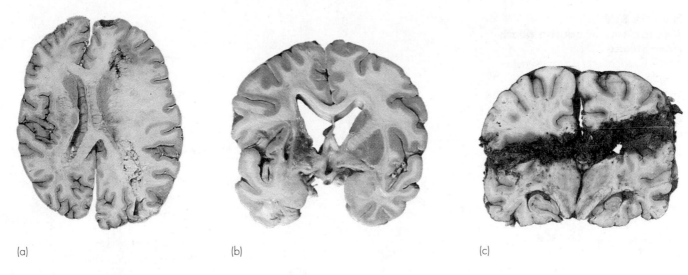

(a)   (b)   (c)

FIGURE **15.1**
Three damaged human brains
(**a**) Brain of a person who died immediately after a stroke. Note the swelling on the right side.
(**b**) Brain of a person who survived for a long time after a stroke. Note the cavities on the left side,
where many cells were lost. (**c**) Brain of a person who suffered a gunshot wound and died immediately.   Source: Courtesy of Dana Copeland.

If one of your relatives had a stroke at home and you called a hospital, what advice would you probably get? As recently as the 1980s, the staff would have been in no great hurry to see the patient, because they had little to offer anyway. They were likely to recommend keeping the patient warm and providing tranquilizers or similar medications to lower blood pressure for the next few days or weeks. We now know that those procedures actually made the condition worse. Today, it is possible to reduce the effects of a stroke if physicians intervene within one to three hours—perhaps as much as six, but the quicker the better.

Strokes kill neurons in two waves. First, cells in the immediate vicinity of the ischemia or hemorrhage die quickly. We still have little prospect of protecting those cells. Second, cells in the **penumbra** (Latin for *partial shadow*), the region that surrounds the immediate damage, are threatened and may die over the next few days (Ginsberg, 1995a; Hsu, Sik, Gallyas, Horváth, & Buzsáki, 1994; Jonas, 1995). With quick intervention, physicians may save those cells.

In ischemia, cells in the penumbra lose much but not all of their oxygen and glucose supplies. In hemorrhage, they are flooded with excess oxygen, calcium, and other blood products that would ordinarily enter very slowly. After either ischemia or hemorrhage, penumbra cells are invaded by waste products from the dead or dying cells in the area of direct damage. Potassium ions begin to accumulate outside neurons in the penumbra, because the sodium-potassium pump does not have as much energy as usual. **Edema** (accumulation of fluid) forms in the area because the blood-brain

barrier has broken down. The combination of potassium buildup and edema causes glia cells to dump much of the glutamate and other neurotransmitters they had been storing (Billups & Attwell, 1996; Ginsberg, 1995b). The excess glutamate overstimulates the neurons, making it even more difficult for their sodium-potassium pumps to keep pace. Sodium, calcium, and zinc ions gradually accumulate inside neurons, swelling the membrane (in some cases even bursting it) and interfering with normal chemical processes within the cell (Koh et al., 1996; Zinkland, Thompson, Salama, & Patel, 1992). As neurons die, glia cells proliferate, removing waste products and dead neurons. Figure 15.2 summarizes this process. The main point of this figure is that both ischemia and hemorrhage kill neurons by overstimulating them.

Researchers now know a number of ways to decrease cell death, and the main issue is to determine which methods are most effective and practical. One way is to use clot-busting drugs that restore blood flow as quickly as possible to the brain after ischemia (Barinaga, 1996). (Those drugs are, of course, useless after a hemorrhage.) Another method is to use drugs that block activity at glutamate synapses, increase it at inhibitory GABA synapses, or prevent calcium or zinc from entering neurons (Koh et al., 1996; Lubitz, Carter, Beenhakker, Lin, & Jacobson, 1995; Myseros & Bullock, 1995; Sharkey & Butcher, 1994). Nerve growth factor and other neurotrophins also minimize the loss of neurons, through unknown mechanisms (Barinaga, 1996; Choi-Lundberg et al., 1997; Levivier, Przedborski, Bencsics, & Kang, 1995). In animal studies, the most

FIGURE **15.2**
Mechanisms of neuron death after stroke
Procedures that can preserve neurons include removing the blood clot, blocking excitatory synapses, stimulating inhibitory synapses, blocking the flow of calcium and zinc, and cooling the brain.

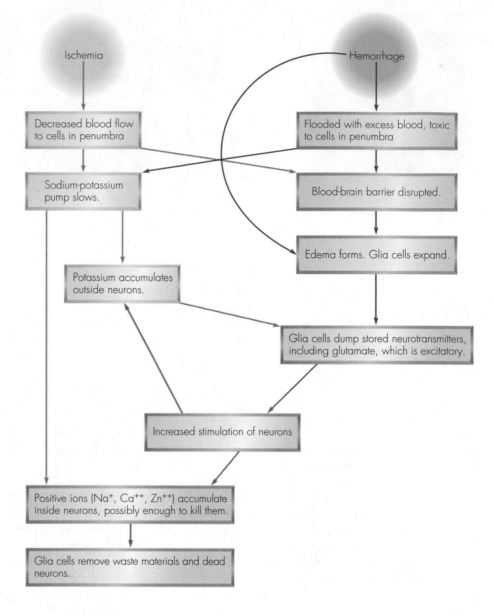

effective method found so far is to cool the brain. A cooled brain has less activity, lower energy needs, and less risk of overstimulation than does a brain at normal temperature. Protection of neurons is greatest if brain temperature is lowered from 37°C to 29°C, beginning within 30 minutes after ischemia and continuing for the next 24 hours (Barone, Feuerstein, & White, 1997; Colbourne & Corbett, 1995). The smaller, later, or briefer the decrease in temperature, the less benefit.

Assessment of Brain-Damaged Patients

Any study of recovery requires repeated measurements of the impaired behaviors. The results are useful not only for research purposes but also for planning a treat-

ment program and for identifying what a person with brain damage can and cannot do. (Can he or she return to work or school? Drive a car?)

Neuropsychologists have a wide variety of tests to assess abilities and disabilities. If they know someone's problem area from the start, they can choose tests accordingly. For example, they might concentrate on visual tests with one patient and language tests with another. In most cases, however, they start with a whole battery of tests to measure vision, hearing, manual dexterity, overall intelligence, language, memory, abstract thinking, and so forth (Lezak, 1995). A neuropsychologist also observes the person for signs of unusual impulsivity, either excessive or deficient emotional expression, inadequate social responsiveness, and other symptoms of impairment. Ideally, the neuropsychologist moves beyond identifying the person's weaknesses, trying to understand the reasons behind them. For example, two patients might have the same low score on a test of naming objects, one because of a language problem and the other because of perceptual problems (Delis, Kramer, Fridlund, & Kaplan, 1990). Additional tests help clarify the patient's abilities and limitations.

Any statement about how brain damage has impaired the person's behavior implies a comparison. Ideally, one would like to compare the person's behavior before and after the damage, but seldom if ever does a neuropsychologist have adequate data on previous behavior. A low test score might not indicate damage in a person who had never performed well; an apparently normal score might indicate damage in someone who had previously performed at a superior level. In many cases friends and relatives can provide useful information about previous performance. A neuropsychologist can also compare scores across tests. A pattern of scoring in the normal-to-high range on most tests and very badly on a few is usually a sign of damage.

A neuropsychologist is torn between competing goals. On the one hand, it is helpful to conduct as many tests as possible, to explore what the person can and cannot do, and why. On the other hand, a very long series of tests will fatigue, bore, or discourage most patients. Spreading the tests over two or more days helps, but even so, an alert psychologist notices when the patient is no longer alert, and halts the testing.

The Precarious Nature of Recovery

Someone with a sore foot may be able to walk just about normally under most conditions, but limp badly when carrying a heavy load uphill. Similarly, those who have recovered from brain damage vary enormously in their performance from one time to another (Stuss, Pogue, Buckle, & Bondar, 1994). They deteriorate visibly after a little fatigue or stress that would hardly affect a normal person.

How Stress Impairs Recovered Behavior

Someone whose behavior recovers after a stroke may deteriorate again, temporarily, after a couple of beers or a tiring day, or toward the end of a long testing session (Fleet & Heilman, 1986). The behavior of brain-damaged rats also deteriorates under stress or fatigue. In a cool room, both a normal rat and a rat that has recovered from lateral hypothalamic damage increase their food intake. (Digesting food generates body heat.) If the room gets colder, the normal rat eats even more, but the brain damaged rat may fail to eat altogether, especially if only dry food and water are available (Snyder & Stricker, 1985).

Immediate effect: Sensory neglect. Rat ignores sensory stimulus on the opposite side of the body.

Later effect: Sensory extinction. Rat responds first on the normal side. It responds to the string on the opposite side later.

Still later: Rat responds to both sides equally *unless* the environment is changed or the rat is stressed.

FIGURE **15.3**
Recovery from damage to one hemisphere

After damage to one side of the cerebral cortex, especially the parietal cortex, both humans and rats pay less attention to stimuli on the opposite side of the body, and may ignore it altogether. This reaction is known as **sensory neglect** (see Figure 15.3). After partial recovery, they respond to stimuli on both sides of the body, but they respond first to the side opposite the normal hemisphere. People at this stage of recovery can describe what they see on the weaker side of the body only if they see nothing on the normal side; if they see something on both sides, they describe only what they see on the normal side (Baylis, Driver, & Rafal, 1993). This tendency for a stimulus on the normal side to overwhelm a stimulus on the impaired side is known as **sensory extinction.**

Eventually, both people and rats respond to stimuli on both sides equally. For example, a rat with strings tied to both forelimbs works equally hard at trying to remove each of them. However, under mild stress or after a slight change in the environment, the rat loses its recovered behavior. If the experimenter simply turns on the lights or opens the cage door, the rat temporarily goes back to paying more attention to the normal side (Schallert & Whishaw, 1984). Presumably, humans also revert to sensory neglect or sensory extinction under conditions of stress or environmental changes that would scarcely affect a normal individual.

The Loss of Recovered Behavior in Old Age

A recovered rat also deteriorates more in old age than normal rats do. In rats, as in humans, a certain number of neurons die throughout life, especially in old age. This natural loss can magnify the effects of a brain lesion long after an individual seems to have recovered from it. By the time a rat that has recovered from lateral hypothalamic damage is 2 years old (old age for a rat), it begins to lose its recovered feeding and drinking behaviors and its responsiveness to sensory stimuli.

Eventually, the rat returns to a condition approximating its behavior just after the lesion (Schallert, 1983).

In one study, investigators compared World War II veterans who suffered brain injuries during the war with veterans who suffered other kinds of injuries. In the 1950s, about ten years after the war, while they were still young men, the brain-injured veterans scored almost as high as the others on the Army General Classification Test (a kind of IQ test). But by the 1980s, as they were approaching retirement age, the brain-injured men showed a significant decline in performance, while the other men were performing about the same as they had 30 years earlier (Corkin, Rosen, Sullivan, & Clegg, 1989). (See Figure 15.4.)

Imagine how this principle might apply to a degenerative condition, such as Parkinson's disease. A young person might suffer many mild traumas to the brain, either from blows to the head or exposure to toxins. Each injury itself is minor, the young brain can compensate, and no symptoms are apparent at the time. Many years later, however, the loss of neurons that naturally occurs in old age may combine with the previously hidden effects of early damage to produce major deficits (Schallert, 1983). The degenerative condition unmasks damage that had occurred much earlier.

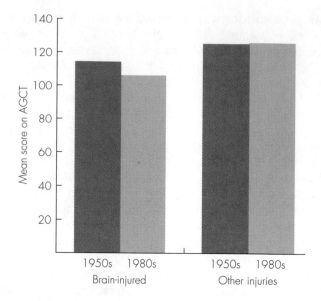

FIGURE **15.4**

Deterioration of brain-injured men in old age

Brain-injured World War II veterans performed slightly below other veterans on IQ tests in the 1950s; they deteriorated significantly over the next 30 years, whereas the other veterans did not. Source: Data from Corkin, Rosen, Sullivan, & Clegg, 1989.

Adjustments and Potential Recovery After Brain Damage

How can someone recover lost behaviors after brain damage, given that the brain cannot replace the lost neurons? A simple assumption is that another part of the brain takes over the functions of the damaged area, but this assumption is valid only in a limited sense. When someone who has injured her left leg walks on her right leg and crutches, the arms and right leg are simply performing their own functions in a new way, not really taking over the function of the damaged leg. Similarly, after damage to the motor cortex in one hemisphere, the motor cortex of the remaining hemisphere will develop some control of the ipsilateral limb (Chollet & Weiller, 1994). It is not really duplicating the function of the damaged area; it is merely making greater use of the weak ipsilateral pathways that already existed.

Structural changes in the surviving neurons can partially restore lost functions, or the person can learn new ways to solve old problems. Let us consider some of the mechanisms of recovery.

Learned Adjustments in Behavior

Much of the recovery that takes place after brain damage is learned; the brain-damaged individual makes better use of unimpaired abilities. For example, some-

one who has lost vision in all but the center of the visual field may learn to move his or her head back and forth to compensate for the loss in peripheral vision (Marshall, 1985).

A brain-damaged person or animal may also learn to use abilities that at first appeared to be lost but actually were just impaired. For example, it is possible to eliminate most of the sensory information from a leg by cutting the sensory nerves from that leg to the spinal cord (see Figure 15.5). The animal loses sensation from the affected body parts, but it can still control the muscles. Such a limb is referred to as **deafferented.** Although the animal *can* still control the muscles of the deafferented limb, it seldom uses them. For example, monkeys with a deafferented limb do not spontaneously use it for walking, picking up objects, or any other voluntary behaviors (Taub & Berman, 1968). Investigators initially assumed that the monkey could not use the limb because of the lack of sensory feedback. In a later experiment, however, they cut the afferent nerves of both forelimbs; despite this more extensive damage, the monkey regained use of both deafferented limbs. It could walk moderately fast, climb upward or sideways on the walls of metal cages, and even pick up a raisin between its thumb and forefinger. Apparently, a monkey fails to use one deafferented forelimb only because walking on three limbs is easier than moving the impaired limb. When both limbs are deafferented, the monkey is forced to use both.

Similarly, many people with brain damage find it easier, especially at first, to struggle along without even

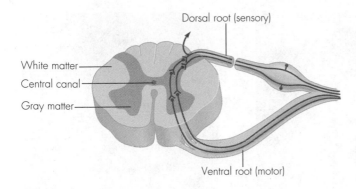

FIGURE 15.5
Cross section through the spinal cord
A cut through the dorsal root (as shown) deprives the animal of touch sensations from part of the body, while leaving the motor nerves intact.

trying to use an impaired ability. Many of them are capable of more than they are doing and more than they realize they can do. Therapy for brain-damaged people sometimes focuses on showing them how much they already can do and encouraging them to practice those skills.

Diaschisis

Behavioral deficit after brain damage reflects more than just the loss of cells. Ordinarily, axons from each neuron provide stimulation that helps to keep other neurons active. When a neuron dies, the neurons that depended on it for input become less active. For example, after damage to an area in the right hemisphere, the corresponding area in the left hemisphere becomes temporarily less active also (Perani, Vallar, Paulesu, Alberoni, & Fazio, 1993). **Diaschisis** (di-AS-ki-sis, from a Greek term meaning *to shock throughout*) refers to the decreased activity of surviving neurons after other neurons are damaged (Feeney & Baron, 1986).

If diaschisis is an important contributor to behavioral deficits following brain damage, then stimulant drugs should promote recovery. In a series of experiments, D. M. Feeney and colleagues measured the behavioral effects of cortical damage in rats and cats. Depending on the location of the damage, the animals showed impairments in either coordinated movement or depth perception. Injecting amphetamine (which increases dopamine and norepinephrine activity) significantly enhanced the behaviors, and animals that practiced the behaviors under the influence of amphetamine showed long-lasting benefits. Injecting the drug haloperidol (which blocks most of the same synapses) impaired behavioral recovery (Feeney & Sutton, 1988; Feeney, Sutton, Boyeson, Hovda, & Dail, 1985; Hovda & Feeney, 1989; Sutton, Hovda, & Feeney, 1989). Other experimenters have found that daily use of benzodi-

azepine tranquilizers, such as diazepam (Valium), for the first three weeks after brain damage can completely prevent behavioral recovery (Schallert, Hernandez, & Barth, 1986).

These results have implications for the treatment of stroke patients. People who have just suffered strokes or other brain damage are often given various kinds of tranquilizers to control blood pressure, but these probably also interfere with behavioral recovery (Boyeson, Callister, & Cavazos, 1992). The research on diaschisis indicates that physicians should use such drugs as sparingly as possible.

The Regrowth of Axons

Although a destroyed cell body cannot be replaced, damaged axons do grow back under certain circumstances. A neuron of the peripheral nervous system has its cell body in the spinal cord and an axon that extends into the periphery. When such an axon is crushed, the degenerated portion grows back toward the periphery at a rate of about 1 mm per day. If it is myelinated, the regenerating axon follows the myelin path back to its original target. If the axon was cut instead of crushed, the myelin on the two sides of the cut may not line up correctly, and the regenerating axon may not have a sure path to follow. A sensory nerve finds its way to a sensory receptor, and a motor nerve finds its way to a muscle (Brushart, 1993); still, a motor nerve may attach to the wrong muscle, as Figure 15.6 illustrates.

Within the mature mammalian brain or spinal cord, damaged axons regenerate over insignificant distances, if at all. Therefore, paralysis caused by spinal cord injury is permanent. However, after a cut through the optic nerve or the spinal cord of certain fish species, enough axons regenerate across the cut to restore fairly normal functioning (Bernstein & Gelderd, 1970; Rovainen, 1976; Scherer, 1986; Selzer, 1978).

Why do damaged axons regenerate in the central and peripheral nervous systems of fish and in the peripheral nervous system of mammals, but not in the central nervous system of mammals? Researchers have considered a number of possibilities. One is that a cut through the adult mammalian spinal cord results in too much scar tissue. A number of attempts have been made to inhibit the formation of scar tissue, but none has led to any reliable recovery from spinal-cord damage (e.g., McMasters, 1962).

Another part of the explanation is chemical. Adult mammalian axons do not under any circumstances grow as readily as fetal axons (Rosario, Aldskogius, Carlstedt, & Sidman, 1993). Furthermore, in adult mammals, both the central and peripheral nervous systems form proteins that inhibit axon growth. After damage to a peripheral nerve, the glia cells in the periphery manufacture chemicals that overcome the usual

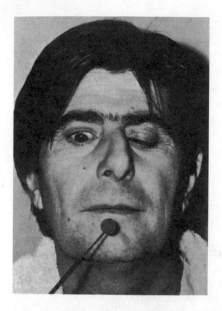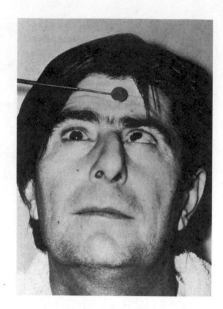

FIGURE **15.6**

What can happen if damaged axons regenerate to incorrect muscles

Damaged axons to the muscles of the patient's right eye regenerated but attached incorrectly. When he looks down, his right eyelid opens wide instead of closing like the other eyelid. His eye movements are frequently misaimed, and he has trouble moving his right eye upward or to the left.
Source: Thomas, 1988.

growth-inhibiting proteins, but glia cells in the CNS do not (Bähr & Przyrembel, 1995). In one study, investigators found that injecting an antibody to the growth-inhibiting proteins caused axons to grow across a subtotal cut through a rat's spinal cord. As a result, the rats regained partial control of their hindlegs (Bregman et al., 1995). Such chemicals may someday help humans recover from *hemiplegia*, one-sided paralysis caused by a cut partway through the spinal cord. (When the human spinal cord is cut all the way through, the separated halves pull so far apart that no axon could bridge the gap.)

Sprouting

After damage to a set of axons, the cells that had received input from them react to the loss by secreting chemicals such as nerve growth factor, which we encountered back in Chapter 5 (Van der Zee, Fawcett, & Diamond, 1992). Those chemicals induce nearby uninjured axons to form new branches, or **collateral sprouts,** that attach to the vacant synapses (see Figure 15.7). Gradually, over several months, the sprouts fill in most of the vacated synapses. For example, after loss of about half of the cells in a rat's *locus coeruleus* (a hindbrain area), the brain shows an enormous drop in the number of synapses that the locus coeruleus supplies to the forebrain. Over the next six months, the surviving axons sprout enough to restore almost completely normal input (Fritschy & Grzanna, 1992).

Sprouting is probably a normal condition, not one that occurs only in response to brain damage (Cotman & Nieto-Sampedro, 1982). The brain is constantly losing old synapses and sprouting new ones to replace them.

In some cases, when one axon is removed, an unrelated axon sprouts to occupy the vacant synapse. This kind of sprouting is probably either useless or harmful, because it is providing inappropriate information. In other cases, however, the sprouts come from closely related axons. For example, after damage to the connections to the left hippocampus from the left entorhinal cortex (the nearest part of the cerebral cortex), sprouts develop from the right entorhinal cortex. Their development takes a few days, about the same time as recovery of the behaviors (Kolb, 1995). Furthermore, after behavioral recovery has occurred, damage to the sprouted path from the right entorhinal cortex greatly impairs the behavior (Ramirez, McQuilkin, Carrigan, MacDonald, & Kelley, 1996). This result is probably the strongest evidence for the beneficial effects of sprouting. Furthermore, recovery from brain damage is enhanced by **gangliosides** (a class of glycolipids—that is, combined carbohydrate and fat molecules), which enhance collateral sprouting (Sabel, Slavin, & Stein, 1984).

Denervation Supersensitivity

A postsynaptic cell that is deprived of synaptic input for a long time becomes more sensitive to the neurotrans-

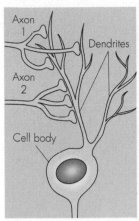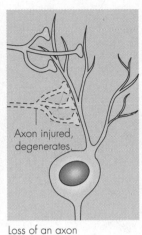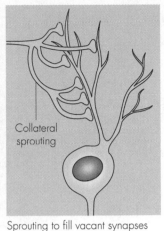

FIGURE **15.7**
Collateral sprouting

At first | Loss of an axon | Sprouting to fill vacant synapses

mitter. For example, a normal muscle cell responds to the neurotransmitter acetylcholine only at the neuromuscular junction. If the axon is cut, or if it is inactive for days, the muscle cell builds additional receptors, becoming sensitive to acetylcholine over a wider area of its surface (Johns & Thesleff, 1961; Levitt-Gilmour & Salpeter, 1986). The same process occurs in neurons. Heightened sensitivity to a neurotransmitter after the destruction of incoming axons is known as **denervation supersensitivity** (Glick, 1974). Heightened sensitivity as a result of inactivity by incoming axons is called **disuse supersensitivity.** The mechanisms of supersensitivity are not yet well understood. A neuron deprived of its usual stimulation increases its number of

receptors (Kostrzewa, 1995), but not in proportion to the amount of supersensitivity (LaHoste & Marshall, 1993). Evidently, supersensitivity depends on additional changes within the cell.

One way to demonstrate denervation supersensitivity is to remove dopamine synapses selectively by injecting **6-hydroxydopamine (6-OHDA)** into relevant parts of the brain. Because 6-OHDA is chemically similar to dopamine and norepinephrine, the neurons that release these neurotransmitters recognize 6-OHDA, absorb it, and die after it is oxidized into toxic chemicals. As Figure 15.8 shows, after an injection of 6-OHDA to one side of the brain, postsynaptic cells react to the decreased dopamine input by increasing their number of

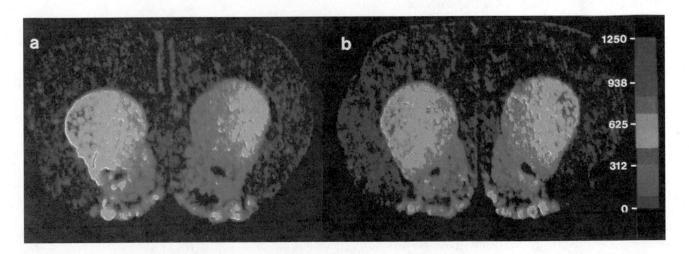

FIGURE **15.8**
Responses of dopamine receptors to decreased input
In these autoradiography slides, red indicates the highest amount of radioactive binding, followed by yellow, green, and blue. **(a)** An injection of 6-OHDA destroyed dopamine axons in the hemisphere on the left. In response, that hemisphere developed an increased number of D_2 receptors, as indicated by increased binding of a radioactive drug that attaches to those receptors. **(b)** Rats in another group also received a 6-OHDA lesion to one hemisphere, but they then received daily injections of a drug that blocks D_2 receptors. Here, D_2 receptors increased equally in both hemispheres.   Source: LaHoste & Marshall, 1989.

FIGURE **15.9**
Demonstration of denervation supersensitivity
Injecting 6-OHDA destroys axons that release dopamine on one side of the brain. Later, amphetamine stimulates only the intact side of the brain because it cannot cause axons to release dopamine on the damaged side. Apomorphine stimulates the damaged side more strongly because it directly stimulates dopamine receptors, which have become supersensitive on that side.   Source: Data from Marshall, Drew, & Neve, 1983.

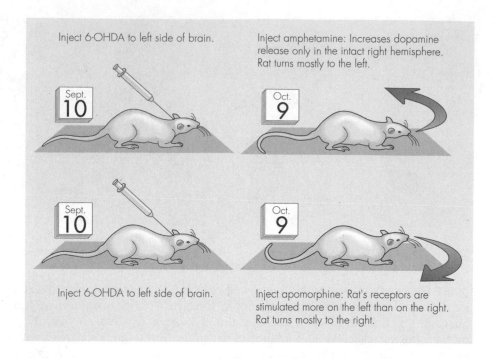

Inject 6-OHDA to left side of brain.

Inject amphetamine: Increases dopamine release only in the intact right hemisphere. Rat turns mostly to the left.

Inject 6-OHDA to left side of brain.

Inject apomorphine: Rat's receptors are stimulated more on the left than on the right. Rat turns mostly to the right.

dopamine receptors on that side (LaHoste & Marshall, 1989).

Such changes contribute to recovery by increasing neurons' responses to the limited amount of dopamine that remains. In one study, experimenters injected 6-OHDA on one side of rats' brains, damaging dopamine neurons on that side only (see Figure 15.9). They waited weeks for postsynaptic neurons to become supersensitive to dopamine. Then they injected the rats with either amphetamine or apomorphine. Amphetamine causes dopamine-containing axons to release more neurotransmitter. Because one side of the brain was lacking dopamine axons, the amphetamine stimulated only the intact side of the brain, causing the rats to turn in one direction. (With stimulation in the right hemisphere, the animal is more responsive to stimuli on the left, so it circles to the left toward the damaged side.) **Apomorphine** is a morphine derivative that directly stimulates dopamine receptors. Because of denervation supersensitivity, apomorphine strongly stimulates the damaged side of the brain, so rats are more responsive to stimuli on the right, and therefore turn *away from* the damaged side of the brain (Marshall, Drew, & Neve, 1983). These results (shown in Figure 15.9) indicate that the denervated side of the brain has become supersensitive to dopamine and to drugs that stimulate dopamine receptors.

Denervation supersensitivity helps explain why people can lose most of their dopamine-containing axons from the substantia nigra before they begin to show symptoms of Parkinson's disease (Zigmond, Abercrombie, Berger, Grace, & Stricker, 1990). After some of the axons are lost, the remaining axons compensate by increasing their release of dopamine. After still further loss, the receptors on the postsynaptic membrane develop denervation supersensitivity. Such compensation can delay the symptoms of Parkinson's disease until someone has lost more than 75 percent of the original axons, sometimes as much as 80 or 90 percent.

Reorganization of Sensory Representations

As we saw in Chapter 5, experiences can modify the connections within the cerebral cortex. Recall that after someone has played a stringed instrument for many years, the somatosensory cortex has an enlarged representation of the fingers of the left hand. On a smaller scale, after monkeys repeatedly pick up a small object with their fingers, the motor cortex representation of those fingers increases, slightly and temporarily (Nudo, Milliken, Jenkins, & Merzenich, 1996). In Braille proofreaders, the brain representation of the index finger is measurably larger at the end of a workday than at the same time on a vacation day (Pascual-Leone, Wasserman, Sadato, & Hallett, 1995). These changes may reflect collateral sprouting, but given their rapid speed, they are more likely to represent increased responses by the postsynaptic neurons. Sensory axons produce strong effects on some neurons and subthreshold effects on neighboring neurons, so a mere adjustment of synaptic strength could alter the brain representation of a sensory signal (Das & Gilbert, 1995).

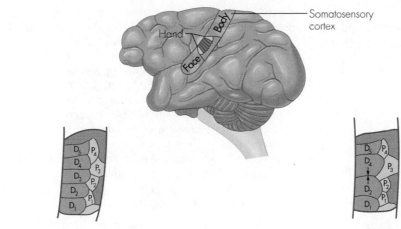

FIGURE **15.10**
Somatosensory cortex of a monkey after a finger amputation
Note that the cortical area previously responsive to the third finger (D$_3$) becomes responsive to the second and fourth fingers (D$_2$ and D$_4$) and part of the palm (P$_3$).   Source: From Kaas, Merzenich, & Killackey, 1983.

(a) Normal (before amputation)   (b) After amputation of 3rd digit

Even greater and more permanent synaptic reorganization can occur after permanent loss of sensation from a body part. For example, Figure 15.10a shows the representation in the primary somatosensory cortex of touch stimuli of the hand of a normal monkey. In one study, experimenters amputated finger 3 in an owl monkey. The cortical cells that used to respond to information from that finger now had no input. As time passed, more and more of them became responsive to finger 2, finger 4, or part of the palm, until eventually the cortex had the pattern of responsiveness we see in Figure 15.10b (Kaas, Merzenich, & Killackey, 1983; Merzenich et al., 1984).

For many years, neuroscientists assumed that cortical reorganization was limited to displacements of an axon's representation over about 1 mm or so—a realistic estimate of how far a cortical axon's branches might extend. Then came a surprise. Investigators recorded from the cerebral cortices of monkeys that had each had an entire limb deafferented 12 years previously, and found that the large stretch of cortex previously responsive to that limb had become responsive to the face (Pons et al., 1991). At first, this result was stunning and puzzling, as it was implausible that axons in the face area of the cortex had grown sprouts to a cortical area 10 to 14 mm away. Later researchers found that after amputation of a hand or limb, axons form sprouts not only in the cortex but also in the spinal cord and brain stem (Florence & Kaas, 1995). Cortical cell responsiveness reflects all the changes in the sensory path, not just in the cortex itself.

Are the changes in the cerebral cortex after an amputation beneficial? Probably not. People who have substantial cortical changes after an amputation generally experience painful phantom-limb sensations (Flor et al., 1995). The amputation-induced changes are probably just an extreme and detrimental aspect of what is ordinarily a beneficial process—the slight readjustments of brain representation that accord with use and disuse of body parts.

Table 15.1 summarizes the mechanisms we have discussed that may contribute to recovery from brain damage.

TABLE **15.1**

Mechanisms of Recovery from Brain Damage

1. Learned adjustments in behavior
2. Return to normal functioning by undamaged neurons: reduction of diaschisis
3. Regeneration of damaged axons (occurs in the central and peripheral nervous systems of fish; occurs only in the peripheral nervous systems of mature mammals)
4. Changes at synapses in the brain: sprouting and denervation supersensitivity

IN **CLOSING**

Brain Damage and Recovery

In contrast to the multiple ways we have of replacing or temporarily compensating for the loss of blood or skin cells, our mechanisms of recovering from nervous-system damage are strikingly meagre and unreliable. Even the responses that do occur, such as collateral sprouting of axons or reorganization of sensory representations, are helpful in some cases and harmful in others. It is tempting to speculate that we did not evolve many mechanisms of recovery from brain damage because, through most of our evolutionary history, a brain-damaged individual was not likely to survive long enough to recover. Today, modern medicine keeps brain- or spinal-cord-damaged people alive for many years, and we need continuing research on how to improve artificially the modest recovery mechanisms that we have.

Summary

1. Strokes, a common cause of brain damage in old age, kill neurons by overstimulation. A sudden blow to the head is a more common cause of brain damage in young people. (p. 402)

2. Neuropsychologists use a variety of tests to determine what a brain-damaged person can and cannot do, and why. (p. 402)

3. People and animals that have recovered from brain damage are more likely than normal individuals to deteriorate under stress or in old age. (p. 403)

4. Much recovery from brain damage does not require structural changes in the brain; it depends on learned changes in behavior to take advantage of the skills that remain, even if they are impaired. (p. 404)

5. After brain damage, neurons that are remote from the site of damage may become inactive because they receive less input than usual. Behavioral recovery from brain damage depends partly on increased activity by these remote neurons; stimulant drugs can facilitate activity in surviving cells. (p. 405)

6. A cut axon may regenerate in the peripheral nervous system of a mammal and in either the central or peripheral nervous system of certain fish. One reason for this difference is that the adult mammalian nervous system produces proteins that inhibit the growth of axons. (p. 405)

7. When one set of axons dies, neighboring axons may, under certain conditions, sprout new branches to innervate the vacant synapses. (p. 406)

8. If many of the axons innervating a postsynaptic neuron die or become inactive, the neuron may become responsive to other axons. (p. 407)

Review Questions

1. In what way is ischemia different from hemorrhage? In what ways do they produce similar effects on the brain? (p. 400)

2. Besides closed-head injury and stroke, what are some other causes of human brain damage? (p. 400)

3. If a patient's level of performance before brain damage is unknown, what pattern of test results can nevertheless indicate probable brain damage? (p. 403)

4. In what ways is a person or animal that has recovered from brain damage different from one that has never suffered brain damage? (p. 403)

5. What shows that brain-damaged animals are sometimes capable of behaviors that they do not spontaneously engage in? Describe one example. (p. 404)

6. The drug haloperidol is given to many patients suffering from a variety of psychological disorders. Why would it be unwise to administer haloperidol to a recent stroke victim? (p. 405)

7. Explain why axons may fail to regenerate across a cut through the mammalian spinal cord. (p. 405)

8. What is the evidence that collateral sprouting sometimes assists recovery from brain damage? (p. 406)

9. What conditions produce denervation supersensitivity? (p. 407)

10. When the sensory cortex reorganizes its connections following loss of sensation from a finger, what happens to the sensations from neighboring parts of the hand? (p. 409)

Thought Question

1. Ordinarily, patients with Parkinson's disease move very slowly, if at all. However, during an emergency (such as a fire in the building), they sometimes move rapidly and vigorously. Suggest a possible explanation.

Suggestions for Further Reading

DeMille, A. (1981). *Reprieve: A memoir.* Garden City, NY: Doubleday. A stroke victim's own account of her stroke and recovery from it, with interpolated commentary by a neurologist, Fred Plum.

Kolb, B. (1995). *Brain plasticity and behavior.* Mahwah, NJ: Erlbaum. Excellent discussion of research on what recovers after brain damage, and what does not, and why, and how.

Terms

stroke (or **cerebrovascular accident**)   brain damage caused when a blood clot or other obstruction interrupts the flow of blood to a brain area (p. 400)

ischemia   local insufficiency of blood because a blood clot or other obstruction has closed an artery (p. 400)

hemorrhage   excess blood flow to an area because an artery has ruptured (p. 400)

penumbra   an area of endangered cells surrounding an area of primary damage (p. 401)

edema   accumulation of fluid (p. 401)

sensory neglect   ignoring stimuli on the side of the body opposite an area of brain damage (p. 403)

sensory extinction   tendency to respond first and more strongly to stimuli on the same side of the body as brain damage, as opposed to stimuli on the opposite side (p. 403)

deafferent   having had the sensory nerves removed from a body part (p. 404)

diaschisis decreased activity of surviving neurons after other neurons are damaged (p. 405)

collateral sprout newly formed branch from an uninjured axon that attaches to a synapse vacated when another axon was destroyed (p. 406)

ganglioside molecule composed of carbohydrates and fats (p. 406)

denervation supersensitivity increased sensitivity of a postsynaptic cell after removal of an axon that formerly innervated it (p. 407)

disuse supersensitivity increased sensitivity of a postsynaptic cell after a period of decreased input by incoming axons (p. 407)

6-hydroxydopamine (6-OHDA) chemical that destroys neurons that release dopamine or norepinephrine (p. 407)

apomorphine morphine derivative that stimulates dopamine receptors (p. 408)

Factors Influencing Recovery

Why do two individuals with apparently the same brain damage differ in the extent of their recovery? Sometimes it is because they are of different ages or because the injuries developed at different rates. In other cases, different therapies produce different outcomes.

Effects of Age

According to the **Kennard principle,** named after Margaret Kennard, who first stated it (Kennard, 1938), recovery will be more extensive after brain damage early in life than after similar damage later. For example, a 2-year-old who loses the entire left hemisphere will probably develop nearly normal speech, whereas an older child with similar damage will regain less speech, and an adult will recover still less (Satz, Strauss, & Whitaker, 1990).

The problem with the Kennard principle is that it does not apply to very many cases. The effects of early brain damage may be greater than, less than, or the same as the effects of later damage, depending on the location of the damage and the tested behavior (Kolb, 1995). In some cases, an infant recovers better than an adult from one type of lesion, but neither recovers at all from a slightly larger lesion or a lesion in a slightly different location (Málková, Mishkin, & Bachevalier, 1995; Shupert, Cornwell, & Payne, 1993). In other cases, especially if the damage occurs prenatally or in the first half-year of life, infants suffer far more severe consequences than adults. Poor nutrition or exposure to alcohol or other drugs can disrupt brain development in infancy far more drastically than in an older child or adult (O'Leary & Boll, 1984). We can identify several possible reasons why brain damage produces different results at different ages.

Altered Connections of Spared Neurons

Infant neurons have greater potential than adult neurons do for collateral sprouting of axons (McWilliams & Lynch, 1983, 1984), dendritic branching (Kolb & Gibb, 1993), and redirection of axons whose normal target is unavailable. For example, suppose that the superior colliculus on the left side of an infant hamster's brain is damaged before the optic nerve has reached it. When the optic nerve does reach the damaged area, its axons cross through it and attach to the superior colliculus on the right side instead (see Figure 15.11). The hamster then shows some spatial orientation toward what it sees in the right visual field. Unfortunately, it orients in the wrong direction. That is, a hamster that sees something on the right turns to the left. It is as if the right superior colliculus interprets all input as coming from the left visual field as usual (Schneider & Jhaveri, 1974). This example shows that early brain damage can lead to a different pattern of connections than adult damage, and not necessarily a better pattern.

Effects on Still Developing Neurons

In normal development, the immature brain produces many more neurons and synapses than will survive to adulthood, as we saw in Chapter 5. As development proceeds, many extra neurons and connections are lost. Early damage to one set of neurons can affect the survival and connections of other immature neurons.

For example, after one hemisphere of an infant rat brain is removed, the other hemisphere increases in thickness (Kolb, Sutherland, & Whishaw, 1983). Evidently, neurons of one hemisphere compete with neurons of the other hemisphere; if one hemisphere is damaged, a greater percentage of cells in the opposite hemisphere can survive. In contrast, after removal of

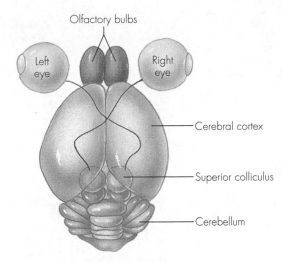

Normal pattern of innervation of hamster superior colliculus

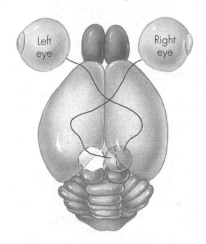

Pattern of innervation if left superior colliculus is destroyed in newborn

FIGURE **15.11**
Axon growth after infant brain damage
If the superior colliculus of a newborn hamster is destroyed on one side, the axons that normally innervate the damaged side go to the opposite superior colliculus.   Source: Based on results of Schneider & Jhaveri, 1974.

the anterior portion of the infant cortex, the posterior portion develops less than normal (Kolb & Holmes, 1983). Apparently, the survival of neurons in the posterior cortex requires interaction with neurons in the anterior cortex, so damage to the anterior cortex affects the behavior of infant rats more than it does the behavior of adults.

Here is another example of early damage producing either excellent recovery or severe deficits, depending on its location. Patricia Goldman, studying infant monkeys, found that damage to the **orbital frontal cortex** (an anterior area of the prefrontal cortex) produces deficits on the delayed alternation task, which requires

alternating between choosing an object on the left and choosing an object on the right. This deficit is quite clear at age 1 year; however, by age 2 years, the behavior improves considerably. Monkeys suffering the same brain damage at a later age show far less recovery (Goldman, 1976; Miller, Goldman, & Rosvold, 1973). Evidently, early damage to the orbital frontal cortex prompts later developing areas to change their organization in a way that compensates for the damage.

In contrast, damage to the **dorsolateral prefrontal cortex** of an infant monkey produces at first only a moderate deficit on the delayed alternation task. One year after the injury, it performs surprisingly well, almost as well as a normal 1-year-old monkey. When tested two years after the lesion, however, the brain-damaged monkey shows clear behavioral deficits (Goldman, 1971). That is, the behavioral deficit actually increases over time. The apparent explanation rests on the fact that the dorsolateral prefrontal cortex is slow to mature. The infant lesion produces little effect by age 1 year because a healthy dorsolateral prefrontal cortex does not do much at that age. But by age 2 years, when that area should start assuming some important functions, the damage begins to make a difference. Figure 15.12 summarizes these results. We shall return to this point in Chapter 16: Some investigators believe that schizophrenia is associated with early damage to the dorsolateral prefrontal cortex, but that because of the slow maturation of this area, the effects do not become fully evident until adolescence or early adulthood.

Slow-Onset and Rapid-Onset Lesions

A monkey suffers permanent loss of fine movements after sudden damage to the motor cortex on both sides of its brain. However, if the damage occurs in several stages, with a couple of weeks to recover from one small brain injury before the next one occurs, the monkey may continue to walk and to carry on other activities even after massive cumulative damage to the cortex (Travis & Woolsey, 1956). This phenomenon, called the **serial-lesion effect,** occurs after some kinds of brain damage and not others. Part of the explanation is that collateral sprouting is more extensive after a series of small lesions than after one large lesion (Ramirez et al., 1996). Perhaps a few normal connections that survive after a partial lesion guide the development of the sprouts, or perhaps the normal connections sustain the healthy functioning of the postsynaptic neurons.

Another part of the explanation for the serial-lesion effect is that during gradual damage an individual can learn better ways of using the surviving abilities. For

FIGURE **15.12**
Delayed effects of brain damage in infant monkeys
After damage to the dorsolateral prefrontal cortex, monkeys seem relatively unimpaired at age 1 year but are more severely impaired later, when this area ordinarily matures. After damage to the orbital frontal cortex, monkeys show a clear behavioral impairment at first but substantial recovery later.   Source: Based on Goldman, 1976.

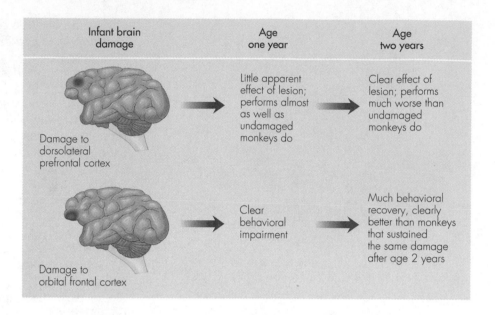

example, in one experiment rats with bilateral damage to their somatosensory and motor cortex displayed a variety of sensory and motor impairments, from which they recovered only slightly. After unilateral damage to the same areas, they displayed unilateral impairments from which they substantially recovered—but only if they were allowed to practice the behaviors. If they then sustained damage on the opposite side of the brain, the behaviors that recovered after the first damage remained intact (deCastro & Zrull, 1988). Evidently, the rats recovered from the first damage largely through a learning process. (Indeed, collateral sprouting occurs much more readily in animals that have relevant experiences during the delays between operations, so collateral sprouting and new learning may turn out to be different names for the same thing.)

Therapies

After someone suffers brain damage, physicians, physical therapists, and others try to help the person recover. Although therapy today consists almost entirely of supervised practice of the impaired behaviors, direct brain interventions may become possible.

Behavioral Interventions

You may fail to find a book that you know the library used to have, either because the book is lost or because the library has lost its record of the book's location. Similarly, brain-damaged people and animals may seem to have forgotten a particular skill, either because they have actually lost it or because they cannot find it. Therapists help brain-damaged people find their lost skills or learn to use their remaining abilities more effectively. For example, some people with frontal-lobe damage behave in socially inappropriate ways, using obscene language, failing to wash themselves, or making lewd overtures to strangers. Therapists may provide positive reinforcement for polite speech, good grooming, and self-restraint. The brain-damaged people gradually recover the social skills that they appeared to have lost (McGlynn, 1990).

Similarly, a brain-damaged animal that seems to have forgotten a learned skill may still retain it in some hidden manner. After damage to its visual cortex, a rat that had previously learned to approach a white card instead of a black card for food chose randomly between the two cards. Had the rat forgotten the discrimination completely? Evidently not, because it could much more easily relearn to approach the white card than it could learn to approach the black card (LeVere & Morlock, 1973). Apparently, some of the original learning survived the brain damage. (See Figure 15.13.)

Thomas LeVere (1975) proposed that such a lesion does not destroy the memory engram but merely impairs the rat's ability to find it. When the rat reacquires the skill, it is actually relocating or reaccessing the original memory. Moreover, the reaccessing process is not impaired by a drug that greatly impedes the learning of new tasks (Davis & LeVere, 1979).

Similarly, humans who have suffered brain damage may have trouble accessing certain skills and memories. Just as a monkey that has no sensation in one arm may try to get by without using it, a person who has an impaired sensory system may try to do without it

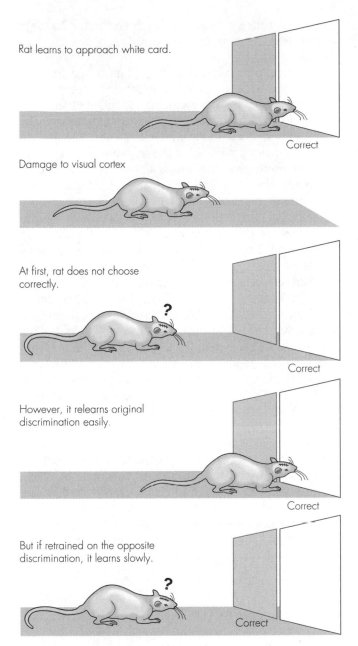

Rat learns to approach white card.

Correct

Damage to visual cortex

At first, rat does not choose correctly.

?

Correct

However, it relearns original discrimination easily.

Correct

But if retrained on the opposite discrimination, it learns slowly.

?

Correct

FIGURE 15.13
Memory impairment after cortical damage
Brain damage impairs retrieval of a memory but does not destroy it completely.   Source: Based on LeVere & Morlock, 1973.

(LeVere, 1980). The task of physical therapists, occupational therapists, and speech therapists is to prod brain-damaged patients into practicing their impaired skills instead of ignoring them.

In an experiment that supports this approach to therapy, N. D. LeVere and T. E. LeVere (1982) trained rats with visual-cortex lesions on a discrimination task that included both brightness and tactile cues. For one group of rats, the brightness and tactile stimuli were redundant; the rats could solve the problem by responding to either stimulus. This group solved the task rapidly but paid attention only to the tactile stimuli. If they were presented with only brightness stimuli, they responded randomly. For a second group of rats, the tactile stimuli were irrelevant; they could solve the problem only on the basis of brightness. This group took much longer than normal rats to solve the problem because their attention to the tactile stimuli distracted them from the relevant visual cues, but they did eventually solve it. In short, rats with visual-cortex lesions can learn about visual stimuli, but they are impaired if other stimuli are available (Davis & LeVere, 1982). To help humans with similar brain damage, therapists should either simplify the problem by removing distracting stimuli or teach the individual to concentrate on the relevant stimuli.

Drugs

Several drugs have been shown to aid recovery from brain damage in animals. So far, we do not know their effect on humans.

Nimodipine, a drug that prevents calcium from entering cells, improves memory for visual learning tasks in rats with visual-cortex lesions (LeVere, Ford, & Sandin, 1992; LeVere, 1993). Calcium blockers administered before brain damage produce modest benefits, presumably by preventing a toxic rush of calcium into neurons. Calcium blockers produce greater benefits if administered after brain damage, presumably by improving cellular functioning. Recall from Chapter 13 that calcium blockers can improve learning and memory by preventing inappropriate stimulation at NMDA-type glutamate synapses.

Several studies indicate that gangliosides (which, as we have seen, may enhance collateral sprouting) promote the restoration of damaged brains. The fact that they adhere to neuron membranes suggests that they contribute to the recognition of one neuron by another in early development, guiding axons to the correct locations to form synapses. Daily injections of gangliosides aid the recovery of behavior after several kinds of brain damage (Cahn, Borziex, Aldinio, Toffano, & Cahn, 1989; Ramirez et al., 1987a, 1987b; Sabel, Slavin, & Stein, 1984). Exactly how they do so is not yet known.

Brain Grafts

At the risk of sounding Frankensteinian, could surgeons replace dead brain cells by transplanting healthy cells from someone else? Grafts of brain tissue encounter only limited risk of tissue rejection. Perhaps because the blood-brain barrier protects the brain from foreign substances, the immune system is less active in the brain than elsewhere (Nicholas & Arnason, 1992); it is also possible to give drugs that suppress rejection of the transplanted tissue. The grafted brain tissue grows, however, only if it comes from a fetus.

In a pioneering study, M. J. Perlow and colleagues (1979) injected the chemical 6-OHDA into rats to make lesions in the substantia nigra in one hemisphere. The substantia nigra is the part of the brain that degenerates in Parkinson's disease; each rat developed movement abnormalities on one side of the body only. After the movement abnormalities stabilized, the experimenters transplanted the substantia nigra from rat fetuses into the damaged brains. The grafts survived in 29 of the 30 rats that received them, making synapses in varying numbers. Four weeks after the grafts were implanted, most recipients had recovered much of their normal movement. Control animals that suffered the same brain damage without receiving grafts showed little or no behavioral recovery.

Inspired by this report, other investigators tried transplanting fetal tissue to reverse the effects of many types of brain damage, producing successful effects in some cases but not in others (Fisher & Gage, 1993). Ordinarily, scientists recommend that any experimental procedure be extensively tested with laboratory animals before it is tried on humans, but in this case the temptation was too great. People in the late stages of Parkinson's disease and other degenerative conditions are willing to try almost anything, and so are their physicians. After all, they have little to lose.

But if surgeons are to transplant brain tissue, who will be the donors? Several early studies used tissue from the patient's own adrenal gland. Although that tissue is not composed of neurons, it produces and releases dopamine, the transmitter that is deficient in the brains of Parkinson's patients. Unfortunately, the adrenal gland transplants produced little if any benefit for most patients (see, for example, Backlund et al., 1985).

It is also possible to transplant brain tissue taken from aborted fetuses. Benefits of such surgery have varied from weak to moderate, but they do not constitute a cure (Hoffer et al., 1992; Kordower et al., 1996; Landau, 1993). The operation is a difficult one, requiring for each patient brain tissue from at least 6 or 7 aborted fetuses, age 6 to 9 weeks post conception. Many observers—even those who do not object to abortion itself—question whether the modest benefits are worth the effort. At best, the procedure requires more research (Kupsch, Oertel, Earl, & Sautter, 1995).

One way to avoid needing multiple aborted human fetuses is to grow cells in tissue culture, genetically alter them so that they produce large quantities of L-dopa, and then transplant them into the brain. The drawback to this approach has been that the altered cells often cause tumors. Research continues on ways to improve the benefits while reducing the dangers (Snyder, 1994).

Another possibility is to transplant tissue from fetuses of another species. Although this idea may sound extreme, physicians have indeed transplanted substantia nigra tissue from the brains of pig fetuses into the brains of patients with Parkinson's disease. The investigators have not yet reported the amount of benefit, but a postmortem examination of one patient, who died seven months after the transplant for unrelated reasons, found that substantial numbers of transplanted pig neurons survived and made synapses with the human neurons (Deacon et al., 1997). We shall eagerly await word on the long-term consequences of such surgery.

The research on brain transplants has raised yet another possibility for treatment. In several experiments, the transplanted tissue failed to survive but the recipient showed behavioral recovery anyway. Evidently, the transplanted tissue releases trophic factors that stimulate axon and dendrite growth in the surrounding areas of the recipient's own brain (Bohn, Cupit, Marciano, & Gash, 1987; Dunnett, Ryan, Levin, Reynolds, & Bunch, 1987; Ensor, Morley, Redfern, & Miles, 1993). Further research has demonstrated that brain injections of neurotrophins can significantly benefit brain-damaged rats and monkeys, presumably by enhancing the growth of axons and dendrites (Gash et al., 1996; Kolb, Cote, Ribeiro-da-Silva, & Cuello, 1997). Unfortunately, because neurotrophins do not cross the blood-brain barrier, they must be implanted surgically. Still, the possibility remains that researchers may develop new drugs that do cross the barrier and mimic the effects of neurotrophins.

IN CLOSING

Prospects for Recovery

One measure of how far we have come is that the big question in this field is no longer *whether* we shall someday have good therapies for brain-damaged patients, but *what* those treatments will be. Will the answer be transplant of fetal tissues? Or will it be implantation of neurotrophins, or drugs with related effects that cross the blood-brain barrier, or calcium blockers, or gangliosides, or yet other possibilities? Researchers do not have the answers now, but they have reason to be optimistic for the future.

Summary

1. Recovery from brain damage may be better or worse in infants than in adults, depending on a number of circumstances. (p. 412)
2. After early damage to the dorsolateral prefrontal cortex, the behavior of monkeys seems normal at age 1 year (when the structure would be immature anyway) but deteriorates at age 2 years (when it ordinarily becomes mature). (p. 413)
3. Recovery is sometimes better if the damage develops in several stages, instead of all at once, either because of increased collateral sprouting or because experience after a partial lesion helps reorganize the surviving tissues. (p. 413)
4. Therapy for brain-damaged people consists mostly of helping them practice the abilities that have been impaired but not destroyed. (p. 414)
5. Drugs that enhance memory or guide axonal growth promote recovery after certain kinds of brain damage. (p. 415)
6. Animal experiments suggest the possibility of transplanting fetal brain grafts as a therapy for brain damage. However, results with humans have had mixed results, and a search for better methods continues. (p. 415)

Review Questions

1. Why might the effects of brain damage differ between infants and adults? Give more than one reason and evidence for each. (p. 412)
2. What are the usual methods and goals of therapy for people with brain damage? (p. 414)
3. What kind of donor must be used in brain graft experiments if the transplanted tissue is to survive and make connections? (p. 416)

Thought Question

1. For the people who have had fetal cells transplanted into their brains, what behavioral tests would you recommend to evaluate the effectiveness of the procedure?

Suggestion for Further Reading

Stein, D. G., Brailowsky, S., & Will, B. (1995). *Brain repair.* New York: Oxford University Press. Excellent nontechnical discussion of the prospects for enhancing recovery from brain damage.

Terms

Kennard principle generalization (not always correct) that it is easier to recover from brain damage early in life than later (p. 412)

orbital frontal cortex an anterior area of the prefrontal cortex (p. 413)

dorsolateral prefrontal cortex area of the prefrontal cortex (p. 413)

serial-lesion effect tendency for recovery to be more successful after a series of small lesions than after a single, large lesion (p. 413)

MOOD DISORDERS AND SCHIZOPHRENIA

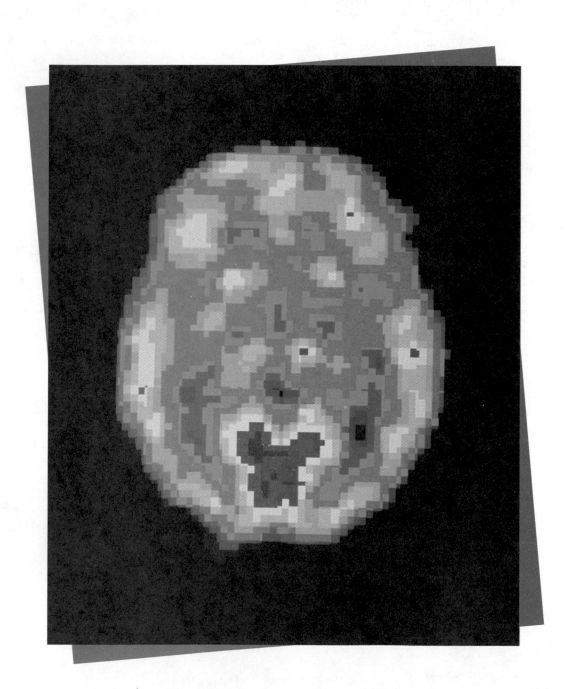

CHAPTER **SIXTEEN**

MAIN**IDEAS**

1. Mood disorders and schizophrenia result from numerous biological and environmental influences.
2. Various drugs used for treating depression and schizophrenia alter transmission at various types of synapses. The drugs' effectiveness suggests that the disorders may be caused in part by problems affecting particular neurotransmitters.
3. A number of nonpharmaceutical biological treatments, including electroconvulsive shock, changes in sleep patterns, exposure to bright light, and lithium salts, are also effective against certain kinds of mood disorder.
4. Schizophrenia may be the result of genetic or other problems that impair early development of the brain.

Until the late 1860s, people with aphasia were considered mentally ill. After physicians discovered that aphasia is caused by brain damage, those patients were treated by neurologists instead of psychiatrists. Similarly, after physicians discovered that general paresis, a type of intellectual deterioration, is a symptom of the third stage of syphilis infection (see Figure 16.1), people with this problem became neurological patients rather than psychiatric patients. Apparently, as soon as we find a neurological basis for a psychiatric disorder, we hesitate to call it a mental illness.

If we found neurological bases for all psychological disorders, would psychiatrists and clinical psychologists go out of business? No. Psychotherapy (talking with a psychotherapist) can help people suffering from aphasia, general paresis, or even a broken leg. Evidence accumulating since about 1950 indicates that anxiety, obsessive-compulsive disorder, sleep disorders, violent behavior, and many other psychological disorders have biological aspects. Psychotherapists have learned to coordinate psychotherapy with biological therapy, but they still find ample demand for psychotherapy. The presence of biological contributors to a disorder does not deny the importance of experiential contributors.

In this chapter, we examine some disorders that in many cases become so severe that they absolutely dominate a person's life. Researchers disagree, sometimes sharply, about the relative importance of biological and environmental factors. Here we emphasize the biological components; *Biological Psychology* is, after all, the title of this book. But this emphasis does not imply that other aspects are unimportant.

FIGURE **16.1**
Brain damage associated with general paresis
General paresis is the final stage of syphilis. Many of the gyri in the cerebral cortex are shrunken.   Source: Courtesy of Dana Copeland.

Mood Disorders

You might imagine that we would all be better off if we could never feel sad, but the evidence indicates the contrary. Antonio Damasio (1994) examined a man who, as a result of prefrontal damage, felt almost no emotions, including sadness and anger. Far from being purely rational, he frequently made amazingly stupid decisions, losing his job, his family, and his savings. When tested in the laboratory, he had no trouble predicting the probable outcomes of various decisions. For example, when asked what would happen if he cashed a check and the bank teller handed him too much money, he knew the probable consequences of either returning it or walking away with it. He also knew the probable consequences of various actions he might take after damaging someone's property. But he admitted, "And after all this, I still wouldn't know what to do" (Damasio, 1994, p. 49). Because he felt so little emotion, he could not even imagine feeling good or bad about various outcomes. He knew that one action would win him approval and another would get him in trouble, but it was not obvious to him that approval would feel better than trouble, or that he would prefer one to the other.

In short, the capacity to feel sad is useful. However, when sadness is extremely prolonged or severe, it interferes with productive living.

Major Depressive Disorder

Almost everyone feels somewhat depressed at times—sad, discouraged, lacking in energy. The difference between ordinary depression and major depression is a matter of intensity and duration. People with a **major depression** feel sad and helpless every day for weeks at a time. They have no energy, feel worthless, contemplate suicide, have trouble sleeping, get little pleasure from sex (Nofzinger et al., 1993) or food, and in many cases can hardly even imagine being happy again. Major depression is diagnosed about twice as often in women as in men. It can occur at any time from adolescence to old age, with a peak frequency in the 25–44-year age range. According to a survey of more than 8,000 U.S. adults, about 19 percent of all people suffer psychiatrically significant depression at least once in their lives (Kessler et al., 1994).

Triggering Depressed Episodes

Most depressed people can point to a life event that seemed to precipitate their depression, or at least to aggravate it. Most also have evidence of genetic or other biological predispositions to depression. The most severe episodes occur when someone who has always been a little depressed, perhaps because of a biological predisposition, then has a traumatic experience. One study found that the stress of caring for a child with a disability did not increase the probability of the mother's becoming depressed, but it intensified any depression that she did have (Breslau & Davis, 1986).

Depression is generally episodic, not constant. Someone may feel normal for weeks, months, or years between episodes of depression. A variety of events alter the timing and intensity of depressive episodes. (They are like dust that causes an asthmatic person to sneeze: The dust did not cause the asthma; it just triggered its expression.) Hormonal changes are one example. Of all women admitted for depression to one psychiatric hospital, 41 percent entered on the day before or the first day of menstruation (Abramowitz, Baker, & Fleischer, 1982). Similarly, a certain amount of depression is common just after giving birth. Most women experience "the blues" for a day or two after delivery because of pain, emotional upheaval, the inconvenience of hospital care, and possibly hormonal changes. About 20 percent experience a moderately serious **postpartum depression**—that is, a depression after giving birth. About 1 woman in 1,000 enters a more serious, long-lasting depression (Hopkins, Marcus, & Campbell,

1984). In most cases, however, she was already predisposed to depression and may have suffered several previous episodes unrelated to childbirth (Schöpf, Bryois, Jonquière, & Le, 1984).

Abnormalities of Hemispheric Dominance

Studies of normal people have found a fairly strong relationship between happy mood and increased activity in the left prefrontal cortex (Jacobs & Snyder, 1996). Most depressed people have decreased activity in the left and increased activity in the right prefrontal cortex (Davidson, 1984; Starkstein & Robinson, 1986). When trying to solve cognitive problems, depressed people's eyes gaze to the left, not to the right as in most people (Lenhart & Katkin, 1986).

Many people with left-hemisphere damage become seriously depressed; fewer people do after damage to the right hemisphere (Bolla-Wilson, Robinson, Starkstein, Boston, & Price, 1989). In rare cases, people with right-hemisphere damage become manic (Robinson, Boston, Starkstein, & Price, 1988). Overall, the evidence suggests that left-hemisphere damage or inactivity is associated with depression. We shall return to this point when we discuss the effects of electroconvulsive shock to the left or right hemisphere.

Genetics

Ten to 20 percent of the parents, brothers, and sisters of depressed patients have mood disorders themselves (Smeraldi, Kidd, Negri, Heimbuch, & Melica, 1979; Weissman et al., 1984). Furthermore, adopted children who become depressed have, on the average, more biological relatives who are depressed than depressed adoptive relatives (Wender et al., 1986).

So far, researchers have not identified a particular gene that is strongly linked to depression, and they are more likely to find general risk genes than genes specifically for depression. Having a close relative with depression increases one's risk not only of depression but also of alcoholism, other substance abuse, and anxiety disorders (Kendler et al., 1995).

Viruses

A few cases of depression may be linked to a viral infection called **Borna disease.** As recently as the 1980s, Borna disease was known to infect only the brains of European farm animals. Gradually, investigators discovered that a much greater variety of species are vulnerable, over a much wider geographic range. In severe cases, the virus is fatal; in milder cases, it is noted mostly by its behavioral effects, such as periods of frantic activity alternating with periods of inactivity.

Many viruses are passed between humans and other species, although the effects on humans may be quite different, or even undetectable. In 1985, investigators reported the results of a blood test given to 370 humans (Amsterdam et al., 1985). Only 12 people tested positive for Borna disease virus, but *all 12 were suffering from major depression or bipolar disorder.* These 12 were a small percentage of the 265 depressed people tested; still, it is significant that *none* of the 105 nondepressed people tested positive for the virus.

A few years passed while virologists improved their methods for measuring the presence of the Borna virus. In the early 1990s, thousands of people were examined on three continents. The Borna virus was found in about 2 percent of normal people, 30 percent of severely depressed patients, and 13–14 percent of people with certain chronic brain diseases (Bode, Ferszt, & Czech, 1993; Bode, Riegel, Lange, & Ludwig, 1992). In another study, depressed patients were tested repeatedly. In some of them, the number of Borna disease antigens increased during the weeks of greatest depression and decreased when the symptoms declined (Bode, Zimmerman, Ferszt, Steinbach, & Ludwig, 1995). Obviously, more research is necessary, but these data suggest a relationship between the Borna virus and depression.

Antidepressant Drugs

It is logical to assume that investigators would first figure out the causes of a psychological disorder and then develop a treatment to address it. The actual sequence has frequently been the opposite: First, investigators find a drug or other therapy that appears to be helpful, and then they infer what the underlying cause of the disorder must have been. Like many other psychiatric drugs, antidepressants were discovered by accident (see Digression 16.1), and they have increased our understanding of depression rather than the other way around.

After the earliest antidepressant drugs were developed in the 1950s, several investigators independently and almost simultaneously noted that they all increased the activity at catecholamine synapses in the brain (Garattini & Valzelli, 1960; MacLean, 1962; Stein, 1962). They therefore inferred that depression might be related to deficient stimulation at dopamine and norepinephrine synapses.

Today's antidepressant drugs fall into three major categories: tricyclics, MAOIs, and "second-generation" antidepressants, also known as selective serotonin reuptake inhibitors. (See Figure 16.2.) The **tricyclics** (such as imipramine, trade name Tofranil) operate by

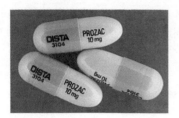

FIGURE **16.2**
Fluoxetine (Prozac) pills
Tricyclic drugs block the reuptake of catecholamines and serotonin by presynaptic terminals. Monoamine oxidase inhibitors
block the breakdown of catecholamines and serotonin after their
release into the synaptic cleft. The effects of second-generation
antidepressants, such as Prozac, are more limited to a single
neurotransmitter.

preventing the presynaptic neuron from reabsorbing
catecholamines or serotonin after releasing them; thus,
the neurotransmitters remain longer in the synaptic
cleft and continue stimulating the postsynaptic cell.

The **monoamine oxidase inhibitors (MAOIs)**
(such as phenelzine, trade name Nardil) block the enzyme *monoamine oxidase (MAO),* which metabolizes
catecholamines and serotonin into inactive forms.
When MAOIs block this enzyme, released neurotransmitter molecules remain longer than usual at the
synapse without being inactivated; they therefore stim-

ulate the postsynaptic cell more than usual. The tricyclics are generally more helpful than the MAOIs for
most depressed patients; however, MAOIs are helpful
for many patients who do not respond to tricyclics
(Thase, Trivedi, & Rush, 1995).

The **second-generation antidepressants,** or **selective serotonin reuptake inhibitors,** are similar to tricyclics but are specific to the neurotransmitter serotonin. For example, fluoxetine (trade name Prozac)
blocks the reuptake of serotonin by the presynaptic terminal. Fluoxetine and similar drugs have more limited
and predictable side effects than those drugs that affect
four or more neurotransmitters (Feighner et al., 1991).
Tricyclics may produce dizziness, drowsiness, blurred
vision, rapid heartbeat, dry mouth, and excessive
sweating, often so severely that people have to quit taking the drug or reduce their dose to an ineffective level.
Fluoxetine, however, ordinarily produces only mild
nausea or headache. The milder the side effects, the
larger the dose a person can take, and therefore the
greater the benefits are likely to be. The use of fluoxetine has been controversial because of claims that it occasionally provokes suicidal thoughts or violent behavior. Those claims are surprising; recall from Chapter 12
that violence is generally associated with *decreased*
serotonin activity, whereas fluoxetine *increases* serotonin activity. And, indeed, follow-up studies have
found that people taking fluoxetine are much more

DIGRESSION **16.1**

Accidental Discoveries of Psychiatric Drugs

We like to think that basic science comes first and that applied science or technology later applies the discoveries of basic science to solve practical problems. Yet the history of drug
therapies, particularly in psychiatry, includes many examples
of useful drugs stumbled upon by accident that researchers
then had to study to explain their success.

Disulfiram, for example, was originally used in the manufacture of rubber. Someone noticed that workers in a certain
rubber factory developed a distaste for alcohol and traced the
cause to disulfiram, which had altered the workers' metabolism so they became ill after drinking any alcohol. Disulfiram,
now better known by the trade name Antabuse, is often prescribed for people who are trying to avoid alcohol.

Iproniazid was originally marketed as rocket fuel. Eventually, someone discovered that it was useful therapy for tuberculosis. Later, while experimenting on its effects in treating tuberculosis, someone discovered that it was an effective
antidepressant (Klerman, 1975).

The use of bromides to control epilepsy was originally
based on a theory, but the theory was all wrong (Friedlander,

1986; Levitt, 1975). People in the 1800s who believed that
masturbation caused epilepsy thought that bromides reduced
sexual drive. Therefore, the reasoning went, bromides should
reduce epilepsy. It turns out that bromides do relieve epilepsy,
but for altogether different reasons.

For decades, the search for new psychiatric drugs was a
matter of haphazardly testing as many chemicals as possible,
first on laboratory animals and then on humans. For example,
investigators looking for new tranquilizers would seek out
drugs that decreased rats' avoidance of stimuli associated
with shock. (A drug that decreased avoidance presumably decreased fear.) Today, because we largely understand how
tranquilizers and other drugs affect synapses, drug researchers no longer have to test nearly so many compounds
on animals. They start by synthesizing chemicals with properties similar to those of drugs already in use, evaluating new
chemicals in test tubes or tissue samples until they find one
with a potential for stronger or more specific effects on neurotransmission.

likely to experience a decrease in aggressiveness than an increase (Fuller, 1996).

Implications for the physiology of depression Now that we know what kinds of drugs relieve depression, we can infer what brain abnormalities produce depression, right? Unfortunately, it is not that simple. Disorders of serotonin and norepinephrine synapses apparently contribute in some way to depression, but we do not know how they (and no doubt others as well) produce the final outcome.

Explaining the time course of the drugs' effectiveness is a major research problem. For example, a tricyclic drug quickly blocks reuptake of both serotonin and catecholamines. A little later, but still within the first few hours, the excess neurotransmitter that has accumulated in the synaptic cleft stimulates the **autoreceptors** on the presynaptic terminal, decreasing further release of the neurotransmitter. In other words, the initial effects of the drug are self-limiting; it prolongs the presence of serotonin and catecholamines in the synapse, but thereby decreases their further release. As still more time passes, the prolonged stimulation of the autoreceptors desensitizes them, restoring something close to the original rate of release (Antelman, Chiodo, & DeGiovanni, 1982; Sulser, Gillespie, Mishra, & Manier, 1984). Meanwhile, the prolonged stimulation of the postsynaptic receptors gradually decreases their sensitivity, and alters the activity of second messengers in complex ways that researchers have just begun to investigate. So, is the combined result increased or decreased stimulation of the postsynaptic cells? And why is behavior affected so slowly? Some people note a response within a few days, but the benefits continue to increase for at least two to three weeks.

You may be understandably confused at this point; researchers themselves are confused. What do all these results tell us about the underlying causes of depression? Primarily, they imply that the mechanisms are more complex than simply having too much or too little of a particular neurotransmitter. We must await new research to clarify both how the drugs work and what causes depression in the first place.

Other Therapies

Antidepressant drugs have provided safe, effective, relatively inexpensive help for a great many people, but about one-third of depressed patients do not respond to them. Cognitive, behavioral, and interpersonal psychotherapies are also beneficial to many patients, although to date no one has found a way to predict which patient will respond best to which treatment (Persons, Thase, & Crits-Christoph, 1996). Successful psychotherapy is most likely to produce long-lasting relief (Evans et al., 1992); even people who respond well to medication have a risk of relapse within weeks or months after they stop taking the drugs. However, psychotherapy is more expensive and time-consuming than drug therapies, and it, too, fails for many patients. Therapists have also developed several other kinds of treatment.

Electroconvulsive therapy **Electroconvulsive therapy (ECT)** has had a stormy history (Fink, 1985). It originated with the observation that among certain people who suffer from both epilepsy and schizophrenia, an increase in the symptoms of one disorder is often associated with a decrease in the symptoms of the other (Trimble & Thompson, 1986). In the 1930s, a Hungarian physician, Ladislas Meduna, intentionally induced convulsive seizures in schizophrenic patients to see whether this would relieve their symptoms. Soon other physicians were doing the same, using a large dose of insulin to induce the seizures. Insulin shock is a dreadful experience, however, and very difficult to control. An Italian physician, Ugo Cerletti, after years of experimentation with animals, developed a method of inducing seizures with an electric shock through the head (Cerletti & Bini, 1938). Electroconvulsive therapy is quick, and most patients awaken from it calmly and do not remember it.

Although ECT proved to be only occasionally beneficial in treating schizophrenia, psychiatrists who tested it with other disorders discovered that it did seem to help many depressed patients, although they had no explanation for its success. It became a common treatment for depression. Its overuse and misuse, especially during the 1950s, gave it a bad reputation. Some patients were given ECT a hundred times or more, without their consent, even when it appeared to be ineffective.

When antidepressant drugs became available in the late 1950s, the use of ECT declined rapidly. However, as it became clear in the 1970s that not all depressed patients respond well to the drugs, ECT made a partial comeback. It is used today only with informed consent, usually for patients who have not responded to any of the antidepressant drugs (Scovern & Kilmann, 1980; Weiner, 1979). It is also sometimes recommended for patients with strong suicidal tendencies, because it works faster than antidepressant drugs: Feeling better in one week instead of two may be the difference between life and death.

ECT is usually applied every other day for about two weeks, sometimes longer. Patients are given muscle relaxants or anesthetics to minimize discomfort and the possibility of injury (Figure 16.3). Because the shock is much less intense than in earlier years, the risk of provoking a heart attack is very low for healthy young to middle-aged patients, although it is higher for elderly patients.

FIGURE **16.3**
Electroconvulsive therapy (ECT)
In contrast to the practices of an earlier era, ECT today is administered with muscle relaxants or anesthetics to minimize discomfort. It can be used only if the patient gives informed consent.

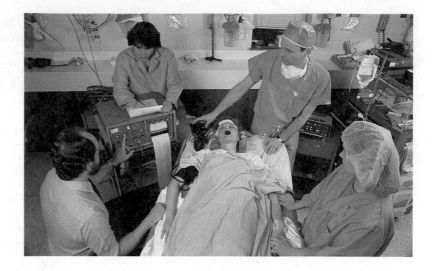

The most common side effect of ECT is memory loss, but if physicians administer the shock to the right hemisphere only, the antidepressant effects still occur and memory remains normal (McElhiney et al., 1995). Because depression is associated with decreased activity of the left hemisphere, right-hemisphere ECT may either promote a better balance of activity between the two hemispheres or somehow enhance activity in the left hemisphere.

Medical commissions in both the United States and Great Britain have concluded that ECT is both safe and effective (Fink, 1985). According to one extensive review of the literature, 80 percent of all severely depressed patients respond well to ECT, whereas only 64 percent respond well to tricyclic drugs and even fewer to MAOIs (Janicak et al., 1985). The benefits are not permanent, however; about half of those who respond well to ECT relapse into depression within six months unless they are given drugs or other therapies to prevent it (Riddle & Scott, 1995).

Half a century after the introduction of ECT, no one is yet sure how it relieves depression. It stimulates the production of additional dopamine type D_1 and D_2 receptors in the nucleus accumbens (Smith, Lindefors, Hurd, & Sharp, 1995), decreases the number of norepinephrine receptors at postsynaptic cells (Kellar & Stockmeier, 1986; Lerer & Shapira, 1986), and exerts a wide variety of other effects. We do not know, however, which effect is most critical therapeutically.

Altered sleep patterns Most depressed people, especially those who are middle-aged or older, experience sleep abnormalities that suggest a disorder of their biological rhythms. Recall from Chapter 9 that a normal nondepressed person who goes to bed at the normal time first enters REM sleep about 80 minutes after falling asleep; the amount of REM sleep remains low for the first half of the night and increases in the second half. That trend is controlled by the time of day, not by how long the person has been asleep. Someone who usually falls asleep at 11 P.M. but is up until 3 A.M. on a given night is likely to enter REM sleep rapidly, because REM sleep is related to circadian rhythms, as reflected by changes in body temperature (see Figure 16.4). REM sleep occupies a small percentage of total sleep while body temperature is declining and a larger percentage while body temperature is rising (Czeisler, Weitzman, Moore-Ede, Zimmerman, & Knauer, 1980).

Most depressed people enter REM sleep within 45 minutes after going to bed at their normal time, but for them body temperature may already be starting to rise at that time, as Figure 16.4 illustrates. REM sleep begins early and may occupy a great deal of sleep time. Most depressed people sleep restlessly, awaken early, and cannot get back to sleep. During the day, they feel drowsy. As they recover from depression, their sleep improves also (Dew et al., 1996).

Several means of adjusting sleep habits can alleviate depression (Gillin, 1983). One promising method is to have the person go to sleep earlier than usual, in phase with his or her temperature cycle. Sleep begins at, say, 6 P.M., when the temperature cycle is at about the point it is in nondepressed people at 11 P.M.; after 8 hours of sleep the person awakens at 2 A.M. On each succeeding night, the person goes to sleep half an hour later, until bedtime is at 11 P.M. or some other satisfactory point. In short, therapists treat the depressed patient like someone who is having trouble adjusting to a change in time zones. The result is a relief from depression that lasts for months (Sack, Nurnberger, Rosenthal, Ashburn, & Wehr, 1985).

Another approach is to keep the person awake all night, which produces a rapid relief from depression (Pflug, 1973). Why this is effective is not known; furthermore, the benefits last only a day or two, and depressed patients frankly hate the treatment. REM sleep

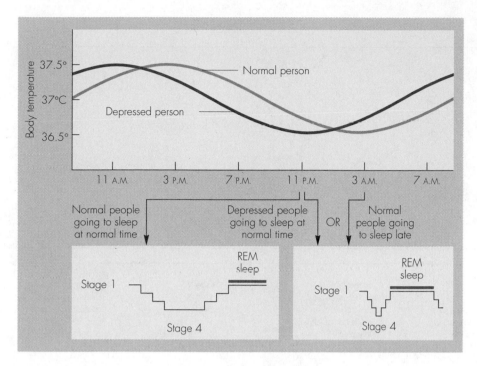

FIGURE **16.4**
Sleep, REM, and the circadian rhythm of body temperature
Nondepressed people going to bed at their normal time get much stage 4 sleep for the first few hours and increasing amounts of REM sleep later in the night. Most depressed people have circadian rhythms that are advanced by several hours; when they go to sleep at 11 P.M., they sleep as a normal person would at about 3 A.M.   Source: Bottom graphs adapted from Hobson, 1989.

deprivation can also relieve depression; the therapist awakens the person whenever signs of REM appear (Vogel, Thompson, Thurmond, & Rivers, 1973). The benefits develop gradually but can last from days to weeks. Again, how the effect works is not known. For nondepressed people, sleep deprivation or REM deprivation makes mood worse, not better (Roy-Byrne, Uhde, & Post, 1986).

Bipolar Disorder

Depression is either a unipolar or a bipolar disorder. People with **unipolar disorder** experience only one pole, or extreme; they vary between feeling normal and feeling depressed. People with **bipolar disorder**—also known as **manic-depressive disorder**—alternate between the poles of depression and its opposite, **mania,** which is characterized by restless activity, excitement, laughter, a mostly happy mood, rambling speech, and loss of inhibitions. In extreme cases, manic people are dangerous to themselves and others. Figure 16.5 represents the rise and fall of a manic episode in one hospitalized patient.

A cycle from depression to mania and back to depression again may last only a few days or for a year or more (Bunney, Murphy, Goodwin, & Borge, 1972). Some people's cycles are so regular that one can predict their manic and depressive episodes long in advance (Richter, 1938, 1957b, 1957c), as Figure 16.6

shows. About 1 person in 1,000 is diagnosed with bipolar disorder, but many more have mild, undiagnosed, and untreated cases. The mean age of onset is the late 20s.

The rate of glucose metabolism is a good indicator of overall brain activity, and it varies as a function of mania and depression, as seen in Figure 16.7. During mania, activity is higher than normal. During depression, it is lower than normal, especially in the left frontal lobe (Baxter et al., 1985) and parts of the temporal and parietal lobes (Sackeim et al., 1990).

Genetics

Modern methods of biochemical analysis have enabled researchers to identify the genes responsible for Huntington's disease, Alzheimer's disease, and many other conditions. Research on bipolar disorder has yielded apparent linkage to genes on chromosomes 4, 6, 11, 13, 15, and 18 (Blackwood et al., 1996; Egeland et al., 1987; Freimer et al., 1996; Ginns et al., 1996). Some of these may be false leads, but it is also possible that many genes have similar effects.

Treatments

Lithium salts are the most effective known therapy for bipolar disorder and for certain cases in which a person alternates regularly between depression and normal mood. The effectiveness of lithium was discovered by

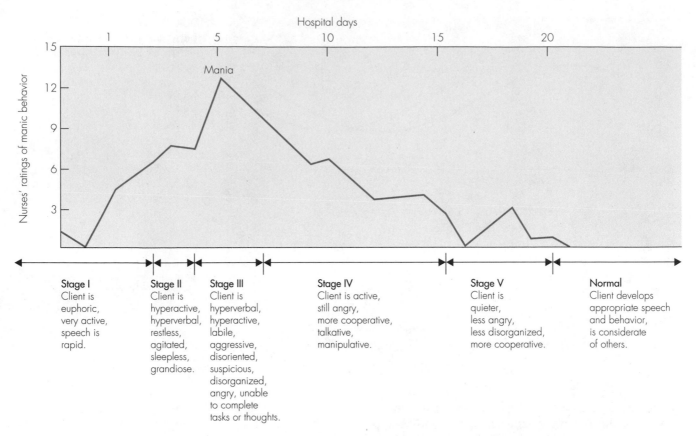

Hospital days

Stage I
Client is
euphoric,
very active,
speech is
rapid.

Stage II
Client is
hyperactive,
hyperverbal,
restless,
agitated,
sleepless,
grandiose.

Stage III
Client is
hyperverbal,
hyperactive,
labile,
aggressive,
disoriented,
suspicious,
disorganized,
angry, unable
to complete
tasks or thoughts.

Stage IV
Client is active,
still angry,
more cooperative,
talkative,
manipulative.

Stage V
Client is
quieter,
less angry,
less disorganized,
more cooperative.

Normal
Client develops
appropriate speech
and behavior,
is considerate
of others.

FIGURE **16.5**
Observations of a three-week manic episode
Source: From Janosik & Davies, 1987.

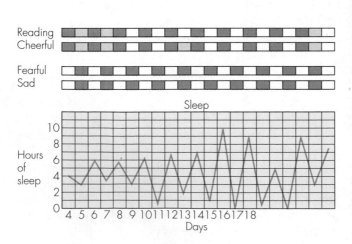

FIGURE **16.6**
Records for a woman with rapid-cycling bipolar disorder
Blue means "definitely," light blue means "somewhat," and white means "no" for each category. Note that days of cheerfulness and reading alternated with days of fearfulness and sadness. Note also that she slept well on her cheerful days and poorly on her sad days.   Source: Based on Richter, 1938.

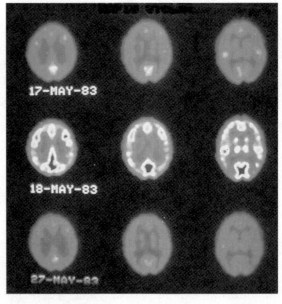

FIGURE **16.7**
PET scans for a bipolar patient
Horizontal planes through three levels of the brain are shown for each day. On May 17 and May 27, when the patient was depressed, brain metabolic rates were low. On May 18, when the patient was in a cheerful, hypomanic mood, the brain metabolic rate was high. Red indicates the highest metabolic rate, followed by yellow, green, and blue.   Source: Courtesy of L. R. Baxter, Jr.

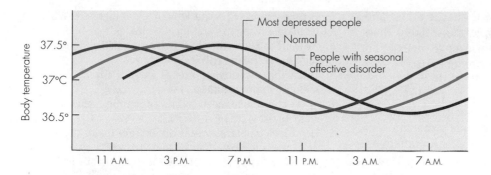

FIGURE **16.8**
Circadian rhythms for normal, depressed, and SAD people
Note that SAD patients are phase-delayed, whereas most other depressed patients are phase-advanced.

accident. An Australian investigator, J. F. Cade, who believed that uric acid would be therapeutically useful for treating mania and depression, mixed uric acid with a lithium salt to help it dissolve and then gave the solution to patients. It was indeed helpful, although investigators eventually realized that the lithium was the effective agent.

Lithium keeps the mood of a bipolar patient steady. With continued use, it prevents a relapse into either mania or depression. The use of lithium must be regulated carefully, however. The therapeutic dose is not much less than the dose that produces toxic effects. However, people who take lithium within the recommended doses suffer no ill effects, even after many years of treatment (Schou, 1997). Nevertheless, a pregnant patient should probably suspend her lithium treatment for the sake of her baby's development (Teixeira, Lopes, & Secoli, 1995).

How lithium relieves bipolar disorder is still not known. Because it alleviates both mania and depression—opposite states—its effects cannot be achieved simply by increasing or decreasing the activity at a particular type of synapse. Therapeutic doses of lithium produce complex effects on several second-messenger systems and thereby affect activity in many neuronal pathways (Manji, Potter, & Lenox, 1995). Presumably, these effects somehow bring fluctuating brain systems into stability. Certainly, much still remains to be learned.

About one-fifth to one-third of bipolar patients fail to respond satisfactorily to lithium. In these cases, many therapists have had good results with anticonvulsant drugs, such as carbamazepine. As with lithium, we do not know how the anticonvulsants relieve bipolar disorder.

Seasonal Affective Disorder

An uncommon form of depression is **seasonal affective disorder,** conveniently abbreviated **SAD.** Most people who live in nontropical latitudes feel happier and more active in the summer, when there are many hours of sunlight, than they do in winter (Madden, Heath, Rosenthal, & Martin, 1996). For some people, these responses are so strong that they become seriously depressed in the winter and somewhat manic in the summer. A few people show the opposite pattern, becoming depressed in summer (Faedda et al., 1993).

SAD is most common and severe in regions closest to the poles, where the nights are very long in winter and very short in summer. Some patients who are depressed every winter in their far northern homes suffer no such depression if they spend the winter in, say, southern California (Pande, 1985; Rosenthal et al., 1984). In many ways, SAD differs from other types of depression; for example, SAD patients have phase-delayed sleep and temperature rhythms, unlike most other depressed patients, whose rhythms are phase-advanced (Teicher et al., 1997). (See Figure 16.8.)

It is possible to treat SAD with very bright lights (for example, 2,500 lux). The person sits in front of the lights for an hour or more before the sun rises or after it sets, thus artificially creating a longer period of daylight. Some research suggests that artificial light has its greatest antidepressant effect early in the morning (Sack et al., 1990); other research indicates that morning and evening light are equally effective (Wirz-Justice et al., 1993); still other research indicates that bright light is helpful even in the middle of the day (Penev, Zee, & Turek, 1997). Researchers do not agree on what causes seasonal affective disorder or why bright light alleviates it.

IN**CLOSING**

The Biology of Mood Swings

Do you feel sad because of events that have happened to you or because of your brain chemistry? Both. Indeed, your experiences of events *are* changes in your brain state; you cannot have one without the other. The better question is: Are some people more likely than others to become depressed because of a preexisting condition in their brain structure or chemistry? The answer to that one is "probably." It is difficult to get from "probably" to "definitely," because it is difficult to do research on human moods. At each stage in life, brain structure and chemistry alter one's reactions to events, and experience in turn alters the brain, affecting the reaction to the next event. To study an adult brain is to face a challenge analogous to watching a few minutes in the middle of a complex movie and trying to guess how events led up to that point.

Summary

1. People with major depression feel sad, helpless, and lacking in energy for weeks at a time. For most, depression occurs as a series of episodes, each triggered by life events or biological changes. (p. 420)
2. Major depression is associated with decreased activity in the left frontal cortex and increased activity in the right. (p. 421)
3. Depression is apparently linked to genes that increase the risk of a variety of disorders, not just depression. Some cases of depression are apparently related to infection with Borna disease virus. (p. 421)
4. Three kinds of antidepressant drugs are in wide use: tricyclics, MAOIs, and second-generation antidepressants. The mechanisms by which drugs relieve depression are as yet only partly understood. (p. 421)
5. Other therapies for depression include cognitive psychotherapy, electroconvulsive therapy, and altered sleep patterns. (p. 423)
6. Several genes have been tentatively linked to bipolar disorder, in which people alternate between two extremes, depression and mania. Lithium salts are usually effective in relieving the disorder, although we are not yet sure why. (p. 425)
7. Seasonal affective disorder is marked by recurrent depression in one season, generally winter. It can be relieved by exposure to bright lights. (p. 427)

Review Questions

1. Are completely unemotional people more rational in their decision making than the rest of us? (p. 420)
2. What kinds of events increase the intensity of depression, although they do not cause the underlying predisposition to depression? (p. 420)
3. What are three major types of antidepressant drugs, and what are their effects on synapses? (p. 421)
4. How quickly do antidepressants affect the synapses? How quickly do they relieve depression? (p. 423)

5. For what kind of patient is ECT recommended? What are its main advantages and disadvantages? (p. 423)
6. How are the procedures for delivering ECT different today than in the 1950s? (p. 423)
7. What modification of the procedure for ECT reduces memory impairment? (p. 424)
8. What changes in sleep habits sometimes relieve depression? (p. 424)
9. How does bipolar disorder differ from major depression, and how is it most often treated? (p. 425)
10. In what parts of the world are people least likely to experience seasonal affective disorder? (p. 427)

Thought Questions

1. It has been suggested that ECT relieves depression by causing people to forget the events that caused it. What is the evidence against that hypothesis?
2. Certain people suffer from what they describe as "post-Christmas depression," a feeling of letdown after all the excitement of the holiday season. What other explanation can you offer?

Suggestions for Further Reading

Damasio, A. (1994). *Descartes' error.* New York: Putnam. Fascinating discussion of the usefulness of emotions, including fear and sadness.

Heston, L. L. (1992). *Mending minds.* New York: W. H. Freeman. A nontechnical description of contemporary, drug-oriented psychiatry. Chapters 1 and 2 deal with mood disorders.

Lickey, M. E., & Gordon, B. (1991). *Medicine and mental illness.* New York: W. H. Freeman. Discussion of drugs in the treatment of depression and other psychological disorders.

Terms

major depression   state of feeling sad, helpless, and lacking in energy and pleasure for weeks at a time (p. 420)

postpartum depression   depression after giving birth (p. 420)

Borna disease   viral infection that affects the nervous system, producing results that range from exaggerated activity fluctuations to death (p. 421)

tricyclic   drug that prevents the presynaptic neuron that releases catecholamine or serotonin molecules from reabsorbing them (p. 421)

monoamine oxidase inhibitor (MAOI)   drug that blocks the enzyme monoamine oxidase (p. 422)

second-generation antidepressant or **selective serotonin reuptake inhibitor**   antidepressant drug that blocks reuptake of the neurotransmitter serotonin (p. 422)

autoreceptor   presynaptic receptor that responds to the neurotransmitter released by the presynaptic cell itself (p. 423)

electroconvulsive therapy (ECT)   electrically inducing convulsion in an attempt to relieve depression or other disorders (p. 423)

unipolar disorder   mood disorder with only one extreme (or pole), generally depression (p. 425)

bipolar disorder or **manic-depressive disorder**   condition in which a person alternates between the two poles of mania and depression (p. 425)

mania   condition of restless activity, excitement, laughter, mostly happy mood, and few inhibitions (p. 425)

lithium   an element whose salts are often used as a therapy for bipolar disorder (p. 425)

seasonal affective disorder (SAD)   period of depression that reoccurs seasonally, usually in the winter (p. 427)

Schizophrenia

Here is a conversation between two people diagnosed with schizophrenia (Haley, 1959):

A: Do you work at the air base?

B: You know what I think of work. I'm 33 in June, do you mind?

A: June?

B: 33 years old in June. This stuff goes out the window after I live this, uh—leave this hospital. So I can't get my vocal cords back. So I lay off cigarettes. I'm in a spatial condition, from outer space myself. . . .

A: I'm a real spaceship from across.

B: A lot of people talk that way, like crazy, but "Believe It or Not," by Ripley, take it or leave it—alone—it's in the *Examiner,* it's in the comic section, "Believe It or Not," by Ripley, Robert E. Ripley, believe it or not, but we don't have to believe anything, unless I feel like it. Every little rosette—too much alone.

A: Yeah, it could be possible.

B: I'm a civilian seaman.

A: Could be possible. I take my bath in the ocean.

B: Bathing stinks. You know why? 'Cause you can't quit when you feel like it. You're in the service.

People with schizophrenia say and do things that other people (including most other people with schizophrenia) find difficult to understand. The causes of the disorder are still not well understood, but they apparently include a large biological component.

Characteristics

Schizophrenia is a severe disorder characterized both by deteriorating ability to function in everyday life and by some combination of hallucinations, delusions, thought disorder, movement disorder, and inappropriate emotional expressions. The *Diagnostic and Statistical Manual of Mental Disorders, Fourth Edition (DSM-IV)* provides a more complete formal description (American Psychiatric Association, 1994). Affected people vary considerably in both their behavioral symptoms and their biological characteristics. For some, hallucinations and delusions are prominent; thought disorders are dominant for others; some have clear signs of brain damage, and others do not. Investigators are still not sure whether schizophrenia is a single disorder or a family of loosely related disorders (Heinrichs, 1993; Iacono & Grove, 1993).

Schizophrenia was originally called *dementia praecox,* which is Latin for "premature deterioration of the mind." In 1911, Eugen Bleuler introduced the term *schizophrenia,* which has been preferred ever since. Although schizophrenia is Greek for "split mind," it is *not* the same thing as *multiple personality,* a condition in which a person alternates between one personality and another. A person with schizophrenia has only one personality. The split in the schizophrenic mind is between the emotional and intellectual aspects of the person: What the person expresses—or fails to express—emotionally is often at odds with what the person is saying.

Behavioral Symptoms

Schizophrenia is characterized by **positive symptoms** (behaviors that are present that should be absent) and **negative symptoms** (behaviors that are absent that should be present). The typical negative symptoms are deficits of social interaction, emotional expression, and speech. Negative symptoms tend to be stable over time and unresponsive to most drugs and other therapies. Positive symptoms, which are usually more sporadic, fall into two clusters that do not correlate strongly with each other (Andreasen, Arndt, Alliger, Miller, & Flaum,

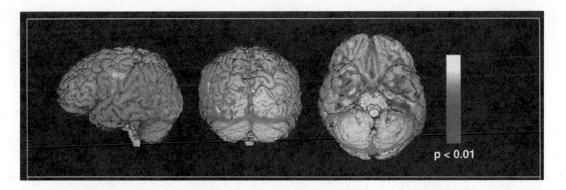

FIGURE **16.9**
Brain areas activated during hallucinations
Researchers made PET scans of the brain of a schizophrenic patient during
both auditory and visual hallucinations, and compared the activity to his resting
state. Yellow indicates areas of greatest activation and red is next greatest.
Note the widespread areas of activation; note also the lack of activation in
Broca's area, where we might have expected activity if the hallucinations were
due to inner speech.   Source: Silbersweig et al., 1995.

1995). The *psychotic* cluster consists of **delusions** (unfounded beliefs, such as the conviction that one is being persecuted severely or that invaders from outer space are trying to control one's behavior) and **hallucinations** (abnormal sensory experiences, such as hearing voices when no one else is speaking). PET scans have determined that hallucinations occur during periods of increased activity in the thalamus, hippocampus, basal ganglia, and prefrontal cortex (Silbersweig et al., 1995). (See Figure 16.9.)

The *disorganized* cluster of positive symptoms consists of inappropriate emotions (expressing great happiness or sadness for no apparent reason), bizarre behaviors, and thought disorders. The most typical **thought disorder** of schizophrenia is a difficulty understanding and using abstract concepts. For example, a schizophrenic person would take literally a proverb such as "When the cat is away, the mice will play." Schizophrenic people also fail to organize their thoughts, associating ideas loosely, as in a dream.

Schizophrenia can be either acute or chronic. An **acute** condition has a sudden onset and good prospects for return to normality in a short time. A **chronic** condition has a gradual onset and a long-term course. There may be improvement, but it is likely to be slow and incomplete.

Before antischizophrenic drugs became available in the mid-1950s, most schizophrenic people were confined to mental hospitals, where they generally deteriorated for the rest of their lives. Today, many people with schizophrenia manage to live normally with the aid of drugs and outpatient treatment, and many others live normal lives most of the time, with an occasional need for hospitalization.

Demographic Data

It is difficult to diagnose schizophrenia. There are many borderline cases, and it is possible to confuse schizophrenia with several other disorders. (See Digression 16.2.) Consequently, statistics on the prevalence of schizophrenia cannot be precise. According to one large survey of U.S. adults, about 1.3 percent of all people will suffer from schizophrenia at some point in their lives (Kendler, Gallagher, Abelson, & Kessler, 1996). Many other people, perhaps another 1 percent of the population, will develop a milder *schizoid* condition. Schizophrenia occurs in all ethnic groups and about equally in men and women, although on the average it develops at an earlier age in men. It is reported 10 to 100 times more often in the United States and Europe than in most Third World countries (Torrey, 1986), although part of the discrepancy could be due to differences in diagnostic standards and record keeping. Within the United States, schizophrenia is more common in impoverished areas than in wealthy areas.

Genetics

Here we have a peculiar situation. For some years now, researchers have made the convincing case that schizophrenia depends partly on a genetic predisposition. However, despite serious efforts to get beyond that point, we still do not know how many genes are involved, how they exert their influence, or how they interact with environmental factors.

The Evidence

People with schizophrenia are more likely than others are to have relatives with schizophrenia, as shown in Figure 16.10 (Gottesman, 1991). Similarity within a family indicates only that genetics is a possible factor, however. The link between schizophrenia and genetics rests on other, stronger kinds of evidence.

Twin studies   When one monozygotic twin is schizophrenic, there is about a 50 percent probability of the other twin becoming schizophrenic also, and an additional possibility of other serious disturbances, including borderline schizophrenia (Kendler & Robinette, 1983). However, if one dizygotic twin is schizophrenic, the other twin has only about a 15 percent probability of schizophrenia (Kendler, 1983; McGuffin, Farmer, Gottesman, Murray, & Reveley, 1984). That is, for monozygotic twins there is a 50 percent **concordance** (agreement) for schizophrenia, and a 15 percent concordance for dizygotic twins. Furthermore, twin pairs who are really monozygotic, but thought they weren't, are more concordant for schizophrenia than twin pairs who thought they were, but really aren't (Kendler, 1983). That is, *being* monozygotic is more critical than *being treated as* monozygotic.

Curiously, the concordance rate for schizophrenia between monozygotic twins is related to the concordance rate for handedness. Some monozygotic twins are mirror images of one another in appearance, and one is right-handed and the other is left-handed (Segal, 1984). Among pairs of monozygotic twins who are both right-handed, the schizophrenia concordance rate is 92 percent. But among pairs in which one twin is right-handed and the other is left-handed, the concordance rate is only 25 percent (Boklage, 1977).

DIGRESSION 16.2

Differential Diagnosis of Psychological Disorders

Suppose you are a psychiatrist, and you meet a patient who has recently deteriorated in everyday functioning and has hallucinations, delusions, thought disorder, and disorganized speech. You are ready to enter a diagnosis of schizophrenia and begin treatment, right?

Not so fast. According to *DSM-IV* (American Psychiatric Association, 1994), before making a diagnosis of schizophrenia one must first rule out other conditions that might produce similar symptoms. A **differential diagnosis** is one that identifies a condition as distinct from all similar conditions. Here are a few conditions that can resemble schizophrenia.

- *Mood disorder with psychotic features.* Depressed people sometimes have hallucinations and delusions, especially delusions of guilt or failure.
- *Prolonged substance abuse.* Symptoms resembling paranoid schizophrenia can result from drug abuse, especially if someone uses large amounts over weeks or months. Drugs likely to produce such effects include amphetamine, methamphetamine, cocaine, LSD, and phencyclidine ("angel dust"). Substance abuse is more likely than schizophrenia to produce temporary symptoms, and more likely to produce visual hallucinations.
- *Brain damage.* Lesions to the temporal or prefrontal cortex can produce symptoms resembling schizophrenia. Presumably, no competent therapist would confuse schizophrenia with the effects of a stroke, but one might easily overlook the possibility of a brain tumor.
- *Undetected hearing deficits.* Sometimes someone who is starting to have trouble hearing thinks that everyone else is whispering, and therefore starts to worry, "They're whispering because they're talking about me!" If the only problem is delusions of persecution, it is wise to check the person's hearing.
- *Huntington's disease.* In the later stages of Huntington's disease, people suffer hallucinations, delusions, and disordered thinking. You might think that no one would confuse Huntington's disease with schizophrenia, but sometimes the psychological symptoms become prominent before the motor impairments do. And, after all, catatonic schizophrenia includes motor abnormalities, so a mixture of psychological and motor symptoms could represent either schizophrenia or Huntington's disease. Huntington's disease usually starts at a later age than schizophrenia, but not always. A family medical history usually calls attention to the possibility of Huntington's disease, but some people are adopted or for other reasons do not know their history.
- *Nutritional abnormalities.* Niacin deficiency can produce hallucinations and delusions (Hoffer, 1973); so can prolonged deficiency of vitamin C or an allergy to milk proteins (not the same thing as lactose intolerance). Celiac disease, an inflammation of the upper small intestine, often caused by or at least aggravated by a reaction to wheat gluten, leads to poor absorption of nutrients, and sometimes hallucinations and delusions that can be alleviated by a gluten-free diet (Singh & Kay, 1976). Most psychiatrists consider dietary deficiencies or allergies to be a rare cause of schizophrenic reactions, but if we almost never test for the possibility, how do we know?

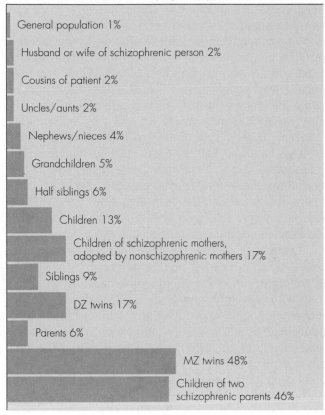

Percent developing schizophrenia

General population 1%

Husband or wife of schizophrenic person 2%

Cousins of patient 2%

Uncles/aunts 2%

Nephews/nieces 4%

Grandchildren 5%

Half siblings 6%

Children 13%

Children of schizophrenic mothers, adopted by nonschizophrenic mothers 17%

Siblings 9%

DZ twins 17%

Parents 6%

MZ twins 48%

Children of two schizophrenic parents 46%

FIGURE 16.10
Probabilities of developing schizophrenia
The closer the genetic relationship to someone with schizophrenia, the higher the probability of developing it oneself. Source: Data from Gottesman, 1991.

Adopted children who develop schizophrenia When an adopted child develops schizophrenia, the adopting relatives are as a rule psychologically normal, but a high percentage of the biological relatives have schizophrenia. One Danish study found schizophrenia in 12.5 percent of the immediate biological relatives and in none of the adopting relatives (Kety et al., 1994). A child of schizophrenic parentage who is adopted by a normal couple is more likely to develop schizophrenia than is a child of normal parents who has an adopted parent with schizophrenia (Wender, Rosenthal, Kety, Schulsinger, & Welner, 1974). These data point to either genetics or prenatal environment as a determining factor in schizophrenia.

In rare cases, an adopted child has a **paternal half-sibling** who is also adopted. Paternal half-siblings have the same father but different mothers; they are more closely related than cousins but less closely related than full brother and sister. Another Danish study found 63 adopted schizophrenics with paternal half-siblings who were adopted by other families. Eight of

the 63 half-siblings had schizophrenia also—a concordance well above the approximately 1 percent prevalence of schizophrenia in the population (Kety, 1977). Note that because these children had different mothers, they did not share a common environment even before birth.

(*A note in passing:* Much of the best genetic and epidemiological research comes from Denmark and other Scandinavian countries, because they have a long history of excellent medical record keeping.)

Children of people with schizophrenia and their twins
Suppose one twin has schizophrenia and the other does not, and that both twins eventually become parents. What is the risk of schizophrenia in their children? To test this question, researchers have gone through the medical records in Norway and Denmark and found that the children of the twin without schizophrenia have almost the same risk of schizophrenia as do the children of the twin with schizophrenia (Gottesman & Bertelson, 1989; Kringlen & Cramer, 1989).

What do these data mean? Apparently, both twins inherited genes that predispose a person to schizophrenia. Some unknown influence caused those genes to produce schizophrenia in one twin and not the other, but both twins can pass the genes to their children. These data indicate that genes are not the whole explanation of schizophrenia; clearly, someone with genes for schizophrenia may avoid developing it. They also suggest that people without genes for schizophrenia seldom develop it. (If purely environmental factors caused schizophrenia in a twin with no genes for schizophrenia, the other twin would not be likely to have schizophrenic children.)

Unanswered Questions

Although research indicates an important genetic influence on schizophrenia, a number of questions remain. *What* gene or genes increase the risk of schizophrenia, and *how?* Although we know which genes are linked to Huntington's disease, Alzheimer's disease, and many other conditions, the search for genes relevant to schizophrenia continues. Although a number of researchers have isolated genes that appeared to be linked to schizophrenia in a particular population (e.g., Straub et al., 1995), so far the results have not been consistently replicable. Part of the problem is that many people are misclassified. Twin studies tell us that many people who have the gene(s) fail to develop schizophrenia, and we know that many people with other disorders are incorrectly diagnosed as having schizophrenia. It is also possible that schizophrenia emerges from the combined effects of several genes, no one of which produces schizophrenic effects by itself.

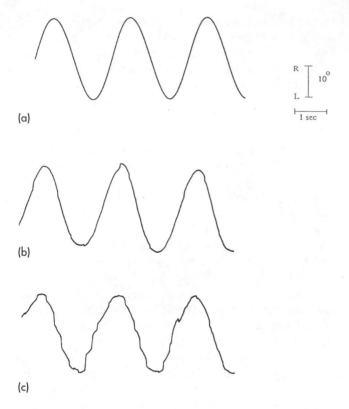

FIGURE 16.11

Pursuit eye movements of people with and without schizophrenia

(**a**) Movement of a visual target. (**b**) Eye movements of a person without schizophrenia, following the target. (**c**) Eye movements of a person with schizophrenia. Note that the person with schizophrenia has clearly apparent but not gross deficits. The eyes stay close to the target but lag frequently and make occasional backward movements.   Source: Sereno & Holzman, 1993.

A second issue: On the average, people with schizophrenia have fewer children than most other people. So what maintains the gene at such a high frequency in the population? Why hasn't natural selection depleted it? One hypothesis is that schizophrenia results from a combination of two or more genes; perhaps each gene is maintained in the population because it is beneficial by itself, even though in combination it is harmful.

The Search for Behavioral Markers

One way to facilitate the search for possible schizophrenia genes is to find a biological marker that identifies people with the predisposing genes, independently of whether they are actually diagnosed with schizophrenia. Such a marker would also help therapists identify people who are at risk and perhaps let them develop interventions to prevent or minimize the condition.

One possible marker is an impairment of pursuit eye movements. We make two kinds of eye movements: A **saccadic eye movement** shifts suddenly from one target to another. When you read this page, your eyes jump from one fixation point to another by saccades. A **pursuit eye movement** focuses on a moving object. Most people with schizophrenia have deficits in their pursuit eye movements; either the eyes stop moving while the target continues, or the eyes make a saccadic movement that takes them off the target (Sereno & Holzman, 1993). (See Figure 16.11.) They have such difficulties both before they start drug treatment (Lieberman et al., 1993) and after drugs relieve the symptoms. Pursuit eye movements are also impaired in many of their close relatives (Keefe et al., 1997). These results support the hypothesis that abnormal pursuit eye movements indicate vulnerability to schizophrenia.

Pursuit eye movements are not, however, a sufficiently accurate marker by themselves; they are linked to conditions other than schizophrenia, and not everyone with schizophrenia has abnormal pursuit eye movements. Many people with schizophrenia have nonschizophrenic relatives who have attention problems (Keefe et al., 1997), moderately impaired scores on neuropsychological tests (Cannon et al., 1994), deficits in spatial working memory (Park, Holzman, & Goldman-Rakic, 1995), and weak habituation to a repeated tone (Hollister, Mednick, Brennan, & Cannon, 1994). Each of these by itself is at best a moderately accurate marker for vulnerability to schizophrenia, so a combination of scores might prove more useful.

The Neurodevelopmental Hypothesis

According to the **neurodevelopmental hypothesis** now popular among biomedical researchers, schizophrenia is due in large part to abnormalities in the prenatal (before birth) or neonatal (newborn) development of the nervous system, which lead to subtle but important abnormalities of brain anatomy and major abnormalities in behavior (Weinberger, 1996). The hypothesis holds that stressful experiences can aggravate the symptoms and that supportive relatives and friends can decrease them, but environmental factors by themselves do not cause schizophrenia.

The evidence for the neurodevelopmental hypothesis is that (1) in addition to genetics, several kinds of prenatal or neonatal abnormalities that impair brain development are linked to later schizophrenia; (2) people with schizophrenia have a number of minor brain abnormalities that apparently originate early in life; and (3) it is plausible that certain abnormalities of early brain development could produce behavioral abnormalities in adulthood.

Prenatal and Neonatal Abnormalities of Development

Many people with schizophrenia who do not have affected relatives showed abnormalities before or shortly after birth that might have affected their brain development. One set of investigators examined the birth records of people who later developed schizophrenia and found a larger-than-normal number of "nonoptimal signs," such as extensive maternal bleeding during pregnancy, prolonged labor, complications during delivery, low birth weight, low head circumference at birth, and disproportionality between body length and weight at birth (Hultman, Öhman, Cnattingius, Wieselgren, & Lindström, 1997). Most babies have one or two such signs, but those with seven or more (of a possible 34) were likely to develop schizophrenia later.

Schizophrenia has also been linked to problems in early or middle pregnancy. During the winter of 1944–45, near the end of World War II, Germany blockaded the Netherlands, which depended heavily on imported food. The Dutch people endured a near-starvation diet until the Allies liberated them in May. Women who were in the earliest stage of pregnancy during the starvation period gave birth to a high percentage of babies who later developed schizophrenia (Susser et al., 1996).

If a mother is Rh-negative and her baby is Rh-positive, a small amount of the baby's Rh-positive blood factor may, beginning in the second trimester, leak into the mother's blood supply, triggering an immunological rejection response. The response is weak with the woman's first Rh-positive baby but stronger during later pregnancies, and it is more intense with boy than with girl babies. Second- and later-born boy babies with Rh incompatibility have an increased risk of hearing deficits, mental retardation, and several other problems, and about twice the usual probability of schizophrenia (Hollister, Laing, & Mednick, 1996).

Further evidence that the risk may be traced to prenatal difficulties stems from the **season-of-birth effect:** the tendency for people born in winter to have a slightly greater probability of developing schizophrenia than people born at other times of the year (Bradbury & Miller, 1985). This tendency occurs only in nontropical climates (where the weather changes by season), and it is particularly pronounced for schizophrenics who have no schizophrenic relatives. Whereas a family with several schizophrenic members has a fairly high probability of schizophrenia for any child, in other families, the probability of schizophrenia is generally low but increases for children born in the winter (Bradbury & Miller, 1985).

What might account for the season-of-birth effect? The likeliest hypothesis is viral infection. Viral epi-

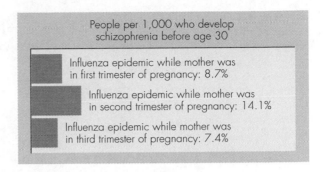

FIGURE **16.12**
Schizophrenia after an influenza epidemic
The probability of schizophrenia is greatest if the epidemic occurred during the second trimester of the mother's pregnancy. Source: Data from Mednick, Machon, & Huttunen, 1990.

demics are most common in fall. Therefore, the reasoning goes, during a fall epidemic, many pregnant women become infected with a virus that impairs a crucial stage of brain development in babies who will be born in the winter. A virus that affects the mother does not cross the placenta, and there is no evidence of viral damage in the brains of people with schizophrenia (Taller et al., 1996). However, a viral infection gives the mother a fever, and the fetal brain is extremely vulnerable to heat damage. A mere 1.5°C fever slows the division of fetal neurons, and a 3°C fever kills them (Laburn, 1996). (Exercise during pregnancy does not overheat the abdomen and is not dangerous to the fetus.)

To test the possible role of viral infections, investigators have asked whether the season-of-birth effect is particularly strong after a major fall epidemic. The answer is apparently yes. For example, Europe had a major influenza epidemic in the fall of 1957, and babies who were born three months later eventually developed schizophrenia at a rate almost twice as high as usual (Mednick, Machon, & Huttunen, 1990). (See Figure 16.12.) When a viral epidemic occurred at some time other than fall, the incidence of schizophrenia increased for babies born three months later (Barr, Mednick, & Munk-Jorgensen, 1990; Torrey, Rawlings, & Waldman, 1988). Almost any viral infection is dangerous; the risk of schizophrenia increases after epidemics of influenza, measles, polio, and chicken pox. However, all the reported effects have been small, and we need to examine more data before drawing any firm conclusions.

Mild Brain Abnormalities

In accord with the neurodevelopmental hypothesis, some people with schizophrenia (not all) show mild abnormalities of brain development. MRI scans indi-

FIGURE **16.13**
Coronal sections for identical twins
Left: Brain of the twin who has schizophrenia. *Right:* Brain of the twin who does not. Note that the ventricles (near the center of each brain) are larger in the twin with schizophrenia.
Source: Photos courtesy of E. F. Torrey & M. F. Casanova/NIMH.

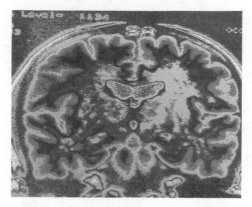
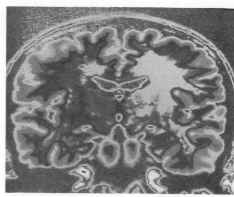

cate that in people with schizophrenia, the cerebral cortex and the overall forebrain are slightly smaller than in healthy control subjects of the same age (Benes, 1995; Brown et al., 1986; Kareken et al., 1995; Turetsky et al., 1995). Researchers have also found thalamic abnormalities, which may be related to attentional difficulties (Andreasen et al., 1994) and larger-than-normal ventricles (Zipursky, Lim, Sullivan, Brown, & Pfefferbaum, 1992). The ventricles are fluid-filled spaces; they become enlarged after a loss of neurons. (See Figure 16.13.) All these anatomical characteristics vary, as, of course, do behavioral symptoms. Brain anatomy is generally most abnormal in people with the greatest social and cognitive deficits.

On a variety of neuropsychological tests, schizophrenic patients tend to show deficits of memory and attention similar to those of people with damage to the temporal or prefrontal cortex (Beatty, Jocic, Monson, & Katzung, 1994; Park, Holzman, & Goldman-Rakic, 1995; Saykin et al., 1994; Seidman et al., 1995). The areas with the most consistent signs of abnormality include the cortical areas that mature most slowly, such as the dorsolateral prefrontal cortex (Pearlson, Petty, Ross, & Tien, 1996). Those areas may be slightly smaller than normal, and their activity does not increase during memory tasks, as it does in other people (Berman, Torrey, Daniel, & Weinberger, 1992; Dolan et al., 1995). As you might expect, people with schizophrenia perform poorly on memory tasks (Goldberg, Weinberger, Berman, Pliskin, & Podd, 1987).

At a microscopic level, some researchers have found fewer than the normal number of neurons in various cortical areas (Benes, Davidson, & Bird, 1986), whereas others have found neurons that are smaller than normal (Selemon, Rajkowska, & Goldman-Rakic, 1995). There are also miscellaneous indications of abnormal neuronal development. During an early stage of brain maturation, certain developing neurons migrate through layers of white matter to reach their normal destination in the cerebral cortex. In some people with schizophrenia, many of those neurons apparently failed

to complete the journey; they remain throughout life deep in the white matter (Akbarian et al., 1996a). Also, some neurons that reach their normal locations fail to arrange themselves in the neat, orderly manner typical of normal brains (Benes & Bird, 1987). (See Figures 16.14 and 16.15.) The details of abnormal development remain to be established, but it is noteworthy that many schizophrenic patients have abnormal amounts of cell-recognition molecules that guide the migration of neurons and axons during early development (Honer et al., 1997; Poltorak et al., 1997).

Studies have found no significant differences in the brains of younger and older schizophrenic patients (Andreasen et al., 1990; Selemon, Rajkowska, & Goldman-Rakic, 1995). Furthermore, autopsies of schizophrenic brains have revealed no proliferation of glia cells, which ordinarily increase in damaged areas (Benes, 1995). Researchers therefore conclude that schizophrenia is not associated with gradual brain damage in adulthood, as is Parkinson's disease and Huntington's disease. Instead, the brain abnormalities probably occur early in life, either from genetic causes or because of problems during pregnancy.

Early Development and Later Psychopathology

One question may have struck you by now. How can we reconcile the evidence for abnormalities of early brain development with the fact that the symptoms of schizophrenia usually become prominent between ages 20 and 30? The time course may not be so puzzling as it seems at first (Weinberger, 1996). The areas that most consistently show signs of abnormality are the ones that mature most slowly. As discussed in Chapter 15, infant monkeys with damage in the dorsolateral prefrontal cortex behave normally at first and gradually become impaired later, when the dorsolateral prefrontal cortex would ordinarily become mature. The same kind of damage in human infants might produce more seri-

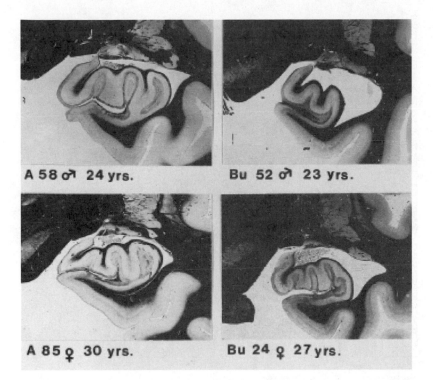

FIGURE **16.14**
The hippocampus of normal people (left) and people with schizophrenia (right)
Notice the atrophy of the brains on the right.
Source: From Bogerts, Meertz, & Schönfeldt-Bausch, 1985; photos courtesy of B. Bogerts.

FIGURE **16.15**
Hippocampal disorganization in schizophrenia
The cells of a normal person (top) show an orderly arrangement; those of someone with schizophrenia (bottom) appear more haphazard and disorganized.   Source: Photos courtesy of Arnold Scheibel.

ous behavioral problems in late adolescence and young adulthood than it did in early childhood. Thus, particular kinds of early brain damage may lead to delayed effects on psychological well-being.

The current status of the neurodevelopmental hypothesis is best described as plausible, but not firmly established. Many studies link schizophrenia to probable prenatal damage and mild brain abnormalities, but the effects are small, vary from one sample of patients to another, and are often subject to alternative interpretations (Weinberger, 1996). Additional research will be necessary to test the hypothesis more thoroughly.

Neurotransmitters and Drugs

Since the discovery of antischizophrenic drugs in the 1950s, much research has confirmed a connection between schizophrenia and the dopamine synapses of the brain. Still, the exact nature of that abnormality remains uncertain.

FIGURE **16.16**
Dopamine-blocking effects of antipsychotic drugs

Drugs along the horizontal axis are arranged in terms of the average daily dose prescribed for schizophrenic patients. (Horizontal lines indicate common ranges of dosage.) Along the vertical axis is the amount required of each drug to block postsynaptic dopamine receptors to a certain degree. A drug's effectiveness in blocking dopamine synapses is almost perfectly correlated with its ability to control schizophrenia.
Source: From Seeman, Lee, Chau-Wong, & Wong, 1976.

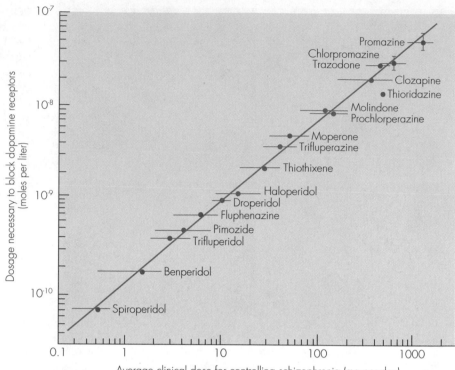

Drugs That Can Provoke Schizophrenic Symptoms

Large, frequent doses of certain drugs can induce **substance-induced psychotic disorder,** characterized by hallucinations and delusions. The main differences between drug-induced psychosis and schizophrenia are that victims of the drug-induced states often report visual hallucinations, whereas schizophrenic people seldom do, and that a drug-induced psychosis is usually temporary (Ellinwood, 1969; Sato, 1992). A psychotic reaction is likely after extensive use of stimulant drugs such as amphetamine, methamphetamine, or cocaine. The fact that all these drugs stimulate dopamine synapses seems to support the **dopamine hypothesis of schizophrenia,** the idea that schizophrenia results from excess activity at certain dopamine synapses. However, the results are equally compatible with the **glutamate hypothesis of schizophrenia,** according to which the underlying problem is deficient activity at certain glutamate synapses. In many brain areas, dopamine inhibits glutamate release; in others, glutamate excites neurons that dopamine inhibits. Thus, increased dopamine activity would have many of the same effects as decreased glutamate activity. Furthermore, the drug *phencyclidine* ("angel dust"), which inhibits glutamate receptors, produces symptoms that mimic schizophrenia even more closely than the dopamine stimulants do. Curiously, phencyclidine pro-

duces little if any psychotic response in preadolescents; the potential for such effects emerges later, as does the likelihood of schizophrenia (Olney & Farger, 1995).

Drug Therapies

In the 1950s researchers discovered that the drug **chlorpromazine** (trade name Thorazine) helps to relieve schizophrenia. Previously, few schizophrenic patients who entered a mental hospital ever left. Chlorpromazine and related drugs can halt the course of the disease, especially if treatment is begun early. The way drugs control schizophrenia is similar to the way insulin controls diabetes. The medication must be taken regularly, or the symptoms are likely to return.

Researchers later discovered many other **antipsychotic** or **neuroleptic drugs.** Most of them belong to two chemical families: the **phenothiazines,** which include chlorpromazine, and the **butyrophenones,** which include **haloperidol** (trade name Haldol). Figure 16.16 illustrates the correlation between the therapeutic effects of various drugs and their ability to block postsynaptic dopamine receptors. For each drug, researchers determined the mean dose prescribed for schizophrenic patients (displayed along the horizontal axis). Presumably, drugs such as spiroperidol (at the lower left in the figure) are prescribed in the lowest doses because minimal amounts are effective; larger doses of drugs such as chlorpromazine are needed to achieve the same effect. The investigators also determined what dose of each drug is necessary to block dopamine receptors (displayed along the vertical axis). As the figure shows, the more effective a given drug is at blocking dopamine receptors, the more effective it is for relieving schizophrenia (Seeman, Lee, Chau-Wong, & Wong, 1976). These results support the dopamine hypothesis of schizophrenia, but they are equally compatible with the glutamate hypothesis. (If the original problem is deficient glutamate, one way to remedy the situation would be to block the dopamine synapses that inhibit glutamate release.) Furthermore, a number of antipsychotic drugs both stimulate glutamate synapses, especially the NMDA type, and block dopamine synapses (Banerjee, Zuck, Yablonsky-Alter, & Lidsky, 1995).

Side Effects and the Search for Improved Drugs

Most investigators in this field believe that antipsychotic drugs are beneficial because they decrease the activity of dopamine neurons in the **mesolimbocortical system,** a set of neurons that project from the midbrain tegmentum to the limbic system. However, the drugs also decrease the activity of other dopamine neurons, which are responsible for movement. Consequently, the drugs produce a combination of desired and undesired effects.

The most serious of the unpleasant side effects is **tardive dyskinesia** (TARD-eev dis-kih-NEE-zhee-uh), tremors and other involuntary movements that increase over years on medication, especially in people who have taken large doses and in people who get the weakest therapeutic benefits (Chakos et al., 1996). Tardive dyskinesia may result from denervation supersensitivity (Chapter 15): Prolonged blockage of dopamine transmission causes the postsynaptic neurons to increase in sensitivity and respond vigorously to even small amounts of dopamine. Slight stimulation of these highly responsive synapses causes bursts of involuntary movements. Antipsychotic drugs apparently do not increase the number of dopamine receptors (Andersson et al., 1990), but there are other mechanisms by which denervation supersensitivity could occur.

Once tardive dyskinesia emerges, it is very persistent. Consequently, the best solution is to prevent it in the first place. Certain new drugs called *atypical antipsychotics,* such as clozapine, show much promise for alleviating schizophrenia with little risk of tardive dyskinesia. They block dopamine activity in the pathways to the prefrontal cortex but have less effect in the basal ganglia, the area presumably relevant to tardive dyskinesia (White & Wang, 1983). (See Figure 16.17.) Unlike

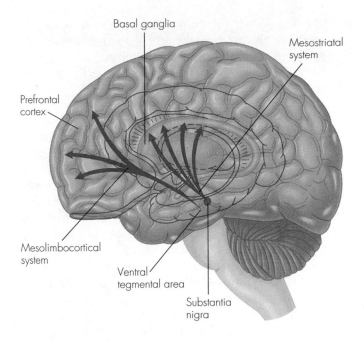

FIGURE **16.17**
Two major dopamine pathways
The mesolimbocortical system is apparently responsible for the symptoms of schizophrenia; the path to the basal ganglia is probably responsible for tardive dyskinesia, a movement disorder. Source: Based on Valzelli, 1980.

most antipsychotic drugs, clozapine blocks dopamine type D_4 receptors more than D_2; it also blocks serotonin type 5-HT_2 receptors and produces benefits in many patients who do not respond to other antipsychotic drugs. Unfortunately, clozapine produces side effects of its own, including a decrease in white blood cells that leaves the person vulnerable to infections. At present, each antipsychotic drug has advantages and disadvantages; the search for better drugs continues.

Neurotransmitters and Their Receptors

Although drugs that block dopamine receptors alleviate schizophrenia, the underlying problem cannot be anything so simple as excess production and release of dopamine. Dopamine and its metabolites are generally found in approximately normal levels in people with schizophrenia (Jaskiw & Weinberger, 1992). However, amphetamine induces a greater release of dopamine in schizophrenic people than in others, on the average, so evidently schizophrenic people have a greater capacity for release (Breier et al., 1997). Studies of dopamine receptors have yielded complicated results. Evidently, the density of dopamine type D_2 receptors is about normal, but that of type D_1 is lower than normal, and the levels of D_3 and D_4 are about twice as high as normal (Gurevich et al., 1997; Murray et al., 1995; Okubo et al.,

1997). We do not yet know whether the receptor abnormalities are the original problem, or whether they develop in compensation for different amounts of dopamine release in various brain areas. Researchers have found no relationship between schizophrenia and the genes that code for dopamine receptors.

The brains of schizophrenic people also release lower-than-normal amounts of the neurotransmitters GABA and glutamate (Akbarian et al., 1995; Benes, Vincent, Marie, & Khan, 1996; Tsai et al., 1995), and the glutamate receptors in the prefrontal cortex are altered in form (Akbarian et al., 1996b). Because any abnormality in one neurotransmitter is likely to affect others as well, it is difficult to infer whether the original problem is in dopamine, glutamate, or other synapses.

A further complication is the time it takes for antipsychotic drugs to be effective. Although the drugs block dopamine receptors almost at once, their effects on behavior build up gradually over two or three weeks. Like antidepressants, antipsychotic drugs probably induce gradual changes in both the pattern of release by the presynaptic neuron and the sensitivity of the postsynaptic neuron.

IN **CLOSING**

The Biology of Complex Psychological Disorders

The present is an exciting time for researchers studying the biological basis of schizophrenia and other psychological disorders. Very clearly, all the answers are not yet in, but just as clearly, progress is occurring. Every research project offers hope of another step toward greater understanding.

How plausible is the prospect of a totally biological explanation for a complex psychological disorder? There is room for disagreement on this issue, and we cannot know the answer until we have more information. It is worth emphasizing, however, that even a strictly biological explanation of the underlying problem would leave a major role for experience. Just as a computer with a hardware bug may function either badly or almost normally, depending on the software, the behavior of someone with mild genetic or neurodevelopmental abnormalities will be better in some environments and worse in others.

Summary

1. Positive symptoms of schizophrenia (characteristics not present in most other people) include hallucinations, delusions, inappropriate emotions, bizarre behaviors, and thought disorder. (p. 430)

2. Negative symptoms (normal characteristics absent in people with schizophrenia) include deficits of social interaction, emotional expression, and speech. (p. 430)

3. Studies of twins and adopted children indicate a genetic predisposition to schizophrenia, although not everyone with the gene develops the condition. Researchers have not conclusively identified the relevant genes or determined what they do. (p. 432)

4. Many relatives of schizophrenic patients have behaviors that may be markers for the underlying gene, such as impaired pursuit eye movements. (p. 434)

5. According to the neurodevelopmental hypothesis, either genes or difficulties early in life impair brain development in ways that lead to behavioral abnormalities beginning in early adulthood. (p. 434)

6. The probability of schizophrenia is higher than average for those who were subjected to prenatal malnutrition, Rh incompatibility, or maternal fever. (p. 435)

7. Some people with schizophrenia show mild abnormalities of early brain development, which do not increase during adulthood. (p. 435)

8. A number of self-administered drugs that stimulate dopamine synapses or inhibit glutamate synapses can eventually induce symptoms that resemble schizophrenia. (p. 438)

9. Drugs that relieve schizophrenia block dopamine synapses, stimulate glutamate synapses, or both. Because dopamine and glutamate have opposite effects in many brain areas, the results are equally compatible with the hypothesis that schizophrenia reflects excess dopamine activity and the hypothesis that it reflects deficient glutamate activity. (p. 438)

10. Prolonged use of antipsychotic drugs may produce tardive dyskinesia, a movement disorder. (p. 439)

11. People with schizophrenia have apparently normal levels of dopamine release and a mixture of increased and decreased expression of various dopamine receptors. They also have lower-than-normal release of GABA and glutamate. (p. 439)

Review Questions

1. Describe the thought disorder of a typical schizophrenic person. (p. 431)

2. If someone has hallucinations and delusions, what diagnoses should a therapist consider other than schizophrenia? (p. 432)

3. If a schizophrenic person has a nonschizophrenic twin, is the nonschizophrenic twin likely to have children who eventually develop schizophrenia? What conclusions follow from this answer? (p. 433)

4. What behaviors are more common among the relatives of schizophrenic patients than among other people? (p. 434)

5. What is the season-of-birth effect, and what is a promising hypothesis for it? (p. 435)

6. Which brain areas are most likely to show abnormal development in schizophrenic patients? (p. 435)

7. If, as proposed, schizophrenia is due to early abnormal brain development, why do behavioral symptoms not become prominent until much later? (p. 436)

8. Why are so many results equally compatible with the dopamine hypothesis and the glutamate hypothesis? (p. 438)

9. What are the advantages and disadvantages of clozapine? (p. 439)

10. How long does it take for an antipsychotic drug to alter activity at the synapses? How long does it take to alter behavior? (p. 440)

Thought Questions

1. With some illnesses, a patient who at first fails to respond is offered higher and higher doses of medication. However, if a schizophrenic patient does not respond to antipsychotic drugs, it is generally not a good idea to increase them. Why not?

2. Long-term use of antipsychotic drugs can induce tardive dyskinesia. However, if a person with tardive dyskinesia stops taking the drugs, the symptoms actually grow worse, at least temporarily. Why?

Suggestions for Further Reading

Gottesman, I. I. (1991). *Schizophrenia genesis*. New York: W. H. Freeman. Discussion of the causes of schizophrenia, with emphasis on genetics.

Heston, L. L. (1992). *Mending minds*. New York: W. H. Freeman. A nontechnical description of contemporary, drug-oriented psychiatry. Chapter 3 covers schizophrenia.

Terms

schizophrenia disorder characterized both by a deteriorating ability to function in everyday life and by some combination of hallucinations, delusions, thought disorder, movement disorder, and inappropriate emotional expressions (p. 430)

positive symptom presence of a behavior not seen in normal people (p. 430)

negative symptom absence of a behavior ordinarily seen in normal people (p. 430)

delusion belief that other people regard as unfounded, such as the belief that one is being severely persecuted (p. 431)

hallucination sensory experience that does not correspond to reality (p. 431)

thought disorder impaired thinking, such as difficulty understanding and using abstract concepts (p. 431)

acute having a sudden onset and a strong possibility of ending quickly (p. 431)

chronic having a gradual onset and long duration (p. 431)

concordance agreement (A pair of twins is concordant for a trait if both of them have it or if neither has it.) (p. 432)

differential diagnosis identification of a condition as distinct from all similar conditions (p. 432)

paternal half-siblings people who have the same father but different mothers (p. 433)

saccadic eye movement sudden shift of the eyes from one target to another (p. 434)

pursuit eye movement eye movement that follows a moving target (p. 434)

neurodevelopmental hypothesis proposal that schizophrenia is due in large part to abnormalities in the prenatal or neonatal development of the nervous system, which lead to subtle but important abnormalities of brain anatomy and major abnormalities in behavior (p. 434)

season-of-birth effect tendency for people born in winter to have a greater probability of developing schizophrenia than people born in other seasons (p. 435)

substance-induced psychotic disorder condition provoked by large, repeated doses of a drug, which resembles schizophrenia and includes hallucinations and delusions (p. 438)

dopamine hypothesis of schizophrenia proposal that schizophrenia is due to excess activity at certain dopamine synapses (p. 438)

glutamate hypothesis of schizophrenia proposal that schizophrenia is due to deficient activity at certain glutamate synapses (p. 438)

chlorpromazine first drug found to relieve schizophrenia (p. 438)

antipsychotic or **neuroleptic drug** drug that relieves schizophrenia (p. 438)

phenothiazine class of neuroleptic drugs that includes chlorpromazine (p. 438)

butyrophenone class of neuroleptic drugs that includes haloperidol (p. 438)

haloperidol a common neuroleptic drug (p. 438)

mesolimbocortical system set of neurons that project from the midbrain tegmentum to the limbic system (p. 439)

tardive dyskinesia side effect of neuroleptic drugs characterized by tremors and other involuntary movements (p. 439)

Mind and Brain

MAIN**IDEAS**

1. Philosophers and neuroscientists have long considered the relationship between mind and brain. Nearly all now reject the common assumption that the mind exists independently of the physical brain.
2. Determining which brain activities correspond to which experiences is philosophically easy, though scientifically difficult. The harder philosophical question is why, in a universe of matter and energy, consciousness exists at all.

After completing a course titled "Brain and Behavior," a Stanford sophomore named Andrew Bradley (1997) captured the essence of a deep philosophical problem, one that I hope you have contemplated also:

I am composed of water, neurons and energy. I am also composed of ideas, dreams and ethics. By drawing the microscope of science intensely close to the interface shared by these two states, "Brain and Behavior" makes one ponder what it means to be a human and to realize the amazing circumstances that are life.

At the close of the introduction to this text, I remarked, "Biological psychology is a very ambitious field. We are setting out to explain as much as we can of psychology in strictly biological, physical terms." As you know by now, the explanations are still incomplete, littered with "maybe," "probably," and "this part to be filled in later." Nevertheless, researchers are making steady progress. Biological explanations of behavior and experience are better developed than they were even a few years ago and, just as important, researchers have rejected many hypotheses that once seemed reasonable. (Scientific progress occurs as much in its rejections as in its acceptances.) Biological psychologists are not only ambitious, but also optimistic.

But if everything is explained in terms of physical mechanisms, what happens to the concept of mind? We all feel, rightly or wrongly, that we deliberately decide what to do, that our conscious thought processes control our behavior, or at least certain parts of it.

Classical Positions on the Mind–Brain Relationship

Many philosophers have addressed the **mind–body** or **mind–brain problem:** What is the relationship between the mind and the brain? The most popular view is, no doubt, **dualism,** the belief that mind and body are different kinds of substance that somehow interact. The French philosopher René Descartes defended dualism but recognized the vexing issue of how an immaterial mind could influence a physical brain. He proposed that mind and brain interact at a single point in space, which he suggested was the pineal gland, the smallest unpaired structure he could find in the brain.

Although Descartes gets credit for the first explicit defense of dualism, he hardly originated the idea. Nearly all of us, myself included, began as dualists (except for the part about the pineal gland). We grew up convinced that our thoughts control our actions, and when we were told that the brain controls behavior, we reacted, "Well, okay, then the brain communicates with the mind, and the mind controls the brain."

Although dualism is a belief that is very hard to shake, nearly all philosophers and scientists who have much to say about it reject it, preferring instead some form of **monism,** the belief that the universe consists of only one kind of existence. Various forms of monism are possible, including the following:

- **Materialism:** the view that only the physical world exists, and that mental events are at most a meaningless and accidental by-product of physical processes
- **Mentalism:** the view that only the mind really exists, and that the physical world exists only in our imagination, or perhaps only in the mind of God
- **Identity position:** the view that mental processes are the same thing as certain kinds of brain processes, but described in different terms

Most philosophers and neuroscientists today favor some version of the identity position. By this view, what you and I experience as consciousness *is* brain activity; one does not exist separately from the other. In a sense, then, your mind *does* control your behavior, but only because mind is *the same thing* as brain activity—or at least as certain kinds of brain activity. (You are not conscious of everything that happens in your brain.) Mind emerges from certain organizations of matter and energy, just as the properties of water emerge from a compound of hydrogen and oxygen.

(Does a belief in monism mean that we are lowering our evaluation of mind to the merely material? Maybe not. Maybe we are elevating our concept of the material world.)

Why would neuroscientists and philosophers insist that mind is fully equivalent to brain activity? The strongest reason comes from physics. According to the law of conservation of matter and energy, the only way to accelerate any of the matter or transform any of the energy in your body is to act upon it with other matter or energy. Therefore, if the mind moves the body, then the mind itself must be matter or energy.

The second reason for equating mind with brain activity is that doing so has been a fruitful research strategy. If the mind is whatever is left over after we have explained the brain functions, then its role is gradually getting smaller and smaller, and indeed "mind" becomes little more than a name we give to the gaps in our brain science.

Continuing Problems

Has monism been proved correct? No. In fact, scientists seldom regard any theory as proved, except in mathematics. Nevertheless, the arguments in favor of monism are compelling. Until and unless someone explains how a nonphysical entity could influence the physical world, I recommend that you be very cautious about how you use the term *mind.* You can certainly talk about mind or consciousness if you understand those terms to refer to a product of or synonym for brain activity. But if by *mind* you imply a ghostlike something that has neither matter nor energy and yet influences matter and energy, do not underestimate the physical and philosophical arguments that can be marshaled against you (Dennett, 1991).

If we accept some version of the monist position, have we then solved the mind–brain problem? Hardly. The question remains, *why* is there any such thing as consciousness? One way to clarify that question is by rephrasing it: Could someone build a supercomputer that mimics all the functions of the human brain? If so, would that machine be conscious? If not, why are we?

Philosophers addressing the mind–brain relationship distinguish the easy problems from the hard problem. The **easy problems** pertain to which brain activity is associated with which experience or behavior. For example, researchers were solving easy problems when they determined that activity in the central amygdala corresponds to fear, and that activity in the middle temporal cortex is essential to perceiving visual motion. These problems are not really easy to solve; they require enormous amounts of careful research. They are easy only in the sense that they raise no serious philosophical issues.

The **hard problem,** on the other hand, is the question of why and how any kind of brain activity is associated with consciousness. Never mind whether anxiety depends on the amygdala or the pineal gland; why is it related to *any* part of the brain? Physical activity in the brain *appears* to be different from consciousness, and saying they are the same thing does not make the problem go away. Daniel Dennett (1991) argues in *Consciousness Explained* that the hard problem really consists of an enormous number of easy problems. Once we fully answer all the easy problems, the hard problem will go away. Maybe. Dennett is very persuasive, and yet it is difficult to be convinced that the hard problem has been solved.

The problem in doing research on mind–body relationships is that consciousness is not observable. Although I am directly aware of my own conscious mind, and you of yours, we cannot observe each other's. Indeed, none of us can be certain that anyone else is conscious at all. I infer that other people are conscious because they look and act much as I do. Chimpanzees are less like us, but close enough that I infer that they are conscious, too. What about rats? Fish? Squid? Houseflies? Computers? Rocks? Each of us reaches a point of hesitation or doubt, and we don't all reach it at the same point. I don't know whether houseflies are conscious, and furthermore I don't know how I could determine the answer. You can see why it is so difficult to determine the relationship of consciousness to the physical brain.

Several people have told me that they originally became neuroscientists because they were fascinated with the mind–brain problem and hoped to contribute to its solution, even in a small way. In the meantime, the best we can do is to solve the easy problems as well as possible. As you have seen, we now know that losing various parts of the brain means losing parts of the mind. We also know that stimulating certain brain activities can evoke certain experiences or behavioral tendencies. *Why* there is such a close relationship between brain and experience may elude us, but at least we continue to explore and document the connection. If Dennett is right that answering the easy problems does answer the hard problem, then great. Even if not, research findings have important applications of their own, and should at least improve our philosophical musings about the hard question.

Summary

1. Dualism, the popular view that the mind exists separately from the brain, faces the apparently fatal difficulty that the matter and energy of the brain can be influenced only by other matter and energy. (p. 444)

2. Nearly all philosophers and scientists who have addressed the mind–brain problem favor some version of monism, the belief that the universe consists of only one kind of substance. That substance could be either material (materialism) or mental (mentalism), or a combination of both (identity position). (p. 444)

3. Even if we accept the identity position, as most neuroscientists do, the hard question remains: Why is there such a thing as conscious experience at all, and why does it emerge from certain kinds of brain activity? (p. 444)

Suggestion for Further Reading

Dennett, D. C. (1991). *Consciousness explained*. Boston: Little, Brown. Although Dennett may or may not have explained consciousness, he has dealt with the mind–brain issue in a deep and provocative manner.

Terms

mind–body or **mind–brain problem**   question of how the mind is related to the brain (p. 444)

dualism   belief that the mind exists independently of the brain and exerts some control over it (p. 444)

monism   theory that only one kind of substance exists in the universe (not separate physical and mental substances) (p. 444)

materialism   belief that the brain is a machine and that consciousness is irrelevant to its functioning (p. 444)

mentalism   theory that the physical world exists only to the extent that a conscious mind perceives it (p. 444)

identity position   belief that the mind is the same thing as brain activity, described in different terms (p. 444)

easy problems   philosophically unchallenging questions of which brain activity is associated with which experience or behavior (p. 444)

hard problem   philosophical question of why and how any kind of brain activity is associated with consciousness (p. 444)

Brief, Basic Chemistry

MAIN**IDEAS**

1. All matter is composed of a limited number of elements that combine in endless ways.
2. Atoms, the component parts of an element, consist of protons, neutrons, and electrons. Most atoms can gain or lose electrons, or share them with other atoms.
3. The chemistry of life is predominantly the chemistry of carbon compounds.

Introduction

To understand certain aspects of biological psychology, particularly the action potential and the molecular mechanisms of synaptic transmission, you need to know a little about chemistry. If you have taken a high school or college course and remember the material reasonably well, you should have no trouble with the chemistry in this text. If your knowledge of chemistry is pretty hazy, this appendix will help. (If you plan to take other courses in biological psychology, you should study as much biology and chemistry as possible.)

Elements and Compounds

If you look around, you will see an enormous variety of materials—dirt, water, wood, plastic, metal, cloth, glass, your own body. Every object is composed of a small number of basic building blocks. If a piece of wood catches fire, it breaks down into ashes, gases, and water vapor. The same is true of your body. An investigator could take those ashes, gases, and water and break them down by chemical and electrical means into carbon, oxygen, hydrogen, nitrogen, and a few other materials. Eventually, however, the investigator arrives at a set of materials that cannot be broken down further: Pure carbon or pure oxygen, for example, cannot be converted into anything simpler, at least not by ordinary chemical means. (High-power bombardment with subatomic particles is another story.) The matter we see is composed of **elements** (materials that cannot be broken down into other materials) and **compounds** (materials made up by combining elements).

Chemists have found 92 elements in nature, and they have constructed more in the laboratory. (Actually, one of the 92—technetium—is so rare as to be virtually unknown in nature.) Figure A.1, the periodic table, lists each of these elements. Of these, only a few are important for life on Earth. Table A.1 shows the elements commonly found in the human body.

Note that each element has a one- or two-letter abbreviation, such as O for oxygen, H for hydrogen, and Ca for calcium. These are internationally accepted symbols that facilitate communication among chemists who speak different languages. For example, element number 19 is called potassium in English, potassio in Italian, kālijs in Latvian, and draslík in Czech. But chemists in all countries use the symbol K (from *kalium,* the Latin word for *potassium*). Similarly, the symbol for sodium is Na (from *natrium,* the Latin word for *sodium*), and the symbol for iron is Fe (from the Latin word *ferrum*).

A compound is represented by the symbols for the elements that compose it. For example, NaCl stands for sodium chloride (common table salt). H_2O, the symbol for water, indicates that water consists of two parts of hydrogen and one part of oxygen.

Atoms and Molecules

A block of iron can be chopped finer and finer until it is divided into tiny pieces that cannot be broken down any further. Those pieces are called **atoms.** Every element is composed of atoms. A compound, such as water, can also be divided into tinier and tinier pieces. The smallest possible piece of a compound is called a **molecule.** A molecule of water can be further decomposed into two atoms of hydrogen and one atom of oxygen, but when that happens the compound is broken and is no longer water. A molecule is the smallest piece of a compound that retains the properties of the compound.

An atom is composed of subatomic particles, including protons, neutrons, and electrons. A proton has a positive electrical charge, a neutron has a neutral charge, and an electron has a negative charge. The nucleus of an atom—its center—contains one or more protons plus a number of neutrons. Electrons are found in the space around the nucleus. Because an atom has the same number of protons as electrons, the electrical charges balance out. (Ions, which we shall consider in a moment, have an imbalance of positive and negative charges.)

The difference between one element and another is in the number of protons in the nucleus of the atom. Hydrogen has just one proton, for example, and oxygen has eight. The number of protons is the **atomic number** of the element; in the periodic table it is recorded at the top of the square for each element. The number at the bottom is the element's **atomic weight,** which indicates the weight of an atom relative to the weight of one

TABLE A.1

The Elements That Compose Almost All of the Human Body

Element	Symbol	Percent by Weight in Human Body
Oxygen	O	65
Carbon	C	18
Hydrogen	H	10
Nitrogen	N	3
Calcium	Ca	2
Phosphorus	P	1.1
Potassium	K	0.35
Sulfur	S	0.25
Sodium	Na	0.15
Chlorine	Cl	0.15
Magnesium	Mg	0.05
Iron	Fe	Trace
Copper	Cu	Trace
Iodine	I	Trace
Fluorine	F	Trace
Manganese	Mn	Trace
Zinc	Zn	Trace
Selenium	Se	Trace
Molybdenum	Mo	Trace

Periodic Table of the Elements

Period																		

Alkali Metals 1 IA

Noble Gases 18 VIIIA

Halogens 17 VIIA

Alkaline Earth Metals 2 IIA

Transition Elements

Inner Transition Elements

| 1 IA | 2 IIA | 3 IIIB | 4 IVB | 5 VB | 6 VIB | 7 VIIB | 8 VIIIB | 9 VIIIB | 10 VIIIB | 11 IB | 12 IIB | 13 IIIA | 14 IVA | 15 VA | 16 VIA | 17 VIIA | 18 VIIIA |

Period 1
1 **H** hydrogen 1.008
2 **He** helium 4.003

Period 2
3 **Li** lithium 6.941
4 **Be** beryllium 9.012
5 **B** boron 10.81
6 **C** carbon 12.011
7 **N** nitrogen 14.007
8 **O** oxygen 16.0
9 **F** fluorine 18.999
10 **Ne** neon 20.179

Period 3
11 **Na** sodium 22.99
12 **Mg** magnesium 24.305
13 **Al** aluminum 26.982
14 **Si** silicon 28.085
15 **P** phosphorous 30.974
16 **S** sulfur 32.060
17 **Cl** chlorine 35.453
18 **Ar** argon 39.948

Period 4
19 **K** potassium 39.098
20 **Ca** calcium 40.08
21 **Sc** scandium 44.955
22 **Ti** titanium 47.90
23 **V** vanadium 50.941
24 **Cr** chromium 51.996
25 **Mn** manganese 54.938
26 **Fe** iron 55.847
27 **Co** cobalt 58.933
28 **Ni** nickel 58.70
29 **Cu** copper 63.546
30 **Zn** zinc 65.38
31 **Ga** gallium 69.72
32 **Ge** germanium 72.59
33 **As** arsenic 74.922
34 **Se** selenium 78.96
35 **Br** bromine 79.904
36 **Kr** krypton 83.80

Period 5
37 **Rb** rubidium 85.468
38 **Sr** strontium 87.62
39 **Y** yttrium 88.906
40 **Zr** zirconium 91.22
41 **Nb** niobium 92.906
42 **Mo** molybdenum 95.940
43 **Tc** technetium (97)
44 **Ru** ruthenium 101.07
45 **Rh** rhodium 102.905
46 **Pd** palladium 106.40
47 **Ag** silver 107.868
48 **Cd** cadmium 112.41
49 **In** indium 114.82
50 **Sn** tin 118.69
51 **Sb** antimony 121.75
52 **Te** tellurium 127.60
53 **I** iodine 126.904
54 **Xe** xenon 131.30

Period 6
55 **Cs** cesium 132.905
56 **Ba** barium 137.33
57 **La** lanthanum 138.906
72 **Hf** hafnium 178.49
73 **Ta** tantalum 180.948
74 **W** tungsten 183.85
75 **Re** rhenium 186.207
76 **Os** osmium 190.20
77 **Ir** iridium 192.22
78 **Pt** platinum 195.09
79 **Au** gold 196.967
80 **Hg** mercury 200.59
81 **Tl** thallium 204.37
82 **Pb** lead 207.20
83 **Bi** bismuth 208.980
84 **Po** polonium (209)
85 **At** astatine (210)
86 **Rn** radon (222)

Period 7
87 **Fr** francium (223)
88 **Ra** radium 226.025
89 **Ac** actinium (227)
104 **Rf/Db** rutherfordium/dubnium (261)
105 **Ha/Jl** hahnium/joliotium (262)
106 **Sg/Rf** seaborgium/rutherfordium (263)
107 **Ns/Bh** nielsbohrium/bohrium (262)
108 **Hs/Hn** hassium/hahnium (265)
109 **Mt** meitnerium (266)
110 **Uun** ununnilium (269)
111 **Uuu** unununium (272)
112 **Uub** ununbium (277)

† Lanthanides 6
58 **Ce** cerium 140.12
59 **Pr** praseodymium 140.908
60 **Nd** neodymium 144.24
61 **Pm** promethium (145)
62 **Sm** samarium 150.40
63 **Eu** europium 151.96
64 **Gd** gadolinium 157.25
65 **Tb** terbium 158.925
66 **Dy** dysprosium 162.50
67 **Ho** holmium 164.93
68 **Er** erbium 167.26
69 **Tm** thulium 168.934
70 **Yb** ytterbium 173.04
71 **Lu** lutetium 174.97

‡ Actinides 7
90 **Th** thorium 232.038
91 **Pa** protactinium 231.036
92 **U** uranium 238.029
93 **Np** neptunium (237)
94 **Pu** plutonium (244)
95 **Am** americium (243)
96 **Cm** curium (247)
97 **Bk** berkelium (247)
98 **Cf** californium (251)
99 **Es** einsteinium (254)
100 **Fm** fermium (257)
101 **Md** mendelevium (258)
102 **No** nobelium (255)
103 **Lr** lawrencium (260)

Key
atomic number — 1
symbol of element — **H**
element name — hydrogen
atomic weight — 1.008

FIGURE **A.1**
The periodic table of chemistry

It is called "periodic" because certain properties show up at periodic intervals. For example, the column from lithium down consists of metals that readily form salts. The column at the far right consists of gases that do not readily form compounds. The names and symbols for elements 104–108 are in dispute. Elements 110–112 have only tentative names and symbols.

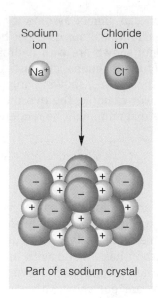

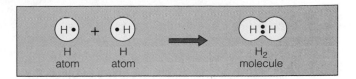

FIGURE **A.3**
Structure of a hydrogen molecule
A hydrogen atom has one electron; in the compound, the two atoms share the two electrons equally.

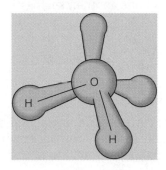

FIGURE **A.2**
The crystal structure of sodium chloride
Each sodium ion is surrounded by chloride ions, and each chloride ion is surrounded by sodium ions; no ion is bound to any other single ion in particular.

FIGURE **A.4**
Structure of a water molecule
The oxygen atom shares a pair of electrons with each hydrogen atom. Oxygen holds the electrons more tightly, making the oxygen part of the molecule more negatively charged than the hydrogen part of the molecule.

proton. A proton has a weight of one unit, a neutron has a weight just trivially greater than one, and an electron has a weight just trivially greater than zero. The atomic weight of the element is the number of protons in the atom plus the average number of neutrons. For example, most hydrogen atoms have one proton and no neutrons; a few atoms per thousand have one or two neutrons, giving an average atomic weight of 1.008. Sodium ions have 11 protons; most also have 12 neutrons, and the atomic weight is slightly less than 23. (Can you figure out the number of neutrons in the average potassium atom? Refer to Figure A.1.)

Ions and Chemical Bonds

An atom that has gained or lost one or more electrons is called an **ion.** For example, if sodium and chloride come together, the sodium atoms readily lose one electron each and the chloride atoms gain one each. The result is a set of positively charged sodium ions (indicated Na^+) and negatively charged chloride ions (Cl^-). Potassium atoms, like sodium atoms, tend to lose an electron and to become positively charged ions (K^+); calcium ions tend to lose two electrons and gain a double positive charge (Ca^{++}).

Because positive charges attract negative charges, sodium ions attract chloride ions. When dry, sodium and chloride form a crystal structure, as Figure A.2

shows. (In water solution, the two kinds of ions move about haphazardly, occasionally attracting one another but then pulling apart.) The attraction of positive ions for negative ions forms an **ionic bond.** In other cases, instead of transferring an electron from one atom to another, some pairs of atoms share electrons with each other, forming a **covalent bond.** For example, two hydrogen atoms bind as shown in Figure A.3, and two hydrogen atoms bind with an oxygen atom as shown in Figure A.4. Atoms that are attached by a covalent bond cannot move independently of one another.

Reactions of Carbon Compounds

Living organisms depend on the enormously versatile compounds of carbon. Because of the importance of these compounds for life, the chemistry of carbon is known as organic chemistry.

Carbon atoms form covalent bonds with hydrogen, oxygen, and a number of other elements. They also form covalent bonds with other carbon atoms. Two carbon atoms may share from one to three pairs of electrons. Such bonds can be indicated as follows:

C—C   Two atoms share one pair of electrons.
C=C   Two atoms share two pairs of electrons.
C≡C   Two atoms share three pairs of electrons.

Each carbon atom ordinarily forms four covalent bonds, either with other carbon atoms, with hydrogen atoms, or with other atoms. Many biologically important compounds include long chains of carbon compounds linked to one another, such as:

Note that each carbon atom has a total of four bonds, counting each double bond as two. In some molecules, the carbon chain loops around to form a ring:

Ringed structures are common in organic chemistry. To simplify the diagrams, chemists often omit the hydrogen atoms. You can simply assume that each carbon atom in the diagram has four covalent bonds and that all the bonds not shown are with hydrogen atoms. To further simplify the diagrams, chemists often omit the carbon atoms themselves, showing only the carbon-to-carbon bonds. For example, the two molecules shown in the previous diagram might be rendered as follows:

If a particular carbon atom has a bond with some atom other than hydrogen, the diagram shows the exception. For example, in each of the two molecules diagrammed below, one carbon has a bond with an oxygen atom, which in turn has a bond with a hydrogen atom. All the bonds that are not shown are carbon–hydrogen bonds.

Figure A.5 illustrates some carbon compounds that are critical for animal life. Purines and pyrimidines form the central structure of DNA and RNA, the chemicals responsible for heredity. Proteins, fats, and carbohydrates are the primary types of fuel that the body uses. Figure A.6 displays the chemical structures of seven neurotransmitters that are extensively discussed in this text.

FIGURE **A.5**
Structures of some important biological molecules
The R in the protein represents a point of attachment for various chains that differ from one amino acid to another.

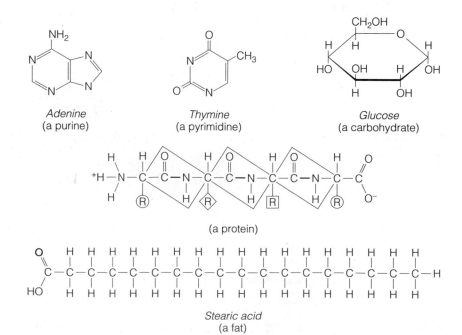

Adenine
(a purine)

Thymine
(a pyrimidine)

Glucose
(a carbohydrate)

(a protein)

Stearic acid
(a fat)

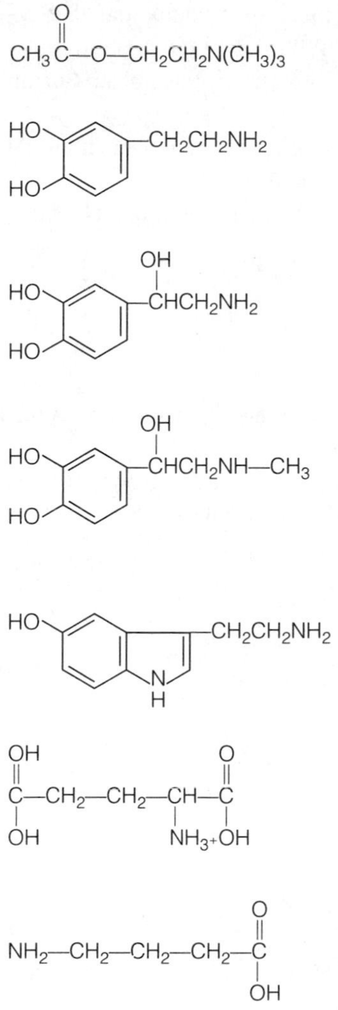

FIGURE **A.6**
Chemical structures of seven abundant neurotransmitters

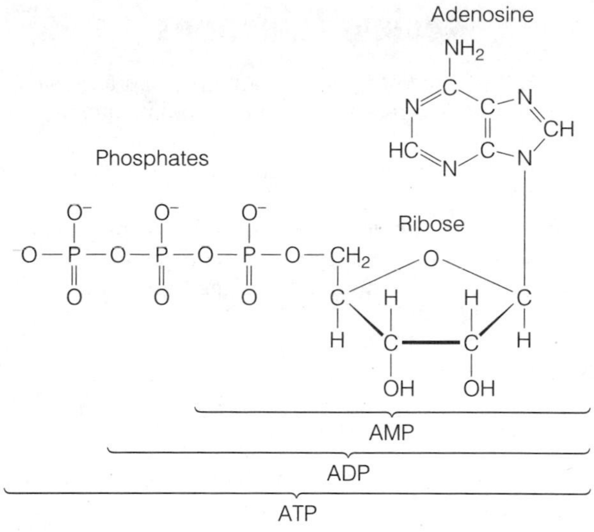

The figure shows chemical structures labeled: Acetylcholine, Dopamine, Norepinephrine, Epinephrine, Serotonin (5-hydroxytryptamine), Glutamate, GABA (γ-amino-butyric acid)

FIGURE **A.7**
ATP, composed of adenosine, ribose, and three phosphates
ATP can lose one phosphate group to form ADP (adenosine diphosphate) and then lose another one to form AMP (adenosine monophosphate). Each time it breaks off a phosphate group, it releases energy.

Chemical Reactions in the Body

A living organism is an immensely complicated, coordinated set of chemical reactions. Life requires that the rate of each reaction be carefully regulated. In many cases, one reaction produces a chemical that enters into another reaction, which produces another chemical that enters into another reaction, and so forth. If any one of those reactions is too rapid compared to the others, the chemical it produces will accumulate to possibly harmful levels. If a reaction is too slow, it will not produce enough product and the next reaction will be stalled.

Enzymes are proteins that control the rate of chemical reactions. Each reaction is controlled by a particular enzyme. Enzymes are a type of catalyst. A catalyst is any chemical that facilitates a reaction among other chemicals, without being altered itself in the process.

The Role of ATP

The body relies on **ATP (adenosine triphosphate)** as its main way of sending energy where it is needed (Figure A.7). Much of the energy derived from food goes into forming ATP molecules that eventually provide energy for the muscles and other body parts.

ATP consists of adenosine bound to ribose and three phosphate groups (PO_3). Phosphates form high-energy covalent bonds. That is, a large amount of energy is required to form the bonds and a large amount of energy is released when they break. ATP can break off one or two of its three phosphates to provide energy.

Summary

1. Matter is composed of 92 elements that combine to form an endless variety of compounds. (p.447)
2. An atom is the smallest piece of an element. A molecule is the smallest piece of a compound that maintains the properties of the compound. (p. 447)
3. The atoms of some elements can gain or lose an electron, thus becoming ions. Positively charged ions attract negatively charged ions, forming an ionic bond. (p. 449)
4. In some cases two or more atoms may share electrons, thus forming a covalent bond. (p. 449)
5. Enzymes are proteins that promote and control certain chemical reactions in the body. (p. 451)
6. The principal carrier of energy in the body is a chemical called ATP. (p. 451)

Review Questions

1. What is the difference between an atom and a molecule? What is the difference between an atom and an ion? (p. 447)
2. What are the most abundant elements in the human body? (p. 447)
3. What does the atomic number of an element represent? What does the atomic weight represent? (p. 447)
4. What kind of bonds do carbon atoms form—ionic or covalent? (p. 449)

Terms

element   material that cannot be broken down into other materials (p. 447)

compound   material made by combining elements (p. 447)

atom   piece of an element that cannot be divided any further (p. 447)

molecule   smallest possible piece of a compound that retains the properties of the compound (p. 447)

atomic number   number of protons in the nucleus of an atom (p. 447)

atomic weight   number indicating the weight of an atom relative to a weight of one for a proton (p. 447)

ion   atom that has gained or lost one or more electrons (p. 449)

ionic bond   chemical attraction between two ions of opposite charge (p. 449)

covalent bond   chemical bond between two atoms that share electrons (p. 449)

enzyme   protein that controls the rate of chemical reactions in the body (p. 451)

ATP (adenosine triphosphate)   a chemical the body uses as its main way of delivering energy where it is needed (p. 451)

Society for Neuroscience Policies on the Use of Animals and Human Subjects in Neuroscience Research

Policy on the Use of Animals in Neuroscience Research

The Policy on the Use of Animals in Neuroscience Research affects a number of the Society's functions that involve making decisions about animal research conducted by individual members. These include the scheduling of scientific presentations at the Annual Meeting, the review and publication of original research papers in *The Journal of Neuroscience,* and the defense of members whose ethical use of animals in research is questioned by antivivisectionists. The responsibility for implementing the policy in each of these areas will rest with the relevant administrative body (Program Committee, Publications Committee, Editorial Board, and Committee on Animals in Research, respectively), in consultation with Council.

Introduction

The Society for Neuroscience, as a professional society for basic and clinical researchers in neuroscience, endorses and supports the appropriate and responsible use of animals as experimental subjects. Knowledge generated by neuroscience research on animals has led to important advances in the understanding of diseases and disorders that affect the nervous system and in the development of better treatments that reduce suffering in humans and animals. This knowledge also makes a critical contribution to our understanding of ourselves, the complexities of our brains, and what makes us human. Continued progress in understanding how the brain works and further advances in treating and curing disorders of the nervous system require investigation of complex functions at all levels in the living nervous system. Because no adequate alternatives exist, much of this research must be done on animal subjects. The Society takes the position that neuroscientists have an obligation to contribute to this progress through responsible and humane research on animals.

Several functions of the Society are related to the use of animals in research. A number of these involve decisions about research conducted by individual members of the Society, including the scheduling of scientific presentations at the Annual Meeting, the review and publication of original research papers in *The Journal of Neuroscience,* and the defense of members whose ethical use of animals in research is questioned by antivivisectionists. Each of these functions, by establishing explicit support of the Society for the research of individual members, defines a relationship between the Society and its members. The purpose of this document is to outline the policy that guides that relationship. Compliance with the following policy will be an important factor in determining the suitability of research for presentation at the Annual Meeting or for publication in *The Journal of Neuroscience,* and in situations where the Society is asked to provide public and active support for a member whose use of animals in research has been questioned.

General Policy

Neuroscience research uses complicated, often invasive methods, each of which is associated with different problems, risks, and specific technical considerations.

An experimental method that would be deemed inappropriate for one kind of research may be the method of choice for another kind of research. It is therefore impossible for the Society to define specific policies and procedures for the care and use of all research animals and for the design and conduct of every neuroscience experiment.

The U.S. *Public Health Service Policy on Humane Care and Use of Laboratory Animals* (PHS Policy) and the *Guide for the Care and Use of Laboratory Animals* (the Guide) describe a set of general policies and procedures designed to ensure the humane and appropriate use of live vertebrate animals in all forms of biomedical research. The Society finds the policies and procedures set forth in the PHS Policy and the Guide to be both necessary and sufficient to ensure a high standard of animal care and use and adopts them as its official "Policy on the Use of Animals in Neuroscience Research" (Society Policy). All Society members are expected to conduct their animal research in compliance with the Society Policy and are required to verify that they have done so when submitting abstracts for presentation at the Annual Meeting or manuscripts for publication in *The Journal of Neuroscience*. Adherence to the Society Policy is also an important step toward receiving help from the Society in responding to questions about a member's use of animals in research. A complete description of the Society's policy and procedures for defending members whose research comes under attack is given in the Society's *Handbook for the Use of Animals in Neuroscience Research.*

Local Committee Review

An important element of the Society Policy is the establishment of a local committee that is charged with reviewing and approving all proposed animal care and use procedures. In addition to scientists experienced in research involving animals and a veterinarian, the membership of this local committee should include an individual who is not affiliated with the member's institution in any other way. In reviewing a proposed use of animals, the committee should evaluate the adequacy of institutional policies, animal husbandry, veterinary care, and the physical plant. Specific attention should be paid to proposed procedures for animal procurement, quarantine and stabilization, separation by species, disease diagnosis and treatment, anesthesia and analgesia, surgery and postsurgical care, and euthanasia. The review committee also should ensure that procedures involving live vertebrate animals are designed and performed with due consideration of their relevance to human or animal health, the advancement of knowledge, or the good of society. This review and approval of a member's use of live vertebrate animals in research by a local committee is an essential component of the Society Policy. Assistance in developing appropriate animal care and use procedures and establishing a local review committee can be obtained from the documents listed below and from the Society.

Other Laws, Regulations, and Policies

In addition to complying with the policy described above, Regular Members (i.e., North American residents) of the Society must also adhere to all relevant national, state, or local laws and/or regulations that govern their use of animals in neuroscience research. Thus, U.S. members must observe the U.S. Animal Welfare Act (as amended in 1985) and its implementing regulations from the U.S. Department of Agriculture. Canadian members must abide by the *Guide to the Care and Use of Experimental Animals,* and members in Mexico must comply with the *Reglamento de la Ley General de Salud en Materia de Investigacion para la Salud* of the Secretaria de Salud (published on Jan. 6, 1987). Similarly, in addition to complying with the laws and regulations of their home countries, Foreign Members of the Society should adhere to the official Society Policy outlined here.

Recommended References

"Anesthesia and paralysis in experimental animals." *Visual Neuroscience,* 1:421–426. 1984.

The Biomedical Investigator's Handbook for Researchers Using Animal Models. 1987. Foundation for Biomedical Research, 818 Connecticut Ave., N.W., Suite 303, Washington, D.C. 20006.

Guide for the Care and Use of Laboratory Animals, 7th edition. 1996. NRC (National Research Council), Institute of Laboratory Animal Resources, National Academy of Sciences, 2101 Constitution Ave., N.W., Washington, D.C. 20418.

Guide to the Care and Use of Experimental Animals, 2nd edition, vol. 1. 1993. Canadian Council on Animal Care, 350 Albert St., Suite 315, Ottawa, Ontario, Canada K1R 1B1.

Handbook for the Use of Animals in Neuroscience Research. 1991. Society for Neuroscience, 11 Dupont Circle, N.W., Suite 500, Washington, D.C. 20036.

OPRR Public Health Service Policy on Humane Care and Use of Laboratory Animals (revised Sept. 1986). Office for Protection from Research Risks, NIH, 6100 Executive Blvd., Suite 3B01-MSC 7507, Rockville, MD 20892-7507.

Preparation and Maintenance of Higher Mammals During Neuroscience Experiments. Report of a National Institutes of Health Workshop. NIH Publication No. 91-3207, March 1991. National Eye Institute, Bldg. 31, Rm. 6A47, Bethesda, MD 20892.

Seventh Title of the Regulations of the General Law of Health, Regarding Health Research. In: *Laws and Codes of Mexico*. Published in the Porrua Collection, 12th updated edition, pp. 430–431. Porrua Publishers, Mexico, 1995.

The following principles, based largely on the PHS *Policy on Humane Care and Use of Laboratory Animals*, can be a useful guide in the design and implementation of experimental procedures involving laboratory animals.

Animals selected for a procedure should be of an appropriate species and quality and the minimum number required to obtain valid results.

Proper use of animals, including the avoidance or minimization of discomfort, distress, and pain, when consistent with sound scientific practices, is imperative.

Procedures with animals that may cause more than momentary or slight pain or distress should be performed with appropriate sedation, analgesia, or anesthesia. Surgical or other painful procedures should not be performed on unanesthetized animals paralyzed by chemical agents.

Postoperative care of animals shall be such as to minimize discomfort and pain and, in any case, shall be equivalent to accepted practices in schools of veterinary medicine.

Animals that would otherwise suffer severe or chronic pain or distress that cannot be relieved should be painlessly killed at the end of the procedure or, if appropriate, during the procedure. If the study requires the death of the animal, the animal must be killed in a humane manner.

Living conditions should be appropriate for the species and contribute to the animals' health and comfort. Normally, the housing, feeding, and care of all animals used for biomedical purposes must be directed by a veterinarian or other scientist trained and experienced in the proper care, handling, and use of the species being maintained or studied. In any case, appropriate veterinary care shall be provided.

Exceptions to these principles require careful consideration and should only be made by an appropriate review group such as an institutional animal care and use committee.

Policy on the Use of Human Subjects in Neuroscience Research

Experimental procedures involving human subjects must have been conducted in conformance with the policies and principles contained in the Federal Policy for the Protection of Human Subjects (United States Office of Science and Technology Policy) and in the Declaration of Helsinki. When publishing a paper in *The Journal of Neuroscience* or submitting an abstract for presentation at the Annual Meeting, authors must sign a statement of compliance with this policy.

Recommended References

Declaration of Helsinki. (Adopted in 1964 by the 18th World Medical Assembly in Helsinki, Finland, and revised by the 29th World Medical Assembly in Tokyo in 1975.) In: *The Main Issue in Bioethics Revised Edition*. Andrew C. Varga, Ed. New York: Paulist Press, 1984.

Federal Policy for the Protection of Human Subjects; Notices and Rules. *Federal Register*. Vol. 56, No. 117 (June 18, 1991), pp. 28002–28007.

References

Numbers or letters in parentheses following citations indicate the chapter or appendix in which a reference is cited.

Aboitiz, F. (1996). Does bigger mean better? Evolutionary determinants of brain size and structure. *Brain, Behavior and Evolution, 47,* 225-245. (5)

Abramov, I., Gordon, J., Hendrickson, A., Hainline, L., Dobson, V., & LaBossiere, E. (1982). The retina of the newborn human infant. *Science, 217,* 265-267. (6)

Abramowitz, E. S., Baker, A. H., & Fleischer, S. F. (1982). Onset of depressive psychiatric crises and the menstrual cycle. *American Journal of Psychiatry, 139,* 475-478. (16)

Adamec, R. E., Stark-Adamec, C., & Livingston, K. E. (1980). The development of predatory aggression and defense in the domestic cat (*Felis catus*): 3. Effects on development of hunger between 180 and 365 days of age. *Behavioral and Neural Biology, 30,* 435-447. (12)

Adams, D. B., Gold, A. R., & Burt, A. D. (1978). Rise in female-initiated sexual activity at ovulation and its suppression by oral contraceptives. *New England Journal of Medicine, 299,* 1145-1150. (11)

Adkins, E. K., & Adler, N. T. (1972). Hormonal control of behavior in the Japanese quail. *Journal of Comparative and Physiological Psychology, 81,* 27-36. (11)

Adkins-Regan, E. (1988). Sex hormones and sexual orientation in animals. *Psychobiology, 16,* 335-347. (11)

Adolphs, R., Damasio, H., Tranel, D., & Damasio, A. R. (1996). Cortical systems for the recognition of emotion in facial expressions. *Journal of Neuroscience, 16,* 7678-7687. (12)

Adolphs, R., Tranel, D., Damasio, H., & Damasio, A. (1994). Impaired recognition of emotion in facial expressions following bilateral damage to the human amygdala. *Nature, 372,* 669-672. (12)

Adolphs, R., Tranel, D., Damasio, H., & Damasio, A. (1995). Fear and the human amygdala. *Journal of Neuroscience, 15,* 5879-5891. (12)

Advokat, C., & Kutlesic, V. (1995). Pharmacotherapy of the eating disorders: A commentary. *Neuroscience and Biobehavioral Reviews, 19,* 59-66. (10)

Aggleton, J. P., Blindt, H. S., & Rawlins, J. N. P. (1989). Effects of amygdaloid and amygdaloid-hippocampal lesions on object recognition and spatial working memory in rats. *Behavioral Neuroscience, 103,* 962-974. (13)

Ahima, R. S., Prabakaran, D., Mantzoros, C., Qu, D., Lowell, B., Maratos-Flier, E., & Flier, J. S. (1996). Role of leptin in the neuroendocrine response to fasting. *Nature, 382,* 250-252. (10)

Ahlskog, J. E., & Hoebel, B. G. (1973). Overeating and obesity from damage to a noradrenergic system in the brain. *Science, 182,* 166-169. (10)

Ahlskog, J. E., Randall, P. K., & Hoebel, B. G. (1975). Hypothalamic hyperphagia: Dissociation form hyperphagia following destruction of noradrenergic neurons. *Science, 190,* 399-401. (10)

Akbarian, S., Kim, J. J., Potkin, S. G., Hagman, J. O., Tafazzoli, A., Bunney, W. E. Jr., & Jones, E. G. (1995). Gene expression for glutamic acid decarboxylase is reduced without loss of neurons in prefrontal cortex of schizophrenics. *Archives of General Psychiatry, 52,* 258-266. (16)

Akbarian, S., Kim, J. J., Potkin, S. G., Hetrick, W. P., Bunney, W. E. Jr., & Jones, E. G. (1996a). Maldistribution of interstitial neurons in prefrontal white matter of the brains of schizophrenic patients. *Archives of General Psychiatry, 53,* 425-436. (16)

Akbarian, S., Sucher, N. J., Bradley, D., Tafazzoli, A., Trinh, D., Hetrick, W. P., Potkin, S. G., Sandman, C. A., Bunney, W. E. Jr., & Jones, E. G. (1996b). Selective alterations in gene expression for NMDA receptor subunits in prefrontal cortex of schizophrenics. *Journal of Neuroscience, 16,* 19-30. (16)

Alberts, J. R. (1978). Huddling by rat pups: Group behavioral mechanisms of temperature regulation and energy conservation. *Journal of Comparative and Physiological Psychology, 92,* 231-245. (10)

Albright, T. D. (1992). Form-cue invariant motion processing in primate visual cortex. *Science, 255,* 1141-1143. (6)

Aldrich, M. S. (1993). Narcolepsy. *Neurology, 42* (Suppl. 6), 34-43. (9)

Alexander, J. T., Cheung, W. K., Dietz, C. B., & Leibowitz, S. F. (1993).

Meal patterns and macronutrient intake after peripheral and PVN injections of the α_2-receptor antagonist idazoxan. *Physiology & Behavior, 53,* 623-630. (10)

Allison, T., & Cicchetti, D. V. (1976). Sleep in mammals: Ecological and constitutional correlates. *Science, 194,* 732-734. (9)

Allison, T., & Goff, W. R. (1968). Sleep in a primitive mammal, the spiny anteater. *Psychophysiology, 5,* 200-201. (9)

Almli, C. R., Fisher, R. S., & Hill, D. L. (1979). Lateral hypothalamus destruction in infant rats produces consummatory deficits without sensory neglect or attenuated arousal. *Experimental Neurology, 66,* 146-157. (10)

Alper, J. (1991). Outfoxing the foxes. *Science, 253,* 741. (1)

Al-Rashid, R. A. (1971). Hypothalamic syndrome in acute childhood leukemia. *Clinical Pediatrics, 10,* 53-54. (10)

Altner, H. (1978). Physiology of taste. In R. F. Schmidt (Ed.), *Fundamentals of sensory physiology* (pp. 218-227). New York: Springer-Verlag. (7)

Alvarado, M. C., & Rudy, J. W. (1995). A comparison of kainic acid plus colchicine and biotenic acid-induced hippocampal formation damage on four configural tasks in rats. *Behavioral Neuroscience, 109,* 1052-1062. (13)

American Medical Association. (1988). *Use of animals in biomedical research.* (1)

American Psychiatric Association. (1994). *Diagnostic and statistical manual of mental disorders* (4th ed.). Washington, DC: American Psychiatric Association. (16)

Amoore, J. E. (1977). Specific anosmia and the concept of primary odors. *Chemical Senses and Flavor, 2,* 267-281. (7)

Amsterdam, J. D., Winokur, A., Dyson, W., Herzog, S., Gonzalez, F., Rott, R., & Koprowski, H. (1985). Borna disease virus. *Archives of General Psychiatry, 42,* 1093-1096. (16)

Amzica, F., & Steriade, M. (1996). Progressive cortical synchronization of ponto-geniculo-occipital potentials during rapid eye movement sleep. *Neuroscience, 72,* 309-314. (9)

Anderson, B., & Harvey, T. (1996). Alterations in cortical thickness and neuronal density in the frontal cortex of Einstein, Albert. *Neuroscience Letters, 210,* 161-164. (5)

Andersson, U., Eckernäs, S.-Å., Hartvig, P., Ulin, J., Långström, B., & Häggström, J.-E. (1990). Striatal binding of ^{11}C-NMSP studied with positron emission tomography in patients with persistent tardive dyskinesia: No evidence for altered dopamine D_2 receptor binding. *Journal of Neural Transmission, 79,* 215-226. (16)

Andreasen, N. C. (1988). Brain imaging: Applications in psychiatry. *Science, 239,* 1381-1388. (4)

Andreasen, N. C., Arndt, S., Alliger, R., Miller, D., & Flaum, M. (1995). Symptoms of schizophrenia: Methods, meanings, and mechanisms. *Archives of General Psychiatry, 52,* 341-351. (16)

Andreasen, N. C., Arndt, S., Swayze, V. W. II, Cizadlo, T., Flaum, M., O'Leary, D., Ernhardt, J. C., & Yuh, W. T. C. (1994). Thalamic abnormalities in schizophrenia visualized through magnetic resonance image averaging. *Science, 266,* 294-298. (16)

Andreasen, N. C., Swayze, V. W. II, Flaum, M., Yates, W. R., Arndt, S., & McChesney, C. (1990). Ventricular enlargement in schizophrenia evaluated with computed tomographic scanning. *Archives of General Psychiatry, 47,* 1008-1015. (16)

Antelman, S. M., Chiodo, L. A., & DeGiovanni, L. A. (1982). Antidepressants and dopamine autoreceptors: Implications for both a novel means of treating depression and understanding bipolar illness. *Advances in Biochemical Psychopharmacology, 31,* 121-132. (16)

Antin, J., Gibbs, J., Holt, J., Young, R. C., & Smith, G. P. (1975). Cholecystokinin elicits the complete behavioral sequence of satiety in rats. *Journal of Comparative and Physiological Psychology, 89,* 784-790. (10)

Antrobus, J. S. (1986). Dreaming: Cortical activation and perceptual thresholds. *Journal of Mind and Behavior, 7,* 193-211. (9)

Apostolakis, E. M., Garai, J., Fox, C., Smith, C. L., Watson, S. J., Clark, J. H., & O'Malley, B. W. (1996). Dopaminergic regulation of progesterone receptors: Brain D5 dopamine receptors mediate induction of lordosis by D1-like agonists in rats. *Journal of Neuroscience, 16,* 4823-4834. (11)

Appley, M. H. (1991). Motivation, equilibrium, and stress. In R. Dienstbier (Ed.), *Nebraska symposium on motivation 1990* (pp. 1-67). Lincoln, NE: University of Nebraska Press. (11)

Arkin, A. M., Toth, M. F., Baker, J., & Hastey, J. M. (1970). The frequency of sleep talking in the laboratory among chronic sleep talkers and good dream recallers. *Journal of Nervous and Mental Disease, 151,* 369-374. (9)

Armstrong, D., Dunn, J. K., Antalffy, B., & Trivedi, R. (1995). Selective dendritic alterations in the cortex of Rett syndrome. *Journal of Neuropathology and Experimental Neurology, 54,* 195-201. (5)

Armstrong, D. M., & Marple-Horvat, D. E. (1996). Role of the cerebellum and motor cortex in the regulation of visually controlled locomotion. *Canadian Journal of Physiology and Pharmacology, 74,* 443-455. (8)

Arnold, A. P., & Breedlove, S. M. (1985). Organizational and activational effects of sex steroids on brain and behavior: A reanalysis. *Hormones and Behavior, 19,* 469-498. (11)

Arnsten, A. F. T., Cai, J. X., & Goldman-Rakic, P. S. (1995). Dopamine D2 receptor mechanisms contribute to age-related cognitive decline: The effects of quinpirole on memory and motor performance in monkeys. *Journal of Neuroscience, 15,* 3429-3439. (13)

Aronson, B. D., Johnson, K. A., Loros, J. J., & Dunlap, J. C. (1994). Negative feedback defining a circadian clock: Autoregulation of the clock gene *frequency. Science, 263,* 1578-1584. (9)

Arvidson, K., & Friberg, U. (1980). Human taste: Response and taste bud number in fungiform papillae. *Science, 209,* 807-808. (7)

Asanuma, H. (1981). The pyramidal tract. In V. B. Brooks (Ed.), *Handbook of physiology: Section 1: The nervous system, Volume 2. Motor control* (Pt. 1, pp. 703-733). Bethesda, MD: American Physiological Society. (8)

Aserinsky, E., & Kleitman, N. (1955). Two types of ocular motility occurring in sleep. *Journal of Applied Physiology, 8,* 1-10. (9)

Attardi, D. G., & Sperry, R. W. (1963). Preferential selection of central pathways by regenerating optic fibers. *Experimental Neurology, 7,* 46-64. (5)

Attenburrow, M. E. J., Dowling, B. A., Sargent, P. A., Sharpley, A. L., & Cowen, P. J. (1995). Melatonin phase advances circadian rhythm. *Psychopharmacology, 121,* 503-505. (9)

Aylward, E. H., Harris, G. J., Hoehn-Saric, R., Barta, P. E., Machlin, S. R., & Pearlson, G. D. (1996). Normal caudate nucleus in obsessive-compulsive disorder assessed by quantitative neuroimaging. *Archives of General Psychiatry, 53,* 577-584. (12)

Babich, F. R., Jacobson, A. L., Bubash, S., & Jacobson, A. (1965). Transfer of a response to naive rats by injection of ribonucleic acid extracted from trained rats. *Science, 149,* 656-657. (13)

Backlund, E.-O., Granberg, P.-O., Hamberger, B., Sedvall, G., Seiger, A., & Olson, L. (1985). Transplantation of adrenal medullary tissue to striatum in parkinsonism. In A. Björklund & U. Stenevi (Eds.), *Neural grafting in the mammalian CNS* (pp. 551-556). Amsterdam: Elsevier. (15)

Baddeley, A. D., & Hitch, G. J. (1994). Developments in the concept of working memory. *Neuropsychology, 8,* 485-493. (13)

Baghdoyan, H. A., Spotts, J. L., & Snyder, S. G. (1993). Simultaneous pontine and basal forebrain microinjections of carbachol suppress REM sleep. *Journal of Neuroscience, 13,* 229-242. (9)

Bähr, M., & Przyrembel, C. (1995). Myelin from peripheral and central nervous system is a nonpermissive substrate for retinal ganglion cell axons. *Experimental Neurology, 134,* 87-93. (15)

Bailey, J. M., & Bell, A. P. (1993). Familiality of female and male homosexuality. *Behavior Genetics, 23,* 313-322. (11)

Bailey, J. M., & Benishay, D. S. (1993). Familial aggregation of female sexual orientation. *American Journal of Psychiatry, 150,* 272-277. (11)

Bailey, J. M., & Pillard, R. C. (1991). A genetic study of male sexual orientation. *Archives of General Psychiatry, 48,* 1089-1096. (11)

Bailey, J. M., Pillard, R. C., Neale, M. C., & Agyei, Y. (1993). Heritable factors influence sexual orientation in women. *Archives of General Psychiatry, 50,* 217-223. (11)

Bailey, J. M., Willerman, L., & Parks, C. (1991). A test of the maternal stress theory of human male homosexuality. *Archives of Sexual Behavior, 20,* 277-293. (11)

Ballard, P. A., Tetrud, J. W., & Langston, J. W. (1985). Permanent human parkinsonism due to 1-methyl-4-phenyl-1,2,3,6-tetrahydropyridine (MPTP). *Neurology, 35,* 949-956. (8)

Banerjee, S. P., Zuck, L. G., Yablonsky-Alter, E., & Lidsky, T. I. (1995). Glutamate agonist activity: Implications for antipsychotic drug action and schizophrenia. *NeuroReport, 6,* 2500-2504. (16)

Banks, M. S., Aslin, R. N., & Letson, R. D. (1975). Sensitive period for the development of human binocular vision. *Science, 190,* 675-677. (6)

Barbizet, J. (1970). *Human memory and its pathology.* San Francisco: W. H. Freeman. (14)

Bard, P. (1929). The central representation of the sympathetic system. *Archives of Neurology and Psychiatry, 22,* 230-246. (12)

Bard, P. (1934). On emotional expression after decortication with some remarks on certain theoretical views. *Psychological Review, 41,* 309-329. (12)

Barinaga, M. (1996). Finding new drugs to treat stroke. *Science, 272,* 664-666. (15)

Barnes, B. M. (1996 Sept./Oct.). Sang froid. *The Sciences, 36* (5), 13-14. (9)

Barone, F. C., Feuerstein, G. Z., & White, R. F. (1997). Brain cooling during transient focal ischemia provides complete neuroprotection. *Neuroscience and Biobehavioral Reviews, 21,* 31-44. (15)

Barr, C. E., Mednick, S. A., & Munk-Jorgensen, P. (1990). Exposure to influenza epidemics during gestation and adult schizophrenia. *Archives of General Psychiatry, 47,* 869-874. (16)

Barth, D. S., & MacDonald, K. D. (1996). Thalamic modulation of high-frequency oscillating potentials in auditory cortex. *Nature, 383,* 78-81. (4)

Bartoshuk, L. M. (1991). Taste, smell, and pleasure. In R. C. Bolles (Ed.) *The hedonics of taste* (pp. 15-28). Hillsdale, NJ: Lawrence Erlbaum. (7)

Bartoshuk, L. M., Gentile, R. L., Moskowitz, H. R., & Meiselman, H. L. (1974). Sweet taste induced by miracle fruit (*Synsephalum dulcificum*). *Physiology & Behavior, 12,* 449-456. (7)

Bartoshuk, L. M., Lee, C.-H., & Scarpellino, R. (1972). Sweet taste of water induced by artichoke (*Cynara scolymus*). *Science, 178,* 988-990. (7)

Basbaum, A. I., & Fields, H. L. (1984). Endogenous pain control systems: Brainstem spinal pathways and endorphin circuitry. *Annual Review of Neuroscience, 7,* 309-338. (7)

Basil, J. A., Kamil, A. C., Balda, R. P., & Fite, K. V. (1996). Differences in hippocampal volume among food storing corvids. *Brain, Behavior and Evolution, 47,* 156-164. (13)

Bastien, C., & Campbell, K. (1992). The evoked K-complex: All-or-none phenomenon? *Sleep, 15,* 236-245. (9)

Baum, A., Gatchel, R. J., & Schaeffer, M. A. (1983). Emotional, behavioral, and physiological effects of chronic stresss at Three Mile Island. *Journal of Consulting & Clinical Psychology, 51,* 565-582. (12)

Baum, M. J., Tobet, S. A., Cherry, J. A., & Paredes, R. G. (1996). Estrogenic control of preoptic area development in a carnivore, the ferret. *Cellular and Molecular Neurobiology, 16,* 117-128. (11)

Baum, M. J., & Vreeburg, J. T. M. (1973). Copulation in castrated male rats following combined treatment with estradiol and dihydrotestosterone. *Science, 182,* 283-285. (11)

Baxendale, S., Abdulla, S., Elgar, G., Buck, D., Berks, M., Micklem, G., Durbin, R., Bates, G., Brenner, S., Beck, S., & Lehrach, H. (1995). Comparative sequence analysis of the human and pufferfish Huntington's disease genes. *Nature Genetics, 10,* 67-75. (8)

Baxter, L. R., Phelps, M. E., Mazziotta, J. C., Schwartz, J. M., Gerner, R. H., Selin, C. E., & Sumida, R. M. (1985). Cerebral metabolic rates for glucose in mood disorders. *Archives of General Psychiatry, 42,* 441-447. (16)

Baxter, L. R. Jr., Schwartz, J. M., Bergman, K. S., Szuba, M. P., Guze, B. H., Mazziotta, J. C., Alazraki, A., Selin, C. E., Ferng, H.-K., Munford, P., & Phelps, M. E. (1992). Caudate glucose metabolic rate changes with both drug and behavior therapy for obsessive-compulsive disorder. *Archives of General Psychiatry, 49,* 681-689. (12)

Baxter, M. G., Bucci, D. J., Gorman, L. K., Wiley, R. G., & Gallagher, M. (1995). Selective immunotoxic lesions of basal forebrain cholinergic cells: Effects on learning and memory in rats. *Behavioral Neuroscience, 109,* 714-722. (13)

Bayer, S. A. (1985). Neuron production in the hippocampus and olfactory bulb of the adult rat brain: Addition or replacement? *Annals of the New York Academy of Sciences, 457,* 163-172. (2)

Baylis, G. C., Driver, J., & Rafal, R. D. (1993). Visual extinction and stimulus repetition. *Journal of Cognitive Neuroscience, 5,* 453-466. (15)

Beach, F. A., Buehler, M. G., & Dunbar, I. F. (1982). Competitive behavior in male, female, and pseudohermaphroditic female dogs. *Journal of Comparative and Physiological Psychology, 96,* 855-874. (11)

Beatty, W. W., Jocic, Z., Monson, N., & Katzung, V. M. (1994). Problem solving by schizophrenic and schizoaffective patients on the Wisconsin and California Card Sorting Tasks. *Neuropsychology, 8,* 49-54. (16)

Beck, K. D., Valverde, J., Alexi, T., Poulsen, K., Moffat, B., Vandlen, R. A., Rosenthal, A., & Hefti, F. (1995). Mesencephalic dopaminergic neurons protected by GDNF from axotomy-induced degeneration in the adult brain. *Nature, 373,* 339-341. (5)

Becker, H. C. (1988). Effects of the imidazobenzodiazepine Ro15-4513 on the stimulant and depressant actions of ethanol on spontaneous locomotor activity. *Life Sciences, 43,* 643-650. (12)

Behrmann, M., & Moscovitch, M. (1994). Object-centered neglect in patients with unilateral neglect: Effects of left-right coordinates of objects. *Journal of Cognitive Neuroscience, 6,* 1-6. (4)

Békésy, G.—See von Békésy, G.

Belichenko, P. V., & Dahlström, A. (1995). Studies on the 3-dimensional architecture of dendritic spines and varicosities in human cortex by confocal laser scanning microscopy and Lucifer Yellow microinjections. *Journal of Neuroscience Methods, 57,* 55-61. (5)

Bellugi, U., Poizner, H., & Klima, E. S. (1983). Brain organization for language: Clues from sign aphasia. *Human Neurobiology, 2,* 155-170. (14)

Bellugi, U., Wang, P. P., & Jernigan, T. L. (1994). Williams syndrome: An unusual neuropsychological profile. In S. H. Broman & J. Grafman (Eds.), *Atypical cognitive deficits in developmental disorders* (pp. 23-56). Hillsdale, NJ: Lawrence Erlbaum. (14)

Benca, R. M., Obermeyer, W. H., Thisted, R. A., & Gillin, J. C. (1992). Sleep and psychiatric disorders. *Archives of General Psychiatry, 49,* 651-668. (9)

Benes, F. M. (1995). Is there a neuroanatomic basis for schizophrenia? An old question revisited. *The Neuroscientist, 1,* 104-115. (16)

Benes, F. M., & Bird, E. D. (1987). An analysis of the arrangement of neurons in the cingulate cortex of schizophrenic patients. *Archives of General Psychiatry, 44,* 608-616. (16)

Benes, F. M., Davidson, J., & Bird, E. D. (1986). Quantitative cytoarchitectural studies of the cerebral cortex of schizophrenics. *Archives of General Psychiatry, 43,* 31-35. (16)

Benes, F. M., Turtle, M., Khan, Y., & Farol, P. (1994). Myelination of a key relay zone in the hippocampal formation occurs in the human brain during childhood, adolescence, and adulthood. *Archives of General Psychiatry, 51,* 477-484. (5)

Benes, F. M., Vincent, S. L., Marie, A., & Khan, Y. (1996). Up-regulation of GABA$_A$ receptor binding on neurons of the prefrontal cortex in schizophrenic subjects. *Neuroscience, 75,* 1021-1031. (16)

Benington, J. H., & Heller, H. C. (1995). Monoaminergic and cholinergic modulation of REM-sleep timing in rats. *Brain Research, 681,* 141-146. (9)

Benjamin, J., Li, L., Patterson, C., Greenberg, B. D., Murphy, D. L., & Hamer, D. H. (1996). Population and familial association between the D4 dopamine receptor gene and measures of Novelty Seeking. *Nature Genetics, 12,* 81-84. (3)

Berenbaum, S. A., & Hines, M. (1992). Early androgens are related to childhood sex-typed toy preferences. *Psychological Science, 3,* 203-206. (11)

Berger, R. J., & Phillips, N. H. (1995). Energy conservation and sleep. *Behavioural Brain Research, 69,* 65-73. (9)

Berman, K. F., Torrey, E. F., Daniel, D. G., & Weinberger, D. R. (1992). Regional cerebral blood flow in monozygotic twins discordant and concordant for schizophrenia. *Archives of General Psychiatry, 49,* 927-934. (16)

Bernardis, L. L., & Bellinger, L. L. (1996). The lateral hypothalamic area revisited: Ingestive behavior. *Neuroscience and Biobehavioral Reviews, 20,* 189-287. (10)

Bernstein, J. J., & Gelderd, J. B. (1970). Regeneration of the long spinal tracts in the goldfish. *Brain Research, 20,* 33-38. (15)

Berridge, K. C. (1996). Food reward: Brain substrates of wanting and liking. *Neuroscience and Biobehavioral Reviews, 20,* 1-25. (3)

Berridge, K. C., & Robinson, T. E. (1995). The mind of an addicted brain: Neural sensitization of wanting versus liking. *Current Directions in Psychological Science, 4,* 71-76. (3)

Berridge, K. C., Venier, I. L., & Robinson, T. E. (1989). Taste reactivity analysis of 6-hydroxydopamine-induced aphagia: Implications for arousal and anhedonia hypotheses of dopamine function. *Behavioral Neuroscience, 103*, 36-45. (10)

Bettencourt, B. A., & Miller, N. (1996). Gender differences in aggression as a function of provocation: A meta-analysis. *Psychological Bulletin, 119*, 422-447. (12)

Biben, M. (1979). Predation and predatory play behaviour of domestic cats. *Animal Behaviour, 27*, 81-94. (12)

Billington, C. J., & Levine, A. S. (1992). Hypothalamic neuropeptide Y regulation of feeding and energy metabolism. *Current Opinion in Neurobiology, 2*, 847-851. (10)

Billups, B., & Attwell, D. (1996). Modulation of non-vesicular glutamate release by pH. *Nature, 379*, 171-174. (15)

Black, D. W., Noyes, R. Jr., Goldstein, R. B., & Blum, N. (1992). A family study of obsessive-compulsive disorder. *Archives of General Psychiatry, 49*, 362-368. (12)

Blackwell, A., & Bates, E. (1995). Inducing agrammatic profiles in normals: Evidence for the selective vulnerability of morphology under cognitive resource limitation. *Journal of Cognitive Neuroscience, 7*, 228-257. (14)

Blackwood, D. H. R., He, L., Morris, S. W., McLean, A., Whitton, C., Thomson, M., Walker, M. T., Woodburn, K., Sharp, C. M., Wright, A. F., Shibasaki, Y., St. Clair, D. M., Porteous, D. J., & Muir, W. J. (1996). A locus for bipolar affective disorder on chromosome 4p. *Nature Genetics, 12*, 427-430. (16)

Blake, R., & Hirsch, H. V. B. (1975). Deficits in binocular depth perception in cats after alternating monocular deprivation. *Science, 190*, 1114-1116. (6)

Blass, E. M., Shide, D. J., Zaw-Mon, C., & Sorrentino, J. (1995). Mother as shield: Differential effects of contact and nursing on pain responsivity in infant rats—Evidence for nonopioid mediation. *Behavioral Neuroscience, 109*, 342-353. (7)

Bliss, T. V. P., & Lømo, T. (1973). Long-lasting potentiation of synaptic transmission in the dentate area of the anaesthetized rabbit following stimulation of the perforant path. *Journal of Physiology* (London), *232*, 331-356. (13)

Bloch, G. J., Butler, P. C., & Kohlert, J. G. (1996). Galanin microinjected into the medial preoptic nucleus facilitates female- and male-typical sexual behaviors in the female rat. *Physiology & Behavior, 59*, 1147-1154. (11)

Bloch, G. J., & Mills, R. (1995). Prepubertal testosterone treatment of neonatally gonadectomized male rats: Defeminization and masculinization of behavioral and endocrine function in adulthood. *Neuroscience and Biobehavioral Reviews, 19*, 187-200. (11)

Bloch, G. J., Mills, R., & Gale, S. (1995). Prepubertal testosterone treatment of female rats: Defeminization of behavioral and endocrine function in adulthood. *Neuroscience and Biobehavioral Reviews, 19*, 177-186. (11)

Block, B. A., Finnerty, J. R., Stewart, A. F. R., & Kidd, J. (1993). Evolution of endothermy in fish: Mapping physiological traits on a molecular phylogeny. *Science, 260*, 210-214. (10)

Blum, D. (1994). *The monkey wars.* New York: Oxford University Press. (1)

Blum, K., Cull, J. G., Braverman, E. R., & Comings, D. E. (1996). Reward deficiency syndrome. *American Scientist, 84*, 132-145. (3)

Bode, L., Ferszt, R., & Czech, G. (1993). Borna disease virus infection and affective disorders in man. *Archives of Virology, Suppl. 7*, 159-167. (16)

Bode, L., Riegel, S., Lange, W., & Ludwig, H. (1992). Human infections with Borna disease virus: Seroprevalence in patients with chronic diseases and healthy individuals. *Journal of Medical Virology, 36*, 309-315. (16)

Bode, L., Zimmerman, W., Ferszt, R., Steinbach, F., & Ludwig, H. (1995). Borna disease virus genome transcribed and expressed in psychiatric patients. *Nature Medicine, 1*, 232-236. (16)

Bodian, D. (1962). The generalized vertebrate neuron. *Science, 137*, 323-326. (2)

Bogardus, C., Lillioja, S., Ravussin, E., Abbott, W., Zawadzki, J. K., Young, A., Knowler, W. C., Jacobowitz, R., & Moll, P. P. (1986). Familial dependence of the resting metabolic rate. *New England Journal of Medicine, 315*, 96-100. (10)

Bogerts, B., Meertz, E., & Schönfeldt-Bausch, R. (1985). Basal ganglia and limbic system pathology in schizophrenia. *Archives of General Psychiatry, 42*, 784-791. (16)

Bohn, M. C., Cupit, L., Marciano, F., & Gash, D. M. (1987). Adrenal medulla grafts enhance recovery of striatal dopaminergic fibers. *Science, 237*, 913-916. (15)

Boivin, D. B., Duffy, J. F., Kronauer, R. E., & Czeisler, C. A. (1996). Dose-response relationships for resetting of human circadian clock by light. *Nature, 379*, 540-542. (9)

Boklage, C. E. (1977). Schizophrenia, brain asymmetry development, and twinning: Cellular relationship with etiological and possibly prognostic implications. *Biological Psychiatry, 12*, 19-35. (16)

Bolla-Wilson, K., Robinson, R. G., Starkstein, S. E., Boston, J., & Price, T. R. (1989). Lateralization of dementia of depression in stroke patients. *American Journal of Psychiatry, 146*, 627-634. (16)

Booth-Kewley, S., & Friedman, H. S. (1987). Psychological predictors of heart disease: A quantitative review. *Psychological Bulletin, 101*, 343-362. (12)

Boring, E. G. (1950). *A history of experimental psychology* (2nd ed.). New York: Appleton-Century-Crofts. (14)

Borod, J. C., Koff, E., Lorch, M., & Nicholas, M. (1986). The expression and perception of facial emotion in brain-damaged patients. *Neuropsychologia, 24*, 169-180. (14)

Bouma, H., & Legein, C. P. (1977). Foveal and parafoveal recognition of letters and words by dyslexics and by average readers. *Neuropsychologia, 15*, 69-80. (14)

Bowmaker, J. K., & Dartnall, H. J. A. (1980). Visual pigments of rods and cones in a human retina.

Journal of Physiology (London), *298*, 501-511. (6)

Boyeson, M. G., Callister, T. R., & Cavazos, J. E. (1992). Biochemical and behavioral effects of a sensorimotor cortex injury in rats pretreated with the noradrenergic neurotoxin DSP-4. *Behavioral Neuroscience, 106*, 964-973. (15)

Braak, H., Braak, E., Yilmazer, D., Schultz, C., de Vos, R. A. I., & Jansen, E. N. H. (1995). Nigral and extranigral pathology in Parkinson's disease. *Journal of Neural Transmission, Suppl. 46*, 15-31. (8)

Bradbury, T. N., & Miller, G. A. (1985). Season of birth in schizophrenia: A review of evidence, methodology, and etiology. *Psychological Bulletin, 98*, 569-594. (16)

Bradley, A. (1997). Learning curve. *Stanford, 25*, 42. (Epilogue)

Bradshaw, J. L., & Nettleton, N. C. (1981). The nature of hemispheric specialization in man. *Behavioral and Brain Sciences, 4*, 51-91. (14)

Brambilla, F., Brunetta, M., Draisci, A., Peirone, A., Perna, G., Sacerdote, P., Manfredi, B., & Panerai, A. E. (1995). T-lymphocyte concentrations of cholecystokinin-8 and beta-endorphin in eating disorders: II. Bulimia nervosa. *Psychiatry Research, 59*, 51-56. (10)

Braus, H. (1960). *Anatomie des Menschen, 3. Band: Periphere Leistungsbahnen II. Centrales Nervensystem, Sinnesorgane. 2. Auflage* [Human anatomy: Vol. 3. Peripheral pathways II. Central nervous system, sensory organs (2nd ed.)]. Berlin: Springer-Verlag. (4, 7)

Breedlove, S. M. (1992). Sexual dimorphism in the vertebrate nervous system. *Journal of Neuroscience, 12*, 4133-4142. (11)

Bregman, B. S., Kunkel-Bagden, E., Schnell, L., Dai, H. N., Gao, D., & Schwab, M. E. (1995). Recovery from spinal cord injury mediated by antibodies to neurite growth inhibitors. *Nature, 378*, 498-501. (15)

Breier, A., Su, T.-P., Saunders, R., Carson, R. E., Kolachana, B. S., deBartolemeis, A., Weinberger, D. R., Weisenfeld, N., Malhotra, A. K., Eckelman, W. C., & Pickar, D. (1997). Schizophrenia is associated with elevated amphetamine-indiced synaptic dopamine concentrations: Evidence from a novel positron emission tomography method. *Proceedings of the National Academy of Sciences, USA, 94*, 2569-2574. (16)

Breslau, N., & Davis, G. C. (1986). Chronic stress and major depression. *Archives of General Psychiatry, 43*, 309-314. (16)

Brewerton, T. D. (1995). Toward a unified theory of serotonin dysregulation in eating and related disorders. *Psychoneuroendocrinology, 20*, 561-590. (10)

Bridgeman, B., & Staggs, D. (1982). Plasticity in human blindsight. *Vision Research, 22*, 1199-1203. (6)

Bronson, F. H. (1974). Pheromonal influences on reproductive activities in rodents. In M. C. Birch (Ed.), *Pheromones* (pp. 344-365). Amsterdam: North Holland. (7)

Brooks, D. C., & Bizzi, E. (1963). Brain stem electrical activity during deep sleep. *Archives Italiennes de Biologie, 101*, 648-665. (9)

Brooks, D. J. (1995). The role of the basal ganglia in motor control: Contributions from PET. *Journal of the Neurological Sciences, 128*, 1-13. (8)

Brooks, J. H., & Reddon, J. R. (1996). Serum testosterone in violent and nonviolent young offenders. *Journal of Clinical Psychology, 52*, 475-483. (12)

Broughton, R., Billlings, R., Cartwright, R., Doucette, D., Edmeads, J., Edwardh, M., Ervin, F., Orchard, B., Hill, R., & Turrell, G. (1994). Homicidal somnambulism: A case report. *Sleep, 17*, 253-264. (9)

Brown, G. L., Ebert, M. H., Goyer, P. F., Jimerson, D. C., Klein, W. J., Bunney, W. E., & Goodwin, F. K. (1982). Aggression, suicide, and serotonin: Relationships of CSF amine metabolites. *American Journal of Psychiatry, 139*, 741-746. (12)

Brown, J. R., Ye, H., Bronson, R. T., Dikkes, P., & Greenberg, M. E. (1996). A defect in nurturing in mice lacking the immediate early gene *fos B. Cell, 86*, 297-309. (11)

Brown, R., Colter, N., Corsellis, N., Crow, T. J., Frith, C., Jagoe, R., Johnstone, E. C., & Marsh, L. (1986). Postmortem evidence of structural brain changes in schizophrenia. *Archives of General Psychiatry, 43*, 36-42. (16)

Brownell, K. D., Greenwood, M. R. C., Stellar, E., & Shrager, E. E. (1986). The effects of repeated cycles of weight loss and regain in rats. *Physiology & Behavior, 38*, 459-464. (10)

Brunelli, S. A., Shindledecker, R. D., & Hofer, M. A. (1987). Behavioral responses of juvenile rats (*Rattus norvegicus*) to neonates after infusion of maternal blood plasma. *Journal of Comparative Psychology, 101*, 47-59. (11)

Brushart, T. M. F. (1993). Motor axons preferentially reinnervate motor pathways. *Journal of Neuroscience, 13*, 2730-2738. (15)

Bruyer, R., Dupuis, M., Ophoven, E., Rectem, D., & Reynaert, C. (1985). Anatomical and behavioral study of a case of asymptomatic callosal agenesis. *Cortex, 21*, 417-430. (14)

Brysbaert, M., Vitu, F., & Schroyens, W. (1996). The right visual field advantage and the optimal viewing position effect: On the relation between foveal and parafoveal word recognition. *Neuropsychology, 10*, 385-395. (14)

Buck, L. B. (1996). Information coding in the vertebrate olfactory system. *Annual Review of Neuroscience, 19*, 517-544. (7)

Buck, L., & Axel, R. (1991). A novel multigene family may encode odorant receptors: A molecular basis for odor recognition. *Cell, 65*, 175-187. (7)

Buell, S. J., & Coleman, P. D. (1981). Quantitative evidence for selective dendritic growth in normal human aging but not in senile dementia. *Brain Research, 214*, 23-41. (2)

Bundgaard, M. (1986). Pathways across the vertebrate blood brain barrier: Morphological viewpoints. *Annals of the New York Academy of Sciences, 481*, 7-19. (2)

Bunney, W. E. Jr., Murphy, D. L., Goodwin, F. K., & Borge, G. F. (1972). The "switch process" in manic-depressive illness. *Archives of General Psychiatry, 27*, 295-302. (16)

Burke, J. R., Enghild, J. J., Martin, M. E., Jou, Y.-S., Myers, R. M.,

Roses, A. D., Vance, J. M., & Strittmatter, W. J. (1996). Huntingtin and DRPLA proteins selectively interact with the enzyme GAPDH. *Nature Medicine, 2,* 347-350. (8)

Burn, D. J., Mark, M. H., Playford, E. D., Maraganore, D. M., Zimmerman, T. R. Jr., Duvoisin, R. C., Harding, A. E., Marsden, C. D., & Brooks, D. J. (1992). Parkinson's disease in twins studied with ^{18}F-dopa and positron emission tomography. *Neurology, 42,* 1894-1900. (8)

Burr, D. C., Morrone, M. C., & Ross, J. (1994). Selective suppression of the magnocellular visual pathway during saccadic eye movements. *Nature, 371,* 511-513. (6)

Burton, R. F. (1994). *Physiology by numbers.* Cambridge, England: Cambridge University Press. (10)

Buss, D. M. (1994). The strategies of human mating. *American Scientist, 82,* 238-249. (1)

Butera, P. C., Xiong, M., Davis, R. J., & Platania, S. P. (1996). Central implants of dilute estradiol enhance the satiety effects of CCK-8. *Behavioral Neuroscience, 110,* 823-830. (10)

Butterfield, P. G., Valanis, B. G., Spencer, P. S., Lindeman, C. A., & Nutt, J. G. (1993). Environmental antecedents of young-onset Parkinson's disease. *Neurology, 43,* 1150-1158. (8)

Buxbaum, L. J., & Coslett, H. B. (1996). Deep dyslexic phenomena in a letter-by-letter reader. *Brain and Language, 54,* 136-167. (14)

Cadoret, R. J., Yates, W. R., Troughton, E., Woodworth, G., & Steward, M. A. (1995). Genetic-environmental interaction in the genesis of aggressivity and conduct disorders. *Archives of General Psychiatry, 52,* 916-924. (12)

Cahill, L., Babinsky, R., Markowitsch, H. J., & McGaugh, J. L. (1995). The amygdala and emotional memory. *Nature, 377,* 295-296. (12, 13)

Cahn, R., Borziex, M.-G., Aldinio, C., Toffano, G., & Cahn, J. (1989). Influence of monosialoganglioside inner ester on neurologic recovery after global cerebral ischemia in monkeys. *Stroke, 20,* 652-656. (15)

Cajal, S. R. (1937). Recollections of my life. *Memoirs of the American Philosophical Society, 8.* (Original work published 1901-1917.) (2)

Calamandrei, G., & Keverne, E. B. (1994). Differential expression of *fos* protein in the brain of female mice dependent on pup sensory cues and maternal experience. *Behavioral Neuroscience, 108,* 113-120. (11)

Calandrei, G., & Alleva, E. (1995). Neuronal growth factors, neurotrophins, and memory deficiency. *Behavioural Brain Research, 66,* 129-132. (5)

Campbell, C. B. G., & Hodos, W. (1991). The *scala naturae* revisited: Evolutionary scales and anagenesis in comparative psychology. *Journal of Comparative Psychology, 105,* 211-221. (5)

Campbell, S. S., & Tobler, I. (1984). Animal sleep: A review of sleep duration across phylogeny. *Neuroscience & Biobehavioral Reviews, 8,* 269-300. (9)

Campeau, S., & Davis, M. (1995). Involvement of the central nucleus and basolateral complex of the amygdala in fear conditioning measured with fear-potentiated startle in rats trained concurrently with auditory and visual conditioned stimuli. *Journal of Neuroscience, 15,* 2301-2311. (12)

Campfield, L. A., Smith, F. J., Guisez, Y., Devos, R., & Burn, P. (1995). Recombinant mouse OB protein: Evidence for a peripheral signal linking adiposity and central neural networks. *Science, 269,* 546-552. (10)

Canavan, A. G. M., Sprengelmeyer, R., Diener, H.-C., & Hömberg, V. (1994). Conditional associative learning is impaired in cerebellar disease in humans. *Behavioral Neuroscience, 108,* 475-485. (4)

Cannon, T. D., Zorilla, L. E., Shtasel, D., Gur, R. E., Gur, R. C., Marco, E. J., Mobert, P., & Price, R. A. (1994). Neuropsychological functioning in siblings discordant for schizophrenia and healthy volunteers. *Archives of General Psychiatry, 51,* 651-661. (16)

Cannon, W. B. (1929). Organization for physiological homeostasis. *Physiological Reviews, 9,* 399-431. (10)

Cannon, W. B. (1942). "Voodoo" death. *American Anthropologist, 44,* 169-181. (12)

Caramazza, A. (1995). Interview with Alfonso Caramazza. *Journal of Cognitive Neuroscience, 7,* 303-309. (14)

Carani, C., Zini, D., Baldini, A., Della Casa, L., Ghizzani, A., & Marrama, P. (1990). Effects of androgen treatment in impotent men with normal and low levels of free testosterone. *Archives of Sexual Behavior, 19,* 223-234. (11)

Carlezon, W. A. Jr., & Wise, R. A. (1996). Rewarding actions of phencyclidine and related drugs in nucleus accumbens shell and frontal cortex. *Journal of Neuroscience, 16,* 3112-3122. (3)

Carpenter, G. A., & Grossberg, S. (1984). A neural theory of circadian rhythms: Aschoff's rule in diurnal and nocturnal mammals. *American Journal of Physiology, 247,* R1067-R1082. (9)

Carter, C. S. (1992). Hormonal influences on human sexual behavior. In J. B. Becker, S. M. Breedlove, & D. Crews (Eds.), *Behavioral endocrinology* (pp. 131-142). Cambridge, MA: MIT Press. (11)

Carvell, G. E., & Simons, D. J. (1996). Abnormal tactile experience early in life disrupts active touch. *Journal of Neuroscience, 16,* 2750-2757. (7)

Cassaday, H. J., & Rawlins, J. N. P. (1995). Fornix-fimbria section and working memory deficits in rats: Stimulus complexity and stimulus size. *Behavioral Neuroscience, 109,* 594-606. (13)

Castellucci, V. F., & Kandel, E. R. (1974). A quantal analysis of the synaptic depression underlying habituation of the gill-withdrawal reflex in *Aplysia. Proceedings of the National Academy of Sciences, USA, 71,* 5004-5008. (13)

Castellucci, V. F., Pinsker, H., Kupfermann, I., & Kandel, E. (1970). Neuronal mechanisms of habituation and dishabituation of the gill-withdrawal reflex in *Aplysia. Science, 167,* 1745-1748. (13)

Catchpole, C. K., & Slater, P. J. B. (1995). *Bird song: Biological themes and variations.* Cambridge, England: Cambridge University Press. (Intro)

Catterall, W. A. (1984). The molecular basis of neuronal excitability. *Science, 223,* 653-661. (2)

Celebrini, S., & Newsome, W. T. (1995). Microstimulation of extrastriate area MST influences performance on a direction discrimination task. *Journal of Neurophysiology, 73,* 437-448. (6)

Cerletti, U., & Bini, L. (1938). L'Elettroshock [Electroshock]. *Archivio Generale di Neurologia e Psichiatria e Psicoanalisi, 19,* 266-268. (16)

Chakos, M. H., Ma, J., Alvir, J., Woerner, M. G., Koreen, A., Geisler, S., Mayerhoff, D., Sobel, S., Kane, J. M., Borenstein, M., & Lieberman, J. A. (1996). Incidence and correlates of tardive dyskinesia in first episode of schizophrenia. *Archives of General Psychiatry, 53,* 313-319. (16)

Chandra, V., Bharucha, N. E., & Schoenberg, B. S. (1984). Mortality data for the U.S. for deaths due to and related to twenty neurologic diseases. *Neuroepidemiology, 3,* 149-168. (8)

Chase, C. (1993, July/August). Intersexual rights. *The Sciences, 33* (4), 3. (11)

Chase, T. N., Wexler, N. S., & Barbeau, A. (1979). *Advances in neurology: Vol. 23. Huntington's disease.* New York: Raven. (8)

Chehab, F. F., Mounzih, K., Lu, R., & Lim, M. E. (1997). Early onset of reproductive function in normal female mice treated with leptin. *Science, 275,* 88-90. (10)

Chen, C. C., David, A. S., Nunnerly, H., Michell, M., Dawson, J. L., Berry, H., Dobbs, J., & Fahy, T. (1995). Adverse life events and breast cancer: Case-control study. *British Medical Journal, 311,* 1527-1530. (12)

Cheour-Luhtanen, M., Alho, K., Sainio, K., Rinne, T., Reinikainen, K., Pohjavuoir, M., Renlund, M., Aaltonen, O., Eerola, O., & Näätänen, R. (1996). The ontogenetically earliest discriminative response of the human brain. *Psychophysiology, 33,* 478-481. (14)

Chiara, C., Pompeiano, M., & Tononi, G. (1996). Neuronal gene expression in the waking state: A role for the locus coeruleus. *Science, 274,* 1211-1215. (9)

Chiueh, C. C. (1988). Dopamine in the extrapyramidal motor function: A study based upon the MPTP-induced primate model of parkinsonism. *Annals of the New York Academy of Sciences, 515,* 226-248. (8)

Choi-Lundberg, D. L., Lin, Q., Chang, Y.-N., Chiang, Y. L., Hay, C. M., Mohajeri, H., Davidson, B. L., & Bohn, M. C. (1997). Dopaminergic neurons protected from degeneration by GDNF gene therapy. *Science, 275,* 838-841. (15)

Chollet, F., & Weiller, C. (1994). Imaging recovery of function following brain injury. *Current Opinion in Neurobiology, 4,* 226-230. (15)

Chugani, H. T., & Phelps, M. E. (1986). Maturational changes in cerebral function in infants determined by ^{18}FDG positron emission tomography. *Science, 231,* 840-843. (5)

Cicone, N., Wapner, W., Foldi, N. S., Zurif, E., & Gardner, H. (1979). The relation between gesture and language in aphasic communication. *Brain and Language, 8,* 324-349. (14)

Citron, M., Westaway, D., Xia, W., Carlson, G., Diehl, T., Levesque, G., Johnson-Wood, K., Lee, M., Seubert, P., Davis, A., Kholodenko, D., Motter, R., Sherrington, R., Perry, B., Yao, H., Strome, R., Lieberburg, I., Rommens, J., Kim, S., Schenk, D., Fraser, P., St. George Hyslop, P., & Selkoe, D. J. (1997). Mutant presenilins of Alzheimer's disease increase production of 42-residue amyloid β-protein in both transfected cells and transgenic mice. *Nature Medicine, 3,* 67-72. (13)

Claes, S., Van Zand, K., Legius, E., Dom, R., Malfroid, M., Baro, F., Godderis, J., & Cassiman, J.-J. (1995). Correlations between triplet repeat expansion and clinical features in Huntington's disease. *Archives of Neurology, 52,* 749-753. (8)

Clark, R. E., & Lavond, D. G. (1993). Reversible lesions of the red nucleus during acquisition and retention of a classically conditioned behavior in rabbits. *Behavioral Neuroscience, 107,* 264-270. (13)

Clarke, S., Assal, G., & deTribolet, N. (1993). Left hemisphere strategies in visual recognition, topographical orientation and time planning. *Neuropsychologia, 31,* 99-113. (14)

Cleary, L. J., Hammer, M., & Byrne, J. H. (1989). Insights into the cellular mechanisms of short-term sensitization in *Aplysia.* In T. J. Carew & D. B. Kelley (Eds.), *Perspectives in neural systems and behavior* (pp. 105-119). New York: Alan R. Liss. (13)

Clohessy, A. B., Posner, M. I., Rothbart, M. K., & Veccra, S. P. (1991). The development of inhibition of return in early infancy. *Journal of Cognitive Neuroscience, 3,* 345-350. (6)

Cloninger, C. R., Bohman, M., & Sigvardsson, S. (1981). Inheritance of alcohol abuse: Cross-fostering analysis of adopted men. *Archives of General Psychiatry, 38,* 861-868. (3)

Cohen, B., Novick, D., & Rubinstein, M. (1996). Modulation of insulin activities by leptin. *Science, 274,* 1185-1188. (10)

Cohen, J. D., Noll, D. C., & Schneider, W. (1993). Functional magnetic resonance imaging: Overview and methods for psychological research. *Behavior Research Methods, Instruments, & Computers, 25,* 101-113. (4)

Cohen, N. J., Eichenbaum, H., Deacedo, B. S., & Corkin, S. (1985). Different memory systems underlying acquisition of procedural and declarative knowledge. *Annals of the New York Academy of Sciences, 444,* 54-71. (13)

Cohen, S., & Herbert, T. B. (1996). Health psychology: Psychological factors and physical disease from the perspective of human psychoneuroimmunology. *Annual Review of Psychology, 47,* 113-142. (12)

Cohen, S., Kaplan, J. R., Cunnick, J. E., Manuck, S. B., & Rabin, B. S. (1992). Chronic social stress, affiliation, and cellular immune response in nonhuman primates. *Psychological Science, 3,* 301-304. (12)

Cohen, S., & Williamson, G. M. (1991). Stress and infectious disease in humans. *Psychological Bulletin, 109,* 5-24. (12)

Cohen-Cory, S., & Fraser, S. E. (1995). Effects of brain-derived neurotrophic factor on optic axon branching and remodeling *in vivo*. *Nature, 378,* 192-196. (5)

Cohen-Tannoudji, M., Babinet, C., & Wassef, M. (1994). Early determination of a mouse somatosensory cortex marker. *Nature, 368,* 460-463. (5)

Colbourne, F., & Corbett, D. (1995). Delayed postischemic hypothermia: A six-month survival study using behavioral and histological assessments of neuroprotection. *Journal of Neuroscience, 15,* 7250-7260. (15)

Cole, J. (1995). *Pride and a daily marathon.* Cambridge, MA: MIT Press. (8)

Coleman-Mesches, K., Salinas, J. A., & McGaugh, J. L. (1996). Unilateral amygdala inactivation after training attenuates memory for reduced reward. *Behavioural Brain Research, 77,* 175-180. (12)

Comings, D. E., & Amromin, G. D. (1974). Autosomal dominant insensitivity to pain with hyperplastic myelinopathy and autosomal dominant indifference to pain. *Neurology, 24,* 838-848. (7)

Compton, D. M., Dietrich, K. L., Smith, J. S., & Johnson, S. D. (1995). Animal rights activism and animal welfare concerns in the academic setting: Levels of activism and the perceived importance of research with animals. *Psychological Reports, 76,* 23-31. (1)

Considine, R. V., Sinha, M. K., Heiman, M. L., Kriauciunas, A., Stephens, T. W., Nyce, M. R., Ohannesian, J. P., Maarco, C. C., McKee, L. J., Bauer, T. L., & Caro, J. F. (1996). Serum immunoreactive-leptin concentrations in normal-weight and obese humans. *New England Journal of Medicine, 334,* 292-295. (10)

Cooper, S. J., Dourish, C. T., & Barber, D. J. (1990). Reversal of the anorectic effect of (+)-fenfluramine in the rat by the selective cholecystokinin receptor antagonist MK-329. *British Journal of Pharmacology, 99,* 65-70. (10)

Corder, E. H., Saunders, A. M., Strittmatter, W. J., Schmechel, D. E., Gaskell, P. C., Small, G. W., Roses, A. D., Haines, J. L., & Pericak-Vance, M. A. (1993). Gene dose of apolipoprotein E type 4 allele and the risk of Alzheimer's disease in late onset families. *Science, 261,* 921-923. (13)

Coren, S., & Porac, C. (1977). Fifty centuries of right-handedness: The historical record. *Science, 198,* 631-632. (14)

Corkin, S. (1984). Lasting consequences of bilateral medial temporal lobectomy: Clinical course and experimental findings in H. M. *Seminars in Neurology, 4,* 249-259. (13)

Corkin, S., Amaral, D. G., González, R. G., Johnson, K. A., & Hyman, B. T. (1997). H. M.'s medial temporal lobe lesion: Findings from magnetic resonance imaging. *Journal of Neuroscience, 17,* 3964-3979. (13)

Corkin, S., Rosen, T. J., Sullivan, E. V., & Clegg, R. A. (1989). Penetrating head injury in young adulthood exacerbates cognitive decline in later years. *Journal of Neuroscience, 9,* 3876-3883. (15)

Cornelissen, P., Richardson, A., Mason, A., Fowler, S., & Stein, J. (1995). Contrast sensitivity and coherent motion detection measured at photopic luminance levels in dyslexics and controls. *Vision Research, 35,* 1483-1494. (14)

Coss, R. G., Brandon, J. G., & Globus, A. (1980). Changes in morphology of dendritic spines on honeybee calycal interneurons associated with cumulative nursing and foraging experiences. *Brain Research, 192,* 49-59. (5)

Coss, R. G., & Globus, A. (1979). Social experience affects the development of dendritic spines and branches on tectal interneurons in the jewel fish. *Developmental Psychobiology, 12,* 347-358. (5)

Cotman, C. W., & Nieto-Sampedro, M. (1982). Brain function, synapse renewal, and plasticity. *Annual Review of Psychology, 33,* 371-401. (15)

Courchesne, E., Townsend, J., Akshoomoff, N. A., Saitoh, O., Yeung-Courchesne, R., Lincoln, A. J., James, H. E., Haas, R. H., Schreibman, L., & Lau, L. (1994). Impairment in shifting attention in autistic and cerebellar patients. *Behavioral Neuroscience, 108,* 848-865. (4)

Cowey, A., & Stoerig, P. (1995). Blindsight in monkeys. *Nature, 373,* 247-249. (6)

Craig, A. D., Bushnell, M. C., Zhang, E.-T., & Blomqvist, A. (1994). A thalamic nucleus specific for pain and temperature sensation. *Nature, 372,* 770-773. (7)

Crair, M. C., & Malenka, R. C. (1995). A critical period for long-term potentiation at thalamocortical synapses. *Nature, 375,* 325-328. (6)

Crawley, J. N. (1990). Coexistence of neuropeptides and "classical" neurotransmitters. *Annals of the New York Academy of Sciences, 579,* 233-245. (3)

Cremers, C. W. R. J., & van Rijn, P. M. (1991). Acquired causes of deafness in childhood. *Annals of the New York Academy of Sciences, 630,* 197-202. (7)

Crenshaw, A. G., Fridén, J., Thornell, L.-E., & Hargens, A. R. (1991). Extreme endurance training: Evidence of capillary and mitochondria compartmentalization in human skeletal muscle. *European Journal of Applied Physiology, 63,* 173-178. (8)

Critchley, H. D., & Rolls, E. T. (1996). Hunger and satiety modify the responses of olfactory and visual neurons in the primate orbitofrontal cortex. *Journal of Neurophysiology, 75,* 1673-1686. (10)

Culebras, A., & Moore, J. T. (1989). Magnetic resonance findings in REM sleep behavior disorder. *Neurology, 39,* 1519-1523. (9)

Cummings, J. L. (1995). Anatomic and behavioral aspects of frontal-subcortical circuits. *Annals of the New York Academy of Sciences, 769,* 1-13. (13)

Cummings, J. L., & Victoroff, J. I. (1990). Noncognitive neuropsychiatric syndromes in Alzheimer's disease. *Neuropsychiatry, Neuropsychology, & Behavioral Neurology, 3,* 140-158. (13)

Cutler, W. B., Preti, G., Krieger, A., Huggins, G. R., Garcia, C. R., & Lawley, H. J. (1986). Human axillary secretions influence women's menstrual cycles: The role of donor extract from men. *Hormones and Behavior, 20,* 463-473. (7)

Cynader, M., & Chernenko, G. (1976).

Abolition of direction selectivity in the visual cortex of the cat. *Science, 193,* 504-505. (6)

Czeisler, C. A., Weitzman, E. D., Moore-Ede, M. C., Zimmerman, J. C., & Knauer, R. S. (1980). Human sleep: Its duration and organization depend on its circadian phase. *Science, 210,* 1264-1267. (9, 16)

Dabbs, J. M. Jr., Carr, T. S., Frady, R. L., & Riad, J. K. (1995). Testosterone, crime, and misbehavior among 692 male prison inmates. *Personality and Individual Differences, 18,* 627-633. (12)

Dabbs, J. M., & Morris, R. (1990). Testosterone, social class, and antisocial behavior in a sample of 4,462 men. *Psychological Science, 1,* 209-211. (12)

Dale, N., Schacher, S., & Kandel, E. R. (1988). Long-term facilitation in *Aplysia* involves increase in transmitter release. *Science, 239,* 282-285. (13)

Dalton, K. (1968). Ante-natal progesterone and intelligence. *British Journal of Psychiatry, 114,* 1377-1382. (11)

Damasio, A. R. (1994). *Descartes' error.* New York: G. P. Putnam's sons. (16)

Damasio, H., Grabowski, T. J., Tranel, D., Hichwa, R. D., & Damasio, A. R. (1996). A neural basis for lexical retrieval. *Nature, 380,* 499-505. (14)

Darba, S., Balada, F., Garau, A., Gatell, P., Sala, J., & Marti-Carbonell, M. A. (1995). Perinatal alterations of thyroid hormones and behaviour in adult rats. *Behavioural Brain Research, 68,* 159-164. (5)

Darian-Smith, C., & Gilbert, C. D. (1995). Topographic reorganization in the striate cortex of the adult cat and monkey is cortically mediated. *Journal of Neuroscience, 15,* 1631-1647. (6)

Das, A., & Gilbert, C. D. (1995). Long-range horizontal connections and their role in cortical reorganization revealed by optical recording of cat primary visual cortex. *Nature, 375,* 780-784. (15)

Daum, I., Ackermann, H., Schugens, M. M., Reimold, C., Dichgans, J., & Birbaumer, N. (1993). The cerebellum and cognitive functions in humans. *Behavioral Neuroscience, 107,* 411-419. (8)

Davidson, R. J. (1984). Affect, cognition, and hemispheric specialization. In C. E. Izard, J. Kagan, & R. B. Zajonc (Eds.), *Emotions, cognition, & behavior* (pp. 320-365). Cambridge, England: Cambridge University Press. (16)

Davis, C., Kennedy, S. H., Ralevski, E., Dionne, M., Brewer, H., Neitzert, C., & Ratusny, D. (1995). Obsessive compulsiveness and physical activity in anorexia nervosa and high-level exercising. *Journal of Psychosomatic Research, 39,* 967-976. (10)

Davis, G. A. (1993). *A survey of adult aphasia and related language disorders.* Englewood Cliffs, NJ: Prentice-Hall. (14)

Davis, H. (1996). Underestimating the rat's intelligence. *Cognitive Brain Research, 3,* 291-298. (5)

Davis, J. D., Smith, G. P., & Kung, T. M. (1994). Abdominal vagotomy alters the structure of the ingestive behavior of rats ingesting liquid diet. *Behavioral Neuroscience, 108,* 767-779. (10)

Davis, N., & LeVere, T. E. (1979). Recovery of function after brain damage: Different processes and the facilitation of one. *Physiological Psychology, 7,* 233-240. (15)

Davis, N., & LeVere, T. E. (1982). Recovery of function after brain damage: The question of individual behaviors or functionality. *Experimental Neurology, 75,* 68-78. (15)

Dawkins, R. (1989). *The selfish gene* (new edition). Oxford, England: Oxford University Press. (1)

Dawson, T. M., & Dawson, V. L. (1995). Nitric oxide: Actions and pathological roles. *The Neuroscientist, 1,* 7-18. (3)

Deacon, S., & Arendt, J. (1996). Adapting to phase shifts, II. Effects of melatonin and conflicting light treatment. *Physiology & Behavior, 59,* 675-682. (9)

Deacon, T., Schumacher, J., Dinsmore, J., Thomas, C., Palmer, P., Kott, S., Edge, A., Penney, D., Kassissieh, S., Dempsey, P., & Isacson, O. (1997). Histological evidence of fetal pig neural cell survival after transplantation into a patient with Parkinson's disease. *Nature Medicine, 3,* 350-353. (15)

Deacon, T. W. (1990a). Problems of ontogeny and phylogeny in brain-size evolution. *International Journal of Primatology, 11,* 237-282. (5)

Deacon, T. W. (1990b). Rethinking mammalian brain evolution. *American Zoologist, 30,* 629-705. (5)

Deacon, T. W. (1992). Brain-language coevolution. In J. A. Hawkins & M. Gell-Mann (Eds.), *The evolution of human languages* (pp. 49-83). Reading, MA: Addison-Wesley. (5, 14)

Deacon, T. W. (1997). *The symbolic species.* New York: W. W. Norton (5)

DeArmond, S. J., Fusco, M. M., & Dewey, M. M. (1974). *Structure of the human brain.* New York: Oxford University Press. (10)

deCastro, J. M., & Zrull, M. C. (1988). Recovery of sensorimotor function after frontal cortex damage in rats: Evidence that the serial lesion effect is due to serial recovery. *Behavioral Neuroscience, 102,* 843-851. (15)

DeCoursey, P. (1960). Phase control of activity in a rodent. *Cold Spring Harbor symposia on quantitative biology, 25,* 49-55. (9)

de Jong, W. W., Hendriks, W., Sanyal, S., & Nevo, E. (1990). The eye of the blind mole rat (*Spalax ehrenbergi*): Regressive evolution at the molecular level. In E. Nevo & O. A. Reig (Eds.), *Evolution of subterranean mammals at the organismal and molecular levels* (pp. 383-395). New York: Alan R. Liss (9)

Del Cerro, M. C. R., Perez Izquierdo, M. A., Rosenblatt, J. S., Johnson, B. M., Pacheco, P., & Komisaruk, B. R. (1995). Brain 2-deoxyglucose levels related to maternal behavior-inducing stimuli in the rat. *Brain Research, 696,* 213-220. (11)

Delgado, J. M. R. (1981). Neuronal constellations in aggressive behavior. In L. Valzelli & L. Morgese (Eds.), *Aggression and violence: A psycho/biological and clinical approach* (pp. 82-98). Milan, Italy: Edizioni Saint Vincent. (12)

Deliagina, T. G., Orlovsky, G. N., & Pavlova, G. A. (1983). The capacity for generation of rhythmic oscillations is distributed in the lumbosacral spinal cord of the cat. *Experimental Brain Research, 53,* 81-90. (8)

Delis, D. C., Kramer, J. H., Fridlund, A. J., & Kaplan, E. (1990). A cognitive science approach to neuropsychological assessment. In P. McReynolds, J. C. Rosen, & G. J. Chelune (Eds.), *Advances in Psychological Assessment* (pp. 101-132). New York: Plenum. (15)

Della Salla, S., Baddeley, A., Papagno, C., & Spinnler, H. (1995). Dual-task paradigm: A means to examine the central executive. *Annals of the New York Academy of Sciences, 769,* 161-171. (13)

Delville, Y., Mansour, K. M., & Ferris, C. F. (1996). Testosterone facilitates aggression by modulating vasopressin receptors in the hypothalamus. *Physiology & Behavior, 60,* 25-29. (12)

Dement, W. (1960). The effect of dream deprivation. *Science, 131,* 1705-1707. (9)

Dement, W. (1972). *Some must watch while some must sleep.* San Francisco: W. H. Freeman. (9)

Dement, W. C. (1990). A personal history of sleep disorders medicine. *Journal of Clinical Neurophysiology, 7,* 17-47. (9)

Dement, W., Ferguson, J., Cohen, H., & Barchas, J. (1969). Non-chemical methods and data using a biochemical model: The REM quanta. In A. J. Mandell & M. P. Mandell (Eds.), *Psychochemical research in man* (pp. 275-325). New York: Academic Press. (9)

Dement, W., & Kleitman, N. (1957a). Cyclic variations in EEG during sleep and their relation to eye movements, body motility, and dreaming. *Electroencephalography and Clinical Neurophysiology, 9,* 673-690. (9)

Dement, W., & Kleitman, N. (1957b). The relation of eye movements during sleep to dream activity: An objective method for the study of dreaming. *Journal of Experimental Psychology, 53,* 339-346. (9)

Dement, W., & Wolpert, E. A. (1958). The relation of eye movements, body motility, and external stimuli to dream content. *Journal of Experimental Psychology, 55,* 543-553. (9)

De Michele, G., Filla, A., Marconi, R., Volpe, G., D'Alessio, A., Scala, R., Abrosia, G., & Campanella, G. (1995). A genetic study of Parkinson's disease. *Journal of Neural Transmission, Supp. 45,* 21-25. (8)

Dennett, D. C. (1991). *Consciousness explained.* Boston, MA: Little, Brown, and Co. (6, Epilogue)

DeSimone, J. A., Heck, G. L., & Bartoshuk, L. M. (1980). Surface active taste modifiers: A comparison of the physical and psychophysical properties of gymnemic acid and sodium lauryl sulfate. *Chemical Senses, 5,* 317-330. (7)

DeSimone, J. A., Heck, G. L., Mierson, S., & DeSimone, S. K. (1984). The active ion transport properties of canine lingual epithelia in vitro. *Journal of General Physiology, 83,* 633-656. (7)

Desimone, R. (1991). Face-selective cells in the temporal cortex of monkeys. *Journal of Cognitive Neuroscience, 3,* 1-8. (6)

Desimone, R., Albright, T. D., Gross, C. G., & Bruce, C. (1984). Stimulus-selective properties of inferior temporal neurons in the macaque. *Journal of Neuroscience, 4,* 2051-2062. (6)

D'Esposito, M., & Grossman, M. (1996). The physiological basis of executive function and working memory. *The Neuroscientist, 2,* 345-352. (13)

D'Esposito, M., Detre, J. A., Alsop, D. C., Shin, R. K., Atlas, S., & Grossman, M. (1995). The neural basis of the central executive system of working memory. *Nature, 378,* 279-281. (13)

Deutsch, J. A., & Ahn, S. J. (1986). The splanchnic nerve and food intake regulation. *Behavioral and Neural Biology, 45,* 43-47. (10)

Deutsch, J. A., Young, W. G., & Kalogeris, T. J. (1978). The stomach signals satiety. *Science, 201,* 165-167. (10)

DeValois, R. L., & Jacobs, G. H. (1968). Primate color vision. *Science, 162,* 533-540. (6)

Devane, W. A., Dysarz, F. A. III, Johnson, M. R., Melvin, L. S., & Howlett, A. C. (1988). Determination and characterization of a cannabinoid receptor in rat brain. *Molecular Pharmacology, 34,* 605-613. (3)

Devor, M. (1996). Pain mechanisms. *The Neuroscientist, 2,* 233-244. (7)

Dew, M. A., Reynolds, C. F. III, Buysse, D. J., Houck, P. R., Hoch, C. C., Monk, T. H., & Kupfer, D. J. (1996). Electroencephalographic sleep profiles during depression. *Archives of General Psychiatry, 53,* 148-156. (16)

DeWeerd, P., Gattass, R., Desimone, R., & Ungerleider, L. G. (1995). Responses of cells in monkey visual cortex during perceptual filling-in of an artificial scotoma. *Nature, 377,* 731-734. (6)

Deyo, R., Straube, K. T., & Disterhoft, J. F. (1989). Nimodipine facilitates associative learning in aging rabbits. *Science, 243,* 809-811. (1)

DeYoe, E. A., Felleman, D. J., Van Essen, D. C., & McClendon, E. (1994). Multiple processing streams in occipitotemporal visual cortex. *Nature, 371,* 151-154. (6)

Diamond, I. T. (1979). The subdivisions of neocortex: A proposal to revise the traditional view of sensory, motor, and association areas. *Progress in Psychobiology and Physiological Psychology, 8,* 1-43. (4)

Diamond, I. T. (1983). Parallel pathways in the auditory, visual, and somatic systems. In G. Macchi, A. Rustioni, & R. Spreafico (Eds.), *Somatosensory integration in the thalamus* (pp. 251-272). Amsterdam: Elsevier. (4)

Diamond, M. (1982). Sexual identity, monozygotic twins reared in discordant sex roles and a BBC follow-up. *Archives of Sexual Behavior, 11,* 181-186. (11)

Diamond, M., & Sigmundson, H. K. (1997). Sex reassignment at birth: Long-term review and clinical implications. *Archives of Pediatrics and Adolescent Medicine, 151,* 298-304. (11)

Diamond, M. C., Scheibel, A. B., Murphy, G. M., & Harvey, T. (1985). On the brain of a scientist: Albert Einstein. *Experimental Neurology, 88,* 198-204. (5)

Diamond, S. (1994). Head pain. *Clinical Symposia, 46* (3), 1-34. (7)

Dias, R., Robbins, T. W., & Roberts, A. C. (1996). Dissociation in prefrontal cortex of affective and attentional shifts. *Nature, 380,* 69-72. (4)

Dichgans, J. (1984). Clinical symptoms of cerebellar dysfunction and their topodiagnostic significance. *Human Neurobiology, 2,* 269-279. (8)

DiMarzo, V., Fontana, A., Cadas, H., Schinelli, S., Cimino, G., Schwartz, J.-C., & Piomelli, D. (1994). Formation and inactivation of endogenous cannabinoid anandamide in central neurons. *Nature, 372,* 686-691. (3)

Dimond, S. J. (1979). Symmetry and asymmetry in the vertebrate brain. In D. A. Oakley & H. C. Plotkin (Eds.), *Brain, behaviour, and evolution* (pp. 189-218). London: Methuen. (14)

DiPelligrino, G., & Wise, S. P. (1991). A neurophysiological comparison of three distinct regions of the primate frontal lobe. *Brain, 114,* 951-978. (8)

Dolan, R. J., Fletcher, P., Frith, C. D., Friston, K. J., Frackowiak, R. S. J., & Grasby, P. M. (1995). Dopaminergic modulation of impaired cognitive activation in the anterior cingulate cortex in schizophrenia. *Nature, 378,* 180-182. (16)

Domenici, L., Parisi, V., & Maffei, L. (1992). Exogenous supply of nerve growth factor prevents the effects of strabismus in the rat. *Neuroscience, 51,* 19-24. (6)

Dörner, G. (1974). Sex-hormone-dependent brain differentiation and sexual functions. In G. Dörner (Ed.), *Endocrinology of sex* (pp. 30-37). Leipzig: J. A. Barth. (11)

Dowling, J. E. (1987). *The retina.* Cambridge, MA: Harvard University Press. (6)

Dowling, J. E., & Boycott, B. B. (1966). Organization of the primate retina. *Proceedings of the Royal Society of London, B, 166,* 80-111. (6)

Drachman, D. B. (1978). Myasthenia gravis. *New England Journal of Medicine, 298,* 136-142, 186-193. (8)

Driesen, N. R., & Raz, N. (1995). The influence of sex, age, and handedness on corpus callosum morphology: A meta-analysis. *Psychobiology, 23,* 240-247. (14)

Dronkers, N. F. (1996). A new brain region for coordinating speech articulation. *Nature, 384,* 159-161. (14)

Duara, R., Kushch, A., Gross-Glenn, K., Barker, W. W., Jallad, B., Pascal, S., Loewenstein, D. A., Sheldon, J., Rabin, M., Levin, B., & Lubs, H. (1991). Neuroanatomic differences between dyslexic and normal readers on magnetic resonance imaging scans. *Archives of Neurology, 48,* 410-416. (14)

Dudchenko, P. A., & Taube, J. S. (1997). Correlation between head direction cell activity and spatial behavior on a radial arm maze. *Behavioral Neuroscience, 111,* 3-19. (13)

Dunlap, J. L., Zadina, J. E., & Gougis, G. (1978). Prenatal stress interacts with prepubertal social isolation to reduce male copulatory behavior. *Physiology and Behavior, 21,* 873-875. (11)

Dunnett, S. B., Ryan, C. N., Levin, P. D., Reynolds, M., & Bunch, S. T. (1987). Functional consequences of embryonic neocortex transplanted to rats with prefrontal cortex lesions. *Behavioral Neuroscience, 101,* 489-503. (15)

During, M. J., Ryder, K. M., & Spencer, D. D. (1995). Hippocampal GABA transporter function in temporal-lobe epilepsy. *Nature, 376,* 174-177. (14)

Dyal, J. A. (1971). Transfer of behavioral bias: Reality and specificity. In E. J. Fjerdingstad (Ed.), *Chemical transfer of learned information* (pp. 219-263). New York: American Elsevier. (13)

Dygdalo, N. N., & Kalinina, T. S. (1994). Tyrosine hydroxylase activities in the brains of wild Norway rats and silver foxes selected for reduced aggressiveness towards humans. *Aggressive Behavior, 20,* 453-460. (12)

Dykes, R. W., Sur, M., Merzenich, M. M., Kaas, J. H., & Nelson, R. J. (1981). Regional segregation of neurons responding to quickly adapting, slowly adapting, deep and Pacinian receptors within thalamic ventroposterior lateral and ventroposterior inferior nuclei in the squirrel monkey (*Saimiri sciureus*). *Neuroscience, 6,* 1687-1692. (7)

Ebstein, R. P., Novick, O., Umansky, R., Priel, B., Osher, Y., Blaine, D., Bennett, E. R., Nemanov, L., Katz, M., & Belmaker, R. H. (1996). Dopamine D4 receptor (*D4DR*) exon III polymorphism associated with the personality trait of Novelty Seeking. *Nature Genetics, 12,* 78-80. (3)

Eccles, J. C. (1964). *The physiology of synapses.* Berlin: Springer-Verlag. (3)

Eccles, J. C. (1986). Chemical transmission and Dale's principle. In T. Hökfelt, K. Fuxe, & B. Pernow (Eds.), *Progress in brain research* (Vol. 68, pp. 3-13). Amsterdam: Elsevier. (3)

Edelman, G. M. (1987). *Neural Darwinism.* New York: Basic Books. (5)

Eden, G. F., VanMeter, J. W., Rumsey, J. M., Maisog, J. M., Woods, R. P., & Zeffiro, T. A. (1996). Abnormal processing of visual motion in dyslexia revealed by functional brain imaging. *Nature, 382,* 66-69. (14)

Edinger, J. D., McCall, W. V., Marsh, G. R., Radtke, R. A., Erwin, C. W., & Lininger, A. (1992). Periodic limb movement variability in older DIMS patients across consecutive nights of home monitoring. *Sleep, 15,* 156-161. (9)

Edman, G., Åsberg, M., Levander, S., & Schalling, D. (1986). Skin conductance habituation and cerebrospinal fluid 5-hydroxyindoleacetic acid in suicidal patients. *Archives of General Psychiatry, 43,* 586-592. (12)

Egeland, J. A., Gerhard, D. S., Pauls, D. L., Sussex, J. N., Kidd, K. K., Allen, C. R., Hostetter, A. M., & Housman, D. E. (1987). Bipolar affective disorders linked to DNA markers on chromosome 11. *Nature, 325,* 783-787. (16)

Ehrhardt, A. A., Meyer-Bahlburg, H. F. L., Rosen, L. R., Feldman, J. F., Veridiano, N. P., Zimmerman, I., & McEwen, B. S. (1985). Sexual orientation after prenatal exposure to exogenous estrogen. *Archives of Sexual Behavior, 14,* 57-77. (11)

Ehrhardt, A. A., & Money, J. (1967). Progestin-induced hermaphroditism: IQ and psychosexual identity in a study of ten girls. *Journal of Sex Research, 3,* 83-100. (11)

Eidelberg, E., & Stein, D. G. (1974). Functional recovery after lesions of the nervous system. *Neurosciences Research Program Bulletin, 12,* 191-303. (15)

Eisenstein, E. M., & Cohen, M. J. (1965). Learning in an isolated prothoracic insect ganglion. *Animal Behaviour, 13*, 104-108. (13)

Elbert, T., Pantev, C., Wienbruch, C., Rockstroh, B., & Taub, E. (1995). Increased cortical representation of the fingers of the left hand in string players. *Science, 270*, 305-307. (5)

Ellinwood, E. H. Jr. (1969). Amphetamine psychosis: A multi-dimensional process. *Seminars in Psychiatry, 1*, 208-226. (16)

Elliott, T. R. (1905). The action of adrenalin. *Journal of Physiology* (London), *32*, 401-467. (3)

Ellis, L. (1986). Evidence of neuroandrogenic etiology of sex roles from a combined analysis of human, nonhuman primate and nonprimate mammalian studies. *Personality and Individual Differences, 7*, 519-552. (11)

Ellis, L., & Ames, M. A. (1987). Neurohormonal functioning and sexual orientation: A theory of homosexuality-heterosexuality. *Psychological Bulletin, 101*, 233-258. (11)

Ellis, L., Ames, M. A., Peckham, W., & Burke, D. (1988). Sexual orientation of human offspring may be altered by severe maternal stress during pregnancy. *Journal of Sex Research, 25*, 152-157. (11)

Engel, B. T. (1985). Stress is a noun! No, a verb! No, an adjective! In T. M. Field, P. M. McCabe, & N. Schneiderman (Eds.), *Stress and coping* (pp. 3-12). Hillsdale, NJ: Lawrence Erlbaum. (12)

Ensor, D. M., Morley, J. S., Redfern, R. M., & Miles, J. B. (1993). The activity of an analogue of MPF (β-endorphin 28-31) in a rat model of Parkinson's disease. *Brain Research, 610*, 166-168. (15)

Epstein, A. N. (1983). The neuropsychology of drinking behavior. In E. Satinoff & P. Teitelbaum (Eds.), *Handbook of behavioral neurobiology, Vol. 6: Motivation* (pp. 367-423). New York: Plenum. (10)

Epstein, A. N. (1990). Prospectus: Thirst and salt appetite. In E. M. Stricker (Ed.), *Handbook of behavioral neurobiology, Vol. 10: Neurobiology of food and fluid intake* (pp. 489-512). New York: Plenum. (10)

Erbas, E. A., Meinertzhagen, I. A., & Shaw, S. R. (1991). Evolution in nervous systems. *Annual Review of Neuroscience, 14*, 9-38. (5)

Erickson, C., & Lehrman, D. (1964). Effect of castration of male ring doves upon ovarian activity of females. *Journal of Comparative and Physiological Psychology, 58*, 164-166. (11)

Erickson, C. J., & Zenone, P. G. (1976). Courtship differences in male ring doves: Avoidance of cuckoldry? *Science, 192*, 1353-13 54. (11)

Erickson, R. P., DiLorenzo, P. M., & Woodbury, M. A. (1994). Classification of taste responses in brain stem: Membership in fuzzy sets. *Journal of Neurophysiology, 71*, 2139-2150. (7)

Etcoff, N. L., Freeman, R., & Cave, K. R. (1991). Can we lose memories of faces? Content specificity and awareness in a prosopagnosic. *Journal of Cognitive Neuroscience, 3*, 25-41. (6)

Evans, B. J. W., Drasdo, N., & Richards, I. L. (1994). An investigation of some sensory and refractive visual factors in dyslexia. *Vision Research, 34*, 1913-1926. (14)

Evans, D. A., Funkenstein, H. H., Albert, M. S., Scherr, P. A., Cook, N. R., Chown, M. J., Hebert, L. E., Hennekens, C. H., & Taylor, J. O. (1989). Prevalence of Alzheimer's disease in a community population of older persons. *Journal of the American Medical Association, 262*, 2551-2556. (13)

Evans, M. D., Hollon, S. D., DeRubeis, R. J., Piasecki, J. M., Grove, W. M., Garvey, M. J., & Tuason, V. B. (1992). Differential relapse following cognitive therapy and pharmacotherapy for depression. *Archives of General Psychiatry, 49*, 802-808. (16)

Evarts, E. V. (1979). Brain mechanisms of movement. *Scientific American, 241* (3), 164-179. (8)

Everson, C. A. (1995). Functional consequences of sustained sleep deprivation in the rat. *Behavioural Brain Research, 69*, 43-54. (9)

Faedda, G. L., Tondo, L., Teicher, M. H., Baldessarini, R. J., Gelbard, H. A., & Floris, G. F. (1993). Seasonal mood disorders: Patterns of seasonal recurrence in mania and depression. *Archives of General Psychiatry, 50*, 17-23. (16)

Fan, P. (1995). Cannabinoid agonists inhibit the activation of 5-HT3 receptors in rat nodose ganglion neurons. *Journal of Neurophysiology, 73*, 907-910. (3)

Fan, W., Boston, B. A., Kesterson, R. A., Hruby, V. J., & Cone, R. D. (1997). Role of melanocortinergic neurons in feeding and the *agouti* obesity syndrome. *Nature, 385*, 165-168. (10)

Fantz, R. L. (1963). Pattern vision in newborn infants. *Science, 140*, 296-279. (6)

Farah, M. J. (1990). *Visual agnosia.* Cambridge, MA: MIT Press. (6)

Farah, M. J. (1992). Is an object an object an object? Cognitive and neuropsychological investigations of domain specificity in visual object recognition. *Current Directions in Psychological Science, 1*, 164-169. (6)

Faust, M., Babkoff, H., & Kravetz, S. (1995). Linguistic process in the two cerebral hemispheres: Implications for modularity vs. interactionism. *Journal of Clinical and Experimental Neuropsychology, 17*, 171-192. (14)

Faust, M., Kravetz, S., & Babkoff, H. (1993). Hemispheric specialization or reading habits: Evidence from lexical decision research with Hebrew words and sentences. *Brain and Language, 44*, 254-263. (14)

Feder, H. H. (1981). Estrous cyclicity in mammals. In N. T. Adler (Ed.), *Neuroendocrinology of reproduction* (pp. 279-348). New York: Plenum. (11)

Federman, D. D. (1967). *Abnormal sexual development.* Philadelphia, PA: W. B. Saunders. (11)

Feeney, D. M. (1987). Human rights and animal welfare. *American Psychologist, 42*, 593-599. (1)

Feeney, D. M., & Baron, J.-C. (1986). Diaschisis. *Stroke, 17*, 817-830. (15)

Feeney, D. M., & Sutton, R. L. (1988). Catecholamines and recovery of function after brain damage. In D. G. Stein & B. A. Sabel (Eds.), *Pharmacological approaches to the treatment of brain and spinal cord injury* (pp. 121-142). New York: Plenum. (15)

Feeney, D. M., Sutton, R. L., Boyeson, M. G., Hovda, D. A., & Dail, W. G. (1985). The locus coeruleus and cerebral metabolism: Recovery of function after cerebral injury. *Physiological Psychology, 13,* 197-203. (15)

Feighner, J. P., Gardner, E. A., Johnston, J. A., Batey, S. R., Khayrallah, M. A., Ascher, J. A., & Lineberry, C. G. (1991). Double-blind comparison of bupropion and fluoxetine in depressed outpatients. *Journal of Clinical Psychiatry, 52,* 329-335. (16)

Fendrich, R., Wessinger, C. M., & Gazzaniga, M. S. (1992). Residual vision in a scotoma: Implications for blindsight. *Science, 258,* 1489-1491. (6)

Fendt, M., Koch, M., & Schnitzler, H.-U. (1996). Lesions of the central gray block conditioned fear as measured with the potentiated startle paradigm. *Behavioural Brain Research, 74,* 127-134. (12)

Fentress, J. C. (1973). Development of grooming in mice with amputated forelimbs. *Science, 179,* 704-705. (8)

Ferguson, N. B. L., & Keesey, R. E. (1975). Effect of a quinine-adulterated diet upon body weight maintenance in male rats with ventromedial hypothalamic lesions. *Journal of Comparative and Physiological Psychology, 89,* 478-488. (10)

Ferster, D., Chung, S., & Wheat, H. (1996). Orientation selectivity of thalamic input to simple cells of cat visual cortex. *Nature, 380,* 249-252. (6)

Fettiplace, R. (1990). Transduction and tuning in auditory hair cells. *Seminars in the Neurosciences, 2,* 33-40. (7)

Fils-Aime, M.-L., Eckardt, M. J., George, D. T., Brown, G. L., Mefford, I., & Linnoila, M. (1996). Early-onset alcoholics have lower cerebrospinal fluid 5-hydroxyindoleacetic acid levels than late-onset alcoholics. *Archives of General Psychiatry, 53,* 211-216. (3)

Fin, C., da Cunha, C., Bromberg, E., Schmitz, P. K., Bianchin, M., Medina, J. H., & Izquierdo, I.

(1995). Experiments suggesting a role for nitric oxide in the hippocampus in memory processes. *Neurobiology of Learning and Memory, 63,* 113-115. (13)

Fink, G., Sumner, B. E. H., Rosie, R., Grace, O., & Quinn, J. P. (1996). Estrogen control of central neurotransmission: Effect on mood, mental state, and memory. *Cellular and Molecular Neurobiology, 16,* 325-344. (11)

Fink, G. R., Halligan, P. W., Marshall, J. C., Frith, C. D., Frackowiak, R. S. J., & Dolan, R. J. (1996). Where in the brain does visual attention select the forest and the trees? *Nature, 382,* 626-628. (14)

Fink, M. (1985). Convulsive therapy: Fifty years of progress. *Convulsive Therapy, 1,* 204-216. (16)

Finlay, B. L., & Darlington, R. B. (1995). Linked regularities in the development and evolution of mammalian brains. *Science, 268,* 1578-1584. (5)

Finlay, B. L., & Pallas, S. L. (1989). Control of cell number in the developing mammalian visual system. *Progress in Neurobiology, 32,* 207-234. (5)

Fischer, Hatzidimitriou, G., Wlos, J., Katz, J., & Ricaurte, G. (1995). Reorganization of ascending 5-HT axon projections in animals previously exposed to the recreational drug (±) 3,4-methylenedioxymethamphetamine (MDMA, "ecstasy"). *Journal of Neuroscience, 15,* 5476-5485. (3)

Fisher, L. J., & Gage, F. H. (1993). Grafting in the mammalian central nervous system. *Physiological Reviews, 73,* 583-616. (15)

Fjerdingstad, E. J. (1973). Transfer of learning in rodents and fish. In W. B. Essman & S. Nakajima (Eds.), *Current biochemical approaches to learning and memory* (pp. 73-98). Flushing, NY: Spectrum. (13)

Flatz, G. (1987). Genetics of lactose digestion in humans. *Advances in Human Genetics, 16,* 1-77. (10)

Fleet, W. S., & Heilman, K. M. (1986). The fatigue effect in hemispatial neglect. *Neurology, 36* (Suppl. 1), 258. (15)

Fleming, A. S., & Korsmit, M. (1996). Plasticity in the maternal circuit: Effects of maternal experience on

fos-lir in hypothalamic, limbic, and cortical structures in the postpartum rat. *Behavioral Neuroscience, 110,* 567-582. (11)

Fletcher, P. (1990). Speech and language defects. *Nature, 346,* 226. (14)

Fletcher, R., & Voke, J. (1985). *Defective colour vision.* Bristol, England: Adam Hilger. (6)

Flor, H., Elbert, T., Knecht, S., Wienbruch, C., Pantev, C., Birbaumer, N., Larbig, W., & Taub, E. (1995). Phantom-limb pain as a perceptual correlate of cortical reorganization following arm amputation. *Nature, 375,* 482-484. (7, 15)

Florence, S. L., & Kaas, J. H. (1995). Large-scale reorganization at multiple levels of the somatosensory pathway follows therapeutic amputation of the hand in monkeys. *Journal of Neuroscience, 15,* 8083-8095. (15)

Folkard, S., Hume, K. I., Minors, D. S., Waterhouse, J. M., & Watson, F. L. (1985). Independence of the circadian rhythm in alertness from the sleep/wake cycle. *Nature, 313,* 678-679. (9)

Folstein, S. E., Phillips, J. A. III, Meyers, D. A., Chase, G. A., Abbott, M. H., Franz, M. L. Waber, P. G., Kazazian, H. H. Jr., Conneally, P. M., Hobbs, W., Tanzi, R., Faryniarz, A., Gibbons, K., & Gusella, J. (1985). Huntington's disease: Two families with differing clinical features show linkage to the G8 probe. *Science, 229,* 776-779. (8)

Foltin, R. W., Haney, M., Comer, S. D., & Fischman, M. W. (1996). Effect of fenfluramine on food intake, mood, and performance of humans living in a residential laboratory. *Physiology & Behavior, 59,* 295-305. (10)

Foote, S. L., & Morrison, J. H. (1987). Extrathalamic modulation of cortical function. *Annual Review of Neuroscience, 10,* 67-95. (4)

Forger, N. G., & Breedlove, S. M. (1987). Motoneuronal death during human fetal development. *Journal of Comparative Neurology, 264,* 118-122. (5)

Forman, R. F., & McCauley, C. (1986). Validity of the positive control polygraph test using the field practice model. *Journal of Applied Psychology, 71*, 691-698. (12)

Foster, R. G. (1993). Photoreceptors and circadian systems. *Current Directions in Psychological Science, 2*, 34-39. (9)

Fowler, J. S., Volkow, N. D., Wang, G.-J., Pappas, N., Logan, J., MacGregor, R., Alexoff, D., Shea, C., Schlyer, D., Wolf, A. P., Warner, D., Zezulkova, I., & Cilento, R. (1996). Inhibition of monoamine oxidase B in the brains of smokers. *Nature, 379*, 733-736. (8)

Frangiskakis, J. M., Ewart, A. K., Morris, C. A., Mervis, C. B., Bertrand, J., Robinson, B. F., Klein, B. P., Ensing, G. J., Everett, L. A., Green, E. D., Pröschel, C., Gutowski, N. J., Noble, M., Atkinson, D. L., Odelberg, S. J., & Keating, M. T. (1996). LIM-kinase 1 hemizygosity implicated in impaired visuospatial constructive cognition. *Cell, 86*, 59-69. (14)

Frank, L. G., Weldele, M. L., & Glickman, S. E. (1995). Masculinization costs in hyaenas. *Nature, 377*, 584-585. (11)

Frank, P. W. (1981). A condition for a sessile strategy. *American Naturalist, 118*, 288-290. (8)

Frank, R. A., Mize, S. J. S., Kennedy, L. M., de los Santos, H. C., & Green, S. J. (1992). The effect of *Gymnema sylvestre* extracts on the sweetness of eight sweeteners. *Chemical Senses, 17*, 461-479. (7)

Frankfurt, M. (1994). Gonadal steroids and neuronal plasticity. *Annals of the New York Academy of Sciences, 743*, 45-60. (11)

Frankland, P. W., Josselyn, S. A., Bradwejn, J., Vaccarino, F. J., & Yeomans, J. S. (1997). Activation of amygdala cholecystokinin$_B$ receptors potentiates the acoustic startle response in the rat. *Journal of Neuroscience, 17*, 1838-1847. (12)

Frankland, P. W., & Ralph, M. R. (1995). Circadian modulation in the rat acoustic startle circuit. *Behavioral Neuroscience, 109*, 43-48. (12)

Franz, E. A., Eliassen, J. C., Ivry, R. B., & Gazzaniga, M. S. (1996). Dissociation of spatial and temporal coupling in the bimanual movements of callosotomy patients. *Psychological Science, 7*, 306-310. (14)

Freed, D. M., & Corkin, S. (1988). Rate of forgetting in H. M. : 6-month recognition. *Behavioral Neuroscience, 102*, 823-827. (13)

Freedman, R. D., & Thibos, L. N. (1975). Contrast sensitivity in humans with abnormal visual experience. *Journal of Physiology, 247*, 687-710. (6)

Fregly, M. J., & Rowland, N. E. (1991). Effect of a nonpeptide angiotensin II receptor antagonist, DuP 753, on angiotensin-related water intake in rats. *Brain Research Bulletin, 27*, 97-100. (10)

Freimer, N. B., Reus, V. I., Escamilla, M. A., McInnes, L. A., Spesny, M., Leon, P., Service, S. K., Smith, L. B., Silva, S., Rojas, E., Gallegos, A., Meza, L., Fournier, E., Baharloo, S., Blankenship, K., Tyler, D. J., Batki, S., Vinogradov, S., Weissenbach, J., Barondes, S. H., & Sandkuijl, L. A. (1996). Genetic mapping using haplotype, association and linkage methods suggests a locus for severe bipolar disorder (BP1) at 18q22-q23. *Nature Genetics, 12*, 436-441. (16)

Frese, M., & Harwich, C. (1984). Shiftwork and the length and quality of sleep. *Journal of Occupational Medicine, 26*, 561-566. (9)

Friedburg, D., & Klöppel, K. P. (1996). Frühzeitige Korrektion von Hyperopie und Astigmatismus bie Kindern führt zu besserer Entwicklung des Sehschärfe. *Klinische Monatsblatt der Augenheilkunde, 209*, 21-24. (6)

Friedlander, W. J. (1986). Who was "the father of bromide treatment of epilepsy"? *Archives of Neurology, 43*, 505-507. (16)

Friedman, M. I., & Stricker, E. M. (1976). The physiological psychology of hunger: A physiological perspective. *Psychological Review, 83*, 409-431. (10)

Frisch, R. E. (1983). Fatness, puberty, and fertility: The effects of nutrition and physical training on menarche and ovulation. In J. Brooks-Gunn & A. C. Petersen (Eds.), *Girls at puberty* (pp. 29-49). New York: Plenum. (11)

Frisch, R. E. (1984). Body fat, puberty and fertility. *Biological Reviews, 59*, 161-188. (11)

Fritsch, G., & Hitzig, E. (1870). Über die elektrische Erregbarkeit des

Grosshirns [Concerning the electrical stimulability of the cerebrum]. *Archiv für Anatomie Physiologie und Wissenschaftliche Medicin*, 300-332. (1, 8)

Fritschy, J.-M., & Grzanna, R. (1992). Degeneration of rat locus coeruleus neurons is not accompanied by an irreversible loss of ascending projections. *Annals of the New York Academy of Sciences, 648*, 275-278. (15)

Fuller, R. K., & Roth, H. P. (1979). Disulfiram for the treatment of alcoholism: An evaluation in 128 men. *Annals of Internal Medicine, 90*, 901-904. (3)

Fuller, R. W. (1996). The influence of fluoxetine on aggressive behavior. *Neuropsychopharmacology, 14*, 77-81. (16)

Fuster, J. M. (1989). *The prefrontal cortex* (2nd ed.). New York: Raven Press. (4)

Gabrieli, J. D. E., Corkin, S., Mickel, S. F., & Growdon, J. H. (1993). Intact acquisition and long-term retention of mirror-tracing skill in Alzheimer's disease and in global amnesia. *Behavioral Neuroscience, 107*, 899-910. (13)

Gabrieli, J. D. E., McGlinchey-Berroth, R., Carrillo, M. C., Gluck, M. A., Cermak, L. S., & Disterhoft, J. F. (1995). Intact delay-eyeblink classical conditioning in amnesia. *Behavioral Neuroscience, 109*, 819-827. (13)

Gabrielli, W. F. Jr., & Plomin, R. (1985). Drinking behavior in the Colorado adoptee and twin sample. *Journal of Studies on Alcohol, 46*, 24-31. (3)

Galef, B. G. Jr. (1992). Weaning from mother's milk to solid foods: The developmental psychobiology of self-selection of foods by rats. *Annals of the New York Academy of Sciences, 662*, 37-52. (10)

Galin, D., Johnstone, J., Nakell, L., & Herron, J. (1979). Development of the capacity for tactile information transfer between hemispheres in normal children. *Science, 204*, 1330-1332. (14)

Gamse, R., Leeman, S. E., Holzer, P., & Lembeck, F. (1981). Differential effects of capsaicin on the content of somatostatin, substance P, and neurotensin in the nervous system of the rat. *Naunyn-Schmiedeberg's Archives of Pharmacology, 317,* 140-148. (7)

Gao, J.-H., Parsons, L. M., Bower, J. M., Xiong, J., Li, J., & Fox, P. T. (1996). Cerebellum implicated in sensory acquisition and discrimination rather than motor control. *Science, 272,* 545-547. (8)

Garattini, S., & Valzelli, L. (1960). Sulla valutazione farmacologica delle sostanze antidepressive [On the pharmacological validation of antidepressive substances]. In *Le sindromi depressive* (pp. 7-30.) (16)

Gardner, B. T., & Gardner, R. A. (1975). Evidence for sentence constituents in the early utterances of child and chimpanzee. *Journal of Experimental Psychology: General, 104,* 244-267. (14)

Gardner, H., & Zurif, E. B. (1975). *Bee* but not *be:* Oral reading of single words in aphasia and alexia. *Neuropsychologia, 13,* 181-190. (14)

Gash, D. M., Zhang, Z., Ovadia, A., Cass, W. A., Yi, A., Simmerman, L., Russell, D., Martin, D., Lapchak, P. A., Collins, F., Hoffer, B. J., & Gerhardt, G. A. (1996). Functional recovery in parkinsonian monkeys treated with GDNF. *Nature, 380,* 252-255. (15)

Gaze, R. M., & Sharma, S. C. (1970). Axial differences in the reinnervation of the goldfish optic tectum by regenerating optic fibers. *Experimental Brain Research, 10,* 171-181. (5)

Gazzaniga, M. S., LeDoux, J. E., & Wilson, D. H. (1977). Language, praxis, and the right hemisphere: Clues to some mechanisms of consciousness. *Neurology, 27,* 1144-1147. (14)

Geiger, G., Lettvin, J. Y., & Fahle, M. (1994). Dyslexic children learn a new visual strategy for reading: A controlled experiment. *Vision Research, 34,* 1223-1233. (14)

Geiger, G., Lettvin, J. Y., & Zegarra-Moran, O. (1992). Task-determined strategies of visual process. *Cognitive Brain Research, 1,* 39-52. (14)

Gent, J. F., & Bartoshuk, L. M. (1983). Sweetness of sucrose, neohesperidin dihydrochalcone, and saccharin is related to genetic ability to taste the bitter substance 6-n-propylthiouracil. *Chemical Senses, 7,* 265-272. (7)

George, D. T., Nutt, D. J., Walker, W. V., Porges, S. W., Adinoff, B., & Linnoila, M. (1989). Lactate and hyperventilation substantially attenuate vagal tone in normal volunteers. *Archives of General Psychiatry, 46,* 153-156. (12)

Gerrish, C. J., & Alberts, J. R. (1996). Environmental temperature modulates onset of independent feeding: Warmer is sooner. *Developmental Psychobiology, 29,* 483-495. (10)

Geschwind, N. (1970). The organization of language and the brain. *Science, 170,* 940-944. (14)

Geschwind, N. (1972). Language and the brain. *Scientific American, 226* (4), 76-83. (14)

Geschwind, N., & Galaburda, A. M. (1985). Cerebral lateralization: Biological mechanisms, associations, and pathology: I. A hypothesis and a program for research. *Archives of Neurology, 42,* 428-459. (14)

Geschwind, N., & Levitsky, W. (1968). Human brain: Left-right asymmetries in temporal speech region. *Science, 161,* 186-187. (14)

Getchell, T. V., & Getchell, M. L. (1987). Peripheral mechanisms of olfaction: Biochemistry and neurophysiology. In T. E. Finger & W. L. Silver (Eds.), *Neurobiology of taste and smell* (pp. 91-123). New York: John Wiley. (7)

Giancola, P. R. (1995). Evidence for dorsolateral and orbital prefrontal cortical involvement in the expression of aggressive behavior. *Aggressive Behavior, 21,* 431-450. (12)

Gianoulakis, C., Krishnan, B., & Thavundayil, J. (1996). Enhanced sensitivity of pituitary β-endorphin to ethanol in subjects at high risk of alcoholism. *Archives of General Psychiatry, 53,* 250-257. (3)

Gibbs, F. P. (1983). Temperature dependence of the hamster circadian pacemaker. *American Journal of Physiology, 244,* R607-R610. (9)

Gillette, M. U., & McArthur, A. J. (1996). Circadian actions of melatonin at the suprachiasmatic nucleus. *Behavioural Brain Research, 73,* 135-139. (9)

Gillin, J. C. (1983). The sleep therapies of depression. *Progress in Neuro-Psychopharmacology & Biological Psychiatry, 7,* 351-364. (16)

Ginns, E. I., Ott, J., Egeland, J. A., Allen, C. R., Fann, C. S. J., Pauls, D. L., Weissenbach, J., Carulli, J. P., Falls, K. M., Keith, T. P., & Paul, S. M. (1996). A genome-wide search for chromosomal loci linked to bipolar affective disorder in the Old Order Amish. *Nature Genetics, 12,* 431-435. (16)

Ginsberg, M. D. (1995a). Neuroprotection in brain ischemia: An update (Part I). *The Neuroscientist, 1,* 95-103. (15)

Ginsberg, M. D. (1995b). Neuroprotection in brain ischemia: An update (Part II). *The Neuroscientist, 1,* 164-175. (15)

Giros, B., Jaber, M., Jones, S. R., Wightman, R. M., & Caron, M. G. (1996). Hyperlocomotion and indifference to cocaine and amphetamine in mice lacking the dopamine transporter. *Nature, 379,* 606-612. (3)

Giuliani, D., & Ferrari, F. (1996). Differential behavioral response to dopamine D_2 agonists by sexually naive, sexually active, and sexually inactive male rats. *Behavioral Neuroscience, 110,* 802-808. (11)

Gjedde, A. (1984). Blood-brain transfer of galactose in experimental galactosemia, with special reference to the competitive interaction between galactose and glucose. *Journal of Neurochemistry, 43,* 1654-1662. (2)

Glaser, J. H., Etgen, A. M., & Barfield, R. J. (1987). Temporal aspects of ventromedial hypothalamic progesterone action in the facilitation of estrous behavior in the female rat. *Behavioral Neuroscience, 101,* 534-545. (11)

Glaser, R., Rice, J., Speicher, C. E., Stout, J. C., & Kiecolt-Glaser, J. K. (1986). Stress depresses interferon production by leukocytes concomitant with a decrease in natural killer cell activity. *Behavioral Neuroscience, 100,* 675-678. (12)

Glass, A. V., Gazzaniga, M. S., & Premack, D. (1973). Artificial language training in global aphasics. *Neuropsychologia, 11,* 95-103. (14)

Glendenning, K. K., Baker, B. N., Hutson, K. A., & Masterton, R. B.

(1992). Acoustic chiasm V: Inhibition and excitation in the ipsilateral and contralateral projections of LSO. *Journal of Comparative Neurology, 319,* 100-122. (7)

Glick, S. D. (1974). Changes in drug sensitivity and mechanisms of functional recovery following brain damage. In D. G. Stein, J. J. Rosen, & N. Butters (Eds.), *Plasticity and recovery of function in the central nervous system* (pp. 339-372). New York: Academic Press. (15)

Glickman, S. E., Frank, L. G., Licht, P., Yalcinkaya, T., Siiteri, P. K., & Davidson, J. (1992). Sexual differentiation of the female spotted hyena: One of nature's experiments. *Annals of the New York Academy of Sciences, 662,* 135-159. (11)

Gloning, I., Gloning, K., Weingarten, K., & Berner, P. (1954). Über einen Fall mit Alexie der BRAILLEschrift [On a case with alexia for Braille writing]. *Wiener Zeitschrift für Nervenheilkunde, 10,* 260-273. (14)

Goate, A., Chartier-Harlin, M. C., Mullan, M., Brown, J., Crawford, F., Fidani, L., Giuffra, L., Haynes, A., Irving, N., James, L., Mant, R., Newton, P., Rooke, K., Roques, P., Talbot, C., Pericak-Vance, M., Roses, A., Williamson, R., Rossor, M., Owen, M., & Hardy, J. (1991). Segregation of a missense mutation in the amyloid precursor protein gene with familial Alzheimer's disease. *Nature, 349,* 704-706. (13)

Gödecke, I., & Bonhoeffer, T. (1996). Development of identical orientation maps for two eyes without common visual experience. *Nature, 379,* 251-254. (6)

Gold, R. M. (1973). Hypothalamic obesity: The myth of the ventromedial hypothalamus. *Science, 182,* 488-490. (10)

Goldberg, E. (1995). Rise and fall of modular orthodoxy. *Journal of Clinical and Experimental Neuropsychology, 17,* 193-208. (4)

Goldberg, T. E., Weinberger, D. R., Berman, K. F., Pliskin, N. H., & Podd, M. H. (1987). Further evidence for dementia of the prefrontal type in schizophrenia? *Archives of General Psychiatry, 44,* 1008-1014. (16)

Goldman, B. D. (1981). Puberty. In N. T. Adler (Ed.), *Neuroendocrinology of reproduction* (pp. 229-239). New York: Plenum. (11)

Goldman, P. S. (1971). Functional development of the prefrontal cortex in early life and the problem of neuronal plasticity. *Experimental Neurology, 32,* 366-387. (15)

Goldman, P. S. (1976). The role of experience in recovery of function following orbital prefrontal lesions in infant monkeys. *Neuropsychologia, 14,* 401-412. (15)

Goldman, S. A. (1995). Neuronal precursor cells and neurogenesis in the adult forebrain. *The Neuroscientist, 1,* 338-350. (2)

Goldman-Rakic, P.S. (1987). Development of cortical circuitry and cognitive function. *Child Development, 58,* 601-622. (5)

Goldman-Rakic, P. S. (1988). Topography of cognition: Parallel distributed networks in primate association cortex. *Annual Review of Neuroscience, 11,* 137-156. (inside cover, 4)

Goldman-Rakic, P. S. (1994). Specification of higher cortical functions. In S. H. Broman & J. Grafman (Eds.), *Atypical cognitive deficits in developmental disorders* (pp. 3-17). Hillsdale, NJ: Lawrence Erlbaum. (13)

Goldman-Rakic, P. S. (1995a). Cellular basis of working memory. *Neuron, 14,* 477-485. (13)

Goldman-Rakic, P. S. (1995b). Architecture of the prefrontal cortex and the central executive. *Annals of the New York Academy of Sciences, 769,* 71-83. (13)

Goldman-Rakic, P. S., Bates, J. F., & Chafee, M. V. (1992). The prefrontal cortex and internally generated motor acts. *Current Opinion in Neurobiology, 2,* 830-835. (8)

Goldstein, L. A., & Sengelaub, D. R. (1992). Timing and duration of dihydrotestosterone treatment affect the development of motoneuron number and morphology in a sexually dimorphic rat spinal nucleus. *Journal of Comparative Neurology, 326,* 147-157. (11)

Goldstein, M. (1974). Brain research and violent behavior. *Archives of Neurology, 30,* 1-35. (12)

Goodale, M. A. (1996). Visuomotor modules in the vertebrate brain. *Canadian Journal of Physiology and Pharmacology, 74,* 390-400. (8)

Goodale, M. A., Milner, A. D., Jakobson, L. S., & Carey, D. P. (1991). A neurological dissociation between perceiving objects and grasping them. *Nature, 349,* 154-156. (8)

Goodison, T., & Siegel, S. (1995). Learning and tolerance to the intake suppressive effect of cholecystokinin in rats. *Behavioral Neuroscience, 109,* 62-70. (10)

Gopnik, M., & Crago, M. B. (1991). Familial aggregation of a developmental language disorder. *Cognition, 39,* 1-50. (14)

Gordon, J. A., & Stryker, M. P. (1996). Experience-dependent plasticity of binocular responses in the primary visual cortex of the mouse. *Journal of Neuroscience, 16,* 3274-3286. (6)

Gorski, R. A. (1980). Sexual differentiation of the brain. In D. T. Krieger & J. C. Hughes (Eds.), *Neuroendocrinology* (pp. 215-222). Sunderland, MA: Sinauer. (11)

Gorski, R. A. (1985). The 13th J. A. F. Stevenson memorial lecture. Sexual differentiation of the brain: Possible mechanisms and implications. *Canadian Journal of Physiology and Pharmacology, 63,* 577-594. (11)

Gorski, R. A., & Allen, L. S. (1992). Sexual orientation and the size of the anterior commissure in the human brain. *Proceedings of the National Academy of Sciences, USA, 89,* 7199-7202. (11)

Gosler, A. G., Greenwood, J. J. D., & Perrins, C. (1995). Predation risk and the cost of being fat. *Nature, 377,* 621-623. (10)

Gottesman, I. I. (1991). *Schizophrenia genesis.* New York: W. H. Freeman. (16)

Gottesman, I. I., & Bertelson, A. (1989). Confirming unexpressed genotypes for schizophrenia. *Archives of General Psychiatry, 46,* 867-872. (16)

Götz, R., Köster, R., Winkler, C., Raulf, F., Lottspeich, F., Schartl, M., & Thoenen, H. (1993). Neurotrophin-6 is a new member of the nerve growth factor family. *Nature, 372,* 266-269. (5)

Graves, J. A. M. (1994). Mammalian sex-determining genes. In R. V. Short & E. Balaban (Eds.), *The differences between the sexes* (pp. 397-418). Cambridge, England: Cambridge University Press. (11)

Graybiel, A. M., Aosaki, T., Flaherty, A. W., & Kimura, M. (1994). The basal ganglia and adaptive motor control. *Science, 265,* 1826-1831. (4, 8)

Graziadei, P. P. C., & deHan, R. S. (1973). Neuronal regeneration in frog olfactory system. *Journal of Cell Biology, 59,* 525-530. (2)

Graziadei, P. P. C., & Monti Graziadei, G. A. (1985). Neurogenesis and plasticity of the olfactory sensory neurons. *Annals of the New York Academy of Sciences, 457,* 127-142. (2)

Green, D. J., & Gillette, R. (1982). Circadian rhythm of firing rate recorded from single cells in the rat suprachiasmatic brain slice. *Brain Research, 245,* 198-200. (9)

Greenlee, M. W., Lang, H.-J., Mergner, T., & Seeger, W. (1995). Visual short-term memory of stimulus velocity in patients with unilateral posterior brain damage. *Journal of Neuroscience, 15,* 2287-2300. (6)

Greist, J. H., Jefferson, J. W., Kobak, K. A., Katzelnick, D. J., & Serlin, R. C. (1995). Efficacy and tolerability of serotonin transport inhibitors in obsessive-compulsive disorder. *Archives of General Psychiatry, 52,* 53-60. (12)

Gresty, M. A., Bronstein, A. M., Brandt, T., & Dieterich, M. (1992). Neurology of otolith function. *Brain, 115,* 647-673. (7)

Griffin, D. R., Webster, F. A., & Michael, C. R. (1960). The echolocation of flying insects by bats. *Animal Behaviour, 8,* 141-154. (7)

Grisham, W., Castro, J. M., Kashon, M. L., Ward, I. L., & Ward, O. B. (1992). Prenatal flutamide alters sexually dimorphic nuclei in the spinal cord of male rats. *Brain Research, 578,* 69-74. (11)

Gross, C. G., & Graziano, M. S. A. (1995). Multiple representations of space in the brain. *The Neuroscientist, 1,* 43-50. (4)

Gross, C. G., & Sergent, J. (1992). Face recognition. *Current Opinion in Neurobiology, 2,* 156-161. (6)

Grossman, S. P., Dacey, D., Halaris, A. E., Collier, T., & Routtenberg, A. (1978). Aphagia and adipsia after preferential destruction of nerve cell bodies in hypothalamus. *Science, 202,* 537-539. (10)

Gubernick, D. J., & Alberts, J. R. (1983). Maternal licking of young: Resource exchange and proximate controls. *Physiology & Behavior, 31,* 593-601. (11)

Guidotti, A., Ferrero, P., Fujimoto, M., Santi, R. M., & Costa, E. (1986). Studies on endogenous ligands (endocoids) for the benzodiazepine/beta carboline binding sites. *Advances in Biochemical Pharmacology, 41,* 137-148. (12)

Guidotti, A., Forchetti, C. M., Corda, M. G., Konkel, D., Bennett, C. D., & Costa, E. (1983). Isolation, characterization, and purification to homogeneity of an endogenous polypeptide with agonistic action on benzodiazepine receptors. *Proceedings of the National Academy of Sciences, USA, 80,* 3531-3535. (12)

Gurevich, E. V., Bordelon, Y., Shapiro, R. M., Arnold, S. E., Gur, R. E., & Joyce, J. N. (1997). Mesolimbic dopamine D3 receptors and use of antipsychotics in patients with schizophrenia. *Archives of General Psychiatry, 54,* 225-232. (16)

Gusella, J. F., Tanzi, R. E., Anderson, M. A., Hobbs, W., Gibbons, K., Raschtchian, R., Gilliam, T. C., Wallace, M. R., Wexler, N. S., & Conneally, P. M. (1984). DNA markers for nervous system diseases. *Science, 225,* 1320-1326. (A)

Gustafsson, B., & Wigström, H. (1990). Basic features of long-term potentiation in the hippocampus. *Seminars in the Neurosciences, 2,* 321-333. (13)

Guyton, A. C. (1974). *Function of the human body* (4th ed.). Philadelphia: Saunders. (2)

Gwinner, E. (1986). Circannual rhythms in the control of avian rhythms. *Advances in the Study of Behavior, 16,* 191-228. (9)

Habib, M., Gayraud, D., Oliva, A., Regis, J., Salamon, G., & Khalil, R. (1991). Effects of handedness and sex on the morphology of the corpus callosum: A study with brain magnetic resonance imaging. *Brain and Cognition, 16,* 41-61. (14)

Hagman, J. O., Wood, F., Buchsbaum, M. S., Tallal, P., Flowers, L., & Katz, W. (1992). Cerebral brain metabolism in adult dyslexic subjects assessed with positron emission tomography during performance of an auditory task. *Archives of Neurology, 49,* 734-739. (14)

Haimov, I., & Lavie, P. (1996). Melatonin—A soporific hormone. *Current Directions in Psychological Science, 5,* 106-111. (9)

Halaas, J. L, Gajiwala, K. S., Maffei, M., Cohen, S. L., Chait, B. T., Rabinowitz, D., Lallone, R. L., Burley, S. K., & Friedman, J. M. (1995). Weight-reducing effects of the plasma protein encoded by the *obese* gene. *Science, 269,* 543-546. (10)

Haley, J. (1959). An interactional description of schizophrenia. *Psychiatry, 22,* 321-332. (16)

Hall, M. J., Bartoshuk, L. M., Cain, W. S., & Stevens, J. C. (1975). PTC taste blindness and the taste of caffeine. *Nature, 253,* 442-443. (7)

Hamer, D. H., Hu, S., Magnuson, V. L., Hu, N., & Pattatucci, A. M. L. (1993). A linkage between DNA markers on the X chromosome and male sexual orientation. *Science, 261,* 321-327. (11)

Hamilton, W. D. (1964). The genetical evolution of social behavior (I and II). *Journal of Theoretical Biology, 7,* 1-16; 17-52. (1)

Hamann, S. B., & Squire, L. R. (1995). On the acquisition of new declarative knowledge in amnesia. *Behavioral Neuroscience, 109,* 1027-1044. (13)

Harasty, J., Double, K. L., Halliday, G. M., Kril, J. J., & McRitchie, D. A. (1997). Language-associated cortical regions are proportionally larger in the female brain. *Archives of Neurology, 54,* 171-176. (14)

Hari, R. (1994). Human cortical functions revealed by magnetoencephalography. *Progress in Brain Research, 100,* 163-168. (4)

Harper, C. G., & Kril, J. J. (1993). Neuropathological changes in alcoholics. In W. A. Hunt & S. J. Nixon (Eds.), *Alcohol-induced brain damage* (NIAAA Research

Monograph 22) (pp. 39-69). Rockville, MD: U.S. Department of Health and Human Services. (3)

Harris, G. C., & Aston-Jones, G. (1994). Involvement of D$_2$ dopamine receptors in the nucleus accumbens in the opiate withdrawal syndrome. *Nature, 371*, 155-157. (3)

Harris, K. M., & Stevens, J. K. (1989). Dendritic spines of CA1 pyramidal cells in the rat hippocampus: Serial electron microscopy with reference to their biophysical characteristics. *Journal of Neuroscience, 9*, 2982-2997. (2)

Harris, R. A., Brodie, M. S., & Dunwiddie, T. V. (1992). Possible substrates of ethanol reinforcement: GABA and dopamine. *Annals of the New York Academy of Sciences, 654*, 61-69. (3)

Hart, B. L. (Ed.) (1976). *Experimental psychobiology.* San Francisco: W. H. Freeman. (10)

Hartline, H. K. (1949). Inhibition of activity of visual receptors by illuminating nearby retinal areas in the limulus eye. *Federation Proceedings, 8*, 69. (6)

Hayman, C. A. G., & Macdonald, C. A. (1993). The role of repetition and associative interference in new semantic learning in amnesia: A case experiment. *Journal of Cognitive Neuroscience, 5*, 375-389. (13)

He, S., Cavanagh, P., & Intiligator, J. (1996). Attentional resolution and the locus of visual awareness. *Nature, 383*, 334-337. (6)

Healy, S. D., & Krebs, J. R. (1996). Food storing and the hippocampus in paridae. *Brain, Behavior and Evolution, 47*, 195-199. (13)

Hebb, D. O. (1949). *Organization of behavior.* New York: Wiley. (inside cover, 13)

Heeb, M. M., & Yahr, P. (1996). C-fos immunoreactivity in the sexually dimorphic area of the hypothalamus and related brain regions of male gerbils after exposure to sex-related stimuli or performance of specific sexual behaviors. *Neuroscience, 72*, 1049-1071. (11)

Heffner, R. S., & Heffner, H. E. (1982). Hearing in the elephant (*Elephas maximus*): Absolute sensitivity, frequency discrimination, and sound localization. *Journal of Comparative and Physiological Psychology, 96*, 926-944. (7)

Heinrichs, R. W. (1993). Schizophrenia and the brain. *American Psychologist, 48*, 221-233. (16)

Heller, W., & Levy, J. (1981). Perception and expression of emotion in right-handers and left-handers. *Neuropsychologia, 19*, 263-272. (14)

Hennig, R., & Lømo, T. (1985). Firing patterns of motor units in normal rats. *Nature, 314*, 164-166. (8)

Herkenham, M. (1992). Cannabinoid receptor localization in brain: Relationship to motor and reward systems. *Annals of the New York Academy of Sciences, 654*, 19-32. (3)

Herkenham, M., Lynn, A. B., de Costa, B. R., & Richfield, E. K. (1991). Neuronal localization of cannabinoid receptors in the basal ganglia of the rat. *Brain Research, 547*, 267-274. (3)

Herkenham, M., Lynn, A. B., Little, M. D., Johnson, M. R., Melvin, L. S., de Costa, B. R., & Rice, K. C. (1990). Cannabinoid receptor localization in brain. *Proceedings of the National Academy of Sciences, USA, 87*, 1932-1936. (4)

Herman, L. M., Pack, A. A., & Morrel-Samuels, P. (1993). Representational and conceptual skills of dolphins. In H. L. Roitblat, L. M. Herman, & P. E. Nachtigall (Eds.), *Language and communication: Comparative perspectives* (pp. 403-442). Hillsdale, NJ: Lawrence Erlbaum. (14)

Hernandez, L., Murzi, E., Schwartz, D. H., & Hoebel, B. G. (1992). Electrophysiological and neurochemical approach to a hierarchical feeding organization. In P. Bjorntorp & B. N. Brodoff (Eds.), *Obesity* (pp. 171-183). Philadelphia, PA: J. B. Lippincott. (10)

Herrero, S. (1985). *Bear attacks: Their causes and avoidance.* Piscataway, NJ: Winchester. (7, 10)

Herrmann, K., & Shatz, C. J. (1995). Blockade of action potential activity alters initial arborization of thalamic axons within cortical layer 4. *Proceedings of the National Academy of Sciences, USA, 92*, 11244-11248. (5)

Hettinger, T. P., & Frank, M. E. (1992). Information processing in mammalian gustatory systems. *Current Opinion in Neurobiology, 2*, 469-478. (7)

Hibbard, L. S., McGlone, J. S., Davis, D. W., & Hawkins, R. A. (1987). Three-dimensional representation and analysis of brain energy metabolism. *Science, 236*, 1641-1646. (4)

Hickok, G., Bellugi, U., & Klima, E. S. (1996). The neurobiology of sign language and its implications for the neural basis of language. *Nature, 381*, 699-702. (14)

Higley, J. D., Mehlman, P. T., Higley, S. B., Fernald, B., Vickers, J., Lindell, S. G., Taub, D. M., Suomi, S. J., & Linnoila, M. (1996). Excessive mortality in young free-ranging male nonhuman primates with low cerebrospinal fluid 5-hydroxyindoleacetic acid concentrations. *Archives of General Psychiatry, 53*, 537-543. (12)

Hillis, A. E., & Caramazza, A. (1995). Cognitive and neural mechanisms underlying visual and semantic processing: Implications from "optic aphasia." *Journal of Cognitive Neuroscience, 7*, 457-478. (14)

Hines, M., Davis, F. C., Coquelin, A., Goy, R. W., & Gorski, R. A. (1985). Sexually dimorphic regions in the medial preoptic area and the bed nucleus of the stria terminalis of the guinea pig brain: A description and an investigation of their relationship to gonadal steroids in adulthood. *Journal of Neuroscience, 5*, 40-47. (11)

Hines, M., & Kaufman, F. R. (1994). Androgen and the development of human sex-typical behavior: Rough-and-tumble play and sex of preferred playmates in children with congenital adrenal hyperplasia (CAH). *Child Development, 65*, 1042-1053. (11)

Hiscock, M., Israelian, M., Inch, R., Jacek, C., & Hiscock-Kalil, C. (1995). Is there a sex difference in human laterality? II. An exhaustive survey of visual laterality studies from six neuropsychology journals. *Journal of Clinical and Experimental Neuropsychology, 17*, 590-610. (14)

Hitchcock, J. M., & Davis, M. (1991). Efferent pathway of the amygdala involved in conditioned fear as measured with the fear-potentiated startle paradigm. *Behavioral Neuroscience, 105*, 826-842. (12)

Hobson, J. A. (1989). *Sleep.* New York: Scientific American Library. (16)

Hobson, J. A., & McCarley, R. W. (1977). The brain as a dream state generator: An activation-synthesis hypothesis of the dream process. *American Journal of Psychiatry, 134,* 1335-1348. (9)

Hockfield, S., & Kalb, R. G. (1993). Activity-dependent structural changes during neuronal development. *Current Opinion in Neurobiology, 3,* 87-92. (6)

Hoebel, B. G. (1988). Neuroscience and motivation: Pathways and peptides that define motivational systems. In R. C. Atkinson, R. J. Herrnstein, G. Lindzey, & R. D. Luce (Eds.), *Stevens' handbook of experimental psychology* (2nd ed.) (pp. 547-625). New York: John Wiley. (10)

Hoebel, B. G., & Hernandez, L. (1993). Basic neural mechanisms of feeding and weight regulation. In A. J. Stunkard & T. A. Wadden (Eds.), *Obesity: Theory and therapy* (2nd ed.) (pp. 43-62). New York: Raven Press. (10)

Hoffer, A. (1973). Mechanism of action of nicotinic acid and nicotinamide in the treatment of schizophrenia. In D. Hawkins & L. Pauling (Eds.), *Orthomolecular psychiatry* (pp. 202-262). San Francisco: W. H. Freeman. (16)

Hoffer, B. J., Leenders, K. L., Young, D., Gerhardt, G., Zerbe, G. O., Bygdeman, M., Seiger, A., Olson, L., Strömberg, I., & Freedman, R. (1992). Eighteen-month course of two patients with grafts of fetal dopamine neurons for severe Parkinson's disease. *Experimental Neurology, 118,* 243-252. (15)

Hoffman, P. L., Tabakoff, B., Szabó, G., Suzdak, P. D., & Paul, S. M. (1987). Effect of an imidazobenzodiazepine, Ro15-4513, on the incoordination and hypothermia produced by ethanol and pentobarbital. *Life Sciences, 41,* 611-619. (12)

Hökfelt, T., Johansson, O., & Goldstein, M. (1984). Chemical anatomy of the brain. *Science, 225,* 1326-1334. (3)

Hollister, J. M., Laing, P., & Mednick, S. A. (1996). Rhesus incompatibility as a risk factor for schizophrenia in male adults. *Archives of General Psychiatry, 53,* 19 24. (16)

Hollister, J. M., Mednick, S. A., Brennan, P., & Cannon, T. D. (1994). Impaired autonomic nervous system habituation in those at genetic risk for schizophrenia. *Archives of General Psychiatry, 51,* 552-558. (16)

Holloway, R. L. (1996). Toward a synthetic theory of human brain evolution. In J.-P. Changeux & J. Chavaillon (Eds.), *Origins of the human brain* (pp. 42-54). Oxford, England: Clarendon Press. (5)

Honer, W. G., Falkai, P., Young, C., Wang, T., Xie, J., Bonner, J., Hu, L., Boulianne, G. L., Luo, Z., & Trimble, W. S. (1997). Cingulate cortex synaptic terminal proteins and neural cell adhesion molecules in schizophrenia. *Neuroscience, 78,* 99-110. (16)

Hoover, J. E., & Strick, P. L. (1993). Multiple output channels in the basal ganglia. *Science, 259,* 819-821. (8)

Hopfield, J. J. (1995). Pattern recognition computation using action potential timing for stimulus representation. *Nature, 376,* 33-36. (6)

Hopkins, J., Marcus, M., & Campbell, S. B. (1984). Postpartum depression: A critical review. *Psychological Bulletin, 95,* 498-515. (16)

Hoptman, M. J., & Davidson, R. J. (1994). How and why do the two cerebral hemispheres interact? *Psychological Bulletin, 116,* 195-219. (14)

Hoptman, M. J., & Levy, J. (1988). Perceptual asymmetries in left- and right-handers for cartoon and real faces. *Brain & Cognition, 8,* 178-188. (14)

Hore, J. (1996). Motor control, excitement, and overarm throwing. *Canadian Journal of Physiology and Pharmacology, 74,* 385-389. (8)

Horn, C. C., Tordoff, M. G., & Friedman, M. I. (1996). Does ingested fat produce satiety? *American Journal of Physiology, 270,* R761-R765. (10)

Horne, J. A. (1988). *Why we sleep.* Oxford, England: Oxford University Press. (9)

Horne, J. A. (1992). Sleep and its disorders in children. *Journal of Child Psychology & Psychiatry & Allied Disorders, 33,* 473-487. (9)

Horne, J. A., & Minard, A. (1985). Sleep and sleepiness following a behaviourally "active" day. *Ergonomics, 28,* 567-575. (9)

Horridge, G. A. (1962). Learning of leg position by the ventral nerve cord in headless insects. *Proceedings of the Royal Society of London, B, 157,* 33-52. (13)

Horton, J. C., & Hocking, D. R. (1996). An adult-like pattern of ocular dominance columns in striate cortex of newborn monkeys prior to visual experience. *Journal of Neuroscience, 16,* 1791-1807. (6)

Hovda, D. A., & Feeney, D. M. (1989). Amphetamine-induced recovery of visual cliff performance after bilateral visual cortex ablation in cats: Measurements of depth perception thresholds. *Behavioral Neuroscience, 103,* 574-584. (15)

Howland, H. C., & Sayles, N. (1984). Photorefractive measurements of astigmatism in infants and young children. *Investigative Ophthalmology and Visual Science, 25,* 93-102. (6)

Hsu, M., Sik, A., Gallyas, F., Horváth, Z., & Buzsáki, G. (1994). Short-term and long-term changes in the postischemic hippocampus. *Annals of the New York Academy of Sciences, 743,* 121-140. (15)

Hubel, D. H. (1963, November). The visual cortex of the brain. *Scientific American, 209* (5), 54-62. (6)

Hubel, D. H., & Wiesel, T. N. (1959). Receptive fields of single neurons in the cat's striate cortex. *Journal of Physiology, 148,* 574-591. (6)

Hubel, D. H., & Wiesel, T. N. (1965). Binocular interaction in striate cortex of kittens reared with artificial squint. *Journal of Neurophysiology, 28,* 1041-1059. (6)

Hubel, D. H., & Wiesel, T. N. (1977). Functional architecture of macaque monkey visual cortex. *Proceedings of the Royal Society of London, B, 198,* 1-59. (6)

Hudspeth, A. J. (1985). The cellular basis of hearing: The biophysics of hair cells. *Science, 230,* 745-752. (7)

Hugdahl, K. (1996). Brain laterality— beyond the basics. *European Psychologist, 1,* 206-220. (14)

Hughes, H. C., Nozawa, G., & Kitterle, F. (1996). Global precedence, spatial frequency channels, and the statistics of natural images.

Journal of Cognitive Neuroscience,
8, 197-230. (6)

Hull, E. M., Bitran, D., Pehek, E. A.,
Warner, R. K., Band, L. C., &
Holmes, G. M. (1986). Dopaminergic control of male sex behavior
in rats: Effects of an intracere-
brally-infused agonist. *Brain research, 370,* 73-81. (11)

Hull, E. M., Du, J., Lorrain, D. S., &
Matuszewich, L. (1995). Extracellular dopamine in the medial
preoptic area: Implications for
sexual motivation and hormonal
control of copulation. *Journal of
Neuroscience, 15,* 7465-7471. (11)

Hull, E. M., Du, J., Lorrain, D. S., &
Matuszewich, L. (1997). Testosterone, preoptic dopamine, and
copulation in male rats. *Brain
Research Bulletin,* (11)

Hull, E. M., Eaton, R. C., Markowski,
V. P., Moses, J., Lumley, L. A., &
Loucks, J. A. (1992). Opposite
influence of medial preoptic D1
and D2 receptors on genital reflexes: Implications for copulation. *Life Sciences, 51,* 1705-1713.
(11)

Hull, E. M., Eaton, R. C., Moses, J., &
Lorrain, D. (1993). Copulation
increases dopamine activity in the
medial preoptic area of male rats.
Life Sciences, 52, 935-940. (11)

Hultman, C. M., Öhman, A., Cnattingius, S., Wieselgren, I.-M., &
Lindström, L. H. (1997). Prenatal
and neonatal risk factors for
schizophrenia. *British Journal of
Psychiatry, 170,* 128-133. (16)

Humphrey, P. P. A., Hartig, P., &
Hoyer, D. (1993). A proposed new
nomenclature for 5-HT receptors.
*Trends in Pharmacological Sci-
ences, 14,* 233-236. (3)

Hunt, E., Streissguth, A. P., Kerr, B., &
Carmichael-Olson, H. (1995).
Mothers' alcohol consumption
during pregnancy: Effects on
spatial-visual reasoning in 14-
year-old children. *Psychological
Science, 6,* 339-342. (5)

Hunter, W. S. (1923). *General Psychology* (rev. ed.). Chicago: University
of Chicago Press. (4)

Huntington's Disease Collaborative
Research Group. (1993). A novel
gene containing a trinucleotide
repeat that is expanded and unstable on Huntington's disease chromosomes. *Cell, 72,* 971-983. (8)

Hurvich, L. M., & Jameson, D. (1957).
An opponent-process theory of
color vision. *Psychological Review,
64,* 384-404. (6)

Hyman, B. T., Van Hoesen, G. W.,
Damasio, A. R., & Barnes, C. L.
(1984). Alzheimer's disease: Cell-
specific pathology isolates the
hippocampal formation. *Science,
225,* 1168-1170. (13)

Hynd, G. W., & Semrud-Clikeman, M.
(1989). Dyslexia and brain morphology. *Psychological Bulletin,
106,* 447-482. (14)

Iacono, W. G., & Grove, W. M. (1993).
Schizophrenia reviewed: Toward
an integrative genetic model.
Psychological Science, 4, 273-276.
(16)

Iadecola, C. (1993). Regulation of the
cerebral microcirculation during
neural activity: Is nitric oxide the
missing link? *Trends in Neurosciences, 16,* 206-214. (4)

Iggo, A., & Andres, K. H. (1982). Morphology of cutaneous receptors.
Annual Review of Neuroscience, 5,
1-31. (7)

Imamura, K., Mataga, N., & Mori, K.
(1992). Coding of odor molecules
by mitral/tufted cells in rabbit
olfactory bulb. I. Aliphatic compounds. *Journal of Neurophysiology, 68,* 1986-2002. (7)

Imperato-McGinley, J., Guerrero, L.,
Gautier, T., & Peterson, R. E.
(1974). Steroid 5 alpha-reductase
deficiency in man: An inherited
form of male pseudohermaphroditism. *Science, 186,* 1213-1215.
(11)

Innocenti, G. M. (1980). The primary
visual pathway through the corpus callosum: Morphological and
functional aspects in the cat.
*Archives Italiennes de Biologie,
118,* 124-188. (14)

Innocenti, G. M., & Caminiti, R.
(1980). Postnatal shaping of callosal connections from sensory
areas. *Experimental Brain Research, 38,* 381-394. (14)

Inouye, S. T., & Kawamura, H. (1979).
Persistence of circadian rhythmic-
ity in a mammalian hypothalamic
"island" containing the suprachiasmatic nucleus. *Proceedings of
the National Academy of Sciences,
USA, 76,* 5962-5966. (9)

Irwin, M., Daniels, M., Risch, S. C.,
Bloom, E., & Weiner, H. (1988).
Plasma cortisol and natural killer
cell activity during bereavement.
Biological Psychiatry, 24, 173-178.
(12)

Isaacson, R. L. (1972). Hippocampal
destruction in man and other
animals. *Neuropsychologia, 10,* 47-
64. (13)

Ito, M. (1984). *The cerebellum and
neural control.* New York: Raven
Press. (8)

Ito, M. (1989). Long-term depression.
*Annual Review of Neuroscience,
12,* 85-102. (13)

Ivry, R. B., & Diener, H. C. (1991).
Impaired velocity perception in
patients with lesions of the cerebellum. *Journal of Cognitive Neuroscience, 3,* 355-366. (8)

Ivy, G. O., & Killackey, H. P. (1981).
The ontogeny of the distribution
of callosal projection neurons in
the rat parietal cortex. *Journal of
Comparative Neurology, 195,* 367-
389. (14)

Iwamura, Y. Iriki, A., & Tanaka, M.
(1994). Bilateral hand representation in the postcentral somatosensory cortex. *Nature, 369,* 554-556.
(7)

Izquierdo, I. (1995). Role of the hippocampus, amygdala, and entorhinal cortex in memory storage
and expression. In J. L. McGaugh,
F. Bermúdez-Rattoni, & R. A.
Prado-Alcalá (Eds.), *Plasticity in
the central nervous system* (pp. 41-
56). Mahwah, NJ: Lawrence Erlbaum. (13)

Izquierdo, I., & Medina, J. H. (1995).
Correlation between the pharma-
cology of long-term potentiation
and the pharmacology of memory.
*Neurobiology of Learning and
Memory, 63,* 19-32. (13)

Jacobs, B., Schall, M., & Scheibel,
A. B. (1993). A quantitative dendritic analysis of Wernicke's area
in humans. II. Gender,
hemispheric, and environmental
factors. *Journal of Comparataive
Neurology, 327,* 97-111. (5, 14)

Jacobs, B., & Scheibel, A. B. (1993). A
quantitative dendritic analysis of
Wernicke's area in humans. I.
Lifespan changes. *Journal of Comparative Neurology, 327,* 83-96. (2)

Jacobs, B. L. (1987). How hallucinogenic drugs work. *American Scientist, 75,* 386-392. (3)

Jacobs, G. D., & Snyder, D. (1996). Frontal brain asymmetry predicts affective style in men. *Behavioral Neuroscience, 110,* 3-6. (16)

Jacobs, G. H. (1993). The distribution and nature of colour vision among the mammals. *Biological Reviews, 68,* 413-471. (6)

Jancsó, G., Kiraly, E., & Jancsó-Gábor, A. (1977). Pharmacologically induced selective degeneration of chemosensitive primary sensory neurones. *Nature, 270,* 741-743. (7)

Janicak, P. G., Davis, J. M., Gibbons, R. D., Ericksen, S., Chang, S., & Gallagher, P. (1985). Efficacy of ECT: A meta-analysis. *American Journal of Psychiatry, 142,* 297-302. (16)

Janosik, E. H., & Davies, J. L. (1986). *Psychiatric mental health nursing.* Boston: Jones & Bartlett. (16)

Janowsky, J. S., Oviatt, S. K., & Orwell, E. S. (1994). Testosterone influences spatial cognition in older men. *Behavioral Neuroscience, 108,* 325-332. (11)

Jansen, A. S. P., Nguyen, X. V., Karpitskiy, V., Mettenleiter, T. C., & Loewy, A. D. (1995). Central command neurons of the sympathetic nervous system: Basis of the fight-or-flight response. *Science, 270,* 644-646. (12)

Jarrard, L. E. (1995). What does the hippocampus really do? *Behavioural Brain Research, 71,* 1-10. (13)

Jarrard, L. E., Okaichi, H., Steward, O., & Goldschmidt, R. B. (1984). On the role of hippocampal connections in the performance of place and cue tasks: Comparisons with damage to hippocampus. *Behavioral Neuroscience, 98,* 946-954. (13)

Jaskiw, G. E., & Weinberger, D. R. (1992). Dopamine and schizophrenia—a cortically corrective perspective. *Seminars in the Neurosciences, 4,* 179-188. (16)

Jenner, P. (1990). Parkinson's disease: Clues to the cause of cell death in the substantia nigra. *Seminars in the Neurosciences, 2,* 117-126. (8)

Jerison, H. J. (1985). Animal intelligence as encephalization. *Philosophical Transactions of the Royal Society of London, B, 308,* 21-35. (5)

Jernigan, T. L., & Bellugi, U. (1994). Neuroanatomical distinctions between Williams and Down syndromes. In S. H. Broman & J. Grafman (Eds.), *Atypical cognitive deficits in developmental disorders* (pp. 57-66). Hillsdale, NJ: Lawrence Erlbaum. (14)

Johns, T. R., & Thesleff, S. (1961). Effects of motor inactivation on the chemical sensitivity of skeletal muscle. *Acta Physiologica Scandinavica, 51,* 136-141. (15)

Johnson, L. C. (1969). Physiological and psychological changes following total sleep deprivation. In A. Kales (Ed.), *Sleep: Physiology & pathology* (pp. 206-220). Philadelphia: Lippincott. (9)

Johnson, M. H., Posner, M. I., & Rothbart, M. K. (1991). Components of visual orienting in early infancy: Contingency learning, anticipatory looking, and disengaging. *Journal of Cognitive Neuroscience, 3,* 335-344. (6)

Johnson, M. T. V., Kipnis, A. N., Coltz, J. D., Gupta, A., Silverstein, P., Zwiebel, F., & Ebner, T. J. (1996). Effects of levodopa and viscosity on the velocity and accuracy of visually guided tracking in Parkinson's disease. *Brain, 119,* 801-813. (8)

Johnson, S. C., Pinkston, J. B., Bigler, E. D., & Blatter, D. D. (1996). Corpus callosum morphology in normal controls and traumatic brain injury: Sex differences, mechanisms of injury, and neuropsychological correlates. *Neuropsychology, 10,* 408-415. (5)

Johnson, W. G., & Wildman, H. E. (1983). Influence of external and covert food stimuli on insulin secretion in obese and normal subjects. *Behavioral Neuroscience, 97,* 1025-1028. (10)

Joly, E., Mucke, L., & Oldstone, M. B. A. (1991). Viral persistence in neurons explained by lack of major histocompatibility class I expression. *Science, 253,* 1283-1285. (2)

Jonas, S. (1995). Prophylactic pharmacologic neuroprotection against focal cerebral ischemia. *Annals of the New York Academy of Sciences, 765,* 21-25. (15)

Jones, H. S., & Oswald, I. (1968). Two cases of healthy insomnia. *Electroencephalography and Clinical Neurophysiology, 24,* 378-380. (9)

Jordan, H. A. (1969). Voluntary intragastric feeding. *Journal of Comparative and Physiological Psychology, 68,* 498-506. (10)

Jorgensen, R. S., Johnson, B. T., Kolodziej, M. E., & Schreer, G. E. (1996). Elevated blood pressure and personality: A meta-analytic review. *Psychological Bulletin, 120,* 293-320. (12)

Joyner, A. L., & Guillemot, F. (1994). Gene targeting and development of the nervous system. *Current Opinion in Neurobiology, 4,* 37-42. (4)

Just, M. A., Carpenter, P. A., Keller, T. A., Eddy, W. F., & Thulborn, K. R. (1996). Brain activation modulated by sentence comprehension. *Science, 274,* 114-116. (14)

Kaas, J. H. (1983). What, if anything, is SI? Organization of first somatosensory area of cortex. *Physiological Reviews, 63,* 206-231. (7)

Kaas, J. H. (1989). Why does the brain have so many visual areas? *Journal of Cognitive Neuroscience, 1,* 121-135. (5)

Kaas, J. H. (1995). The evolution of isocortex. *Brain, Behavior and Evolution, 46,* 187-196. (5)

Kaas, J. H., Merzenich, M. M., & Killackey, H. P. (1983). The reorganization of somatosensory cortex following peripheral nerve damage in adult and developing mammals. *Annual Review of Neuroscience, 6,* 325-356. (15)

Kaas, J. H., Nelson, R. J., Sur, M., Lin, C.-S., & Merzenich, M. M. (1979). Multiple representations of the body within the primary somatosensory cortex of primates. *Science, 204,* 521-523. (4)

Kales, A., & Kales, J. D. (1984). *Evaluation and treatment of insomnia.* New York: Oxford. (9)

Kales, A., Scharf, M. B., & Kales, J. D. (1978). Rebound insomnia: A new clinical syndrome. *Science, 201,* 1039-1041. (9)

Kalsner, S. (1990). Heteroreceptors, autoreceptors, and other terminal sites. *Annals of the New York Academy of Sciences, 604,* 1-6. (3)

Kamarck, T., & Jennings, J. R. (1991). Biobehavioral factors in sudden cardiac death. *Psychological Bulletin, 109*, 42-75. (12)

Kandel, E. R., & Schwartz, J. H. (1982). Molecular biology of learning: Modulation of transmitter release. *Science, 218*, 433-443. (13)

Kaplan, M. S. (1985). Formation and turnover of neurons in young and senescent animals: An electromicroscopic and morphometric analysis. *Annals of the New York Academy of Sciences, 457*, 173-192. (2)

Kareken, D. A., Gur, R. C., Mozley, D., Mozley, L. H., Saykin, A. J., Shtasel, D. L., & Gur, R. E. (1995). Cognitive functioning and neuroanatomic volume measures in schizophrenia. *Neuropsychology, 9*, 211-219. (16)

Karmiloff-Smith, A., Klima, E., Bellugi, U., Grant, J., & Baron-Cohen, S. (1995). Is there a social module? Language, face processing, and theory of mind in individuals with Williams syndrome. *Journal of Cognitive Neuroscience, 7*, 196-208. (14)

Karni, A., Tanne, D., Rubenstein, B. S., Askenasy, J. J. M., & Sagi, D. (1994). Dependence on REM sleep of overnight improvement of a perceptual skill. *Science, 265*, 679-682. (9)

Karno, M., Golding, J. M., Sorenson, S. B., & Burnam, A. (1988). The epidemiology of obsessive-compulsive disorder in five US communities. *Archives of General Psychiatry, 45*, 1094-1099. (12)

Karrer, T., & Bartoshuk, L. (1991). Capsaicin desensitization and recovery on the human tongue. *Physiology & Behavior, 49*, 757-764. (7)

Kaye, W. H., Berrettini, W., Gwirtsman, H., & George, D. T. (1990). Altered cerebrospinal fluid neuropeptide Y and peptide YY immunoreactivity in anorexia and bulimia nervosa. *Archives of General Psychiatry, 47*, 548-556. (10)

Keefe, R. S. E., Silverman, J. M., Mohs, R. C., Siever, L. J., Harvey, P. D., Friedman, L., Roitman, S. E. L., DuPre, R. L., Smith, C. J., Schmeidler, J., & Davis, K. L. (1997). Eye tracking, attention, and schizotypal symptoms in nonpsychotic relatives of patients with schizophrenia. *Archives of General Psychiatry, 54*, 169-176. (16)

Keele, S. W., & Ivry, R. (1990). Does the cerebellum provide a common computation for diverse tasks? *Annals of the New York Academy of Sciences, 608*, 179-207. (8)

Kellar, K. J., & Stockmeier, C. A. (1986). Effects of electroconvulsive shock and serotonin axon lesions on beta-adrenergic and serotonin-2 receptors in rat brain. *Annals of the New York Academy of Sciences, 462*, 76-90. (16)

Kendler, K. S. (1983). Overview: A current perspective on twin studies of schizophrenia. *American Journal of Psychiatry, 140*, 1413-1425. (16)

Kendler, K. S., Gallagher, T. J., Abelson, J. M., & Kessler, R. C. (1996). Lifetime prevalence, demographic risk factors, and diagnostic validity of nonaffective psychosis as assessed in a U.S. community sample. *Archives of General Psychiatry, 53*, 1022-1031. (16)

Kendler, K. S., & Robinette, C. D. (1983). Schizophrenia in the National Academy of Sciences–National Research Council twin registry—A 16-year update. *American Journal of Psychiatry, 140*, 1551-1563. (16)

Kendler, K. S., Walters, E. E., Neale, M. C., Kessler, R. C., Heath, A. C., & Eaves, L. J. (1995). The structure of the genetic and environmental risk factors for six major psychiatric disorders in women. *Archives of General Psychiatry, 52*, 374-383. (16)

Kennard, C., Lawden, M., Morland, A. B., & Ruddock, K. H. (1995). Colour identification and colour constancy are impaired in a patient with incomplete achromatopsia associated with prestriate cortical lesions. *Proceedings of the Royal Society of London, B, 260*, 169-175. (6)

Kennard, M. A. (1938). Reorganization of motor function in the cerebral cortex of monkeys deprived of motor and premotor areas in infancy. *Journal of Neurophysiology, 1*, 477-496. (15)

Kerr, D. S., & Abraham, W. C. (1995). Cooperative interactions among afferents govern the induction of homosynaptic long-term depression in the hippocampus. *Proceedings of the National Academy of Sciences USA, 92*, 11637-11641. (13)

Kessler, R. C., McGonagle, K. A., Zhao, S., Nelson, C. B., Hughes, M., Eshleman, S., Wittchen, H.-U., & Kendler, K. S. (1994). Lifetime and 12-month prevalence of *DSM-III-R* psychiatric disorders in the United States. *Archives of General Psychiatry, 51*, 8-19. (16)

Kety, S. S. (1977). Genetic aspects of schizophrenia: Observations on the biological and adoptive relatives of adoptees who became schizophrenic. In E. S. Gershon, R. H. Belmaker, S. S. Kety, & M. Rosenbaum (Eds.), *The impact of biology on modern psychiatry* (pp. 195-206). New York: Spectum Publication (16)

Kety, S. S., Wender, P. H., Jacobson, B., Ingraham, L. J., Jansson, L., Faber, B., & Kinney, D. K. (1994). Mental illness in the biological and adoptive relatives of schizophrenic adoptees. *Archives of General Psychiatry, 51*, 442-455. (16)

Kiecolt-Glaser, J. K., & Glaser, R. (1993). Mind and immunity. In D. Goleman & J. Gurin (Eds.), *Mind/body medicine* (pp. 39-61). Yonkers, NY: Consumer Reports Books. (12)

Killackey, H. P. (1990). Neocortical expansion: An attempt toward relating phylogeny and ontogeny. *Journal of Cognitive Neuroscience, 2*, 1-17. (5)

Killackey, H. P., & Chalupa, L. M. (1986). Ontogenetic change in the distribution of callosal projection neurons in the postcentral gyrus of the fetal rhesus monkey. *Journal of Comparative Neurology, 244*, 331-348. (14)

Killeffer, F. A., & Stern, W. E. (1970). Chronic effects of hypothalamic injury. *Archives of Neurology, 22*, 419-429. (10)

Kim, D.-S., & Bonhoeffer, T. (1994). Reverse occlusion leads to a precise restoration of orientation preference maps in visual cortex. *Nature, 370*, 370-372. (6)

King, B. M., Smith, R. L., & Frohman, L. A. (1984). Hyperinsulinemia in rats with ventromedial hypothalamic lesions: Role of hyperphagia. *Behavioral Neuroscience, 98,* 152-155. (10)

Kingstone, A., & Gazzaniga, M. S. (1995). Subcortical transfer of higher order information: More illusory than real? *Neuropsychology, 9,* 321-328. (14)

Kinnamon, J. C. (1987). Organization and innervation of taste buds. In T. E. Finger and W. L. Silver (Eds.), *Neurobiology of taste and smell* (pp. 277-297). New York: John Wiley. (7)

Kinomura, S., Larsson, J., Gulyás, B., & Roland, P. E. (1996). Activation by attention of the human reticular formation and thalamic intralaminar nuclei. *Science, 271,* 512-515. (9)

Kinsbourne, M., & McMurray, J. (1975). The effect of cerebral dominance on time sharing between speaking and tapping by preschool children. *Child Development, 46,* 240-242. (14)

Kirkwood, A., Lee, H.-K., & Bear, M. F. (1995). Co-regulation of long-term potentiation and experience-dependent synaptic plasticity in visual cortex by age and experience. *Nature, 375,* 328-331. (6)

Klein, D. F. (1993). False suffocation alarms, spontaneous panics, and related conditions. *Archives of General Psychiatry, 50,* 306-317. (12)

Klein, T., Martens, H., Dijk, D.-J., Kronauer, R. E., Seely, E. W., & Czeisler, C. A. (1993). Circadian sleep regulation in the absence of light perception: Chronic non-24-hour circadian rhythm sleep disorder in a blind man with a regular 24-hour sleep-wake schedule. *Sleep, 16,* 333-343. (9)

Kleinschmidt, A., Bear, M. F., & Singer, W. (1987). Blockade of "NMDA" receptors disrupts experience-dependent plasticity of kitten striate cortex. *Science, 238,* 355-358. (13)

Kleitman, N. (1963). *Sleep and wakefulness* (rev. ed.). Chicago: University of Chicago Press. (9)

Klerman, G. L. (1975). Relationships between preclinical testing and therapeutic evaluation of antidepressive drugs: The importance of new animal models for theory and practice. In A. Sudilovsky, S. Gershon, & B. Beer (Eds.), *Predictability in psychopharmacology* (pp. 159-178). New York: Raven. (16)

Kluger, M. J. (1991). Fever: Role of pyrogens and cryogens. *Physiological Reviews, 71,* 93-127. (10)

Klüver, H., & Bucy, P. C. (1939). Preliminary analysis of functions of the temporal lobes in monkeys. *Archives of Neurology and Psychiatry, 42,* 979-1000. (4)

Knight, G. P., Fabes, R. A., & Higgins, D. A. (1996). Concerns about drawing causal inferences from meta-analyses: An example in the study of gender differences in aggression. *Psychological Bulletin, 119,* 410-421. (12)

Knoll, J. (1993). The pharmacological basis of the beneficial effects of (−) deprenyl (selegiline) in Parkinson's and Alzheimer's diseases. *Journal of Neural Transmission, Suppl. 40,* 69-91. (8)

Koch, C., & Zador, A. (1993). The function of dendritic spines: Devices subserving biochemical rather than electrical compartmentalization. *Journal of Neuroscience, 13,* 413-422. (2)

Kodama, J., Fukushima, M., & Sakata, T. (1978). Impaired taste discrimination against quinine following chronic administration of theophylline in rats. *Physiology & Behavior, 20,* 151-155. (7)

Koh, J.-Y., Suh, S. W., Gwag, B. J., He, Y. Y., Hsu, C. Y., & Choi, D. W. (1996). The role of zinc in selective neuronal death after transient global cerebral ischemia. *Science, 260,* 1013-1016. (15)

Kolb, B. (1995). *Brain plasticity and behavior.* Mahwah, NJ: Lawrence Erlbaum. (15)

Kolb, B., Cote, S., Ribeiro-da-Silva, A., & Cuello, A. C. (1997). Nerve growth factor treatment prevents dendritic atrophy and promotes recovery of function after cortical injury. *Neuroscience, 76,* 1139-1151. (15)

Kolb, B., & Gibb, R. (1993). Possible anatomical basis of recovery of function after neonatal frontal lesions in rats. *Behavioral Neuroscience, 107,* 799-811. (15)

Kolb, B., & Holmes, C. (1983). Neonatal motor cortex lesions in the rat: Absence of sparing of motor behaviors and impaired spatial learning concurrent with abnormal cerebral morphogenesis. *Behavioral Neuroscience, 97,* 697-709. (15)

Kolb, B., Sutherland, R. J., & Whishaw, I. Q. (1983). Abnormalities in cortical and subcortical morphology after neonatal neocortical lesions in rats. *Experimental Neurology, 79,* 223-244. (15)

Kolb, B., & Taylor, L. (1981). Affective behavior in patients with localized cortical excisions: Role of lesion site and side. *Science, 214,* 89-90. (14)

Koller, W. C. (1992). How accurately can Parkinson's disease be diagnosed? *Neurology, 42* (Suppl. 1), 6-16. (8)

Komisaruk, B. R., Adler, N. T., & Hutchison, J. (1972). Genital sensory field: Enlargement by estrogen treatment in female rats. *Science, 178,* 1295-1298. (11)

Konishi, M. (1995). Neural mechanisms of auditory image formation. In M. S. Gazzaniga (Ed.), *The cognitive neurosciences* (pp. 269-277). Cambridge, MA: MIT Press. (7)

Kordower, J. H., Rosenstein, J. M., Collier, T. J., Burke, M. A., Chen, E. Y., Li, J. M., Martel, L., Levey, A. E., Mufson, E. J., Freeman, T. B., & Olanow, C. W. (1996). Functional fetal nigral grafts in a patient with Parkinson's disease: Chemoanatomic, ultrastructural and metabolic studies. *Journal of Comparative Neurology, 370,* 203-230. (15)

Kornhuber, H. H. (1974). Cerebral cortex, cerebellum, and basal ganglia: An introduction to their motor functions. In F. O. Schmitt & F. G. Worden (Eds.), The neurosciences: Third study program (pp. 267-280). Cambridge, MA: MIT Press. (8)

Kostrzewa, R. M. (1995). Dopamine receptor supersensitivity. *Neuroscience and Biobehavioral Reviews, 19,* 1-17. (15)

Kraly, F. S. (1990). Drinking elicited by eating. *Progress in Psychobiology and Physiological Psychology, 14,* 67-133. (10)

Kraly, F. S., Kim, Y.-M., Dunham, L. M., & Tribuzio, R. A. (1995). Drinking after intragastric NaCl without increase in systemic plasma osmolality in rats. *American Journal of Physiology, 269,* R1085-R1092. (10)

Kringlen, E., & Cramer, G. (1989). Offspring of monozygotic twins discordant for schizophrenia. *Archives of General Psychiatry, 46,* 873-877. (16)

Kruesi, M. J. P., Hibbs, E. D., Zahn, T. P., Keysor, C. S., Hamburger, S. D., Bartko, J. J., & Rapoport, J. L. (1992). A 2-year prospective follow-up of children and adolescents with disruptive behavior disorders. *Archives of General Psychiatry, 49,* 429-435. (12)

Krupa, D. J., Thompson, J. K., & Thompson, R. F. (1993). Localization of a memory trace in the mammalian brain. *Science, 260,* 989-991. (13)

Krupa, D. J., & Thompson, R. F. (1995). Inactivation of the superior cerebellar peduncle blocks expression but not acquisition of the rabbit's classically conditioned eye-blink response. *Proceedings of the National Academy of Sciences, USA, 92,* 5097-5101. (13)

Krupa, D. J., Weng, J., & Thompson, R. F. (1996). Inactivation of brainstem motor nuclei blocks expression but not acquisition of the rabbit's classically conditioned eyeblink response. *Behavioral Neuroscience, 110,* 219-227. (13)

Kryger, M. (Ed.), with perspectives by C. Guilleminault, J. D. Parkes, M. Dahlitz, M. Mitler, M. Erman, & R. Hajdukovic. (1993). Amphetamines and narcolepsy. *Sleep, 16,* 199-206. (9)

Kujala, T., Alho, K., Kekoni, J., Hämäläinen, H., Reinikainen, K., Salonen, O., Standertskjöld-Norderstam, C.-G., & Näätänen, R. (1995). Auditory and somatosensory event-related brain potentials in early blind humans. *Experimental Brain Research, 104,* 519-526. (5)

Kupfermann, I. (1994). Neural control of feeding. *Current Opinion in Neurobiology, 4,* 869-876. (10)

Kupfermann, I., Castellucci, V., Pinsker, H., & Kandel, E. (1970). Neuronal correlates of habituation and dishabituation of the gill withdrawal reflex in *Aplysia. Science, 167,* 1743-1745. (13)

Kupsch, A., Oertel, W. H., Earl, C. D., & Sautter, J. (1995). Neuronal transplantation and neurotrophic factors in the treatment of Parkinson's disease—update February 1995. *Journal of Neural Transmission, Suppl. 46,* 193-207. (8, 15)

Kurahashi, T., Lowe, G., & Gold, G. H. (1994). Suppression of odorant responses by odorants in olfactory receptor cells. *Science, 265,* 118-120. (7)

Kuypers, H. G. J. M. (1989). Motor system organization. In G. Adelman (Ed.), *Neuroscience year* (pp. 107-110). Boston: Birkhäuser. (8)

LaBar, K. S., & LeDoux, J. E. (1996). Partial disruption of fear conditioning in rats with unilateral amygdala damage: Correspondence with unilateral temporal lobectomy in humans. *Behavioral Neuroscience, 110,* 991-997. (12)

LaBar, K. S., LeDoux, J. E., Spencer, D. D., & Phelps, E. A. (1995). Impaired fear conditioning following unilateral temporal lobectomy in humans. *Journal of Neuroscience, 15,* 6846-6855. (12)

Laburn, H. P. (1996). How does the fetus cope with thermal challenges? *News in Physiological Sciences, 11,* 96-100. (16)

Lague, L., Raiguel, S., & Orban, G. A. (1993). Speed and direction selectivity of macaque middle temporal neurons. *Journal of Neurophysiology, 69,* 19-39. (6)

LaHoste, G. J., & Marshall, J. F. (1989). Non-additivity of D$_2$ receptor proliferation induced by dopamine denervation and chronic selective antagonist administration: Evidence from quantitative autoradiography indicates a single mechanism of action. *Brain Research, 502,* 223-232. (15)

LaHoste, G. J., & Marshall, J. F. (1993). New concepts in dopamine receptor plasticity. *Annals of the New York Academy of Sciences, 702,* 183-196. (15)

LaMantia, A.-S., & Purves, D. (1989). Development of glomerular pattern visualized in the olfactory bulbs of living mice. *Nature, 341,* 646-649. (5)

Lamb, T. D., & Pugh, E. N. Jr. (1990). Physiology of transduction and adaptation in rod and cone pho-

toreceptors. *Seminars in the Neurosciences, 2,* 3-13. (6)

Land, M. F., & Fernald, R. D. (1992). The evolution of eyes. *Annual Review of Neuroscience, 15,* 1-29. (6)

Landau, W. M. (1993). Clinical neuromythology X. Faithful fashion: Survival status of the brain transplant cure for parkinsonism. *Neurology, 43,* 644-649. (15)

Landis, D. M. D. (1987). Initial junctions between developing parallel fibers and Purkinje cells are different from mature synaptic junctions. *Journal of Comparative Neurology, 260,* 513-525. (3)

Landolt, H.-P., Werth, E., Borbély, A. A., & Dijk, D.-J. (1995). Caffeine intake (200 mg) in the morning affects human sleep and EEG power spectra at night. *Brain Research, 675,* 67-74. (9)

Lang, R. A., Flor-Henry, P., & Frenzel, R. R. (1990). Sex hormone profiles in pedophilic and incestuous men. *Annals of Sex Research, 3,* 59-74. (11)

Langworthy, R. A., & Jennings, J. W. (1972). Oddball, abstract olfactory learning in laboratory rats. *Psychological Record, 22,* 487-490. (5)

Lashley, K. S. (1929). *Brain mechanisms and intelligence.* Chicago: University of Chicago Press. (13)

Lashley, K. S. (1930). Basic neural mechanisms in behavior. *Psychological Review, 37,* 1-24. (inside cover)

Lashley, K. S. (1950). In search of the engram. *Symposia of the Society for Experimental Biology, 4,* 454-482. (13)

Lashley, K. S. (1951). The problem of serial order in behavior. In L. A. Jeffress (Ed.), *Cerebral mechanisms in behavior* (pp. 112-136). New York: John Wiley & Sons. (8)

Lassonde, M., Bryden, M. P., & Demers, P. (1990). The corpus callosum and cerebral speech lateralization. *Brain and Language, 38,* 195-206. (14)

Laudenslager, M. L. (1976). Proportional hypothalamic control of behavioral thermoregulation in the squirrel monkey. *Physiology & Behavior, 17,* 383-390. (10)

Laurent, J.-P., Cespuglio, R., & Jouvet, M. (1974). Dèlimitation des voies ascendantes de l'activité pontogéniculo-occipitale chez le chat [Demarcation of the ascending paths of ponto-geniculo-occipital activity in the cat]. *Brain Research, 65,* 29-52. (9)

Lavin, J. H., Wittert, G., Sun, W.-M., Horowitz, M., Morley, J. E., & Read, N. W. (1996). Appetite regulation by carbohydrate: Role of blood glucose and gastrointestinal hormones. *American Journal of Physiology, 271,* E209-E214. (10)

LeDoux, J. E., Iwata, J., Cicchetti, P., & Reis, D. J. (1988). Different projections of the central amygdaloid nucleus mediate autonomic and behavioral correlates of conditioned fear. *Journal of Neuroscience, 8,* 2517-2529. (12)

Lee, Y., Walker, D., & Davis, M. (1996). Lack of a temporal gradient of retrograde amnesia following NMDA-induced lesions of the basolateral amygdala assessed with the fear-potentiated startle paradigm. *Behavioral Neuroscience, 110,* 836-839. (12)

Lehrman, D. S. (1964). The reproductive behavior of ring doves. *Scientific American, 211* (5), 48-54. (11)

Leibowitz, S. F., & Alexander, J. T. (1991). Analysis of neuropeptide Y-induced feeding: Dissociation of Y_1 and Y_2 receptor effects on natural meal patterns. *Peptides, 12,* 1251-1260. (10)

Leibowitz, S. F., Alexander, J. T., Cheung, W. K., & Weiss, G. F. (1993). Effects of serotonin and the serotonin blocker metergoline on meal patterns and macronutrient selection. *Pharmacology Biochemistry & Behavior, 45,* 185-194. (10)

Leibowitz, S. F., Hammer, N. J., & Chang, K. (1981). Hypothalamic paraventricular nucleus lesions produce overeating and obesity in the rat. *Physiology & Behavior, 27,* 1031-1040. (10)

Leibowitz, S. F., Weiss, G. F., & Suh, J. S. (1990). Medial hypothalamic nuclei mediate serotonin's inhibitory effect on feeding behavior. *Pharmacology Biochemistry & Behavior, 37,* 735-742. (10)

LeMagnen, J. (1981). The metabolic basis of dual periodicity of feeding in rats. *Behavioral and Brain Sciences, 4,* 561-607. (10)

Lenhart, R. E., & Katkin, E. S. (1986). Psychophysiological evidence for cerebral laterality effects in a high-risk sample of students with subsyndromal bipolar depressive disorder. *American Journal of Psychiatry, 143,* 602-607. (16)

Lentz, T. L., Burrage, T. G., Smith, A. L., Crick, J., & Tignor, G. H. (1982). Is the acetylcholine receptor a rabies virus receptor? *Science, 215,* 182-184. (12)

Leonard, C. M., Lombardino, L. J., Mercado, L. R., Browd, S. R., Breier, J. I., & Agee, O. F. (1996). Cerebral asymmetry and cognitive development in children: A magnetic resonance imaging study. *Psychological Science, 7,* 89-95. (14)

Leopold, D. A., & Logothetis, N. K. (1996). Activity changes in early visual cortex reflect monkeys' percepts during binocular rivalry. *Nature, 379,* 549-553. (6)

Lerer, B., & Shapira, B. (1986). Neurochemical mechanisms of mood stabilization. *Annals of the New York Academy of Sciences, 462,* 367-375. (16)

Lesse, S. (1984). Psychosurgery. *American Journal of Psychotherapy, 38,* 224-228. (4)

Lester, L. S., & Fanselow, M. S. (1985). Exposure to a cat produces opioid analgesia in rats. *Behavioral Neuroscience, 99,* 756-759. (7)

Lettvin, J. Y., Maturana, H. R., McCulloch, W. S., & Pitts, W. H. (1959). What the frog's eye tells the frog's brain. *Proceedings of the Institute of Radio Engineers, 47,* 1940-1951. (7)

LeVay, S. (1991). A difference in hypothalamic structure between heterosexual and homosexual men. *Science, 253,* 1034-1037. (11)

LeVay, S. (1993). *The sexual brain.* Cambridge, MA: MIT Press. (11)

Levenson, R. W., Oyama, O. N., & Meek, P. S. (1987). Greater reinforcement from alcohol for those at risk: Parental risk, personality risk, and sex. *Journal of Abnormal Psychology, 96,* 242-253. (3)

Leventhal, A. G., Thompson, K. G., Liu, D., Zhou, Y., & Ault, S. J. (1995). Concomitant sensitivity to orientation, direction, and color of cells in layers 2, 3, and 4 of monkey striate cortex. *Journal of Neuroscience, 15,* 1808-1818. (6)

LeVere, N. D., & LeVere, T. E. (1982). Recovery of function after brain damage: Support for the compensation theory of the behavioral deficit. *Physiological Psychology, 10,* 165-174. (15)

LeVere, T. E. (1975). Neural stability, sparing and behavioral recovery following brain damage. *Psychological Review, 82,* 344-358. (15)

LeVere, T. E. (1980). Recovery of function after brain damage: A theory of the behavioral deficit. *Physiological Psychology, 8,* 297-308. (15)

LeVere, T. E. (1993). Recovery of function after brain damage: The effects of nimodipine on the chronic behavioral deficit. *Psychobiology, 21,* 125-129. (15)

LeVere, T. E., Ford, K., & Sandin, M. (1992). Recovery of function after brain damage: The benefits of diets supplemented with the calcium channel blocker nimodipine. *Psychobiology, 20,* 219-222. (15)

LeVere, T. E., & Morlock, G. W. (1973). Nature of visual recovery following posterior neodecortication in the hooded rat. *Journal of Comparative and Physiological Psychology, 83,* 62-67. (15)

Levi-Montalcini, R. (1987). The nerve growth factor 35 years later. *Science, 237,* 1154-1162. (5)

Levi-Montalcini, R. (1988). *In praise of imperfection.* New York: Basic books. (5)

Levin, E. D., & Rose, J. E. (1995). Acute and chronic nicotine interactions with dopamine systems and working memory performance. *Annals of the New York Academy of Sciences, 757,* 245-252. (3)

Levine, B., Hardwick, J. M., Trapp, B. D., Crawford, T. O., Bollinger, R. C., & Griffin, D. E. (1991). Antibody-mediated clearance of alphavirus infection from neurons. *Science, 254,* 856-860. (2)

Levine, J. D., Fields, H. L., & Basbaum, A. I. (1993). Peptides and the primary afferent nociceptor. *Journal of Neuroscience, 13,* 2273-2286. (7)

Levitsky, D. A., & Strupp, B. J. (1995). Malnutrition and the brain: Changing concepts, changing concerns. *Journal of Nutrition, 125* (8 Suppl.), S2212-S2220. (5)

Levitt, R. A. (1975). *Psychopharmacology.* Washington, DC: Hemisphere. (16)

Levitt-Gilmour, T. A., & Salpeter, M. M. (1986). Gradient of extrajunctional acetylcholine receptors early after denervation of mammalian muscle. *Journal of Neuroscience, 6,* 1606-1612. (15)

Levitzki, A. (1988). From epinephrine to cyclic AMP. *Science, 241,* 800-806. (3)

Levivier, M., Przedborski, S., Bencsics, C., & Kang, U. J. (1995). Intrastriatal implantation of fibroblasts genetically engineered to produce brain-derived neurotrophic factor prevents degeneration of dopaminergic neurons in a rat model of Parkinson's disease. *Journal of Neuroscience, 15,* 7810-7820. (15)

Levy, J. (1983). Language, cognition, and the right hemisphere: A response to Gazzaniga. *American Psychologist, 38,* 538-541. (14)

Levy, J., Heller, W., Banich, M. T., & Burton, L. A. (1983). Asymmetry of perception in free viewing of chimeric faces. *Brain and Cognition, 2,* 404-419. (14)

Levy, J., Nebes, R. D., & Sperry, R. W. (1971). Expressive language in the surgically separated minor hemisphere. *Cortex, 7,* 49-58. (14)

Levy-Lahad, E., Wijsman, E. M., Nemens, E., Anderson, L., Goddard, K. A. B., Weber, J. L., Bird, T. D., & Schellenberg, G. D. (1995). A familial Alzheimer's disease locus on chromosome 1. *Science, 269,* 970-973. (13)

Lewis, E. R., Everhart, T. E., & Zeevi, Y. Y. (1969). Studying neural organization in *Aplysia* with the scanning electron microscope. *Science, 165,* 1140-1143. (3)

Lewis, V. G., Money, J., & Epstein, R. (1968). Concordance of verbal and nonverbal ability in the adrenogenital syndrome. *Johns Hopkins Medical Journal, 122,* 192-195. (11)

Lewy, A. J., Ahmed, S., & Sack, R. L. (1996). Phase shifting the human circadian clock using melatonin. *Behavioural Brain Research, 73,* 131-134. (9)

Lezak, M. D. (1995). *Neuropsychological assessment* (3rd ed.). New York: Oxford University Press. (15)

Li, X.-J., Li, S.-H., Sharp, A. H., Nucifora, F. C. Jr., Schilling, G., Lanahan, A., Worley, P., Snyder, S. H., & Ross, C. A. (1995). A huntingtin-associated protein enriched in brain with implications for pathology. *Nature, 378,* 398-402. (8)

Liao, D., Hessler, N. A., & Malinow, R. (1995). Activation of postsynaptically silent synapses during pairing-induced LTP in CA1 region of hippocampal slice. *Nature, 375,* 400-404. (13)

Licinio, J., Wong, M. L., & Gold, P. W. (1996). The hypothalamic-pituitary-adrenal axis in anorexia nervosa. *Psychiatry Research, 62,* 75-83. (10)

Lieberman, J. A., Jody, D., Alvir, J. M. J., Ashtari, M., Levy, D. L., Bogerts, B., Degreef, G., Mayerhoff, D. I., & Cooper, T. (1993). Brain morphology, dopamine, and eye-tracking abnormalities in first-episode schizophrenia. *Archives of General Psychiatry, 50,* 357-368. (16)

Lin, J.-S., Hou, Y., Sakai, K., & Jouvet, M. (1996). Histaminergic descending inputs to the mesopontine tegmentum and their role in the control of cortical activation and wakefulness in the cat. *Journal of Neuroscience, 16,* 1523-1537. (9)

Lin, X. Y., & Glanzman, D. L. (1994). Hebbian induction of long-term potentiation of Aplysia sensorimotor synapses: Partial requirement for activation of an NMDA-related receptor. *Proceedings of the Royal Society of London, B, 255,* 215-221. (13)

Lindberg, N. O., Coburn, C., & Stricker, E. M. (1984). Increased feeding by rats after subdiabetogenic streptozotocin treatment: A role for insulin in satiety. *Behavioral Neuroscience, 98,* 138-145. (10)

Lindsay, P. H., & Norman, D. A. (1972). *Human information processing.* New York: Academic Press. (7)

Lindstrom, J. (1979). Autoimmune response to acetylcholine receptors in myasthenia gravis and its animal model. *Advances in Immunology, 27,* 1-50. (3)

Liu, G., & Tsien, R. W. (1995). Properties of synaptic transmission at single hippocampal synaptic boutons. *Nature, 375,* 404-408. (3)

Livingstone, M. S. (1988, January). Art, illusion and the visual system. *Scientific American, 258* (1), 78-85. (6)

Livingstone, M. S., & Hubel, D. (1988). Segregation of form, color, movement, and depth: Anatomy, physiology, and perception. *Science, 240,* 740-749. (6)

Livingstone, M. S., Rosen, G. D., Drislane, F. W., & Galaburda, A. M. (1991). Physiological and anatomical evidence for a magnocellular defect in developmental dyslexia. *Proceedings of the National Academy of Sciences, USA, 88,* 7943-7947. (14)

Loewenstein, W. R. (1960, August). Biological transducers. *Scientific American, 203* (2), 98-108. (7)

Loewi, O. (1960). An autobiographic sketch. *Perspectives in Biology, 4,* 3-25. (3)

Logan, C. G., & Grafton, S. T. (1995). Functional anatomy of human eyeblink conditioning determined with regional cerebral glucose metabolism and positron-emission tomography. *Proceedings of the National Academy of Sciences, USA, 92,* 7500-7504. (13)

London, E. D., Cascella, N. G., Wong, D. F., Phillips, R. L., Dannals, R. F., Links, J. M., Herning, R., Grayson, R., Jaffe, J. H., & Wagner, H. N. (1990). Cocaine-induced reduction of glucose utilization in human brain. *Archives of General Psychiatry, 47,* 567-574. (3)

Long, N. C. (1996). Evolution of infectious disease: How evolutionary forces shape physiological responses to pathogens. *News in Physiological Sciences, 11,* 83-90. (10)

Loring, D. W., Meador, K. J., Lee, G. P., Murro, A. M., Smith, J. R., Flanigin, H. F., Gallagher, B. B., & King, D. W. (1990). Cerebral language lateralization: Evidence from intracarotid amobarbital testing. *Neuropsychologia, 28,* 831-838. (14)

Lott, I. T. (1982). Down's syndrome, aging, and Alzheimer's disease: A clinical review. *Annals of the New York Academy of Sciences, 396,* 15-27. (13)

Lowe, J., & Carroll, D. (1985). The effects of spinal injury on the intensity of emotional experience. *British Journal of Clinical Psychology, 24,* 135-136. (12)

Lubitz, D. K. J. E., Carter, M. F., Been-hakker, M., Lin, R. C.-S., & Jacob-son, K. A. (1995). Adenosine: A prototherapeutic concept in neu-rodegeneration. *Annals of the New York Academy of Sciences, 765,* 163-178. (15)

Lund, R. D., Lund, J. S., & Wise, R. P. (1974). The organization of the retinal projection to the dorsal lateral geniculate nucleus in pig-mented and albino rats. *Journal of Comparative Neurology, 158,* 383-404. (6)

Lundy-Ekman, L., Ivry, R., Keele, S., & Woolacott, M. (1991). Timing and force control deficits in clumsy children. *Journal of Cognitive Neuroscience, 3,* 367-376. (8)

Lurito, J. T., Georgakopoulos, T., & Georgopoulos, A. P. (1991). Cogni-tive spatial-motor processes. 7. The making of movements at an angle from a stimulus direction: Studies of motor cortical activity at the single cell and population levels. *Experimental Brain Re-search, 87,* 562-580. (8)

Lykken, D. T., McGue, M., Tellegen, A., & Bouchard, T. J. (1992). Emergenesis: Genetic traits that may not run in families. *American Psychologist, 47,* 1565-1577. (1)

Lyman, C. P., O'Brien, R. C., Greene, G. C., & Papafrangos, E. D. (1981). Hibernation and longevity in the Turkish hamster *Mesocricc tus brandti. Science, 212,* 668-670. (9)

Lynch, J. C. (1980). The functional organization of posterior parietal association cortex. *The Behavioral and Brain Sciences, 3,* 485-534. (4)

Lyons, M. J., True, W. R., Eisen, S. A., Goldberg, J., Meyer, J. M., Faraone, S. V., Eaves, L. J., & Tsuang, M. T. (1995). Differential heritability of adult and juvenile antisocial traits. *Archives of Gen-eral Psychiatry, 52,* 906-915. (12)

Lytle, L. D., Messing, R. B., Fisher, L., & Phebus, L. (1975). Effects of long-term corn consumption on brain serotonin and the response to electric shock. *Science, 190,* 692-694. (12)

Macdonald, R. L., Weddle, M. G., & Gross, R. A. (1986). Benzodi-azepine, b-carboline, and barbitu-rate actions on GABA responses. *Advances in Biochemical Psycho-pharmacology, 41,* 67-78. (12)

MacFarlane, J. G., Cleghorn, J. M., & Brown, G. M. (1985a). Melatonin and core temperature rhythms in chronic insomnia. In G. M. Brown & S. D. Wainwright (Eds.), *The pineal gland: Endocrine aspects* (pp. 301-306). New York: Perga-mon. (9)

MacFarlane, J. G., Cleghorn, J. M., & Brown, G. M. (1985b, September). *Circadian rhythms in chronic insomnia.* Paper presented at the 4th World Congress of Biological Psychiatry, Philadelphia. (9)

MacLean, P. D. (1949). Psychosomatic disease and the "visceral brain": Recent developments bearing on the Papez theory of emotion. *Psychosomatic Medicine, 11,* 338-353. (12)

MacLean, P. D. (1954). Studies on limbic system ("visceral brain") and their bearing on psychoso-matic problems. In E. D. Wit-tkower & R. A. Cleghorn (Eds.), *Recent developments in psychoso-matic medicine* (pp. 101-125). Philadelphia: Lippincott. (12)

MacLean, P. D. (1958). Contrasting functions of limbic and neocorti-cal systems of the brain and their relevance to psychophysiological aspects of medicine. *American Journal of Medicine, 25,* 611-626. (12)

MacLean, P. D. (1962). Neurophysiolo-gie. In *Monoamines et système nerveux central* (pp. 269-276). Geneva: Georg a Cie, 1962. (16)

MacLean, P. D. (1970). The limbic brain in relation to the psychoses. In P. Black (Ed.), *Physiological correlates of emotion* (pp. 129-146). New York: Academic Press. (12)

MacLusky, N. J., & Naftolin, F. (1981). Sexual differentiation of the cen-tral nervous system. *Science, 211,* 1294-1303. (11)

Macphail, E. M. (1985). Vertebrate intelligence: The null hypothesis. *Philosophical Transactions of the Royal Society of London, B, 308,* 37-51. (5)

Maes, M., Scharpé, S., Verkerk, R., D'Hondt, P., Peeters, D., Cosyns, P., Thompson, P., De Meyer, F., Wauters, A., & Neels, H. (1995).
Seasonal availability in plasma L-tryptophan availability in healthy volunteers. *Archives of General Psychiatry, 52,* 937-946. (12)

Madden, P. A. F., Heath, A. C., Rosen-thal, N. E., & Martin, N. G. (1996). Seasonal changes in mood and behavior. *Archives of General Psychiatry, 53,* 47-55. (16)

Mahowald, M. W., & Schenck, C. H. (1992). Dissociated states of wakefulness and sleep. *Neurology, 42* (Suppl. 6), 44-52. (9)

Malamed, F., & Zaidel, E. (1993). Language and task effects on lateralized word recognition. *Brain and Language, 45,* 70-85. (14)

Málková, L., Mishkin, M., & Bacheva-lier, J. (1995). Long-term effects of selective neonatal temporal lobe lesions on learning and memory in monkeys. *Behavioral Neuro-science, 109,* 212-226. (15)

Mallick, H., Manchanda, S. K., & Ku-mar, V. M. (1996). β-Adrenergic modulation of male sexual behav-ior elicited from the medial preop-tic area in rats. *Behavioural Brain Research, 74,* 181-187. (11)

Manfredi, M., Stocchi, F., & Vacca. L. (1995). Differential diagnosis of parkinsonism. *Journal of Neural Transmission, Suppl. 45,* 1-9. (8)

Mangiapane, M. L., & Simpson, J. B. (1980). Subfornical organ: Fore-brain site of pressor and dipso-genic action of angiotensin II. *American Journal of Physiology, 239,* R382-R389. (10)

Manji, H. K., Potter, W. Z., & Lenox, R. H. (1995). Signal transduction pathways. *Archives of General Psychiatry, 52,* 531-543. (16)

Mann, J. J., Arango, V., & Underwood, M. D. (1990). Serotonin and suici-dal behavior. *Annals of the New York Academy of Sciences, 600,* 476-485. (12)

Maquet, P., Peters, J.-M., Aerts, J., Delfiore, G., Degueldre, C., Luxen, A., & Franck, G. (1996). Func-tional neuroanatomy of human rapid-eye-movement sleep and dreaming. *Nature, 383,* 163-166. (9)

Mark, V. H., & Ervin, F. R. (1970). *Violence and the brain.* New York: Harper & Row. (12)

Markham, C. H., & Diamond, S. G. (1981). Evidence to support early levodopa therapy in Parkinson disease. *Neurology, 31,* 124-131. (8)

Markram, H., & Tsodyks, M. (1996). Redistribution of synaptic efficacy between neocortical pyramidal neurons. *Nature, 382,* 807-810. (13)

Marks, G. A., Shaffery, J. P., Oksenberg, A., Speciale, S. G., & Roffwarg, H. P. (1995). A functional role for REM sleep in brain maturation. *Behavioural Brain Research, 69,* 1-11. (9)

Marler, P., & Nelson, D. (1992). Neuroselection and song learning in birds: Species universals in a culturally transmitted behavior. *Seminars in the Neurosciences, 4,* 415-423. (5)

Marshall, J. F. (1985). Neural plasticity and recovery of function after brain injury. *International Review of Neurobiology, 26,* 201-247. (15)

Marshall, J. F., Drew, M. C., & Neve, K. A. (1983). Recovery of function after mesotelencephalic dopaminergic injury in senescence. *Brain Research, 259,* 249-260. (15)

Martin, A., Wiggs, C. L., Ungerleider, L. G., & Haxby, J. V. (1996). Neural correlates of category-specific knowledge. *Nature, 379,* 649-652. (14)

Martin, A. R. (1977). Junctional transmission. II. Presynaptic mechanisms. In E. R. Kandel (Ed.), *Handbook of physiology* (Sect. 1, Vol. 1, Pt. 1, pp. 329-355). Bethesda, MD: American Physiological Society. (3)

Martin, R. C., & Blossom-Stach, C. (1986). Evidence of syntactic deficits in a fluent aphasic. *Brain and Language, 28,* 196-234. (14)

Martin, R. D. (1996). Scaling of the mammalian brain: The maternal energy hypothesis. *News in Physiological Sciences, 11,* 149-156. (5)

Martinez, J. L., & Derrick, B. E. (1996). Long-term potentiation and learning. *Annual Review of Psychology, 47,* 173-203. (13)

Martinez-Vargas, M. C., & Erickson, C. J. (1973). Some social and hormonal determinants of nest-building behaviour in the ring dove (*Streptopelia risoria*). *Behaviour, 45,* 12-37. (11)

Mason, D. A., & Frick, P. J. (1994). The heritability of antisocial behavior: A meta-analysis of twin and adoption studies. *Journal of Psychopathology and Behavioral Assessment, 16,* 301-323. (12)

Masterton, B., Heffner, H., & Ravizza, R. (1969). The evolution of human hearing. *Journal of the Acoustical Society of America, 45,* 966-985. (7)

Mattay, V. S., Berman, K. F., Ostrem, J. L., Esposito, G., Van Horn, J. D., Bigelow, L. B., & Weinberger, D. R. (1996). Dextroamphetamine enhances "neural network-specific" physiological signals: A positron-emission tomography rCBF study. *Journal of Neuroscience, 15,* 4816-4822. (3)

May, P. R. A., Fuster, J. M., Haber, J., & Hirschman, A. (1979). Woodpecker drilling behavior: An endorsement of the rotational theory of impact brain injury. *Archives of Neurology, 36,* 370-373. (15)

Mayer, A. D., & Rosenblatt, J. S. (1979). Hormonal influences during the ontogeny of maternal behavior in female rats. *Journal of Comparative and Physiological Psychology, 93,* 879-898. (11)

Mayer, A. D., & Rosenblatt, J. S. (1984). Postpartum changes in maternal responsiveness and nest defense in *Rattus norvegicus. Journal of Comparative Psychology, 98,* 177-188. (11)

Mayer, J. (1953). Glucostatic mechanism of regulation of food intake. *New England Journal of Medicine, 249,* 13-16. (10)

McBurney, D. H., & Bartoshuk, L. M. (1973). Interactions between stimuli with different taste qualities. *Physiology & Behavior, 10,* 1101-1106. (7)

McCarley, R. W., & Hobson, J. A. (1977). The neurobiological origins of psychoanalytic dream theory. *American Journal of Psychiatry, 134,* 1211-1221. (9)

McCarley, R. W., & Hoffman, E. (1981). REM sleep, dreams, and the activation-synthesis hypothesis. *American Journal of Psychiatry, 138,* 904-912. (9)

McClintock, M. K. (1971). Menstrual synchrony and suppression. *Nature, 229,* 244-245. (7)

McConnell, J. V. (1962). Memory transfer through cannibalism in planarians. *Journal of Neuropsychiatry, 3* (Suppl. 1), 42-48. (13)

McConnell, S. K. (1992). The genesis of neuronal diversity during development of cerebral cortex. *Seminars in the Neurosciences, 4,* 347-356. (5)

McCormick, D. A. (1989). Acetylcholine: Distribution, receptors, and actions. *Seminars in the Neurosciences, 1,* 91-101. (3)

McCormick, D. A., & Thompson, R. F. (1984). Cerebellum: Essential involvement in the classically conditioned eyelid response. *Science, 223,* 296-299. (13)

McElhiney, M. C., Moody, B. J., Steif, B. L., Prudic, J., Devanand, D. P., Nobler, M. S., & Sackeim, H. A. (1995). Autobiographical memory and mood: Effects of electroconvulsive therapy. *Neuropsychology, 9,* 501-517. (16)

McGaugh, J. L. (1990). Significance and remembrance: The role of neuromodulatory systems. *Psychological Science, 1,* 15-25. (13)

McGaugh, J. L., Cahill, L., Parent, M. B., Mesches, M. H., Coleman-Mesches, K., & Salinas, J. A. (1995). Involvement of the amygdala in the regulation of memory storage. In J. L. McGaugh, F. Bermúdez-Rattoni, & R. A. Prado-Alcalá (Eds.), *Plasticity in the central nervous system* (pp. 17-39). Mahwah, NJ: Lawrence Erlbaum Associates. (13)

McGaughy, J., Kaiser, T., & Sarter, M. (1996). Behavioral vigilance following infusions of 192 IgG-saporin into the basal forebrain: Selectivity of the behavioral impairment and relation to cortical AChE-positive fiber density. *Behavioral Neuroscience, 110,* 247-265. (13)

McGinnis, M. Y., Williams, G. W., & Lumia, A. R. (1996),. Inhibition of male sex behavior by androgen receptor blockade in preoptic area or hypothalamus, but not amygdala or septum. *Physiology & Behavior, 60,* 783-789. (11)

McGlynn, S. M. (1990). Behavioral approaches to neuropsychological rehabilitation. *Psychological Bulletin, 108,* 420-441. (15)

McGuffin, P., Farmer, A. E., Gottesman, I. I., Murray, R. M., & Reveley, A. M. (1984). Twin concordance for operationally defined schizophrenia. *Archives of General Psychiatry, 41,* 541-545. (16)

McHugh, P. R., & Moran, T. H. (1985). The stomach: A conception of its dynamic role in satiety. *Progress in Psychobiology and Physiological Psychology, 11,* 197-232. (10)

McKinnon, W., Weisse, C. S., Reynolds, C. P., Bowles, C. A., & Baum, A. (1989). Chronic stress, leukocyte-subpopulations, and humoral response to latent viruses. *Health Psychology, 8,* 389-402. (12)

McLean, S., Skirboll, L. R., & Pert, C. B. (1985). Comparison of substance P and enkephalin distribution in rat brain: An overview using radioimmunocytochemistry. *Neuroscience, 14,* 837-852. (7)

McManus, I. C., & Bryden, M. P. (1991). Geschwind's theory of cerebral lateralization: Developing a formal, causal model. *Psychological Bulletin, 110,* 237-253. (14)

McMasters, R. E. (1962). Regeneration of the spinal cord in the rat: Effects of Piromen and ACTH upon the regenerative capacity. *Journal of Comparative Neurology, 119,* 113-121. (15)

McMinn, M. R. (1984). Mechanisms of energy balance in obesity. *Behavioral Neuroscience, 98,* 375-393. (10)

McWilliams, J. R., & Lynch, G. (1983). Rate of synaptic replacement in denervated rat hippocampus declines precipitously from the juvenile period to adulthood. *Science, 221,* 572-574. (15)

McWilliams, J. R., & Lynch, G. (1984). Synaptic density and axonal sprouting in rat hippocampus: Stability in adulthood and decline in late adulthood. *Brain Research, 294,* 152-156. (15)

Meberg, P. J., Barnes, C. A., McNaughton, B. L., & Routtenberg, A. (1993). Protein kinase C and F1/GAP-43 gene expression in hippocampus inversely related to synaptic enhancement lasting 3 days. *Proceedings of the National Academy of Sciences, USA, 90,* 12050-12054. (13)

Meddis, R., Pearson, A. J. D., & Langford, G. (1973). An extreme case of healthy insomnia. *EEG and Clinical Neurophysiology, 35,* 213-214. (9)

Mednick, S. A., Machon, R. A., & Huttunen, M. O. (1990). An up-date on the Helsinki influenza project. *Archives of General Psychiatry, 47,* 292. (16)

Mehiel, R. (1991). Hedonic-shift conditioning with calories. In R. C. Bolles (Ed.), *The hedonics of taste* (pp. 107-126). Hillsdale, NJ: Lawrence Erlbaum. (10)

Meiran, N., & Jelicic, M. (1995). Implicit memory in Alzheimer's disease: A meta-analysis. *Neuropsychology, 9,* 291-303. (13)

Meisel, R. L., Dohanich, G. P., & Ward, I. L. (1979). Effects of prenatal stress on avoidance acquisition, open-field performance and lordotic behavior in male rats. *Physiology & Behavior, 22,* 527-530. (11)

Meister, M., Wong, R. O. L., Baylor, D. A., & Shatz, C. J. (1991). Synchronous bursts of action potentials in ganglion cells of the developing mammalian retina. *Science, 252,* 939-943. (5)

Melzack, R., & Wall, P. D. (1965). Pain mechanisms: A new theory. *Science, 150,* 971-979. (7)

Menco, B. (1992). Ultrastructural studies on membrane, cytoskeletal, mucous, and protective compartments in olfaction. *Microscopy Research and Technique, 22,* 215-224. (7)

Mendell, L. M. (1995). Neurotrophic factors and the specification of neural function. *The Neuroscientist, 1,* 26-34. (5)

Merton, P. A. (1972). How we control the contraction of our muscles. *Scientific American, 226* (5), 30-37. (8)

Merzenich, M. M., Nelson, R. J., Stryker, M. P., Cynader, M. S., Schoppman, A., & Zook, J. M. (1984). Somatosensory cortical map changes following digit amputation in adult monkeys. *Journal of Comparative Neurology, 224,* 591-605. (15)

Mesches, K. C., & McGaugh, J. L. (1995). Differential effects of pretraining inactivation of the right or left amygdala on retention of inhibitory avoidance training. *Behavioral Neuroscience, 109,* 642-647. (12)

Mesulam, M.-M. (1995). Cholinergic pathways and the ascending reticular activating system of the human brain. *Annals of the New York Academy of Sciences, 757,* 169-179. (4, 9)

Mezzanotte, W. S., Tangel, D. J., & White, D. P. (1992). Waking genioglossal electromyogram in sleep apnea patients versus normal controls (a neuromuscular compensatory mechanism). *Journal of Clinical Investigation, 89,* 1571-1579. (9)

Migeon, B. R., Dunn, M. A., Thomas, G., Schmeckpeper, B. J., & Naidu, S. (1995). Studies of X inactivation and isodisomy in twins provide further evidence that the X chromosome is not involved in Rett syndrome. *American Journal of Human Genetics, 56,* 647-653. (5)

Miles, F. A., & Evarts, E. V. (1979). Concepts of motor organization. *Annual Review of Psychology, 30,* 327-362. (8)

Miller, E. A., Goldman, P. S., & Rosvold, H. E. (1973). Delayed recovery of function following orbital prefrontal lesions in infant monkeys. *Science, 182,* 304-306. (15)

Miller, N. E. (1985). The value of behavioral research on animals. *American Psychologist, 40,* 423-440. (1)

Miller, W. C., & DeLong, M. R. (1988). Parkinsonian symptomatology: An anatomical and physiological analysis. *Annals of the New York Academy of Sciences, 515,* 287-302. (8)

Millhorn, D. E., Bayliss, D. A., Erickson, J. T., Gallman, E. A., Szymeczek, C. L., Czyzyk-Krzeska, M., & Dean, J. B. (1989). Cellular and molecular mechanisms of chemical synaptic transmission. *American Journal of Physiology, 257* (6 Part 1), L289-L310. (3)

Milner, B. (1959). The memory defect in bilateral hippocampal lesions. *Psychiatric Research Reports, 11,* 43-58. (13)

Milner, B., Corkin, S., & Teuber, H-L. (1968). Further analysis of the hippocampal amnesic syndrome: 14-year follow-up study of H. M. *Neuropsychologia, 6,* 215-234. (13)

Mirenowicz, J., & Schultz, W. (1996). Preferential activation of midbrain dopamine neurons by appetitive rather than aversive stimuli. *Nature, 379,* 449-451. (3)

Moeller, F. G., Dougherty, D. M., Swann, A. C., Collins, D., Davis, C. M., & Cherek, D. R. (1996). Tryptophan depletion and aggressive responding in healthy males. *Psychopharmacology, 126,* 97-103. (12)

Mogil, J. S., Sternberg, W. F., & Liebeskind, J. C. (1993). Studies of pain, stress and immunity. In C. R. Chapman & K. M. Foley (Eds.), *Current & emerging issues in cancer pain: Research & practice* (pp. 31-47). New York: Raven Press. (7, 12)

Money, J. (1967). Sexual problems of the chronically ill. In C. W. Wahl (Ed.), *Sexual problems: Diagnosis and treatment in medical practice* (pp. 266-287). New York: Free Press. (8)

Money, J. (1970). Matched pairs of hermaphrodites: Behavioral biology of sexual differentiation from chromosomes to gender identity. *Engineering and Science (Cal Tech), 33,* 34-39. (11)

Money, J., & Ehrhardt, A. A. (1968). Prenatal hormonal exposure: Possible effects on behaviour in man. In R. P. Michael (Ed.), *Endocrinology and human behaviour* (pp. 32-48). London: Oxford University Press. (11)

Money, J., & Ehrhardt, A. A. (1972). *Man & woman, boy & girl.* Baltimore, MD: Johns Hopkins University Press. (11)

Money, J., & Lewis, V. (1966). IQ, genetics and accelerated growth: Adrenogenital syndrome. *Bulletin of the Johns Hopkins Hospital, 118,* 365-373. (11)

Money, J., & Schwartz, M. (1978). Biosocial determinants of gender identity differentiation and development. In J. B. Hutchison (Ed.), *Biological determinants of sexual behaviour* (pp. 765-784). Chichester, England: John Wiley. (11)

Monti-Bloch, L., & Grosser, B. I. (1991). Effect of putative pheromones on the electrical activity of the human vomeronasal organ and olfactory epithelium. *Journal of Steroid Biochemistry and Molecular Biology, 39,* 573-582. (7)

Monti-Bloch, L., Jennings-White, C., Dolberg, D. S., & Berliner, D. L. (1994). The human vomeronasal system. *Psychoneuroendocrinology, 19,* 673-686. (7)

Moorcroft, W. H. (1993). *Sleep, dreaming, & sleep disorders* (2nd ed.). Lanham, MD: University Press of America. (9)

Moore, T., Rodman, H. R., Repp, A. B., & Gross, C. G. (1995). Localization of visual stimuli after striate cortex damage in monkeys: Parallels with human blindsight. *Proceedings of the National Academy of Sciences USA, 92,* 8215-8218. (6)

Moore-Ede, M. C., Czeisler, C. A., & Richardson, G. S. (1983). Circadian timekeeping in health and disease. *New England Journal of Medicine, 309,* 469-476. (9)

Morgan, C. A. III, Grillon, C., Southwick, S. M., Davis, M., & Charney, D. S. (1995). Fear-potentiated startle in posttraumatic stress disorder. *Biological Psychology, 38,* 378-385. (12)

Morgan, C. A. III, Grillon, C., Southwick, S. M., Davis, M., & Charney, D. S. (1996). Exaggerated acoustic startle reflex in Gulf War veterans with posttraumatic stress disorder. *American Journal of Psychiatry, 153,* 64-68. (12)

Mori, K., Mataga, N., & Imamura, K. (1992). Differential specificities of single mitral cells in rabbit olfactory bulb for a homologous series of fatty acid odor molecules. *Journal of Neurophysiology, 67,* 786-789. (7)

Morley, J. E. (1995). The role of peptides in appetite regulation across species. *American Zoologist, 35,* 437-445. (10)

Morley, J. E., Bartness, T. J., Gosnell, B. A., & Levine, A. S. (1985). Peptidergic regulation of feeding. *International Review of Neurobiology, 27,* 207-298. (10)

Morley, J. E., Levine, A. S., Grace, M., & Kneip, J. (1985). Peptide YY (PYY), a potent orexigenic agent. *Brain Research, 341,* 200-203. (10)

Morris, J. F., & Pow, D. V. (1993). New anatomical insights into the inputs and outputs from hypothalamic magnocellular neurons. *Annals of the New York Academy of Sciences, 689,* 16-33. (11)

Morris, J. S., Frith, C. D., Perrett, D. I., Rowland, D., Young, A. W., Calder, A. J., & Dolan, R. J. (1996). A differential neural response in the human amygdala to fearful and happy expressions. *Nature, 383,* 812-815. (12)

Morris, M., Lack, L., & Dawson, D. (1990). Sleep-onset insomniacs have delayed temperature rhythms. *Sleep, 13,* 1-14. (9)

Morrison, A. R., Sanford, L. D., Ball, W. A., Mann, G. L., & Ross, R. J. (1995). Stimulus-elicited behavior in rapid eye movement sleep without atonia. *Behavioral Neuroscience, 109,* 972-979. (9)

Morrow, L., Ratcliff, G., & Johnston, C. S. (1986). Externalising spatial knowledge in patients with right hemispheric lesions. *Cognitive Neuropsychology, 2,* 265-273. (14)

Moruzzi, G., & Magoun, H. W. (1949). Brain stem reticular formation and activation of the EEG. *Electroencephalography and Clinical Neurophysiology, 1,* 455-473. (9)

Moscovitch, M. (1985). Memory from infancy to old age: Implications for theories of normal and pathological memory. *Annals of the New York Academy of Sciences, 444,* 78-96. (13)

Moscovitch, M. (1989). Confabulation and the frontal systems: Strategic versus associative retrieval in neuropsychological theories of memory. In H. L. Roediger III, & F. I. M. Craik (Eds.), *Varieties of memory and consciousness: Essays in honour of Endel Tulving* (pp. 133-160). Hillsdale, NJ: Lawrence Erlbaum. (13)

Moscovitch, M. (1992). Memory and working-with-memory: A component process model based on modules and central systems. *Journal of Cognitive Neuroscience, 4,* 257-267. (13)

Moscovitch, M., & Winocur, G. (1995). Frontal lobes, memory, and aging. *Annals of the New York Academy of Sciences, 769,* 119-150. (13)

Moss, C. F., & Simmons, A. M. (1986). Frequency selectivity of hearing in the green treefrog, *Hyla cinerea. Journal of Comparative Physiology, A, 159,* 257-266. (7)

Moyer, K. E. (1974). Sex differences in aggression. In R. C. Friedman, R. M. Richart, & R. L. VandeWiele (Eds.), *Sex differences in behavior* (pp. 335-372). New York: Wiley. (12)

Mrosovsky, N. (1990). *Rheostasis: The physiology of change*. New York: Oxford University Press. (10)

Munk, M. H. J., Roelfsema, P. R., König, P., Engel, A. K., & Singer, W. (1996). Role of reticular activation in the modulation of intracortical synchronization. *Science, 272,* 271-274. (9)

Murphy, M. G., & O'Leary, J. L. (1973). Hanging and climbing functions in raccoon and sloth after total cerebellectomy. *Archives of Neurology, 28,* 111-117. (8)

Murphy, M. R., Checkley, S. A., Seckl, J. R., & Lightman, S. L. (1990). Naloxone inhibits oxytocin release at orgasm in man. *Journal of Clinical Endocrinology and Metabolism, 71,* 1056-1058. (11)

Murray, A. M., Hyde, T. M., Knable, M. B., Herman, M. M., Bigelow, L. B., Carter, J. M., Weinberger, D. R., & Kleinman, J. E. (1995). Distribution of putative D4 dopamine receptors in postmortem striatum from patients with schizophrenia. *Journal of Neuroscience, 15,* 2186-2191. (16)

Murrell, J., Farlow, M., Ghetti, B., & Benson, M. D. (1991). A mutation in the amyloid precursor protein associated with hereditary Alzheimer's disease. *Science, 254,* 97-99. (13)

Myers, J. J., & Sperry, R. W. (1985). Interhemispheric communication after section of the forebrain commissures. *Cortex, 21,* 249-260. (14)

Myseros, J. S., & Bullock, R. (1995). The rationale for glutamate antagonists in the treatment of traumatic brain injury. *Annals of the New York Academy of Sciences, 765,* 262-271. (15)

Nadel, L. (1992). Multiple memory systems: What and why. *Journal of Cognitive Neuroscience, 4,* 179-188. (13)

Nader, K., Bechara, A., Roberts, D. C. S., & van der Kooy, D. (1994). Neuroleptics block high- but not low-dose heroin place preferences: Further evidence for a two-system model of motivation. *Behavioral Neuroscience, 108,* 1128-1138. (3)

Nagahara, A. H., Otto, T., & Gallagher, M. (1995). Entorhinal-perirhinal lesions impair performance of rats on two versions of place learning in the Morris water maze. *Behavioral Neuroscience, 109,* 3-9. (13)

Naggert, J. K., Fricker, L. D., Varlamov, O., Nishina, P. M., Rouille, Y., Steiner, D. F., Carroll, R. J., Paigen, B. J., & Leiter, E. H. (1995). Hyperproinsulinaemia in obese *fat/fat* mice associated with a carboxypeptidase E mutation which reduces enzyme activity. *Nature Genetics, 10,* 135-142. (10)

Nakamura, K., & Kubota, K. (1995). Mnemonic firing of neurons in the monkey temporal pole during a visual recognition memory task. *Journal of Neurophysiology, 74,* 162-178. (13)

Nakanishi, S. (1992). Molecular diversity of glutamate receptors and implications for brain function. *Science, 258,* 597-603. (13)

Nakashima, Y., Kuwamura, T., & Yogo, Y. (1995). Why be a both-ways sex changer? *Ethology, 101,* 301-307. (11)

Nathans, J., Davenport, C. M., Maumenee, I. H., Lewis, R. A., Hejtmancik, J. F., Litt, M., Lovrien, E., Weleber, R., Bachynski, B., Zwas, F., Klingaman, R., & Fishman, G. (1989). Molecular genetics of human blue cone monochromacy. *Science, 245,* 831-838. (6)

Nathans, J., Piantanida, T. P., Eddy, R. L., Shows, T. B., & Hogness, D. S. (1986). Molecular genetics of inherited variations in human color vision. *Science, 232,* 203-210. (6)

Nebes, R. D. (1974). Hemispheric specialization in commissurotomized man. *Psychological Bulletin, 81,* 1-14. (14)

Neitz, J., & Jacobs, G. H. (1986). Reexamination of spectral mechanisms in the rat (*Rattus norvegicus*). *Journal of Comparative Psychology, 100,* 21-29. (6)

Nelson, D. O., & Prosser, C. L. (1981). Intracellular recordings from thermosensitive preoptic neurons. *Science, 213,* 787-789. (10)

Nelson, R. J., Demas, G. E., Huang, P. L., Fishman, M. C., Dawson, V. L., Dawson, T. M., & Snyder, S. H. (1995). Behavioural abnormalities in male mice lacking neuronal nitric oxide synthase. *Nature, 378,* 383-386. (12)

Netter, F. H. (1983). *CIBA collection of medical illustrations: Vol. 1. Nervous system.* New York: CIBA. (11)

Nicholas, M. K., & Arnason, B. G. W. (1992). Immunologic responses in central nervous system transplantation. *Seminars in the Neurosciences, 4,* 273-283. (15)

Nicklas, W. J., Saporito, M., Basma, A., Geller, H. M., & Heikkila, R. E. (1992). Mitochondrial mechanisms of neurotoxicity. *Annals of the New York Academy of Sciences, 648,* 28-36. (8)

Nicoll, R. A., & Madison, D. V. (1982). General anesthetics hyperpolarize neurons in the vertebrate central nervous system. *Science, 217,* 1055-1057. (2)

Nicoll, R. A., & Malenka, R. C. (1995). Contrasting properties of two forms of long-term potentiation in the hippocampus. *Nature, 377,* 115-118. (13)

Nieuwenhuys, R., Voogd, J., & vanHuijzen, C. (1988). *The human central nervous system* (3rd rev. ed.). Berlin: Springer-Verlag. (4, 10)

Nishimura, F., Nishihara, M., Torii, K., & Takahashi, M. (1996). Changes in responsiveness to serotonin on rat ventromedial hypothalamic neurons after food deprivation. *Physiology & Behavior, 60,* 7-12. (10)

Nofzinger, E. A., Thase, M. E., Reynolds, C. F. III, Frank, E., Jennings, J. R., Garamoni, G. L., Fasiczka, A. L., & Kupfer, D. J. (1993). Sexual function in depressed men: Assessment by self-report, behavioral, and nocturnal penile tumescence measures before and after treatment with cognitive behavior therapy. *Archives of General Psychiatry, 50,* 24-30. (16)

North, R. A. (1989). Neurotransmitters and their receptors: From the clone to the clinic. *Seminars in the Neurosciences, 1,* 81-90. (3)

North, R. A. (1992). Cellular actions of opiates and cocaine. *Annals of the New York Academy of Sciences, 654,* 1-6. (3)

Nottebohm, F. (1985). Neuronal replacement in adulthood. *Annals of the New York Academy of Sciences, 457,* 143-161. (2)

Nudo, R. J., Milliken, G. W., Jenkins, W. M., & Merzenich, M. M. (1996). Use-dependent alterations of movement representations in primary motor cortex of adult squirrel monkeys. *Journal of Neuroscience, 16,* 785-807. (15)

Numan, M., & Numan, M. J. (1994). Expression of fos-like immunoreactivity in the preoptic area of maternally behaving virgin rats. *Behavioral Neuroscience, 108,* 379-394. (11)

Nutt, D. J. (1989). Altered central α_2-adrenoceptor sensitivity in panic disorder. *Archives of General Psychiatry, 46,* 165-169. (12)

O'Dowd, B. F., Lefkowitz, R. J., & Caron, M. G. (1989). Structure of the adrenergic and related receptors. *Annual Review of Neuroscience, 12,* 67-83. (3)

Ojemann, J. G., Ojemann, G. A., & Lettich, E. (1992). Neuronal activity related to faces and matching in human right nondominant temporal cortex. *Brain, 115,* 1-13. (6)

O'Keefe, J. (1993). Hippocampus, theta, and spatial memory. *Current Opinion in Neurobiology, 3,* 917-924. (13)

O'Keefe, J., & Burgess, N. (1996). Geometric determinants of the place fields of hippocampal neurons. *Nature, 381,* 425-434. (13)

Okubo, Y., Suhara, T., Suzuki, K., Kobayashi, K., Inoue, O., Terasaki, O., Someya, Y., Sassa, T., Sudo, Y., Matsushima, E., Iyo, M., Tateno, Y., & Toru, M. (1997). Decreased prefrontal dopamine D_1 receptors in schizophrenia revealed by PET. *Nature, 385,* 634-636. (16)

Olds, J. (1958). Satiation effects in self-stimulation of the brain. *Journal of Comparative and Physiological Psychology, 51,* 675-678. (3)

Olds, J. (1962). Hypothalamic substrates of reward. *Physiological Reviews, 42,* 554-604. (3)

Olds, J., & Milner, P. (1954). Positive reinforcement produced by electrical stimulation of the septal area and other regions of the rat brain. *Journal of Comparative and Physiological Psychology, 47,* 419-428. (3)

O'Leary, A. (1990). Stress, emotion, and human immune function. *Psychological Bulletin, 108,* 363-382. (12)

O'Leary, D. S., & Boll, T. J. (1984). Neuropsychological correlates of

early generalized brain dysfunction in children. In C. R. Almli & S. Finger (Eds.), *Early brain damage* (pp. 215-229). Orlando, FL: Academic Press. (15)

Olney, J. W., & Farger, N. B. (1995). Glutamate receptor dysfunction and schizophrenia. *Archives of General Psychiatry, 52,* 998-1007. (16)

Olson, D. J., Kamil, A. C., Balda, R. P., & Nims, P. J. (1995). Performance of four seed-caching corvid species in operant tests of nonspatial and spatial memory. *Journal of Comparative Psychology, 109,* 173-181. (13)

Olton, D. S., & Papas, B. C. (1979). Spatial memory and hippocampal function. *Neuropsychologia, 17,* 669-682. (13)

Olton, D. S., Walker, J. A., & Gage, F. H. (1978). Hippocampal connections and spatial discrimination. *Brain Research, 139,* 295-308. (13)

O'Neal, M. F., Means, L. W., Poole, M. C., & Hamm, R. J. (1996). Estrogen affects performance of ovariectomized rats in a two-choice water-escape working memory task. *Psychoneuroendocrinology, 21,* 51-65. (11)

Overman, W. H., Bachevalier, J., Schuhmann, E., & Ryan, P. (1996). Cognitive gender differences in very young children parallel biologically based cognitive gender differences in monkeys. *Behavioral Neuroscience, 110,* 673-684. (5)

Overman, W. H., Pate, B. J., Moore, K., & Peuster, A. (1996). Ontogeny of place learning in children as measured in the radial arm maze, Morris search task, and open field task. *Behavioral Neuroscience, 110,* 1205-1228. (13)

Paez, X., Stanley, B. G., & Leibowitz, S. F. (1993). Microdialysis analysis of norepinephrine levels in the paraventricular nucleus in association with food intake at dark onset. *Brain Research, 606,* 167-170. (10)

Page, G. G., Ben-Eliyahu, S., Yirmiya, R., & Liebeskind, J. C. (1993). Morphine attenuates surgery-induced enhancement of metastatic colonization in rats. *Pain, 54,* 21-28. (7)

Pande, A. C. (1985). Light-induced hypomania. *American Journal of Psychiatry, 142,* 1126. (16)

Pandey, G. N., Pandey, S. C., Dwivedi, Y., Sharma, R. P., Janicak, P. G., & Davis, J. M. (1995). Platelet serotonin-2A receptors: A potential biological marker for suicidal behavior. *American Journal of Psychiatry, 152,* 850-855. (12)

Papez, J. W. (1937). A proposed mechanism of emotion. *Archives of Neurology and Psychiatry, 38,* 725-743. (12)

Pappone, P. A., & Cahalan, M. D. (1987). *Pandinus imperator* scorpion venom blocks voltage-gated potassium channels in nerve fibers. *Journal of Neuroscience, 7,* 3300-3305. (2)

Park, S., Holzman, P. S., & Goldman-Rakic, P. S. (1995). Spatial working memory deficits in the relatives of schizophrenic patients. *Archives of General Psychiatry, 52,* 821-828. (16)

Parker, G. H. (1922). *Smell, taste, and allied senses in the vertebrates.* Philadelphia: Lippincott. (7)

Parsons, O. A. (1993). Impaired neuropsychological cognitive functioning in sober alcoholics. In W. A. Hunt & S. J. Nixon (Eds.), *Alcohol-induced brain damage* (NIAAA Research Monograph 22) (pp. 173-194). Rockville, MD: U.S. Department of Health and Human Services. (3)

Pascual-Leone, A., Wasserman, E. M., Sadato, N., & Hallett, M. (1995). The role of reading activity on the modulation of motor cortical outputs to the reading hand in braille readers. *Annals of Neurology, 38,* 910-915. (15)

Passingham, R. E. (1979). Brain size and intelligence in man. *Brain, behavior, and evolution, 16,* 253-270. (5)

Patrick, C. J., & Iacono, W. G. (1989). Psychopathy, threat, and polygraph test accuracy. *Journal of Applied Psychology, 74,* 347-355. (12)

Paulson, O. B., & Newman, E. A. (1987). Does the release of potassium from astrocyte endfeet regulate cerebral blood flow? *Science, 237,* 896-898. (4)

Paus, T., Marrett, S., Worsley, K. J., & Evans, A. C. (1995). Extraretinal modulation of cerebral blood flow in the human visual cortex: Implications for saccadic suppression. *Journal of Neurophysiology, 74,* 2179-2183. (6)

Peachey, J. E., & Naranjo, C. A. (1983). The use of disulfiram and other alcohol-sensitizing drugs in the treatment of alcoholism. *Research Advances in Alcohol and Drug Problems, 7,* 397-431. (3)

Pearcey, S. M., Docherty, K. J., & Dabbs, J. M. Jr. (1996). Testosterone and sex role identification in lesbian couples. *Physiology & Behavior, 60,* 1033-1035. (11)

Pearlson, G. D., Petty, R. G., Ross, C. A., & Tien, A. Y. (1996). Schizophrenia: A disease of heteromodal association cortex? *Neuropsychopharmacology, 14,* 1-17. (16)

Pedersen, C. A., Caldwell, J. D., Walker, C., Ayers, G., & Mason, G. A. (1994). Oxytocin activates the postpartum onset of rat maternal behavior in the ventral tegmentum and medial preoptic areas. *Behavioral Neuroscience, 108,* 1163-1171. (11)

Pedersen, C. A., Johns, J. M., Musiol, I., Perez-Delgado, M., Ayers, G., Faggin, B., & Caldwell, J. D. (1995). Interfering with somatosensory stimulation from pups sensitizes experienced, postpartum rat mothers to oxytocin antagonist inhibition of maternal behavior. *Behavioral Neuroscience, 109,* 980-990. (11)

Pellegrino, L. J., Pellegrino, A. S., & Cushman, A. J. (1979). *A stereotaxic atlas of the rat brain* (2nd ed.). New York: Plenum. (4)

Pellis, S. M., O'Brien, D. P., Pellis, V. C., Teitelbaum, P., Wolgin, D. L., & Kennedy, S. (1988). Escalation of feline predation along a gradient from avoidance through "play" to killing. *Behavioral Neuroscience, 102,* 760-777. (12)

Pellymounter, M. A., Cullen, M. J., Baker, M. B., Hecht, R., Winters, D., Boone, T., & Collins, F. (1995). Effects of the *obese* gene product on body weight regulation in *ob/ob* mice. *Science, 269,* 540-543. (10)

Penev, P. D., Zee, P. C., & Turek, F. W. (1997). Serotonin in the spotlight. *Nature, 385,* 123. (16)

Penfield, W. (1955). The permanent record of the stream of consciousness. *Acta Psychologica, 11,* 47-69. (13)

Penfield, W., & Milner, B. (1958). Memory deficit produced by bilateral lesions in the hippocampal zone. *Archives of Neurology and Psychiatry, 79,* 475-497. (13)

Penfield, W., & Perot, P. (1963). The brain's record of auditory and visual experience. *Brain, 86,* 595-696. (13)

Penfield, W., & Rasmussen, T. (1950). *The cerebral cortex of man.* New York: Macmillan. (4)

Pepperberg, I. M. (1981). Functional vocalizations by an African grey parrot. *Zeitschrift für Tierpsychologie, 55,* 139-160. (14)

Pepperberg, I. M. (1993). Cognition and communication in an African Grey parrot (*Psittacus erithacus*): Studies on a nonhuman, nonprimate, nonmammalian subject. In H. L. Roitblat, L. M. Herman, & P. E. Nachtigall (Eds.), *Language and communication: Comparative perspectives* (pp. 221-248). Hillsdale, NJ: Lawrence Erlbaum. (14)

Pepperberg, I. M. (1994). Numerical competence in an African gray parrot (*Psittacus erithacus*). *Journal of Comparative Psychology, 108,* 36-44. (14)

Perani, D., Vallar, G., Paulesu, E., Alberoni, M., & Fazio, F. (1993). Left and right hemisphere contributions to recovery form neglect after right hemisphere damage— An [18F]FDG PET study of two cases. *Neuropsychologia, 31,* 115-125. (15)

Percy, A. K. (1995). Rett syndrome. *Current Opinion in Neurology, 8,* 156-160. (5)

Pericak-Vance, M. A., Bebout, J. L., Gaskell, P. C. Jr., Yamaoka, L. H., Hung, W.-Y., Alberts, M. J., Walker, A. P., Bartlett, R. J., Haynes, C. A., Welsh, K. A., Earl, N. L., Heyman, A., Clark, C. M., & Roses, A. D. (1991). Linkage studies in familial Alzheimer disease: Evidence for chromosome 19 linkage. *American Journal of Human Genetics, 48,* 1034-1050. (13)

Perez, E. A. (1995). Review of the preclinical pharmacology and comparative efficacy of 5-hydroxytryptamine-3 receptor antago-

nists for chemotherapy-induced emesis. *Journal of Clinical Oncology, 13,* 1036-1043. (3)

Perlow, M. J., Freed, W. J., Hoffer, B. J., Seiger, A., Olson, L., & Wyatt, R. J. (1979). Brain grafts reduce motor abnormalities produced by destruction of nigrostriatal dopamine system. *Science, 204,* 643-647. (15)

Persichetti, F., Srinidhi, J., Kanaley, L., Ge, P., Myers, R. H., D'Arrigo, K., Barnes, G. T., McDonald, M. E., Vonsattel, J.-P., Gusella, J. F., & Bird, E. D. (1994). Huntington's disease CAG trinucleotide repeats in pathologically confirmed postmortem brains. *Neurobiology of Disease, 1,* 159-166. (8)

Persons, J. B., Thase, M. E., & Crits-Christoph, P. (1996). The role of psychotherapy in the treatment of depression. *Archives of General Psychiatry, 53,* 283-290. (16)

Pert, C. B., & Snyder, S. H. (1973). The opiate receptor: Demonstration in nervous tissue. *Science, 179,* 1011-1014. (3, 7)

Pesold, C., & Treit, D. (1995). The central and basolateral amygdala differentially mediate the anxiolytic effect of benzodiazepines. *Brain Research, 671,* 213-221. (12)

Petersen, S. E., Fox, P. T., Posner, M. I., Mintun, M., & Raichle, M. E. (1988). Positron emission tomographic studies of the cortical anatomy of single-word processing. *Nature, 331,* 585-589. (14)

Pfaus, J. G., Damsma, G., Wenkstern, D., & Fibiger, H. C. (1995). Sexual activity increases dopamine transmission in the nucleus accumbens and striatum of female rats. *Brain Research, 693,* 21-30. (11)

Pflug, B. (1973). Therapeutic aspects of sleep deprivation. In W. P. Koella & P. Levin (Eds.), *Sleep: Physiology, biochemistry, psychology, pharmacology, clinical implications* (pp. 185-191). Basel: Karger. (16)

Phelps, M. E., & Mazziotta, J. C. (1985). Positron emission tomography: Human brain function and biochemistry. *Science, 228,* 799-809. (4)

Phillips, R. G., & LeDoux, J. E. (1992). Differential contribution of amygdala and hippocampus to cued and contextual fear conditioning.

Behavioral Neuroscience, 106, 274-285. (12)

Pillon, B., Ertle, S., Deweer, B., Sarazin, M., Agid, Y., & Dubois, B. (1996). Memory for spatial location is affected in Parkinson's disease. *Neuropsychologia, 34,* 77-85. (8)

Pincus, J. H., & Tucker, G. J. (1985). *Behavioral neurology* (3rd ed.). New York: Oxford University Press. (7)

Pinel, J. P. J., Treit, D., & Rovner, L. I. (1977). Temporal lobe aggression in rats. *Science, 197,* 1088-1089. (12)

Pinker, S. (1996). Facts about human language relevant to its evolution. In J.-P. Changeux & J. Chavaillon (Eds.), *Origins of the human brain* (pp. 262-283). Oxford, England: Clarendon Press. (14)

Pi-Sunyer, X., Kissileff, H. R., Thornton, J., & Smith, G. P. (1982). C-terminal octapeptide of cholecystokinin decreases food intake in obese men. *Physiology & Behavior, 29,* 627-630. (10)

Plaut, D. C. (1995). Double dissociation without modularity: Evidence from connectionist neuropsychology. *Journal of Clinical and Experimental Neuropsychology, 17,* 291-321. (4)

Plomin, R., Corley, R., DeFries, J. C., & Fulker, D. (1990). Individual differences in television viewing in early childhood: Nature as well as nurture. *Psychological Science, 1,* 371-377. (1)

Plomin, R., Owen, M. J., & McGuffin, P. (1994). The genetic basis of complex human behaviors. *Science, 264,* 1733-1739. (1)

Poling, A., Schlinger, H., & Blakely, E. (1988). Failure of the partial inverse benzodiazepine agonist Ro15-4513 to block the lethal effects of ethanol in rats. *Pharmacology Biochemistry & Behavior, 31,* 945-947. (12)

Pollatsek, A., Bolozky, S., Well, A. D., & Rayner, K. (1981). Asymmetries in the perceptual span for Israeli readers. *Brain and Language, 14,* 174-180. (14)

Poltorak, M., Wright, R., Hemperly, J. J., Torrey, E. F., Issa, F., Wyatt, R. J., & Freed, W. J. (1997). Monozygotic twins discordant for schizophrenia are discordant for N-CAM and L1 in CSF. *Brain Research, 751,* 152-154. (16)

Pomeranz, B. H. (1989). Transcutaneous electrical nerve stimulation (TENS). In G. Adelman (Ed.), *Neuroscience year* (pp. 161-164). Boston: Birkhäuser. (7)

Pons, T. P., Garraghty, P. E., Ommaya, A. K., Kaas, J. H., Taub, E., & Mishkin, M. (1991). Massive cortical reorganization after sensory deafferentation in adult macaques. *Science, 252,* 1857-1860. (15)

Pontieri, F. E., Tanda, G., Orzi, F., & DiChiara, G. (1996). Effects of nicotine on the nucleus accumbens and similarity to those of addictive drugs. *Nature, 382,* 255-257. (2)

Pope, H. G., & Katz, D. L. (1994). Psychiatric and medical effects of anabolic-androgenic steroid use. *Archives of General Psychiatry, 51,* 375-382. (11)

Posner, M. I., Petersen, S. E., Fox, P. T., & Raichle, M. E. (1988). Localization of cognitive operations in the human brain. *Science, 240,* 1627-1631. (14)

Posner, S. F., Baker, L., Heath, A., & Martin, N. G. (1996). Social contact, social attitudes, and twin similarity. *Behavior Genetics, 26,* 123-133. (1)

Potegal, M. (1994). Aggressive arousal: The amygdala connection. In M. Potegal & J. F. Knutson (Eds.), *The dynamics of aggression* (pp. 73-111). Hillsdale, NJ: Lawrence Erlbaum. (12)

Potegal, M., Ferris, C., Hebert, M., Meyerhoff, J. M., & Skaredoff, L. (1996). Attack priming in female Syrian golden hamsters is associated with a *c-fos* coupled process within the corticomedial amygdala. *Neuroscience, 75,* 869-880. (12)

Potegal, M., Hebert, M., DeCoster, M., & Meyerhoff, J. L. (1996). Brief, high-frequency stimulation of the corticomedial amygdala induces a delayed and prolonged increase of aggressiveness in male Syrian golden hamsters. *Behavioral Neuroscience, 110,* 401-412. (12)

Pothos, E., Rada, P., Mark, G. P., & Hoebel, B. G. (1991). Dopamine microdialysis in the nucleus accumbens during acute and chronic morphine, naloxone-precipitated withdrawal and clonidine treatment. *Brain Research, 566,* 348-350. (3)

Preilowski, B. (1975). Bilateral motor interaction: Perceptual-motor performance of partial and complete split-brain patients. In K. J. Zülch, O. Creutzfeldt, & G. C. Galbraith (Eds.), *Cerebral localization* (pp. 115-132). New York: Springer Verlag. (14)

Premack, A. J. (1976). *Why chimps can read.* New York: Harper & Row. (14)

Premack, A. J., & Premack, D. (1972). Teaching language to an ape. *Scientific American, 227* (4), 92-99. (14)

Preti, G., Cutler, W. B., Garcia, C. R., Huggins, G. R., & Lawley, H. J. (1986). Human axillary secretions influence women's menstrual cycles: The role of donor extract of females. *Hormones and Behavior, 20,* 474-482. (7)

Pritchard, T. C., Hamilton, R. B., Morse, J. R., & Norgren, R. (1986). Projections of thalamic gustatory and lingual areas in the monkey, *Macaca fascicularis. Journal of Comparative Neurology, 244,* 213-228. (7)

Provine, R. R. (1979). "Wing-flapping" develops in wingless chicks. *Behavioral and Neural Biology, 27,* 233-237. (8)

Provine, R. R. (1981). Wing-flapping develops in chickens made flightless by feather mutations. *Developmental Psychobiology, 14,* 481-486. (8)

Provine, R. R. (1984). Wing-flapping during development and evolution. *American Scientist, 72,* 448-455. (8)

Provine, R. R. (1986). Yawning as a stereotyped action pattern and releasing stimulus. *Ethology, 72,* 109-122. (Intro, 8)

Provine, R. R. (1996). Laughter. *American Scientist, 84,* 38-45. (Intro)

Provine, R. R., & Westerman, J. A. (1979). Crossing the midline: Limits of early eye-hand behavior. *Child Development, 50,* 437-441. (14)

Puce, A., Allison, T., Gore, J. C., & McCarthy, G. (1995). Face-sensitive regions in human extrastriate cortex studied by functional MRI.

Journal of Neurophysiology, 74, 1192-1199. (6)

Purves, D., & Hadley, R. D. (1985). Changes in the dendritic branching of adult mammalian neurones revealed by repeated imaging *in situ. Nature, 315,* 404-406. (2)

Purves, D., & Lichtman, J. W. (1980). Elimination of synapses in the developing nervous system. *Science, 210,* 153-157. (5)

Quadagno, D. M., Briscoe, R., & Quadagno, J. S. (1977). Effect of perinatal gonadal hormones on selected nonsexual behavior patterns: A critical assessment of the non-human and human literature. *Psychological Bulletin, 84,* 62-80. (11)

Rabey, J. M. (1995). Second generation of dopamine agonists: Pros and cons. *Journal of Neural Transmission, Suppl. 45,* 213-224. (8)

Rada, P., Pothos, E., Mark, G. P., & Hoebel, B. G. (1991). Microdialysis evidence that acetylcholine in the nucleus accumbens is involved in morphine withdrawal and in its treatment with clonidine. *Brain Research, 561,* 354-356. (3)

Rafal, R., Smith, J., Krantz, J., Cohen, A., & Brennan, C. (1990). Extrageniculate vision in hemianopic humans: Saccade inhibition by signals in the blind field. *Science, 250,* 118-121. (6)

Ragozzino, M. E., Unick, K. E., & Gold, P. E. (1996). Hippocampal acetylcholine release during memory testing in rats: Augmentation by glucose. *Proceedings of the National Academy of Sciences, USA, 93,* 4693-4698. (13)

Ragsdale, D. S., McPhee, J. C., Scheuer, T., & Catterall, W. A. (1994). Molecular determinants of state-dependent block of Na$^+$ channels by local anesthetics. *Science, 265,* 1724-1728. (2)

Rainnie, D. G., Grunze, H. C. R., McCarley, R. W., & Greene, R. W. (1994). Adenosine inhibition of mesopontine cholinergic neurons: Implications for EEG arousal. *Science, 263,* 689-692. (9)

Raisman, G. (1991). Glia, neurons, and plasticity. *Annals of the New York Academy of Sciences, 633,* 209-213. (2)

Rakic, P. (1985). DNA synthesis and cell division in the adult primate brain. *Annals of the New York Academy of Sciences, 457,* 193-211. (2)

Rakic, P., & Lidow, M. S. (1995). Distribution and density of monoamine receptors in the primate visual cortex devoid of retinal input from early embryonic stages. *Journal of Neuroscience, 15,* 2561-2574. (6)

Ralph, M. R., Foster, R. G., Davis, F. C., & Menaker, M. (1990). Transplanted suprachiasmatic nucleus determines circadian period. *Science, 247,* 975-978. (9)

Ralph, M. R., & Menaker, M. (1988). A mutation of the circadian system in golden hamsters. *Science, 241,* 1225-1227. (9)

Ramachandran, V. S. (1992). Filling in gaps in perception: Part 1. *Current Directions in Psychological Science, 1,* 199-205. (6)

Ramachandran, V. S., Rogers-Ramachandran, D., & Cobb, S. (1995). Touching the phantom limb. *Nature, 377,* 489-490. (7)

Raming, K., Krieger, J., Strotman, J., Boekhoff, I., Kubick, S., Baumstark, C., & Breer, H. (1993). Cloning and expression of odorant molecules. *Nature, 361,* 353-356. (7)

Ramirez, J. J., Fass, B., Karpiak, S. E., & Steward, O. (1987a). Ganglioside treatments reduce locomotor hyperactivity after bilateral lesions of the entorhinal cortex. *Neuroscience Letters, 75,* 283-287. (15)

Ramirez, J. J., Fass, B., Kilfoil, T., Henschel, B., Grones, W., & Karpiak, S. E. (1987b). Ganglioside-induced enhancement of behavioral recovery after bilateral lesions of the entorhinal cortex. *Brain Research, 414,* 85-90. (15)

Ramirez, J. J., McQuilkin, M., Carrigan, T., MacDonald, K., & Kelley, M. S. (1996). Progressive entorhinal cortex lesions accelerate hippocampal sprouting and spare spatial memory in rats. *Proceedings of the National Academy of Sciences, USA, 93,* 15512-15517. (15)

Ramirez, V. D., Zheng, J., & Siddique, K. M. (1996). Membrane receptors for estrogen, progesterone, and testosterone in the rat brain: Fantasy or reality. *Cellular and Molecular Neurobiology, 16,* 175-198. (11)

Ramsay, D. J., & Thrasher, T. N. (1990). Thirst and water balance. In E. M. Stricker (Ed.), *Handbook of behavioral neurobiology, Vol. 10: Neurobiology of food and fluid intake* (pp. 353-386). New York: Plenum Press. (10)

Randolph, C., Tierney, M. C., & Chase, T. N. (1995). Implicit memory in Alzheimer's disease. *Journal of Clinical and Experimental Neuropsychology, 17,* 343-351. (13)

Ranson, S. W., & Clark, S. L. (1959). *The anatomy of the nervous system: Its development and function* (10th ed.). Philadelphia: W. B. Saunders Co. (4)

Rapoport, S. I., & Robinson, P. J. (1986). Tight-junctional modification as the basis of osmotic opening of the blood-brain barrier. *Annals of the New York Academy of Sciences, 481,* 250-267. (2)

Rausch, G., & Scheich, H. (1982). Dendritic spine loss and enlargement during maturation of the speech control system in the mynah bird (*Gracula religiosa*). *Neuroscience Letters, 29,* 129-133. (5)

Rauschecker, J. P. (1995). Developmental plasticity and memory. *Behavioural Brain Research, 66,* 7-12. (5)

Rauschecker, J. P., Tian, B., & Hauser, M. (1995). Processing of complex sounds in the macaque nonprimary auditory cortex. *Science, 268,* 111-114. (7)

Raymond, J. L., Lisberger, S. G., & Mauk, M. D. (1996). The cerebellum: A neuronal learning machine? *Science, 272,* 1126-1131. (8)

Recht, L. D., Lew, R. A., & Schwartz, W. J. (1995). Baseball teams beaten by jet lag. *Nature, 377,* 583. (9)

Rechtschaffen, A., & Bergmann, B. M. (1995). Sleep deprivation in the rat by the disk-over-water method. *Behavioural Brain Research, 69,* 55-63. (9)

Reeves, A. G., & Plum, F. (1969). Hyperphagia, rage, and dementia accompanying a ventromedial hypothalamic neoplasm. *Archives of Neurology, 20,* 616-624. (10)

Refinetti, R., & Carlisle, H. J. (1986a). Complementary nature of heat production and heat intake during behavioral thermoregulation in the rat. *Behavioral and Neural Biology, 46,* 64-70. (10)

Refinetti, R., & Carlisle, H. J. (1986b). Effects of anterior and posterior hypothalamic temperature changes on thermoregulation in the rat. *Physiology & Behavior, 36,* 1099-1103. (10)

Refinetti, R., & Menaker, M. (1992). The circadian rhythm of body temperature. *Physiology & Behavior, 51,* 613-637. (9)

Regan, T. (1986). The rights of humans and other animals. *Acta Physiologica Scandinavica, 128* (Suppl. 554), 33-40. (1)

Reichling, D. B., Kwiat, G. C., & Basbaum, A. I. (1988). Anatomy, physiology, and pharmacology of the periaqueductal gray contribution to antinociceptive controls. In H. L. Fields & J.-M. Besson (Eds.), *Progress in brain research* (Vol. 77, pp. 31-46). Amsterdam: Elsevier. (7)

Reinisch, J. M. (1981). Prenatal exposure to synthetic progestins increases potential for aggression in humans. *Science, 211,* 1171-1173. (11)

Reisenzein, R. (1983). The Schachter theory of emotion: Two decades later. *Psychological Bulletin, 94,* 239-264. (12)

Ren, K., Thomas, D. A., & Dubner, R. (1995). Nerve growth factor alleviates a painful peripheral neuropathy in rats. *Brain Research, 699,* 286-292. (5)

Ressler, K. J., Sullivan, S. L., & Buck, L. B. (1994). A molecular dissection of spatial patterning in the olfactory system. *Current Opinion in Neurobiology, 4,* 588-596. (7)

Reynolds, C. A., Baker, L. A., & Pedersen, N. L. (1996). Models of spouse similarity: Applications to fluid ability measured in twins and their spouses. *Behavior Genetics, 26,* 73-88. (1)

Richter, C. P. (1922). A behavioristic study of the activity of the rat. *Comparative Psychology Monographs, 1,* 1-55. (9)

Richter, C. P. (1936). Increased salt appetite in adrenalectomized rats. *American Journal of Physiology, 115,* 155-161. (10)

Richter, C. P. (1938). Two-day cycles of alternating good and bad behavior in psychotic patients. *Archives of Neurology and Psychiatry, 39,* 587-598. (16)

Richter, C. P. (1950). Taste and solubility of toxic compounds in poisoning of rats and humans. *Journal of Comparative and Physiological Psychology, 43,* 358-374. (7, 10)

Richter, C. P. (1957a). On the phenomenon of sudden death in animals and man. *Psychosomatic Medicine, 19,* 191-198. (12)

Richter, C. P. (1957b). Behavior and metabolic cycles in animals and man. In P. H. Hoch & J. Zubin (Eds.), *Experimental psychopathology* (pp. 34-54). New York: Grune & Stratton. (16)

Richter, C. P. (1957c). Hormones and rhythms in man and animals. In G. Pincus (Ed.), *Recent progress in hormone research* (Vol. 13, pp. 105-159). New York: Academic Press. (16)

Richter, C. P. (1967). Psychopathology of periodic behavior in animals and man. In J. Zubin & H. F. Hunt (Eds.), *Comparative psychopathology* (pp. 205-227). New York: Grune & Stratton. (9)

Richter, C. P. (1975). Deep hypothermia and its effect on the 24-hour clock of rats and hamsters. *Johns Hopkins Medical Journal, 136,* 1-10. (9)

Richter, C. P., & Langworthy, O. R. (1933). The quill mechanism of the porcupine. *Journal für Psychologie und Neurologie, 45,* 143-153. (4)

Riddle, D. R., Lo, D. C., & Katz, L. C. (1995). NT-4-mediated rescue of lateral geniculate neurons from effects of monocular deprivation. *Nature, 378,* 189-191. (6)

Riddle, W. J. R., & Scott, A. I. F. (1995). Relapse after successful electroconvulsive therapy: The use and impact of continuation antidepressant drug treatment. *Human Psychopharmacology, 10,* 201-205. (16)

Riley, J. N., & Walker, D. W. (1978). Morphological alterations in hippocampus after long-term alcohol consumption in mice. *Science, 201,* 646-648. (3)

Rinn, W. E. (1984). The neuropsychology of facial expression: A review of the neurological and psycholog-

ical mechanisms for producing facial expressions. *Psychological Bulletin, 95,* 52-77. (8, 14)

Robbins, T. W., & Everitt, B. J. (1995). Arousal systems and attention. In M. S. Gazzaniga (Ed.), *The cognitive neurosciences* (pp. 703-720). Cambridge, MA: MIT Press. (9)

Roberts, F. D., Newcomb, P. A., Trentham-Dietz, A., & Storer, B. E. (1996). Self-reported stress and risk of breast cancer. *Cancer, 77,* 1089-1093. (12)

Roberts, W. W., & Nagel, J. (1996). First-order projections activated by stimulation of hypothalamic sites eliciting attack and flight in rats. *Behavioral Neuroscience, 110,* 509-527. (12)

Robillard, T. A. J., & Gersdorff, M. C. H. (1986). Prevention of pre- and perinatal acquired hearing defects, Part I: Study of causes. *Journal of Auditory Research, 26,* 207-237. (7)

Robins, L. N., Helzer, J. E., Weissman, M. M., Orvaschel, H., Gruenberg, E., Burke, J. D. Jr., & Regier, D. A. (1984). Lifetime prevalence of specific psychiatric disorders in three sites. *Archives of General Psychiatry, 41,* 949-958. (12)

Robinson, R. G., Boston, J. D., Starkstein, S. E., & Price, T. R. (1988). Comparison of mania and depression after brain injury: Causal factors. *American Journal of Psychiatry, 145,* 172-178. (16)

Roe, A. W., & Ts'o, D. Y. (1995). Visual topography in primate V2: Multiple representation across functional stripes. *Journal of Neuroscience, 15,* 3689-3715. (6)

Rogers, J., & Morrison, J. H. (1985). Quantitative morphology and regional and laminar distributions of senile plaques in Alzheimer's disease. *Journal of Neuroscience, 5,* 2801-2808. (13)

Rolls, E. T. (1995). Central taste anatomy and neurophysiology. In R. L. Doty (Ed.), *Handbook of olfaction and gustation* (pp. 549-573). New York: Dekker. (7)

Rolls, E. T. (1996) The representation of space in the primate hippocampus, and its relation to memory. In K. Ishikawa, J. L. McGaugh, and H. Sakata (Eds.), *Brain processes and memory* (pp. 203-227). Amsterdam: Elsevier. (13)

Rome, L. C., Loughna, P. T., & Goldspink, G. (1984). Muscle fiber activity in carp as a function of swimming speed and muscle temperature. *American Journal of Psychiatry, 247*, R272-R279. (8)

Romer, A. S. (1962). *The vertebrate body.* Philadelphia, PA: Saunders. (5)

Roozendaal, B., Carmi, O., & McGaugh, J. L. (1996). Adrenocortical suppression blocks the memory-enhancing effects of amphetamine and epinephrine. *Proceedings of the National Academy of Sciences, USA, 93*, 1429-1433. (13)

Rosario, C. M., Aldskogius, H., Carlstedt, T., & Sidman, R. L. (1993). Differentiation and axonal outgrowth pattern of fetal dorsal root ganglion cells orthotopically allografted into adult rats. *Experimental Neurology, 120*, 16-31. (15)

Rose, J. E., Brugge, J. F., Anderson, D. J., & Hind, J. E. (1967). Phase-locked response to low-frequency tones in single auditory nerve fibers of the squirrel monkey. *Journal of Neurophysiology, 30*, 769-793. (7)

Rosenblatt, J. S. (1967). Nonhormonal basis of maternal behavior in the rat. *Science, 156*, 1512-1514. (11)

Rosenblatt, J. S. (1970). Views on the onset and maintenance of maternal behavior in the rat. In L. R. Aronson, E. Tobach, D. S. Lehrman, & J. S. Rosenblatt (Eds.), *Development and evolution of behavior* (pp. 489-515). San Francisco: W. H. Freeman. (11)

Rosenstein, D. L., Kalogeris, K. T., Kalafut, M., Malley, J., & Rubinow, D. R. (1996). Peripheral measures of arginine, vasopressin, atrial natriuretic peptide and adrenocorticotropic hormone in premenstrual syndrome. *Psychoneuroendocrinology, 21*, 347-359. (11)

Rosenthal, N. E., Sack, D. A., Gillin, C. J., Lewy, A. J., Goodwin, F. K., Davenport, Y., Mueller, P. S., Newsome, D. A., & Wehr, T. A. (1984). Seasonal affective disorder. *Archives of General Psychiatry, 41*, 72-80. (16)

Rosenzweig, M. R., & Bennett, E. L. (1996). Psychobiology of plasticity: Effects of training and experience on brain and behavior. *Behavioural Brain Research, 78*, 57-65. (5)

Rosvold, H. E., Mirsky, A. F., & Pribram, K. H. (1954). Influence of amygdalectomy on social behavior in monkeys. *Journal of Comparative and Physiological Psychology, 47*, 173-178. (12)

Rovainen, C. M. (1976). Regeneration of Müller and Mauthner axons after spinal transection in larval lampreys. *Journal of Comparative Neurology, 168*, 545-554. (15)

Rovee-Collier, C., Kupersmidt, J., O'Brien, L., Collier, G., & Tepper, V. (1991). Behavioral thermoregulation and immobilization: Conflicting demands for survival. *Journal of Comparative Psychology, 105*, 232-242. (10)

Rowland, N. (1980). Drinking behavior: Physiological, neurological, and environmental factors. In T. M. Toates & T. R. Halliday (Eds.), *Analysis of motivational processes* (pp. 39-59). London: Academic Press. (10)

Roy, A., DeJong, J., & Linnoila, M. (1989). Cerebrospinal fluid monoamine metabolites and suicidal behavior in depressed patients. *Archives of General Psychiatry, 46*, 609-612. (12)

Roy-Byrne, P. P., Uhde, T. W., & Post, R. M. (1986). Effects of one night's sleep deprivation on mood and behavior in panic disorder. *Archives of General Psychiatry, 43*, 895-899. (16)

Rozin, P. (1990). Getting to like the burn of chili pepper. In B. G. Green, J. R. Mason, & M. R. Kare (Eds.), *Chemical senses,* (Vol. 2, pp. 231-269). New York: Marcel Dekker. (10)

Rozin, P. (1996). Towards a psychology of food and eating: From motivation to module to model to marker, morality, meaning, and metaphor. *Current Directions in Psychological Science, 5*, 18-24. (10)

Rozin, P., & Kalat, J. W. (1971). Specific hungers and poison avoidance as adaptive specializations of learning. *Psychological Review, 78*, 459-486. (10, 13)

Rozin, P., & Pelchat, M. L. (1988). Memories of mammaries: Adaptations to weaning from milk. *Progress in Psychobiology and Physiological Psychology, 13*, 1-29. (10)

Rozin, P., & Schull, J. (1988). The adaptive-evolutionary point of view in experimental psychology. In R. C. Atkinson, R. J. Herrnstein, G. Lindzey, & R. D. Luce (Eds.), *Stevens' handbook of experimental psychology (2nd ed.), Vol. 1: Perception and motivation* (pp. 503-546). (13)

Rozin, P., & Vollmecke, T. A. (1986). Food likes and dislikes. *Annual Review of Nutrition, 6*, 433-456. (10)

Rozin, P., & Zellner, D. (1985). The role of Pavlovian conditioning in the acquisition of food likes and dislikes. *Annals of the New York Academy of Sciences, 443*, 189-202. (10)

Rubens, A. B., & Benson, D. F. (1971). Associative visual agnosia. *Archives of Neurology, 24*, 305-316. (6)

Rudy, J. W., & Sutherland, R. J. (1995). Configural association theory and the hippocampal formation: An appraisal and reconfiguration. *Hippocampus, 5*, 375-389. (13)

Rumbaugh, D. M. (Ed.) (1977). *Language learning by a chimpanzee: The Lana Project.* New York: Academic Press. (14)

Rumbaugh, D. M. (1990). Comparative psychology and the great apes: Their competency in learning, language, and numbers. *Psychological Record, 40*, 15-39. (14)

Rumbaugh, D. M., Savage Rumbaugh, E. S., & Washburn, D. A. (1996). Toward a new outlook on primate learning and behavior: Complex learning and emergent processes in comparative perspective. *Japanese Psychological Research, 38*, 113-125. (5)

Rusak, B. (1977). The role of the suprachiasmatic nuclei in the generation of circadian rhythms in the golden hamster, *Mesocricetus auratus. Journal of Comparative Physiology, A, 118*, 145-164. (9)

Rusak, B., & Zucker, I. (1979). Neural regulation of circadian rhythms. *Physiological Reviews, 59*, 449-526. (9)

Rush, D., & Callahan, K. R. (1989). Exposure to passive cigarette smoking and child development: A critical review. *Annals of the New York Academy of Sciences, 562*, 74-100. (5)

Russell, M. J., Switz, G. M., & Thompson, K. (1980). Olfactory influences on the human menstrual cycle. *Pharmacology, Biochemistry, and Behavior, 13*, 737-738. (7)

Saad, W. A., Luiz, A. C., Camargo, L. A. A., Renzi, A., & Manani, J. V. (1996). The lateral preoptic area plays a dual role in the regulation of thirst in the rat. *Brain Research Bulletin, 39*, 171-176. (10)

Sabel, B. A., Slavin, M. D., & Stein, D. G. (1984). GM₁ ganglioside treatment facilitates behavioral recovery from bilateral brain damage. *Science, 225*, 340-342. (15)

Sack, D. A., Nurnberger, J., Rosenthal, N. E., Ashburn, E., & Wehr, T. A. (1985). Potentiation of antidepressant medications by phase advance of the sleep-wake cycle. *American Journal of Psychiatry, 142*, 606-608. (16)

Sack, R. L., Lewy, A. J., White, D. M., Singer, C. M., Fireman, M. J., & Vandiver, R. (1990). Morning vs. evening light treatment for winter depression. *Archives of General Psychiatry, 47*, 343-351. (16)

Sackeim, H. A., Prohovnik, I., Moeller, J. R., Brown, R. P., Apter, S., Prudic, J., Devanand, D. P., & Mukherjee, S. (1990). Regional cerebral blood flow in mood disorders. I. Comparison of major depressives and normal controls at rest. *Archives of General Psychiatry, 47*, 60-70. (16)

Sackeim, H. A., Putz, E., Vingiano, W., Coleman, E., & McElhiney, M. (1988). Lateralization in the processing of emotionally laden information, I. Normal functioning. *Neuropsychiatry, Neuropsychology, and Behavioral Neurology, 1*, 97-110. (14)

Sadato, N., Pascual-Leone, A., Grafman, J., Ibañez, V., Deiber, M.-P., Dold, G., & Hallett, M. (1996). Activation of the primary visual cortex by Braille reading in blind subjects. *Nature, 380*, 526-528. (5)

Sakai, R. R., & Epstein, A. N. (1990). Dependence of adrenalectomy-induced sodium appetite on the action of angiotensin II in the brain of the rat. *Behavioral Neuroscience, 104*, 167-176. (10)

Sakimura, K., Katsuwada, T., Ito, I., Manabe, T., Takayama, C., Kushiya, E., Yagi, T., Aizawa, S., Inoue, Y., Sugiyama, H., & Mishina, M. (1995). Reduced hippocampal LTP and spatial learning in mice lacking NMDA receptor ε1 subunit. *Nature, 373*, 151-155. (13)

Salmelin, R., Hari, R., Lounasmaa, O. V., & Sams, M. (1994). Dynamics of brain activation during picture naming. *Nature, 368*, 463-465. (4)

Sanberg, P. R., & Coyle, J. T. (1984). Scientific approaches to Huntington's disease. *CRC Critical Reviews in Clinical Neurobiology, 1*, 1-44. (8)

Sanders, R. J. (1989). Sentence comprehension following agenesis of the corpus callosum. *Brain and Language, 37*, 59-72. (14)

Sanders, S. K., & Shekhar, A. (1995). Anxiolytic effects of chlordiazepoxide blocked by injection of GABAₐ and benzodiazepine receptor antagonists in the region of the anterior basolateral amygdala of rats. *Biological Psychiatry, 37*, 473-476. (12)

Sanderson, W. C., Rapee, R. M., & Barlow, D. H. (1989). The influence of an illusion of control on panic attacks induced via inhalation of 5.5% carbon dioxide-enriched air. *Archives of General Psychiatry, 46*, 157-162. (12)

Sanes, J. N., Donoghue, J. P., Thangaraj, V., Edelman, R. R., & Warach, S. (1995). Shared neural substrates controlling hand movements in human motor cortex. *Science, 268*, 1775-1777. (8)

Sanes, J. R. (1993). Topographic maps and molecular gradients. *Current Opinion in Neurobiology, 3*, 67-74. (5)

Sáry, G., Vogels, R., & Orban, G. A. (1993). Cue-invariant shape selectivity of macaque inferior temporal neurons. *Science, 260*, 995-997. (6)

Satinoff, E. (1964). Behavioral thermoregulation in response to local cooling of the rat brain. *American Journal of Physiology, 206*, 1389-1394. (10)

Satinoff, E. (1991). Developmental aspects of behavioral and reflexive thermoregulation. In H. N. Shanir, G. A. Barr, & M. A. Hofer (Eds.), *Developmental psychobiology: New methods and changing concepts* (pp. 169-188). New York: Oxford University Press. (10)

Satinoff, E., McEwen, G. N. Jr., & Williams, B. A. (1976). Behavioral fever in newborn rabbits. *Science, 193*, 1139-1140. (10)

Satinoff, E., & Rutstein, J. (1970). Behavioral thermoregulation in rats with anterior hypothalamic lesions. *Journal of Comparative and Physiological Psychology, 71*, 77-82. (10)

Satinoff, E., Valentino, D., & Teitelbaum, P. (1976). Thermoregulatory cold-defense deficits in rats with preoptic/anterior hypothalamic lesions. *Brain Research Bulletin, 1*, 553-565. (10)

Sato, M. (1992). A lasting vulnerability to psychosis in patients with previous methamphetamine psychosis. *Annals of the New York Academy of Sciences, 654*, 160-170. (16)

Sato, M. A., Yada, M. M., & De Luca, L. A. Jr. (1996). Antagonism of the renin-angiotensin system and water deprivation-induced NaCl Intake in rats. *Physiology & Behavior, 60*, 1099-1104. (10)

Satz, P., Strauss, E., & Whitaker, H. (1990). The ontogeny of hemispheric specialization: Some old hypotheses revisited. *Brain and Language, 38*, 596-614. (15)

Saudou, F., Amara, D. A., Dierich, A., LeMeur, M., Ramboz, S., Segu, L., Buhot, M.-C., & Hen, R. (1994). Enhanced aggressive behavior in mice lacking 5-HT₁ᵦ receptor. *Science, 265*, 1875-1878. (12)

Savage-Rumbaugh, E. S. (1990). Language acquisition in a nonhuman species: Implications for the innateness debate. *Developmental Psychobiology, 23*, 599-620. (14)

Savage-Rumbaugh, E. S. (1991). Language learning in the bonobo: How and why they learn. In N. A. Kresnegor, D. M. Rumbaugh, R. L. Schiefelbusch, & M. Studdert-Kennedy (Eds.), *Biological and behavioral determinants of language development* (pp. 209-233). Hillsdale, NJ: Lawrence Erlbaum. (14)

Savage-Rumbaugh, E. S. (1993). Language learnability in man, ape, and dolphin. In H. L. Roitblat, L. M. Herman, & P. E. Nachtigall (Eds.), *Language and communication: comparative perspectives* (pp. 457-473). Hillsdale, NJ: Lawrence Erlbaum. (14)

Savage-Rumbaugh, E. S., Murphy, J., Sevcik, R. A., Brakke, K. E., Williams, S. L., & Rumbaugh, D. M. (1993). Language comprehension in ape and child. *Monographs of the Society for Research in Child Development, 58, serial no. 233. (14)

Savage-Rumbaugh, E. S., Sevcik, R. A., Brakke, K. E., & Rumbaugh, D. M. (1992). Symbols: Their communicative use, communication, and combination by bonobos (Pan paniscus). In L. P. Lipsitt & C. Rovee-Collier (Eds.), Advances in infancy research (Vol. 7, pp. 221-278). Norwood, NJ: Ablex. (14)

Saykin, A. J., Shtasel, D. L., Gur, R. E., Kester, D. B., Mozley, L. H., Stafiniak, P., & Gur, R. C. (1994). Neuropsychological deficits in neuroleptic naive patients with first-episode schizophrenia. Archives of General Psychiatry, 51, 124-131. (16)

Scammell, T. E., Elmquist, J. K., Griffin, J. D., & Saper, C. B. (1996). Ventromedial preoptic prostaglandin-E$_2$ activates fever-producing autonomic pathways. Journal of Neuroscience, 16, 6246-6254. (10)

Schacher, S., Castellucci, V. F., & Kandel, E. R. (1988). cAMP evokes long-term facilitation in Aplysia sensory neurons that requires new protein synthesis. Science, 240, 1667-1669. (13)

Schacter, D. L. (1983). Amnesia observed: Remembering and forgetting in a natural environment. Journal of Abnormal Psychology, 92, 236-242. (13)

Schacter, D. L. (1985). Priming of old and new knowledge in amnesic patients and normal subjects. Annals of the New York Academy of Sciences, 444, 41-53. (13)

Schallert, T. (1983). Sensorimotor impairment and recovery of function in brain-damaged rats: Reappearance of symptoms during old age. Behavioral Neuroscience, 97, 159-164. (15)

Schallert, T., Hernandez, T. D., & Barth, T. M. (1986). Recovery of function after brain damage: Severe and chronic disruption by diazepam. Brain Research, 379, 104-111. (15)

Schallert, T., & Whishaw, I. Q. (1984). Bilateral cutaneous stimulation of the somatosensory system in hemidecorticate rats. Behavioral Neuroscience, 98, 518-540. (15)

Scheibel, A. B. (1983). Dendritic

changes. In B. Reisberg (Ed.), Alzheimer's disease (pp. 69-73). New York: Free Press. (13)

Scheibel, A. B. (1984). A dendritic correlate of human speech. In N. Geschwind & A. M. Galaburda (Eds.), Cerebral Dominance (pp. 43-52). Cambridge, MA: Harvard University Press. (4)

Scheich, H., & Zuschratter, W. (1995). Mapping of stimulus features and meaning in gerbil auditory cortex with 2-deoxyglucose and c-fos antibodies. Behavioural Brain Research, 66, 195-205. (7)

Schellenberg, G. D., Bird, T. D., Wijsman, E. M., Orr, H. T., Anderson, L., Nemens, E., White, J. A., Bonnycastle, L., Weber, J. L., Alonso, M. E., Potter, H., Heston, L. L., & Martin, G. M. (1992). Genetic linkage evidence for a familial Alzheimer's disease locus on chromosome 14. Science, 258, 668-671. (13)

Schenck, C. H., & Mahowald, M. W. (1996). Long-term, nightly benzodiazepine treatment of injurious parasomnias and other disorders of disrupted nocturnal sleep in 170 adults. American Journal of Medicine, 100, 333-337. (9)

Scherer, S. S. (1986). Reinnervation of the extraocular muscles in goldfish is nonselective. Journal of Neuroscience, 6, 764-77 3. (15)

Scheuner, D., Eckman, C., Jensen, M., Song, X., Citron, M., Suzuki, N., Bird, T. D., Hardy, J., Hutton, M., Kukull, W., Larson, E., Levy-Lahad, E., Viitanen, M., Peskind, E., Poorkaj, P., Schellenberg, G., Tanzi, R., Wasco, W., Lannfelt, L., Selkoe, D., & Younkin, S. (1996). Secreted amyloid β-protein similar to that in the senile plaques of Alzheimer's disease is increased in vivo by the presenilin 1 and 2 and APP mutations linked to familial Alzheimer's disease. Nature Medicine, 2, 864-870. (13)

Schiffman, S. S. (1983). Taste and smell in disease. New England Journal of Medicine, 308, 1275-1279, 1337-1343. (7)

Schiffman, S. S., & Erickson, R. P. (1971). A psychophysical model for gustatory quality. Physiology & Behavior, 7, 617-633. (7)

Schiffman, S. S., & Erickson, R. P. (1980). The issue of primary tastes versus a taste continuum.

Neuroscience & Biobehavioral Reviews, 4, 109-117. (7)

Schiffman, S. S., Lockhead, E., & Maes, F. W. (1983). Amiloride reduces the taste intensity of Na$^+$ and Li$^+$ salts and sweeteners. Proceedings of the National Academy of Sciences, USA, 80, 6136-6140. (7)

Schiffman, S. S., McElroy, A. E., & Erickson, R. P. (1980). The range of taste quality of sodium salts. Physiology & Behavior, 24, 217-224. (7)

Schiller, F. (1979). Paul Broca. Berkeley: University of California Press. (14)

Schlaug, G., Jäncke, L., Huang, Y., & Steinmetz, H. (1995). In vivo evidence of structural brain asymmetry in musicians. Science, 267, 699-701. (5)

Schmid, A., Koch, M., & Schnitzler, H.-U. (1995). Conditioned pleasure attenuates the startle response in rats. Neurobiology of Learning and Memory, 64, 1-3. (12)

Schmidt, J. T., Cicerone, C. M., & Easter, S. S. (1977). Expansion of the half retinal projection to the tectum in goldfish: An electrophysiological and anatomical study. Journal of Comparative Neurology, 177, 257-278. (5)

Schmidt, W. J. (1995). Balance of transmitter activities in the basal ganglia loops. Journal of Neural Transmission, Suppl. 46, 67-76. (8)

Schneider, B. A., Trehub, S. E., Morrongiello, B. A., & Thorpe, L. A. (1986). Auditory sensitivity in preschool children. Journal of the Acoustical Society of America, 79, 447-452. (7)

Schneider, G. E., & Jhaveri, S. R. (1974). Neuroanatomical correlates of spared or altered function after brain lesions in the newborn hamster. In D. G. Stein, J. J. Rosen, & N. Butters (Eds.), Plasticity and recovery of function in the central nervous system (pp. 65-109). New York: Academic Press. (15)

Schöpf, J., Bryois, C., Jonquière, M., & Le, P. K. (1984). On the nosology of severe psychiatric post-partum disorders. European Archives of Psychiatry and Neurological Sciences, 234, 54-63. (16)

Schou, M. (1997). Forty years of lithium treatment. Archives of General Psychiatry, 54, 9-13. (16)

Schuckit, M. A., & Smith, T. L. (1996). An 8-year follow-up of 450 sons of alcoholic and control subjects. *Archives of General Psychiatry, 53,* 202-210. (3)

Schulkin, J. (1991). *Sodium hunger: The search for a salty taste.* Cambridge, England: Cambridge University Press. (10)

Schwartz, J. C., Giros, B., Martres, M.-P., & Sokoloff, P. (1992). The dopamine receptor family: Molecular biology and pharmacology. *Seminars in the Neurosciences, 4,* 99-108. (3)

Schwartz, J. M., Stoessel, P. W., Baxter, L. R. Jr., Martin, K. M., & Phelps, M. E. (1996). Systematic changes in cerebral glucose metabolic rate after successful behavior modification treatment of obsessive-compulsive disorder. *Archives of General Psychiatry, 53,* 109-113. (12)

Schwartz, M. F. (1995). Re-examining the role of executive functions in routine action production. *Annals of the New York Academy of Sciences, 769,* 321-335. (4)

Schwartz, W. J., & Gainer, H. (1977). Suprachiasmatic nucleus: Use of ^{14}C-labeled deoxyglucose uptake as a functional marker. *Science, 197,* 1089-1091. (9)

Scott, T. R. (1987). Coding in the gustatory system. In T. E. Finger & W. L. Silver (Eds.), *Neurobiology of taste and smell* (pp. 355-378). New York: John Wiley. (7)

Scott, T. R. (1992). Taste: The neural basis of body wisdom. In A. P. Simopoulos (Ed.), *Nutritional triggers for health and in disease* (pp. 1-39). Basel: Karger. (7)

Scott, T. R., & Plata-Salaman, C. R. (1991). Coding of taste quality. In T. V. Getchell et al. (Eds.), *Smell and taste in health and disease* (pp. 345-368). New York: Raven Press. (7)

Scovern, A. W., & Kilmann, P. R. (1980). Status of electroconvulsive therapy: Review of the outcome literature. *Psychological Bulletin, 87,* 260-303. (16)

Scoville, W. B., & Milner, B. (1957). Loss of recent memory after bilateral hippocampal lesions. *Journal of Neurology, Neurosurgery, and Psychiatry, 20,* 11-21. (13)

Seeley, R. J., Kaplan, J. M., & Grill, H. J. (1995). Effect of occluding the pylorus on intraoral intake: A test of the gastric hypothesis of meal termination. *Physiology & Behavior, 58,* 245-249. (10)

Seeman, P., Lee, T., Chau-Wong, M., & Wong, K. (1976). Antipsychotic drug doses and neuroleptic/ dopamine receptors. *Nature, 261,* 717-719. (16)

Segal, N. (1984). Asymmetries in monozygotic twins. *American Journal of Psychiatry, 141,* 1638. (16)

Seidman, L. J., Oscar-Berman, M., Kalinowski, A. G., Ajilore, O., Kremen, W. S., Faraone, S., & Tsuang, M. T. (1995). Experimental and clinical neuropsychological measures of prefrontal dysfunction in schizophrenia. *Neuropsychology, 9,* 481-490. (16)

Sejnowski, T. J., Chattarji, S., & Stanton, P. K. (1990). Homosynaptic long-term depression in hippocampus and neocortex. *Seminars in the Neurosciences, 2,* 355-363. (13)

Selemon, L. D., Rajkowska, G., & Goldman-Rakic, P. S. (1995). Abnormally high neuronal density in the schizophrenic cortex. *Archives of General Psychiatry, 52,* 805-818. (16)

Selzer, M. E. (1978). Mechanisms of functional recovery and regeneration after spinal cord transection in larval sea lamprey. *Journal of Physiology, 277,* 395-408. (15)

Sereno, A. B., & Holzman, P. S. (1993). Express saccades and smooth pursuit eye movement function in schizophrenic, affective disorder, and normal subjects. *Journal of Cognitive Neuroscience, 5,* 303-316. (16)

Sershen, H., Toth, E., Lajtha, A., & Vizi, E. S. (1995). Nicotine effects on presynapatic receptor interactions. *Annals of the New York Academy of Sciences, 757,* 238-244. (8)

Shadlen, M. N., & Newsome, W. T. (1996). Motion perception: Seeing and deciding. *Proceedings of the National Academy of Sciences, USA, 93,* 628-633. (8)

Shah, A., & Lisak, R. P. (1993). Immunopharmacologic therapy in myasthenia gravis. *Clinical Neuropharmacology, 16,* 97-103. (8)

Shapiro, B. E., & Danly, M. (1985). The role of the right hemisphere in the control of speech prosody in propositional and affective contexts. *Brain and Language, 25,* 19-36. (14)

Shapiro, C. M., Bortz, R., Mitchell, D., Bartel, P., & Jooste, P. (1981). Slow-wave sleep: A recovery period after exercise. *Science, 214,* 1253-1254. (9)

Shapley, R. (1995). Parallel neural pathways and visual function. In M. S. Gazzaniga (Ed.), *The cognitive neurosciences* (pp. 315-324). Cambridge, MA: MIT Press. (6)

Sharkey, J., & Butcher, S. P. (1994). Immunophilins mediate the neuroprotective effects of FK506 in focal cerebral ischaemia. *Nature, 371,* 336-339. (15)

Shatz, C. J. (1992, September). The developing brain. *Scientific American, 267* (9), 60-67. (5)

Shatz, C. J. (1996). Emergence of order in visual-system development. *Proceedings of the National Academy of Sciences, USA, 93,* 602-608. (6)

Sherin, J. E., Shiromani, P. J., McCarley, R. W., & Saper, C. B. (1996). Activation of ventrolateral preoptic neurons during sleep. *Science, 271,* 216-219. (9)

Sherrington, C. S. (1906). *The integrative action of the nervous system.* New York: Scribner's. (2nd ed.). New Haven, CT: Yale University Press, 1947. (3)

Sherrington, R., Rogaev, E. I., Liang, Y., Rogaeva, E. A., Levesque, G., Ikeda, M., Chi, H., Lin, C., Li, G., Holman, K., Tsuda, T., Mar, L., Foncin, J.-F., Bruni, A. C., Montesi, M. P., Sorbi, S., Rainero, I., Pinessi, L., Nee, L., Chumakov, I., Pollen, D., Brookes, A., Sanseau, P., Polinsky, R. J., Wasco, W., DaSilva, H. A. R., Haines, J. L., Pericak-Vance, M. A., Tanzi, R. E., Roses, A. D., Fraser, P. E., Rommens, J. M., & St. George-Hyslop, P. H. (1995). Cloning of a gene bearing missense mutations in early-onset familial Alzheimer's disease. *Nature, 375,* 754-760. (13)

Sherwin, B. B. (1994). Estrogenic effects on memory in women. *Annals of the New York Academy of Sciences, 743,* 213-231. (11)

Shields, S. A. (1983). Development of autonomic nervous system responsivity in children: A review of the literature. *International Journal of Behavioral Development, 6,* 291-319. (12)

Shik, M. L., & Orlovsky, G. N. (1976). Neurophysiology of locomotor automatism. *Physiological Reviews, 56,* 465-501. (8)

Shimamura, A. P., Janowsky, J. S., & Squire, L. R. (1990). Memory for the temporal order of events in patients with frontal lobe lesions and amnesic patients. *Neuropsychologia, 28,* 803-813. (13)

Shirley, S. G., & Persaud, K. C. (1990). The biochemistry of vertebrate olfaction and taste. *Seminars in the Neurosciences, 2,* 59-68. (7)

Shoulson, I. (1990). Huntington's disease: Cognitive and psychiatric features. *Neuropsychiatry, Neuropsychology, and Behavioral Neurology, 3,* 15-22. (8)

Shozu, M., Akasofu, K., Harada, T., & Kubota, Y. (1991). A new cause of female pseudohermaphroditism: Placental aromatase deficiency. *Journal of Clinical Endocrinology and Metabolism, 72,* 560-566. (11)

Shupert, C., Cornwell, P., & Payne, B. (1993). Differential sparing of depth perception, orienting, and optokinetic nystagmus after neonatal versus adult lesions of cortical areas 17, 18, and 19 in the cat. *Behavioral Neuroscience, 107,* 633-650. (15)

Shutts, D. (1982). *Lobotomy: Resort to the knife.* New York: Van Nostrand Reinhold. (4)

Siegel, A., & Pott, C. B. (1988). Neural substrates of aggression and flight in the cat. *Progress in Neurobiology, 31,* 261-283. (12)

Siegel, J. M. (1995). Phylogeny and the function of REM sleep. *Behavioural Brain Research, 69,* 29-34. (9)

Siegel, J. M., Nienhuis, R., Fahringer, H. M., Paul, R., Shiromani, P., Dement, W. C., Mignot, E., & Chiu, C. (1991). Neuronal activity in narcolepsy: Identification of cataplexy-related cells in the medial medulla. *Science, 252,* 1315-1318. (9)

Siegel, L. S., Share, D., & Geva, E. (1995). Evidence for superior orthographic skills in dyslexics. *Psychological Science, 6,* 250-254. (14)

Silbersweig, D. A., Stern, E., Frith, C., Cahill, C., Holmes, A., Grootoonk, S., Seaward, J., McKenna, P., Chua, S. E., Schnorr, L., Jones, T., & Frackowiak, R. S. J. (1995). A functional neuroanatomy of hallucinations in schizophrenia. *Nature, 378,* 176-179. (16)

Silinsky, E. M. (1989). Adenosine derivatives and neuronal function. *Seminars in the Neurosciences, 1,* 155-165. (3)

Sillito, A. M., Jones, H. E., Gerstein, G. L., & West, D. C. (1994). Feature-linked synchronization of thalamic relay cell firing induced by feedback from the visual cortex. *Nature, 369,* 479-482. (6)

Silvestri, R., de Domenico, P., Raffaele, M., Mento, G., & DiPerri, R. (1991). Sleep in central nervous system disorders: An up to date. *Acta Neurologica, 13,* 577-589. (9)

Simansky, K. J. (1996). Serotonergic control of the organization of feeding and satiety. *Behavioural Brain Research, 73,* 37-42. (10)

Singer, W. (1986). Neuronal activity as a shaping factor in postnatal development of visual cortex. In W. T. Greenough & J. M. Jusaska (Eds.), *Developmental neuropsychobiology* (pp. 271-293). Orlando, FL: Academic Press. (6)

Singh, M. M., & Kay, S. R. (1976). Wheat gluten as a pathogenic factor in schizophrenia. *Science, 191,* 401-402. (16)

Sirigu, A., Grafman, J., Bressler, K., & Sunderland, T. (1991). Multiple representations contribute to body knowledge processing. Evidence from a case of autopagnosia. *Brain, 114,* 629-642. (7)

Sjöström, M., Friden, J., & Ekblom, B. (1987). Endurance, what is it? Muscle morphology after an extremely long distance run. *Acta Physiologica Scandinavica, 130,* 513-520. (8)

Sjöström, M., Johansson, C., & Lorentzon, R. (1988). Muscle pathomorphology in m. quadriceps of marathon runners. Early signs of strain disease or functional adaptation? *Acta Physiologica Scandinavica, 132,* 537-542. (8)

Skaggs, W. E., & McNaughton, B. L. (1996). Replay of neuronal firing sequences in rat hippocampus during sleep following spatial

experience. *Science, 271,* 1870-1873. (9)

Sklar, L. S., & Anisman, H. (1981). Stress and cancer. *Psychological Bulletin, 89,* 369-406. (12)

Slob, A. K., Bax, C. M., Hop, W. C. J., Rowland, D. L., & van der Werff ten Bosch, J. J. (1996). Sexual arousability and the menstrual cycle. *Psychoneuroendocrinology, 21,* 545-558. (11)

Smale, L., Holekamp, K. E., Weldele, M., Frank, L. G., & Glickman, S. E. (1995). Competition and cooperation between litter-mates in the spotted hyaena, *Crocuta crocuta. Animal Behaviour, 50,* 671-682. (11)

Smeraldi, E., Kidd, K. K., Negri, F., Heimbuch, R., & Melica, A. M. (1979). Genetic studies of affective disorders. In J. Obiols, C. Ballús, E. González Monclús, & J. Pujol (Eds.), *Biological psychiatry today* (pp. 60-65). Amsterdam: Elsevier/North Holland Biomedical Press. (16)

Smith, B. K., York, D. A., & Bray, G. A. (1996). Effects of dietary preference and galanin administration in the paraventricular or amygdaloid nucleus on diet self-selection. *Brain Research Bulletin, 39,* 149-154. (10)

Smith, C. (1995). Sleep states and memory processes. *Behavioural Brain Research, 69,* 137-145. (9)

Smith, C. A. D., Gough, A. C., Leigh, P. N., Summers, B. A., Harding, A. E., Maranganore, D. M., Sturman, S. G., Schapira, A. H. V., Williams, A. C., Spurr, N. K., & Wolf, C. R. (1992). Debrisoquine hydroxylase gene polymorphism and susceptibility to Parkinson's disease. *Lancet, 339,* 1375-1377. (8)

Smith, C. U. M. (1996). *Elements of molecular neurobiology.* Chichester, England: John Wiley. (2, 3)

Smith, D. V., VanBuskirk, R. L., Travers, J. B., & Bieber, S. L. (1983). Coding of taste stimuli by hamster brain stem neurons. *Journal of Neurophysiology, 50,* 541-558. (7)

Smith, D. V., & van der Klaauw, N. J. (1995). The perception of saltiness is eliminated by NaCl adaptation: Implications for gustatory transduction and coding. *Chemical Senses, 20,* 545-557. (7)

Smith, L. T. (1975). The interanimal transfer phenomenon: A review. *Psychological Bulletin, 81,* 1078-1095. (13)

Smith, S., Lindefors, N., Hurd, Y., & Sharp, T. (1995). Electroconvulsive shock increases dopamine D_1 and D_2 receptor mRNA in the nucleus accumbens of the rat. *Psychopharmacology, 120,* 333-340. (16)

Snyder, E. Y. (1994). Grafting immortalized neurons to the CNS. *Current Opinion in Neurobiology, 4,* 742-751. (15)

Snyder, G. L., & Stricker, E. M. (1985). Effects of lateral hypothalamic lesions on food intake of rats during exposure to cold. *Behavioral Neuroscience, 99,* 310-322. (15)

Soltesz, I., Smetters, D. K., & Mody, I. (1995). Tonic inhibition originates from synapses close to the soma. *Nature, 14,* 1273-1283. (3)

Somero, G. N. (1996). Temperature and proteins: Little things can mean a lot. *News in Physiological Sciences, 11,* 72-77. (10)

Somjen, G. G. (1988). Nervenkitt: Notes on the history of the concept of neuroglia. *Glia, 1,* 2-9. (2)

Sontheimer, H. (1995a). Glial influences on neuronal signaling. *The Neuroscientist, 1,* 123-126. (2)

Sontheimer, H. (1995b). Glial neuronal interactions: A physiological perspective. *The Neuroscientist, 1,* 328-337. (2)

Spence, S., Shapiro, D., & Zaidel, E. (1996). The role of the right hemisphere in the physiological and cognitive components of emotional processing. *Psychophysiology, 33,* 112-122. (12)

Sperry, R. W. (1943). Visuomotor coordination in the newt (*Triturus viridescens*) after regeneration of the optic nerve. *Journal of Comparative Neurology, 79,* 33-55. (5)

Sperry, R. W. (1961). Cerebral organization and behavior. *Science, 133,* 1749-1757. (14)

Spiegel, T. A. (1973). Caloric regulation of food intake in man. *Journal of Comparative and Physiological Psychology, 84,* 24-37. (10)

Spoont, M. R. (1992). Modulatory role of serotonin in neural information processing: Implications for human psychopathology. *Psychological Bulletin, 112,* 330-350. (12)

Spurzheim, J. G. (1908). *Phrenology* (rev. ed.). Philadelphia: Lippincott. (4)

Squire, L. R. (1992). Memory and the hippocampus: A synthesis from findings with rats, monkeys, and humans. *Psychological Review, 99,* 195-231. (13)

Squire, L. R., Amaral, D. G., & Press, G. A. (1990). Magnetic resonance imaging of the hippocampal formation and mammillary nuclei distinguish medial temporal lobe and diencephalic amnesia. *Journal of Neuroscience, 10,* 3106-3117. (13)

Stanford, L. R. (1987). Conduction velocity variations minimize conduction time differences among retinal ganglion cell axons. *Science, 238,* 358-360. (2, 6)

Stanford, S. C. (1995). Central noradrenergic neurones and stress. *Pharmacology & Therapeutics, 68,* 297-342. (12)

Stanley, B. G., & Gillard, E. R. (1994). Hypothalamic neuropeptide Y and the regulation of eating behavior and body weight. *Current Directions in Psychological Science, 3,* 9-15. (10)

Stanley, B. G., Schwartz, D. H., Hernandez, L., Leibowitz, S. F., & Hoebel, B. G. (1989). Patterns of extracellular 5-hydroxyindoleacetic acid (5-HIAA) in the paraventricular hypothalamus (PVN): Relation to circadian rhythm and deprivation-induced eating behavior. *Pharmacology, Biochemistry, & Behavior, 33,* 257-260. (10)

Starke, K. (1981). *Presynaptic receptors. Annual Review of Pharmacology and Toxicology, 21,* 7-30. (3)

Starkstein, S. E., & Robinson, R. G. (1986). Cerebral lateralization in depression. *American Journal of Psychiatry, 143,* 1631. (16)

Starr, C., & Taggart, R. (1989). *Biology: The unity and diversity of life.* Belmont, CA: Wadsworth. (4, 7, 8, 11)

Stein, B. E., & Meredith, M. A. (1993). *The merging of the senses.* Cambridge, MA: MIT Press. (7)

Stein, L. (1962). Effects and interactions of imipramine, chlorpromazine, reserpine, and amphetamine on self-stimulation: Possible neurophysiological basis of depression. In J. Wortis (Ed.), *Recent advances in biological psychiatry* (Vol. 4, pp. 288-308). New York: Plenum. (16)

Stephens, T. W., Basinski, M., Bristow, P. K., Bue-Valleskey, J. M., Burgett, S. G., Craft, L., Hale, J., Hoffman, J., Hsiung, H. M., Kriauciunas, A., MacKellar, W., Rosteck, P. R. Jr., Schoner, B., Smith, D., Tinsley, F. C., Zhang, W.-Y., & Heiman, M. (1995). The role of neuropeptide Y in the antiobesity action of the *obese* gene product. *Nature, 377,* 530-532. (10)

Stockman, E. R., Callaghan, R. S., Gallagher, C. A., & Baum, M. J. (1986). Sexual differentiation of play behavior in the ferret. *Behavioral Neuroscience, 100,* 563-568. (11)

Stone, V. E., Nisenson, L., Eliassen, J. C., & Gazzaniga, M. S. (1996). Left hemisphere representations of emotional facial expressions. *Neuropsychologia, 34,* 23-29. (14)

Straub, R. E., MacLean, C. J., O'Neill, F. A., Burke, J., Murphy, B., Duke, F., Shinkwin, R., Webb, B. T., Zhang, J., Walsh, D., & Kendler, K. S. (1995). A potential vulnerability locus for schizophrenia on chromosome 6p24-22: Evidence for genetic heterogeneity. *Nature, 11,* 287-293. (16)

Strichartz, G., Rando, T., & Wang, G. K. (1987). An integrated view of the molecular toxinology of sodium channel gating in excitable cells. *Annual Review of Neuroscience, 10,* 237-267. (2)

Stricker, E. M. (1969). Osmoregulation and volume regulation in rats: Inhibition of hypovolemic thirst by water. *American Journal of Physiology, 217,* 98-105. (10)

Stricker, E. M. (1983). Thirst and sodium appetite after colloid treatment in rats: Role of the renin-angiotensinaldosterone system. *Behavioral Neuroscience, 97,* 725-737. (10)

Stricker, E. M., Swerdloff, A. F., & Zigmond, M. J. (1978). Intrahypothalamic injections of kainic acid produce feeding and drinking deficits in rats. *Brain Research, 158,* 470-473. (10)

Strittmatter, W. J., & Roses, A. D.

(1995). Apolipoprotein E: Emerging story in the pathogenesis of Alzheimer's disease. *The Neuroscientist, 1*, 298-306. (13)

Stryker, M. P., & Sherk, H. (1975). Modification of cortical orientation selectivity in the cat by restricted visual experience: A reexamination. *Science, 190*, 904-906. (6)

Stryker, M. P., Sherk, H., Leventhal, A. G., & Hirsch, H. V. B. (1978). Physiological consequences for the cat's visual cortex of effectively restricting early visual experience with oriented contours. *Journal of Neurophysiology, 41*, 896-909. (6)

Strzelczuk, M., & Romaniuk, A. (1996). Fear induced by the blockade of GABA$_A$-ergic transmission in the hypothalamus of the cat: Behavioral and neurochemical study. *Behavioural Brain Research, 72*, 63-71. (12)

Stunkard, A. J., Sorensen, T. I. A., Hanis, C., Teasdale, T. W., Chakraborty, R., Schull, W. J., & Schulsinger, F. (1986). An adoption study of human obesity. *New England Journal of Medicine, 314*, 193-198. (10)

Stuss, D. T., & Benson, D. F. (1984). Neuropsychological studies of the frontal lobes. *Psychological Bulletin, 95*, 3-28. (4)

Stuss, D. T., Pogue, J., Buckle, L., & Bondar, J. (1994). Characterization of stability of performance in patients with traumatic brain injury: Variability and consistency on reaction time tests. *Neuropsychology, 8*, 316-324. (15)

Südhof, T. C. (1995). The synaptic vesicle cycle: A cascade of protein-protein interactions. *Nature, 375*, 645-653. (3)

Sugita, Y. (1996). Global plasticity in adult visual cortex following reversal of visual input. *Nature, 380*, 523-526. (6)

Sulser, F., Gillespie, D. D., Mishra, R., & Manier, D. H. (1984). Desensitization by antidepressants of central norepinephrine receptor systems coupled to adenylate cyclase. *Annals of the New York Academy of Sciences, 430*, 91-101. (16)

Susser, E., Neugebauer, R., Hoek, H. W., Brown, A. S., Lin, S., Labovitz, D., & Gorman, J. M. (1996). Schizophrenia after prenatal famine. *Archives of General Psychiatry, 53*, 25-31. (16)

Sutton, R. L., Hovda, D. A., & Feeney, D. M. (1989). Amphetamine accelerates recovery of locomotor function following bilateral frontal cortex ablation in rats. *Behavioral Neuroscience, 103*, 837-841. (15)

Suzdak, P. D., Glowa, J. R., Crawley, J. N., Schwartz, R. D., Skolnick, P., & Paul, S. M. (1986). A selective imidazobenzodiazepine antagonist of ethanol in the rat. *Science, 234*, 1243-1247. (12)

Swaab, D. F., & Fliers, E. (1985). A sexually dimorphic nucleus in the human brain. *Science, 228*, 1112-1115. (11)

Swaab, D. F., & Hofman, M. A. (1990). An enlarged suprachiasmatic nucleus in homosexual men. *Brain Research, 537*, 141-148. (11)

Swaab, D. F., Slob, A. K., Houtsmuller, E. J., Brand, T., & Zhou, J. N. (1995). Increased number of vasopressin neurons in the suprachiasmatic nucleus (SCN) of 'bisexual' adult male rats following perinatal treatment with the aromatase blacker ATD. *Developmental Brain Research, 85*, 273-279. (11)

Swan, H., & Schatte, C. (1977). Antimetabolic extract from the brain of the hibernating ground squirrel *Citellus tridecemlineatus*. *Science, 195*, 84-85. (9)

Szél, Á., Röhlich, P., Caffé, A. R., Juliusson, B., Aguirre, G., & van Veen, T. (1992). Unique topographic separation of two spectral classes of cones in the mouse retina. *Journal of Comparative Neurology, 325*, 327-342. (6)

Szymusiak, R. (1995). Magnocellular nuclei of the basal forebrain: Substrates of sleep and arousal regulation. *Sleep, 18*, 478-500. (9)

Taddese, A., Nah, S. Y., & McCleskey, E. W. (1995). Selective opioid inhibition of small nociceptive neurons. *Science, 270*, 1366-1369. (7)

Taghavi, E., Menkes, D. B., Howard, R. C., Mason, P. A., Shaw, J. P., & Spears, G. F. S. (1995). Premenstrual syndrome: A double-blind controlled trial of desipramine and methylscopolamine. *International Clinical Psychopharmacology, 10*, 119-122. (11)

Takeuchi, A. (1977). Junctional transmission: I. Postsynaptic mechanisms. In E. R. Kandel (Ed.), *Handbook of physiology, Section 1: Neurophysiology, Vol. 1, Cellular biology of neurons* (Pt. 1, pp. 295-327). Bethesda, MD: American Physiological Society. (3)

Takeuchi, A. H., & Hulse, S. H. (1993). Absolute pitch. *Psychological Bulletin, 113*, 345-361. (5)

Talbot, J. D., Marrett, S., Evans, A. C., Meyer, E., Bushnell, M. C., & Duncan, G. H. (1991). Multiple representations of pain in human cerebral cortex. *Science, 251*, 1355-1358. (7)

Taller, A. M., Asher, D. M., Pomeroy, K. L., Eldadah, B. A., Godec, M. S., Falkai, P. G., Bogert, B., Kleinman, J. E., Stevens, J. R., & Torrey, E. F. (1996). Search for viral nucleic acid sequences in brain tissues of patients with schizophrenia using nested polymerase chain reaction. *Archives of General Psychiatry, 53*, 32-40. (16)

Tanaka, K., Sugita, Y., Moriya, M., & Saito, H.-A. (1993). Analysis of object motion in the ventral part of the medial superior temporal area of the macaque visual cortex. *Journal of Neurophysiology, 69*, 128-142. (6)

Tanaka, Y., Kamo, T., Yoshida, M., & Yamadori, A. (1991). 'So-called' cortical deafness. *Brain, 114*, 2385-2401. (7)

Tanji, J., & Shima, K. (1994). Role for supplementary motor area cells in planning several movements ahead. *Nature, 371*, 413-416. (8)

Taub, E., & Berman, A. J. (1968). Movement and learning in the absence of sensory feedback. In S. J. Freedman (Ed.), *The neuropsychology of spatially oriented behavior* (pp. 173-192). Homewood, IL: Dorsey. (15)

Teicher, M. H., Glod, C. A., Magnus, E., Harper, D., Benson, G., Krueger, K., & McGreenery, C. E. (1997). Circadian rest-activity disturbances in seasonal affective disorder. *Archives of General Psychiatry, 54*, 124-130. (16)

Teitelbaum, P. (1955). Sensory control of hypothalamic hyperphagia.

Journal of Comparative and Physiological Psychology, 48, 156-163. (10)

Teitelbaum, P. (1961). Disturbances in feeding and drinking behavior after hypothalamic lesions. In M. R. Jones (Ed.), *Nebraska symposia on motivation 1961* (pp. 39-69). Lincoln, NE: University of Nebraska Press. (10)

Teitelbaum, P. & Epstein, A. N. (1962). The lateral hypothalamic syndrome. *Psychological Review, 69,* 74-90. (10)

Teitelbaum, P., Pellis, V. C., & Pellis, S. M. (1991). Can allied reflexes promote the integration of a robot's behavior? In J. A. Meyer & S. W. Wilson (Eds.), *From animals to animats: Simulation of animal behavior* (pp. 97-104). Cambridge, MA: MIT Press/Bradford Books. (8)

Teixeira, N. A., Lopes, R. C. M., & Secoli, S. R. (1995). Developmental toxicity of lithium treatment at prophylactic levels. *Brazilian Journal of Medicine and Biological Research, 28,* 230-239. (16)

Telvi, L., Leboyer, M., Chiron, C., Feingold, J., & Ponsot, G. (1994). Is Rett syndrome a chromosome breakage syndrome? *American Journal of Medical Genetics, 51,* 602-605. (5)

Tempel, D. L., Leibowitz, K. J., & Leibowitz, S. F. (1988). Effects of PVN galanin on macronutrient selection. *Peptides, 9,* 309-314. (10)

Terman, G. W., & Liebeskind, J. C. (1986). Relation of stress-induced analgesia to stimulation-produced analgesia. *Annals of the New York Academy of Sciences, 467,* 300-308. (7)

Terman, G. W., Shavitt, Y., Lewis, J. W., Cannon, J. T., & Liebeskind, J. C. (1984). Intrinsic mechanisms of pain inhibition: Activation by stress. *Science, 226,* 1270-1277. (7)

Terrace, H. S., Petitto, L. A., Sanders, R. J., & Bever, T. G. (1979). Can an ape create a sentence? *Science, 206,* 891-902. (14)

Tessier-Lavigne, M., & Goodman, C. S. (1996). The molecular biology of axon guidance. *Science, 274,* 1123-1133. (5)

Tetrud, J. W., Langston, J. W., Garbe, P. L., & Ruttenber, A. J. (1989). Mild parkinsonism in persons exposed to 1-methyl-4-phenyl-1,2,3,6-tetrahydropyridine (MPTP). *Neurology, 39,* 1483-1487. (8)

Thapar, A., Gottesman, I. I., Owen, M. J., O'Donovan, M. C., & McGuffin, P. (1994). The genetics of mental retardation. *British Journal of Psychiatry, 164,* 747-758. (5)

Thase, M. E., Trivedi, M. H., & Rush, A. J. (1995). MAOIs in the contemporary treatment of depression. *Neuropsychopharmacology, 12,* 185-219. (16)

Thibaut, F., Cordier, B., & Kuhn, J.-M. (1996). Gonadotrophin hormone releasing hormone agonist in cases of severe paraphilia: A lifetime treatment? *Psychoneuroendocrinology, 21,* 411-419. (11)

Thomas, P. K. (1988). Clinical aspects of PNS regeneration. In S. G. Waxman (Ed.), *Advances in neurology* (Vol. 47, pp. 9-29). New York: Raven Press. (15)

Thomas, R. K. (1996). Investigating cognitive abilities in animals: Unrealized potential. *Cognitive Brain Research, 3,* 157-166. (5)

Thompson, R. F. (1986). The neurobiology of learning and memory. *Science, 233,* 941-947. (13)

Ticku, M. K., & Kulkarni, S. K. (1988). Molecular interactions of ethanol with GABAergic system and potential of Ro15-4513 as an ethanol antagonist. *Pharmacology Biochemistry & Behavior, 30,* 501-510. (12)

Tinbergen, N. (1951). *The study of instinct.* Oxford, England: Oxford University Press. (Intro, 1)

Tinbergen, N. (1973). The search for animal roots of human behavior. In N. Tinbergen, *The animal in its world* (Vol. 2, pp. 161-174). Cambridge, MA: Harvard University Press. (1)

Tippin, J., & Henn, F. A. (1982). Modified leukotomy in the treatment of intractable obsessional neurosis. *American Journal of Psychiatry, 139,* 1601-1603. (4)

Tobias, P. V. (1996). The brain of the first hominids. In J.-P. Changeux & J. Chavaillon (Eds.). *Origins of the human brain* (pp. 61-81). Oxford, England: Clarendon Press. (5)

Tomac, A., Lindqvist, E., Lin, L.-F. H., Ögren, S. O., Young, D., Hoffer, B. J., & Olson, L. (1995). Protection and repair of the nigrostriatal dopaminergic system by GDNF *in vivo. Nature, 373,* 335-339. (5)

Tootell, R. B. H., Reppas, J. B., Kwong, K. K., Malach, R., Born, R. T., Brady, T. J., Rosen, B. R., & Belliveau, J. W. (1995). Functional analysis of human MT and related visual cortical areas using magnetic resonance imaging. *Journal of Neuroscience, 15,* 3215-3230. (6)

Torrey, E. F. (1986). Geographic variations in schizophrenia. In C. Shagass, R. C. Josiassen, W. H. Bridger, K. J. Weiss, D. Stoff, & G. M. Simpson (Ed.), *Biological Psychiatry 1985* (pp. 1080-1082). New York: Elsevier. (16)

Torrey, E. F., Rawlings, R., & Waldman, I. N. (1988). Schizophrenic births and viral diseases in two states. *Schizophrenia Research, 1,* 73-77. (16)

Tosini, G., & Menaker, M. (1996). Circadian rhythms in cultured mammalian retina. *Science, 272,* 419-421. (9)

Travers, S. P., Pfaffmann, C., & Norgren, R. (1986). Convergence of lingual and palatal gustatory neural activity in the nucleus of the solitary tract. *Brain Research, 365,* 305-320. (7)

Travis, A. M., & Woolsey, C. N. (1956). Motor performance of monkeys after bilateral partial and total cerebral decortications. *American Journal of Physical Medicine, 35,* 273-310. (15)

Trevarthen, C. (1974). Cerebral embryology and the split brain. In M. Kinsbourne & W. L. Smith (Eds.), *Hemispheric disconnection and cerebral function* (pp. 208-236). Springfield, IL: Charles C. Thomas. (14)

Trimble, M. R., & Thompson, P. J. (1986). Neuropsychological and behavioral sequelae of spontaneous seizures. *Annals of the New York Academy of Sciences, 462,* 284-292. (16)

Trivers, R. L. (1985). *Social evolution.* Menlo Park: Benjamin/Cummings. (1)

Trottier, Y., Devys, D., Imbert, G., Saudou, F., An, I., Lutz, Y., Weber, C., Agid, Y., Hirsch, E. C., & Mandel, J.-L. (1995). Cellular localization of the Huntington's disease protein and discrimination of the normal and mutated form. *Nature, 10,* 104-110. (8)

Tsai, G., Passani, L. A., Slusher, B. S., Carter, R., Baer, L., Kleinman, J. E., & Coyle, J. T. (1995). Abnormal excitatory neurotransmitter metabolism in schizophrenic brains. *Archives of General Psychiatry, 52,* 829-836. (16)

Ts'o, D. Y., & Gilbert, C. D. (1988). The organization of chromatic and spatial interactions in the primate striate cortex. *Journal of Neuroscience, 8,* 1712-1727. (6)

Ts'o, D. Y., & Roe, A. W. (1995). Functional compartments in visual cortex: Segregation and interaction. In M. S. Gazzaniga (Ed.), *The cognitive neurosciences* (pp. 325-337). Cambridge, MA: MIT Press. (6)

Tu, G. C., & Israel, Y. (1995). Alcohol consumption by Orientals in North America is predicted largely by a single gene. *Behavior Genetics, 25,* 59-65. (1)

Tucker, D. M. (1981). Lateral brain function, emotion, and conceptualization. *Psychological Bulletin, 89,* 19-46. (14)

Tucker, D. M., Luu, P., & Pribram, K. H. (1995). Social and emotional self-regulation. *Annals of the New York Academy of Sciences, 769,* 213-239. (4)

Turetsky, B., Cowell, P. E., Gur, R. C., Grossman, R. I., Shtasel, D. L., & Gur, R. E. (1995). Frontal and temporal lobe brain volumes in schizophrenia. *Archives of General Psychiatry, 52,* 1061-1070. (16)

Turton, M. D., O'Shea, D., Gunn, I., Beak, S. A., Edwards, C. M. B., Meeran, K., Choi, S. J., Taylor, G. M., Heath, M. M., Lambert, P. D., Wilding, J. P. H., Smith, D. M., Ghatei, M. A., Herbert, J., & Bloom, S. R. (1996). A role for glucagon-like peptide-1 in the central regulation of feeding. *Nature, 379,* 69-72. (10)

Uchino, B. N., Cacioppo, J. T., & Kiecolt-Glaser, J. K. (1996). The relationship between social support and physiological processes: A review with emphasis on underlying mechanisms and implications for health. *Psychological Bulletin, 119,* 488-531. (12)

Udin, S. B., & Scherer, W. J. (1990). Restoration of the plasticity of binocular maps by NMDA after the critical period in *Xenopus. Science, 249,* 669-672. (13)

Udry, J. R., & Morris, N. M. (1968). Distribution of coitus in the menstrual cycle. *Nature, 220,* 593-596. (11)

Unwin, N. (1995). Acetylcholine receptor channel imaged in the open state. *Nature, 373,* 37-43. (3)

Uwano, T., Nishijo, H., Ono, T., & Tamura, R. (1995). Neuronal responsiveness to various sensory stimuli, and associative learning in the rat amygdala. *Neuroscience, 68,* 339-361. (12)

Vaillant, G. E., & Milofsky, E. S. (1982). The etiology of alcoholism. *American Psychologist, 37,* 494-503. (3)

Valvo, A. (1971). *Sight restoration after long-term blindness.* New York: American Foundation for the Blind. (6)

Valzelli, L. (1973). The "isolation syndrome" in mice. *Psychopharmacologia, 31,* 305-320. (12)

Valzelli, L. (1980). *An approach to neuroanatomical and neurochemical psychophysiology.* Torino, Italy: C. G. Edizioni Medico Scientifiche. (10, 16)

Valzelli, L., & Bernasconi, S. (1979). Aggressiveness by isolation and brain serotonin turnover changes in different strains of mice. *Neuropsychobiology, 5,* 129-135. (12)

Vandenbergh, J. G. (1987). Regulation of puberty and its consequences on population dynamics of mice. *American Zoologist, 27,* 891-898. (11)

Van der Zee, C. E. E. M., Fawcett, J., & Diamond, J. (1992). Antibody to NGF inhibits collateral sprouting of septohippocampal fibers following entorhinal cortex lesion in adult rats. *Journal of Comparative Neurology, 326,* 91-100. (15)

Van Essen, D. C., & DeYoe, E. A. (1995). Concurrent processing in the primate visual cortex. In M. S. Gazzaniga (Ed.), *The cognitive neurosciences* (pp. 383-400). Cambridge, MA: MIT Press. (6)

Van Goozen, S. H. M., Frijda, N. H., Wiegant, V. M., Endert, E., & Van de Poll, N. E. (1996). The premen-
strual phase and reactions to aversive events: A study of hormonal influences on emotionality. *Psychoneuroendocrinology, 21,* 479-497. (11)

Van Hoesen, G. W. (1993). The modern concept of association cortex. *Current Opinion in Neurobiology, 3,* 150-154. (4)

Van Hoesen, G. W., Hyman, B. T., & Damasio, A. R. (1991). Entorhinal cortex pathology in Alzheimer's disease. *Hippocampus, 1,* 1-8. (13)

Van Zoeren, J. G., & Stricker, E. M. (1977). Effects of preoptic, lateral hypothalamic, or dopamine-depleting lesions on behavioral thermoregulation in rats exposed to the cold. *Journal of Comparative and Physiological Psychology, 91,* 989-999. (10)

Vargha-Khadem, F., & Passingham, R. E. (1990). Speech and language deficits. *Nature, 346,* 226. (14)

Vautrin, J. (1994). Vesicular or quantal and subquantal transmitter release. *News in Physiological Sciences, 9,* 59-64. (3)

Verrey, F., & Beron, J. (1996). Activation and supply of channels and pumps by aldosterone. *News in Physiological Sciences, 11,* 126-133. (10)

Victor, M., Adams, R. D., & Collins, G. H. (1971). *The Wernicke-Korsakoff syndrome.* Philadelphia: F. A. Davis. (13)

Viitala, J., Korpimäki, E., Palokangas, P., & Koivula, M. (1995). Attraction of kestrels to vole scent marks visible in ultraviolet light. *Nature, 373,* 425-427. (6)

Virkkunen, M., DeJong, J., Bartko, J., Goodwin, F. K., & Linnoila, M. (1989). Relationship of psychobiological variables to recidivism in violent offenders and impulsive fire setters. *Archives of General Psychiatry, 46,* 600-603. (12)

Virkkunen, M., Eggert, M., Rawlings, R., & Linnoila, M. (1996). A prospective follow-up study of alcoholic violent offenders and fire setters. *Archives of General Psychiatry, 53,* 523-529. (12)

Virkkunen, M., Nuutila, A., Goodwin, F. K., & Linnoila, M. (1987). Cerebrospinal fluid monoamine metabolite levels in male arsonists. *Archives of General Psychiatry, 44,* 241-247. (12)

Vizi, E. S. (1984). *Non-synaptic interactions between neurons: Modulation of neurochemical transmission.* Chichester, England: John Wiley. (3)

Vogel, G. W., Thompson, F. C. Jr., Thurmond, A., & Rivers, B. (1973). The effect of REM deprivation on depression. In W. P. Koella & P. Levin (Eds.), *Sleep: Physiology, biochemistry, psychology, pharmacology, clinical implications* (pp. 191-195). Basel: Karger. (16)

Volavka, J. (1990). Aggression, electroencephalography, and evoked potentials: A critical review. *Neuropsychiatry, Neuropsychology, and Behavioral Neurology, 3,* 249-259. (12)

Volkow, N. D., Ding, Y.-S., Fowler, J. S., Wang, G.-J., Logan, J., Gatley, J. S., Dewey, S., Ashby, C., Lieberman, J., Hitzemann, R., & Wolf, A. P. (1995). Is methylphenidate like cocaine? *Archives of General Psychiatry, 52,* 456-463. (3)

Vollhardt, L. T. (1991). Psychoneuroimmunology: A literature review. *American Journal of Orthopsychiatry, 61,* 35-47. (12)

von Békésy, G. (1956). Current status of theories of hearing. *Science, 123,* 779-783. (7)

von der Heydt, R. (1995). Form analysis in visual cortex. In M. S. Gazzaniga (Ed.), *The cognitive neurosciences* (pp. 365-382). Cambridge, MA: MIT Press. (6)

Waisbren, S. R., Brown, M. J., de Sonneville, L. M. J., & Levy, H. L. (1994). Review of neuropsychological functioning in treated phenylketonuria: An information-processing approach. *Acta Paediatrica, 83* (Suppl. 407), 98-103. (1)

Wald, G. (1968). Molecular basis of visual excitation. *Science, 162,* 230-239. (6)

Waldvogel, J. A. (1990). The bird's eye view. *American Scientist, 78,* 342-353. (6)

Waller, N. G., Kojetin, B. A., Bouchard, T. J. Jr., Lykken, D. T., & Tellegen, A. (1990). Genetic and environmental influences on religious interests, attitudes, and values: A study of twins reared apart and together. *Psychological Science, 1,* 138-142. (1)

Wallesch, C.-W., Henriksen, L., Kornhuber, H.-H., & Paulson, O. B. (1985). Observations on regional cerebral blood flow in cortical and subcortical structures during language production in normal man. *Brain and Language, 25,* 224-233. (14)

Wallman, J., & Pettigrew, J. D. (1985). Conjugate and disjunctive saccades in two avian species with contrasting oculomotor strategies. *Journal of Neuroscience, 5,* 1418-1428. (6)

Wan, R.-Q., Pang, K., & Olton, D. S. (1994). Hippocampal and amygdaloid involvement in nonspatial and spatial working memory in rats: Effects of delay and interference. *Behavioral Neuroscience, 108,* 866-882. (13)

Wang, H.-W., Wysocki, C. J., & Gold, G. H. (1993). Induction of olfactory receptor sensitivity in mice. *Science, 260,* 998-1000. (7)

Wang, Q., Schoenlein, R. W., Peteanu, L. A., Mathies, R. A., & Shank, C. V. (1994). Vibrationally coherent photochemistry in the femtosecond primary event of vision. *Science, 266,* 422-424. (6)

Wang, T., Okano, Y., Eisensmith, R., Huang, S. Z., Zeng, Y. T., Wilson, H. Y. L., & Woo, S. L. (1989). Molecular genetics of phenylketonuria in Orientals: Linkage disequilibrium between a termination mutation and haplotype 4 of the phenylalanine hydroxylase gene. *American Journal of Human Genetics, 45,* 675-680. (1)

Warach, S. (1995). Mapping brain pathophysiology and higher cortical function with magnetic resonance imaging. *The Neuroscientist, 1,* 221-235. (4)

Ward, I. L. (1977). Exogenous androgen activates female behavior in noncopulating, prenatally stressed male rats. *Journal of Comparative and Physiological Psychology, 91,* 465-471. (11)

Ward, I. L., & Reed, J. (1985). Prenatal stress and prepubertal social rearing conditions interact to determine sexual behavior in male rats. *Behavioral Neuroscience, 99,* 301-309. (11)

Ward, I. L., Ward, B., Winn, R. J., & Bielawski, D. (1994). Male and female sexual behavior potential of male rats prenatally exposed to the influence of alcohol, stress, or both factors. *Behavioral Neuroscience, 108,* 1188-1195. (11)

Ward, I. L., & Ward, O. B. (1985). Sexual behavior differentiation: Effects of prenatal manipulations in rats. In N. Adler, D. Pfaff, & R. W. Goy (Eds.), *Handbook of behavioral neurobiology,* Vol. 7 (pp. 77-98). New York: Plenum Press. (11)

Ward, O. B., Monaghan, E. P., & Ward, I. L. (1986). Naltrexone blocks the effects of prenatal stress on sexual behavior differentiation in male rats. *Pharmacology Biochemistry & Behavior, 25,* 573-576. (11)

Watson, C. G., Tilleskjor, C., Kucala, T., & Jacobs, L. (1984). The birth seasonality effect in nonschizophrenic psychiatric patients. *Journal of Clinical Psychology, 40,* 884-888. (16)

Watts, A. G., Kelly, A. B., & Sanchez-Watts, G. (1995). Neuropeptides and thirst: The temporal response of corticotropin-releasing hormone and neurotensin/neuromedin N gene expression in rat limbic forebrain neurons to drinking hypertonic saline. *Behavioral Neuroscience, 109,* 1146-1157. (10)

Waxman, S. G., & Ritchie, J. M. (1985). Organization of ion channels in the myelinated nerve fiber. *Science, 228,* 1502-1507. (2)

Webb, W. B. (1974). Sleep as an adaptive response. *Perceptual and Motor Skills, 38,* 1023-1027. (9)

Weber-Fox, C. M., & Neville, H. J. (1996). Maturational constraints on functional specializations for language processing: ERP and behavioral evidence in bilingual speakers. *Journal of Cognitive Neuroscience, 8,* 231-256. (14)

Weinberger, D. R. (1996). On the plausibility of "the neurodevelopmental hypothesis" of schizophrenia. *Neuropsychopharmacology, 14,* 1S-11S. (16)

Weinberger, N. M., Javid, R., & Lepan, B. (1995). Heterosynaptic long-term facilitation of sensory-evoked responses in the auditory cortex by stimulation of the magnocellular medial geniculate body in guinea pigs. *Behavioral Neuroscience, 109,* 10-17. (13)

Weindl, A. (1973). Neuroendocrine

aspects of circumventricular organs. In W. F. Ganong & L. Martini (Eds.), *Frontiers in neuroendocrinology 1973* (pp. 3-32). New York: Oxford University Press. (10)

Weiner, R. D. (1979). The psychiatric use of electrically induced seizures. *American Journal of Psychiatry, 136,* 1507-1517. (16)

Weiskrantz, L., Warrington, E. K., Sanders, M. D., & Marshall, J. (1974). Visual capacity in the hemianopic field following a restricted occipital ablation. *Brain, 97,* 709-728. (6)

Weiss, P. (1924). Die funktion transplantierter amphibienextremitäten. Aufstellung einer resonanztheorie der motorischen nerventätigkeit auf grund abstimmter endorgane [The function of transplanted amphibian limbs. Presentation of a resonance theory of motor nerve action upon tuned end organs]. *Archiv für Mikroskopische Anatomie und Entwicklungsmechanik, 102,* 635-672. (5)

Weissman, M. M., Gershon, E. S., Kidd, K. K., Prusoff, B. A., Leckman, J. F., Dibble, E., Hamovit, J., Thompson, D., Pauls, D. L., & Guroff, J. J. (1984). Psychiatric disorders in the relatives of probands with affective disorders. *Archives of General Psychiatry, 41,* 13-21. (16)

Weller, L., Weller, A., & Avinir, O. (1995). Menstrual synchrony: Only in women who are close friends? *Physiology & Behavior, 58,* 883-889. (7)

Weltzin, T. E., Fernstrom, M. H., & Kaye, W. H. (1994). Serotonin and bulimia nervosa. *Nutrition Reviews, 52,* 399-408. (10)

Wender, P. H., Kety, S. S., Rosenthal, D., Schulsinger, F., Ortmann, J., & Lunde, I. (1986). Psychiatric disorders in the biological and adoptive families of adopted individuals with affective disorders. *Archives of General Psychiatry, 43,* 923-929. (16)

Wender, P. H., Rosenthal, D., Kety, S. S., Schulsinger, F., & Welner, J. (1974). Crossfostering: A research strategy for clarifying the role of genetic and experiential factors in the etiology of schizophrenia. *Archives of General Psychiatry, 30,* 121-128. (16)

Westbrook, G. L. (1994). Glutamate receptor update. *Current Opinion in Neurobiology, 4,* 337-346. (3)

Westbrook, G. L., & Jahr, C. E. (1989). Glutamate receptors in excitatory neurotransmission. *Seminars in the Neurosciences, 1,* 103-114. (3)

Westerink, B. H. C. (1995). Brain microdialysis and its application for the study of animal behavior. *Behavioral Brain Research, 70,* 103-124. (4)

Whitam, F. L., Diamond, M., & Martin, J. (1993). Homosexual orientation in twins: A report on 61 pairs and three triplet sets. *Archives of Sexual Behavior, 22,* 187-206. (11)

White, D. P., Gibb, T. J., Wall, J. M., & Westbrook, P. R. (1995). Assessment of accuracy and analysis time of a novel device to monitor sleep and breathing in the home. *Sleep, 18,* 115-126. (9)

White, F. J., & Wang, R. Y. (1983). Differential effects of classical and atypical antipsychotic drugs on A9 and A10 dopamine neurons. *Science, 221,* 1054-1057. (16)

Whitman, B. W., & Packer, R. J. (1993). The photic sneeze reflex: Literature review and discussion. *Neurology, 43,* 868-871. (8)

Wiborg, I. M., & Dahl, A. A. (1996). Does brief dynamic psychotherapy reduce the relapse rate of panic disorder? *Archives of General Psychiatry, 53,* 689-694. (12)

Wichmann, T., Vitek, J. L., & DeLong, M. R. (1995). Parkinson's disease and the basal ganglia: Lessons from the laboratory and from neurosurgery. *The Neuroscientist, 1,* 236-244. (8)

Wiesel, T. N. (1982). Postnatal development of the visual cortex and the influence of environment. *Nature, 299,* 583-591. (6)

Wiesel, T. N., & Hubel, D. H. (1963). Single-cell responses in striate cortex of kittens deprived of vision in one eye. *Journal of Neurophysiology, 26,* 1003-1017. (6)

Wiggins, S., Whyte, P., Huggins, M., Adam, S., Theilman, J., Bloch, M., Sheps, S. B., Schechter, M. T., & Hayden, M. R., for the Canadian collaborative study of predictive testing. (1992). The psychological consequences of predictive testing for Huntington's disease. *New*

England Journal of Medicine, 327, 1401-1405. (8)

Wild, H. M., Butler, S. R., Carden, D., & Kulikowski, J. J. (1985). Primate cortical area V4 important for colour constancy but not wavelength discrimination. *Nature, 313,* 133-135. (6)

Wilkins, W. K., & Wakefield, J. (1995). Brain evolution and neurolinguistic preconditions. *Behavioral and Brain Sciences, 18,* 161-226. (5)

Willerman, L., Schultz, R., Rutledge, J. N., & Bigler, E. D. (1991). *In vivo* brain size and intelligence. *Intelligence, 15,* 223-228. (5)

Williams, C. L. (1986). A reevaluation of the concept of separable periods of organizational and activational actions of estrogens in development of brain and behavior. *Annals of the New York Academy of Sciences, 474,* 282-292. (11)

Williams, C. L., & McGaugh, J. L. (1993). Reversible lesions of the nucleus of the solitary tract attenuate the memory-modulating effects of posttraining epinephrine. *Behavioral Neuroscience, 107,* 955-962. (13)

Williams, R. W., & Herrup, K. (1988). The control of neuron number. *Annual Review of Neuroscience, 11,* 423-453. (2)

Willingham, D. B., Koroshetz, W. J., & Peterson, E. W. (1996). Motor skills have diverse neural bases: Spared and impaired skill acquisition in Huntington's disease. *Neuropsychology, 10,* 315-321. (8)

Wilson, B. A., Baddeley, A. D., & Kapur, N. (1995). Dense amnesia in a professional musician following herpes simplex virus encephalitis. *Journal of Clinical and Experimental Neuropsychology, 17,* 668-681. (13)

Wilson, C., Nomikos, G. G., Collu, M., & Fibiger, H. C. (1995). Dopaminergic correlates of motivated behavior: Importance of drive. *Journal of Neuroscience, 15,* 5169-5178. (10)

Wilson, D. S., & Sober, E. (1994). Reintroducing group selection to the human behavioral sciences. *Behavioral and Brain Sciences, 17,* 585-654. (1)

Wilson, J. D., George, F. W., & Griffin, J. E. (1981). The hormonal control of sexual development. *Science, 211,* 1278-1284. (11)

Wilson, M. A., & McNaughton, B. L. (1994). Reactivation of hippocampal ensemble memories during sleep. *Science, 265,* 676-679. (9)

Wilson, M. I., & Daly, M. (1996). Male sexual proprietariness and violence against wives. *Current Directions in Psychological Science, 5,* 2-7. (1)

Winfree, A. T. (1983). Impact of a circadian clock on the timing of human sleep. *American Journal of Physiology, 245,* R497-R504. (9)

Winson, J. (1993). The biology and function of rapid eye movement sleep. *Current Opinion in Neurobiology, 3,* 243-248. (9)

Wirz-Justice, A., Graw, P., Kräuchi, K., Gisin, B., Jochum, A., Arendt, J., Fisch, H.-U., Buddeberg, C., & Pöldinger, W. (1993). Light therapy in seasonal affective disorder is independent of time of day or circadian phase. *Archives of General Psychiatry, 50,* 929-937. (16)

Wise, R. A. (1996). Addictive drugs and brain stimulation reward. *Annual Review of Neuroscience, 19,* 319-340. (3)

Wise, R. A., & Bozarth, M. A. (1987). A psychomotor stimulant theory of addiction. *Psychological Review, 94,* 469-492. (3)

Witelson, S. F. (1985). The brain connection: The corpus callosum is larger in left-handers. *Science, 229,* 665-668. (14)

Witelson, S. F., Glezer, I. I., & Kigar, D. L. (1995). Women have greater density of neurons in posterior temporal cortex. *Journal of Neuroscience, 15,* 3418-3428. (5, 14)

Witelson, S. F., & Pallie, W. (1973). Left hemisphere specialization for language in the newborn: Neuroanatomical evidence of asymmetry. *Brain, 96,* 641-646. (14)

Wong, G. T., Gannon, K. S., & Margolskee, R. F. (1996). Transduction of bitter and sweet taste by gustducin. *Nature, 381,* 796-800. (7)

Wong-Riley, M. T. T. (1989). Cytochrome oxidase: An endogenous metabolic marker for neuronal activity. *Trends in Neurosciences, 12,* 94-101. (2)

Woodruf-Pak, D. S., Lavond, D. G., & Thompson, R. F. (1985). Trace conditioning: Abolished by cerebellar nuclear lesions but not

lateral cerebellar cortex aspirations. *Brain Research, 348,* 249-260. (13)

Woodruff-Pak, D. S., Papka, M., & Ivry, R. B. (1996). Cerebellar involvement in eyeblink classical conditioning in humans. *Neuropsychology, 10,* 443-458. (13)

Woodworth, R. S. (1934). *Psychology* (3rd ed.). New York: Henry Holt and Company. (2)

Wulfeck, B., & Bates, E. (1991). Differential sensitivity to errors of agreement and word order in Broca's aphasia. *Journal of Cognitive Neuroscience, 3,* 258-272. (14)

Wurtman, J. J. (1985). Neurotransmitter control of carbohydrate consumption. *Annals of the New York Academy of Sciences, 443,* 145-151. (3)

Yalcinkaya, T. M., Siiteri, P. K., Vigne, J.-L., Licht, P., Pavgi, S., Frank, L. G., & Glickman, S. E. (1993). A mechanism for virilization of female spotted hyenas in utero. *Science, 260,* 1929-1931. (11)

Yamamoto, T. (1984). Taste responses of cortical neurons. *Progress in Neurobiology, 23,* 273-315. (7)

Yarsh, T. L., Farb, D. H., Leeman, S. E., & Jessell, T. M. (1979). Intrathecal capsaicin depletes substance P in the rat spinal cord and produces prolonged thermal analgesia. *Science, 206,* 481-483. (7)

Yeomans, J. S., & Frankland, P. W. (1996). The acoustic startle reflex: neurons and connections. *Brain Research Reviews, 21,* 301-314. (12)

Yoon, M. (1971). Reorganization of retinotectal projection following surgical operations on the optic tectum in goldfish. *Experimental Neurology, 33,* 395-411. (5)

Yost, W. A., & Nielsen, D. W. (1977). *Fundamentals of hearing.* New York: Holt, Rinehart, & Winston. (7)

Young, A. B. (1995). Huntington's disease: Lessons from and for molecular neuroscience. *The Neuroscientist, 1,* 51-58. (8)

Young, B. J., & Leaton, R. N. (1996). Amygdala central nucleus lesions attenuate acoustic startle stimulus-evoked heart rate changes in

rats. *Behavioral Neuroscience, 110,* 228-237. (12)

Young, M. P., & Yamane, S. (1992). Sparse population coding of faces in the inferotemporal cortex. *Science, 256,* 1327-1331. (6)

Young, W. C., Goy, R. W., & Phoenix, C. H. (1964). Hormones and sexual behavior. *Science, 143,* 212-218. (11)

Yuasa, J., Hirano, S., Yamagata, M., & Noda, M. (1996). Visual projection map specified by topographic expression of transcription factors in the retina. *Nature, 382,* 632-635. (5)

Zaidel, D., & Sperry, R. W. (1977). Some long-term motor effects of cerebral commissurotomy in man. *Neuropsychologia, 15,* 193-204. (14)

Zald, D. H., & Kim, S. W. (1996). Anatomy and function of the orbital frontal cortex, I: Anatomy, neurocircuitry, and obsessive-compulsive disorder. *Journal of Neuropsychiatry and Clinical Neurosciences, 8,* 125-138. (12)

Zeigler, H. P., Jacquin, M. F., & Miller, M. G. (1985). Trigeminal orosensation and ingestive behavior in the rat. *Progress in Psychobiology and Physiological Psychology, 11,* 63-196. (10)

Zeki, S. (1980). The representation of colours in the cerebral cortex. *Nature, 284,* 412-418. (6)

Zeki, S. (1983). Colour coding in the cerebral cortex: The responses of wavelength-selective and colour-coded cells in monkey visual cortex to changes in wavelength composition. *Neuroscience, 9,* 767-781. (6)

Zeki, S. (1993). The visual association cortex. *Current Opinion in Neurobiology, 3,* 155-159. (4)

Zeki, S., & Shipp, S. (1988). The functional logic of cortical connections. *Nature, 335,* 311-317. (6)

Zhang, Y., Proenca, R., Maffei, M., Barone, M., Leopold, L., & Friedman, J. M. (1994). Positional cloning of the mouse *obese* gene and its human homologue. *Nature, 372,* 425-432. (10)

Zhuo, M., Hu, Y., Schultz, C., Kandel, E. R., & Hawkins, R. D. (1994).

Role of guanylyl cyclase and cGMP-dependent protein kinase in long-term potentiation. *Nature, 368,* 635-639. (13)

Zigmond, M. J., Abercrombie, E. D., Berger, T. W., Grace, A. A., & Stricker, E. M. (1990). Compensations after lesions of central dopaminergic neurons: Some clinical and basic implications. *Trends in Neurosciences, 13,* 290-296. (8, 15)

Zihl, J., von Cramon, D., & Mai, N. (1983). Selective disturbance of movement vision after bilateral brain damage. *Brain, 106,* 313-340. (6)

Zilles, K., Armstrong, E., Moser, K. H., Schleicher, A., & Stephan, H. (1989). Gyrification in the cerebral cortex of primates. *Brain, Behavior, and Evolution, 34,* 143-150. (5)

Zinkland, W. C., Thompson, C., Salama, A. I., & Patel, J. (1992). Excitatory amino acid-evoked calcium influx and calcium-dependent neurotoxicity in rat cortical cultures. *Annals of the New York Academy of Sciences, 648,* 355-357. (15)

Zipursky, R. B., Lim, K. O., Sullivan, E. V., Brown, B. W., & Pfefferbaum, A. (1992). Widespread cerebral gray matter volume deficits in schizophrenia. *Archives of General Psychiatry, 49,* 195-205. (16)

Zuckerman, M. (1995). Good and bad humors: Biochemical bases of personality and its disorders. *Psychological Science, 6,* 325-332. (3)

Zurif, E. B. (1980). Language mechanisms: A neuropsychological perspective. *American Scientist, 68,* 305-311. (14)

Zwislocki, J. J. (1981). Sound analysis in the ear: A history of discoveries. *American Scientist, 69,* 184-192. (7)

Credits

Chapter 2: 27: Figure 2.5 from "Dendritic Spines of CA1 Pyramidal Cells in the Rat Hippocampus: Serial Electron Microscopy with Reference to their Biophysical Characteristics," by K. M. Harris and J. K. Stevens, 1989, *Journal of Neuroscience, 9,* pp. 2982–2997. Copyright © 1989 Society for Neuroscience. Reprinted by permission. **29:** Figure 2.8, Part e, from R. G. Coss, *Brain Research,* October 1982. Reprinted by permission of R. G. Coss. **31:** Figure 2.10 reprinted by permission from "Changes in Dendritic Branching of Adult Mammalian Neurons Revealed by Repeated Imaging in Situ," by D. Purves and R. D. Hadley, *Nature, 315,* pp. 404–406. Copyright © 1985 Macmillan Magazines Ltd. Reprinted by permission of D. Purves and Macmillan Magazines Ltd.

Chapter 3: 60: Figure 3.12a, adapted from "Autoimmune Response to Acetylcholine Receptors in Myasthenia Gravis and Its Animal Model," by J. Lindstrom. In H. G. Kunkel and F. J. Dixon, Eds., *Advances in Immunology, 27,* p. 10. Copyright © 1979 Academic Press. Reprinted by permission.

Chapter 4: 82: Figure 4.6 from *Biology: The Unity and Diversity of Life,* 5th Edition, by C. Starr and R. Taggart, p. 340. Copyright © 1989 Wadsworth Publishing Company. Reprinted by permission. **94:** Figure 4.17 from *The Anatomy of the Nervous System* by S. W. Ranson and S. L. Clark, 1959. Reprinted by permission of W. B. Saunders Co. **96:** Figure 4.21 adapted from *The Cerebral Cortex of Man* by W. Penfield and T. Rasmussen. Copyright © 1950 Macmillan Publishing Co., Inc. Renewed 1978 by Theodore Rasmussen. Reprinted by permission. **98:** Figure 4.23 after *The Prefrontal Cortex* by J. M. Fuster, 1989. Copyright 1989 Raven Press. Reprinted by permission. **103:** Figure 4.27 from *A Stereotaxic Atlas of the Rat Brain,* Second Edition, by L. J. Pellegrino, A. S. Pellegrino, and A. J. Cushman, 1979. Copyright © 1979 Plenum Publishing. Reprinted by permission. **108:** Figure 4.30 reprinted from *Neuroscience: From the Molecular to the Cognitive,* by R. Hari, 1994, p. 165, with kind permission from Elsevier Science-NL, Sara Burgerhartstraat 25, 1055 KV Amsterdam, The Netherlands.

Chapter 5: 119: Figure 5.6 from "Motoneuronal Death in the Human Fetus," by N. G. Forger and S. M. Breedlove, *Journal of Comparative Neurology, 264,* pp. 118–122. Copyright © 1987 Alan R. Liss, Inc. Reprinted by permission of N. G. Forger. **124:** Figure 5.13 from "Elimination of Synapses in the Developing Nervous System," by D. Purves and J. W. Lichtman, 1980, *Science, 210,* pp. 153–157. Copyright © 1980 by the AAAS. Reprinted by permission. **126:** Figure 5.16 reprinted with permission from "Increased Cortical Representation of the Fingers of the Left Hand in String Players," by T. Elbert, C. Pantev, C. Wienbruch, B. Rockstroh, and E. Taub, *Science, 270,* pp. 305–307. Copyright © 1995 American Association for the Advancement of Science. **132:** Figure 5.20 reprinted with permission from "Linked Regularities in the Development and Evolution of Mammalian Brains," by B. L. Finlay and R. B. Darlington, 1995, *Science, 268,* pp. 1578–1584. Copyright © 1995 American Association for the Advancement of Science. **133:** Figure 5.21 based on "Animal Intelligence as Encephalization," by H. J. Jerison, *Philosophical Transactions of the Royal Society of London, B 308,* pp. 21–35, 1985. Reprinted by permission of the Royal Society and H. J. Jerison. **134:** Figure 5.22 from "Primate Language and Cognition: Common Ground," by D. Rumbaugh, Fall 1995, *Social Research, 62,* p. 717. Copyright © 1995 New School for Social Research. **137:** Figure 5.24 from "Problems of Ontogeny and Phylogeny in Brain-Size Evolution," by T. W. Deacon, 1990, *Journal of Primatology, 11,* pp. 237–282. Copyright © 1990 Plenum Publishing. Reprinted by permission. **138:** Figure 5.25 from "Brain-Language Coevolution," by T. W. Deacon. In J. A. Hawkins & M. Gell-Mann, Eds., *The Evolution of Human Languages,* pp. 49–83. Copyright © 1992 Addison-Wesley. Reprinted by permission of T. W. Deacon.

Chapter 6: 145: Figure 6.4a, based on "Organization of the Primate Retina," by J. E. Dowling and B. B. Boycott, *Proceedings of the Royal Society of London,* B, 1966, 166, pp. 80–111. Used by permission of the Royal Society of London and John Dowling. **150:** Figure 6.9 adapted from "Visual Pigments of Rods and Cones in a Human Retina," by J. K. Bowmaker and H. J. A. Dartnall, *Journal of Physiology,* 298, pp. 501–511. Reprinted by permission. **162:** Figure 6.22 top, from "Receptive Fields of Single Neurons in the Cat's Striate Cortex," by D. H. Hubel and T. N. Wiesel, 1959, *Journal of Physiology,* 148, pp. 574–591. Copyright Cambridge University Press, UK. Reprinted by permission. **164:** Figure 6.25 from "The Visual Cortex of the Brain," by David H. Hubel, November 1963, *Scientific American,* 209, 5, p. 62. Copyright © Scientific American, Inc.

Chapter 7: 185: Figure 7.7 adapted from "Mapping of Stimulus Features and Meaning in Gerbil Auditory Cortex with 2-Deoxyglucose and c-Fos Antibodies," by H. Scheich and W. Zuschratter, *Behavioral Brain Research,* 66, pp. 195–205. Copyright © 1995 with kind permission from Elsevier Science-NL, Sara Burgerhartstraat 25, 1055 KV Amsterdam, The Netherlands. **193:** Figure 7.14 from *Biology: The Unity and Diversity of Life,* 5th Edition, by C. Starr and R. Taggart, p. 338. Copyright © 1989 Wadsworth Publishing Co. Reprinted by permission.

Chapter 8: 214: Figure 8.3 from *Biology: The Unity and Diversity of Life,* 5th Edition, by C. Starr and R. Taggart, p. 331. Copyright © 1989 Wadsworth Publishing Company. Reprinted by permission. **214:** Figure 8.4 from *Biology: The Unity and Diversity of Life,* 5th Edition, by C. Starr and R. Taggart, p. 395. Copyright © 1989 Wadsworth Publishing Company. Reprinted by permission. **229:** Figure 8.15 from "Cognitive Spatial-Motor

Process 7. The Making of Movements . . .," by J. T. Lurito, T. Georgakopoulos, and A. P. Georgopoulos, 1991, *Experimental Brain Research, 87,* pp. 562–580. Copyright © 1991 Springer-Verlag New York Publishers. Reprinted by permission. **234:** Figure 8.18 from "Mortality Data for the U.S. for Deaths Due to and Related to Twenty Neurologic Diseases," by V. Chandra, N. E. Bharucha, and B. S. Shoenberg, 1984, *Neuroepidemiology, 3,* pp. 149–168. Reprinted by permission of S. Karger AG, Basel and V. Chandra. **235:** Figure 8.20 from "Dopamine in the Extrapyramidal Motor Function: A Study Based Upon the MPTP-Induced Primate Model of Parkinsonism," by C. C. Chiueh, 1988, *Annals of the New York Academy of Sciences, 515,* p. 223. Reprinted by permission.

Chapter 9: 243: Figure 9.1 from "Phase Control of Activity in a Rodent," by P. J. DeCoursey, *Cold Spring Harbor Symposia on Quantitative Biology,* 1960, 25:49–55. Reprinted by permission of Cold Spring Harbor Laboratory and P. J. DeCoursey. **243:** Figure 9.2 from "Sleep-Onset Insomniacs Have Delayed Temperature Rhythms," by M. Morris, L. Lack, and D. Dawson, *Sleep,* 1990, 13:1–14. Reprinted by permission. **244:** Figure 9.3 from *Sleep and Wakefulness* by N. Kleitman. Copyright © 1963 by the University of Chicago. **254:** Figure 9.11 polysomnograph records provided by T. E. LeVere. **257:** Figure 9.13 from "Ontogenetic Development of Human Sleep-Dream Cycle," by H. P. Roffwarg, J. N. Muzio, and W. C. Dement, *Science,* 1966, *152:*604–609. Copyright 1966 by the AAAS. Reprinted by permission.

Chapter 10: 288: Figure 10.18 reprinted by permission of the University of Nebraska Press from "Disturbances in Feeding and Drinking Behavior After Hypothalamic Lesions," by P. Teitelbaum, pp. 39–69, in M. R. Jones, Ed., 1961, *Nebraska Symposium on Motivation.* Copyright © 1961 by the University of Nebraska Press. Copyright © renewed 1989 by the University of Nebraska Press.

Chapter 11: 298: Figure 11.1 from *Biology: The Unity and Diversity of Life,* Fifth Edition, by C. Starr and R. Taggart. Copyright © 1989 Wadsworth Publishing Company. Reprinted by permission. **300:** Figure 11.2 from *Biology: The Unity and Diversity of Life,* Fifth Edition, by C. Starr and R. Taggart. Copyright © 1989 Wadsworth Publishing Company. Reprinted by permission. **301:** Figure 11.4 from *Biology: The Unity and Diversity of Life,* Fifth Edition, by C. Starr and R. Taggart. Copyright © 1989 Wadsworth Publishing Company. Reprinted by permission. **301:** Figure 11.5 from *Biology: The Unity and Diversity of Life,* Fifth Edition, by C. Starr and R. Taggart. Copyright © 1989 Wadsworth Publishing Company. Reprinted by permission. **302:** Figure 11.6 from *Biology: The Unity and Diversity of Life,* Fifth Edition, by C. Starr and R. Taggart. Copyright © 1989 Wadsworth Publishing Company. Reprinted by permis-

sion. **302:** Figure 11.7 from *Biology: The Unity and Diversity of Life,* Fifth Edition, by C. Starr and R. Taggart. Copyright © 1989 Wadsworth Publishing Company. Reprinted by permission. **302:** Figure 11.8 from *Biology: The Unity and Diversity of Life,* Fifth Edition, by C. Starr and R. Taggart. Copyright © 1989 Wadsworth Publishing Company. Reprinted by permission. **309:** Figure 11.13 from "Rise in Female-Initiated Sexual Activity at Ovulation and its Suppression by Oral Contraceptives," by D. B. Adams, A. R. Gold and A. D. Burt, 1978, *New England Journal of Medicine, 299,* pp. 1145–1150. Reprinted by permission from *The New England Journal of Medicine.* **320:** Figure 11.20 reprinted with permission from "A Difference in Hypothalamic Structure Between Heterosexual and Homosexual Men," by S. LeVay, *Science, 253,* pp. 1034–1037. Copyright © 1991 American Association for the Advancement of Science. **320:** Figure 11.21 reprinted with permission from "A Difference in Hypothalamic Structure Between Heterosexual and Homosexual Men," by S. LeVay, *Science, 253,* pp. 1034–1037. Copyright © 1991 American Association for the Advancement of Science.

Chapter 12: 325: Figure 12.2 redrawn from "Studies on Limbic Systems 'Visceral Brain', and Their Bearing on Psychosomatic Problems," by P. D. MacLean. In E. D. Wittkower and R. A. Cleghorn, Eds., *Recent Developments in Psychosomatic Medicine.* Copyright 1954 Sir Isaac Pitman & Sons, Ltd. Used by permission of J. B. Lippincott Co. and Sir Isaac Pitman & Sons, Ltd. **340:** Figure 12.12 from "Fear and the Human Amygdala," by R. Adolphs, D. Tranel, H. Damasio, and A. Damasio, *Journal of Neuroscience, 15,* pp. 5879–5891. Copyright © 1995 Oxford University Press. Reprinted by permission.

Chapter 13: 356: Figure 13.8 after "Dendritic Changes," by A. B. Scheibel, p. 70. In B. Reisberg, Ed., *Alzheimer's Disease,* 1983, Free Press. **365:** Figure 13.16 based on "Learning of Leg Position by the Ventral Nerve Cord in Headless Insects," by G. A. Horridge, *Proceedings of the Royal Society of London,* B, 1962, 157, pp. 33–52. Used by permission of the Royal Society of London and G. A. Horridge. **366:** Figure 13.19 redrawn from "Neuronal Mechanisms of Habituation and Dishabituation of the Gill-Withdrawal Reflex in Aplysia," by V. Castellucci, H. Pinsker, I. Kupfermann, and E. R. Kandel, *Science,* 1970, *167,* pp. 1745–1748. Copyright © 1970 by the AAAS. Used by permission of AAAS and V. Castellucci.

Chapter 14: 378: Figure 14.4 from "Subcortical Transfer of Higher Order Information: More Illusory than Real?" by A. Kingstone and M. S. Gazzaniga, 1995, *Neuropsychology, 9,* pp. 321–328. Copyright © 1995 by the American Psychological Association. Reprinted with permission. **381:** Figure 14.7 from "Human Brain: Left-Right Asymmetries in Temporal Speech Region," by N. Geschwind and W. Levitsky, 1968, *Science, 161,* pp. 186–187. Copyright © 1968 by the

AAAS. Reprinted by permission of AAAS and N. Geschwind. **394:** Figure 14.16 from "Williams Syndrome: An Unusual Neuropsychological Profile," by U. Bellugi, P. P. Wang, and T. L. Jernigan. In S. H. Broman and J. Grafman, Eds., *Atypical Cognitive Deficits in Developmental Disorders.* Copyright © 1987 Lawrence Erlbaum. Reprinted by permission. **396:** Figure 14.17 reprinted from "Task-Determined Strategies of Visual Process," by G. Geiger, J. Y. Lettvin, and O. Zegarra-Moran, 1992, *Cognitive Brain Research, 1,* pp. 39–52, 1992 with kind permission of Elsevier Science-NL, Sara Burgerhartstraat 25, 1055 KV Amsterdam, The Netherlands.

Chapter 15: 409: Figure 15.10 redrawn by permission from *The Annual Review of Neuroscience, Volume 6,* copyright 1983 by Annual Reviews, Inc. Used by permission of Annual Reviews, Inc. and Jon H. Kaas.

Chapter 16: 425: Figure 16.4 bottom graphs adapted from *Sleep* by J. Allan Hobson, Scientific American Library, 1989. Reprinted by permission of W. H. Freeman and Company. **426:** Figure 16.5 from *Psychiatric Mental Health Nursing* by E. Janosik and J. Davies, p. 173. Copyright © 1986 Boston: Jones and Bartlett Publishers. Reprinted with permission. **426:** Figure 16.6 based on "Two-Day Cycles of Alternating Good and Bad Behavior in Psychotic Patients," by C. P. Richter, 1938, *Archives of Neurology and Psychiatry, 39,* pp. 587–598. Copyright © 1938 American Medical Association. Reprinted by permission. **434:** Figure 16.11 from "Express Saccades and Smooth Pursuit Eye Movement Function in Schizophrenic Affective Disorder and Normal Subjects," by A. B. Sereno and P. S. Holzman, 1993, *Journal of Cognitive Neuroscience, 5,* pp. 303–316. Copyright © 1993 MIT Press. Reprinted by permission. **438:** Figure 16.16 from "Antipsychotic Drug Doses and Neuroleptic/Dopamine Receptors," by P. Seeman, T. Lee, M. Chau-Wong, and K. Wong, 1976, *Nature, 261,* pp. 717–719. Copyright © 1976 Macmillan Magazines Limited. Reprinted by permission of Nature and Phillip Seeman.

Appendix B: 453: Excerpts from "Policies on the Use of Animals and Human Subjects in Neuroscience Research," Society for Neuroscience. Reprinted by permission.

Endsheet Quotations: Beach, F. A., 1988, "In memoriam: Frank A. Beach." *Hormones and Behavior, 22,* 419–443; and personal communication. **Cannon, W. B.,** 1945, *The way of an investigator.* New York: Norton. **Dement, W. C.,** 1972, *Some must watch while some must sleep.* San Francisco: W. H. Freeman. **Geschwind, N.,** 1965, "Disconnexion syndromes in animals and man." *Brain, 88,* 237–294, 585–644. **Goldman-Rakic, P. S.,** 1988, "Topography of cognition: Parallel distributed networks in primate association cortex." *Annual Review of Neuroscience, 11,* 137–156 (p. 152). **Hebb, D. O.,** 1949, *Organization of behavior,* p. xiii. New York: John Wiley & Sons. **Hubel, D.:**

personal communication. **Ito, M.:** personal communication. **Kandel, E. R.:** personal communication. **Lashley, K. S.,** 1930, "Basic neural mechanisms in behavior." *Psychology Review, 37,* 1–24. **Levi-Montalcini, R.,** 1988, *In praise of imperfection,* p. 94. New York: Basic Books. **Levy, J.:** personal communication. **McGaugh, J. L.:** personal communication. **Pert, C.:** personal communication. **Ramón y Cajal,** S., 1937, "Recollections of my life." *Memoirs of the American Philosophical Society,* 8, parts 1 and 2. **Richter, C. P.:** personal communication. **Rumbaugh, D.,** and **S. Savage-Rumbaugh:** personal communication. **Shatz, C. J.:** personal communication. **Sherrington, C. S.,** 1941, *Man on his nature,* p. 104. New York: Macmillan. **Sperry, R. W.,** 1975, "In search of psyche." In F. G. Worden, J. P. Swazey, & G. Adelman, Eds., *The neurosciences: Paths of discovery,* pp. 425–434. Cambridge, MA: MIT Press. **Wiesel, T. N.,** 1982, "Postnatal development of the visual cortex and the influence of environment." *Nature, 299,* 583–591.

Photo Credits

Introduction: xxii, Courtesy of the Cincinnati Zoo; **2,** left, Steve Maslowski/Photo Researchers; **2,** right, Frank Siteman/Stock Boston; **3,** Gregory Dimijian/Photo Researchers.

Chapter 1: 4, Biophoto Associates/Science Source/Photo Researchers; **11,** F. J. Hiersche/Okapia/Photo Researchers; **13,** Owen Franken/Stock Boston; **19,** Courtesy of the Foundation for Biomedical Research; **20,** top left, Gontier/Photo Researchers; **20,** left center, David M. Barron/Animals Animals; **20,** left bottom, Hank Morgan/Science Source/Photo Researchers; **20,** right top, G. J. Bernard/Animals Animals; **20,** right bottom, Frans Lanting/Photo Researchers.

Chapter 2: 22, CNRI/SPL/Photo Researchers; **26,** Courtesy of Dr. Robert Jacobs, Colorado College; **30,** top, Nancy Kedersha/UCLA/SPL/Photo Researchers; **30,** bottom, Nancy Kedersha/UCLA/SPL/Photo Researchers; **37,** Fritz Goro

Chapter 3: 46, Omikron/Science Source/Photo Researchers; **58,** left, Micrograph courtesy of Dennis M. D. Landis; **58,** right, From "Studying neural organization in Aplysia with the scanning electron microscope" by E. R. Lewis et al., *Science,* 1969, 165:1142. Copyright 1969 by the AAAS. Reprinted by permission of AAAS and E. R. Lewis; **60,** Victor Englebert/Photo Researchers; **68,** From "Cocaine-induced reduction of glucose utilization in human brain" by E. D. London et al., *Archives of General Psychiatry,* 1990, 47:567–574. Copyright 1990, American Medical Association. Used by permission of AMA and E. D. London.

Chapter 4: 76, Hank Morgan/Rainbow; **81,** left, Manfred Kage/Peter Arnold, Inc.; **81,**

right, Manfred Kage/Peter Arnold, Inc.; **86,** Courtesy of Dr. Dana Copeland; **89,** Courtesy of Dr. Dana Copeland; **93,** Courtesy of Dr. Dana Copeland; **93,** Courtesy of Dr. Dana Copeland; **102,** Provided by James W. Kalat; **104,** Martin Rotker/Photo Researchers; **106,** right, Dan McCoy/Rainbow; **107,** Dan McCoy/Rainbow; **108,** Courtesy of Michael E. Phelps and John C. Mazziotta, University of California, Los Angeles, School of Medicine; **109,** left, Burt Glinn/Magnum; **109,** right, Courtesy of Karen Berman and Daniel Weinberger, National Institute of Mental Health.

Chapter 5: 112, Geoff Tompkinson/SPL/ Photo Researchers; **114,** top, Doug Goodman/Monkmeyer Press; **114,** bottom, Courtesy of Dr. Dana Copeland; **117,** From F. M. Benes, M. Turtle, Y. Khan, & Faral. "Myelination of a key relay zone in the hippocampal formation," *Archives of General Psychiatry,* 51:477–484. Copyright 1994 American Medical Association; **118,** From "Development of glomerular pattern visualized in the olfactory bulbs of living mice" by A. S. LaMantia and D. Purves, *Nature,* 1989, 341:646–649. Reprinted by permission from Nature. Copyright 1989 Macmillan Magazines Ltd. Photo courtesy of Dale Purves; **125,** From "Spine stems on tectal interneurons are shortened by social stimulation," by R. G. Coss and A. Globus, *Science,* 1978, 200:787-790. Copyright 1978 by the AAAS. Reprinted by permission of AAAS and Richard G. Coss. **127,** George Steinmetz; **131,** Photo by David Hinds, courtesy of Sharon L. Cummings, Ph.D., University of California, Davis; **137,** left, FPG International; **137,** right, Courtesy of Dr. Thomas Harvey.

Chapter 6: 140, Tom McHugh/Photo Researchers; **144,** Chase Smith; **145,** bottom, Ed Reschke; **148,** right, Micrograph courtesy of E. R. Lewis, F. S. Werblin, and Y. Y. Zeevi; **151,** right, West Rim Enterprises; **154,** From *The Retina* by John E. Dowling, 1987, Belknap Press of Harvard University Press. Micrograph by M. Tachibana and A. Kaneko. Reprinted by permission of John E. Dowling; **155,** Don Wong/Science Source/Photo Researchers; **159,** left, 1997 Artists Right Society ARS, New York, ADAGP, Paris; **159,** right, 1997 Artists Rights Society ARS, New York, ADAGP, Paris; **175,** Courtesy of Helmut V. Hirsch.

Chapter 7: 178, Chip Henderson/Tony Stone Images; **182,** By permission of A. J. Hudspeth. Photos courtesy of A. J. Hudspeth, R. Jacobs, P. Leake, and M. Miller; **192,** Ed Reschke; **195,** left, From "Multiple representations of pain in human cerebral cortex," *Science,* 251:1355–1358. Used by permission of Dr. Jeanne D. Talbot, Université de Montreal; **195,** right, Coco McCoy/ Rainbow; **201,** SIU/Peter Arnold, Inc.

Chapter 8: 210, Brian Bailey/Tony Stone Images; **212,** Jerry Wachter/Focus on Sports; **213,** left top, Ed Reschke; **213,** center top, Ed Reschke; **213,** right top, Ed

Reschke; **213,** bottom, Ed Reschke; **215,** Bill Curtsinger; **219,** left, Johnny Johnson/Natural Selection; **219,** right, L. West/The National Audubon Society/Photo Researchers; **227,** From "Shared neural substrates controlling hand movements in human motor cortex," by J. Sanes, J. Donoghue, V. Thangaraj, R. Edelman, & S. Warach, *Science,* 1995, 268:1774–1778. Copyright 1995 by AAAS. Reprinted by permission of AAAS and J. Sanes; **235,** From "Dopamine in the extrapyramidal motor function: A study based upon the MPTP-induced primate model of Parkinsonism" by C. C. Chiueh, 1998, *Annals of the New York Academy of Sciences,* 515:226–248. Reprinted by permission of the New York Academy of Sciences and C. C. Chiueh; **237,** Courtesy of Robert E. Schmidt, Washington University.

Chapter 9: 240, Norbert Wu; **247,** top, From "Suprachiasmatic nucleus: Use of 14-C-labeled deoxyglucose uptake as a functional marker" by W. J. Schwartz and H. Gainer, *Science,* 1977, 197:1089–1091. Copyright by the AAAS. Used by permission of AAAS and W. J. Schwartz; **247,** bottom, Eviatar Nevo; **253,** Photo from Richard Nowitz; **257,** Tom McHugh/Photo Researchers; **264,** From A. R. Morrison, L. D. Sanford, W. A. Ball, G. L. Mann, and R. J. Ross 1995, "Stimulus-elicited behavior in rapid eye movement sleep without atonia." *Behavioral Neuroscience,* 109:972–979.

Chapter 10: 268, Jeff Lepore/Photo Researchers; **273,** Johnny Johnson/Animals Animals; **274,** A. Cosmos Blank/NAS/ Photo Researchers; **276,** Leonard Lee Rue III/Animals Animals; **276,** James Simon/Photo Researchers; **281,** Gunter Ziesler/Bruce Coleman; **288,** Yoav Levy/Phototake; **290,** Stephen Dalton/Photo Researchers; **291,** John Sholtis/The Rockefeller University; **292,** From "Peptide YY PYY, , a potent orexigenic agent" by J. E. Morley, A. S. Levine, M. Grace and J. Kneip, *Brain Research,* 1985, 341:200–203.

Chapter 11: 296, Gerry Ellis/Nature Photography; **305,** Courtesy of Kay E. Holekamp; **311,** From "A defect in nurturing in mice lacking the immediate early gene fosB," by J. R. Brown, H. Ye, R. T. Bronson, P. Dikkes, and M. E. Greenberg, *Cell,* 1996, 86:297–309; **311,** From J. R. Brown et al., 1996; **316,** From *Abnormal Sexual Development* by D. D. Federman, 1967. Used by permission of W. B. Saunders Company; **319,** From "Sex-hormone-dependent brain differentiation and sexual functions" by G. Dorner, in G. Dorner Ed., *Endocrinology of sex.* Copyright 1975 by permission of Johann Ambrosius Barth; **320,** From "A difference in hypothalamic structure between heterosexual and homosexual men" by S. LeVay, *Science,* 1991, 253:1034–1037. Copyright 1991 by the AAAS.

Name Index

George, F. W., 304
Georgopoulos, A. P., 229
Gerrish, C. J., 274
Gersdorff, M. C. H., 185
Gerstein, G. L., 168
Geschwind, Norman, 381, 382–384, 389, 395
Getchell, M. L., 205
Getchell, T. V., 205
Geva, E., 395
Ghetti, B., 355
Giancola, P. R., 335
Gianoulakis, C., 73
Gibb, R., 412
Gibb, T. J., 265
Gibbs, F. P., 246
Gibbs, J., 283
Gilbert, C. D., 160, 173, 408
Gillard, E. R., 291
Gillespie, D. D., 423
Gillette, M. U., 249
Gillette, R., 246
Gillin, J. A., 264
Gillin, J. C., 424
Ginns, E. I., 425
Ginsberg, M. D., 401
Giros, B., 63, 68
Giuliani, D., 308
Gjedde, A., 33
Glanzman, D. L., 370
Glaser, J. H., 306
Glaser, R., 328, 330
Glass, A. V., 389
Glendenning, K. K., 184
Glezer, I. I., 136, 384
Glick, S. D., 407
Glickman, S. E., 305
Globus, A., 125
Gloning, I., 96
Gloning, K., 96
Goate, A., 355
Cödecke, I., 172
Goff, W. R., 257
Gold, A. R., 309
Gold, C. H., 205, 207
Gold, P. E., 351
Gold, P. W., 293
Gold, R. M., 288
Goldberg, E., 104
Goldberg, Rube, 181
Goldberg, T. E., 436
Golding, J. M., 337
Goldman, B. D., 310
Goldman, Patricia, 413, 414
Goldman, S. A., 30
Goldman-Rakic, P. S., 98, 114, 228, 351, 352, 361, 434, 436
Goldschmidt, R. B., 357
Goldspink, G., 214
Goldstein, L. A., 306
Goldstein, M., 58, 333
Goldstein, R. B., 337
Golgi, Camillo, 26
Goodale, M. A., 228
Goodman, C. S., 121
Goodwin, F. K., 335, 425
Gopnik, M., 394
Gordon, J. A., 172
Gore, J. C., 165
Gorman, L. K., 356
Gorski, R. A., 303, 304, 306, 319
Gosler, A. G., 290
Gosnell, B. A., 287
Gottesman, I. I., 127, 432, 433

Götz, R., 118
Gougis, G., 319
Goy, R. W., 303, 306
Grabowski, T. J., 393
Grace, A. A., 408
Grace, M., 291, 292
Grace, O., 310
Grafman, J., 193
Grafton, S. T., 349
Grant, J., 395
Graves, J. A. M., 303
Graybiel, A. M., 88, 226
Graziadei, P. P. C., 31
Graziano, M. S. A., 96
Green, D. J., 246
Green, S. J., 202
Greenberg, M. E., 311
Greene, G. C., 250
Greene, R. W., 262
Greenlee, M. W., 166
Greenwood, J. J. D., 290
Greenwood, M. R. C., 291
Greist, J. H., 337
Gresty, M. A., 190
Griffin, D. R., 179
Griffin, J. D., 273
Griffin, J. E., 304
Grill, H. J., 284
Grillon, C., 338
Grisham, W., 306
Gross, C. G., 96, 147, 165
Gross, R. A., 341
Grossberg, S., 243
Grosser, B. I., 206
Grossman, M., 352
Grossman, S. P., 287
Grove, W. M., 430
Growdon, J. H., 355
Grunze, H. C. R., 262
Grzanna, R., 406
Gubernick, D. J., 312
Guerrero, L., 316
Guidotti, A., 341
Guillemot, F., 103
Guisez, Y., 291
Gulyás, B., 260
Gurevich, E. V., 439
Gusella, J. F., 237
Gustafsson, B., 368
Guyton, A. C., 36
Gwinner, E., 242
Gwirtsman, H., 294

Haber, J., 400
Habib, M., 382
Hadley, R. D., 31
Hagman, J. O., 395
Haimov, I., 248, 249
Halaas, J. L., 291
Halaris, A. E., 287
Haley, J., 430
Hall, M. J., 203
Hallett, M., 408
Halliday, G. M., 384
Hamer, D. H., 318
Hamilton, R. B., 203
Hamilton, W. D., 14
Hamm, R. J., 310
Hammer, M., 367
Hammer, N. J., 289
Haney, M., 293
Harada, T., 315
Harasty, J., 384
Hargens, A. R., 215

Hari, R., 107
Harper, C. G., 73
Harris, G. C., 69
Harris, K. M., 27
Harris, R. A., 67
Hart, B. L., 286
Hartig, P., 63
Hartline, H. K., 156
Harvey, T., 136
Harvey, Thomas, 137
Harwich, C., 245
Hastey, J. M., 266
Hauser, M., 185
Hawkins, R. A., 105
Hawkins, R. D., 368
Haxby, J. V., 393
Hayman, C. A. G., 353
He, S., 164
Healy, S. D., 359
Heath, A., 9
Heath, A. C., 427
Hebb, Donald, 349, 350, 351
Hebert, M., 332
Heck, G. L., 202, 203
Heeb, M. M., 307
Heffner, H. E., 187
Heffner, R. S., 187
Heikkila, R. E., 234
Heilman, K. S., 403
Heimbuch, R., 421
Heinrichs, R. W., 430
Heller, H. C., 263
Heller, W., 379
Helmholtz, Hermann von, 149
Hendriks, W., 246
Henn, F. A., 99
Hennig, R., 215
Henriksen, L., 392, 393
Herbert, T. B., 329
Hering, Ewald, 150
Herkenham, M., 71, 84
Herman, L. M., 388
Hernandez, L., 287, 289, 292
Hernandez, T. D., 405
Herrero, S., 179
Herrmann, K., 126
Herron, J., 382
Herrup, K., 24
Hessler, N. A., 368
Hettinger, T. P., 203
Hibbard, L. S., 105
Hichwa, R. D., 393
Hickock, G., 390
Higgins, D. A., 333
Higley, J. D., 335
Hill, D. L., 287
Hillis, A. E., 392
Hind, J. E., 183
Hinds, David, 131
Hines, M., 303, 306
Hirano, S., 122
Hirsch, H. V. B., 174
Hirschman, A., 400
Hiscock, M., 383
Hiscock-Kalil, C., 383
Hitch, G. J., 351
Hitchcock, J. M., 339
Hitzig, Eduard, 226
Hobson, J. A., 258, 425
Hockfield, S., 172
Hocking, D. R., 172
Hodos, I., 130
Hoebel, B. G., 68, 286, 287, 288, 289, 292, 293

Hofer, M. A., 311
Hoffer, A., 416
Hoffer, B. J., 432
Hoffman, E., 258
Hoffman, P. L., 342
Hofman, M. A., 319
Hogness, D. S., 151
Hökfelt, T., 58
Holekamp, K. E., 305
Hollister, J. M., 434, 435
Holloway, R. L., 136
Holmes, C., 413
Holt, J., 283
Holzer, P., 195
Holzman, P. S., 434, 436
Hömberg, V., 85
Honer, W. G., 436
Hoover, J. E., 224
Hop, W. C. J., 309
Hopfield, J. J., 143
Hopkins, J., 420
Hoptman, M. J., 375, 379
Hore, J., 212
Horn, C. C., 284
Horne, J. A., 249, 256, 264
Horridge, G. A., 364, 365
Horton, J. C., 172
Horváth, Z., 401
Hou, Y., 261, 262
Houtsmuller, E. J., 319
Hovda, D. M., 405
Howland, H. C., 174
Howlett, A. C., 71
Hoyer, D., 63
Hsu, M., 401
Hu, N., 318
Hu, S., 318
Hu, Y., 368
Huang, Y., 126
Hubel, David H., 158, 159, 161, 162, 163, 164, 172, 174
Hudspeth, A. J., 182
Hugdahl, K., 375
Huggins, G. R., 206
Hughes, H. C., 164
Hull, E. M., 307, 308
Hulse, S. H., 126
Hultman, C. M., 435
Hume, K. I., 244
Humphrey, P. P. A., 63
Hunt, E., 127
Huntington's Disease Collaborative Research Group, 238
Hurd, Y., 424
Hurvich, L. M., 150
Hutchison, J., 306
Hutson, K. A., 184
Huttunen, M. O., 435
Hyman, B. T., 356
Hynd, G. W., 395

Iacono, W. G., 326, 430
Iadecola, C., 109
Iggo, A., 191
Imamura, K., 208
Imperato-McGinley, J., 316
Inch, R., 383
Innocenti, G. M., 375, 382
Inouye, S. T., 246
Intiligator, J., 164
Iriki, A., 192
Irwin, M., 330
Isaacson, R. L., 357
Israel, Y., 9

Subject/Glossary Index

Analgesia relief from pain, 197–198

Anandamide a naturally-occurring brain chemical that stimulates the same receptors as cannabinoids, 71*f*, 71

Androgen a class of steroid hormones more abundant in males than in females for most species, 299*t*, 299–300, 303, 305, 315–316, 316*f*

Androgen insensitivity condition in which a person lacks the mechanism that enables androgens to bind to genes in a cell's nucleus, 315–316, 316*f*

Androstenedione, 305

Anesthetic drugs, 24, 40

"Angel dust". See Phencyclidine

Angiotensin II hormone that constricts the blood vessels, 278, 279, 298

Animal research, 17–21, 18*f*, 453–455

Anomia inability to remember the names of objects, 391

Anorexia nervosa condition in which a person refuses to eat adequately, 293

Anosmia, 207

Antabuse trade name for disulfiram, a drug that prevents the breakdown of acetaldehyde into acetic acid, and which therefore causes people to get sick if they drink alcohol, 73–74, 422

Antagonist drug that blocks the effects of a neurotransmitter, or anything that counteracts the effects of something else, 65

Antagonistic muscle muscle that moves a limb in the opposite direction from some other muscle (for example, an extensor is an antagonist of a flexor), 213–214, 214*f*

Anterior toward the front end, 80*t*

Anterior commissure set of axons that connects the hemispheres in the anterior part of the cerebral cortex; smaller than the corpus callosum, 93, 382, 383*f*

Anterior pituitary portion of the pituitary gland, which releases growth hormone, prolactin, follicle-stimulating hormone, luteinizing hormone, adrenocorticotropic hormone, and thyroid-stimulating hormone, 299*t*, 300–302, 302*f*

Anterograde amnesia loss of memories for events that happened after brain damage or some other event, 352

Antibody Y-shaped protein that fits onto an antigen and weakens it or marks it for destruction, 329

Anticonvulsant drugs, 427

Antidepressant drugs, 65, 421–423

Antidiuretic hormone (ADH) (also known as vasopressin) pituitary hormone that raises blood pressure and enables the kidneys to reabsorb water and therefore to secrete highly concentrated urine, 277, 301, 302*f*, 310

Antigen protein on the surface of a microorganism, in response to which the immune system generates antibodies, 329

Antihistamine drugs, 262

Antipsychotic drug drug that relieves schizophrenia, 66, 438

Anvil. See Incus

Anxiety, 339–341, 341*f*, 342

Apex one end of the cochlea, farthest from the point where the stirrup meets the cochlea, 183

Aphasia lack of language abilities, 389–393, 390*f*, 390*t*, 391*t*, 392*f*, 393*f*

Aplysia, 364–367, 366*f*, 367*f*

Apomorphine morphine derivative that stimulates dopamine receptors, 408*f*, 408

Apoptosis, 118

Areas V1-V5. See V1-V5

Aromatic compounds, 305

Arousal, 260–262, 351

Artificial selection change in the frequencies of various genes in a population because of a breeder's selection of desired individuals for mating purposes, 12

Aspartame, 336

Associativity tendency for pairing with a stronger input to enhance the later effectiveness of a weaker input, 367

Astigmatism blurring of vision for lines in one direction because of the nonspherical shape of the eye, 174–175, 175*f*

Astrocyte (astroglia) a relatively large, star-shaped glia cell, 30*f*, 30

Atom piece of an element that cannot be divided any further, 447

Atomic number number of protons in the nucleus of an atom, 447

Atomic weight number indicating the weight of an atom relative to a weight of one for a proton, 447, 449

ATP adenosine triphosphate, a chemical the body uses as its main way of delivering energy where it is needed; also used as a neurotransmitter, 451*f*, 451

Attack behaviors, 306, 310, 332–336, 334*f*, 336*f*

Attention deficit disorder (ADD) condition marked by impulsiveness and poor control of attention, 68

Atypical antipsychotic drugs, 439

Audition, 180–188
chemical coding, 200–201
deafness, 185–186
ear structure, 181*f*, 181–182, 182*f*
nature of sound, 180*f*, 180
pitch perception, 182–185, 183*f*, 184*f*, 185*f*
and schizophrenia, 432
sound localization, 186*f*, 186–187, 187*f*
and temporal lobe, 97

Autism, 85

Autonomic nervous system set of neurons that regulates functioning of the internal organs, 78, 81–83, 325–326

Autoradiography method of injecting a radioactively labeled chemical and then mapping the distribution of radiation in the brain, 105

Autoreceptor presynaptic receptor that responds to the neurotransmitter released by the presynaptic cell itself, 61–62, 423

Autosomal gene gene on any of the chromosomes other than the sex chromosomes (X and Y), 7

Axon a single fiber that extends from a neuron, 27, 28. See also Impulse conduction
and action potential, 38–40, 41
and arousal, 260
and brain damage recovery, 405–406, 406*f*, 412, 413*f*
competition among, 124
corpus callosum, 374*f*, 374–375, 382
fornix, 88
growth of, 118
and lateralization, 382
and learning, 363
and movement, 212–213, 213*f*, 229
and neurotransmitter transport, 57
pathfinding, 119–123, 120*f*, 121*f*, 123*f*, 124*f*
and sympathetic nervous system, 81, 82
visual system, 154–155

Axon hillock a swelling of the soma, the point where the axon begins, 28, 41

Babinski reflex reflexive flexion of the big toe when the sole of the foot is stimulated, 218

Ballistic movement motion that proceeds as a single organized unit that cannot be redirected once it begins, 217

Barbiturate class of drugs used as anticonvulsants, sedatives, and tranquilizers, 340

Baroreceptor receptor that detects the blood pressure in the largest blood vessels, 278–279

Basal forebrain forebrain area anterior and dorsal to the hypothalamus; includes cell clusters that promote wakefulness and other cell clusters that promote sleep, 261, 262, 356

Basal ganglia set of subcortical forebrain structures including the caudate nucleus, putamen, and globus pallidus, 87–88, 88*f*, 337
and movement, 86, 224, 226*f*, 226
and tardive dyskinesia, 439

Basal metabolism rate of energy use while the body is at rest, used largely for maintaining a constant body temperature, 132, 270

Base the part of the tympanic membrane closest to the stirrup, 183

Basilar membrane floor of the scala media, within the cochlea, 182, 183*f*

B cell type of leukocyte that matures in the bone marrow, 329, 330

BDNF. See Brain-derived neurotrophic factor

Behavioral medicine field that considers the influence on people's health of their eating and drinking habits, smoking, stress, exercise, and other behavioral variables, 327

Bell-Magendie Law observation that the dorsal roots of the spinal cord carry sensory information and that the ventral roots carry motor information toward the muscles and glands, 80

Benzodiazepine class of widely used antianxiety drugs, 340–341, 341*f*

β—endorphin, 197, 299*t*

Binocular vision sight based on simultaneous stimulation of two eyes, 172*f*, 172

Biological clock internal mechanism for controlling rhythmic variations in a behavior, 243–246, 247*f*, 248–249

Biological explanations of behavior, 2–3

Biological psychology study of the physiological and evolutionary principles underlying behavior, 1

brain, 284, 292–293, 293t, 294, 298, 340

Choroid plexus, 90

Chromosome strand of DNA bearing the genes, 6, 7, 303

Chronic conditions conditions having a gradual onset and long duration, 431

Cilia, 204, 205

Cingulate gyrus, 86

Circadian rhythm repeating on a rhythm of approximately one day, 242, 242–243, 243f, 264–265, 265f, 319–320. *See also* Wakefulness/sleep cycles
and mood disorders, 424–425, 425f, 427

Circannual rhythm repeating on a rhythm of approximately one year, 242

Circumcision, 316

Classical conditioning type of conditioning produced by the pairing of two stimuli, one of which evokes an automatic response, 346, 347f, 348f, 348, 349, 363

Clomipramine, 337

Clozapine, 439

CNS. *See* Central nervous system

Cocaine strong stimulant drug that blocks the reuptake of dopamine by the presynaptic neuron, 68f, 68, 84, 438

Cochlea structure in the inner ear, containing auditory receptors, 182

Coding the one-to-one correspondence between some aspect of the physical stimulus and some aspect of the nervous system's activity, 142f, 142

Cognition, 310, 380

Cold remedies, 83

Collateral sprout newly formed branch from an uninjured axon that attaches to a synapse vacated when another axon was destroyed, 406, 407f, 412, 415

Color blindness, 150–151, 154

Color constancy ability to recognize the color of an object despite changes in lighting, 166

Color vision, 149f
chemical coding, 200
color blindness, 150–151, 154
and concurrent pathways, 159f, 160
theories of, 149–150, 150f, 151f
and visual receptors, 147
and visual system, 165–166

Column collection of cortical neurons, arranged perpendicular to the surface of the cortex, all of which respond to similar aspects of the stimulus, 80t, 94f, 94, 163, 164f

Combination pill, 309

Complex cell cell type of the visual cortex that responds best to a light stimulus of a particular shape anywhere in its receptive field; its receptive field cannot be mapped into fixed excitatory and inhibitory zones, 161, 162f, 162t, 163f

Compound material made up by combining elements, 447

Computerized axial tomography (CT scan) method of visualizing a living brain by injecting a dye into the blood and then passing X rays through the head and recording them by detectors on the other side, 105–106, 106f

COMT catechol-o-methyltransferase, an enzyme that metabolizes catecholamines, 63, 65

Concentration gradient difference in concentration of a solute across some distance, 36, 37, 39–40

Concordance agreement (A pair of twins is concordant for a trait if both of them have it or if neither has it.), 432

Conditioned response (CR) response evoked by a conditioned stimulus as a result of the pairing of that stimulus with an unconditioned stimulus, 346

Conditioned stimulus (CS) stimulus that comes to evoke a particular response only after the pairing of that stimulus with an unconditioned stimulus, 346

Conduction aphasia, 392

Conductive deafness hearing loss that occurs if the bones of the middle ear fail to transmit sound waves properly to the cochlea, 186

Cone one type of receptor in the retina, specialized for color vision and detailed vision, 147, 149. *See also* Visual receptors

Confabulation a made-up story or answer, such as one offered by an amnesic patient to fill in a gap in memory, 355

Configural conditioning, 358

Consciousness, 445

Consolidation formation and strengthening of long-term memories, 350–351

Contralateral on the opposite side of the body (left or right), 80t

Cooperativity tendency for nearly simultaneous stimulation by two or more axons to produce more LTP than stimulation by just one, 367

Coronal plane (frontal plane) a plane that shows brain structures as they would be seen from the front, 80t, 86f

Corpus callosum large set of axons that connects the two hemispheres of the cerebral cortex, 93, 374f, 374–375
damage to, 375–376, 377f
development of, 382
sex differences, 384

Corpus luteum, 309

Cortical blindness, 95

Corticospinal fluid (CSF). *See* Cerebrospinal fluid

Corticosterone, 299t, 299, 351

Cortisol hormone released by the adrenal cortex that elevates blood sugar and enhances metabolism, 293, 299t, 299, 310, 328

Covalent bond chemical bond between two atoms that share electrons, 449

CR. *See* Conditioned response

Cranial nerve part of a set of nerves controlling sensory and motor information of the head, connecting to nuclei in the medulla, pons, midbrain, or forebrain, 84t, 84, 84–85, 85f

Craniosacral nervous system. *See* Parasympathetic nervous system

Crib death. *See* Sudden infant death syndrome

Critical period time early in development during which some event (such as an experience or the presence of a hormone) has a long-lasting effect (synonym: sensitive period)
and long-term potentiation, 370
and sex differences, 303–305, 306
and sexual orientation, 318–319
and vision, 173, 174, 175

Cross-adaptation reduced response to one stimulus because of recent exposure to some other stimulus, 202

Crossing over exchange of parts between two chromosomes during replication, 7

Cross-tolerance tolerance to one drug because of exposure to a different drug, 342

CS. *See* Conditioned stimulus

CSF. *See* Cerebrospinal fluid

CT scan. *See* Computerized axial tomography

Curare, 60

CVA. *See* Cerebrovascular accident

Cyclic AMP, 60, 299

Cyproterone, 308

Cytokines chemicals released by the immune system that cross the blood-brain barrier and influence neuronal function, 329

Cytoplasm fluid inside the cell membrane but outside the nucleus, 25

Cytosine, 10

DA. *See* Dopamine

Dairy products, 282f, 282

Dale's law, 58

DBI. *See* Diazepam-binding inhibitor

Deafferent to remove the sensory nerves from a body part, 404, 405f

Deafness, 185–186, 391

Declarative memory memory that a person can state, identifying it as a memory (opposite: procedural memory), 353, 355, 358

Delayed matching-to-sample task task in which an animal sees an object and then after a delay must choose the object matching the sample, 357, 358

Delayed nonmatching-to-sample task task in which an animal sees an object and then after a delay must choose the object not matching the sample, 357–358, 358f

Delayed-response task assignment in which an animal must respond on the basis of a signal it remembers but which is no longer present, 98, 351–352

Delusion belief that other people regard as unfounded, such as the belief that one is severely persecuted, 431

Dendrite thin, widely branching fiber that emanates from a neuron, 26–27, 28
and brain damage recovery, 412
changes in, 31f, 31
growth of, 116, 125f, 125, 128
impulse conduction, 43
and language, 391
and learning, 368

Dendritic spine short outgrowth along the dendrites, 27f, 27, 125f, 125

Denervation supersensitivity increased sensitivity by a postsynaptic cell after removal of an axon that formerly innervated it, 406–408, 407f, 408f, 439

Deoxyribonucleic acid (DNA) the chemical that composes the chromosomes, 10f, 10, 11f

Depolarization reduction in the level of polarization across a membrane, 38–39, 40, 41, 43, 49. *See also* Action potential

Deprenyl drug that inhibits the enzyme monoamine oxidase B; found to slow the progress of Parkinson's disease, 236

Depression
  and eating disorders, 293
  major depressive disorder,
    420–425
  and Parkinson's disease, 233
  and steroids, 301
Depth perception, 159f, 160,
  166, 173–174
Dermatome area of skin connected to a particular spinal
  nerve, 192, 193f
DES. *See* Diethylstilbestrol
DHT, 316
Diabetes, 6, 285f, 285, 291
Diaschisis decreased activity of
  surviving neurons after
  other neurons are damaged,
  405
Diazepam, 340
**Diazepam-binding inhibitor
  (DBI)** brain protein that
  blocks the behavioral effects
  of diazepam and other
  benzodiazepines, 341
Diet, 282–283. *See also* Digestive
  system; Eating regulation
  and brain size, 135
  and neurotransmitter synthe-
    sis, 56
  and schizophrenia, 432
  and serotonins, 336
Diethylstilbestrol (DES) a
  synthetic estrogen, 319
Dieting, 291
Differential diagnosis identification of a condition in distinction from all similar
  conditions, 432
Differentiation formation of the
  axon and dendrites that
  gives a neuron its distinctive shape, 116
Digestive system, 281f, 281–284.
  See also Eating regulation
Dihydrotestosterone, 306
Disinhibition, 52
Disorganization symptoms, 431
Distal located more distant from
  the point of origin or attachment, 80t
Disulfiram. *See* Antabuse
Disuse supersensitivity increased sensitivity by a
  post-synaptic cell after a
  period of decreased input
  by incoming axons, 407
Dizygotic twin fraternal (non-
  identical) twin, 8, 432
DNA deoxyribonucleic acid, the
  chemical that composes the
  chromosomes, 10f, 10, 11f
Dolphins, 388
Dominant gene gene that exerts
  noticeable effects even in an
  individual who has only
  one copy of the gene per
  cell, 6
Dopa chemical precursor of
  dopamine and other catecholamines, 65
Dopamine chemical that acts as
  a neurotransmitter, one of
  the catecholamines
  and blood-brain barrier, 31

and denervation supersensitiv-
    ity, 407f, 407–408, 408f
  and depression, 424
  drug effects on, 65, 66, 67–69,
    70–71, 72
  and eating regulation, 293t
  and learning, 368
  neurotransmitter receptors,
    63, 69–70, 70f
  and Parkinson's disease,
    233–234, 235f, 236
  and schizophrenia, 438f, 438,
    439f, 439–440
  and sex hormones, 307–308,
    310
  synthesis of, 57f
**Dopamine hypothesis of schiz-
  ophrenia** hypothesis that
  schizophrenia is due to
  excess activity at certain
  dopamine synapses, 438f,
  438, 439f, 439–440
Dorsal toward the back, away
  from the ventral (stomach)
  side. The top of the human
  brain is considered dorsal
  because that is its position
  in four-legged animals, 78,
  79f, 80t
Dorsal root ganglion set of
  sensory neuron somas on
  the dorsal side of the spinal
  cord, 80
Dorsolateral prefrontal cortex
  area of the prefrontal cortex, 263, 413, 436
Dorsolateral tract a path of
  axons in the spinal cord
  from the ipsilateral hemisphere of the brain, controlling movements of p
  eripheral muscles, 229, 230f
Dorsomedial thalamus, 354
Double dissociation of function
  demonstration that one
  lesion impairs behavior A
  more than it impairs behavior B, while a second lesion
  impairs behavior B more
  than it impairs behavior A,
  104
Down syndrome, 355
Dreaming, 255, 258, 263, 266
Drug effects on synaptic transmission, 65–74, 66f, 69f.
  See also Drugs; *specific
  drugs*
  alcohol, 72–74
  antidepressant, 65, 421–423
  caffeine, 72
  hallucinogenic drugs, 71–72,
    72f
  marijuana, 71f, 71, 84
  MDMA, 72
  nicotine, 68
  opiate drugs, 68–69, 70–71,
    84
  phencyclidine, 69
  and receptor variations, 69–70
  and reinforcement studies,
    66–67
  stimulant drugs, 67–68, 68f,
    84
  variations in, 65–66

Drugs. *See also* Alcohol; Alco-
    holism; Drug effects on
    synaptic transmission;
    specific drugs
  anesthetic, 24, 40
  antidepressant, 65, 421–423
  antihistamine, 262
  for bipolar disorder, 426–427
  for brain damage recovery, 415
  cold remedies, 83
  designer, 236
  for myasthenia gravis, 233
  and neurotransmitter inactiva-
    tion, 63
  and Parkinson's disease, 234
  and schizophrenia, 432,
    437–439, 438f
  and sex hormones, 308
  tranquilizers, 265, 340–341,
    341f, 342
Dualism belief that the mind
  exists independent of the
  brain and exerts some
  control over it, 444
Duodenum part of the small
  intestine adjoining the
  stomach, 284
Dynorphin, 197, 293t
Dyslexia a specific reading
  difficulty in a person with
  adequate vision and at least
  average skills in academic
  areas other than reading,
  395–396, 396f

Ears, 181f, 181–182, 182f
Easy problems philosophically
  unchallenging questions of
  which brain activity is
  associated with which
  experience or behavior, 444
Eating regulation, 281–294
  and digestive system, 281f,
    281–284, 283–284
  disorders, 293–294
  and genetics, 290–291
  and glucose, 284–286
  and hypothalamus, 286f,
    286–289, 287f, 288f, 289f,
    289t
  and neurotransmitters,
    291–293, 292f, 293t, 294
  and taste, 283
Echidnas, 257
"Ecstasy," 72
ECT. *See* Electroconvulsive
  therapy
Edema excessive fluid build-up
  in the intercellular spaces of
  the body, 401
EEG. *See* Electroencephalograph
Efferent axon a neuron that
  carries information away
  from a structure, 29f, 29
Efficacy tendency of a drug to
  activate a particular kind of
  receptor, 65
Elderly people. *See* aging
Electrical gradient difference in
  electrical potential across
  some distance, 36, 37, 38f,
  39
**Electroconvulsive therapy
  (ECT)** electrically inducing

a convulsion in an attempt
    to relieve depression or
    other disorders, 423–424,
    424f
Electroencephalograph (EEG)
  device that records the
  electrical activity of the
  brain through electrodes on
  the scalp, 107, 253, 254f
Element material that cannot be
  broken down into other
  materials, 447t, 447, 448f
Emotion, 324–328. *See also* Stress
  and attack behaviors, 332
  and autonomic nervous sys-
    tem arousal, 325–326
  and health, 327–328
  and lateralization, 379f, 379
  and limbic system, 324f,
    324–325, 325f
Encephalitis, 234
End bulbs. *See* Presynaptic
  terminal
Endocrine gland organ that
  produces and releases
  hormones, 87, 298f, 298
Endogenous circadian rhythm
  self-generated rhythm that
  lasts about a day, 242,
  242–243, 243f, 264–265,
  265f, 319–320. *See also*
  Wakefulness/sleep cycles
  and mood disorders, 424–425,
  425f, 427
Endogenous circannual rhythm
  self-generated rhythm that
  lasts about a year, 242
Endoplasmic reticulum a network of thin tubes within a
  cell that transport newly
  synthesized proteins to
  other locations, 25
Endorphin category of neurotransmitters that stimulate
  the same receptors as opiates, 68–69, 70, 197
Endothelial cells, 32
Endozepine brain protein that
  blocks the behavioral effects
  of benzodiazepines, 341
End-stopped cell cell of the
  visual cortex that responds
  best to stimuli of a precisely
  limited type, anywhere in a
  large rec eptive field, with a
  strong inhibitory field at
  one end of its field. (Also
  known as a hypercomplex
  cell.), 161, 162t, 163f
Engram the physical representation of learning, 346, 348f,
  348–349, 350f
Entorhinal cortex, 356, 370
Environment, 8–9, 11, 234–235,
  272. *See also* Experience
Enzyme protein that controls
  the rate of chemical reactions in the body, 10, 451
Epilepsy a condition characterized by repeated episodes of
  excessive, synchronized
  neural activity, mainly
  because of decreased release of the inhibitory

transmitter GABA, 325, 335, 340, 375, 377, 422, 423

Epinephrine chemical that acts as a neurotransmitter, one of the catecholamines, 57*f*, 298, 299*t*, 351

EPSP excitatory postsynaptic potential, a subthreshold depolarization of the postsynaptic membrane, 49–50, 51–52, 366

Escape behaviors, 336–341, 342

Estradiol one type of estrogen, 293*t*, 303, 305–306, 309, 310

Estrogen a class of steroid hormones more abundant in females than in males for most species, 299*t*, 299–300, 303, 304–306, 309, 310

Ether, 40

Ethical issues, 10–11, 17–21, 453–455

Ethnic differences
  in acetaldehyde metabolization problems, 9
  in Parkinson's disease, 233, 234*f*
  in PKU, 8

Ethyl alcohol (or ethanol) the type of alcohol that people drink (in contrast to methyl alcohol, isopropyl alcohol, and others), 73

Evoked potential electrical activity recorded from the brain, usually via electrodes on the scalp, in response to sensory stimuli, 107

Evolution change in the frequencies of various genes in a population over generations, 2, 11–14
  and animal research, 17
  brain, 130*f*, 130–138
  and eating regulation, 293
  evolutionary trees, 11–12, 12*f*
  and hair erection, 2, 83
  and language, 386–389, 387*f*, 388*f*
  and motor programs, 219
  and sleep, 250, 251*f*, 256, 257

Evolutionary explanation hypothesis that relates a structure or a behavior to the evolutionary history of a species, 2. *See also* Evolution

Evolutionary theory of sleep concept that the function of sleep is to conserve energy at times of relative inefficiency, 250

Excitatory postsynaptic potential (EPSP) graded depolarization of a neuron, 49–50, 51–52, 366

Experience. *See also* Environment
  and brain development, 124–127, 125*f*, 126*f*
  and food selection, 283
  and long-term potentiation, 370

and neuron structure, 30
and therapies, 419
and visual development, 172–175, 173*f*, 175*f*

Explicit memory deliberate recall of information that one recognizes as a memory, detectable by direct testing such as asking a person to describe a past event (opposite: implicit memory), 354, 355, 358

Extensor muscle muscle that extends a limb, 214*f*, 214

Eyes, 143–144, 144*f*, 145*f*, 146–147. *See also* Vision

Fast-twitch muscle muscle that produces fast contractions but fatigues rapidly, 215

Fatigue, 40

Fear, 336–340, 337*f*, 338*f*

Feature detector neuron whose responses indicate the presence of a particular feature, 164

Fetal alcohol syndrome condition resulting from prenatal exposure to alcohol and marked by decreased alertness, hyperactivity, varying degrees of mental retardation, motor problems, heart defects, and facial abnormalities, 127*f*, 127

Fever, 273, 435

Finger-to-nose test, 223

Fish, 120, 214–215, 405

Fissure a long, deep sulcus, 80*t*

Flexor muscle muscle that draws an extremity, such as an arm, toward the trunk of the body, 213–214, 214*f*

Fluent aphasia. *See* Wernicke's aphasia

Fluoxetine, 422–423

Fluvoxamine, 337

fMRI. *See* Functional magnetic resonance imaging

Focus (in the context of epilepsy) a damaged or malfunctioning area of the brain from which an epileptic seizure originates, 325, 335, 377

Follicle-stimulating hormone (FSH) pituitary hormone that promotes the growth of follicles in the ovary, 299*t*, 309, 310

Food. *See* Diet

Forebrain the most anterior part of the brain, including the cerebral cortex and other structures, 86*f*, 86, 261, 262, 287, 436

Fornix tract of axons connecting the hippocampus with the hypothalamus and other areas, 88

Fovea center of the retina, point at which receptors are most densely packed, 143–144, 147–148, 148*t*

Free-running rhythm circadian or circannual rhythm that is not being periodically reset by light or other cues, 243

Frequency the number of sound waves per second, 180, 182–184

Frequency theory concept that pitch perception depends on differences in frequency of action potentials by auditory neurons, 182–184, 183*f*

Frontal lobe one of the lobes of the cerebral cortex, 98–99

Frontal lobotomy. *See* Prefrontal lobotomy

Frontal plane (coronal plane) a plane that shows brain structures as they would be seen from the front, 80*t*

FSH. *See* Follicle-stimulating hormone

Functional explanation description of why a structure or behavior evolved as it did, 2, 3, 14

Functional magnetic resonance imaging (fMRI) a modified version of MRI that measures energies released by hemoglobin molecules in an MRI scan, and then determines the brain areas receiving the greatest supply of blood and oxygen, 109–110

GABA gamma amino butyric acid, a neurotransmitter that generally, perhaps always, acts as an inhibitor
  drug effects on, 68–69, 70–71, 73
  and escape behaviors, 340–341, 341*f*
  and ionotropic effects, 59
  and sleep, 262
  and stroke, 481

GABA$_A$ receptor complex structure that includes a site that binds GABA as well as sites that bind other chemicals that modify the sensitivity of the GABA site, 340–341, 341*f*, 342

Galvanic skin response (GSR) measure of the electrical conductance of the skin, 326

Ganglion (plural: **ganglia**) a cluster of neuron cell bodies, usually outside the CNS (as in the sympathetic nervous system), or any cluster of neurons in an invertebrate species, 80*t*, 80, 81

Ganglion cell type of neuron within the eye, 144, 145*f*, 146, 154, 155. *See also* Vision

Ganglioside molecule composed of carbohydrates and fats, 406, 415

Gases, 56

Gate theory assumption that stimulation of certain nonpain axons in the skin or in the brain can inhibit transmission of pain messages in the spinal cord, 196, 198

Gender identity the sex with which a person identifies, 314–317, 315*f*, 316*f*

Gender role the activities and dispositions that a particular society encourages for one sex or the other, 14, 314

Gene a physical particle that determines some aspect of inheritance, 6. *See also* Genetics

Gene-knockout approach, 103

Gene localization, 10–11, 238

General anesthetic chemical that depresses brain activity as a whole, 40

Generalized seizure an epileptic seizure that spreads quickly across neurons over a large portion of both hemispheres of the brain, 377

Generator potential local depolarization or hyperpolarization of a neuron membrane, 142

Genetics, 6–11, 7*f*, 11*f*
  and alcoholism, 7, 9, 10, 69, 73
  and Alzheimer's disease, 355
  and attack behaviors, 333
  and behavior, 9–10
  biochemistry, 10–11
  and bipolar disorder, 425
  and depression, 421
  and eating regulation, 290–291
  gene-knockout approach, 103
  and handedness, 382
  heritability, 8–10, 8–9, 70, 234, 237–238
  and intelligence, 135
  and language, 394*f*, 394–395
  Mendelian, 6–8
  and neurotransmitter receptors, 70
  and schizophrenia, 431–434, 433*f*
  and sexual orientation, 317*f*, 317–318, 318*f*

Glia a type of cell in the nervous system that (unlike neurons) does not conduct impulses to other cells, 24, 29–31, 401

Globus pallidus one of the structures of the basal ganglia, 87, 224

Glomeruli, 116, 118*f*

GLP-1. *See* Glucagon-like peptide

Glucagon pancreatic hormone that stimulates the liver to convert stored glycogen to glucose, 284, 285*f*, 292, 299*t*

Glucagon-like peptide (GLP-1), 292, 293*t*

and sleep, 262
and stress, 328*f*, 328
and thirst, 278
and vision, 155
Hypovolemia lower than normal blood volume, 278
Hypovolemic thirst thirst provoked by low blood volume, 278*f*, 278, 279*t*

Identity position belief that the mind is the same thing as brain activity, described in different terms, 444
Imipramine, 421–422
Immune system set of structures that protects the body against viruses and bacteria, 328–330, 329*f*
Immunohistochemistry method of using the immune system to label particular types of tissues, 105
Implicit memory influence of recent experience on memory, even if one does not recognize that influence or realize that one is using memory at all (opposite: explicit memory), 354, 355
Impotence inability to have an erection, 308
Impulse conduction, 35–44. *See also* Action potential
local neurons, 43–44
resting potentials, 35–38, 38*f*, 40
Incus one of the small bones of the middle ear; also known as the anvil, 181–182
Infant amnesia tendency for people to recall few specific events that occurred before about age 4 or 5 years, 360
Infants
alpha-fetoprotein, 305–306
amnesia, 360
brain damage recovery, 412–413, 413*f*, 414*f*
lateralization, 382
reflexes, 218, 336–337
sleep, 256, 257*f*
vision, 171*f*, 171–172
Inferior below another part, 80*t*
Inferior colliculus part of the auditory system located in the midbrain, 85
Inferior temporal cortex portion of the cortex where neurons are highly sensitive to complex aspects of the shape of visual stimuli within very large receptive fields, 164–165
Influenza, 435*f*
Inhibitory postsynaptic potential (IPSP) temporary hyperpolarization of a membrane, 50–51
Inner-ear deafness hearing loss that results from damage to the cochlea, the hair cells, or the auditory nerve, 185–186

Insomnia lack of sleep, leaving the person feeling poorly rested the following day, 264–265, 265*f*
Institutional Animal Care and Use Committees, 21
Insulin hormone that increases the conversion of glucose into stored fat and facilitates the transfer of glucose across the cell membrane, 56, 299*t*, 423
and eating regulation, 284–286, 285*f*, 286*f*
Intelligence, 133–135, 134*f*, 136, 137*f*
Interleukin-1, 273
Interneuron a neuron that receives information from other neurons and sends it to either motor neurons or interneurons, 28, 80
Intersex individual whose sexual development is intermediate between male and female, 314–316, 315*f*
Interstitial nucleus 3, 320*f*, 320
Intrinsic neuron a neuron whose axons and dendrites are all confined within a given structure, 29
Invertebrates, 27, 363–367, 366*f*, 367*f*
Ion atom that has gained or lost one or more electrons, 449. *See also* Ion channels; *specific ions*
Ion channels, 36, 37*f*, 37–38, 39, 40. *See also* Action potential
Ionic bond chemical attraction between two ions of opposite charge, 449
Ionotropic effect synaptic effect that depends on the rapid opening of some kind of gate in the membrane, 59*f*, 59, 60*f*
Iproniazid, 422
Ipsilateral on the same side of the body (left or right), 80*t*
IPSP inhibitory postsynaptic potential, a temporary hyperpolarization of a membrane, 50–51
Ischemia local insufficiency of blood because a blood clot or other obstruction has closed an artery, 400

James-Lange theory notion that physiological states cause emotions, not vice versa, 326
Jet lag disruption of biological rhythms caused by travel across time zones, 245*f*, 245

K-complex sharp high-amplitude negative wave followed by a smaller, slower positive wave, 253
Kennard principle generalization (not always correct) that it is easier to recover

from brain damage early in life than later in life, 412
Kenyon cell, 29*f*
Kidney, 299*t*
Kin selection selection for a genetic trait that benefits one's relatives, 14
Klüver-Bucy syndrome condition in which monkeys with damaged temporal lobes fail to display normal fears and anxieties, 97, 334
Koniocellular cells, 159
Korsakoff's syndrome type of brain damage caused by thiamine deficiency, characterized by apathy, confusion, and memory impairment, 24, 33, 354–355

Labeled-line theory concept that each receptor responds to a limited range of stimuli and has a direct line to the brain, 200
Lactase enzyme necessary for lactose metabolism, 282
Lactose the sugar in milk, 282*f*, 282
Lamarckian evolution discredited theory that evolution proceeds through the inheritance of acquired characteristics, 13
Lamina (plural: laminae) a layer of cell bodies separated from other cell bodies by a layer of fibers, 80*t*, 93–94, 94*f*
Language, 386–397
and brain damage, 389–393, 390*f*, 390*t*, 391*t*, 392*f*, 393*f*
dyslexia, 395–396, 396*f*
and evolution, 386–389, 387*f*, 388*f*
genetic abnormalities, 394*f*, 394–395
and lateralization, 381
Lateral toward the side, away from the midline, 80*t*
Lateral geniculate a nucleus of the thalamus; part of the visual system, 154
Lateral hypothalamus area of the hypothalamus in which damage impairs eating and drinking, 261, 286*f*, 286–287, 287*f*
Lateral inhibition restraint of activity in one neuron by activity in a neighboring neuron, 155–158, 156*f*, 157*f*
Lateral interpositus nucleus a nucleus of the cerebellum critical for classical conditioning of the eyeblink response in rabbits, 348–349
Lateralization division of labor or specializations between the two hemispheres of the brain, 374–384
corpus callosum, 374*f*, 374–376, 377*f*

and depression, 421
development of, 381*f*, 381–382, 383*f*
and electroconvulsive therapy, 424
and handedness, 382–384, 384*f*
hemisphere functions, 378–380, 379*f*, 380*f*
split-brain people, 375–378, 378*f*, 379
Lateral preoptic area portion of the hypothalamus that includes some cells that facilitate drinking and some that inhibit it, 278
Law of specific nerve energies principle that any activity by a particular nerve always conveys the same kind of information to the brain, 143
Lazy eye (amblyopia ex anopsia) a condition in which a child uses just one eye for vision, while ignoring the other eye, 173
L-dopa chemical precursor of dopamine and other catecholamines, 236, 416
Learning, 346–349. *See also* Memory
and brain size, 134–135
classical and operant conditioning, 346, 347*f*, 348*f*, 348, 349
engrams, 346, 348*f*, 348–349, 350*f*
Hebbian synapses, 363
invertebrate research, 363–367, 366*f*, 367*f*
long-term potentiation, 367–368, 369*f*, 370
and neuron structural changes, 31
Lens structure within the eye that can focus light by increasing or decreasing its thickness, 143
Leptin peptide released by fat cells; tends to decrease eating, 291–292
Lesion damage to a structure, 103–104
Leu-enkephalin a chain of five amino acids believed to function as a neurotransmitter that inhibits pain, 196
Leukocyte white blood cell, a component of the immune system, 273, 328–329
LH. *See* Lateral hypothalamus; Luteinizing hormone
Librium, 340
Life, defined, 269
Limbic system interconnected set of subcortical structures in the forebrain, including the hypothalamus, hippocampus, amygdala, olfactory bulb, septum, other small structures, and parts of the thalamus and cerebral cortex, 86*f*, 86

Night terror experience of intense anxiety during sleep, from which a person awakens screaming in terror, 266

Nimodipine, 415

Nissl stain, 104

Nitric oxide a gas that acts as a neurotransmitter, 56, 58, 109, 368

NMDA receptor glutamate receptor that also responds to N-methyl-D-aspartate, 368, 370, 415

NMR (nuclear magnetic resonance). *See* Magnetic resonance imaging

NO. *See* Nitric oxide

Nociceptin, 197

Node of Ranvier short unmyelinated section of axon between segments of myelin, 42*f*, 42

Nonfluent aphasia. *See* Broca's aphasia

Non-REM sleep (NREM) sleep stages other than REM sleep, 255, 266

Noradrenaline. *See* Norepinephrine

Norepinephrine chemical that acts as a neurotransmitter, one of the catecholamines, 57*f*, 298, 299*t*
and depression, 424
drug effects on, 65, 66*f*, 68
and eating regulation, 293*t*
and premenstrual syndrome, 310
and sexual behavior, 307
and sympathetic nervous system, 83

Novocain, 40

NPY. *See* Neuropeptide Y

NREM sleep. *See* non-REM sleep

NTS. *See* Nucleus of the tractus solitarius

Nuclear magnetic resonance method of imaging a living brain by using a magnetic field and a radio frequency field to make atoms with odd atomic weights all rotate in the same direction and then removing those fields and measuring the energy the atoms release, 106, 107*f*, 135

Nuclei of the cerebellum clusters of neurons in the interior of the cerebellum, which send axons to motor-controlling areas outside the cerebellum, 224

Nucleus a cluster of neurons within the central nervous system, or a structure within a cell that contains the chromosomes, 25, 84

Nucleus accumbens small subcortical brain area that is rich in dopamine receptors and evidently a major part of the brain's reinforcement system, 66, 67*f*, 69

Nucleus of the tractus solitarius (NTS) area in the medulla that receives input from taste receptors, 203, 287

NutraSweet, 336

Nutrition. *See* Diet

Obesity, 265, 286, 291, 292

Object permanence task, 114

Obsessive-compulsive disorder psychological disorder characterized by intrusive thoughts and urges to perform repetitive acts, 293, 337

Occipital lobe one of the four lobes of the cerebral cortex, 95, 263

6-OHDA. *See* 6-Hydroxydopamine

Olfaction sense of smell, 88, 204–208, 205*f*, 207*f*

Olfactory bulb a forebrain structure that receives most of its input from the olfactory cells, 86, 133, 205

Olfactory cell neuron responsible for smell, located on the olfactory epithelium in the rear of the nasal air passages, 204

Olfactory receptors, 30–31, 204–207

Oligodendrocyte glia cell that surrounds and insulates certain axons in the vertebrate brain and spinal cord, 30*f*, 30

Omnivore animal that eats both meat and plants, 282

Ondansetron, 69

Onset insomnia difficulty falling asleep, 264

Ontogenetic explanation description of how a structure or a behavior develops, 2

Operant conditioning type of conditioning in which reinforcement or punishment changes the future probabilities of a given behavior, 346, 347*f*

Opiate drugs class of drugs that stimulate endorphin receptors in the nervous system, 68–69, 70–77, 84
and pain, 196, 197, 198

Opioid mechanisms systems responsive to opiate drugs and similar chemicals, 196

Opponent-process theory notion that we perceive color in terms of paired opposites: white versus black, red versus green, and blue versus yellow, 150, 151*f*

Optic aphasia, 392

Optic chiasm point at which parts of the optic nerves cross to the opposite side of the brain, 375

Optic nerve the second cranial nerve, a band of axons from the ganglion cells of the retina to the brain, 146

Orbital frontal cortex an anterior area of the prefrontal cortex, 413

Orbital prefrontal cortex, 337*f*, 337

Organizing effect long-lasting effect of a hormone that is present during a critical period early in development, 303–306, 304*f*

Organ of Corti the array of hair cells attached to the basilar membrane in the cochlea of the inner ear, 181*f*

Organum vasculosum laminae terminalis. *See* OVLT

Orientation (of a visual stimulus) the angle (such as vertical or horizontal) of a bar of light in the visual field, 161, 162*f*

Osmotic pressure tendency of water to flow across a semipermeable membrane from the area of low solute concentration to the area of high solute concentration, 277*f*, 277

Osmotic thirst thirst that results from an increase in the concentration of solutes in the body, 277*f*, 277–278, 279*t*

Otolith organ an organ responsible for vestibular sensation, 190, 191*f*

Oval window a membrane of the inner ear, adjacent to the stirrup, 181–182

Ovary female gonad that produces eggs, 299*t*, 303

OVLT organum vasculosum laminae terminalis, a brain structure on the border of the third ventricle, highly sensitive to the osmotic pressure of the blood, 277*f*, 278

Oxytocin hormone released by the posterior pituitary; also used as a neurotransmitter in the brain; important for sexual and parental behaviors, 299*t*, 301, 302*f*, 308, 311, 312

Pacinian corpuscle a receptor that responds to a sudden displacement of the skin or high-frequency vibration on the skin, 191, 192*f*

Pain, 194–198, 196*f*, 197*f*

Pancreas, 299*t*

Panic disorder condition characterized by occasional attacks of extreme fear, breathlessness, heart palpitations, fatigue, and dizziness, 337

Pan paniscus, 387–388, 388*f*

Panting, 271

Papilla structure on the surface of the tongue containing taste buds, 201*f*, 201

Paradoxical sleep a stage of sleep characterized by complete relaxation of the large muscles but high activity in the brain; synonym for REM sleep, 254. *See also* REM sleep

Parallel fiber axon that runs perpendicular to the planes of the Purkinje cells in the cerebellum, 224, 368

Paraquat, 234, 235*f*

Parasympathetic nervous system (PNS) system of nerves innervating the internal organs, tending to conserve energy, 81–82, 325

Parathyroid gland, 299*t*

Parathyroid hormone, 299*t*

Paraventricular nucleus (PVN) area of the hypothalamus which controls secretion of vasopressin; also limits meal size, 278, 289, 291, 292*f*

Parental behavior, 310–312, 311*f*

Parietal lobe one of the lobes of the cerebral cortex, 96–97, 97*f*

Parkinson's disease malady caused by damage to a dopamine pathway, resulting in slow movements, difficulty initiating movements, rigidity of the muscles, and tremors, 233–237, 234*f*
and denervation supersensitivity, 408
and dopamine, 31
and movement, 217
substantia nigra deterioration, 85
treatments, 236–237, 416

Parrots, 388*f*, 388–389

Partial penetrance tendency of a gene to be expressed only under certain circumstances, 6–7

Partial seizure epileptic seizure that begins in a focus somewhere in the brain and then spreads to nearby areas in just one hemisphere, 377

Parvocellular neuron small-celled neuron of the visual system that is sensitive to color differences and visual details, 159*t*, 159–160

Paternal half-siblings people who have the same father but different mothers, 433

PCP. *See* Phencyclidine

Penetrance the degree of expression of a gene, 6–7

Penis, 306, 316–317

Penumbra an area of endangered cells surrounding an area of primary damage, 401

Peptide chain of amino acids, 56, 57

Peptide hormone hormone composed of a chain of amino acids, 299, 300*f*

Peptide neurotransmitter a neurotransmitter composed of a chain of amino acids, 56, 57

Peptide YY (PYY), 294

Periaqueductal gray area of the brain stem that is rich in enkephalin synapses, 197*f*, 197

Perikaryon. *See* Cell body

Periodic limb movement disorder repeated involuntary movement of the legs and sometimes arms during sleep, 266

Periovulatory period time just before and after the release of the ovum, time when fertility is highest, 309

Peripheral nervous system (PNS) nerves outside the brain and spinal cord, 78

Peripheral vision, 147–148, 148*t*

Permeability the ability of an ion to cross a membrane, 36

Personality, 63, 69–70, 70*f*

PET. *See* Positron-emission tomography

Petit mal seizure (or *absence seizure*) type of generalized seizure in which the person stares unresponsively for a period of seconds, making no sudden movements, except perhaps for eye blinking or a drooping of the head, 377

PET scan positron-emission tomography, a method of mapping activity in a living brain by recording the emission of radioactivity from injected chemicals, 107–108, 108*f*, 262

PGO wave pattern of high-amplitude electrical potentials that occurs first in the pons, then in the lateral geniculate, and finally in the occipital cortex, 263*f*, 263

Phantom limb a sensation that feels like a body part even after that part has been amputated, 193–194, 194*f*, 409

Phencyclidine (PCP) drug that blocks certain glutamate synapses, 69, 438. *See also* Hallucinogenic drugs

Phenelzine, 422

Phenothiazine a class of antipsychotic drugs including chlorpromazine, 438

Phenylalanine, 8–9, 336

Phenylketonuria (PKU) inherited inability to metabolize phenylalanine, leading to mental retardation unless the afflicted person stays on a strict low-phenylalanine diet throughout childhood, 8–9

Phenylthiocarbamide (PTC), 6

Pheromone odorous chemical released by one animal that affects the behavior of other members of the same species, 206

Phonological loop aspect of working memory that stores auditory information, including (for humans) words, 351–352

Phosphates, 451*f*, 451

Photopigment chemical in the rods and cones that releases energy when struck by light, 148

Phrenology nineteenth-century theory that personality types are related to bumps on the skull, 101*f*, 101–102

Physiological explanation concept that relates an activity to how the brain and other organs of the body function, 2

Pineal gland a small unpaired hormone-releasing gland inside the brain, 248, 299*t*

Pinna the fleshy and cartilaginous structure at the exterior of the ear, 181

Pitch the experience that corresponds to the frequency of a sound, 180, 182–185, 183*f*, 184*f*, 185*f*

Pituitary gland endocrine gland attached to the hypothalamus; its secretions regulate the activity of many other hormonal glands, 87, 272*f*, 299*t*, 300–302, 302*f*

PKU. *See* Phenylketonuria

Place theory concept that pitch perception depends on which part of the inner ear has cells with the greatest activity level, 182–184

Planum temporale area of the temporal cortex that for most people is larger in the left hemisphere than in the right hemisphere, 381*f*, 381

Plaque structure formed from degenerating axons and dendrites in the brains of people with Alzheimer's disease, 356*f*, 356

Plasma membrane. *See* Membrane

PNS. *See* Parasympathetic nervous system; Peripheral nervous system

POA. *See* Preoptic area

Poikilotherm animal that maintains the body at approximately the same temperature as the environment (synonym: endotherm), 270–271

Polarization an electrical gradient across a membrane, 36

Polygraph test, 326*f*, 326

Polysomnograph a combination of EEG and eye-movement records, and sometimes other data, for a sleeping person, 254*f*, 255

Pons hindbrain structure, anterior or ventral to the medulla, 85, 262

Positive symptom presence of a behavior not seen in normal people, 430–431

Positron-emission tomography a method of mapping activity in a living brain by recording the emission of radioactivity from injected chemicals, 107–108, 108*f*, 262

Postcentral gyrus gyrus of the cerebral cortex just posterior to the central gyrus; a primary projection site for touch and other body sensations, 96, 126

Posterior toward the rear end, 80*t*

Posterior parietal cortex area important for using visual and somatosensory cues to guide movement, 228

Posterior pituitary portion of the pituitary gland, 299*t*, 301

Postganglionic axons, 81, 82–83

Postpartum depression depression after giving birth, 420–421

Postsynaptic neuron neuron on the receiving end of a synapse, 49, 58, 69, 123, 363

denervation supersensitivity, 406–408

Posttraumatic stress disorder condition characterized by periodic outbursts of anxiety, panic, or depression provoked by reminders of a traumatic experience, 338

Potassium ions, 36–37, 40*f*, 40, 203, 367. *See also* Ion channels; Sodium-potassium pump

Precentral gyrus gyrus of the cerebral cortex just anterior to the central sulcus; a primary point of origin for axons of the pyramidal system of motor control, 98

Prefrontal cortex the most anterior portion of the frontal lobe of the cerebral cortex, 98*f*, 98, 99

brain damage recovery, 413
and memory, 98, 351–352, 354
and movement, 228
and sleep, 263

Prefrontal lobotomy surgical disconnection of the prefrontal cortex from the rest of the brain, 98, 99

Premenstrual syndrome, 310

Premotor cortex area of the frontal cortex, just anterior to the primary motor cortex, active during the planning of a movement, 228

Preoptic area brain area adjacent to the anterior hypothalamus, important for temperature control, 271, 272–273, 307

Presymptomatic test exam to predict the onset of a disease, conducted before any symptoms appear, 237–238

Presynaptic neuron neuron on the releasing end of a synapse, 49

Presynaptic receptor receptor located on the terminal at the tip of an axon, 61*f*, 61–62, 72

Presynaptic terminal the tip of an axon, the point from which the axon releases chemicals, 27, 58

Primary auditory cortex area in the temporal lobes in which cells respond best to tones of a particular frequency, 184*f*, 184–185, 185*f*

Primary motor cortex area of the frontal cortex just anterior to the central sulcus; a primary point of origin for axons of the pyramidal system of motor control, 226–229, 227*f*, 229*f*, 230*f*

Primary somatosensory cortex. *See* Postcentral gyrus

Primary visual cortex (V1) area of the cortex responsible for the first stage of visual processing, 95, 160

Primate member of the mammalian order that includes humans, monkeys, apes, and their relatives

brain organization, 137*f*, 138*f*
brain size, 131–132, 134*f*
language, 386–388, 387*f*
sex differences, 136

Priming phenomenon that seeing or hearing a word or words increases the probability that a person will soon use those same words, 354

Procedural memory memory of how to do something (opposite: declarative memory), 353, 355

Progesterone hormone that prepares the uterus for the implantation of a fertilized ovum, 299*t*, 299–300, 306, 309

Prolactin a hormone released by the anterior pituitary that stimulates lactation in mammary glands, 299*t*

Proliferation the production of new cells, 116

Propagation of the action potential transmission of an action potential down an axon, 41*f*, 41–42

Proprioceptor receptor that is sensitive to the position and movement of a part of the body, 215–217, 216*f*